Hi, may you enjoy

"La Fée captures the aroma and taste that great writers and artists such as Rimbaud, Toulouse-Lautrec, and Vincent Van Gogh enjoyed at the end of the 19th Century"

Marie-Claude Delahaye,
world-renowned absinthe expert and historian

ABSINTHE SUPERIEURE

in many a fine cocktail...

George Rowley
30.8.2017

Difford's Guide

TO

COCKTAILS

TWELFTH EDITION

FOR DISCERNING DRINKERS

Before continuing please be aware that:
• This guide is intended for adults of legal drinking age
• Consumption of alcohol in excess can be harmful to your health
• The sugar levels in some cocktails may mask their alcohol content
• Do not consume alcoholic cocktails and drive or operate machinery
• Great care should be exercised when combining flames and alcohol
• Consumption of raw and unpasteurised eggs may be harmful to health and should not be consumed by infants, small children, pregnant women, the elderly or any persons who may be immunocompromised. Please only use pasteurised eggs and egg products.
• Please follow the alcohol content guidelines for drinks in this guide where a 'shot' is equal to 30ml of alcohol at most, and beware that a 25ml measure of spirit at 40% alc./vol. is equal to one unit of alcohol.
• Women who are trying to conceive or who are pregnant are advised to avoid alcohol.
• Please take extreme care when using either dry ice or nitrous oxide. We do not recommend using liquid nitrogen for the preparation of cocktails.

We did it
Recipes and words Simon Difford
Photography and design Dan Malpass
Publisher and director Paloma Alos
We all work for Odd Firm of Sin Limited.
www.diffordsguide.com
We proudly printed this book in the United Kingdom.

ISBN: 978-0-9576815-3-8
Twelfth edition published 2016

Don't blame us

The views expressed in this publication are not necessarily the views of Odd Firm of Sin Limited (the publisher).

While every effort is made to ensure the accuracy of information contained in this publication at the time of going to press, no responsibility will be accepted for errors or omissions. Odd Firm of Sin Limited and Simon Difford specifically disclaim responsibility for any adverse effects that may result from the use or application of the recipes and information contained in this book.

The advice and strategies contained herein may not be suitable for your situation.

Difford's Guide

TO

COCKTAILS

TWELFTH EDITION

FOR DISCERNING DRINKERS

WRITTEN BY

SIMON DIFFORD

Introduction

CAFE
PACIFICO

66
The ultimate cocktail
book – simple, clear
and totally doable.
Everyone needs
diffordsguide Cocktails
on their bookshelf.
99

JAMIE OLIVER

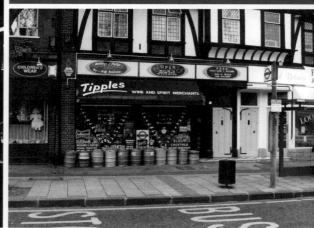

I started making cocktails in my kitchen at home back in 1990 when I owned an off-licence in Hayes in South London. I supplied numerous local restaurants and bars, particularly specialising in harder to obtain liqueurs and spirits. A few doors down the street from my shop was, and still is, a American Diner called Dillinger's and this was the first cocktail bar I supplied. As requests came for various flavoured syrups, liqueurs I'd not heard of, and tinned cream of coconut, so my interest in the cocktails these ingredients were used in grew.

Years later, 1997 to be precise, my interest in the subject had grown to the extent that I re-mortgaged our family home (again) to launch CLASS. Mailed to bars across the UK, the title of this monthly magazine was an acronym of Cocktail, Liqueur And Speciality Spirit, which broadly summed up its content. It was the success of this magazine that led me to meet Dick Bradsell, now sadly departed, he was the most important bartending influence in the UK since the Savoy's Harry Cradock in the 1930s. Over numerous sessions in bars and experimental cocktail evenings at my apartment with Dick I learned that his drinks were great drinks because he perfected and then recorded recipes.

If I was in a bar with Dick and a bartender made him a particularly good rendition of a classic cocktail, he would ask for the recipe and compare it to his own. If it was better, then he'd tweak his recipe or adopt the newly discovered formula.

I have followed Dick's example and asked for recipes in many of the world's best bars and I'd like to take this opportunity to thank the hundreds of bartenders who have shared their recipes with me. I have also harvested recipes from vintage cocktail books and I study most of the new cocktail books as they are released to see what I can learn from my peers. This book is a compendium of these recipes with an additional ten percent that I have personally created (look for 'yours truly' in the origin).

Sadly, most bartenders have a limited opportunity to travel and have little opportunity to seek out and test new recipes. Over the last 19 years I've managed to make a career out of doing just that. Few people have visited more bars and I doubt anyone has made more cocktails. OK, I'm sure many bartenders have mixed more drinks, but I have made more different recipes – there are 3,000 in this book alone and I have mixed and sampled every one of them – some numerous times over, trying different ratios. I then remake every cocktail again for Dan Malpass, friend and designer of this publication since 1999, to photograph.

If you find that one of the recipes in this book is your own, then hopefully I have credited you accordingly. I have modified the proportions of some recipes to (in my opinion) improve their balance, to simplify, or to avoid obscure or outdated ingredients. Some recipes originally used brands of alcohol other than those that I now recommend. And I recommend ingredients which I think are good quality and widely available. When crediting a recipe, I usually add the word "adapted" when I have made such changes. Hopefully my adaptations are for the better and I have respected the soul of such cocktails.

Despite tweaking, some recipes are simply better than others – my own included; so I have assigned a score to each cocktail on a scale of one to five (according to my own tastes), indicating the score with stars above the name of each drink.

Do you know a better version of a cocktail in the book? Is one of your creations worth including in the next edition? If so, then please email me your recipes to simon@diffordsguide.com.

Between editions of this book I continually update our website, diffordsguide.com, and I urge you to check here for new recipes, additional information and videos. Please also subscribe to our free weekly email by registering at diffordsguide.com.

In the words of Churchill, "I have taken more out of alcohol than it has taken out of me." I wish the same for you and hope you enjoy the world of cocktails has much as I have and do.

Cheers.

Simon Difford

Key Ingredients

THE KEY INGREDIENTS AND FRIDGE & PANTRY ESSENTIALS

VODKA

GIN

RUM

TEQUILA

SCOTCH WHISKY

COGNAC

BOURBON

TRIPLE SEC

APRICOT LIQUEUR

ELDERFLOWER LIQUEUR

BERRY LIQUEUR

DRY VERMOUTH

SWEET VERMOUTH

CHAMPAGNE

LEMONS

LIMES

ORANGES

PINK GRAPEFRUITS

STRAWBERRIES

RASPBERRIES

MINT

BASIL LEAVES

BANANAS

BLUEBERRIES

GRAPES (RED AND WHITE)

CUCUMBER

CRANBERRY JUICE

PRESSED PINEAPPLE JUICE

TOMATO
JUICE

PRESSED
APPLE JUICE

COLA

SODA WATER

GINGER ALE

GINGER BEER

TONIC WATER

LEMONADE

LIME CORDIAL

ANGOSTURA
BITTERS

ORANGE
BITTERS

EGGS

MILK

SINGLE
CREAM

MARASCHINO
CHERRIES

SUGAR
SYRUP

DEMERARA
SUGAR SYRUP

POMEGRANATE
(GRENADINE) SYRUP

RUNNY
HONEY

AGAVE
SYRUP

TEA

COFFEE
(FILTER & ESPRESSO)

ENGLISH ORANGE
MARMALADE

WORCESTERSHIRE
SAUCE

BLACK PEPPER

TABLE SALT

CELERY SALT

CARDAMOM
PODS

CLOVES

NUTMEG

Basic Equipment

As with most pastimes, a bewildering array of bartending equipment is available but watch a bartender at work and you'll find they use very few pieces of equipment. The vast majority of cocktails need either shaking or stirring so you can pretty much get by with just a shaker and long handled barspoon. Ideally you'd also have a mixing glass but you can just stir in the tin.

However, if you have the following 20 or so items you pretty much have the full pro-bartending kit. I've not arranged them in any particular order of importance but I have left the blender till last as if on a budget it's the one item I'd forego, and with it blended drinks.

1. COCKTAIL SHAKER

You can shake a cocktail using a jam jar. You can also start a fire with a couple of sticks but it's easier and quicker to use a match. Similarly, why would you want to shake a cocktail in something like a jam jar when the piece of equipment designed for the job is so affordable?

Cocktail shakers are made in numerous shapes and sizes but there are two basic designs – 'two-piece' and 'three-piece' shakers. You will need one or the other. Three-piece shakers are generally easier for beginners to master and have the added benefit of having a built-in strainer, whereas a separate hawthorn strainer will also be required when using a two-piece shaker.

THREE-PIECE COCKTAIL SHAKERS

Three-piece shakers are also called 'Standard' or 'Cobbler' shakers, they comprise of three sections:

1. Flat-bottomed, conical base or 'can'
2. Built-in strainer mid-section
3. Top cap or lid which seals the shaker

In 1872, the first patent for a cobbler-style three-piece shaker was granted in the United States. This style of shaker is preferred by Japanese bartenders and practitioners of the hard-shake due to their relatively small capacity limiting travel of the ingredients and ice inside.

Three-piece shakers with built-in strainers pour more slowly than two-piece shakers, especially if the drink being poured contains the pulp of muddled fruit. However, we recommend this style of shaker for home, non-professional use due to its ease of use.

TWO-PIECE COCKTAIL SHAKERS

As the name suggests a two-piece shaker consists of two flat-bottomed cones, one larger than the other. The large cone, or 'can', is made of stainless steel or silver plated steel while the smaller cone can be glass, stainless steel or even plastic. If the smaller cone is glass the pair are collectively known as a 'Boston Shaker', and if metal then you have what's known as a 'French Shaker'.

I recommend 'tin and tin' (French) two-piece shakers over 'glass and tin' (Boston) shakers. If you do opt for glass then don't buy a Boston shaker that relies on a rubber ring to seal. Cocktail Kingdom, Alessi and WMF shakers seal without needing to thump and open with ease. But however good your two-piece shaker, these devices demand an element of skill and practice for a new user to become proficient. See page 33 for how to use.

1A. HAWTHORNE STRAINER

If you opted for a two-piece shaker then I'd suggest you also acquire a hawthorne strainer. These have a spring which runs around their circumference to help catch particles of ice and fruit created by the violent act of shaking. They also often have 'lugs' which rest on the rim of the shaker to hold the strainer in position when being used. Most designs of hawthorne strainer incorporate a ridge or finger rest, which when pushed serves to secure the sprung-loaded gap between the strainer and the side of the shaker, so allowing finer particles to be caught.

2. MIXING GLASS

There is much debate among bartenders as to the best vessel to use for stirring, with some preferring glass to metal. Scientific experiments by New York-based Dave Arnold,

prove that metal heats up and cools down quickly, and in doing so uses minimal energy, so having little effect on the temperature of the finished cocktail. In contrast, heavy glass stirring/mixing glasses have more thermal mass, so absorb more energy from the drink being mixed. The heavier they are, the more energy they will absorb. Pre-chilling or freezing such glasses mitigates this effect and, according to Dave, "makes them as good as, or better than, an un-chilled metal shaker".

Mixing glasses come in a multitude of shapes and sizes and, bearing in mind the above, heavy Japanese cut-glass stirring glasses stored in a refrigerator or ideally a freezer are now favoured in most high-end bars. If a specially designed lipped mixing glass is not available, a Boston glass (the glass half of a Boston shaker) or even the base of a standard shaker, will suffice.

3. STIRRING SPOON

There are almost as many different styles of bar spoon on the market as there are stirring glasses. Some have spiralling stems, some have flat ends and others three-pronged fork ends. The key thing is for your spoon to have a long stem so it will reach down to the base of the glass.

4. JULEP STRAINER

Julep strainers are best described as being perforated metal spoons which are slightly smaller than hawthorne strainers so allowing them to fit inside mixing glasses. They are said to take their name from Kentucky gentlemen who would historically hold them over a Mint Julep to keep the ice and mint from their moustaches.

To strain from my mixing glass I use Cocktail Kingdom's Antique-Style Hawthorne Strainer. Based on a strainer patented back in 1892, as the name suggests this is a hawthorne strainer rather than a julep strainer but it is designed to fit large and standard mixing glasses.

5. FINE STRAINER

I'm firmly in the camp that believe that shaken drinks should be fine strained to remove the tiny ice shards which otherwise float like scum on the surface of shaken cocktails. That said, I'd rather have ice scum than have to use a ridiculously small 'tea strainer' with an overly fine sieve. See diffordsguide.com for the perfect fine strainer, a tool that's also useful for removing pith and pips from citrus juice.

6. MEASURE

Please don't try to make any of the cocktails in this book without an accurate measure. Or if you do don't blame me if they taste unbalanced. Use a jigger, thimble measure, medicine measure or even a shot glass, but ideally use a graduated measure such as the handy plastic mini angled measuring jug made by OXO Good Grips.

7. PARING KNIFE

You'll need a sharp knife for cutting fruit for squeezing, and preparing garnishes. I love Japanese carbon steel knives but prolonged contact with citrus attacks their carbon steel, turning it black. A good stainless steel knife will do but I prefer ceramic knives such as those made by Kyocera. But beware, razor sharp ceramic knives will not stand flexing or twisting motions and cannot be used for cutting hard objects. An ideal blade length is around 13cm (5 inch) as this is long enough to tackle a large pineapple or melon.

8. CUTTING BOARD

Food hygiene used to point towards the use of polyethylene plastic boards, but while these will stand up to sanitising in hot temperatures and harsh cleaning products, the thin grooves left in these boards harbour bacteria. It is not uncommon to see white cutting boards turned black in bars and if you do I'd recommend drinking elsewhere.

Avoid glass cutting boards or indeed any such hard surface which will blunt your knives. Properly cared-for wooden boards are a traditional, attractive and practical choice. Wipe them regularly with antibacterial cleaner and rub the board with coarse salt at the end of a bar shift before a thorough clean. Revive the wood with regular doses of food-grade mineral oil (poppyseed oil or linseed oil, not vegetable or olive oils).

Many chefs are now using rubber cutting boards as they are durable enough to withstand cleaning in hot water and yet are kind to knives. Unlike wooden or plastic boards they also have the advantage of not needing to be placed on a damp cloth to stop them slipping. Rubber cutting boards are more expensive than wood but last much longer, so are worth the investment.

9. SWIVEL PEELER

So called because their blades swivel so they present at the correct cutting angle, these are chiefly designed for peeling potatoes, carrots and such like in the kitchen but they are also perfect for slicing long thin slivers of citrus peel, termed 'twists'.

There are two designers of these peelers, one with the blade in line with the handle and the other with the blade horizontal to the handle, sometimes called 'Y peelers' due to their shape. I much prefer the type with the blade in line with the handle and favour those made by OXO Good Grips.

10. CHANNEL KNIFE & CITRUS ZESTER

I've a number of zesters and channel (canal) knives and apart from cutting the odd horse's neck rarely use any of them. Even then you can cut a horses neck with a swivel peeler as above. However, channel knives cost less than a tenner and if investing I recommend the OXO Good Grips model illustrated here.

11. CITRUS JUICER

Let's face it, Jamie Oliver uses his hands so pretty much any citrus juicer will do. However, the best cheap juicers are the hand-held hinged type that bartenders tend to call "Mexican elbows" (Mexicans don't). Department stores sell these in various colours, green for lime, yellow for lemon and orange for oranges (you guessed it). You don't need a trio or sizes – a lime will happily sit in either the lemon or orange sized device. If you're flush with cash then I'd opt for a lever action pillar press such as those made by Hamilton Beach or Olympus (formerly called OrangeX).

12. WAITER'S FRIEND CORKSCREW

I would love to claim that I use a Chateau Laguiole Master Sommelier (pronounced 'Shato Layol') but like so many others, I actually own, and have lost, numerous cheap Waiter's Friends which double as cork screw and bottle opener. Model 60 – double lever at waitersfriend.co.uk does the job.

13. ICE RECEPTACLE

If working in a cocktail bar then I'd hope you have a built-in insulated or even refrigerated ice-chest with drainage. Sadly these don't feature in your average domestic kitchen so I recommend using a 14 litre insulated plastic cool box. Ideally put mesh in the bottom to allow melted water to drain. The ice will last longer if it's not sat in a pool of water.

Buy bags of ice as required and empty into your cool box when making cocktails so enabling you to scoop ice from the box into your shaker. Cool boxes are also handy for transporting ice to a party.

14. ICE SCOOP

Now you've an ice-chest, or at least a cool box, so you'll need an ice scoop. I use three ice scoops: one monster-size plastic one for taking ice from my ice-machine; a 12oz aluminium scoop for scooping cubed ice in my shaker or mixing glass; and a 6oz aluminium scoop for crushed ice – the latter chosen because its small size is better for channelling crushed ice into glasses.

15. MUDDLER

Jokes about phallic-looking muddlers aside, all you need is a long, round shaft such as a rolling pin. Elegantly shaped wooden muddlers look great but due to storing in my continually water flushed dipper-well (luxury built into my

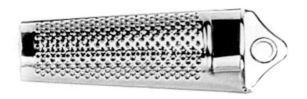

bar) I tend to use a more contemporary looking and robust stainless steel and plastic muddler.

16. NUTMEG GRATER

When selecting a nutmeg grater perhaps look for the type which also has a compartment for storing your nutmeg. That way you know where the nutmeg is.

17. POWDER SHAKER

A shaker with a fine mesh of the type used in coffee shops to dust cappuccinos is perfect for applying powdered chocolate and cinnamon over the surface of cocktails.

18. LINEN GLASS CLOTHS

My mum calls these "tea towels" and they are more essential to bartending than any other item mentioned here. To best dry and leave glasses streak-free, wash at the hottest your machine will allow and don't use fabric conditioner. Glass cloths are not only used for polishing glasses, keep one to hand or tied to your waist to wipe water and juice from your hands as you work.

19. WOODEN MALLET & LEWIS BAGS

In ideal world you'd have a crushed ice machine or even a mechanical ice-crusher but arguably a mallet & Lewis bag make better crushed ice as the bag absorbs moisture from the ice. Alternatively, you can crush cubed ice by wrapping in one of the linen cloths above and bashing with a heavy muddler or rolling pin. You can also use a food processer to crush ice but it's not the best thing for the blades.

20. LIPPED SAUCEPAN

Not only handy for heating your soup but perfect for making sugar syrup and flavoured sugar syrups such as pomegranate (grenadine).

21. BLENDER

You'll need a blender for all those Frozen Daiquiris and Piña Coladas so choose one with a large capacity and a powerful motor. Vitamix (www.vitamix.com) may not be the best-looking but they are certainly powerful and tough. Your average domestic blender will not have the power to crush ice so you'll need to use crushed ice. However, a Vitamix will pulverise large cubes of ice straight from the freezer. Judge your blender by the power (wattage) of its electric motor rather than how slick the stainless steel design looks on your countertop.

22. THE BAG

Professional photographers' equipment bags are perfect for storing and carrying bar equipment. The one pictured by Tamrac (tamrac.com) is the one I use and features padded sections originally designed to house camera lenses but which are deep enough to accommodate shakers, mixing glasses and glassware. An abundance of front and side pockets, designed for holding lens caps and other paraphernalia snugly house bar spoons, measures, strainers and smaller bar tools. Visit any professional camera store and you'll find a large range of such bags.

Glassware

GLASSWARE

Cocktails are something of a luxury. You don't just ping a cap and pour – they take a degree of time and skill to mix, so deserve a decent and appropriate glass.

Before you start, check your glassware is clean and free from chips, watermarks and lipstick. Always handle glasses by the base or the stem to avoid leaving finger marks and never put your fingers inside a glass.

Ideally, glassware should be chilled in a freezer prior to use. This is particularly important for Martini, Coupe, Nick & Nora and Flute glasses in which drinks are usually served 'up', without ice. Allow 20 to 30 minutes to sufficiently chill a glass in the freezer. If you don't have a freezer to hand then you can chill glasses by filling them with ice (ideally crushed, not cubed) and topping up with water. Leave the glass to cool while you prepare the drink, then discard the ice and water once you are ready to pour. This method is quicker than chilling in the freezer but not nearly as effective.

Conversely, to warm a glass ready for a hot cocktail, place a bar spoon in the glass and fill it with hot water. Then discard the water and pour in the drink. Only then should you remove the spoon, which is there to help disperse the shock of the heat.

There are thousands of differently shaped glasses, but if you own those mentioned here you will have a glass to suit practically every drink and occasion. Failing that, a set of Collins, Coupe and Old-fashioned or Rocks glasses, and possibly Flutes if you fancy champagne cocktails, will allow you to serve the majority of drinks in this book.

COUPE / COUPETTE / CHAMPAGNE SAUCER

Known in cocktail circles as a Coupe, Champagne Saucers are perfect for serving straight-up drinks. Urban myth has it that the original Coupe glass was moulded in the shape of Marie Antoinette's left breast. Sadly, the truth is the glass was invented in England in 1663, long before the reign of the queen. Although I am the proud owner of a pair of Coupes shaped after British model Kate Moss' left breast – but that's another story… .Modern Coupes are widely available but search out vintage examples. Store in a freezer to ensure well chilled prior to use.
Capacity to brim: 7oz / 20cl

MARTINI

The curvy Coupe has made the angular v-shaped lines of the classic Martini glass look a tad dated but somehow a Martini is not a Martini when served in a rounded glass. A Martini glass should be no bigger than 7oz / 20cl, as a true Martini warms up too much in the time it takes to drink a larger one. Keep Martini glasses in a freezer so they are well chilled before use.
Capacity to brim: 7oz / 20cl

NICK & NORA

These dainty stemmed elongated glasses date from the 1930s, tend to be smaller than the more commonplace curvy breast-shaped Coupe and can be a third of the size of a 80s Martini lunch-style angular Martini glass. Reminiscent of speakeasies, Nick & Nora glasses are and can be used for pretty much any drink served in a

Coupe. Store in a refrigerator or ideally a freezer so they are well chilled before use. Named after Nick and Nora Charles, a fictional couple created by Dashiell Hammett in his novel The Thin Man. Nick is an alcoholic private detective married to Nora, a wealthy Nob Hill heiress. The film portrays the glamorous couple enjoying 1930s cocktail culture. The book and its characters were later adapted for a series of movies (1934-1947), radio (1940s), television (1950s) and as a Broadway musical.

Capacity to brim: 4oz-6oz / 17cl-18cl

OLD-FASHIONED

Another glass whose name refers to the best-known drink served in it, it is also great for enjoying spirits such as whisky. Choose a luxuriously large glass with a thick heavy base and a flat ground rim.

Capacity to brim: 11oz / 32cl

DOUBLE OLD-FASHIONED

Sometimes referred to as DOF glasses, Double Old-Fashioned are simply extra-large Old-Fashioned glasses. They are synonymous with tiki drinks such as the Mai Tai where their large volume capacity allows for a generously sized drink to be served with crushed ice.

Capacity to brim: 12oz-16oz / 35cl-47cl

ROCKS GLASS

Basically a utilitarian Old-Fashioned glass, but stronger with thicker glass and rim, often made from toughened glass so better suited to drinks that require muddling in the glass. A hardy glass, if there is such a thing.

Capacity to brim: 9oz-11oz / 27cl-32cl

COLLINS GLASS

Named after the Collins cocktail, the name 'Collins' is something of a catch-all term for tall slim straight sided glasses. Not to be confused with the similar, slightly squatter and broader, and importantly smaller, 'hi-ball' glass. A 12oz Collins glass will suffice for cocktails and perfectly accommodates a 330ml bottle of beer or soda. However, many favour the use of larger 14oz glasses.

Capacity to brim: 12oz - 14oz / 35cl – 41cl

HIGHBALL OR HI-BALL GLASS

Tall and narrow (in proportion to its height) with straight or slightly flaring sides. As David Embury says in his The Fine Art of Mixing Drinks, "Don't expect to have the Highball which you order at a bar served in anything larger than a Sour glass unless you order a double. It is a decidedly generous bar that gives you a full 2-ounce drink in a Highball. Two ounces of liquor in a 14 or 16 ounce glass filled with ice and carbonated beverage would more nearly resemble the traditional Sunday-school lemonade than a Highball." Ideally use 8oz (235ml) Hi-ball glasses as these are the optimal size for both highballs and fizzes. Use frozen or at least chilled.

Capacity to brim: 6oz-10oz / 18cl-30cl

SLING GLASS

Reminiscent of a pilsner beer glass, these tall elegant glasses are perfect for long drinks and can be used in place of a Collins glass. The Sling is named after its own category of cocktails and is most identified with the Singapore Sling.

Capacity to brim: 11oz / 32cl

BOSTON / PINT GLASS

A tall, heavy conical glass with a thick rim which, depending on how you view it, is either designed for serving beer or to be combined with a Boston tin to form a shaker. It can also be used as a mixing glass for stirred drinks.
Capacity to brim: 17oz / 48cl

JULEP CUP

Traditionally, Mint Julep cocktails are served in these short conical-shaped cups. The best ones are silver or pewter but stainless steel versions are more commonplace. They should be stored in the freezer, but even when used at room temperature the crushed ice used when serving a Mint Julep will ensure a thick frost forms, coating the outside of the cup.
Capacity to brim: 12oz-13oz / 35cl-38cl

MULE MUG

Usually engraved with a kicking mule, these small copper mugs were originally, and are still used to serve vodka-based Moscow Mule Cocktails. Now, just about any cocktail topped with ginger beer and served in a copper mug has 'Mule' in its name.
Capacity to brim: 12oz / 35cl

TIKI MUG

Coming in all shapes and sizes but most commonly tall and tubular, these ceramic mugs with a glossy glaze are usually embellished with totem pole-like tiki idols or shaped liked figurines.
Capacity to brim: 14oz-22oz / 41cl-65cl

COPITA / SHERRY GLASS

A small stemmed wine glass which tapers inwards towards the rim to concentrate the aromas inside. Not to be confused with similarly sized Sour glasses below which taper out from the stem.
Capacity to brim: 4oz-4.5oz / 12cl-13cl

SOUR GLASS

This small glass is narrow at the stem and tapers out to a wider lip. As the name would suggest, it is used for serving sours straight-up. Many favour serving sours over ice in an Old-Fashioned glass but any of the sour recipes in this book can be strained and served 'up' in this glass.
Capacity to brim: 3-5oz / 9cl-15cl

FLUTE GLASS

Flutes are perfect for serving champagne cocktails as their tall, slim elegant design helps maintain the wine's fizz. Be sure to chill well before use.
Capacity to brim: 6oz / 17cl

GOBLET/ WINE GLASS

Not often used for cocktails, but worth having, if for no other reason than to enjoy your wine. An 11oz glass is big enough to be luxurious. Thin glasses with flat ground rims (rather than rounded) are even more luxurious.
Capacity to brim: 11oz / 32cl

SNIFTER GLASS / BRANDY BALLOON

Perhaps best-known as a 'Brandy Balloon', the bigger the bowl, the more luxurious the glass appears. Use to enjoy cocktails and deluxe aged spirits such as cognac. Fashion has it that cocktails served in Snifter glasses are often lightly warmed.

Capacity to brim: 12oz / 35cl

SHOT GLASS

Shot glasses come in all shapes and sizes. You'll need small ones if you're sensible and big ones if you're not. If you are serving layered shots then choose tall, thin glasses to accentuate the thickness of each layer.

Capacity to brim (pictured glass): 2oz / 6cl

TODDY GLASS

Frequently referred to as a 'liqueur coffee glass', which is indeed its main use, this glass was popularised by the Irish Coffee. Toddy glasses are designed to withstand heat and usually have a stem or a handle on the side, allowing hot drinks to be comfortably held.

Capacity to brim: 8.5oz / 25cl

ABSINTHE GLASS

Tall, wide rimmed, footed glasses, often with a dose line, bulge or bubble roughly a quarter of the way up from the foot to indicate how much absinthe to pour (typically 1oz to 1¼oz dose).

Capacity to brim: 8oz-11oz / 24cl-33cl

TEA CUP

It's not just the great British cup of tea that is served from such vessels with many cocktails, usually served chilled, presented in a tea cup – perhaps a reference to alcoholic drinks being served in tea cups during Prohibition to disguise the fact that they were alcoholic.

Capacity to brim: 6oz-8oz / 18cl-24cl

MARGARITA GLASS

Named after the eponymous cocktail, this curvy glass shaped like an upside-down sombrero hat is still predominately used for serving Margaritas. Its rim cries out for salt. Consider using a more modestly shaped and sized Coupe.

Capacity to brim: 8oz / 24cl

POCO GRANDE / PIÑA COLADA GLASS

Sometimes referred to as a Piña Colada glass, the Poco Grande is a big-bowled glass and is commonly used for frozen drinks (served with crushed ice). It screams out for a pineapple wedge, a cherry and possibly a paper parasol as well.

Capacity to brim: 14oz / 40cl

HURRICANE GLASS

Similarly shaped but taller and much larger than a Poco Grande glass, Hurricane glasses resemble the glass of a Hurricane lamp, hence the name. These glasses are synonymous with the eponymously named drink – indeed it is rare to see anything other than a Hurricane cocktail served in this ridiculously large glass. Capacity to brim: 20oz / 60cl

Bartending Basics

BARTENDING BASICS

By definition, any drink which is described as a cocktail contains more than one ingredient. So if you are going to make cocktails you have to know how to combine these various liquids. Firstly, as in cooking, there is a correct order in which to prepare things, and, with few exceptions, it runs as follows:

1. Select glass and chill or pre-heat (if required)
2. Prepare garnish (if required)
3. Pour ingredients into mixing receptacle
4. Add ice (if required)
5. Mix ingredients (shake, stir, blend etc.)
6. Strain (or pour) into glass
7. Add pre-prepared garnish (if required)
8. Serve to guest or enjoy yourself

Unlike cooking where there are a myriad of preparation methods to master, there are essentially only eight different ways to combine the ingredients that comprise a cocktail:

1. Shake
2. Stir
3. Blend
4. Build
5. Throw
6. Roll
7. Swizzle
8. Layer

At the heart of every cocktail lies at least one of these methods, so understanding these terms is fundamental.

1. SHAKING

Shaking not only mixes a drink, it also chills, dilutes and aerates it. Along with stirring, shaking is the most common technique employed to mix cocktails. Shaking is very simple and if you are new to cocktail making, then please continue reading. However, if you are an experienced bartender then I suggest you skip to 'Advanced cocktail shaking tips, myths and lessons'.

COCKTAIL SHAKING BASICS

When following a cocktail recipe and you see the phrase "shake with ice and strain" or similar, you should place all the required ingredients in a cocktail shaker with cubed ice and shake briskly – in a similar manner to agitating the metal ball in a can of spray-paint. Shake for around 12 seconds then strain the liquid into the glass, leaving the ice behind in the shaker.

The temperature and dilution achieved by shaking is just as important to the resulting cocktail as using the right proportions of each ingredient. If you use too little or wet ice it will melt too quickly in the shaker, producing an over-diluted drink – so always use fresh ice and fill your shaker two-thirds full with ice.

Losing your grip whilst shaking is likely to make a mess and a flying shaker could injure a bystander, so always hold the shaker firmly with two hands and never shake fizzy ingredients (unless in a minute proportion to the rest of the drink).

Shakers come in numerous different sizes and designs but in essence there are two types of shakers: three-piece shakers and two-piece shakers. Please refer to the previous equipment chapter to establish which of these two types of shaker you have.

HOW TO USE A THREE-PIECE COCKTAIL SHAKER:

1. Combine all ingredients in the base of the shaker.

2. Fill two-thirds full with ice.

3. Place the top and cap firmly on the base.

4. Pick up the closed shaker with one hand on the top, securing the cap, and the other gripping the bottom, and shake vigorously. The cap should always be on the top when shaking and should point away from guests.

5. After shaking briskly for around 12 seconds, lift off the cap, hold the shaker by its base with one finger securing the top and pour the drink through the built-in strainer.

HOW TO USE A TWO-PIECE COCKTAIL SHAKER

If using a two-piece shaker for the first time I strongly recommend you refer to the cocktail area of diffordsguide.com where you will find a video of me demonstrating how to use a two-piece shaker. However, if you're not online then follow these instructions.

1. Combine ingredients in the glass (or smaller of the two cans).

2. Fill the large can with ice and using one quick motion you can bring the tin filled with ice down on the smaller tin without losing any ice or spilling your drink. However, if you prefer to play safe then pour the contents of the small tin into the large ice-filled tin before sealing. Lightly tap the top with the palm of your hand to create a seal between the two parts.

3. Lift shaker with one hand on the top and the other gripping the base and shake vigorously. The smaller can (or glass) should always be on the top when shaking and should point away from guests.

4. After shaking for around 12 seconds, hold the larger can in one hand and break the seal between the two halves of the shaker by tapping the base can with the palm of your other hand at the point where it meets the upper can (or glass).

5. Before pouring, place a strainer with a coiled rim (also known as a hawthorne strainer) over the top of the can and

strain the mixture into the glass, leaving the ice behind.

6. The ice used during shaking is now spent and should simply be dumped.

The used empty shaker should be rinsed with cold water before making the next drink.

SHAKE WITH CUBED ICE

I recommend always shaking with cubed ice. However, if shaking with large chunks of ice hacked off an ice block (block ice) then a longer shake will be required to achieve the same dilution due to the reduced service area of the ice. Conversely, if shaking with crushed ice then the extra surface area will result in increased dilution.

2. STIRRING

Stirring is the most basic way of mixing a cocktail. You might not give much thought to a technique used to stir a cup of tea or even a pot of paint, but somehow cocktails deserve a little more reverence.

There is much debate among bartenders as to the best vessel to use for stirring, with some preferring glass to metal. Scientific experiments by Dave Arnold, prove that metal heats up and cools down quickly, and in doing so uses minimal energy, so having little effect on the temperature of the finished cocktail. In contrast, heavy glass mixing glasses have more thermal mass, so absorb more energy from the drink being mixed. The heavier they are, the more energy they will absorb. Pre-chilling or freezing such glasses mitigates this effect and, according to Dave, "makes them as good as, or better than, an un-chilled metal shaker".

If a cocktail recipe calls for you to 'stir with ice and strain', then you should:

1. Ideally pre-chill both your mixing glass and serving glass in a refrigerator or freezer. However, if this is not possible, you will need to chill them by first filling with ice and then topping with water. Stir the ice and water in the glass as if mixing a drink before dumping the contents.

2. Measure your ingredients into your chilled mixing glass and then fill two-thirds with ice. Bartending myth used to have it that adding ice last would better control dilution, as the ice would not be melting as you measured in the ingredients. However, science (Dave Arnold) has shown that leaving the ingredients on ice for as much as a minute has little effect on either dilution or the temperature of the final cocktail.

3. Hold the bar spoon between your thumb and the first two fingers of your dominant hand with the spoon's shaft running between your middle finger and ring finger.

4. Slide the bowl of the spoon down the inside edge of the glass until it almost touches the base of the glass.

5. Keeping your arm, and to an extent your wrist still, use your fingers to pull the spoon towards and then away from you, aiming to hit the quarter hour marks on an imaginary clock-face inside your mixing glass. As the spoon runs around so it will spin the ice and liquid in the glass, while spinning on its own axis in your fingers.

6. Stir briskly for about 30-45 seconds – this should account for at least 50 revolutions.

7. Place your strainer into or over the mixing glass (see 'straining') and strain into your chilled serving glass. If the recipe calls for the drink to be served over ice then you should ice your glass first. Never use the ice from the mixing glass in the drink itself.

8. The ice used during stirring is now spent and should be dumped, or alternatively can be left in the mixing glass to keep it chilled ready for the next drink. If the latter, remember to dump the ice and rinse the glass with cold water before making the next drink

STIRRING VS. SHAKING A COCKTAIL

Stirring and shaking obviously result in the various ingredients being mixed together, but both actions also cool and dilute the cocktail being mixed. The key difference between the two mixing methods is that the violent action of shaking achieves the same results quicker. The same degree of cooling and dilution can be achieved with 15 to 20 seconds of shaking as opposed to 90 to 120 seconds of stirring. With few exceptions, (most notably the Old Fashioned) drinks are not stirred for longer than 30 to 45 seconds, so do not end up as cold or as diluted as if they had been shaken.

Why stir then? Stirring merely chills and dilutes a cocktail whereas shaking additionally changes its texture. The ice, being violently shaken about inside the shaker, also aerates the drink producing tiny air bubbles, which are held in suspension in the liquid, giving the cocktail a cloudy appearance. Stirring, on the other hand, has the benefit of delivering a crystal-clear cocktail.

Hence, bartending 'law' has it that drinks made with only clear ingredients should be stirred and drinks with cloudy ingredients such as citrus juice, milk or cream should be shaken. Laws are, of course, made to be broken, and while it is true that any drink which can be stirred can also be shaken – and occasionally might even be better for it (should, for example, a Vodkatini be shaken or stirred?) – drinks containing egg white, cream and, to an extent, milk, should always be shaken.

STRAINING

When straining a shaken drink, a hawthorne strainer tends to be used, but when straining a stirred drink it is traditional to use a julep strainer (see page 19). Both designs of strainer allow the liquid to be poured from the shaker/mixing glass while retaining the spent ice.

Whichever design of strainer you are using you should position the strainer over the top of (if using a hawthorne), or inside of (if using a julep strainer) the shaker or mixing glass. Your forefinger be pressing down on the strainer to hold in place with your thumb at the front of the shaker/mixing glass and your remaining three fingers around the back. Lift and pour.

FINE/DOUBLE-STRAINING

Most cocktails that are served 'straight up' – without ice – benefit from an additional strain, over and above the standard hawthorne strain. This 'fine strain' (sometimes also called a 'double strain') removes even the smallest fragments of fruit and fine flecks of ice which can float to the surface and spoil the appearance of a drink. This is not usually necessary when a drink has been stirred (or rolled).

Fine straining is achieved by simply holding a fine sieve, like a tea strainer, between the shaker and the glass. Some misguided souls believe that straining a shaken drink removes air trapped in the liquid, so affecting mouth feel and reducing the thickness of any foamy head. Rest assured, the holes in the strainer are small enough to capture ice crystals but not air, so please always fine strain when shaking.

3. BLENDING

When a cocktail recipe calls for you to 'blend with ice', place all ingredients and ice into a blender and blend until a smooth, even consistency is achieved. Ideally, you should use crushed ice, as this lessens wear on the blender and ensures lumps of ice don't make it through to the served drink.

Place liquid ingredients in the blender first, adding the ice last. If you have a variable speed blender, always start slowly and build up speed. You'll need around a 6oz scoops worth of ice. Add too much and your blended drink will be too thick and resemble a sorbet. Too little ice and your drink will be thin and watery.

4. BUILDING

The term 'build' simply refers to combining the ingredients within the glass in which the cocktail will be served - think Gin and Tonic.

When building a long drink containing a fizzy ingredient, particularly champagne, it pays to pour some of the fizzy ingredients first, then pour the flat ingredients and finally top with the balance of the fizzy ingredient. Pouring the flat ingredients over the foaming fizzy ingredient knocks the foam back. The balance of the sparkling ingredients should be poured last to ensure a foaming head. This method is much quicker than pouring the flat ingredients first and merely 'topping up' with the all the sparkling ingredient in one pour. It also better mixes the ingredients as they are poured into the glass so avoiding the need to stir, which is detrimental to carbonation. Hence this method also produces a fizzier drink.

5. THROWING

Sometimes also referred to as the 'cuban roll' but not to be confused with simply rolling the cocktail shaker over and over (see overleaf), 'throwing' offers more dilution and aeration than simply stirring, but is more gentle than shaking. It is achieved by simply pouring the ingredients from one container to another.

Any drink can be 'thrown' but this method is particularly effective when making drinks with wine based ingredients such as vermouth and sherry as it enhances aeration and releases aromatics. The aim is create tiny air bubbles which give a textural element in a way that stirring and shaking can't. Stirring should not produce bubbles and shaking creates larger bubbles. To experience the benefits of throwing a drink compare stirred and thrown versions of Manhattan and Bamboo cocktails.

To quote Stuart Hudson, a proponent of the art of throwing, "Throwing is incredibly easy - if you can catch a ball you'll be able to throw. It's physically gentle, balletic and elegant, and while shaking causes injuries and is tough on the body, throwing can be kept up as a lifelong skill."

HOW TO THROW

1. Select your two vessels. Shaker tins are easier to use than mixing glasses due to the steel rim producing a cleaner pour. Ideally use two large base shakers rather than a small tin from a shaker set. In Barcelona bartenders predominantly use specially made throwing glasses that have a very precise lip but these are still harder to use than a pair of tins.

2. Assemble your ingredients in one of the vessels with ice. This will be the 'top vessel'. Don't use too much ice or you won't be able to control the top container but you need to 2/3rds fill with ice as the drink will be in contact with it for only half the time.

3. Choose a julep or hawthorne strainer that will nestle inside the top vessel at an angle of about 45° so allowing liquid to be poured back into the vessel over the strainer.

4. Hold the top vessel high above your head in your right-hand.

5. Using your left hand, hold the second 'catching vessel' near the brim between your thumb and middle finger so the vessel can pivot between your fingers. This will allow you to take the catching vessel down almost as far as your knees.

6. Raise the 'catching vessel' up to meet the top vessel and pour from the top vessel into the catching vessel. Throwing is all about letting the liquid fall from high to low, after all, liquid obeys the laws of gravity. Don't start the throw with the vessels at mid-height and try and raise one and lower the other. Start with both cups at the top and let the catching hand drop down. If you try and do it any other way you will spill the liquid.

7. Start pouring slowly and control the speed at which the liquid falls. If you bring your hand down too quickly you will end up chasing the liquid around. Be sure to watch the catching vessel as you lower it. Don't look at the top vessel. Concentrate on the one you're lowering.

8. Holding the catching vessel at a slight angle so the falling liquid hits the inside edge of the tin will help prevent splashing.

9. Increase the distance between the two vessels as you pour while keeping the top vessel aloft and continue watching the catching vessel as it is lowered. You should be at your maximum reach with about a third of the liquid left in the top vessel. This allows the last of the liquid to aerate the drink with the maximum fall. As you get to the last of the liquid it starts to break into droplets. When you see this happening, straighten your catching vessel so the last droplets fall directly into the drink rather than hitting the edge of the vessel. This pulls oxygen down into the drink and opens it.

10. Then pour the partially mixed cocktail back into the first ice-filled container and repeat the process. Four to five throws create the best result. Watch the liquid and you will be able to see the fine bubbles as you pour and you'll get a feel for when it's ready. If you are using large cubes of colder ice you may need six or seven throws in order to achieve the 30 to 35% dilution you are looking for.

6. ROLLING OR TUMBLING

Mixing a cocktail by 'rolling' is pretty self-explanatory. Instead of violently moving the shaker back and forth it is tumbled over and over in a circular motion between the two hands. While the drink is mixed in the shaker it is a very gentle way to mix and chill a drink.

The best-known example of a drink which benefits from being rolled rather than shaken is a Bloody Mary. Rolling maintains the thick mouthfeel of the tomato juice. Conversely, shaking a Bloody Mary destroys the thick texture of the tomato juice so producing a very thin drink.

7. SWIZZLING

To 'swizzle' a drink is simply to stir it using a particular tool and action. This style of drink mixing originated in the Caribbean and originally a twig with a few forked branches was used. Today 'swizzlesticks' are usually made of metal or plastic and have several blades or fingers attached to the base at right angles to the shaft, although some bartending suppliers still sell Caribbean wooden swizzle sticks.

Genuine wooden swizzle sticks come from Quararibea Turbinata trees which are native to the eastern Caribbean and such is the Quararibea Turbinata's repute in this area that it is commonly called the Swizzlestick Tree.

To swizzle, simply immerse the blades of your swizzle stick into the drink. (Swizzled drinks are served with crushed ice.) Hold the shaft between the palms of both hands and rotate the stick rapidly by sliding your hands back and forth against it. If you do not have a bona fide swizzle stick, use a bar spoon in the same manner.

8. LAYERING

Layering isn't strictly mixing. To the contrary, the idea here is to float each ingredient on its predecessor without the ingredients merging at all – think B52.

As the name suggests, layered drinks include layers of different ingredients, often with contrasting colours. This effect is achieved by carefully pouring each ingredient into the glass so that it floats on its predecessor.

The success of this technique is dependent on the density (specific gravity) of the liquids used. As a rule of thumb, the less alcohol and the more sugar an ingredient contains, the heavier it is. The heaviest ingredients should be poured first and the lightest last. Syrups are non-alcoholic and contain a lot of sugar so are usually the heaviest ingredient. Liqueurs, which are high in sugar and lower in alcohol than spirits, are generally the next heaviest ingredient. The exception to this rule is cream and cream liqueurs, which can float.

One brand of a particular liqueur may be heavier or lighter than another. The relative temperatures of ingredients may also affect their ability to float or sink. Hence, a degree of experimentation is inevitable when creating layered drinks.

Layering can be achieved in one of two ways. The first involves pouring liquid down the spiral handle of a bar spoon, keeping the flat, disc-shaped end of the spoon over the surface of the drink. Alternatively you can hold the bowl end of a bar spoon (or a soup spoon) in contact with the side of the glass and over the surface of the drink and pour slowly over it. Specially designed tools are also available that mimic the action of pouring down a flat ended barspoon as these tools also spread and cushion the affect the falling liquid has it hits the surface of the drink.

The term 'float' refers to layering the final ingredient of a cocktail on to its surface.

Additional techniques

ADDITIONAL TECHNIQUES & RECOMMENDATIONS

MUDDLING

Muddling means pummelling fruits, herbs and/or spices with a muddler (a blunt tool similar to a pestle) so as to crush them and release their flavour. You can also use a rolling pin. Just as you would use a pestle and mortar, push down on the muddler with a twisting action.

Only attempt to muddle in the base of a shaker or a suitably sturdy glass. Never attempt to muddle hard, unripe fruits in a glass as the pressure required could break the glass. I've witnessed a bartender slash his hand open on a broken glass while muddling and can't over-emphasize how careful you should be.

MEASURING

Balancing each ingredient within a cocktail is key to making a great drink. Therefore the accuracy with which ingredients are measured is critical to the finished cocktail.

In this guide, we've expressed the measures of each ingredient in 'shots'. Ideally, a shot is 25ml or one US fluid ounce, measured in a standard jigger. (You can also use a clean medicine measure or even a small shot glass.) Whatever your chosen measure, it should have straight sides to enable you to accurately judge fractions of a shot. Look for measures which are graduated in ounces and marked with quarter and half ounces.

The measure 'spoon' refers to a bar spoon, which is slightly larger than a standard teaspoon. Personally, I measure in fluid ounces and count a slightly under-filled flat bar spoon as ⅛ of an ounce.

Some bartenders attempt to measure shots by counting time and estimating the amount of liquid flowing through a bottle's spout. This is known as 'free-pouring' and in unskilled hands can be terribly inaccurate. I strongly recommend the use of a physical measure and a great deal of care.

Fellow Europeans who find 'shots' and fluid ounces decidedly imperial should work to the following rough conversion table (1 US fluid ounce is actually 29.574ml but the below rule-of-thumbs are much simpler to follow):

2 shots = 2oz = 60ml
1¾ shot = 1¾oz = 52.5ml
1½ shots = 1½oz = 45ml
1 shot = 1oz = 30ml
¾ shot = ¾oz = 22.5ml
⅔ shot = ⅔oz = 20ml
½ shot = ½oz = 15ml
⅓ shot = ⅓oz = 10ml
¼ shot = ¼oz = 7.5ml
⅛ shot = ⅛oz = 3.75ml

ICE

A plentiful supply of fresh ice is essential to making good cocktails.

When buying bagged ice, avoid the hollow, tubular kind and thin wafers. Instead, look for large, solid cubes of ice. We recommend a Kold Draft (kold-draft.com) or Hoshizaki (hoshizaki.com) ice machine to produce large (inch/25mm square) solid cubes.

When filling ice cube trays, use bottled or filtered water to avoid the taste of chlorine often apparent in municipal water supplies. Your ice should be dry, almost sticky to the touch. Avoid 'wet' ice that has started to thaw.

Whenever serving a drink over ice, always fill the glass with ice, rather than just adding a few cubes. This not only makes the drink much colder, but the ice lasts longer and so does not dilute into the drink.

Never use ice in a cocktail shaker twice, even if it's to mix the same drink as before. You should always discard ice after straining the drink and use fresh ice to fill the glass if so required. Pouring shaken ice straight into the glass with the liquid will result in an overly diluted drink which will not be as cold as one where the drink is strained over fresh ice.

Unless otherwise stated, all references to ice in this book mean cubed ice. If crushed ice is required for a particular recipe, the recipe will state 'crushed ice'. This is available

commercially. Alternatively, you can crush cubed ice in an ice-crusher or simply bash a Lewis bag or tea towel of cubed ice with a rolling pin.

If a glass is broken near your ice stocks, melt the ice with warm water, clean the container and re-stock with fresh ice. If this occurs in a busy bar and you are not immediately able to clean the ice chest, mark it as being contaminated with a liberal coating of red grenadine syrup and draw ice from another station.

FLAME

The terms 'ignite', 'flame' or 'flambé' mean that a drink should be set alight. Please exercise extreme care when setting fire to drinks. Be particularly careful not to knock over a lit drink and never attempt to carry a drink which is still alight. Before drinking, cover the glass so as to suffocate the flame and be aware that the rim of the glass may be hot.

EGGS IN COCKTAILS

Egg white adds viscosity and mouthfeel to cocktails and drinks such as sours only taste their best when made with fresh eggs. However, raw eggs can be hazardous to health so you may decide it is safer to use commercially produced pasteurised egg white, particularly if you are infirm or pregnant (but then you probably shouldn't be drinking cocktails anyway).

Unfortunately egg white in cocktails gives off an aroma not unlike dog breath or a damp dog's coat. This should be masked with a few drops of bitters dropped onto the drink's foamy head, expressing citrus zest oils (twist) over the drink or by dusting with chocolate, nutmeg or cinnamon.

Too much egg white in a cocktail is detrimental and half the yolk of a small egg is plenty. I tend to crack eggs and separate their white into a small plastic squeeze bottle and then use this to squeeze the desired amount of egg white into each cocktail. It pays to shake the bottle before use to slightly loosen the egg whites. Refrigerate the bottle and use within 48 hours or preferably sooner.

I'm sure I've suffered more upset stomachs from drinking too much alcohol than I have as a result of bad eggs. That said, it's worth taking steps to reduce the risk of salmonella poisoning and therefore please adhere to the following dos and don'ts.

1. Use small or medium eggs rather than large sized eggs. Don't worry about the colour of the shell as this isn't an indication of quality or the bird's feed, it's dictated by the breed of bird.

2. If in the UK only use eggs marked with the Lion Quality stamp. These have been laid by hens vaccinated against salmonella.

3. Preferably use organic eggs as they are laid by hens who have been reared in the most humane way possible. Everything from their housing, freedom of movement and food is strictly governed. After organic, free-range is the next best environment for a hen to be raised and then barn eggs. Lastly caged eggs rank as the most inhuman way to farm hens.

4. Store your eggs in a sealed box in the refrigerator. Storing in a box prevents smells permeating through the shells and flavouring the egg. Conversely you may want to place citrus peels, spices, truffles or teas in the box to flavour your eggs.

5. Use eggs well before their use-by-date.

6. Always wash the shell of an egg under running hot water prior to cracking and using.

7. Test the freshness of an egg by placing in water. A fresh egg will sink but a stale one will float.

Don't consume raw eggs if:

1. You are uncertain about their freshness.

2. There is a crack or flaw in the shell.

3. They don't wobble when rolled across a flat surface.

4. The egg white is watery instead of gel-like.

5. The egg yolk is not convex and firm.

6. The egg yolk bursts easily.

7. They smell foul.

8. Don't consume raw eggs at all if you are pregnant or have a weak immune system or other health issues.

Advanced Bartending

ADVANCED COCKTAIL SHAKING TIPS, MYTHS & LESSONS

There's more to shaking a cocktail than you might think. I've been mixing up cocktails for over 25 years and changed little until 2009 when Dave Arnold, then of New York's French Culinary Institute, and Eben Klemm, a much respected bartending friend of his, presented The Science of Shaking at that year's Tales of the Cocktail. Dave expands on this and his subsequent research in his excellent book 'Liquid Intelligence', and much of the following is drawn from his work.

1. USE STAINLESS STEEL RATHER THAN GLASS

Stainless steel heats up and cools down quickly, and in doing so uses minimal energy, so having little effect on the temperature of the finished cocktail. In contrast, heavy Boston glasses have more thermal mass, so absorb more energy from the drink being shaken. Hence, while Boston glass and tin shakers are good for demonstrating how to mix cocktails I prefer to use a 'tin and tin' two-piece shaker. (Three piece cobbler shakers are slower to use and in my view are inferior tools for professional use.)

2. AVOID MAKING A SPLASH

I've noticed that most bartenders assemble their cocktail in the smaller tin of a two-piece shaker and then also scoop their ice into this smaller tin. This risks the drink splashing the scoop so contaminating the ice when the scoop is returned to the ice-chest. It also limits the amount of ice going into the shaker compared to scooping the ice into the larger tin.

Ideally combine the ingredients in the smaller tin and then add ice to the larger tin. If you use one quick motion you can bring the tin filled with ice down on the smaller tin without losing any ice or spilling your drink. However, if you prefer to play safe then pour the contents of the small tin into the large ice-filled tin before sealing.

3. IT DOESN'T MATTER HOW YOU SHAKE

Dave Arnold's experiments have proven that no matter how you shake and pretty much whatever kind of ice you use, as long as you shake vigorously for 12 seconds, you'll produce a drink between -5°C/23°F and -8°C/18°F (differences mostly dependent on construction of shaker, its temperature and alcohol strength of cocktail) with very much the same dilution. Dance around as much as you like but different shaking techniques make no difference to the end temperature or dilution. And that includes the Japanese hard shake.

4. SHAKING FOR LONGER WON'T MAKE IT COLDER OR MORE DILUTE

The effect of a large amount of ice being forced back and forth through a relatively small amount of liquid in a cocktail shaker is such an efficient way of cooling that after around 12 seconds thermal equilibrium is reached, between -5°C/23°F and -8°C/18°F (more alcoholic drinks can be colder due to alcohol freezing at a lower temperature than water). Continuing to shake after this point is reached will make very little difference to the temperature or dilution of the drink.

5. TEMPERATURE OF ICE

Ice taken straight from a freezer is usually around -18°C/-4°F depending on the freezer. The ice used in most bars is comparatively warm being little under freezing point, 0°C/32°F. Some of the chilling action from the freezer ice will come from its low temperature as heat is conducted from the liquid to the ice, but most of the chilling affect – as much as eight times as more – is due to heat energy provided by the liquid being used to melt the ice (known as fusion).

So ice straight from a freezer will chill a drink marginally quicker than ice from an ice-machine, but that difference is small and hardly matters as when shaking as thermal equilibrium is quickly reached (as explained above). Consequently ice straight from the freezer has little benefit on temperature when used in a shaker compared to ice from a machine. However, the two different types of ice have dramatically different effects on dilution.

6. WET ICE & DILUTION

Ice taken straight from a freezer has a dry surface, and if your freezer is cold enough, when touched will stick to your finger as the ice freezes the moisture on your skin. Conversely, even while still sat inside an ice machine the ice used in most bars is wet due to the surfaces of the ice melting – let alone once it has sat in an ice-chest for 20 minutes having been carried from the machine in a bucket.

It's obvious that the comparatively dry freezer ice will produce less dilution in a shaken cocktail than the wet ice from a machine. That thin layer of water on each surface of the ice cube immediately adds to the volume of liquid in the shaker, so increasing the ratio of liquid to ice and giving the ice more liquid to chill. Hence the ice melts quicker as it chills the increased volume of liquid producing more liquid. And so it goes on.

So it is beneficial to use ice straight from a freezer and I like to shovel ice from my machine into thick bags which I put in the chest freezer next to the machine. I fill my ice-chest with ice from the freezer, replenishing the freezer from the machine as I go.

Even if you are stuck with using wet melting ice then you can dry it. Using salad spinner seems a little over zealous. Instead use a two-piece shaker and pour your ingredients into the small tin (déjà vu from 2 above). Put the ice in the large tin and place a strainer over the ice-filled large tin, upend, agitate and violently lower and raise the strainer covered upended tin to allow most of the water on the ice to drain away. Then introduce the ice to the other ingredients and shake.

7. SIZE OF ICE CUBE

So long as your ice is dry (see above) then the size of ice cube has little effect on the level of dilution – be that tubular ice, chunky cubes from a Hoshizaki or Kold-Draft machine, or even boulders hacked from block ice. Crushed ice is another matter…

8. NEVER SHAKE WITH CRUSHED ICE

Shaking with crushed ice will produce dramatically higher levels of dilution than shaking with cubed ice. And the amount of that dilution is hard to predict due to crushed ice having such a large surface area and accelerated melt speed.

9. CONTROLLED ADDITIONAL DILUTION

A drink shaken with dry surface ice (see above) will gain around 20% dilution from the ice during shaking but some drinks, such as the Daiquiri, benefit from higher levels of dilution. Some bartenders achieve this by shaking such cocktails with a combination of cubes and crushed ice. Levels of dilution produced by this method tend to be inconsistent. It is much better to use ice straight from a freezer and add a measured amount of chilled water as an additional ingredient. Hence, in my recipes it is common to see "½ shot of chilled water (omit if wet ice)" as the last ingredient.

10. TEXTURE OF A SHAKEN DRINK

Shaking aerates a cocktail – evident by the tiny air bubbles visible in the drink and the foam that forms on the surface. These air bubbles add a discernible texture not produced by stirring. Sadly these air bubbles dissipate quickly and with them this texture is lost. Hence, shaken drinks should be consumed soon after they have been strained into the glass.

Some ingredients produce and retain aeration, and with it texture, better than others. Try to whip plain water into a foam, or come to that any spirit, and what little aeration is produced immediately dissipates. That's because water molecules are electrically attracted to each other so won't spread out to form bubbles unless something is added that weakens their attraction to each other.

Conversely, whipping or shaking pineapple juice always produces thick lasting foam. Lime and lemon juice also works well but be warned, while straining to remove pulp does not adversely affect citrus fruits' ability to hold aeration, clarification will kill it due to the plants pectin and other polysaccharides being removed.

Milk and cream are also good texturisers, as is milk whey which has the same foaming effect without tasting of milk or curdling when used in acidic drinks. However, due to its high protein content (around 10%) egg white is the king of the cocktail foam.

The size of ice cube you use will have a dramatic effect on the texture of the finished shaken drink – the bigger the cube the better the texture. Shaking with one huge chunk of ice produces the best texture but does not yield enough dilution, so ideally hit a happy medium (as recommended by Dave Arnold) by shaking with one large cube and several smaller cubes. Also consider adding a little egg white to all your shaken drinks.

11. DRY SHAKE & THE REVERSE DRY SHAKE

When making drinks containing cream and eggs it is common practice among many bartenders to first shake the mixture without ice, before shaking the drink a second time with ice. This practice is known as 'dry shaking' and the theory is that first shaking without ice, and so at a higher temperature, better allows the drink to emulsify producing more aeration and a thicker foam on top of the finished cocktail.

Some bartenders also place a spring from a hawthorne strainer in the shaker during the first 'dry shake' as this acts as a whisk inside the shaker when the drink is shaken.

Dry shaking does indeed produce more foam than conventional shaking with ice. But not as much as 'reverse dry shaking' does. Aristotelis Papadopoulos (Telis to his friends) from Thessaloniki in Greece lays claim to discovering the benefits of this technique. Combine all your ingredients in the shaker and shake conventionally with ice. Then open your shaker and strain liquid back into the smaller tin (supposing you've followed my advice and use a two-piece shaker). Discard ice left in large tin. Reseal shaker and shake again without ice. Then pour your drink into the glass through a fine strainer to catch any curdled egg and the chalaza (the tissue that connects the yolk to the shell's membrane).

12. THE OPENING

Banging a two-piece shaker on the bar to open is decidedly amateurish and when witnessed is usually the prelude to a bad drink. Similarly hitting the shaker with your elbow to break the seal may have once been an accepted flair move but now seems somewhat passé. Even tapping with the palm of your hand is looking slow and dated compared to breaking the seal by pushing the smaller tin diagonally with your thumb. But however you open your shaker, be sure you can confidently open your shaker.

INFUSION AND MACERATION

Alcohol's ability to draw out flavoursome substances from herbs and spices by infusion and then preserve those flavours has been used since the Middle Ages – originally by monks to produce potions with perceived health benefits – water of life. Today infusion/maceration is used to flavour spirits.

Infusion simply involves immersing herbs, spices, nuts or fruit in alcohol and leaving to soak until the desired flavours have leached out. The same applies to macerating, but as the name implies, in this case the botanicals being infused are first broken up/sliced/diced to expose a larger surface area, so allowing the alcohol to leach flavour from more of the botanical's cells.

Motion, heat and pressure can be used to increase the rate of extraction. Motion can be as simple as shaking a bottle in which something is being infused every few hours, or in commercial applications infusion often takes place in revolving tanks. Heating, (leaving in a warm place), helps break open the botanical's cells, so allowing the alcohol to more easily extract flavour while pressure forces the alcohol into the botanical being infused.

Beware of the speed and degree of extraction. A common mistake is to allow over extraction by adding too much of the flavouring substance or leaving it in the alcohol for too long. Tea, for example, infuses very quickly and starts releasing unwanted bitter tannins after just five minutes while vanilla pods can be left for days and hard substances such as nuts left for weeks.

FOAMS

Some cocktails benefit from being served with a foam float, the aroma and flavour of which usually contrasts with that of the drink beneath, so adding complexity. Foams are usually made in and dispensed from cream whipping siphons.

Gelatin, egg white (or another form of protein such as Hy-foamer) is added to the flavoured mixture so when the siphon is charged with nitrous oxide this reacts with the protein to produce a foam. Popular base ingredients include cold tea, fruit juice and champagne, but the foam can be made using pretty much any liquid provided it is not oily and the alcohol content is below 20%, and ideally under 10% alc./vol.. Both the ingredients and the charged siphon should be stored in a refrigerator as the colder the foam, the thicker it will be when discharged and the longer it will last on the drink.

When making your foam mixture allow one egg white per 200ml of liquid or one sheet of gelatin leaf per 500ml. Some advocate adding a small amount of gelatin leaf even if using egg as it produces a finer, longer lasting foam. Sugar syrup (possibly flavoured) or another sweetener such as honey should be used in your foam recipe as this amplifies the flavour of the foam. If using fruit juice then strain out any pulp with a fine strainer or cheesecloth.

Only fill your siphon to two-thirds capacity to ensure room for the gas to react then screw closed to seal. Charge with one nitrous oxide cartridge for a 500ml siphon and two cartridges if a litre capacity. Store in the refrigerator and leave for the nitrous oxide to react with the protein for at least 30 minutes before dispensing.

Nitrous oxide (N2O), the key to these foams, is commonly known as laughing gas and is a colourless non-flammable gas with a pleasant, slightly sweet smell. Its nickname refers to the stimulating effects of inhaling it, which include spontaneous laughter, slight hallucinations and an analgesic effect. It is used in motorsport to boost power (nitrous oxide kit), and in surgery and dentistry as an analgesic. A 50/50 mixture of nitrous oxide and oxygen

('gas and air') is commonly used during childbirth. Nitrous oxide is a powerful greenhouse gas and you add to its global warming effect when opening a bag of potato chips as the gas is used to displace staleness-inducing oxygen in snack food packaging.

WARNING

Inhaling nitrous oxide directly from a whipped cream charger or tank poses very serious health risks. These include potential lung collapse due to the high pressure and frostbite since the gas is very cold when released. I'm not suggesting you try this, but most recreational nitrous oxide users discharge the gas into a balloon before inhaling. Nitrous oxide can also cause mild nausea or dizziness and is unsafe to inhale while standing as you are likely to fall. I should also add that the possession of and recreational use of nitrous oxide is a criminal offence in much of the US and other areas of the world.

SMOKES & SMOKERS

Originally used as a preservative, chefs commonly use smoke to flavour food and a chef's smoker can also be used to flavour cocktails.

Resembling a battery-powered bong, chef's smokers use an electric fan to draw air through a fire chamber with a gauze base and expel the smoke created through a plastic tube which can be bubbled through your cocktail or dispensed into a jar/shaker/mixing glass containing the cocktail.

A large range of fine wood shavings cut for use in smokers are available with maple, apple and hickory wood most popular. Dried spices, leaf teas and even essential oil soaked cotton wool can also be burnt.

Be warned, the flavour of smoke is very pervasive and over exposure can ruin a good drink in the same manner as over use of bitters. Turn on the motor before attempting to light as the fan will help draw the flame into the chamber and aid ignition. Once lit chef's smokers produce a lot of smoke so have your drink ready to be smoked, ensure

adequate ventilation of the room and beware of smoke alarms. It's essential to clean smokers regularly to prevent the resins generated during burning clogging up the device and also impairing the flavours emitted by the smoke.

FAT-WASHING

Made famous by the Benton's Old Fashioned created by Don Lee at PDT in New York City, which uses bourbon flavoured smoky bacon fat, fat-washing is a method of flavouring any spirit with a variety of fatty foods including meats, fish, cheeses and butter.

Grill/melt the food with heat, drain off the fat emitted and pour into a bottle of spirit via a fine strainer to remove unwanted particulates. Seal the bottle, shake and place in a refrigerator to solidify the fat, shaking occasionally. Leave for a week to allow the fat's flavour to infuse into the spirit.

Lastly clarify by straining the cold liquid first through a fine strainer and then a cheesecloth. The spirit will have taken on the flavour of the fat and also acquired a silky mouthfeel.

TOASTING AND CARAMELISATION

Natural sugars in foods can be caramelised by heating with a chef's blow-torch (also called a crème brûlée burner due to the best known dish which benefits from caramelisation). Caramelisation changes the flavour of foods such as fruit and nuts which can be used as a garnish or muddled into the drink.

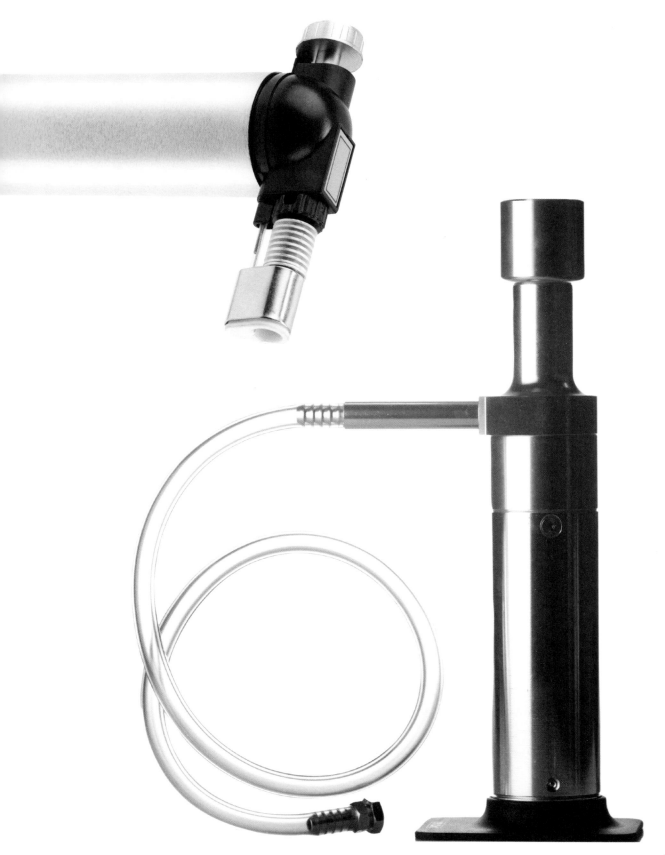

Garnishing

GARNISHING

Garnishes are used to decorate cocktails and are often anchored to the rim of the glass. Strictly speaking, garnishes should be edible and can comprise anything from banana chunks, strawberries or redcurrants to coffee beans, confectionery, basil leaves and slices of fresh ginger. The correct garnish will often enhance the aroma and flavour, as well as the look, of a drink.

When deciding on what to garnish your cocktail with, use the ingredients within the drink as inspiration. For example, if a drink is made using lime juice, then a lime wedge is a safe option.

Fruit selected for high juice yields may not be ideal for garnishes. For example, larger limes juice well but smaller limes make more attractive garnishes. Whatever fruit you use, it should be unblemished and washed prior to use. Cut citrus fruits have a maximum shelf life of 24 hours when refrigerated.

ZEST TWIST

This term refers to affecting the aroma and so perceived flavour of a drink by releasing the aromatic oils from a strip of citrus zest – lemon, lime, orange or grapefruit.

Using a knife or peeler, cut a ½inch (12mm) wide length of zest from an un-waxed, cleaned fruit so as to leave just a little of the white pith. Hold it over the top of the cocktail with the thumb and forefinger of each hand, coloured side down. Turn one end clockwise and the other anti-clockwise so as to twist the peel and force some of its oils over the surface of the drink.

Some then like to wipe the zest around the rim of the glass to deposit any flavoursome oils left on the surface of the peel, while others maintain this merely makes the edge of the glass taste bitter. You also have the option to discard the spent zest, drop it onto the surface of the drink or mount it on the glass rim.

Citrus twists can also be thin, string-like lengths of zest cut with a channel (canella) knife and wrapped around a stirring rod to make a spring-like garnish, which is then slid off the stirrer and into the drink. Such thinly cut string-like twists can also be tied into a knot.

Whatever your twist, it should be cut from thoroughly cleaned citrus fruit without blemishes of spots on its skin. Ideally, zests should be cut fresh for each drink but if this is not possible then kept pre-cut refrigerated. Store in a sealed plastic box with some moist paper towel, but even then, once cut their shelf life is little more than one day.

FLAMED ZEST TWIST

A flamed zest twist is a dramatic variation on the usual citrus zest twist and involves burning the aromatic oils emitted from citrus fruit zest as they are expressed over the surface of a drink. Lemons and limes are sometimes treated in this way but oranges are most popular and give the best results. Firm, thick-skinned navel oranges are best.

You will need to cut a large coin-shaped disc or as wide a strip of zest as you can – wider than you would for a standard twist. Hold the cut zest, peel side down, between the thumb and forefinger about four inches above the drink. In your other hand, ignite a match or lighter, then pinch the peel by its edges so that its oils squirt through the flame towards the surface of the drink - there should be a flash as the oils ignite.

APPLE SLICE

An apple slice garnish is quick, easy and looks great. Simply slice an apple finely using a mandolin and float the resulting disc on the surface of your drink. Apple slices look better and are more buoyant when dehydrated (see overleaf). Alternatively cut a thicker slice and mount either the whole slice or a fraction of the slice on the glass rim by means of diagonal cut in the slice. Apple slices are best cut to order as the cut fruit turns brown very quickly. You can prevent this oxidation by coating the cut sides with citrus juice.

APPLE WEDGE

Apple wedges can easily be secured to the rim of a glass – cut a wedge that is a maximum ¾in thick and slice diagonally to centre to allow placement on glass rim. Alternatively, just drop the garnish into the drink – this is particularly effective in tall drinks. The fruit should be firm and fresh, not brown or bruised, and the skin should be left on.

APPLE CHEVRON

Using a quarter of an apple, cut wafer-thin slices down into the fruit, but not all the way through – stop about a centimetre from the end of the apple wedge. Cut 5 or 6 slices into the fruit and then ease out these slices into a fan. Leave the skin of the apple on.

CARAMELISED AND DEHYDRATED APPLE DISCS

These are more time-consuming but worth the effort. Slice an apple finely using a mandolin. Then either coat the slices in sugar syrup or blanch them by dipping them into a simmering pan containing three parts granulated sugar and two parts water. Whichever option you choose, drain off the excess liquid and lay the slices on a baking tray lined with greaseproof paper. Place in a dehydrator or in an oven set to 85ºC (185ºF) and bake for about three hours, until the discs are crisp and golden. You can store these in an air-tight container in the refrigerator for up to a fortnight.

APRICOT SLICE

Use either whole dried apricots or a slice of apricot and cut a slit into centre of fruit (rather than the skin side) to allow placement on the glass rim.

BANANA SLICE

Fruit should not be either green, bruised or overripe. Some like to remove the skin, whereas others prefer to leave on for both appearance and ease of use. Cut a slit into centre of fruit to allow placement on glass rim.

BERRY SKEWERS

Berries such as blackberries, raspberries, strawberries and blueberries make an attractive and tasty garnish. Use fruit that is ripe but firm and not mushy. Berries can either be floated on the top of a drink or skewered (usually in threes for health, wealth and happiness) kebab-style on a cocktail stick and placed across the top of the glass.

CELERY STICKS

Celery sticks may be placed in drinks as stirring rods, as is typical in a Bloody Mary. Choose firm sticks without bruises and cut to a length several inches longer than your glass, so when placed inside it protrudes over the rim. Angled cuts tend to be more attractive than simply chopping at 90° to the stem. Leave a little of the bushy leaves on, if possible.

CHERRIES

Fresh cherries make a tasty and attractive garnish but luxurious maraschino cherries such as Luxardo are more desirable. If using fresh fruit, use cherries which are ripe but firm and not mushy. It is common to cut a slit in cherries to allow them to be secured to the glass rim or spear with cocktail sticks/picks.

CHOCOLATE DUST

The instruction 'dust with chocolate' refers to a fine coating of cocoa powder on the surface of a drink – à la cappuccinos. The chocolate layer needs to remain very fine so as not to sink into the drink. Use cocoa powder, rather than grated chocolate and consider applying with a chocolate duster or through a fine sieve.

CHOCOLATE RIM

Wipe a cut orange slice around the outside rim of glass to leave a line of juice with which to stick powder to glass (rather than lime juice when using salt). Also see 'salt rim' on page 66.

CINNAMON DUST

The instruction 'dust with cinnamon' refers to a fine coating of the spice on the surface of a drink. If using powdered cinnamon, use sparingly so the layer does not become too thick and so sink into drink. Better to use a whole cinnamon stick and a fine grater to ensure the dusting is very light.

CINNAMON & SUGAR RIM

Wipe a thin strip of sugar syrup around the outside rim of your glass and then roll this in a saucer containing a mixture of cinnamon powder and caster sugar. Also see 'salt rim' on page 66.

CINNAMON STICKS

These are often placed whole into hot drinks and toddies. There are several lengths of dried cinnamon stick available, so ensure that cinnamon is longer than the glass you are serving in.

CHILLI

A small red eye chilli, with a diagonal slice to allow it to sit firmly on the rim of the glass, looks good, smells good but is probably best not consumed – each to their own. Take the usual precautions when handling chillies and similarly warn drinkers.

COFFEE BEANS

Simply float three coffee beans on the surface of the drink. Why three? The number signifies health, wealth and happiness and is said to bestow good luck on the drinker.

CUCUMBER SLICE

Use fresh, moist, crisp cucumber as either a slice or stick. Slices can be cut thin enough to float on the surface of the drink, or, cut thicker, slit and secured to the glass rim.

CUCUMBER STICK

To make a stick, cut a length of cucumber to suit the glass (it should either sit an inch above the rim of the glass or fit exactly) then cut lengthways into $\frac{1}{8}$ segments leaving skin on. These can be used as a stirrer, much like a celery stick.

FLAMING ZEST BOAT

Not only does this potentially dangerous garnish add to the theatrical style of Tiki drinks, but people's inner child find floating fire boats strangely alluring. Make a zest boat by chopping a lime or lemon lengthwise into four and scraping away the flesh from one wedge. Float your boat on top of the drink and carefully pour in its cargo of high-strength spirit -usually over-proof rum (for example Pusser's Navy rum). Lastly, and very carefully, ignite the rum. Fire boats constitute a fire hazard. Please be careful and:

1. Only use a fraction of a shot of rum or it will burn for ages.
2. Be aware that the flame may be blue and so almost invisible.
3. Don't move the glass, let alone attempt to drink from it, until the flame is out.
4. Don't blame us if your bar/home/life goes up in smoke.

FLOWERS & PETALS

Flowers and petals set afloat on a drink make for an attractive garnish. Ensure the flowers used are edible and have not been sprayed. Suitable varieties include Dendrobium Orchids, Pansies, certain Rose varieties, Nasturtiums, Marigolds and Violets.

FRUIT STICK

A fruit stick consists of one or more pineapple cubes and a maraschino cherry skewered kebab-style on a cocktail stick or specially designed plastic or wooden pick. Popularly used to garnish Tiki-style drinks, the creation of the fruit stick is credited to Victor Jules Bergeron (A.K.A. Trader Vic) in the early 1930s.

Cut pineapple into quarters from top to bottom and remove woody core. Further cut into ½ inch or 1 centimetre cubes. Do not use overripe or mushy fruit. Cut pineapple kept refrigerated (in a sealed box with a moist paper towel) will stay fresh for up to a day but it is of course preferable to cut to order.

GRAPES

Grapes can be a simple and effective garnish. Either drop them into the drink or push three onto a cocktail stick and balance across the rim of the glass.

GRATED CHOCOLATE

To sprinkle chocolate on the surface of a drink you can either shave chocolate using a vegetable peeler or dust with powder using a chocolate shaker with a fine mesh. Alternatively, crumble a Cadbury's Flake bar, in which case ensure fragments are small enough to prevent them sinking into drink.

HORSE'S NECK PEEL

This is usually used to garnish the drink of the same name and is basically a long strip of peel cut in a continuous spiral and placed so as to overhang the rim of the glass. Lemon is most commonly used but a Horse's Neck can also be made from oranges and limes.

To achieve this hold a lemon lying horizontally in your hand with one end facing you. Use a canelle knife to cut into the far end of the fruit and pull towards you ¼inch. Then turn the cut 90 degrees and start cutting around the lemon so that a ½inch wide strip is left between the channels you cut. The strip left spiralling around the lemon that will form your Horse's Neck. Using a small knife, carefully cut this strip from the lemon leaving as much of the white pith behind. This is placed in the glass spiralling up from the bottom to the top with the 'head' hooked over the rim of the glass. Place the ice inside the spiral before pouring your drink.

KIWI SLICE

Kiwi fruit slices prettily. Clean the fruit, peel and slice using a slit in the side to secure to the rim of the glass.

LEMON SLICE

Sometimes referred to as a 'lemon wheel' this is one of the truly classic garnishes. Wash fruit thoroughly and preferably use un-waxed lemons with uniform yellow skin (without green or brown discolouration).

Cut ⅜ inch thick slices across the width of the fruit discarding both ends (poles). Slice to centre for placement on glass rim. Preferably cut as required or store cut fruit for a maximum of six hours.

LEMON WEDGE

Wedges of lemons are often squeezed into drinks or fixed to the side of the glass as a garnish. A lemon wedge is an eighth segment of the fruit. Wash fruit thoroughly and preferably use un-waxed lemons with uniform yellow skin (without green or brown discolouration). Cut the 'knobs' from either pole of the fruit, slice the fruit in half lengthwise, then cut each half into four equal wedges lengthwise. Cut a slit into the pointed flesh of each wedge to enable placement on glass rim. Preferably cut as required or store cut fruit for a maximum of six hours.

LIME SLICE

Sometimes referred to as a 'lime wheel'. Wash fruit thoroughly and preferably use un-waxed limes with uniform green skin (without yellow or brown discolouration). Cut ⅜ inch thick slices across the width of the fruit discarding both ends (poles). Slice to centre for placement on glass rim. Preferably cut as required or store cut fruit for a maximum of six hours.

LIME WEDGE

Fix lime wedge on side of glass or squeeze and drop into drink. A wedge is a sixth, or with large limes, an eighth segment of the fruit. The lime should have green skin without yellow or brown discolouration. Cut the 'knobs' from the top and bottom poles of the fruit, slice the fruit in half lengthwise, then cut each half into three (or for eighths, four) equal wedges lengthwise.

There are numerous ways to cut a slit into the fruit to fix onto glass but the most popular is by cutting into the pointed flesh at an angle. Lime wedges should be used within six hours of being cut and preferably cut as required.

MANGO

Fresh mango is not generally used as a garnish. However, you can cut the flesh into cubes and skewer them on a cocktail stick or fix a long thin wedge on the glass rim. Alternatively garnish mango cocktails with slices of dried mango on a stick.

MARASCHINO CHERRIES

Maraschino cherries were originally fresh cherries marinated in maraschino liqueur and such cherries are still made and available from producers such as Luxardo. However, nowadays the term often refers to preserved, sweetened cherries dyed bright red with food colouring and usually almond-flavoured.

Blue and yellow dyed maraschino cherries are also available and typically the green ones are peppermint-flavoured (think green crème de menthe) while the blue ones are orange-flavoured (think blue curaçao). That said, in the US, it would appear they all have the same almond-maraschino flavour regardless of the colour. Shame.

Stemmed maraschino cherries, as the name suggests, retain their stems to make a more attractive garnish (those with dexterous tongues can amaze their friends by tying said stems in a knot while in their mouths).

Maraschino cherries should be refrigerated and left in their own syrup/liqueur which should be saved as it is often used in recipes such as a Sweet Manhattan. Drop cherry into drink or skewer on a stick.

MINT LEAF / SPRIG

A simple leaf or mint sprig atop a cocktail adds colour and a wonderful fresh fragrance.

Mint is a perennial herb which grows in most temperate parts of the world. The varieties which non-botanists call 'mint' belong to the genus mentha. Mentha species include apple mint, curly mint, pennyroyal, peppermint, pineapple mint, spearmint and water or bog mint.

The various different species of mint are equally diverse in their appearance and flavour. No matter what the variety, mint always has a square stem and grows symmetrically with leaves arranged in opposite pairs from the stem.

Spearmint, or garden mint, is the most common kind and you may well find it growing in your garden. Peppermint is the second most common and its leaves are valued for their pungent oil which is used to flavour confectionery, desserts and liqueurs such as crème de menthe.

The main visible difference between peppermint and spearmint is in the leaves. Spearmint leaves have a crinkly surface and seem to grow straight out of the plant's main stem, while peppermint leaves have a smoother surface and individual stems. Which type of mint you choose to use in drinks is largely a matter of personal taste: some particularly seeking out mentha nemorosa for Mojitos.

Growing your own mint, be it spearmint, peppermint or otherwise is easy – but be sure to keep it in a container or it will overrun your garden. Either buy a plant or place a sprig in a glass of water. When it roots, pot it in a large, shallow tub with drainage holes. Place bricks under the tub to prevent the roots from growing through the holes. Mint likes to grow in moist soil so keep well-watered.

Treat cut mint stems like fresh flowers and cut the tip of the stems off to ensure the stems are able to take up water. Then soak the mint in water at 10 to 15°C (50 to 60°F) for 10 minutes to clean and revitalise. Remove from the water.

To prepare mint for bar use pick off all but the top 6 leaves from each stem so leaving a mint sprig with a long bare stem. Trim the sprig stems to your desired uniform length and place in a jar of water as you would fresh flowers.

Then either place on your bar top or for prolonged storage place the jar of sprigs in a plastic bag, seal and place standing in a refrigerator.

The leaves should be stored in a sealed plastic box between layers of moist paper towel and stored in the refrigerator.

When using mint leaves to garnish a drink, boost the olfactory effect by smacking the mint lightly between your hands before you drop onto the surface of the drink or drape over the edge of the rim.

When selecting a mint sprig for garnish, hit the sprig against your glass to release its aroma, plant into the drink and consider dusting with the sprig with icing sugar.

NUTMEG DUST

The instruction 'dust with nutmeg' refers to a fine coating of the spice on the surface of a drink. It is preferable to grate fresh nutmeg as the powdered kind lacks flavour. Use a very fine grater and ensure that no one area becomes too heavily covered and so sinks into the drink.

OLIVES

The 'Oliver' from the 'Oliver Twist' duo classically graces a Dry Martini. It is essential to wash olives thoroughly to prevent oil from spoiling the appearance of a drink. Only remove sufficient olives required for a particular session from the jar. Olives should be refrigerated and left in the oil or brine in which they were packaged. This brine may be used in a Dirty Martini.

ONIONS

Onions should be stored and left in the oil or brine in which they were packaged and only removed from the jar when required. Small white cocktail onions are most notably used to garnish a Gibson Martini.

ORANGE SLICE

Orange slices (or wheels) can be used whole in the drink or speared with cocktail sticks and cherries to make sails. It's also common to cut the slices in half. Select (preferably un-waxed) fruit without brown discolouration and wash thoroughly. Cut ⅜ inch thick slices and store for a maximum of six hours or better, cut as required.

PAPER PARASOL (UMBRELLA)

A cocktail parasol is a miniature paper umbrella with cardboard ribs and a toothpick stem. It tends to be used to garnish rum-based or Tiki cocktails and is thought to have originally been introduced in the early 1930s by Don the Beachcomber at his Beachcomber restaurant in Hollywood, USA. Their purpose is ostensibly to shield delicate ice cubes from the rays of the sun, but they have attained a kitsch, iconic status.

PASSION FRUIT BOAT

Despite its name, the fruit of love is remarkably ugly and garnishing can be a challenge. The two best garnishes utilising this fruit are 1) to float half a fruit like a boat on the surface of your drink, or 2) if your cocktail uses crushed ice, cut a quarter of passion fruit and place it on the surface of the ice

PEACH SLICE/WEDGE

Peaches should be firm but not mushy and the skin should remain on. Wash and cut wedges a maximum ¾ inch / 2cm thick and slice diagonally to allow placement on glass rim.

PEAR SLICE/WEDGE

Slices of pear can look great on the rim of a Martini glass. However, they oxidise very quickly, and should be rubbed with lemon juice to prevent this.

PHYSALIS

Leave fruit whole with leaves and stalks but wash before use. Carefully open the leaves and gently fold back against the stem and turn the stem and leaves in the opposite direction of the fruit half-a-turn. Then make a diagonal incision across the bottom of the fruit to facilitate placement on glass rim.

PINEAPPLE WEDGE

No Piña Colada or truly tropical cocktail is properly dressed without a wedge of pineapple, preferably with a maraschino cherry spiked into it. Cut the pineapple into ½ inch or 1cm thick rings and cut each ring into wedges as if cutting a cake, avoiding the woody core. A knife slit in the side of the wedge allows you to anchor it to the rim of a glass. The skin adds to the appearance of this garnish so should remain on, but golden is preferable to green. Do not use overripe or mushy fruit and either cut as required or store for maximum of one day.

SAIL

A sail is a whole slice (or wheel) of citrus fruit, usually orange, served on a cocktail stick 'mast' and so known as a 'sail'. Usually the circular slice of fruit is folded around a maraschino cherry and the cocktail stick is skewered through both pieces of fruit.

SALT/SUGAR RIM

Some recipes call for the rim of the glass to be coated with salt, sugar or other ingredients such as desiccated coconut or chocolate: you will need to moisten the rim first before the ingredient will hold. When using salt, wipe a cut wedge of lime around the outside edge of the rim, then roll the outside edge through a saucer of salt. (Use sea salt rather than iodised salt as the flavour is less 'biting'.) For sweet ingredients like sugar and chocolate, either use an orange slice as you would a lime wedge or moisten a sponge or paper towel with a suitable liqueur and run it around the outside edge of the glass.

Whatever you are using to rim the glass should cling to the outside edge only. Remember, garnishes are not a cocktail ingredient but an optional extra to be consumed by choice. They should not contaminate your cocktail. If some of your garnishes become stuck to the inside edge of the glass, remove excess using a fresh fruit wedge or a paper towel.

It is good practice to salt or sugar only half or two-thirds of the rim of a glass. This allows the drinker the option of avoiding the salt or sugar. If you rim glasses some hours prior to use, the lime juice or liqueur will dry, leaving a crust of salt or sugar crystals around the rim. The glasses can then be placed in a refrigerator to chill ready for use. If not kept ice cold, the juice and sugar can run down the glass.

A piece of equipment with the unfortunate name 'rimmer' has three sections: one with a sponge for water or lime juice; one containing sugar; and a third containing salt. Beware, as this encourages dipping the glass onto a moist sponge and then into the garnish, and so contaminating the inside of the glass.

SPICY BEANS

Canadian readers will be well aware of these long, thin pickled beans. They are a popular alternative to celery in those parts as a garnish for 'Caesar' cocktails, a Canadian twist on the Bloody Mary. They originate with Blaze Denoon, who started picking beans in Vancouver in 1995. For more information, see blazesbeans.com.

STAR ANISE

Star anise is the star-shaped pericarp of Illicium verum, a small native evergreen tree of southwest China. This dried spice is frequently floated on the surface of anise-flavoured drinks (so those who dislike this flavour should consider themselves warned).

STAR FRUIT

Star fruit can be floated on the top of the drink and a wafer-thin slice should be cut to ensure the fruit does not sink. Otherwise a thicker slice can also be placed on the rim of the glass. Cut a slice of star fruit about ¼inch or ½cm thick and cut a slit diagonally to centre to allow placement on glass rim.

STRAWBERRY FAN

Cut wafer-thin slices into strawberry and spear with a cocktail stick. Spread the slices apart to create a fan.

Recipes

OUR RECIPES EXPLAINED

New
Indicates a new drink

Cocktail name ——— **ATTA BOY COCKTAIL (NEW)** ⊶

Key
Indicates which drinks can be made
using our 14 key ingredients

Grade ———
Drinks are graded as:
1 star = Disgusting
5+ stars = Outstanding

★ ★ ★ ★ ⯪

Glass: Coupe
Garnish: Orange zest twist
Method: STIR all ingredients with ice and strain into
chilled glass.

Glass ———
For glassware shapes and names see
page 26

2	shots	**Rutte Dry Gin**
1	shot	**Martini Extra Dry vermouth**
⅓	shot	**Pomegranate / grenadine syrup (2:1)**

Ingredients
Recipes are laid out in the order we
recommend adding to glass or shaker

Garnish ———
For full information on garnishes see
page 58

Shot
Ideally a shot equals 30ml or 1oz but
could be a shot glass or bottle cap

Origin: Adapted from a recipe in Harry Craddock's
1930 The Savoy Cocktail Book.
Comment: The orange zest twist makes or breaks this
classic, which when properly balanced lets the gin
shine with the sweet pomegranate notes of the
grenadine obvious but not in your face.

Method ———
See pages 32-41 for tips on how to
shake, stir etc

Comment
Indication of taste

Origin
When, where and who created
recipes

71

1862

★★★★☆

Glass: Martini
Garnish: Orange zest twist (discarded) & Luxardo Maraschino cherry
Method: SHAKE all ingredients with ice and strain back into shaker. DRY SHAKE (without ice) to emulsify and fine strain into chilled glass.

2½ shots   Bacardi Carta Blanca light rum
¾ shot   Romate Fino sherry
¼ shot   Luxardo Maraschino liqueur
¼ shot   Freshly squeezed lemon juice
¼ shot   Sugar syrup (2 sugar to 1 water)
1 dash   Angostura Aromatic Bitters
½ fresh   Egg white

Origin: Adapted from a drink created in 2008 by Scott Ingram at MC Bar, Abode Hotel, Glasgow, Scotland. The name is a reference to the year when Facundo M. Bacardi established his first distillery.
Comment: Fantastically complex with notes of rum, maraschino, sherry and orange.

57 T-BIRD SHOT

★★★★☆

Glass: Shot
Garnish: None
Method: SHAKE all ingredients with ice and fine strain into chilled glass.

½ shot   Ketel One Vodka
½ shot   Grand Marnier Cordon Rouge
½ shot   Disaronno Originale amaretto

Origin: A 57 T-bird, or 1957 Ford Thunderbird to give it its full title, immortalised in the Beach Boys' song 'Fun Fun Fun', was the classic car for any 1950s teenager. Top down, radio up, girl next to you...

THE 75

★★★★½

Glass: Martini
Garnish: Star anise
Method: SHAKE all ingredients with ice and fine strain into chilled glass.

2 shots   Calvados brandy
1 shot   Rutte Dry Gin
¼ shot   Le Fée Parisienne absinthe
¼ shot   Pomegranate / grenadine syrup (2:1)
½ shot   Chilled water (omit if wet ice)

Origin: Like the French 75, this was named after the celebrated 75, a French 75mm field gun developed during the 1890s and used by the French army during the First World War and beyond. The gun was unusually lethal due to its fast rate of fire.
Comment: Hardened palates will appreciate this fantastically dry, aromatic and complex cocktail.

8TH DAY (MOCKTAIL)

★★★½☆

Glass: Collins
Garnish: Lime wedge & ginger slice
Method: SHAKE all ingredients with ice and fine strain into ice-filled glass.

2½ shots   Cold jasmine tea
¾ shot   Freshly squeezed lime juice
¼ shot   Ginger sugar syrup
Top with   Lemonade/Sprite/7-Up

Origin: Discovered in 2009 at Cloud 23, Manchester, England.
Comment: Jasmine, lime, ginger and lemon – refreshing and complex.

A.B.C. COCKTAIL

★★★★½

Glass: Martini (small)
Garnish: Lemon zest twist & Luxardo Maraschino cherry
Method: TEAR mint and place in shaker. Add other ingredients, SHAKE with ice and fine strain into chilled glass.

7 fresh   Mint leaves
1 shot   Tawny port
1 shot   Martell VSOP Médaillon cognac
¼ shot   Luxardo Maraschino liqueur
⅛ shot   Sugar syrup (2 sugar to 1 water)

Origin: Vintage cocktail of unknown origin.
Comment: Wonderfully delicate. Mint gives subtle freshness to the classic port and brandy combo.

A.J.

★★★★☆

Glass: Martini
Garnish: Dust with cinnamon powder
Method: SHAKE all ingredients with ice and fine strain into chilled glass.

2 shots   Calvados brandy
2 shots   Freshly squeezed pink grapefruit juice
½ shot   Sugar syrup (2 sugar to 1 water)

Origin: The initials in the name stand for 'applejack', the American style of apple brandy this drink was originally based upon.
Comment: Amazingly simple and beautifully balanced. I hope you like apple brandy as much as I do.

A1 COCKTAIL

★★★½☆

Glass: Martini
Garnish: Orange zest twist
Method: SHAKE all ingredients with ice and fine strain into chilled glass.

1½ shots   Rutte Dry Gin
1 shot   Grand Marnier Cordon Rouge
¼ shot   Freshly squeezed lemon juice
⅛ shot   Pomegranate / grenadine syrup (2:1)

Origin: In W.J. Tarling's 1937 'Café Royal Cocktail Book' this cocktail is accompanied by the notation, 'Invented by Albert'. The recipe stated is '1 dash lemon juice, 1/3 Grand Marnier, 2/3 Dry Gin, Dash Grenadine.'
Comment: The richness of Grand Marnier balances lemon juice in this classic gin-led drink. A dash of grenadine provides the pink hue.

ABACAXI RICAÇO

★★★★☆

Glass: Pineapple shell (frozen)
Garnish: Cut a straw sized hole in the top of the pineapple shell & replace it as a lid
Method: Cut the top off a small pineapple and carefully scoop out the flesh from the base to leave a shell with 12mm (½ inch) thick walls. Place the shell in a freezer to chill. Remove the hard core from the pineapple flesh and discard; roughly chop the remaining flesh, add other ingredients and **BLEND** with one 12oz scoop of crushed ice. Pour into the pineapple shell and serve with straws. (The flesh of one pineapple blended with the following ingredients will fill at least two shells).

1	whole	Pineapple (fresh)
3	shots	Bacardi Carta Oro rum
¾	shot	Freshly squeezed lime juice
½	shot	Granulated sugar

Origin: Adapted from David Embury's 1948 'The Fine Art of Mixing Drinks'. Pronounced 'Ah-bah-Kah-shee Rich-kah-So', the Portuguese name of this Brazilian drink literally translates as 'Extra Delicious Pineapple'.
Comment: Looks and tastes great but is a load of hassle to make.

ABBEY MARTINI

★★★½☆

Glass: Martini
Garnish: Orange zest twist
Method: SHAKE all ingredients with ice and fine strain into chilled glass.

2	shots	Rutte Dry Gin
1	shot	Martini Rosso vermouth
1	shot	Freshly squeezed orange juice
3	dash	Angostura Aromatic Bitters

Origin: This 1930s classic cocktail is closely related to the better known Bronx.
Comment: A dry, orangey, herbal, gin-laced concoction.

ABSINTHE COCKTAIL #1

★★★½☆

Glass: Coupe
Garnish: Mint leaf
Method: SHAKE all ingredients with ice and fine strain into chilled glass.

1 shot Le Fée Parisienne absinthe
1 shot Chilled water
¼ shot Sugar syrup
(2 sugar to 1 water)

Origin: Dr. Ordinaire perfected his recipe for absinthe in 1792 and from day one it required the addition of water and sugar to make it palatable.
Comment: Absinthe tamed and served straight-up.

ABSINTHE COCKTAIL #2

★★★½☆

Glass: Martini
Garnish: Lemon zest twist
Method: SHAKE all ingredients with ice and fine strain into chilled glass.

1	shot	Le Fée Parisienne absinthe
¼	shot	Marie Brizard Anisette
1	dash	Angostura Aromatic Bitters
1½	shots	Chilled water (reduce if wet ice)

Origin: Adapted from Jerry Thomas' 1887 'Bartender's Guide'.
Comment: This aniseed-flavoured mix tastes surprisingly tame but includes a shot of the notorious green fairy.

ABSINTHE COOLER (NEW)

★★★½☆

Glass: Collins
Garnish: Grapes
Method: SHAKE first 5 ingredients with ice and strain into ice-filled glass. **TOP** with ginger ale.

4 fresh Basil leaves
1½ shots Le Fée Parisienne absinthe
1 shot St-Germain elderflower liqueur
1 shot Freshly squeezed lime juice
¼ shot Sugar syrup
(2 sugar to 1 water)
Top with Ginger ale

Comment: The basil is subdued, as is the elderflower with absinthe being the predominant flavour – although not domineeringly so.

ABSINTHE DRIP COCKTAIL #1 (FRENCH METHOD)

★★★☆☆

Glass: Absinthe glass or old-fashioned
Garnish: None
Method: POUR absinthe into glass. **PLACE** cube of sugar on a slotted absinthe spoon resting across the top of the glass. Using a bottle of chilled mineral water with a small hole in the cap, **DRIP** water over the sugar so it dissolves and drips into the glass. Traditionally the same amount of sugar is added as water but I find full strength absinthe requires more dilution. Add ice, stir and serve.

1½	shots	Le Fée Parisienne absinthe
2	shots	Chilled water
1	cube	Granulated sugar

Origin: This is the traditional method of serving absinthe. It was common until shortly before the First World War, when the drink was banned in most countries.
Comment: Patience is a virtue. Slow dripping of the water is essential to dissolve the entire sugar cube and give the drink enough sweetness to balance the absinthe.

ABSINTHE DRIP COCKTAIL #2 (CZECH METHOD)

★★★☆☆

Glass: Absinthe glass or old-fashioned
Garnish: None
Method: **PLACE** sugar cube on a slotted absinthe spoon resting across the top of the glass. **POUR** the absinthe over the sugar cube into the glass. **LIGHT** the absinthe soaked cube and leave to burn and caramelise. Using a bottle of chilled mineral water with a small hole in the cap, **DRIP** water over what's left of the sugar so it dissolves and drips into the glass. Add ice, stir and serve.

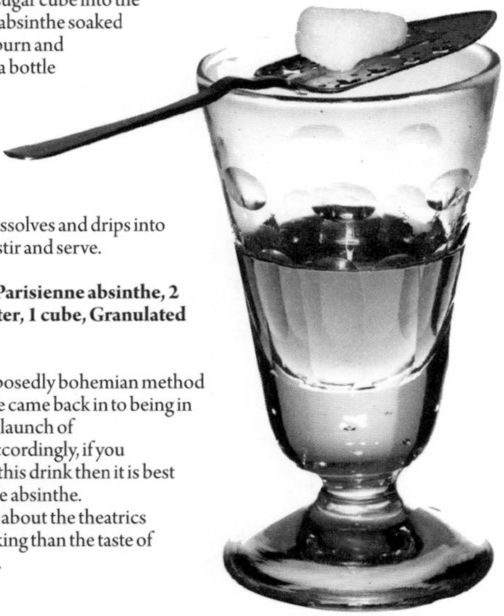

1½ shots Le Fée Parisienne absinthe, 2 shots Chilled water, 1 cube, Granulated sugar

Origin: This supposedly bohemian method of serving absinthe came back in to being in 1998 with the UK launch of Hill's Absinthe. Accordingly, if you are going to make this drink then it is best to use a Czech style absinthe.
Comment: More about the theatrics involved in its making than the taste of the finished drink.

ABSINTHE DROP

★★★☆☆

Glass: Old-fashioned
Garnish: None
Method: **STIR** all ingredients and strain into ice-filled glass.

1 shot **Le Fée Parisienne absinthe**
¼ shot **Marie Brizard Anisette**
2 shots **Chilled water**

Origin: Vintage cocktail of unknown origin.
Comment: A fix for aniseed addicts.

ABSINTHE FRAPPÉ

★★★★☆

Glass: Old-fashioned
Garnish: Mint sprig
Method: **SHAKE** all ingredients with ice and fine strain into glass filled with crushed ice. **CHURN** (stir) and serve with straws.

1½ shots **Le Fée Parisienne absinthe**
½ shot **Marie Brizard Anisette**
1½ shots **Chilled water**
¼ shot **Sugar syrup (2 sugar to 1 water)**

Origin: Created in 1874 by Cayetano Ferrer at Aleix's Coffee House, New Orleans, which consequently became known as The Absinthe Room. Today the establishment is fittingly known as the Old Absinthe House.
Comment: Aniseed and the fire of absinthe moderated by sugar and ice but still a dangerous combination.

ABSINTHE GIMLET

★★★½☆

Glass: Coupe
Garnish: Lime wedge
Method: **SHAKE** all ingredients with ice and fine strain into chilled glass.

1½ shots **Rutte Dry Gin**
½ shot **Le Fée Parisienne absinthe**
½ shot **Rose's lime cordial**
¼ shot **Freshly squeezed lime juice**
½ shot **Chilled water**

Origin: Created by Tara Garnell at the Cabinet Room, London, England after making Charles Vexenat's Green Beast.
Comment: A herbal riff on Charles Schumann's Gimlet (see Gimlet #2)

ABSINTHE ITALIANO COCKTAIL

★★★☆☆

Glass: Martini
Garnish: Lemon zest twist
Method: **SHAKE** all ingredients with ice and fine strain into chilled glass.

1 shot **Le Fée Parisienne absinthe**
½ shot **Marie Brizard Anisette**
¼ shot **Luxardo Maraschino liqueur**
1½ shots **Chilled water** (reduce if wet ice)

Origin: A long lost classic.
Comment: Liqueurs sweeten and tame the absinthe burn in this milky green concoction.

ABSINTHE MAKES THE HEART GROW FONDER (NEW)

★★★★½

Glass: Coupe
Garnish: Flamed orange zest twist
Method: **SHAKE** all ingredients with ice and fine strain into chilled glass.

1½ shots **Rutte Dry Gin**
¼ shot **Le Fée Parisienne absinthe**
⅓ shot **Luxardo Maraschino liqueur**
⅛ shot **Cherry Heering Liqueur**
⅛ shot **Campari Bitter**
¾ shot **Freshly squeezed pink grapefruit juice**
⅛ shot **Sugar syrup (2 sugar to 1 water)**
½ shot **Chilled water** (omit if wet ice)

Origin: Adaptation of a recipe by Scott Diaz, Seattle, WA, USA.
Comment: Absinthe and gin delicately lead this subtle cherry flavoured cocktail. Campari adds more colour than flavour while pink grapefruit freshens.

ABSINTHE MARTINI

★★★★☆

Glass: Martini
Garnish: Star anise
Method: **STIR** all ingredients with ice and strain into chilled glass.

2½ shots **Rutte Dry Gin**
½ shot **Martini Extra Dry vermouth**
⅛ shot **Le Fée Parisienne absinthe**

Comment: A classic Gin Martini made aniseed fresh with a dash of absinthe.

ABSINTHE SOUR

★★★½☆

Glass: Old-fashioned
Garnish: Lemon zest twist
Method: SHAKE all ingredients with ice and strain back into shaker. **DRY SHAKE** (without ice) to emulsify and fine strain into chilled glass.

1 shot Le Fée Parisienne absinthe
1 shot Sugar syrup (2 sugar to 1 water)
1 shot Freshly squeezed lemon juice
½ fresh Egg white

Comment: A touch of the sours for absinthe lovers.

ABSINTHE SPECIAL COCKTAIL

★★★☆☆

Glass: Martini
Garnish: Lemon zest twist
Method: SHAKE all ingredients with ice and fine strain into chilled glass.

1 shot Le Fée Parisienne absinthe
¼ shot Rutte Dry Gin
¼ shot Marie Brizard Anisette
2 dash Angostura Aromatic Bitters
1 dash Angostura Orange Bitters
1½ shots Chilled water (reduce if wet ice)

Origin: A long lost classic.
Comment: Tongue-numbingly strong in flavour and alcohol.

ABSINTHE SUISESSE

★★★☆☆

Glass: Old-fashioned
Garnish: Mint sprig
Method: SHAKE all ingredients with ice and strain into glass filled with crushed ice.

1½ shots Le Fée Parisienne absinthe
½ shot Almond (orgeat) syrup
1 fresh Egg white
½ shot Milk
½ shot Single cream / half-and-half

Origin: New Orleans 1930s.
Comment: Absinthe smoothed with cream and sweet almond.

ABSINTHE WITHOUT LEAVE

★★½☆☆

Glass: Shot
Garnish: None
Method: Refrigerate ingredients then **LAYER** in chilled glass by carefully pouring in the following order.

¾ shot Pisang Ambon liqueur
¾ shot Baileys Irish cream liqueur
½ shot Le Fée Parisienne absinthe

Origin: Discovered in 2003 at Hush, London, England.
Comment: This green and brown stripy shot is easy to layer but not so easy to drink.

ABSOLUTELY FABULOUS

★★★★☆

Glass: Flute
Garnish: Strawberry
Method: SHAKE first two ingredients with ice and strain into glass. **TOP** with champagne.

1 shot Ketel One Vodka
2 shots Cranberry juice
Top with G.H. Mumm Cordon Rouge Champagne

Origin: Created in 1999 at Monte's Club, London, England, and named after the 'Absolutely Fabulous' television series.
Comment: Easy to quaff – Patsy would love it.

ACAPULCO

★★★½☆

Glass: Collins
Garnish: Pineapple wedge
Method: SHAKE all ingredients with ice and strain into ice-filled glass.

1 shot Patrón reposado tequila
1 shot Bacardi Carta Oro rum
1 shot Freshly squeezed pink grapefruit juice
2½ shots Fresh pressed pineapple juice
½ shot Sugar syrup (2 sugar to 1 water)

Comment: An innocuous, fruity mixture laced with tequila and rum.

ACAPULCO DAIQUIRI

★★★★☆

Glass: Martini
Garnish: Lime wedge
Method: DRY SHAKE (without ice) all ingredients to emulsify. Add ice, **SHAKE** again and fine strain into chilled glass.

1½ shots Bacardi Carta Blanca light rum
½ shot De Kuyper Triple Sec
¾ shot Freshly squeezed lemon juice
¾ shot Rose's lime cordial
½ fresh Egg white

Comment: A smooth, yet citrus-rich Daiquiri.

ACE

★★★½☆

Glass: Martini
Garnish: Luxardo Maraschino cherry
Method: DRY SHAKE (without ice) all ingredients to emulsify. Add ice, **SHAKE** again and fine strain into chilled glass.

2 shots Rutte Dry Gin
½ shot Pomegranate / grenadine syrup (2:1)
½ shot Single cream / half-and-half
½ shot Milk
½ fresh Egg white

Comment: Pleasant, creamy, sweetened gin. Add more pomegranate syrup to taste.

ACE OF CLUBS DAIQUIRI

★★★★⯪

Glass: Martini
Garnish: Dust with chocolate powder
Method: SHAKE all ingredients with ice and fine strain into chilled glass.

½	shot	White crème de cacao liqueur
2	shots	Bacardi Carta Oro rum
½	shot	Freshly squeezed lime juice
⅛	shot	Sugar syrup (2 sugar to 1 water)

Origin: Created in the 1930s at a Bermudian nightclub of the same name.
Comment: A Daiquiri with a hint of chocolate.

ACHILLES HEEL

★★★★☆

Glass: Collins
Garnish: Apple slice
Method: SHAKE all ingredients with ice and strain into ice-filled glass.

2	shots	Zubrówka bison vodka
¼	shot	Chambord Liqueur
¼	shot	Peachtree peach schnapps
1	shot	Pressed apple juice
½	shot	Freshly squeezed lemon juice

Origin: Created in 2005 at Koba, Brighton, England.
Comment: If you like French Martinis you'll love this semi-sweet Tatanka.

ACT OF VIOLETS

★★★⯪☆

Glass: Coupe
Garnish: Dust with grated nutmeg
Method: DRY SHAKE all ingredients (without ice). SHAKE again with ice and fine strain into chilled glass.

2	shots	Rutte Dry Gin
⅓	shot	Martini Extra Dry vermouth
⅔	shot	Benoit Serres crème de violette
⅔	shot	Freshly squeezed lemon juice
2	dash	Angostura Aromatic Bitters
½	fresh	Egg white

Origin: Created in 2009 by Ryan Chetiyawardana at Bramble Bar and Lounge, Edinburgh, Scotland. Originally based on Martin Miller's gin, this cocktail won the brand's UK Lost and Stolen competition.
Comment: Silky berry fruit fortified with gin and balanced with lemon juice and dry vermouth.

ADAM & EVE

★★★★☆

Glass: Old-fashioned
Garnish: Lemon zest twist
Method: SHAKE all ingredients with ice and strain into ice filled glass.

2	shots	Bourbon whiskey
½	shot	Galliano L'Autentico liqueur
¼	shot	Sugar syrup (2 sugar to 1 water)
3	dash	Angostura Aromatic Bitters

Comment: Lovers of the Sazerac will appreciate this herbal, bourbon-laced concoction.

ADAM & EVE #2

★★★⯪☆

Glass: Martini
Garnish: Raspberries & lemon zest twist
Method: SHAKE all ingredients with ice and fine strain into chilled glass.

1 shot Rutte Dry Gin
1 shot Martell VSOP Médaillon cognac
1 shot Freshly squeezed lemon juice
1 shot Lejay crème de Cassis de Dijon

Comment: Fruity but not too sweet.

ADDINGTON

★★★★★

Glass: Martini
Garnish: Orange zest twist
Method: SHAKE first two ingredients with ice and fine strain into chilled glass. TOP with just the merest squirt of soda from chilled siphon.

2	shots	Martini Rosso vermouth
1	shot	Martini Extra Dry vermouth
Top with		Soda from siphon

Origin: Vintage cocktail of unknown origin.
Comment: Substituting vermouths, such as Martini Reserva Rubino, dramatically alters the character of this cocktail.

ADDISON

★★★★⯪☆

Glass: Martini
Garnish: Luxardo Maraschino cherry
Method: STIR all ingredients with ice and fine strain into chilled glass.

1½ shots Rutte Dry Gin
1½ shots Martini Rosso vermouth

Comment: Basically a very wet Sweet Martini.

ADELAIDE SWIZZLE

★★★★☆

Glass: Collins
Garnish: Lime slice
Method: POUR
ingredients into chilled glass
and half fill with crushed ice.
SWIZZLE with a swizzle
stick (or churn with a
barspoon). Add more
crushed ice to fill and
SWIZZLE some more.
Serve with straws.

**2 shots Bacardi Carta
Blanca light rum
¾ shot Taylor's Velvet
Falernum liqueur
½ shot Freshly squeezed
lime juice
2 dash Peychaud's
aromatic bitters**

Origin: This is the signature
cocktail at Café Adelaide's
Swizzle Stick Bar, New
Orleans, USA. There it is
made with a liquid poured
from a plain bottle marked
'top secret' but, having tried a
drop, we're sure it's
Falernum.
Comment: A slightly pink,
dry, spicy long drink with
rum and a hint of cloves and
lime.

ADIOS

★★★★☆

Glass: Shot
Garnish: None
Method: Refrigerate ingredients then **LAYER** in
chilled glass by carefully pouring in the order shown
here.

¾	shot	Coffee liqueur
¾	shot	Patrón reposado tequila

Comment: Surprisingly tasty with a potent agave
reminder of what you've just knocked back.

ADIOS AMIGOS COCKTAIL 🔑

★★★★☆

Glass: Martini
Garnish: Lemon zest twist
Method: SHAKE all ingredients with ice and fine
strain into chilled glass.

1	shot	Bacardi Carta Blanca light rum
½	shot	Martell VSOP Médaillon cognac
½	shot	Rutte Dry Gin
½	shot	Martini Extra Dry vermouth
¼	shot	Freshly squeezed lime juice
¼	shot	Sugar syrup (2 sugar to 1 water)
½	shot	Chilled water (omit if wet ice)

Origin: Adapted from Victor Bergeron's 'Trader Vic's
Bartender's Guide' (1972 revised edition).
Comment: To quote Victor Bergeron, "You know that
adios means good-bye. You drink two or three of these,
and it's adios, believe me, it's adios."

ADONIS

★★★★☆

Glass: Martini
Garnish: Orange zest twist
Method: STIR all ingredients with ice and strain into
chilled glass.

2	shots	Romate Fino sherry
1	shot	Martini Rosso vermouth
2	dash	Angostura Orange Bitters

Origin: Thought to have been created in 1886 to
celebrate the success of a Broadway musical.
Comment: A surprisingly delicate, dry, aromatic
oldie.

THE AFFILIATE (NEW)

★★★★☆

Glass: Old fashioned
Garnish: Orange zest twist
Method: STIR all ingredients with ice and strain into
ice-filled glass.

1½	shot	Bacardi Carta Ocho aged rum
¾	shot	Romate fino sherry
¾	shot	Cherry Heering liqueur
2	dash	Angostura Aromatic bitters
2	dash	Orange bitters

Origin: Created in 2013 by Charles Joly at The Aviary,
Chicago, USA.
Comment: Judicious dashing of orange bitters and
hitting the correct dilution will make or break this
drink, which is a fine balance between aged rum and
rich cherry liqueur versus dry fino sherry and aromatic
bitters.

AFFINITY 🔑

★★★★★

Glass: Coupe
Garnish: Luxardo Maraschino cherry or lemon zest twist.
Method: STIR all
ingredients with
ice and strain
into chilled
glass.

**1 shot Dewar's
12yo Scotch
whisky
1 shot Martini
Rosso vermouth
1 shot Martini Extra
Dry vermouth
1 dash Angostura
Aromatic Bitters**

Origin: Fashionable in the 1920s.
Comment: Aperitif-style cocktail
which when shaken has an almost
creamy, soft, mouthfeel. Stir, as the
recipe originally intended and the
Scotch notes are more pronounced.
I prefer mine shaken.

AFFOGATO COCKTAIL (NEW)

Glass: Martini
Garnish: Float 3 coffee beans
Method: **BLEND** all ingredients with three cubes ice.

1½ shots	Bepi Tosolini Grappa di Moscato
½ shot	Coffee liqueur
½ shot	Dark crème de cacao liqueur
1 shot	Espresso coffee (freshly made & hot)
1 scoop	Vanilla ice cream

Origin: Created in 2013 by yours truly for Jamie's Italian Bars.
Comment: Based on the classic Italian dessert of the same name, this after dinner cocktail blends coffee and chocolate with ice-cream, appropriately fortified with a splash of grappa.

AFTER EIGHT

Glass: Shot
Garnish: None
Method: **SHAKE** all ingredients with ice and fine strain into chilled glass.

½ shot	Ketel One Vodka
½ shot	White crème de cacao liqueur
½ shot	Green crème de menthe liqueur

Comment: Looks like mouthwash but tastes like liquid After Eight chocolates. This makes for a great finish to a meal. Dessert and after dinner minty drink in one.

AFTER SIX SHOT

Glass: Shot
Garnish: None
Method: Refrigerate ingredients then **LAYER** in chilled glass by carefully pouring in the order shown here.

½ shot	Coffee liqueur
½ shot	Giffard Menthe Pastille liqueur
½ shot	Baileys Irish cream liqueur

Comment: A layered, creamy, coffee and mint shot.

AFTERBURNER

Glass: Snifter
Garnish: None
Method: **POUR** all ingredients into glass, swirl to mix, Flambé and then extinguish flame. Please take care and beware of hot glass rim.

1 shot	Giffard Menthe Pastille liqueur
½ shot	White overproof rum
1 shot	Coffee liqueur

Comment: A surprisingly smooth and moreish peppermint-laced drink.

AGED HONEY DAIQUIRI

Glass: Martini
Garnish: Lime wedge
Method: **STIR** honey with rum in base of shaker until honey dissolves. Add lime juice and water, **SHAKE** with ice and fine strain into chilled glass.

2 shots	Bacardi Carta Ocho aged rum
1½ spoon	Runny honey
½ shot	Freshly squeezed lime juice
½ shot	Chilled water

Comment: Sweet honey replaces sugar syrup in this natural Daiquiri. Try experimenting with different honeys. We favour orange blossom honey.

AGENT ORANGE

Glass: Old-fashioned
Garnish: Orange zest twist
Method: **SHAKE** all ingredients with ice and strain into ice-filled glass.

1 shot	Ketel One Vodka
½ shot	Grand Marnier Cordon Rouge
½ shot	De Kuyper Triple Sec
2 shots	Freshly squeezed orange juice

Comment: Fresh orange is good for you. This has all of the flavour but few of the health benefits.

AGGRAVATION

Glass: Old-fashioned
Garnish: Dust with grated nutmeg
Method: **SHAKE** all ingredients with ice and strain into ice-filled glass.

2 shots	Dewar's 12yo Scotch whisky
¾ shot	Coffee liqueur
¾ shot	Single cream / half-and-half
¾ shot	Milk
¼ shot	Sugar syrup (2 sugar to 1 water)

Comment: If you like Scotch and enjoy creamy drinks, you'll love this.

AGUA DE CUBA

Glass: Flute
Garnish: Watermelon wedge

Method: **MUDDLE** watermelon in base of shaker. Add other ingredients, **SHAKE** with ice and fine strain into chilled glass.

2 slice	Fresh watermelon
2 shots	Bacardi Carta Blanca light rum
⅔ shot	Taylor's Velvet Falernum liqueur
⅔ shot	Freshly squeezed lemon juice

Origin: Adapted from a drink created in 2010 by Joey Medrington at Tigerlily, Edinburgh, Scotland.
Comment: A light summery rum-based drink with fresh watermelon and subtle clove spice.

AIR MAIL

★★★★☆

Glass: Collins
Garnish: Mint sprig
Method: SHAKE first four ingredients with ice and fine strain into ice-filled glass. TOP with champagne.

2 shots Bacardi Carta Oro rum
¼ shot Honey sugar syrup
½ shot Freshly squeezed lime juice
½ shot Freshly squeezed orange juice
Top with G.H. Mumm Cordon Rouge Champagne

Origin: Adapted from a classic recipe, which first appears in the 1949 Esquire's 'Handbook for Hosts'. This is a potent drink and the name could be a reference to airmail being the quickest way of getting a letter from A to B.
Comment: This old classic is basically a Honeysuckle served long and topped with champagne, rum, honey and a touch of citrus freshness make this one of the better champagne cocktails.

AKU AKU

★★★★☆

Glass: Martini
Garnish: Pineapple wedge, Luxardo Maraschino cherry and mint sprig
Method: BLEND all ingredients with 12oz scoop of crushed ice. Serve with short straws.

1 shot Bacardi Carta Blanca light rum
½ shot Peachtree peach schnapps
1½ shots Fresh pressed pineapple juice
½ shot Sugar syrup (2 sugar to 1 water)
¾ shot Freshly squeezed lime juice
10 fresh Mint leaves

Origin: Adapted from Victor Bergeron's 'Trader Vic's Bartender's Guide' (1972 revised edition)
Comment: This Tiki classic looks a little like frozen stagnant pond water but tastes minty fresh and rather good.

ALABAMA SLAMMER #1

★★★☆☆

Glass: Martini
Garnish: Orange zest twist
Method: SHAKE all ingredients with ice and fine strain into chilled glass.

1½ shots Ketel One Vodka
¾ shot Southern Comfort liqueur
1 shot Freshly squeezed orange juice
¼ shot Pomegranate / grenadine syrup (2:1)

Comment: None of the ingredients come from Alabama and the drink is served too long to slam. However, it's a good, rhythmic, rhyming name, if a little naff these days.

ALABAMA SLAMMER #2

★★★☆☆

Glass: Old-fashioned
Garnish: Peach slice
Method: SHAKE all ingredients with ice and strain into ice-filled glass.

1½ shots Southern Comfort liqueur
½ shot Disaronno Originale amaretto
½ shot Sloe Gin liqueur
2 shots Freshly squeezed orange juice
¾ shot Freshly squeezed lemon juice

Comment: Rich in flavour and quite sweet with a citrus bite. Surprisingly peachy!

ALABAZAM

★★★★☆

Glass: Collins
Garnish: Lemon slice
Method: SHAKE first five ingredients with ice and strain into ice-filled glass. TOP with soda.

2 shots Martell VSOP Médaillon cognac
1 shot Grand Marnier Cordon Rouge
1 shot Freshly squeezed lemon juice
½ shot Sugar syrup (2 sugar to 1 water)
1 dash Angostura Orange Bitters (optional)
Top with Soda (club soda)

Origin: Recipe adapted from William Schmidt's 1892 'The Flowing Bowl'.
Comment: Beware – this long fruity number packs a cognac charged punch.

ALAMAGOOZLUM COCKTAIL

★★★★☆

Glass: Martini
Garnish: Pineapple wedge
Method: DRY SHAKE (without ice) all ingredients to emulsify. Add ice, SHAKE again and fine strain into chilled glass.

1 shot Rutte Old Simon oude jenever
¾ shot Yellow Chartreuse liqueur
¾ shot White overproof rum
¼ shot Grand Marnier Cordon Rouge
¾ shot Sugar syrup (2 sugar to 1 water)
1 shot Chilled water
¼ shot Angostura Aromatic Bitters
¼ fresh Egg white (optional)

Origin: Adapted from David A. Embury's 1948 'Fine Art of Mixing Drinks', where he writes, "This cocktail is supposed to have been a speciality of the elder Morgan of the House of Morgan, which goes to prove as a bartender he was an excellent banker."
Comment: Even Mr Embury would approve of this version. Overproof Jamaican rum and copious amounts of bitters make this drink.

ALAN'S APPLE BREEZE 0—🔑

★★★½☆

Glass: Collins
Garnish: Apple wedge
Method: SHAKE all ingredients with ice and strain into ice-filled glass.

2	shots	Bacardi Carta Blanca light rum
½	shot	De Kuyper XO Apricot Brandy
1½	shots	Pressed apple juice
1½	shots	Cranberry juice
½	shot	Freshly squeezed lime juice
¼	shot	Sugar syrup (2 sugar to 1 water)

Origin: Created in 2002 by Alan Johnston at Metropolitan, Glasgow, Scotland.
Comment: A sweet, tangy version of the Apple Breeze.

ALASKA #1 (SAVOY RECIPE)

★★★★☆

Glass: Martini
Garnish: Orange zest twist
Method: SHAKE all ingredients with ice and fine strain into chilled glass.

2½	shots	Rutte Dry Gin
¾	shot	Yellow Chartreuse liqueur
1	shot	Romate Fino sherry
3	dash	Angostura Orange Bitters

Origin: In his 1930 'The Savoy Cocktail Book', Harry Craddock writes, "so far as can be ascertained this delectable potion is NOT the staple diet of the Esquimaux. It was probably first thought of in South Carolina – hence its name."
Comment: We've added a shot of dry sherry as recommended by David Embury in his 1948 'Fine Art of Mixing Drinks'.

ALASKA #2

★★★☆☆

Glass: Martini
Garnish: Luxardo Maraschino cherry
Method: SHAKE all ingredients with ice and fine strain into chilled glass.

2	shots	Rutte Dry Gin
1½	shots	Freshly squeezed lemon juice
½	shot	Sugar syrup (2 sugar to 1 water)
¼	shot	Lejay crème de cassis de Dijon

Comment: The original recipe suggests adding the cassis separately after the drink is strained into the glass so it sinks. Looks great but the resulting drink is very sour until the cassis is stirred in.

ALASKAN COCKTAIL

★★★½☆

Glass: Martini
Garnish: Lemon zest twist (discarded) & mint leaf
Method: STIR all the ingredients with ice and strain into chilled glass.

2½	shots	Rutte Dry Gin
¾	shot	Yellow Chartreuse liqueur
¾	shot	Chilled water (omit if wet ice)

Origin: Contemporary version of the Alaska.
Comment: This very punchy drink benefits from dilution. The result will appeal to gin and Chartreuse fans.

ALBERTO MARTINI

★★★★☆

Glass: Coupe
Garnish: Orange zest twist
Method: STIR all ingredients with ice and strain into chilled glass.

1¼	shots	Rutte Dry Gin
1¼	shots	Martini Extra Dry vermouth
1	shot	Romate Fino sherry
½	shot	De Kuyper Triple Sec

Origin: In W.J. Tarling's 1937 'Café Royal Cocktail Book' the invention of this cocktail is credited to A.J. Smith.
Comment: Dry, complex and aromatic. An equal parts gin and vermouth Martini with a good dose of fino sherry and a splash of triple sec.

ALCATRAZ (NEW)

★★★★½

Glass: Old fashioned
Garnish: Orange zest twist
Method: STIR all ingredients with ice and strain into ice-filled glass.

1½	shot	Patrón Anejo tequila
¾	shot	Romate Oloroso sherry
½	shot	Suze Saveur d'Autrefois
¼	shot	Del Maguey Vida Mezcal
1	spoon	Agave nectar
2	dash	Fee Brothers Aztec Chocolate bitters

Origin: Adapted from a recipe created in 2015 by Christin Wagner at La Petite Grocery, New Orleans, USA. Recipe courtesy of Gary 'gaz' Regan's Ardent Spirits.
Comment: Dry and lightly bitter, this tequila-based sipper makes for a great aperitif cocktail.

ALESSANDRO

★★★☆☆

Glass: Martini
Garnish: Lemon zest twist
Method: SHAKE all ingredients with ice and fine strain into chilled glass.

¾	shot	Rutte Dry Gin
¾	shot	Black sambuca liqueur
¾	shot	Milk
¾	shot	Single cream / half-and-half

Comment: Hints of aniseed, elderflower and gin emerge from this grey, creamy drink.

ALEXANDER

★★★★½

Glass: Coupe
Garnish: Dust with grated nutmeg
Method: SHAKE all ingredients with ice and strain back into shaker. DRY SHAKE (without ice) and fine strain into chilled glass.

1½	shot	Rutte Dry Gin
1	shot	White crème de cacao liqueur
¾	shot	Single cream / half-and-half
¼	fresh	Egg white (optional)

Origin: The original Alexander, equal parts gin, crème de cacao and cream, is thought to have originated in the twentieth century, certainly before 1915, evidenced by an equal parts recipe appearing in Hugo Ensslin's 1916 *Recipes for Mixed Drinks*.

Historian Barry Popik's website (barrypopik.com) lists several plausible origins for this drink. The first being a cutting from page 11 of the news section of the 3rd October 1915 Philadelphia (PA) Inquirer. "The head bartender has even gone so far as to invent an Alexander cocktail, which he is reserving to be served during the World Series." This referred to The Racquet Club and the 1915 World Series which was won by Boston beating Philadelphia. The bartender created the drink in honour of Philadelphia pitcher Grover Cleveland Alexander (1887-1950).

Alternatively, a 21st March 1929 newspaper column by New York columnist Walter Winchell links the origin of the Alexander cocktail to Troy Alexander, a bartender at a New York pre-Prohibition lobster restaurant called Rector's and claims that Troy created his eponymously named cocktail for a dinner celebrating a successful advertising campaign.

The advertisement depicted Phoebe Snow, a fictitious railway traveller, wearing a snow-white dress featured in an advertising campaign for the Delaware, Lackawanna and Western Railroad (DL&W) to promote the company's use of clean-burning anthracite to fuel its locomotives.

Coal-fuelled trains frequently covered travellers with black soot but DL&W owned vast anthracite mines in Pennsylvania so could legitimately claim that their passengers' clothes would arrive clean after a long journey. The first advertisement depicted an image of Phoebe Snow, supposedly a young New York socialite who frequently travelled to Buffalo, New York wearing a white dress and a short poem:

Says Phoebe Snow
about to go
upon a trip to Buffalo
"My gown stays white
from morn till night
Upon the Road of Anthracite"

The popular advertisements first appeared at the turn of the 20th century and ran for nearly seventy years. Phoebe became one of America's most recognized advertising mascots. The Alexander became a Prohibition favourite as the cream and nutmeg garnish helped disguise the rough taste of homemade 'bathtub' gin.

It took around two decades for the brandy based Alexander to emerge and the first written reference to a brandy-based rather than gin-based Alexander I've been able to find appears in W. J. Tarling's 1937 *Café Royal Cocktail Book - Coronation Edition*.

Tellingly in his 1946 *The Rowing Bartender*, Bill Kelly writes under his recipe for a Brandy Alexander, "P.S. The boys during prohibition used gin."

The inevitable arrival of the brandy-based Alexander may have been impeded by Prohibition, but it quickly went on to dominate. I wonder if the present reawakened interest in gin will once again see the original gin-based Alexander re-emerge?

Comment: This gin-laced creamy Alexander has sadly slipped from popularity, partly knocked by its successors, particularly the Brandy Alexander.

ALEXANDER THE GREAT

★★★★½

Glass: Martini
Garnish: Dust with grated nutmeg
Method: SHAKE all ingredients with ice and strain back into shaker. **DRY SHAKE** (without ice) and fine strain into chilled glass.

1½	shot	Ketel One Vodka
½	shot	Coffee liqueur
½	shot	White crème de cacao liqueur
¾	shot	Single cream / half-and-half
¼	fresh	Egg white (optional)

Comment: A tasty combination of coffee, chocolate and cream, laced with vodka.

ALEXANDER'S BIG BROTHER

★★★½☆

Glass: Martini
Garnish: Physalis (cape gooseberry)
Method: SHAKE all ingredients with ice and fine strain into chilled glass.

1½	shots	Rutte Dry Gin
¼	shot	De Kuyper Triple Sec
¾	shot	Blue curaçao liqueur
¾	shot	Milk
¾	shot	Single cream / half-and-half

Comment: Orangey in taste and creamy blue in colour - mildly better than pink for the macho out there.

ALEXANDER'S SISTER

★★★½☆

Glass: Martini
Garnish: Dust with freshly grated nutmeg
Method: SHAKE all ingredients with ice and strain back into shaker. **DRY SHAKE** (without ice) and fine strain into chilled glass.

1½	shot	Rutte Dry Gin
½	shot	Green crème de menthe
¾	shot	Single cream / half-and-half
⅛	shot	Sugar syrup (2 sugar to 1 water)
¼	fresh	Egg white (optional)

Comment: A green minty thing for dairy lovers.

ALEXANDRA

★★★½☆

Glass: Martini
Garnish: Dust with freshly grated nutmeg
Method: SHAKE all ingredients with ice and strain back into shaker. **DRY SHAKE** (without ice) and fine strain into chilled glass.

1½ shot Pusser's Navy rum
1 shot Coffee liqueur
1 shot Single cream / half-and-half
¼ fresh Egg white (optional)

Comment: Surprisingly potent and spicy, despite the ladylike name.

ALFONSO

★★★½☆

Glass: Flute
Garnish: Lemon zest twist
Method: Coat sugar cube with bitters and drop into glass. **POUR** Dubonnet and then champagne into chilled glass.

1	cube	Granulated sugar
4	dash	Angostura Aromatic Bitters
½	shot	Dubonnet Red
Top with		G.H. Mumm Cordon Rouge Champagne

Origin: Named after the deposed Spanish king Alfonso XIII, who first tasted this drink while exiled in France.
Comment: Herbal variation on the classic Champagne Cocktail

B
C
D
E
F
G
H
I
J
K
L
M
N
O
P
Q
R
S
T
U
V
W
X
Y
Z

ALFONSO MARTINI

★★★★☆

Glass: Martini
Garnish: Orange zest twist
Method: SHAKE all ingredients with ice and fine
strain into a chilled glass.

½ shot   **Rutte Dry Gin**
1 shot   **Grand Marnier Cordon Rouge**
½ shot   **Martini Extra Dry vermouth**
¼ shot   **Martini Rosso vermouth**
2 dash   **Angostura Aromatic Bitters**
½ shot   **Chilled water** (omit if wet ice)

Origin: Adapted from Victor Bergeron's 'Trader Vic's
Bartender's Guide' (1972 revised edition).
Comment: Dry yet slightly sweet with hints of orange,
gin and warm spice.

ALGERIA

★★★★½

Glass: Martini
Garnish: Orange zest twist
Method: SHAKE all ingredients with ice and fine
strain into chilled glass.

2 shots   **BarSol Mosto Verde Italia pisco**
½ shot   **De Kuyper Triple Sec**
½ shot   **De Kuyper XO Apricot Brandy**
¾ shot   **Chilled water**

Origin: Modern adaptation of a classic.
Comment: Pisco, apricot and orange combine
wonderfully in this medium dry, balanced cocktail
with a tangy bite.

ALGONQUIN

★★★★☆

Glass: Old-fashioned
Garnish: Pineapple wedge & Luxardo Maraschino
cherry
Method: MUDDLE pineapple in base of shaker. Add
other ingredients, SHAKE with ice and fine strain into
ice-filled glass.

½ ring   **Pineapple (fresh)**
     (cored, skinned and chopped)
1½ shots   **Straight rye whiskey**
¾ shot   **Martini Extra Dry vermouth**
1 dash   **Peychaud's aromatic bitters**

Origin: One of several classic cocktails accredited to
New York City's Algonquin Hotel in the 1930s. Its true
origins are lost in time.
Comment: A dry aromatic aperitif-style of cocktail. If
you don't want this drink frothy then stir instead of shake.

ALICE MINE

★★★★☆

Glass: Martini
Garnish: Orange zest twist
Method: STIR all ingredients with ice and strain into
chilled glass.

1 shot   **Grand Marnier Cordon Rouge**
½ shot   **Rutte Dry Gin**
½ shot   **Martini Extra Dry vermouth**
¼ shot   **Martini Rosso vermouth**
1 dash   **Angostura Aromatic Bitters**

Origin: Vintage cocktail of unknown origin.
Comment: A Medium Dry Martini with luscious
orange notes.

ALIEN SECRETION

★★★½☆

Glass: Collins
Garnish: Pineapple wedge & Luxardo Maraschino
cherry
Method: SHAKE all ingredients with ice and strain
into ice-filled glass.

2 shots   **Ketel One Vodka**
½ shot   **Midori Green Melon liqueur**
½ shot   **Coconut rum liqueur**
3 shots   **Fresh pressed pineapple juice**

Origin: One of many 80s cocktails with a dodgy name.
Comment: Lime green and fruity but all too
drinkable, with a distinct bite despite its mild
sweetness.

ALL WHITE FRAPPÉ

★★★½☆

Glass: Old-fashioned
Garnish: Lemon zest twist
Method: BLEND ingredients with 6oz scoop of
crushed ice. Pour into glass and serve with short straws.

1 shot   **Luxardo sambuca dei cesari**
1 shot   **White crème de cacao liqueur**
1 shot   **Giffard Menthe Pastille liqueur**
1 shot   **Freshly squeezed lemon juice**

Comment: Aniseed, chocolate, peppermint and
lemon juice are an unlikely but tasty combination for
summer afternoons.

ALLEGROTTINI

★★★½☆

Glass: Martini
Garnish: Orange zest twist
Method: SHAKE all the ingredients with ice and fine
strain into chilled glass.

1½ shots   **Ketel One Citroen vodka**
¾ shot   **De Kuyper Triple Sec**
¼ shot   **Martini Extra Dry vermouth**
¾ shot   **Freshly squeezed orange juice**
¼ shot   **Freshly squeezed lime juice**

Origin: Discovered in 2005 at the Four Seasons
Hotel, Prague, Czech Republic.
Comment: Strongly citrus but dry rather than bitter.

ALMOND MARTINI #1

★★★★☆

Glass: Martini
Garnish: Sink three almonds
Method: SHAKE all ingredients with ice and fine
strain into chilled glass.

2 shots   **Ketel One Vodka**
½ shot   **Freshly squeezed lemon juice**
½ shot   **Almond (orgeat) syrup**
1 shot   **Pressed apple juice**
2 dash   **Peach bitters** (optional)

Origin: Created in 2004 by Matt Pomeroy at Baltic,
London, England.
Comment: Almond inspired with hints of apple and
lemon juice.

ALMOND MARTINI #2

★★★★☆

Glass: Martini
Garnish: Sink three almonds
Method: **SHAKE** all ingredients with ice and fine strain into chilled glass.

2 shots Ketel One Vodka
¾ shot Disaronno Originale amaretto
¼ shot Martini Extra Dry vermouth
¾ shot Chilled water (omit if wet ice)

Origin: Created in 2005 by yours truly.
Comment: A delicate, almond flavoured Vodka Martini.

ALMOND OLD FASHIONED

★★★★½

Glass: Old-fashioned
Garnish: Orange zest twist
Method: **STIR** one shot of tequila with two ice cubes in a glass. Add amaretto, agave syrup, bitters and two more ice cubes. Stir some more then add another two ice cubes and the remaining tequila. Stir lots more so as to melt ice then add more ice. The melting and stirring in of ice cubes is essential to the dilution and taste of the drink.

2 shots Patrón reposado tequila
¼ shot Disaronno Originale amaretto
¼ shot Agave syrup
3 dash Angostura Orange Bitters

Origin: Created in 2005 by Mark Prat at Maze, London, England.
Comment: One to please fans of both tequila and the Old Fashioned drinks genre.

ALMOND PINA COLADA (NEW)

★★★★☆

Glass: Collins
Garnish: Pineapple wedge
Method: **SHAKE** all ingredients with ice and strain into ice-filled glass.

2 shots Bacardi Carta Blanca light rum
½ shot Disaronno Originale amaretto
2½ shots Fresh pressed pineapple juice
¾ shot Freshly squeezed lime juice
⅓ shot Almond (orgeat) syrup

Comment: As the name suggests this tall shaken cocktail has strong flavours of pineapple and almond.

AMALIA

★★★★☆

Glass: Coupe
Garnish: Pineapple foam
Method: **SHAKE** all ingredients with ice and fine strain into chilled glass.

2 shots Bacardi Carta Blanca light rum
¾ shot Freshly squeezed lemon juice
¼ shot Sugar syrup (2 sugar to 1 water)
1 shot Sauvignon blanc white wine
⅛ shot Gooseberry & mint cordial

Origin: Created in 2008 by Sam Dean, Mobar, Nottingham England.
Comment: Sip a gooseberry and mint influenced lemon Daiquiri though a foam topping.

AMANTE PICANTE

★★★½☆

Glass: Martini
Garnish: Cucumber slices
Method: **MUDDLE** cucumber and coriander (cilantro). Add other ingredients, **SHAKE** with ice and fine strain into chilled glass.

2 slice English cucumber peeled
2 sprig Coriander (cilantro) leaves
1½ shots Patrón reposado tequila
1 shot Freshly squeezed lime juice
½ shot Agave syrup
2 dash Green Tabasco Sauce

Origin: Created in 2008 by Francesco Lafranconi of Southern Wine & Spirits USA.
Comment: So green and fresh that it must be good for you as well as tasting great.

AMARETTO SOUR

★★★★☆

Glass: Old-fashioned
Garnish: Lemon slice & cherry on stick (sail)
Method: **DRY SHAKE** (without ice) all ingredients to emulsify. Add ice, **SHAKE** again and strain into ice-filled glass.

2 shots Disaronno Originale amaretto
1 shot Freshly squeezed lemon juice
½ fresh Egg white
1 dash Angostura Aromatic Bitters

Comment: Sweet 'n' sour - frothy with an almond buzz. Three dashes (12 drops) of Angostura bitters help balance the drink and add an extra burst of flavour.

AMARETTO SOUR II (MORGENTHALER FORMULA)

★★★★½

Glass: Old-fashioned
Garnish: Lemon zest twist (discarded) & Luxardo Maraschino Cherries on stick.

Method: **SHAKE** all ingredients with ice and strain back into shaker. **DRY SHAKE** (without ice) and pour into ice-filled glass.

1½ shots Disaronno Originale amaretto
1 shot Bourbon whiskey
1 shot Freshly squeezed lemon juice
½ fresh Egg white

Origin: Adapted from a drink created in 2012 by Jeffrey Morgenthaler in Oregon, USA. Jeffrey's original formula called for 3/4 shot cask-strength bourbon and additionally used 1 spoon of sugar syrup.
Comment: As the name suggests, this drink is dominated by amaretto, with lemon juice providing the sour balancing element and a slug of bourbon giving backbone.

STAR RATINGS EXPLAINED

★★★★★+	OUTSTANDING	★★★★★	EXCEPTIONAL
★★★★½	EXCELLENT	★★★★☆	RECOMMENDED
★★★½☆	COMMENDED	★★★☆☆	MEDIOCRE
★★½☆☆	DISAPPOINTING	★★☆☆☆	PRETTY AWFUL
★½☆☆☆	SHAMEFUL	★☆☆☆☆	DISGUSTING

AMARITA

★★★☆☆

Glass: Martini
Garnish: Length of lime peel
Method: SHAKE all ingredients with ice and fine strain into chilled glass.

1½ shots Patrón reposado tequila
¾ shot Aperol Aperitivo
½ shot Freshly squeezed lime juice
3 dash Grapefruit bitters

Origin: Created in 2007 by Neyah White, San Francisco USA.
Comment: Tequila predominates in this fairly bitter drink.

AMATITAN TWIST

★★★★★

Glass: Coupe
Garnish: Grapefruit zest twist
Method: STIR all ingredients with ice and strain into chilled glass.

2 shots Patrón añejo tequila
¼ shot Luxardo Maraschino liqueur
¼ shot Yellow Chartreuse liqueur
2 dash Grapefruit bitters

Origin: Created in 2010 by Dave West at Trio Bar and Grill, Leeds, England.
Comment: The sublime taste of great añejo tequila mellowed and delicately flavoured with maraschino, chartreuse and grapefruit bitters.

AMBER

★★★★☆

Glass: Collins
Garnish: Dust with grated nutmeg & apple wedge
Method: MUDDLE ginger in base of shaker. Add other ingredients, **SHAKE** with ice and strain into glass filled with crushed ice.

4 slice Fresh root ginger (thumbnail sized)
1½ shots Zubrówka bison vodka
4 shots Pressed apple juice
½ shot Sugar syrup (2 sugar to 1 water)
½ shot Apple Schnapps liqueur

Origin: Created in 2001 by Douglas Ankrah for Akbar at the Red Fort, Soho, London, England.
Comment: A fantastic combination of adult flavours in a long, thirst-quenching drink. Also great served up.

AMBER NECTAR

★★★★☆

Glass: Coupe
Garnish: Lemon zest twist
Method: STIR honey with scotch in base of shaker until honey dissolves. Add other ingredients, **SHAKE** with ice and strain into ice-filled glass.

2 shots Dewar's 12yo Scotch whisky
¼ shot Islay single malt Scotch whisky
2 spoon Runny honey
1 shot Martini Extra Dry vermouth

Origin: Adapted by yours truly from a drink discovered in Amsterdam during 2013, originally based on vodka with honey liqueur, the honey cried out for scotch and then some Islay single malt. It's called the Amber Nectar after all.
Comment: Honey lifts and enhances this blend of scotch, single Islay malt and dry vermouth.

AMBER NEGRONI (NEW)

★★★★☆

Glass: Old-fashioned
Garnish: Orange slice
Method: STIR all ingredients with ice and strain into ice-filled glass.

1 shot Martell VSOP Médaillon cognac
1 shot Byrrh Grand Quinquina
1 shot Amer Picon
½ shot Suze Saveur d'Autrefois

Origin: Created in January 2015 by Matthias Lataille at the Cabinet Room, London, England using Martell V.S.O.P. cognac.
Comment: This very serious Negroni has great depth of flavour with mocha coffee and bitter gentian.

AMBER ROOM #1

★★★★☆

Glass: Martini
Garnish: Lemon zest twist (discarded) & Luxardo Maraschino cherry
Method: SHAKE all ingredients with ice and fine strain into chilled glass.

1½ shots Rutte Dry Gin
½ shot Green Chartreuse liqueur
½ shot Martini Rosso vermouth
2 dash Angostura Orange Bitters
½ shot Chilled water (omit if wet ice)

Origin: This vintage cocktail originated from a layered or 'pousse-café' style drink called a Bijou. The original drink was so named after the French word meaning 'jewel' due to its trio of ingredients being coloured after the three most precious jewels: diamond (gin), ruby (sweet vermouth) and emerald (Green Chartreuse).

Shake rather than layer and the colours combine to make this an aptly named amber coloured drink.
Comment: Serious and packed with bold flavours. Fellow Chartreuse fans will approve.

AMBER ROOM #2

★★★★½

Glass: Martini
Garnish: Lemon zest twist
Method: STIR all ingredients with ice and strain into chilled glass.

1½ shots	Rutte Dry Gin
1 shot	Martini Extra Dry vermouth (originally Ambre)
¼ shot	St-Germain elderflower liqueur
1 dash	Angostura Orange Bitters

Origin: Created in 2007 by Stephan Berg, Munich, Germany.
Comment: A subtle, delicately floral Martini.

AMBROSIA

★★★★☆

Glass: Flute
Garnish: None
Method: SHAKE first 4 ingredients with ice and strain into glass, **TOP** with champagne.

1 shot	Martell VSOP Médaillon cognac
1 shot	Calvados brandy
¼ shot	De Kuyper Triple Sec
¼ shot	Freshly squeezed lemon juice
Top with	G.H. Mumm Cordon Rouge Champagne

Comment: Dry, fortified champers with a hint of apple.

AMBROSIO CUP (NEW)

★★★★½

Glass: Coupe
Garnish: Mint leaf
Method: SHAKE first 6 ingredients with ice and fine strain into chilled glass. **TOP** with soda water.

8 fresh Mint leaves
¾ shot Capucana cachaça
¾ shot Zubrówka bison vodka
¾ shot San León Manzanilla sherry
½ shot Freshly squeezed lime juice
½ shot Sugar syrup (2 sugar to 1 water)
1 shot Soda (club soda)

Origin: Created in 2013 by Ann Robinson at PDT, New York City, USA
Comment: Cachaça, Bison Grass vodka and San León Manzanilla sherry combine harmoniously and are freshened with mint and lime in this refreshing cocktail.

AMERICAN BEAUTY #1

★★★★½

Glass: Martini
Garnish: Rose petal
Method: SHAKE first 6 ingredients with ice and fine strain into chilled glass. Then use the back of a spoon to help **FLOAT** red wine over drink.

2½ shots Martell VSOP Médaillon cognac
½ shot Martini Extra Dry
½ shot Giffard Menthe Pastille liqueur
½ shot Freshly squeezed orange juice
½ shot Pomegranate / grenadine syrup (2:1)
¼ shot Shiraz red wine
¾ shot Chilled water

Origin: Adapted from a recipe in David A. Embury's 1948 'Fine Art of Mixing Drinks'.
Comment: Both fresh and refreshing. A subtle hint of peppermint gives zing to this cognac-based cocktail.

AMERICAN BEAUTY #2

★★★½☆

Glass: Martini
Garnish: Mint leaf
Method: SHAKE first five ingredients with ice and fine strain into chilled glass. Use the back of a soup spoon to **FLOAT** port over drink.

1 shot	Martell VSOP Médaillon cognac
1 shot	Martini Extra Dry vermouth
¼ shot	Giffard Menthe Pastille liqueur
1 shot	Freshly squeezed orange juice
½ shot	Pomegranate / grenadine syrup (2:1)
½ shot	Tawny port

Origin: Adapted from Victor Bergeron's 'Trader Vic's Bartender's Guide' (1972 revised edition).
Comment: Invigorating and peppermint-fresh yet sophisticated and complex.

AMERICAN PIE COCKTAIL

★★★★☆

Glass: Martini
Garnish: Apple wedge
Method: SHAKE all ingredients with ice and fine strain into chilled glass.

1½ shots	Bourbon whiskey
½ shot	Apple Schnapps liqueur
½ shot	Lejay Crème de Myrtille liqueur
¾ shot	Cranberry juice
½ shot	Pressed apple juice
¼ shot	Freshly squeezed lime juice

Origin: Adapted from a recipe discovered at Oxo Tower Restaurant & Bar, London, England.
Comment: This berry and apple pie has a tangy bite.

AMERICANA 🗝

★★★☆☆

Glass: Flute
Garnish: Peach slice
Method: Coat sugar cube with bitters and drop into glass. **POUR** bourbon and then champagne into chilled glass.

1	cube	Granulated sugar
4	dash	Angostura Aromatic Bitters
½	shot	Bourbon whiskey
Top with		G.H. Mumm Cordon Rouge Champagne

Comment: The Wild West take on the classic Champagne Cocktail.

AMERICANO

★★★★½

Glass: Collins
Garnish: Orange slice
Method: **POUR** Campari and vermouth into ice-filled glass and **TOP** with soda. Stir and serve with straws.

2 shots Campari Bitter
2 shots Martini Rosso vermouth, Top with Soda (club soda)

Origin: First served in the 1860s in Gaspare Campari's bar in Milan, this was originally known as the 'Milano-Torino' as Campari came from Milano (Milan) and sweet vermouth from Torino (Turin). It was not until Prohibition that the Italians noticed an influx of Americans who enjoyed the drink and so dubbed it Americano.
Comment: A bitter, fizzy, long refreshing drink, which you'll love if you like Campari.

AMPERSAND COCKTAIL

★★★★★☆

Glass: Coupe
Garnish: Orange zest twist
Method: **STIR** all ingredients with ice and strain into chilled glass.

1	shot	Old Tom gin
1	shot	Martell VSOP Médaillon cognac
1	shot	Martini Rosso vermouth
⅛	shot	Grand Marnier Cordon Rouge
1	dash	Angostura Orange Bitters

Origin: First published in A. S. Crockett's 1935 'The Old Waldorf-Astoria Bar Book'. The name may be a reference to the '&' in Martini & Rossi, likely the brand of vermouth originally used.
Comment: A brandy influenced wet, sweet Martini with a hint of orange.

AMSTERDAM COCKTAIL

★★★★½

Glass: Martini
Garnish: Orange zest twist
Method: **SHAKE** all ingredients with ice and fine strain into chilled glass.

2	shots	Rutte Old Simon oude jenever
1	shot	De Kuyper Triple Sec
1	shot	Freshly squeezed orange juice
3	dash	Angostura Orange Bitters

Origin: Adapted from Victor Bergeron's 'Trader Vic's Bartender's Guide' (1972 revised edition).
Comment: Very orange, dry but wonderfully smooth.

THE ANCIENT DAIQUIRI

★★★☆☆

Glass: Martini
Garnish: None
Method: **SHAKE** all ingredients with ice and fine strain into chilled glass.

1	shot	Bacardi Carta Blanca light rum
½	shot	Drambuie liqueur
½	shot	Green Chartreuse liqueur
¾	shot	Freshly squeezed lime juice
¼	shot	Vanilla sugar syrup

Origin: Created in 2008 by Lewis Jaffrey, Drambuie's Global Brand Ambassador and according to Lewis it is so named due to the ingredients having a combined age over 650 years.
Comment: Herbal liqueurs heavily influence this Daiquiri twist.

ANDEAN DUSK COCKTAIL (NEW)

★★★★½

Glass: Flute
Garnish: Drop cold red grape into drink
Method: **MUDDLE** grapes in base of shaker. Add next 3 ingredients, **SHAKE** with ice and fine strain into chilled glass. **TOP** with champagne.

3	fresh	Red grapes
1	shot	BarSol Mosto Verde Italia pisco
½	fresh	Freshly squeezed lemon juice
¼	shot	Sugar syrup (2 sugar to 1 water)
Top with		G.H. Mumm Brut Rosé Champagne

Comment: Dry biscuity champagne adds sparkle to sweet red grapes while pisco fortifies and adds complex distilled grape flavours.

ANEJO HIGHBALL

★★★★☆

Glass: Collins
Garnish: Orange & lime slices
Method: **SHAKE** first four ingredients with ice and strain into ice-filled glass.

2	shots	Bacardi Carta Ocho aged rum
1	shot	Orange Curaçao liqueur
1	shot	Freshly squeezed lime juice
1	dash	Angostura Aromatic Bitters
Top with		Gosling's Stormy Ginger Beer

Origin: Created in the late 1990s by Dale DeGroff, New York City, USA.
Comment: Orange and rum with a hint of ginger spice. Long and thirst-quenching.

ANEJO MANHATTAN

★★★⯪☆

Glass: Martini
Garnish: Salami
wrapped cherry on a
pick
Method: STIR all
ingredients with ice and strain
into chilled glass.

2 shots Patrón añejo tequila
½ shot Martini Rosso vermouth
¼ shot Licor 43 liqueur
1 dash Angostura Aromatic Bitters
1 dash Angostura Orange Bitters

Origin: Created by Ryan Magarian, Seattle, USA.
Comment: Tequila dominates this dry, serious
Manhattan-like cocktail

ANGEL FACE

★★★★⯪

Glass: Martini
Garnish: Apple wedge
Method: STIR all ingredients with ice and fine strain
into a chilled glass.

1	shot	**Rutte Dry Gin**
1	shot	**Calvados brandy**
1	shot	**De Kuyper XO Apricot Brandy**
½	shot	**Chilled water** (omit if wet ice)

Origin: Adapted from Harry Craddock's 1930 'The
Savoy Cocktail Book'.
Comment: Rich apricot and apple with a backbone of
botanical gin. Balanced rather than dry or sweet.

This drink looks better when stirred but the original
1930 recipe is shaken and we think it tastes better for it
- that is unless you add some water to increase the
dilution of the stirred recipe.

ANGEL JUICE

★★★⯪☆

Glass: Martini
Garnish: Apple fan
Method: DRY SHAKE (without ice) all ingredients
to emulsify. Add ice, **SHAKE** again and fine strain into
chilled glass.

1	shot	**Pear flavoured vodka**
½	shot	**St-Germain elderflower liqueur**
½	shot	**Sauvignon blanc white wine**
½	shot	**Pressed apple juice**
¼	shot	**Sugar syrup (2 sugar to 1 water)**
½	shot	**Freshly squeezed lime juice**
½	fresh	**Egg white**

Origin: Created in 2008 by Jay Decker at Paramount,
London, England.
Comment: Pear and elderflower lead this fruity drink.

THE ANGEL WORE RED (NEW)

★★★★⯪

Glass: Collins
Garnish: Lemon zest twist
Method: STIR first 3 ingredients with ice. **POUR**
beer into ice-filled glass and then strain stirred
ingredients into glass and lightly stir.

1⅔	shots	**Martini Bianco vermouth**
⅔	shot	**Campari Bitter**
⅓	shot	**Giffard Menthe Pastille liqueur**
2	shots	**Peroni lager**

Origin: Adapted from a drink created in 2015 by
Dominic Whisson at the American Bar, The Savoy
Hotel, London, England.
Comment: A most unusual combination of classic
Italian red bitter liqueur, bianco vermouth, crème de
menthe and lager combine brilliantly in this refreshing
aperitif.

ANGEL'S DRAFT

★★★★⯪

Glass: Coupe
Garnish: Grapefruit zest twist
(discarded) & mint leaf
Method: SHAKE all ingredients
with ice and strain back into
shaker. **DRY SHAKE** (without
ice) to emulsify and fine strain
into chilled glass.

1½ shots Bacardi Carta Blanca
light rum
¼ shot Yellow Chartreuse liqueur
½ shot Freshly squeezed lime juice
¼ shot Agave syrup
1 dash Grapefruit bitters
3 fresh Mint leaves
¼ fresh Egg white

Origin: Adapted from the Bacardi
legacy UK winning drink of 2010
by Matthew Dakers. He created
this drink in 2009 at The Hoxton
Pony, London, England.
Comment: A refreshing, minty,
light cocktail with herbal
complexity.

ANGEL'S SHARE #1

★★★★⯪

Glass: Martini
Garnish: Orange zest twist
Method: STIR heaped spoon of orange marmalade
with cognac in base of shaker until marmalade
dissolves. Add other ingredients, **SHAKE** with ice and
fine strain into chilled glass.

1	spoon	**English orange marmalade**
2	shots	**Martell VSOP Médaillon cognac**
¼	shot	**Licor 43 liqueur**
½	shot	**Freshly squeezed lemon juice**
¼	shot	**Sugar syrup (2 sugar to 1 water)**

Origin: Created in 2005 by Milo Rodriguez, London.
Comment: Tangy citrus fruit and cognac smoothed
with a hint of vanilla.

ANGEL'S SHARE #2

★★★★⯪

Glass: Snifter
Garnish: None
Method: POUR the Chartreuse into glass and coat the inside of the glass with the liqueur by tilting and rotating it. **DISCARD** excess liqueur. Carefully set the liqueur on the inside of the glass alight and allow it to **BURN** for a few seconds. Extinguish flame by placing a saucer over the glass, add other ingredients and **SWIRL** to mix. Beware of hot glass rim.

¼	shot	Green Chartreuse liqueur
1½	shots	Martell VSOP Médaillon cognac
¾	shot	Nocello walnut liqueur
½	shot	Tawny port

Origin: Adapted from a recipe created in 2005 by Jacques Bezuidenhout at Harry Denton's Starlight Room, San Francisco, USA.
Comment: A fabulous drink, especially when VEP Chartreuse, family reserve cognac and 20 year old tawny port are used as per the original Starlight Room recipe.

ANIS'TINI

★★★★☆

Glass: Martini
Garnish: Star anise
Method: MUDDLE star anise in base of shaker. Add other ingredients, **SHAKE** with ice and fine strain into chilled glass.

2	dried	Star anise
1	shot	Ketel One Vodka
¾	shot	Black sambuca liqueur
½	shot	Pernod anise
1½	shots	Chilled water (reduce if wet ice)

Origin: Discovered in 2002 at Lot 61, New York City, USA
Comment: Specs of star anise are evident in this aniseedy Martini.

ANIS-THETIC

★★★★⯪☆

Glass: Old-fashioned
Garnish: Mint sprig & absinthe mist from atomiser
Method: SHAKE all ingredients and fine strain into an empty chilled glass.

12	fresh	Mint leaves
2	shots	Bourbon whiskey
¼	shot	Giffard Menthe Pastille liqueur
¼	shot	Bénédictine D.O.M. liqueur
⅛	shot	Marie Brizard Anisette
⅛	shot	Sugar syrup (2 sugar to 1 water)
3	dash	Angostura Aromatic Bitters
3	dash	Peychaud's aromatic bitters
¼	shot	Chilled water (omit if wet ice)

Origin: Adapted from a drink created in 2009 by Danny Murphy at the Met Bar, London, England. Originally made with homemade anis syrup and without crème de menthe.
Comment: As the name suggests, this bourbon-based drink is fresh breath-tastic.

ANITA'S ATTITUDE ADJUSTER

★★★☆☆

Glass: Sling
Garnish: Lemon slice & cherry on stick (sail)
Method: SHAKE first seven ingredients with ice and strain into ice-filled glass. **TOP** with champagne and gently stir.

½	shot	De Kuyper Triple Sec
½	shot	Patrón reposado tequila
½	shot	Bacardi Carta Blanca light rum
½	shot	Rutte Dry Gin
½	shot	Ketel One Vodka
½	shot	Freshly squeezed lime juice
½	shot	Sugar syrup (2 sugar to 1 water)
Top with		G.H. Mumm Cordon Rouge Champagne

Comment: Anita has a problem - she's indecisive when it comes to choosing base spirits.

THE ANSONIA

★★★★☆

Glass: Coupe
Garnish: Luxardo Maraschino cherry

Method: STIR all ingredients with ice and strain into chilled glass.

2	shots	Dewar's 12yo Scotch whisky
½	shot	Martini Rosso vermouth
¼	shot	Luxardo Maraschino liqueur
⅛	shot	Le Fée Parisienne absinthe

Origin: Adapted from a recipe by Charles Christopher in his 1934 ' Pioneers of Mixing at Elite Bars' and named after a luxurious residential hotel on Manhattan's Upper West Side. The Ansonia was built in 1904 and was the permanent home of the rich and famous including baseball player Babe Ruth, composer Igor Stravinsky, writer Theodore Dreiser and operatic tenor Enrico Caruso.

The first air-conditioned hotel in New York, the hotel's opulence was legendary and included a lobby pool and fountain which was home to a family of live seals. The original recipe called for dashes of Ojen bitters rather than absinthe. However, absinthe was banned in the USA at the time and Ojen was a Spanish brand of absinthe, so this was a way to communicate use of absinthe to other bartenders without highlighting the fact to authorities.
Comment: Scotch with delicate notes of sweet vermouth, maraschino and absinthe. Subtle and refined.

ANTE

★★★★☆

Glass: Martini
Garnish: Orange zest twist
Method: STIR all ingredients with ice and strain into chilled glass.

2	shots	Calvados brandy
½	shot	De Kuyper Triple Sec
1	shot	Dubonnet Red
2	dash	Angostura Aromatic Bitters

Origin: Recipe adapted from one discovered in 2006 on drinkboy.com.
Comment: Medium dry, complex spiced apple with hints of orange.

APACHE

★★★☆☆

Glass: Shot
Garnish: None
Method: Refrigerate ingredients then **LAYER** in chilled glass by carefully pouring in the following order.

¾ shot   **Coffee liqueur**
½ shot   **Midori Green Melon liqueur**
½ shot   **Baileys Irish cream liqueur**

Comment: A coffee, melon and whiskey cream layered shot.

APEROL SPRITZ

★★★★⯪

Glass: Old-fashioned
Garnish: Orange slice
Method: **POUR** ingredients into ice-filled glass in the following order and lightly stir.

3 shots   **Soave wine**
2 shots   **Aperol Aperitivo**
Top with   **Soda (club soda)**

Origin: Popular in northern Italy, especially in Venice and the Veneto region where it is pronounced "Spriss". (From the German verb Spritzen, meaning spray or splash). This aperitif cocktail's origins date back to the end of the 19th century when Venice was still part of the Austrian Empire, and is based on the Austrian Spritzer, a combination of equal parts white wine and soda water. It is made with the traditional white wines of the Veneto region, Pinot Grigio or Soave and sometimes with Prosecco.
Comment: Slightly sweetened, herbal flavoured and diluted wine. Those of you with a sweet tooth may like to try equal parts wine and Aperol with a splash of soda. Surprisingly it's the wine that dries this drink as Aperol is relatively sweet.

APHRODISIAC

★★★☆☆

Glass: Collins
Garnish: Apple slice
Method: **MUDDLE** ginger in base of shaker. Add other ingredients, **SHAKE** with ice and fine strain into ice-filled glass.

2 slice   **Fresh root ginger (thumbnail sized)**
2 shots   **Vanilla infused Ketel One vodka**
½ shot   **Green Chartreuse liqueur**
2½ shots   **Pressed apple juice**
1½ shots   **Sauvignon blanc white wine**

Origin: Created in 2002 by Yannick Miserieux at The Fifth Floor Bar, London, England.
Comment: As strong in flavour as it is high in alcohol.

APPILY MARRIED ⊙━┅

★★★★⯪

Glass: Martini
Garnish: Cinnamon & sugar rim
Method: **STIR** honey with vodka in base of shaker until honey dissolves. Add apple juice, **SHAKE** with ice and fine strain into chilled glass.

2 spoon   **Runny honey**
2½ shots   **Ketel One Vodka**
½ shot   **Pressed apple juice**

Origin: Created in 2005 by yours truly.
Comment: Apple and honey are indeed a marriage made in heaven, especially when laced with grainy vodka notes.

APPLE & BLACKBERRY SPRITZ (NEW)

★★★★☆

Glass: Rocks
Garnish: Blackberry and apple wedge
Method: **POUR** prosecco and liqueurs into glass. Add ice. Top with soda.

3 shots   **Prosecco sparkling wine**
1 shot   **Sour apple liqueur**
1 shot   **Lejay Crème de Mûre liqueur**
Top with   **Soda (club soda)**

Origin: Created in 2013 by yours truly for Jamie's Italian Bars.
Comment: The name aptly describes the drink.

APPLE & ELDERFLOWER COLLINS

★★★★☆

Glass: Collins
Garnish: Lemon slice
Method: **SHAKE** first 4 ingredients with ice and strain into ice-filled glass. **TOP** with soda, stir and serve with straws.

1½ shots   **Rutte Dry Gin**
1 shot   **St-Germain elderflower liqueur**
1 shot   **Apple Schnapps liqueur**
1 shot   **Freshly squeezed lime juice**
Top with   **Soda (club soda)**

Origin: Created in 2004 by yours truly, London, England.
Comment: A John Collins with lime in place of lemon and sweetened with apple and elderflower liqueurs.

APPLE BLACK ROYAL (NEW)

★★★★⯪

Glass: Flute
Garnish: Blackberry on rim
Method: **SHAKE** first 3 ingredients with ice and strain into chilled glass. **TOP** with champagne.

½ shot   **Lejay Crème de Mûre liqueur**
¼ shot   **Sour apple liqueur**
¾ shot   **Calvados brandy**
Top with   **G.H. Mumm Brut Rosé Champagne**

Origin: Created in 2015 by yours truly at the Cabinet Room, London, England.
Comment: Richly flavoured apple and blackberry fruit liqueurs, bolstered and fortified with calvados, charged and given character with rose champagne.

APPLE BLOSSOM COCKTAIL

★★★★⯪

Glass: Martini
Garnish: Apple wedge
Method: **SHAKE** all ingredients with ice and fine strain into chilled glass.

2 shots   **Calvados brandy**
2 shots   **Martini Rosso vermouth**

Origin: Adapted from Victor Bergeron's 'Trader Vic's Bartender's Guide' (1972 revised edition).
Comment: Stupidly simple to mix but complex to the taste. Spiced and concentrated apple.

APPLE BRANDY SOUR

★★★★⯪

Glass: Old-fashioned
Garnish: Lemon slice & cherry on stick (sail)
Method: DRY SHAKE (without ice) all ingredients to emulsify. Add ice, **SHAKE** again and strain into ice-filled glass.

2	shots	Calvados brandy
1	shot	Freshly squeezed lemon juice
¾	shot	Sugar syrup (2 sugar to 1 water)
3	dash	Angostura Aromatic Bitters
½	fresh	Egg white

Comment: Sour by name - balanced sweet and sour apple by nature.

APPLE BREEZE

★★★★☆

Glass: Collins
Garnish: Apple wedge
Method: SHAKE all ingredients with ice and strain into ice-filled glass.

2	shots	Zubrówka bison vodka
2½	shots	Pressed apple juice
1½	shots	Cranberry juice

Comment: More interesting than the better known Sea Breeze.

APPLE BUCK

★★★★☆

Glass: Collins
Garnish: Apple wedge
Method: SHAKE first four ingredients with ice and strain into ice-filled glass. **TOP** with ginger ale.

1½	shots	Calvados brandy
½	shot	Sour apple liqueur
1	shot	Pressed apple juice
½	shot	Freshly squeezed lime juice
Top with		Ginger ale

Origin: Adapted from a drink created in 2004 by Wayne Collins.
Comment: A refreshing long number with a taste reminiscent of cider.

APPLE CART

★★★★☆

Glass: Martini
Garnish: Apple wedge
Method: SHAKE all ingredients with ice and fine strain into chilled glass.

1½	shots	Calvados brandy
1	shot	De Kuyper Triple Sec
1	shot	Freshly squeezed lemon juice
½	shot	Chilled water (omit if wet ice)

Origin: This classic cocktail is an adaptation of the even older Sidecar.
Comment: A serious combination of apple with orange and sweet with sour.

APPLE CRUMBLE COCKTAIL #2

★★★★☆

Glass: Martini
Garnish: Dust with cinnamon powder
Method: SHAKE all ingredients with ice and fine strain into chilled glass.

2	shots	Tuaca liqueur
½	shot	Freshly squeezed lemon juice
2	shots	Pressed apple juice

Origin: Created in 2002 by Eion Richards at Bond's Bar, London, England.
Comment: Easy to make and equally easy to drink.

APPLE FOOL

★★★★☆

Glass: Coupe
Garnish: Float dehydrated apple slice
Method: SHAKE all ingredients with ice and fine strain into chilled glass.

5	fresh	Basil leaves
1½	shots	Patrón reposado tequila
½	shot	Green Chartreuse liqueur
1	shot	Freshly squeezed ruby grapefruit juice
¾	shot	Freshly squeezed lime juice
½	shot	Sugar syrup (2 sugar to 1 water)

Origin: Adapted from a drink created by Aisha Sharpe, New York City, USA.
Comment: This drink looks like it is going to be good for you, it's fresh and enlivening

APPLE MAC

★★★★☆

Glass: Martini
Garnish: Apple slice
Method: SHAKE all ingredients with ice and fine strain into chilled glass.

2	shots	Dewar's 12yo Scotch whisky
1½	shots	Pressed apple juice
½	shot	Stone's green ginger wine

Origin: A 2004 riff on the classic Whisky Mac by yours truly, London, England.
Comment: Scotch, ginger and apple are a threesome made in heaven.

APPLE MANHATTAN #1

★★★★☆

Glass: Martini
Garnish: Dehydrated apple slice
Method: STIR all ingredients with ice and strain into chilled glass.

2	shots	Bourbon whiskey
1½	shots	Apple Schnapps liqueur
½	shot	Martini Rosso vermouth

Origin: Our take on a drink created by David Marsden at First on First in New York City and latterly popularised by Dale DeGroff.
Comment: Rusty gold in colour, this is a flavoursome threesome for bourbon lovers.

APPLE MANHATTAN #2

★★★★☆

Glass: Martini
Garnish: Apple wedge
Method: STIR all ingredients with ice and strain into chilled glass.

2 shots Bourbon whiskey
¾ shot Apple Schnapps liqueur
¼ shot De Kuyper Triple Sec
½ shot Martini Rosso vermouth

Origin: Created in Sweden by Asa Nevestveit and Robert Sorman at Grill, Stockholm, Sweden.
Comment: Exactly as billed, a Manhattan with a hint of apple.

APPLE MARTINI # 2

★★★★☆

Glass: Martini
Garnish: Apple wedge
Method: SHAKE all ingredients with ice and fine strain into chilled glass.

1½ shots Ketel One Vodka
1 shot Apple Schnapps liqueur
2 shots Pressed apple juice

Comment: There are as many different recipes for this drink as there are varieties of apple and brands of apple liqueur: this one was popular in the UK during the Noughties.

APPLE MARTINI (SIMPLE)

★★★★☆

Glass: Martini
Garnish: Luxardo Maraschino cherry
Method: SHAKE all ingredients with ice and fine strain into chilled glass.

2 shots Ketel One Vodka
1¾ shots Pressed apple juice
¼ shot Sugar syrup (2 sugar to 1 water)

Origin: Formula by yours truly in 2004.
Comment: This is subtitled 'simple' for good reason but, if freshly pressed juice is used, it's as good if not better than other Apple Martini recipes.

APPLE MOJITO

★★★★☆

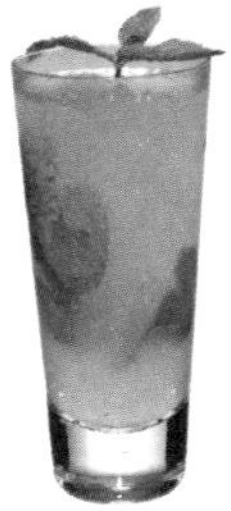

Glass: Collins
Garnish: Mint sprig
Method: Lightly **MUDDLE** (just to bruise) mint in base of glass. Add other ingredients, half fill glass with crushed ice and **CHURN** (stir) with bar spoon. Fill glass to brim with more crushed ice and **CHURN** some more. Serve with straws.

12 fresh Mint leaves
2 shots Bacardi Carta Blanca light rum
1 shot Apple Schnapps liqueur
1 shot Freshly squeezed lime juice

Origin: Recipe by yours truly in 2005.
Comment: An enduring classic given a touch of apple. Those with a sweet tooth may want to add more apple liqueur or even a dash of sugar syrup.

THE APPLE ONE

★★★★☆

Glass: Collins
Garnish: Apple slice & mint leaf
Method: SHAKE all ingredients with ice and fine strain into glass filled with crushed ice.

2 shots Bourbon whiskey
¾ shot St-Germain elderflower liqueur
¾ shot Pressed apple juice
½ shot Freshly squeezed lime juice

Origin: Adapted from a recipe created in 2008 by Vincenzo Marianella at Doheny, Los Angeles, USA.
Comment: Whiskey, elderflower and apple with a refreshing burst of citrus.

APPLE PIE COCKTAIL

★★★★☆

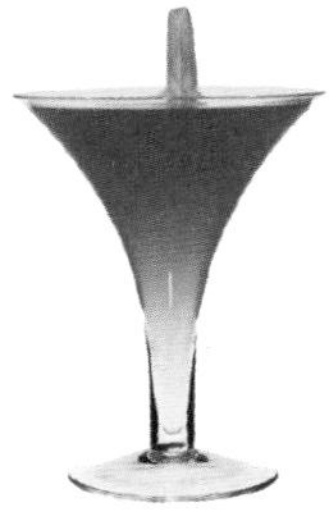

Glass: Martini
Garnish: Apple wedge
Method: SHAKE all ingredients with ice and fine strain into chilled glass.

1½ shots Zubrówka bison vodka
½ shot Cinnamon schnapps
2 shots Pressed apple juice
1 shot Cranberry juice

Origin: Created in 2000 by Alexia Pau Barrera at Sand Bar, Clapham, England.
Comment: There's a good hit of cinnamon in this apple pie.

APPLE SPRITZ

★★★★☆

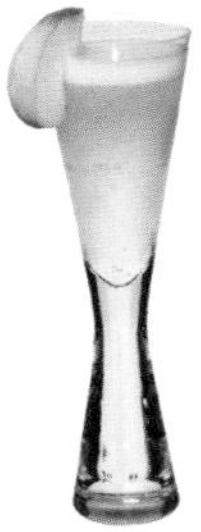

Glass: Flute
Garnish: Peach slice
Method: POUR first 2 ingredients into glass then **TOP** with champagne.

¾ shot Apple Schnapps liqueur
¼ shot Peachtree peach schnapps
Top with G.H.Mumm Cordon Rouge Champagne

Origin: Discovered in 2003 at Paramount Hotel, New York City, USA.
Comment: Sweet, fruity champagne.

APPLE STRUDEL #2

★★★★½

Glass: Coupe
Garnish: Cinnamon & sugar rim
Method: SHAKE all ingredients with ice and fine strain into chilled glass.

1½ shots Vanilla infused Ketel One vodka
½ shot Dewar's 12yo Scotch whisky
½ shot Apple Schnapps liqueur
½ shot Martini Extra Dry vermouth
½ shot Pressed apple juice
¼ shot Sugar syrup (2 sugar to 1 water)

Origin: Created in 2006 by yours truly, London, England.
Comment: Apple, vanilla and a hint of Scotch - reminiscent of the dessert but a good deal drier.

APPLE VIRGIN MOJITO (MOCKTAIL)

★★★★☆☆

Glass: Collins
Garnish: Mint sprig
Method: PLACE mint, lemon, lime and sugar in glass. Half fill glass with crushed ice and CHURN (stir). Add more crushed ice to fill glass. Add apple juice, top with soda and CHURN some more. Serve with straws.

12	fresh	Mint leaves
½	shot	Freshly squeezed lemon juice
½	shot	Freshly squeezed lime juice
¾	shot	Sugar syrup (2 sugar to 1 water)
3	shots	Pressed apple juice
Top with		Soda (club soda)

Origin: Created in 2002 by Tony Conigliaro at Isola, London, England.
Comment: A very refreshing driver's option.

APPLE, CUCUMBER & ELDERFLOWER CUP

★★★★☆

Glass: Martini
Garnish: Cucumber slices
Method: MUDDLE cucumber in base of shaker. Add other ingredients, SHAKE with ice and fine strain into chilled glass.

1	inch	English cucumber peeled
2	shots	Zubrówka bison vodka
½	shot	St-Germain elderflower liqueur
½	shot	Pressed apple juice

Origin: Discovered in 2007 at Public Restaurant, New York City, USA.
Comment: Apple and Zubrówka is a magic combination, as is apple and elderflower. Here these flavoursome combinations are enhanced and freshened by cucumber.

APPLEJACK RABBIT

★★★★☆

Glass: Jam jar
Garnish: Cinnamon stick and dust with freshly grated cinnamon
Method: SHAKE all ingredients with ice and strain into ice-filled jar.

1½ shots Applejack brandy (bonded)
½ shot Maple syrup
1 shot Freshly squeezed orange juice
¾ shot Freshly squeezed lemon juice

Origin: This on the rocks and jarred version of the Savoy book's classic is adapted from a drink discovered in 2009 by Dino Koletsas at Bourne & Hollingsworth, London, England.
Comment: Apple brandy sweetened by maple syrup, soured by lemon and lengthened with orange.

APPLEJACK RABBIT COCKTAIL

★★★★☆☆

Glass: Coupe
Garnish: Lemon zest twist
Method: SHAKE all ingredients with ice and fine strain into chilled glass.

1 ¾ shots Applejack brandy (bonded)
¼ shot Maple syrup
¾ shot Freshly squeezed orange juice
½ shot Freshly squeezed lemon juice

Origin: This drink is usually credited to Harry Craddock's 1930 'The Savoy Cocktail Book' which specifies: one hooker of applejack, the juice of one lemon, the juice of one orange and one hooker of maple syrup. In his 1948 'Fine Art of Mixing Drinks', David A. Embury writes, "This drink is also sometimes, for no reason at all, called the Applejack Dynamite. The same cocktail made with a gin base plus a dash of Angostura is called the Old Vermont." Incidentally, Embury's recipe is: 6 part applejack (1 1/2 shots), 1 part lemon juice (1/4 shot), 1 part orange juice (1/4 shot) and 1 part maple syrup (1/4 shot).
Comment: Stewed apple with citrus and a faint toffee apple finish.

APPLESINTH

★★★★☆

Glass: Old-fashioned
Garnish: Apple wedge
Method: SHAKE all ingredients with ice and strain into glass filled with crushed ice.

1	shot	Le Fée Parisienne absinthe
1	shot	Apple Schnapps liqueur
2	shots	Pressed apple juice
¾	shot	Freshly squeezed lime juice
½	shot	Sugar syrup (2 sugar to 1 water)

Origin: Created in 1999 by Alex Kammerling, London, England.
Comment: Hints of apple and liquorice combine to make a very moreish cocktail.

APRICOT COSMO

★★★★☆

Glass: Martini
Garnish: Apricot slice
Method: STIR apricot preserve with vodka until preserve dissolves. Add other ingredients, SHAKE with ice and fine strain into chilled glass.

2	shots	Ketel One Vodka
1	spoon	Apricot jam (preserve)
1	shot	Cranberry juice
¼	shot	Sugar syrup (2 sugar to 1 water)
½	shot	Freshly squeezed lime juice
2	dash	Angostura Orange Bitters

Origin: Created in 2004 at Aura Kitchen & Bar, London, England.
Comment: The apricot preserve adds a flavoursome tang to the contemporary classic.

APRICOT FIZZ

★★★⯪☆

Glass: Collins
Garnish: Lemon wedge
Method: **SHAKE** first three ingredients with ice and strain into ice-filled glass. **TOP** with soda water.

2	shots	De Kuyper XO Apricot Brandy
1	shot	Freshly squeezed orange juice
½	shot	Freshly squeezed lime juice
Top with		Soda from siphon

Comment: This low-alcohol, refreshing cocktail is perfect for a summer afternoon.

APRICOT LADY SOUR

★★★⯪☆

Glass: Old-fashioned
Garnish: Lemon slice & cherry on stick (sail)
Method: **DRY SHAKE** (without ice) all ingredients to emulsify. Add ice, **SHAKE** again and strain into ice-filled glass.

1½	shots	Bacardi Carta Blanca light rum
1	shot	De Kuyper XO Apricot Brandy
1	shot	Freshly squeezed lemon juice
¼	shot	Sugar syrup (2 sugar to 1 water)
½	fresh	Egg white

Comment: This seemingly soft and fluffy, apricot flavoured drink hides a most unladylike rum bite.

APRICOT MANGO COCKTAIL

★★★★⯪

Glass: Martini
Garnish: Mango slice
Method: **SHAKE** all ingredients with ice and fine strain into glass.

1½	shots	Rutte Dry Gin
¾	shot	De Kuyper XO Apricot Brandy
¾	shot	Mango purée
½	shot	Freshly squeezed lemon juice
½	shot	Sugar syrup (2 sugar to 1 water)
2	dash	Angostura Orange Bitters

Origin: Originally named Apricot Mango Martini this drink was created during the fresh fruit Martini craze that swept through London's bars in the mid 1990s. Name and recipe updated by yours truly in September 2014.
Comment: Just as it says on the tin. Rich tropical and orchard fruit, but not overly sweet with balancing lemon citrus acidity, orange bitters and underlying gin botanical complexity.

APRICOT RICKEY

★★★★☆

Glass: Collins (small 8oz)
Garnish: Length of lime peel
Method: **SHAKE** first three ingredients with ice and strain into ice-filled glass. **TOP** with soda.

1	shot	Rutte Dry Gin
1	shot	De Kuyper XO Apricot Brandy
½	shot	Freshly squeezed lime juice
Top with		Soda (club soda)

Comment: Light, fruity and refreshing, if a little on the sweet side.

APRICOT SOUR

★★★★☆

Glass: Old-fashioned
Garnish: Lemon zest twist
Method: **STIR** apricot jam (preserve) with bourbon until it dissolves. Add other ingredients, **SHAKE** with ice and fine strain into ice-filled glass.

2	spoon	Apricot jam (preserve)
1½	shots	Bourbon whiskey
½	shot	De Kuyper XO Apricot Brandy
1	shot	Pressed apple juice
½	shot	Freshly squeezed lemon juice

Origin: Created in 2005 by Wayne Collins for Maxxium UK.
Comment: Short and fruity.

APRIL SHOWER

★★★★☆

Glass: Martini
Garnish: Orange zest twist
Method: **SHAKE** all ingredients with ice and fine strain into chilled glass.

2	shots	Martell VSOP Médaillon cognac
½	shot	Bénédictine D.O.M. liqueur
1½	shots	Freshly squeezed orange juice

Comment: This mustard coloured, medium dry, cognac-based drink harnesses the uniquely herbal edge of Bénédictine.

AQUARIUS

★★★⯪☆

Glass: Old-fashioned
Garnish: None
Method: **SHAKE** all ingredients with ice and strain into ice-filled glass.

2	shots	Dewar's 12yo Scotch whisky
1	shot	Cherry Heering Liqueur
1½	shots	Cranberry juice

Comment: A sweet cherry edge is balanced by the dryness of cranberry and Scotch.

ARCHIBALD PERISCOPE

★★★★☆

Glass: Collins
Garnish: Long bendy straw
Method: **SHAKE** first three ingredients with ice and fine strain into chilled glass. **TOP** with soda and then carefully **FLOAT** Rioja wine.

2	shots	Rutte Dry Gin
1	shot	Peachtree peach schnapps
¾	shot	Sauvignon blanc white wine
¾	shot	Chilled water
½	shot	Rioja red wine

Origin: Adapted (considerably) from a drink discovered in 2009 at Albert & Pearl, Islington, London, England.
Comment: Slightly sweet, long and refreshing. To quote the menu at Albert & Pearl where we discovered this cocktail, "a sight for sore eyes".

ARGENTINA COCKTAIL

★★★★☆

Glass: Martini
Garnish: Orange zest twist
Method: **STIR** all ingredients with ice and strain into chilled glass.

1 shot **Rutte Dry Gin**
1 shot **Martini Extra Dry vermouth**
¼ shot **De Kuyper Triple Sec**
¼ shot **Bénédictine D.O.M. liqueur**
1 dash **Angostura Orange Bitters**
1 dash **Angostura Aromatic Bitters**

Comment: A wet martini softened by liqueur and given a hint of citrus and spice.

ARGHA NOAH

★★★★☆

Glass: Old-fashioned
Garnish: Orange zest twist
Method: **STIR** all ingredients with ice and strain into ice-filled glass.

2 shots **Bacardi Carta Ocho aged rum**
⅛ shot **Honey sugar syrup**
¼ shot **Drambuie liqueur**
⅛ shot **Romate Oloroso sherry**
½ shot **Cranberry juice**

Origin: Created in January 2009 by yours truly at the Cabinet Room, London, England.
Comment: Delicately spiced, honeyed and sherried aged rum.

ARISITIOL COCKTAIL (NEW)

★★★★½

Glass: Coupe
Garnish: Mint leaf
Method: Lightly **MUDDLE** mint in base of stirring glass. Add other ingredients, **STIR** with ice and strain into chilled glass.

3 fresh **Mint leaves**
1½ shots **Rutte Dry Gin**
1 shot **Skinos Mastiha**
1½ shots **Birch water**
4 drop **Bob's Bitters Peppermint bitters** (optional)

Origin: Created in August 2015 by yours truly at the Cabinet Room, London, England.
Comment: The thinking man's mixed drink, this is based on gin with the distinctive flavour of Greek mastiha and lengthened with birch water.

ARMILLITA CHICO

★★★½☆

Glass: Martini (large 10oz)
Garnish: Lime wedge
Method: **BLEND** all ingredients with 12oz scoop crushed ice.

2 shots **Patrón reposado tequila**
1 shot **Freshly squeezed lime juice**
½ shot **Pomegranate / grenadine syrup (2:1)**
2 dash **Orange flower water**

Comment: Similar to a frozen Margarita but more subtle and dry.

ARMY & NAVY

★★★★☆

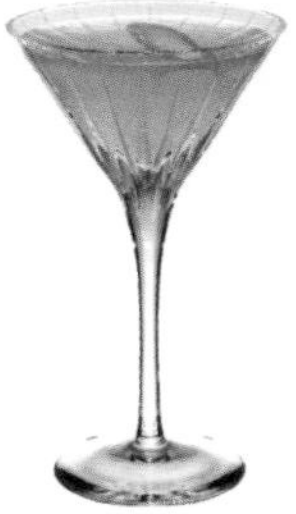

Glass: Martini
Garnish: Lemon zest twist
Method: **SHAKE** all ingredients with ice and fine strain into chilled glass.

2 shots **Rutte Dry Gin**
½ shot **Freshly squeezed lemon juice**
¼ shot **Almond (orgeat) syrup**
½ shot **Chilled water** (omit if wet ice)

Origin: This old classic was originally made to an 8:4:4 formula but we have borrowed this 8:2:1 formula from David A. Embury's 1948 'Fine Art of Mixing Drinks' (he describes the original formulation as "horrible").
Comment: Almond and lemon flavoured gin. Subtle, citrusy and dry.

ARMY MARTINI

★★★★☆

Glass: Martini
Garnish: Mint leaf
Method: **SHAKE** all ingredients with ice and fine strain into chilled glass.

2½ shots **Rutte Dry Gin**
¼ shot **Martini Rosso vermouth**
¼ shot **Pomegranate / grenadine syrup (2:1)**

Comment: This rosé Martini is harder than it looks - perhaps why the name?

ARNAUD MARTINI

★★★★☆

Glass: Martini
Garnish: Blackberries
Method: **STIR** all ingredients with ice and strain into chilled glass.

1 shot **Rutte Dry Gin**
1 shot **Martini Extra Dry vermouth**
1 shot **Lejay Crème de Cassis de Dijon**

Origin: A classic cocktail named after the pre-war stage actress Yvonne Arnaud.
Comment: An interesting balance of blackcurrant, vermouth and gin. Sweet palate and dry finish.

ARNOLD PALMER (MOCKTAIL)

★★★★☆

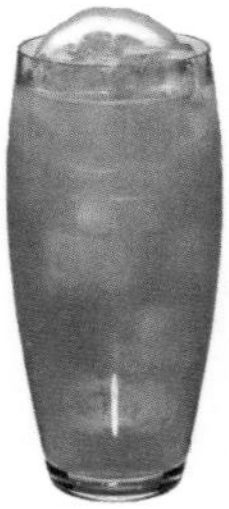

Glass: Collins
Garnish: Lemon slice
Method: **SHAKE** all ingredients with ice and strain into ice-filled glass.

3 shots **Cold English breakfast tea**
2 shots **Freshly squeezed lemon juice**
1 shot **Sugar syrup (2 sugar to 1 water)**

Origin: A popular drink throughout the United States. Named after and said to be a favourite of the legendary golfer.
Comment: Real lemon iced tea. Balanced and wonderfully refreshing.

ARTIST'S SPECIAL (NEW)

★★★★⯪

Glass: Coupe
Garnish: Redcurrant bunch laid across rim
Method: SHAKE all ingredients with ice and fine strain into chilled glass.

1½ shots Teeling Small Batch Irish whiskey
1½ shots Romate Oloroso sherry
½ shot Freshly squeezed lemon juice
¼ shot Red currant (groseille) syrup

Origin: A voraciously pink Parisian special from the 1920s, this cocktail first appears in Harry and Wynn's 'Barflies and Cocktails' in 1927. Three years later the Artist's Special then featured in 'The Savoy Cocktail Book'. Harry Craddock wrote of it: "This is the genuine 'Ink of Inspiration' imbibed at the Bal Bullier, Paris. The recipe is from the Artist's Club, Rue Pigalle, Paris."
Comment: Irish whiskey is often matured in Romate Oloroso sherry seasoned casks so it's no surprise that whiskey and sherry blend harmoniously in this cocktail, with lemon tartness balanced by rich red currant syrup.

ASIAN GINGER COCKTAIL

★★★★☆

Glass: Martini
Garnish: Fresh ginger slice
Method: MUDDLE ginger in base of shaker. Add other ingredients, SHAKE with ice and fine strain into chilled glass.

2 slice Fresh root ginger (thumbnail sized)
2¼ shots Junmai ginjō sake
1½ shots Ketel One Vodka
¼ shot Sugar syrup (2 sugar to 1 water)

Origin: Adapted from a recipe created in 2004 by Chris Langan of Barnomadics.
Comment: Lightly spiced with ginger, distinctly oriental in character.

ASIAN MARY

★★★★☆

Glass: Collins
Garnish: Lemongrass
Method: MUDDLE ginger in base of shaker and add vodka. Squeeze wasabi paste onto bar spoon and STIR with vodka and ginger until dissolved. Add other ingredients, SHAKE with ice and fine strain into ice-filled glass.

3 slice Fresh root ginger (thumbnail sized)
3 pea Wasabi paste
3 shots Ketel One Citroen vodka
1 spoon Soy sauce
½ shot Freshly squeezed lemon juice
4 shots Tomato juice

Comment: An aptly named Bloody Mary with plenty of Asian spice.

ASTOR

★★★★☆

Glass: Martini
Garnish: Lemon zest twist
Method: SHAKE all ingredients with ice and fine strain into chilled glass.

1¼ shots Rutte Dry Gin
1 shot Swedish Punch liqueur
¼ shot Freshly squeezed lemon juice
¼ shot Freshly squeezed orange juice

Origin: Recipe adapted from Albert Stevens Crockett's 1931 'The Old Waldorf-Astoria Bar Book' where the recipe is accompanied by the following notation, "Perhaps [named] after William Waldorf, who built the original Waldorf. However, chances are, it originated either at the old Astor House or the Astor Hotel, and took its name from its bar of nativity."
Comment: Citrus and the tang of Swedish punch add a distinctive flavour to gin in this tasty vintage cocktail.

ASTORIA

★★★★☆

Glass: Martini
Garnish: Lemon zest twist
Method: STIR all ingredients with ice and strain into chilled glass.

1 shot Old Tom gin
2 shots Martini Extra Dry vermouth
2 dash Angostura Orange Bitters

Origin: Recipe adapted from Albert Stevens Crockett's 1931 'The Old Waldorf-Astoria Bar Book' where the recipe is accompanied by the following notation, "After the big annex to the Old Waldorf, which at its opening, in 1897, became the main part of the establishment."

William Waldorf Astor built the original Waldorf Hotel, which opened in 1893, next door to his aunt's home, on the site of his father's mansion and today's Empire State Building. John Astor persuaded his aunt to move uptown and then built the Astor Hotel. The two hotels were connected and the combined Waldorf-Astoria became the largest hotel in the world at the time.
Comment: An Old Tom based super wet (two-thirds vermouth to one-third gin) Martini with a slug of orange bitters and served with a twist.

B
C
D
E
F
G
H
I
J
K
L
M
N
O
P
Q
R
S
T
U
V
W
X
Y
Z

ATHOLL BROSE

★★★★★

Glass: Coupe
Garnish: Dust with grated nutmeg
Method: Prepare oatmeal water by soaking three heaped tablespoons of oatmeal in half a mug of warm water. Stir and leave to stand for fifteen minutes. Then strain to extract the creamy liquid and discard what's left of the oatmeal.

To make the drink, **STIR** honey with Scotch until honey dissolves. Add other ingredients, **SHAKE** with ice and fine strain into chilled glass.

2	spoon	Runny honey (heather)
2	shots	Dewar's 12yo Scotch whisky
1½	shots	Oatmeal water
¼	shot	Drambuie liqueur
¼	shot	Disaronno Originale amaretto
½	shot	Single cream / half-and-half

Origin: Our adaptation of a Scottish classic.

Legend has it that Atholl Brose was created by the Earl of Atholl in 1475 when he was trying to capture Iain MacDonald, Lord of the Isles and leader of a rebellion against the king. Hearing rumours that MacDonald was drawing his drinking water from a small well, the Earl ordered it to be filled with honey, whisky and oatmeal. MacDonald lingered at the well enjoying the concoction and was captured.
Comment: Forget the porridge and kick start your day with a Atholl Brose.

ATOMIC DOG

★★★☆☆

Glass: Collins
Garnish: Pineapple wedge & Luxardo Maraschino cherry
Method: **SHAKE** all ingredients with ice and strain into ice-filled glass.

1½	shots	Bacardi Carta Blanca light rum
¾	shot	Midori Green Melon liqueur
¾	shot	Coconut rum liqueur
2½	shots	Fresh pressed pineapple juice
¾	shot	Freshly squeezed lemon juice

Comment: A long, refreshing tropical drink with melon, coconut and pineapple juice.

ATTA BOY COCKTAIL (NEW)

★★★★☆

Glass: Coupe
Garnish: Orange zest twist
Method: **STIR** all ingredients with ice and strain into chilled glass.

2	shots	Rutte Dry Gin
1	shot	Martini Extra Dry vermouth
⅓	shot	Pomegranate / grenadine syrup (2:1)

Origin: Adapted from a recipe in Harry Craddock's 1930 The Savoy Cocktail Book.
Comment: The orange zest twist makes or breaks this classic, which when properly balanced lets the gin shine with the sweet pomegranate notes of the grenadine obvious but not in your face.

ATTITUDE ADJUSTER

★★★☆☆

Glass: Hurricane
Garnish: Orange slice & cherry on stick (sail)
Method: **SHAKE** first 3 ingredients with ice and strain into ice-filled glass. **TOP** with Coca-Cola then **DRIZZLE** orange and coffee liqueurs.

2	shots	Rutte Dry Gin
1	shot	De Kuyper Triple Sec
¾	shot	Freshly squeezed lime juice
Top with		Coca-Cola
¼	shot	Grand Marnier Cordon Rouge
¼	shot	Coffee liqueur

Comment: We've simplified and tried to improve this somewhat dodgy but popular cocktail. Sorry, we failed!

THE ATTY COCKTAIL

★★★★☆

Glass: Martini
Garnish: Lemon zest twist
Method: **SHAKE** all ingredients with ice and fine strain into chilled glass.

2¼	shots	Rutte Dry Gin
¾	shot	Martini Extra Dry vermouth
¼	shot	Benoit Serres créme de violette
¼	shot	Le Fée Parisienne absinthe

Origin: Adapted from Harry Craddock's 1930 'The Savoy Cocktail Book'.
Comment: Dry and aromatic with floral hints and aniseed notes.

AULD ALLIANCE

★★★☆☆

Glass: Collins
Garnish: Lemon slice
Method: **SHAKE** first 4 ingredients with ice and strain into ice-filled glass. **TOP** with lemonade.

1½	shots	Dewar's 12yo Scotch whisky
¾	shot	Freshly squeezed lemon juice
½	shot	De Kuyper Triple Sec
¼	shot	Sugar syrup (2 sugar to 1 water)
Top with		Lemonade (English-style)

Comment: An orange-influenced whisky sour served long and refreshing.

AUNT AGATHA

★★★☆☆

Glass: Old-fashioned
Garnish: Orange zest twist
Method: **SHAKE** first 3 ingredients with ice and strain into glass filled with crushed ice. **DASH** bitters over surface.

1½	shots	Pusser's Navy Rum (54.5%)
2	shots	Freshly squeezed orange juice
1	shot	Fresh pressed pineapple juice
3	dash	Angostura Aromatic Bitters

Origin: Aunt Agatha was Bertie Wooster's terrifying aunt in P.G. Wodehouse's books.
Comment: A most unusual looking, tropical tasting concoction.

AUNT EMILY

★★★★☆

Glass: Martini
Garnish: Apricot slice
Method: **SHAKE** all ingredients with ice and fine strain into chilled glass.

1½	shots	**Rutte Dry Gin**
1½	shots	**Calvados brandy**
¾	shot	**De Kuyper XO Apricot Brandy**
¾	shot	**Freshly squeezed orange juice**
⅛	shot	**Pomegranate / grenadine syrup (2:1)**

Origin: A forgotten classic.
Comment: Aunt Emily is onto something as these ingredients combine to make a stylish fruity Martini.

AUNTIE'S HOT XMAS PUNCH

★★★★☆

Glass: Toddy
Garnish: Cinnamon stick
Method: **POUR** all ingredients into glass and stir. **MICROWAVE** for a minute (vary time depending on your microwave oven), stir again and serve.

1½	shots	**Romate Pedro Ximénez sherry**
2¼	shots	**Martell VSOP Médaillon cognac**
¾	shot	**Freshly squeezed lemon juice**
3	shots	**Pressed apple juice**
4	dash	**Peychaud's aromatic bitters**

Origin: Created by yours truly. 'Auntie' is a nickname for the BBC and the drink uses the traditional punch proportions of 1 sour, 2 sweet, 3 strong and 4 weak.
Comment: A fruity seasonal warmer.

AUTUMN COCKTAIL

★★★★☆

Glass: Martini
Garnish: Orange zest twist
Method: Cut passion fruit in half and scoop out flesh into shaker. Add other ingredients, **SHAKE** with ice and fine strain into chilled glass.

1	fresh	**Passion fruit**
2	shots	**Zubrówka bison vodka**
1	shot	**Pressed apple juice**
½	shot	**Passion fruit syrup**
½	fresh	**Egg white**

Origin: Created in 2004 by yours truly and inspired by Max Warner's excellent Autumn Punch.
Comment: An easy drinking, smooth, fruity cocktail with grassy hints courtesy of bison vodka.

AUTUMN LEAVES

★★★★½

Glass: Old-fashioned
Garnish: Orange zest twist
Method: **STIR** all ingredients with ice and strain into ice-filled glass.

1	shot	**Straight rye whiskey**
1	shot	**Calvados brandy**
1	shot	**Martini Rosso vermouth**
¼	shot	**Strega liqueur**
2	dash	**Angostura Aromatic Bitters**

Origin: Created in 2008 by Jeffrey Morgenthaler at Bel Ami Lounge, Oregon, USA. Jeffrey's original recipe calls for Carpano Antica Formula.
Comment: Whiskey, apple brandy, vermouth and herbal liqueur combine delightfully.

AUTUMN PUNCH

★★★★½

Glass: Sling
Garnish: Physalis (cape gooseberry)
Method: Cut passion fruit in half and scoop out flesh into shaker. Add vodka, passion fruit syrup, pear and lemon juice, **SHAKE** with ice and strain into ice-filled glass. **TOP** with champagne.

1	fresh	**Passion fruit**
2	shots	**Zubrówka bison vodka**
¼	shot	**Passion fruit syrup**
1	shot	**Pressed pear juice**
½	shot	**Freshly squeezed lemon juice**
Top with		**G.H. Mumm Cordon Rouge Champagne**

Origin: Created in 2001 by Max Warner at Baltic Bar, London, England.
Comment: Autumnal in colour with a wonderful meld of complementary flavours.

AVALANCHE SHOT

★★½☆☆

Glass: Shot
Garnish: None
Method: Refrigerate ingredients then **LAYER** in chilled glass by carefully pouring in the following order.

½	shot	**Coffee liqueur**
½	shot	**White crème de cacao liqueur**
½	shot	**Southern Comfort liqueur**

Comment: Rich, smooth and sticky - peculiarly, this has an almost nutty taste.

AVENUE

★★★★☆

Glass: Martini
Garnish: Orange zest twist
Method: Cut passion fruit in half and scoop flesh into shaker. Add other ingredients, **SHAKE** with ice and fine strain into chilled glass.

1	fresh	**Passion fruit**
1	shot	**Bourbon whiskey**
1	shot	**Calvados brandy**
¼	shot	**Pomegranate / grenadine syrup (2:1)**
⅛	shot	**Orange flower water**
1	dash	**Angostura Orange Bitters**
½	shot	**Chilled water** (omit if wet ice)

Origin: Adapted from W.J. Tarling's 1937 'Café Royal Bar Book'.
Comment: Passion fruit and orange flavours, laced with apple brandy and bourbon. Fruity yet dry.

STAR RATINGS EXPLAINED

★★★★★+	OUTSTANDING	★★★★★	EXCEPTIONAL
★★★★½	EXCELLENT	★★★★☆	RECOMMENDED
★★★½☆	COMMENDED	★★★☆☆	MEDIOCRE
★★½☆☆	DISAPPOINTING	★★☆☆☆	PRETTY AWFUL
★½☆☆☆	SHAMEFUL	★☆☆☆☆	DISGUSTING

Aviation Cocktail

The Aviation is a classic gin based cocktail which is shaken and served straight-up. It is basically a Gin Sour but with lemon juice sourness balanced by sweet maraschino liqueur and sometimes also crème de violet liqueur, rather than simply sugar syrup.

The Aviation cocktail first appears in print in Hugo R. Ensslin's 1916 'Recipes for Mixed Drinks'. Ensslin was the head bartender at New York's Hotel Wallick and is widely credited for creating the cocktail.

Aviation Cocktail (Hugo R. Ensslin's recipe)
"1/3 Lemon juice, 2/3 El Bart gin, 2 dashes Maraschino, 2 dashes Crème de Violette. Shake well in mixing glass with cracked ice, strain and serve."

The above recipe is a tad on the sour side being light on gin and heavy on lemon juice, so in my Aviation recipe I have balanced Ensslin's proportions by simply upping the gin by ¼ shot and reducing the lemon juice by ¼ shot. The result is better balanced and reveals the delicate floral flavours of crème de violette.

So named due to the crème de violette giving the cocktail a pale sky-blue colour, the Aviation dates from the early age of aeronautics when air travel was a glamorous luxury that only the rich could afford. The brand of crème de violette used is crucial to the look and taste of this cocktail and personally I favour Benoit Serres Liqueur de la Violette.

Crème de violette has never been the most widely distributed of liqueurs so many, including Harry Craddock in his 1930 Savoy Cocktail Book, simply omit it from the recipe.

Aviation Cocktail (Harry Craddock's recipe)
"1/3 Lemon juice, 2/3 Dry Gin, 2 dashes Maraschino liqueur. Shake well and strain into a cocktail glass."

Although no longer strictly an Aviation Cocktail, the combination of gin, lemon juice and maraschino does produce a cocktail with a flavour reminiscent of Ensslin's original, albeit without the subtle blue hue or floral notes of crème de violette. However, Craddock's recipe is very sour and lacks subtlety so my adapted recipe uses a lot less lemon juice.

Popular in the 1940s, the Blue Moon cocktail is an Aviation with gin, lemon juice and Crème Yvette liqueur (or crème de violette) but without maraschino. The recipe appears on the back label of Crème Yvette bottles dating from the period.

The Blue Moon (Crème Yvette label recipe)
"as originated by "Oscar of the Waldorf"
¼ Crème Yvette, ¾ Dry Gin, Ice, shake, serve in cocktail glasses."

In his The Cocktailian column in the San Francisco Chronicle (27 September 2007) Gary 'gaz' Regan revealed his riff on the classic Aviation. Called the Moonlight Cocktail, this is basically an Aviation but with triple sec in place of maraschino and lime instead of lemon juice.

Moonlight Cocktail (Gaz Regan's recipe)
"1½ oz Gin (Beefeater, Plymouth or Tanqueray), ½ oz Cointreau, ½ oz Crème de violette, ½ oz Fresh lime juice.
Instructions: Fill a cocktail shaker two-thirds full of ice and add all of the ingredients. Shake for approximately 15 seconds, and strain into a chilled Champagne flute."

Gaz used lime juice because he didn't have any lemons at the time but in my adaptation of Gaz's recipe I've mellowed the lime sourness by using a combination of both lime and lemon juice.

My own Biggles Aviation uses gin as a base but is far removed from the classic Aviation with ginger liqueur replacing maraschino and/or crème de violette. Back in 2006 when launching St-Germain liqueur I also created an elderflower riff of the Aviation called The Elder Aviator.

AVIATION COCKTAIL (DIFFORD'S RECIPE)

★★★★★

Glass: Martini
Garnish: Lemon zest twist (& optional sugar rim)
Method: **SHAKE** all ingredients with ice and fine strain into chilled glass.

1¾ shots **Rutte Dry Gin**
½ shot **Luxardo Maraschino liqueur**
¼ shot **Benoit Serres créme de violette**
½ shot **Freshly squeezed lemon juice**
¼ shot **Chilled water** (omit if wet ice)

Origin: My yours truly adaptation of Hugo R. Ensslin's Aviation Cocktail in his 1916 'Recipes for Mixed Drinks'.
Comment: Benefits from a long shake. Citrus, floral gin with a slightly sour finish.

AVIATION COCKTAIL (HARRY CRADDOCK'S RECIPE)

★★★★½

Glass: Martini
Garnish: Luxardo Maraschino cherry (& optional sugar rim)
Method: **SHAKE** all ingredients with ice and fine strain into chilled glass.

1¾ shots **Rutte Dry Gin**
¾ shot **Luxardo Maraschino liqueur**
½ shot **Freshly squeezed lemon juice**
¼ shot **Chilled water** (omit if wet ice)

Origin: A well-established vintage cocktail.
Comment: This is a fantastic, tangy cocktail and dangerously easy to drink - too many of these and you really will be flying.

AVIATOR #1

★★★★☆

Glass: Martini
Garnish: Lemon zest twist
Method: **SHAKE** first 4 ingredients with ice and fine strain into chilled glass. **POUR** cassis into centre of drink (it should sink).

2 shots **Rutte Dry Gin**
½ shot **Luxardo Maraschino liqueur**
½ shot **Freshly squeezed lemon juice**
½ fresh **Egg white**
¼ shot **Lejay crème de cassis de Dijon**

Comment: An Aviation with egg white and a dash of cassis in the bottom but is actually better and more balanced when the cassis is shaken with the other ingredients.

AVIATOR #2

★★★½☆

Glass: Martini
Garnish: Lemon zest twist
Method: **STIR** all ingredients with ice and strain into chilled glass.

1 shot **Rutte Dry Gin**
1 shot **Martini Extra Dry vermouth**
1 shot **Martini Rosso vermouth**
1 shot **Dubonnet Red**

Origin: A classic cocktail of unknown origin.
Comment: Bittersweet herbal notes of vermouth with a subtle hint of gin.

AWOL

★★★★☆

Glass: Shot
Garnish: None
Method: LAYER in chilled glass by carefully pouring ingredients in the following order. Then FLAME drink and allow to burn for no more than ten seconds before extinguishing flame and consuming. Take extreme care and beware of hot glass.

½ shot   Midori Green Melon liqueur
½ shot   Ketel One Vodka
½ shot   Fresh pressed pineapple juice
½ shot   White overproof rum

Origin: Created in 1993 by Lane Zellman at Louis XVI Restaurant, St. Louis Hotel, New Orleans, USA.
Comment: A strong but surprisingly palatable shot.

B & B

★★★★☆

Glass: Old-fashioned
Garnish: Lemon zest twist
Method: STIR ingredients with ice and strain into ice-filled glass.

2 shots   Bénédictine D.O.M. liqueur
2 shots   Martell VSOP Médaillon cognac

Origin: Said to have been created in 1937 by a bartender at New York's famous 21 Club – "Never let the truth get in the way of a good story."
Comment: Honeyed and spiced cognac.

B & T

★★★★☆

Glass: Martini
Garnish: Lime zest twist
Method: SHAKE all ingredients with ice and fine strain into chilled glass.

2 shots   Patrón reposado tequila
1 shot   Bénédictine D.O.M. liqueur

Origin: Adapted from a drink created in 2007 by Neyah White, San Francisco, USA. Originally this consisted of equal parts served unchilled in a brandy glass and using anejo tequila.
Comment: Delicately spiced and slightly sweetened tequila.

B-52 FROZEN

★★★★☆

Glass: Old-fashioned
Garnish: Crumbled Cadbury's Flake bar
Method: BLEND ingredients with 6oz scoop of crushed ice. Pour into glass and serve with straws.

1 shot   Baileys Irish cream liqueur
1 shot   Grand Marnier Cordon Rouge
1 shot   Coffee liqueur

Comment: The classic shot blended with ice.

B-52 SHOT

★★★★☆

Glass: Shot
Garnish: None
Method: Refrigerate ingredients then LAYER in chilled glass by carefully pouring in the following order.

½ shot   Coffee liqueur
½ shot   Baileys Irish cream liqueur
½ shot   Grand Marnier Cordon Rouge

Origin: Named after B-52 bombers in Vietnam.
Comment: Probably the best-known and most popular shot.

B-53 SHOT

★★★☆☆

Glass: Shot
Garnish: None
Method: Refrigerate ingredients then LAYER in chilled glass by carefully pouring in the following order.

½ shot   Coffee liqueur
½ shot   Baileys Irish cream liqueur
½ shot   Ketel One Vodka

Comment: Why settle for a 52 when you can go one better?

B-54 SHOT

★★★☆☆

Glass: Shot
Garnish: None
Method: Refrigerate ingredients then LAYER in chilled glass by carefully pouring in the following order.

½ shot   Disaronno Originale amaretto
½ shot   Coffee liqueur
½ shot   Baileys Irish cream liqueur

Comment: Layered and sticky - but nice.

B-55 SHOT

★★★☆☆

Glass: Shot
Garnish: None
Method: Refrigerate ingredients then LAYER in chilled glass by carefully pouring in the following order.

½ shot   Coffee liqueur
½ shot   Baileys Irish cream liqueur
½ shot   Le Fée Parisienne absinthe

Comment: The latest and scariest of the B-something range of layered shots.

B2C2

★★★⯪☆

Glass: Martini
Garnish: Orange zest twist
Method: **SHAKE** first 3 ingredients with ice and strain into ice-filled glass. **TOP** with champagne.

1	shot	Martell VSOP Médaillon cognac
1	shot	Bénédictine D.O.M. liqueur
1	shot	De Kuyper Triple Sec
Top with		G.H. Mumm Cordon Rouge Champagne

Origin: Named after this cocktail's four ingredients and created in France during World War II by American soldiers using booty liberated from retreating Germans. B2=brandy (cognac) and Benedictine, C2= Cointreau (triple sec) and champagne.
Comment: Strong and sweet.

B5200

★★★☆☆

Glass: Shot
Garnish: None
Method: Refrigerate ingredients then **LAYER** in chilled glass by carefully pouring in the following order.

½	shot	Coffee liqueur
½	shot	Baileys Irish cream liqueur
½	shot	Pusser's Navy Rum (54.5%)

Origin: Discovered in 2003 at Circus Bar, London, England.
Comment: Layering this drink is as easy as inflating a life jacket - drink a few and you'll need one.

BABY BLUE COCKTAIL

★★★⯪☆

Glass: Martini
Garnish: Orange zest twist
Method: **SHAKE** all ingredients with ice and fine strain into chilled glass.

2	shots	Rutte Dry Gin
¾	shot	Blue curaçao liqueur
¾	shot	Freshly squeezed pink grapefruit juice
¾	shot	Fresh pressed pineapple juice

Comment: Turquoise blue, easy drinking, fruity gin.

BABY GUINNESS

★★★⯪☆

Glass: Shot
Garnish: None
Method: Refrigerate ingredients then **LAYER** in chilled glass by carefully pouring in the following order.

| 1 | shot | Coffee liqueur |
| ½ | shot | Baileys Irish cream liqueur |

Comment: Looks like a miniature pint of Guinness stout.

BABY WOO WOO

★★★☆☆

Glass: Shot
Garnish: Lime wedge
Method: **SHAKE** all ingredients with ice and fine strain into chilled glass.

½	shot	Ketel One Vodka
½	shot	Peachtree peach schnapps
½	shot	Cranberry juice

Comment: Pink, sweet and all too easy to shoot.

BACARDI COCKTAIL

★★★★⯪

Glass: Martini
Garnish: Luxardo Maraschino cherry
Method: **SHAKE** all ingredients with ice and fine strain into chilled glass.

2	shots	Bacardi Carta Blanca light rum
½	shot	Freshly squeezed lime juice
¼	shot	Pomegranate / grenadine syrup (2:1)
⅛	shot	Sugar syrup (2 sugar to 1 water)
½	shot	Chilled water

Origin: The Bacardi Cocktail originated in Cuba in 1917 and quickly grew in popularity with the growth of the cocktail culture in the USA after Prohibition, so much so that it became known simply as 'the Bacardi'.

There are two schools of thought over the original ingredients, some believe it was originally simply a Daiquiri, containing rum, lime juice, and sugar but made using Bacardi rum and that the now ubiquitous grenadine version originated in New York sometime after Prohibition. Others hold that the grenadine was there at conception, after all the earliest known Daiquiri recipe was made with Bacardi rum. However, the number of vintage cocktail books listing a Bacardi Cocktail without grenadine would seem to back up the inclusion of grenadine being a later addition.

Like the Daiquiri, The Bacardi Cocktail was sometimes served frozen and talking about this iced version, Jack Doyle, former barman at Sloppy Joe's in Key West, then Bacardi Imports Inc barman in New York, explained, "The secret to the iced version was to shake the flaked iced until it looked like sherbet." This technique became known as frappe.

As the Bacardi Cocktail rapidly grew in popularity a small number of establishments neglected to use Bacardi rum as the base ingredient, despite the brand being fundamental to the drink's name and flavour. In 1936, this led the Bacardi Company to take the Barbizon-Plaza Hotel and the Wivel Restaurant in West Fifty-Fourth Street to court in New York City to ensure that when a customer asked for 'Bacardi' by name they were given Bacardi Rum, so protecting the company's trademark.

Bacardi's case at New York's Supreme Court involved the premise that theirs was a unique rum and Bacardi family members traveled from Cuba to New York to appear as witnesses. Even Enrique Schueg, the third President of the Bacardi Company, took to the witness stand. When asked by Justice Walsh, "Well, how is this Bacardi Rum of yours made?" he replied, "Oh! That is my secret." Despite this secrecy, after deliberation, Justice John L. Walsh eventually affirmed that "Bacardi Rum is unique and uncopyable" and issued a ruling that a Bacardi Cocktail must legally be made with rum manufactured by the Compania Ron Bacardi.
Comment: This classic salmon-pinky drink perfectly combines and balances the light rum with the rich sourness of lime juice and the sweetness of pomegranate syrup.

BACARDI SPECIAL ⚷

★★★★★

Glass: Martini
Garnish: Luxardo Maraschino cherry
Method: SHAKE all ingredients with ice and fine strain into chilled glass.

1½	shots	Bacardi Carta Blanca light rum
¾	shot	Rutte Dry Gin
½	shot	Freshly squeezed lime juice
¼	shot	Pomegranate / grenadine syrup (2:1)
⅛	shot	Sugar syrup (2 sugar to 1 water)
½	shot	Chilled water (omit if wet ice)

Origin: Adapted from Harry Craddock's 1930 'The Savoy Cocktail Book' which also has the following notation to this vintage adaptation of the 'Bacardi Cocktail', "Made famous by Karl K. Kitchen, the well-known New York Newspaper Columnist."
Comment: Hit the perfect proportions and you will strike a wondrous balance of flavoursome rum, gin botanicals, limey sourness and fruity sweetness.

BACCIO PUNCH

★★★☆☆

Glass: Collins
Garnish: Orange & lemon slices
Method: SHAKE first three ingredients with ice and strain into ice-filled glass. **TOP** with champagne and soda water. Lightly stir and serve with straws.

1½	shots	Rutte Dry Gin
¾	shot	Marie Brizard Anisette
1½	shots	Freshly squeezed pink grapefruit juice
1½	shots	G.H. Mumm Cordon Rouge Champagne
¾	shot	Soda (club soda)

Origin: The origin of this vintage cocktail is unknown but it in Italian its name means 'kiss'.
Comment: A classic for aniseed lovers only.

BAHAMA MAMA

★★★★☆

Glass: Collins
Garnish: Pineapple wedge & Luxardo Maraschino cherry
Method: SHAKE all ingredients with ice and strain into ice-filled glass.

¾	shot	Pusser's Navy Rum (54.5%)
¾	shot	Bacardi Carta Ocho aged rum
1	shot	Coconut rum liqueur
1¾	shots	Freshly squeezed orange juice
2½	shots	Fresh pressed pineapple juice
3	dash	Angostura Aromatic Bitters

Comment: A tropical, fruity number laced with rum.

BAHAMAS DAIQUIRI

★★★★½

Glass: Martini
Garnish: Pineapple wedge
Method: SHAKE all ingredients with ice and fine strain into chilled glass.

1½	shots	Pot still Jamaican rum
¾	shot	Coconut rum liqueur
¼	shot	Coffee liqueur
1½	shots	Fresh pressed pineapple juice
½	shot	Freshly squeezed lime juice

Origin: Adapted from the Bahamas Martini created in 2002 by Yannick Miseriaux at the Fifth Floor Bar, Harvey Nichols, London, England.
Comment: Totally tropical with a sweet tangy edge.

BAHIA

★★★★½☆

Glass: Collins
Garnish: Pineapple wedge, Luxardo Maraschino cherry & mint sprig
Method: BLEND all ingredients with 12oz scoop crushed ice and serve with straws.

2½	shots	Bacardi Carta Blanca light rum
½	shot	Coco Re'al Cream of Coconut
3	shots	Fresh pressed pineapple juice

Origin: Bahia is one of the 26 states of Brazil. It is also a pre-Prohibition drink containing dry vermouth, sherry, absinthe and bitters. This more recent Piña Colada style offering has more mass market appeal.
Comment: If you like Piña Coladas but are too embarrassed to order one then this drink is for you.

BAJAN DAIQUIRI

★★★★☆

Glass:
Garnish: Lime wedge
Method: SHAKE all ingredients with ice and fine strain into chilled glass.

2	shots	Bacardi Carta Oro rum
½	shot	Taylor's Velvet Falernum liqueur
¾	shot	Freshly squeezed lime juice
½	shot	Chilled water (omit if wet ice)

Origin: Created in 2006 by yours truly, London, England.
Comment: A full-flavoured Daiquiri with clove spice.

BAJAN MOJITO

★★★★☆

Glass: Collins
Garnish: Passion fruit & mint sprig
Method: Cut passion fruit in half and scoop flesh into glass. Add mint and gently **MUDDLE** (just to bruise mint). Add rum, lime juice and crushed ice. **CHURN** (stir) drink in glass to mix. **DRIZZLE** passion fruit liqueur and serve with straws.

1	fresh	Passion fruit
8	fresh	Mint leaves
2	shots	Bacardi Carta Oro rum
½	shot	Freshly squeezed lime juice
½	shot	Sugar syrup (2 sugar to 1 water)
¼	shot	Passoa Liqueur

Origin: Adapted from a recipe by Wayne Collins, London, England.
Comment: A laid-back fruity, slightly sweet Mojito.

BAJAN PASSION

★★★★☆

Glass: Martini
Garnish: Passion fruit
Method: Cut passion fruit in half and scoop flesh into shaker. Add other ingredients, **SHAKE** with ice and fine strain into chilled glass.

1	fresh	Passion fruit
1½	shots	Bacardi Carta Oro rum
½	shot	De Kuyper XO Apricot Brandy
1	shot	Freshly squeezed lime juice
¼	shot	Sugar syrup (2 sugar to 1 water)
¼	shot	Vanilla sugar syrup

Origin: Created in 2004 by Wayne Collins for Maxxium UK.
Comment: A Daiquiri laced with fruit and spice.

BAJITO

★★★★⯪

Glass: Collins
Garnish: Mint sprig
Method: Lightly **MUDDLE** mint and basil in glass just enough to bruise. Add rum, sugar and lime juice. Half fill glass with crushed ice and **CHURN** (stir) with bar spoon. Add more crushed ice and **CHURN** some more. Continue adding crushed ice and churning until glass is full.

6	fresh	Mint leaves
6	fresh	Basil leaves
2	shots	Bacardi Carta Blanca light rum
1	shot	Freshly squeezed lime juice
¼	shot	Sugar syrup (2 sugar to 1 water)

Origin: Discovered in 2004 at Excelsior Bar, Boston, USA.
Comment: Basically a Mojito with basil as well as mint.

BALABUSHKA

★★★⯪☆

Glass: Martini
Garnish: Apple slice
Method: **SHAKE** all ingredients with ice and fine strain into chilled glass.

1½	shots	Ketel One Vodka
½	shot	De Kuyper Triple Sec
½	shot	Freshly squeezed lemon juice
1	shot	Pressed apple juice
⅛	shot	Almond (orgeat) syrup

Origin: Created in 2001 by Julien Escot at Langdon Hall Hotel, Cambridge, Ontario, Canada. Named in homage to George Balabushka, the legendary billiards cue maker.
Comment: This vodka-based cocktail has flavours of apple, lemon, orange and almond.

BALALAIKA

★★★★☆

Glass: Martini
Garnish: Orange zest twist
Method: **SHAKE** all ingredients with ice and fine strain into chilled glass.

1¼	shots	Ketel One Vodka
1¼	shots	De Kuyper Triple Sec
1¼	shots	Freshly squeezed lemon juice

Comment: Richly flavoured with orange and lemon.

BALD EAGLE

★★★★⯪

Glass: Martini
Garnish: Salt rim
Method: **SHAKE** all ingredients with ice and fine strain into chilled glass.

2	shots	Patrón reposado tequila
¾	shot	Freshly squeezed pink grapefruit juice
½	shot	Cranberry juice
¼	shot	Freshly squeezed lime juice
¼	shot	Freshly squeezed lemon juice
¼	shot	Sugar syrup (2 sugar to 1 water)

Origin: Created for yours truly in 2001 by Salvatore Calabrese at The Lanesborough Hotel's Library Bar, London, England.
Comment: If you like tequila and you like your drinks on the sour side, this is for you.

BALD EAGLE SHOT

★★⯪☆☆

Glass: Shot
Garnish: None
Method: Refrigerate ingredients then **LAYER** in chilled glass by carefully pouring in the following order.

½	shot	Giffard Menthe Pastille liqueur
¾	shot	Patrón reposado tequila

Comment: Minty tequila - fresh breath tastic.

BALLET RUSSE

★★★★⯪☆

Glass: Martini
Garnish: Lime wedge
Method: **SHAKE** all ingredients with ice and fine strain into chilled glass.

2	shots	Ketel One Vodka
¾	shot	Lejay crème de cassis de Dijon
1	shot	Freshly squeezed lime juice
¼	shot	Sugar syrup (2 sugar to 1 water)

Comment: Intense sweet blackcurrant balanced by lime sourness.

BALM COCKTAIL

★★★★⯪☆

Glass: Martini
Garnish: Olive on stick
Method: **SHAKE** all ingredients with ice and fine strain into chilled glass.

3	shots	San León Manzanilla sherry
½	shot	De Kuyper Triple Sec
⅛	shot	Allspice pimento dram liqueur
½	shot	Freshly squeezed orange juice
1	dash	Angostura Orange Bitters

Origin: Adapted from Harry Craddock's 1930 ' The Savoy Cocktail Book'.
Comment: Medium dry sherry flavoured with orange and subtle spice.

BALTIC SPRING PUNCH

★★★★☆

Glass: Collins
Garnish: Peach wedge on rim
Method: **MUDDLE** peach in base of shaker. Add other ingredients, **SHAKE** with ice and fine strain into ice-filled glass.

1	fresh	Ripe peach (skinned and diced)
1½	shots	Rose petal liqueur
½	shot	Freshly squeezed lemon juice
¼	shot	Sugar syrup (2 sugar to 1 water)
Top with		G.H. Mumm Cordon Rouge Champagne

Origin: Created in 2002 at Baltic, London, England.
Comment: Sweet and fruity with champagne sparkle. It's peachy!

BALTIMORE EGG NOG

★★★☆☆

Glass: Wine
Garnish: Dust with grated nutmeg
Method: Vigorously **SHAKE** all ingredients with ice and fine strain into chilled glass.

1	shot	Martell VSOP Médaillon cognac
1	shot	Gosling's Black Seal dark rum
½	shot	Verdelho madeira (medium dry)
1	fresh	Eggs (white & yolk) (white & yolk beaten together)
½	shot	Sugar syrup (2 sugar to 1 water)
½	shot	Single cream / half-and-half
½	shot	Milk

Origin: One of the most famous flip-style drinks.
Comment: A rich meal of a drink with a whole egg and cream - fortified with cognac, rum and madeira.

BAMBOO #1

★★★★☆

Glass: Martini
Garnish: Orange zest twist
Method: STIR all ingredients with ice and strain into chilled glass.

2	shots	Romate Fino sherry
2	shots	Martini Extra Dry vermouth
¼	shot	De Kuyper Triple Sec
3	dash	Angostura Orange Bitters

Origin: A classic and all but forgotten cocktail from the 1940s.
Comment: For sophisticated palates only.

BAMBOO #2

★★★★☆

Glass: Martini
Garnish: Toasted almonds
Method: STIR all ingredients with ice and strain into ice-filled glass.

2	shots	Romate Fino sherry
1	shot	Martini Extra Dry vermouth
1	shot	Martini Rosso vermouth

Origin: Adapted from Harry Craddock's 1930 'The Savoy Cocktail Book'.
Comment: The combination of vermouth and fino makes for a fabulously complex cocktail.

BAMBOO COCKTAIL (DIFFORD'S 'PERFECT' RECIPE) (NEW)

★★★★★

Glass: Coupe
Garnish: Orange zest twist
Method: STIR all ingredients with ice and strain into chilled glass.

1	shot	Romate Fino sherry
1	shot	Martini Extra Dry vermouth
1	shot	Martini Rosso vermouth
1	dash	Angostura Orange Bitters

Origin: Adapted from numerous other Bamboo recipes by yours truly on 2nd August 2014 at the Cabinet Room, London, England.
Comment: Sweet vermouth counters dry sherry with dry vermouth further enhancing the vinous flavours and balance. Orange bitters and an orange zest twist add citrus freshness and enhances the delicate bittersweet balance.

BANANA BLISS

★★★★☆

Glass: Martini
Garnish: Orange zest twist
Method: STIR all ingredients with ice and strain into chilled glass.

2	shots	Martell VSOP Médaillon cognac
1	shot	Crème de banane liqueur
½	shot	Chilled water (omit if wet ice)
2	dash	Angostura Orange Bitters

Comment: Crème de banane and cognac go shockingly well together.

BANANA BOOMER

★★★★☆

Glass: Martini
Garnish: Banana chunk
Method: SHAKE all ingredients with ice and strain into chilled glass.

1	shot	Ketel One Vodka
1	shot	Crème de banane liqueur
½	shot	De Kuyper XO Apricot Brandy
½	shot	Cherry Heering Liqueur
¾	shot	Freshly squeezed orange juice
¾	shot	Fresh pressed pineapple juice

Comment: Fortified bubble gum for the young at heart.

BANANA COLADA

★★★★☆

Glass: Hurricane
Garnish: Banana chunk
Method: BLEND ingredients with 12oz scoop of crushed ice. Pour into glass and serve with straws.

2	shots	Bacardi Carta Blanca light rum
½	shot	Crème de banane liqueur
4	shots	Fresh pressed pineapple juice
1	fresh	Banana (peeled)
1	shot	Coco Re'al Cream of Coconut

Comment: Don't skimp, use a whole banana per drink for real flavour.

BANANA COW

★★★☆☆

Glass: Collins
Garnish: Banana chunk
Method: BLEND all ingredients with 12oz scoop crushed ice and serve with straws.

1	shot	Bacardi Carta Blanca light rum
3	shots	Milk
½	shot	Sugar syrup (2 sugar to 1 water)
1	dash	Angostura Aromatic Bitters
1	dash	Vanilla extract
1	fresh	Banana (peeled)

Origin: Created by Victor J. Bergeron. This recipe is adapted from his 'Trader Vic's Bartender's Guide (1972 revised edition)'.
Comment: Trader Vic writes of his drink, "the world's finest, greatest, oh-so good peachy hangover special. This'll do when nothing else will." We think Vic is somewhat overselling this malty banana meal of a drink.

BANANA DAIQUIRI

★★★⯪☆

Glass: Hurricane
Garnish: Banana chunk
Method: BLEND ingredients with 12oz scoop of crushed ice. Pour into glass and serve with straws.

2	shots	Bacardi Carta Blanca light rum
1	shot	Crème de banane liqueur
½	shot	Freshly squeezed lime juice
1	fresh	Banana (peeled)

Comment: A tangy banana disco drink that's not too sweet.

BANANA FLAMBÉ

★★★★☆

Glass: Old-fashioned
Garnish: Cinnamon stick
Method: In a shallow dish flambé half a split banana with orange juice, sugar and cinnamon. **FLAMBÉ** until the banana softens completely and the orange juice reduces. Add cognac and flambé further. **MUDDLE** banana in the base of shaker, add other ingredients, **SHAKE** with ice and fine strain into chilled glass.

½ fresh Banana (peeled)
1 shot Freshly squeezed orange juice
1 spoon Granulated sugar
2 pinch Ground cinnamon
½ shot Martell VSOP Médaillon cognac
1½ shots Ketel One Vodka
½ shot Capucana cachaça
½ shot Freshly squeezed lemon juice
¼ shot Sugar syrup (2 sugar to 1 water)

Origin: Created in 2008 by Mauricio 'Tony' Harion from Mixing Bar Consulting, Belo Horizonte, Brazil.
Comment: As Tony says "it's worth it".

BANANA SMOOTHIE (ALCOHOLIC)

★★★★☆

Glass: Sling
Garnish: Banana chunk
Method: BLEND ingredients with 12oz scoop of crushed ice. Pour into glass and serve immediately with straws.

2	shots	Ketel One Vodka
1½	shots	Yoghurt liqueur
3	spoon	Runny honey
½	fresh	Banana (peeled)
½	shot	Crème de banane liqueur
1	shot	Pressed apple juice

Origin: Created in 2011 by yours truly at the Cabinet Room, London, England.
Comment: Packed with fruit, this creamy banana flavoured shake is 'hardened' with a double measure of vodka.

BANANA SMOOTHIE (MOCKTAIL)

★★★★⯪

Glass: Hurricane
Garnish: Banana chunk
Method: BLEND ingredients with 12oz scoop of crushed ice. Pour into glass and serve immediately with straws.

7	spoon	Natural yoghurt
3	spoon	Runny honey
1	fresh	Banana (peeled)
3	shots	Pressed apple juice

Origin: Created in 2005 by Lisa Ball, London, England.
Comment: Serve with breakfast cereal and you'll be set up for the day. The high fresh banana content means this drink will quickly turn brown if left. This can be countered by adding fresh lemon juice and balancing with more honey but this detracts from the fresh banana flavour.

BANANAS & CREAM

★★★★☆

Glass: Collins
Garnish: Banana chunk
Method: BLEND ingredients with 12oz scoop of crushed ice. Pour into glass and serve with straws.

2	shots	Crème de banane liqueur
1	shot	Disaronno Originale amaretto
1	shot	Baileys Irish cream liqueur
1	shot	Single cream / half-and-half
2	shots	Milk

Comment: Banana and cream frappé with hints of almond. One for a summer afternoon.

BANDERA

★★★★☆

Glass: Shot
Garnish: None
Method: POUR tequila and lime juice into separate shot (caballitos) glasses. To make Sangrita to fill third glass, **SHAKE** rest of ingredients with ice and fine strain into glass. Instruct drinker to sip from all three glasses alternatively.

2	shots	Patrón silver tequila
2	shots	Freshly squeezed lime juice
½	shot	Tomato juice
½	shot	Pomegranate juice
¼	shot	Freshly squeezed orange juice
½	shot	Freshly squeezed lime juice
⅛	shot	Pomegranate / grenadine syrup (2:1)
2	drop	Tabasco hot pepper sauce
2	dash	Worcestershire sauce
1	pinch	Salt
1	grind	Black pepper

Origin: A popular and classic way of serving tequila in Mexico. Sangrita means 'little blood' in Spanish and the drink is served with tequila in practically every bar in Mexico.
Comment: In Mexico the quality of the homemade Sangrita can make or break a bar. The Sangrita in this trio is spicy and slightly sweet.

BANOFFEE COCKTAIL

★★★★☆

Glass: Martini
Garnish: Dust with chocolate powder
Method: MUDDLE banana in base of shaker. Add other ingredients, **SHAKE** with ice and fine strain into chilled glass.

¼	fresh	Banana (peeled)
1½	shots	Vanilla infused Ketel One vodka
¾	shot	Butterscotch liqueur
¾	shot	Crème de banane liqueur
1	spoon	Maple syrup
½	shot	Milk
½	shot	Single cream / half-and-half

Origin: Adapted from a recipe created in 2002 by Barrie 'Snood' Wilson, Zinc Bar & Grill, Edinburgh, Scotland.
Comment: Thick and rich, one for after the cheese course.

BARBARA WEST

★★★★☆

Glass: Martini
Garnish: Lemon zest twist
Method: SHAKE all ingredients with ice and fine strain into chilled glass.

2	shots	Rutte Dry Gin
1	shot	Romate Amontillado sherry
½	shot	Freshly squeezed lemon juice
¼	shot	Sugar syrup (2 sugar to 1 water)
2	dash	Angostura Aromatic Bitters

Origin: A classic from the 1930s.
Comment: Well-balanced but for serious gin and sherry drinkers only.

BARBARY COAST

★★★★☆

Glass: Martini
Garnish: Dust with grated nutmeg
Method: SHAKE all ingredients with ice and fine strain into chilled glass.

1	shot	Dewar's 12yo Scotch whisky
1	shot	Rutte Dry Gin
1	shot	White crème de cacao liqueur
½	shot	Single cream / half-and-half
½	shot	Milk

Origin: A Prohibition era cocktail (1920-1933) of unknown origin.
Comment: Chocolaty, creamy and smooth without smothering the spirits.

BARNACLE BILL

★★★☆☆

Glass: Old-fashioned
Garnish: Mint sprig
Method: SHAKE all ingredients with ice and strain into glass filled with crushed ice.

½	shot	Yellow Chartreuse liqueur
½	shot	Parfait Amour liqueur
½	shot	Pernod anise
½	shot	Chilled water (omit if wet ice)

Origin: Adapted from Victor Bergeron's ' Trader Vic's Bartender's Guide (1972 revised edition)'.
Comment: This sweet drink is best enjoyed after a meal on a warm night.

BARNEY BARNATO COCKTAIL

★★★★☆

Glass: Martini
Garnish: Lemon zest twist
Method: STIR all ingredients with ice and strain into chilled glass.

1½	shots	Dubonnet Red
1½	shots	Martell VSOP Médaillon cognac
¼	shot	Grand Marnier Cordon Rouge
1	dash	Angostura Aromatic Bitters

Origin: This cocktail is named after Barney Barnato, who was born Barnett Issacs in 1852 in the Whitechapel slum of London and traded on his Jewish-Cockney wit and humour. With only a box of cigars to his name, in 1873 Barney fled poverty to join his brother in the South African diamond rush and changed his name. He formed the Barnato Diamond Mining Company and within ten years he had become a millionaire. He and his brother were eventually forced to sell out to Cecil John Rhodes for $5,338,650, then the single largest cheque that had been written. The fortune was little compensation for being beaten in the battle to control the Cape diamond mines - Rhodes went on to form the now mighty De Beers.

After a brief spell in South African politics Barnato died in 1897 when he was lost overboard near the island of Madeira, whilst on a passage home to England. It is still questioned as to whether he jumped, fell or was pushed. His body was recovered but the mysterious circumstances of his death were never resolved. He is buried at Willesden Jewish Cemetery, London.

His vast fortune was divided between his family, including his sister Sarah and her husband Abraham Rantzen, great-grandparents of English TV presenter Esther Rantzen. Another beneficiary was his son, Woolf Barnato, who used part of this inheritance to become one of the so-called Bentley Boys racing drivers in the 1920s.

This recipe is adapted from Harry Craddock's 1930 'The Savoy Cocktail Book' which calls for a now defunct South African product called Caperitif. We have used Dubonnet Red in its place, but some consider white vermouth or aromatised wine a better substitute.
Comment: Orange always works when mixed with cognac and here Dubonnet also tames and adds an aromatic wine complexity.

BARNUM (WAS RIGHT)

★★★☆☆

Glass: Martini
Garnish: Lemon zest twist
Method: SHAKE all ingredients with ice and fine strain into chilled glass.

2	shots	Rutte Dry Gin
1	shot	De Kuyper XO Apricot Brandy
½	shot	Freshly squeezed lemon juice
2	dash	Angostura Aromatic Bitters
½	shot	Chilled water (omit if wet ice)

Origin: A 1930s classic resurrected by Ted Haigh in his 2004 book ' Vintage Spirits & Forgotten Cocktails'.
Comment: A classic cocktail flavour combination that still pleases.

BARTENDER'S MARTINI

★★★★☆

Glass: Martini
Garnish: Orange zest twist
Method: SHAKE all ingredients with ice and fine strain into chilled glass.

1	shot	Rutte Dry Gin
1	shot	Romate Fino sherry
1	shot	Dubonnet Red
1	shot	Martini Extra Dry vermouth
½	shot	Grand Marnier Cordon Rouge

Comment: This classic cocktail resembles an aromatic Martini. Hints of sherry and orange are followed by a dry finish.

BARTENDER'S ROOT BEER

★★★★☆

Glass: Collins
Garnish: Lime wedge
Method: POUR first three ingredients into ice-filled glass and TOP with cola.

1	shot	Galliano L'Autentico liqueur
1	shot	Coffee liqueur
¼	shot	Freshly squeezed lime juice
Top with		Coca-Cola

Comment: Not quite the root of all evil, but tasty all the same.

BASIL & HONEY DAIQUIRI

★★★★★

Glass: Martini
Garnish: Basil leaf
Method: STIR honey and rum in base of shaker until honey dissolves. Add other ingredients, SHAKE with ice and fine strain into chilled glass.

2	spoon	Runny honey
2½	shots	Bacardi Carta Blanca light rum
3	fresh	Basil leaves
½	shot	Freshly squeezed lime juice

Origin: Created in 2005 by yours truly, London, England.
Comment: Basil adds dry vegetable notes to a honeyed Daiquiri.

BASIL BEAUTY

★★★★☆

Glass: Martini
Garnish: Pineapple wedge
Method: Cut passion fruit in half and scoop flesh into shaker. Add other ingredients, SHAKE with ice and fine strain into chilled glass.

1	whole	Passion fruit
3	fresh	Basil leaves
2	shots	Ketel One Citroen vodka
2	shots	Fresh pressed pineapple juice
¼	shot	Freshly squeezed lime juice
½	shot	Coconut syrup

Origin: Created in 1999 by Wayne Collins, London, England
Comment: Pineapple and passion fruit laced with citrus vodka and infused with hints of lime, basil and coconut.

BASIL BRAMBLE SLING

★★★★⯪

Glass: Sling
Garnish: Mint sprig
Method: MUDDLE basil in base of shaker. Add rest of ingredients, SHAKE with ice and strain into ice-filled glass. Serve with straws.

7	fresh	Basil leaves
2	shots	Rutte Dry Gin
1½	shots	Freshly squeezed lemon juice
½	shot	Sugar syrup (2 sugar to 1 water)
½	shot	Lejay Crème de Mûre liqueur

Origin: Created in 2003 by Alexandra Fiot at Lonsdale House, London, UK.
Comment: Wonderfully refreshing and balanced.

BASIL GIMLET

★★★★⯪

Glass: Martini
Garnish: Lime wedge
Method: SHAKE all ingredients with ice and fine strain into chilled glass.

2½	shots	Rutte Dry Gin
¼	shot	Freshly squeezed lime juice
1½	shots	Rose's lime cordial
3	shots	Basil leaves

Origin: Adapted from a drink discovered in 2006 at Stella, Boston, USA
Comment: Tangy, citrus fresh and balanced.

BASIL GRANDE

★★★★☆

Glass: Martini
Garnish: Strawberry
Method: MUDDLE strawberries and basil leaves in shaker base. Add other ingredients, SHAKE with ice and fine strain into glass. Dust with black pepper.

4	fresh	Small ripe strawberries (hulled)
4	fresh	Basil leaves
¾	shot	Ketel One Vodka
¾	shot	Chambord Liqueur
¾	shot	Grand Marnier Cordon Rouge
1½	shots	Cranberry juice

Origin: Created in 2001 by Jamie Wilkinson at Living Room, Manchester, England.
Comment: Fruity, with interest courtesy of the basil and a grind of pepper.

STAR RATINGS EXPLAINED

★★★★★+ OUTSTANDING	★★★★★ EXCEPTIONAL
★★★★⯪ EXCELLENT	★★★★☆ RECOMMENDED
★★★⯪☆ COMMENDED	★★★☆☆ MEDIOCRE
★★⯪☆☆ DISAPPOINTING	★★☆☆☆ PRETTY AWFUL
★⯪☆☆☆ SHAMEFUL	★☆☆☆☆ DISGUSTING

BASIL MARY

★★★★☆

Glass: Collins
Garnish: Basil leaf
Method: SHAKE all ingredients with ice and fine strain into ice-filled glass.

7	fresh	Basil leaves
2	shots	Pepper-infused Ketel One vodka
4	shots	Tomato juice
8	drop	Tabasco hot pepper sauce
½	shot	Tawny port
4	dash	Worcestershire sauce
½	spoon	Horseradish sauce
2	pinch	Celery salt
2	grind	Black pepper
½	shot	Freshly squeezed lemon juice

Origin: Discovered in 2004 at Indigo Yard, Edinburgh, Scotland.
Comment: A particularly spicy Mary with a herbal twist.

BASILIAN

★★★★☆

Glass: Collins
Garnish: Lime slice & basil leaf
Method: MUDDLE cucumber and basil in base of shaker. Add next four ingredients, SHAKE with ice and fine strain into ice-filled glass. TOP with ginger ale.

1	inch	English cucumber peeled
5	fresh	Basil leaves
2	shots	Capucana cachaça
¾	shot	Grand Marnier Cordon Rouge
½	shot	Freshly squeezed lime juice
¼	shot	Sugar syrup (2 sugar to 1 water)
Top with		Ginger ale

Origin: Created in 2005 by Duncan McRae at Dragonfly, Edinburgh, Scotland.
Comment: Vegetable notes with hints of orange and ginger. Healthy tasting!

BASILICO

★★★★☆

Glass: Old-fashioned
Garnish: Basil leaf
Method: MUDDLE basil in base of shaker. Add other ingredients, SHAKE with ice and strain into glass filled with crushed ice.

7	fresh	Basil leaves
2	shots	Ketel One Vodka
½	shot	Pallini Limoncello
½	shot	Freshly squeezed lemon juice
½	shot	Sugar syrup (2 sugar to 1 water)

Origin: Discovered in 2004 at Atlantic Bar & Grill, London, England.
Comment: A lemon Caipirovska with basil.

BATANGA 🔑

★★★★☆

Glass: Collins
Garnish: Salt rim
Method: POUR ingredients into ice-filled glass, stir and serve with straws.

2	shots	Patrón reposado tequila
½	shot	Freshly squeezed lime juice
Top with		Coca-Cola

Origin: Created in 1961 by the legendary Don Javier Delgado Corona, owner/bartender of La Capilla (The Chapel) in Tequila, Mexico. Mixing cocktails in his eighties, Don Javier is noted for ritualistically stirring his drinks with a knife.

The Batanga is a very popular drink in Mexico, helped by being featured in an advertising campaign by El Tequileño, a tequila distilled close to Don Javier's bar.
Comment: Basically a Cuba Libre made with tequila in place of rum. An improvement.

BATIDA (NEW)

★★★★☆

Glass: Collins
Garnish: Lime wedge
Method: SHAKE all ingredients with ice and strain into glass filled with crushed ice. Or alternatively, BLEND all ingredients with crushed ice.

1⅔	shots	Capucana cachaça
2	shots	Coconut water
1	shot	Condensed milk
¼	shot	Freshly squeezed lime juice

Origin: Originating from Brazil, in Portuguese, batida means shaken or milkshake. Along with the Caipirinha, the Batida could be considered the country's national drink. Both drinks are based on Brazil's national spirit, cachaça. This recipe by Jorge Balbontin of Vantguard, Barcelona, Spain.
Comment: Thick and creamy with fortifying underlying cachaça spirit.

BATIDA DE ABACAXI

★★★★☆

Glass: Collins
Garnish: Pineapple wedge
Method: SHAKE all ingredients with ice and strain into ice-filled glass.

2	shots	Capucana cachaça
2½	shots	Fresh pressed pineapple juice
1	shot	Condensed milk
½	shot	Sugar syrup (2 sugar to 1 water)

Origin: The Batida (meaning 'shake') is a traditional Brazilian drink and 'Abacaxi' means pineapple in Portuguese, the official language of Brazil.

Batida is a broad term for a drink usually containing fresh fruit, sugar and/or sweetened condensed milk (leite condensado). They are often blended with crushed ice or shaken and served over crushed ice.
Comment: This easy crowd pleaser is creamy, fruity and to taste - only vaguely alcoholic.

BATIDA DE BANANA

★★★⯪☆

Glass: Collins
Garnish: Banana chunk
Method: BLEND ingredients with 12oz scoop of crushed ice. Pour into glass and serve with straws.

2	shots	Capucana cachaça
1	fresh	Banana (peeled)
1	shot	Condensed milk

Origin: The Batida (meaning 'shake') is a traditional Brazilian drink.
Comment: So thick that this is something of a liquid dessert - surprisingly yummy.

BATIDA DE CARNEVAL

★★★⯪☆

Glass: Collins
Garnish: Mango slice
Method: BLEND all ingredients with 12oz scoop crushed ice and serve with straws.

2	shots	Capucana cachaça
2	shots	Mango purée
1	shot	Freshly squeezed orange juice
1	shot	Condensed milk

Origin: The Batida (meaning 'shake') is a traditional Brazilian drink and 'Carneval' means mango in Portuguese, the official language of Brazil.
Comment: So thick and fruity this easy, smoothie-style drink is something of a meal in itself - a three-course dessert that is.

BATIDA DE COCO

★★★☆☆

Glass: Collins
Garnish: Dust with grated nutmeg
Method: BLEND ingredients with 12oz scoop of crushed ice. Pour into glass and serve with straws.

2	shots	Capucana cachaça
2	shots	Coco Re'al Cream of Coconut
1	shot	Condensed milk

Origin: Literally meaning a shake of coconut, this is a traditional Brazilian drink.
Comment: As the name would suggest this is literally an alcoholic coconut-flavoured shake.

BATIDA DE GOIABA

★★★☆☆

Glass: Collins
Garnish: Mango slice
Method: SHAKE all ingredients with ice and strain into glass filled with crushed ice.

2	shots	Capucana cachaça
2½	shots	Guava juice
1	shot	Condensed milk

Origin: The Batida (meaning 'shake') is a traditional Brazilian drink and 'Goiaba' means guava in Portuguese, the official language of Brazil.
Comment: An alcoholic guava-flavoured shake.

BATIDA DE MILHO VERDE

★★★⯪☆

Glass: Collins
Garnish: Dust with cinnamon powder
Method: BLEND all ingredients with 12oz scoop crushed ice. Serve with straws.

2½	shots	Capucana cachaça
70	gram	Sweetcorn (canned)
1½	shots	Condensed milk

Origin: A classic Brazilian drink.
Comment: Quite possibly your first sweetcorn cocktail.

BATIDA DE MORANGO

★★★☆☆

Glass: Collins
Garnish: Strawberry
Method: BLEND all ingredients with 12oz scoop crushed ice. Serve with straws.

2	shots	Capucana cachaça
12	fresh	Small ripe strawberries (hulled)
1	shot	Lejay Crème de Fraise liqueur
½	shot	Condensed milk

Origin: The Batida (meaning 'shake') is a traditional Brazilian drink and 'Morango' means strawberry in Portuguese, the official language of Brazil.
Comment: Strawberry milkshake laced with cachaça.

BATIDA ROSA

★★★★⯪

Glass: Collins
Garnish: Pineapple wedge
Method: POUR soda water into ice-filled glass. **SHAKE** other ingredients with ice and strain into ice-filled and soda charged glass.

2	shots	Soda (club soda)
2	shots	Capucana cachaça
1	shot	Fresh pressed pineapple juice
1	shot	Freshly squeezed lemon juice
¾	shot	Pomegranate / grenadine syrup (2:1)

Origin: Adapted from a drink created in 2008 by Jeffrey Morgenthaler at Bel Ami Lounge, Oregon, USA.
Comment: Fruity and tropical. A tall refreshing drink for a hot evening or an afternoon beside the pool.

BAY BREEZE

★★★⯪☆

Glass: Collins
Garnish: Pineapple wedge
Method: SHAKE all ingredients with ice and strain into ice-filled glass.

2	shots	Ketel One Vodka
1½	shots	Cranberry juice
2½	shots	Fresh pressed pineapple juice

Comment: Pink, fluffy, sweet and easy to drink.

A B C D E F G H I J K L M N O P Q R S T U V W X Y Z

BAZOOKA

★★★½☆☆

Glass: Shot
Garnish: None
Method: SHAKE all ingredients with ice and fine strain into chilled glass.

¾ shot Southern Comfort liqueur
½ shot Crème de banane liqueur
⅛ shot Pomegranate / grenadine syrup (2:1)
¼ shot Single cream / half-and-half

Comment: A sticky, pink shot.

BBC

★★★★½

Glass: Martini
Garnish: Dust with grated nutmeg
Method: SHAKE all ingredients with ice and fine strain into chilled glass.

1 shots Martell VSOP Médaillon cognac
1 shot Bénédictine D.O.M. liqueur
1 shot Single cream / half-and-half

Comment: Brandy and Bénédictine (a classic combo) smoothed with cream. Drier than you might expect.
Origin: Thought to have originated in the UK in the late 1970s and named, not after the British Broadcasting Company, but its ingredients: Brandy, Bénédictine and Cream.

BBC COCKTAIL

★★★★☆

Glass: Old-fashioned
Garnish: Apple fan
Method: STIR all ingredients with ice and strain into ice-filled glass.

2 shots Bacardi Carta Ocho aged rum
½ shot Becherovka (Carlsbad Becher)
1 dash Wormwood bitters

Origin: Created in 2009 by Marian Beke at the Artesian Bar, London, England. The Artesian Bar sits in the Langham Hotel opposite the BBC's Broadcasting House. Indeed, the BBC moved into the Langham after the Broadcasting House was bombed during the Second World War ...they stayed almost 20 years.
Comment: Based on the classic B & B cocktail with rum replacing brandy and Becherovka in place of Bènèdictine.

BE-TON

★★★★½☆

Glass: Collins
Garnish: Lime wedge
Method: POUR Becherovka into ice-filled glass, then TOP with tonic water and stir.

2 shots Becherovka (Carlsbad Becher)
Top with Tonic Water

Origin: Becherovka (or Carlsbad Becher as it's sometimes known) is the Czech national liqueur. Matured in oak, it contains cinnamon, cloves, nutmeg and other herbs.
Comment: This spicy drink is the Czech Republic's answer to the Gin 'n' Tonic and could be considered the national drink.

BEACH BLONDE

★★★★☆

Glass: Collins
Garnish: Banana chunk
Method: BLEND ingredients with 12oz scoop of crushed ice. Pour into glass and serve with straws.

½ fresh Banana (peeled)
3 shots Warninks Advocaat liqueur
1 shot White overproof rum
3 shots Freshly squeezed orange juice

Origin: Created in 2002 by Alex Kammerling, London, England.
Comment: Fruity, creamy holiday drinking.

BEACH ICED TEA 🔑

★★★½☆

Glass: Sling
Garnish: Lemon slice
Method: SHAKE all ingredients with ice and strain into ice-filled glass.

½ shot Bacardi Carta Blanca light rum
½ shot Rutte Dry Gin
½ shot Ketel One Vodka
½ shot Patrón reposado tequila
½ shot De Kuyper Triple Sec
1 shot Freshly squeezed lemon juice
½ shot Sugar syrup (2 sugar to 1 water)
3 shots Cranberry juice

Comment: A Long Island Iced Tea with cranberry juice instead of cola.

BEACHCOMBER

★★★★☆

Glass: Martini
Garnish: Lime wedge
Method: SHAKE all ingredients with ice and fine strain into chilled glass.

2 shots Bacardi Carta Blanca light rum
½ shot De Kuyper Triple Sec
¾ shot Freshly squeezed lime juice
¼ shot Luxardo Maraschino liqueur
½ shot Chilled water (omit if wet ice)

Origin: Adapted from Patrick Gavin Duffy's 1956 ' The Official Mixer's Manual' .
Comment: A Daiquiri with the addition of a dash of triple sec and maraschino.

BEACHCOMBER'S DAIQUIRI 🔑

★★★★☆

Glass: Martini
Garnish: Lime slice
Method: BLEND all ingredients with one 6oz scoop crushed ice and serve with straws.

2 shots Bacardi Carta Blanca light rum
1 shot De Kuyper Triple Sec
¾ shot Freshly squeezed lime juice
¼ shot Sugar syrup (2 sugar to 1 water)

Origin: Created by Ernest Raymond Beaumont-Gantt, A.K.A. Don The Beachcomber at his bar in Hollywood, California, USA.
Comment: Basically a frozen rum margarita.

BEACHCOMBER'S RUM BARREL

★★★⯪☆

Glass: Rum barrel mug or pint glass
Garnish: Pineapple wedge, Luxardo Maraschino cherry & mint sprig
Method: BLEND all ingredients with 12oz scoop crushed ice and serve with straws.

2	shots	Bacardi Carta Blanca light rum
2	shots	Pot still Jamaican rum
1	shot	Freshly squeezed orange juice
1	shot	Fresh pressed pineapple juice
1	shot	Freshly squeezed pink grapefruit juice
¾	shot	Freshly squeezed lime juice
½	shot	Honey sugar syrup
¼	shot	Pomegranate / grenadine syrup (2:1)
¼	shot	Allspice pimento dram liqueur
¼	shot	Taylor's Velvet Falernum liqueur
⅛	shot	Le Fée Parisienne absinthe
1	dash	Angostura Aromatic Bitters

Origin: Created by Ernest Raymond Beaumont-Gantt, A.K.A. Don The Beachcomber at his bar in Hollywood, California, USA.
Comment: A foamy head hides a tasty (and be warned) rum laced, tangy fruity drink.

BEAM-ME-UP SCOTTY

★★⯪☆☆

Glass: Shot
Garnish: None
Method: Refrigerate ingredients then **LAYER** in chilled glass by carefully pouring in the following order.

½	shot	Coffee liqueur
½	shot	Crème de banane liqueur
½	shot	Baileys Irish cream liqueur

Comment: Coffee, banana and creamy whiskey. Very sweet but not too offensive and easy to layer.

BEARSKIN MARTINI

★★★★☆

Glass: Martini
Garnish: Two Kalamata olives
Method: STIR all ingredients with ice and strain into chilled glass.

2½	shots	Ketel One Vodka
⅛	shot	Kümmel
⅛	shot	Martini Extra Dry vermouth

Comment: A caraway influenced Martini.

BEAUTIFUL LADY

★★★★☆

Glass: Martini
Garnish: Grated chocolate
Method: STIR first 2 ingredients with ice and strain into chilled glass. **FLOAT** thin layer of lightly whipped cream.

1½	shots	Chocolate Spirit
¾	shot	Cherry Heering Liqueur
Float		Single cream / half-and-half

Origin: Created in 2010 by Klaus St. Rainer at Schumann's Bar Munich, Germany.
Comment: This dessert-style drink with cherry and chocolate combined under a layer of cream is reminiscent of a black forest gateau.

THE BEAUTY BENEATH

★★★★☆

Glass: Martini
Garnish: Orange zest twist
Method: STIR all ingredients with ice and strain into a chilled glass.

1¾	shots	Bacardi Carta Ocho aged rum
½	shot	Martini Rosso vermouth
½	shot	Campari Bitter
½	shot	De Kuyper Triple Sec
1	dash	Angostura Aromatic Bitters

Origin: Created in 2008 by Jeffrey Morgenthaler at Bel Ami Lounge, Oregon, USA.
Comment: Orange dominates this bitter-sweet Manhattan, come Daiquiri, come Negroni.

BEBBO COCKTAIL

★★★★⯪

Glass: Coupe
Garnish: Lemon zest twist
Method: STIR honey with gin in base of shaker until honey dissolves. Add other ingredients, **SHAKE** with ice and fine strain into chilled glass.

2 spoon	Runny honey
1½ shots	Rutte Dry Gin
¾ shot	Freshly squeezed lemon juice
½ shot	Blood orange juice
¼ shot	Chilled water (omit if wet ice)

Origin: A long lost relation of the Bee's Knees revived thanks to Ted Haigh's 2004 book 'Vintage Spirits & Forgotten Cocktails'. Although not classically called for, this is best made with blood orange juice. We've also knocked back the lemon juice by 25% from the original recipe.
Comment: Fresh, clean and fruity with honeyed notes. Choose your honey wisely.

BEE STING

★★★★☆

Glass: Collins
Garnish: Apple slice
Method: STIR honey with whiskey in base of shaker until honey dissolves. Add tequila and apple juice, **SHAKE** with ice and strain into ice-filled glass. **TOP** with a splash of ginger ale

1	shot	Straight rye whiskey
1	spoon	Runny honey
1	shot	Patrón reposado tequila
2	shots	Pressed apple juice
Top with		Ginger ale

Origin: Discovered in 2005 at The Royal Exchange Grand Café & Bar, London, England.
Comment: A delicately spiced, long, refreshing drink.

BEE'S KNEES #1

★★★★☆

Glass: Martini
Garnish: Orange zest twist
Method: STIR honey with rum until honey dissolves. Add other ingredients, SHAKE with ice and fine strain into chilled glass.

1¼	shots	Bacardi Carta Blanca light rum
1¼	shots	Pusser's Navy Rum (54.5%)
2	spoon	Runny honey
1	shot	Freshly squeezed orange juice
½	shot	Milk
½	shot	Single cream / half-and-half

Comment: Smooth and orangey to start, with a rum and honey finish.

BEE'S KNEES #2 🔑

★★★★⯪

Glass: Martini
Garnish: Orange zest twist
Method: In base of shaker STIR honey with gin until honey dissolves. Add lemon and orange juice, SHAKE with ice and fine strain into chilled glass.

2	shots	Rutte Dry Gin
3	spoon	Runny honey
1	shot	Freshly squeezed lemon juice
1	shot	Freshly squeezed orange juice

Origin: Adapted from David Embury's 1948 'The Fine Art Of Mixing Drinks'.
Comment: This honeyed citrus concoction really is the bee's knees.

BEE'S KNEES #3 🔑

★★★★⯪

Glass: Martini
Garnish: Lemon zest twist
Method: In base of shaker STIR honey with gin until honey dissolves. Add lemon juice, SHAKE with ice and fine strain into chilled glass.

2	shots	Rutte Dry Gin
3	spoon	Runny honey
¾	shot	Freshly squeezed lemon juice

Comment: The combination of honey and lemon suggests flu relief but don't wait for an ailment before trying this soothing concoction.

BEETLE JEUSE

★★★★☆

Glass: Collins
Garnish: Mint sprig
Method: Lightly MUDDLE mint in base of shaker just enough to bruise. Add other ingredients, SHAKE with ice and strain into ice-filled glass.

7	fresh	Mint leaves
1	shot	Green Chartreuse liqueur
1	shot	Zubrówka bison vodka
3½	shots	Pressed apple juice
¼	shot	Passion fruit syrup

Origin: Created in 2003 by Milo Rodriguez at Raoul's Bar, Oxford, and named after Beetlejuice, the Tim Burton black comedy about a young couple whose premature death leads them to a series of bizarre afterlife exploits.
Comment: Long and refreshing with a flavour reminiscent of caramelised apple.

BEETROOT & VANILLA DAIQUIRI (NEW)

★★★★☆

Glass: Coupe
Garnish: Lime wedge
Method: SHAKE all ingredients with ice and fine strain into chilled glass.

2½	shots	Bacardi Carta Oro rum
¾	shot	Beetroot juice
½	shot	Freshly squeezed lime juice
½	shot	Vanilla sugar syrup

Origin: Adapted from a recipe created in 2014 by Josh Powell at Bar44, Penarth, Wales.
Comment: Just what it says on the tin, only the beetroot pervades this otherwise classic Daiquiri more than the vanilla. Perhaps also consider using vanilla infused rum.

BEGGAR'S BANQUET

★★★★☆

Glass: Collins
Garnish: Orange slice
Method: SHAKE first four ingredients with ice and strain into ice-filled glass. TOP with beer.

2	shots	Bourbon whiskey
1	shot	Freshly squeezed lemon juice
¾	shot	Maple syrup
2	dash	Angostura Aromatic Bitters
Top with		Fuller's Chiswick Bitter

Origin: Created in 2010 by Aisha Sharpe, New York City, USA.
Comment: If using a 12oz glass you'll know you have great ice if when strained into glass you have sufficient room for a good 1-2 shots of beer.

BEJA FLOR COCKTAIL

★★★★☆

Glass: Martini
Garnish: Banana chunk
Method: SHAKE all ingredients with ice and fine strain into chilled glass.

2	shots	Capucana cachaça
1	shot	De Kuyper Triple Sec
1	shot	Crème de banane liqueur
½	shot	Freshly squeezed lemon juice

Comment: Sharp and quite dry but with a sweet banana twang.

BELLA DONNA DAIQUIRI

★★★★⯪

Glass: Martini
Garnish: Cinnamon powder rim
Method: SHAKE all ingredients with ice and fine strain into chilled glass.

1½	shots	Gosling's Black Seal dark rum
1½	shots	Disaronno Originale amaretto
½	shot	Freshly squeezed lemon juice
¼	shot	Sugar syrup (2 sugar to 1 water)
½	shot	Chilled water (omit if wet ice)

Origin: Adapted from a drink discovered in 2003 at Bellagio, Las Vegas, USA.
Comment: Back in 2003, this was the hit cocktail for Difford's Guide staff at the Bellagio, Las Vegas, after working at the Nightclub & Bar Beverage Convention. Try one and see why.

BELLINI (DIFFORD'S RECIPE)

★★★★⯪

Glass: Flute
Garnish: Peach slice
Method: SHAKE first three ingredients with ice and fine strain into chilled glass. Add prosecco and gently stir.

2	shots	Peach purée
½	shot	Crème de pêche (peach) liqueur
¼	shot	Freshly squeezed lemon juice
Top with		Prosecco sparkling wine

Origin: It has long been traditional in Italy to marinade fresh peaches in wine and the Bellini draws on this tradition, combining prosecco wine with puréed white peaches.

Giuseppe Cipriani created this drink at Harry's Bar, Venice, in 1945, fourteen years after he opened his tiny place on the edge of the Grand Canal, not far from Piazza San Marco.

Cipriani named his cocktail after the 15th-century Venetian painter Giovanni Bellini due to the drink's pink hue and the painter's penchant for using rich pinks on his canvases.

Like many other legendary bars around the world, Harry's owes some of its notoriety to being patronised by probably the world's greatest drinker, Ernest Hemingway. It was also the haunt of Sinclair Lewis, Orson Welles, F. Scott Fitzgerald and Dorothy Parker, and continues to attract celebrities to this day. But you don't have to be a celebrity to go to Harry's Bar. Cocktail aficionados from around the world make pilgrimages to the birthplace of the Bellini to sample the original recipe.

White peaches are in season in Italy from May to September, so in Venice those bars that insist on only using fresh peaches rather than frozen purée sell the drink between May and October.
Comment: It's hard not to like this blend of peaches and sparkling wine.

BELLINI PEACH SPRITZ (NEW)

★★★★☆

Glass: Rocks
Garnish: Lemon wheel or peach wedge.
Method: POUR ingredients into ice-filled glass.

3	shots	Prosecco sparkling wine
1¼	shots	Peach purée
¼	shot	Freshly squeezed lemon juice
½	shot	Peachtree peach schnapps
Top with		Soda (club soda)

Origin: Created in 2013 by yours truly for Jamie's Italian Bars.
Comment: Basically a Bellini served on the rocks.

BELLINI-TINI

★★★★☆

Glass: Martini
Garnish: Peach slice
Method: SHAKE all ingredients with ice and fine strain into chilled glass.

2	shots	Ketel One Vodka
½	shot	Peachtree peach schnapps
2	shots	Peach purée
3	dash	Peach bitters

Comment: Peachy! Based on the Bellini, funnily enough.

BENDING BLADES COCKTAIL (NEW)

★★★★⯪

Glass: Coupe
Garnish: Lemon zest twist
Method: STIR all ingredients with ice and strain into chilled glass.

1½	shots	Patrón silver tequila
½	shot	Suze Saveur d'Autrefois
½	shot	San León Manzanilla sherry
¾	shot	Pink grapefruit (pamplemousse) liqueur
¾	shot	Chilled water (omit if wet ice)

Origin: Adapted from a recipe created in 2015 by Christopher Day at General Lee's, Los Angeles, USA.
Comment: This tequila based cocktail is bitter before turning bittersweet, then finishes with a long bitter finish. It won't be for everybody but for those who appreciate the flavour of gentiane liqueur will appreciate this drink for its simplicity and originality.

BÉNÉDICTINE CONVERSION

★★★★⯪

Glass: Coupe
Garnish: Thyme sprig
Method: STIR all ingredients with ice and strain into chilled glass.

1½	shots	Patrón reposado tequila
½	shot	Del Maguey VIDA mezcal
⅓	shot	Bénédictine D.O.M. liqueur
½	shot	Thyme liqueur
¾	shot	Chilled water (reduce if wet ice)

Comment: Tequila and mezcal based with herbal and liqueur and thyme.

THE BENNETT COCKTAIL (NEW)

★★★★⯪

Glass: Coupe
Garnish: Float dehydrated lime wheel
Method: SHAKE all ingredients with ice and strain into a chilled glass.

2 Rutte Dry Gin
¾ Freshly squeezed lime juice
½ Sugar syrup (2 sugar to 1 water)
2 dashes Angostura aromatic bitters
½ Chilled water (omit if wet ice)

Comment: Judicious dashing of bitters makes or breaks this riff on the classic Gimlet.
Origin: Adapted from a recipe created in 2015 by Meaghan Dorman at The Bennett, New York City, USA.

BENNY & HOT

★★★★⯪☆

Glass: Toddy
Garnish: Lemon slice
Method: POUR ingredients into warmed glass.

2   shots   **Bénédictine D.O.M. liqueur**
4   shots   **Boiling water**

Origin: Burnley Miner's Club in North West England is, somewhat bizarrely, thought to be the world's biggest single account for sales of Bénédictine. Its 700-odd members consume around 48 bottles each week. This conspicuous liqueur consumption dates back to after the Second World War when the men of the 11th battalion of the East Lancashire regiment were based in Normandy. They discovered the local liqueur, Bénédictine D.O.M., which they drank as a grog with hot water. This became known as a 'Benny and Hot' and its popularity travelled home with the troops to Lancashire towns such as Accrington and Burnley.

At Burnley Miner's Club the Benny & Hot is served 50/50 Bénédictine D.O.M. liqueur and hot water with a squeeze of lemon juice. We have not visited the club and it was Ludovic Miazga, Bénédictine's charismatic French brand ambassador, who recounted the serve he discovered while visiting the club. We must have looked skeptical because he was emphatic. "No bullshit," he said, before adding: "Excuse my French". It's not every day you hear an actual Frenchman say "Excuse my French." So it must be true.
Comment: Make this winter warmer to the classic 'Burnley' 50:50 proportions and it can be a tad rich, hence the 1:2 proportions used here.

BENSONHURST

★★★★⯪

Glass: Coupe
Garnish: Luxardo Maraschino cherry
Method: STIR all ingredients with ice and strain into chilled glass.

2   shots   **Straight rye whiskey**
¼   shot   **Luxardo Maraschino liqueur**
1   shot   **Martini Extra Dry vermouth**
⅛   shot   **Cynar**

Origin: Adapted from a drink created in 2006 by Chad Solomon and named after a neighbourhood close to his home in Brooklyn, New York City, USA.
Comment: This Manhattan-like drink is one of many to emerge since 2006 taking their inspiration from the Brooklyn cocktail.

BENTLEY

★★★★☆

Glass: Old-fashioned
Garnish: Orange zest twist
Method: STIR all ingredients with ice and strain into empty glass

1½ **shots**   **Calvados brandy**
1½ **shots**   **Dubonnet Red**
2   **dash**   **Peychaud's aromatic bitters** (optional)

Origin: Adapted from Harry Craddock's 1930 'The Savoy Cocktail Book'.
Comment: Dry, spiced wine impregnated with apple - pretty damn good.

BENTON'S OLD FASHIONED

★★★★★

Glass: Rocks
Garnish: Orange twist
Method: STIR bourbon and maple syrup in base of mixing glass until syrup dissolves. Add bitters and ice and **STIR** again. Strain into ice-filled glass.

*To make the fat washed bourbon: Grill 4 slices of bacon to obtain 30ml/1oz of warm fat (originally Benton's bacon was used but any extra-smoky bacon will suffice) and pour this into a 70cl of bourbon (in a 75cl bottle). Leave to infuse at room temperature for a day before placing bottle in a freezer to solidify the fat. Then clarify the bourbon by straining into a clean bottle.

2 shots **Bourbon whiskey** (bacon fat washed)
¼ shot **Maple syrup**
2 dash **Angostura Aromatic Bitters**

Origin: Created in 2008 by Don Lee at Manhattan's exclusive and elusive PDT bar. PDT is short for 'Please Don't Tell' and perhaps the most famous of New York's numerous bars modeled on Prohibition speakeasies.
Comment: Even vegetarians like bacon and everybody likes Old Fashioneds.

BERLIN SOUR

★★★★☆

Glass: Sour or Martini/Coupette
Garnish: Lemon slice & cherry on stick (sail)
Method: SHAKE all ingredients with ice and fine strain into chilled glass.

2   shots   **Kümmel**
½   shot   **Luxardo Maraschino liqueur**
1   shot   **Freshly squeezed lemon juice**
¼   shot   **Sugar syrup** (2 sugar to 1 water)

Origin: Created in 2009 by Thorsten Pannek at Hilton, Frankfurt, Germany.
Comment: The sweet powerful flavours of kummel and maraschino liqueurs are tamed and harnessed in this sour.

BERMONDSEY MINUTE (NEW)

★★★★★⯪

Glass: Coupe
Garnish: Lemon and orange zest (discarded) & float 3 coffee beans
Method: STIR all ingredients with ice and strain into chilled glass.

2   shots   **Patrón reposado tequila**
⅔   shot   **Carpano Antica Formula**
¼   shot   **Luxardo Maraschino liqueur**
¼   shot   **Lavender sugar syrup**
½   shot   **Chilled water**

Origin: Created in Bermondsey, London in 2014 by yours truly and adapted from the New York Minute, originally by Luke Whearty at Der Raum, Melbourne.
Comment: Tequila and lavender are a match made in heaven, made more complex with herbal wine notes from the vermouth, aromatised by delicately fruity maraschino cherry.

BERMUDA COCKTAIL

★★★★☆

Glass: Martini
Garnish: Orange zest twist
Method: SHAKE all ingredients with ice and fine strain into chilled glass.

2	shots	Rutte Dry Gin
½	shot	Peachtree peach schnapps
½	shot	Freshly squeezed orange juice
¼	shot	Pomegranate / grenadine syrup (2:1)

Origin: Adapted from Victor Bergeron's 'Trader Vic's Bartender's Guide' (1972 revised edition).
Comment: Gin with a sweetening touch of peach, orange and pomegranate.

BERMUDA ROSE COCKTAIL

★★★★☆

Glass: Martini
Garnish: Apricot slice
Method: SHAKE all ingredients with ice and fine strain into chilled glass.

2	shots	Rutte Dry Gin
½	shot	De Kuyper XO Apricot Brandy
¼	shot	Pomegranate / grenadine syrup (2:1)
½	shot	Chilled water (omit if wet ice)

Origin: Adapted from Victor Bergeron's 'Trader Vic's Bartender's Guide' (1972 revised edition).
Comment: Delicate, floral and aromatic. A hint of sweetness but not so as to offend.

BERMUDA RUM SWIZZLE

★★★★☆

Glass: Collins
Garnish: Pineapple wedge & Luxardo Maraschino cherry
Method: POUR ingredients into glass and two-thirds fill with crushed ice. SWIZZLE with a swizzle stick or CHURN (stir) with a bar spoon. Fill glass with more crushed ice and repeat. Serve with straws.

1	shot	Bacardi Carta Oro rum
1	shot	Gosling's Black Seal dark rum
¾	shot	Taylor's Velvet Falernum liqueur
1	shot	Fresh pressed pineapple juice
1	shot	Freshly squeezed orange juice
½	shot	Freshly squeezed pink grapefruit juice
½	shot	Freshly squeezed lime juice
¼	shot	Freshly squeezed lemon juice
2	dash	Angostura Aromatic Bitters

Origin: This recipe is adapted from one by Del Pedro, originally from Bermuda but now resident in New York City. It came my way (in 1997) courtesy of LeNell Smothers, and apparently it originally heralds from the Swizzle Inn in Bermuda where their rather appropriate slogan is "Swizzle Inn, Swagger Out".
Comment: Your five-a-day fruits in a glass, laced with pungent rums and spice infused sweet Falernum.

BERNICE

★★★½☆

Glass: Coupe
Garnish: Mint sprig
Method: SHAKE all ingredients with ice and fine strain into chilled glass.

2	shots	Ketel One Vodka
¾	shot	Freshly squeezed lime juice
¼	shot	Galliano L'Autentico liqueur
½	shot	Sugar syrup (2 sugar to 1 water)

Origin: Adapted from a drink in Ted Saucier's 1951 book, "Bottoms Up!".
Comment: Vodka and lime with sweet herbal peppermint courtesy of Galliano.

BERRY BLAST (MOCKTAIL) (NEW)

★★★★½

Glass: Collins
Garnish: Mint sprig & lemon slice
Method: SHAKE all ingredients with ice and strain into ice-filled glass.

8	fresh Raspberries
¾ shot	Freshly squeezed lemon juice
¾ shot	Passion fruit syrup
2 shots	Cold English breakfast tea
2 shots	Cranberry juice

Origin: Adapted from a drink created at Jamie's Italian Bars.
Comment: As the name suggests this non-alcoholic long drink is loaded with berry fruit, presented over the light tannins of a black tea base with a splash of passion fruit syrup adding flavour and a hint of balancing sweetness.

BERRY CAIPIRINHA

★★★★☆

Glass: Old-fashioned
Garnish: None
Method: MUDDLE lime and berries in base of glass. Add other ingredients and fill glass with crushed ice. CHURN drink with bar spoon and serve with short straws.

¾	fresh	Lime (fresh whole) (chopped wedges)
3	fresh	Raspberries
3	fresh	Blackberries
2	shots	Capucana cachaça
¾	shot	Sugar syrup (2 sugar to 1 water)

Comment: A fruity version of the popular Brazilian drink.

BERRY SMASH (MOCKTAIL)

★★★★☆

Glass: Old-fashioned
Garnish: Seasonal berries
Method: SHAKE all ingredients with ice and strain into glass filled with crushed ice.

7	fresh	Raspberries
3	fresh	Blackberries
2	shots	Cranberry juice
1	shot	Pressed apple juice
½	shot	Freshly squeezed lemon juice
¼	spoon	Honey sugar syrup

Comment: Red berries with a splash of apple juice and honey served over crushed ice.

BETSY ROSS

★★★★☆

Glass: Coupe
Garnish: Orange zest twist
Method: STIR all ingredients with ice and strain into chilled glass.

1½	shots	Martell VSOP Médaillon cognac
1½	shots	Ruby port
½	shot	Orange Curaçao liqueur
2	dash	Angostura Aromatic Bitters

Comment: Deep burgundy red and boozy and based on the classic combination of port and brandy, this is a drink to finish a night with. (Benefits from some dilution so stir well.)

BETTER & BETTER (NEW)

★★★★☆

Glass: Old-fashioned
Garnish: Lemon zest twist
Method: STIR all ingredients with ice and strain into ice-filled glass.

1½	shots	Del Maguey VIDA mezcal
½	shot	Pot still Jamaican rum
½	shot	Taylor's Velvet Falernum liqueur

Origin: Created in 2012 by Richard Boccato at Dutch Kills, Long Island City, NY, USA.
Comment: Initially strong and punchy, but as the name suggests, as the ice melts dilution makes this drink better and better.

BETWEEN DECKS 0━🗝

★★★★☆

Glass: Collins
Garnish: Pineapple wedge, Luxardo Maraschino cherry & mint sprig
Method: SHAKE all ingredients with ice and strain into ice-filled glass.

2½	shots	Rutte Dry Gin
1	shot	Freshly squeezed orange juice
1	shot	Cranberry juice
½	shot	Freshly squeezed lime juice
¼	shot	Sugar syrup (2 sugar to 1 water)
½	shot	Chilled water (omit if wet ice)

Origin: Adapted from Victor Bergeron's 'Trader vic's Bartender's Guide' (1972 revised edition).
Comment: We've upped the ante on this drink with more gin and less fruit than the original. So beware.

BETWEEN THE SHEETS #1 (DIFFORD'S FORMULA) 0━🗝

★★★★☆

Glass: Martini
Garnish: Lemon zest twist
Method: SHAKE all ingredients with ice and fine strain into chilled glass.

¾	shot	Bacardi Carta Blanca light rum
¾	shot	Martell VSOP Médaillon cognac
¾	shot	De Kuyper Triple Sec
¼	shot	Freshly squeezed lemon juice
⅛	shot	Sugar syrup (2 sugar to 1 water)
½	shot	Chilled water (omit if wet ice)

Origin: Created in the early 1930s (during Prohibition) by Harry MacElhone of Harry's New York Bar in Paris, and derived from the Sidecar.
Comment: Classic proportions to this drink are most often quoted as being: 1 rum, 1 cognac, 1 triple sec and 1/4 lemon juice but three shots of 40% alcohol and a splash of lemon juice make for a tart drink which should not be undertaken lightly. The formula above maintains the essential flavour and ingredients of the classic recipe but is a little more approachable.

BETWEEN THE SHEETS #2 (WONDRICH'S FORMULA)

★★★★★

Glass: Martini
Garnish: Orange zest twist (flamed)
Method: SHAKE all ingredients with ice and fine strain into chilled glass.

1	shot	Martell VSOP Médaillon cognac
½	shot	Bénédictine D.O.M. liqueur
½	shot	De Kuyper Triple Sec
¼	shot	Freshly squeezed lemon juice
½	shot	Chilled water (omit if wet ice)

Origin: Formula adapted from recipe by David Wondrich. We've cut the lemon by a third, and when using dry cubed ice, we add a splash of water.
Comment: Bénédictine takes the place of rum in this variation on a classic.

BEUSER & ANGUS SPECIAL

★★★★☆

Glass: Old-fashioned
Garnish: Orange zest twist
Method: SHAKE all ingredients with ice and fine strain into glass filled with crushed ice.

1¾	shots	Green Chartreuse liqueur
½	shot	Luxardo Maraschino liqueur
¾	shot	Freshly squeezed lime juice
⅛	shot	Sugar syrup (2 sugar to 1 water)
1	whole	Eggs (white & yolk)
3	dash	Orange flower water

Origin: Created by Gonçalo de Sousa Monteiro of Berlin, Germany who was inspired to make this drink for two fellow 'Travelling Mixologists', Bastian Heuser and Angus Winchester.
Comment: A floral, aromatic and herbal Chartreuse flip.

BEVERLY HILLS HOTEL COCKTAIL

★★★★☆

Glass: Martini
Garnish: Rosemary sprig
Method: **SHAKE** all ingredients with ice and fine strain into chilled glass.

2 shots Rutte Dry Gin
1 shot St-Germain elderflower liqueur
1 shot Freshly squeezed pink grapefruit juice

Origin: Adapted from a drink created in 2007 by Philip Spee at The Beverly Hills Hotel, California, USA.
Comment: Dry, but not oppressively so. Zingy grapefruit with gin complexity and delicate floral notes.

BEVERLY HILLS ICED TEA

★★★½☆

Glass: Sling
Garnish: Lime zest twist
Method: **SHAKE** first five ingredients with ice and strain into ice-filled glass. **TOP** with champagne and gently stir.

¾ shot Rutte Dry Gin
¾ shot Ketel One Vodka
1 shot De Kuyper Triple Sec
½ shot Freshly squeezed lime juice
½ shot Sugar syrup (2 sugar to 1 water)
Top with G.H. Mumm Cordon Rouge Champagne

Comment: Very strong and refreshing.

BG3

★★★½☆

Glass: Collins
Garnish: Lemon wedge

Method: **SHAKE** first 3 ingredients with ice and strain into ice-filled glass. **Top with** bitter lemon and lightly stir.

2 shots Rutte Old Simon oude jenever
1 shot De Kuyper Triple Sec
2 dash Angostura Orange Bitters
Top with Bitter lemon

Comment: A long, refreshing drink combining the full-bodied flavours of genever with sweet orange and bitter lemon.

BIARRITZ

★★★½☆

Glass: Old-fashioned
Garnish: Orange slice & cherry on stick (sail)
Method: **SHAKE** all ingredients with ice and strain into ice-filled glass.

2 shots Martell VSOP Médaillon cognac
1 shot Grand Marnier Cordon Rouge
¾ shot Freshly squeezed lemon juice
3 dash Angostura Aromatic Bitters
½ fresh Egg white

Comment: Basically a brandy sour with a little something extra from the orange liqueur.

BIBLICAL SIDECAR

★★★★☆

Glass: Coupe
Garnish: Orange zest twist
Method: **MUDDLE** cloves in base of shaker. Add other ingredients, **SHAKE** with ice and fine strain into chilled glass.

1 dried Clove
2 shots Martell VSOP Médaillon cognac
½ shot Grand Marnier Cordon Rouge
¼ shot King's Ginger Liqueur
¾ shot Freshly squeezed orange juice

Origin: A Christmas cocktail created in October 2011 by yours truly at the Cabinet Room, London, England.
Comment: Cognac and freshly squeezed orange juice warmed with ginger and clove spice.

BICARDAR

★★★★☆

Glass: Martini
Garnish: Lemon zest twist
Method: **STIR** all ingredients with ice and strain into chilled glass.

2 shots Bacardi Carta Blanca light rum
¼ shot De Kuyper XO Apricot Brandy
¼ shot Luxardo Maraschino liqueur
⅛ shot Freshly squeezed lemon juice
1 dash Angostura Orange Bitters
¼ shot Chilled water (omit if wet ice)

Origin: Created in 2008 by Kashi Forootani at Seattle Hotel, Brighton, England.
Comment: Subtle and delicate with hints of apricot, cherry, lemon and orange.

BIGGLES AVIATION

★★★★½

Glass: Martini
Garnish: Fresh ginger & lime wheels
Method: **SHAKE** all ingredients with ice and strain into chilled glass.

2 shots Rutte Dry Gin
½ shot King's Ginger Liqueur
½ shot Freshly squeezed lemon juice
¼ shot Sugar syrup (2 sugar to 1 water)
¼ shot Chilled water (omit if wet ice)

Origin: Created in 2008 by yours truly at the Cabinet Room, London, England.
Comment: A ginger influenced Aviation named after the fictional book 'Biggles in Borneo' about WWII flying heroes Ginger, Algy and Biggles. Inspired by the ginger used in Canton ginger liqueur being sourced from Borneo.

BIGGLES SIDECAR

★★★★✦

Glass: Martini
Garnish: Fresh ginger & lemon slices
Method: SHAKE all ingredients with ice and fine strain into chilled glass.

2	shots	Martell VSOP Médaillon cognac
½	shot	King's Ginger Liqueur
½	shot	Freshly squeezed lemon juice
¼	shot	Sugar syrup (2 sugar to 1 water)
1	dash	Peychaud's aromatic bitters
½	shot	Chilled water (omit if wet ice)

Origin: Created in 2008 by yours truly at the Cabinet Room, London, England. As a kid I was a Biggles reader.
Comment: The idea was to make a riff on an Aviation (see Biggles Aviation) but ginger cries out for cognac so we also ended up with this ginger Sidecar.

BIJOU COCKTAIL (DIFFORD'S RECIPE)

★★★★✦

Glass: Coupe
Garnish: Lemon zest twist (discarded) & Luxardo Maraschino cherry

Method: STIR all ingredients with ice and strain into chilled glass.

1¼	shots	Rutte Dry Gin
¾	shot	Green Chartreuse liqueur
1¼	shots	Martini Rosso vermouth
1	dash	Angostura Orange Bitters
¼	shot	Chilled water (omit if wet ice)

Origin: Recipe adapted from Harry Johnson's 1900 Bartender's Manual which calls for "1/3 wine glass Chartreuse (green); 1/3 wine glass vermouth (Italian); 1/3 wine glass of Plymouth gin; 1 dash orange bitters".

The Bijou first appeared in C. F. Lawor's 1895 book The Mixicologist as equal parts gin, Grand Marnier and sweet vermouth.

Comment: It is not uncommon to see this drink stipulated with equal parts gin, Chartreuse and sweet vermouth, as called for in Harry Johnson's Bartender's Manual. In fact that's the norm. Equal parts works, but it makes for a drink strong enough to drop a rhinoceros with Chartreuse overly dominant (and I love Chartreuse).

The level of booze in this drink makes dilution key, so don't hesitate to up the amount of water if using huge chunks of ice fresh out the freezer.

BIJOU COCKTAIL (INSPIRED BY LAWOR'S 1895 RECIPE) (NEW)

★★★★✦

Glass: Coupe
Garnish: Orange zest twist
Method: STIR all ingredients with ice and strain into a chilled glass.

1½	shots	Rutte Dry Gin
¾	shot	Grand Marnier liqueur
¾	shot	Martini Rosso sweet vermouth

Comment: A boozy sipper of a cocktail that's medium dry with honeyed richness. Gin based with orange zesty freshness and sweet vermouth adding deep herbal complexity. A great after-dinner cocktail that also works well on-the-rocks.
AKA: Not to be confused with the more commonplace equal parts gin, Chartreuse and vermouth Bijou which first appeared in Harry Johnson's 1900 Bartender's Manual.

Origin: Adapted from the original equal parts gin, Grand Marnier and sweet vermouth recipe in C. F. Lawor's 1895 book The Mixicologist in which he describes this as "a delicious drink." Handily adding, "Grand Marnier can also be served in a pony-glass like any liqueur." Remember, Louis-Alexandre Marnier-Lapostolle only created Grand Marnier 15 years earlier and it must have taken a while for the new liqueur to find its way from France to the Grand Hotel in Cincinnati where Lawor worked, so he was commenting on what was then an exciting new product.

BIJOU SHOT

★★★☆☆

Glass: Shot
Garnish: None
Method: Carefully LAYER ingredients in the following order.

½	shot	Martini Rosso vermouth
½	shot	Green Chartreuse liqueur
½	shot	Rutte Dry Gin

Origin: This vintage layered, or 'pousse-café' style drink is named after the French for 'jewel', apparently a reference to its trio of ingredients having the colours of the three most precious jewels: diamond (gin), ruby (sweet vermouth) and emerald (Green Chartreuse).

If all the ingredients, and so the colours, are mixed together the result is a rather better 'Bijou #1', also aptly named Amber Dream due to its colour. If I were you I wouldn't bother with this layered drink, grab a stirring glass and enjoy an Amber Dream.
Comment: A shot loaded with bold flavours best suited to fans of Chartreuse.

BIKINI MARTINI

★★★★☆

Glass: Martini
Garnish: Orange zest twist
Method: SHAKE all ingredients with ice and fine strain into chilled glass.

2	shots	Rutte Dry Gin
¼	shot	Peachtree peach schnapps
¾	shot	Blue curaçao liqueur
¼	shot	Freshly squeezed lemon juice
½	shot	Chilled water (omit if wet ice)

Origin: Adapted from a cocktail created in 1999 by Dick Bradsell for an Agent Provocateur swimwear launch.

The bikini swimsuit was named after Bikini Atoll, where A-bombs were tested after World War II, on the basis that such a revealing garment would cause as much shock as a thermonuclear device.
Comment: A vivid blue combination of lemon, orange and peach laced with gin.

BINGO

★★★☆☆

Glass: Collins
Garnish: Lemon slice
Method: SHAKE first four ingredients with ice and strain into ice-filled glass. TOP with soda water.

1	shot	Ketel One Vodka
1	shot	Grand Marnier Cordon Rouge
1	shot	De Kuyper XO Apricot Brandy
½	shot	Freshly squeezed lemon juice
Top with		Soda (club soda)

Comment: Refreshing, fruity long drink.

THE BIRD IS THE WORD NO.1

★★★★☆

Glass: Coupe
Garnish: Lemon zest twist
Method: SHAKE all ingredients with ice and fine strain into chilled glass.

1½ shots Patrón reposado tequila
1 shot Yellow Chartreuse liqueur
½ shot De Kuyper XO Apricot Brandy
1 shot Freshly squeezed lemon juice

Origin: Adapted from a drink created in May 2010 by Fraser Campbell at Tony Starrs Kitten Club, Melbourne, Australia.
Comment: To quote Fraser Campbell, the drinks creator, "influenced primarily by "The Last Word" with hints of "Yellow Parrot" ...and a tequila base."

THE BIRD IS THE WORD NO.2

★★★★☆

Glass: Coupe
Garnish: Luxardo Maraschino cherry
Method: SHAKE all ingredients with ice and fine strain into chilled glass.

¾	shot	Bepi Tosolini Grappa di Moscato
¾	shot	Green Chartreuse liqueur
½	shot	Luxardo Maraschino liqueur
½	shot	Freshly squeezed lime juice
1	dash	Bob's Chocolate bitters
½	shot	Chilled water (omit if wet ice)

Origin: Adapted from a drink discovered at Salon 39, Copenhagen, Denmark.
Comment: A grappa based 'Last Word' by way of Denmark.

BISCOTTI SPRITZ (NEW)

★★★★☆

Glass: Old-fashioned
Garnish: Biscotti biscuit across top of glass
Method: POUR prosecco and liqueurs into glass. Add ice. Top with soda.

3	shots	Prosecco sparkling wine
1	shot	Hazelnut liqueur
1	shot	Butterscotch liqueur
Top with		Soda (club soda)

Origin: Created in 2013 for Jamie's Italian Bar.
Comment: Hazelnut and butterscotch liqueurs flavour this Prosecco based spritz. Great when complemented by a biscotti biscuit.

BISHOP

★★★★☆

Glass: Toddy
Garnish: Dust with grated nutmeg
Method: Use a heatproof glass and preheat by filling with boiling water. **MUDDLE** cloves in the base of shaker. Add boiling water and **STIR** in honey and other ingredients. Fine strain into glass. (Consider heating in **MICROWAVE** for twenty seconds to boost temperature).

7	dried	Clove
2	spoon	Runny honey
3	shots	Boiling water
2½ shots		Tawny port
1	shot	Freshly squeezed orange juice

Origin: Our quick 'n' easy take on this variation of the 18th century Negus - reputedly a favourite of the writer Dr. Johnson. The traditional recipe begins with studding an orange with cloves and roasting it in the oven.
Comment: A flavoursome and warming variation on mulled wine.

BISON SOUR

★★★★☆

Glass: Old-fashioned
Garnish: Lemon zest twist
Method: SHAKE all ingredients with ice and strain into ice-filled glass.

2 shots Zubrówka bison vodka
1 shot Freshly squeezed lemon juice
½ shot Sugar syrup (2 sugar to 1 water)
1 pinch Ground cinnamon
½ fresh Egg white

Comment: A flavour enhanced vodka sour.

BISTRO SIDECAR

★★★★☆

Glass: Martini
Garnish: Lemon zest twist
Method: SHAKE all ingredients with ice and fine strain into chilled glass.

1½ shots		Martell VSOP Médaillon cognac
½	shot	Tuaca liqueur
½	shot	Hazelnut liqueur
¼	shot	Freshly squeezed lemon juice
¼	shot	Freshly squeezed orange juice

Origin: Adapted from a recipe by chef Kathy Casey Food Studios, Seattle, USA. Kathy's original recipe called for a sugar rim and tangerine juice.
Comment: Although significantly twisted from the classic, this is still recognisably a Sidecar in style.

BITCHES BREW

★★★★☆

Glass: Sour or Martini / Coupette
Garnish: Dust with grated nutmeg
Method: DRY SHAKE all ingredients without ice.
Add ice, **SHAKE** again and fine strain into chilled glass.

1	shot	Martinique blanc rhum agricole
1	shot	Bacardi Carta Ocho aged rum
1	shot	Freshly squeezed lime juice
½	shot	Allspice pimento dram liqueur
½	shot	Sugar syrup (2 Demerara sugar to 1 water)
1	shot	Eggs (white & yolk)

Origin: Created in 2008 by Daniel Eun at PDT, New
York City, USA.
Comment: This flavoursome flip-style drink comes
served with a hint of Caribbean spice.

BITCHES' BREW COCKTAIL (DIFFORD'S RECIPE) (NEW)

★★★★⯪

Glass: Coupe
Garnish: Orange zest twist and Luxardo maraschino
cherry
Method: STIR all ingredients with ice and strain into
ice-filled glass.

1	shot	Byrrh Grand Quinquina
¾	shot	Rutte Old Simon oude jenever
¾	shot	Ketel One Vodka
¾	shot	India pale ale beer

Origin: Named due to its beer and Byrrh aperitif base and
after the track by Miles Davis. Created by yours truly on 21st
February 2015 at the Cabinet Room, London, England.
Comment: Beer has never tasted so complex - sweet
aperitif, dry hoppy IPA beer, bready jenever and
cleansing vodka.

BITTER GRAPEFRUIT

★★★⯪☆

Glass: Martini
Garnish: Grapefruit zest twist
Method: SHAKE all ingredients with ice and fine
strain into chilled glass.

1½	shots	Ketel One Vodka
½	shot	Aperol Aperitivo
1	shot	Martini Rosso vermouth
½	shot	Freshly squeezed pink grapefruit juice

Origin: Discovered in 2007 at Public Restaurant,
New York City, USA.
Comment: Grapefruit influenced and Negroni in style.

BITTER IN BRAZIL (NEW)

★★★★⯪

Glass: Old-fashioned
Garnish: Orange zest twist
Method: STIR all ingredients with ice and strain into
ice-filled glass (preferably large chunk of block ice).

1½	shots	Capucana cachaça
¾	shot	Orange Curaçao liqueur
¾	shot	Carpano Punt E Mes
⅛	shot	Sugar syrup (2 sugar to 1 water)
½	spoon	Fernet Branca
½	shot	Chilled water

Origin: Adapted from a recipe created at The Citizen
Wine Bar, Worcester, Massachusetts, USA.
Comment: Cachaça based and bittersweet with orange
accents and Fernet Branca contributing subtle bitterness.

BITTER LADY

★★★★☆

Glass: Martini
Garnish: Grapefruit zest twist
Method: SHAKE all ingredients with ice and fine
strain into chilled glass.

1½	shots	Rutte Dry Gin
1	spoon	Runny honey
¼	shot	Campari Bitter
½	shot	Freshly squeezed lemon juice
½	fresh	Egg white

Origin: Adapted from a drink created by Mickael
Perron from Bar Now On.
Comment: We have dramatically cut the Campari and
lemon in Mickael's original recipe to make a much
lighter drink.

BITTER SWEET SYMPHONY 🔑

★★★⯪☆

Glass: Martini
Garnish: Apricot slice
Method: SHAKE all ingredients with ice and fine
strain into chilled glass.

½	shot	Ketel One Vodka
1	shot	De Kuyper Triple Sec
1	shot	De Kuyper XO Apricot Brandy
½	shot	Freshly squeezed lime juice
1½	shots	Freshly squeezed pink grapefruit juice

Origin: Adapted from a drink created in 2003 by
Wayne Collins for Maxxium UK.
Comment: This roller coaster ride of bitter and sweet
mainly features apricot and grapefruit.

BITTEREST PILL

★★★⯪☆

Glass: Shot
Garnish: None
Method: Refrigerate ingredients then **LAYER** in
chilled glass by carefully pouring in the following
order.

½	shot	Ketel One Vodka
½	shot	Campari Bitter
½	shot	Passion fruit syrup

Origin: Created by Alex Kammerling, London,
England.
Comment: The bitterness of Campari, toned down by
passion fruit sugar syrup.

BLACK & TAN

★★★⯪☆

Glass: Pint
Garnish: None
Method: POUR lager into chilled glass then **FLOAT**
Guinness on top.

| ½ | pint | Budweiser Budvar |
| ½ | pint | Guinness stout |

Origin: It's likely that the term "black and tan"
originated in England, where different beers have been
blended since at least the seventeenth century. The
earliest written usage of the term in this context is from
1881.
Comment: A layered drink with Lager downstairs and
Guinness upstairs. If poured correctly these two beers
make a perfect "black and tan" layer in the glass.

BLACK & VELVET

★★★★☆

Glass: Boston
Garnish: None
Method: POUR cider into chilled glass then FLOAT Guinness on top.

½ pint   Medium dry cider
½ pint   Guinness stout

Comment: Cider downstairs, Guinness upstairs

BLACK 'N' BLUE CAIPIROVSKA

★★★★☆

Glass: Old-fashioned
Garnish: None
Method: MUDDLE berries in base of glass. Add other ingredients. Fill glass with crushed ice and CHURN (stir) with bar spoon. Serve with straws.

6 fresh   Blackberries
10 fresh   Blueberries
2 shots   Ketel One Vodka
½ shot   Freshly squeezed lime juice
¾ shot   Sugar syrup (2 sugar to 1 water)

Comment: A great fruity twist on the regular Caipirovska.

BLACK BISON MARTINI

★★★★☆

Glass: Martini
Garnish: Apple wedge
Method: SHAKE all ingredients with ice and fine strain into chilled glass.

2 shots   Rutte Dry Gin
½ shot   Apple Schnapps liqueur
1½ shots   Pressed apple juice
¼ shot   Martini Extra Dry vermouth

Origin: Adapted from a drink discovered in 2001 at Oxo Tower Bar, London, England.
Comment: A fragrant cocktail with a dry finish. As the name suggests, also works well with Zubrowka Bison vodka in place of gin.

BLACK DIAMOND

★★★★☆

Glass: Martini
Garnish: Dust with grated white chocolate
Method: SHAKE all ingredients with ice and fine strain into chilled glass.

1¼ shots   Bacardi Carta Blanca light rum
1¼ shots   Dark crème de cacao liqueur
1¼ shots   Espresso coffee (freshly made & hot)

Origin: Created in March 2004 by yours truly, London, England.
Comment: This flavoursome mix of coffee and chocolate is further enhanced if vanilla-infused rum is used.

BLACK FEATHER ⚷

★★★★☆

Glass: Martini
Garnish: Lemon zest twist
Method: STIR all ingredients with ice and strain into chilled glass.

2 shots   Martell VSOP Médaillon cognac
½ shot   De Kuyper Triple Sec
1 shot   Martini Extra Dry vermouth
1 dash   Angostura Aromatic Bitters

Origin: Adapted from a drink created in 2000 by Robert Hess and published on drinkboy.com
Comment: Rounded cognac notes with a hint of orange. For dry, adult palates.

BLACK FOREST GATEAU

★★★★☆

Glass: Martini
Garnish: Dust with chocolate powder
Method: SHAKE first four ingredients with ice and strain into chilled glass. FLOAT cream on drink.

2 shots   Ketel One Vodka
¾ shot   Chambord Liqueur
¾ shot   Lejay Crème de Fraise liqueur
¼ shot   Lejay crème de cassis de Dijon
1 shot   Single cream / half-and-half

Origin: Created in 2002 at Hush, London, England.
Comment: Dessert by name and dessert by nature. Wonderfully moreish, naughty but very nice.

BLACK JACK (NEW)

★★★★☆

Glass: Coupe
Garnish: Lemon twist (discarded) & Black Jack chew
Method: STIR all ingredients with ice and strain into chilled glass.

1½ shots   Byrrh Grand Quinquina
½ shot   Le Fée Parisienne absinthe
½ shot   Amer Picon
½ shot   De Kuyper Triple Sec
4 drop   Bob's Bitters Liquorice Bitters
¾ shot   Chilled water (omit if wet ice)

Comment: For us Brits this cocktail rekindles memories of the tuck shop and a black tongue from chewing on far too many Black Jacks. Happily booze now takes the place of the sugar rush.

BLACK JACK COCKTAIL

★★★★☆

Glass: Martini
Garnish: Lemon zest twist
Method: STIR all ingredients with ice and strain into chilled glass.

1½ shots   Rutte Dry Gin
½ shot   Kirschwasser eau de vie
½ shot   Lejay crème de cassis de Dijon
¾ shot   Chilled water (omit if wet ice)

Origin: The name Black Jack traditionally refers to a water bottle made from air dried leather. When the leather was dried it tended to turn black.
Comment: More burgundy than black but dark fruits of the forest dominate this medium dry cocktail.

BLACK JACK SHOT

★★★☆☆

Glass: Shot
Garnish: None
Method: Refrigerate ingredients then **LAYER** in chilled glass by carefully pouring in the following order.

¾ shot **Black sambuca liqueur**
¾ shot **Jack Daniel's Old No.7 Brand**

Comment: Whiskey sweetened with sambuca.

BLACK JAPAN

★★⊟☆☆

Glass: Collins
Garnish: None
Method: **POUR** melon liqueur into chilled glass then float Guinness on top.

1½ shots **Midori Green Melon liqueur**
Float **Guinness stout**

Origin: Black Japan is the name of a protective lacquer applied to metal.
Comment: This student-style drink will appeal to those with youthful exuberance and a sweet tooth.

BLACK MAGIC

★★★★☆

Glass: Flute
Garnish: Black grapes
Method: **MUDDLE** grapes in base of shaker. Add liqueur, **SHAKE** with ice and fine strain into chilled glass. **TOP** with champagne.

12 fresh **Red grapes**
½ shot **Grand Marnier Cordon Rouge**
Top with **G.H. Mumm Cordon Rouge Champagne**

Comment: More peachy in colour than black but balanced and tasty. Not sweet.

BLACK MUSSEL

★★★⊟☆

Glass: Flute
Garnish: Orange zest twist (discarded)
Method: **POUR** first two ingredients into glass and **TOP** with champagne.

½ shot **Blue curaçao liqueur**
¼ shot **Lejay crème de cassis de Dijon**
Top with **G.H. Mumm Cordon Rouge Champagne**

Comment: Blue curaçao adds a hint of orange to a Kir Royale.

BLACK ROSE

★★★★⊟

Glass: Old-fashioned
Garnish: Lemon zest twist
Method: **STIR** all ingredients with ice and strain into (empty - no ice) chilled glass.

1 shot **Bourbon whiskey**
1 shot **Martell VSOP Médaillon cognac**
¼ shot **Pomegranate / grenadine syrup (2:1)**
3 dash **Peychaud's aromatic bitters**
1 dash **Angostura Aromatic Bitters**

Comment: Sazerac-like but easier for the uninitiated.

BLACK RUSSIAN

★★★⊟☆

Glass: Old-fashioned
Garnish: Lemon slice & cherry on stick (sail)
Method: **STIR** all ingredients with ice and strain into ice-filled glass.

2 shots **Ketel One Vodka**
¾ shot **Coffee liqueur**

Origin: Thought to have been created circa 1949 by Gustav Tops, a hotel bartender in Brussels. Set against the start of the Cold War, the drink is said to have been inspired by Perle Skirvin Mesta, the U.S. ambassador to Luxembourg (1949-1953) and rich American socialite who the term 'hostess with the mostess' was coined for due to her lavish parties.

As well as this cocktail, Perle was the inspiration for Irving Berlin's musical 'Call Me Madam' and several books, including her own autobiography, Perle: My Story, published in 1960.
Comment: This popular cocktail is often served topped with cola, when it becomes a Colorado Bulldog.

BLACK SPRING (NEW)

★★★★☆

Glass: Collins
Garnish: 3 Luxardo cherries on stick
Method: **STIR** first 3 ingredients with ice and strain into ice-filled glass. **TOP** with ginger beer and lightly stir.

1 shot **Straight rye whiskey**
1 shot **Byrrh Grand Quinquina**
1 shot **Amaro liqueur**
2½ shots **Gosling's Stormy Ginger Beer**

Origin: Believed to originate from Denver, USA.
Comment: Ginger spice with a bittersweet fruity rye bread bite.

BLACK STRAP

★★★★☆

Glass: Martini
Garnish: Orange zest twist
Method: **STIR** all ingredients with ice and strain into chilled glass.

2 shots **Gosling's Black Seal dark rum**
½ shot **Bénédictine D.O.M. liqueur**
½ shot **Dark crème de cacao liqueur**
2 drop **Tabasco hot pepper sauce**

Origin: Adapted from a recipe created in 2007 by Neyah White, San Francisco, USA.
Comment: This drink benefits from the dilution, which comes with a lengthy stir.

BLACK TIE

★★★★☆

Glass: Old-fashioned
Garnish: Physalis (cape gooseberry)
Method: **SHAKE** all ingredients with ice and strain into ice-filled glass.

1	shot	**Bacardi Carta Ocho aged rum**
½	shot	**Bacardi Carta Blanca light rum**
½	shot	**De Kuyper Triple Sec**
¼	shot	**Almond (orgeat) syrup**
½	spoon	**Black strap molasses**
¾	shot	**Freshly squeezed lime juice**
⅛	shot	**Sugar syrup (2 sugar to 1 water)**

Origin: Adapted from a drink created by Mark Lynch at Green 19, Dublin, Ireland.
Comment: Depending on the sweetness of your molasses, you may not need to add sugar syrup.

BLACK VELVET

★★★½☆

Glass: Flute
Garnish: Shamrock (or mint leaf)
Method: Slowly **POUR** ingredients into chilled glass and gently stir.

3½ shots	**Guinness stout**
Top with	**G.H. Mumm Cordon Rouge Champagne**

Origin: Thought to have originated in 1861 at Brook's Club, London although some credit the Shelbourne Hotel, Dublin, Ireland. What is certain is that this drink was created at the time when Britain was mourning the death of HRH Prince Albert, husband of Queen Victoria.

The Black Velvet is often served to commemorate Saint Patrick's Day but is more fittingly served on 14th December as this is the day Prince Albert died of typhoid fever in 1861. Devastated, the Queen wore black for the rest of her life so this drink's shrouding of champagne is most appropriate.

In his 1948 'Fine Art of Mixing Drinks', David A. Embury writes of this drink, "I was first introduced to Black Velvet at the home of a very dear friend of mine in Montreal and I received one of the greatest of all the drinking surprises of my whole life. The combination of champagne and stout sounds terrifying - something like molasses and horseradish. Actually, it's excellent. The champagne cuts the heavy, syrupy consistency of the stout, and the stout takes the sharp, tart edge off the champagne. Each is the perfect complement of the other. Be sure, however, that you use (a) a good bottle of stout, (b) an extra-dry champagne - preferably a brut or nature."
Comment: Full-flavoured stout and delicate champagne are an unlikely combination but this classic has stood the test of time. Some may wish to add a barspoon of sugar syrup.

BLACKBEARD

★★★☆☆

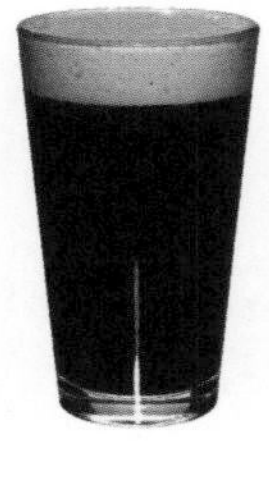

Glass: Pint
Garnish: None
Method: **POUR** ingredients in glass and serve.

2	shots	**Bacardi Carta Blanca light rum**
½	unit	**Guinness stout**
Top with		**Coca-Cola**

Origin: Thought to have originated in Stirling, Scotland, during the late 1990s.
Comment: Something of a student drink, this tastes better than it sounds.

BLACKTHORN COCKTAIL

★★★★☆

Glass: Martini
Garnish: Lemon zest twist
Method: **STIR** all ingredients with ice and strain into chilled glass.

1½ shots Rutte Dry Gin
¾ shot Kirschwasser eau de vie
¾ shot Dubonnet Red

Comment: This drink benefits from a long, chilling and diluting stir. The result is a Martini-style, fruity but dry.

BLACKTHORN ENGLISH

★★★½☆

Glass: Martini
Garnish: Orange zest twist
Method: **SHAKE** all ingredients with ice and fine strain into chilled glass.

1½	shots	**Sloe Gin liqueur**
1	shot	**Rutte Dry Gin**
¾	shot	**Martini Rosso vermouth**
3	dash	**Angostura Orange Bitters**
½	shot	**Chilled water** (omit if wet ice)

Origin: A vintage classic whose origins are unknown.
Comment: A fruit influenced yet dry and classic Martini.

BLACKTHORN IRISH

★★★★½

Glass: Coupe
Garnish: Lemon zest twist
Method: **STIR** first 4 ingredients with ice and strain into chilled glass. Dash abinsthe into surface of drink and then stroke barspoon once through drink (rather than stir in).

1½	shot	**Teeling Small Batch Irish whiskey**
¾	shot	**Martini Extra Dry Vermouth**
¾	shot	**Martini Rosso Vermouth**
2	dash	**Bokers bitters**
3	dash	**Le Fée Parisienne absinthe**

Comment: The original equal parts whiskey and dry vermouth recipe is way too dry, so in time for Saint Patrick's Day 2016 we experimented and concluded that splitting the vermouth proportion evenly between dry and sweet vermouths was the 'perfect' solution, producing an aromatic balanced cocktail with faint hints of anise from the absinthe.
Origin: This cocktail first appeared (as Black Thorn Irish) in Harry Johnson's 1900 *Bartender's Manual* where he stipulates "3 or 4 dashes of absinthe; 3 or 4 dashes of bitters (Boker's genuine only); 1/2 wine glass of French vermouth; 1/2 wine glass of Irish whiskey."

BLADE RUNNER

★★★★☆

Glass: Collins
Garnish: Pineapple wedge & Luxardo Maraschino cherry
Method: **SHAKE** all ingredients with ice and strain into ice-filled glass.

2 shots Bacardi Carta Blanca light rum
½ shot Pot still Jamaican rum
2½ shots Fresh pressed pineapple juice
¼ shot Sugar syrup (2 sugar to 1 water)
2 dash Angostura Aromatic Bitters
½ shot Freshly squeezed lime juice

Origin: Discovered in 2005 at Zoulou Bar, Berlin, Germany.
Comment: Tangy and fruity but not too sweet.

BLANCHE CORPSE REVIVER (NEW)

★★★★☆

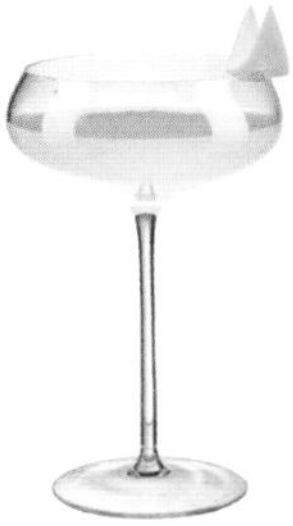

Glass: Coupe
Garnish: Lemon zest twist
Method: **SHAKE** all ingredients with ice and fine strain into chilled glass.

¾ shot La Fée Absinthe Blanche
¾ shot De Kuyper Triple Sec
¾ shot Lillet Blanc
¾ shot Freshly squeezed lemon juice
¼ shot Sugar syrup (2 sugar to 1 water)
½ shot Chilled water

Origin: Adapted from a recipe created in 2013 by Stephen Quainton at B.Y.O.C. Bar, Brighton, England.
Comment: Blanche absinthe sits surprisingly well in this riff on the classic Corpse Reviver.

BLANCHE REFRESHER (NEW)

★★★★☆

Glass: Goblet
Garnish: Strings of lemon zest
Method: **SHAKE** first 3 ingredients with ice and strain into glass filled with crushed ice. Drizzle Green Chartreuse all over the top of the drink.

1 shot La Fée Absinthe Blanche
1 shot Taylor's Velvet Falernum liqueur
1 shot Freshly squeezed lemon juice
½ shot Green Chartreuse liqueur

Origin: Adapted from a recipe created in 2013 by Stephen Quainton at B.Y.O.C. Bar, Brighton, England.
Comment: Challenging ingredients, including a whole shot of absinthe, combine to make a very approachable, aptly refreshing cocktail.

BLING! BLING!

★★★★½

Glass: Shot
Garnish: None
Method: **MUDDLE** raspberries in base of shaker. Add vodka, lime and sugar, **SHAKE** with ice and fine strain into glass. **TOP** with champagne.

7 fresh Raspberries
½ shot Ketel One Vodka
½ shot Freshly squeezed lime juice
¼ shot Sugar syrup (2 sugar to 1 water)
Top with G.H. Mumm Cordon Rouge Champagne

Origin: Created in 2001 by Phillip Jeffrey at the GE Club, London, England.
Comment: An ostentatious little number.

BLINKER

★★★★☆

Glass: Coupe
Garnish: Lemon zest twist
Method: **SHAKE** all ingredients with ice and fine strain into chilled glass.

2 shots Bourbon whiskey
¼ shot Pomegranate / grenadine syrup (2:1)
1 shot Freshly squeezed pink grapefruit juice

Origin: First published in Patrick Gavin Duffy's 1934 The Official Mixer's Manual.
Comment: Back in the 1930s David Embury wrote of this drink, "One of a few cocktails using grapefruit juice. Not particularly good but not too bad." How times have changed!

BLINKER (HAWKSMOOR'S RIFF) (NEW)

★★★★½

Glass: Coupe
Garnish: Lemon zest twist
Method: **SHAKE** all ingredients with ice and fine strain into chilled glass.

2 shot Straight rye whiskey
½ shot Freshly squeezed pink grapefruit juice
3 fresh Raspberries
¼ shot Sugar syrup (2 sugar to 1 water)

Comment: The original Blinker from Patrick Gavin Duffy's 1934 *The Official Mixer's Manual* uses grenadine but Hawksmoor have switched this for a few fresh raspberries and a dash of sugar syrup, turning a good drink into a great cocktail.
Origin: Adapted from a recipe discovered in 2013 at Hawksmoor, Spitalfields, London, England.

Blood and Sand cocktail

Probably the best-known Scotch whisky based cocktail, the Blood & Sand is traditionally made with equal parts Scotch whisky, cherry brandy, sweet vermouth and orange juice, shaken and served straight-up. Created in 1922, the drink is named after Rudolph Valentino's Blood & Sand bullfighter movie which was released the same year.

Based on the 1909 Spanish novel Blood and Sand (Sangre y arena) by Vicente Blasco Ibáñez and the play by Thomas Cushing, the silent film was a box office hit. It tells the dramatic story of Juan Gallardo (Valentino), a poor village boy who grows up to become one of the greatest matadors in Spain. He marries his childhood sweetheart, the beautiful and virtuous Carmen, but once rich and famous is seduced by a wealthy widow. They embark on a torrid affair, but feeling guilty he tries to end the affair. Furious at his rejection, his lover exposes their affair to his wife. Distracted and depressed he becomes reckless in the arena and somewhat predictably is killed in a bullfight. However, in true Hollywood style, just moments before his death, he manages to reconcile with his wife Carmen who is naturally grief stricken. The end.

Who was inspired by the film to make the cocktail is unknown, but it first appears in Harry Craddock's '1930 The Savoy Cocktail Book'. The deep amber red cherry brandy is said to represent the blood and the orange juice the sand.

The Blood and Sand is one of those cocktails which started as being equal proportions and has pretty much remained so. It works but is perhaps a tad sweet with the cherry brandy slightly dominating the Scotch. If making late at night I like to double the scotch so:
1½ shot Scotch whisky
¾ shot Cherry brandy
¾ shot Sweet vermouth
¾ shot Orange juice

The discovery that blood orange juice is far superior to navel orange juice (but freshly squeezed navel orange is superior to any packaged orange juice) led me to create the Bloody Blood & Sand. In doing so I also introduced a splash of Islay malt to help the Scotch stand up to the other big flavoured ingredients.

This got me thinking about the cherry brandy and the Straits Sling, so I tried 50% cherry brandy and 50% kirsch eau-de-vie. That worked so I applied the same logic to the vermouth and the drink also became 'perfect', resulting in my Perfectly Straight Blood & Sand.

I came across the excellent Dutch Blood and Sand, made with jenever at London's Satan's Whiskers bar where they add a dash of lemon juice and simple syrup to their equal parts Blood & Sand.

BLOOD AND SAND (CLASSIC FORMULA)

★★★★☆

Glass: Martini
Garnish: Orange zest twist
Method: SHAKE all ingredients with ice and fine strain into chilled glass.

¾ shot Dewar's 12yo Scotch whisky
¾ shot Cherry Heering Liqueur
¾ shot Martini Rosso vermouth
¾ shot Freshly squeezed orange juice

Comment: One of the best classic Scotch cocktails but a tad on the sweet side. Said by many to be the Scotch-based cocktail that Scotch haters will like.

BLOOD AND SAND (DIFFORD'S RECIPE)

★★★★★

Glass: Coupe
Garnish: Orange zest twist (discarded) & Luxardo Maraschino cherry
Method: SHAKE all ingredients with ice and fine strain into chilled glass.

1 shot Dewar's 12yo Scotch whisky
¾ shot Cherry Heering Liqueur
¾ shot Martini Rosso vermouth
1 shot Blood orange juice
⅛ shot Islay single malt Scotch whisky

Comment: The equal parts (scotch, cherry brandy, sweet vermouth and orange juice) formula from the 1930 'The Savoy Cocktail Book' is the accepted classic Blood & Sand recipe but results in a cocktail that's a tad sweet for hardened whisky drinkers. This is dryer and fresher with slightly increased amounts of Scotch and orange juice. Those who like Scotch and a slightly drier drink might also appreciate the additional spoon of Islay malt.

BLOOD ORANGE COCKTAIL

★★★★½

Glass: Coupe
Garnish: Orange zest twist
Method: SHAKE all ingredients with ice and fine strain into chilled glass.

1½ shots Rutte Dry Gin
½ shot Campari Bitter
½ shot Martini Extra Dry vermouth
1 shot Blood orange juice

Origin: Adapted from a drink created in 2008 by Jeffrey Morgenthaler at Bel Ami Lounge, Oregon, USA.
Comment: Full-on tangy fresh blood orange with a subtle gin back bone, Campari and dry vermouth add complexity.

BLOOD ORANGE MARGARITA (NEW)

★★★★½

Glass: Old-fashioned
Garnish: Half salt rim and blood orange slice
Method: SHAKE all ingredients with ice and strain into ice-filled glass.

1½ shots Patrón Silver tequila
¾ shot De Kuyper Triple Sec
¼ shot Campari Bitter
¾ shot Blood orange juice
¾ shot Freshly squeezed lime juice
¼ shot Sugar syrup (2 sugar to 1 water)

Origin: Created in 2000 by Ben Davidson in Sydney, Australia.
Comment: Notes of tequila, orangey triple sec, bittersweet Campari, blood orange and lime juice all sit in perfect kilter in this tasty riff on the classic Margarita.

BLOOD SAGE

★★★★½

Glass: Martini
Garnish: Sage leaf
Method: MUDDLE orange and sage in base of shaker. Add other ingredients, **SHAKE** with ice and fine strain into chilled glass.

½ shot Blood orange juice
2 fresh Sage leaves
2 shots Rutte Dry Gin
¾ shot Freshly squeezed lime juice
½ shot Sugar syrup (2 sugar to 1 water)
½ fresh Egg white

Origin: Adapted from a drink created by Ryan Magarian, Seattle, USA.
Comment: Sage combines wonderfully with gin and orange in this beautifully balanced drink.

BLOODED KNEES COCKTAIL (NEW)

★★★★★

Glass: Coupe
Garnish: Orange zest twist
Method: SHAKE all ingredients with ice and fine strain into chilled glass.

2	shots	Rutte Dry Gin
3	spoon	Runny honey
¾	shot	Blood orange juice
¾	shot	Freshly squeezed lemon juice

Origin: Adapted from the classic Bee's Knees, made bloody by the use of blood orange juice.
Comment: Tart lemon and orange citrus notes are balanced by rich and flavoursome honey with gin fortifying and adding botanical complexity.

BLOODHOUND #1

★★★★⯪☆

Glass: Martini
Garnish: Raspberries
Method: MUDDLE raspberries in base of shaker. Add other ingredients, SHAKE with ice and fine strain into chilled glass.

6	fresh	Raspberries
2	shots	Rutte Dry Gin
¾	shot	Martini Extra Dry vermouth
¾	shot	Martini Rosso vermouth
¼	shot	Luxardo Maraschino liqueur

Origin: Unknown but in his 1922 'Mixing Cocktails', Harry McElhone credits the Duke of Manchester with this drinks creation. However, in his 1907 'World Drinks', William Boothby lists a Bloodhound, as does Tom Bullock in his 1917 'The Ideal Bartender'.
Comment: Looks like fruity disco drink fodder but is actually surprising dry and strong.

BLOODHOUND #2

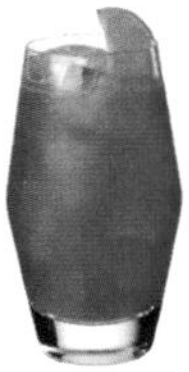

★★★★⯪☆

Glass: Collins
Garnish: Lime wedge
Method: SHAKE all ingredients with ice and strain into ice-filled glass.

1	shot	Ketel One Vodka
2	shots	Campari Bitter
3	shots	Freshly squeezed pink grapefruit juice

Comment: A dry, tart, refreshing long drink.

BLOODY BLOOD & SAND (NEW)

★★★★★

Glass: Coupe
Garnish: Orange zest twist
Method: SHAKE all ingredients with ice and fine strain into chilled glass.

¾	shot	Dewar's 12yo Scotch whisky
½	shot	Islay single malt Scotch whisky
¾	shot	Cherry Heering Liqueur
¾	shot	Martini Rosso vermouth
1	shot	Blood orange juice

Origin: Created in March 2014 by yours truly at the Cabinet Room, London, England.
Comment: A Blood & Sand with the smoky influence of Islay single malt whisky and the rounding citrus notes of blood orange juice.

BLOODY BRONX COCKTAIL

★★★★⯪

Glass: Coupe
Garnish: Luxardo Maraschino cherry
Method: SHAKE all ingredients with ice and fine strain into chilled glass.

1 ¾	shots	Rutte Dry Gin
½	shot	Martini Rosso vermouth
¼	shot	Martini Extra Dry vermouth
1	shot	Blood orange juice

Origin: Adapted from the classic Bronx Cocktail, created in 1906 by Johnny Solon, a bartender at New York's Waldorf-Astoria Hotel, and named after the newly opened Bronx Zoo.
Comment: A Bronx made 'bloody' by the use of blood oranges. Fruity yet dry with botanical notes both from the vermouth and the gin.

BLOODY CAESAR

★★★★☆

Glass: Collins
Garnish: Pickled bean
Method: ROCK rather than shake all ingredients in a shaker with ice and fine strain into ice-filled glass.

2 shots Ketel One Vodka
4 shots Mott's Clamato juice
½ shot Freshly squeezed lemon juice
7 drop Tabasco hot pepper sauce
3 dash Worcestershire sauce
2 pinch Celery salt
2 grind Black pepper

Origin: Created by Walter Chell in 1969 to celebrate the opening of Marco's Italian restaurant at the Calgary Inn, Canada. Walter was inspired by the flavours of Spaghetti Vongole (spaghetti with clams) and named the drink after the Roman emperor.
Comment: A peculiarly Canadian fishy twist on the classic Bloody Mary.

BLOODY JOSEPH

★★★⯪☆

Glass: Collins
Garnish: Celery stick
Method: ROCK rather than shake all ingredients in a shaker with ice and fine strain into ice-filled glass.

2	shots	Dewar's 12yo Scotch whisky
4	shots	Tomato juice
½	shot	Freshly squeezed lemon juice
8	drop	Tabasco hot pepper sauce
4	dash	Worcestershire sauce
½	spoon	Horseradish sauce
2	pinch	Celery salt
2	grind	Black pepper

Comment: A Bloody Mary with whisky.

BLOODY MARIA

★★★★☆

Glass: Collins
Garnish: Salt & pepper rim plus celery stick
Method: SHAKE all ingredients with ice and strain into ice-filled glass.

2	shots	Patrón reposado tequila
4	shots	Tomato juice
½	shot	Freshly squeezed lemon juice
8	drop	Tabasco hot pepper sauce
4	dash	Worcestershire sauce
½	spoon	Horseradish sauce
½	shot	Tawny port
2	pinch	Celery salt
2	grind	Black pepper

Comment: Tequila adds a very interesting kick to the classic Bloody Mary.

BLOODY MARU

★★★★☆

Glass: Collins
Garnish: Lemongrass
Method: ROCK rather than shake all ingredients in a shaker with ice and fine strain into ice-filled glass.

4	shots	Junmai ginjō sake
½	shot	Freshly squeezed lemon juice
8	drop	Tabasco hot pepper sauce
4	dash	Worcestershire sauce
2	pinch	Celery salt
2	grind	Black pepper

Comment: A Bloody Mary based on sake.

Bloody Mary cocktail

Whatever the precise story behind this fantastic drink, Bloody Mary recipes are as personal as for Martinis. Purists will only use pepper sauce, worcestershire sauce, salt and lemon to spice up tomato juice and vodka but everything from oysters to V8 can be added.

Our recommended Bloody Mary recipe calls for vodka, tomato juice, pepper sauce, worcestershire sauce, black pepper and celery salt. These are now common ingredients to almost all modern day Bloody Marys. Our recipe also uses lemon juice to add freshness and its inclusion is becoming the norm. My own version of the Bloody Mary uses all these ingredients with a little sugar to balance the addition of lemon juice and amplify the flavours of the other ingredients. I also add sherry and bell pepper juice to contribute more flavour and freshness.

Other variations include:
Asian Mary (with wasabi, ginger & soy sauce)
Bloody Bull (with beef consommé)
Bloody Caesar (with clam juice)
Bloody Joseph (with Scotch whisky)
Bloody Maria (with tequila)
Bloody Maru (with sake)
Bloody Shame (without alcohol)
Bullshot (with beef bouillon)
Cubanita (with rum)
Red Snapper (with gin)

A Bloody Mary tastes better if the tomato juice retains some viscosity. Thin/dilute tomato juice detracts from the drink, no matter how balanced and perfectly spiced to suit the drinker's taste. Shaking tends to detrimentally affect viscosity so it's

better to simply turn the shaker over and over, rather than shaking, using a motion that is often referred to as a Cuban roll. I recommend 20 revolutions with fresh ice by which time the outside of the shaker should be thoroughly frosted.

There is also debate as to whether it is best to serve a Bloody Mary with or without ice. The answer is with ice, but that ice should come straight from a freezer. Ice-machine ice is too wet, even when taken straight from the machine. A long single column of ice made in a mould is ideal as this will keep the drink cold but give minimal dilution.

History

The creation of the Bloody Mary is often credited to Fernand Petiot in the 1920s while a young bartender at Harry's New York Bar in Paris. However, it appears he simply spiced up an existing and well-established combo of vodka and tomato juice while working at the St. Regis Hotel during the 1940s. The originator of savoury blend of vodka and tomato juice was probably George Jessel, Hollywood star of the 1920s-1950s, and it looks likely that he also christened his favourite drink Bloody Mary.

Written by Jack McGarry, you can read what is surely the most comprehensive history of the Bloody Mary on diffordsguide.com.

BLOODY MARY (DIFFORD'S RECIPE)

★★★★★

Glass: Collins
Garnish: Grate pepper over drink and place celery stick in glass (optional salt & pepper rim)
Method: MUDDLE pepper in base of shaker. Add other ingredients, ROLL rather than shake with ice and strain into ice-filled glass. (Use double frozen ice freshly from freezer to fill glass.)

½	ring	Yellow bell pepper (chopped)
2	shots	Ketel One Vodka
3	shots	Tomato juice
½	shot	Romate Amontillado sherry
½	shot	Freshly squeezed lemon juice
¼	shot	Sugar syrup (2 sugar to 1 water)
2	pinch	Celery salt
3	grind	Black pepper
10	drop	Tabasco hot pepper sauce
4	dash	Worcestershire sauce

Origin: Created in 2007 by yours truly at the Cabinet Room, London, England.
Comment: A Bloody Mary Cocktail with a hint of bell pepper freshness and a touch of sherry.

BLOODY MARY (MODERN RECIPE)

★★★★☆

Glass: Collins
Garnish: Celery stick (optional salt & pepper rim)
Method: ROLL rather than shake all ingredients with ice and strain into ice-filled glass. (Use double frozen ice freshly from freezer to fill glass.)

2	shots	Ketel One Vodka
4	shots	Tomato juice
½	shot	Freshly squeezed lemon juice
8	drop	Tabasco hot pepper sauce
4	dash	Worcestershire sauce
2	grind	Black pepper
1	pinch	Celery salt

Origin: For the full history and other information please see our full entry of the Bloody Mary cocktail.
Comment: The classic brunch cocktail.

BLOODY NEGRONI (NEW)

★★★★★

Glass: Old-fashioned
Garnish: Blood orange slice
Method: SHAKE all ingredients with ice and strain into ice-filled glass.

¾ shot   **Rutte Dry Gin**
¾ shot   **Campari Bitter**
¾ shot   **Martini Rosso vermouth**
¾ shot   **Blood orange juice**

Origin: I'm sure someone came up with this combo years before but made by yours truly February 2014 at the Cabinet Room, London England.
Comment: A classic Negroni consists of equal parts gin, Campari and sweet vermouth garnished with an orange slice. When in season, a splash of blood orange juice adds a refreshing citrusy tang.

BLOODY SHAME (MOCKTAIL)

★★★★½☆

Glass: Collins
Garnish: Celery stick
Method: ROCK rather than shake all ingredients in a shaker with ice and fine strain into ice-filled glass.

5 shots   **Tomato juice**
½ shot   **Freshly squeezed lemon juice**
8 drop   **Tabasco hot pepper sauce**
4 dash   **Worcestershire sauce**
½ spoon   **Horseradish sauce**
2 pinch   **Celery salt**
2 grind   **Black pepper**

Comment: Somehow missing something.

BLOOMSBURY MARTINI

★★★★☆

Glass: Martini
Garnish: Lemon zest twist
Method: STIR all ingredients with ice and strain into chilled glass.

2 shots   **Rutte Dry Gin**
½ shot   **Licor 43 liqueur**
½ shot   **Martini Extra Dry vermouth**
2 dash   **Peychaud's aromatic bitters**

Origin: Adapted from a drink created in 2003 by Robert Hess and published on drinkboy.com
Comment: This pinky/rusty drink benefits from a good long stir but the result is an aromatic, medium dry, spicy vanilla Martini.

BLUE BIRD

★★★☆☆

Glass: Martini
Garnish: Orange zest twist
Method: SHAKE all ingredients with ice and fine strain into chilled glass.

2 shots   **Rutte Dry Gin**
1 shot   **Blue curaçao liqueur**
¾ shot   **Freshly squeezed lemon juice**
¼ shot   **Almond (orgeat) syrup**

Origin: Thought to have been created in the late 1950s in Montmartre, Paris, France.
Comment: A blue rinsed, orange washed, gin based 'tini' that benefits from being sweetened with almond rather than plain syrup.

BLUE BLAZER

★★★★☆

Glass: Snifter
Garnish: Lemon zest twist
Method: The drink involves setting whisky alight and pouring it between two silver tankards, creating an arc of flame.

WARNING - please practice with water first to perfect your method. Stand on a non-flammable floor and have suitable fire-fighting equipment nearby. The following recipe makes two drinks.

You will need two large silver-plated tankards with handles. Preheat these with boiling water and warm the whisky. **POUR** the whisky into one tankard and fresh boiling water into the other. Ignite the whisky using a long match and while still blazing pour the whisky into the other tankard. Then mix ingredients by pouring them from one tankard to the other. The foolhardy increase the distance between the tankards as they pour, thus creating a spectacular long blue flame between the two. Jerry Thomas is said to have held the tankards at a meter's distance from each other. Extinguish flame by covering flaming tankard with base of the other tankard, pour into glass and sweeten to taste by stirring in powdered sugar.

4 shots Dewar's 12yo Scotch whisky
4 shots Boiling water
1 spoon Powdered sugar

Origin: This spectacular serve was created by Jerry Thomas, author of the first bartending book and travelling performance bartender. Thomas was a master of showmanship; he used solid silver bar tools and cups embellished with precious stones and metals. He understood the importance of putting on a show when making drinks and people traveled to see his 'act' as much as they did to try his legendary cocktails.

Nicknamed the 'Professor' due to his ability to deal "with the fanciest orders imaginable", Thomas developed his signature 'Blue Blazer' drink whilst working at the El Dorado, a gambling saloon in San Francisco during the gold rush. Legend has it that Thomas would only make the drink if the outside temperature was 10°C (50°F) or below, making an exception to this rule if the person ordering was suffering with a cold or the flu, whose symptoms the drink was to alleviate.

The story of its creation says that a huge gruff man stormed into the bar Thomas was working in and (quoting from an account by Herber Asbury in 1928) said: "Bar-keep! Fix me up some hell-fire that'll shake me right down to my gizzard!" Thomas then proceeded to pour ignited whisky and boiling water between two cups. In Asbury's story the man drank the cocktail and said "He done it. Right down to my gizzard! Yes, sir, right down to my gizzard!"

President Ulysses S. Grant witnessed Thomas perform this spectacle and was apparently so impressed that he presented him with a cigar. In his 1862 ' Bartender's Guide' Thomas wrote: "A beholder gazing for the first time upon an experienced artist, compounding this beverage, would naturally come to the conclusion that it was a nectar for Pluto rather than Bacchus."
Comment: The showy way to make a simple hot whisky punch.

BLUE EYED MARTINI

★★★★½☆

Glass: Martini
Garnish: Lemon zest twist
Method: STIR all ingredients with ice and strain into chilled glass.

1½ shots   **Ketel One Vodka**
½ shot   **Rutte Dry Gin**
⅛ shot   **Blue curaçao liqueur**
¼ shot   **Martini Extra Dry vermouth**

Comment: A blue rinsed Vodka Martini.

BLUE HAWAII

★★★★☆

Glass: Collins
Garnish: Pineapple wedge,
Luxardo Maraschino cherry &
paper parasol
Method: POUR blue curaçao into
ice-filled glass. **SHAKE** the sugar
syrup, pineapple and lime juice
with ice and strain into ice filled
glass so it forms a layer (carefully
pour so floats on previous layer)
over blue curaçao. Lastly **FLOAT**
rum on top of drink.

½ shot Blue curaçao liqueur
3 shots Fresh pressed
pineapple juice
1 shot Freshly squeezed
lime juice
½ shot Sugar syrup
(2 sugar to 1 water)
1½ shots Bacardi Carta Blanca
light rum

Origin: Created in 1957 by Harry
Yee at Henry Kaiser's Hawaiian
Village Hotel (latterly the Hilton)
in Waikiki, Oahu, Hawaii. The
drink is named after the hit song
from the 1937 Bing Crosby film,
Waikiki Wedding, and not after
what is generously described as a
"musical-comedy" Elvis Presley
1961 film of the same name.
Comment: Aloha!

BLUE HAWAIIAN

★★★☆☆

Glass: Hurricane
Garnish: Pineapple wedge & Luxardo Maraschino
cherry
Method: BLEND ingredients with 12oz scoop of
crushed ice. Pour into glass and serve with straws.

2	shots	Bacardi Carta Blanca light rum
1	shot	Blue curaçao liqueur
1½	shots	Coco Re'al Cream of Coconut
3	shots	Fresh pressed pineapple juice
¼	shot	Freshly squeezed lemon juice

Origin: Probably created by Don the Beachcomber in
Los Angeles, USA.
Comment: A blue rinsed Piña Colada.

BLUE LAGOON

★★★☆☆

Glass: Collins
Garnish: Orange slice
Method: BLEND ingredients with 12oz scoop of
crushed ice. Pour into glass and serve with straws.

1	shot	Rutte Dry Gin
1	shot	Ketel One Vodka
1	shot	Blue curaçao liqueur
1	shot	Freshly squeezed lime juice
1	shot	Sugar syrup (2 sugar to 1 water)

Origin: Created in 1960 by Andy MacElhone (son of
Harry) at Harry's New York Bar, Paris, France.
Comment: Better than the film - not hard!

BLUE LASSI

★★★★☆

Glass: Coupe
Garnish: Orange zest twist (discarded) & mint leaf
Method: SHAKE all ingredients with ice and fine
strain into chilled glass.

1½	shots	Ketel One Vodka (infused with vanilla)
1½	shots	Yoghurt liqueur
½	shot	Blue curaçao liqueur
2	dash	Rose water

Origin: Created in 2011 by yours truly at the Cabinet
Room, London, England.
Comment: Baby blue creamy yoghurt with vanilla
infused vodka, orange liqueur and aromatic rose water.

BLUE MARGARITA

★★★★☆

Glass: Coupe
Garnish: Lime slice
Method: BLEND all ingredients with one 12oz scoop
crushed ice. Serve with straws.

2	shots	Patrón reposado tequila
1	shot	Blue curaçao liqueur
1	shot	Freshly squeezed lime juice
½	shot	Sugar syrup (2 sugar to 1 water)

Comment: As the name suggests, a Margarita, only
blue. This 'Disco Drink' look scary but tastes pretty
good.

BLUE MONDAY

★★★★☆

Glass: Old-fashioned
Garnish: Orange zest twist
Method: SHAKE all
ingredients with ice and fine
strain into chilled glass.

1½ shots Ketel One
Citroen vodka
¾ shot Blue
curaçao liqueur
½ shot De Kuyper
Triple Sec
½ shot Martini Extra Dry
vermouth
2 dash Angostura Orange
Bitters

Origin: Adapted from
Harry Craddock's 1930 'The
Savoy Cocktail Book'. His
recipe called for ¼ triple sec
liqueur, ¾ vodka and 1 dash
blue food colouring. The Blue
Monday also appears in
Patrick Gavin Duffy's 1934 '
The Official Mixer's Manual'.
Comment: Disco blue but
medium dry with a
bittersweet orange taste.

BLUE MOON COCKTAIL (1940'S RECIPE)

★★★★☆

Glass: Coupe
Garnish: Raspberries
Method: SHAKE all ingredients with ice and fine strain into chilled glass.

2 shots Rutte Dry Gin
½ shot Benoit Serres
crème de violette
½ shot Freshly squeezed
lemon juice
½ fresh Egg white (optional)

Origin: This cocktail is said to have been created around 1940 by Oscar Tschirky at Waldorf-Astoria Hotel in Manhattan, New York, USA. Better known as "Oscar of the Waldorf", he was maître d'hôtel at Waldorf-Astoria and is also credited for inventing the Waldorf salad and Eggs Benedict. Although he never worked as a chef, capitalising on his reputation at the hotel, he also authored a cocktail book.

The Blue Moon cocktail was lost for decades, due to production of Créme Yvette ceasing in 1969, but thanks to Créme Yvette's 2010 relaunch, has been rediscovered. Incidentally, blue moon is an astronomical term for the second of two full moons to occur in the same calendar months.
Comment: A relation of the Aviation Cocktail, this drink features on the back label of Créme Yvette bottles dating from the 1940s. Now once again available, consequently this liqueur is more identified with the Blue Moon than crème de violette, which appears in some other versions of the Blue Moon.

When made with crème de violette (use ¾ shot) the drink is indeed a blue-grey colour, as befits its name. However, when made with Crème Yvette (you'll only need a ½ shot) the drink is more pink than blue, so leading me to think that it was originally made with crème de violette.

BLUE MOON COCKTAIL (DALE DEGROFF'S RECIPE)

★★★★☆

Glass: Coupe
Garnish: Sage leaf & blueberry
Method: Lightly **MUDDLE** blueberry in base of shaker (to break skin). Add vodka and one heaped spoon of oolong tea and stir in base of shaker for 60 seconds (or leave to steep for ten minutes). Add other ingredients, **SHAKE** with ice and fine strain into chilled glass.

1 fresh Blueberries
2 shots Ketel One Vodka
1 spoon Oolong tea
½ shot St-Germain elderflower liqueur
¾ shot Freshly squeezed lemon juice
½ shot Agave syrup
1 fresh Sage leaves

Origin: Adapted from a recipe created in 2010 by Dale DeGroff, New York, USA. Blue moon is an astronomical term for the second of two full moons to occur in the same calendar month.
Comment: A hint of blueberry fruit with oolong tea, elderflower, sage and lemon.

BLUE MOUNTAIN COCKTAIL

★★★★☆

Glass: Martini
Garnish: Orange zest twist (discarded) & coffee beans
Method: SHAKE all ingredients with ice and fine strain into chilled glass.

1½ shots Bacardi Carta Ocho aged rum
½ shot Ketel One Vodka
½ shot Coffee liqueur
1½ shots Freshly squeezed orange juice

Comment: A balanced wake-up call where the blue mountain means coffee and freshly squeezed orange juice.

BLUE PASSION

★★★½☆

Glass: Old-fashioned
Garnish: Orange zest twist
Method: SHAKE all ingredients with ice and strain into glass filled with crushed ice. If serving over cubed ice use this recipe: 1½ light white rum, ¾ blue curaçao, ¾ lime juice and ½ sugar syrup.

1 shot Bacardi Carta Blanca light rum
1 shot Blue curaçao liqueur
1¾ shots Freshly squeezed lime juice
1 shot Sugar syrup (2 sugar to 1 water)

Comment: Sweet and sour and turquoise blue.

BLUE RIBAND

★★★☆☆

Glass: Martini
Garnish: Luxardo Maraschino cherry
Method: STIR all ingredients with ice and strain into chilled glass.

2 shots Rutte Dry Gin
1 shot De Kuyper Triple Sec
1 shot Blue curaçao liqueur

Origin: The 'Blue Riband' was awarded to the liner that made the fastest Atlantic crossing. This cocktail is thought to have been created on one of these ships.
Comment: A sweetened, blue rinsed, orange and gin Martini.

BLUE TRAIN

★★★½☆

Glass: Coupe
Garnish: Orange wedge on rim

Method: SHAKE all ingredients with ice and fine strain into chilled glass.

2 shots Rutte Dry Gin
¾ shot De Kuyper Triple Sec
½ shot Blue curaçao liqueur
¾ shot Freshly squeezed lemon juice

Comment: Yup, it's blue, slightly sweet and orange flavoured.

BLUE VELVET MARGARITA

★★★★☆

Glass: Coupe
Garnish: Lime wedge
Method: SHAKE all ingredients with ice and fine strain into chilled glass.

2	shots	Patrón reposado tequila
½	shot	De Kuyper Triple Sec
½	shot	Blue curaçao liqueur
1	shot	Freshly squeezed lime juice

Origin: Discovered in 2005 at Velvet Margarita Cantina, Los Angeles, USA.
Comment: May look lurid but is a surprisingly tasty Margarita.

BLUEBERRY COCKTAIL #1

★★★⯪☆

Glass: Martini
Garnish: Lemon zest twist (discarded) & blueberries
Method: MUDDLE blueberries in base of shaker. Add other ingredients, SHAKE with ice and fine strain into chilled glass.

20	fresh	Blueberries
2	shots	Ketel One Vodka
¼	shot	Lejay Crème de Myrtille liqueur
⅛	shot	Sugar syrup (2 sugar to 1 water)

Comment: Rich blueberry fruit fortified with grainy vodka. Not too sweet.

BLUEBERRY COCKTAIL #2

★★★★☆

Glass: Martini
Garnish: Blueberries
Method: MUDDLE blueberries in base of shaker. Add other ingredients, SHAKE with ice and fine strain into chilled glass.

24	fresh	Blueberries
2	shots	Ketel One Vodka
¼	shot	Sugar syrup (2 sugar to 1 water)
¾	shot	Sauvignon blanc white wine

Comment: Rich blueberry fruit fortified with vodka made more interesting by a splash of wine.

BLUEBERRY DAIQUIRI

★★★★☆

Glass: Martini
Garnish: Blueberries
Method: MUDDLE blueberries in base of shaker. Add other ingredients, SHAKE with ice and fine strain into chilled glass.

20	fresh	Blueberries
2	shots	Bacardi Carta Blanca light rum
½	shot	Lejay Crème de Myrtille liqueur
¼	shot	Freshly squeezed lime juice

Origin: Created in 2002 by yours truly, London, England.
Comment: Blueberry juice and liqueur lengthens and sweetens an otherwise classic Daiquiri.

BLUEBERRY TEA

★★★★☆

Glass: Toddy
Garnish: Lemon wedge & cinnamon stick
Method: POUR first two ingredients into glass, top up with tea and stir.

¾	shot	Disaronno Originale amaretto
¾	shot	Grand Marnier Cordon Rouge
Top with		Hot English breakfast tea

Comment: This does indeed taste just as described on the tin.

BLUSHIN' RUSSIAN

★★★★☆

Glass: Martini
Garnish: Float 3 coffee beans
Method: SHAKE all ingredients with ice and fine strain into chilled glass.

1	shot	Ketel One Vodka
½	shot	Disaronno Originale amaretto
1	shot	Coffee liqueur
1	shot	Single cream / half-and-half

Comment: A White Russian with a hint of almond.

BOBBY BURNS COCKTAIL (CRADDOCK'S RECIPE)

★★★★⯪

Glass: Coupe
Garnish: Lemon zest twist & side of shortbread
Method: STIR all ingredients with ice and strain into chilled glass.

2 shots Dewar's 12yo Scotch whisky
1 shot Martini Rosso vermouth
¼ shot Bénédictine D.O.M. liqueur

Origin: Recipe adapted from Harry Craddock's 1930, The Savoy Cocktail Book which calls for equal parts vermouth and Scotch with three dashes of Bénédictine. Craddock writes of this drink, "One of the very best Whisky Cocktails. A very fast mover on Saint Andrew's Day."

This drink is named after and commemorates Robert Burns (1759-1796): poet, balladeer and Scotland's favourite son. On the 25th January Scots honour the great man's presumed birthday on what has become known as Burns Night with poem readings, the ritualistic serving of haggis and a few drams.
Comment: Rich and slightly sweet, laced with spice liqueur and a good dram. The ritualistic serving of haggis and a dram or two.

BOBBY BURNS COCKTAIL (CROCKETT'S RECIPE)

★★★★⯪

Glass: Old-fashioned
Garnish: Luxardo Maraschino cherry
Method: POUR absinthe into ice-filled glass. **TOP** with water and leave to stand. Separately **STIR** Scotch, vermouth and bitters with ice. **DISCARD** contents of glass (absinthe, water and ice) and fill with fresh ice. **STRAIN** contents of mixing glass into ice-filled absinthe-coated glass.

2	shots	Dewar's 12yo Scotch whisky
1	shot	Martini Rosso vermouth
1	dash	Angostura Orange Bitters
½	shot	Le Fée Parisienne absinthe

Origin: Recipe adapted from Albert Stevens Crockett's 1931 'The Old Waldorf-Astoria Bar Book' where the drink is listed as "Robert Burns" accompanied by the following notation, "It may have been named after the celebrated Scotsman. Chances are, however, that it was christened in honour of a cigar salesman, who 'bought' in the Old Bar [at the Waldorf-Astoria]."

Cocktail historian, Gary 'gaz' Regan discovered that in the 1923 edition of 'Valentine's Manual of Old New York', a book edited by Henry Collins Brown, there is a picture with the following description:

"The island plot at corner of 42nd Street, and Broadway in 1880, now occupied by the 'Times' building, after the demolition of the Pabst restaurant and brownstone houses."

The scene includes billboards advertising Bergen Beach, the Castle Square Opera Company, and the Lyceum Theatre, which was playing The Moth and the Flame at the time but as gaz points out, "Most interesting, though, is the shop that stands in the foreground of the picture. The words on the awning proclaim, Robert Burns Cigars."

As gaz explained in his Drinks Bulletin, "Albert Stevens Crockett might well have been correct when he said that the drink could have been named for a cigar salesman, but 'Robert Burns' was the name of a brand of cigar, and although it's very possible that the guy who owned this shop went by the same name, it's more likely that The Robert Burns cocktail that was created at the old Waldorf was named for the shop, as a nod to the owner. The old Waldorf Astoria [which stood on the site of today's Empire State Building] didn't open until 1893, some 13 years after the aforementioned picture was taken, but it's not a big stretch to think that the cigar vendor was still in business when the hotel opened, and the Robert Burns brand of cigars was still on the market in the 1960s, or maybe later."

Thanks gaz.
Comment: Scotch and vermouth with added interest courtesy of absinthe and orange bitters.

BOBBY BURNS COCKTAIL (EMBURY'S RECIPE)

★★★★⯪

Glass: Coupe
Garnish: Lemon zest twist
Method: STIR all ingredients with ice and strain into chilled cocktail glass

2	shots	Dewar's 12yo Scotch whisky
1	shot	Martini Rosso vermouth
¼	shot	Drambuie liqueur
2	dash	Peychaud's aromatic bitters

Origin: Recipe adapted from David A. Embury's 1953 'Fine Art of Mixing Drinks', in which he writes of this drink, "Peychaud, somehow seems to blend better than Angostura with the Scotch. Benedictine is sometimes used in place of Drambuie. However, the Drambuie is preferable because it is made with a Scotch whisky base."
Comment: This version of the Bobby Burns is rarely seen, it is worthy of a trial.

BOBBY DE NIRO

★★★⯪☆

Glass: Martini
Garnish: Apricot slice
Method: STIR jam with gin until jam is dissolved. Add other ingredients, **SHAKE** with ice and fine strain into chilled glass.

1	spoon	Apricot jam (preserve)
2	shots	Rutte Dry Gin
¼	shot	De Kuyper XO Apricot Brandy
½	shot	Freshly squeezed lemon juice
1	dash	Angostura Orange Bitters

Origin: Adapted from a drink discovered in 2008 at Westbourne House, London, England.
Comment: An apricot twist on the Casino cocktail.

BOHEMIAN ICED TEA

★★★★⯪

Glass: Old-fashioned
Garnish: Lemon zest twist
Method: STIR all ingredients with ice and strain into ice-filled glass.

1½	shots	Becherovka (Carlsbad Becher)
½	shot	Ketel One Vodka
½	shot	Old Krupnik
½	shot	Peachtree peach schnapps
2½	shots	Cold Earl Grey tea

Origin: Created by Alex Kammerling at Detroit, London, England. Originally stirred in a tea pot and served in tea cups.
Comment: A fruity and refreshing drink with surprising flavours.

BOHEMIAN MARTINI

★★★★⯪

Glass: Martini
Garnish: Caperberry
Method: STIR all ingredients with ice and strain into chilled glass.

2½	shots	Rutte Dry Gin
½	shot	Martini Extra Dry vermouth

Origin: Created at LAB Bar, London, England. Named after Cafe Boheme, the restaurant practically opposite, where the LAB crew would go for sustenance after a shift.
Comment: A gin Martini garnished with a caperberry.

BOILERMAKER

★★★★⯪

Glass: Shot
Garnish: None
Method: POUR whiskey to brim of shot glass and then manoeuvre shot glass so it is held tight up against the inside base of an upturned Boston glass. Then quickly flip the Boston glass over so that the bourbon is trapped in the now upside-down shot glass. Now pour beer into Boston glass over the whiskey filled shot glass.

1	shot	Bourbon whiskey
1	pint	Budweiser Budvar

Origin: Unknown but in his book 'The Joy of Mixology' Gary Regan credits steelworkers in western Pennsylvania.
Comment: When you get to the end of the beer the shot glass lifts and the whiskey is released as a chaser.

BOLERO

★★★★☆☆

Glass: Martini
Garnish: Apple slice
Method: STIR all ingredients with ice and strain into chilled glass.

1½ shots	Bacardi Carta Blanca light rum
¾ shot	Calvados brandy
¼ shot	Martini Rosso vermouth

Origin: A classic of unknown origins.
Comment: A dry, challenging drink for modern palates. Be sure to stir well as dilution is key.

BOLERO SOUR 🗝

★★★★☆

Glass: Old-fashioned
Garnish: Orange & lime zest twists (discarded)
Method: SHAKE all ingredients with ice and fine strain into an ice-filled glass.

1	shot	Bacardi Carta Blanca light rum
1	shot	Martell VSOP Médaillon cognac
½	shot	Freshly squeezed orange juice
1	shot	Freshly squeezed lime juice
½	shot	Sugar syrup (2 sugar to 1 water)
½	fresh	Egg white

Origin: Adapted from David A. Embury's 1948 'The Fine Art of Mixing Drinks'.
Comment: A beautifully balanced, flavoursome medley of sweet and sour.

BOLSHOI PUNCH

★★★★☆

Glass: Old-fashioned
Garnish: None
Method: SHAKE all ingredients with ice and strain into glass filled with crushed ice.

1½ shots	White overproof rum
1	shot	Lejay crème de cassis de Dijon
¾	shot	Freshly squeezed lime juice
½	shot	Sugar syrup (2 sugar to 1 water)

Comment: An innocuous-seeming pink classic - richly flavoured and easy to drink.

THE BOMB (NEW)

★★★★☆

Glass: Coupe
Garnish: Orange zest twist
Method: SHAKE all ingredients with ice and fine strain into chilled glass.

1½ shots	Romate Amontillado sherry
½	shot	De Kuyper Triple Sec
¾	shot	Freshly squeezed orange juice
⅛	shot	Allspice pimento dram liqueur
1	dash	Angostura Orange Bitters

Origin: Adapted from a recipe in Stan Jones' 1977 'Jones Complete Bar Guide'.
Comment: A sherry-led aperitif cocktail. Don't be put off by its murky appearance.

BOMBAY LASSI COCKTAIL

★★★★☆

Glass: Martini
Garnish: Mint sprig
Method: MUDDLE cardamom in base of shaker. Add other ingredients, **SHAKE** with ice and fine strain into chilled glass.

1	whole	Cardamom pod
1½ shots	Ketel One Vodka (infused with vanilla)
1½ shots	Yoghurt liqueur
½	shot	King's Ginger Liqueur
¼	shot	Freshly squeezed lemon juice

Origin: Created in 2011 by yours truly at the Cabinet Room, London, England.
Comment: Creamy vanilla yet balanced rather than sweet with hints of cardamom, ginger and lemon.

BOMBAY NO. 2

★★★★☆

Glass: Coupe
Garnish: Orange zest twist
Method: STIR all ingredients with ice and fine strain into chilled glass.

1½ shots	Martell VSOP Médaillon cognac
¼	shot	De Kuyper Triple Sec
¾	shot	Martini Extra Dry vermouth
¾	shot	Martini Rosso vermouth
⅛	shot	Le Fée Parisienne absinthe

Origin: Adaptation from Harry Craddock's 1930 'The Savoy Cocktail Book'.
Comment: A smooth, complex, Sazerac-style Martini.

BOMBER

★★★★☆

Glass: Collins
Garnish: Lime wedge
Method: SHAKE first three ingredients with ice and strain into ice-filled glass. **TOP** with ginger beer, stir and serve with straws.

1	shot	Bacardi Carta Blanca light rum
1	shot	Bacardi OakHeart Spiced Rum
1	shot	Freshly squeezed lime juice
Top with	Gosling's Stormy Ginger Beer

Origin: Created in 1998 by the B. Bar crew at The Reading Festival, England
Comment: Cross between a Moscow Mule and a Cuba Libre.

BON BON

★★★★☆

Glass: Martini
Garnish: Lemon zest twist
Method: SHAKE all ingredients with ice and fine strain into chilled glass.

1	shot	Vanilla infused Ketel One vodka
½	shot	Butterscotch liqueur
¾	shot	Pallini Limoncello
¾	shot	Freshly squeezed lemon juice
¼	shot	Sugar syrup (2 sugar to 1 water)
½	shot	Chilled water (omit if wet ice)

Origin: Adapted from a drink discovered in 2001 at LAB Bar, London, England.
Comment: Relive your youth and the taste of those big round sweets in this bitter-sweet, lemony cocktail.

BONAPARTE COCKTAIL (NEW)

★★★★½

Glass: Collins
Garnish: Orange slice
Method: POUR chilled soda water into ice-filled glass. Add freshly brewed hot espresso coffee so it layers on the sparkling water. Lastly pour the Mandarine Napoleon liqueur (the tasty part of the Bonaparte) which will sink through the coffee layer, pulling the drink together while leaving the coffee's crema on the surface.

3	shots	Soda (club soda)
1	shot	Espresso coffee (freshly made & hot)
1½	shots	Mandarine Napoléon liqueur

Origin: Created 20th February 2014 by yours truly at the Cabinet Room, London, England.
Comment: Zesty mandarin orange and espresso coffee served as a tall refreshing cocktail.

BONNIE PRINCE CHARLES

★★★★☆

Glass: Martini
Garnish: Lime wedge
Method: SHAKE all ingredients with ice and fine strain into chilled glass.

2¼	shots	Martell VSOP Médaillon cognac
¾	shot	Drambuie liqueur
¾	shot	Freshly squeezed lime juice

Origin: Recipe to proportions found in Victor Bergeron's 'Trader Vic's Bartender's Guide' (1972 revised edition)
Comment: Honeyed, spiced cognac with a touch of citrus. But is it fit for a Prince?

BONSONI

★★★½☆

Glass: Martini
Garnish: Orange zest twist
Method: STIR all ingredients with ice and strain into chilled glass.

2	shots	Martini Rosso vermouth
½	shot	Fernet Branca
¾	shot	Chilled water (omit if wet ice)

Origin: Vintage cocktail of unknown origin.
Comment: Vermouth tames Fernet but will still only appeal to those with suitably old-school palates.

BOOMERANG

★★★½☆

Glass: Martini
Garnish: Luxardo Maraschino cherry
Method: SHAKE all ingredients with ice and fine strain into chilled glass.

1½	shots	Bourbon whiskey
¼	shot	Luxardo Maraschino liqueur
¾	shot	Martini Extra Dry vermouth
¾	shot	Martini Rosso vermouth
½	shot	Freshly squeezed lemon juice
½	shot	Sugar syrup (2 sugar to 1 water)
2	dash	Angostura Aromatic Bitters

Comment: A very Sweet Manhattan with lemon juice.

BOOZY SUZIE (NEW)

★★★★½

Glass: Coupe
Garnish: Pink grapefruit zest twist (discarded) & 3 spots of Peychaud's bitters drawn through foamy head
Method: SHAKE all ingredients with ice and strain back into shaker. **DRY SHAKE** (without ice) and fine strain into chilled glass.

1½	shots	Ketel One Vodka
½	shot	Suze Saveur d'Autrefois
½	shot	Martini Bianco
⅓	shot	Sugar syrup (2 sugar to 1 water)
¼	shot	Freshly squeezed pink grapefruit juice
2	dash	Peychaud's aromatic bitters
¼	fresh	Egg white

Origin: Created in August 2015 by yours truly at the Cabinet Room, London, England.
Comment: Bittersweet gentian is the prevalent flavour (hence the 'Suzie' name), toned down by bianco vermouth and freshened with pink grapefruit over a fortifying grainy vodka base. Peychaud's subtly adds it's distinctive flavour.

BORA BORA BREW (MOCKTAIL)

★★½☆☆

Glass: Collins
Garnish: Pineapple wedge
Method: SHAKE all ingredients with ice and strain into ice-filled glass.

3	shots	Fresh pressed pineapple juice
⅛	shot	Pomegranate / grenadine syrup (2:1)
Top with		Ginger ale

Comment: Fruity and frothy ginger beer.

BORDER HOP (NEW)

★★★½☆

Glass: Toddy
Garnish: Dried apple slice
Method: POUR all ingredients into warmed glass and stir.

2	shots	Dewar's 12yo Scotch whisky
1	shot	Pressed apple juice
¼	shot	Maple syrup
5	shots	Boiling water

Comment: Scotch whisky and apple juice, lightly sweetened with maple syrup and charged with boiling water.

BORDERLINE

★★★½☆

Glass: Martini
Garnish: Orange zest twist
Method: SHAKE all ingredients with ice and fine strain into chilled glass.

2	shots	Bourbon whiskey
½	shot	Freshly squeezed lemon juice
½	shot	Maple syrup
¾	shot	Carpano Punt E Mes

Origin: Created in 2004 by James Mellor at Mint Leaf, London, England.
Comment: Bourbon sweetened with maple syrup, soured by lemon and made more complex by vermouth.

BOSOM CARESSER

★★★★☆

Glass: Martini
Garnish: Orange zest twist (discarded)
Method: **SHAKE** all ingredients with ice and fine strain into chilled glass.

2 shots Martell VSOP Médaillon cognac
½ shot Grand Marnier Cordon Rouge
½ shot Verdelho madeira (medium dry)
¼ shot Pomegranate / grenadine syrup (2:1)
1 fresh Egg yolk

Comment: No bosoms to hand, then caress your throat.

BOSSA NOVA #1

★★★★☆

Glass: Collins
Garnish: Lime slice
Method: **SHAKE** all ingredients with ice and strain into ice-filled glass.

2 shots Bacardi Carta Blanca light rum
¾ shot De Kuyper XO Apricot Brandy
¾ shot Galliano L'Autentico liqueur
2 shots Pressed apple juice
¾ shot Freshly squeezed lime juice

Origin: Named after the Brazilian dance which in turn comes from the Portuguese 'bossa', meaning 'tendency', and 'nova', meaning 'new'.
Comment: Apple with the added zing of rum, Galliano, apricot and lime juice.

BOSSA NOVA #2

★★★½☆

Glass: Collins
Garnish: None
Method: **SHAKE** all ingredients with ice and strain into ice-filled glass.

2 shots Bacardi Carta Blanca light rum
½ shot De Kuyper XO Apricot Brandy
½ shot Galliano L'Autentico liqueur
2 shots Fresh pressed pineapple juice
½ shot Freshly squeezed lemon juice

Comment: Long and frothy with fruity rum and subtle anis notes. Not too sweet.

BOSTON

★★★½☆

Glass: Martini
Garnish: Apricot slice
Method: **SHAKE** all ingredients with ice and fine strain into chilled glass.

1¾ shots Rutte Dry Gin
1 shot De Kuyper XO Apricot Brandy
1 shot Freshly squeezed lemon juice
¼ shot Sugar syrup (2 sugar to 1 water)
⅛ shot Pomegranate / grenadine syrup (2:1)

Comment: Gin laced tangy fruit.

BOSTON DELUXE

★★★★☆

Glass: Coupe
Garnish: Saffron fronds
Method: **DRY SHAKE** all ingredients (without ice). **SHAKE** with ice and fine strain into chilled glass.

1½ shots Bourbon whiskey
¾ shot Freshly squeezed lemon juice
¾ shot Freshly squeezed orange juice
½ shot Saffron syrup (2:1 sugar syrup heated with saffron fronds)
2 dash Angostura Orange Bitters
½ fresh Egg white

Origin: Created in 2012 by Nicolas Kröger at the Rivoli Bar, Ritz Hotel, London, England.
Comment: A spiced, citrusy take on a bourbon sour.

BOSTON FLIP

★★★★☆

Glass: Goblet
Garnish: Dust with grated nutmeg
Method: **SHAKE** all ingredients with ice and fine strain into chilled glass.

2 shots Bourbon whiskey
2 shots Verdelho madeira (medium dry)
¼ shot Sugar syrup (2 sugar to 1 water)
1 fresh Eggs (white & yolk)

Comment: A good dusting of freshly grated nutmeg makes this old school drink.

BOSTON TEA PARTY

★★★☆☆

Glass: Collins
Garnish: Orange slice
Method: **SHAKE** first ten ingredients with ice and strain into ice-filled glass. **TOP** with cola.

½ shot Ketel One Vodka
½ shot Dewar's 12yo Scotch whisky
½ shot De Kuyper Triple Sec
½ shot Pusser's Navy Rum (54.5%)
½ shot Rutte Dry Gin
½ shot Patrón reposado tequila
½ shot Martini Extra Dry vermouth
½ shot Freshly squeezed orange juice
1 shot Freshly squeezed lime juice
½ shot Sugar syrup (2 sugar to 1 water)
Top with Coca-Cola

Origin: Named after the revolt by early US settlers against the imposition of tax by the British Crown, which became the War of Independence.
Comment: Almost every speedrail spirit plus a splash of orange, lime and coke.

BOULEVARD

★★★★☆

Glass: Martini
Garnish: Orange zest twist (discarded) & Luxardo Maraschino cherry
Method: **STIR** all ingredients with ice and strain into chilled glass.

2½ shots Bourbon whiskey
½ shot Grand Marnier Cordon Rouge
1 shot Martini Extra Dry vermouth
2 dash Angostura Orange Bitters

Origin: A classic of unknown origins.
Comment: A Manhattan-style cocktail which takes no prisoners.

BOULEVARDIER COCKTAIL

★★★★½

Glass: Old-fashioned
Garnish: Lemon or orange zest twist
Method: STIR all ingredients with
ice and strain into ice-filled glass.

1½ shots Bourbon whiskey
1 shot Martini Rosso
vermouth
1 shot Campari Bitter

Origin: The Boulevardier was
made for Erskine Gwynne by
Harry McElhone at his Harry's
New York Bar in Paris and the
drink appears in his 1927 book,
Barflies and Cocktails.

Like Harry, Erskine Gwynne was
an American expatriate, but he
was also a socialite, nephew of
railroad tycoon Alfred
Vanderbilt and most
importantly for this story, edited
a monthly magazine called The
Boulevardier, hence the drink's
name.
Comment: Basically a Negroni
with bourbon replacing gin. A
combo which Negroni lovers
should try.

BOUQUET

★★★½☆

Glass: Martini
Garnish: Lemon zest twist
Method: SHAKE all ingredients with ice and fine
strain into chilled glass.

1	spoon	Runny honey
2	shots	Rutte Dry Gin
½	shot	Freshly squeezed lemon juice
¼	shot	Rose syrup
½	shot	Chilled water

Origin: Adapted from a drink created in 2005 by Alex
Pacumbo at Cocoon, London, England.
Comment: Rose delicately flavours gin with a sweet
and sour balance provided by honey and lemon.

BOURBON BLUSH

★★★★½

Glass: Martini
Garnish: Strawberry on rim
Method: MUDDLE strawberries in base of shaker.
Add other ingredients, **SHAKE** with ice and fine strain
into chilled glass.

3	fresh	Small ripe strawberries (hulled)
2	shots	Bourbon whiskey
¾	shot	Lejay Crème de Framboise liqueur
¼	shot	Maple syrup

Origin: Created in 2003 by Simon King at MJU at
Millennium Hotel, London, England.
Comment: Fresh strawberry, raspberry liqueur and
maple syrup combine brilliantly with bourbon in this
cocktail.

BOURBON COOKIE

★★★★☆

Glass: Old-fashioned
Garnish: Dust with cinnamon powder
Method: SHAKE all ingredients with ice and strain
into ice-filled glass.

2	shots	Bourbon whiskey
½	shot	Single cream / half-and-half
½	shot	Milk
½	shot	Passion fruit syrup
½	shot	Butterscotch liqueur

Origin: Created in 2002 by Andres Masso, London,
England.
Comment: Looks tame but packs a flavoursome
punch.

BOURBON CRUSTA

★★★★½

Glass: Flute
Garnish: Find a lemon which fits into a
small wineglass tightly enough to act as a
watertight extension to the glass. Cut off
both ends of the fruit and carefully remove
the pulp to leave a barrel-shaped shell of
skin. Place in the top of the glass. Wet the
edge of the glass and exposed fruit shell
with sugar syrup and dip in caster sugar to
frost the edge of both peel and glass. Leave
for a couple of hours to form a hard crust.
Method: SHAKE all ingredients with ice
and fine strain into pre-prepared glass.

2 shots Bourbon whiskey
¼ shot De Kuyper Triple Sec
⅛ shot Luxardo Maraschino liqueur
½ shot Freshly squeezed lemon juice
¼ shot Sugar syrup (2 sugar to 1 water)
2 dash Angostura Orange Bitters
½ shot Chilled water (omit if wet ice)

Comment: Beautifully balanced bourbon
and fresh lemon.

BOURBON MILK PUNCH

★★★★½

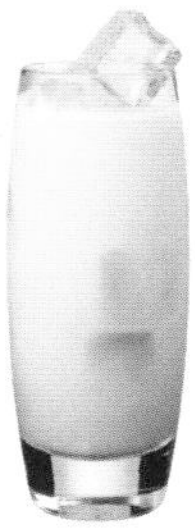

Glass: Collins
Garnish: Dust with grated nutmeg
Method: SHAKE all ingredients with ice and strain
into ice-filled glass.

1½	shots	Bourbon whiskey
¼	shot	Sugar syrup (2 sugar to 1 water)
4	shots	Milk
⅛	shot	Vanilla extract

Origin: This classic was popular during America's
Prohibition era and is still widely served in New Orleans
where it is commonly consumed with Sunday brunch.
Comment: Truly the milk of the Gods! Delicate
bourbon with a touch of vanilla. Balanced rather than
sweet and milky rather than creamy.

BOURBON RENEWAL

★★★½☆

Glass: Old-fashioned
Garnish: Seasonal berries
Method: **SHAKE** all ingredients with ice and strain into ice-filled glass.

2	shots	Bourbon whiskey
1	shot	Freshly squeezed lemon juice
½	shot	Lejay crème de cassis de Dijon
¼	shot	Sugar syrup (2 sugar to 1 water)
1	dash	Angostura Aromatic Bitters

Origin: Created in 2008 by Jeffrey Morgenthaler at Bel Ami Lounge, Oregon, USA.
Comment: Fruit supplements rather than dominates Bourbon in this easy long drink.

BOURBON SKIN ⚷

★★★★☆

Glass: Toddy
Garnish: Large orange zest twist
Method: Place barspoon in warmed glass. **POUR** all ingredients into warmed glass and **STIR**.

2	shots	Bourbon whiskey
3	shots	Boiling water
¼	shot	Sugar syrup (2 sugar to 1 water)

Origin: The only difference between a 'skin' and a 'toddy' is the addition of citrus peel to a skin.
Comment: Hot, watered down bourbon stirred with orange oils. Simple but very tasty.

BOURBON SMASH ⚷

★★★½☆

Glass: Collins
Garnish: Lime slice
Method: **MUDDLE** raspberries in base of shaker. Add other ingredients, **SHAKE** with ice and fine strain into ice-filled glass.

12	fresh	Raspberries
4	fresh	Mint leaves
2½	shots	Bourbon whiskey
3	shots	Cranberry juice
1	shot	Freshly squeezed lime juice
½	shot	Sugar syrup (2 sugar to 1 water)
2	dash	Angostura Aromatic Bitters

Comment: This refreshing long drink has a sharp edge that adds to its appeal.

BOURBONELLA

★★★★☆

Glass: Martini
Garnish: Luxardo Maraschino cherry
Method: **STIR** all ingredients with ice and fine strain into chilled glass.

1¾	shots	Bourbon whiskey
¾	shot	De Kuyper Triple Sec
¾	shot	Martini Extra Dry vermouth
¼	shot	Pomegranate / grenadine syrup (2:1)
3	dash	Peychaud's aromatic bitters

Comment: If you like bourbon, you'll love this fruity Manhattan.

BOXCAR ⚷

★★★½☆

Glass: Martini
Garnish: Sugar rim
Method: **SHAKE** all ingredients with ice and fine strain into chilled glass.

2	shots	Rutte Dry Gin
½	shot	De Kuyper Triple Sec
¾	shot	Freshly squeezed lime juice
⅛	shot	Pomegranate / grenadine syrup (2:1)
½	fresh	Egg white

Comment: A White Lady in a sugar-rimmed glass with the addition of a dash of grenadine and substituting lemon juice for lime.

BRADFORD

★★★★☆

Glass: Martini
Garnish: Chilled olive on stick or lemon zest twist
Method: **SHAKE** all ingredients with ice and fine strain into chilled glass.

2½	shots	Rutte Dry Gin
½	shot	Martini Extra Dry vermouth
3	dash	Angostura Orange Bitters (optional)

Origin: A Bradford is a Martini which is shaken rather than stirred. Like the Martini itself, the origin of the Bradford is lost in time. However, In Harry Johnson's 1900 edition of his *Bartender's Manual* he includes two Martini recipes – one simply titled "Martini Cocktail" and the other "Bradford à la Martini" – crucially the Martini is stirred while the Bradford is shaken.
Comment: More approachable than a stirred Dry Martini and downright soft compared to a Naked Martini.

BRAINSTORM

★★★★½

Glass: Coupe
Garnish: Orange zest twist
Method: **STIR** all ingredients with ice and strain into chilled glass.

2	shot	Teeling Small Batch Irish whiskey
½	shot	Bénédictine D.O.M.
½	shot	Martini Extra Dry vermouth

Comment: Dry vermouth balances the sweet notes of Bénédictine over a boozy Irish whisky base.
Origin: This classic from the 1920s first appears in Harry Craddock's 1930 *The Savoy Cocktail Book*.

BRAMBLE

★★★★☆

Glass: Old-fashioned
Garnish: Blackberries & lemon slice
Method: **SHAKE** first three ingredients with ice and strain into glass filled with crushed ice. **DRIZZLE** liqueur over drink to create a 'bleeding' effect in the glass. Serve with short straws.

2	shots	Rutte Dry Gin
1	shot	Freshly squeezed lemon juice
½	shot	Sugar syrup (2 sugar to 1 water)
½	shot	Lejay Crème de Mûre liqueur

Origin: Created in the mid-80s by Dick Bradsell at Fred's Club, Soho, London, England.
Comment: One of the best and most popular drinks created in the 1980s.

BRAMBLETTE

★★★★½☆

Glass: Martini
Garnish: Orange zest twist
Method: SHAKE all ingredients with ice and fine strain into chilled glass.

2	shots	Rutte Dry Gin
1	shot	Benoit Serres créme de violette
¾	shot	Freshly squeezed lemon juice
¼	shot	Sugar syrup (2 sugar to 1 water)

Comment: A martini style drink with a floral, gin-laced palate.

BRANDY ALEXANDER

★★★★★½

Glass: Coupe
Garnish: Dust with freshly grated nutmeg
Method: SHAKE all ingredients with ice and strain back into shaker. **DRY SHAKE** (without ice) and fine strain into chilled glass.

1½	shot	Martell VSOP Médaillon cognac
½	shot	Dark crème de cacao liqueur
½	shot	White crème de cacao liqueur
¾	shot	Single cream / half-and-half
½	fresh	Egg white (optional)

Comment: This after dinner classic is rich, creamy and subtly chocolaty.
Origin: Originally known as *Alexander #2*, the Brandy Alexander is thought to have been created sometime during the 1930s, certainly prior to 1937 when it first appears in print. This classic blend of brandy and chocolate smoothed with cream is based on the original Alexander calling for gin as its base. As to whom substituted brandy in place of gin is lost in time.

BRANDY BLAZER ⚷

★★★★½☆

Glass: Snifter
Garnish: Lemon & orange zest twists
Method: POUR cognac into a warmed glass and rest the bowl of the glass on an old-fashioned glass so it lies on its side supported by the rim. **FLAME** the cognac and carefully move the glass back to an upright position sitting normally on your work surface. **POUR** in hot water (this will extinguish any remaining flame) and sugar. Stir, garnish and serve.

2	shots	Martell VSOP Médaillon cognac
2	shots	Boiling water
¼	shot	Sugar syrup (2 sugar to 1 water)

Origin: A variation on 'Professor' Jerry Thomas' Blue Blazer which involved theatrically pouring ignited brandy between two mugs. Please don't try this at home, kids.
Comment: One way to warm your winter nights.

BRANDY BUCK

★★★★½☆

Glass: Collins
Garnish: Lemon wedge
Method: SHAKE first 3 ingredients with ice and strain into ice-filled glass. **TOP** with ginger ale and serve with straws.

2½	shots	Martell VSOP Médaillon cognac
¼	shot	Grand Marnier Cordon Rouge
¼	shot	Freshly squeezed lemon juice
Top with		Ginger ale

Comment: Lemon juice adds balance to the sweet ginger ale. Cognac provides the backbone.

BRANDY COCKTAIL

★★★★☆

Glass: Martini
Garnish: Lemon zest twist
Method: SHAKE all ingredients with ice and fine strain into chilled glass.

5 fresh Mint leaves
2 shots Martell VSOP Médaillon cognac
¼ shot Grand Marnier Cordon Rouge
¼ shot Sugar syrup (2 sugar to 1 water)
1 dash Angostura Aromatic Bitters

Origin: Vintage cocktail of unknown origin.
Comment: Subtle mint and citrus lightly flavour the cognac.

BRANDY CRUSTA

★★★★½

Glass: Flute
Garnish: Some merely shove a wide long piece of lemon peel around the inside of the glass rim, leaving the drinker to push the peel down into the glass in order to sip from the drink. Instead I prefer the peel to become a watertight extension to the glass.

Find a lemon which fits snugly in the top of a small wine, flute or sour glass. Cut off both ends of the fruit and carefully remove the pulp to leave a barrel-shaped shell of skin. Place in the top of the glass. Wet the edge of the glass and exposed fruit shell with sugar syrup and dip in caster sugar to frost the edge of both peel and glass. Leave for a couple of hours to form a hard crust that helps secure the peel.
Method: SHAKE all ingredients with ice and fine strain into pre-prepared glass.

1¾	shots	Martell VSOP Médaillon cognac
¼	shot	De Kuyper Triple Sec
¼	shot	Luxardo Maraschino liqueur
½	shot	Freshly squeezed lemon juice
¼	shot	Sugar syrup (2 sugar to 1 water)
2	dash	Angostura Aromatic Bitters
½	shot	Chilled water (omit if wet ice)

Origin: Created in the 1850s by Joseph Santini, an Italian from Trieste, in New Orleans, USA, either at the City Exchange in the French Quarter, or at his Jewel of the South saloon on Gravier Street in the American Quarter which he opened in 1855. The name refers to the crust of sugar around the rim.

Regarded by many as the forerunner to the Sidecar and, by extension, the Margarita, crusted sugar rim and all. The Brandy Crusta is a veritable member of cocktail royalty, so much so that it proudly takes its place as the fourth drink to be illustrated in the world's first cocktail book, Jerry Thomas' 1862 ' Bar-Tender's Guide' where Santini is wrongly credited as being of Spanish origins and spelt Santana.
Comment: This old classic zings with fresh lemon and is beautifully balanced by the cognac base.

BRANDY DAISY

★★★★★☆

Glass: Small wine glass
Garnish: Seasonal berries & mint sprig
Method: **STIR** first 4 ingredients with ice and strain into glass filled with crushed ice. **TOP** with a splash of soda and briefly stir.

1½	shot	Martell VSOP Médaillon cognac
⅔	shot	Yellow Chartreuse
½	shot	Freshly squeezed lemon juice
⅓	shot	Sugar syrup (2 sugar to 1 water)
1	shot	Soda water

Comment: Yellow Chartreuse notes show through strongly in this short refreshing drink, with cognac providing the base flavour and lemon juice contributing freshening citrus balance.
Origin: The Brandy Daisy appears in Jerry Thomas' 2nd edition of his *Bar-tender's Guide* (1887) and then the 2nd edition of Harry Johnson's *Bartenders Manual* (1888). Tellingly both bartenders omit the Brandy Daisy, and indeed Daisies in general from their first editions. We prefer Johnson's recipe.

BRANDY FIX

★★★★★☆

Glass: Old-fashioned
Garnish: Lemon zest twist
Method: **SHAKE** all ingredients with ice and strain into ice-filled glass.

2	shots	Martell VSOP Médaillon cognac
½	shot	Fresh pressed pineapple juice
½	shot	Freshly squeezed lemon juice
¼	shot	Sugar syrup (2 sugar to 1 water)
⅛	shot	Yellow Chartreuse liqueur

Comment: This wonderful classic is on the tart side of well balanced.

BRANDY FIZZ

★★★★☆

Glass: Collins (small 8oz)
Garnish: Lemon slice
Method: **SHAKE** first three ingredients with ice and fine strain into chilled glass (without ice). **TOP** with soda.

2	shots	Martell VSOP Médaillon cognac
½	shot	Freshly squeezed lemon juice
¼	shot	Sugar syrup (2 sugar to 1 water)
Top with		Soda from siphon

Comment: A refreshing and tasty dry drink: cognac and lemon balanced with a little sugar and lengthened with soda.

BRANDY FLIP 0━━

★★★★★☆

Glass: Martini
Garnish: Dust with grated nutmeg
Method: **SHAKE** all ingredients with ice and fine strain into chilled glass.

1½	shots	Martell VSOP Médaillon cognac
¼	shot	Sugar syrup (2 sugar to 1 water)
¼	shot	Single cream / half-and-half
1	fresh	Eggs (white & yolk)

Origin: A forgotten classic.
Comment: A serious alternative to advocaat for those without raw egg inhibitions.

BRANDY MILK PUNCH

★★★★☆

Glass: Collins
Garnish: Dust with grated nutmeg
Method: **SHAKE** all ingredients with ice and strain into ice-filled glass.

1½	shots	Martell VSOP Médaillon cognac
4	shots	Milk
¼	shot	Sugar syrup (2 sugar to 1 water)
⅛	shot	Vanilla extract

Origin: A classic which was popular during America's Prohibition era and dates back to colonial times. It is still widely served in New Orleans where it is commonly consumed with Sunday brunch.
Comment: This traditional New Orleans hangover cure beats your bog-standard vanilla milkshake.

BRANDY SMASH 0━━

★★★★☆

Glass: Old-fashioned
Garnish: Mint sprig
Method: Lightly **MUDDLE** mint in base of shaker just enough to bruise. Add other ingredients, **SHAKE** with ice and fine strain into ice-filled glass.

7	fresh	Mint leaves
2	shots	Martell VSOP Médaillon cognac
¼	shot	Sugar syrup (2 sugar to 1 water)

Origin: A classic from the 1850s.
Comment: Sweetened cognac flavoured with mint. Simple but beautiful.

BRANDY SOUR 0━━

★★★★★☆

Glass: Old-fashioned
Garnish: Lemon slice & cherry on stick (sail)
Method: **SHAKE** all ingredients with ice and strain into ice-filled glass.

2	shots	Martell VSOP Médaillon cognac
1	shot	Freshly squeezed lemon juice
½	shot	Sugar syrup (2 sugar to 1 water)
3	dash	Angostura Aromatic Bitters
½	fresh	Egg white

Comment: After the Whisky Sour, this is the most requested sour. Try it and you'll see why - but don't omit the egg white.

BRASS MONKEY 0━━

★★★★☆

Glass: Collins
Garnish: Lemon slice
Method: **SHAKE** all ingredients with ice and strain into ice-filled glass.

1	shot	Bacardi Carta Blanca light rum
1	shot	Ketel One Vodka
2½	shots	Freshly squeezed lemon juice
1	shot	Sugar syrup (2 sugar to 1 water)

Comment: Tangy, alcoholic, almost sherbet-like lemonade.

BRASS RAIL

★★★★⯨

Glass: Martini
Garnish: Physalis (cape gooseberry)
Method: SHAKE all ingredients with ice and fine strain into chilled glass.

2	shots	Bacardi Carta Blanca light rum
½	shot	Bénédictine D.O.M. liqueur
½	shot	Freshly squeezed lemon juice
2	shots	Sugar syrup (2 sugar to 1 water)
½	fresh	Egg white
1	dash	Angostura Orange Bitters
½	shot	Chilled water (omit if wet ice)

Origin: Adapted from a recipe by Tony Abou-Ganim. He was inspired by his late cousin Helen David's penchant for a nightcap after a special occasion; her favourite was Bénédictine. This drink is named after Helen's bar the Brass Rail in Port Huron. Helen's memory is commemorated in the 'Helen David Spirit Award' which is given for lifetime achievement at the annual Tales of the Cocktail.
Comment: Rather like a Daiquiri, yet subtly sweetened and spiced.

BRAZEN MARTINI

★★★★☆

Glass: Martini
Garnish: Orange zest twist
Method: STIR all ingredients with ice and strain into chilled glass.

2½	shots	Zubrówka bison vodka
¼	shot	Parfait Amour liqueur

Comment: Not for the faint hearted - a great combination of grassy bison vodka with violet Parfait Amour.

BRAZIL 66 COCKTAIL (NEW)

★★★★⯨

Glass: Old-fashioned
Garnish: Lime wedge
Method: SHAKE all ingredients with ice and strain into ice-filled glass.

1½	shots	Capucana cachaça
½	shot	De Kuyper Triple Sec
½	shot	Freshly squeezed orange juice
¼	shot	Sugar syrup (2 sugar to 1 water)
½	shot	Freshly squeezed lime juice
½	shot	Chilled water (omit if wet ice)

Origin: Adapted from a drink created at Absinthe, San Francisco, USA

Back in 1966 Brazil had much to be bitter about. The country's team had done well in the two previous World Cups and in their first match in the 1966 Cup against Bulgaria, Pele, already the world's most famous footballer, became the first player to score in three World Cups with a goal from a free kick. The Bulgarians spent the rest of the match fouling Pele resulting in him being unable to play in Brazil's next game against Hungary. Without their star player Brazil lost, meaning they needed a win in their next and final group game against Portugal. The Portuguese players followed the bad example set by the Bulgarians and repeatedly fouled Pele resulting in him hobbling through much of the game. The Bulgarians won and Brazil were eliminated from the World cup at the group stage.
Comment: Reminiscent of an orange influenced Caipirinha.

BRAZILIAN BERRY

★★★★☆

Glass: Old-fashioned
Garnish: Mint sprig
Method: MUDDLE fruit in base of shaker. Add other ingredients, SHAKE with ice and fine strain into glass filled with crushed ice. Serve with straws.

4	fresh	Blackcurrants
3	fresh	Raspberries
1½	shots	Sauvignon blanc white wine
1	shot	Capucana cachaça
1	shot	Lejay crème de cassis de Dijon

Origin: Created in 2002 by Dan Spink at Browns, St Martin's Lane, London, England.
Comment: This drink combines wine, cachaça and rich berry fruits.

BRAZILIAN COFFEE

★★★⯨☆

Glass: Toddy
Garnish: Coffee beans
Method: BLEND ingredients with 6oz scoop of crushed ice. Pour into glass and serve with straws.

1	shot	Capucana cachaça
1	shot	Single cream / half-and-half
2	shots	Espresso coffee (freshly made & hot)
¾	shot	Sugar syrup (2 sugar to 1 water)

Comment: Strong coffee and plenty of sugar are essential in this Brazilian number.

BRAZILIAN COSMOPOLITAN

★★★⯨☆

Glass: Martini
Garnish: Orange zest twist
Method: SHAKE all ingredients with ice and fine strain into chilled glass.

1	shot	Capucana cachaça
1	shot	De Kuyper Triple Sec
1½	shots	Cranberry juice
½	shot	Freshly squeezed lime juice

Comment: The distinctive character of cachaça bursts through the fruit in this twist on the contemporary classic.

BRAZILIAN MONK

★★★⯨☆

Glass: Hurricane
Garnish: Crumbled Cadbury's Flake bar
Method: BLEND ingredients with 12oz scoop of crushed ice. Pour into glass and serve with straws.

1	shot	Hazelnut liqueur
1	shot	Coffee liqueur
1	shot	Dark crème de cacao liqueur
3	scoop	Vanilla ice cream

Comment: Nutty and rich dessert in a glass.

BRAZILIAN NAIL

★★★★☆

Glass: Old-fashioned
Garnish: Lime zest twist
Method: **STIR** all ingredients with ice and strain into ice-filled glass.

1½ shots   Capucana cachaça
½ shot   Dewar's 12yo Scotch whisky
¾ shot   Drambuie liqueur

Origin: Created in 2010 by Jamie Stephenson, Manchester, England.
Comment: A rift on the classic Rusty Nail using cachaça as the main base spirit with a hint of Scotch maintaining its lineage to the Drambuie Nail family.

BREAKFAST AT TERRELL'S

★★★★☆

Glass: Flute
Garnish: Kumquat
Method: **SHAKE** first four ingredients with ice and strain into chilled glass. **TOP** with champagne.

¾ shot   Single cream / half-and-half
¾ shot   Mandarine Napoléon liqueur
¾ shot   Freshly squeezed orange juice
⅛ shot   Sugar syrup (2 sugar to 1 water)
Top with   G.H. Mumm Cordon Rouge Champagne

Origin: Created by Jamie Terrell for the late Philip Holzberg at Vinexpo, Bordeaux, France, 1999.
Comment: This creamy orange champagne cocktail is almost as smooth as a Sgroppino.

BREAKFAST CLUB 0━┱

★★★★★

Glass: Martini
Garnish: Lemon zest twist
Method: **STIR** honey and marmalade with rum until dissolved. Add tea, **SHAKE** with ice and fine strain into chilled glass.

1 spoon   English orange marmalade
1 spoon   Runny honey
2 shots   Bacardi Carta Blanca light rum
1 shot   Cold Lapsang Souchong tea

Origin: Recipe discovered in 2008 courtesy of DrinkBoy.com.
Comment: Slightly smoky with incredible depth of flavour. A perfectly balanced delight.

BREAKFAST GIMLET 0━┱

★★★★☆

Glass: Martini
Garnish: Basil leaf
Method: **STIR** marmalade with gin in base of shaker to dissolve marmalade. Add lemon juice and lime cordial, **SHAKE** with ice and fine strain into chilled glass.

2½ shots   Rutte Dry Gin
¼ shot   Rose's lime cordial
2 spoon   English orange marmalade
¼ shot   Freshly squeezed lemon juice

Origin: Created by yours truly at the Cabinet Room, London, England.
Comment: Orange marmalade both justifies the 'breakfast' prefix and adds complexity to this gimlet.

BREAKFAST IN MANHATTAN

★★★★⯪

Glass: Coupe
Garnish: Orange zest twist
Method: **STIR** marmalade with bourbon to dissolve marmalade. Add other ingredients, **STIR** with ice and fine strain into chilled glass.

1 spoon   English orange marmalade
2 shots   Bourbon whiskey
½ shot   Martini Rosso vermouth
1 dash   Angostura Orange Bitters

Origin: Discovered in 2009 at Bentley's, Dublin, Ireland.
Comment: The British Breakfast Martini comes to Manhattan.

BREAKFAST MARTINI 0━┱

★★★★★

Glass: Martini
Garnish: Orange zest twist & slice of toast on rim
Method: **STIR** marmalade with gin in base of shaker until it dissolves. Add other ingredients, **SHAKE** with ice and fine strain into chilled glass.

1 spoon   English orange marmalade (fine sliced)
1⅔ shots   Rutte Dry Gin
½ shot   De Kuyper Triple Sec
½ shot   Freshly squeezed lemon juice

Origin: This now world famous drink was created in the late 1990s by bartender, raconteur and long term President of the United Kingdom Bartender's Guild, Salvatore Calabrese. Being of proud Italian descent, Salvatore usually has little more than a swift espresso for breakfast. However, one morning, Sue his English wife, insisted he sit down for breakfast and served up toast and marmalade. Salvatore came up with the idea for his Breakfast Martini while enjoying the tangy preserve covered toast and took the jar to work with him. Later that day, at London's Library Bar in the Lanesborough Hotel he perfected his signature cocktail.

Salvatore's Breakfast Martini has since inspired bartenders around the world to create their own cocktails using preserves such as jam and marmalade. Coincidentally, Harry Craddock's 1930 ' The Savoy Cocktail Book' includes a recipe to a ' Marmalade Cocktail', very similar to Salvatore's Breakfast Martini. However, Salvatore says that the inspiration to his drink, which is simply a White Lady with marmalade in it, was the hearty English breakfast and not the classic English bartending book.
Comment: The success or failure of this tangy drink is partly reliant on the quality of marmalade used.

BRIDGETOWN DAIQUIRI

★★★★☆

Glass: Coupe
Garnish: Grapefruit wedge

Method: **SHAKE** all ingredients with ice and fine strain into chilled glass.

2 shots   Bacardi Carta Oro rum
½ shot   Luxardo Maraschino liqueur
½ shot   Sugar syrup (2 sugar to 1 water)
½ shot   Freshly squeezed ruby grapefruit juice
½ shot   Freshly squeezed lime juice

Origin: Unknown.
Comment: Delicate and very slightly sweet with maraschino liqueur brilliantly balancing grapefruit juice.

BRIGHTON PUNCH

★★★★☆

Glass: Collins
Garnish: Pineapple wedge
Method: SHAKE all ingredients with ice and fine strain into chilled glass.

1½	shots	Bourbon whiskey
1½	shots	Bénédictine D.O.M. liqueur
1½	shots	Martell VSOP Médaillon cognac
2½	shots	Fresh pressed pineapple juice
2	shots	Freshly squeezed lemon juice

Origin: Popular in the bars of Berlin, Germany.
Comment: Don't bother trying the version with orange juice but do try halving the quantities and serving up. Served long or short this is beautifully balanced.

BRITS SPRITZ (NEW)

★★★★☆

Glass: Collins
Garnish: Squeeze grapefruit wedge into drink & add cucumber slice
Method: POUR all ingredients into ice-filled glass and stir.

2	shots	Prosecco sparkling wine
1	shot	Kamm & Sons
1	shot	St-Germain elderflower liqueur
2	shots	Soda (club soda)

Origin: Created by Alex Kammerling of Kamm & Sons, this is the brand's signature cocktail.
Comment: An elderflower Spritz with depth of flavour and British character courtesy of Kamm & Sons.

BROADMOOR COCKTAIL

★★★★½

Glass: Martini
Garnish: Orange zest twist (flamed)
Method: SHAKE all ingredients with ice and fine strain into chilled glass.

2	shots	Dewar's 12yo Scotch whisky
½	shot	Green Chartreuse liqueur
½	shot	Sugar syrup (2 sugar to 1 water)
4	dash	Angostura Orange Bitters

Origin: Created in 2001 by Swedish bartender Andreas Noren at The Player, London, England and popularised at Milk & Honey, London, England. Named after the infamous British mental institution.
Comment: Beautifully simple and seriously complex.

BROKEN SPUR

★★★☆☆

Glass: Martini
Garnish: Dust with grated nutmeg
Method: SHAKE all ingredients with ice and fine strain into chilled glass.

3	shots	Dry white port
¼	shot	Rutte Dry Gin
¼	shot	Martini Rosso vermouth
⅛	shot	Marie Brizard Anisette
1	fresh	Egg yolk

Origin: Vintage cocktail of unknown origin.
Comment: Smooth rather than creamy and only lightly alcoholic. Perhaps one after a boozy dinner?

BRONX #1 (ORIGINAL) 🔑

★★★★☆

Glass: Martini
Garnish: Orange zest twist (discarded) & Luxardo Maraschino cherry
Method: SHAKE all ingredients with ice and fine strain into chilled glass.

1½ shots Rutte Dry Gin
¾ shot Martini Extra Dry vermouth
¾ shot Martini Rosso vermouth
1 shot Freshly squeezed orange juice

Origin: Created in 1906 by Johnny Solon, a bartender at New York's Waldorf-Astoria Hotel (the Empire State Building occupies the site today), and named after the newly opened Bronx Zoo. This is reputedly the first cocktail to use fruit juice.

In his 1935, ' The Old Waldorf-Astoria' book, A.S. Crockett published what he says is
"Solon's own story of the Creation - of the Bronx: We had a cocktail in those days called the Duplex, which had a pretty fair demand. One day, I was making one for a customer when in came Traverson, head waiter of the Empire Room - the main dining room in the original Waldorf. A Duplex was composed of equal parts of French [dry] and Italian [sweet] Vermouth, shaken up with squeezed orange peel, or two dashes of Orange Bitters. Traverson said, "Why don't you get up a new cocktail? I have a customer who says you can't do it." "Can't I?" I replied. "Well", I finished the Duplex I was making, and a thought came to me. I poured into a mixing glass the equivalent of two jiggers of Gordon Gin. Then I filled the jigger with orange juice, so that it made one-third of orange and two-thirds of gin. Then into the mixture I put a dash of each Italian and French Vermouth, shaking the thing up. I didn't taste it myself, but I poured it into a cocktail glass and handed it to Traverson and said: "You are a pretty good judge. (He was.) See what you think of that." Traverson tasted it. Then he swallowed it whole.

" 'By God!' he said, you've really got something new! That will make a big hit. Make me another and I will take it back to that customer in the dining room. Bet you'll sell a lot of them. Have you got plenty of oranges? If you haven't, you had better stock up, because I'm going to sell a lot of those cocktails during lunch.

"The demand for Bronx cocktails started that day. Pretty soon we were using a whole case of oranges a day. And then several cases.

"The name? No, it wasn't really named directly after the borough or the river so-called. I had been at the Bronx Zoo a day or so before, and saw, of course, a lot of beasts I had never known. Customers used to tell me of the strange animals they saw after a lot of mixed drinks. So when Traverson said to me, as he started to take the drink in to the customer, "What'll I tell him is the name of this drink?" I thought of those animals, and said: "Oh, you can tell him it is a 'Bronx.'"
Comment: A serious, dry, complex cocktail. Less bitter than many of its era, but still challenging to more tender modern palates.

BRONZE ADONIS

★★★★☆

Glass: Martini
Garnish: Lemon zest twist
Method: STIR all ingredients with ice and strain into a chilled glass.

1½	shots	Romate Fino sherry
1½	shots	Noilly Ambre vermouth
½	shot	San León Manzanilla sherry
2	dash	Angostura Orange Bitters

Origin: Created in 2008 by Julian de Féral at The East Rooms, London, England.
Comment: A simple yet fabulous twist on the Adonis.

A B C D E F G H I J K L M N O P Q R S T U V W X Y Z

Brooklyn Cocktail

Named after the New York borough, the Brooklyn Cocktail was inspired by the already established and popular Manhattan and Bronx cocktails of its neighbouring boroughs.

The Brooklyn first appears in print in Jacob. A. Grohusko's 1908 'Jack's Manual' as follows:

"Brooklyn Cocktail, 1 dash Amer Picon Bitters, 1 dash Maraschino, 50% rye whiskey, 50% Ballor Vermouth, Fill glass with ice, Stir and strain. Serve."

Jacob 'Jack' Grohusko lived in Hoboken, New Jersey and was the head bartender at Baracca's Restaurant in Wall Street, lower Manhattan. His only tenuous link with Brooklyn was that the owner of Baracca's was a Brooklynite. No matter, he put the borough on the cocktail map and in 1914, Jacques Straub included a version of the drink using French [dry] vermouth rather than Italian [sweet] in his 'Straub's Manual of Mixed Drinks'. You'll also find the Brooklyn in Harry Cradock's 1930 'Savoy Cocktail Book' made with 2/3 Canadian Club whisky and 1/3 French vermouth alongside dashes of Amer Picon and Maraschino. In his 1933 'Official Mixer's Manual', Patrick Gavin Duffy also opts for the 2/3 rye whiskey to 1/3 French vermouth formula.

In his 2015 'Updated and Revised Imbibe', drinks historian David Wondrich comments that, "Grohusko's original, with its Italian [sweet] vermouth, is far better than the version that has come down to us, which uses French vermouth [dry], something that experts at the time felt mixed poorly with whiskey."

Sadly, Amer Picon is little distributed outside of its domestic French market and, for better or worse, its recipe was changed back in the 1940s so all we can make today is a modern interpretation of Grohusko's 1908 recipe. That original recipe may have been equal parts Italian vermouth and rye, or 50% French and Italian vermouth and rye - with dashes of Amer Picon and maraschino, both are better than any of the one-third to two-thirds versions we've tried.

BROOKLYN (GROHUSKO'S ORIGINAL) (NEW)

★★★★★

Glass: Coupe
Garnish: Luxardo maraschino cherry
Method: **STIR** all ingredients with ice and strain into chilled glass.

1½ shots Straight rye whiskey
1½ shots Martini Rosso vermouth
⅛ shot Amer Picon
⅛ shot Luxardo Maraschino liqueur
¾ shot Chilled water

Comment: Despite the generous dose of Italian 'sweet' vermouth, rye whiskey shines in this harmonious Manhattan-like dry cocktail.

BROOKLYN (PERFECT) (NEW)

★★★★★½

Glass: Coupe
Garnish: Luxardo maraschino cherry
Method: **STIR** all ingredients with ice and strain into chilled glass.

1½ shots Straight rye whiskey
½ shot Martini Extra Dry vermouth
½ shot Martini Rosso vermouth
⅓ shot Amer Picon
⅓ shot Luxardo Maraschino liqueur
¾ shot Chilled water (omit if wet ice)

Comment: A perfect Manhattan with bittersweet French amero rather than aromatic bitters and a balancing dash of sweet maraschino liqueur.

BROOKLYN (ST GEORGE VERSION)

★★★★☆

Glass: Martini
Garnish: Luxardo Maraschino cherry
Method: **STIR** all ingredients with ice and strain into chilled glass.

2 shots Bourbon whiskey
½ shot Martini Extra Dry vermouth
½ shot Martini Rosso vermouth
¼ dash Luxardo Maraschino liqueur
2 dash Angostura Aromatic Bitters

Origin: Thought to have originated at the St George Hotel, Brooklyn, New York City, USA.

In his 1948 'The Fine Art of Mixing Drinks', David Embury says of the Brooklyn, "You will note that the Brooklyn is nothing but a Dry Manhattan with a dash of maraschino. It is supposed to be a specialty of that grand old Brooklyn hotel, the St. George. I would be willing to wager, however, that even in Brooklyn there are at least five to ten times as many Manhattans consumed as there are Brooklyns. Try both and you will understand why."
Comment: Basically a 'perfect' bourbon-based Manhattan with a generous dash of maraschino liqueur. The lack of Amer Picon in this recipe as well as the use of bourbon rather than rye whiskey means it's not what's now generally recognised as being a Brooklyn.

BROOKLYN COCKTAIL

★★★★½

Glass: Coupe
Garnish: Luxardo Maraschino cherry
Method: **STIR** all ingredients with ice and strain into chilled glass.

1½ shots Straight rye whiskey
1½ shots Martini Extra Dry vermouth
⅓ shot Amer Picon
⅓ shot Luxardo Maraschino liqueur
¾ shot Chilled water (omit if wet ice)

Origin: One of the Manhattan variations named after New York's five states.
Comment: Perhaps my favourite of the many renditions of the Brooklyn cocktail due to being bone dry, yet made approachable by faint sweet maraschino notes and bittersweet Amer Picon herbal complexity.

BROOKLYN GODFATHER

★★★★½

Glass: Martini
Garnish: Luxardo Maraschino cherry
Method: **STIR** all ingredients with ice and strain into chilled glass.

2 shots Bourbon whiskey
½ shot Disaronno Originale amaretto
½ shot Martini Extra Dry vermouth
¼ shot Martini Rosso vermouth

Comment: Described by some as being a Brooklyn but perhaps more a bourbon whiskey-based Godfather with vermouth.

BROWN BOMBER COCKTAIL (NEW)

★★★★☆

Glass: Coupe
Garnish: Luxardo Maraschino cherry
Method: STIR all ingredients with ice and strain into chilled glass.

1⅔ shots	Bourbon whiskey
⅔ shot	Byrrh Grand Quinquina
½ shot	Suze Saveur d'Autrefois
¾ shot	Chilled water (omit if wet ice)

Comment: Faintly reminiscent of a Manhattan with underlying gentian bitterness and the rich berry red notes of Byrrh.

BROWN DERBY

★★★★★

Glass: Coupe
Garnish: Grapefruit zest twist

Method: SHAKE all ingredients with ice and fine strain into chilled glass.

1½ shots Bourbon whiskey
1 shot Freshly squeezed pink grapefruit juice
¼ shot Maple syrup

Origin: Named after The Brown Derby chain of restaurants in Los Angeles, California. The original restaurant opened in 1926 at 3427 Wilshire Boulevard and was iconic due to the building being shaped like a man's derby hat. The chain was started by Robert H. Cobb and Herbert Somborn (a former husband of film star Gloria Swanson).
Comment: Maple syrup combines wonderfully with bourbon and balances grapefruit sourness to make a short drink that's equally as enticing at the beginning or end of a night.

BRUBAKER OLD-FASHIONED

★★★★☆

Glass: Old-fashioned
Garnish: Lemon zest twist
Method: STIR malt extract in glass with Scotch until malt extract dissolves. Add ice and one shot of Scotch and stir. Add remaining Scotch, sugar and Angostura and stir some more. Add more ice and keep stirring so that ice dilutes the drink.

2	spoon	Malt extract
2	shots	Dewar's 12yo Scotch whisky
¼	shot	Sugar syrup (2 sugar to 1 water)
3	dash	Angostura Aromatic Bitters

Origin: Created in 2003 by Shelim Islam at the GE Club, London, England. Shelim named this drink after a horse in the sports section of a paper (also a film made in the seventies starring Robert Redford).
Comment: If you like Scotch you should try this extra malty dram. After all that stirring you'll deserve one.

BRUISED POMEGRANATE (NEW)

★★★★⯪

Glass: Coupe
Garnish: Orange zest twist (discarded) & Luxardo maraschino cherry
Method: THROW all ingredients with ice and strain into chilled glass.

1½ shots	Straight rye whiskey
1½ shots	Byrrh Grand Quinquina
⅛ shot	Pomegranate / grenadine syrup (2:1)
1 dash	Le Fée Parisienne absinthe
1 dash	Angostura Orange Bitters
4 drop	Bob's Chocolate bitters
1 pinch	Salt
¾ shot	Chilled water

Origin: Created in August 2015 by yours truly at the Cabinet Room, London, England.
Comment: This cocktail sits somewhere in the East River between a Manhattan and a Brooklyn with some Thames Estuary thrown in.

BRUNSWICK

★★★★⯪

Glass: Old-fashioned
Garnish: Orange slice & cherry on stick (sail)
Method: SHAKE first 3 ingredients with ice and fine strain into ice-filled glass. **FLOAT** claret on drink.

2	shots	Straight rye whiskey
¾	shot	Freshly squeezed lemon juice
½	shot	Sugar syrup (2 sugar to 1 water)
¾	shot	Claret red wine

Origin: Recipe adapted from the 1935 'The Old Waldorf-Astoria Bar Book' in which Albert S. Crocket writes of this drink, "Invented at the Old Hotel Brunswick, once a resort for Fashion, and situated on the north side of Madison Square."
Comment: Has the good looks and also the flavour profile to back them up.

BUBBLEGUM SHOT

★★★☆☆

Glass: Shot
Garnish: None
Method: SHAKE all ingredients with ice and fine strain into chilled glass.

½	shot	Midori Green Melon liqueur
½	shot	Disaronno Originale amaretto
¼	shot	Single cream / half-and-half

Comment: As the name suggests, this tastes a little like bubble gum.

THE BUCK / GIN BUCK 🔑

★★★⯪☆

Glass: Collins
Garnish: Lemon wedge
Method: POUR first two ingredients into ice-filled glass and **TOP** with ginger ale. Stir and serve with straws.

2½ shots Rutte Dry Gin
½ shot Freshly squeezed lemon juice
Top with Ginger ale

Comment: The Buck can be improved by adding a dash of liqueur appropriate to the spirit base. E.g. add a dash of Grand Marnier to a Brandy Buck.

BUCK'S FIZZ ⬤⚷

★★★☆☆

Glass: Flute
Garnish: None
Method: POUR ingredients into chilled glass and gently stir.

2 shots Freshly squeezed orange juice
Top with G.H. Mumm Cordon Rouge Champagne

Origin: Created in 1921 by Mr McGarry, first bartender at the Buck's Club, London.
Comment: Not really a cocktail and not that challenging, but great for brunch.

BUCKEYE ⬤⚷

★★★★⯪

Glass: Martini
Garnish: Black olive
Method: STIR all ingredients with ice and strain into chilled glass.

2½ shots Rutte Dry Gin
½ shot Martini Extra Dry vermouth

Comment: A standard Dry Martini - but a Buckeye is always garnished with a black olive instead of a green one.

BUENA VIDA

★★★★☆

Glass: Old-fashioned
Garnish: Pineapple wedge
Method: SHAKE all ingredients with ice and strain into glass filled with crushed ice.

2 shots Patrón reposado tequila
1¾ shots Freshly squeezed pink grapefruit juice
¾ shot Fresh pressed pineapple juice
3 dash Angostura Aromatic Bitters
½ shot Vanilla sugar syrup

Origin: Adapted from a drink created in 2011 by Lee Clinton.
Comment: The fruits combine brilliantly with the tequila and spice comes courtesy of Angostura.

BULL SHOT

★★★⯪☆

Glass: Collins
Garnish: Celery salt rim
Method: SHAKE all ingredients with ice and strain into ice-filled glass.

2 shots Ketel One Vodka
4 shots Cold beef bouillon
½ shot Freshly squeezed lemon juice
3 dash Worcestershire sauce
3 dash Tabasco hot pepper sauce
1 pinch Salt
1 grind Black pepper

Comment: Cow broth replaces tomato in this Mary for carnivorous drinkers.

BULL'S BLOOD

★★★★⯪

Glass: Martini
Garnish: Orange zest twist
Method: SHAKE all ingredients with ice and fine strain into chilled glass.

½ shot Bacardi Carta Blanca light rum
1 shot Martell VSOP Médaillon cognac
1 shot Grand Marnier Cordon Rouge
1½ shots Freshly squeezed orange juice

Comment: Orange fruitiness fortified with cognac and white rum. Fruity but dry.

BULL'S MILK

★★★⯪☆

Glass: Collins
Garnish: None
Method: SHAKE all ingredients with ice and strain into ice-filled glass.

1 shot Bacardi Carta Blanca light rum
1½ shots Martell VSOP Médaillon cognac
4 shots Milk
½ shot Maple syrup

Comment: Dark spirits tamed by thick maple syrup and milk.

BULLDOG

★★★⯪☆

Glass: Collins
Garnish: None
Method: SHAKE first 4 ingredients with ice and strain into ice-filled glass. **TOP** with cola, stir and serve with straws.

1 shot Bacardi Carta Blanca light rum
1 shot Coffee liqueur
1½ shots Milk
1½ shots Single cream / half-and-half
Top with Coca-Cola

Comment: Surprisingly nice - cola cuts through the cream.

BULLDOG HIGHBALL ⬤⚷

★★★☆☆

Glass: Collins
Garnish: Orange slice
Method: SHAKE first two ingredients with ice and strain into ice-filled glass. **TOP** with ginger ale and lightly stir. Serve with straws.

2 shots Rutte Dry Gin
1½ shots Freshly squeezed orange juice
Top with Ginger ale

Comment: Light and easy drinking. Gin and orange lightly spiced with ginger.

BULLFROG #1

★★★☆☆

Glass: Collins
Garnish: Luxardo Maraschino cherry
Method: SHAKE all ingredients with ice and strain into glass filled with crushed ice.

1½ shots   Ketel One Vodka
¾ shot   Giffard Menthe Pastille liqueur
1 shot   Single cream / half-and-half
1 shot   Milk

Comment: Tastes of mint ice-cream.

BULLFROG #2

★★★☆☆

Glass: Collins
Garnish: Lime wedge
Method: POUR vodka and lime into ice-filled glass and TOP with lemonade.

2 shots   Ketel One Vodka
½ shot   Freshly squeezed lime juice
Top with   Lemonade / Sprite / 7-Up

Comment: Long, dry and fresh.

BUSHRANGER

★★★★☆

Glass: Martini
Garnish: Orange zest twist

Method: STIR all ingredients with ice and stain into ice-filled glass.

1½ shots   Bacardi Carta Blanca light rum
1½ shots   Dubonnet Red
2 dash   Angostura Aromatic Bitters

Origin: Unknown. Originally, in the early years of the British settlement of Australia, Bushrangers were runaway convicts who had the survival skills necessary to use the Australian bush as a refuge from the authorities. The term then evolved as the Australian term for a highwayman.
Comment: Slightly sweet, this complex cocktail combines flavours of red wine with subtle herbal notes and is fortified with light rum.

BUSHWICK

★★★★½

Glass: Coupe
Garnish: None
Method: STIR all ingredients with ice and strain into a chilled glass.

2 shots   Straight rye whiskey
¾ shot   Martini Rosso vermouth
¼ shot   Luxardo Maraschino liqueur
¼ shot   Amer Picon

Origin: Created in 2009 by Phil Ward at Mayahuel New York City, USA. This riff on the Brooklyn is named after Bushwick, a neighbourhood in the north east of the New York City borough of Brooklyn.
Comment: This Italian-American blend is better and even more gripping than Godfather II.

THE BUSINESS 0—⚷

★★★★½

Glass: Coupe
Garnish: Lime zest twist
Method: SHAKE all ingredients with ice and fine strain into chilled glass.

2 shots   Rutte Dry Gin
½ shot   Honey water (3 honey to 1 water)
½ shot   Freshly squeezed lime juice

Origin: Adapted from a drink discovered at London's Milk & Honey.
Comment: A Bee's Knees with lime juice. It's snappier with lime instead of lemon.

BUTTERCUP COCKTAIL (NEW)

★★★★½

Glass: Coupe
Garnish: Lemon zest on rim (not sprayed) nestling Werther's Original butter candy
Method: STIR all ingredients with ice and strain into chilled glass.

2 shots   Rutte Old Simon oude jenever
¾ shot   Butterscotch liqueur
¾ shot   Martini Rosso vermouth

Origin: My adaptation of a recipe I discovered in January 2014 in Amsterdam, Netherlands.
Comment: When made to the original specification: 1 shot jenever, 1 shot butterscotch liqueur and ¾ shot sweet vermouth, this drink has a great flavour but lacks depth of flavour. Hence the formula above which is heavy on the jenever with equal parts butterscotch liqueur and sweet vermouth. It's even better when an oude jevever is used rather than a jonge as this amplifies the butterscotch notes.

Beware, the original recipe calls for a lemon zest twist garnish but the lemon oils overpower the butterscotch, so if you use a slither of lemon skin to fix our choice of a Werther's Original to the rim, then don't express the lemon's oils over the drink.

Don't be tempted to use buttercup flowers as a garnish as they are poisonous. They are also poisonous when eaten by livestock but their acrid taste and the blistering of the mouth they cause mean that animals don't tend to eat them. Interestingly, the toxins degrade when dried, so hay containing dried buttercups is safe for animals to eat.

BUTTERFLY COCKTAIL 0—⚷

★★★★☆

Glass: Martini
Garnish: Lemon zest twist
Method: MUDDLE grapes in base of shaker. Add other ingredients and fine strain into chilled glass.

8 fresh   Seedless white grapes
3 fresh   Basil leaves
3 fresh   Mint leaves
1½ shots   Ketel One Vodka
¼ shot   St-Germain elderflower liqueur
¼ shot   Freshly squeezed lemon juice

Origin: Created by Alex Kammerling, London, England.
Comment: Light and refreshing but with citrus complexity.

BUZZARD'S BREATH

★★★☆☆

Glass: Hurricane
Garnish: Pineapple wedge
Method: BLEND ingredients with 12oz scoop of crushed ice. Pour into glass and serve with straws.

2½ shots   Capucana cachaça
1   shot   Coco Re'al Cream of Coconut
2   shots   Fresh pressed pineapple juice
¼   shot   Single cream / half-and-half

Comment: A Piña Colada made with cachaça.

BYCULLA

★★★★☆

Glass: Martini
Garnish: Fresh ginger slice
Method: SHAKE all ingredients with ice and fine strain into chilled glass.

1   shot   Romate Fino sherry
1   shot   Tawny port
½   shot   Grand Marnier Cordon Rouge
½   shot   King's Ginger Liqueur
½   shot   Chilled water (omit if wet ice)

Origin: An adaptation of a vintage cocktail recipe of unknown origin. Believed to be named after a neighbourhood in South Mumbai, India.
Comment: Claret-cum-mulled wine, but hold out for the warming ginger finish.

BYRRH & BEER ON-THE-ROCKS (NEW)

★★★★★

Glass: Old-fashioned
Garnish: Orange zest twist
Method: POUR ingredients into ice-filled glass and stir.

2   shots   Byrrh Grand Quinquina
2   shots   Fuller's Chiswick Bitter

Origin: Created by yours truly on 14th March 2015 at the Cabinet Room, London, England.
Comment: I love a good beer and I love Byrrh – a marriage made in Bermondsey. Best served as an aperitif cocktail.

BYRRH CASSIS (NEW)

★★★★☆

Glass: Collins
Garnish: Orange slice
Method: POUR all ingredients into ice-filled glass in the following order and lightly stir.

3½ shots   Soda (club soda)
1½ shots   Byrrh Grand Quinquina
¾   shot   Lejay crème de cassis de Dijon

Origin: Adapted from a recipe in Harry Craddock's 1930 'The Savoy Cocktail Book'.
Comment: Rich berry and red wine flavours are lengthened and enlivened with sparkling water.

BYRRH COCKTAIL (NEW)

★★★★☆

Glass: Coupe
Garnish: Orange zest twist (discarded) & Luxardo maraschino cherry
Method: STIR all ingredients with ice and strain into chilled glass.

1⅓ shots   Canadian blended whisky
1⅓ shots   Byrrh Grand Quinquina
1⅓ shots   Lillet Blanc
1   dash   Peach bitters

Origin: Adapted from a recipe in Harry Craddock's 1930 'The Savoy Cocktail Book'.
Comment: Canadian blended whisky provides the backbone over which layers of complex French aromatised wine are layered.

BYRRH SPECIAL (NEW)

★★★★☆

Glass: Coupe
Garnish: Lemon zest twist
Method: STIR ingredients with ice and strain into chilled glass.

1½ shots   Byrrh Grand Quinquina
1½ shots   Old Tom gin

Origin: Adapted from a recipe in Harry Craddock's 1930 'The Savoy Cocktail Book'.
Comment: The botanicals in gin combine brilliantly with Byrrh to create a cocktail that works as well as an aperitif as it does a digestive.

BYZANTINE

★★★★☆

Glass: Collins
Garnish: Basil leaf
Method: MUDDLE basil in base of shaker. Add other ingredients apart from tonic water, **SHAKE** with ice and strain into ice-filled glass. **TOP** with tonic water.

6   fresh   Basil leaves
1½ shots   Rutte Dry Gin
½   shot   Passion fruit syrup
½   shot   Lime & lemongrass cordial
2   shots   Fresh pressed pineapple juice
Top with   Tonic Water

Origin: Created in 2001 by Douglas Ankrah for Akbar, Soho, London, England.
Comment: This fruity, herbal drink is even better made the way Douglas originally intended, with basil infused gin instead of muddled leaves.

C C KAZI

★★★★☆

Glass: Martini
Garnish: Lime wedge
Method: SHAKE all ingredients with ice and fine strain into chilled glass.

1¾ shots   Patrón reposado tequila
1¾ shots   Cranberry juice
½   shot   Freshly squeezed lime juice
¼   shot   Sugar syrup (2 sugar to 1 water)

Comment: A Rude Cosmo without the liqueur.

THE C&C

★★★☆☆

Glass: Shot
Garnish: None
Method: LAYER by carefully pouring ingredients in the following order.

¾ shot De Kuyper Triple Sec
¾ shot Martell VSOP Médaillon cognac

Comment: The initial heat of brandy is chased and extinguished by sweet orange liqueur.

CABLE CAR

★★★★☆

Glass: Martini
Garnish: Cinnamon & sugar rim
Method: SHAKE all ingredients with ice and fine strain into chilled glass.

2 shots Bacardi OakHeart
Spiced Rum
1 shot De Kuyper Triple Sec
½ shot Freshly squeezed
lemon juice
¼ shot Sugar syrup
(2 sugar to 1 water)
½ fresh Egg white

Origin: Created in 1996 by Tony Abou-Ganim at the Starlight Room, a nightclub and cocktail lounge atop San Francisco's Sir Francis Drake Hotel. The Nob Hill cable cars pass by the bar, hence its catchphrase 'between the stars and the cable cars'. Some say that Cory Reistad created the Cable Car but this is what Tony says of such claims, "Cory Reistad did indeed work at the Starlight Room with me although not as a member of the opening team. All the menus were created by myself and yes other bartenders were encouraged to participate but the Cable Car was one of my creations which did indeed go on the menu and was created in 1996."

Tony's original 1996 recipe: 1 1/2oz Captain Morgan Spiced Rum, 3/4oz Marie Brizard orange curacao and 1 1/2oz fresh lemon sour mix (which is made with 2 parts fresh squeezed, filtered lemon juice with 1 part simple syrup).
Comment: Vanilla and spice from the rum interact with the orange liqueur in this balanced, Daiquiri style drink.

CABLEGRAM

★★★★☆

Glass: Collins
Garnish: Candied ginger
Method: SHAKE all ingredients with ice and fine strain into ice-filled glass. **TOP** with soda.

2 shots Straight rye whiskey
¾ shot Ginger sugar syrup
½ shot Freshly squeezed lime juice
Top with Soda (club soda)

Origin: Adapted from a drink created in 2009 by Eric Alperin at The Varnish, Los Angeles, USA.
Comment: Whiskey and ginger with a fresh zing of lime.

CACHAÇA DAIQUIRI

★★★★☆

Glass: Martini
Garnish: Lime wedge
Method: SHAKE all ingredients with ice and fine strain into chilled glass.

2 shots Capucana cachaça
½ shot Freshly squeezed lime juice
¼ shot Sugar syrup (2 sugar to 1 water)
½ shot Chilled water (omit if wet ice)

Comment: Might be in a cocktail glass but it tastes like a Caipirinha.

CACTUS BANGER

★★★★☆

Glass: Martini
Garnish: Lime wedge
Method: SHAKE all ingredients with ice and fine strain into chilled glass.

1 shot Patrón reposado tequila
1 shot Grand Marnier Cordon Rouge
2 shots Freshly squeezed orange juice
½ shot Freshly squeezed lime juice

Comment: A golden, sunny looking and sunny tasting drink.

CACTUS JACK

★★★★☆

Glass: Martini
Garnish: Pineapple leaf
Method: SHAKE all ingredients with ice and fine strain into chilled glass.

1 shot Patrón reposado tequila
¾ shot Blue curaçao liqueur
1¼ shots Freshly squeezed orange juice
1 shot Fresh pressed pineapple juice
½ shot Freshly squeezed lemon juice

Comment: Vivid in colour, this orange led, Tequila based drink has a balanced sweet and sourness.

CAFÉ GATES

★★★★☆

Glass: Toddy
Garnish: Coffee beans
Method: Place bar spoon in glass, **POUR** first three ingredients and top up with coffee, then float cream by pouring over the back of a spoon.

¾ shot Grand Marnier Cordon Rouge
¾ shot Coffee liqueur
¾ shot Dark crème de cacao liqueur
Top with Filter coffee (hot)
¾ shot Single cream / half-and-half

Comment: Chocolate orange with coffee and cream.

CAIPIGINGER

★★★½☆

Glass: Old-fashioned
Garnish: Lime zest twist (discarded) & lime wedge
Method: **MUDDLE** ginger in base of shaker. Add other ingredients, **SHAKE** with ice and strain into glass filled with crushed ice. Serve with straws.

2	shots	Capucana cachaça
2	slice	Fresh root ginger (thumbnail sized)
1	shot	Freshly squeezed lime juice
¾	shot	Sugar syrup (2 sugar to 1 water)

Comment: A ginger spiced take on the Caipirinha

CAIPIRINHA #1 (BRAZILIAN SERVE)

★★★★½

Glass: Old-fashioned
Garnish: None
Method: **MUDDLE** lime in the base of a robust glass to release the juices and oils in its skin. Pour cachaça and sugar into glass, add ice and **STIR**. Serve with straws.

¾	fresh	Lime (fresh whole) (chopped wedges)
2	shots	Capucana cachaça
½	shot	Sugar syrup (2 sugar to 1 water)

Origin: Pronounced 'Kie-Pur-Reen-Yah', the name of this traditional Brazilian cocktail literally translates as 'little countryside drink'. It is made by muddling 'limon sutil' limes, which are native to Brazil and mixing with sugar and cachaça. Be sure to muddle in a sturdy, non-breakable glass. In Britain and other 'new' cachaça markets it is common practice to serve this drink with crushed ice but in Brazil it is usually served with cubed ice. Capirinhas and variations on the theme are staples in cachaçarias, traditional Brazilian bars which specialise in cachaça.
Comment: You are probably used to this drink being served with crushed ice but until you have tried it with cubed ice you have not really tried a Caipirinha.

CAIPIRINHA #2 (CONTEMPORARY SERVE)

★★★★☆

Glass: Old-fashioned
Garnish: Serve with 2 short straws
Method: **MUDDLE** lime wedges in the base of shaker to release juice and oils in its skin. Add cachaça and sugar. **SHAKE** with 6oz scoop crushed ice and pour all without straining into glass.

¾	fresh	Lime (fresh whole) (chopped wedges)
2	shots	Capucana cachaça
½	shot	Sugar syrup (2 sugar to 1 water)

Origin: In its native Brazil it is usual to serve this drink with cubed ice but the drink travelled to the UK at a time when the use of crushed ice was fashionable and so in this and other 'new' cachaça markets use of crushed ice has become the norm.
Comment: There is much debate among bartenders as to whether granulated sugar or sugar syrup and if brown or white sugar should be used when making this drink. Those who favour granulated sugar argue that muddling with the abrasive crystals helps extract the oils from the lime's skin. Personally, I hate the crunch of sugar as inevitably not all the granulated sugar dissolves. Whether you should use brown or white sugar to make your syrup is another question. I prefer mine made the way it is in its native Brazil, with white sugar.

CAIPIRISSIMA 🔑

★★★★½

Glass: Old-fashioned
Garnish: Serve with 2 short straws
Method: **MUDDLE** lime wedges in the base of shaker to release juice and oils in its skin. Add rum and sugar. **SHAKE** with 6oz scoop crushed ice and pour all without straining into glass.

¾	fresh	Lime (fresh whole) (chopped wedges)
2	shots	Bacardi Carta Blanca light rum
½	shot	Sugar syrup (2 sugar to 1 water)

Comment: A Daiquiri-like drink made in the style of a Caipirinha.

CAIPIROVSKA 🔑

★★★★☆

Glass: Old-fashioned
Garnish: Serve with 2 short straws
Method: **MUDDLE** lime wedges in the base of shaker to release juice and oils in its skin. Add vodka and sugar. **SHAKE** with 6oz scoop crushed ice and pour all without straining into glass.

¾	fresh	Lime (fresh whole) (chopped wedges)
2	shots	Ketel One Vodka
½	shot	Sugar syrup (2 sugar to 1 water)

Comment: Vodka replaces cachaça in this Caipirinha-style drink.

CAIPIRUVA

★★★★☆

Glass: Old-fashioned
Garnish: None
Method: **MUDDLE** lime wedges and grapes in base of shaker to release juices. Add cachaça and sugar. **SHAKE** with 6oz scoop crushed ice and pour all without straining into glass.

½	fresh	Lime (fresh whole) (chopped wedges)
4	fresh	Seedless white grapes
2	shots	Capucana cachaça
½	shot	Light muscovado sugar syrup (2 sugar to 1 water)

Origin: Created by Dale DeGroff, New York, USA.
Comment: A grape juice laced twist on the Caipirinha.

CAIPIRUVA BACCHANALIA

★★★½☆

Glass: Old-fashioned
Garnish: None
Method: **MUDDLE** lime and grapes in base of shaker to release juices. Add other ingredients, **SHAKE** with 6oz scoop crushed ice and pour all without straining into glass.

½	fresh	Lime (fresh whole) (chopped wedges)
5	fresh	Red grapes
2	shots	Capucana cachaça
1	shot	Honey sugar syrup
¾	shot	Sauternes dessert wine
3	dash	Grapefruit bitters

Origin: Created in 2008 by Julian de Féral at The East Rooms, London, England.
Comment: This twist on Dale's Caipiruva is sweetened by honey and dessert wine.

CAJUN NAIL

★★★★⯪

Glass: Old-fashioned
Garnish: Lemon zest twist (discarded)
Method: POUR absinthe into ice-filled glass, **TOP** with water and leave to stand. Separately **STIR** whiskey, Drambuie and bitters with ice. **DISCARD** contents of glass (absinthe, water and ice) and **STRAIN** stirred drink into empty absinthe-coated glass.

½	shot	Le Fée Parisienne absinthe
1½	shots	Jack Daniel's Old No.7 Brand
1½	shots	Drambuie liqueur
3	dash	Peychaud's aromatic bitters
3	dash	Angostura Aromatic Bitters

Origin: Created in 2010 by yours truly at the Cabinet Room, London, England.
Comment: A riff on the classic Sazerac.

CALIFORNIA ROOT BEER

★★★⯪☆

Glass: Sling
Garnish: Lime wedge
Method: SHAKE first 3 ingredients with ice and strain into ice-filled glass. **TOP** with soda.

1	shot	Ketel One Vodka
½	shot	Coffee liqueur
¾	shot	Galliano L'Autentico liqueur
Top with		Soda (club soda)

Comment: Does indeed taste like root beer.

CALIFORNIAN MARTINI

★★★★☆

Glass: Martini
Garnish: Orange zest twist
Method: STIR all ingredients with ice and strain into chilled glass.

2	shots	Ketel One Vodka
1	shot	Grand Marnier Cordon Rouge
½	shot	Martini Extra Dry vermouth
2	dash	Angostura Orange Bitters

Comment: A medium dry, fragrant orange Martini

CALL ME OLD-FASHIONED 🔑

★★★★⯪

Glass: Old-fashioned
Garnish: Orange zest twist
Method: STIR sugar syrup and bitters with two ice cubes in a glass. Add 1½ shots of cognac and two more ice cubes. **STIR** some more and add another two ice cubes and another shot of cognac. Stir lots more and add more ice.

2½	shots	Martell VSOP Médaillon cognac
¼	shot	Sugar syrup (2 sugar to 1 water)
2	dash	Angostura Aromatic Bitters

Origin: Created in 2001 by yours truly, London, England.
Comment: An Old-Fashioned made with cognac instead of whiskey. Works well.

CALVADOS COCKTAIL

★★★★⯪

Glass: Martini
Garnish: Orange zest twist
Method: SHAKE all ingredients with ice and fine strain into chilled glass.

1½	shots	Calvados brandy
¾	shot	De Kuyper Triple Sec
1½	shots	Freshly squeezed orange juice
2	dash	Angostura Orange Bitters

Origin: Adapted from Harry Craddock's 1930 'The Savoy Cocktail Book'.
Comment: Tangy orange with an alcoholic apple bite.

CAMERON'S KICK

★★★★☆

Glass: Martini
Garnish: Lemon zest twist
Method: SHAKE all ingredients with ice and fine strain into chilled glass.

1½	shots	Dewar's 12yo Scotch whisky
1½	shots	Teeling Small Batch Irish whiskey
¾	shot	Freshly squeezed lemon juice
½	shot	Almond (orgeat) syrup

Origin: Adapted form Harry Craddock's 1930 ' The Savoy Cocktail Book'.
Comment: Peaty, honeyed whisky with a cleansing hint of lemon, rounded by almond.

CAMPIRINHA

★★★★☆

Glass: Old-fashioned
Garnish: None
Method: MUDDLE lime and grapefruit in base of shaker to release juices. Add other ingredients, **SHAKE** with 6oz scoop crushed ice and pour all without straining into glass.

½	fresh	Lime (fresh whole) (chopped wedges)
¼	fresh	Ruby red grapefruit (chopped wedges)
2	shots	Campari Bitter
½	shot	Sugar syrup (2 sugar to 1 water)

Origin: Adapted from a drink created in 2006 by Jamie Lawton at Orchid, Auckland, New Zealand.
Comment: This bright red fruit laden drink has the looks to appeal to all but its bitter-sweet flavour is specific to Campari convertees.

CANADIAN APPLE (MOCKTAIL)

★★★★☆

Glass: Collins
Garnish: Apple slice
Method: SHAKE all ingredients with ice and fine strain into ice-filled glass.

3½	shots	Pressed apple juice
1½	shots	Freshly squeezed lemon juice
¾	shot	Maple syrup

Origin: Adapted from a drink discovered in 2005 at the Four Seasons Hotel, Prague, Czech Republic.
Comment: Refreshing and balanced with just the right amount of citrus acidity.

CANARIE

★★★☆☆

Glass: Collins
Garnish: None
Method: POUR pastis and lemon syrup into glass. Serve iced water separately in a small jug (known in France as a 'broc') so the customer can dilute to their own taste (I recommend five shots). Lastly, add ice to fill glass.

1	shot	Ricard Pastis
½	shot	Lemon syrup (glasco citron)
Top with		Chilled water

Origin: Very popular throughout France, this drink is fittingly named after the bird, which is typically bred for its bright yellow plumage.
Comment: The traditional French café drink with a twist of lemon sweetness

CANARY FLIP

★★★★☆

Glass: Martini
Garnish: Lemon zest twist
Method: SHAKE all ingredients with ice and fine strain into chilled glass.

2	shots	Warninks Advocaat liqueur
2	shots	Sauvignon blanc white wine
¾	shot	Freshly squeezed lemon juice

Origin: Created in 2002 by Alex Kammerling, London, England.
Comment: A delightful balance of egg, spirit and wine.

CANCHANCHARA 🗝

★★★☆☆

Glass: Old-fashioned
Garnish: Lemon slice
Method: STIR honey with rum in the glass drink is to be served in. Add lemon juice and ice. **STIR** and serve.

3	spoon	Runny honey
2	shots	Bacardi Carta Blanca light rum
1½	shots	Freshly squeezed lemon juice

Origin: The Cuban forerunner of the Daiquiri, as drunk by Cuban revolutionaries fighting off the Spanish at the end of the nineteenth century. To be really authentic omit the ice. Origin and the recipe from Christine Sismondo's 2005 'Mondo Cocktail'.
Comment: Achieve the perfect balance between sweet honey and sour lemon and this is a great drink.

CANEFLOWER COCKTAIL (NEW)

★★★★☆

Glass: Coupe
Garnish: Orange zest twist
Method: STIR all ingredients with ice and strain into chilled glass.

1½	shots	Capucana cachaça
¾	shot	Aperol Aperitivo
¾	shot	St-Germain elderflower liqueur
¾	shot	Chilled water (omit if wet ice)

Origin: Adapted from a recipe by Jeffrey Morgenthaler, Portland, Oregon, USA
Comment: Rust coloured and bittersweet with cachaça and elderflower.

CANTARITOS

★★★★☆

Glass: Cantaritos clay pot
Garnish: Lime wedge
Method: Submerge pot in cold water to clean the inside and wet the outside clay. This improves the appearance and keeps pot cold. **POUR** ingredients into ice-filled pot, **STIR** and serve with straws.

2 shots Patrón reposado tequila
2 shots Freshly squeezed orange juice
1 shot Freshly squeezed ruby grapefruit juice
¾ shot Freshly squeezed lime juice
1 spoon Salt
Top with Grapefruit Soda

Origin: A cocktail commonly made in bars, cafés and even road side stalls of Jalisco, Mexico. The simple 'cantaritos' clay pot is often used as a disposable take away container.
Comment: Juicy (freshly squeezed orange, grapefruit and lime) and refreshing slightly salty tequila invigorated with sparkling grapefruit soda.

CANTEEN MARTINI

★★★☆☆

Glass: Martini
Garnish: Luxardo Maraschino cherry
Method: SHAKE all ingredients with ice and fine strain into chilled glass.

1½	shots	Bacardi Carta Blanca light rum
½	shot	Disaronno Originale amaretto
1½	shots	Southern Comfort liqueur
½	shot	Freshly squeezed lime juice

Origin: Originally created by Joey Guerra at Canteen, New York City, and adapted by author and columnist Gary Regan.
Comment: Tangy, sweet and sour - Southern Comfort drinkers will love this.

CAPE CODDER 🗝

★★★☆☆

Glass: Old-fashioned
Garnish: Lime wedge
Method: SHAKE all ingredients with ice and strain into ice-filled glass.

2	shots	Ketel One Vodka
3	shots	Cranberry juice
¼	shot	Freshly squeezed lime juice

Origin: Named after the resort on the Massachusetts coast. This fish shaped piece of land is where some of the first Europeans settled in the US. Here they found cranberries, the indigenous North American berry on which this drink is based.
Comment: Dry and refreshing but not particularly interesting.

THE CAPPA COCKTAIL

★★★★½

Glass: Coupe
Garnish: Lemon zest twist

Method: STIR all ingredients with ice and strain into chilled glass.

2 shots Rutte Dry Gin
1½ shots Chevessac Pineau Des Charentes Extra Vieux
½ shot Luxardo Maraschino liqueur

Origin: Adapted from a drink created in 2012 by Franky Marshall at 15 Romolo, San Francisco, USA.
Comment: Dry, balanced and delicate with a balanced marriage of gin, fortified wine and maraschino.

CAPPERCAILLE 🔑

★★★★☆

Glass: Martini
Garnish: Pineapple wedge
Method: STIR honey with whisky until honey dissolves. Add other ingredients, **SHAKE** with ice and fine strain into chilled glass.

2 shots Dewar's 12yo Scotch whisky
½ shot De Kuyper Triple Sec
½ shot De Kuyper XO Apricot Brandy
2 spoon Runny honey
1 shot Fresh pressed pineapple juice
½ shot Freshly squeezed lemon juice

Origin: Created by Wayne Collins for Maxxium UK.
Comment: Wonderfully tangy, fruity Scotch.

CAPRICE

★★★★☆

Glass: Martini
Garnish: Orange zest twist
Method: STIR all ingredients with ice and strain into chilled glass.

1½ shots Rutte Dry Gin
½ shot Bénédictine D.O.M. liqueur
½ shot Martini Extra Dry vermouth
1 dash Angostura Orange Bitters

Comment: A long stir delivers the dilution necessary for this aromatic, spiced Wet Martini.

CAPTAIN COLLINS

★★★½☆

Glass: Collins
Garnish: Orange slice & cherry on stick (sail)
Method: SHAKE first 3 ingredients with ice and strain into ice-filled glass. **TOP** with soda, stir and serve with straws.

2 shots Canadian blended whisky
1 shot Freshly squeezed lemon juice
½ shot Sugar syrup (2 sugar to 1 water)
Top with Soda (club soda)

Origin: Classic Collins variation.
Comment: Sweetened, soured and diluted whisky.

CARAMEL MANHATTAN

★★★★½

Glass: Martini
Garnish: Lemon zest twist (discarded) & pineapple wedge
Method: SHAKE all ingredients with ice and fine strain into chilled glass.

1½ shots Bourbon whiskey
¾ shot Caramel liqueur
½ shot Martini Rosso vermouth
1 shot Fresh pressed pineapple juice
2 dash Peychaud's aromatic bitters

Origin: Adapted from a drink created in 2002 by Nick Strangeway, London, England.
Comment: Flavours combine harmoniously with the character of the bourbon still evident.

CARAVAN

★★★☆☆

Glass: Collins
Garnish: Cherries
Method: POUR ingredients into ice-filled glass. Stir and serve with straws.

3 shots Shiraz red wine
½ shot Grand Marnier Cordon Rouge
Top with Coca-Cola

Origin: Popular in the French Alpine ski resorts.
Comment: A punch-like long drink.

CARDINAL PUNCH

★★★½☆

Glass: Old-fashioned
Garnish: None
Method: POUR cassis into ice-filled glass and top up with wine. Stir and serve with straws.

1 shot Lejay crème de cassis de Dijon
Top with Shiraz red wine

Comment: A particularly fruity red.

CARDINALE

★★★★½

Glass: Old-fashioned
Garnish: Orange slice
Method: STIR all ingredients with ice and strain into ice-filled glass.

1½ shots Rutte Dry Gin
1½ shots Campari Bitter
1½ shots Martini Extra Dry vermouth

Origin: The creation of this Negroni-like drink is credited to the Excelsior Hotel in Rome or Harry's Bar in Venice sometime in the 1930s.
Comment: Lighter than a classic Negroni made with sweet vermouth but even more polarising. This is a love or hate dry, bitter drink.

CARIBBEAN BREEZE

★★★★☆

Glass: Collins
Garnish: Pineapple wedge
Method: SHAKE all ingredients with ice and strain into ice-filled glass.

1¼ shots   Bacardi Carta Blanca light rum
½ shot   Crème de banane liqueur
2½ shots   Fresh pressed pineapple juice
2 shots   Cranberry juice
½ shot   Rose's lime cordial

Comment: A long drink with bags of tangy fruit flavours.

CARIBBEAN PIÑA COLADA

★★★★☆

Glass: Hurricane
Garnish: Pineapple wedge & Luxardo Maraschino cherry
Method: BLEND ingredients with 12oz scoop of crushed ice. Pour into glass and serve with straws.

2 shots   Bacardi Carta Blanca light rum
3 shots   Fresh pressed pineapple juice
½ shot   Coco Re'al Cream of Coconut
4 dash   Angostura Aromatic Bitters
1 pinch   Salt

Comment: Angostura and salt make this a less sticky Colada.

CARIBBEAN PUNCH

★★★★☆

Glass: Collins
Garnish: Lime zest twist
Method: SHAKE all ingredients with ice and strain into glass filled with crushed ice.

2¼ shots   White overproof rum
½ shot   Disaronno Originale amaretto
½ shot   Coconut rum liqueur
¼ shot   Galliano L'Autentico liqueur
¾ shot   Freshly squeezed lemon juice
3 shots   Fresh pressed pineapple juice
¼ shot   Pomegranate / grenadine syrup (2:1)

Comment: Red in colour and innocent looking, this flavoursome drink sure packs a punch.

CARIBE DAIQUIRI

★★★★☆

Glass: Martini
Garnish: Lemon wedge
Method: SHAKE all ingredients with ice and fine strain into chilled glass.

2 shots   Bacardi Carta Blanca light rum
1 shot   Fresh pressed pineapple juice
½ shot   Freshly squeezed lemon juice
¼ shot   Taylor's Velvet Falernum liqueur

Comment: A dry, fruity spicy Daiquiri

CAROL CHANNING

★★★☆☆

Glass: Flute
Garnish: Raspberries
Method: POUR first 2 ingredients into chilled glass. TOP with champagne.

¾ shot   Framboise eau-de-vie
⅔ shot   Lejay Crème de framboise liqueur
Top with   G.H. Mumm Brut
           Cordon Rouge Champagne

Comment: Fortified raspberry and champagne.
Origin: Created in 1984 by Dick Bradsell, London, England. In the Dec-Jan 1998 edition of CLASS magazine (page 7), Dick wrote, "This drink was invented with the help of the shaved milliner Stephen Jones. We named it after the famously large mouthed American comedienne Carol Channing because of her appearance in the film 'Thoroughly Modern Milly'. For some reason she spends much of the time on the screen running about shouting 'raspberries'. I still do not know why!"

"To make, pour 25mls of framboise eau de vie into a champagne flute and add 20mls of crème de framboise liqueur. Top with champagne and garnish with a fresh raspberry. It is sometimes necessary to add a dash of sugar syrup if the liqueur content is not so sweet."

CARROL COCKTAIL

★★★☆☆

Glass: Martini
Garnish: Pickled walnut or onion
Method: STIR all ingredients with ice and strain into chilled glass.

2 shots   Martell VSOP Médaillon cognac
1 shot   Martini Rosso vermouth

Origin: Adapted form Victor Bergeron's 'Trader Vic's Bartender's Guide' (1972 revised edition).
Comment: Aromatic wine and cognac - dry yet easy.

CARROLL GARDENS

★★★★☆

Glass: Coupe
Garnish: Luxardo Maraschino cherry
Method: STIR ingredients over ice and strain into a cocktail glass. Squeeze lemon twist over the drink, wipe the rim with the peel and discard.

2 shots Straight rye whiskey
½ shot Amaro liqueur
⅛ shot Luxardo Maraschino liqueur
½ shot Carpano Punt E Mes

Origin: Created in 2009 by Joaquin Simo at Death and Company, New York City, USA in honour of his neighbourhood, Brooklyn's Carroll Gardens.
Comment: This delightful twist on the Brooklyn is the most Italian American of drinks.

CARTHUSIAN NAIL

★★★★☆

Glass: Old-fashioned
Garnish: Mint sprig
Method: STIR all ingredients with ice and strain into ice-filled glass.

1½ shots	Dewar's 12yo Scotch whisky
¾ shot	Drambuie liqueur
¼ shot	Green Chartreuse liqueur

Origin: Created in 2010 by yours truly at the Cabinet Room, London, England.
Comment: A Chartreuse influenced riff on the classic Rusty Nail.

CARUSO MARTINI

★★★☆☆

Glass: Martini
Garnish: Mint leaf
Method: SHAKE all ingredients with ice and fine strain into chilled glass.

1 shot	Rutte Dry Gin
1 shot	Martini Extra Dry vermouth
1 shot	Green crème de menthe liqueur

Origin: This recipe was adapted form Harry Craddock's 1930 'The Savoy Cocktail Book'. The drink was created at The Savoy for the tenor Enrico Caruso in the early 20th century.
Comment: Emerald Green with full-on mint. Good as a digestif after a tenor-sized meal.

CASABLANCA #1

★★★★☆

Glass: Martini
Garnish: Orange zest twist
Method: SHAKE all ingredients with ice and fine strain into chilled glass.

2 shots	Bacardi Carta Blanca light rum
¾ shot	De Kuyper Triple Sec
¾ shot	Freshly squeezed lime juice
½ shot	Luxardo Maraschino liqueur
½ fresh	Egg white

Origin: Named after Michael Curtiz's 1942 classic starring Bogie and Ingrid Bergman.
Comment: A rum based variation on the White Lady, with zingy citrus and sweet maraschino.

CASABLANCA #2

★★★☆☆

Glass: Martini
Garnish: Dust with grated nutmeg
Method: SHAKE all ingredients with ice and fine strain into chilled glass.

1 shot	Ketel One Vodka
1 shot	Warninks Advocaat liqueur
¼ shot	Galliano L'Autentico liqueur
¼ shot	Freshly squeezed lemon juice
1 shot	Freshly squeezed orange juice
½ shot	Single cream / half-and-half

Comment: Creamy, fruity, alcoholic custard. Different!

CASANOVA

★★★★☆

Glass: Martini
Garnish: Crumbled Cadbury's Flake bar
Method: SHAKE all ingredients with ice and fine strain into chilled glass.

1½ shots	Bourbon whiskey
¾ shot	Coffee liqueur
¾ shot	Verdelho madeira (medium dry)
¾ shot	Milk
¾ shot	Single cream / half-and-half
⅛ shot	Sugar syrup (2 sugar to 1 water)

Comment: Rich, medium-sweet and creamy with a mocha coffee finish.

CASINO #1

★★★★★

Glass: Martini
Garnish: Luxardo Maraschino cherry
Method: SHAKE all ingredients with ice and fine strain into chilled glass.

1½ shots	Rutte Dry Gin
¾ shot	Luxardo Maraschino liqueur
½ shot	Freshly squeezed lemon juice
¼ shot	Chilled water (omit if wet ice)
1 dash	Angostura Orange Bitters

Origin: Recipe adapted from Harry Craddock's 1930 'The Savoy Cocktail Book'.
Comment: Basically an Aviation dried and made more complex with a dash of orange bitters.

CASINO #2

★★★★☆

Glass: Martini
Garnish: Luxardo Maraschino cherry
Method: SHAKE all ingredients with ice and fine strain into chilled glass.

2 shots	Rutte Dry Gin
¾ shot	Luxardo Maraschino liqueur
½ shot	Freshly squeezed lemon juice
½ shot	Freshly squeezed orange juice
1 dash	Angostura Orange Bitters

Origin: Recipe adapted from David A. Embury's 1948 'Fine Art of Mixing Drinks'.
Comment: Basically an Aviation but with a dash of orange juice and orange bitters.

CASSE NOISSETTE

★★★★☆

Glass: Martini
Garnish: Dust with grated nutmeg
Method: SHAKE first 3 ingredients with ice and strain into chilled glass. **FLOAT** thin layer of cream over drink.

1½ shots	Ketel One Vodka
¾ shot	Coffee liqueur
¾ shot	Hazelnut liqueur
¾ shot	Single cream / half-and-half

Origin: Adapted from a drink created in 2001 by Julien Escot at Hotel du Cap-Eden Roc in Cap d'Antibes (France). Casse Noisette won the overall contest at London, Drinks International Bartender's Challenge 2004.
Comment: Sip hazelnut and coffee through a creamy topping. A dessert of a drink.

CASSINI

★★★★✩✩

Glass: Martini
Garnish: Blackberries
Method: SHAKE all ingredients with ice and fine strain into chilled glass.

2	shots	Ketel One Vodka
1½	shots	Cranberry juice
¼	shot	Lejay crème de cassis de Dijon

Origin: Created in 1998 by yours truly, London, England.
Comment: A simple but pleasant berry drink.

CASTRO

★★★★✩✩

Glass: Martini
Garnish: Lime wedge
Method: SHAKE all ingredients with ice and fine strain into chilled glass.

1½	shots	Bacardi Carta Ocho aged rum
¾	shot	Calvados brandy
¼	shot	Freshly squeezed orange juice
½	shot	Freshly squeezed lime juice
¼	shot	Rose's lime cordial
¼	shot	Sugar syrup (2 sugar to 1 water)

Origin: Named after the Cuban.
Comment: Tangy and fruity.

CAUSEWAY

★★★★✩✩

Glass: Collins
Garnish: None
Method: SHAKE first 5 ingredients with ice and strain into ice-filled glass, **TOP** with ginger ale.

2	shots	Teeling Small Batch Irish whiskey
1	shot	Drambuie liqueur
2	dash	Angostura Orange Bitters
4	dash	Angostura Aromatic Bitters
¼	shot	Freshly squeezed lemon juice
Top with		Ginger ale

Origin: Created by David Myers at Titanic, London, England.
Comment: Dry, aromatic long whiskey drink.

CELERY COCKTAIL

★★★★✩

Glass: Martini
Garnish: Salt rim & celery stick
Method: SHAKE all ingredients with ice and fine strain into chilled glass.

2	shots	Ketel One Vodka
¼	shot	Sugar syrup (2 sugar to 1 water)
1¾	shots	Freshly extracted celery juice

Origin: Created by Andreas Tsanos at Momos, London, England in 2001.
Comment: Celery is usually only tasty when loaded with blue cheese. Vodka also seems to make it rather palatable.

CELERY GIMLET

★★★★✩

Glass: Coupe
Garnish: Celery tip & leaf
Method: SHAKE all ingredients with ice and fine strain into chilled glass.

1½	shots	Rutte Dry Gin
1	shot	Freshly extracted celery juice
¼	shot	Green Chartreuse liqueur
⅓	shot	Freshly squeezed lime juice
⅛	shot	Rose's lime cordial
⅛	shot	Chardonnay white wine vinegar
2	dash	Celery bitters

Origin: Created in 2010 by Naren Young at Saxon & Parole, New York City, USA.
Comment: Occupying the ground between the Gimlet and a Shrub with pleasing savoury celery notes adding interest.

CELTIC MARGARITA

★★★★✩

Glass: Coupe
Garnish: Salt rim & lemon wedge
Method: SHAKE all ingredients with ice and fine strain into chilled glass.

2	shots	Dewar's 12yo Scotch whisky
1	shot	De Kuyper Triple Sec
1	shot	Freshly squeezed lemon juice

Origin: Discovered in 2004 at Milk & Honey, London, England.
Comment: A Scotch Margarita - try it, it works.

CEMENT MIXER

★✩✩✩✩

Glass: Shot
Garnish: None
Method: POUR cream liqueur into glass and carefully **LAYER** lime juice so it floats on cream liqueur. Instruct drinker to hold and swirl the drink around in their mouth before swallowing.

| ¾ | shot | Baileys Irish cream liqueur |
| ¾ | shot | Rose's lime cordial |

Comment: When mixed in the mouth, the acid in the lime juice will curdle the cream liqueur causing it to rapidly gain viscosity and stick to the drinkers' teeth, like cement.

CHAM CHAM

★★★★✩✩

Glass: Flute
Garnish: Seasonal berries
Method: POUR liqueur into chilled glass and **TOP** with champagne.

| ½ | shot | Chambord Liqueur |
| Top with | | G.H. Mumm Cordon Rouge Champagne |

Comment: A pleasant blend of fruit and champagne to rival the Kir Royale.

Champagne Cocktail

One of the oldest cocktails, dating back to at least the mid-1800s, the Champagne Cocktail consists of a sugar cube douched in aromatic bitters dropped into the base of a glass, over which is poured a small measure of cognac before the glass is topped up with champagne.

The first written mention of the Champagne Cocktail appears in the catchily titled 'Panama in 1855. An Account of the Panama Rail-road, of the cities of Panama and Aspinwall with sketches of life and characters on the Isthmus by Robert Tomes'. Published 1855 in New York by Harper & Brothers.

On page 61, Tomes writes, "I profess the belief that drinking Champagne cock-tails[sic] before breakfast, and smoking forty cigars daily, to be an immoderate enjoyment of the good things of this world." On the following page he handily goes on to describe in some detail how a Champagne Cocktail is made:

"What shall I drink?" I asked a friend at my side. "A Champagne cock-tail - the most delicious thing in the world - let me make you one", was his response; and he suited the action to the word. A bottle of prime, sparkling 'Mumm' was brought, a refreshing plateful of crystal ice, fresh from Rockland by the last steamer, and rather a medical looking bottle, upon which was written a direct, brief terms, 'Bitters'. My friend, whose benevolent eyes expressed pity for my sufferings, while his lips were eloquent of prospective alleviation to my-self, and of consciousness, the result of long experience, of his own anticipated enjoyment, pounded the crystal ice, with a series of quick, successive blows, pattered it into the tumblers like a shower of hail, dropping in the bitters, which diffused a glow like that of early sunrise, dashed in the sugar, which somewhat clouded the beautiful prospect, and gave what the artists call a dead tint to the mixture; then out popped the eager 'Mumm', and the Champagne cock-tail, thus was perfected, went whirling, roaring, foaming, and flowing down mine and the friendly concocter's thirsty throats."

The above account is interesting as it not only proves that Champagne Cocktails were being made before 1855, but also shows that the drink was originally served in a tumbler over crushed ice, and made with aromatic bitters, sugar syrup and champagne. Interestingly there is no mention of brandy - cognac or otherwise.

In the world's first cocktail book, How to Mix Drinks, or The Bon Vivant's Companion published in 1862, Jerry Thomas also omits the brandy, commonly used in today's recipes. He also serves in a tumbler over broken (crushed) ice. We don't take the instruction to "Shake well" literally and presume he meant stir.

Jerry Thomas' 1862 Champagne Cocktail
"(One bottle of wine to every six large glasses.) (Per glass) ½ teaspoon of sugar, 1 or 2 dashes of bitters, 1 piece of lemon peel. Fill tumbler one-third full of broken ice, and fill balance with wine. Shake well and serve."

By the time Thomas wrote the 1887 edition of his book, fashion and the Champagne Cocktail had obviously moved on. He calls for a goblet rather than a tumbler, and the "broken ice" has been replaced with a "small lump of ice", and the use of a sugar is introduced - much closer to the modern day Champagne Cocktail.

In his 1948 'The Fine Art of Mixing Drinks', David Embury writes, "This drink should be served in a pre-chilled saucer champagne glass. Place a medium-sized loaf of sugar in the glass and saturate it with Angostura bitters - about 2 dashes. Fill with thoroughly chilled champagne. Add a twist of lemon or orange peel, or both."

Embury also added his personal opinion of the drink, "From every point of view, other than cost, this cocktail is a decidedly inferior drink, and no true champagne lover would ever commit the sacrilege of polluting a real vintage champagne by dunking even plain sugar - much less bitters - in it.

So if you must... serve this incongruous mess just for the sake of 'putting on the dog,' then, in the name of all that a true lover of the grape holds sacred, use a cheap domestic champagne or even an artificially carbonated white wine."

David Wondrich has more encouraging words of wisdom, "Don't use loose sugar or try to crush the cube - the whole point isn't so much to sweeten the drink as to create bubbles, which the cube will do as it slowly dissolves. Some prefer an ice cube in theirs, which will (to state the bleeding obvious) prolong the chill at the cost of a certain dilution. Or you can replace the bitters with absinthe and float a tablespoon or so of cognac (good cognac) on top. That's called a Casino Cocktail."

CHAMPAGNE COCKTAIL

★★★☆☆

Glass: Flute
Garnish: Orange zest twist (discarded)
Method: **COAT** sugar cube with bitters and drop into glass. **POUR** cognac over soaked cube, then **TOP** with champagne.

1	cube	**Brown sugar**
3	dash	**Angostura Aromatic Bitters**
1	shot	**Martell VSOP Médaillon cognac**
Top with		**G.H.Mumm Cordon Rouge Champagne**

Comment: An over hyped classic cocktail that gets sweeter as you reach the dissolving cube at the bottom.

CHAMPAGNE CUP

★★★★☆

Glass: Flute
Garnish: Luxardo Maraschino cherry
Method: **STIR** first 3 ingredients with ice and strain into chilled glass. **TOP** with champagne and gently stir.

¾	shot	**Martell VSOP Médaillon cognac**
½	shot	**Grand Marnier Cordon Rouge**
¼	shot	**Maraschino syrup (from cherry jar)**
Top with		**G.H.Mumm Cordon Rouge Champagne**

Comment: Sweet maraschino helps balance this dry drink.

CHAMPAGNE DAISY

★★★☆☆

Glass: Flute
Garnish: Pomegranate wedge
Method: **SHAKE** first 3 ingredients with ice and fine strain into chilled glass, **TOP** with champagne.

1	shot	**Yellow Chartreuse liqueur**
⅛	shot	**Pomegranate / grenadine syrup (2:1)**
1	shot	**Freshly squeezed lemon juice**
Top with		**G.H.Mumm Cordon Rouge Champagne**

Comment: You'll need to like Chartreuse and citrus champagne to appreciate this drink.

CHAMPAGNE MARGUERITE (NEW)

★★★½☆

Glass: Goblet
Garnish: Lemon wedge, edible flowers & seasonal berries
Method: **SHAKE** first 5 ingredients with ice and strain into ice-filled glass. **TOP** with champagne.

1	shot	**Rutte Dry Gin**
⅛	shot	**Luxardo Maraschino liqueur**
⅛	shot	**Almond (orgeat) syrup**
⅔	shot	**Freshly squeezed lemon juice**
¼	shot	**Sugar syrup (2 sugar to 1 water)**
2	shots	**G.H.Mumm Cordon Rouge Champagne**

Origin: Created in January 2014 for Laurent-Perrier by Sean Ware of the London Cocktail Club, London, England.
Comment: A classic cocktail from the 1860's revived in 2014 by Sean Ware of the London Cocktail Club with Demi-Sec champagne. We've used brut but compensated for this with a dash of sugar syrup.

CHAMPAGNE PICK-ME-UP

★★★★☆

Glass: Flute
Garnish: Orange zest twist (discarded)
Method: **SHAKE** first three ingredients with ice and fine strain into chilled glass. **TOP** with champagne.

1 shot Martell VSOP Médaillon cognac
1½ shots Freshly squeezed orange juice
¼ shot Pomegranate / grenadine syrup (2:1)
Top with G.H. Mumm Cordon Rouge Champagne

Origin: There are many versions of this classic cocktail but I have taken this one from Dale DeGroff's 2008 'The Essential Cocktail' where Dale credits this recipe to the Ritz Bar Paris circa 1936.
Comment: A subtle hint of biscuity champagne shines through this very quaffable drink.

CHAMPINO

★★★★☆

Glass: Flute
Garnish: Orange zest twist
Method: **SHAKE** first 2 ingredients with ice and fine strain into chilled glass. **TOP** with champagne.

1 shot Campari Bitter
1 shot Martini Rosso vermouth
Top with G.H. Mumm Cordon Rouge Champagne

Comment: A champagne option for Negroni lovers.

CHAMPS-ELYSEES COCKTAIL

★★★★½

Glass: Coupe
Garnish: Lemon zest twist
Method: **SHAKE** all ingredients with ice and fine strain into chilled glass.

1½ shots Martell VSOP Médaillon cognac
½ shot Green Chartreuse liqueur
¼ shot Freshly squeezed lemon juice
¼ shot Sugar syrup (2 sugar to 1 water)
2 dash Angostura Aromatic Bitters
½ shot Chilled water (omit if wet ice)

Origin: The Champs-Élysées is named after the touristy Parisian boulevard.
Comment: A great after dinner drink for lovers of cognac and Chartreuse.

CHANBANGER COCKTAIL (NEW)

★★★★½

Glass: Coupe
Garnish: Lemon zest twist
Method: **SHAKE** all ingredients with ice and strain into chilled glass.

1½ shots Bacardi Carta Ocho aged rum
⅔ shot Cherry Heering Liqueur
⅓ shot Freshly squeezed lemon juice
¾ shot Freshly squeezed pink grapefruit juice
⅓ shot Sugar syrup (2 sugar to 1 water)

Origin: Created in 2014 by Barney Chan at The Mayor of Scaredy Cat Town, London, England
Comment: Like its creator this drink is hard to classify. A hint of Singapore Sling oriental cherry with some Cuban Daiquiri aged rum and a splash of Papa's grapefruit citrus sourness.

CHANCELLOR

★★★★½

Glass: Martini
Garnish: Orange zest twist
Method: **SHAKE** all ingredients with ice and fine strain into chilled glass.

2 shots Dewar's 12yo Scotch whisky
1 shot Tawny port
½ shot Martini Extra Dry vermouth
¼ shot Sugar syrup (2 sugar to 1 water)
2 dash Angostura Orange Bitters

Origin: A classic of unknown origins.
Comment: Complex and sophisticated Scotch with fruity notes.

CHANTICLEER COCKTAIL

★★★★★

Glass: Coupe
Garnish: Orange zest twist
Method: **DRY SHAKE** all ingredients (without ice). **SHAKE** again with ice and fine strain into chilled glass.

1 shot Rutte Dry Gin
1½ shots Martini Extra Dry vermouth
½ shot De Kuyper Triple Sec
½ fresh Egg white

Origin: Recipe adapted from A.S. Crockett's 1935 'The Old Waldorf-Astoria Bar Book' which originally calls for "orange gin" rather than using an orange liqueur. Crockett handily says of this drink, "Add a Cock's Comb if desired." He also explains that the drink "celebrated the local opening of Edmond Rostand's Chanticler".

Edmond Rostand was a French poet and dramatist, best-known for his play Cyrano de Bergerac. First released in 1910, Chantecler (correct spelling) is a story where the characters are based on barnyard animals, and whose eponymous protagonist is a rooster who believes that his song makes the sun rise.

By all accounts the cocktail is rather better than the play. Incidentally, the 'Chantecler' is actually a breed of chicken developed in the early 20th century by Brother Wilfred Chantelain, a Trappist monk at the Abbey of Notre-Dame du Lac in Canada.
Comment: Wonderfully aromatic orange with a complex balance of gin and vermouth.

CHARENTE COLLINS

★★★★☆

Glass: Collins
Garnish: Mint sprig & orange zest twist
Method: Lightly **MUDDLE** mint in base of shaker (just to bruise). Add other ingredients, **SHAKE** with ice and strain into glass filled with crushed ice. Serve with straws.

5 fresh Mint leaves
2 shots Grand Marnier Cordon Rouge
1 shot St-Germain elderflower liqueur
1 shot Freshly squeezed lemon juice

Origin: Refreshing orange and lemon with a hint of elderflower.
Comment: Created in 2005 by Kieran Bailey, The Light Bar, London, England.

CHARENTE WHITE NEGRONI (NEW)

★★★★⯪

Glass: Old-fashioned
Garnish: Pink grapefruit zest twist
Method: POUR all ingredients into ice-filled glass and STIR.

½	shot	Rutte Dry Gin
½	shot	Martell VSOP Médaillon cognac
1	shot	Suze Saveur d'Autrefois
1	shot	Lillet Blanc

Origin: Created in January 2014 by yours truly and Matthias Lataille at the Cabinet Room, London England.
Comment: A White Negroni with the cognac replacing half of the gin. Fittingly 'Charente' references the Cognac area of France.

CHARLES DAIQUIRI

★★★★⯪

Glass: Martini
Garnish: Lime wedge
Method: SHAKE all ingredients with ice and fine strain into chilled glass.

1	shot	Bacardi Carta Blanca light rum
1	shot	Pusser's Navy Rum (54.5%)
½	shot	De Kuyper Triple Sec
½	shot	Freshly squeezed lime juice
⅛	shot	Sugar syrup (2 sugar to 1 water)
½	shot	Chilled water (omit if wet ice)

Comment: Navy rum and triple sec add special interest to this Daiquiri.

CHARLIE ⚷

★★★★⯪

Glass: Coupe
Garnish: Luxardo Maraschino cherry
Method: STIR all ingredients with ice and strain into chilled glass.

2	shots	Bourbon whiskey
½	shot	Martini Rosso vermouth
¼	shot	Chambord Liqueur
1	dash	Angostura Aromatic Bitters

Origin: Created in 2009 by yours truly at the Cabinet Room, London England and named after Charlotte Ashburner, then Chambord liqueur's UK brand manager.
Comment: A sweet Manhattan-style cocktail.

CHARLIE CHAPLIN COCKTAIL

★★★★☆

Glass: Coupe
Garnish: Apricot wedge
Method: SHAKE all ingredients with ice and fine strain into chilled glass.

¾	shot	De Kuyper XO Apricot Brandy
¾	shot	Sloe Gin liqueur
¾	shot	Freshly squeezed lime juice
¾	shot	Chilled water (omit if wet ice)

Origin: Created and originally served at New York's old Waldorf-Astoria prior to 1920. This recipe is adapted from Albert Stevens Crocketts 1935 'The Old Waldorf-Astoria Bar Book'. The drink is named after Sir Charles Spencer 'Charlie' Chaplin (1889-1977), the English slapstick comic actor of the silent film era, who was at the height of his career when this eponymous cocktail was created.
Comment: Dilution is key to this fruity bitter-sweet cocktail, hence the possible need to add some water depending on your ice.

CHARTREUSE SWIZZLE

★★★★⯪

Glass: Collins
Garnish: Pineapple wedge & Luxardo Maraschino cherry
Method: POUR ingredients into chilled glass and two-thirds fill with crushed ice. SWIZZLE with a swizzle stick (or churn with a barspoon). Add more crushed ice to fill and SWIZZLE some more. Serve with straws.

1¼	shots	Green Chartreuse liqueur
½	shot	Taylor's Velvet Falernum liqueur
2	shots	Fresh pressed pineapple juice
½	shot	Freshly squeezed lime juice

Origin: Created by Marco Dionysos at Tres Agaves, San Francisco, USA.
Comment: A swizzle for people like me - Chartreuse lovers. Best enjoyed on a hot summer's evening.

CHAS

★★★★☆

Glass: Martini
Garnish: Orange zest twist
Method: SHAKE all ingredients with ice and fine strain into chilled glass.

1¾	shots	Bourbon whiskey
½	shot	Bénédictine D.O.M. liqueur
½	shot	Disaronno Originale amaretto
½	shot	De Kuyper Triple Sec
½	shot	Grand Marnier Cordon Rouge

Origin: Created in 2003 by Murray Stenson at Zig Zag Café, Seattle, USA.
Comment: A wonderfully tangy cocktail with great bourbon personality and hints of almond and orange.

CHATHAM HOTEL SPECIAL

★★★★☆

Glass: Martini
Garnish: Dust with grated nutmeg
Method: SHAKE all ingredients with ice and fine strain into chilled glass.

2	shots	Martell VSOP Médaillon cognac
¾	shot	Tawny port
½	shot	Dark crème de cacao liqueur
¼	shot	Single cream / half-and-half
¼	shot	Milk

Origin: This mid-1900s classic from New York's Chatham Hotel was resurrected by Ted Haigh in his 2004 book 'Vintage Spirits & Forgotten Cocktails'.
Comment: Slightly changed proportions and replaced the original lemon zest garnish with a little extra spice.

CHE'S REVOLUTION

★★★★☆

Glass: Martini
Garnish: Pineapple wedge
Method: SHAKE all ingredients with ice and fine strain into chilled glass.

4	fresh	Mint leaves
2	shots	Bacardi Carta Blanca light rum
1½	shots	Fresh pressed pineapple juice
¼	shot	Maple syrup

Origin: Created in 2003 by Ben Reed for the launch party of MJU Bar @ Millennium Hotel, London, England
Comment: Complex and easy drinking with hints of maple syrup and mint amongst the pineapple and rum.

CHEEKY MONKEY

★★★★☆

Glass: Martini
Garnish: Orange zest twist
Method: SHAKE all ingredients with ice and fine strain into chilled glass.

1	shot	Ketel One Vodka
1	shot	Yellow Chartreuse liqueur
1½	shots	Freshly squeezed orange juice
1	dash	Angostura Orange Bitters

Origin: Created in 2001 by Tony Conigliaro at Isola, Knightsbridge, London, England.
Comment: Fire yellow in colour, this drink features the distinctive flavour of Chartreuse with a citrus supporting cast.

CHEEKY VIMTO

★★⯪☆☆

Glass: Boston
Garnish: Don't bother
Method: Pour port into glass and **TOP** with WKD Blue.

2	shots	Ruby port
1	bottle	WKD Original Blue

Origin: So named as this cocktail's flavour resembles the soft drink of the same name. The Cheeky Vimto emerged in Britain in the early-Noughties but became famous in June 2005 when the Daily Mail newspaper reported it as being Welsh singer-songwriter, Charlotte Church's favourite drink. She was then something of a teen diva party animal so the paper used the catchy heading, "Wild Charlotte's binge-drinking shame".
Despite the name, the soft drink Vimto is not an ingredient in this drink, but for the record, it is a sweet purple coloured soft drink containing grape, raspberry and blackcurrant juices and flavoured with herbs and spices. Vimto was created in 1908 in Timperley, Cheshire, England by John Noel Nichols, a wholesaler of spices and medicines.
Comment: A sickly sweet blackcurrant and berry fruit flavoured drink for the undiscerning.

CHELSEA SIDECAR ⊙━

★★★★☆

Glass: Martini
Garnish: Lemon zest twist
Method: SHAKE all ingredients with ice and fine strain into chilled glass.

1½	shots	Rutte Dry Gin
1	shot	De Kuyper Triple Sec
1	shot	Freshly squeezed lemon juice
¼	shot	Sugar syrup (2 sugar to 1 water)

Comment: Gin replaces cognac in this variation on the classic Sidecar.

CHERRUTE

★★★★☆

Glass: Martini
Garnish: Grapefruit zest twist (discarded) & Luxardo Maraschino cherry
Method: SHAKE all ingredients with ice and fine strain into chilled glass.

2	shots	Ketel One Vodka
½	shot	Cherry Heering Liqueur
1½	shots	Freshly squeezed pink grapefruit juice

Origin: Created in the early Noughties by Nicholas P J Snape at Mojo, Leeds, England.
Comment: Sweet cherry brandy balanced by the fruity acidity of grapefruit, laced with vodka.

CHERRY ALEXANDER

★★★★☆

Glass: Coupe
Garnish: Luxardo Maraschino cherry
Method: SHAKE all ingredients with ice and strain back into shaker. **DRY SHAKE** (without ice) and fine strain into chilled glass.

1	shot	Vanilla infused Ketel One vodka
½ s	hot	Cherry Heering liqueur
½	shot	White crème de cacao liqueur
1	shot	Single cream / half-and-half

Comment: A rich Black Forest Gateau like fruity twist on the creamy classic.
Origin: Created by Wayne Collins for Maxxium UK.

CHERRY BLOSSOM

★★★⯪☆

Glass: Martini
Garnish: Luxardo Maraschino cherry
Method: SHAKE all ingredients with ice and fine strain into chilled glass.

¾	shot	Cherry Heering Liqueur
¾	shot	Kirschwasser eau de vie
½	shot	De Kuyper Triple Sec
¼	shot	Maraschino syrup (from cherry jar)
1¼	shots	Freshly squeezed lemon juice

Comment: Bundles of flavour - tangy and moreish.

CHERRY MARINER

★★★★☆

Glass: Martini
Garnish: Luxardo Maraschino cherry
Method: SHAKE all ingredients with ice and fine strain into chilled glass.

2	shots	Rutte Dry Gin
1	shot	Cherry Heering Liqueur
¼	shot	Luxardo Maraschino liqueur
2	dash	Angostura Orange Bitters

Origin: Adapted from a drink created by Mickael Perron from Bar Now On.
Comment: Rich cherry liqueurs fortified by gin and bittered with a hint of orange.

CHERRY MARTINI

★★★★☆

Glass: Martini
Garnish: Lemon zest twist
Method: SHAKE all ingredients with ice and fine strain into chilled glass.

2	shots	Ketel One Citroen vodka
¾	shot	Cherry Heering Liqueur
½	shot	Martini Extra Dry vermouth
½	shot	Chilled water (omit if wet ice)

Origin: Created in 2005 by yours truly, London, England.
Comment: A hint of cherry is balanced by citrus freshness, and dried and deepened by vermouth.

CHERRY MASH SOUR

★★★★☆

Glass: Old-fashioned
Garnish: Lemon zest twist & Luxardo Maraschino cherry
Method: SHAKE all ingredients with ice and strain into ice-filled glass.

2	shots	Jack Daniel's Old No.7 Brand
½	shot	Cherry Heering Liqueur
¾	shot	Freshly squeezed lemon juice
½	shot	Sugar syrup (2 sugar to 1 water)

Origin: Created by Dale DeGroff when Beverage Manager at the Rainbow Room Promenade Bar, New York City, USA.
Comment: The rich flavour of Tennessee whiskey soured with lemon and sweetened with cherry liqueur.

CHICLET DAIQUIRI

★★★½☆

Glass: Martini
Garnish: Banana chunk
Method: BLEND ingredients with a 12oz scoop of crushed ice and serve in large chilled glass.

2½	shots	Bacardi Carta Blanca light rum
½	shot	Crème de banane liqueur
⅛	shot	Giffard Menthe Pastille liqueur
½	shot	Freshly squeezed lime juice
¼	shot	Sugar syrup (2 sugar to 1 water)

Origin: Often found on Cuban bar menus, this was created at La Floridita, Havana.
Comment: A wonderfully refreshing drink on a summer's day with surprisingly subtle flavours.

CHIHUAHUA MARGARITA

★★★½☆

Glass: Martini
Garnish: None
Method: SHAKE all ingredients with ice and fine strain into chilled glass.

2	shots	Patrón reposado tequila
2	shots	Freshly squeezed pink grapefruit juice
⅛	shot	Agave syrup
3	dash	Angostura Aromatic Bitters

Comment: Tequila and grapefruit juice pepped up with Angostura.

CHILCANO DE PISCO (NEW)

★★★★☆

Glass: Collins
Garnish: Lime wedge
Method: POUR all ingredients into ice-filled glass and lightly stir.

2	shots	BarSol Mosto Verde Italia pisco
¼	shot	Freshly squeezed lime juice
3	dash	Amargo Chuncho bitters
3½	shots	Ginger ale

Origin: Not to be confused with a fish soup called chilcano de pescado, the Chilcano de Pisco is a traditional Peruvian way of serving pisco.
Comment: Pisco and ginger ale made more interesting by a splash of lime juice and a few dashes of Amargo Chuncho bitters.

CHILL BILL (NEW)

★★★½☆

Glass: Goblet
Garnish: Lemon slice
Method: POUR all ingredients into ice-filled glass and lightly stir.

| 1⅓ | shots | Kwai Feh lychee liqueur |
| Top with | | Bitter lemon |

Comment: Bitter lemon balances sweet lychee liqueur in this simple and lightly alcoholic long drink.

CHIMAYO

★★★★☆

Glass: Martini
Garnish: Apple slice
Method: SHAKE all ingredients with ice and fine strain into chilled glass.

2	shots	Patrón reposado tequila
½	shot	Lejay crème de cassis de Dijon
¾	shot	Pressed apple juice
¼	shot	Freshly squeezed lemon juice

Origin: Named after El Potrero de Chimayo in northern New Mexico, USA
Comment: Apple juice and cassis take the sting off tequila.

CHIN CHIN

★★★★½

Glass: Flute
Garnish: None
Method: STIR honey with Scotch in base of shaker. Add apple juice, SHAKE with ice and strain into chilled glass. TOP with champagne.

½	spoon	Runny honey
1	shot	Dewar's 12yo Scotch whisky
½	shot	Pressed apple juice
Top with		G.H. Mumm Cordon Rouge Champagne

Origin: Created in 2002 by Tony Conigliaro at Isola, Knightsbridge, London, England.
Comment: Golden honey in colour and also in flavour. An unusual and great tasting Champagne cocktail.

CHINA BEACH

★★★★☆

Glass: Martini
Garnish: Fresh ginger slice
Method: SHAKE all ingredients with ice and fine strain into chilled glass.

1	shot	Ketel One Vodka
1	shot	King's Ginger Liqueur
2	shots	Cranberry juice

Comment: Dry and lightly spiced.

CHINA BLUE

★★★⯪☆

Glass: Collins
Garnish: Orange slice
Method: SHAKE all ingredients with ice and strain into ice-filled glass.

1	shot	Kwai Feh lychee liqueur
1	shot	Blue curaçao liqueur
4	shots	Freshly squeezed pink grapefruit juice

Origin: Emerged in Japan in the late 1990s and still popular along the Pacific Rim.
Comment: Looks sweet, but due to a generous splash of grapefruit is actually balanced and refreshing.

CHINA BLUE COCKTAIL

★★★★☆

Glass: Martini
Garnish: Lychee
Method: SHAKE all ingredients with ice and fine strain into chilled glass.

1	shot	Kwai Feh lychee liqueur
1	shot	Blue curaçao liqueur
2	shots	Freshly squeezed pink grapefruit juice
¼	shot	Freshly squeezed lemon juice

Origin: An almost inevitable short adaptation of the original long drink.
Comment: This simple cocktail with its turquoise colour tastes more adult and interesting than its colour might suggest.

CHINA MARTINI

★★★⯪☆

Glass: Martini
Garnish: Orange zest twist & lychee
Method: STIR all ingredients with ice and fine strain into chilled glass.

1½	shots	Rutte Dry Gin
½	shot	Kwai Feh lychee liqueur
¼	shot	De Kuyper Triple Sec
½	shot	Martini Extra Dry vermouth

Origin: Created in 2004 by Wayne Collins for Maxxium UK.
Comment: A complex, not too sweet lychee Martini.

CHINATO NAIL

★★★★☆

Glass: Old-fashioned
Garnish: Lemon zest twist
Method: STIR all ingredients with ice and strain into ice-filled glass.

2½	shots	Dewar's 12yo Scotch whisky
½	shot	Drambuie liqueur
½	shot	Antica Ricetta Barolo Chinato

Origin: Created in 2012 by yours truly at the Cabinet Room, London, England.
Comment: A riff on the Rusty Nail using Barolo Chinato. Perhaps one for whisky and Negroni fans.

CHINESE COSMOPOLITAN

★★★★☆

Glass: Martini
Garnish: Orange zest twist (flamed)
Method: SHAKE all ingredients with ice and fine strain into chilled glass.

2	shots	Old Krupnik
¾	shot	Kwai Feh lychee liqueur
½	shot	Freshly squeezed lime juice
1	shot	Cranberry juice

Origin: Discovered in 2003 at Raoul's Bar, Oxford, England.
Comment: Oriental in name and style - perhaps a tad sweeter than your standard Cosmo.

CHINESE WHISPER

★★★★☆

Glass: Martini
Garnish: Lemon zest twist
Method: MUDDLE ginger in base of shaker. Add other ingredients, SHAKE with ice and fine strain into chilled glass.

2	slice	Fresh root ginger (thumbnail sized)
2	shots	Ketel One Citroen vodka
1	shot	Kwai Feh lychee liqueur
½	shot	Freshly squeezed lime juice
¼	shot	Ginger sugar syrup

Origin: Adapted from a recipe discovered in 2003 at Oxo Tower Bar, London, England.
Comment: There's more than a whisper of ginger in this spicy Martini.

CHOCOLARITA

★★★★☆

Glass: Coupe
Garnish: Chocolate powder rim
Method: SHAKE all ingredients with ice and fine strain into chilled glass.

2	shots	Patrón reposado tequila
¼	shot	Dark crème de cacao liqueur
¼	shot	Coffee liqueur
1	shot	Freshly squeezed lime juice
¼	shot	Sugar syrup (2 sugar to 1 water)

Origin: Adapted from a recipe discovered in 2005 at Agave, Hong Kong.
Comment: As the name suggests - a Margarita with chocolate and coffee.

CHOCOLATE BISCUIT

★★★⯪☆

Glass: Martini
Garnish: Bourbon biscuit
Method: SHAKE all ingredients with ice and fine strain into chilled glass.

2	shots	Martell VSOP Médaillon cognac
1	shot	Dark crème de cacao liqueur
1	shot	Coffee liqueur

Origin: Created in 1999 by Gillian Stanfield at The Atlantic Bar & Grill, London, England.
Comment: Sweet and rich, with coffee and chocolate - one to chase dessert.

CHOCOLATE MARTINI

★★★★☆

Glass: Martini
Garnish: Chocolate powder rim
Method: SHAKE all ingredients with ice and fine strain into chilled glass.

2	shots	Ketel One Vodka
1	shot	White crème de cacao liqueur
1	shot	Martini Extra Dry vermouth

Comment: Vodka and chocolate made more interesting with a hint of vermouth.

CHOCOLATE MINT MARTINI

★★★★☆

Glass: Martini
Garnish: Chocolate powder rim
Method: STIR all ingredients with ice and strain into chilled glass.

2	shots	Ketel One Vodka
½	shot	Giffard Menthe Pastille liqueur
½	shot	White crème de cacao liqueur
½	shot	Martini Extra Dry vermouth

Comment: An after dinner sweety that tastes of chocolate mints.

CHOCOLATE PUFF

★★★★☆

Glass: Old-fashioned
Garnish: Crumbled Cadbury's Flake bar
Method: SHAKE all ingredients with ice and fine strain into chilled glass.

1	shot	Bacardi Carta Oro rum
1	shot	Dark crème de cacao liqueur
6	spoon	Natural yoghurt
2	twist	Fresh orange
¼	shot	Sugar syrup (2 sugar to 1 water)

Origin: Created by Wayne Collins in 2002 for Maxxium UK.
Comment: Smooth as you like. The orange is surprisingly evident.

CHOCOLATE SAZERAC

★★★★☆

Glass: Old-fashioned
Garnish: Lemon zest twist (discarded) & apple wedge
Method: Fill glass with ice, **POUR** in absinthe, top up with water and leave the mixture to stand in the glass. Separately **STIR** bourbon, cacao, sugar and bitters with ice. Finally discard contents of glass (absinthe, water and ice) and strain contents of shaker into empty absinthe-coated glass.

½	shot	Le Fée Parisienne absinthe
2	shots	Bourbon whiskey
½	shot	White crème de cacao liqueur
¼	shot	Sugar syrup (2 sugar to 1 water)
2	dash	Peychaud's aromatic bitters

Origin: Created in 2005 by Tonin Kacaj at Maze, London, England.
Comment: This twist on the classic Sazerac pairs absinthe, bourbon and chocolate to great effect.

CHOCOLATE SIDECAR

★★★★☆

Glass: Martini
Garnish: Chocolate powder rim
Method: SHAKE all ingredients with ice and fine strain into chilled glass.

1	shot	Martell VSOP Médaillon cognac
1	shot	Dark crème de cacao liqueur
1	shot	Tawny port
1	shot	Freshly squeezed lime juice
½	shot	Sugar syrup (2 sugar to 1 water)

Origin: Created in 2005 by Wayne Collins for Maxxium UK.

CHOCOLATE STINGER

★★★★☆

Glass: Old-fashioned
Garnish: Mint sprig
Method: STIR all ingredients with ice and strain into glass filled with crushed ice.

2	shots	Chocolate Spirit
¾	shot	Giffard Menthe Pastille liqueur

Origin: Adapted from a drink created in 2010 by Klaus St. Rainer at Schumann's Bar, Munich, Germany.
Comment: Chocolate and mint served frappé.

CHRISTMAS CHEER-RE (NEW)

★★★★⯪

Glass: Coupe
Garnish: Orange zest twist (discarded) & Luxardo Maraschino cherry
Method: STIR all ingredients with ice and strain into glass.

1 shot Rutte Old Simon oude jenever
1 shot Cherry Heering Liqueur
1 shot Antica Ricetta Barolo Chinato
½ shot Rutte Dry Gin
¼ shot Luxardo Maraschino liqueur
2 dash Angostura Orange Bitters

Origin: Created in December 2014 by yours truly and christened by Paloma Alos.
Comment: Jenever provides the yuletide spirit base, sweetened and flavoured by cherry liqueur, with Chinato drying and adding wine notes while gin adds freshness and botanical complexity. Maraschino and orange bitters complete this festive tipple.

CHRISTMAS MARGARITA

★★★½☆

Glass: Coupe
Garnish: Orange zest twist
Method: SHAKE all ingredients with ice and fine strain into chilled glass.

1½ shots   **Patrón reposado tequila**
1½ shots   **Cranberry juice**
½ shot   **Freshly squeezed lime juice**
½ shot   **Grand Marnier Cordon Rouge**

Origin: A Christmas cocktail created in October 2011 by yours truly at the Cabinet Room, London, England.
Comment: The Cosmopolitan meets the Margarita in this gloriously pink cocktail.

CHRISTMAS SPECIAL (NEW)

★★★★½

Glass: Old-fashioned
Garnish: Orange zest twist (discarded) and float half shelled walnut
Method: STIR all ingredients with ice and fine strain into ice-filled glass.

2   shots   **Martell VSOP Médaillon cognac**
½ shot   **Romate Pedro Ximénez sherry**
½ shot   **Mandarine Napoléon liqueur**
¼ shot   **Nocello walnut liqueur**

Origin: Created in December 2013 by yours truly and Paloma Alos at the Cabinet Room, London, England.
Comment: The perfect after dinner cocktail at any time of year but particularly appropriate over the festive period due to its ingredients – Romate Pedro Ximénez sherry tastes like Christmas pudding, mandarins are not just for Christmas and walnuts are best cracked whilst watching a Christmas special.

CHRISTMAS VELVET ALEXANDER

★★★★½

Glass: Coupe
Garnish: Orange zest twist (discard) and freshly grated nutmeg
Method: SHAKE all ingredients with ice and fine strain into chilled glass.

1½ shots   **Warninks Advocaat liqueur**
1½ shots   **Rutte Dry Gin**
¾ shot   **Romate Fino sherry**

Origin: A Christmas cocktail created in October 2011 by yours truly at the Cabinet Room, London, England.
Comment: Combining advocaat, gin and fino sherry, this is the ultimate stereotypical Christmas English granny's cocktail.

CHRYSANTHEMUM

★★★★☆

Glass: Martini
Garnish: Orange zest twist
Method: STIR all ingredients with ice and strain into chilled glass.

2   shots   **Martini Extra Dry vermouth**
1   shot   **Bénédictine D.O.M. liqueur**
⅛ shot   **Le Fée Parisienne absinthe**

Origin: In his 1930 'The Savoy Cocktail Book', Harry Craddock writes of this drink: 'Well-known and very popular in the American Bar of the S.S. Europa'.
Comment: Herbal and aromatic, this benefits from the dilution that comes with a good long stir.

CHUBACABRAS DAIQUIRI

★★★☆☆

Glass: Martini
Garnish: Luxardo Maraschino cherry
Method: SHAKE all ingredients with ice and fine-strain into chilled glass.

2   shots   **Bacardi Carta Blanca light rum**
¾ shot   **Freshly squeezed lime juice**
¼ shot   **Almond (orgeat) syrup**
⅛ shot   **Luxardo Maraschino liqueur**
⅛ shot   **Le Fée Parisienne absinthe**
⅛ shot   **Orange flower water**

Origin: Created in 2008 by Marcis Dzelzainis at Quo Vadis, London, England. The name literally translates as 'goat sucker' and is the name given to a mythical Latin American creature that is said to kill goats and other small animals to then suck the blood out of them. The first reported incidences occurred in Puerto Rico in 1995.
Comment: Absinthe, almond, maraschino and orange flower blossom water make for a highly flavoured daiquiri.

CHURCHILL MARTINI

★★★★☆

Glass: Martini
Garnish: Olive
Method: STIR gin with ice while glancing at an unopened bottle of dry vermouth. Strain into chilled glass.

2½ shots   **Rutte Dry Gin**

Origin: Legend has it that Sir Winston Churchill liked his Martinis served without the vermouth actually being added to the drink, just present in the same room.
Comment: Gin served chilled and neat, other than with a little dilution courtesy of melting ice. A great man but not necessarily a great drink.

CHUTES & LADDERS COCKTAIL (NEW)

★★★★½

Glass: Old-fashioned
Garnish: Orange zest twist (discarded)
Method: SHAKE all ingredients with ice and fine strain into ice-filled glass.

1¾ shots Patrón Silver tequila
1 shot Swedish Punch liqueur
1 shot Cocchi Americano Bianco
½ shot Freshly squeezed lime juice

Origin: Adapted from a drink created in 2014 by Frederic Yarm, Russell House Tavern, Cambridge, MA, USA.
Comment: Citrusy tequila-led with Swedish punch and Cocchi Americano rounding and adding their distinctive flavours.

CICADA COCKTAIL

★★★⯪☆

Glass: Martini
Garnish: Dust with grated nutmeg
Method: SHAKE all ingredients with ice and fine strain into chilled glass.

2	shots	Bourbon whiskey
1	shot	Disaronno Originale amaretto
½	shot	Single cream / half-and-half
¾	shot	Sugar syrup (2 sugar to 1 water)

Origin: Those familiar with the Grasshopper cocktail (named for its green colour) will understand why this one is called the Cicada (they're a bit browner).
Comment: Smoothed whiskey with more than a hint of almond.

CIDER APPLE COCKTAIL

★★★★☆

Glass: Martini
Garnish: Apple wedge
Method: SHAKE all ingredients with ice & fine strain into chilled glass.

1½	shots	Calvados brandy
¾	shot	Apple Schnapps liqueur
¾	shot	Freshly squeezed lemon juice
1	shot	Pressed apple juice
¼	shot	Sugar syrup (2 sugar to 1 water)

Origin: Created in 1998 by Jamie Terrell at Lab, London, England.
Comment: As the name suggests, rich cider flavours with a sharp finish.

CIDER APPLE COOLER

★★★★☆

Glass: Collins
Garnish: None
Method: SHAKE all ingredients with ice and strain into ice-filled glass.

2	shots	Calvados brandy
1	shot	Apple Schnapps liqueur
4½	shots	Pressed apple juice

Comment: Not unlike the taste of strong dry cider.

CIDER HOUSE RULES

★★★★☆

Glass: Old-fashioned
Garnish: Apple wedge
Method: SHAKE all ingredients with ice & fine strain into ice-filled glass.

2	shots	Patrón reposado tequila
1½	shots	Pressed apple juice
½	shot	Freshly squeezed lemon juice
¼	shot	Agave syrup
½	spoon	Ground cinnamon

Origin: Created by New York-based Brian Van Flandern, of Creative Cocktail Consultants Corp and named after the double Academy Award winning 1999 film and 1985 novel by John Irving of the same name.
Comment: Margarita-style drink with tequila, lemon and apple juice.

CINDERELLA (MOCKTAIL)

★★⯪☆☆

Glass: Collins
Garnish: Lemon slice
Method: SHAKE first 5 ingredients with ice & strain into ice-filled glass.
TOP with soda water.

2	shots	Freshly squeezed orange juice
1½	shots	Fresh pressed pineapple juice
¾	shot	Freshly squeezed lemon juice
⅛	shot	Pomegranate / grenadine syrup (2:1)
3	dash	Angostura Aromatic Bitters
Top with		Soda (club soda)

Comment: Long, fresh and fruity.

CITRUS CAIPIROVSKA

★★★★☆

Glass: Old-fashioned
Garnish: None
Method: MUDDLE lemon in base of glass. Add other ingredients and fill glass with crushed ice. **CHURN** drink with bar spoon and serve with short straws.

¾	fresh	Lemon
2	shots	Ketel One Citroen vodka
¾	shot	Sugar syrup (2 sugar to 1 water)

Comment: Superbly refreshing balance of sweet and citrus sourness.

CITRUS MARTINI

★★★★☆

Glass: Martini
Garnish: Orange zest twist
Method: SHAKE all ingredients with ice & fine strain into chilled glass.

1½	shots	Ketel One Citroen vodka
¼	shot	De Kuyper Triple Sec
1	shot	Freshly squeezed lemon juice
¼	shot	Sugar syrup (2 sugar to 1 water)
3	dash	Angostura Orange Bitters

Origin: Created by Dick Bradsell at Fred's, London, England, in the late 80s.
Comment: Orange undertones add citrus depth to the lemon explosion.

CITRUS RUM COOLER

★★★★☆

Glass: Collins
Garnish: Orange slice
Method: SHAKE first three ingredients with ice and strain into ice-filled glass. **TOP** with lemonade. Lightly stir and serve with straws.

1	shot	Bacardi Carta Blanca light rum
½	shot	Grand Marnier Cordon Rouge
2	shots	Freshly squeezed orange juice
Top with		Lemonade/Sprite/7-Up

Comment: Light, fruity, easy and very refreshing.

CLAIRVOYANT

★★★★☆

Glass: Martini
Garnish: Orange zest twist
Method: STIR all ingredients with ice & fine strain into chilled glass.

1½ shots	Romate Fino sherry
1½ shots	Martini Extra Dry vermouth
¾ shot	Hazelnut liqueur
1 dash	Angostura Orange Bitters

Origin: Created in 2008 by yours truly in Jerez, Spain and named after Claire Hu, a fellow drinks hack on the same trip who was a fan of hazelnut liqueur.
Comment: A hazelnut flavoured variation on the classic Coronation Cocktail.

CLARA ASTIÉ COCKTAIL

★★★★☆

Glass: Martini
Garnish: Grapefruit zest twist (discarded) & dried apricot
Method: STIR jam with rum until jam dissolves. Add other ingredients, SHAKE with ice and fine strain into chilled glass.

2 shots	Bacardi Carta Blanca light rum
1 spoon	Apricot jam (preserve)
1 shot	Martini Extra Dry vermouth
⅛ shot	Luxardo Maraschino liqueur
1 dash	Grapefruit bitters
½ shot	Chilled water (omit if wet ice)

Origin: Adapted from a drink created in 2008 by Ian McLaren of Bacardi. The name is in tribute to Doña Amalia's Godmother whose bequest revived the fortunes of Don Facundo Bacardi Massó allowing him to establish the rum brand we know today.
Comment: Tangy apricot with hints of maraschino dried by vermouth and fortified by light rum.

CLARET COBBLER

★★★★☆

Glass: Goblet
Garnish: Mint sprig
Method: SHAKE all ingredients with ice & fine strain into glass filled with crushed ice. Serve with straws.

1½ shots	Martell VSOP Médaillon cognac
1 shot	Grand Marnier Cordon Rouge
2½ shots	Shiraz red wine

Origin: My version of a classic Cobbler.
Comment: Fortified and slightly sweetened wine cooled and lengthened by ice.

CLARIDGE COCKTAIL ⚿

★★★★☆

Glass: Martini
Garnish: Lemon zest twist
Method: SHAKE all ingredients with ice & fine strain into chilled glass.

1½ shots	Rutte Dry Gin
1½ shots	Martini Extra Dry vermouth
½ shot	De Kuyper Triple Sec
½ shot	De Kuyper XO Apricot Brandy

Origin: Adapted from Harry Craddock's 1930 'The Savoy Cocktail Book'
Comment: Gin for strength, vermouth for dryness and liqueur to sweeten - an interesting combination.

CLASSIC COCKTAIL

★★★★⯪

Glass: Martini
Garnish: Lemon zest twist (& optional sugar rim)
Method: SHAKE all ingredients with ice and fine strain into chilled glass.

2 shots	Martell VSOP Médaillon cognac
½ shot	Grand Marnier Cordon Rouge
½ shot	Luxardo Maraschino liqueur
½ shot	Freshly squeezed lemon juice
½ shot	Chilled water (omit if wet ice)

Origin: Adapted form Harry Craddock's 1930 'The Savoy Cocktail Book'
Comment: Reminiscent of a Sidecar with Maraschino.

CLAUDINE COCKTAIL (NEW)

★★★★⯪

Glass: Coupe
Garnish: Orange zest twist
Method: STIR all ingredients with ice and strain into chilled glass.

1⅓ shots	Armagnac brandy
⅓ shot	Martini Extra Dry vermouth
⅓ shot	Martini Rosso vermouth
⅓ shot	Byrrh Grand Quinquina
1 dash	Angostura Orange Bitters

Origin: Created in 2015 by Matteo Malisan at 69 Colebrooke Row, London, England.
Comment: Dry and aromatic, the combination of Byrrh and armagnac reveals interesting favours of dried apricot and chocolate.

CLEMENTINE

★★★☆☆

Glass: Shot
Garnish: Sugar coated orange wedge
Method: Refrigerate ingredients then LAYER in chilled glass by carefully pouring in the following order. Instruct drinker to down in one and bite into the wedge.

| ½ shot | Pallini Limoncello |
| ½ shot | Mandarine Napoléon liqueur |

Comment: Short, sweet and very fruity

CLIPPER COCKTAIL ⚿

★★★⯪☆

Glass: Martini
Garnish: Lemon zest twist
Method: SHAKE all ingredients and fine strain into glass filled with crushed ice.

2 shots	Bacardi Carta Blanca light rum
2 shots	Martini Extra Dry vermouth
½ shot	Pomegranate / grenadine syrup (2:1)

Origin: Peggy Guggenheim's biography mentions that this cocktail was served during the 1940s on the Boeing flying boats known as Clippers.
Comment: Light, easy drinking and very refreshing.

CLOCKWORK ORANGE

★★★½☆

Glass: Collins
Garnish: Orange slice
Method: SHAKE all ingredients with ice and strain into ice-filled glass.

1½ shots   **Martell VSOP Médaillon cognac**
1½ shots   **Grand Marnier Cordon Rouge**
3   shots   **Freshly squeezed orange juice**

Comment: Neither as memorable nor as controversial as the film but a pleasant orange drink all the same.

CLOSING ARGUMENT (NEW)

★★★★½

Glass: Coupe
Garnish: Lime zest twist
Method: SHAKE all ingredients with ice and strain into chilled glass.

¾   shot   **Del Maguey VIDA mezcal**
¾   shot   **Green Chartreuse liqueur**
¾   shot   **Luxardo Maraschino liqueur**
¾   shot   **Freshly squeezed lime juice**

Comment: A mezcal-based Last Word. It works! End of argument.

CLOUD 9 (NEW)

★★★★☆

Glass: Coupe
Garnish: Lemon zest peel
Method: STIR all ingredients with ice and strain into chilled glass.

2   shots   **Patrón silver tequila**
¾   shot   **Lillet Blanc**
½   shot   **Suze Saveur d'Autrefois**
½   shot   **Chilled water** (omit if wet ice)

Origin: Adapted from a recipe by Jeremy Oertel, Mayahuel, New York City, USA.
Comment: A trio of big flavours (tequila, Lillet Blanc and gentian liqueur) come together harmoniously.

CLOVER CLUB (HOUSE-MADE)

★★★★½

Glass: Martini
Garnish: Lemon zest twist
Method: SHAKE all ingredients with ice and fine strain into chilled glass.

1½ shots   **Rutte Dry Gin**
1½ spoon   **Raspberry syrup (1 juice to 1 sugar)**
½   shot   **Martini Extra Dry vermouth**
¾   shot   **Freshly squeezed lemon juice**

Origin: Created by Julie Reiner at Clover Club, New York City, USA.
Comment: Fruity, light, well-balanced and easy-drinking.

CLOVER CLUB COCKTAIL NO.3 (DIFFORD'S RECIPE)

★★★★½

Glass: Martini
Garnish: Lemon zest twist (sprayed & discarded)
Method: SHAKE all ingredients with ice and fine strain into chilled glass.

5   fresh   **Raspberries**
1¾ shots   **Rutte Dry Gin**
¼   shot   **Martini Extra Dry vermouth**
¼   shot   **Martini Rosso vermouth**
¼   shot   **Freshly squeezed lemon juice**
¼   shot   **Sugar syrup (2 sugar to 1 water)**
½   fresh   **Egg white**

Origin: Version of a vintage classic by yours truly at the Cabinet Room, London, England.
Comment: Creamy and easy – with notes of raspberry, gin, citrus and delicate spice.

CLOVER CLUB COCKTAIL NO.3 (LOWE'S RECIPE)

★★★★½

Glass: Martini
Garnish: None
Method: SHAKE all ingredients with ice and fine strain into chilled glass.

1   shot   **Rutte Dry Gin**
1   shot   **Martini Extra Dry vermouth**
1   shot   **Freshly squeezed lemon juice**
1   shot   **Raspberry syrup (1 juice to 1 sugar)**
½   fresh   **Egg white**

Origin: Recipe from '1909 Drinks - How to Mix and Serve, by Paul E. Lowe' and courtesy of Dave Wondrich who says this is the earliest Clover Club recipe he has discovered.
Lowe omits the lemon juice in his original recipe but this is thought to be a mistake. Albert Stevens Crockett credits the creation of this cocktail to the Bellevue-Stratford Hotel, Philadelphia in his 1931 'Old Waldorf Bar Days'.
Comment: Balanced and complex with a fruity blast of raspberry - made interesting due to its inclusion of vermouth.

CLOVER LEAF COCKTAIL NO.1 (CLASSIC FORMULA)

★★★★☆

Glass: Martini
Garnish: Mint leaf
Method: SHAKE all ingredients with ice & fine strain into chilled glass.

2   shots   **Rutte Dry Gin**
½   shot   **Freshly squeezed lemon juice**
¼   shot   **Pomegranate / grenadine syrup (2:1)**
½   fresh   **Egg white**

Comment: Smooth, aromatic, fruity and medium sweet.

CLOVER LEAF MARTINI NO.2 (MODERN FORMULA)

★★★★½☆

Glass: Martini
Garnish: Mint leaf
Method: MUDDLE raspberries in base of shaker. Add other ingredients, SHAKE with ice and fine strain into chilled glass.

7   fresh   **Raspberries**
3   fresh   **Mint leaves**
2   shots   **Rutte Dry Gin**
¾   shot   **Freshly squeezed lemon juice**
½   shot   **Pomegranate / grenadine syrup (2:1)**
½   fresh   **Egg white**

Comment: Carpet scaring red, this fruity adaptation perhaps has a wider appeal than the original Clover Leaf.

CLOYSTERS

★★★★☆

Glass: Martini
Garnish: Grapefruit zest twist
Method: SHAKE all ingredients with ice & fine strain into chilled glass.

- 2 shots **Rutte Dry Gin**
- ½ shot **Yellow Chartreuse liqueur**
- ½ shot **Freshly squeezed pink grapefruit juice**
- ¼ shot **Freshly squeezed lemon juice**
- ⅛ shot **Sugar syrup (2 sugar to 1 water)**
- ¼ shot **Chilled water** (omit if wet ice)

Origin: Adapted from a drink created in 2007 by John Deragon at PDT, New York City, USA.
Comment: There's a suitable subtle monastic influence to this complex, gin based, most learned of cocktails.

CLUB COCKTAIL (BUTT'S RECIPE)

★★★★☆

Glass: Martini
Garnish: Luxardo Maraschino cherry
Method: STIR all ingredients with ice & fine strain into chilled glass.

- 2 shots **Bacardi Carta Oro rum**
- ½ shot **Martini Rosso vermouth**
- ½ shot **Martini Extra Dry vermouth**
- ½ shot **Maraschino syrup (from cherry jar)**
- 3 dash **Angostura Aromatic Bitters**
- ¾ shot **Chilled water** (omit if wet ice)

Origin: Adapted from a drink created in 2002 by Michael Butt at Milk & Honey, London, England.
Comment: An aromatic, spirited, classical cocktail.

CLUB COCKTAIL (CRADDOCK'S RECIPE)

★★★★☆

Glass: Martini
Garnish: Chilled olive on stick
Method: SHAKE all ingredients with ice & strain into chilled glass.

- 2 shots **Rutte Dry Gin**
- 1 shot **Martini Rosso vermouth**
- ⅛ shot **Yellow Chartreuse liqueur**

Origin: Adapted form Harry Craddock's 1930 'The Savoy Cocktail Book'.
Comment: A sweet Martini with a hint of Chartreuse.

CLUB COCKTAIL (DIFFORD'S RECIPE) (NEW)

★★★★½

Glass: Coupe
Garnish: Pineapple wedge & Luxardo maraschino cherry
Method: SHAKE all ingredients with ice and fine strain into chilled glass.

- 2 shots **Martell VSOP Médaillon cognac**
- ¼ shot **BarSol Mosto Verde Italia pisco**
- ½ shot **Luxardo Maraschino liqueur**
- ¾ shot **Fresh pressed pineapple juice**
- 2 dash **Peychaud's aromatic bitters**

Origin: I yours truly have simply added a splash of pisco to the classic Club Cocktail which first appeared in W.C. Whitfield's 1939 'Just Cocktails' book.
Comment: Cognac and pisco brandies with maraschino and pineapple adding fruity tropical freshness and a foamy head.

CLUB COCKTAIL (EMBURY'S RECIPE)

★★★★☆

Glass: Martini
Garnish: Orange zest twist
Method: STIR all ingredients with ice and strain into chilled glass.

- 1½ shots **Romate Fino sherry**
- 1½ shots **Tawny port**
- 1 dash **Angostura Orange Bitters**

Origin: In his 1948 'The Fine Art of Mixing Drinks', David A. Embury writes, "Perhaps it would not be too much of an exaggeration to say there are as many Club Cocktails as there are clubs." This example is adapted from the same book.
Comment: Dry and incredibly aromatic. A perfect aperitif.

CLUB COCKTAIL (WHITFIELD'S RECIPE) (NEW)

★★★★½

Glass: Coupe
Garnish: Pineapple wedge & Luxardo maraschino cherry
Method: SHAKE all ingredients with ice and fine strain into chilled glass.

2 shots Martell VSOP Médaillon cognac
½ shot Luxardo Maraschino liqueur
½ shot Fresh pressed pineapple juice
2 dash Peychaud's aromatic bitters

Origin: The Club Cocktail first appeared in W.C. Whitfield's 1939 'Just Cocktails' book (although does not appear in his 1941 Here's How Mixed Drinks by the same Three Mountaineers Inc. publishers).
Comment: Pineapple juice adds fruity tropical freshness and a foamy head, this is fortified with cognac and aromatised with a splash of maraschino cherry liqueur and a couple of dashes of New Orleans bitters.

CLUBLAND COCKTAIL

★★★★☆

Glass: Coupe
Garnish: Orange zest twist
Method: STIR all ingredients with ice & fine strain into chilled glass.

- 1½ shots **Ketel One Vodka**
- 1½ shots **Dry white port**
- 1 dash **Angostura Aromatic Bitters**

Origin: In W.J. Tarling's (Bill Tarling) 1937 'Café Royal Cocktail Book Coronation Edition', the creation of this drink is credited to one A. Mackintosh. Originally made with a brand of port called Clubland, hence this drink's name.
Comment: Go easy on the bitters and this is a complex and rewarding Martini-style drink.

COBBLE HILL

★★★★☆

Glass: Coupe
Garnish: Lemon zest twist (discarded) & cucumber slice
Method: **MUDDLE** cucumber in base of stirring glass. Add other ingredients, **STIR** with ice and fine strain into chilled glass.

2 slice English cucumber peeled
2 shots Straight rye whiskey
½ shot Martini Extra Dry vermouth
½ shot Amaro liqueur

Origin: Created in 2009 by Sam Ross at Milk & Honey, New York City, USA.
Comment: Sam describes this drink as "a summertime Manhattan." It is.

COBBLED RASPBERRY COCKTAIL

★★★★☆

Glass: Martini
Garnish: 3 raspberries on stick
Method: **SHAKE** all ingredients with ice and fine strain into chilled glass.

2	shots	**Ketel One Vodka**
¾	shot	**Shiraz red wine**
¼	shot	**Lejay Crème de Framboise liqueur**
8	fresh	**Raspberries**
⅓	shot	**Sugar syrup (2 sugar to 1 water)**

Origin: Created in 2004 by yours truly, London, England.
Comment: A simple 1990s Raspberry 'Martini' with a splash of wine.

COBBLERS

★★★★☆

Glass: Goblet
Garnish: Mint sprig
Method: **SHAKE** all ingredients with ice and fine strain into glass filled with crushed ice. Serve with straws.

1½	shots	**Martell VSOP Médaillon cognac**
1	shot	**Grand Marnier Cordon Rouge**
2½	shots	**Shiraz red wine**

Origin: Cobblers emerged in the mid 1800s and circa 1880 the bartender Harry Johnson said of the Sherry Cobbler 'This drink is without doubt the most popular beverage in this country, with ladies as well as with gentlemen. It is a very refreshing drink for old and young.'

Cobblers are served with straws in a goblet filled with crushed ice and decorated with fruit and a sprig or two of mint. They are based on spirits and/or wine sweetened with sugar syrup or sweet liqueur. Classically Cobblers contain little or no citrus but modern variations often call for citrus and other fruits to be muddled. We believe it's the lack of citrus that sets Cobblers apart. The best examples of these use the tannin and acidity in the wine to bitter and so balance the drink.

Cobblers are also classically built in the glass. We prefer to shake ours to properly cool and mix them before straining over fresh crushed ice and stirring.

Interestingly, this drink is often cited for heralding in the paper straw which wasn't patented until 1888. Prior to that straws were just that, 'straw', usually rye, or even hollow pasta (macaroni or vermicelli).
Comment: Fortified and slightly sweetened wine cooled and lengthened by ice.

COCO CABANA

★★★½☆

Glass: Martini
Garnish: Pineapple wedge
Method: **SHAKE** all ingredients with ice and fine strain into chilled glass.

½	shot	**Midori Green Melon liqueur**
1½	shots	**Coconut rum liqueur**
2	shots	**Fresh pressed pineapple juice**
¾	shot	**Milk**
¾	shot	**Single cream / half-and-half**

Comment: A sweet, creamy tropical number for Barry Manilow fans.

COCO MILKY WAY COCKTAIL (NEW)

★★★★☆

Glass: Collins
Garnish: Lemon zest & slice of Milky Way chocolate bar
Method: **BLEND** all ingredients with 6oz scoop of crushed ice and pour into glass.

1½	shots	**Capucana cachaça**
⅔	shot	**Fresh pressed pineapple juice**
⅓	shot	**Disaronno Originale amaretto**
⅓	shot	**Hazelnut liqueur**
⅓	shot	**Coconut syrup**
⅓	shot	**Freshly squeezed lemon juice**
⅔	shot	**Single cream / half-and-half**

Origin: Created in 2015 by Daniel Sampere at One Ocean Club, Barcelona, Spain.
Comment: Cachaça laced pineapple, coconut and cream with hints of almond and hazelnut.

COCONUT DAIQUIRI

★★★★☆

Glass: Martini
Garnish: Lime wedge
Method: **SHAKE** all ingredients with ice & fine strain into chilled glass.

2	shots	**Bacardi Carta Blanca light rum**
1	shot	**Coconut rum liqueur**
½	shot	**Freshly squeezed lime juice**
½	shot	**Coconut syrup**
¾	scoop	**Chilled water** (omit if wet ice)

Comment: Classic Daiquiri flavour with a pleasing tropical touch.

COCONUT WATER

★★★★☆

Glass: Coupe
Garnish: None
Method: STIR all ingredients with ice and fine strain into chilled glass.

1 shot **Ketel One Vodka**
2¼ shots **Coconut rum liqueur**
⅛ shot **Coconut syrup**
1¼ shots **Chilled water** (reduce if wet ice)

Origin: Created in 2003 by yours truly, London, England.
Comment: Have you ever drunk from a fresh coconut in the Caribbean? Well, this is London's alcoholic equivalent.

COESSENTIAL

★★★★½

Glass: Coupe
Garnish: Float mint leaf
Method: SHAKE all ingredients with ice and fine strain into chilled glass.

8 fresh Mint leaves
2 shots Ketel One Vodka
½ shot White crème de cacao liqueur
⅛ shot Le Fée Parisienne absinthe

Origin: Created in 2011 by yours truly at the Cabinet Room, London, England.
Comment: To quote from the Oxford English Dictionary, "This is done with the help of the hands of conciousness that extend from the spiritual heart and are coessential to it". It is and John Coe did. Thanks again John, this delicate but aromatic drink is dedicated to you.

COFFEE & VANILLA DAIQUIRI

★★★★☆

Glass: Coupe
Garnish: Coffee beans
Method: SHAKE all ingredients with ice & fine strain into chilled glass.

2 shots **Bacardi Carta Blanca light rum** (vanilla infused)
1 shot **Coffee liqueur**
½ shot **Freshly squeezed lime juice**
⅛ shot **Sugar syrup (2 sugar to 1 water)**
¾ shot **Chilled water** (omit if wet ice)

Origin: Created in 2002 by yours truly, London, England.
Comment: Coffee, vanilla, sweetness and sourness all in harmony.

COFFEE BATIDA

★★★☆☆

Glass: Old-fashioned
Garnish: Coffee beans
Method: BLEND all ingredients with crushed ice and serve with straws

2 shots **Capucana cachaça**
1 shot **Coffee liqueur**
1 shot **Espresso coffee (freshly made & hot)**
½ shot **Sugar syrup (2 sugar to 1 water)**

Comment: Fortunately this caffeine and cachaça laced cocktail tastes a good deal better than it looks.

COFFEE COCKTAIL

★★★★½

Glass: Wine
Garnish: Dust with freshly grated nutmeg
Method: SHAKE all ingredients with ice and fine strain into chilled glass.

2 shots **Tawny port**
1 shot **Martell VSOP Médaillon cognac**
½ shot **Sugar syrup (2 sugar to 1 water)**
1 fresh **Eggs (white & yolk)**

Origin: Recipe adapted from Jerry 'The Professor' Thomas' 1887 'The Bar-tender's Guide'.
Comment: As the anonymous writer of the 1887 edition of the Professor's book comments, "The name of this drink is a misnomer, as coffee and bitters are not to be found among its ingredients, but it looks like coffee when it has been properly concocted."

COGNAC JULEP

★★★★★

Glass: Julep Tin
Garnish: Mint sprig
Method: SHAKE all ingredients with ice and fine strain into julep cup half filled with crushed ice. **CHURN** (stir) the drink with the crushed ice using a bar spoon. Top up the cup with more crushed ice and **CHURN** again. Repeat this process until the drink fills the cup and serve.

12 fresh Mint leaves
2½ shots Martell VSOP Médaillon cognac
⅔ shot Sugar syrup (2 sugar to 1 water)

Origin: Although bourbon is now most commonly associated with the Julep it is probable that it was first made with cognac.
Comment: A deliciously refreshing cocktail. Woody rancio notes in the cognac are freshened by the mint. Those with a dry palate may want to reduce the sugar a touch.

COLA DE MONO

★★★★☆

Glass: Martini
Garnish: Dust with cinnamon powder
Method: MUDDLE cinnamon stick and pisco in base of shaker. Add other ingredients, **SHAKE** with ice and fine strain into a chilled glass.

1 inch   Cinnamon stick
2 shots BarSol Mosto Verde Italia pisco
1 shot   Espresso coffee (freshly made & hot)
1 shot   Coffee liqueur

Origin: Created by yours truly and based on a Chilean drink traditionally consumed at Christmas, the name of which literally translates as 'Tail of Monkey'. The original uses milk and sugar instead of coffee liqueur.
Comment: Coffee and cinnamon - a drink to be savoured after diner.

COLD BLOODED

★★★☆☆

Glass: Old-fashioned
Garnish: Rosemary sprig
Method: MUDDLE rosemary in base of shaker. Add other ingredients, **SHAKE** with ice & fine strain into ice-filled glass.

1 fresh Rosemary sprig
1½ shots Grand Marnier Cordon Rouge
2 shots Cranberry juice
½ shot Freshly squeezed lemon juice
½ shot Sugar syrup (2 sugar to 1 water)

Origin: Adapted from a drink discovered in 2008 on Steve Olson's akawinegeek.com site.
Comment: Red berry, orange and pine.

COLD COMFORT

★★★★☆

Glass: Old-fashioned
Garnish: None
Method: SHAKE all ingredients with ice and strain into ice-filled glass.

2 shots White overproof rum
6 spoon Runny honey
1 shot   Freshly squeezed lime juice

Origin: Discovered in Jamaica in 2001.
Comment: Take at the first sign of a cold, and then retreat under your bed covers. Repeat dose regularly while symptoms persist. Warning - do not consume with other forms of medication.

COLD WHISKY PUNCH (NEW)

★★★★☆

Glass: Old-fashioned
Garnish: Lemon zest twist & seasonal berries
Method: SPRAY lemon zest twists into shaker and drop in. Add other ingredients, **SHAKE** with ice and strain into ice-filled glass.

2 slice Lemon zest
2 shots Dewar's 12yo Scotch whisky
½ shot Freshly squeezed lemon juice
⅓ shot Sugar syrup (2 sugar to 1 water)
1½ shots Chilled water

Origin: The godfather of bartending, Jerry Thomas, offered both a hot and cold version of his Scotch Whisky Punch in his 1862 Bartender's Guide and it is in the cold form that the drink has survived. Modernity dictated that we streamline the recipe and ingredients which originally called for boiling water and an extended chilling period.
Comment: A balanced – not sweet, nor sour or strong – refreshing short whisky cocktail.

COLD WINTER WARMER SOUR

★★★★☆

Glass: Old-fashioned
Garnish: Lemon zest twist (discarded), orange slice & Luxardo Maraschino cherry on stick (sail)
Method: STIR honey with vodka in base of shaker until honey dissolves. Add other ingredients, **SHAKE** with ice and strain back into shaker. **DRY SHAKE** (without ice) and strain into ice-filled glass.

1 spoon Runny honey
1 shot Ketel One Citroen vodka
½ shot Bénédictine D.O.M. liqueur
1 shot Freshly squeezed lemon juice
½ fresh Egg white

Origin: Created in 2006 by yours truly, London, England.
Comment: Flavours reminiscent of a hot toddy but served in a cold sour.

COLLAR & CUFF

★★★★☆

Glass: Toddy
Garnish: Lemon slice
Method: PLACE bar spoon in glass, add ingredients & **STIR.**

2 spoon Runny honey
1 shot Dewar's 12yo Scotch whisky
1 shot King's Ginger Liqueur
1 shot Freshly squeezed lemon juice
Top with Boiling water

Origin: Created in 2003 by yours truly, London, England.
Comment: A ginger infused riff on a toddy.

COLLETTI ROYALE (NEW)

★★★★☆

Glass: Wine
Garnish: Dehydrated blood orange wheel
Method: SHAKE first 6 ingredients with ice and strain into ice-filled glass. **TOP** with Champagne.

1½ shots Patrón reposado tequila
½ shot De Kuyper Triple Sec
½ shot St-Germain elderflower liqueur
½ shot Blood orange juice
½ shot Freshly squeezed lime juice
2 dash Angostura Orange Bitters
1 shot G.H. Mumm Brut Rosé Champagne

Origin: Adapted from a Valentine's drink created in 2013 by Julie Reiner in New York City, USA.
Comment: Sweet and sour and very fruity - like a good Valentine's date.

Collins Cocktail

A Collins is basically a sour cocktail made using a base spirit (most usually gin), lemon juice, sugar and carbonated water, served long over ice in the glass named after it. Collins glasses are tall and round and usually have a capacity of 12 to 16 ounces to their brim.

In his 1948 'Fine Art of Mixing Drinks', David A. Embury, describes the Collins as being "a lemonade made with charged water and spiked with gin or some other liquor." He goes on to say, "Originally there were two brothers only in the Collins family - Tom and John. During recent years, however, numerous cousins have appeared on the scene - Pedro, Pierre, Sandy, Mike, Jack, the Colonel and several others whose first names have not yet been officially recorded in the baptismal registry."

Dutch Collins (with genever/jenever/Hollands)
Captain Collins (with Canadian whisky)
Colonel Collins (with bourbon whiskey)
Jack Collins (with vodka)
Jock or Sandy Collins (with Scotch whisky)
Joe Collins (with vodka)
John Collins (with London dry gin)
Mike Collins (with Irish whiskey)
Pedro Collins (with light white rum)
Pepito Collins (with tequila)
Pierre Collins (with cognac/brandy)
Tom Collins (with old tom gin or London dry gin but ideally old tom)
Vodka Collins (AKA Joe Collins)

Embury explains the confusion/difference between a Tom and John Collins, "The original Collinses were always made with gin but, strangely enough, never with London dry gin - the very liquor that is practically always used in making a Collins today. The Tom Collins was made with Old Tom gin and the John Collins with Holland gin [genever]."

"The adoption of London dry gin as a Collins base gave rise to two schools of nomenclature. With one school it was simply substituted for Old Tom gin in the Tom Collins. The other school, however, preferred to retain the Tom Collins name for the original drink made with Old Tom gin and, since Holland gin was practically never used any more in a Collins, they transferred the John Collins to the Collins made with London dry gin. This accounts for the confusion that exists in present-day books of recipes. In some the Tom recipe calls for Old Tom gin and the John recipe for dry gin, in others the Tom recipe calls for dry gin and the John recipe for Holland gin. Actually, of course, Old Tom gin is merely a sweetened London gin. Consequently, we can make our Tom Collins with either Old Tom or London dry gin, but, if Old Tom gin is used the quantity of sugar should be reduced by about a half."

The creation of the Collins is credited to John Collins, a bartender who worked at Limmer's Hotel, Conduit Street, London. The 'coffee house' of Limmer's Hotel was a true dive bar, popular with sporting types during the 19th century, and famous, according to the 1860s memoirs of a Captain Gronow (a Victorian writer of four observational tomes) for its Gin Punch as early as 1814.

It would appear that the Collins morphed from the Gin Punch, a very popular drink of the day. Whether or not John (or possibly Jim) Collins, head waiter of Limmer's was responsible for first creating/naming the Tom Collins will never be known but he is immortalised in a limerick written by Frank and Charles Sheridan about John Collins:

My name is John Collins, head waiter at Limmer's,
Corner of Conduit Street, Hanover Square,
My chief occupation is filling brimmers
For all the young gentlemen frequenters there.
Mr. Frank always drinks my gin punch when he smokes.

It could be that the special gin-punch for which John Collins of Limmer's was famous went on to become known as the Tom Collins when it was made using Old Tom gin.

An alternative story attributes the drink's creation to a Mr Collins who started work at a New York tavern called the Whitehouse in 1873 and made thirst quenching gin drinks. Another story identifies a different Tom Collins, who worked as a bartender in New Jersey and New York City. There are apparently also versions attributing its creation to San Francisco and Australia, and it is not impossible that the drink evolved in two or more places independently.

Others say that the Tom Collins originated in New York, and takes its name from the Great Tom Collins Hoax which took the city by storm in 1874. This practical joke involved telling a friend that a man named Tom Collins had been insulting them, and that he could be found in a bar some distance away. However, a recipe for the Tom Collins appears in the Steward and Barkeeper's Manual of 1869 so proving the 'Hoax' to be exactly that. So what evidence there is suggests that the Collins was an adaptation of the long popular Gin Punch and that it could well have been created by John Collins at Limmer's.

The original Collins was probably based on genever, then old tom gin and finally London dry gin as fashion changed the style of gin available in London and New York. Each juniper spirit produces a differently styled Collins - all good, though my own preference is for an oude jenever.

COLLINS

★★★★½

Glass: Collins
Garnish: Orange slice & Luxardo Maraschino cherry on stick (sail)
Method: SHAKE first 3 ingredients with ice & strain into ice-filled glass. **TOP** with soda, stir and serve with straws.

2	shots	Rutte Old Simon oude jenever
1	shot	Freshly squeezed lemon juice
½	shot	Sugar syrup (2 sugar to 1 water)
Top with		Soda (club soda)

Comment: Some say the John/Tom Collins was originally made with jenever. So is this the original or an adaptation on the Tom Collins? We will probably never know, but it tastes great.

COLONEL COLLINS

★★★★☆

Glass: Collins
Garnish: Orange slice & cherry on stick (sail)
Method: SHAKE first three ingredients with ice and strain into ice-filled glass. TOP with soda, stir and serve with straws.

2	shots	Bourbon whiskey
1	shot	Freshly squeezed lemon juice
½	shot	Sugar syrup (2 sugar to 1 water)
Top with		Soda (club soda)

Origin: Sweetened, soured and diluted bourbon.
Comment: Classic Collins variation.

COLONEL T

★★★★☆

Glass: Sling
Garnish: Pineapple leaf
Method: SHAKE all ingredients with ice and strain into ice-filled glass.

2	shots	Bourbon whiskey
1	shot	De Kuyper XO Apricot Brandy
2½	shots	Fresh pressed pineapple juice

Comment: Mellow and long with pineapple, apricot and bourbon.

COLONEL'S BIG OPU

★★★★☆

Glass: Collins
Garnish: Orange slice & cherry on stick (sail)
Method: SHAKE first 3 ingredients with ice and strain into ice-filled glass. TOP with champagne and serve with straws.

1 shot Rutte Dry Gin
1 shot De Kuyper Triple Sec
½ shot Freshly squeezed lime juice
Top with G.H. Mumm Cordon Rouge Champagne
1 dash Angostura Orange Bitters

Origin: Adapted from Victor J. Bergeron's and taken from his 'Trader Vic's Bartender's Guide' (1972 revised edition), where he writes "This is one of our old drinks. The colonel's big opu: the colonel's big belly."
Comment: A long, fruity yet dry drink charged with champagne.

THE COLONIAL COOLER

★★★★☆

Glass: Collins
Garnish: Mint sprig and pineapple wedge
Method: STIR first 5 ingredients with ice and strain into ice-filled glass. TOP up with soda.

1½ shots Rutte Dry Gin
1½ shots Martini Rosso vermouth
⅛ shot Grand Marnier Cordon Rouge
⅛ shot Amer Picon
1 dash Angostura Aromatic Bitters
Top with Soda (club soda)

Origin: This recipe is adapted from Charles H. Baker's 1939 'The Gentlemen's Companion' in which Baker explains that he encountered this drink in mid-1920's at the Sandakan Club, North Borneo, during an excursion from the SS Reolute, a round-the-world steamer.

The steamer anchored some 14 miles off shore and Baker and his companions set ashore in two lifeboats, both of which failed to make dry land due to engine trouble. A Borneo prahu "with a sail like a striped butterfly and a gent in a G-string and a headdress" raised the alarm and the adventurers were eventually towed ashore by a British North Borneo Company tug.

"We first went out to the Sandakan Club - there'd be a British Club on Mount Everest if 2 Britishers could stand the cold there! - and had these Coolers, through the courtesy of an American who was sentimental enough to fetch a mint root out with him.

"To 1 jigger of dry gin add the same of Italian vermouth. To this base donate 1 dash of each. Angostura and Amer Picon, and 1 tsp of orange Curaçao. Stir with a goodly lump of ice in a small highball or sour glass, and top off with a squirt of soda garnished with 2 sprigs of mint and a stick of ripe pineapple."
Comment: Basically a Gin and It lengthened with soda and spiced with dashes of Amer Picon, Angostura bitters and orange curaçao.

COLONIAL ROT

★★★☆☆

Glass: Collins
Garnish: Mint sprig
Method: Lightly MUDDLE mint in base of shaker just enough to bruise. Add next 4 ingredients, SHAKE with ice and fine strain into ice-filled glass. TOP with half soda and half lemonade.

7	fresh	Mint leaves
½	shot	Le Fée Parisienne absinthe
1	shot	Ketel One Citroen vodka
½	shot	Sugar syrup (2 sugar to 1 water)
½	shot	Freshly squeezed lime juice
Top with		Lemonade/Sprite/7-Up
Splash		Soda (club soda)

Comment: Long and green with more than a touch of the green fairy.

COLONY

★★★★☆

Glass: Martini
Garnish: Grapefruit zest twist
Method: SHAKE all ingredients with ice and fine strain into chilled glass.

1½ shots Rutte Dry Gin
¾ shot Freshly squeezed pink grapefruit juice
¼ shot Luxardo Maraschino liqueur

Origin: Created during the Prohibition period at New York's Colony speakeasy, possibly by bartender Marco Hattem. The Colony attracted an upmarket Clientele, including the Vanderbilts and Windsors. The liquor was kept in an elevator which would be sent to either that attic or the basement if federal agents raided.
Comment: Grapefruit and maraschino balance each other in this gin based classic.

COLORADO BULLDOG

★★½☆☆

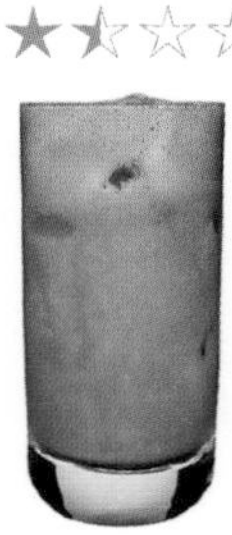

Glass: Collins
Garnish: None
Method: SHAKE first 4 ingredients with ice and strain into ice-filled glass. **TOP** with cola.

1½ shots Ketel One Vodka
1 shot Coffee liqueur
1 shot Single cream / half-and-half
1 shot Milk
Top with Coca-Cola

Comment: This dog's bite is hidden by cream.

COLUMBUS DAIQUIRI

★★★☆☆

Glass: Martini
Garnish: Lime wedge
Method: SHAKE all ingredients with ice and fine strain into chilled glass.

1 shot Bacardi Carta Oro rum
1 shot De Kuyper XO Apricot Brandy
1 shot Freshly squeezed lime juice
½ shot Chilled water (omit if wet ice)

Comment: A tangy, apricot flavoured Daiquiri.

COMET COCKTAIL

★★★★½

Glass: Coupe
Garnish: Grapefruit zest twist
Method: SHAKE all ingredients and strain into chilled glass.

1½ shot Martell V.S.O.P Médaillon cognac
¼ shot De Kuyper Triple sec
¼ shot Drambuie liqueur
1 shot Freshly squeezed grapefruit juice
1 dash Angostura Aromatic Bitters

Comment: This riff on the Sidecar is lighter, less tart, and altogether more approachable than the original, but some may find it lacks the original's cleansing zesty bite.
Origin: Created in 1952 by Eddie "King Cocktail" Clarke at the Albany Club, Albermarle Street, London, England to honour the first ever jet aircraft to fly a commercial route. The *de Havilland DH 106 Comet* was developed and manufactured by de Havilland at its Hatfield Aerodrome, Hertfordshire, England. The Comet 1 prototype, registered G-ALYP ("Yoke Peter") first flew on 27th July 1949. This same aircraft, on 2nd May 1952 took off from London bound for Johannesburg on a scheduled BOAC service as the world's first jetliner flight with fare-paying passengers.

Eddie Clarke's original recipe called for Van der Hum, a South African orange liqueur, undoubtedly selected by Eddie due to the destination of that inaugural flight. The use of equal parts triple sec and Drambuie is an accepted substitution and works well.

COMMODORE #1

★★★★☆

Glass: Martini
Garnish: Luxardo Maraschino cherry
Method: SHAKE all ingredients with ice and fine strain into chilled glass.

2 shots Bacardi Carta Oro rum
½ shot Freshly squeezed lemon juice
¼ shot Sugar syrup (2 sugar to 1 water)
⅛ shot Pomegranate / grenadine syrup (2:1)
½ fresh Egg white

Origin: Adapted from David A. Embury's 1948 'The Fine Art of Mixing Drinks', where he writes, "Another version of the Commodore calls for whisky instead of rum, omits the egg white, and uses orange bitters in place of the grenadine. Obviously, the two Commodores command two different fleets."
Comment: A smooth, sweet Daiquiri with flavoursome rum.

COMMODORE #2

★★★★☆

Glass: Old-fashioned
Garnish: Luxardo Maraschino cherry
Method: SHAKE all ingredients with ice and fine strain into ice-filled glass.

2 shots Bourbon whiskey
¾ shot White crème de cacao liqueur
¼ shot Pomegranate / grenadine syrup (2:1)
½ shot Freshly squeezed lemon juice
2 dash Angostura Aromatic Bitters (optional)

Origin: Recipe adapted from Albert S. Crockett's 1935 'Old Waldorf Bar Days'. The original recipe calls for equal parts lemon juice, bourbon and crème de cacao with a dash of grenadine, and for the drink to be served 'straight-up' - we believe it's better on the rocks.
Comment: Fruity, tangy Bourbon, surprisingly dry despite its sweet ingredients.

CONAN DOYLE

★★★★★

Glass: Old-fashioned
Garnish: Lemon zest twist
Method: STIR all ingredients with ice and strain into ice-filled glass.

2 shots Talisker single malt whisky
¼ shot Taylor's Velvet Falernum liqueur
3 dash Whiskey Barrel Aged Bitters

Origin: Discovered in 2008 at Tonic Bar, Edinburgh, Scotland.
Comment: A literary rift on a Corn'n'Oil - elementary but tasty.

CONGO BLUE

★★★★⯪☆

Glass: Martini
Garnish: Lemon zest twist
Method: SHAKE all ingredients with ice and fine strain into chilled glass.

1¼ shots	Zubrówka bison vodka
½ shot	Midori Green Melon liqueur
½ shot	Lejay Crème de Mûre liqueur
1 shot	Pressed apple juice
¼ shot	Freshly squeezed lemon juice

Origin: Created in 1999 by Marc Dietrich at Atlantic Bar & Grill, London and apparently named after the beauty of the Congo sunset.
Comment: Flavoursome and sweet.

CONTINENTAL SOUR

★★★★☆

Glass: Old-fashioned
Garnish: None
Method: SHAKE first five ingredients with ice and fine strain into ice-filled glass. Finish with port float.

2 shots	Bourbon whiskey
1 shot	Freshly squeezed lemon juice
½ fresh	Sugar syrup (2 sugar to 1 water)
1 dash	Angostura Aromatic Bitters
½ shot	Egg white
¼ shot	Tawny port

Origin: Discovered in May 2010 at Stagger Lee, Berlin, Germany
Comment: A Whiskey Sour made 'continental' by the addition of a splash of port.

COOL MARTINI

★★★⯪☆

Glass: Martini
Garnish: Apple fan
Method: SHAKE all ingredients with ice and fine strain into chilled glass.

1½ shots	Midori Green Melon liqueur
1 shot	Patrón reposado tequila
1½ shots	Cranberry juice

Comment: Tastes nothing like the ingredients - which include melon, tequila and cranberry juice. Try it and see if you taste toffee.

COOL ORCHARD

★★★★☆

Glass: Old-fashioned
Garnish: Pineapple wedge & Luxardo Maraschino cherry
Method: MUDDLE ginger in base of shaker. Add other ingredients, SHAKE with ice and fine strain into ice-filled glass.

2 slice	Fresh root ginger (thumbnail sized)
1½ shots	Bacardi Carta Ocho aged rum
½ shot	Ginger sugar syrup
¼ shot	Almond (orgeat) syrup
1 shot	Fresh pressed pineapple juice
¼ shot	Freshly squeezed lime juice
½ shot	Vanilla schnapps

Origin: Created in 2001 by Douglas Ankrah for Akbar, Soho, London, England
Comment: A great drink with unusual ingredients.

COOLMAN COCKTAIL ⚿

★★★★⯪

Glass: Martini
Garnish: Orange zest twist
Method: SHAKE all ingredients with ice and fine strain into chilled glass.

1¾ shots	Ketel One Vodka
½ shot	De Kuyper Triple Sec
2 shots	Pressed apple juice
¼ shot	Freshly squeezed lemon juice

Origin: Created in 2001 by Jack Coleman at The Library Bar, Lanesborough Hotel, London, England.
Comment: Fragrant and complex. Integrated hints of apple and orange are laced with grassy vodka.

COOPERSTOWN ⚿

★★★☆☆

Glass: Coupe
Garnish: Orange zest twist (discarded) & mint sprig
Method: STIR all ingredients (including mint) with ice and fine strain into chilled glass.

8 fresh	Mint leaves
2½ shots	Rutte Dry Gin
¼ shot	Martini Dry vermouth
¼ shot	Martini Rosso vermouth

Comment: A minty Perfect Martini which is made more widely appreciable by the addition of half a barspoon of sugar syrup.

COPENHAGEN COCKTAIL

★★★★⯪

Glass: Coupe
Garnish: Orange zest twist
Method: SHAKE all ingredients with ice and fine strain into chilled glass.

1⅔ shots	Rutte Old Simon oude jenever
⅔ shot	Cherry Heering Liqueur
⅔ shot	Freshly squeezed lime juice
⅓ shot	Sugar syrup (2 sugar to 1 water)
1 dash	Angostura Aromatic Bitters
⅔ shot	Chilled water (omit if wet ice)

Origin: In August 2009, Cherry Heering, a liqueur from Copenhagen, challenged local bartenders to create a signature cocktail for their city. This winning recipe was created by Gromit Eduardsen at Bar 1105 in Copenhagen, Denmark.
Comment: Bready notes in the jenever combine with the cherry brandy and the lime juice to produce a complex bittersweet, jammy cocktail.

COPPER ILLUSION

★★★★☆

Glass: Old-fashioned
Garnish: Orange zest twist
Method: STIR all ingredients with ice and strain into ice-filled glass.

1½ shots	Rutte Dry Gin
¾ shot	De Kuyper Triple Sec
¾ shot	Campari Bitter

Origin: Unknown but brought to my attention in 2005 courtesy of Angus Winchester.
Comment: Basically a Negroni with liqueur replacing sweet vermouth. Like the Italian classic this is both bitter and sweet.

COQUETAIL AU VANILLA

★★★★☆

Glass: Old-fashioned
Garnish: Luxardo Maraschino cherry
Method: SHAKE all ingredients with ice and strain into glass filled with crushed ice. Serve with straws.

| 2 | shots | Bacardi Carta Blanca (vanilla infused) |
| ¼ | shot | Taylor's Velvet Falernum liqueur |

Origin: An adaptation of a classic by yours truly, London, England.
Comment: This drink may look fluffy and sweet but it's dry and lightly spiced. Perfect for a sunny afternoon.

CORDLESS SCREWDRIVER

★★★☆☆

Glass: Shot
Garnish: Sugar coated orange slice
Method: POUR vodka and champagne into glass and serve. Instruct drinker to down in one and then bite into the orange wedge.

| 1 | shot | Ketel One Oranje |
| Top with | | G.H. Mumm Brut Cordon Rouge champagne |

Comment: A slammer style drink for those looking for a fruity alternative to tequila.

CORN'N'OIL COCKTAIL

★★★★☆

Glass: Old-fashioned
Garnish: Lime zest twist (discarded) & lime slice
Method: STIR all ingredients with ice and strain into-filled glass.

2	shots	Bacardi Carta Oro rum
½	shot	Taylor's Velvet Falernum liqueur
2	dash	Angostura Aromatic Bitters

Origin: Popular in the Caribbean, particularly Barbados and Jamaica, the origins of the Corn'n'Oil are lost in time.
Comment: Rum slightly sweetened and flavoured with the lime and clove flavours of falernum.

THE CORNICHON (NEW)

★★★★☆

Glass: Coupe
Garnish: Cocktail onion and cornichon
Method: STIR all ingredients with ice and strain into chilled glass.

1½	shots	Patrón silver tequila
½	shot	Romate Amontillado sherry
¼	shot	Grand Marnier Cordon Rouge
½	shot	Martini Extra Dry vermouth
¼	shot	Chile liqueur
½	shot	Cranberry juice
½	shot	Chilled water (omit if wet ice)

Origin: Created in August 2015 by yours truly at the Cabinet Room, London, England.
Comment: A cornucopia of flavours with which to get pickled.

CORNWALL NEGRONI

★★★★☆

Glass: Coupe
Garnish: Orange zest twist (flamed)
Method: STIR all ingredients with ice and strain into chilled glass.

2	shots	Rutte Dry Gin
½	shot	Campari Bitter
½	shot	Carpano Punt E Mes
½	shot	Martini Rosso vermouth
1	dash	Angostura Orange Bitters

Origin: Created in 2006 by Philip Ward, New York, USA after attending Gary 'gaz' Regan's Cocktails in the Country workshop in Cornwall-on-Hudson.
Comment: A Negroni style cocktail served up. Heavy on the gin and relatively light on Campari and vermouth. It's a formula that works but like us, you may prefer yours served on the rocks.

COROLVA COCKTAIL

★★☆☆☆

Glass: Coupe
Garnish: None
Method: SHAKE all ingredients with ice and fine strain into chilled glass.

2	shots	Rutte Dry Gin
1	shot	Martini Rosso vermouth
⅛	shot	Le Fée Parisienne absinthe
⅛	shot	Single cream / half-and-half

Comment: Why would you bother mixing these ingredients together to make this drink?

CORONATION

★★★☆☆

Glass: Collins
Garnish: Luxardo Maraschino cherry
Method: STIR first 5 ingredients with ice and strain into ice-filled glass. **TOP** with soda, stir and serve with straws.

1	shot	Romate Fino sherry
2	shots	Sauvignon blanc white wine
¼	shot	Luxardo Maraschino liqueur
1	shot	Martini Extra Dry vermouth
2	dash	Angostura Aromatic Bitters
Top with		Soda (club soda)

Comment: Light and aromatic.

CORONATION COCKTAIL NO.1

★★★★☆

Glass: Coupe
Garnish: Orange zest twist
Method: STIR all ingredients with ice and strain into chilled glass.

1½	shots	Romate Fino sherry
¼	shot	Luxardo Maraschino liqueur
1½	shots	Martini Extra Dry vermouth
2	dash	Angostura Orange Bitters

Origin: Adapted from Harry Craddock's 1930 'The Savoy Cocktail Book'.
Comment: Medium dry and wonderfully aromatic.

CORPSE REVIVER #3

★★★★☆

Glass: Martini
Garnish: Lemon zest twist
Method: SHAKE all ingredients with ice and fine strain into chilled glass.

¾ shot   Rutte Dry Gin
¾ shot   Swedish Punch liqueur
¾ shot   De Kuyper Triple Sec
⅛ shot   Le Fée Parisienne absinthe
¾ shot   Freshly squeezed lemon juice

Origin: Perhaps a touch sweet but the kill or cure alcohol is well masked.
Comment: Adapted from Victor Bergeron's 'Trader Vic's Bartender's Guide' (1972 revised edition).

CORPSE REVIVER COCKTAIL NO.2 (CONTEMPORARY RECIPE)

★★★★☆

Glass: Martini
Garnish: Lemon zest twist
Method: SHAKE all ingredients with ice and fine strain into chilled glass.

¾ shot   Rutte Dry Gin
¾ shot   Yellow Chartreuse liqueur
¾ shot   Lillet Blanc
¾ shot   Freshly squeezed lemon juice
⅛ shot   Le Fée Parisienne absinthe

Origin: A riff on the classic Corpse Reviver No.2 popular with bartenders during the late noughties.
Comment: Yellow Chartreuse replaces triple sec in this riff on the classic Corpse Reviver Cocktail No.2.

CORPSE REVIVER NO.1 #1

★★★☆☆

Glass: Martini
Garnish: Orange zest twist
Method: STIR ingredients with ice and strain into chilled glass.

1½ shots   Martell VSOP Médaillon cognac
¾ shot   Calvados brandy
¾ shot   Martini Rosso vermouth
½ shot   Chilled water (omit if wet ice)

Origin: Created by Frank Meier, Ritz Bar, Paris, France. This recipe was adapted from Harry Craddock's 1930 'The Savoy Cocktail Book', where he writes, "To be taken before 11am, or whenever steam or energy are needed."
Comment: Dry and potent. A 'pick-me-up' hangover cure - or possibly put-you-right-back-down-again!

CORPSE REVIVER NO.1 #2 (GILBERG'S RECIPE)

★★★☆☆

Glass: Martini
Garnish: Lemon zest twist
Method: STIR all ingredients with ice and strain into chilled glass.

2   shots   Calvados brandy
¾   shot   Martell VSOP Médaillon cognac
¾   shot   Martini Rosso vermouth

Origin: In his book 'The Joy of Mixology', Gary Regan recommends this version of the Corpse Reviver, which he writes was originally created in 2001 by Steve Gilberg, publisher of happyhours.com.
Comment: Strong enough to awaken the dead.

CORPSE REVIVER NO.2 #1 (SAVOY RECIPE)

★★★★☆

Glass: Martini
Garnish: Lemon zest twist
Method: SHAKE all ingredients with ice and fine strain into chilled glass.

¾ shot Rutte Dry Gin
¾ shot De Kuyper Triple Sec
¾ shot Lillet Blanc
¾ shot Freshly squeezed lemon juice
⅛ shot Le Fée Parisienne absinthe

Origin: Adapted from 1930 ' The Savoy Cocktail Book' where Harry Craddock says of this drink, "Four of these taken in swift succession will unrevive the corpse again." Harry originally stipulated Kina Lillet as the dry vermouth.
Comment: Well-balanced with zesty lemon and absinthe just shinning above other ingredients.

CORPSE REVIVER NO.BLUE

★★★★☆

Glass: Coupe
Garnish: Lemon zest twist
Method: SHAKE all ingredients with ice and fine strain into chilled glass.

¾ shot   Rutte Dry Gin
¾ shot   Lillet Blanc
¾ shot   Blue curaçao liqueur
1 shot   Freshly squeezed lemon juice
⅛ shot   Le Fée Parisienne absinthe

Origin: Created by Jacob Briars in the noughties, around the time a Facebook group started called 'A Jihad on all Blue Drinks'. This was Jacob's reaction to it. He 'blued' the most popular bartender's drink at the time.
Comment: "Considering it's blue, I quite like it," was the general opinion from across the Cabinet Room bar.

COSMOPOLIS COCKTAIL (NEW)

★★★★☆

Glass: Martini
Garnish: Flamed orange zest
Method: SHAKE all ingredients with ice and strain into chilled glass.

1   shot   Ketel One Vodka
¾   shot   Skinos Mastiha
¾   shot   Cranberry juice
¼   shot   Freshly squeezed lime juice

Comment: A riff on a Cosmopolitan with the distinctive Greek influence of mastiha.

Cosmopolitan Cocktail

The Cosmopolitan is one of those cocktails that has had various incarnations through the ages - some of them, quite probably, independent of one another. During the 1990s, the familiar blend of cranberry, citrus and vodka was one of the most popular cocktails in New York and London.

The first reference to a Cosmopolitan cocktail appears in the 1934 book 'Pioneers of Mixing at Elite Bars'. This Cosmopolitan recipe includes triple sec and is very similar to today's drink, only with lemon in place of lime, gin in place of vodka and raspberry syrup in place of cranberry. The raspberry gives the drink a pale pink appearance not dissimilar from its modern day namesake.

A likely early ancestor of the modern day Cosmopolitan is the Harpoon Cocktail, a drink promoted by Ocean Spray during the 1960s. A 1968 bottle label from Ocean Spray's archives lists the Harpoon as a "new cocktail" with a recipe specifying 2 ounces Ocean Spray cranberry and 1 ounce vodka or light rum served "over the rocks or tall with soda". Ocean Spray's recipe also suggests adding an optional splash of lime or lemon. In 1970, the company updated their Harpoon Cocktail recipe to also list gin as a possible base spirit.

Well over a decade after the Harpoon during the latter half of the 1980s, Cheryl Cook claims to have invented the Cosmopolitan Cocktail while head bartender at The Strand on Washington Avenue, South Beach, Miami. She apparently based her drink on the newly available Absolut Citron vodka and added a splash of triple sec, a dash of Rose's lime and, in her own words, "just enough cranberry to make it oh so pretty in pink". The date often quoted for her claim is 1985, three years prior to the launch of Absolut Citron.

The cosmopolitan made the rounds of gay bars in San Francisco in the late 70s and early 80s. At that time it consisted of vodka with Rose's Lime and Rose's Grenadine and it is this drink that Toby Cecchini says "came to New York and came to me through another bartender who worked at The Odeon called Melisa Huffsmith. It was a ghastly drink and I reformulated it using Citron, which Absolut had just come out with, cranberry juice, and the things we were using at the time to make fresh Margaritas. It was kind of a no brainer. I was 25 years old and I invented the drink to impress the waitresses. I invented the Cosmopolitan as it's known."

In 1996, across town at Manhattan's Rainbow Rooms, bartending legend Dale DeGroff came across the Cosmopolitan, perfected his own recipe, and helped by Madonna and his signature flamed orange zest twist garnish, made the cocktail fashionable.

New York Magazine credited Dale with the drink's invention, other publications followed and he was asked to present it on several television stations. Due to this publicity it is Dale who continues to be most identified with the Cosmopolitan Cocktail.

Dale has never claimed to have invented the Cosmopolitan and in his own 2002 book, 'The Craft of the Cocktail' he explains that while he did not invent the Cosmopolitan, "What I did do was popularize a definitive recipe that became widely accepted as the standard." It was Dale who added the flamboyant flamed orange zest twist.

When the HBO television series, 'Sex and the City' debuted in 1998, its creators decided the Cosmopolitan would be the perfect accompaniment to Carrie Bradshaw's fashionista Manhattan lifestyle. Carrie, Miranda, Charlotte and sexpot Samantha were frequently shown sipping Cosmos and when the series hit the big screen in 2008, the film closed with the girls questioning why they had ever stopped drinking them.

STAR RATINGS EXPLAINED

★★★★★+	OUTSTANDING	★★★★★	EXCEPTIONAL
★★★★½	EXCELLENT	★★★★☆	RECOMMENDED
★★★½☆	COMMENDED	★★★☆☆	MEDIOCRE
★★½☆☆	DISAPPOINTING	★★☆☆☆	PRETTY AWFUL
★½☆☆☆	SHAMEFUL	★☆☆☆☆	DISGUSTING

COSMOPOLITAN COCKTAIL (1934 RECIPE)

★★★★☆

Glass: Martini
Garnish: Orange zest twist
Method: **SHAKE** all ingredients with ice and fine strain into chilled glass.

2 shots Rutte Dry Gin
½ shot De Kuyper Triple Sec
¾ shot Freshly squeezed lemon juice
¼ shot Raspberry syrup (1 juice to 1 sugar)

Origin: Adapted from the Cosmopolitan Cocktail recipe in the 1934 book, 'Pioneers of Mixing at Elite Bars'. This calls for "jigger Gordons' gin, 2 dashes Cointreau, juice of one lemon, teaspoon Raspberry juice", specifying the drink should be shaken and strained into "Glass No.4" (a 3½ oz goblet).
Comment: Reminiscent of a Sidecar and, depending on your syrup, well-balanced.

COSMOPOLITAN COCKTAIL (DALE DEGROFF'S RECIPE)

★★★★☆

Glass: Martini
Garnish: Orange zest twist (flamed)
Method: **SHAKE** all ingredients with ice and fine strain into chilled glass.

1½ shots Ketel One Citroen vodka
½ shot De Kuyper Triple Sec
1 shot Cranberry juice
¼ shot Freshly squeezed lime juice

Origin: This recipe is from Dale's 2002 'The Craft of the Cocktail' where he also explains that while he did not invent the Cosmopolitan, in his own words, "What I did do was popularize a definitive recipe that became widely accepted as the standard."
Comment: This is the definitive Cosmo recipe from the man most associated with the drinks development and popularity.

COSMOPOLITAN COCKTAIL (DIFFORD'S RECIPE)

★★★★½

Glass: Martini
Garnish: Orange zest twist (flamed)
Method: **SHAKE** all ingredients with ice and fine strain into chilled glass.

1 shot Ketel One Vodka
1 shot De Kuyper Triple Sec
1½ shots Cranberry juice
½ shot Freshly squeezed lime juice
1 dash Angostura Orange Bitters (optional)

Comment: A Cosmopolitan should normally be made with citrus vodka but this recipe works just as well with unflavoured vodka and personally, when a good quality cranberry juice is used, I prefer the simplicity of unflavoured vodka in this cocktail.

COSMOPOLITAN COCKTAIL (TOBY CECCHINI'S RECIPE) (NEW)

★★★★☆

Glass: Martini
Garnish: Lime wedge
Method: SHAKE all ingredients with ice and fine strain into chilled glass.

1½ shot Ketel One Citroen vodka
¾ shot De Kuyper Triple Sec
¾ shot Freshly squeezed lime juice
¾ shot Cranberry juice

Origin: The original Cosmopolitan cocktail recipe as created in 1988 by Toby Cecchini at The Odeon in New York City. Toby's recipe used the then newly launched Absolut Citron and Cointreau tripe sec.
Comment: This 2,1,1,1 original Cosmopolitan is slightly on the tart side of balanced with the citrus flavoured vodka shining over the other ingredients.

COSMOPOLITAN DELIGHT

★★★★☆

Glass: Martini
Garnish: Orange zest twist (flamed)
Method: SHAKE all ingredients with ice and fine strain into chilled glass.

1½ shots Martell VSOP Médaillon cognac
½ shot Grand Marnier Cordon Rouge
1¼ shots Shiraz red wine
¼ shot Almond (orgeat) syrup
¾ shot Freshly squeezed lemon juice
¼ shot Sugar syrup (2 sugar to 1 water)

Origin: Adapted from Dale DeGroff's book, 'The Craft of the Cocktail'. He credits the original recipe to a 1902 book by Charlie Paul.
Comment: No relation to the modern Cosmopolitan, this is a mellow, balanced blend of citrus, brandy and red wine.

COVADONGA

★★★☆☆

Glass: Martini
Garnish: Orange slice
Method: SHAKE all ingredients with ice and fine strain into chilled glass.

1½ shots Campari Bitter
1 shot Martini Rosso vermouth
1 shot Freshly squeezed orange juice
½ shot Pomegranate / grenadine syrup (2:1)
5 dash Angostura Aromatic Bitters

Origin: Adapted form Victor Bergeron's 'Trader Vic's Bartender's Guide' (1972 revised edition).
Comment: Sweet, tart and fruity.

COWBOY HOOF MARTINI

★★★★⯪

Glass: Martini
Garnish: Orange zest twist
Method: SHAKE all ingredients (including mint) with ice and fine strain into chilled glass.

5 fresh Mint leaves
2½ shot Rutte Dry Gin
⅙ shot Sugar syrup (2 sugar to 1 water)
2 dash Angostura Orange Bitters

Comment: Lightly sweetened gin shaken with fresh aromatic mint.
Origin: Created in the early 1990s by Dick Bradsell at Detroit, London, England.

COX'S DAIQUIRI

★★★★★

Glass: Martini
Garnish: Cox's apple ring (in memory of Jennings Cox)
Method: SHAKE all ingredients with ice and fine strain into chilled glass.

2½ shots Bacardi Carta Blanca (vanilla infused)
½ shot Freshly squeezed lime juice
1 shot Fresh pressed pineapple juice
¼ shot Vanilla sugar syrup

Origin: One of two cocktails with which I yours truly won 'The Best Daiquiri in London Competition' in 2002. It is named after Jennings Cox, the American mining engineer credited with first creating the Daiquiri.
Comment: Vanilla and pineapple bring out the sweetness of the rum against a citrus background.

CRANAPPLE BREEZE

★★★⯪☆

Glass: Collins
Garnish: Lime slice
Method: SHAKE first five ingredients with ice and strain into ice-filled glass. TOP with ginger ale and stir.

1 shot Ketel One Citroen vodka
1 shot De Kuyper Triple Sec
1 shot Cranberry juice
1 shot Pressed apple juice
½ shot Freshly squeezed lime juice
Top with Ginger ale

Origin: Created in 2002 by Wayne Collins.
Comment: A refreshing cooler for a hot day by the pool.

CRANBERRY & MINT COCKTAIL ⚷

★★★⯪☆

Glass: Martini
Garnish: Cranberries & mint leaf
Method: Lightly MUDDLE mint in base of shaker just enough to bruise. Add other ingredients, SHAKE with ice and fine strain into chilled glass.

8 fresh Mint leaves
2 shots Ketel One Vodka
1½ shots Cranberry juice
¼ shot Pomegranate / grenadine syrup (2:1)

Origin: Created in 2003 by yours truly.
Comment: This little red number combines the dryness of cranberry, the sweetness of grenadine and the fragrance of mint.

CRAPPLE (MOCKTAIL)

★★★½☆

Glass: Collins
Garnish: Lime wedge
Method: **SHAKE** all ingredients with ice and strain into ice-filled glass. Serve with straws.

2½ shots Cranberry juice
2 shots Pressed apple juice
1 shot Freshly squeezed lime juice
½ shot Sugar syrup (2 sugar to 1 water)

Comment: Cranberry, apple and lime. Simple but refreshing and decidedly fruity.

CREAM CAKE

★★★½☆

Glass: Martini
Garnish: Crumbled Cadbury's Flake bar
Method: **SHAKE** all ingredients with ice and fine strain into chilled glass.

1¼ shots Baileys Irish cream liqueur
1¼ shots Peachtree peach schnapps
1¼ shots Disaronno Originale amaretto
1 shot Single cream / half-and-half

Comment: Creamy pleasure for the sweet of tooth.

CREAM SODA COCKTAIL

★★★½☆

Glass: Collins
Garnish: Lemon slice
Method: **SHAKE** first 3 ingredients with ice and strain into ice-filled glass. **TOP** with lemonade and serve with straws.

1½ shots Vanilla infused Ketel One vodka
1 shot Bacardi Carta Blanca light rum
½ shot Licor 43 liqueur
Top with Lemonade/Sprite/7-Up

Origin: Created in 2008 by yours truly at the Cabinet Room, London, England.
Comment: An alcoholic cream soda created for Debbie Rizzo who expressed a desire for just such a thing.

CREAMSICLE

★★★½☆

Glass: Martini
Garnish: Orange zest twist
Method: **SHAKE** all ingredients with ice and fine strain into chilled glass.

1 shot Ketel One Oranje vodka
1 shot Grand Marnier Cordon Rouge
½ shot Single cream / half-and-half
½ shot Milk
¼ shot Sugar syrup (2 sugar to 1 water)

Comment: A creamy orange number with a surprisingly pleasant taste.

CREAMY BEE

★★★★☆

Glass: Martini
Garnish: Cinnamon & sugar rim with raspberry
Method: **SHAKE** all ingredients with ice and fine strain into chilled glass

1½ shots Old Krupnik
½ shot Baileys Irish cream liqueur
½ shot Chambord Liqueur
½ shot Hazelnut liqueur
¼ shot Cinnamon schnapps

Origin: Created in 2002 at Hush, London, England and originally made with cinnamon syrup in place of Goldschläger.
Comment: Creamy cinnamon with hints of honey, nuts and berries.

CREAMY CREAMSICLE

★★★½☆

Glass: Martini
Garnish: None
Method: **SHAKE** all ingredients with ice and fine strain into chilled glass.

½ shot Ketel One Oranje vodka
1¼ shots Disaronno Originale amaretto
1 shot Freshly squeezed orange juice
¾ shot Milk
¾ shot Single cream / half-and-half

Comment: Ultra smooth and creamy. Dessert, anyone?

CREAMY VANILLA COLADA

★★★★½

Glass: Coupe
Garnish: Dust with chocolate powder
Method: **SHAKE** all ingredients with ice and fine strain into chilled glass.

2 shots Bacardi Carta Ocho aged rum
1½ shots Yoghurt liqueur
6 drop Vanilla extract

Origin: Created in 2011 by yours truly at the Cabinet Room, London, England.
Comment: Creamy yoghurt married with aged rum and richly flavoured with vanilla.

CRÈME ANGLAISE COCKTAIL

★★★★☆

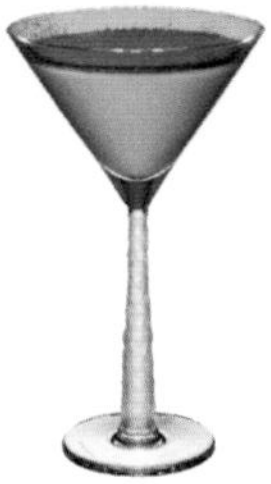

Glass: Martini
Garnish: Dust with chocolate powder
Method: **SHAKE** all ingredients with ice and fine strain into chilled glass.

1 shot Vanilla infused Ketel One vodka
2 shots Warninks Advocaat liqueur
½ shot Single cream / half-and-half

Origin: Created in 2004 by yours truly, London, England.
Comment: Very reminiscent of alcoholic crème anglaise.

CRÈME BRÛLÉE COCKTAIL

★★★⯪☆

Glass: Martini
Garnish: Dust with cinnamon powder
Method: SHAKE all ingredients with ice and fine strain into chilled glass.

2	shots	Vanilla infused Ketel One vodka
½	unit	Caramel liqueur
¾	shot	Licor 43 liqueur
1	shot	Single cream / half-and-half
½	fresh	Egg yolk

Origin: Adapted from a drink created in 2002 by Yannick Miseriaux at the Fifth Floor Bar, London, England.
Comment: OK, so there's no crust, but this does contain egg yolk, caramel, vanilla, sugar and cream. Due to the cinnamon, it even has a brown top.

CRÈME DE CAFÉ

★★★⯪☆

Glass: Old-fashioned
Garnish: None
Method: SHAKE ingredients with ice and strain into ice-filled glass.

¾	shot	Bacardi Carta Oro rum
1	shot	Coffee liqueur
¾	shot	Luxardo sambuca dei cesari
1	shot	Single cream / half-and-half
1	shot	Milk

Comment: Coffee predominates over the creaminess with hints of aniseed and rum.

CREOLE CONTENTMENT

★★★★☆

Glass: Coupe
Garnish: Luxardo Maraschino cherry
Method: STIR all ingredients with ice and strain into chilled glass.

1½	shots	Martell VSOP Médaillon cognac
1	shot	Sercial (dry) Madeira wine
¼	shot	Luxardo Maraschino liqueur
1	dash	Angostura Orange Bitters
½	shot	Chilled water

Origin: Adapted from Charles H. Baker's 1939 ' The Gentlemen's Companion' in which Baker writes, "Creole Contentment, an Insidious Pleasantry from the Charming-Hot-Bed of Intrigue and Culture which is the Pulse of the Great Delta Country - New Orleans.

"This hazard and liability to consistent maidenhood came to our desk through office of a friend whose father once was Episcopal Bishop of Washington, and who writes books about pirates. Don't treat this one lightly, mes amis....

"Of Cognac, Madeira wine and maraschino, take 1 pony; turn this into a bar glass with ice; toss in 1 dash of orange bitters, stir well, pour into a big Manhattan glass or saucer type champagne, and garnish with 3 maraschino cherries; red, green and white... Our personal experience is that it is better to cut the maraschino down by half, stepping up the cognac in that ratio. The business of the 3 cherries, while no doubt a pretty and chivalrous gesture of the feminine victim is, of course, sheerest swank. It is a good drink and needs a little trimming."
Comment: If using a sweeter Madeira such as Verdelho/Rainwater (medium dry) or Bual (medium sweet) you'll need to adjust this finely balanced cocktail. Even Baker himself says says it "needs a little trimming". However, dry Sercial Madeira works best to produce a finely balanced complex cocktail.

CREOLE COSMO

★★★★⯪

Glass: Martini
Garnish: Lime zest twist
Method: SHAKE all ingredients with ice and fine strain into chilled glass.

1	shot	Martinique blanc rhum agricole
1	shot	Clément Creole Shrubb liqueur
1	shot	Cranberry juice
½	shot	Freshly squeezed lime juice

Comment: Dry tangy and more sophisticated than your bog-standard Cosmo.

CREOLE GIMLET

★★★★☆

Glass: Coupe
Garnish: Lime zest twist
Method: STIR all ingredients with ice and strain into chilled glass.

2½	shots	Rutte Dry Gin
½	shot	Taylor's Velvet Falernum liqueur
¼	shot	Rose's lime cordial
1	dash	Peychaud's aromatic bitters

Origin: Created in 2009 by Gonçalo de Sousa Monteiro, Berlin, Germany.
Comment: Falernum adds a touch of Caribbean spice to this Gimlet.

CRIMEA

★★★☆☆

Glass: Martini
Garnish: Coriander leaf
Method: MUDDLE coriander in base of shaker. Add other ingredients, **SHAKE** with ice and fine strain into chilled glass.

5	fresh	Coriander (cilantro) leaves
2	shots	Rutte Dry Gin
1	shot	Pressed apple juice
¼	shot	Freshly squeezed lemon juice
⅛	shot	Sugar syrup (2 sugar to 1 water)
½	shot	Chilled water (omit if wet ice)

Origin: Adapted from a drink discovered in 2006 at Ballroom, London, England.
Comment: Fragrant, herbal gin with a hint of citrus.

CROUCHING TIGER

★★★☆☆

Glass: Shot
Garnish: None
Method: SHAKE all ingredients with ice and fine strain into chilled glass.

¾	shot	Patrón reposado tequila
½	shot	Kwai Feh lychee liqueur

Comment: Tequila and lychee combine harmoniously in this semi-sweet shot.

THE CROW COCKTAIL 🔑

★★★☆☆

Glass: Martini
Garnish: Lemon zest twist
Method: SHAKE all ingredients with ice and fine strain into chilled glass.

2	shots	Dewar's 12 Year Old Scotch whisky
1	shot	Freshly squeezed lemon juice
½	shot	Pomegranate / grenadine syrup (2:1)

Origin: Adapted from Harry Craddock's 1930 'The Savoy Cocktail Book'.
Comment: If you use great syrup and have a penchant for Scotch then you could be pleasantly surprised by this drink.

CROWN STAG

★★★★☆

Glass: Old-fashioned
Garnish: Lemon slice
Method: SHAKE ingredients with ice and strain into ice-filled glass.

1½	shots	Ketel One Vodka
1½	shots	Jägermeister
1	shot	Chambord Liqueur

Comment: A surprisingly workable combination.

CRUEL INTENTION

★★★★☆

Glass: Martini
Garnish: Lime slice
Method: SHAKE all ingredients with ice and fine strain into chilled glass.

2	shots	Bourbon whiskey
¼	shot	De Kuyper XO Apricot Brandy
¼	shot	Disaronno Originale amaretto
1	shot	Fresh pressed pineapple juice
½	shot	Freshly squeezed lime juice

Origin: Discovered in 2005 at The Mansion, Amsterdam, The Netherlands.
Comment: Bourbon with a hint of apricot, almond, pineapple and lime. Hardly cruel!

CRUSHED STRAWBERRY FIZZ

★★★★☆

Glass: Collins (small 8oz)
Garnish: Strawberry
Method: MUDDLE strawberries in base of shaker. Add other ingredients apart from soda, **SHAKE** with ice and fine strain into chilled glass (without ice). **TOP** with soda.

3	fresh	Small ripe strawberries (hulled)
2	shots	Old Tom gin
1	shot	Freshly squeezed lemon juice
½	shot	Sugar syrup (2 sugar to 1 water)
Top with		Soda from siphon

Origin: This Gin Fizz adaptation was created circa 1880 at the St. Nicholas Hotel, New York City.
Comment: Fruity and all too easy to drink. Don't hold back, the lack of ice in this tall drink requires you consume while still cold. But responsibly, of course.

CRUSTAS (GENERIC NAME) 🔑

★★★★☆

Glass: Wine
Garnish: Find a lemon which fits into a small wineglass tightly enough to act as a watertight extension to the glass. Cut off both ends of the fruit and carefully remove the pulp to leave a barrel-shaped shell of skin. Place in the top of the glass. Wet the edge of the glass and exposed fruit shell with sugar syrup and dip in caster sugar to frost the edge of both peel and glass. Leave for a couple of hours to form a hard crust.
Method: SHAKE all ingredients with ice and fine strain into pre-prepared glass.

2	shots	Brandy, whisk(e)y, gin, rum etc.
½	shot	Freshly squeezed lemon juice
¼	shot	Sugar syrup (2 sugar to 1 water)
1	dash	Angostura Aromatic Bitters

Origin: The invention of the Crusta is credited to a Joseph Santina at the Jewel of the South or a Joseph Santini at the City Exchange in New Orleans sometime during the 1840s or 1850s. It first appeared in print as 'The Brandy Crusta' in Jerry Thomas' 1862 'Bartender's Guide'.

Crustas always contain a spirit, lemon juice and sugar - sometimes in the form of a liqueur or liqueurs. They are so named due to their sugar rim, which should be applied hours before the drink is made so that it is dried hard, or indeed crusty, when the drink is served. Crustas are also distinguished by being garnished with a band of orange or lemon zest, and are drunk from the rim of the fruit, rather than the rim of the glass.

As David A. Embury writes in his 1948 'The Fine Art of Mixing Drinks', "The distinguishing feature of the Crusta is that the entire inside of the glass is lined with lemon or orange peel. The drink may be served in either a wineglass or an Old-Fashioned glass, although it is much harder to make the peel fit in the Old-Fashioned glass."

Embury goes on to say, "While the 'Brandy Crusta' is the most common form of this drink, it is, after all, merely a Sour-type drink served in fancy style. Substitution of a different liquor as a base will give a Gin Crusta, a Rum Crusta, an Applejack Crusta, A Whisky Crusta, and so on."
Comment: Some cocktail historians, Ted Haigh included, consider the Crusta the forerunner of the Sidecar and in turn the Margarita. It's a very logical argument.

CRUX

★★★★☆

Glass: Martini
Garnish: Orange zest twist
Method: SHAKE all ingredients and fine strain into chilled glass.

1	shot	Martell VSOP Médaillon cognac
1	shot	De Kuyper Triple Sec
1	shot	Dubonnet Red
1	shot	Freshly squeezed lemon juice

Comment: The 'crux' of the matter is rarely as tasty as this fruity and none too sweet cognac.

Cuba Libre

The Cuba Libre is simply rum and Coca Cola with a squeeze of lime. But there is so much more to this refreshing long drink. Should it contain Angostura bitters? Exactly how much lime juice is just right? And while the drink has a rich heritage there is discourse over exactly when and who christened the combo 'Cuba Libre'.

The Cuba Libre is classically made with two wedges of lime squeezed into the glass with the spent wedges dropped into the drink. Predictably in our recipe we prefer to pour a measured amount of lime - (predicated on the use of a 12 ounce glass filled with inch square ice cubes) we use ¼ shot (7.5ml) with 2 dashes of Angostura bitters, or ½ shot (15ml) if no bitters are added. Our preference is to reduce the amount of lime and use bitters.

In his 1939 'The Gentleman's Companion', Charles H. Baker Jr. calls for the lime to be muddled to extract the oils in the skin. He writes:

"This native Island concoction started by accident and has caught on everywhere throughout the south, has filtered through the north and west. Last summer, for instance, we ran into Kooba Lee-brays 5,000 feet up in the North Carolina Mountains at High Hampton, the year before in Mexico City and Seattle. Last week in Palm Beach and Cat Cay. The only trouble with the drink is that it started by accident and without imagination, has been carried along by the ease of its supply. Under any condition it is too sweet.

"What's to do?...After clinical experimenting for which our insurance carriers heartily dislike us, we tested several variations of the original, with this result: the Improved 'Cuba Libre' consists of 1 big jigger of Carta de Oro Bacardi, the juice of 1 small green lime, and the lime peel after squeezing. Put in a Tom Collins glass, muddle well to get oil worked up over sides of glass, add lots of ice lumps, fill up with a bottle of chilled Coca Cola. Stir up once, and 'salud y pesetas'!"

The Cuba Libre peaked in popularity in America during the 1940s, partly aided by the Andrews Sisters who in 1945 had a hit single with 'Rum and Coca-Cola', named after the drink's ingredients. During the war, all spirits production went over to industrial alcohol - in the absence of whiskey and gin, Americans turned to imported Caribbean rum. Sugar was also rationed so limiting the making of many classic cocktails and affecting production of sodas such as ginger ale. However, Coca-Cola remained readily available.

Like many stories there is more than one version of how the Cuba Libre (free Cuba) was born into the world and by whom it was christened. The following account follows Bacardi's narrative. The rum was the dominant brand of rum on the island at the time (whatever that time was) and it is the brand most often identified with the drink - as in Charles H. Baker's account above.

The Cuba Libre was born out of Cuba's War of Independence with the Spanish, a war in which, like most Cubans, the Bacardi family were involved. In the late 1890s, Cuba's anti-colonial fighters were called the Mambí. Emilio Bacardi, eldest son of Emilio Bacardi, was one of them. He began his military service as aide de camp to Major General Antonio Maceo, Cuba's 'Bronze Titan', fighting the Spanish from Cuba's dense forests, or 'manigua'. During the war he was promoted to colonel, and became known as 'El Coronel'.

The war was scarcely over when, in late 1898 Warren Candler (brother of Asa Candler, then owner of Coca-Cola) sailed for Cuba, the first of twenty such trips. As a result of Warren's visits to Cuba, there in May 1899 the company hired a sales merchant to sell Coca-Cola syrup for use in soda fountains and appointed Jose Parejo, a Havana wine merchant as the Cuban distributor for Coca-Cola.

By 1900 Coca-Cola was both popular and widely available in Cuba so it is not surprising that American soldiers still garrisoned there started ordering Bacardi Cuban Rum and Coke with a squeeze of the ubiquitous lime. One soldier in particular, Captain Russell of the U.S. Signal Corps, is credited with starting this trend when one day in August 1900 he ordered the combination in a Havana bar. Naturally his drink sparked interest from the soldiers around him and before long the entire bar was drinking it. The Captain proposed a toast, 'Por Cuba libre!' in celebration of a 'free Cuba'. Fortunately for posterity, the event is supported by a sworn affidavit from a witness, Fausto Rodriguez.

Rodriguez was a personal messenger to General Wood, appointed the military governor of Cuba after entering Santiago de Cuba on 17th July 1898, after Roosevelt's victory at the battle of San Juan Hill. After the Republic of Cuba was born on 20th May 1902, General Wood left Cuba and Fausto Rodriguez returned to Santiago de Cuba. Sixty-five years later, on 21st December 1964, Rodriguez told Emilito Bacardi the following story, affirmed under oath:

During the period of military intervention, two Americans opened and operated a bar called The American Bar on Neptuno Street, between Consulado and Prado in Havana. It was patronized almost exclusively by American soldiers and by American civilians who worked in the various government offices in Havana.

"In 1899 I was employed as a messenger in the office of the U.S. Army Signal Corps, I became quite friendly with an American whose last name was Russell (I do not remember his given name). He worked in the office of the Chief Signal Officer. Mr Russell frequently took me to The American Bar where we used to drink Bacardi Rum and Coca-Cola.

One afternoon in August 1900, I went to The American Bar with Mr Russell, and he drank his usual Bacardi Rum and Coca-Cola. I just drank Coca-Cola, being only 14 years old. On that occasion, there was a group of American soldiers at the bar, and one of them asked Mr Russell what he was drinking. He told them it was Bacardi Rum and Coca-Cola and suggested they try it, which they did.

The soldiers who drank the Bacardi Rum and Coca-Cola said they liked it, and wanted to know what the drink was called. When Mr Russell told them that the drink did not have a name, one of the soldiers said, "Let's give it a name". Another said, "How about calling it 'Cuba Libre'?" They all agreed and ordered another round of Bacardi Rum and Coca-Cola, calling it a Cuba Libre. To my best knowledge, this is the first time this phrase 'Cuba Libre' has been applied to a drink. Thus, the first Cuba Libre consisted of Bacardi Rum and Coca-Cola.

During the American intervention, the words Cuba Libre - meaning Free Cuba - had a special political significance, and were used a great deal by the Cubans and Americans in Cuba. It seemed quite natural that the American soldiers selected and applied this popular slogan to this drink, which they considered indigenous to Cuba, consisting of Bacardi Rum and Coca-Cola. The name caught on quickly, and has remained popular to the present time." [sic]

This above affidavit was used by Bacardi in a 1960s advertisement and Rodriguez's story was cited in a book by Charles A. Coulombe.

However, some dispute the above turn of events arguing that Coca-Cola wasn't available in Cuba during the Spanish-American war. In his "'For God, Country and Coca-Cola, The Definitive History of the World's Most Popular Soft Drink'" (Orion Business Books 2000), Mark Pendergrast writes (in chapter 5) that Coca Cola was not commercially bottled until 1899 (an earlier 1888 bottling tasted vile so the experiment abandoned and other attempts during the 1890s did not achieve significant distribution). According to page 93, Coca-Cola appointed a sales merchant for Cuba, of fountain syrup not bottles, in May 1899, i.e., a year after the war ended in August 1898 and the U.S. troops, the Rough Riders were pulled out (September 1898).

The book has the following to say about Coca-Cola in Cuba in the 1890s:

p.69: "When the U.S. went to war with Spain in 1898, Thomas became a clerk in a Cuban commissary, where he was impressed by the popularity of a carbonated pineapple drink called Pina Frio. Upon his return to Chattanooga the following year, he decided that perhaps his fortune lay in bottling the popular soda fountain drink, Coca-Cola..." - he then went onto get a bottling contract for parts of the United States, not Cuba."

p.93: "The war was scarcely over when, in late 1898, Warren Candler sailed for Cuba, the first of twenty such visits. Upon his return, he enthusiastically reported that Cuba was "our nearest, neediest, ripest missionary field"...After hearing about this "ripe field" from Warren, Asa promptly enlisted Jose Parejo, a wine merchant, as a Havana wholesaler for Coca-Cola in May of 1899."

According to Wikipedia, "Coca-Cola was sold in bottles for the first time on March 12, 1894. Cans of Coke first appeared in 1955. The first bottling of Coca-Cola occurred in Vicksburg, Mississippi, at the Biedenharn Candy Company in 1891. Its proprietor was Joseph A. Biedenharn. The original bottles were Biedenharn bottles, very different from the much later hobble-skirt design that is now so familiar."

According to The Biedenham Coca-Cola Museum, "Replying to your inquiry in your recent letter, beg to advise that I think it was in the summer of 1894 that we first bottled Coca-Cola at what was then 218-220 Washington Street, Vicksburg, Mississippi."

Reading the above there is little doubt that Coca Cola was available in Cuba in 1900 and that's when Mr Russell is said to have christened the drink 'Cuba Libre'. I guess not all the U.S. troops left Cuba in September 1898. And we all know how hard it is to withdrawal troops after the U.S. and its allies have intervened in another country's conflict!

CUBA LIBRE

★★★★☆

Glass: Collins
Garnish: Lime wedge
Method: POUR ingredients into ice-filled glass and lightly stir.

3	shots	Coca-Cola
2	shots	Bacardi Carta Oro rum
¼	shot	Freshly squeezed lime juice
2	dash	Angostura Aromatic Bitters
Top with		Coca-Cola

Comment: Basically a rum and coke with a squeeze of lime, but Cuba Libre has much more of a ring about it. And it is much more of a drink, the squeeze of lime and dashes of bitters add layers of complexity, balancing the sweetness of the cola.

CUBA PINTADA

★★★½☆

Glass: Collins
Garnish: Lime wedge
Method: **POUR** ingredients in to ice-filled glass, **STIR** and serve with straws.

2 shots Bacardi Carta Blanca light rum
1 shot Coca-Cola
Top with Soda (club soda)

Comment: The name of this popular Cuban drink literally means 'stained Cuba' and there is just enough cola in this rum and soda to stain the drink brown.

CUBAN COCKTAIL NO.2 #1

★★★½☆

Glass: Martini
Garnish: Lemon zest twist
Method: **SHAKE** all ingredients with ice and fine strain into chilled glass.

1½ shots Bacardi Carta Blanca light rum
⅛ shot Luxardo Maraschino liqueur
⅛ shot Pomegranate / grenadine syrup (2:1)
¼ shot Freshly squeezed lemon juice
1 dash Angostura Orange Bitters
½ shot Chilled water (omit if wet ice)

Origin: Adapted from Victor Bergeron's 'Trader Vic's Bartender's Guide' (1972 revised edition).
Comment: Perfumed yet not sweetened rum.

CUBAN COCKTAIL NO.3 #2

★★★½☆

Glass: Martini
Garnish: Lemon zest twist
Method: **SHAKE** all ingredients with ice and fine strain into chilled glass.

1½ shots Bacardi Carta Oro rum
¼ shot Martell VSOP Médaillon cognac
½ shot De Kuyper XO Apricot Brandy
½ shot Freshly squeezed lime juice
1 dash Angostura Orange Bitters
½ shot Chilled water (omit if wet ice)

Origin: Adapted from Victor Bergeron's 'Trader Vic's Bartender's Giude' (1972) revised edition).
Comment: Like much of the caribbean, this drink has French influences. Thank goodness for Admiral Rodney.

CUBAN HEAL

★★★★☆

Glass: Martini
Garnish: Lemon zest twist
Method: **STIR** all ingredients with ice and strain into chilled glass.

2½ shots Bacardi Carta Blanca light rum
¼ shot Cynar
¼ shot Pallini Limoncello
¼ shot Honey sugar syrup
2 dash Peychaud's aromatic bitters

Origin: Created in 2008 by Matthew Keegan at Blanch House, Brighton, England. The ingredients were chosen due to their historically being believed to be remedies.
Comment: Honey-ed and initially sweet with herbal spirity rum notes adding depth.

CUBAN ISLAND

★★★½☆

Glass: Martini
Garnish: Orange zest twist
Method: **SHAKE** all ingredients with ice and fine strain into chilled glass.

2 shots Bacardi Carta Blanca light rum
½ shot Martini Extra Dry vermouth
½ shot Freshly squeezed lemon juice
¼ shot Sugar syrup (2 sugar to 1 water)

Origin: Adapted from a drink discovered in 2005 at Di Vino's, Hong Kong.
Comment: The Daiquiri meets the Wet Martini.

CUBAN LIBERAL

★★★★★

Glass: Coupe
Garnish: Orange zest twist
Method: **SHAKE** all ingredients with ice and fine strain into chilled glass.

1½ shots Bacardi Carta Blanca light rum
1 shot Martini Rosso vermouth
½ spoon Amer Picon
2 dash Angostura Orange Bitters

Origin: Adapted from a drink featured in bar La Florida (El Floridita) Cocktails of 1935.
Comment: Light white rum mellowed by Italian vermouth and made interesting with bittersweet French Amer Picon liqueur.

CUBAN MASTER

★★★☆☆

Glass: Collins
Garnish: None
Method: **SHAKE** all ingredients with ice and fine strain into chilled glass.

1½ shots Bacardi Carta Blanca light rum
1 shot Martell VSOP Médaillon cognac
1½ shots Freshly squeezed orange juice
1½ shots Fresh pressed pineapple juice
½ shot Freshly squeezed lemon juice
¼ shot Sugar syrup (2 sugar to 1 water)

Origin: A classic cocktail discovered in 1999 during a trip to in Cuba.
Comment: Well balanced, wonderfully fruity.

CUBAN SPECIAL

★★★☆☆

Glass: Old-fashioned
Garnish: Orange zest twist
Method: **SHAKE** ingredients with ice and strain into ice-filled glass.

1½ shots Bacardi Carta Blanca light rum
¾ shot De Kuyper Triple Sec
2 shots Fresh pressed pineapple juice
¼ shot Freshly squeezed lime juice

Comment: Not that special, but certainly OK.

CUBANITA

★★★★☆

Glass: Collins
Garnish: Lime wedge
Method: SHAKE all ingredients with ice and strain into ice-filled glass.

2	shots	Bacardi Carta Blanca light rum
3½	shots	Tomato juice
½	shot	Freshly squeezed lemon juice
7	dash	Tabasco hot pepper sauce
4	dash	Worcestershire sauce
½	spoon	Horseradish sauce
2	pinch	Celery salt
2	pinch	Black pepper

Comment: The Bloody Mary returns - this time with rum.

CUBATA 0⚊

★★★⯪☆

Glass: Collins
Garnish: Lime wedge
Method: SHAKE gin and lime with ice and strain into ice-filled glass. TOP with cola and serve with straws.

2	shots	Rutte Dry Gin
½	shot	Freshly squeezed lime juice
Top with		Coca-Cola

Origin: The gin-based equivalent to the rum-based Cuba Libre. This drink is popular in Spain where gin is the dominant spirit.
Comment: Hard to hate but the cola and lime dominate the subtle gin flavours.

CUCUMBER & MINT MARTINI 0⚊

★★★★☆

Glass: Martini
Garnish: Cucumber slices
Method: MUDDLE cucumber and mint in base of shaker. Add other ingredients, SHAKE with ice and fine strain into chilled glass.

2	inch	English cucumber peeled
7	fresh	Mint leaves
2	shots	Ketel One Vodka
1	shot	Pressed apple juice
¼	shot	Sugar syrup (2 sugar to 1 water)

Origin: Created in 2004 by David Ramos in the Netherlands.
Comment: A well balanced fortified salad in a glass - almost healthy.

CUCUMBER MARTINI

★★★★⯪

Glass: Martini
Garnish: Cucumber peel
Method: MUDDLE cucumber in base of shaker. Add other ingredients, SHAKE with ice and strain into glass.

1	shot	Ketel One Vodka
1	shot	Zubrówka bison vodka
2	inch	English cucumber peeled
½	shot	Sugar syrup (2 sugar to 1 water)

Origin: There are many different Cucumber Martini recipes; this is mine.
Comment: Cucumber has never tasted so good.

CUCUMBER SAKE-TINI

★★★★☆

Glass: Martini
Garnish: Cucumber slices
Method: MUDDLE cucumber in base of shaker. Add other ingredients, SHAKE with ice and fine strain into chilled glass.

1½	inch	English cucumber peeled
1½	shots	Ketel One Vodka
1½	shots	Junmai ginjō sake
¼	shot	Sugar syrup (2 sugar to 1 water)

Origin: Created in 2004 by Lisa Ball, London, England.
Comment: Subtle and dry. Cucumber and sake are made for each other.

CULROSS COCKTAIL 0⚊

★★★★☆

Glass: Coupe
Garnish: Orange zest twist
Method: SHAKE all ingredients with ice and fine strain into chilled glass.

1	shot	Bacardi Carta Blanca light rum
1	shot	De Kuyper XO Apricot Brandy
1	shot	Martini Extra Dry
¾	shot	Freshly squeezed lemon juice

Comment: Light rum, aromatic wine served 'up' with the marzipan and almond notes of apricot liqueur. Originally made with Lillet Blanc in place of dry vermouth.

CUMBERSOME

★★★★☆

Glass: Martini
Garnish: Physalis (cape gooseberry)
Method: MUDDLE cucumber in base of shaker. Add other ingredients, SHAKE with ice and strain into a chilled Martini glass.

4	inch	English cucumber peeled
2	shots	Rutte Dry Gin
½	shot	Campari Bitter
1	shot	Freshly squeezed orange juice
½	shot	Sugar syrup (2 sugar to 1 water)

Origin: Created in 2002 by Shelim Islam at the GE Club, London, England.
Comment: Interesting and fresh as you like with a pleasant bitterness.

CUNNINGHAM

★★★★⯪

Glass: Martini
Garnish: Flamed blood orange zest twist and Luxardo maraschino cherry
Method: SHAKE all ingredients with ice and fine strain into a chilled glass.

1¾	shots	Dewar's 12 Year Old Scotch whisky
½	shot	Freshly squeezed lemon juice
½	shot	Blood orange juice
½	shot	Bénédictine D.O.M. liqueur
½	shot	Cherry Heering Liqueur

Origin: Adapted from a recipe created by Marco Dionysos at Tres Agaves, San Francisco, USA and in memory of Johnny Cunningham (1957 - 2003), one of the world's all-time great Scottish fiddlers.
Comment: Reminiscent of a Blood and Sand with Bénédictine and lemon juice replacing sweet vermouth.

CUPPA JOE

★★★★☆

Glass: Martini
Garnish: Lemon zest twist
Method: SHAKE all ingredients with ice and fine strain into chilled glass.

1½ shots   Ketel One Vodka
1½ shots   Espresso coffee (freshly made & hot)
1½ shots   Hazelnut liqueur

Origin: Created in 2003 at Cellar Bar, New York City, USA.
Comment: Nutty coffee fortified with vodka - well balanced.

CURDISH COCKTAIL

★★★★☆

Glass: Martini
Garnish: Lemon zest twist
Method: STIR lemon curd with gin in base of shaker until curd dissolves. Add other ingredients, SHAKE with ice and fine strain into chilled glass.

2   shots   Rutte Dry Gin
2   spoon   Lemon curd
½   shot   Sour apple liqueur
½   shot   Freshly squeezed lime juice

Origin: Created in 2001 by Tadgh Ryan at West Street, London, England.
Comment: Beautifully balanced with the tang of lemon curd.

THE CURRIER

★★★★☆

Glass: Martini
Garnish: Mint leaf
Method: SHAKE all ingredients with ice and fine strain into chilled glass.

1½ shots   Bourbon whiskey
½   shot   Kümmel
¼   shot   Freshly squeezed lime juice
¼   shot   Rose's lime cordial

Origin: Recipe submitted in July 2006 by Murray Stenson at ZigZag Café, Seattle, USA.
Comment: A wonderfully cleansing after dinner cocktail with bourbon and lime plus hints of caraway and fennel courtesy of Kümmel.

CUSTARD TART

★★★★☆

Glass: Shot
Garnish: Physalis (cape gooseberry)
Method: MUDDLE physalis fruits in base of shaker can. Add other ingredients, SHAKE with ice and strain.

3   fresh   Physalis fruits
¾   shot   Bacardi Carta Blanca light rum
½   shot   Warninks Advocaat liqueur
½   shot   Peachtree peach schnapps
¼   shot   Freshly squeezed lime juice

Origin: Created by Alex Kammerling in 2001.
Comment: Custardy, strangely enough.

CVO FIREVAULT

★★★★☆

Glass: Martini
Garnish: Orange zest twist
Method: SHAKE all ingredients with ice and fine strain into chilled glass.

1½ shots   Ketel One Vodka
¾   shot   Campari Bitter
¾   shot   Freshly squeezed orange juice
¾   shot   Fresh pressed pineapple juice

Origin: Discovered in 2005 at CVO Firevault, London, England.
Comment: Fruity yet slightly bitter. Orange predominates with strong bursts of Campari.

CYDER PRESS

★★★★☆

Glass: Martini
Garnish: Apple slice
Method: SHAKE all ingredients with ice and fine strain into chilled glass.

2   shots   Calvados brandy
1   shot   Medium dry cider
½   shot   St-Germain elderflower liqueur
¾   shot   Pressed apple juice

Origin: Created in 2006 by yours truly, London, England.
Comment: Fresh, fermented and distilled apple juice with a hint of elderflower.

D'ARTAGNAN

★★★½☆

Glass: Martini
Garnish: Lemon zest twist
Method: SHAKE first four ingredients with ice and fine strain into chilled glass. TOP with champagne.

½   shot   Armagnac brandy
½   shot   Grand Marnier Cordon Rouge
2   shots   Freshly squeezed orange juice
¼   shot   Sugar syrup (2 sugar to 1 water)
Top with   G.H. Mumm Brut
           Cordon Rouge champagne

Comment: Use genuine freshly pressed juice and you'll have a tasty Mimosa-style drink.

DAIQUIRI AUTHENTICO

★★★★½

Glass: Martini
Garnish: Lime wedge
Method: SHAKE all ingredients with ice and fine strain into chilled glass.

2   shots   Bacardi Carta Blanca light rum
¼   shot   Galliano L'Autentico liqueur
½   shot   Freshly squeezed lime juice
¼   shot   Sugar syrup (2 sugar to 1 water)

Origin: A simplification of a drink created in 2008 by Erik Lorincz at Purple Bar, Sanderson Hotel, London, England.
Comment: A lightly peppermint spiced influenced daiquiri.

DAIQUIRI DE LUXE

★★★★☆

Glass: Martini
Garnish: Lime wedge
Method: SHAKE all ingredients with ice and fine strain into chilled glass.

2	shots	Bacardi Carta Blanca light rum
¼	shot	Rose's lime cordial
½	shot	Freshly squeezed lime juice
¼	shot	Almond (orgeat) syrup
¼	shot	Chilled water (omit if wet ice)

Comment: A classic Daiquiri but with lime cordial and almond syrup replacing sugar as the sweetener.

DAIQUIRI ELIXIR

★★★★★

Glass: Martini
Garnish: Lime wedge
Method: SHAKE all ingredients with ice and fine strain into chilled glass.

2	shots	Bacardi Carta Blanca light rum
½	shot	Freshly squeezed lime juice
¼	shot	Martinique cane sugar syrup
⅛	shot	Green Chartreuse liqueur
½	shot	Chilled water (omit if wet ice)

Origin: A Daiquiri variation by yours truly.
Comment: Freshly pressed sugar cane syrup and the French elixir Chartreuse add complexity to the classic Daiquiri.

Daiquiri Cocktail

Pronounced 'Dye-Ker-Ree', this drink bears a close relationship to the Canchanchara, a 19th century Cuban blend of rum, lemon, honey and water, but the Daiquiris creation is credited to Jennings Stockton Cox, an American engineer at the turn of the 20th century.

In 1898, after Roosevelt's victory at the Battle of San Juan Hill, the Americans began to exploit Cuba's iron-ore mines and Cox led one of the initial exploratory expeditions. Cox and his team worked in the Sierra Maestra Mountains on the south-eastern shore of Cuba where the small town of Daiquiri lies and it was while he was there that he created his classic drink.

The engineers received substantial salaries and generous tobacco rations, after all there had to be some inducements for these qualified engineers to leave secure positions in the USA and brave the threat of yellow fever in Cuba. Thankfully our hero also requested they each received a monthly ration of the local rum, Bacardi Carta Blanca, and noticing that the Cuban workers often mixed Bacardi with their evening coffee, he began to experiment himself.

Drinks legend has it that another engineer called Pagliuchi was viewing mines in the region and met with Cox. During their meeting they set about making a drink from the ingredients Cox had to hand: rum, limes and sugar. Cox's granddaughter recounts a slightly different tale; namely that Cox ran out of gin when entertaining American guests. Wary of serving them straight rum, he added lime and sugar. However Cox came to concoct the drink, the result was sublime.

On page 38 of his 1928 book, 'When it's Cocktail Time in Cuba', Basil Woon writes that this drink was popular with a group who used to meet in Santiago's Venus bar every morning at eight o'clock. "The boys used to have three or four every morning. Most of them worked in the Daiquiri mines, the superintendent of which was a gentleman named Cox - Jennings Cox. One morning in the Venus Cox said: "Boys, we've been drinking this delicious little drink for some time, but we've never named

it. Let's christen it now!" The boys milled around a bit and finally Cox said: "I'll tell you what, lads - we all work at Daiquiri and we all drank this drink first there. Let's call it a Daiquiri."

Woon's account documents the origin and naming of the Daiquiri and unlike many other cocktails where their creation is lost in time, that of the Daiquiri is well substantiated, including the original recipe, recorded by Jennings Cox in his personal diary.

The Daiquiri seems to have travelled back to America with US Admiral Lucius Johnson, who fought in the Spanish-American war of 1898. He introduced the drink to the Army & Navy Club in Washington DC and a plaque in their Daiquiri Lounge records his place in cocktail history.

In his seminal 1948 'Fine Art of Mixing Drinks', David A. Embury writes, "The Daiquiri, like the Old-Fashioned, deserves an even greater popularity than it now enjoys. For example, it is in my opinion, a vastly superior cocktail to the Manhattan, yet most bars sell more Manhattans than Daiquiris. So far as I can ascertain there are two main reasons why more Daiquiris are not sold: The use of inferior rums and the use of improper proportions."

To address those two points...

In his personal diary Jennings Cox records his original Daiquiri recipe (to serve six) as follows: "The juice of six lemons; Six teaspoons full of sugar; Six Bacardi cups ('Carta Blanca'); Two small cups of mineral water; Plenty of crushed ice"

This original recipe and other such historical references specify Bacardi Carta Blanca as the rum used to make a Daiquiri. Thus to make an authentic Daiquiri you should use a light white rum. And as Bacardi purports to be made using the same strain of cultured yeast and recipe as in Jennings Cox's day, then modern day Bacardi Carta Blanca appears a natural first choice. I find that Bacardi has a delicate mushroom/blue cheese note, which adds a distinctive character that I like in the finished drink. In the interest of balanced editorial I should also mention I'm also a fan of El Dorado 3 Year Old in my Daiquiris.

Although Cox's recipe records the use of lemons it is most likely that he is actually referring to limes which are native to Cuba and that the confusion arises due to the common Cuban term for lime being 'limón'. Again to quote from Embury, "Actually lemons are almost unknown in Cuba, whereas lime trees grow in everyone's own yard."

Embury's own recipe calls for sugar syrup and this is something with which I whole-heartedly agree as granulated or caster sugar does not as readily dissolve in cold liquid. If you must insist in 'spooning' rather than pouring your sugar please use a mortar and pestle to first crush caster sugar to a fine powder, often termed 'bar sugar' or 'powdered sugar'.

Better still, make your own sugar syrup by pouring one cup of filtered water into a saucepan and over a very low heat, so as not to even come close to boiling, stir in two cups of caster sugar. Allow to cool, bottle and store in a refrigerator where it will last for a couple of months.

Thus we have our ingredients: Bacardi Carta Blanca, freshly squeezed lime juice and 2:1 (double strength) sugar syrup. Now for the perfect proportions.

London's most famous bartender, Dick Bradsell, originally taught me Embury's 8:2:1 Daiquiri formula and I used to believe this was the best (I still do when making Daiquiris with aged rum.) Embury's 8:2:1 Daiquiri consists: 8 parts (2 shots) white label Cuban rum, 2 parts (1/2 shot) lime juice and 1 part (1/4 shot) sugar syrup.

Some bartenders make Daiquiris according to the classic Margarita formula with twice as much lime and sugar as Embury. Known as the Daiquiri No.1 natural ('countdown' 3:2:1 formula), I have experimented with this but found that while tequila is robust enough to shine above the citrus flavour such a large proportion of lime tends to overpower the more delicate flavours of light rum. However, I do prefer a small increase in lime but in proportion to a similar small increase in the rum. After all a mere two measures of rum would hardly satisfy great Daiquiri drinkers such as Hemingway. Thus I have now settled on my 10:3:2 formula.

Embury's mixing instructions are, "Shake vigorously with plenty of finely crushed ice and strain into chilled cocktail glasses." This is to add dilution, a crucial aspect to mixing a perfect Daiquiri. As crushed ice is so variable in its wetness and so also the amount of dilution it adds to a drink, instead I prefer to shake with large cubes of double frozen ice taken from a freezer with the addition of 1/2 shot iced water. (I refreeze cubed ice produced by ice machine). I aim to shake with such vigour that there is instead some degree of crushed ice left in the shaker when I strain the drink. This makes for an ice-cold Daiquiri with the controlled dilution essential to great straight-up Daiquiris.

A

In my formative Daiquiri drinking years I followed the convention that a Daiquiri No.1 should be served 'straight-up'. However, I have now reverted to drinking my Daiquiris 'on-the-rocks' and interestingly Cox's original recipe suggests that this may also be the way he originally intended the drink to be served.

B

In his diary Cox stipulates, "Put all ingredients in a cocktail shaker and shake well. Do not strain as the glass may be served with some ice." And as Albert S. Crockett notes of this drink in his 1935 "The Old Waldorf-Astoria Bar Book", "Personal preference dictates serving the cocktail with finely shaved ice in the glass."

C

Obviously serving a drink over ice will add dilution so rendering the additional dash of water to my 10:3:2 Daiquiri formula superfluous. Having tried 'up' and 'on-the-rocks' Daiquiris made to the same formula next to each other I have to admit that more nuances are found in the 'up' when compared to 'on-the-rocks'. However, I prefer holding and drinking from a big heavy old-fashioned glass rather than a delicate V-shaped Martini or curvaceous Coupette. Thus I now vary my serve according to mood but with a shot of water added when served 'up' and omitted when served 'on-the-rocks'.

D

E

F

The 'frozen' blended Daiquiri is said to have first been produced by Emilio Gonzalez at the Plaza Hotel in Cuba. However, it was made famous by Constantino (Constante) Ribalagua Vert who presided over the bar at Havana's La Florida (later renamed Floridita to distinguish it from the restaurant of the same name) for some forty years until his death in early December 1952.

G

H

David Embury writes of Havana's Floridita, "This restaurant, at the corner of Obispo and Monserrate streets in Havana, became known as 'La Catedral del Daiquiri' (The Temple of the Daiquiri) and Ribalagua as the Cocktail King - 'El Rey de los Coteleros'". The title was, indeed, well deserved. His limes were gently squeezed with his fingers lest even a drop of the bitter oil from the peel got into the drink; the cocktails were mixed (but not over mixed) in a Waring Blender; the stinging cold drink was strained through a fine sieve into the glass so that not one tiny piece of the ice remained in it. No smallest detail was overlooked in achieving the flawless perfection of the drink.

I

J

K

Ernest Hemingway, the hard-drinking, Nobel prize-winning author, lived in Cuba for years, indulging his passions for fishing, shooting and boozing. In the 30s and the 40s he would often work his way through twelve of the Floridita's frozen Daiquiris - often doubles, renamed 'Papa Dobles' in his honour. The Hemingway Special Daiquiri, which includes grapefruit, was created for him.

L

M

In his book 'Islands in the Stream', Hemingway's hero stares deep into his frozen Daiquiri, and Hemingway writes, "It reminded him of the sea. The frappéd part of the drink was like the wake of a ship and the clear part was the way the water looked when the bow cut it when you were in shallow water over marl bottom. That was almost the exact colour."

N

O

There's nothing like a Frozen Daiquiri to quench your thirst on a hot summer's day and after experimentation I use a 16:6:6:1 formula with the all-important maraschino.

P

When I visited Cuba I quickly learnt that in Cuba you need to ask for a "Natural Daiquiri" if you seek a Daiquiri shaken rather than blended. Wherever you are in the world, when ordering a Daiquiri you need to convey to the bartender exactly what Daiquiri you desire. It is essential you're specific, otherwise ordering just a 'Daiquiri' could result in your being asked, "What flavour would you like - strawberry, banana, mango or pineapple?" In such cases answering "just lime please" often leaves the questioner perplexed.

Q

R

S

To further confuse the ordering of a Daiquiri, the great Ribalagua listed his Daiquiri adaptations as Daiquiri No.2, No.3, No.4 and No.5. Thus a simple 'original' or 'classic' Daiquiri should properly be termed 'Daiquiri No.1' and this can be served either 'Natural' (straight-up), 'On-The-Rocks' (over cubed ice) or 'Frozen' (blended with crushed ice).

T

U

V

W

X

Y

Z

STAR RATINGS EXPLAINED

★★★★★+ OUTSTANDING	★★★★★ EXCEPTIONAL
★★★★☆ EXCELLENT	★★★★☆ RECOMMENDED
★★★☆☆ COMMENDED	★★★☆☆ MEDIOCRE
★★☆☆☆ DISAPPOINTING	★★☆☆☆ PRETTY AWFUL
★☆☆☆☆ SHAMEFUL	★☆☆☆☆ DISGUSTING

DAIQUIRI NO.1 (EL FLORIDITA STYLE)

★★★★☆

Glass: Martini
Garnish: Luxardo Maraschino cherry
Method: BLEND all ingredients with 6oz scoop of crushed ice. Pour into glass and serve.

2	shots	Bacardi Carta Blanca light rum
1/8	shot	Luxardo Maraschino liqueur
1/2	shot	Freshly squeezed lime juice
1/4	shot	Freshly squeezed pink grapefruit juice
1/2	shot	Sugar syrup (2 sugar to 1 water)

Origin: Emilio Gonzalez is said to have first adapted the Natural Daiquiri into this frozen version at the Plaza Hotel in Cuba. However, Constantino Ribalaigua Vert of Havana's Floridita bar made the drink famous in 1912 and today the Floridita is known as 'the cradle of the Daiquiri'.
Comment: Great on a hot day, but the coldness masks much of the flavour evident when this drink is served 'up' or natural.

DAIQUIRI NO.1 FROZEN (DIFFORD'S 16:6:6:1 FORMULA)

★★★★★

Glass: Martini
Garnish: Luxardo Maraschino cherry
Method: BLEND well all ingredients with 6oz scoop of crushed ice. **STRAIN** blended drink through a fine strainer to remove ice fragments.

2	shots	Bacardi Carta Blanca light rum
3/4	shot	Freshly squeezed lime juice
3/4	shot	Sugar syrup (2 sugar to 1 water)
1/8	shot	Luxardo Maraschino liqueur

Comment: Blend with too much ice and you will have a tasteless slushy drink that will give you brain-ache if you drink it too fast. However, made correctly and fine strained this is a superbly refreshing drink on a hot day.

DAIQUIRI NO.1 NATURAL (COUNTDOWN 3:2:1 FORMULA)

★★★★☆

Glass: Martini
Garnish: Lime wedge
Method: SHAKE all ingredients with ice and fine strain into chilled glass.

2¼ shots Bacardi Carta Blanca light rum
1½ shots Freshly squeezed lime juice
¾ shot Sugar syrup (2 sugar to 1 water)
½ shot Chilled water (omit if wet ice)
3 drop Difford's Daiquiri Bitters

Origin: I am indebted to Roger Vilalta who in 2010 at Banker's Bar in Barcelona, Spain made me an excellent daiquiri using this formula.
Comment: Made to the easy-to-remember 3:2:1 Daiquiri (or countdown) formula this balanced but limey daiquiri lacks the poise of my preferred 10:3:2 formula.

DAIQUIRI NO.1 NATURAL (DIFFORD'S 10:3:2 RECIPE) 🗝️

★★★★★

Glass: Martini
Garnish: Lime wedge
Method: Bitter lime zest oils are key to the balance of this drink. Hence, peel your lime before squeezing for juice and then add two slices (cut pole to pole) of lime peel with other ingredients. Then SHAKE with ice and fine strain into chilled glass

2½ shots Bacardi Carta Blanca light rum
¾ shot Freshly squeezed lime juice
½ shot Sugar syrup (2 sugar to 1 water)
½ shot Chilled water (omit if wet ice)
2 slice Lime peel

Comment: Crisp, light and refreshing. Perfectly balanced complexity of flavours.

DAIQUIRI NO.1 NATURAL (EMBURY'S 8:2:1 FORMULA)

★★★★★

Glass: Martini
Garnish: Lime wedge
Method: SHAKE all ingredients with ice and fine strain into chilled glass.

2	shots	Bacardi Carta Ocho aged rum
½	shot	Freshly squeezed lime juice
¼	shot	Sugar syrup (2 sugar to 1 water)
½	shot	Chilled water (omit if wet ice)

Origin: According to David A. Embury's 1948 'Fine Art of Mixing Drinks' the classic proportions of a daiquiri are: 8 parts (2 shots) white label Cuban rum, 2 parts (1/2 shot) lime juice and 1 part (1/4 shot) sugar syrup. I have added the optional addition of water for increased dilution.
Comment: Traditionally a Natural Daiquiri should always be based on light rum but if I should feel like breaking with tradition and using aged rum, I find Embury's 8:2:1 formula works particularly well.

DAIQUIRI NO.1 ON-THE-ROCKS (DIFFORD'S 10:3:2 FORMULA) 🗝️

★★★★★

Glass: Old-fashioned
Garnish: Lime slice & Luxardo Maraschino cherry
Method: SHAKE all ingredients with ice and fine strain into ice-filled glass.

2½	shots	Bacardi Carta Blanca light rum
¾	shot	Freshly squeezed lime juice
½	shot	Sugar syrup (2 sugar to 1 water)

Comment: Light and refreshing. No one flavour predominates - sweet and sour are in harmony with the rum.

DAIQUIRI NO.2 🗝️

★★★★⯪

Glass: Martini
Garnish: Lime wedge
Method: SHAKE all ingredients with ice and fine strain into chilled glass.

2	shots	Bacardi Carta Blanca light rum
⅛	shot	De Kuyper Triple Sec
½	shot	Freshly squeezed orange juice
½	shot	Freshly squeezed lime juice
¼	shot	Sugar syrup (2 sugar to 1 water)

Origin: Created circa 1915 by Constantino (Constante) Ribalaigua Vert at Floridita bar in Havana, Cuba.
Comment: A Daiquiri with subtle orange notes, but far from being a mere Orange Daiquiri.

DAIQUIRI NO.2 (EL FLORIDITA STYLE)

★★★⯪☆

Glass: Martini
Garnish: Lime wedge
Method: SHAKE all ingredients with ice and fine strain into chilled glass.

2	shots	Bacardi Carta Blanca light rum
½	shot	Martini Rosso vermouth
½	shot	Freshly squeezed lime juice
¼	shot	White crème de cacao liqueur
⅛	shot	Pomegranate / grenadine syrup (2:1)

Comment: Like other Daiquiris, this complex version benefits from dilution so consider adding a dash of water.

DAIQUIRI NO.3

★★★★★

Glass: Old-fashioned
Garnish: Lime wedge
Method: SHAKE all ingredients with ice and fine strain into chilled glass.

2 shots Bacardi Carta Blanca light rum
½ shot Freshly squeezed lime juice
½ shot Sugar syrup (2 sugar to 1 water)
¼ shot Freshly squeezed pink grapefruit juice
⅛ shot Luxardo Maraschino liqueur

Origin: Thought to have been created by Constantino (Constante) Ribalaigua Vert at the Floridita bar in Havana, Cuba, circa 1915. If this was invented as early as 1915, then this was the predecessor of the Hemingway Daiquiri, since Hemingway did not arrive in Cuba until 1928.
Comment: A Daiquiri No.1 with a tang of grapefruit and hint of maraschino. Essentially a Hemingway Special Daiquiri (Papa Doble Daiquiri) for folk without the great author's constitution or love of the sours.

DAIQUIRI NO.4 (FLORIDA STYLE)

★★★★☆

Glass: Martini
Garnish: Lime wedge
Method: SHAKE all ingredients with finely crushed ice and strain into chilled glass.

2 shots Bacardi Carta Oro rum
½ shot Lime (fresh whole)
¼ shot Sugar syrup (2 sugar to 1 water)
¼ shot Luxardo Maraschino liqueur
½ shot Chilled water (reduce if wet ice)

Origin: Created by Constantino (Constante) Ribalaigua Vert at the Floridita bar in Havana, Cuba. This recipe is adapted from a 1937 Bar Florida (later renamed Floridita) menu, also in Havana, Cuba.
Comment: Maraschino cherry liqueur flavours this finely balanced golden rum based Daiquiri.

DAIQUIRI NO.5 (PINK DAIQUIRI)

★★★★☆

Glass: Martini
Garnish: Lime wedge
Method: SHAKE all ingredients with ice and fine strain into chilled glass.

2 shots Bacardi Carta Blanca light rum
⅛ shot Luxardo Maraschino liqueur
¼ shot Pomegranate / grenadine syrup (2:1)
½ shot Freshly squeezed lime juice
¼ shot Sugar syrup (2 sugar to 1 water)

Origin: Created by Constantino (Constante) Ribalaigua Vert at the Floridita bar in Havana, Cuba.
Comment: Classically tangy Daiquiri but sweetened with pomegranate syrup and a splash of maraschino.

DAIQUIRI NOIR

★★★★☆

Glass: Martini
Garnish: Mint sprig
Method: Lightly MUDDLE mint in base of shaker. Add other ingredients, SHAKE with ice and fine strain into chilled glass.

7 fresh Mint leaves
2 shots Bacardi Carta Ocho aged rum
½ shot Drambuie liqueur
½ shot Freshly squeezed lime juice
¼ shot Sugar syrup (2 sugar to 1 water)

Origin: Drambuie adds herbal consistency to this minty fresh aged rum Daiquiri.
Comment: Discovered in 2008 at Hugos Bar Pizza, Sydney, Australia.

DAISY CUTTER MARTINI

★★★★☆

Glass: Martini
Garnish: Mint leaf
Method: Lightly MUDDLE mint in base of shaker (just to bruise). Add other ingredients, SHAKE with ice and fine strain into chilled glass.

3 fresh Mint leaves
1½ shots Ketel One Vodka
1 shot St-Germain elderflower liqueur
1 shot Martini Extra Dry vermouth
¼ shot Yellow Chartreuse liqueur

Origin: Created in 2006 by yours truly. Named not for the bomb but after the English cricketing term for a ball bowled so incompetently that it skims along the ground.
Comment: Floral, minty and herbal with a dry finish.

DAISY DUKE ⚷

★★★☆☆

Glass: Old-fashioned
Garnish: Seasonal berries
Method: SHAKE all ingredients with ice and strain into glass filled with crushed ice. Serve with straws.

2 shots Bourbon whiskey
½ shot Pomegranate / grenadine syrup (2:1)
1 shot Freshly squeezed lemon juice

Origin: Created in 2002 by Jake Burger at Townhouse, Leeds, England.
Comment: This bright red drink tastes more adult than it looks.

DAMN IT JIMMY

★★★★☆

Glass: Martini
Garnish: Blue cheese stuffed olives
Method: STIR all ingredients with ice and fine strain into chilled glass.

1½ shots Junmai ginjō sake
1½ shots Bacardi Carta Blanca light rum
¼ shot Romate Fino sherry
¼ shot Martini Extra Dry vermouth
¼ shot Sugar syrup (2 sugar to 1 water)

Origin: Created in August 2008 by yours truly at the Cabinet Room, London, England.
Comment: Delicately flavoured and ever so slightly sweet.

DAMN-THE WEATHER ⚷

★★★☆☆

Glass: Martini
Garnish: Orange zest twist
Method: SHAKE all ingredients with ice and fine strain into chilled glass.

1 shot Rutte Dry Gin
½ shot De Kuyper Triple Sec
1 shot Martini Rosso vermouth
1½ shots Freshly squeezed orange juice

Comment: Gin and herbal notes emerge in this predominantly orange drink.

DAMSON IN DISTRESS

★★★★☆

Glass: Shot
Garnish: None
Method: **SHAKE** all ingredients with ice and fine strain into chilled glass.

1½ shots Damson gin liqueur
½ shot Disaronno Originale amaretto
¼ shot Freshly squeezed lemon juice

Origin: Discovered in 2003 at Hush, London, England.
Comment: Damson and amaretto sharpened by lemon.

THE DANDY (NEW)

★★★★☆

Glass: Coupe
Garnish: Seasonal berries
Method: **STIR** first 3 ingredients with ice and strain into chilled glass. **TOP** with champagne.

2 shots Martell VSOP Médaillon cognac
⅓ shot Bénédictine D.O.M. liqueur
¼ shot Luxardo Maraschino liqueur
1½ shots G.H. Mumm Brut Cordon Rouge champagne

Origin: Adapted from a recipe discovered at Hawksmoor Spitalfields, London in 2014.
Comment: Bénédictine adds both saffron flavour and vivid yellow colour to this cognac based cocktail with maraschino contributing fruity notes. Champagne dries and provides effervescence and body to this well-balanced cocktail.

DANDY COCKTAIL

★★★★½

Glass: Martini
Garnish: Lemon & orange zest twists
Method: **STIR** all ingredients with ice and strain into chilled glass.

1½ shots Bourbon whiskey
½ shot De Kuyper Triple Sec
1½ shots Dubonnet Red
1 dash Angostura Aromatic Bitters

Origin: Adapted from Harry Craddock's 1930 'The Savoy Cocktail Book'.
Comment: This complex Manhattan variant is a well balanced combo of spirit, liqueur and aromatic wine.

DANTES IN FERNET (NEW)

★★★★★

Glass: Coupe
Garnish: Grapefruit zest twist
Method: **SHAKE** all ingredients with ice and fine strain into chilled glass.

1 shot Speyside single malt whisky
⅛ shot Fernet Branca
1 shot Blood orange juice
⅓ shot Maple syrup
1 dash Xocolatl Mole bitters

Origin: Created in September 2013 by Mickaël Lenu, a Frenchman while working at Ancestral bar in Wellington, New Zealand.
Comment: It's obvious that this Blood & Sand-like cocktail contains Fernet Branca, it has an almost smoky herbal influence. Maple syrup is an inspired sweetener and flavour enhancer.

DARK 'N' STORMY

★★★★☆

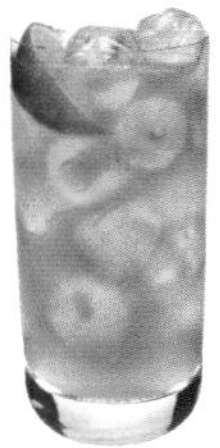

Glass: Collins
Garnish: Lime wedge
Method: **SHAKE** first three ingredients with ice and strain into ice-filled glass. **TOP** with ginger beer, stir and serve with straws.

2 shots Gosling's Black Seal dark rum
1 shot Freshly squeezed lime juice
½ shot Sugar syrup (2 sugar to 1 water)
Top with Gosling's Stormy Ginger Beer

Origin: The national drink of Bermuda, where ginger beer and Gosling's rum are produced.
Comment: This deliciously spicy drink is part of the Mule family - but is distinctive due to the strong flavour of the rum.

DARK DAIQUIRI

★★★★½

Glass: Martini
Garnish: Lime wedge
Method: **SHAKE** all ingredients with ice and fine strain into chilled glass.

1½ shots Bacardi Carta Ocho aged rum
½ shot Pusser's Navy Rum (54.5%)
½ shot Freshly squeezed lime juice
½ shot Sugar syrup (2 sugar to 1 water)
¾ shot Chilled water (omit if wet ice)

Comment: The fine sweet and sour balance of a great Daiquiri with hints of molasses.

DARK'N'STORMY SHOT

★★★½☆

Glass: Shot
Garnish: None
Method: **POUR** the first 3 ingredients into the glass in the following order. Then carefully **FLOAT** rum on the surface of the drink.

¼ shot Freshly squeezed lime juice
¾ shot Gosling's Stormy Ginger Beer
¼ shot King's Ginger Liqueur
½ shot Gosling's Black Seal dark rum

Origin: Adapted from a drink created in 2010 by Simon Fraser and Andrew Holmes at Rumbar, Hamilton, Bermuda - home of the Dark 'n' Stormy.
Comment: Tastes like a bite-sized Dark 'n' Stormy. As 'shots' go is both tasty and restrained on its alcoholic punch.

DARLINGTON

★★★☆☆

Glass: Martini
Garnish: Orange zest twist
Method: **SHAKE** all ingredients with ice and fine strain into chilled glass.

2 shots Rutte Dry Gin
½ shot Calvados brandy
½ shot Blue curaçao liqueur
1 shot Martini Extra Dry vermouth
1 shot Freshly squeezed lemon juice
¼ shot Sugar syrup (2 sugar to 1 water)

Origin: In W.J. Tarling's 1937 Café Royal Cocktail Book (Coronation Edition), the invention of this cocktail is credited to J.B. O'Brien.
Comment: Gin, orange and lemon made Martini-like by a drying splash of vermouth.

DARTH JÄGER

★★★½☆

Glass: Shot
Garnish: None
Method: POUR Jägermeister into shot glass. Place old-fashioned glass over shot glass and **UPEND** to leave full shot glass now upside down in old-fashioned glass. Slowly **POUR** cider into old fashioned glass.

1 shot **Jägermeister**
3 shots **Medium dry cider**

Origin: Created in 2012 by Darren Warburton at Buddha on the Beach bar on Koh Tao island, Thailand.
Comment: This riff on a Jägerbomb leaves the 'Dark Lord' sitting in 'Ciderspace'.

DC MARTINI

★★★★☆

Glass: Martini
Garnish: None
Method: STIR all ingredients with ice and strain into chilled glass.

2 shots **Bacardi Carta Blanca light rum**
¼ shot **Hazelnut liqueur**
¼ shot **White crème de cacao liqueur**
¼ shot **Sugar syrup (2 sugar to 1 water)**
½ shot **Chilled water** (omit if wet ice)

Origin: Discovered in 2000 at Teatro, London, England.
Comment: Vanilla, chocolate and a hint of nut. Add more sugar to taste.

DE BEAUVOIR

★★★★★

Glass: Coupe
Garnish: Orange zest twist

Method: SHAKE all ingredients with ice and fine strain into chilled glass.

1 shot **Straight rye whiskey**
⅔ shot **Hazelnut liqueur**
½ shot **Freshly squeezed lemon juice**
1¾ shots **Beavertown Smog Rocket Smoked Porter**
1 spoon **Brown sugar**
1 dash **Whiskey Barrel Aged Bitters**

Origin: Created in 2013 by Andrea Montague from London, England to win the Difford's Guide Beer-tail Competition for London Cocktail Week 2013 held on Friday 9th August 2013 at the Cabinet Room, London, England.

Named after De Beauvoir Town, an area of north London boundaried by Kingsland Road to the east, Southgate Road to the west, the Regent's Canal in the south and Tottenham Road to the north. The cockney name for the area, Beaverstown, is also the name of the brewery in Hackney whose Smog Rocket porter Andrea used in her winning cocktail.
Comment: Richly flavoured and lusciously bitter sweet with rye whiskey, bitter porter and sour lemon juice balancing hazelnut liqueur and brown sugar.

DE LA LOUISIANE #1

★★★★☆

Glass: Martini
Garnish: Lemon zest twist
Method: STIR all ingredients with ice and strain into chilled glass.

2 shots Bourbon whiskey
¼ shot Bénédictine D.O.M. liqueur
1 dash Angostura Aromatic Bitters
½ shot Chilled water (omit if wet ice)

Origin: The signature cocktail of the Restaurant de la Louisiane in New Orleans which opened in 1881.
Comment: Whiskey with hints of honey and spice.

DE LA LOUISIANE #2 (EQUAL PARTS BOURBON)

★★★★☆

Glass: Martini
Garnish: Luxardo Maraschino cherry
Method: STIR all ingredients with ice and strain into chilled glass.

1 shot **Bourbon whiskey**
1 shot **Bénédictine D.O.M. liqueur**
1 shot **Martini Rosso vermouth**
⅛ shot **Le Fée Parisienne absinthe**
3 dash **Peychaud's aromatic bitters**

Origin: This bourbon rather than rye take on this cocktail is adapted from Stanley Clisby Arthur's 1937 book 'Famous New Orleans Drinks and How to Mix 'Em' in which he wrote, This is the special cocktail served at Restaurant de la Louisiane, one of the famous French restaurants of New Orleans, long the rendezvous of those who appreciate the best in Creole cuisine.
Comment: Full flavoured and complex, yet fairly sweet, with herbal notes and a touch of absinthe.

DE LA LOUISIANE #3

★★★★☆

Glass: Martini
Garnish: Orange zest twist
Method: STIR all ingredients with ice and strain into chilled glass.

1½ shots **Bourbon whiskey**
1 shot **Dubonnet Red**
¼ shot **De Kuyper Triple Sec**
2 dash **Peychaud's aromatic bitters**
½ shot **Chilled water** (omit if wet ice)

Origin: Another variation on this New Orleans classic first served in the early 1930s at Restaurant de la Louisiane in New Orleans.
Comment: Beautifully balanced. This fruity whiskey drink manages to be both approachable and serious.

DE LA LOUISIANE #4

★★★★★

Glass: Coupe
Garnish: Luxardo Maraschino cherry
Method: STIR all ingredients with ice and strain into chilled glass.

1	shot	Straight rye whiskey
½	shot	Bénédictine D.O.M. liqueur
1	shot	Martini Rosso vermouth
⅛	shot	Le Fée Parisienne absinthe
2	dash	Peychaud's aromatic bitters
¾	shot	Chilled water (omit if wet ice)

Origin: Recipe adapted from Stanley Clisby Arthur's 1937 book 'Famous New Orleans Drinks and How to Mix 'Em' in which he wrote, This is the special cocktail served at Restaurant de la Louisiane, one of the famous French restaurants of New Orleans, long the rendezvous of those who appreciate the best in Creole cuisine. La Louisiane cocktail is as out-of-the-ordinary as the many distinctive dishes that grace its menu.
Comment: A rye-based Sweet Manhattan made even sweeter with herbal Bénédictine liqueur and bittered with Peychaud's and absinthe.

Originally made with equal parts rye whiskey, Bénédictine D.O.M and sweet vermouth, unless you have a sweet tooth reducing the liqueur as per this recipe makes for a more balanced drink. This is our favoured version of this famous New Orleans cocktail.

DEAD MAN'S MULE

★★★½☆

Glass: Collins
Garnish: Lime wedge
Method: SHAKE first four ingredients with ice and strain into ice-filled glass. TOP with ginger beer.

¾	shot	Le Fée Parisienne absinthe
¾	shot	Cinnamon schnapps
¾	shot	Almond (orgeat) syrup
½	shot	Freshly squeezed lime juice
Top with		Gosling's Stormy Ginger Beer

Origin: Discovered in 2003 at the Met bar, London, England.
Comment: Strong in every respect. Big, full-on flavours of aniseed, cinnamon and ginger.

DEAD PARROT COLADA (NEW)

★★★★☆

Glass: Collins
Garnish: Small stuffed dead parrot that's passed on, no more, expired and gone to meet 'is maker, a stiff, bereft of life, rests in peace, pushing up the daisies, off the twig, kicked the bucket, shuffled off 'is mortal coil, run down the curtain and joined the bleedin' choir invisible. An ex-parrot. And preferably one with "lovely plumage".
Method: BLEND all ingredients with ice and serve with straws.

1½	shots	Rutte Dry Gin
½	shot	Lysholm Linie Aquavit
½	shot	Blue curaçao liqueur
¼	shot	Luxardo Maraschino liqueur
½	shot	Freshly squeezed lemon juice
1½	shots	Coconut water
½	shot	Sugar syrup (2 sugar to 1 water)

Origin: Created in July 2014 by yours truly after watching Monty Python's famed Dead Parrot Sketch performed by John Cleese and Michael Palin at London's O2

arena. In the sketch, the disgruntled customer Mr Praline (played by Cleese) returns a "Norwegian Blue" parrot to the shopkeeper (Michael Palin) explaining, "That parrot is definitely deceased, and when I purchased it not 'alf an hour ago, you assured me that its total lack of movement was due to it bein' tired and shagged out following a prolonged squawk."

The use of Lysholm Linie Aquavit and the cocktails colour is inspired by the "Norwegian Blue" parrot while gin represents British humour. The coconut and loose colada theme comes from the late 1960s/70s when the sketch was originally performed.
Comment: Gin and delicate maraschino cherry with orange and lemon, coconut and a hint of Norwegian aquavit character.

DEATH BY CHOCOLATE

★★★★☆

Glass: Hurricane
Garnish: Crumbled Cadbury's Flake bar
Method: BLEND all ingredients with two 12oz scoops of crushed ice and serve with straws.

1	shot	Ketel One Vodka
1½	shots	Baileys Irish cream liqueur
1	shot	De Kuyper Dark crème de cacao
3	scoop	Chocolate ice-cream

Comment: Unsophisticated but delicious. Don't be cheap - use deluxe ice cream.

DEATH FLIP

★★★★½

Glass: Coupe
Garnish: Grated Nutmeg

Method: DRY SHAKE all ingredients (without ice). SHAKE again with ice and fine strain into chilled glass.

1	shot	Patrón silver tequila
1	shot	Jägermeister
1	shot	Yellow Chartreuse liqueur
¼	shot	Sugar syrup (2 sugar to 1 water)
1	whole	Egg (white & yolk)

Origin: Created in 2010 by Chris (Hasselhoff) Hysted the Black Pearl, Melbourne, Australia.
Comment: With a whole egg a shot of tequila, Jägermeister and Chartreuse, this is both a Death Flip and your last meal. Challenging herbal and bitter complexity yet with endearing sweet creaminess.

DEATH IN THE AFTERNOON

★★★☆☆

Glass: Flute
Garnish: Rose petal
Method: SHAKE first three ingredients with ice and fine strain into chilled glass. TOP with champagne.

¼	shot	Le Fée Parisienne absinthe
½	shot	Freshly squeezed lemon juice
¼	shot	Sugar syrup (2 sugar to 1 water)
Top with		G.H. Mumm Brut Cordon Rouge champagne

Origin: Created by Ernest Hemingway (not just named after his book), this recipe was the author's contribution to a 1935 cocktail book titled "So Red the Nose, or Breath in the Afternoon". We've toned down the maestro's original recipe a little, as it included a whopping ounce-and-a-half of absinthe.
Comment: Bravado (absinthe) dominates this drink, alongside hints of citrus and biscuity champagne.

DEATH IN THE GULF STREAM

★★★★☆

Glass: Collins
Garnish: Lime wedge
Method: **SHAKE** all ingredients with ice and strain into glass filled with crushed ice. **CHURN** (stir) and add more ice until glass is filled.

2	shots	Rutte Old Simon oude jenever
1	shot	Freshly squeezed lime juice
½	shot	Sugar syrup (2 sugar to 1 water)
4	dash	Angostura Aromatic Bitters
1		grated zest of Lime (fresh whole)

Origin: According to Charles H. Baker's 1946 'The Gentleman's Companion', this libation was a favourite of Ernest Hemingway.

"We got Hemingway's other picker-upper, and liked it. Take a tall thin water tumbler and fill it with finely cracked ice. Lace this broken debris with four good purple splashes of Angostura, add the juice and crushed peel of one green lime, and fill the glass almost full with Holland gin... No sugar, no fancying. It's strong, it's bitter - but so is English ale strong and bitter, in many cases. We don't add sugar to ale, and we don't need sugar in a Death In The Gulf Stream - or at least not more than one teaspoon. Its tartness and its bitterness are its chief charm. It is reviving and refreshing; cools the blood and inspires renewed interest in food, companions and life."
Comment: Remembering that Hemingway was a diabetic so had a very sour tooth, we believe this drink needs more than 'one teaspoon' of sugar. Thus we've added half a shot of sugar syrup to the original recipe. It also benefits from dilution, so be sure to shake well and churn in the glass.

DEATH IN VENICE

★★★★☆

Glass: Flute
Garnish: Orange zest twist
Method: **POUR** Campari and grapefruit bitters into chilled glass and **TOP** with Prosecco.

½	shot	Campari Bitter
2	dash	Grapefruit bitters
Top with		Prosecco sparkling wine

Origin: Created in 2010 by Tony Conigliaro at 69 Colebrooke Row, London, England.
Comment: Something of a cross between the Italian Spritz and Ernest Hemingway's Death in the Afternoon.

DEAUVILLE #1

★★★★☆

Glass: Martini
Garnish: Lemon zest twist
Method: **SHAKE** all ingredients with ice and fine strain into chilled glass.

1	shot	Calvados brandy
1	shot	Martell VSOP Médaillon cognac
¾	shot	De Kuyper Triple Sec
½	shot	Freshly squeezed lemon juice
⅛	shot	Sugar syrup (2 sugar to 1 water)
½	shot	Chilled water (omit if wet ice)

Origin: A classic drink of unknown origin.
Comment: A well-balanced appley twist on the classic Sidecar.

DEAUVILLE #2

★★★★☆

Glass: Martini
Garnish: Lemon zest twist
Method: **SHAKE** all ingredients with ice and fine strain into chilled glass.

1	shot	Calvados brandy
1	shot	Martell VSOP Médaillon cognac
1	shot	De Kuyper Triple Sec
1	shot	Freshly squeezed lemon juice
¼	shot	Sugar syrup (2 sugar to 1 water)

Origin: A classic drink of unknown origin.
Comment: The classic recipe omits the sugar syrup, which makes this drink too sour for my taste. Duly sweetened, it is very much in the Sidecar vein.

DEBONAIR

★★★★☆

Glass: Coupe
Garnish: Lemon zest twist
Method: **STIR** all ingredients with ice and strain into chilled glass.

2½ shots Speyside single malt whisky
1 shot King's Ginger Liqueur

Origin: Created in the 1990s by gaz Regan who in his San Francisco Chronicle 'The Cocktailian' column wrote of this drink, "I gave the formula a series of silly names, and eventually I got really frustrated with it so I looked up "sophisti-cated" in Roget's Thesaurus. The Debonair was born."
Comment: Rich and sophisti-cated, this drink has a zing of ginger spice and citrus from the garnish.

DEEP SOUTH

★★★☆☆

Glass: Old-fashioned
Garnish: Lime wedge
Method: **MUDDLE** ginger in base of shaker. Add other ingredients, **SHAKE** with ice and fine strain into glass filled with crushed ice.

2	slice	Fresh root ginger (thumbnail sized)
1½	shots	Rutte Dry Gin
1½	shots	Freshly squeezed orange juice
¾	shot	Freshly squeezed lime juice

Origin: Discovered in 1999 at AKA Bar, London, England.
Comment: Citrusy with delicate orange and ginger flavours.

DEFENDER COCKTAIL

★★★★★+

Glass: Coupe
Garnish: Orange zest twist
Method: STIR all ingredients with ice and strain into chilled glass.

1½ shots Old Tom gin
1   shot   Martini Rosso vermouth
⅓   shot   Benoit Serres créme de violette
2   dash   Angostura Orange Bitters

Origin: Recipe adapted from 'Old Waldorf Bar Days' published 1931, which said of this drink, "The name of an American yacht which took care of one of Sir Thomas Lipton's early but seemingly endless Shamrocks'". (Shamrock being the name of Sir Thomas Lipton's fleet of America's Cup racing yachts.)
Comment: One of those drinks where the bitter oils from the orange zest twist are crucial to its fine balance.

THE DELICIOUS SOUR

★★★★☆

Glass: Old-fashioned
Garnish: Lemon slice & cherry on stick (sail)
Method: SHAKE all ingredients with ice and strain into ice-filled glass.

2   shots Calvados brandy
1   shot   Crème de pêche (peach) liqueur
1   shot   Freshly squeezed lemon juice
¼   shot   Sugar syrup (2 sugar to 1 water)
½   fresh Egg white
Top with Soda (club soda)

Origin: Adapted from William Schmidt's 1892 book, 'The Flowing Bowl'.
Comment: 'Tis rather.

DELMARVA COCKTAIL NO.1

★★★★☆

Glass: Martini
Garnish: Mint sprig
Method: SHAKE all ingredients with ice and fine strain into chilled glass.

2   shots Bourbon whiskey
½   shot   Martini Extra Dry vermouth
½   shot   Giffard Menthe Pastille liqueur
½   shot   Freshly squeezed lemon juice

Origin: Created by Ted 'Dr. Cocktail' Haigh, who hails from America's Delmarva Peninsula.
Comment: A minty fresh, dry, palate cleanser.

DELMARVA COCKTAIL NO.2

★★★★☆

Glass: Martini
Garnish: Lemon zest twist
Method: SHAKE all ingredients with ice and fine strain into chilled glass.

2   shots Bourbon whiskey
½   shot   Martini Extra Dry vermouth
½   shot   White crème de cacao liqueur
½   shot   Freshly squeezed lemon juice

Origin: Gary Regan adapted Ted Haigh's original Delmarva Cocktail and published this version in his 'Joy of Mixology'.
Comment: Whiskey's distinctive character shines through but is softened and flavoured by chocolate and a hint of citrus.

DELMONICO 0━┉

★★★★☆

Glass: Martini
Garnish: Orange zest twist
Method: STIR all ingredients with ice and strain into chilled glass.

1¼ shots Martell VSOP Médaillon cognac
1½ shots Martini Rosso vermouth
1¼ shots Martini Extra Dry vermouth
3   dash   Angostura Aromatic Bitters

Origin: A classic from the 1930's.
Comment: A perfect Manhattan with cognac substituted for the whiskey.

DELMONICO SPECIAL 0━┉

★★★☆☆

Glass: Martini
Garnish: Orange zest twist
Method: STIR all ingredients with ice and strain into chilled glass.

2¼ shots Rutte Dry Gin
¼   shot   Martell VSOP Médaillon cognac
¾   shot   Martini Extra Dry vermouth
3   dash   Angostura Aromatic Bitters

Origin: A classic from the 1930's.
Comment: A Wet Martini dried with a splash of cognac.

THE DEMOCRAT

★★★☆☆

Glass: Collins
Garnish: Lemon slice
Method: SHAKE with ice and strain into glass filled with crushed ice.

2   shots Bourbon whiskey
½   shot   Crème de pêche (peach) liqueur
½   shot   Honey sugar syrup
1½ shots Freshly squeezed lemon juice

Origin: Created in 2007 by Jon Santer at Bourbon & Branch, San Francisco, USA as 'a kind of ode to the south - a democratic stronghold for so long'.
Comment: The base spirit is inspired by Harry Truman, 33rd President, who only drank bourbon and is considered by many to be the last great Democrat.

DEMPSEY

★★★★☆

Glass: Martini
Garnish: Luxardo Maraschino cherry
Method: SHAKE all ingredients with ice and fine strain into chilled glass.

1½ shots Rutte Dry Gin
1½ shots Calvados brandy
⅛   shot   Le Fée Parisienne absinthe
½   shot   Pomegranate / grenadine syrup (2:1)

Origin: A vintage cocktail of unknown origins.
Comment: Just on the right side of sweet but as hard as nails.

DENNY & ELENI (NEW)

★★★★☆

Glass: Coupe
Garnish: Mint leaf
Method: STIR all ingredients with ice and strain into chilled glass.

1½ shots	Dewar's 12 Year Old Scotch whisky
1 shot	Skinos Mastiha
⅛ shot	Islay single malt Scotch whisky
1 shot	Birch water
8 drop	Bob's Bitters Liquorice Bitters

Origin: Created in August 2015 by yours truly at the Cabinet Room, London, England.
Comment: Named after Denny Kallivoka and Eleni Nikoloulia, our favourite Greek drinks writers, this whisky based cocktail has a healthy glug of mastiha with birch water. It finishes with liquorice and Islay whisky.

DEPTH BOMB

★★★☆☆

Glass: Old-fashioned
Garnish: Lime wedge
Method: SHAKE all ingredients with ice and strain into glass filled with crushed ice.

1 shot	Calvados brandy
1 shot	Martell VSOP Médaillon cognac
¼ shot	Pomegranate / grenadine syrup (2:1)
¾ shot	Freshly squeezed lime juice
½ shot	Sugar syrup (2 sugar to 1 water)

Comment: Brandy and apple brandy benefit from a sour hint of lemon, balanced by grenadine.

DERBY DAIQUIRI

★★★★☆

Glass: Martini
Garnish: Orange zest twist
Method: SHAKE all ingredients with ice and fine strain into chilled glass.

2 shots	Bacardi Carta Blanca light rum
¾ shot	Freshly squeezed orange juice
½ shot	Freshly squeezed lime juice
¼ shot	Sugar syrup (2 sugar to 1 water)

Comment: A fruity twist on the Classic Daiquiri.

DERBY FIZZ

★★★★☆

Glass: Collins (small 8oz)
Garnish: Lemon slice
Method: SHAKE first six ingredients with ice and strain into chilled glass. TOP with soda.

1¾ shots	Bourbon whiskey
1½ shots	Bacardi Carta Blanca light rum
¼ shot	Grand Marnier Cordon Rouge
1 shot	Freshly squeezed lemon juice
½ shot	Sugar syrup (2 sugar to 1 water)
½ fresh	Egg white
Top with	Soda from siphon

Comment: An elongated sour with perfectly balanced strength, sweetness and sourness.

DESERT COOLER

★★★☆☆

Glass: Collins
Garnish: Orange slice
Method: SHAKE first three ingredients with ice and strain into ice-filled glass. TOP with ginger beer.

2 shots	Rutte Dry Gin
¾ shot	Cherry Heering Liqueur
1½ shots	Freshly squeezed orange juice
Top with	Gosling's Stormy Ginger Beer

Comment: Sandy in colour - as its name suggests - with a refreshing bite.

DESHLER COCKTAIL (NEW)

★★★★☆

Glass: Martini
Garnish: Orange zest twist
Method: STIR all ingredients with ice and strain into chilled glass.

1½ shots	Straight rye whiskey
1 shot	Dubonnet Red
½ shot	De Kuyper Triple Sec
2 dash	Peychaud's aromatic bitters

Comment: A dry Manhattan-like cocktail with a hint of orange.

DETROIT ATHLETIC CLUB

★★★★☆

Glass: Coupe
Garnish: Float thin lemon wheel or dehydrated slice of lemon on surface
Method: STIR all ingredients with ice and strain into chilled glass.

2 shots	Teeling Small Batch Irish whiskey
¼ shot	Green Chartreuse liqueur
¼ shot	Martini Rosso vermouth
¼ shot	Taylor's Velvet Falernum liqueur
¾ shot	Chilled water (omit if wet ice)

Origin: Adapted from a drink created in 2010 by Donovan Sornig, Bar Manager at Bol Restaurant, Vail, Colorado. The drink was inspired by The Last Word created at the Detroit Athletic Club which Donovan grew up just four miles away from.
Comment: Irish whiskey with a splash of sweet vermouth, clove rich falernum and the all-important monastic liqueur.

DETROIT MARTINI

★★★★☆

Glass: Martini
Garnish: Mint sprig
Method: SHAKE all ingredients (including mint) with ice and fine strain into chilled glass.

7 fresh	Mint leaves
3 shots	Ketel One Vodka
½ shot	Sugar syrup (2 sugar to 1 water)
⅛ shot	Freshly squeezed lime juice

Origin: Created by Dick Bradsell in the mid 90s and based on his Cowboy Hoof Martini.
Comment: Vodka doused mint with the merest hint of lime. Clean and flavoursome.

DETROPOLITAN

★★★★☆

Glass: Martini
Garnish: Orange zest twist (flamed)
Method: SHAKE all ingredients with ice and fine strain into chilled glass.

1	shot	Ketel One Vodka
½	shot	De Kuyper Triple Sec
1½	shots	Cranberry juice
½	shot	Freshly squeezed lime juice
¼	shot	Lejay crème de cassis de Dijon

Origin: Created at Detroit, London, England.
Comment: Yet another twist on the Cosmopolitan.

DEVIL

★★★⯪☆

Glass: Martini
Garnish: Lemon zest twist
Method: SHAKE all ingredients with ice and fine strain into chilled glass.

2	shots	Tawny port
1½	shots	Martini Extra Dry vermouth
¼	shot	Freshly squeezed lemon juice

Comment: A devil to get out of your carpet but quite dry and aromatic on the palate.

DEVIL'S COCKTAIL

★★★⯪☆

Glass: Martini
Garnish: Lemon zest twist
Method: SHAKE all ingredients with ice and fine strain into a chilled glass.

2	shots	Tawny port
1½	shots	Martini Extra Dry vermouth
¼	shot	Freshly squeezed lemon juice

Origin: Vintage cocktail of unknown origin.
Comment: Lemon predominates with the richness of port fighting to be heard.

DEVIL'S HORN

★★★★☆

Glass: Coupe
Garnish: Two chillies on rim to form devil's horns
Method: MUDDLE chilli in base of shaker. Add other ingredients, SHAKE with ice and fine strain into chilled glass.

1	ring	Red chilli (thin slice)
3	fresh	Raspberries
2	shots	Bacardi Carta Ocho aged rum
¾	shot	Cranberry juice
1	shot	Honey sugar syrup
1	shot	Freshly squeezed lime juice

Origin: Created in 2010 by Roger Vilalta at Banker's Bar, Mandarin Oriental, Barcelona, Spain.
Comment: A great balance of sweetness, sourness and spice.

DEVIL'S MANHATTAN

★★★★☆

Glass: Martini
Garnish: Lemon zest twist
Method: STIR all ingredients with ice and strain into chilled glass.

2	shots	Bourbon whiskey
1	shot	Southern Comfort liqueur
½	shot	Martini Rosso vermouth
3	dash	Peychaud's aromatic bitters

Comment: A sweet Manhattan with a hint of the south.

DEVIL'S SHARE

★★★★☆

Glass: Old-fashioned
Garnish: Orange zest twist
Method: MUDDLE ginger in base of shaker. Add other ingredients, SHAKE with ice and fine strain into ice-filled glass.

2	slice	Fresh root ginger (thumbnail sized)
2	shots	Bourbon whiskey
¾	shot	Freshly squeezed orange juice
1	shot	Freshly squeezed lemon juice
½	shot	Maple syrup

Origin: Created in 2006 by Pete Kendall at Match Bar, London, England.
Comment: Ginger, bourbon and lemon makes for a spicy and tasty little devil.

DIABLE ROUGE

★★★⯪☆

Glass: Martini
Garnish: Seasonal berries
Method: SHAKE all ingredients with ice and fine strain into chilled glass.

2	shots	Ketel One Vodka
2	shots	Fresh pressed pineapple juice
¼	shot	Lejay crème de cassis de Dijon

Comment: Not quite as rouge as the name would suggest. Hard to hate.

DIAMOND DOG

★★★⯪☆

Glass: Old-fashioned
Garnish: Orange slice
Method: SHAKE all ingredients with ice and strain into ice-filled glass.

1	shot	Campari Bitter
1	shot	Martini Extra Dry vermouth
1	shot	Rose's lime cordial
1	shot	Freshly squeezed orange juice

Origin: Discovered in 2005 at Four Seasons George V, Paris, France.
Comment: Bittersweet and refreshingly different.

DIAMOND FIZZ

★★★★☆

Glass: Collins (small 8oz)
Garnish: Lemon slice
Method: SHAKE first three ingredients with ice and strain into chilled glass (without ice). **TOP** with champagne.

2	shots	Rutte Dry Gin
1	shot	Freshly squeezed lemon juice
½	shot	Sugar syrup (2 sugar to 1 water)
Top with		G.H. Mumm Brut Cordon Rouge champagne

Origin: A long lost classic.
Comment: Why top a Fizz with soda when you can use champagne?

DIMI-TINI

★★★★☆

Glass: Martini
Garnish: Grapefruit zest twist
Method: SHAKE all ingredients with ice and fine strain into chilled glass.

7	fresh	Raspberries
2	shots	Ketel One Vodka
¼	shot	Cherry Heering Liqueur
½	shot	Freshly squeezed lime juice
⅛	shot	Sugar syrup (2 sugar to 1 water)

Origin: Adapted from a recipe by Dimitri Lezinska, London, England.
Comment: Like Dimi - this drink's easy to like.

DIAMONDBACK

★★★★⯪

Glass: Coupe
Garnish: Luxardo Maraschino cherry
Method: STIR all ingredients with ice and strain unto chilled glass.

1½	shots	Straight rye whiskey
¾	shot	Applejack brandy (bonded)
¾	shot	Yellow Chartreuse liqueur

Origin: Adapted from Ted Saucier's 1951 'Bottoms Up' book in which the author calls for two parts rye whiskey, one part applejack and one part yellow Chartreuse.
Comment: This potent cocktail marries apple spirit with rye whiskey and rich herbal Chartreuse. A great after dinner tipple.

DINGO

★★★☆☆

Glass: Collins
Garnish: Orange slice
Method: SHAKE all ingredients with ice and strain into ice-filled glass.

1	shot	Bacardi Carta Blanca light rum
1	shot	Bourbon whiskey
½	shot	Disaronno Originale amaretto
2	shots	Freshly squeezed orange juice
1	shot	Freshly squeezed lemon juice
¼	shot	Pomegranate / grenadine syrup (2:1)
¼	shot	Sugar syrup (2 sugar to 1 water)

Comment: Very fruity but with a rum and whiskey kick.

DICKENS' DRY MARTINI

★★★★★

Glass: Martini
Garnish: None
Method: STIR all ingredients with ice and strain into chilled glass.

2½	shots	Rutte Dry Gin
½	shot	Martini Extra Dry vermouth

Comment: A 5:1 Dry Martini served without any garnish (i.e. no olive or twist). The name is a reference to Charles Dicken's novel Oliver Twist.

DINO SOUR

★★★★⯪

Glass: Old-fashioned
Garnish: Lemon slice & cherry on stick (sail)
Method: SHAKE all ingredients with ice and fine strain into chilled glass.

1	shot	Bacardi Carta Blanca light rum
1	shot	Gosling's Black Seal dark rum
1	shot	Freshly squeezed lemon juice
½	shot	Sugar syrup (2 sugar to 1 water)
½	fresh	Egg white

Comment: Two diverse rums combine brilliantly in this classic sour.

DIKI-DIKI

★★★★⯪

Glass: Martini
Garnish: Sugar rim
Method: SHAKE all ingredients with ice and fine strain into chilled glass.

2	shots	Calvados brandy
½	shot	Swedish Punch liqueur
½	shot	Freshly squeezed pink grapefruit juice

Origin: Adapted from Harry Craddock's 1930 'The Savoy Cocktail Book'.
Comment: Fruity yet tart. The sourness is a challenge initially but very rewarding.

DIPLOMAT

★★★★⯪☆

Glass: Old-fashioned
Garnish: Orange zest twist
Method: STIR all ingredients with ice and strain into ice-filled glass.

2	shots	Martini Extra Dry vermouth
1	shot	Martini Rosso vermouth
⅛	shot	Luxardo Maraschino liqueur
2	dash	Angostura Orange Bitters

Origin: Adapted from Harry Craddock's 1930 'The Savoy Cocktail Book'.
Comment: Wonderfully aromatic and dry. Too good to waste on diplomats.

DIRTY BANANA

★★★★☆

Glass: Collins
Garnish: Banana chunk
Method: BLEND all ingredients with 12oz scoop crushed ice. Serve with straws.

1½ shots	Bacardi Carta Blanca light rum
1	shot	Coffee liqueur
1	shot	Crème de banane liqueur
1	shot	Single cream / half-and-half
1	shot	Milk
1	fresh	Banana (peeled)

Origin: A popular cocktail in Jamaica.
Comment: Long, creamy and filling banana drink with a 'dirty' flavour and colour courtesy of coffee liqueur.

DIRTY MARTINI COCKTAIL

★★★½☆

Glass: Martini
Garnish: Olive on stick
Method: STIR all ingredients with ice and strain into a chilled glass.

2½ shots Rutte Dry Gin
¼ shot Olive brine (from jarred olive)
¼ shot Martini Extra Dry vermouth

Origin: Some attribute the creation of this drink to Roosevelt: the 32nd president was a keen home bartender, although his cocktails were reportedly 'horrendous' and there is no evidence that he used olive brine in his Martinis.
Comment: This drink varies from delicious to disgusting, depending on the liquid in your jar of olives. Oil will provide a revolting emulsion: make sure that your olives are packed in brine.

DIRTY SANCHEZ

★★★★☆

Glass: Collins
Garnish: Lime slice
Method: SHAKE first four ingredients with ice and strain into ice-filled glass. **TOP** with ginger beer.

2	shots	Patrón reposado tequila
¾	shot	Agavero liqueur
½	shot	Chambord Liqueur
½	shot	Freshly squeezed lime juice
Top with	Gosling's Stormy Ginger Beer

Origin: Created in 2001 by Phillip Jeffrey and Ian Baldwin at the GE Club, London, England.
Comment: A wonderfully refreshing and complex long summer drink.

DIRTY(ISH) BANANA COCKTAIL (NEW)

★★★★☆

Glass: Collins
Garnish: Banana slice
Method: BLEND all ingredients with 12oz scoop crushed ice.

1½ shots	Capucana cachaça
1	shot	Coffee liqueur
1	shot	Crème de banane liqueur
1	shot	Single cream / half-and-half
½	fresh	Banana (peeled)
1	dash	Angostura Orange Bitters

Origin: Created in 2015 by Jorge Balbontin of Vantguard, Barcelona, Spain.
Comment: Coffee liqueur, banana and cream laced with cachaça and blended to a creamy icy consistency.

DIVINO'S

★★★★☆

Glass: Martini
Garnish: Dust with grated white chocolate
Method: SHAKE all ingredients with ice and fine strain into chilled glass.

½	shot	Ketel One Vodka
2½ shots	Barolo wine
1	shot	De Kuyper Dark crème de cacao

Origin: Discovered in 2005 at DiVino, Hong Kong.
Comment: The chocolate liqueur takes the acidity off the wine without masking its flavour.

DIVISION BELL (NEW)

★★★★½

Glass: Coupe
Garnish: Grapefruit zest twist
Method: SHAKE all ingredients with ice and strain into chilled glass.

1	shot	Del Maguey VIDA mezcal
¾	shot	Aperol
½	shot	Luxardo Maraschino liqueur
¾	shot	Freshly squeezed lime juice

Comment: A mezcal inspired variation of the Last Word with a refreshing, boozy blend of ingredients based on mezcal.
Origin: Created in 2009 by Phil Ward at Mayahuel, New York City, USA.

DIXIE COSMOPOLITAN

★★★☆☆

Glass: Martini
Garnish: Cinnamon & sugar rim with orange zest twist (flamed)
Method: Brake up section of cinnamon and drop into shaker. Add other ingredients, **SHAKE** with ice and fine strain into chilled glass.

2	inch	Cinnamon stick
1	shot	Southern Comfort liqueur
1	shot	De Kuyper Triple Sec
¼	shot	Rose's lime cordial
1½ shots	Cranberry juice

Origin: Created circa 2005 by Matthew Dakers, a globetrotting professional bartender.
Comment: Slightly sweet and somewhat reminiscent of jellybean sweets.

DIXIE DEW

★★★★⯪

Glass: Martini
Garnish: Orange zest twist
Method: SHAKE all ingredients with ice and fine strain into chilled glass.

2	shots	Bourbon whiskey
½	shot	Giffard Menthe Pastille liqueur
½	shot	De Kuyper Triple Sec
¾	shot	Chilled water (omit if wet ice)

Comment: A peppermint fresh, bourbon laced drink.

DNA #1

★★★⯪☆

Glass: Martini
Garnish: Orange zest twist
Method: SHAKE all ingredients with ice and fine strain into chilled glass.

1½ shots		Rutte Dry Gin
¾	shot	De Kuyper XO Apricot Brandy
1	shot	Freshly squeezed lemon juice
¼	shot	Sugar syrup (2 sugar to 1 water)
2	dash	Angostura Orange Bitters

Origin: Created by Emmanuel Audermatte at The Atlantic Bar and Grill, London, England, 1999.
Comment: Slightly sharp and very fruity, but pleasantly so.

DNA #2

★★★☆☆

Glass: Martini
Garnish: Lemon zest twist
Method: SHAKE all ingredients with ice and fine strain into chilled glass.

1	shot	Rutte Dry Gin
1	shot	Damson gin liqueur
¾	shot	De Kuyper XO Apricot Brandy
½	shot	Freshly squeezed lime juice
2	dash	Angostura Aromatic Bitters
½	shot	Chilled water

Origin: Created in 2005 by Tonin Kacaj at Maze, London, England.
Comment: Tangy, fruity and gin laced.

DOCTOR FUNK

★★★⯪☆

Glass: Sling
Garnish: Lime wedge
Method: SHAKE first 6 ingredients with ice and strain into glass filled with crushed ice. **TOP** with soda and serve with straws.

2½ shots		Gosling's Black Seal dark rum
¼	shot	Pernod anise
½	shot	Freshly squeezed lemon juice
¼	shot	Freshly squeezed lime juice
¼	shot	Sugar syrup (2 sugar to 1 water)
¼	shot	Pomegranate / grenadine syrup (2:1)
Top with		Soda (club soda)

Origin: A Tiki drink adapted from one created circa 1937 by Don the Beachcomber.
Comment: Too many and you'll need your very own doctor.

DOCTOR NO.1

★★★★⯪

Glass: Martini
Garnish: Lime zest twist
Method: SHAKE all ingredients with ice and fine strain into chilled glass.

1½ shots		Bacardi Carta Ocho aged rum
1½ shots		Swedish Punch liqueur
¾	shot	Freshly squeezed lime juice

Origin: In David Embury's classic, 'The Fine Art of Mixing Drinks', my hero lists four wildly different drinks using Swedish Punch (also see Doctor No.2, No.3 and No.4). 'Trader Vic's 'Bartender's Guide' lists two variations of a single drink, for which the above is my own recipe.
Comment: Retitled 'Swedish Daiquiri', this could be a hit.

DOCTOR NO.2

★★★★⯪

Glass: Martini
Garnish: Lime zest twist
Method: SHAKE all ingredients with ice and fine strain into chilled glass.

2	shots	Swedish Punch liqueur
1	shot	Freshly squeezed lime juice

Origin: Unknown, but David A. Embury's 1948 Fine Art of Mixing Drinks lists a cocktail called a Doctor No.2 (consisting of equal parts lemon juice, Swedish Punch and gin) and states "This is also known as a Gretta Garbo."
Comment: Lime combines wells with the aromatics spices in Swedish Punch.

DOCTOR NO.3 (NEW)

★★★★☆

Glass: Coupe
Garnish: Orange zest twist
Method: SHAKE all ingredients with ice and fine strain into chilled glass.

1½ shots		Swedish Punch liqueur
¾	shot	Freshly squeezed orange juice
¾	shot	Freshly squeezed lemon juice

Origin: Recipe adapted from David A. Embury's 1948 Fine Art of Mixing Drinks.
Comment: Tangy Swedish Punch freshened with orange and lemon juice.

DOCTOR NO.4 (NEW)

★★★★☆

Glass: Coupe
Garnish: Orange zest twist
Method: SHAKE all ingredients with ice and fine strain into chilled glass.

1½ shots		Swedish Punch liqueur
½	shot	Pot still Jamaican rum
¾	shot	Freshly squeezed lime juice

Origin: Recipe adapted from David A. Embury's 1948 Fine Art of Mixing Drinks.
Comment: A characterful Daiquiri - pungent Jamaican rum combines with tangy Swedish Punch balanced by lime juice.

DOHENY PISCO PUNCH

★★★★☆

Glass: Collins
Garnish: Mint sprig & pineapple slice
Method: Lightly **MUDDLE** (just to bruise) mint in base of shaker. Add next five ingredients, **SHAKE** with ice and strain into ice-filled glass. **TOP** with ginger beer.

12 fresh   Mint leaves
1½ shots   Fresh pressed pineapple juice
2   shots   BarSol Mosto Verde Italia pisco
¾   shot   Freshly squeezed lemon juice
¼   shot   Vanilla sugar syrup
1   dash   Angostura Aromatic Bitters
Top with   Gosling's Stormy Ginger Beer

Origin: Adapted from a drink created in 2007 by Vincenzo Marianello at Doheny, Los Angeles, USA.
Comment: Vincenzo's twist on the San Franciscan classic.

DOLCE HAVANA

★★★★☆

Glass: Martini
Garnish: None
Method: SHAKE all ingredients with ice and fine strain into chilled glass.

1¼ shots   Bacardi Carta Blanca light rum
½   shot   De Kuyper Triple Sec
½   shot   Campari Bitter
1¼ shots   Freshly squeezed orange juice
1¼ shots   Freshly squeezed lime juice
⅛   shot   Sugar syrup (2 sugar to 1 water)

Origin: Created by Fabrizio Musorella in 2000 at the Library Bar, Lanesborough Hotel, London, England.
Comment: A melange of Mediterranean fruit.

DOLCE-AMARO

★★★★☆

Glass: Martini
Garnish: Orange zest twist
Method: STIR all ingredients with ice and strain into chilled glass.

¾   shot   Disaronno Originale amaretto
1½ shots   Campari Bitter
1½ shots   Martini Extra Dry vermouth

Comment: The very apt name translates as 'bittersweet'.

DOLORES #1

★★★★☆

Glass: Martini
Garnish: Lemon zest twist
Method: SHAKE all ingredients with ice and fine strain into chilled glass.

2   shots   Bacardi Carta Ocho aged rum
2   shots   Dubonnet Red
1   shot   Romate Fino sherry

Origin: A classic. Some recipes include a splash of orange juice.
Comment: Aromatic and well balanced, provided you use French-made Dubonnet.

DOLORES #2

★★★★☆

Glass: Martini
Garnish: Dust with grated nutmeg
Method: SHAKE all ingredients with ice and fine strain into chilled glass.

1½ shots   Martell VSOP Médaillon cognac
¾   shot   Cherry Heering Liqueur
¾   shot   White crème de cacao liqueur
1   fresh   Egg white

Comment: A chocolaty after dinner libation.

DON DAISY

★★★★☆

Glass: Martini
Garnish: Lemon zest twist
Method: SHAKE all ingredients with ice and fine strain into chilled glass.

1½ shots   Bacardi Carta Blanca light rum
½   shot   St-Germain elderflower liqueur
½   shot   Martini Extra Dry vermouth
¼   shot   Freshly squeezed lemon juice
¼   shot   Sugar syrup (2 sugar to 1 water)
½   fresh   Egg white

Origin: Created in 2008 by James Tait, UK.
Comment: This zesty, silky smooth and easy drink is laced with light rum.

DON JUAN

★★★★☆

Glass: Martini
Garnish: Orange zest twist
Method: SHAKE all ingredients with ice and fine strain into chilled glass.

1¾ shots   Martell VSOP Médaillon cognac
1   shot   Licor 43 liqueur
1   shot   Freshly squeezed orange juice
½   shot   Milk
½   shot   Single cream / half-and-half

Comment: A lightly creamy orange affair with vanilla spice.

DON'S DELIGHT

★★★★☆

Glass: Martini
Garnish: Lime wedge
Method: SHAKE all ingredients with ice and fine strain into chilled glass.

2   shots   Patrón añejo tequila
½   shot   Bourbon whiskey
⅛   shot   Disaronno Originale amaretto
1¼ shots   Lime (fresh whole)
½   shot   Sugar syrup (2 sugar to 1 water)
1   fresh   Egg white

Origin: Created in 2008 by Brian Van Flandern in New York, USA.
Comment: When made with Don Julio 1942, as this drink originally was, this is another memorable trick by the affable Brian Van Flandern.

DON'S PASSION

★★★½☆

Glass: Coupe
Garnish: Passion fruit
Method: Cut passion fruit in half and scoop out flesh and seeds into shaker. Add next 4 ingredients, **SHAKE** with ice and fine strain into chilled glass. Pour grenadine into centre of drink (should sink to bottom).

1	fresh	Passion fruit
2	shots	Bacardi Carta Blanca light rum
½	shot	Galliano L'Autentico liqueur
1	shot	Freshly squeezed lime juice
½	shot	Freshly squeezed orange juice
¼	shot	Pomegranate / grenadine syrup (2:1)

Origin: Created in 2008 by Symeon White at Avon Gorge Hotel, Bristol, UK.
Comment: Passion fruit and Galliano influence this Bacardi Cocktail style drink.

DONEGAL

★★★★☆

Glass: Martini
Garnish: Orange zest twist
Method: **SHAKE** all ingredients with ice and fine strain into chilled glass.

1½	shots	Teeling Small Batch Irish whiskey
½	shot	Luxardo Maraschino liqueur
½	shot	Mandarine Napoléon liqueur
1¼	shots	Martini Extra Dry vermouth

Comment: Aromatised Irish whiskey with cherry and orange.

DONNA'S CREAMY'TINI

★★★★½☆

Glass: Martini
Garnish: Luxardo Maraschino cherry
Method: **SHAKE** all ingredients with ice and fine strain into chilled glass.

1	shot	Disaronno Originale amaretto
1	shot	Cherry Heering Liqueur
1	shot	De Kuyper Dark crème de cacao
1	shot	Single cream / half-and-half

Origin: Adapted from a drink created in 2002 by Yannick Miseriaux at the Fifth Floor Bar, London, England.
Comment: A fine example of an alcoholic liquid pudding.

DOPO CENA

★★★★☆

Glass: Coupe
Garnish: Cherry
Method: **DRY SHAKE** all ingredients (without ice). **SHAKE** again with ice and fine strain into chilled glass.

1	shot	Disaronno Originale amaretto
1	shot	Kirschwasser eau de vie
½	shot	Luxardo Maraschino liqueur
1	shot	Freshly squeezed lemon juice
1	spoon	Sugar syrup (2 sugar to 1 water)
1	dash	Egg white
1	dash	Angostura Aromatic Bitters

Origin: Created by Adrian Gomes, 10 Dollar Shake, Aberdeen, Scotland.
Comment: Under the white head lies a dessert cocktail with aromatic cherry and marzipan flavours.

DORIAN GRAY

★★★★½☆

Glass: Martini
Garnish: Orange zest twist
Method: **SHAKE** all ingredients with ice and fine strain into chilled glass.

1½	shots	Bacardi Carta Blanca light rum
¾	shot	Grand Marnier Cordon Rouge
1	shot	Freshly squeezed orange juice
¾	shot	Cranberry juice

Origin: Discovered in 1999 at One Aldwych, London, England. It takes its name from Oscar Wilde's novel, in which a socialite's wish to remain as young and charming as his own portrait is granted. Allured by his depraved friend Lord Henry Wotton, Dorian Gray assumes a life of perversion and sin. But every time he sins the painting ages, while Gray stays young and healthy.
Comment: Fruity and rum laced, not overly sweet.

DOROTHY PARKER

★★★★½☆

Glass: Martini
Garnish: Sugar rim
Method: **SHAKE** first 4 ingredients with ice and fine strain into chilled glass. **TOP** with champagne.

1½	shots	Ketel One Citroen vodka
½	shot	De Kuyper Triple Sec
¼	shot	Chambord Liqueur
½	shot	Freshly squeezed lemon juice
Top with		G.H. Mumm Brut Cordon Rouge champagne

Origin: Discovered in 2007 at Town Hall, San Francisco, USA, and named for the wit and drinker.
Comment: Light, fruity and easy to drink.

DOUBLE GRAPE (NEW)

★★★★★½

Glass: Coupe
Garnish: Orange zest twist (discarded) & 2 red grapes
Method: **STIR** ingredients with ice and strain into chilled glass.

1¾	shots	BarSol Mosto Verde Italia pisco
1¾	shots	Byrrh Grand Quinquina
1	dash	Grapefruit bitters

Origin: Created by yours truly at the Cabinet Room, London, England.
Comment: The aromatics of the distilled wine of pisco combine harmoniously with the aromatised wine's sweet grapey notes.

DOUBLE GRAPE COCKTAIL

★★★★★½

Glass: Martini
Garnish: White grapes
Method: **MUDDLE** grapes in base of shaker. Add other ingredients, **SHAKE** with ice and fine strain into chilled glass.

12	fresh	Seedless white grapes
2	shots	Ketel One Vodka
¾	shot	Sauvignon blanc white wine
½	shot	Sugar syrup (2 sugar to 1 water)

Origin: Created in 2004 by yours truly, London, England.
Comment: The wine adds complexity to this simple grape cocktail.

DOUBLE VISION

★★★½☆

Glass: Martini
Garnish: 2 blackcurrants on rim
Method: SHAKE all ingredients with ice and fine strain into chilled glass.

¾	shot	Ketel One Citroen vodka
¾	shot	Raspberry flavoured vodka
¾	shot	Pressed apple juice
¾	shot	Freshly squeezed lime juice
½	shot	Sugar syrup (2 sugar to 1 water)
2	dash	Angostura Aromatic Bitters

Comment: Citrus fresh with apple and red berries.

DOWA

★★★★☆

Glass: Old-fashioned
Garnish: Lime wedge
Method: STIR honey and vodka in base of shaker until honey dissolves. Add lime juice, SHAKE with ice and strain into glass filled with crushed ice. Serve with straws.

2½	shots	Ketel One Vodka
4	spoon	Runny honey
¼	shot	Freshly squeezed lime juice

Origin: This cocktail is particularly popular in upscale hotel bars in Kenya where it is enjoyed by the safari set. The name translates as 'medicine'.
Comment: Very similar to the Caipirovska in its use of vodka, lime and crushed ice: the honey makes the difference.

DOWNHILL RACER

★★★★½

Glass: Martini
Garnish: Pineapple wedge
Method: SHAKE all ingredients with ice and fine strain into chilled glass.

1¾	shots	Bacardi Carta Ocho aged rum
¾	shot	Disaronno Originale amaretto
1½	shots	Fresh pressed pineapple juice

Comment: Aged rum sweetened, softened and flavoured with pineapple and amaretto. A crowd pleaser.

DR ZEUS

★★★★½

Glass: Old-fashioned
Garnish: None
Method: POUR Fernet Branca into ice-filled glass. Separately MUDDLE raisins in base of shaker, add other ingredients and SHAKE with ice. Finally DISCARD contents of glass and strain contents of shaker into the Fernet Branca coated glass.

1	shot	Fernet Branca
20	dried	Raisins
2	shots	Martell VSOP Médaillon cognac
¼	shot	Sugar syrup (2 sugar to 1 water)
⅛	shot	Coffee liqueur
1	dash	Angostura Orange Bitters

Origin: Created by Adam Ennis in 2001 at Isola, Knightsbridge, London, England.
Comment: Not that far removed from a Sazerac cocktail, this is innovative and great tasting.

DRAGON BLOSSOM

★★★☆☆

Glass: Martini
Garnish: Luxardo Maraschino cherry
Method: SHAKE all ingredients with ice and fine strain into chilled glass.

1¾	shots	Rose petal liqueur
¼	shot	Kwai Feh lychee liqueur
¼	shot	Maraschino syrup (from cherry jar)
1¾	shots	Cranberry juice

Comment: Light, aromatic, semi-sweet and distinctly oriental in style.

DRAMATIC MARTINI

★★★½☆

Glass: Martini
Garnish: Dust with grated nutmeg
Method: SHAKE all ingredients with ice and fine strain into chilled glass.

1	shot	Tuaca liqueur
1	shot	Grand Marnier Cordon Rouge
1	shot	Baileys Irish cream liqueur
1	shot	Milk

Comment: Creamy and sweet with orangey, herbal notes.

DREAM COCKTAIL

★★★★☆

Glass: Martini
Garnish: Orange zest twist
Method: SHAKE all ingredients with ice and fine strain into chilled glass.

1½	shots	Martell VSOP Médaillon cognac
¾	shot	De Kuyper Triple Sec
⅛	shot	Marie Brizard Anisette
½	shot	Chilled water (omit if wet ice)

Comment: An after-dinner drink with brandy, orange liqueur and a refreshing burst of aniseed. Double the measure of anisette liqueur if a tad on the sweet side.

DREAMSICLE

★★★½☆

Glass: Martini
Garnish: None
Method: SHAKE first 3 ingredients with ice and fine strain into chilled glass. FLOAT cream.

1½	shots	Coffee liqueur
¾	shot	De Kuyper Triple Sec
1	shot	Freshly squeezed orange juice
¾	shot	Single cream / half-and-half

Comment: Sweet coffee and orange smoothed by a creamy top. A veritable dessert in a glass.

DREAMY DORINI SMOKING MARTINI

★★★★☆

Glass: Coupe
Garnish: Lemon zest twist
Method: STIR all ingredients with ice and strain into chilled glass.

½ shot   **Pernod anise**
½ shot   **Islay single malt Scotch whisky**
2   shots   **Ketel One Vodka**

Origin: Adapted from a recipe created by Audrey Saunders in 2003 at Beacon restaurant, New York, USA.
Comment: As the name implies, this Martini is a good helping of smoky peat. If you like that kind of thing, it's equally dreamy.

DREIKLANG (THREE OF A KIND)

★★★★☆

Glass: Old-fashioned
Garnish: Orange zest twist
Method: STIR sugar syrup with two ice cubes, add xoxolate mole and stir again. Add more ice plus tequila and STIR some more.

2   shots   **Patrón reposado tequila**
½ shot   **Sugar syrup (2 sugar to 1 water)**
5   drop   **Xocolatl Mole bitters**

Origin: Created in 2007 by Heiko Tagawa, Germany.
Comment: Named after the German word for 'three of a kind' due to the trio of flavours encountered in this drink; orange, agave and chocolate.

DRIED MEADOW FLOWER (NEW)

★★★★⯪

Glass: Collins
Garnish: Lemon slice
Method: SHAKE first 4 ingredients with ice and strain into ice-filled glass.

1½ shots   **Patrón reposado tequila**
1   shot   **St-Germain elderflower liqueur**
½ shot   **Suze Saveur d'Autrefois**
½ shot   **Freshly squeezed lemon juice**
Top with   **Soda (club soda)**

Origin: Created in August 2015 by yours truly at the Cabinet Room, London, England.
Comment: Floral elderflower and tequila with a hint of bittersweet gentian and refreshing lemon.

DROWNED OUT

★★★⯪☆

Glass: Collins
Garnish: Lime wedge
Method: POUR ingredients into ice-filled glass, stir and serve with straws.

2   shots   **Pernod anise**
1   shot   **Freshly squeezed lime juice**
Top with   **Ginger ale**

Comment: Ginger combines with aniseed rather than drowning it.

DRY DAIQUIRI

★★★★⯪☆

Glass: Martini
Garnish: Lime wedge
Method: SHAKE all ingredients with ice and fine strain into chilled glass.

2   shots   **Bacardi Carta Ocho aged rum**
½ shot   **Freshly squeezed lime juice**
¼ shot   **Sugar syrup (2 sugar to 1 water)**
⅛ shot   **Campari Bitter**
⅛ shot   **Passion fruit syrup**

Origin: Created in 2007 by Kevin Armstrong, Match Group, London.
Comment: Passion fruit syrup is powerful stuff and a little goes a long way in this drink.

DRY ICE MARTINI

★★★★★

Glass: Martini
Garnish: Orange zest twist
Method: STIR all ingredients with ice and strain into chilled glass.

2   shots   **Ketel One Vodka**
½ shot   **Martini Extra Dry vermouth**
¾ shot   **Icewine**

Origin: Created in 2004 by yours truly in London, England.
Comment: I always see Icewine in duty free shops. It has fabulously rich concentrated flavours due to being made using grapes frozen on the vine in Canada's harsh and early winters. Thanks to Icewine, despite the name, this Martini is slightly honeyed rather than being bone dry.

DRY MARTINI #1 (PREFERRED 5:1 RATIO)

★★★★★

Glass: Martini
Garnish: Chilled olive on stick or lemon zest twist
Method: STIR all ingredients with ice and strain into chilled glass.

2½ shots   **Rutte Dry Gin**
½ shot   **Martini Extra Dry vermouth**
4   drop   **Angostura Orange Bitters** (optional)

Origin: The Martini and its origins is a topic that can raise temperatures among drinks aficionados and, as so often, no one really knows.

Today the drink is a blend of dry gin or vodka with a hint of dry vermouth. Yet it seems to have evolved from the Manhattan via the Martinez, a rather sweet drink based on Dutch genever or Old Tom gin with the addition of sweet vermouth, curaçao and orange bitters. The Martini, like the Martinez, was initially sweet, not dry (hence the need to specify that its descendant was a 'Dry' Martini), and very heavy on the vermouth by modern standards.

Martinis were known in the late 1880s but the Dry Martini most likely appeared with the emergence of the London dry gin style. In 1906 Louis Muckenstrum wrote about a dry Martini Cocktail which, like the Martinez, benefited from curaçao and bitters as well as vermouth. Yet, unlike earlier versions, both the gin and the vermouth were dry. According to Gary Regan, the marketers at Martini & Rosso vermouth were advertising a Dry Martini cocktail heavily at that time.

One myth attributes the creation of the Dry Martini to one Martini di Arma di Taggia, head bartender at New York's Knickerbocker Hotel, in 1911, although this is clearly too late. It is also no longer believed that the name relates to Martini & Henry rifles, the first of which was launched in 1871.

The Dry Martini seems to have got drier and drier over the years. Curaçao rapidly left the drink, but orange bitters remained a usual ingredient until the 1940s (interestingly, these are now coming back into vogue in some bars).

There is some debate as to whether a Martini should be shaken or stirred. It should be stirred. If shaken, it becomes a 'Bradford'. Shaking the drink increases the dilution and introduces air bubbles into the drink, making it taste fresher and colder but making the drink appear cloudy due to the introduction of tiny air bubbles.

Comment: We have chosen a 5:1 ratio as our 'preferred' Dry Martini specification in deference to David Embury who writes of this drink in his "The Fine Art of Mixing Drinks, "After extensive experimentation I have arrived at the ratio of 5 to 1 as the proportion most pleasing to the average palate. Personally I like a ratio of about 7 to 1 even better, and I know some who prefer a ratio as high as 10 to 1."

The proportion of gin to vermouth is a matter of taste; some say 5 to 1, others that one drop is sufficient. I recommend you ask the drinker how they would like their Martini, in the same manner that you might ask how they have their steak.

DRY MARTINI #2 (NAKED 10:1 RATIO)

★ ★ ★ ★ ☆

Glass: Martini
Garnish: Chilled olive on stick or lemon zest twist
Method: POUR water into glass, swirl around to coat and place in freezer for at least two hours, alongside the bottle of gin. Swirl water in glass from time to time until the inside of the glass is covered in a thin layer of ice and the gin is frozen. **POUR** vermouth into icy glass and swirl to coat the ice with vermouth. **POUR** frozen gin into glass and serve immediately.

¼ shot   **Chilled water**
⅛ shot   **Martini Extra Dry vermouth**
2½ shots **Rutte Dry Gin**

Origin: After the Second World War, vermouth proportions in the classic Dry Martini dropped rapidly, and this 'Naked' style of serve began to appear. Traditionally both vermouth and gin had been stirred with ice. In a Naked Martini the merest hint of vermouth is swirled around a well-chilled glass and then frozen gin is poured into the vermouth-coated glass.

The trick to a good Naked Martini is still achieving some dilution by the addition of a splash of water in the glass before freezing. I learnt from Salvatore Calabrese, who originally tended bar at London's Duke's Hotel – famous for its Dry Martinis.
Comment: Dilution is achieved as the water you have frozen in the glass begins to melt. Both glass and gin must be freezing cold so that the temperature masks the strength of the alcohol. Thus the drink does not taste nearly as strong as it is – you have been warned.

DRY MARTINI #3 (3:1 RATIO)

★ ★ ★ ★ ☆

Glass: Martini
Garnish: Chilled olive on stick or lemon zest twist.
Method: STIR all ingredients with ice and strain into chilled glass.

2¼ shots **Rutte Dry Gin**
¾ shot   **Martini Extra Dry vermouth**

Comment: Three to one may be unfair odds in a fight but vermouth shines in this stirred off-dry Martini. Through experimentation we have found that 3:1 Martinis are better stirred rather than shaken. Conversely 15:1 Martinis are better shaken rather than stirred.

DRY MARTINI #4 (EMBURY'S 7:1 RATIO)

★ ★ ★ ★ ★

Glass: Martini
Garnish: Chilled olive on stick or lemon zest twist.
Method: STIR all ingredients with ice and strain into chilled glass.

2½ shots **Rutte Dry Gin**
⅓ shot **Martini Extra Dry vermouth**

Origin: In his 'Fine Art of Mixing Drinks', David Embury writes of this drink "After extensive experimentation I have arrived at the ratio of 5 to 1 as the proportion most pleasing to the average palate. Personally, I like a ratio of about 7 to 1 even better, and I know some who prefer a ratio as high as 10 to 1."
Comment: Readers of Embury will know he had a bone dry palate and Martinis made to his specification are just that, and with the correct dilution, fabulous.

DRY MARTINI #6 (SERVED WET 2:1 RATIO)

★ ★ ★ ★ ☆

Glass: Martini
Garnish: Chilled olive on stick or lemon zest twist
Method: STIR all ingredients with ice and strain into chilled glass.

3 shots   **Rutte Dry Gin**
1½ shots   **Martini Extra Dry vermouth**

Origin: A generous measure of vermouth to two of gin, hence the name 'Wet' Martini.
Comment: Reputed to be a favourite of HRH Prince Charles.

DRY MARTINI #7 (SOPPING WET 2:1.5 RATIO)

★ ★ ★ ★ ☆

Glass: Martini
Garnish: Chilled olive on stick or lemon zest twist
Method: STIR all ingredients with ice and strain into chilled glass.

2 shots   **Rutte Dry Gin**
1½ shots   **Martini Extra Dry vermouth**
1 dash   **Angostura Orange Bitters** (optional)

Comment: Herbal vermouth flavours pervade this Sopping Wet Martini.

DRY MARTINI (MONTGOMERY'S 15:1 RATIO)

★★★★★+

Glass: Martini
Garnish: Orange zest twist
Method: SHAKE all ingredients with ice and fine strain into chilled glass.

2	shots	Rutte Dry Gin
⅛	shot	Martini Extra Dry vermouth
1	dash	Angostura Orange Bitters

Origin: Unknown but this 15:1 gin to vermouth Martini was said to be Ernest Hemingway's favourite formula and is named after British Field Marshall Bernard Montgomery, who it is said, liked the gin in his Martini to outnumber the vermouth in roughly the same ratio as he liked to outnumber his opponents in battle.

Nicknamed 'Monty', Field Marshal Bernard Law Montgomery (1887-1976) fought and was seriously wounded in the First World War and was one of the most notorious British commanders in the Second World War. He commanded allied troops at the Battle of El Alamein and was a key planner of the Normandy D-Day invasion. On 4 May 1945 he took the German surrender at Luneburg Heath in northern Germany.
Comment: Bone dry - a superbly cleansing Martini. Through experimentation we have found that 15:1 Martinis are better shaken rather than stirred. Conversely 3:1 Martinis are better stirred rather than shaken. I also prefer an orange zest twist to the more usual lemon zest or olive.

DRY ORANGE MARTINI

★★★★☆

Glass: Martini
Garnish: Grapefruit zest twist
Method: STIR all ingredients with ice and strain into chilled glass.

2	shots	Rutte Dry Gin
¼	shot	De Kuyper Triple Sec
¾	shot	Martini Extra Dry vermouth
2	dash	Angostura Orange Bitters

Origin: Created in 2003 by Wayne Collins for Maxxium UK.
Comment: Bone dry, orangey, aptly named Martini.

DUBLIN MINSTREL (NEW)

★★★★★

Glass: Coupe
Garnish: Lime zest twist
Method: SHAKE all ingredients with ice and fine strain into chilled glass.

1	shot	Teeling Small Batch Irish whiskey
⅔	shot	Green Chartreuse liqueur
⅔	shot	Luxardo Maraschino liqueur
⅔	shot	Freshly squeezed lime juice

Origin: Created by yours truly 12th February 2015 at the Cabinet Room, London, England.
Comment: A riff on the classic Last Word cocktail substituting Irish whiskey for gin. Named after Frank Fogarty, a vaudeville performer known as the The Dublin Minstrel. Fogarty is referenced in Ted Saucier's 1951 'Bottoms Up!' book as introducing the Last Word to the Detroit Athletic Club around 1920 and is possibly who the Last Word was originally named after.

DUBLINER COCKTAIL

★★★★☆

Glass: Martini
Garnish: Luxardo Maraschino cherry
Method: STIR all ingredients with ice and strain into chilled glass.

2	shots	Teeling Small Batch Irish whiskey
½	shot	Grand Marnier Cordon Rouge
½	shot	Martini Rosso vermouth
1	dash	Angostura Orange Bitters

Origin: Adapted from a recipe by Gary & Mardee Regan in 1999 in New York, USA.
Comment: A Manhattan variation calling for Irish whiskey instead of bourbon or rye, mixed with equal parts sweet vermouth, orange liqueur and a dash of orange bitters - ideally Regan's Orange Bitters.

THE DUBONNET COCKTAIL #1

★★★★☆

Glass: Old-fashioned
Garnish: Lemon zest twist
Method: STIR all ingredients with ice and strain into ice-filled glass.

1½	shots	Rutte Dry Gin
1½	shots	Dubonnet Red
¼	shot	Freshly squeezed lemon juice

Origin: A classic that was popular in Britain during the 1920s.
Comment: Simple yet complex. Dry and aromatic.

THE DUBONNET COCKTAIL #2

★★★½☆

Glass: Martini
Garnish: Lemon zest twist
Method: SHAKE all ingredients with ice and fine strain into chilled glass.

1½	shots	Rutte Dry Gin
1½	shots	Dubonnet Red
¼	shot	Freshly squeezed lemon juice

Origin: Vintage cocktail of unknown origin.
Comment: Gin and Dubonnet with a hint of citrus. Be sure your Dubonnet is the French stuff.

DULCHIN

★★★★½

Glass: Martini
Garnish: Orange zest twist
Method: SHAKE all ingredients with ice and fine strain into chilled glass.

2	shots	BarSol Mosto Verde Italia pisco
½	shot	Grand Marnier Cordon Rouge
½	shot	De Kuyper XO Apricot Brandy
¼	shot	Rose's lime cordial
¼	shot	Pomegranate / grenadine syrup (2:1)
¾	shot	Chilled water (omit if wet ice)

Comment: This dry, amber coloured, fruity cocktail carries a pisco punch.

THE DUNAWAY

★★★★☆

Glass: Coupe
Garnish: Lemon zest twist (discarded)
Method: STIR all ingredients with ice and strain into chilled glass.

2¼ shots   Romate Fino sherry
½   shot   Cynar
¼   shot   Luxardo Maraschino liqueur
2   dash   Angostura Aromatic Bitters

Origin: Created in 2010 by Misty Kalkofen at Drink, Boston, USA.
Comment: A dry sherry-rich aperitif cocktail.

DURANGO

★★★☆☆

Glass: Collins
Garnish: Orange slice
Method: SHAKE first three ingredients with ice and strain into ice-filled glass. TOP with soda.

2   shots   Patrón reposado tequila
¾   shot   Disaronno Originale amaretto
1   shot   Freshly squeezed pink grapefruit juice
Top with   Soda (club soda)

Comment: This sandy coloured drink makes tequila, amaretto and grapefruit into unlikely but harmonious bedfellows.

DUTCH BLOOD AND SAND

★★★★☆

Glass: Coupe
Garnish: Orange zest twist
Method: SHAKE all ingredients with ice and fine strain into chilled glass.

1   shot   Rutte Old Simon oude jenever
¾   shot   Martini Rosso vermouth
¾   shot   Cherry Heering Liqueur
¾   shot   Freshly squeezed orange juice

Comment: A light fragrant style of the classic cocktail usually Scotch whisky based.

DUTCH BREAKFAST COCKTAIL

★★★★☆

Glass: Martini
Garnish: Orange zest twist
Method: SHAKE all ingredients with ice and fine strain into chilled glass.

1½ shots   Warninks Advocaat liqueur
1½ shots   Rutte Dry Gin
1   shot   Freshly squeezed lemon juice
¼   shot   Sugar syrup (2 sugar to 1 water)
⅛   shot   Galliano L'Autentico liqueur

Origin: Created in 2002 by Alex Kammerling, London, England.
Comment: A tasty, aromatic, almost creamy alternative to a fry-up.

DUTCH COUNT NEGRONI

★★★★☆

Glass: Old-fashioned
Garnish: Orange slice
Method: POUR ingredients into ice-filled glass and STIR.

1   shot   Rutte Old Simon oude jenever
1   shot   Campari Bitter
1   shot   Martini Rosso vermouth

Origin: Discovered in 2011 at Vesper Bar, Amsterdam, The Netherlands.
Comment: Jenever's flavoursome character adds malty notes to an otherwise traditional Negroni.

DUTCH COURAGE

★★★★☆

Glass: Collins
Garnish: Lemon slice
Method: SHAKE all ingredients with ice and strain into ice-filled glass.

1   shot   Rutte Dry Gin
1   shot   Warninks Advocaat liqueur
¾   shot   Freshly squeezed lemon juice
3   shots   Pressed apple juice

Origin: Created in 2002 by Alex Kammerling, London, England.
Comment: A refreshing alternative to a traditional English lemonade.

DUTCH MARTINI

★★★★☆

Glass: Martini
Garnish: Olive on stick
Method: STIR all ingredients with ice and strain into chilled glass.

2   shots   Ketel One Vodka
¼   shot   Rutte Old Simon oude jenever
⅛   shot   Orange Curaçao liqueur
⅛   shot   Martini Extra Dry vermouth

Comment: A modern twist on the classic Dr Martini inspired by a vintage bartender. In his 1882 'New and Improved Bartender's Manual' Harry Johnson's Martini Cocktail recipe calls for "a dash of curaçao or absinthe, if required."

DUTCH MASTER

★★★★☆

Glass: Martini
Garnish: White grapes
Method: STIR all ingredients with ice and strain into chilled glass.

2   shots   Ketel One Vodka
⅛   shot   Romate Fino sherry
⅛   shot   St-Germain elderflower liqueur
1   shot   Tonic Water

Origin: Created in 2007 by Bruce Borthwick in Fife, Scotland.
Comment: It's a vodka and tonic but not like you know it.

DUTCH WORD

★★★★☆

Glass: Martini
Garnish: Lime zest twist (discarded) & lime wedge on rim
Method: **SHAKE** all ingredients with ice and fine strain into chilled glass.

1 shot **Rutte Old Simon oude jenever**
⅔ shot **Green Chartreuse liqueur**
⅔ shot **Luxardo Maraschino liqueur**
⅔ shot **Freshly squeezed lime juice**

Origin: Created in December 2010 by yours truly at the Cabinet Room, London, England.
Comment: A genever-based variation to the classic Last Word cocktail.

DYEVITCHKA

★★★★☆

Glass: Martini
Garnish: Orange zest twist
Method: **SHAKE** all ingredients with ice and fine strain into chilled glass.

1 shot **Ketel One Vodka**
1 shot **De Kuyper Triple Sec**
½ shot **Freshly squeezed lime juice**
¼ shot **Sugar syrup (2 sugar to 1 water)**
1½ shots **Fresh pressed pineapple juice**

Comment: Pineapple replaces cranberry in this Cosmo-like cocktail.

EARL GREY FIZZ

★★★★☆

Glass: Flute
Garnish: Lemon zest twist
Method: **SHAKE** first three ingredients with ice and strain into chilled glass. **TOP** with champagne.

1 shot **Ketel One Vodka**
½ shot **Cold Earl Grey tea**
¼ shot **Sugar syrup (2 sugar to 1 water)**
Top with **G.H. Mumm Brut Cordon Rouge champagne**

Origin: Created in 2002 by Henry Besant at Lonsdale House, London, England.
Comment: Looks like a glass of champagne but has a well judged little extra something.

EARL GREY MARTEANI

★★★★½

Glass: Martini
Garnish: Lemon zest twist
Method: **SHAKE** all ingredients with ice and fine strain into chilled glass.

2 shots **Rutte Dry Gin** (tea infused)
¾ shot **Freshly squeezed lemon juice**
½ fresh **Egg white**
½ shot **Sugar syrup (2 sugar to 1 water)**

Origin: Adapted from a drink created in 2000 by Audrey Saunders at Bemelmans Bar at the Carlyle, New York City.
Comment: A fantastic and very English drink created by a New Yorker. The gin botanicals combine wonderfully with the flavours and tannins of the tea.

EAST 8 HOLD-UP COCKTAIL (NEW)

★★★★☆

Glass: Old-fashioned
Garnish: Pineapple & lime wedges
Method: **SHAKE** all ingredients with ice and strain into ice-filled glass.

1½ shots **Ketel One Vodka**
½ shot **Aperol Aperitivo**
⅔ shot **Fresh pressed pineapple juice**
½ shot **Freshly squeezed lime juice**
¼ shot **Sugar syrup (2 sugar to 1 water)**
⅛ shot **Passion fruit syrup**

Origin: Created in 2010 by Kevin Armstrong at Milk & Honey, London. The name comes from the part of London where Kevin lived, E8, an area where muggings were commonplace.

One night Keven had just dropped Sam Jeveons off during their taxi ride home and Sam stopped to take a leak. While pissing against a wall with his trousers dropped around his feet, a guy came up behind him, stepped on his trousers and told him to hand over his wallet. Sam ended up chasing the guy with trousers around his ankles. The episode became known as the East 8 Hold Up.
Comment: Vodka based, fruity and bittersweet with pineapple and passion fruit.

EAST INDIA #1

★★★★★

Glass: Martini
Garnish: Orange zest twist
Method: **SHAKE** all ingredients with ice and fine strain into chilled glass.

2½ shots **Martell VSOP Médaillon cognac**
⅛ shot **Grand Marnier Cordon Rouge**
⅛ shot **Luxardo Maraschino liqueur**
¼ shot **Pomegranate / grenadine syrup (2:1)**
1 dash **Angostura Aromatic Bitters**

Origin: The first mention of an East India appears in Harry Johnson's 1882 'Bartender's Manual'. This slightly different and rather better recipe is adapted from Ted Haigh's 'Vintage Spirits & Forgotten Cocktails'.
Comment: Wonderfully complex and rounded - a serious drink for serious drinkers.

EAST INDIA #2

★★★★½

Glass: Martini
Garnish: Orange zest twist & dust with grated nutmeg
Method: **SHAKE** all ingredients with ice and fine strain into chilled glass.

1½ shots **Martell VSOP Médaillon cognac**
¾ shot **Grand Marnier Cordon Rouge**
1½ shots **Fresh pressed pineapple juice**
2 dash **Angostura Aromatic Bitters**

Origin: Another version of the East India classic, thought to originate with Frank Meier at the Ritz Bar, Paris.
Comment: A rich but bitter short drink based on cognac.

EAST INDIA HOUSE

★★★★☆

Glass: Martini
Garnish: Lemon zest twist
Method: SHAKE all ingredients with ice and fine strain into chilled glass.

2	shots	Martell VSOP Médaillon cognac
½	shot	Bacardi Carta Ocho aged rum
½	shot	De Kuyper Triple Sec
½	shot	Fresh pressed pineapple juice
2	dash	Angostura Orange Bitters

Origin: I've adapted this recipe from a classic cocktail which is thought to have been created in the 19th century by Harry Johnson: I've doubled the quantities of everything but cognac.
Comment: Dry and challenging - rewarding for some.

EAST INDIAN

★★★★⯪

Glass: Martini
Garnish: Olive on stick
Method: STIR all ingredients with ice and strain into chilled glass.

2	shots	Romate Fino sherry
2	shots	Martini Extra Dry vermouth
¼	shot	Sugar syrup (2 sugar to 1 water)
3	dash	Angostura Orange Bitters

Comment: Dry and pretty flat (like much of India) but perfectly balanced with subtle hints of orange zest.

EAST MEETS WEST JULEP

★★★⯪☆

Glass: Old-fashioned
Garnish: Mint sprig & pomegranate seeds
Method: SHAKE all ingredients with ice and fine strain into glass filled with crushed ice.

¾	shot	Pomegranate juice
7	fresh	Mint leaves
2	shots	Bourbon whiskey
½	shot	Honey sugar syrup
¼	shot	Pomegranate / grenadine syrup (2:1)

Origin: Adapted from a drink created in 2008 by Nidal Ramini at Montgomery Place, London, England.
Comment: Reminiscent of honeyed Mint Julep with pomegranate fruit.

EAST VILLAGE ATHLETIC CLUB

★★★★☆

Glass: Martini
Garnish: Lime wedge
Method: SHAKE all ingredients with ice and fine strain into chilled glass.

¾	shot	Patrón silver tequila
¾	shot	Yellow Chartreuse liqueur
¾	shot	Grand Marnier Cordon Rouge
¾	shot	Freshly squeezed lemon juice

Origin: The Last Word, a vintage cocktail classic, was first documented in Ted Saucier's Bottoms Up in 1951 where its creation was attributed to the Detroit Athletic Club. In 2008 the folk at New York's PDT tinkered with the recipe to create this drink named after their own hood.
Comment: Essentially a Last Word with tequila instead of gin.

EASTER COCKTAIL

★★★★⯪

Glass: Coupe
Garnish: Dust with chocolate powder or crumbled Cadbury's Flake bar with mini chocolate eggs in orange zest nest on rim.
Method: MUDDLE cardamom pods in base of shaker. Add other ingredients, SHAKE with ice and strain back into shaker. DRY SHAKE (without ice) and fine strain into chilled glass.

4	whole	Cardamom pod
2	shot	Vanilla infused Ketel One vodka
1	shot	White crème de cacao liqueur
¼	shot	Sugar syrup (2 sugar to 1 water)
½	shot	Chilled water
½	fresh	Egg white

Comment: Chocolate cocktail with extra interest thanks to vanilla and cardamom.
Origin: Created in 2003 by Simon King at MJU Bar, Millennium Hotel, London, England. The egg white was our addition to Simon's recipe - it seemed appropriate to add egg given this is an Easter Cocktail. We also added the orange zest nest of chocolate eggs.

EASTERN COCKTAIL

★★★★☆

Glass: Martini
Garnish: Japanese ume plum
Method: SHAKE all ingredients with ice and fine strain into chilled glass.

2	shots	Ketel One Vodka
1½	shots	Choya Umeshu plum liqueur
1	shot	Pressed apple juice

Origin: Created in 2003 by Chris Langan, Barnomadics, Scotland.
Comment: Light, fragrant and fruity - distinctly oriental.

EASTERN PROMISE

★★★★☆

Glass: Martini
Garnish: Lemon zest twist
Method: SHAKE all ingredients with ice and fine strain into chilled glass.

2	shots	Ketel One Vodka
¼	shot	De Kuyper XO Apricot Brandy
½	shot	Rose syrup
½	shot	Freshly squeezed lemon juice
½	shot	Chilled water (omit if wet ice)

Origin: Adapted from a drink discovered in 2004 at Oxo Tower Bar, London, England.
Comment: Citrus dominates this drink but the result is floral rather than tart.

STAR RATINGS EXPLAINED

★★★★★⁺ OUTSTANDING	★★★★★ EXCEPTIONAL
★★★★⯪ EXCELLENT	★★★★☆ RECOMMENDED
★★★⯪☆ COMMENDED	★★★☆☆ MEDIOCRE
★★⯪☆☆ DISAPPOINTING	★★☆☆☆ PRETTY AWFUL
★⯪☆☆☆ SHAMEFUL	★☆☆☆☆ DISGUSTING

EASTERN PROMISES

★★★★☆

Glass: Coupe
Garnish: Mandarin zest

Method: SHAKE all ingredients with ice and fine strain into chilled glass.

2	shots	Bacardi Carta Blanca light rum
½	shot	Martini Rosso vermouth
1	shot	Freshly squeezed orange juice
⅓	shot	Freshly squeezed lime juice
⅓	shot	Sugar syrup (2 sugar to 1 water)
2	dash	Peychaud's aromatic bitters

Origin: Created in 2011 by Simone Caporale at Artesian at the Langham Hotel, London, England.
Comment: This rum-based drink was apparently inspired by the golden age of the cocktail, with aromatic mandarin, tart lime, bittersweet vermouth resulting in an elegant cocktail with a complex finish.

EASTERN RASPBERRY SIDECAR

★★★★☆

Glass: Martini
Garnish: Sugar rim & raspberry
Method: MUDDLE raspberries in base of shaker. Add other ingredients, **SHAKE** with ice and fine strain into chilled glass.

7 fresh Raspberries
1 shot Martell VSOP Médaillon cognac
1 shot Junmai ginjō sake
½ shot De Kuyper Triple Sec
½ shot Sugar syrup (2 sugar to 1 water)
½ shot Freshly squeezed lemon juice

Origin: Created by Ryan Magarian, Seattle, USA.
Comment: Refreshing, fruity, easy drinking.

EASTERN SIN

★★★☆☆

Glass: Martini
Garnish: Pineapple wedge
Method: SHAKE all ingredients with ice and fine strain into chilled glass.

1½	shots	Dewar's 12 Year Old Scotch whisky
1½	shots	Cherry Heering Liqueur
½	shot	De Kuyper Triple Sec
½	shot	Martini Rosso vermouth
½	shot	Fresh pressed pineapple juice

Origin: In W.J. Tarling's 1937 Café Royal Cocktail Book the invention of this cocktail is credited to J. Stoneham. I have cut the amount of cherry brandy by a third compared to the Café Royal formula.
Comment: Fruity and slightly sweet but toned by a hint of Scotch.

EASTSIDE GIMLET

★★★★½

Glass: Coupe
Garnish: Mint leaf & cucumber slice
Method: MUDDLE cucumber in base of shaker. Add gin, lime juice and sugar syrup, **SHAKE** with ice and fine strain into chilled glass. **TOP** with a splash of soda.

2 slice Cucumber (English)
8 fresh Mint leaves
2 shot Rutte Dry Gin
¾ shot Freshly squeezed lime juice
½ shot Sugar syrup (2 sugar to 1 water)
½ shot Soda water (club soda)

Comment: A riff on the Southside using cucumber – an ingredient originally inspired by Hendrick's Gin having recently launched when this gin cocktail was first created.
Origin: Created in 2004 by George Delgado at Libation, New York City, USA – originally as a long drink. Christy Pope took the Eastside to Milk & Honey where this now popular straight-up version was created.

EASY SPEAK

★★★★½

Glass: Old-fashioned
Garnish: Lemon zest twist
Method: STIR all ingredients with ice and strain into chilled glass (without ice).

2	shots	Bourbon whiskey
¾	shot	Cynar
¼	shot	Sugar syrup (2 sugar to 1 water)

Origin: Created in 2012 by Scott Diaz, Beverage & Cafe Manager at Elliott's Oyster House & Seafood Café, Seattle, USA.
Comment: Originally with a few dashes if chocolate bitters but this drink has enough complexity without the extra bitterness.

EASY TIGER

★★★★☆

Glass: Martini
Garnish: Orange zest twist
Method: MUDDLE ginger in base of shaker. Add honey and tequila, and **STIR** until honey is dissolved. Add other ingredients, **SHAKE** with ice and fine strain into chilled glass.

2	slice	Fresh root ginger (thumbnail sized)
2	spoon	Runny honey
2	shots	Patrón reposado tequila
1	shot	Freshly squeezed lime juice
¾	shot	Chilled water (omit if wet ice)

Origin: Created in 1999 by Alex Kammerling.
Comment: Tangy and zesty with rich honey and ginger.

A B C D E F G H I J K L M N O P Q R S T U V W X Y Z

ECLIPSE

★★★★☆

Glass: Collins
Garnish: Raspberries & mint sprig
Method: **MUDDLE** raspberries in base of shaker. Add other ingredients, **SHAKE** with ice and strain into glass filled with crushed ice. Serve with straws.

12 fresh	Raspberries
2 shots	Bourbon whiskey
1 shot	Chambord Liqueur
½ shot	Freshly squeezed lime juice
2 shots	Cranberry juice

Origin: Signature cocktail at the chain of Eclipse Bars, London, England.
Comment: A fruity summer cooler which I challenge anyone not to like.

EDEN

★★★★☆

Glass: Collins
Garnish: Orange zest twist
Method: **SHAKE** first three ingredients with ice and strain into ice-filled glass. **TOP** with tonic water.

2 shots	Ketel One Vodka
½ shot	St-Germain elderflower liqueur
1½ shots	Pressed apple juice
Top with	Tonic Water

Origin: Created in 2003 by Sylvian Solignac at Citrus, London, England.
Comment: Orange zest predominates in a long, refreshing drink that's perfect for warm days.

EDEN COCKTAIL

★★★☆☆

Glass: Martini
Garnish: Orange zest twist
Method: **SHAKE** all ingredients with ice and fine strain into chilled glass.

2½ shots	Rutte Dry Gin
½ shot	Parfait Amour liqueur
¼ shot	Freshly squeezed lemon juice
¼ shot	Rose water
¼ shot	Chilled water (omit if wet ice)

Origin: Adapted from a recipe discovered in 2003 at Oxo Tower Bar, London, England.
Comment: Rich purple in colour with rose, vanilla, almond, citrus and gin.

EDISON'S MEDICINE COCKTAIL (NEW)

★★★★☆

Glass: Coupe
Garnish: Float basil leaf
Method: **SHAKE** all ingredients with ice and fine strain into chilled glass.

6 fresh	Basil leaves
1½ shots	Capucana cachaça
½ shot	Yellow Chartreuse liqueur
¾ shot	Freshly squeezed lime juice
½ shot	Agave syrup
½ shot	Chilled water (omit if wet ice)

Origin: Adapted from a 2011 recipe created by Pete Gugni at The Bedford, Chicago, USA
Comment: Cachaça leads with basil and Chartreuse herbal notes, zesty lime and agave richness.

EGG CUSTARD COCKTAIL

★★★☆☆

Glass: Martini
Garnish: Dust with grated nutmeg
Method: **SHAKE** all ingredients with ice and fine strain into chilled glass.

1½ shots	Ketel One Vodka
1 shot	Warninks Advocaat liqueur
½ shot	Vanilla infused Ketel One vodka
½ shot	Bourbon whiskey
¼ shot	Sugar syrup (2 sugar to 1 water)

Origin: Created in 2002 by Alex Kammerling, London, England.
Comment: As custardy as the name would suggest but surprisingly potent.

EGGNOG #1 (COLD)

★★★☆☆

Glass: Collins
Garnish: Dust with grated nutmeg
Method: **SHAKE** all ingredients with ice and strain into ice-filled glass.

2½ shots	Martell VSOP Médaillon cognac
½ shot	Sugar syrup (2 sugar to 1 water)
1 fresh	Eggs (white & yolk)
½ shot	Single cream / half-and-half
2 shots	Milk

Comment: Lightly flavoured alcoholic egg custard. Also try swapping dark rum for the cognac.

EGGNOG #2 (HOT)

★★★★☆

Glass: Toddy
Garnish: Dust with grated nutmeg
Method: **POUR** ingredients into heatproof glass and **STIR** thoroughly. **HEAT** in microwave oven for a minute (adjust time as appropriate to your oven) and **STIR** again. Alternatively, mix and warm in pan over heat - do not boil.

2½ shots	Martell VSOP Médaillon cognac
½ shot	Sugar syrup (2 sugar to 1 water)
1 fresh	Eggs (white & yolk)
½ shot	Single cream / half-and-half
2 shots	Milk

Comment: A warming, spicy and filling meal in a glass.

EIGHTEEN '97

★★★★☆

Glass: Martini
Garnish: Orange zest twist (discarded) & white grapes
Method: **MUDDLE** kumquats in base of shaker. Add next three ingredients, shake and fine strain into a chilled glass. **FLOAT** wine.

5 fresh	Kumquats (chopped)
1½ shots	Bepi Tosolini Grappa di Moscato
1¼ shots	St-Germain elderflower liqueur
¼ shot	Sugar syrup (2 sugar to 1 water)
¼ shot	Merlot red wine

Origin: Created in 2008 by Raffaello Dante at Salvatore's at FIFTY, London, England.
Comment: Looks great and, with the citrus freshness of kumquat combined with the oily character of grappa, it also tastes great.

EL BURRO

★★★★☆

Glass: Collins
Garnish: Lime slice
Method: **SHAKE** first 4 ingredients with ice and strain into ice-filled glass. **TOP** with ginger beer.

2 shots Patrón reposado tequila
½ shot Freshly squeezed lime juice
¼ shot Sugar syrup (2 sugar to 1 water)
3 dash Angostura Aromatic Bitters
Top with Gosling's Stormy Ginger Beer

Origin: Created by Henry Besant and Andres Masso, London, England. The name of this Mexican version of the Moscow Mule translates from Spanish as 'The Donkey'.
Comment: Ginger spice and tequila soured with lime.

EL COCO

★★★★☆

Glass: Martini
Garnish: Lime zest twist
Method: **STIR** all ingredients with ice and fine strain into chilled glass.

2 shots Bacardi Carta Blanca light rum
1 shot Coconut water
¼ shot Sugar syrup (2 sugar to 1 water)
⅛ shot Freshly squeezed lime juice

Origin: Created in 2008 by Richard Hunt at Mahiki, London, England and named after the coconut palm outside the original Bacardi distillery in Santiago de Cuba.
Comment: Rum and coconut water with the merest hint of lime.

EL DIABLO COCKTAIL

★★★★☆

Glass: Collins
Garnish: Lime wedge
Method: **SHAKE** first 3 ingredients with ice and strain into ice-filled glass. **TOP** with ginger beer.

2 shots Patrón reposado tequila
¾ shot Lejay crème de cassis de Dijon
1 shot Freshly squeezed lime juice
Top with Gosling's Stormy Ginger Beer

Origin: Thought to have originated in California during the 1940's. The name translates as 'The Devil'.
Comment: The tequila, red fruit and ginger aren't exactly a subtle combination but it is one that has proved both popular and enduring.

EL MEDITERRANEO (NEW)

★★★★½

Glass: Coupe
Garnish: Drip 5 drops of olive oil on top
Method: **SHAKE** all ingredients with ice and fine strain into chilled glass. (There's no need to muddle basil if good ice and shake.)

3 fresh Basil leaves
1⅔ shots Bacardi Carta Blanca light rum
⅓ shot Skinos Mastiha
⅔ shot Freshly squeezed lemon juice
⅓ shot Sugar syrup (2 sugar to 1 water)

Origin: Created in 2015 by Jad Ballout, Bar Manager at Central Station Boutique Bar in Beirut, Lebanon. El Mediterráneo was the winning Lebanese entry to the 2015 Bacardi Legacy cocktail competition.
Jad was apparently inspired by two existing popular cocktails, the Mint Julep and the Gin Basil Smash while the mastiha liqueur adds a Mediterranean touch. The drops of olive oil on top of the drink not only reflect Mediterranean cuisine but were inspired by the fact that Don Facundo, the creator of Bacardi, used to sell his first homemade rum in recycled olive oil tins.
Comment: A little mastiha greatly influences this delicately flavoured cocktail that is reminiscent of a very light lemon Daiquiri flavoured with mastiha and basil.

EL MOMENTO PERFECTO

★★★★☆

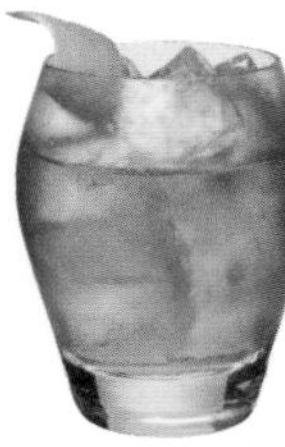

Glass: Old-fashioned
Garnish: Lemon zest twist
Method: **STIR** over cubed ice and julep strain into heavy old fashioned glass over fresh ice.

1½ shots Bacardi Carta Blanca light rum
⅔ shot Lillet Blanc
⅔ shot Byrrh Grand Quinquina
⅓ shot Campari Bitter
1 spoon English orange marmalade

Origin: Adapted from a drink created in 2011 by Daniel Bovey at Sahara Bar, Reading, England.
Comment: A rum and marmalade Negroni-like drink.

EL PRESIDENTE #2

★★★½☆

Glass: Martini
Garnish: Lime zest twist
Method: **SHAKE** all ingredients with ice and fine strain into chilled glass.

2 shots Bacardi Carta Blanca light rum
1 shot Martini Extra Dry vermouth
1 dash Angostura Aromatic Bitters

Comment: Bone dry. Rather like a rum based, old school Martini.

EL PRESIDENTE #3

★★★☆☆

Glass: Martini
Garnish: Orange zest twist
Method: **SHAKE** all ingredients with ice and fine strain into chilled glass.

2 shots Bacardi Carta Blanca light rum
1 shot Martini Extra Dry vermouth
½ shot De Kuyper Triple Sec
¼ shot Pomegranate / grenadine syrup (2:1)

Origin: Adapted from Victor Bergeron's 'Trader Vic's Bartender's Guide' (1972 revised edition). Vic writes of this drink, "This is the real recipe".
Comment: A sweeter version of El Presidente #2.

EL PRESIDENTE #4

★★★★☆

Glass: Martini
Garnish: Orange zest twist
Method: **STIR** all ingredients with ice and strain into chilled glass.

1½ shots Bacardi Carta Blanca light rum
½ shot De Kuyper Triple Sec
¾ shot Martini Extra Dry vermouth

Comment: Dry, but not bone dry, with balanced fruit from the triple sec and vermouth.

EL PRESIDENTE NO.1 #1

★★★★☆

Glass: Martini
Garnish: Lime wedge
Method: SHAKE all ingredients with ice and fine stain into chilled glass.

2	shots	Bacardi Carta Blanca light rum
¾	shot	Fresh pressed pineapple juice
½	shot	Freshly squeezed lime juice
¼	shot	Pomegranate / grenadine syrup (2:1)

Origin: Classic variation on the Daiquiri, of unknown origin.
Comment: Rum and pineapple combine wonderfully and the Daiquiri is the king of cocktails.

EL PRESIDENTE NO.1 #2

★★★★★

Glass: Coupe
Garnish: Orange zest twist
Method: SHAKE all ingredients with ice and fine strain into chilled glass.

2	shots	Bacardi Carta Blanca light rum
1	shot	Martini Extra Dry vermouth
¼	shot	Pomegranate / grenadine syrup (2:1)

Comment: This rose pink tinted coloured drink harnesses a delicate balance between light rum and vermouth with a touch of pomegranate fruity sweetness.

EL TORADO

★★★★☆

Glass: Martini
Garnish: Apple slice
Method: SHAKE all ingredients with ice and fine strain into chilled glass.

2	shots	Patrón reposado tequila
½	shot	Martini Extra Dry vermouth
1½	shots	Pressed apple juice

Origin: Popular throughout Mexico.
Comment: Dry, sophisticated and fruity, with tequila body.

ELDER & WISER

★★★★☆

Glass: Old-fashioned
Garnish: Lemon zest twist
Method: SHAKE all ingredients with ice and fine strain into ice-filled glass.

2	shots	Bourbon whiskey
1	shot	St-Germain elderflower liqueur
1	shot	Pressed apple juice

Origin: Created in 2006 by yours truly and named for its original base, Wiser's Canadian whisky.
Comment: Apple and elderflower combine wonderfully with bourbon.

ELDER AVIATOR

★★★★☆

Glass: Martini
Garnish: Lemon zest twist
Method: SHAKE all ingredients with ice and fine strain into chilled glass.

2	shots	Rutte Dry Gin
½	shot	St-Germain elderflower liqueur
¼	shot	Luxardo Maraschino liqueur
½	shot	Freshly squeezed lemon juice
½	shot	Chilled water (omit if wet ice)

Origin: Created in 2006 by yours truly, London, England.
Comment: A floral riff on the classic Aviation.

ELDER FASHION (NEW)

★★★★☆

Glass: Old-fashioned
Garnish: Grapefruit zest twist
Method: POUR all ingredients into ice-filled glass and **STIR**.

2	shots	Rutte Dry Gin
¾	shot	St-Germain elderflower liqueur
2	dash	Orange bitters

Comment: Boozy and cleansing with gin, floral elderflower with zesty citrus.
Origin: Created by Phil Ward (2007), Death & Co, New York, USA

ELDER FASHIONED

★★★★☆

Glass: Old-fashioned
Garnish: Orange zest twist
Method: STIR one shot of bourbon with two ice cubes in a glass. Add elderflower liqueur, orange bitters and two more ice cubes. **STIR** some more and add another two ice cubes and the rest of the bourbon. **STIR** lots more and add more ice.

2	shots	Bourbon whiskey
¾	shot	St-Germain elderflower liqueur
1	dash	Angostura Orange Bitters

Origin: Created in 2006 by yours truly, London, England.
Comment: Whiskey and elderflower served in the Old-Fashioned style. The elderflower liqueur smooths the bourbon.

ELDER SOUR

★★★★☆

Glass: Old-fashioned
Garnish: Lemon slice & cherry on stick (sail)
Method: SHAKE all ingredients with ice and strain back into shaker. **DRY SHAKE** (without ice) and strain into ice-filled glass.

2	shots	St-Germain elderflower liqueur
1	shot	Freshly squeezed lime juice
½	fresh	Egg white
1	dash	Angostura Orange Bitters (optional)

Origin: Created in 2006 by yours truly, London, England.
Comment: So smooth it's almost fluffy. A great after-dinner drink.

ELDERFLOWER COLLINS #1

★★★★☆

Glass: Collins
Garnish: Physalis (cape gooseberry)
Method: SHAKE first 4 ingredients with ice and strain into ice-filled glass. **TOP** with soda.

2	shots	**Rutte Dry Gin**
½	shot	**St-Germain elderflower liqueur**
1	shot	**Freshly squeezed lemon juice**
⅛	shot	**Sugar syrup (2 sugar to 1 water)**
Top with		**Soda (club soda)**

Comment: A hint of elderflower adds interest to the classic Collins cocktail - long, balanced and refreshing.

ELDERFLOWER COLLINS #2

★★★★☆

Glass: Collins
Garnish: Lemon slice
Method: SHAKE first four ingredients with ice and strain into ice-filled glass. **TOP** with soda.

2	shots	**Ketel One Citroen vodka**
⅛	shot	**Luxardo Maraschino liqueur**
¼	shot	**St-Germain elderflower liqueur**
¾	shot	**Freshly squeezed lemon juice**
Top with		**Soda (club soda)**

Comment: Long and refreshing with a floral, cherry and citrus flavour.

ELDERFLOWER COSMO

★★★★½

Glass: Martini
Garnish: Lime zest twist
Method: SHAKE all ingredients with ice and fine strain into chilled glass.

1½	shots	**Ketel One Vodka**
1	shot	**St-Germain elderflower liqueur**
½	shot	**Fresh pressed pineapple juice**
¼	shot	**Freshly squeezed lime juice**

Origin: Created in 2006 by yours truly, London, England.
Comment: Despite the absence of citrus vodka, orange liqueur and cranberry, this delicate blend is still Cosmopolitan-esque in style.

ELDERFLOWER DAIQUIRI

★★★★☆

Glass: Martini
Garnish: Lime wedge
Method: SHAKE all ingredients with ice and fine strain into chilled glass.

2	shots	**Bacardi Carta Blanca light rum**
1	shot	**St-Germain elderflower liqueur**
½	shot	**Freshly squeezed lime juice**

Origin: Created in 2006 by yours truly, London, England.
Comment: Elderflower liqueur adds floral interest to the classic Daiquiri.

ELDERFLOWER GIN FIZZ

★★★★☆

Glass: Collins (small 8oz)
Garnish: Lemon slice & mint sprig
Method: SHAKE first three ingredients with ice and fine strain into chilled glass (without ice). **TOP** with soda.

2	shots	**Rutte Dry Gin**
¾	shot	**Freshly squeezed lemon juice**
1	shot	**St-Germain elderflower liqueur**
Top with		**Soda from siphon**

Comment: Go easy with the size of Collins glass you use or this drink with become over diluted. Due to the lack of ice in the serve also ensure the soda is well chilled and preferably use a frozen bottle of gin.

ELDERFLOWER MANHATTAN

★★★★½

Glass: Martini
Garnish: Luxardo Maraschino cherry
Method: SHAKE all ingredients with ice and fine strain into chilled glass.

2	shots	**Bourbon whiskey**
1	shot	**St-Germain elderflower liqueur**
½	shot	**Martini Extra Dry vermouth**
2	dash	**Angostura Aromatic Bitters**

Origin: Created in 2006 by yours truly, London, England.
Comment: Elderflower replaces sweet vermouth in this floral Manhattan.

ELDERFLOWER MARTINI #1

★★★★☆

Glass: Martini
Garnish: Lime zest twist
Method: SHAKE all ingredients with ice and fine strain into chilled glass.

2	shots	**Zubrówka bison vodka**
1	shot	**St-Germain elderflower liqueur**
½	shot	**Martini Extra Dry vermouth**

Comment: This veritable shrubbery is both floral and grassy with dry borders.

ELDERFLOWER MARTINI #2

★★★★½

Glass: Martini
Garnish: Lemon zest twist
Method: SHAKE all ingredients with ice and fine strain into chilled glass.

1	shot	**Zubrówka bison vodka**
1	shot	**Ketel One Vodka**
1	shot	**St-Germain elderflower liqueur**
½	shot	**Martini Extra Dry vermouth**

Comment: Dry but not bone dry with aromatic hints of grass and elderflower.

ELDERFLOWER MOJITO

★★★★⯪

Glass: Collins
Garnish: Mint sprig
Method: Lightly **MUDDLE** (just to bruise) mint in base of glass. Add other ingredients, half fill glass with crushed ice and **CHURN** (stir) with bar spoon. Fill glass to brim with more crushed ice and churn some more. Serve with straws.

12 fresh   **Mint leaves**
2 shots   **Bacardi Carta Blanca light rum**
1 shot   **St-Germain elderflower liqueur**
1 shot   **Freshly squeezed lime juice**

Comment: The enduring classic benefits from a touch of elderflower.

ELECTRO BATIDA (NEW)

★★★★☆

Glass: Coconut shell or Collins glass
Garnish: Desiccated coconut and dehydrated lime
Method: **SHAKE** all ingredients with ice and strain into ice-filled coconut shell or collins glass.

2 shots   **Capucana cachaça**
⅓ shot   **Del Maguey VIDA mezcal**
3 shots   **Coconut water**
¼ shot   **Roasted hazelnut sugar syrup**
⅓ shot   **Freshly squeezed lime juice**
¼ shot   **Sugar syrup (2 sugar to 1 water)**

Origin: Adapted from a drink created in 2014 by Jorge Balbontin, Vantguard Brand Development Manager.
Comment: Cachaça and coconut water with a touch of hazelnut, lime and subtly smoky mezcal.

ELEGANTE MARGARITA

★★★★⯪

Glass: Coupe
Garnish: Lime wedge & salt rim (optional)
Method: **SHAKE** all ingredients with ice and fine strain into chilled glass.

1½ shots   **Patrón reposado tequila**
½ shot   **De Kuyper Triple Sec**
½ shot   **Rose's lime cordial**
¾ shot   **Freshly squeezed lime juice**
½ shot   **Sugar syrup (2 sugar to 1 water)**

Origin: Created in 1999 by Robert Plotkin and Raymon Flores of BarMedia, USA.
Comment: One of the best Margarita recipes around. Richly endowed with flavour.

ELIXIR

★★★★☆

Glass: Collins
Garnish: Mint sprig
Method: Lightly **MUDDLE** mint in base of shaker. Add next 3 ingredients, **SHAKE** with ice and strain into ice-filled glasses. **TOP** with soda, stir and serve with straws.

7 fresh   **Mint leaves**
1½ shots   **Green Chartreuse liqueur**
1 shot   **Sugar syrup (2 sugar to 1 water)**
¾ shot   **Freshly squeezed lime juice**
Top with   **Soda (club soda)**

Origin: Created in 2003 by Gian Franco Pola for Capannina in Cremona and Coconuts in Rimini, Italy.
Comment: A minty, herbal, refreshing summer drink.

ELIXIRITA

★★★★☆

Glass: Martini
Garnish: None
Method: **SHAKE** all ingredients with ice and fine strain into chilled glass.

2 shots   **Patrón reposado tequila**
1 shot   **Lime (fresh whole)**
½ shot   **Agave syrup**
¼ shot   **Martell VSOP Médaillon cognac**

Origin: Created in 2007 by H. Joseph Ehrmann, this is the signature Margarita at his bar 'Elixir' in San Francisco, USA. He dedicated it to the Boston College Eagles.
Comment: Basically a Tommy's Margarita with a splash of cognac served straight-up.

ELK MARTINI

★★★⯪☆

Glass: Martini
Garnish: Lemon zest twist
Method: **STIR** all ingredients with ice and fine strain into chilled glass.

1 shot   **Rutte Dry Gin**
1 shot   **La Vieille Prune plum brandy**
¼ shot   **Martini Extra Dry vermouth**

Origin: Adapted from Harry Craddock's 1930 'The Savoy Cocktail Book'.
Comment: Craddock calls for this drink to be shaken, but in this instance stirring seems more in order.

ELLE FOR LEATHER

★★★★⯪

Glass: Collins
Garnish: Vanilla pod
Method: **SHAKE** first 4 ingredients with ice and strain into glass filled with crushed ice. **TOP** with champagne.

1½ shots   **Dewar's 12 Year Old Scotch whisky**
1 shot   **Vanilla schnapps**
¼ shot   **Freshly squeezed lemon juice**
⅛ shot   **Sugar syrup (2 sugar to 1 water)**
Top with   **G.H. Mumm Brut Cordon Rouge champagne**

Origin: Created in 2001 by Reece Clark at Hush Up, London, England.
Comment: A long, cool champagne cocktail pepped up with Scotch whisky and vanilla schnapps. Easy drinking - yet adult.

ELLE LOVES COCKTAIL (NEW)

★★★★⯪

Glass: Coupe
Garnish: Dried rose petals
Method: **SHAKE** all ingredients with ice and fine strain into chilled glass.

1½ shots   **Bacardi Carta Blanca light rum** (vanilla infused)
1 shot   **Wine Rose - White Zinfandel**
1¼ shots   **Fresh pressed pineapple juice**
¼ shot   **Pomegranate / grenadine syrup (2:1)**

Origin: Created 30-January-2014 by yours truly at the Cabinet Room as a Valentine's Day drink.
Comment: Fruity, very slightly sweet and suitably pink in colour.

ELYSIAN

★★★★☆

Glass: Martini
Garnish: Apple slice
Method: STIR all ingredients with ice and strain into chilled glass.

2	shots	Calvados brandy
½	shot	Martini Rosso vermouth
½	shot	Martini Extra Dry vermouth
¼	shot	Maple syrup
3	dash	Angostura Aromatic Bitters
3	dash	Peychaud's aromatic bitters

Origin: Created in 2004 by Mickael Perron at Millbank Lounge Bar, London, England.
Comment: Dry and aromatic, although not for all tastes.

EMBASSY COCKTAIL

★★★☆☆

Glass: Martini
Garnish: Orange zest twist
Method: SHAKE all ingredients with ice and fine strain into chilled glass.

1	shot	Martell VSOP Médaillon cognac
1	shot	Bacardi Carta Blanca light rum
1	shot	De Kuyper Triple Sec
¾	shot	Freshly squeezed lime juice
1	dash	Angostura Aromatic Bitters

Origin: Created in 1930 at the famous Embassy Club speakeasy in Hollywood, USA.
Comment: Bone dry - one for hardened palates.

EMERALD MARTINI

★★★★☆

Glass: Martini
Garnish: Lemon & lime zest twists (discarded) & mint leaf
Method: STIR all ingredients with ice and strain into chilled glass.

1	shot	Green Chartreuse liqueur
1	shot	Chilled water
2	shots	Lime flavoured vodka

Origin: Discovered in 2005 at Bugsy's Prague, Czech Republic.
Comment: A serious drink that's rammed with alcohol and flavour.

EMERSON

★★★½☆

Glass: Coupe
Garnish: Luxardo Maraschino cherry on stick
Method: SHAKE all ingredients with ice and fine strain into chilled glass.

2	shots	Old Tom gin
1	shot	Martini Rosso vermouth
¾	shot	Freshly squeezed lemon juice
⅓	shot	Luxardo Maraschino liqueur

Origin: Recipe adapted from Albert Stevens Crockett's 1931 The Old Waldorf-Astoria Bar Book.
Comment: The botanical notes of old tom with herbal vermouth, zesty lime and sweet maraschino. Balanced but old-school.

EMPEROR'S MEMOIRS

★★★★☆

Glass: Collins
Garnish: Orange & lemon zest twists
Method: SHAKE first 4 ingredients with ice and strain into ice-filled glass. TOP with ginger beer.

1	shot	Rutte Dry Gin
½	shot	Carpano Punt E Mes
¼	shot	Ginger cordial (non-alcoholic)
¼	shot	Freshly squeezed lemon juice
Top with		Gosling's Stormy Ginger Beer

Origin: Created in 2001 by Douglas Ankrah for Akbar, Soho, London, England.
Comment: Not particularly alcoholic, but strong in a gingery, spicy way.

EMPIRE COCKTAIL

★★★☆☆

Glass: Martini
Garnish: Apricot slice
Method: SHAKE all ingredients with ice and fine strain into chilled glass.

1½	shots	Rutte Dry Gin
¾	shot	Calvados brandy
¾	shot	De Kuyper XO Apricot Brandy

Origin: Adapted from Harry Craddock's 1930 'The Savoy Cocktail Book'.
Comment: Apricot dried by gin and apple brandy.

ENCANTADO

★★★★☆

Glass: Martini
Garnish: Mint sprig
Method: SHAKE all ingredients with ice and fine strain into chilled glass.

1½	shots	Patrón reposado tequila
½	shot	Martell VSOP Médaillon cognac
½	shot	Peachtree peach schnapps
½	shot	Chambord Liqueur
½	shot	Freshly squeezed lime juice

Comment: Essentially a Margarita with a hint of peach and raspberry. Not too sweet.

ENCHANTED

★★★½☆

Glass: Collins
Garnish: Mint sprig
Method: MUDDLE grapes in base of shaker. Add next three ingredients, SHAKE with ice and fine strain into ice-filled glass. TOP with ginger ale.

7	fresh	Seedless white grapes
1½	shots	Martell VSOP Médaillon cognac
½	shot	Kwai Feh lychee liqueur
½	shot	Freshly squeezed lime juice
Top with		Ginger ale

Origin: Created by Wayne Collins, UK.
Comment: Light, fruity and easy drinking with lychee and ginger dominating.

ENGLISH BREAKFAST COCKTAIL 🗝

★★★★⯪

Glass: Martini
Garnish: Orange zest twist
Method: SHAKE all ingredients with ice and fine strain into chilled glass.

1	shot	Rutte Dry Gin
1	shot	St-Germain elderflower liqueur
1	shot	Cold English breakfast tea
½	shot	Freshly squeezed lemon juice

Origin: Created in 2006 by yours truly, London, England.
Comment: Light and fragrant with black tea, elderflower and the botanical influence of gin.

ENGLISH CHANNEL

★★★★⯪

Glass: Martini
Garnish: Lemon zest twist
Method: SHAKE all ingredients with ice and fine strain into chilled glass.

¾	shot	Grand Marnier Cordon Rouge
¾	shot	Bénédictine D.O.M. liqueur
2	shots	Cold Earl Grey tea

Origin: Adapted from a drink discovered in 2005 at Bellini, Auckland, New Zealand.
Comment: The earl grey tannins balance the spice and orange in the liqueurs to make a harmonious aperitif.

ENGLISH GARDEN 🗝

★★★★☆

Glass: Collins
Garnish: Cucumber slices
Method: SHAKE all ingredient with ice and fine strain into ice-filled glass.

2	shots	Rutte Dry Gin
2½	shots	Pressed apple juice
1	shot	St-Germain elderflower liqueur
½	shot	Freshly squeezed lime juice

Comment: Quintessentially English in flavour - anyone for tennis?

ENGLISH MARMALADE (NEW)

★★★★★

Glass: Coupe
Garnish: Orange zest twist
Method: STIR marmalade with gin in base of shaker so as to dissolve marmalade. Add other ingredients, SHAKE with ice and fine strain into chilled glass.

1	spoon	English orange marmalade
2	shots	Rutte Dry Gin
¼	shot	Campari Bitter
½	shot	Freshly squeezed lemon juice
1	dash	Angostura Orange Bitters

Origin: Adapted from a recipe discovered in 2013 at Hawksmoor, Spitalfields, London, England.
Comment: The addition of Campari and aromatic bitters to the classic recipe from the 1930 Savoy Cocktail Book, lifts the Marmalade Cocktail to a new level of bittersweet complexity.

ENGLISH MARTINI

★★★★⯪

Glass: Martini
Garnish: Rosemary sprig
Method: Strip rosemary leaves from stem and MUDDLE in base of shaker. Add other ingredients, SHAKE with ice and fine strain into chilled glass.

1	fresh	Rosemary sprig
2½	shots	Rutte Dry Gin
1	shot	St-Germain elderflower liqueur

Origin: Adapted from a drink created in 2003 at MJU, Millennium Hotel, London, England.
Comment: Rosemary and sweet elderflower combine wonderfully with the gin botanicals to make an interesting and approachable Martini.

ENGLISH ROSE

★★★★☆

Glass: Martini
Garnish: Luxardo Maraschino cherry
Method: STIR all ingredients with ice and strain into chilled glass.

1¾	shots	Rutte Dry Gin
½	shot	Parfait Amour liqueur
¾	shot	Martini Extra Dry vermouth
¼	shot	Freshly squeezed lemon juice
⅛	shot	Pomegranate / grenadine syrup (2:1)

Comment: A dry, complex, gin laced drink. Stir well.

ENRICO PALAZZO (NEW)

★★★★★

Glass: Coupe
Garnish: Grapefruit zest twist
Method: STIR all ingredients with ice and strain into carbonator. CARBONATE and pour into chilled glass.

1½	shots	Bourbon whiskey
1	shot	Martini Rosso vermouth
¾	shot	Aperol Aperitivo
¼	shot	Suze Saveur d'Autrefois
2	dash	Grapefruit bitters

Comment: A bittersweet Manhattan-style lightly sparkling cocktail.

ENTENTE CORDIALE COCKTAIL (NEW)

★★★★☆

Glass: Coupe
Garnish: Lemon zest twist
Method: STIR all ingredients with ice and fine strain into chilled glass.

1½	shots	Rutte Dry Gin
⅔	shot	De Kuyper XO Apricot Brandy
½	shot	Martini Extra Dry vermouth
1	dash	Angostura Orange Bitters

Comment: This gin laced cocktail is flavoured with apricot liqueur which is balanced and made more complex by dry vermouth. A dash of orange bitters and a light lemon zest twist subtly serve to unify all. (Go easy with the bitters and zest.)

THE ENTWISTLE

★★★½☆

Glass: Coupe
Garnish: Dust with cinnamon powder
Method: **STIR** calvados with maple syrup to dissolve syrup. Add other ingredients, **STIR** with ice and strain into chilled glass.

1	spoon	**Maple syrup**
2	shots	**Calvados brandy**
½	shot	**Campari Bitter**
½	shot	**Apple Schnapps liqueur**

Origin: Updated from a drink discovered in 2010 at Rye, San Francisco, USA.
Comment: Complex and bitter-sweet with a cidery base courtesy of apple spirit and apple liqueur with sweet maple syrup balancing bitter Campari.

ENTWISTLE'S ERROR

★★★★☆

Glass: Collins
Garnish: Lemon slice
Method: **SHAKE** first two ingredients with ice and strain into ice-filled glass. **TOP** with tonic water.

2	shots	**Bacardi Carta Ocho aged rum**
½	shot	**Freshly squeezed lemon juice**
Top with		**Tonic Water**

Comment: Richly flavoured - an elongated long aged daiquiri-like cocktail.

ENVY

★★★★☆

Glass: Martini
Garnish: Star fruit
Method: **SHAKE** all ingredients with ice and fine strain into chilled glass.

½	shot	**Ketel One Vodka**
2	shots	**Midori Green Melon liqueur**
1	shot	**Peachtree peach schnapps**
¾	shot	**Hazelnut liqueur**
¼	shot	**Freshly squeezed lime juice**

Comment: Green with melon, oh, and a hint of hazelnut. A tad on the sweet side.

EPESTONE DAIQUIRI

★★★★☆

Glass: Martini
Garnish: Lime wedge
Method: **SHAKE** all ingredients with ice and fine strain into chilled glass.

2	shots	**Bacardi Carta Blanca light rum**
½	shot	**Lejay crème de cassis de Dijon**
½	shot	**Freshly squeezed lime juice**
½	shot	**Chilled water** (omit if wet ice)

Comment: A pleasant, maroon coloured, blackcurrant flavoured Daiquiri.

EPIPHANY

★★★½☆

Glass: Martini
Garnish: Seasonal berries
Method: **SHAKE** all ingredients with ice and fine strain into chilled glass.

1¾	shots	**Bourbon whiskey**
½	shot	**Lejay Crème de Mûre liqueur**
2	shots	**Pressed apple juice**

Origin: Created in 2004 by Naomi Young at Match, London, England.
Comment: Not sure what a fruity bourbon drink has to do with the manifestation of Christ.

EPISCOPAL

★★★★½

Glass: Old-fashioned
Garnish: None
Method: **STIR** ingredients with ice and fine strain into chilled glass.

1½	shots	**Green Chartreuse liqueur**
¾	shot	**Yellow Chartreuse liqueur**

Origin: A well-established drink promoted by the marketeers at Chartreuse and named due to the combining of the clerical colours of yellow and green.
Comment: My favourite way to enjoy Chartreuse. Especially good when made with V.E.P Chartreuse.

ESCALATOR COCKTAIL

★★★★½

Glass: Martini
Garnish: Pear slice
Method: **SHAKE** all ingredients with ice and fine strain into chilled glass.

1	shot	**Poire William eau de vie**
½	shot	**Zubrówka bison vodka**
2	shots	**Pressed apple juice**
⅛	shot	**Sugar syrup (2 sugar to 1 water)**

Origin: Created in 2002 by Kevin Connelly, England. It's called an escalator because the 'apples and pears', rhyming slang for 'stairs', are shaken.
Comment: This orchard-fresh concoction was originally made with Korte Palinka (Hungarian pear schnapps).

ESMERALDA COCKTAIL (NEW)

★★★★½

Glass: Coupe
Garnish: Lime wedge
Method: **SHAKE** all ingredients with ice and fine strain into chilled glass.

1¾	shots	**Capucana cachaça**
⅓	shot	**Islay single malt Scotch whisky**
½	shot	**St-Germain elderflower liqueur**
½	shot	**Freshly squeezed lime juice**
¼	shot	**Sugar syrup (2 sugar to 1 water)**
¾	shot	**Chilled water** (omit if wet ice)

Origin: Adapted from a recipe originally created by Ben Sandrof at Drink, Boston, USA.
Comment: Cachaça, lime and elderflower with a smoky hit of Islay whisky.

ESPECIAL DAY

★★★★½

Glass: Martini
Garnish: Blackberries & lemon zest twist (discarded)
Method: MUDDLE blackberries in base of shaker.
Add other ingredients, **SHAKE** with ice and fine strain into chilled glass.

3	fresh	Blackberries
2	shots	Bacardi Carta Blanca light rum
½	shot	Martini Rosso vermouth
¾	shot	Lejay Crème de Mûre liqueur
½	shot	Fresh pressed pineapple juice
3	dash	Peychaud's aromatic bitters

Origin: Created in 2005 by Tonin Kacaj at Maze, London, England.
Comment: Beautifully balanced, aromatic, rum laced and fruity.

ESPRESSO DAIQUIRI 🗝

★★★★☆

Glass: Martini
Garnish: Coffee beans
Method: SHAKE all ingredients with ice and fine strain into chilled glass.

2	shots	Bacardi Carta Blanca light rum
1¾	shots	Espresso coffee (freshly made & hot)
½	shot	Sugar syrup (2 sugar to 1 water)

Comment: Rum based twist on the ubiquitous Espresso Martini.

Espresso Martini

Likened to a vodka & Red Bull for the discerning, the caffeine loaded Espresso Martini consists of generous shots of vodka and espresso with coffee liqueur and a dash of sugar. Although not a true Martini, and these days often served in a coupe rather than a V-shaped glass, the Espresso Martini is perhaps the best-known of contemporary classic cocktails to emerge from the 1990s.

Like every cocktail, an Espresso Martini is only as good as its ingredients. So you'll need a decent vodka and freshly made espresso coffee. The crema (creamy foam) on top of the coffee is key to the success and appearance of the finished cocktail. It may seem perverse to pour a steaming hot shot of espresso coffee into a shaker and then immediately shake with ice, rather than using cold/iced coffee, but let the coffee cool and so the crema die and you'll kill the cocktail. As with an espresso, the amount of sugar required to balance this cocktail is very much down to the tastes of the individual drinker but the ½ shot of coffee liqueur and ¼ shot of sugar used in our Espresso Martini recipe suits the average palate.

Espresso Martinis are usually garnished with three coffee beans floating on the creamy surface of the drink. The floating of three beans comes from the traditional serving of Sambuca in Italy where the three beans are called 'con la mosca', meaning "with the fly". The three beans represent health, wealth and happiness.

In addition to the three coffee beans I also like to express a lemon zest over the surface of the drink and then discard the zest (rather than use as a garnish). The lemon oils do negatively affect the foam but the lemony aroma adds considerably to the drink.

The drink we know today as the Espresso Martini started life as the far more fittingly titled Vodka Espresso. Created in 1983 by Dick Bradsell at the Soho Brasserie, London for a customer who'd asked for a drink to "wake her up, and fk her up." When asked as to exactly why he settled on that drink that day, Dick

told me: "The coffee machine at the Soho Brasserie was right next to the station where I served drinks. It was a nightmare, as there were coffee grounds everywhere, so coffee was very much on my mind. And it was all about vodka back then - it was all people were drinking."

Dick's original recipe called for vodka, sugar syrup, two types of coffee liqueur and freshly made espresso. As the eighties turned into the nineties people were still drinking vodka but this was the decade of the neo Martini – any cocktail served in a V-shaped glass and based on vodka was considered a 'Martini' and such neo Martinis were what bar goers ordered. Dick tweaked and re-christened his Vodka Espresso to the then more desirably named Espresso Martini. Finally, to complete his trilogy of coffee cocktails, in 1998 Dick renamed his creation Pharmaceutical Stimulant and served it on-the-rocks at the then newly opened Pharmacy in Notting Hill where Damian Hurst artwork hung and Dick was Bar Manager (the site is now a Waitrose store).

So Vodka Espresso, Espresso Martini and Pharmaceutical Stimulant are essentially the same drink which morphed over a couple of decades to suit the tastes of a changing audience and situation.

ESPRESSO MARTINI

★★★★★

Glass: Martini
Garnish: Lemon zest twist (discarded) plus float 3 coffee beans on surface
Method: SHAKE all ingredients with ice and fine strain into chilled glass.

1½	shots	Ketel One Vodka
1½	shots	Espresso coffee (freshly made & hot)
½	shot	Coffee liqueur
¼	shot	Sugar syrup (2 sugar to 1 water)

Comment: Forget the 'Vodka Red Bull', this is the cocktail connoisseur's way of combining caffeine and vodka.

ESQUIRE #1

★★★★☆

Glass: Martini
Garnish: Orange zest twist
Method: SHAKE all ingredients with ice and fine strain into chilled glass.

2	shots	Bourbon whiskey
¾	shot	Grand Marnier Cordon Rouge
¾	shot	Freshly squeezed orange juice
1	dash	Angostura Aromatic Bitters
½	shot	Chilled water

Comment: Spicy bourbon laden with orange fruit.

ESQUIRE #2

★★★½☆

Glass: Martini
Garnish: Blackberries
Method: STIR all ingredients with ice and strain into chilled glass.

1½	shots	Ketel One Vodka
¾	shot	Raspberry flavoured vodka
¾	shot	Parfait Amour liqueur

Origin: Created in the 1990's by Dick Bradsell for Esquire Magazine.
Comment: One for hardened Martini drinkers.

ESTES

★★★★☆

Glass: Collins
Garnish: Raspberries & lime zest strips
Method: MUDDLE raspberries in base of shaker. Add other ingredients, **SHAKE** with ice and fine strain into glass filled with crushed ice.

1¾ shots	Patrón reposado tequila
½ shot	Chambord Liqueur
1¾ shots	Cranberry juice
½ shot	Agave syrup
¾ shot	Freshly squeezed lime juice
7 fresh	Raspberries

Origin: Created in 2005 by Henry Besant and Andres Masso, London, England, and named in honour of Tomas Estes, the official Tequila Ambassador in Europe.
Comment: This rich, fruity long drink is a real crowd pleaser.

ESTILO VIEJO

★★★★½

Glass: Old-fashioned
Garnish: Lime zest twist
Method: STIR half of the tequila with two ice cubes in a glass. Add agave syrup and Angostura and two more ice cubes. Stir some more and add another two ice cubes and the rest of the tequila. Stir lots more and add more ice. The melting and stirring of the ice is essential to the dilution and taste of the drink.

2½ shots	Patrón reposado tequila
½ shot	Agave syrup
3 dash	Angostura Aromatic Bitters

Origin: The name of this drink literally translates from Spanish as 'Old Style'. It is basically a Tequila Old-fashioned.
Comment: Even better when made with añejo tequila.

EVERY-BODY'S IRISH COCKTAIL

★★★☆☆

Glass: Martini
Garnish: Green maraschino cherry
Method: SHAKE all ingredients with ice and fine strain into chilled glass.

2 shots	Teeling Small Batch Irish whiskey
½ shot	Green Chartreuse liqueur
¼ shot	Green crème de menthe liqueur

Origin: In his 1930 ' The Savoy Cocktail Book', Harry Craddock writes of this drink, "Created to mark, and now in great demand on, St. Patrick's Day."
Comment: Like the Incredible Hulk, this drink packs a dangerous green punch.

EVITA

★★★½☆

Glass: Martini
Garnish: Orange zest twist
Method: SHAKE all ingredients with ice and fine strain into chilled glass.

2 shots	Ketel One Vodka
½ shot	Midori Green Melon liqueur
1 shot	Freshly squeezed orange juice
½ shot	Freshly squeezed lime juice

Comment: A tangy, lime green, medium-sweet combination of melon, orange and lime.

EXOTIC PASSION

★★★½☆

Glass: Collins
Garnish: Pineapple wedge & strawberry
Method: SHAKE all ingredients with ice and strain into ice-filled glass.

1½ shots	Ketel One Vodka
¾ shot	Lejay Crème de Fraise
¾ shot	Passoa Liqueur
1½ shots	Fresh pressed pineapple juice
1½ shots	Freshly squeezed pink grapefruit juice

Comment: Bittersweet and floral - one for the poolside.

EXTRADITION

★★★★☆

Glass: Old-fashioned
Garnish: Strawberry
Method: MUDDLE strawberries in base of shaker. Add other ingredients, **SHAKE** with ice and fine strain into ice-filled glass.

3 fresh	Small ripe strawberries (hulled)
2 shots	BarSol Mosto Verde Italia pisco
2 shots	Pressed apple juice
¾ shot	Passion fruit syrup

Origin: Created in 2001 by Francis Timmons at Detroit, London, England.
Comment: A light, fruity drink for a summer afternoon.

F-16 SHOT

★★★☆☆

Glass: Shot
Garnish: Luxardo Maraschino cherry
Method: Refrigerate ingredients then **LAYER** in chilled glass by carefully pouring in the order listed.

½ shot	Baileys Irish cream liqueur
½ shot	Bacardi Carta Blanca light rum
½ shot	Coffee liqueur

Origin: Named for the F-16 jet and closely related to the B-52.
Comment: May not break the sound barrier but at least it layers well.

FACUNDO'S FLARE

★★★½☆

Glass: Martini
Garnish: None
Method: SHAKE all ingredients with ice and fine strain into chilled glass.

1½ shots	Bacardi Carta Blanca light rum
½ shot	Aperol Aperitivo
1 shot	Freshly squeezed orange juice
½ shot	Vanilla sugar syrup
2 dash	Peach bitters
½ fresh	Egg white

Origin: Created by Bruce Hamilton at Tigerlily, Edinburgh, Scotland.
Comment: So smooth this drink is almost creamy. Vanilla dominates with fruity hints of rum.

FAIR & WARMER COCKTAIL 0━

★★★☆☆

Glass: Martini
Garnish: Orange zest twist
Method: SHAKE all ingredients with ice and fine strain into chilled glass.

2	shots	Bacardi Carta Blanca light rum
½	shot	De Kuyper Triple Sec
1	shot	Martini Rosso vermouth

Origin: Adapted from Harry Craddock's 1930 'The Savoy Cocktail Book'.
Comment: Sure to warm and fairly good.

FAIRBANKS COCKTAIL NO.1 0━

★★★☆☆

Glass: Martini
Garnish: Luxardo Maraschino cherry
Method: SHAKE all ingredients with ice and fine strain into chilled glass.

1	shot	Rutte Dry Gin
1	shot	De Kuyper XO Apricot Brandy
1	shot	Martini Extra Dry vermouth
¼	shot	Freshly squeezed lemon juice
¼	shot	Pomegranate / grenadine syrup (2:1)
½	shot	Chilled water (omit if wet ice)

Origin: Adapted from Harry Craddock's 1930 'The Savoy Cocktail Book'.
Comment: Apricot liqueur dominates this cocktail but the dry vermouth and dilution save from excessive sweetness.

FAIRY CREAM (NEW)

★★★★½

Glass: Coupe
Garnish: Dust with freshly grated nutmeg
Method: SHAKE all ingredients with ice and fine strain into chilled glass.

1¼	shots	Le Fée Parisienne absinthe
1¼	shots	Single cream / half-and-half
¾	shot	De Kuyper Dark crème de cacao
½	shot	White crème de cacao liqueur

Origin: Created in 2010 by Dick Bradsell, London, England.
Comment: Absinthe, the green fairy, sits majestically with cream and chocolate in this indulgent after-dinner cocktail.

FAIRY SUGAR MAMA (NEW)

★★★½☆

Glass: Coupe
Garnish: Lemon twist (discarded) & mint leaf pegged to rim
Method: SHAKE all ingredients with ice and fine strain into chilled glass.

1	shot	Le Fée Parisienne absinthe
1⅔	shots	Fresh pressed pineapple juice
¾	shot	Freshly squeezed lime juice
⅔	shot	Almond (orgeat) syrup
⅓	shot	Campari Bitter

Origin: Created in 2014 by Andy Mil at the London Cocktail Club, London, England.
Comment: Fruit juice, almond syrup and the bold flavours of Campari mask a whole shot of absinthe in this baby pink drink.

FALCONI

★★★★☆

Glass: Martini
Garnish: Orange zest twist
Method: STIR all ingredients with ice and strain into chilled glass.

2	shots	Straight rye whiskey
1	shot	Martini Extra Dry vermouth
1	shot	Tawny port
1	dash	Angostura Orange Bitters

Comment: Dry and subtly aromatic.

FALLEN ANGEL

★★★☆☆

Glass: Martini
Garnish: Mint leaf
Method: SHAKE all ingredients with ice and fine strain into chilled glass.

2	shots	Rutte Dry Gin
1	shot	Freshly squeezed lemon juice
¼	shot	Green crème de menthe liqueur
¼	shot	Sugar syrup (2 sugar to 1 water)

Origin: Vintage cocktail of unknown origin.
Comment: Gin laced lime and fresh mint. A somewhat acquired taste.

FALLEN LEAVES

★★★★½

Glass: Coupe
Garnish: Lemon zest twist
Method: STIR all ingredients with ice and strain into chilled glass.

1½	shots	Calvados brandy
1½	shots	Martini Rosso vermouth
½	shot	Martini Extra Dry vermouth
¼	shot	Martell VSOP Médaillon cognac

Origin: Created in 1982 by Charles Schumann in Munich, Germany, and first published in his book 'American Bar'.
Comment: Suitably autumnal in colour. The vermouths and brandies are presented in harmony.

FANCY BRANDY 0━

★★★½☆

Glass: Martini
Garnish: Lemon zest twist
Method: SHAKE all ingredients with ice and fine strain into chilled glass.

2	shots	Martell VSOP Médaillon cognac
¼	shot	De Kuyper Triple Sec
⅛	shot	Sugar syrup (2 sugar to 1 water)
1	dash	Angostura Aromatic Bitters
½	shot	Chilled water (omit if wet ice)

Origin: Adapted from a recipe by Charles Schumann, Munich, Germany, and published in his 'American Bar'. Very similar to Jerry Thomas' Fancy Brandy Cocktail, published in his 1862 edition.
Comment: The appropriately named brandy based drink benefits from dilution, hence my addition of a splash of water.

A B C D E F G H I J K L M N O P Q R S T U V W X Y Z

FANCY DRINK

★★★½☆

Glass: Sling
Garnish: Lemon slice & kumquat
Method: **SHAKE** first three ingredients with ice and strain into ice-filled glass. **TOP** with bitter lemon.

1 shot **Grand Marnier Cordon Rouge**
1 shot **Bacardi Carta Blanca light rum**
2 shots **Freshly squeezed pink grapefruit juice**
Top with **Bitter lemon**

Comment: Tasty tart! Refreshingly sour.

FANCY FREE

★★★★½

Glass: Martini
Garnish: Luxardo Maraschino cherry
Method: **SHAKE** all ingredients with ice and fine strain into chilled glass.

2 shots **Bourbon whiskey**
½ shot **Luxardo Maraschino liqueur**
2 dash **Angostura Aromatic Bitters**
2 dash **Angostura Orange Bitters**
½ shot **Chilled water** (omit if wet ice)

Comment: Aromatised, tamed bourbon.

FANDANGO

★★★★☆

Glass: Coupe
Garnish: Mint sprig
Method: **STIR** all ingredients with ice and fine strain into ice-filled glass.

1¼ shots **Rutte Dry Gin**
1¼ shots **Ketel One Vodka**
1 shot **Yellow Chartreuse liqueur**
½ shot **Chilled water** (omit if wet ice)

Origin: Recipe adapted from a book titled 'Cocktails de Paris RIP' which was published in Paris in 1929.
Comment: A heady mix of gin, vodka and the distinctive herbal flavour of Chartreuse.

FANHATTAN

★★★★☆

Glass: Martini
Garnish: Fig wedge
Method: **STIR** all ingredients with ice and fine strain into chilled glass.

2 shots **Bourbon whiskey**
½ shot **Carpano Punt E Mes**
½ shot **Crème de Figue (fig) liqueur**
1 dash **Angostura Aromatic Bitters**

Origin: Created in 2010 by Dan Richards of Host Academy, UK.
Comment: Twist on a Manhattan for fig lovers.

FANTASIA (MOCKTAIL)

★★★½☆

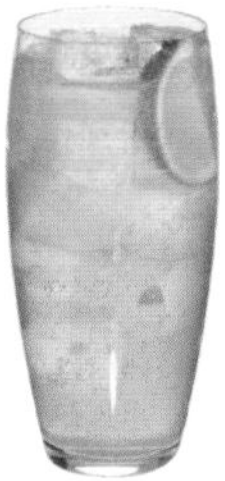

Glass: Collins
Garnish: Lime wedge
Method: **SHAKE** first four ingredients with ice and strain into ice-filled glass. **TOP** with lemonade, stir and serve with straws.

¼ shot **Freshly squeezed lime juice**
¼ shot **Freshly squeezed lemon juice**
¼ shot **Sugar syrup (2 sugar to 1 water)**
5 dash **Angostura Aromatic Bitters**
Top with **Lemonade/Sprite/7-Up**

Origin: Discovered in 2004 at Claris Hotel, Barcelona, Spain.
Comment: A Spanish twist on the popular Australian LLB.

FAT SAILOR

★★★★☆

Glass: Old-fashioned
Garnish: Lime wedge
Method: **SHAKE** all ingredients with ice and strain into glass filled with crushed ice.

1½ shots **Bacardi Carta Oro rum**
¾ shot **Pusser's Navy Rum (54.5%)**
¼ shot **Coffee liqueur**
½ shot **Freshly squeezed lime juice**
1 shot **Rose's lime cordial**

Origin: Tiki style drink of unknown origin.
Comment: A tasty, suitably calorie laden, rum concoction.

FAT TIRE

★★★★☆

Glass: Old-fashioned
Garnish: Orange zest twist
Method: **SHAKE** all ingredients with ice and fine strain into ice-filled glass.

1½ shots Bacardi Carta Ocho aged rum
1 shot Amaro liqueur
½ shot Freshly squeezed orange juice
½ shot Fresh pressed pineapple juice

Origin: Discovered in San Francisco in 2006, hence the American spelling of 'tyre'.
Comment: This flavourful, bittersweet aperitif won't be to everyone's taste.

FEATHER DUSTER CRUSTA

★★★★☆

Glass: Martini
Garnish: Find a lemon which fits into a small wineglass tightly enough to act as a watertight extension to the glass. Cut off both ends of the fruit and carefully remove the pulp to leave a barrel-shaped shell of skin. Place in the top of the glass. Wet the edge of the glass and exposed fruit shell with sugar syrup and dip in caster sugar to frost the edge of both peel and glass. Leave for a couple of hours to form a hard crust.
Method: SHAKE all ingredients with ice and fine strain into chilled glass.

1½ shots	Calvados brandy
½ shot	Luxardo Maraschino liqueur
¾ shot	Freshly squeezed pink grapefruit juice
½ shot	Freshly squeezed lemon juice
¼ shot	Passion fruit syrup
¼ shot	Pomegranate / grenadine syrup (2:1)
2 dash	Peychaud's aromatic bitters

Origin: Created in 2006 by Gregor de Gruyther at Ronnie Scott's, London, England. It is 'quite a light Crusta', hence the name.
Comment: In Gregor's own words, based on the father of the Sidecar, the granddad of the Margarita, Laydeez an' Gennulmen! The Brandy Crusta.

FEN ELLA

★★★★☆

Glass: Coupe
Garnish: Fresh fennel
Method: MUDDLE fennel in stirring glass. Add other ingredients, STIR with ice and fine strain into ice-filled glass.

15 dried	Fennel seeds
2 shots	Dewar's 12 Year Old Scotch whisky
½ shot	Apple Schnapps liqueur
⅛ shot	Sugar syrup (2 sugar to 1 water)
⅛ shot	Ricard Pastis
½ shot	Chilled water (omit if wet ice)

Origin: Created in July 2013 by yours truly at the Cabinet Room, London, England.
Comment: Fennel and pastis freshen and delicately flavour Scotch with the merest hint of apple. Best made by infusing the fennel with the scotch whisky for a week or so rather than muddling.

FERNANDO

★★★★☆

Glass: Coupe
Garnish: None
Method: STIR all ingredients with ice and strain into chilled glass.

1 shot	Martini Extra Dry vermouth
1 shot	Martini Rosso vermouth
¼ shot	Galliano L'Autentico liqueur
⅛ shot	Fernet Branca

Origin: Drink adapted from one discovered in 2010 at Employees Only, New York City, USA. Originally based only on bianco vermouth with no dry vermouth.
Comment: An unusually vermouth based herbal cocktail - very fresh and aromatic.

FIBBER MCGEE

★★★★☆

Glass: Coupe
Garnish: Grapefruit zest twist
Method: SHAKE all ingredients with ice and fine strain into chilled glass.

2 shots	Rutte Dry Gin
1 shot	Martini Rosso vermouth
1 shot	Freshly squeezed pink grapefruit juice
2 dash	Angostura Aromatic Bitters

Comment: Delicately flavoured, bitter-sweet grapefruit and sweet vermouth fortified with gin.

FIENDTINI

★★★★☆

Glass: Martini
Garnish: Gherkin
Method: STIR all ingredients with ice and strain into chilled glass.

2½ shots	Rutte Dry Gin
½ shot	Martini Extra Dry vermouth
¼ shot	Chilled water

Comment: A gin Martini 'dirtied' with pickled gherkin brine and garnished with a pickled gherkin.

FIESTA

★★★★☆

Glass: Martini
Garnish: Pomegranate seeds
Method: SHAKE all ingredients with ice and fine strain into chilled glass.

1 shot	Bacardi Carta Blanca light rum
1 shot	Calvados brandy
1 shot	Martini Extra Dry vermouth
⅛ shot	Freshly squeezed lime juice
⅛ shot	Pomegranate / grenadine syrup (2:1)

Comment: With the right amount of quality pomegranate syrup, this is a great drink.

FIFTH AVENUE SHOT

★★☆☆☆

Glass: Shot
Garnish: None
Method: Refrigerate ingredients then LAYER in chilled glass by carefully pouring in the following order.

½ shot	De Kuyper Dark crème de cacao
½ shot	De Kuyper XO Apricot Brandy
½ shot	Single cream / half-and-half

Comment: A sweet, apricot and chocolate creamy shot.

FIFTH DEGREE

★★★½☆

Glass: Martini
Garnish: Lemon zest twist
Method: STIR Campari with ice (to coat ice and glass) and then strain to discard excess. Add other ingredients, **STIR** with coated ice and strain into chilled glass.

⅛ shot Campari Bitter
2 shots Ketel One Vodka
1 shot Martini Rosso vermouth
¼ shot Luxardo Maraschino liqueur

Origin: Created in 2008 and promoted by Diageo's Reserve Brands division. Apparently this drink was inspired by the classic Martinez.
Comment: Bitter sweet.

FIFTY-FIFTY DRY MARTINI #8 (1:1 RATIO)

★★★★☆

Glass: Martini
Garnish: Olive on stick
Method: SHAKE all ingredients with ice and fine strain into chilled glass.

1½ shots Rutte Dry Gin
1½ shots Martini Extra Dry vermouth

Origin: Adapted from Harry Craddock's 1930 'The Savoy Cocktail Book'.
Comment: A very 'wet' but wonderfully dry Martini which demands an olive, not a twist. Before you start - Craddock calls for it to be shaken.

FIG SUPREME

★★★½☆

Glass: Old-fashioned
Garnish: Fig wedge
Method: Scoop out the flesh of figs and **MUDDLE** in base of shaker. Add other ingredients, **SHAKE** with ice and fine strain into glass filled with crushed ice.

2 fresh Figs
2 shots Patrón añejo tequila
½ shot Freshly squeezed lime juice
¼ shot Grand Marnier Cordon Rouge
¼ shot Pomegranate / grenadine syrup (2:1)

Origin: Created by Salvatore Calabrese at Salvatore At Fifty, London, England.
Comment: Fig and pomegranate add an extra dimension to this Margarita-style cocktail.

FILTHY DIRTY MARTINI

★★★☆☆

Glass: Martini
Garnish: Chilled olives on stick & lemon zest twist
Method: STIR all ingredients with ice and fine strain into chilled glass.

2 shots Rutte Dry Gin
¼ shot Martini Extra Dry vermouth
⅛ shot Freshly squeezed lime juice
⅛ shot Olive brine (from jarred olive)

Comment: However hard you think you are, this one's harder.

FINAL WARD

★★★★☆

Glass: Martini
Garnish: Lemon zest twist
Method: SHAKE all ingredients with ice and fine strain into chilled glass.

¾ shot Straight rye whiskey
¾ shot Green Chartreuse liqueur
¾ shot Luxardo Maraschino liqueur
¾ shot Freshly squeezed lemon juice

Origin: Adapted from a drink created in 2007 by Phil Ward at Death & Co., New York City, USA.
Comment: The Last Word is classically made with gin, maraschino, Chartreuse and lime juice. In this twist, whiskey replaces the gin, and Mr Ward switches citrus fruits from lime to lemon.

FINE & DANDY

★★★½☆

Glass: Martini
Garnish: Lemon zest twist
Method: SHAKE all ingredients with ice and fine strain into chilled glass.

1¾ shots Rutte Dry Gin
¾ shot De Kuyper Triple Sec
½ shot Freshly squeezed lemon juice
¼ shot Sugar syrup (2 sugar to 1 water)
½ shot Chilled water (omit if wet ice)
1 dash Angostura Aromatic Bitters

Comment: A gin based drink that's soured with lemon and sweetened with orange liqueur.

FINITALY

★★★★☆

Glass: Martini
Garnish: Raspberries
Method: SHAKE all ingredients with ice and fine strain into chilled glass.

1½ shots Ketel One Vodka
½ shot Chambord Liqueur
½ shot Martini Rosso vermouth
¾ shot Chilled water (omit if wet ice)

Origin: Created by Michael Mahe at Hush, London, England.
Comment: A simple, berry led Martini.

FINO FLIP

★★★★½

Glass: Coupe
Garnish: 3 drops of Angostura bitters.
Method: SHAKE all ingredients with ice and fine strain into chilled glass.

3 shots Romate Fino sherry
½ shot Sugar syrup (2 sugar to 1 water)
3 dash Angostura Aromatic Bitters
1 fresh Egg yolk

Origin: Unknown
Comment: Salty tang of fino balanced and given extra richness by the egg.

FIREMAN'S SOUR

★★★★⯪

Glass: Old-fashioned
Garnish: Orange slice & cherry on stick (sail)
Method: SHAKE all ingredients with ice and strain into ice-filled glass.

2	shots	Bacardi Carta Blanca light rum
1	shot	Freshly squeezed lime juice
½	shot	Pomegranate / grenadine syrup (2:1)
½	fresh	Egg white

Origin: Circa 1930s, USA.
Comment: Smooth and balanced with great rum character. Lime fresh and fruity sweet.

FIRST OF JULY

★★★★☆

Glass: Martini
Garnish: Apple slice & blackberry
Method: MUDDLE blackberries in base of shaker. Add other ingredients, **SHAKE** with ice and fine strain into chilled glass.

4	fresh	Blackberries
2	shots	Calvados brandy
1	shot	Chambord Liqueur
2	shots	Freshly squeezed pink grapefruit juice

Origin: Created on 1st of July by David Guidi at Morton's, London, England.
Comment: Rich blackberry fruit with a hint of grapefruit acidity.

FISH HOUSE PUNCH #1

★★★★★

Glass: Collins
Garnish: Lemon slice & dust with grated nutmeg
Method: SHAKE all ingredients with ice and strain into ice-filled glass.

1	shot	Martell VSOP Médaillon cognac
1	shot	Bacardi Carta Oro rum
¾	shot	Crème de pêche (peach) liqueur
¾	shot	Freshly squeezed lemon juice
¼	shot	Sugar syrup (2 sugar to 1 water)
2	shots	Chilled water

Origin: Probably the most famous of all punch recipes this is believed to have originated at a Philadelphia fishing and social club called the 'State in Schuylkill Fishing Corporation' which was established in 1732 with a club house built on the banks of Pennsylvania's Schuylkill River (pronounced Skoo-kul). When the drink was first made here is unknown but drinks historian David Wondrich says the first written reference to the Fish House Punch appeared in 1794.

Others say it was first made in 1848 by Shippen Willing of Philadelphia to celebrate women being allowed into the Fish House for the first time for a Christmas Party. Whatever the origin, as with all traditional punch recipes, this would have originally been mixed in larger quantities and served from a punch bowl. Many modern variations use soda water (club soda) in place of mineral water. The inclusion of peach liqueur is a modern substitute for the traditional barrel-aged peach brandy. However, some believe the Schuylkill original omitted peach entirely.

The following poem may be recited when serving a Fish House Punch.

There's a little place just out of town,
Where, if you go to lunch,
They'll make you forget your mother-in-law
With a drink called Fish-House Punch.
Comment: This fruit laced mix is neither too sweet, nor too strong. It is perfect.

FISH HOUSE PUNCH #2

★★★★⯪

Glass: Collins
Garnish: Lemon slice & dust with grated nutmeg
Method: SHAKE all ingredients with ice and strain into ice-filled glass.

1	shot	Martell VSOP Médaillon cognac
1	shot	Bacardi Carta Blanca light rum
1	shot	Crème de pêche (peach) liqueur
1½	shots	Cold English breakfast tea
1	shot	Freshly squeezed lemon juice
¼	shot	Sugar syrup (2 sugar to 1 water)

Comment: Over the decades the recipe the Fish House Punch has constantly morphed. The inclusion of cold tea is a contemporary adaptation.

FITZGERALD

★★★★☆

Glass: Old-fashioned
Garnish: Lemon wedge
Method: SHAKE all ingredients with ice and strain into ice-filled glass.

2	shots	Rutte Dry Gin
½	shot	Sugar syrup (2 sugar to 1 water)
1	shot	Freshly squeezed lemon juice
2	dash	Angostura Aromatic Bitters

Origin: Adapted from a drink created in the early 1990s by Dale DeGroff at the Rainbow Room, New York City, USA.
Comment: A gin sour without the egg white.

FIX (GENERIC NAME)

★★★★☆

Glass: Old-fashioned
Garnish: Seasonal fruit
Method: SHAKE all ingredients with ice and strain into ice-filled glass.

2 shots Brandy, whisk(e)y, gin, rum etc.
1 shot Freshly squeezed lemon juice
1 shot Fruit juice (often pineapple)
½ shot Sugar syrup (2 sugar to 1 water)

Origin: A Fix is a classic style of drink that constitutes of a spirit, lemon juice, and some kind of sweet fruit served short.
Comment: Match the juice and spirit and this formula works every time.

FIZZ (GENERIC NAME)

★★★★☆

Glass: Collins (small 8oz)
Garnish: None
Method: **SHAKE** first four ingredients with ice and strain into chilled glass (no ice in glass). **TOP** with soda dispensed from a siphon.

2	shots	**Brandy, whisk(e)y, gin, rum etc.**
1	shot	**Freshly squeezed lemon or lime juice**
½	shot	**Sugar syrup (2 sugar to 1 water)**
½	fresh	**Egg white** (optional)
Top with		**Soda from siphon**

Origin: Like the Collins, this mid-19th century classic is basically a sour lengthened with carbonated water and at first glance there is little difference between a Fizz and a Collins. However, there are several distinguishing features.

A Collins should be served in at least a 12 ounce, and ideally a 14 ounce tall glass, while that used for a Fizz should be no bigger than eight ounces. A Collins should be served in an ice-filled glass, while a Fizz should be served in a chilled glass without ice.

A Fizz should also be made using carbonated water from a siphon in preference to soda from bottles or cans. The burst of pressure from the siphon helps build a bubbly head while the tiny bubbles generated give off carbonic acid, benefiting the flavour and the mouth-feel of the drink.

For proportions we have turned to David A. Embury's seminal 1948 ' The Fine Art of Mixing Drinks'. He recommends: "1 - or a little less sweet (sugar, fruit syrup, or liqueur), 2 sour (lime or lemon juice), 3 - or a little more - strong (spirituous liquor), and 4 weak (charged water and ice). ' We've interpreted this as follows: 2 shots spirit (gin, whiskey, vodka, brandy), 1 shot lemon or lime juice, 1/2 shot sugar syrup, topped up with soda. We've added half a fresh egg white, which technically makes the drink a 'Silver Fizz'.
Comment: We recommend the Derby Fizz with its combination of liqueur and spirits over these more traditional versions.

FIZZ Á LA VIOLETTE

★★★★☆

Glass: Collins (small 8oz)
Garnish: None
Method: 1/ Flash **BLEND** first 6 ingredients without ice (to emulsify mix). Then pour contents of blender into shaker and **SHAKE** with ice. Strain into chilled glass (no ice in glass) and **TOP** with soda from siphon.

Alternatively: 2/ **SHAKE** first 6 ingredients with ice and strain back into shaker. **DRY SHAKE** (without ice) and strain into chilled glass (no ice). **TOP** with soda water from siphon.

1½	shots	**Old Tom gin**
¼	shot	**Benoit Serres créme de violette**
1	shot	**Freshly squeezed lemon juice**
½	shot	**Sugar syrup (2 sugar to 1 water)**
1	shot	**Single cream / half-and-half**
1	shot	**Egg white**
Top with		**Soda from siphon**

Origin: An adaptation of the Ramos Fizz. In his 1939 'The Gentleman's Companion', Charles H. Baker Jr. credits this drinks creation to Ahmed Soliman a manufacturer and seller of Perfume Essences in the Khan el Kalili Bazaar, Cairo.
Comment: A delicate floral drink that is so creamy smooth that it is almost fluffy.

FLAME OF LOVE MARTINI

★★★½☆

Glass: Martini
Garnish: Orange zest twist (flamed)
Method: Pour sherry into chilled glass, swirl to coat inside and discard excess. Using a match or lighter, express and ignite the oils from the orange peel so the burnt oil coats the inside of the sherry-coated glass. **SHAKE** the vodka with ice and fine strain into the coated glass.

3 twist Orange peel
2 shots Ketel One Vodka
¼ shot Romate Fino sherry

Origin: Created at Chasen's, a legendary Hollywood restaurant that opened in 1936 and was a haunt of movie stars and even royalty until its eventual demise in 1995. The memorabilia that decorated the restaurant was held in storage and in 1997 Maud and Dave Chasen's grandson opened another Chasen's on Beverly Hills' Cañon Drive which sadly failed due to a lack of patróns.

During the original Chasen's heyday its star-studded clientele enjoyed drinks created by its noted bartender Pepe Ruiz. Of these the Flame of Love is his most famous creation, partly due to its originally being made for Dean Martin. The legend of this drink is further embellished by Dean dragging his old pal Frank Sinatra to Chasen's to try the drink. The story goes that Frank was so impressed that he ordered one for everyone in the place.
Comment: Bone dry but fresh and most definitely citrusy.

FLAMING DR PEPPER

★★☆☆☆

Glass: Boston & shot
Garnish: None
Method: **POUR** beer into Boston glass. Layer amaretto and rum in chilled shot glass by carefully pouring amaretto and then rum. **IGNITE** the rum and carefully lift shot glass then drop (bottom first) into Boston glass.

1	pint	**Budweiser Budvar**
½	shot	**Disaronno Originale amaretto**
½	shot	**White overproof rum**

Origin: So named as the end result resembles the taste of the proprietary Dr Pepper soft drink. This drink inspired an episode of The Simpsons featuring a similar drink titled the 'Flaming Homer' and later the 'Flaming Moe' (after the programme's bartender).
Comment: Please consider the likelihood of burning yourself while attempting to lift the flaming shot into the beer.

FLAMING FERRARI

★★☆☆☆

Glass: Shot
Garnish: Assistant to help the drinker consume the concoction
Method: Step 1: **LAYER** the first four ingredients by carefully pouring in order into a Martini glass. Step 2: In two shot glasses **POUR** the remaining two ingredients separately. Step 3: **IGNITE** the contents of the Martini glass. Give two long straws to the drinker and instruct them to drink the contents of the Martini glass in one go. As they do so, slowly **POUR** the contents of the two shot glasses into the flaming Martini glass.

½	shot	Pomegranate / grenadine syrup (2:1)
1	shot	Galliano L'Autentico liqueur
1	shot	Black sambuca liqueur
1	shot	Green Chartreuse liqueur
1	shot	Grand Marnier Cordon Rouge
1	shot	Pusser's Navy Rum (54.5%)

Origin: Created by the late Thai Dang, owner of Nam Long le Shaker, Old Brompton Road, London, England.
Comment: Not recommended if you want to remember the rest of the evening and please be careful - alcohol and fire is a risky combination.

FLAMINGO #1

★★★★☆

Glass: Martini
Garnish: Banana chunk
Method: **SHAKE** all ingredients with ice and fine strain into chilled glass.

1	shot	Bourbon whiskey
¾	shot	Crème de banane liqueur
1½	shots	Freshly squeezed orange juice
¾	shot	Freshly squeezed lemon juice
½	fresh	Egg white

Comment: It's not pink but it has bourbon, banana, orange and lemon smoothed with egg white.

FLAMINGO #2

★★★★☆

Glass: Martini
Garnish: Star fruit
Method: **SHAKE** all ingredients with ice and fine strain into chilled glass.

2	shots	Bacardi Carta Ocho aged rum
1½	shots	Fresh pressed pineapple juice
½	shot	Freshly squeezed lime juice
⅛	shot	Pomegranate / grenadine syrup (2:1)

Origin: Classic of unknown origins.
Comment: A tasty, pink drink with a frothy top.

FLATLINER

★★☆☆☆

Glass: Shot
Garnish: None
Method: **POUR** sambuca into chilled glass. **LAYER** tequila by carefully pouring over sambuca. Lastly **DRIP** pepper sauce onto drink. This will sink through the tequila to form an orange line on top of the sambuca.

¾	shot	Luxardo sambuca dei cesari
¾	shot	Patrón reposado tequila
8	drop	Tabasco hot pepper sauce

Comment: A serious combination of sweetness, strength and heat. Looks weird and tastes weirder.

FLIP COCKTAIL (GENERIC RECIPE)

★★★★☆

Glass: Sour or Martini / Coupette
Garnish: Dust with grated nutmeg
Method: **SHAKE** all ingredients with the ice and fine strain into chilled glass.

2	shots	Brandy, whisk(e)y, gin, rum etc.
1	shot	Sugar syrup (2 sugar to 1 water)
1	fresh	Eggs (white & yolk)
½	shot	Single cream / half-and-half

Origin: Flips basically consist of any fortified wine or liquor shaken with a whole egg and sweetened with sugar. They can also contain cream and are typically garnished with a dusting of nutmeg and served in a sour glass or small Martini glass. They can be served hot or cold.

The very first Flips, which emerged as early as the late 1600s, consisted of a tankard of ale to which a mixture made from sugar, eggs and spices was added before being heated with a red-hot iron poker from the fire. Later they came to mean any fortified wine or liquor shaken with a whole egg and sweetened with sugar.
Comment: I favour creamy, spicy, bourbon based Flips.

FLIP WILLIAMS

★★★★☆

Glass: Sour or Martini / Coupette
Garnish: Dust with grated nutmeg
Method: **SHAKE** all ingredients with ice and fine strain into chilled glass.

1½	shots	Bourbon whiskey
¾	shot	Poire William pear liqueur
¼	shot	Sugar syrup (2 sugar to 1 water)
½	shot	Single cream / half-and-half
2	dash	Angostura Aromatic Bitters
1	fresh	Egg yolk

Origin: Created in 2007 by Julian de Feral at Milk & Honey, London, England.
Comment: Velvety smooth with hints of whiskey and pear.

FLIPPING GOOD

★★★★☆

Glass: Sour or Martini / Coupette
Garnish: Dust with grated nutmeg
Method: **SHAKE** all ingredients with ice and strain back into shaker. **DRY SHAKE** (without ice) and fine strain into chilled glass.

2	shots	Bacardi Carta Ocho aged rum
½	shot	Sugar syrup (2 sugar to 1 water)
½	shot	Single cream / half-and-half
1	fresh	Egg yolk

Origin: Created in December 2008 by yours truly at the Cabinet Room, London, England.
Comment: Basically an aged rum flip with the sugar level reduced and egg white omitted.

A B C D E F G H I J K L M N O P Q R S T U V W X Y Z

THE FLIRT

★★★½☆

Glass: Martini
Garnish: Lipstick on rim
Method: **SHAKE** all ingredients with ice and fine strain into chilled glass.

2 shots **Patrón reposado tequila**
¾ shot **De Kuyper XO Apricot Brandy**
¾ shot **Freshly squeezed lime juice**
1 shot **Cranberry juice**

Origin: Created in 2002 by Dick Bradsell at Lonsdale House, London, England.
Comment: A fruity drink to upset glass washers throughout the land.

FLIRTINI #1

★★★★☆

Glass: Martini
Garnish: Pineapple wedge
Method: **SHAKE** all ingredients with ice and fine strain into chilled glass.

2 shots **Ketel One Vodka**
¼ shot **Chambord Liqueur**
1½ shots **Fresh pressed pineapple juice**

Origin: Made famous on television's Sex and the City. Said to have been created in 2003 for Sarah Jessica Parker at Guastavinos, New York City, USA.
Comment: It's a French Martini - hard not to like.

FLIRTINI #2

★★★★☆

Glass: Martini
Garnish: Luxardo Maraschino cherry
Method: **SHAKE** first 3 ingredients with ice and fine strain into chilled glass. **TOP** with champagne.

¾ shot **Ketel One Vodka**
¾ shot **De Kuyper Triple Sec**
2 shots **Fresh pressed pineapple juice**
Top with **G.H. Mumm Brut Cordon Rouge champagne**

Origin: Adapted from a recipe by the New York bartender Dale DeGroff.
Comment: A flirtatious little number that slips down easily.

THE FLO ZIEGFELD

★★★½☆

Glass: Martini
Garnish: Pineapple wedge
Method: **SHAKE** all ingredients with ice and fine strain into chilled glass.

2 shots **Rutte Dry Gin**
1 shot **Fresh pressed pineapple juice**
¼ shot **Sugar syrup (2 sugar to 1 water)**

Origin: Named after Florenz Ziegfeld, the Broadway Impresario, whose widow released the recipe for the 1946 'Stork Club Bar Book'.
Comment: The original recipe omits sugar but was probably made with sweetened pineapple juice.

FLORADORA (NEW)

★★★★☆

Glass: Collins
Garnish: Raspberry and lime wedge
Method: **SHAKE** first three ingredients with ice and strain into ice-filled glass. **TOP** with ginger ale and lightly stir.

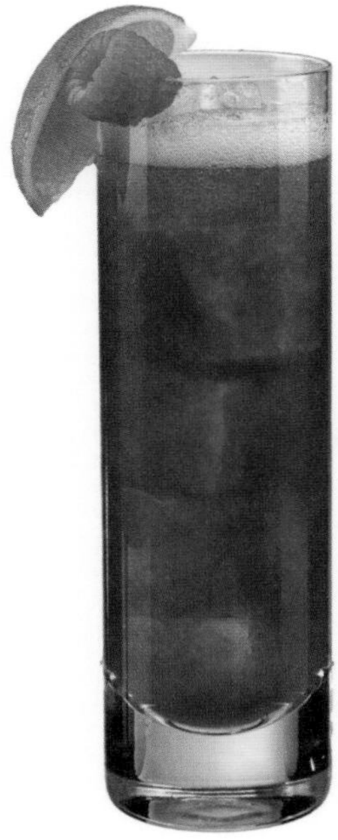

1¾ shots Rutte Dry Gin
¾ shot Freshly squeezed lime juice
¾ shot Lejay Crème de Framboise
Top with Ginger ale

Origin: Dating from the turn of the 20th century, this drink is named after a successful musical which originally opened in London in 1899 and then Broadway the following year. The show was famous for its double sextet, 'Tell Me Pretty Maiden' and chorus line of 'Florodora Girls'.
Comment: This pink, gin-based drink is light and fruity with lime juice balancing sweet raspberry liqueur and lengthened with ginger ale.

FLORAL MARTINI

★★★★☆

Glass: Martini
Garnish: Edible flower
Method: **STIR** all ingredients with ice and fine strain into chilled glass.

2 shots **Rutte Dry Gin**
½ shot **St-Germain elderflower liqueur**
½ shot **Martini Extra Dry vermouth**
¼ shot **Rose water**
½ shot **Chilled water** (omit if wet ice)

Origin: Adapted from a drink created in 2003 at Zander Bar, London, England.
Comment: This aptly named gin Martini is soft but dry.

FLORENCE FIZZ (NEW)

★★★½☆

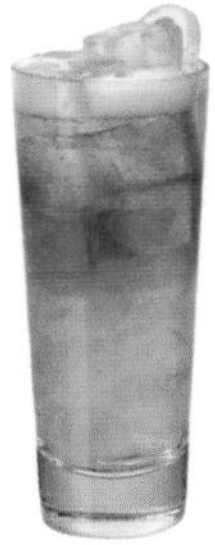

Glass: Collins
Garnish: Half lemon slice
Method: **POUR** Limoncello, lemon juice and elderflower cordial into glass. Add crushed ice and **LAYER** pomegranate juice. Add more crushed ice and **TOP** with prosecco.

¾ shot **Pallini Limoncello**
½ shot **Freshly squeezed lemon juice**
½ shot **Elderflower cordial**
1½ shots **Pomegranate juice**
2 shots **Prosecco sparkling wine**

Origin: Adapted from a popular drink on the menu of Jamie's Italian restaurant and bar chain.
Comment: Very fruity with a refreshing tang of limoncello and lemon juice topped with Prosecco.

FLORIDA COCKTAIL (MOCKTAIL) 🔑

★★★☆☆

Glass: Collins
Garnish: Orange slice & cherry on stick (sail)
Method: SHAKE first 4 ingredients with ice and strain into ice-filled glass, **TOP** with soda.

1	shot	Freshly squeezed pink grapefruit juice
2	shots	Freshly squeezed orange juice
½	shot	Freshly squeezed lemon juice
¼	shot	Sugar syrup (2 sugar to 1 water)
Top with		Soda (club soda)

Comment: The Florida sun shines through this fruity, refreshing drink.

FLORIDA DAIQUIRI

★★★★⯪

Glass: Martini
Garnish: Luxardo Maraschino cherry
Method: SHAKE all ingredients with ice and fine strain into chilled glass.

2	shots	Bacardi Carta Blanca light rum
½	shot	Freshly squeezed lime juice
¼	shot	Sugar syrup (2 sugar to 1 water)
½	shot	Freshly squeezed pink grapefruit juice
⅛	shot	Luxardo Maraschino liqueur
¾	shot	Chilled water (omit if wet ice)

Comment: This classic blend of rum, lime and sugar, but with a hint of freshly squeezed grapefruit juice and maraschino. A user-friendly version of a Hemingway Special.

FLORIDA SLING

★★★☆☆

Glass: Sling
Garnish: Redcurrants
Method: SHAKE all ingredients with ice and strain into ice-filled glass.

2	shots	Rutte Dry Gin
¼	shot	Cherry Heering Liqueur
2	shots	Fresh pressed pineapple juice
¾	shot	Freshly squeezed lemon juice
¼	shot	Pomegranate / grenadine syrup (2:1)

Comment: A tall, pink, dumbed down Singapore Sling.

FLORIDITA MARGARITA 🔑

★★★★☆

Glass: Coupe
Garnish: Lime wedge & salt rim (optional)
Method: SHAKE all ingredients with ice and fine strain into chilled glass.

1½	shots	Patrón reposado tequila
½	shot	De Kuyper Triple Sec
½	shot	Cranberry juice
¼	shot	Rose's lime cordial
1½	shots	Freshly squeezed pink grapefruit juice
¾	shot	Freshly squeezed lime juice
½	shot	Sugar syrup (2 sugar to 1 water)

Origin: Created in 1999 by Robert Plotkin and Raymon Flores of BarMedia, USA.
Comment: A blush coloured, Margarita-style drink with a well-matched amalgamation of flavours.

FLOWER POWER MARTINI

★★★★⯪

Glass: Martini
Garnish: Orange zest twist
Method: SHAKE all ingredients with ice and fine strain into chilled glass.

2	shots	Rutte Dry Gin
½	shot	St-Germain elderflower liqueur
½	shot	Martini Extra Dry vermouth
¼	shot	Benoit Serres créme de violette

Origin: Created in 2007 by yours truly, London, England.
Comment: A Dry Martini served super-wet with even more flower power than Austin Powers.

FLUFFY DUCK

★★★⯪☆

Glass: Collins
Garnish: Orange slice
Method: SHAKE first 4 ingredients with ice and strain into ice-filled glass. **TOP** with soda.

1½	shots	Rutte Dry Gin
1½	shots	Warninks Advocaat liqueur
1	shot	De Kuyper Triple Sec
1	shot	Freshly squeezed orange juice
Top with		Soda (club soda)

Comment: Light, creamy and easy drinking. The gin's character prevents it from being too fluffy.

FLUTTER

★★★★⯪

Glass: Martini
Garnish: Orange zest twist
Method: SHAKE all ingredients with ice and fine strain into chilled glass.

2	shots	Patrón reposado tequila
1	shot	Coffee liqueur
1¼	shots	Fresh pressed pineapple juice

Origin: Created in 2003 by Tony Coningliaro at Lonsdale House, London, England.
Comment: The three ingredients combine brilliantly.

FLY LIKE A BUTTERFLY

★★★★☆

Glass: Martini
Garnish: Orange zest twist
Method: SHAKE all ingredients with ice and fine strain into chilled glass.

1	shot	Martini Extra Dry vermouth
1	shot	Martini Rosso vermouth
½	shot	Dubonnet Red
½	shot	Freshly squeezed orange juice

Origin: Created by yours truly, this is my take on a classic cocktail called a 'Lovely Butterfly' made with the same ingredients.
Comment: This light, aromatic, sweet and sour beauty has a grown-up, quinine-rich flavour but lacks the 'sting like a bee' finish.

FLY ME THE FLIP TO FRANCE (NEW)

★★★★½

Glass: Coupe
Garnish: Orange zest twist
Method: **SHAKE** all ingredients with ice and fine strain into chilled glass.

1½ shots Byrrh Grand Quinquina
¾ shot Rutte Dry Gin
¾ shot Campari Bitter
⅕ shot Grapefruit sugar syrup (2:1)
1 whole Eggs (white & yolk)

Origin: Adapted from a recipe created in 2015 by Ben Campbell at the Alchemist, Manchester, England.

FLYING DUTCHMAN

★★★★☆

Glass: Martini
Garnish: Orange zest twist
Method: **STIR** all ingredients with ice and strain into chilled glass.

2½ shots Rutte Old Simon oude jenever
¼ shot De Kuyper Triple Sec
2 dash Angostura Orange Bitters
¾ shot Chilled water

Comment: A Martini with more than a hint of orange.

FLYING FRENCHMAN (ABSINTHE ESPRESSO MARTINI) (NEW)

★★★★½

Glass: Coupe
Garnish: Float star anise
Method: **SHAKE** all ingredients with ice and fine strain into chilled glass.

1 shot Le Fée Parisienne absinthe
1 shot Coffee liqueur
1 shot Espresso coffee (freshly made & hot)

Origin: Adapted from a drink created in 2014 for La Fée Parisienne by Andy Mil at the London Cocktail Club. Andy's recipe originally called for Patrón XO Café and an additional 15ml of sugar syrup.
Comment: Best described as an energy cocktail on steroids - equal parts absinthe, coffee liqueur and espresso. However, unlike most caffeine laden energy drinks the Flying Frenchman is very tasty.

FLYING GRASSHOPPER

★★★½☆

Glass: Martini
Garnish: Chocolate powder rim & mint leaf
Method: **SHAKE** all ingredients with ice and fine strain into chilled glass.

1 shot Ketel One Vodka
¾ shot White crème de cacao liqueur
¾ shot Single cream / half-and-half
¾ shot Milk
½ shot Green crème de menthe liqueur

Comment: A Grasshopper with vodka - tastes like a choc mint ice cream.

FLYING SCOTSMAN

★★★★☆

Glass: Old-fashioned
Garnish: Orange zest twist
Method: **STIR** all ingredients with ice and strain into ice-filled glass.

2 shots Dewar's 12 Year Old Scotch whisky
2 shots Martini Rosso vermouth
¼ shot Sugar syrup (2 sugar to 1 water)
3 dash Angostura Aromatic Bitters

Comment: Sweetened Scotch with plenty of spice: like a homemade whisky liqueur.

FLYING TIGRE COCTEL

★★★★☆

Glass: Martini
Garnish: Orange zest twist
Method: **SHAKE** all ingredients with ice and fine strain into chilled glass.

1¾ shots Bacardi Carta Blanca light rum
¾ shot Rutte Dry Gin
¼ shot Sugar syrup (2 sugar to 1 water)
⅛ shot Pomegranate / grenadine syrup (2:1)
3 dash Angostura Aromatic Bitters
¾ shot Chilled water (omit if wet ice)

Origin: Adapted from a recipe in the 1949 edition of Esquire's 'Handbook for Hosts'. The drink is credited to an unnamed Captain serving in the US Marines, Amphibious Group Seven, at Santiago de Cuba in 1942.
Comment: Light, aromatic and complex - one to sip.

FOG CUTTER #1

★★★★☆

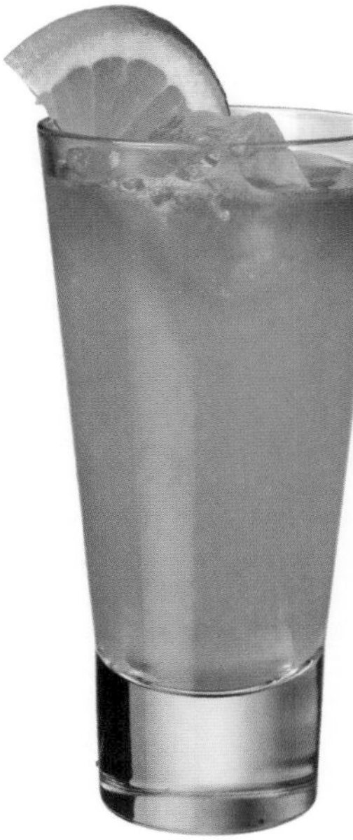

Glass: Collins
Garnish: Orange slice
Method: **SHAKE** first 6 ingredients with ice and strain into ice-filled glass. **FLOAT** sherry on top of drink and serve without straws.

1½ shots Bacardi Carta Blanca light rum
¾ shot Martell VSOP Médaillon cognac
½ shot Rutte Dry Gin
1½ shots Freshly squeezed orange juice
½ shot Freshly squeezed lemon juice
½ shot Almond (orgeat) syrup
½ shot Romate Amontillado sherry

Origin: A version of what became a Tiki classic, sometimes credited to Trader Vic and/or Don the Beachcomber. In his 'Bartender's Guide' (1972 revised edition) Vic remarks, "Fog Cutter, hell. After two of these, you won't even see the stuff".
Comment: Don't be fooled by the innocuous colour. This long, fruity drink packs a serious kick.

FOG CUTTER #2

★★★★⯪

Glass: Old-fashioned
Garnish: Orange slice
Method: SHAKE first 5 ingredients with ice and strain into glass filled with crushed ice. **DRIZZLE** cherry brandy over drink and serve with straws.

1	shot	Bacardi Carta Blanca light rum
½	shot	Martell VSOP Médaillon cognac
½	shot	Rutte Dry Gin
½	shot	Freshly squeezed lime juice
¼	shot	Sugar syrup (2 sugar to 1 water)
¼	shot	Cherry Heering Liqueur

Comment: A well balanced (neither too strong nor too sweet), short, fruity drink which is reminiscent of the modern day Bramble.

FOGERTY

★★★★☆

Glass: Coupe
Garnish: Orange zest twist
Method: STIR all ingredients with ice and strain into chilled glass.

2	shots	Straight rye whiskey
½	shot	Campari Bitter
¼	shot	Lejay crème de cassis de Dijon
2	dash	Angostura Orange Bitters

Origin: Adapted from a drink created in 2010 by Ryan 'Jesus' Fitzgerald at Beretta San Francisco, USA.
Comment: This well-balanced cocktail was originally based on straight rye but we prefer with bourbon.

FOGHORN COCKTAIL (NEW)

★★★★☆

Glass: Coupe
Garnish: Lemon zest twist
Method: STIR all ingredients with ice and strain into chilled glass.

1½	shots	Rutte Dry Gin
½	shot	De Kuyper Triple Sec
¾	shot	Lillet Blanc
3	dash	Le Fée Parisienne absinthe
¾	shot	Chilled water (omit if wet ice)

Comment: Triple sec sweetens dry gin with zesty orange, Lillet adds dry complex wine notes and a few dashes of absinthe contribute subtle anise and fennel.

FORBIDDEN FRUITS

★★★★☆

Glass: Collins
Garnish: Seasonal berries
Method: MUDDLE berries in base of shaker. Add next three ingredients, **SHAKE** with ice and strain into glass filled with crushed ice. **TOP** with ginger beer.

4	fresh	Blueberries
4	fresh	Blackberries
4	fresh	Raspberries
4	fresh	Small ripe strawberries (hulled)
2	shots	Bacardi Carta Blanca light rum
1	shot	Freshly squeezed lime juice
½	shot	Sugar syrup (2 sugar to 1 water)
Top with		Gosling's Stormy Ginger Beer

Origin: Created in 2001 by Andres Masso at Lab Bar, London, England.
Comment: Long and fruity with something of a bite.

FORD COCKTAIL (NEW)

★★★★★

Glass: Coupe
Garnish: Orange zest twist
Method: STIR all ingredients with ice and strain into chilled glass.

2	shots	Old Tom gin
1	shot	Martini Extra Dry vermouth
⅓	shot	Bénédictine D.O.M. liqueur
2	dash	Angostura Orange Bitters

Origin: Adapted from a recipe in George J Kappeler's 1900 book, Modern American Drinks.
Comment: The Ford Cocktail is a Martini-style cocktail sweetened by both the use of old tom gin and Bénédictine D.O.M. liqueur (not B&B) served 'wet' with a generous splash of dry vermouth. The orange bitters and zest are essential to the drink's success.

THE FORMOSA

★★★⯪☆

Glass: Martini
Garnish: Orange zest twist
Method: STIR all ingredients with ice and strain into chilled glass.

2	shots	Junmai ginjō sake
2	shots	Dry white port

Comment: Light and easy to drink. Wine-like.

FORT LAUDERDALE 〇━🗝

★★★☆☆

Glass: Martini
Garnish: Orange zest twist
Method: SHAKE all ingredients with ice and fine strain into chilled glass.

1½	shots	Bacardi Carta Blanca light rum
½	shot	Martini Rosso vermouth
1	shot	Freshly squeezed orange juice
¼	shot	Freshly squeezed lime juice

Comment: Rum, vermouth, lime and orange form a challenging combination in this golden drink.

FOSBURY FLIP

★★★★⯪

Glass: Collins
Garnish: Apricot slice
Method: SHAKE all ingredients with ice and strain into ice-filled glass.

2	shots	Bacardi Carta Ocho aged rum
¾	shot	De Kuyper XO Apricot Brandy
¾	shot	Hazelnut liqueur
2	shots	Freshly squeezed orange juice
⅔	shot	Freshly squeezed lime juice
⅛	shot	Pomegranate / grenadine syrup (2:1)
1	fresh	Egg yolk

Origin: Adapted from a drink created in 2002 by Salvatore Calabrese at the Library Bar, Lanesborough Hotel, London, England, for Kirsten Fosbury. The Fosbury Flop is the style of high jump used by almost all successful high jumpers today and introduced by the American Dick Fosbury, who won the Gold Medal at the 1968 Olympic Games.
Comment: This richly flavoured, velvety drink is almost custardy in consistency but with a refreshing hint of lime.

FOUR ACES

★★★★⯪

Glass: Old-fashioned
Garnish: Basil leaf
Method: MUDDLE grapes in base of shaker. Add next five ingredients, **SHAKE** with ice and fine strain into ice-filled glass. **TOP** with soda water, stir and serve with straws.

6	fresh	Seedless white grapes
1½	shots	Ketel One Vodka
½	shot	Freshly squeezed lime juice
½	shot	King's Ginger Liqueur
¼	shot	Sugar syrup (2 sugar to 1 water)
4	fresh	Basil leaves (torn)

Origin: Created in 2009 by Damian Windsor at The Roger Room, Los Angeles, USA. Inspired by Table 8, Los Angeles.
Comment: A summery, light, superbly balanced herbal fruit cocktail. Originally made with Luksusowa.

FOUR LEAF CLOVER

★★★★⯪

Glass: Martini
Garnish: Physalis (cape gooseberry)
Method: MUDDLE clove in base of shaker. Add other ingredients, **SHAKE** with ice and fine strain into chilled glass.

1	dried	Clove
2	shots	Bacardi Carta Blanca light rum
1	shot	Pressed apple juice
¾	shot	Freshly squeezed lime juice
½	shot	Honey sugar syrup

Origin: Created in 2008 by Denis Broci at Maze bar & Restaurant, London, England.
Comment: Originally based on vodka but seemed a shame not to try it as a Daiquiri.

FOUR SKIN DAIQUIRI (NEW)

★★★★⯪

Glass: Coupe
Garnish: Lime wedge on rim
Method: SHAKE all ingredients with ice and fine strain into chilled glass.

1½ shots Bacardi Carta Blanca light rum
1¼ shots Skinos Mastiha
½ shot Freshly squeezed lime juice
¾ shot Birch water

Origin: Created in August 2015 by yours truly at the Cabinet Room, London, England.
Comment: Daiquiri's are refreshing but this mastiha influenced example is particularly so. As 'four' the name, well it's a Daiquiri with four ingredients, including mastiha and the brand we used was Skinos, so appropriate, we think you'll agree.

FOUR W DAIQUIRI

★★★★☆

Glass: Martini
Garnish: Grapefruit wedge
Method: SHAKE all ingredients with ice and fine strain into chilled glass.

2	shots	Bacardi Carta Oro rum
1½	shots	Freshly squeezed pink grapefruit juice
2	dash	Angostura Aromatic Bitters
¾	shot	Maple syrup
½	shot	Chilled water (omit if wet ice)

Origin: My version of an old drink created by Herb Smith and popularised by his friend Oscar at the Waldorf, New York City. The drink was named in honour of the Duke of Windsor and his bride, formerly Wallis Warfield Simpson. The four 'W's stand for Wallis Warfield Windsor Wallop
Comment: The oomph of rum, the sourness of grapefruit and the richness of maple syrup, all aromatised by bitters.

FOURTH OF JULY COCKTAIL

★★★☆☆

Glass: Martini
Garnish: Dust with cinnamon powder
Method: POUR bourbon and Galliano into warm glass, **IGNITE** and sprinkle cinnamon while flaming. **SHAKE** last three ingredients with ice and strain into glass over extinguished bourbon and Galliano base.

1 shot Bourbon whiskey
1 shot Galliano L'Autentico liqueur
1 pinch Ground cinnamon
1 shot Coffee liqueur
1 shot Freshly squeezed orange juice
1 shot Single cream / half-and-half

Comment: More a stage show than a cocktail but rich and tasty all the same.

FOURTH OF JULY SHOT

★★⯪☆☆

Glass: Shot
Garnish: None
Method: Refrigerate ingredients then **LAYER** in chilled glass by carefully pouring in the following order.

¼	shot	Pomegranate / grenadine syrup (2:1)
½	shot	Blue curaçao liqueur
½	shot	Ketel One Vodka

Comment: Looks cool... tastes less so!

FOXY LADY

★★★★☆

Glass: Coupe
Garnish: Strawberry

Method: DRY SHAKE all ingredients (without ice). **SHAKE** again with ice and strain to chilled cocktail glass.

1½ shots Rutte Dry Gin
½ shot Lejay Crème de Fraise
¾ shot Freshly squeezed lemon juice
⅓ shot Sugar syrup (2 sugar to 1 water)
½ fresh Egg white

Origin: Adapted from a drink created in 2005 by Nicolas Skovgaard at Fox Hotelbar, Copenhagen, Denmark. Nicolas revised this recipe in 2013 to use chamomile tea infused gin.
Comment: Best described as a strawberry gin sour, the herbal botanicals in the gin combine well with the sweet strawberry.

FRANCO RUSSIAN PUNCH (NEW)

★★★★☆

Glass: Collins
Garnish: Lemon wedge, raspberry & blackberry
Method: SHAKE first four ingredients with ice and strain into ice-filled glass. **TOP** with champagne and lightly stir.

1 shot Ketel One Vodka
⅔ shot Chambord Liqueur
2 fresh Raspberries
½ shot Freshly squeezed lemon juice
4 shots G.H. Mumm Brut Cordon Rouge champagne

Origin: Created in January 2014 for Laurent-Perrier by Sean Ware of the London Cocktail Club, London, England.
Comment: This long refreshing berry and champagne cocktail is a riff on Dick Bradsell's Russian Spring Punch.

FRANCOPHILE MARTINI

★★★★☆

Glass: Martini
Garnish: Pineapple wedge
Method: SHAKE all ingredients with ice and fine strain into chilled glass.

1 shot Rutte Dry Gin
1 shot Ketel One Vodka
½ shot Chambord Liqueur
½ shot Martini Extra Dry vermouth
1 shot Fresh pressed pineapple juice

Origin: Created in June 2011 by yours truly at the Cabinet Room, London, England.
Comment: A simple variation on the vodka-based 'French Martini' adding gin and dry vermouth to help justify its 'martini' name.

FRANK SULLIVAN COCKTAIL

★★★☆☆

Glass: Martini
Garnish: Lemon zest twist & sugar rim
Method: SHAKE all ingredients with ice and fine strain into chilled glass.

1 shot Martell VSOP Médaillon cognac
1 shot De Kuyper Triple Sec
1 shot Martini Extra Dry vermouth
1 shot Freshly squeezed lemon juice

Origin: Adapted from Harry Craddock's 1930 'The Savoy Cocktail Book'.
Comment: A Sidecar made dry with the vermouth. It needs the sweet rim.

FRANKENJACK COCKTAIL

★★★★☆

Glass: Martini
Garnish: Orange zest twist
Method: SHAKE all ingredients with ice and fine strain into chilled glass.

1½ shots Rutte Dry Gin
½ shot De Kuyper XO Apricot Brandy
½ shot De Kuyper Triple Sec
1½ shots Martini Extra Dry vermouth

Origin: Adapted from Harry Craddock's 1930 'The Savoy Cocktail Book'.
Comment: Dry and sophisticated.

FRANKLIN DRY MARTINI

★★★★★

Glass: Martini
Garnish: Two olives on stick
Method: STIR vermouth with ice and strain to **DISCARD** excess, leaving the glass and ice coated with vermouth. **POUR** gin over vermouth coated ice, **STIR** and strain into chilled glass.

2½ shots Rutte Dry Gin
½ shot Martini Extra Dry vermouth

Comment: A Dry Martini named after Franklin Roosevelt and garnished with two olives.

FREDDY FUDPUCKER

★★★☆☆

Glass: Collins
Garnish: Orange slice
Method: SHAKE all ingredients with ice and strain into ice-filled glass.

2 shots Patrón reposado tequila
½ shot Galliano L'Autentico liqueur
3½ shots Freshly squeezed orange juice

Comment: A Harvey Wallbanger made with tequila in place of vodka. It's usual to build this drink and 'float' Galliano over the top. However, as the Galliano sinks anyway it is better shaken.

FREE TOWN

★★★★☆

Glass: Martini
Garnish: Luxardo Maraschino cherry
Method: SHAKE all ingredients with ice and fine strain into chilled glass.

2	shots	Bacardi Carta Blanca light rum
1	shot	Tawny port
½	shot	Sugar syrup (2 sugar to 1 water)
2	dash	Peychaud's aromatic bitters

Origin: Created in 2004 by Alexandra Fiot at Lonsdale, London, England.
Comment: Great for sipping after dinner.

FRENCH 75 COCKTAIL

★★★★☆

Glass: Flute
Garnish: Lemon zest twist
Method: SHAKE first three ingredients with ice and strain into chilled glass. **TOP** with champagne.

1½	shots	Rutte Dry Gin
½	shot	Freshly squeezed lemon juice
¼	shot	Sugar syrup (2 sugar to 1 water)
Top with		G.H. Mumm Brut Cordon Rouge champagne

Origin: Legend has it that the drink was created by Harry MacElhone at his Harry's American Bar, Paris, in 1925 and was named after the 75mm Howitzer field gun used by the French army during the First World War (1914 to 1918). However, like other drinks in the first (1919) edition of Harry's own book, ' The ABC of Mixing Drinks', he credits the drink to Macgarry of Buck's Club, London, England.

This drink's creation is now sometimes attributed to the USA during the Prohibition era (1920-1933). Although the Howitzer was mounted on American tanks, our issues with the American origin theory are that the Great War was well over by the time Prohibition started and we question whether an American, now or then, would name a drink after a metric measurement. Being Brits, we favour The French 75 being an English drink that grew in popularity in France during the Prohibition era and found its way to the US with returning officers.
Comment: Fresh, clean, sophisticated - very drinkable and hasn't dated.

FRENCH 76

★★★★☆

Glass: Flute
Garnish: Luxardo Maraschino cherry
Method: SHAKE first 3 ingredients with ice and strain into chilled glass. **TOP** with champagne.

1	shot	Ketel One Vodka
½	shot	Freshly squeezed lemon juice
¼	shot	Sugar syrup (2 sugar to 1 water)
Top with		G.H. Mumm Brut Cordon Rouge champagne

Comment: A Vodka Sour topped with champagne. Works well.

FRENCH 77

★★★★☆

Glass: Flute
Garnish: Lemon zest twist
Method: POUR first two ingredients into chilled glass, and **TOP** with champagne.

1	shot	St-Germain elderflower liqueur
¼	shot	Freshly squeezed lemon juice
Top with		G.H. Mumm Brut Cordon Rouge champagne

Origin: I created this twist on the classic French 75 in 2006.
Comment: Elderflower liqueur adds flavour to champagne while a splash of lemon juice balances the sweetness.

FRENCH 125 (NEW)

★★★★☆

Glass: Flute
Garnish: Lemon zest twist
Method: SHAKE first three ingredients with ice and strain into chilled glass. **TOP** with champagne.

1½	shot	Martell VSOP Médaillon cognac
½	shot	Freshly squeezed lemon juice
⅓	shot	Sugar syrup (2 sugar to 1 water)
Top with		G.H. Mumm Brut Cordon Rouge champagne

Comment: A champagne charged cognac sour. Enlivening and refreshing.
Origin: A cognac based version of the French 75 which was named after the 75mm Howitzer field gun used by the French army during the First World War. This cognac version is appropriately named after another gun, the tank mounted Soviet 2A46 (also called D-81T) 125mm/L48 smoothbore cannon.

FRENCH BISON-TINI

★★★★☆

Glass: Martini
Garnish: Raspberries
Method: SHAKE all ingredients with ice and fine strain into chilled glass.

2	shots	Zubrówka bison vodka
¼	shot	Chambord Liqueur
2	shots	Fresh pressed pineapple juice

Comment: A French Martini with the distinctive taste of Żubrówka.

FRENCH COCKTAIL

★★★★½

Glass: Martini
Garnish: Pineapple wedge
Method: SHAKE all ingredients with ice and fine strain into chilled glass.

2	shots	Martell VSOP Médaillon cognac
1½	shots	Fresh pressed pineapple juice
½	shot	Chambord Liqueur

Origin: Created in June 2011 by yours truly at the Cabinet Room, London, England.
Comment: A simple riff on the 'French Martini' swapping the usual vodka for the more French cognac. Fruity and easy drinking.

FRENCH CONNECTION

★★★½☆

Glass: Old-fashioned
Garnish: Lemon zest twist
Method: STIR all ingredients with ice and strain into ice-filled glass.

| 2 | shots | Martell VSOP Médaillon cognac |
| 1 | shot | Disaronno Originale amaretto |

Comment: The apricot and almond notes in amaretto combine perfectly with cognac in this simple drink.

FRENCH DAIQUIRI

★★★★½

Glass: Martini
Garnish: Pineapple wedge
Method: SHAKE all ingredients with ice and fine strain into chilled glass.

2½	shots	Bacardi Carta Blanca light rum
½	shot	Chambord Liqueur
½	shot	Freshly squeezed lime juice
1½	shots	Fresh pressed pineapple juice
3	dash	Difford's Daiquiri Bitters

Origin: Created in 2009 by yours truly at the Cabinet Room, London, England for Charlotte Ashburner, then UK brand manager of Chambord liqueur.
Comment: A classic Daiquiri made fruity with the addition of black raspberry liqueur and pineapple juice.

FRENCH DAISY

★★★½☆

Glass: Martini
Garnish: Lemon zest twist
Method: SHAKE first four ingredients with ice and fine strain into chilled glass. **TOP** with champagne.

1	shot	Martell VSOP Médaillon cognac
½	shot	Lejay crème de cassis de Dijon
½	shot	St-Germain elderflower liqueur
1	shot	Freshly squeezed lemon juice
Top with		G.H. Mumm Brut Cordon Rouge champagne

Origin: Adapted from a drink created by Wayne Collins, London, England.
Comment: Rich blackcurrant with hints of elderflower, citrus and champagne. Slightly sweet.

FRENCH LEAVE

★★★☆☆

Glass: Collins
Garnish: Orange slice
Method: SHAKE all ingredients with ice and strain into ice-filled glass.

1½	shots	Ketel One Vodka
½	shot	Pernod anise
3½	shots	Freshly squeezed orange juice

Comment: An easy drinking blend of vodka, anise and orange juice.

FRENCH MAID

★★★★½

Glass: Collins
Garnish: Mint sprig speared cucumber slice
Method: MUDDLE cucumber in base of shaker. Add next 5 ingredients, **SHAKE** with ice and fine strain into ice-filled glass. **TOP** with ginger beer.

3 slice English
cucumber peeled
8 fresh Mint leaves
1½ shots Martell VSOP
Médaillon cognac
½ shot Taylor's Velvet
Falernum liqueur
¾ shot Freshly squeezed
lime juice
⅓ shot Sugar syrup
(2 sugar to 1 water)
1 shot Gosling's Stormy
Ginger Beer

Origin: Created in autumn 2008 by Jim Meehan at PDT, New York, USA.
Comment: As Jim Meeham said when he gave us this recipe, "This hybrid of Audrey Saunders Gin Gin Mule substitutes cognac for gin and adds falernum and cucumber. Milk & Honey barman Sam Ross has a similar drink made with Bourbon dubbed the Kentucky Maid: consider this her spicy French sister."

French Martini

The French Martini is one of a few contemporary classic cocktails that is known worldwide and enjoyed by a wide cross section of consumers – not just cocktail aficionados. And despite what you may have heard, the drink was not invented by Chambord as part of some mass marketing campaign. Although it would be hard to deny that the French Martini has done a lot for the fortunes of that "black raspberry liqueur".

A simple combination of three ingredients: pineapple, vodka and black raspberry liqueur but as with other simple drinks, several formulations prevail.

Obviously named for its use of French raspberry liqueur and the fact that it is served in a V-shaped glass, the French Martini was invented in the late 1980s in New York at one of restauranteur Keith McNally's bars. Although it does not actually contain vermouth and is a touch on the fruity sweet side (depending on how much liqueur you add), during the late 1980s and 90s cocktail renaissance, pretty much any drink served in a V-shaped glass was named Martini.

By 1996 the French Martini was on the menu at McNally's renowned Balthazar in SoHo, New York. In London the drink was made at the Met Bar, then the favoured hangout of the glitterati and a bar which championed fruity vodka based cocktails christened 'fresh fruit Martinis'.

Many modern day bartenders started their careers making dozens of French Martinis every night so it's understandable that it's not a drink that's revered by many bartenders. However, the French Martini has its virtues and by adjusting the proportions of the ingredients can be tailored to suit almost every palate.

FRENCH MARTINI 🔑

★★★★☆

Glass: Martini
Garnish: Pineapple wedge
Method: SHAKE all ingredients with ice and fine strain into chilled glass.

2	shots	Ketel One Vodka
½	shot	Chambord Liqueur
1½	shots	Fresh pressed pineapple juice

Comment: Raspberry and pineapple laced with vodka. Easy drinking and very fruity.

FRENCH MOJITO 🔑

★★★★⯪

Glass: Collins
Garnish: Raspberries & mint sprig
Method: Lightly MUDDLE mint in base of glass (just to bruise). Add rum, liqueur and lime juice. Half-fill glass with crushed ice and CHURN (stir) with bar spoon. Continue to add crushed ice and churn until drink is level with glass rim.

12	fresh	Mint leaves
2	shots	Bacardi Carta Blanca light rum
½	shot	Chambord Liqueur
1	shot	Freshly squeezed lime juice
¼	shot	Sugar syrup (2 sugar to 1 water)

Comment: A classic Mojito with a hint of berry fruit.

FRENCH MULE 🔑

★★★★☆

Glass: Collins
Garnish: Mint sprig
Method: SHAKE first 4 ingredients with ice and strain into ice-filled glass. TOP with ginger beer, stir and serve with straws.

2	shots	Martell VSOP Médaillon cognac
1	shot	Freshly squeezed lime juice
1	shot	Sugar syrup (2 sugar to 1 water)
3	dash	Angostura Aromatic Bitters
Top with		Gosling's Stormy Ginger Beer

Comment: This French answer to the vodka based Moscow Mule uses cognac to make a more flavoursome, long, refreshing drink.

FRENCH SHERBERT 🔑

★★★⯪☆

Glass: Martini
Garnish: Orange zest twist
Method: SHAKE all ingredients with ice and fine strain into chilled glass.

1	shot	Rutte Dry Gin
1	shot	De Kuyper Triple Sec
1	shot	Freshly squeezed orange juice
1	shot	Freshly squeezed lime juice

Comment: Not particulary French or sherbety - just a fresh orange wake up call.

FRENCH SPRING PUNCH

★★★★☆

Glass: Sling
Garnish: Strawberry
Method: SHAKE first 4 ingredients with ice and strain into ice-filled glass. TOP with champagne and serve with straws.

1	shot	Martell VSOP Médaillon cognac
½	shot	Lejay Crème de Framboise liqueur
½	shot	Freshly squeezed lemon juice
¼	shot	Sugar syrup (2 sugar to 1 water)
Top with		G.H. Mumm Brut Cordon Rouge champagne

Origin: Created by Dick Bradsell and Rodolphe Sorel at Match EC1, London, England, during the late 1990's.
Comment: Not as popular as the Russian Spring Punch but still a modern day London classic.

FRENCH TEAR #1

★★★★☆

Glass: Martini
Garnish: Pineapple wedge
Method: SHAKE all ingredients with ice and fine strain into chilled glass.

1¾	shots	Bacardi Carta Blanca light rum
¾	shot	Grand Marnier Cordon Rouge
2	shots	Fresh pressed pineapple juice

Origin: Discovered in 2000 at Quo Vadis, London, England.
Comment: Light, flavoursome, easy drinking. Altogether very gluggable.

FRESA BATIDA

★★★⯪☆

Glass: Collins (small 8oz)
Garnish: Strawberry
Method: MUDDLE strawberries in base of shaker. Add other ingredients, SHAKE with ice and strain into glass filled with crushed ice.

2½	shots	Capucana cachaça
½	shot	Freshly squeezed lemon juice
½	shot	Sugar syrup (2 sugar to 1 water)
7	fresh	Small ripe strawberries (hulled)

Origin: The Batida is a traditional Brazilian style of drink and 'Fresa' means strawberry in Portuguese, the official language of Brazil.
Comment: A long, very refreshing strawberry drink laced with cachaça.

FRESCA

★★★⯪☆

Glass: Martini
Garnish: Lemon zest twist
Method: SHAKE first 4 ingredients with ice and fine strain into chilled glass. TOP with lemonade.

1½	shots	Ketel One Citroen vodka
½	shot	Chambord Liqueur
1	shot	Freshly squeezed pink grapefruit juice
½	shot	Freshly squeezed lemon juice
Top with		Lemonade/Sprite/7-Up

Comment: The sweet, fizzy topping is essential to lengthen and balance this drink.

FRESCA NOVA

★★★½☆

Glass: Flute
Garnish: Orange slice
Method: SHAKE first four ingredients with ice and fine strain into chilled glass. Slowly **TOP** with champagne.

1½	shots	**Grand Marnier Cordon Rouge**
¾	shot	**Freshly squeezed orange juice**
¼	shot	**Sugar syrup (2 sugar to 1 water)**
1	shot	**Single cream / half-and-half**
Top with		**G.H. Mumm Brut Cordon Rouge champagne**

Origin: Created by Jamie Terrell for Phillip Holzberg at Vinexpo 1999.
Comment: Cream, orange and champagne work surprisingly well.

FRESH COCKTAIL (NEW)

★★★★☆

Glass: Coupe
Garnish: Cucumber slice
Method: MUDDLE cucumber in base of shaker. Add other ingredients, **SHAKE** with ice and fine strain into chilled glass.

1	inch	**English cucumber peeled** (chopped)
1	shot	**Rutte Dry Gin**
1	shot	**Skinos Mastiha**
⅕	shot	**Freshly squeezed lemon juice**
⅛	shot	**Sugar syrup (2 sugar to 1 water)**
1	dash	**Angostura Aromatic Bitters**

Comment: The distinctive fresh flavour of mastiha paired with cucumber, gin and lemon juice.

FRESH MARTINI (NEW)

★★★★½

Glass: Coupe
Garnish: Mint leaf
Method: STIR all ingredients with ice and strain into chilled glass.

2	shots	**Rutte Dry Gin**
½	shot	**Skinos Mastiha**
⅓	shot	**Giffard Menthe Pastille liqueur**
¾	shot	**Martini Bianco**
5	drop	**Bob's Bitters Peppermint bitters**

Origin: Created 19th April 2015 by yours truly at the Cabinet Room, London, England.
Comment: The perfect digestif Martini. Mastiha and white crème de menthe - both renowned for their digestive properties - add cooling freshness to this wet, lightly sweetened Martini.

STAR RATINGS EXPLAINED

★★★★★+	OUTSTANDING	★★★★★	EXCEPTIONAL
★★★★½	EXCELLENT	★★★★☆	RECOMMENDED
★★★½☆	COMMENDED	★★★☆☆	MEDIOCRE
★★½☆☆	DISAPPOINTING	★★☆☆☆	PRETTY AWFUL
★½☆☆☆	SHAMEFUL	★☆☆☆☆	DISGUSTING

FRESH WHITE LADY COCKTAIL (NEW)

★★★★½

Glass: Coupe
Garnish: Lemon zest twist (discarded) & mint sprig
Method: SHAKE all ingredients with ice and strain back into shaker. **DRY SHAKE** without ice and strain into chilled glass.

1	shot	**Rutte Dry Gin**
¾	shot	**De Kuyper Triple Sec**
¾	shot	**Skinos Mastiha**
¾	shot	**Freshly squeezed lemon juice**
4	dash	**Bob's Bitters Peppermint bitters**
½	fresh	**Egg white**

Origin: Created by yours truly in August 2015 at the Cabinet Room, London, England. Inspired after making the same drink with white crème de menthe (Minty White Lady) and wondering how it would be with mastiha.
Comment: Skinos and peppermint bitters bring minty freshness to this riff on the classic White Lady.

FRIDA'S BROW

★★★★☆

Glass: Martini
Garnish: Dust with cinnamon powder
Method: SHAKE all ingredients with ice and fine strain into chilled glass.

2	shots	**Patrón reposado tequila**
½	shot	**White crème de cacao liqueur**
¼	shot	**Pomegranate / grenadine syrup (2:1)**
½	shot	**Single cream / half-and-half**
½	shot	**Milk**

Origin: Discovered in 2005 at Velvet Margarita Cantina, Los Angeles, USA.
Comment: Creamy, sweetened tequila with hints of chocolate.

FRISCO SOUR

★★★★☆

Glass: Old-fashioned
Garnish: Orange slice & cherry on stick (sail)
Method: SHAKE all ingredients and strain into ice-filled glass.

2 shots Bourbon whiskey
½ shot Bénédictine D.O.M. liqueur
½ shot Freshly squeezed lemon juice
¼ shot Sugar syrup (2 sugar to 1 water)
½ fresh Egg white

Comment: A bourbon rich sour with monastic herbal notes.

FRISKY BISON

★★★★⯪

Glass: Martini
Garnish: Apple slice
Method: Lightly **MUDDLE** mint in base of shaker (just to bruise). Add other ingredients, **SHAKE** with ice and fine strain into chilled glass.

7	fresh	Mint leaves
2	shots	Zubrówka bison vodka
1	shot	Apple Schnapps liqueur
1	shot	Pressed apple juice
½	shot	Freshly squeezed lime juice
¼	shot	Sugar syrup (2 sugar to 1 water)

Origin: Created by Tony Kerr in 1999 at Mash & Air in Manchester, England.
Comment: Sweet 'n' sour, fruity, minty and fresh.

FROTH BLOWER COCKTAIL 🗝

★★★★⯪

Glass: Martini
Garnish: Lemon zest twist (discarded)
Method: **SHAKE** all ingredients with ice and fine strain into chilled glass.

2	shots	Rutte Dry Gin
¼	shot	Pomegranate / grenadine syrup (2:1)
1	fresh	Egg white

Origin: Adapted from Harry Craddock's 1930 'The Savoy Cocktail Book'.
Comment: Salmon-pink and very frothy but surprisingly complex and tasty.

FROUPE COCKTAIL

★★★★☆

Glass: Martini
Garnish: Orange zest twist
Method: **STIR** all ingredients with ice and strain into chilled glass.

1½	shots	Martell VSOP Médaillon cognac
1½	shots	Martini Rosso vermouth
¼	shot	Bénédictine D.O.M. liqueur

Origin: Adapted from Harry Craddock's 1930 'The Savoy Cocktail Book'.
Comment: A bittersweet, herbal old-school drink that's in line for rediscovery.

FROZEN MARGARITA 🗝

★★★★☆

Glass: Coupe
Garnish: Luxardo Maraschino cherry
Method: **BLEND** all ingredients with 6oz scoop of crushed ice. Serve heaped in the glass and with straws.

1½	shots	Patrón reposado tequila
¾	shot	De Kuyper Triple Sec
¾	shot	Freshly squeezed lime juice
½	shot	Sugar syrup (2 sugar to 1 water)

Comment: Citrus freshness with the subtle agave of tequila served frozen.

FRUIT & NUT COCKTAIL

★★★★☆

Glass: Martini
Garnish: Orange zest twist & almond flakes
Method: **SHAKE** all ingredients with ice and fine strain into chilled glass.

1	shot	Vanilla infused Ketel One vodka
½	shot	Romate Pedro Ximénez sherry
1	shot	Hazelnut liqueur
1	shot	Cranberry juice
½	shot	Freshly squeezed orange juice

Origin: Created in 2004 by yours truly.
Comment: A rich Christmas pudding of a cocktail.

FRUIT CUP

★★★★⯪

Glass: Collins
Garnish: Lemon, orange & strawberry slices, mint sprig & borage in drink
Method: **SHAKE** first 4 ingredients with ice and strain into ice-filled glass. Add garnish. **TOP** with ginger ale and cola and lightly stir.

1 shot Rutte Dry Gin
1 shot Orange Curaçao liqueur
1 shot Martini Rosso vermouth
2 dash Angostura Aromatic Bitters
1 shot Coca-Cola
1½ shots Ginger ale

Origin: Created in 2011 by yours truly in an attempt to improve on a Pimm's Cup.
Comment: A refreshing fruity long summery drink, reminiscent of home-made Pimms.

FRUIT CUP SPRITZ (NEW)

★★★★⯪

Glass: Old-fashioned
Garnish: Half orange slice, lemon slice & mint sprig
Method: **POUR** ingredients into ice-filled glass.

3	shots	Prosecco sparkling wine
¾	shot	Martini Bianco
½	shot	De Kuyper Triple Sec
½	shot	Martini Rosso vermouth
Top with		Soda (club soda)

Origin: Created in 2013 by yours truly for Jamie's Italian Bar.
Comment: A light summery spritz with flavours reminiscent of Pimm's.

FRUIT PASTEL

★★★½☆

Glass: Martini
Garnish: Half sugared rim and Fruit Pastille sweets
Method: SHAKE all ingredients with ice and fine strain into chilled glass.

1½	shots	Ketel One Citroen vodka
½	shot	Parfait Amour liqueur
½	shot	Apple Schnapps liqueur
¼	shot	Freshly squeezed lime juice
⅛	shot	Sugar syrup (2 sugar to 1 water)

Origin: Created in late October 2005 by Darren Thrush at the fourth floor Cafe and Bar at Harvey Nichols, Leeds, England. To quote Darren, "The martini glass must have a sugared rim to enhance the presentation and the sweet concept. What's amazing about this concept is that the colour represents what is probably everybody's favourite flavour fruit pastille - the blackcurrant one."
Comment: Tastes distinctly like a Fruit Pastille sweet.

FRUIT SOUR

★★★★☆

Glass: Old-fashioned
Garnish: Lemon zest twist
Method: SHAKE all ingredients with ice and strain into ice-filled glass.

1	shot	Bourbon whiskey
1	shot	De Kuyper Triple Sec
1	shot	Freshly squeezed lemon juice
½	shot	Egg white

Comment: An orange influenced, sweet and sour whiskey cocktail.

FRUIT TREE DAIQUIRI

★★★★☆

Glass: Martini
Garnish: Grapefruit wedge & Luxardo Maraschino cherry
Method: SHAKE all ingredients with ice and fine strain into chilled glass.

2	shots	Bacardi Carta Blanca light rum
¾	shot	De Kuyper XO Apricot Brandy
¾	shot	Freshly squeezed pink grapefruit juice
¾	shot	Freshly squeezed lime juice
¼	shot	Maraschino syrup (from cherry jar)
½	shot	Chilled water (omit if wet ice)

Comment: A restrained Papa Doble with apricot liqueur.

FU MANCHU DAIQUIRI

★★★★☆

Glass: Collins
Garnish: Pineapple wedge
Method: SHAKE all ingredients with ice and fine strain into chilled glass.

2	shots	Bacardi Carta Blanca light rum
1	shot	Freshly squeezed lime juice
½	shot	Sugar syrup (2 sugar to 1 water)
¼	shot	De Kuyper Triple Sec
¼	shot	Giffard Menthe Pastille liqueur
¾	shot	Chilled water (omit if wet ice)

Origin: Adapted from a recipe in David A. Embury's 1948 ' Fine Art of Mixing Drinks'.
Comment: A natural Daiquiri with a refreshing, clean, citrusy, minty edge.

FUEGO MANZANA NO.2

★★★★☆

Glass: Martini
Garnish: Small red chilli
Method: MUDDLE chilli in base of shaker. Add other ingredients, **SHAKE** with ice and fine strain into chilled glass.

1	inch	Red chilli (thin slice)
2	shots	Patrón reposado tequila
½	shot	Apple Schnapps liqueur
1	shot	Pressed apple juice
½	shot	Freshly squeezed lime juice
⅛	shot	Sugar syrup (2 sugar to 1 water)

Origin: Created by Danny Smith at Che, London, England, initially using rum instead of tequila. 'Fuego Manzana' is Spanish for Fire Apple.
Comment: A hint of chilli heat adds interest to an Apple Margarita, creating a full flavoured contemporary classic.

FULL CIRCLE

★★★★☆

Glass: Collins
Garnish: Pineapple wedge
Method: Cut pomegranate in half and juice with a spinning citrus juicer. **SHAKE** all ingredients with ice and fine strain into ice-filled glass.

3	shots	Pomegranate juice
2	shots	Rutte Dry Gin
¾	shot	Fresh pressed pineapple juice

Origin: Adapted from a drink discovered in 2004 at Mandarin Oriental, New York City, USA. The name is a reference to the bar's location - Columbus Circle, where the world's first one-way rotary system (roundabout) was implemented in 1904.
Comment: Fruity and easy drinking, yet with complexity from the gin.

FULL MONTE

★★★★☆

Glass: Sling
Garnish: Lemon slice
Method: SHAKE first eight ingredients with ice and strain into ice-filled glass. **TOP** with champagne, lightly stir and serve with straws.

½ shot Bacardi Carta Blanca light rum
½ shot Rutte Dry Gin
½ shot Ketel One Vodka
½ shot Patrón silver tequila
½ shot Luxardo Maraschino liqueur
1 shot Freshly squeezed lemon juice
¼ shot Sugar syrup (2 sugar to 1 water)
2 dash Angostura Aromatic Bitters
Top with G.H. Mumm Brut Cordon
Rouge champagne

Origin: Created by Audrey Saunders at Pegu Club, New York City, USA.
Comment: Champagne replaces cola and maraschino liqueur replaces triple sec in this sophisticated adaptation of a Long Island Iced Tea.

FUMIGATOR FLIP

★★★½☆

Glass: Sour or Martini/Coupette
Garnish: Dust with grated nutmeg & Luxardo Maraschino cherry
Method: WASH chilled glass with whisky (swirl to coat inside and shake to discard excess). **SHAKE** other ingredients with ice and fine strain into whisky coated chilled glass.

¼	shot	Islay single malt Scotch whisky
2	shots	Bacardi Carta Ocho aged rum
1	shot	Cherry Heering Liqueur
⅛	shot	Sugar syrup (2 sugar to 1 water)
½	shot	Single cream / half-and-half
1	fresh	Egg yolk

Origin: Created in 2008 by Julian de Feral at Bureau, London, England.
Comment: Subtle notes, smoky malt with rum and cherry, smoothed by egg and cream.

FUNKY MONKEY

★★★★☆

Glass: Coconut shell or Collins glass
Garnish: Toasted coconut strips
Method: BLEND all ingredients with 12oz scoop of crushed ice and serve with straws.

1	shot	Bacardi Carta Oro rum
¾	shot	Crème de banane liqueur
¾	shot	White crème de cacao liqueur
1	shot	Coco Re'al Cream of Coconut
1	shot	Single cream / half-and-half
1	shot	Milk
1	fresh	Banana (peeled)

Origin: Created in 1998 by Tony Abou-Ganim, Las Vegas, USA.
Comment: Be sure to use a ripe or even over-ripe banana in this tropical style drink.

FUR COLLAR 0‑🗝

★★★★☆

Glass: Coupe
Garnish: Orange zest twist
Method: SHAKE all ingredients with ice and fine strain into chilled glass.

2	shots	Ketel One Vodka
½	shot	De Kuyper XO Apricot Brandy
¾	shot	Freshly squeezed orange juice

Origin: Adapted from a drink in Ted Saucier's 1951 book, 'Bottoms Up!'
Comment: Apricot brandy adds fruity zinginess to what otherwise would be a Screwdriver served 'up'.

FUZZY NAVEL

★★½☆☆

Glass: Collins
Garnish: Lemon slice
Method: SHAKE all ingredients with ice and strain into ice-filled glass.

2	shots	Peachtree peach schnapps
4	shots	Freshly squeezed orange juice

Origin: A not very well regarded but extremely well known cocktail whose origins are lost.
Comment: The hairy version is a slightly more interesting, drier, less fluffy concoction. So why have a fluffy navel when you can have a hairy one?

G & TEA 0‑🗝

★★★★☆

Glass: Collins
Garnish: Lemon slice
Method: SHAKE first 3 ingredients with ice and strain into ice-filled glass. **TOP** with tonic water.

1½	shots	Rutte Dry Gin
1	shot	St-Germain elderflower liqueur
1	shot	Cold English breakfast tea
Top with		Tonic Water

Origin: Created in 2006 by yours truly, London, England.
Comment: Dry, floral, long and refreshing.

G. G AND G

★★★★☆

Glass: Old-fashioned
Garnish: Grapefruit zest twist
Method: SHAKE all ingredients with ice and fine strain into an ice-filled rocks glass.

1½	shots	Rutte Dry Gin
1	shot	Galliano L'Autentico liqueur
1	shot	Freshly squeezed pink grapefruit juice
2	dash	Angostura Orange Bitters

Origin: Adapted from a recipe by Ago Perrone, Connaught Hotel, London, England.
Comment: Pine fresh gin notes combine with aniseed and herbal notes, freshened by pink grapefruit and toned by dashes of orange bitters.

GALVANISED NAIL

★★★★☆

Glass: Martini
Garnish: Lemon zest twist
Method: SHAKE all ingredients with ice and fine strain into chilled glass.

2	shots	Dewar's 12 Year Old Scotch whisky
½	shot	Drambuie liqueur
¼	shot	St-Germain elderflower liqueur
½	shot	Pressed apple juice
¼	shot	Freshly squeezed lemon juice

Origin: Created in 2003 by yours truly, taking inspiration from the Rusty Nail.
Comment: Scotch and honeyed spice with a hint of apple and elderflower plus some lemon freshness.

GAMBLE

★★★½☆

Glass: Old-fashioned
Garnish: Grapefruit slice
Method: SHAKE all ingredients with ice and fine strain into glass filled with crushed ice.

1	shot	Sloe Gin liqueur
1	shot	Rutte Dry Gin
1	shot	Freshly squeezed pink grapefruit juice
¼	shot	Sugar syrup (2 sugar to 1 water)
½	shot	Cherry Heering Liqueur

Origin: Created in April 2011 by Matt Donnelly at the Bacchus Pub and Kitchen, London. To quote Matt, "The drink is called a 'Gamble' due to the fact I gambled on changing 'The Bramble'."
Comment: An easy drinking, gin-laced, fruity summery drink.

GAME SET MATCH (NEW)

★★★★⯪

Glass: Coupe
Garnish: Half lemon slice & Luxardo Maraschino cherry on stick
Method: STIR all ingredients with ice and strain into chilled glass.

2 shots Bourbon whiskey
½ shot Carpano Antica Formula
½ shot Cynar
2 dash Angostura Aromatic Bitters
1 dash Angostura Orange Bitters

Origin: Created in 2013 by Juan 'J.P.' Caceres-Rojas while working in Washington D.C., USA.
Comment: A Sweet Manhattan with Cynar and orange bitters. What's not to like?

GANSEVOORT FIZZ

★★★⯪☆

Glass: Collins
Garnish: Lemon slice
Method: SHAKE first 4 ingredients with ice and strain into ice-filled glass. TOP with soda.

2 shots Bacardi Carta Ocho aged rum
1 shot Drambuie liqueur
1 shot Freshly squeezed lemon juice
2 dash Peychaud's aromatic bitters
Top with Soda (club soda)

Origin: Created for 5 Ninth in Manhattan and originally published in David Wondrich's 2005 'Killer Cocktails'.
Comment: A potent, flavoursome herbal cooler based on aged rum.

GARDEN DELIGHT (NEW)

★★★⯪☆

Glass: Collins
Garnish: Gently roll muddler over rosemary sprig to release aromas before adding to glass
Method: Place two long slices of cucumber into ice-filled glass. Add melon liqueur and gin and stir. TOP with tonic water and stir again.

2 slice English cucumber peeled
1 shot Midori Green Melon liqueur
1 shot Rutte Dry Gin
Top with Tonic Water

Origin: Created in 2014 by Manuel Terron, Midori Global Brand ambassador.
Comment: Slightly sweet, light, fruity and summery.

GARDEN, GRAIN & GRAPE

★★★★⯪

Glass: Coupe
Garnish: Mint sprig
Method: MUDDLE grapes in base of shaker. Add other ingredients, DRY SHAKE (without ice). SHAKE again with ice and fine strain into chilled glass.

5 fresh Seedless white grapes
1½ shots Ketel One Vodka
¾ shot Sauvignon blanc white wine
1 dash Egg white (optional)

Origin: Adapted from a drink created in 2012 by Mal Spence at Blythswood Square Hotel, Glasgow, Scotland.
Comment: Pale green lime with frothy white head, this delicate wine and grape flavoured drink is laced with a large splash of vodka.

GARIBALDI

★★★☆☆

Glass: Collins
Garnish: Orange slice
Method: POUR Campari into ice-filled glass. TOP with orange juice, stir and serve with straws.

2 shots Campari Bitter
Top with Freshly squeezed orange juice

Origin: Appears on cocktail lists throughout Italy. Named after the famous revolutionary general who helped liberate and reunify Italy.
Comment: Reminiscent of red grapefruit juice.

GATOR BITE

★★★⯪☆

Glass: Coupe
Garnish: Salt rim
Method: SHAKE all ingredients with ice and fine strain into chilled glass.

1 shot Green Chartreuse liqueur
1½ shots De Kuyper Triple Sec
1 shot Freshly squeezed lime juice
¾ shot Sugar syrup (2 sugar to 1 water)

Comment: Looks like a Margarita, but instead of tequila features the unique taste of Chartreuse. Yup, it bites.

GAUGUIN

★★★☆☆

Glass: Old-fashioned
Garnish: Luxardo Maraschino cherry
Method: BLEND all ingredients with 6oz crushed ice and serve with straws.

2 shots Bacardi Carta Blanca light rum
½ shot Freshly squeezed lime juice
½ shot Freshly squeezed lemon juice
½ shot Passion fruit syrup

Comment: The passion fruit shines through in this drink, which is very much a frozen Daiquiri in style.

GE BLONDE

★★★★☆

Glass: Martini
Garnish: Apple wedge
Method: SHAKE all ingredients with ice and fine strain into chilled glass.

1¾ shots	Dewar's 12 Year Old Scotch whisky
1¼ shots	Sauvignon blanc white wine
1 shot	Pressed apple juice
½ shot	Sugar syrup (2 sugar to 1 water)
¼ shot	Freshly squeezed lemon juice

Origin: A combined effort by the staff of London's GE Club in January 2002, this was named by Linda, a waitress at the club who happens to be blonde. She claimed the name was inspired by the cocktail's straw colour.
Comment: This delicate drink demands freshly pressed apple juice and flavoursome Scotch with subtle peat.

GEISHA MAR-TEA-KNEE

★★★★☆

Glass: Martini
Garnish: Open tea pearl
Method: SHAKE all ingredients with ice and fine strain into chilled glass.

1½ shots	Rutte Dry Gin
¾ shot	Zen green tea liqueur
1 shot	Cold jasmine tea

Origin: Created in the USA in 2006.
Comment: Surprisingly fresh and light, this starts slightly sweet but finishes with refreshing bitter tannins. Tea pearls - hand-rolled balls of tea leaves - make a wonderful garnish.

GENERAL HARRISON'S NOGG

★★★★★

Glass: Old-fashioned
Garnish: Dust with freshly grated nutmeg
Method: Using an especially designed 'fizz' shaker (such as Perlini) that's designed to be carbonated. SHAKE all ingredients with ice and strain into glass (without ice). Be sure to shake well to completely emulsify the egg.

1½ shots	Calvados brandy
2 shots	Medium dry cider
½ shot	Sugar syrup (2 sugar to 1 water)
2 dash	Dale DeGroff's Pimento Bitters
1 fresh	Eggs (white & yolk)

Origin: We were sent this recipe by Dale DeGroff in December 2012 who said: "A personal favourite, adapted from a recipe from Jerry Thomas' 1862 edition of How to Mix Drinks: a totally different take on eggnog – made as a single-serve drink it includes a raw egg, so you need to shake the hell out of it."

This cocktail is named after General William Henry Harrison, the American president to hold office for the shortest period. He was elected 4th March 1841 and died a month to the day later of pneumonia. Harrison was known for his drinking and cider was one of his preferred tipples. It is said that this eggnog was his favourite drink.
Comment: A whole raw egg contributes body to this filling, flavoursome, wintry, delicate cocktail. The retained CO2 fizz of the cider adds essential body and balancing acidy but demands the use of a specialised shaker.

GENNARO'S SIDECAR (NEW)

★★★★☆

Glass: Coupe
Garnish: Orange zest twist
Method: SHAKE all ingredients with ice and fine strain into chilled glass.

1½ shots	Martell VSOP Médaillon cognac
1 shot	De Kuyper Triple Sec
½ shot	Pallini Limoncello
½ shot	Freshly squeezed lemon juice
½ shot	Chilled water (omit if wet ice)

Origin: Adapted from a popular drink on the menu of Jamie's Italian restaurant and bar chain.
Comment: This Difford version of the established Jamie's Italian Gennaro's Sidecar is predictably more boozy than the original but retains the balance between sweet limoncello liqueur and tart lemon juice.

GENTLE BREEZE (MOCKTAIL) 🔑

★★★☆☆

Glass: Collins
Garnish: Lime wedge
Method: POUR ingredients into ice-filled glass, stir and serve with straws.

| 4 shots | Cranberry juice |
| 2 shots | Freshly squeezed pink grapefruit juice |

Comment: A Seabreeze without the hard stuff.

GENTLEMAN'S AGREEMENT

★★★★☆

Glass: Collins
Garnish: Orange zest twist
Method: SHAKE first 3 ingredients with ice and strain into ice-filled glass. TOP with soda.

2½ shots	Jack Daniel's Old No.7 Brand
½ shot	Almond (orgeat) syrup
½ shot	Freshly squeezed lemon juice
Top with	Soda (club soda)

Origin: A cocktail used by Brown-Forman to promote Gentleman Jack.
Comment: Amaretto-like almond flavours with Tennessee whiskey balanced with fresh lemon juice and lengthened with refreshing soda.

GEORGETOWN PUNCH

★★★★☆

Glass: Collins
Garnish: Pineapple wedge
Method: SHAKE all ingredients with ice and fine strain into ice-filled glass.

1 shot	Bacardi Carta Blanca light rum
¾ shot	Gosling's Black Seal dark rum
1½ shots	Coconut rum liqueur
1 shot	Cranberry juice
1 shot	Fresh pressed pineapple juice
¾ shot	Freshly squeezed lime juice

Origin: Adapted from a drink discovered in 2005 at Degrees, Washington DC, USA.
Comment: A Tiki-style, fruity rum punch.

GEORGIA MINT JULEP

★★★★⯪

Glass: Collins
Garnish: Mint sprig
Method: Lightly **MUDDLE** (only to bruise) mint in base of shaker. Add other ingredients, **SHAKE** with ice and strain into chilled glass half filled with crushed ice. **CHURN** (stir) the drink using a bar spoon. Top up the glass with more crushed ice and churn again. Continue adding crushed ice and churning until the drink meets the rim of the glass. Serve with two long straws.

12 fresh	Mint leaves
2½ shots	Bourbon whiskey
1 shot	Peachtree peach schnapps
⅛ shot	Sugar syrup (2 sugar to 1 water)
3 dash	Angostura Aromatic Bitters

Origin: This classic was originally made with peach brandy in place of peach liqueur. It is also sometimes made with apricot brandy.
Comment: Bourbon, peach and mint are flavours that combine harmoniously.

THE GETAWAY (AKA CYNAR DAIQUIRI)

★★★★⯪

Glass: Coupe
Garnish: Lime wedge on rim
Method: SHAKE all ingredients with ice and fine strain into chilled glass.

1½ shots	Bacardi Carta Ocho aged rum
½ shot	Cynar
¼ shot	Freshly squeezed lemon juice
¼ shot	Freshly squeezed lime juice
¼ shot	Sugar syrup (2 sugar to 1 water)

Origin: Adapted from a drink created in 2012 by Wayne Curtis at The Passenger, Washington D.C., USA.
Comment: The bitter vegetal taste of Cynar turns this Daiquiri into a digestif.

GIBSON DRY MARTINI 🗝

★★★★⯪

Glass: Martini
Garnish: Two cocktail onions on stick
Method: STIR all ingredients with ice and strain into chilled glass.

2½ shot	Rutte Dry Gin
½ shot	Martini Extra Dry Vermouth

Comment: A classic Dry Martini with cocktail onions in place of an olive or a twist.
Origin: Today a Gibson is a Dry Martini served with two onions. Charles Dana Gibson produced hugely popular pen-and-ink drawings between the 1890s and 1930s. His illustrations of girls were as iconic as modern-day supermodels, and it is said this drink was named after the well-endowed Gibson Girls, hence the two onions. Gibson was a member of New York's The Players Club and a bartender there by the name of Charley Connolly is credited for at least adding the garnish, if not actually creating the drink.

However, recipes for the Gibson without onions appear in both the 1914 *Drinks* by Jacques Straub and in Tom Bullock's 1917 *The Ideal Bartender* with the recipe for a Martini-like drink called a L.P.W. specifying "Add a pickled onion and serve." Bullock also includes a cocktail called a "Onion Cocktail" with old tom gin, Italian vermouth "and no bitters" with the instruction "Strain and serve with an onion."

Gimlet cocktail

Classically the Gimlet is a simple 50-50 mix of gin and lime cordial but the rise in vodka's popularity during the 1990s and early noughties saw vodka frequently used in place of gin to make a Gimlet. As gin has recently regained ground on vodka so it has reclaimed its rightful place in the Gimlet. Modern, drier palates have also caused the proportion of lime cordial used in a Gimlet to dwindle.

The story behind the Gimlet

In 1747, James Lind, a Scottish surgeon, discovered that consumption of citrus fruits helped prevent scurvy, one of the most common illnesses on board ship. We now understand that scurvy is caused by a Vitamin C deficiency and that it is the vitamins in citrus fruit which help ward off the condition. In 1867, the Merchant Shipping Act made it mandatory for all British ships to carry rations of lime juice for the crew.

Lauchlin Rose, the owner of a shipyard in Leith, Scotland, had been working to solve the problem of how to keep citrus juice fresh for months on board ship. In 1867 he patented a process for preserving fruit juice without alcohol. To give his product wider appeal he sweetened the mixture, packaged it in an attractive bottle and named it 'Rose's Lime Cordial'.

Once the benefits of drinking lime juice became more broadly known, British sailors consumed so much of the stuff, often mixed with their daily ration of rum and water ('grog'), that they became affectionately known as 'Limeys'. While the ratings drunk rum, their officers drink gin so naturally mixed Rose's lime cordial with gin to make Gimlets. Hence, the creation of the Gimlet is the result of circumstance rather than clever mixing of ingredients, and that's the way it tastes if you try an un-chilled (they had no ice) 50-50 Gimlet. However, stirred over ice, mixed to more balanced proportions and the result is divine. Gin and lime just work, that's why it's the garnish of choice for G&Ts.

As for the name, a 'gimlet' was a small tool used to tap the barrels of spirits which were carried on British Navy ships: this could be the origin of the drink's name. Another story cites a naval doctor, Rear-Admiral Sir Thomas Desmond Gimlette (1857-1943), who is said to have mixed gin with lime 'to help the medicine go down'. Although credible, it is not substantiated in his obituary in The Times, 6 October 1943, nor his entry in Who Was Who 1941-1950, and we guess pretty much every doctor in the Navy spurted a similar mantra at the time.

GIMLET (SCHUMANN'S RECIPE) 🗝

★★★★⯪

Glass: Martini
Garnish: Luxardo Maraschino cherry
Method: SHAKE all ingredients with ice and fine strain into chilled glass.

2½ shots	Rutte Dry Gin
¼ shot	Freshly squeezed lime juice
1¼ shots	Rose's lime cordial

Origin: A shaken twist on an already established drink by the famous bartender and cocktail author Charles Schumann of Munich, Germany.
Comment: Generously laced with gin and wonderfully tart.

STAR RATINGS EXPLAINED

★★★★★⁺ OUTSTANDING	★★★★★ EXCEPTIONAL
★★★★⯪ EXCELLENT	★★★★☆ RECOMMENDED
★★★⯪☆ COMMENDED	★★★☆☆ MEDIOCRE
★★⯪☆☆ DISAPPOINTING	★★☆☆☆ PRETTY AWFUL
★⯪☆☆☆ SHAMEFUL	★☆☆☆☆ DISGUSTING

GIMLET COCKTAIL (CHARLES H. BAKER'S 1939 RECIPE) (NEW)

★★★★☆

Glass: Coupe
Garnish: Lime wedge
Method: STIR all ingredients with ice and strain into chilled glass.

2   shots   Rutte Dry Gin
¼   shot   Sugar syrup (2 sugar to 1 water)
⅛   shot   Rose's lime cordial
¾   shot   Chilled water

Origin: Adapted from recipe first published by Charles H. Baker Jr. in his 1946 'Gentleman's Companion'.
Comment: Boozy and very subtly flavoured and edging very slightly towards being sweet.

GIMLET COCKTAIL (DIFFORD'S RECIPE)

★★★★★

Glass: Coupe
Garnish: Express 3 lime zests into glass before pouring drink. Lime wedge on rim.
Method: SHAKE all ingredients with ice and fine strain into chilled glass.

1½ shots Rutte dry gin
½ shot Rutte Old Simon oude jenever
¼ shot Sugar syrup (2 sugar to 1 water)
⅛ shot Freshly squeezed lemon juice
⅛ shot Freshly squeezed lime juice
½ shot Chilled water

Origin: This version of the classic Gimlet by yours truly at the Cabinet Room, London, England.
Comment: The Gimlet is usually stirred but unless you've super strained your freshly squeezed citrus juice then even if stirred this cocktail won't be perfectly clear. So do as Harry Craddock directs in his 1930 Savoy Cocktail book and use some elbow grease to shake and invigorate this upper decks cocktail.

GIN & FRENCH

★★★★☆

Glass: Old-fashioned
Garnish: Lemon slice
Method: STIR all ingredients with ice and strain into ice-filled glass.

2   shots   Rutte Dry Gin
2   shots   Martini Extra Dry vermouth

Origin: Traditionally Italian vermouth was sweet while French vermouth was dry. Hence this drink is simply gin and dry vermouth.
Comment: Bone dry but botanically rich.

GIN & IT

★★★★★

Glass: Old-fashioned
Garnish: Orange slice (if served straight-up use a lemon zest twist)
Method: STIR all ingredients with ice and strain into ice-filled glass.

1¾ shots   Rutte Dry Gin
1¾ shots   Martini Rosso vermouth
1   dash   Angostura Orange Bitters

Origin: The name is short for 'Gin and Italian', a reference to the sweet vermouth, which was traditionally Italian while French vermouth was dry.

In his ' Craft of the Cocktail', Dale DeGroff states that the Gin and IT was originally known as a 'Sweet Martini' and as such was a popular drink during the 1880s and 1890s at the Hoffman House and other New York bars. Later it became known as 'Gin & Italian', until during Prohibition it was shortened to 'Gin & IT'.

The Gin & IT made its way to London during Prohibition in America and due to the British love of gin, the Gin & IT became a very popular drink and staple pub serve. Its popularity waned with both that of vermouth and gin in the late 1980s but is now ripe for discovery by a new generation of gin and vermouth drinkers.
Comment: Remembering both vermouth and gin are flavoured with similar botanicals, they obviously have an affinity for each other. This drink may be simple but made with a full-bodied Vermouth di Torino it's a fabulously tasty combination of botanicals, wine and spirit.

GIN & JUICE

★★★☆☆

Glass: Collins
Garnish: Orange slice
Method: SHAKE all ingredients with ice and strain into ice-filled glass.

2   shots   Rutte Dry Gin
2½ shots   Freshly squeezed orange juice
1½ shots   Freshly squeezed pink grapefruit juice

Origin: Possibly the inspiration behind the Top 10 single 'Gin and Juice' by rapper Snoop Doggy Dogg, from his debut album 'Doggystyle'.
Comment: Gin and fruit juice. OK, but nothing to sing about.

GIN & SIN

★★★★☆

Glass: Martini
Garnish: Orange zest twist
Method: SHAKE all ingredients with ice and fine strain into chilled glass.

2   shots   Rutte Dry Gin
1   shot   Freshly squeezed orange juice
½   shot   Freshly squeezed lemon juice
¼   shot   Pomegranate / grenadine syrup (2:1)
½   shot   Chilled water (omit if wet ice)

Comment: This is one of those drinks that benefits from a little dilution to prevent the citrus and gin becoming too aggressive.

GIN & TONIC

★★★★⯪

Glass: Collins
Garnish: Lime wedge
Method: POUR ingredients into ice-filled glass and serve.

| 2 | shots | Rutte Dry Gin |
| Top with | | Tonic Water |

Origin: The precise origin of the G&T is lost in the mists of time. Gin (or at least a grain based juniper spirit) was drunk for medicinal reasons from the 1600s onwards. Quinine, the pungent bark extract which gives tonic its distinctive bitterness, had been used against malaria for even longer. The first known quinine-based tonics were marketed during the 1850's.

The popularity of tonic in the British colonies, especially India, is clear. Schweppes launched their first carbonated quinine tonic in 1870, branding it Indian Tonic Water. The ladies and gentlemen of the Raj also drank phenomenal quantities of gin. It is therefore accepted that gin and tonic emerged in India during the second half of the nineteenth century and was drunk partly to ward off malaria.
Comment: This might not be considered a cocktail by most, but it is actually classified as a Highball. Whatever, it's one of the simplest and best drinks ever devised, hence its lasting popularity.

GIN ATOMIC

★★★⯪☆

Glass: Collins
Garnish: Lemon zest twist
Method: Lightly MUDDLE (just to bruise) basil in base of shaker. Add other ingredients apart from tonic, SHAKE with ice and strain into ice-filled glass. TOP with tonic water and serve with straws.

3	fresh	Basil leaves
2	shots	Rutte Dry Gin
1	shot	St-Germain elderflower liqueur
½	shot	Freshly squeezed lemon juice
2	dash	Lemon bitters (optional)
Top with		Tonic Water

Origin: Created in 2007 by Brendan Mainini at The Ambassador Bar, San Francisco, USA.
Comment: A nuclear gin and tonic - or at least, one that simply radiates flavour.

GIN BASIL SMASH/GIN PESTO

★★★★⯪

Glass: Old-fashioned
Garnish: 3 Basil sprigs
Method: Gently muddle basil in base of SHAKER with Gin (and ideally leave to stand for 10 minutes). Add other ingredients, SHAKE with ice and fine strain into ice-filled glass.

12	fresh	Basil leaves
2	shots	Rutte Dry Gin
¾	shot	Freshly squeezed lemon juice
⅓	shot	Sugar syrup (2 sugar to 1 water)

Origin: Adapted from a drink created in July 2008 by Jörg Meyer at Bar Le Lion, Hamburg, Germany. Jörg originally blogged that his new creation was called a Gin Pesto but it quickly became better known as the Gin Basil Smash.
Comment: Jörg says: better too much, than not enough, basil in this drink. He also specifies that the basil is muddled rather than just broken by the action of shaking as this produces a greener drink. Lazily, I prefer them just shaken as this seems to produce a fresher-tasting drink. Whichever method you employ, you'll find the flavours of basil combine wonderfully in this gin sour.

GIN BERRY

★★★⯪☆

Glass: Martini
Garnish: Lime zest twist
Method: SHAKE all ingredients with ice and fine strain into chilled glass.

1½	shots	Rutte Dry Gin
½	shot	Chambord Liqueur
½	shot	Freshly squeezed lime juice
1½	shots	Cranberry juice

Origin: Adapted from a drink created in 2004 by Chris Lacey, UK.
Comment: Berry flavours combine harmoniously with gin - what an appropriate name.

GIN COCKTAIL

★★★★☆

Glass: Martini
Garnish: Lemon zest twist
Method: STIR all ingredients with ice and fine strain into chilled glass.

2½	shots	Rutte Dry Gin
⅛	shot	De Kuyper Triple Sec
⅛	shot	Sugar syrup (2 sugar to 1 water)
2	dash	Angostura Aromatic Bitters

Origin: A classic that was already well-established when Jerry Thomas recorded his version of the recipe in 1862.
Comment: A pink gin made more approachable by a splash of triple sec and sugar syrup.

GIN COLHEITA (NEW)

★★★★⯪

Glass: Coupe
Garnish: Lemon zest twist
Method: THROW (pour from one vessel to another from a height) all ingredients with ice and strain into chilled glass.

2	shots	Rutte Dry Gin
1	shot	Verdelho madeira (medium dry)
¼	shot	Freshly squeezed lemon juice
⅓	shot	Pomegranate / grenadine syrup (2:1)

Origin: Created on 20th August 2014 by yours truly to accompany 'Beef, Juniper and Pistachio Canapés' for the EBLEX Quality Standard Mark Scheme for beef and lamb. Tasty meat and a tasty cocktail.
Comment: The quality and style of your madeira is crucial to the success and balance of this cocktail - don't skimp – buy a colheita.

GIN DAISY

★★★★☆

Glass: Goblet
Garnish: Luxardo Maraschino cherry
Method: SHAKE all ingredients with ice and strain into glass filled with crushed ice. CHURN (stir) drink with ice and serve with straws.

2	shots	Rutte Dry Gin
¼	shot	Yellow Chartreuse liqueur
¼	shot	Freshly squeezed lemon juice
¼	shot	Pomegranate / grenadine syrup (2:1)

Origin: A classic Daisy variation.
Comment: If correctly made this serious, gin dominated cocktail should be blush, not pink.

GIN DAISY #2 (JERRY THOMAS STYLE)

★★★★☆

Glass: Martini
Garnish: Seasonal berries
Method: SHAKE first four ingredients with ice and fine strain into chilled glass. TOP with a splash of soda from a siphon.

1½ shots Rutte Old Simon oude jenever
½ shot Grand Marnier Cordon Rouge
¾ shot Freshly squeezed lemon juice
¼ shot Sugar syrup (2 sugar to 1 water)
1 splash Soda from siphon

Origin: The origins of the Daisy are lost in time but the first written reference to it is in an 1866 novel called 'Gay Life in New York, or Fast Men and Grass Widows' by Henry Llewellyn Williams. This recipe is adapted from Jerry Thomas' 1876 'How to Mix Drinks'.
Comment: The rich style of genever combines wonderfully with orange liqueur in this balanced classic.

GIN DAISY #3 (MODERN LONG STYLE) 0━━

★★★★☆

Glass: Collins
Garnish: Seasonal berries
Method: SHAKE first 3 ingredients with ice and strain into ice-filled glass. TOP with soda and serve with straws.

2 shots Rutte Dry Gin
1 shot Freshly squeezed lemon juice
½ shot Pomegranate / grenadine syrup (2:1)
Top with Soda (club soda)

Origin: Daisies can be served in a goblet filled with crushed ice, straight-up or as in this case in a Collins glass.
Comment: Fruit and botanicals served long and refreshing.

GIN FIX 0━━

★★★★☆

Glass: Goblet
Garnish: Lemon slice
Method: SHAKE all ingredients with ice and strain into glass with crushed ice. CHURN (stir) drink with ice and serve with straws.

2 shots Rutte Dry Gin
1 shot Freshly squeezed lemon juice
½ shot Sugar syrup (2 sugar to 1 water)

Origin: The fix is an old classic that's very similar to the Daisy.
Comment: A Gin Sour served over crushed ice in a goblet.

GIN FIXED 0━━

★★★★☆

Glass: Martini
Garnish: Lemon slice
Method: SHAKE all ingredients with ice and strain into glass with crushed ice. CHURN (stir) drink with ice and serve with straws.

2 shots Rutte Dry Gin
¼ shot De Kuyper Triple Sec
1 shot Fresh pressed pineapple juice
½ shot Freshly squeezed lemon juice
¼ shot Sugar syrup (2 sugar to 1 water)

Comment: Sweet and sour with a spirity pineapple twang.

GIN FIZZ 0━━

★★★★☆

Glass: Collins (small 8oz)
Garnish: Lemon slice & mint sprig
Method: SHAKE first three ingredients with ice and strain into chilled glass (without ice). TOP with soda.

2 shots Rutte Dry Gin
1 shot Lemon
½ shot Sugar syrup (2 sugar to 1 water)
Top with Soda from siphon

Origin: A mid-19th century classic.
Comment: Everyone has heard of this clean, refreshing, long drink but few have actually tried it.

GIN GARDEN 0━━

★★★★☆

Glass: Martini
Garnish: Cucumber slices
Method: MUDDLE cucumber in base of shaker. Add other ingredients, SHAKE with ice and fine strain into chilled glass.

1 inch English cucumber peeled
2 shots Rutte Dry Gin
1 shot St-Germain elderflower liqueur
1 shot Pressed apple juice

Origin: Adapted from a drink that Dan Warner at Zander and Tobias Blazquez Garcia at Steam collaborated on in London, England, in 2001.
Comment: A veritable English shrubbery with flowers, fruit and vegetables flourishing in harmony.

GIN GENIE

★★★★☆

Glass: Collins
Garnish: Mint sprig
Method: Lightly MUDDLE mint in base of shaker (just to bruise). Add other ingredients, SHAKE with ice and strain into glass filled with crushed ice.

8 fresh Mint leaves
1½ shots Rutte Dry Gin
1 shot Sloe Gin liqueur
1 shot Freshly squeezed lemon juice
½ shot Sugar syrup (2 sugar to 1 water)

Origin: Adapted from a drink created in 2002 by Wayne Collins, UK.
Comment: A fruit-led long drink for gin-loving Bowie fans.

A
B
C
D
E
F
G
H
I
J
K
L
M
N
O
P
Q
R
S
T
U
V
W
X
Y
Z

GIN GIN

★★★★½☆

Glass: Old-fashioned
Garnish: Lemon zest twist
Method: STIR all ingredients with ice and strain into ice-filled glass.

| 2 | shots | Rutte Dry Gin |
| 1 | shot | Stone's green ginger wine |

Comment: Gin and ginger - as simple as that. Surprisingly good.

GIN GIN MULE

★★★★☆

Glass: Collins
Garnish: Lime wedge & mint sprigs
Method: MUDDLE ginger in base of shaker. Add next 4 ingredients, **SHAKE** with ice and fine strain into ice-filled glass. **TOP** with ginger beer.

2	slice	Fresh root ginger (thumbnail sized)
2	shots	Rutte Dry Gin
½	shot	Freshly squeezed lime juice
¼	shot	Sugar syrup (2 sugar to 1 water)
12	fresh	Mint leaves
Top with		Gosling's Stormy Ginger Beer

Origin: Adapted from a drink created in 2000 by Audrey Saunders at Beacon, New York City, USA.
Comment: Fresh ginger, mint and the herbal notes from gin make this much more than just another take on the Moscow Mule.

GIN PUNCH #1 ☗

★★★★½

Glass: Collins
Garnish: Lemon slice
Method: SHAKE all ingredients with ice and stain into ice-filled glass.

2	shots	Rutte Dry Gin
¾	shot	Freshly squeezed lemon juice
¾	shot	Sugar syrup (2 sugar to 1 water)
2	shots	Chilled water
1	dash	Angostura Aromatic Bitters

Origin: This is a version of the drink for which Limmer's Hotel in London was most famed: a Captain Gronow recalled it in his 1860s memoirs as one of the top, if filthy and seedy, sporting hangouts of 1814, thanks in part to its 'famous gin-punch'. A bartender named John Collins worked there later in the 19th century, and was famous enough to inspire a limerick, so many believe he created the Collins, which is similar to gin punch, although the drink is not named in the rhyme which goes as follows:

My name is John Collins,
head waiter at Limmer's,
Corner of Conduit Street,
Hanover Square,
My chief occupation is filling brimmers
For all the young gentlemen frequenters there.
Comment: Light and refreshing, akin to alcoholic real lemonade.

GIN PUNCH #2

★★★★☆

Glass: Collins
Garnish: Seasonal berries
Method: SHAKE all ingredients with ice and strain into ice-filled glass. Serve with straws.

3	shots	Rutte Old Simon oude jenever
½	shot	Freshly squeezed lemon juice
¼	shot	Raspberries
¼	shot	Sugar syrup (2 sugar to 1 water)
¼	shot	Freshly squeezed orange juice
⅛	shot	Fresh pressed pineapple juice
⅛	shot	Luxardo Maraschino liqueur
2	shots	Chilled water

Origin: Adapted from Hebert Asbury's 1928 reprint of Jerry Thomas' 1862, 'How to Mix Drinks', or 'The Bon Vivant's Companion.'
Comment: Easy on the palate yet incredibly complex. Linseed oil notes of genever shine through.

GIN RICKEY ☗

★★★★☆

Glass: Collins (small 8oz)
Garnish: Length of lime peel
Method: SHAKE first three ingredients with ice and strain into ice-filled glass. **TOP** with soda.

2	shots	Rutte Dry Gin
½	shot	Freshly squeezed lime juice
¼	shot	Sugar syrup (2 sugar to 1 water)
Top with		Soda (club soda)

Origin: Believed to have been created by bartender George A. Williamson in 1880 at Shoomaker's Bar in Washington DC and named after Colonel Joe Rickey, who it is said Williamson witnessed squeeze lime into his whisky before topping his drink with soda. Coincidentally or not, Colonel Rickey went on to become a major importer of limes into the US.

The Gin Rickey cocktail first appeared in print in Harry Johnson's 1882 'Bartenders Manual' where Harry calls for a "medium size fizz glass" to be used with " 1 or 2 pieces of ice; squeeze the juice of 1 good-sized lime or 2 small ones; 1 wine glass of Tom or Holland gin if required; Fill up glass with club soda, carbonic or selters if required, and serve with a spoon."

Many confuse the Rickey and the Collins. For the record a Rickey is made with lime juice and a Collins with lemon juice. A Rickey is also usually served in a shorter glass than a Collins but that difference is secondary.
Comment: Clean, sharp and refreshing.

GIN SALAD DRY MARTINI

★★★★★

Glass: Martini
Garnish: 3 chilled olives and 2 cocktail onions
Method: STIR all ingredients with ice and strain into chilled glass.

2½	shots	Rutte Dry Gin
½	shot	Martini Extra Dry vermouth
1	dash	Angostura Orange Bitters (optional)

Comment: A Gin Salad is made like a regular Dry Martini but with three olives and two cocktail onions as garnish. They should be pushed onto the stick in the following order: olive-onion-olive-onion-olive.

GIN SLING

★★★★☆

Glass: Sling
Garnish: Lemon slice
Method: SHAKE first 3 ingredients with ice and fine strain into ice-filled glass. **TOP** with soda water.

2	shots	Rutte Dry Gin
½	shot	Freshly squeezed lemon juice
¼	shot	Sugar syrup (2 sugar to 1 water)
Top with		Soda (club soda)

Origin: 'Sling' comes from the German word 'schlingen', meaning 'to swallow' and is a style of drink which was popular from the late 1700s.
Comment: Sugar balances the citrus juice, the spirit fortifies and the carbonate lengthens.

GIN SOUR

★★★★½

Glass: Old-fashioned
Garnish: Lemon slice & cherry on stick (sail)
Method: SHAKE all ingredients with ice and strain into ice-filled glass.

2	shots	Rutte Dry Gin
1	shot	Freshly squeezed lemon juice
½	shot	Sugar syrup (2 sugar to 1 water)
½	fresh	Egg white
3	dash	Angostura Aromatic Bitters

Comment: This 4:2:8 formula is a tad sourer than the classic sour proportions of 3:4:8: three quarter part of the sour ingredient (lemon juice), one part of the sweet ingredient (sugar syrup) and two parts of the strong ingredient (gin).

GIN TWIST

★★★★½

Glass: Toddy
Garnish: Lemon zest twist
Method: POUR ingredients into pre-warmed glass and **STIR.**

1½	shots	Rutte Dry Gin
¾	shot	Freshly squeezed lemon juice
½	shot	Sugar syrup (2 sugar to 1 water)
Top with		Boiling water

Origin: This classic English cocktail dates back to at least the early 1800s and was so popular at the time that it is frequently referred to in novels and periodicals from the time. In Sir Walter Scott's 1823 novel St Ronan's Well, the character Captain MacTurk says, "Sir Binco, I will beg the favour of your company to the smoking-room, where we may have a cigar and a glass of gin-twist; and we will consider how the honour of the company must be supported and upholden upon the present conjuncture."

William Makepeace Thackeray mentions the Gin Twist in his 1869 ' Miscellanies: The Book of Snobs. Sketches and Travels in London'. "About eleven men in white neckcloths drop in from dinner-parties, and show their lacquered boots and shirt-studs with a little complacency - and at midnight, after the theatres, the young rakes and viveurs come swaggering in, and call loudly for Gin-Twist."
Comment: Gin botanicals flavour this delicate citrusy, warming drink.

GIN-GER & TONIC

★★★★☆

Glass: Collins
Garnish: Lime wedge
Method: MUDDLE ginger in base of shaker, add gin and sugar, **SHAKE** with ice and strain into ice-filled glass. **TOP** with tonic water.

2	slice	Fresh root ginger (thumbnail sized)
2	shots	Rutte Dry Gin
¼	shot	Sugar syrup (2 sugar to 1 water)
Top with		Tonic Water

Comment: A dry, refreshing long drink for those that like their G&Ts gingered.

GIN-GER TOM

★★★★☆

Glass: Collins
Garnish: Orange slice & cherry on stick (sail)
Method: MUDDLE ginger in base of shaker. Add other ingredients, **SHAKE** with ice and fine strain into ice filled glass.

2	slice	Fresh root ginger (thumbnail sized)
2	shots	Rutte Dry Gin
1	shot	Freshly squeezed lime juice
½	shot	Sugar syrup (2 sugar to 1 water)
Top with		Soda (club soda)

Origin: Adapted from a drink created in 2003 by Jamie Terrell at Lab, London, England.
Comment: A Tom Collins with lime and ginger - very refreshing.

GINGER COCKTAIL

★★★★☆

Glass: Martini
Garnish: Slice root ginger
Method: MUDDLE ginger in base of shaker. Add other ingredients, **SHAKE** with ice and fine strain into chilled glass.

2	slice	Fresh root ginger (thumbnail sized)
2	shots	Ketel One Vodka
¾	shot	Stone's green ginger wine
¾	shot	Pressed apple juice
½	shot	Freshly squeezed lime juice
¼	shot	Sugar syrup (2 sugar to 1 water)

Origin: Discovered in 2003 at Hurricane Bar and Grill, Edinburgh, Scotland.
Comment: This Martini may be served chilled but its flavour is distinctly warming.

GINGER COSMO

★★★★☆

Glass: Martini
Garnish: Fresh ginger slice
Method: SHAKE all ingredients with ice and fine strain into glass.

2	shots	Ketel One Citroen vodka
¾	shot	King's Ginger Liqueur
1¼	shots	Cranberry juice
¼	shot	Freshly squeezed lime juice
⅛	shot	Sugar syrup (2 sugar to 1 water)

Origin: Emerged during 2002 in New York City.
Comment: Just what it says on the tin - your everyday Cosmo given extra vitality courtesy of a hint of ginger spice.

GINGER COSMOS

★★★⯪☆

Glass: Collins
Garnish: Basil leaf
Method: MUDDLE ginger and basil in base of shaker. Add other ingredients, SHAKE with ice and fine strain into glass filled with crushed ice. Stir and serve with straws.

2	slice	Fresh root ginger (thumbnail sized)
5	fresh	Basil leaves
2	shots	Rutte Dry Gin
1½	shots	Fresh pressed pineapple juice
1½	shots	Pressed apple juice
¼	shot	Freshly squeezed lime juice
¼	shot	Sugar syrup (2 sugar to 1 water)

Origin: Created in 2003 by Massilimiliano Greco at Zander, London, England. 'Cosmos' is a reference to the botanical name for pineapple, Ananas comosus.
Comment: Warming ginger spice in a very cooling, fruity drink.

GINGER FROST

★★★⯪☆

Glass: Coupe
Garnish: Fresh ginger slice
Method: DRY SHAKE (without ice) all ingredients. SHAKE again with ice and strain into chilled glass.

1½	shots	Ketel One Vodka
½	shot	Freshly squeezed lemon juice
¼	shot	Sugar syrup (2 sugar to 1 water)
¾	shot	Freshly squeezed orange juice
½	fresh	Egg white
¾	shot	King's Ginger Liqueur

Comment: Freshly squeezed lemon and orange juices, spiced with ginger and laced with vodka.

GINGER MARGARITA

★★★★☆

Glass: Coupe
Garnish: Lime wedge
Method: SHAKE all ingredients with ice and fine strain into chilled glass.

2	shots	Patrón reposado tequila
1	shot	King's Ginger Liqueur
1	shot	Freshly squeezed lime juice

Comment: A Margarita spiced with ginger.

GINGER MOJITO 🍸⚷

★★★★☆

Glass: Collins
Garnish: Mint sprig
Method: MUDDLE ginger in base of shaker. Add mint and lightly MUDDLE (just to bruise). Add next three ingredients, SHAKE with ice and fine strain into glass filled with crushed ice. TOP with ginger ale.

3	slice	Fresh root ginger (thumbnail sized)
12	fresh	Mint leaves
2	shots	Bacardi Carta Blanca light rum
½	shot	Freshly squeezed lime juice
½	shot	Sugar syrup (2 sugar to 1 water)
Top with		Ginger ale

Comment: A spiced variation on the classic Mojito.

GINGER MOJITO (MOCKTAIL) (NEW)

★★★★⯪

Glass: Collins
Garnish: Mint sprig
Method: POUR first 2 ingredients into glass. Add lime wedges (cut in half) & mint leaves. Add crushed ice and CHURN (stir). TOP with soda and CHURN again.

¾	shot	Freshly squeezed lime juice
½	shot	Sugar syrup (2 sugar to 1 water)
3	wedge	Lime (fresh whole)
12	fresh	Mint leaves
Top with		Soda (club soda)

Origin: Adapted from a popular drink on the menu of Jamie's Italian restaurant and bar chain.
Comment: This Mojito may lack alcohol, indeed it's alcohol free, but it's refreshing, balanced and tasty nonetheless.

GINGER NUT

★★★⯪☆

Glass: Collins
Garnish: Lemon wedge
Method: POUR ingredients into ice-filled glass and stir.

1½	shots	Ketel One Citroen vodka
1½	shots	Hazelnut liqueur
Top with		Gosling's Stormy Ginger Beer

Comment: A long, refreshing meld of strong flavours.

GINGER PUNCH

★★★⯪☆

Glass: Collins
Garnish: Lime wedge
Method: MUDDLE ginger in base of shaker. Add honey and rum and STIR until honey is dissolved. Add lime juice and sugar, SHAKE with ice and fine strain into ice-filled glass. TOP with ginger ale.

2	slice	Fresh root ginger (thumbnail sized)
2	spoon	Runny honey
2½	shots	Bacardi Carta Oro rum
¾	shot	Freshly squeezed lime juice
¼	shot	Sugar syrup (2 sugar to 1 water)
Top with		Ginger ale

Comment: A ginger spiced rum punch.

GINGER SNAP

★★★★☆

Glass: Collins
Garnish: Lemon zest twist
Method: SHAKE first five ingredients with ice and strain into an ice-filled glass. TOP with soda and serve with straws.

1½	shots	Rutte Dry Gin
½	shot	King's Ginger Liqueur
½	shot	De Kuyper Triple Sec
½	shot	Freshly squeezed lemon juice
1	dash	Angostura Aromatic Bitters
Top with		Soda (club soda)

Origin: Created in 2007 by Gary Regan, New York, USA.
Comment: This balanced Gin Collins is sweetened by ginger and orange liqueurs.

A B C D E F G H I J K L M N O P Q R S T U V W X Y Z

GINGERBREAD COCKTAIL

★★★★☆

Glass: Martini
Garnish: Fresh ginger slice
Method: SHAKE all ingredients with ice and fine strain into into chilled glass.

1½ shots Bourbon whiskey
¾ shot Butterscotch liqueur
¾ shot Stone's green ginger wine
2 shots Pressed apple juice

Origin: Created by yours truly in 2004.
Comment: Sticky, warming and spicy.

GINGERBREAD MARTINI (NEW)

★★★★½

Glass: Coupe
Garnish: Gingerbread or ginger cookie
Method: STIR all ingredients with ice and strain into chilled glass.

2 shots Ketel One Vodka
1 shot Martini Extra Dry vermouth
¼ shot Disaronno Originale amaretto
¼ shot Gingerbread sugar syrup

Origin: Created in December 2014 by yours truly at the Cabinet Room, London, England.
Comment: A soaking wet Vodka Martini with a festive dose of almond and gingerbread.

GIUSEPPE'S HABIT

★★★★☆

Glass: Martini
Garnish: Star anise
Method: Spray the oils from the two lemon zest twists into the cocktail shaker, wipe them around the rim of the glass and drop them into the shaker, **SHAKE** with ice and fine strain into chilled glass.

2 fresh Lemon zest
1½ shots Galliano L'Autentico liqueur
¾ shot Hazelnut liqueur
¾ shot De Kuyper Triple Sec
1¼ shots Pressed apple juice

Origin: Created in 2002 by Leon Stokes at Zinc Bar & Grill, Birmingham, England,
Comment: An intriguing drink that combines hazelnut, orange, apple, aniseed and peppermint.

GIVE ME A DIME

★★★★☆

Glass: Martini
Garnish: Crumbled Cadbury's Flake bar
Method: SHAKE all ingredients with ice and fine strain into chilled glass.

1½ shots White crème de cacao liqueur
1½ shots Butterscotch liqueur
1½ shots Single cream / half-and-half

Comment: Creamy, sweet and tasty.

GIVE ME FEVER (NEW)

★★★★½

Glass: Coupe
Garnish: Flamed lemon zest twist
Method: SHAKE first 6 ingredients with ice and strain into chilled glass. Top with a splash of tonic water.

1 shot Rutte Dry Gin
½ shot Del Maguey VIDA mezcal
½ shot Freshly squeezed lime juice
¼ shot Freshly squeezed lemon juice
¾ shot De Kuyper Triple Sec
⅛ shot Lavender sugar syrup
½ shot Tonic Water

Origin: Created 3rd May 2014 by yours truly at the Cabinet Room, London, England while 'Fever' by Peggy Lee was playing.
Comment: This drink combines the fever quenching G&T with medicinal lavender and flavoursome mezcal from the Mexican territories where us Brits are susceptible to fever... bom, bom, bom ... give me fever. What a lovely way to burn.

GL'AMOUR COCKTAIL (NEW)

★★★★½

Glass: Coupe
Garnish: Edible flower or dried rose petals
Method: SHAKE all ingredients with ice and fine strain into chilled glass.

1½ shots Martell VSOP Médaillon cognac
1 shot Chambord Liqueur
⅔ shot Freshly squeezed lemon juice
¼ shot Sugar syrup (2 sugar to 1 water)
⅛ shot Rose water
½ shot Egg white

Comment: Berry richness fortified with cognac and balanced with lemon juice. A dash of sugar adds richness while egg white smooths.

GLAD EYE COCKTAIL

★★★☆☆

Glass: Martini
Garnish: Star anise
Method: SHAKE all ingredients with ice and fine strain into chilled glass.

1½ shots Le Fée Parisienne absinthe
1 shot Giffard Menthe Pastille liqueur
1 shot Chilled water (reduce if wet ice)

Origin: Adapted from Harry Craddock's 1930 'The Savoy Cocktail Book'.
Comment: This minty aniseed cocktail takes more than its colour from the green fairy.

GLENN'S BRIDE

★★★★⯪

Glass: Martini
Garnish: Orange zest twist
Method: SHAKE all ingredients with ice and fine strain into chilled glass.

2	shots	Bourbon whiskey
1	shot	St-Germain elderflower liqueur
2	dash	Angostura Aromatic Bitters
¼	shot	Rose water

Origin: Adapted from a drink created in 2005 by Julian Gibbs, England.
Comment: This serious, bourbon based cocktail ranks alongside the Sazerac in its aromatic complexity.

GLOOM CHASER COCKTAIL #1

★★★⯪☆

Glass: Martini
Garnish: Orange zest twist
Method: SHAKE all ingredients with ice and strain into chilled glass.

¾	shot	Grand Marnier Cordon Rouge
¾	shot	De Kuyper Triple Sec
1	shot	Freshly squeezed lemon juice
¼	shot	Pomegranate / grenadine syrup (2:1)
1	shot	Chilled water (reduce if wet ice)

Origin: Adapted from Harry Craddock's 1930 'The Savoy Cocktail Book'.
Comment: A sunny coloured drink for happy souls. And sweet orange and pomegranate soured with lemon would make anyone happy.

GLOOM CHASER COCKTAIL #2

★★★⯪☆

Glass: Martini
Garnish: Seasonal berries
Method: SHAKE all ingredients with ice and strain into chilled glass.

2	shots	Rutte Dry Gin
1	shot	Martini Extra Dry Vermouth
½	shot	La Fee Parisienne absinthe
¼	shot	Pomegranate / grenadine syrup (2:1)
½	shot	Chilled water (reduce if wet ice)

Origin: Adapted from David A. Embury's 1948 'Fine Art of Mixing Drinks'.
Comment: A little absinthe goes a long way and may even chase your gloom away.

GLOOM LIFTER

★★★★☆

Glass: Coupe
Garnish: Lemon wedge
Method: DRY SHAKE all ingredients (without ice). SHAKE again with ice and fine strain into chilled glass.

1½	shots	Teeling Small Batch Irish whiskey
½	shot	Martell VSOP Médaillon cognac
⅓	shot	Pomegranate / grenadine syrup (2:1)
1	shot	Freshly squeezed lemon juice
¼	shot	Sugar syrup (2 sugar to 1 water)
½	fresh	Egg white

Comment: An Irish whiskey and cognac sour served straight-up.

GLORIA ⬤─🗝

★★★⯪☆

Glass: Flute
Garnish: Lemon zest twist
Method: SHAKE first 3 ingredients with ice and fine strain into chilled glass. TOP with champagne.

1	shot	Patrón reposado tequila
½	shot	Freshly squeezed lemon juice
½	shot	Sugar syrup (2 sugar to 1 water)
Top with		G.H. Mumm Brut Cordon Rouge champagne

Comment: A tequila sour topped with champagne or a tequila French 75.

GODFATHER COCKTAIL

★★★⯪☆

Glass: Old-fashioned
Garnish: Garnish with a twist of orange.
Method: STIR all ingredients with ice and strain into ice-filled glass.

| 2 | shots | Dewar's 12 Year Old Scotch whisky |
| 1 | shot | Disaronno Originale amaretto |

Comment: Scotch diluted and sweetened with almond - simple but good.

GODFREY

★★★★☆

Glass: Old-fashioned
Garnish: Blackberries
Method: MUDDLE blackberries in base if shaker. Add other ingredients, SHAKE with ice and fine strain into glass filled with crushed ice.

6	fresh	Blackberries
1½	shots	Martell VSOP Médaillon cognac
½	shot	Grand Marnier Cordon Rouge
¼	shot	Lejay Crème de Mûre liqueur
¼	shot	Freshly squeezed lemon juice
¼	shot	Sugar syrup (2 sugar to 1 water)

Origin: Created by Salvatore Calabrese at the Library Bar, Lanesborough Hotel, London, England.
Comment: Well balanced with a rich blackberry flavour.

GOLD MEDALION

★★★⯪☆

Glass: Martini
Garnish: Orange zest twist (flamed)
Method: SHAKE all ingredients with ice and fine strain into chilled glass.

1½	shots	Martell VSOP Médaillon cognac
1	shot	Galliano L'Autentico liqueur
1½	shots	Freshly squeezed orange juice
¼	shot	Freshly squeezed lime juice
½	fresh	Egg white (optional)

Comment: Gold by name and golden in colour. Frothy, orange fresh and cognac based.

GOLD RUSH

★★★★½

Glass: Old-fashioned
Garnish: Lemon zest twist (discarded) & lemon wedge
Method: SHAKE all ingredients with ice and fine strain into ice-filled glass.

2	shot	Bourbon whiskey
¾	shot	Freshly squeezed lemon juice
¾	shot	Honey water (3:1)

Comment: A Whiskey Sour made with honey syrup in place of sugar.
Origin: Recipe envisaged by T. J. Siegel one night in 2001 at Milk & Honey, New York City, USA where it was first made by Sasha Petraske.

THE GOLD RUSH

★★★★½

Glass: Coupe
Garnish: Luxardo Maraschino cherry
Method: SHAKE all ingredients with ice and fine strain into chilled glass.

1½	shots	King's Ginger Liqueur
1	shot	Bourbon whiskey
¼	shot	Freshly squeezed lime juice
¼	shot	Freshly squeezed lemon juice

Comment: The name refers to this sweet 'n' sour, zesty ginger drinks golden hue. Bourbon provides the base while lemon and lime balance the flavoursome sweet ginger liqueur

GOLDEN BRONX

★★★½☆

Glass: Martini
Garnish: Luxardo Maraschino cherry
Method: SHAKE all ingredients with ice and fine strain into chilled glass.

2 shots Rutte Dry Gin
¼ shot Martini Extra Dry vermouth
¼ shot Martini Rosso vermouth
1 shot Freshly squeezed orange juice
⅛ shot Sugar syrup (2 sugar to 1 water)
1 fresh Egg yolk

Origin: A vintage cocktail adapted from the classic Bronx Cocktail, created in 1906 by Johnny Solon, a bartender at New York's Waldorf-Astoria Hotel, and named after the newly opened Bronx Zoo.
Comment: A Bronx made 'golden' by the addition of egg yolk.

GOLDEN CADILLAC

★★★½☆

Glass: Martini
Garnish: Dust with grated nutmeg
Method: SHAKE all ingredients with ice and fine strain into chilled glass.

1	shot	White crème de cacao liqueur
½	shot	Galliano L'Autentico liqueur
1½	shots	Freshly squeezed orange juice
½	shot	Single cream / half-and-half
½	shot	Milk
2	dash	Angostura Orange Bitters

Origin: To quote the bar's own website (poorreds.com), "Poor Red's is world famous for its Golden Cadillacs. Cadillacs are a blended drink of Galliano liqueur, half and half, white créme de cacao and ice, most delicious! We are the largest consumer of Galliano in the world. Also famous for our award winning barbecued ribs."
Comment: This shaken recipe includes orange juice and this gives the otherwise anaemic looking drink its namesake golden hue. The addition of orange bitters helps balance the drink and boost the orange flavour.

GOLDEN DAWN

★★★★☆

Glass: Martini
Garnish: Orange zest twist
Method: SHAKE first five ingredients with ice and fine strain into chilled glass. Carefully POUR grenadine into centre of drink so that it sinks to create a sunrise effect.

¾	shot	Rutte Dry Gin
1	shot	Calvados brandy
1	shot	De Kuyper XO Apricot Brandy
1	shot	Freshly squeezed orange juice
2	dash	Angostura Aromatic Bitters
⅛	shot	Pomegranate / grenadine syrup (2:1)

Origin: Created in September 1930 by Tom Buttery at the Berkeley Hotel, London, England. There are now many versions of this classic drink (David Embury's 'The Fine Art of Mixing Drinks' lists three) but this is my favourite.
Comment: Although it spoils the sunrise effect, this drink is less tart if the syrup lying on the bottom is stirred into the drink (or, better, included when shaking).

GOLDEN FIZZ #1

★★★½☆

Glass: Collins (small 8oz)
Garnish: Lemon slice & mint sprig
Method: SHAKE first four ingredients with ice and fine strain into chilled glass. TOP with soda.

2	shots	Rutte Dry Gin
1	shot	Freshly squeezed lemon juice
½	shot	Sugar syrup (2 sugar to 1 water)
1	fresh	Egg yolk
Top with		Soda from siphon

Origin: Mid-19th Century classic.
Comment: You may have some raw egg inhibitions to conquer before you can enjoy this drink.

GOLDEN FIZZ #2

★★★★☆

Glass: Collins
Garnish: Orange slice & mint sprig
Method: STIR honey with gin in base of shaker until honey dissolves. Add next three ingredients, **SHAKE** with ice and strain into ice-filled glass. **TOP** with lemonade.

2	spoon	Runny honey
1½	shots	Rutte Dry Gin
1	shot	De Kuyper Triple Sec
1	shot	Freshly squeezed pink grapefruit juice
¼	shot	Freshly squeezed lemon juice
Top with		Lemonade / Sprite / 7-Up

Origin: Adapted from a drink created by Wayne Collins, UK.
Comment: More cloudy white than golden but a pleasant, refreshing long drink all the same.

GOLDEN GIRL

★★★★☆

Glass: Martini
Garnish: Grated orange zest
Method: SHAKE all ingredients with ice and fine strain into chilled glass.

1¼	shots	Bacardi Carta Ocho aged rum
1	shot	Fresh pressed pineapple juice
1	shot	Tawny port
¼	shot	Sugar syrup (2 sugar to 1 water)
1	fresh	Eggs (white & yolk)

Origin: Created by Dale DeGroff, New York City, USA. I've slightly increased the proportions of rum and port from Dale's original recipe.
Comment: This appropriately named velvety drink is a refined dessert in a glass.

GOLDEN IVY

★★★★☆

Glass: Coupe
Garnish: Orange zest twist
Method: STIR all ingredients with ice and strain into chilled glass.

2 shots Martell VSOP Médaillon cognac
½ shot Muscat wine
1 shot Cranberry juice

Origin: A Christmas cocktail created in October 2011 by yours truly at the Cabinet Room, London, England.
Comment: Cognac stirred with rich berry flavours of muscat wine along with the relatively dry berry flavour of cranberry.

GOLDEN MAC

★★★★⯪☆

Glass: Old-fashioned
Garnish: Orange zest twist
Method: MUDDLE ginger in base of shaker. Add honey and Scotch and **STIR** until honey dissolves. Add other ingredients, **SHAKE** with ice and fine strain into ice-filled glass.

2	slice	Fresh root ginger (thumbnail sized)
2	spoon	Runny honey
2	shots	Dewar's 12 Year Old Scotch whisky
¼	shot	Hazelnut liqueur
¼	shot	Butterscotch liqueur

Origin: Adapted from a drink discovered in 2003 at Golden Mac, Glasgow, Scotland.
Comment: Looks, and even tastes golden.

GOLDEN NAIL

★★★★☆

Glass: Old-fashioned
Garnish: Orange zest twist
Method: STIR all ingredients with ice and strain into ice-filled glass.

1½	shots	Bourbon whiskey
¾	shot	Southern Comfort liqueur
2	dash	Peychaud's aromatic bitters

Comment: A warming taste of southern hospitality.

GOLDEN RETRIEVER

★★★★⯪

Glass: Martini
Garnish: Orange zest twist
Method: STIR all ingredients with ice and strain into chilled glass.

1	shot	Bacardi Carta Blanca light rum
1	shot	Green Chartreuse liqueur
1	shot	Licor 43 liqueur

Origin: Created in 2002 by Dick Bradsell at Alfred's, London, England.
Comment: This powerful straw yellow cocktail offers a myriad of flavours. Benefits from the dilution of a long stir.

GOLDEN SCREW

★★★★⯪☆

Glass: Flute
Garnish: Physalis (cape gooseberry)
Method: POUR all ingredients into chilled glass and lightly stir.

½	shot	Martell VSOP Médaillon cognac
½	shot	De Kuyper XO Apricot Brandy
1	shot	Freshly squeezed orange juice
Top with		G.H. Mumm Brut Cordon Rouge champagne

Comment: A favourite with the Midas and others whose budgets extend beyond a Buck's Fizz or a Mimosa.

GOLDEN SHOT

★★★☆☆

Glass: Shot
Garnish: None
Method: Refrigerate ingredients then **LAYER** in chilled glass by carefully pouring in the following order.

½ shot   Drambuie liqueur
½ shot   Baileys Irish cream liqueur
½ shot   Dewar's 12 Year Old Scotch whisky

Comment: A whisky based layered shot with plenty of character.

GOLDEN SLIPPER

★★★★☆

Glass: Martini
Garnish: Apricot slice
Method: SHAKE all ingredients with ice and fine strain into chilled glass.

1½ shots   Yellow Chartreuse liqueur
1½ shots   De Kuyper XO Apricot Brandy
1   fresh   Egg yolk

Comment: Rich in colour and equally rich in flavour. A dessert with a punch.

GOLDEN WAVE

★★★★☆

Glass: Sling
Garnish: Pineapple wedge
Method: BLEND all ingredients with a 12oz scoop of crushed ice and serve with straws.

1   shot   Bacardi Carta Blanca light rum
½ shot   De Kuyper Triple Sec
½ shot   Taylor's Velvet Falernum liqueur
1   shot   Fresh pressed pineapple juice
¾ shot   Freshly squeezed lemon juice

Origin: A Tiki drink created in 1969 by Jose 'Joe' Yatco at China Trader, California, USA.
Comment: Rum laced fruit served long and cold with crushed ice.

GOLF COCKTAIL

★★★★☆

Glass: Martini
Garnish: Orange zest twist
Method: STIR all ingredients with ice and strain into chilled glass.

2   shots   Rutte Dry Gin
1   shot   Martini Extra Dry vermouth
1   dash   Angostura Aromatic Bitters

Comment: A 'wet' Martini with bitters.

GOOD HOPE PLANTATION RUM PUNCH

★★★★☆

Glass: Old-fashioned
Garnish: Luxardo Maraschino cherry
Method: SHAKE first four ingredients with ice and strain into glass filled with crushed ice. **TOP** with soda.

1   shot   Pot still Jamaican rum
1   shot   De Kuyper Triple Sec
1   shot   Grand Marnier Cordon Rouge
1   shot   Freshly squeezed lime juice
Top with   Soda (club soda)

Origin: Originally made at the Good Hope Hotel, Falmouth, Jamaica. The Good Hope is an 18th Century country house set in a 2,000-acre plantation high in the lush landscape of Cockpit Country near Montego Bay.
Comment: A classic citrus laced, big flavoured, punch.

GOODY-GOODY

★★★☆☆

Glass: Martini
Garnish: Orange zest twist
Method: SHAKE all ingredients with ice and fine strain into chilled glass.

2 shots Rutte Dry Gin
1 shot Dubonnet Red
¼ shot Freshly squeezed lemon juice
½ shot Yellow Chartreuse liqueur

Origin: In W.J. Tarling's 1937 'Café Royal Cocktail Book Coronation Edition' the invention of this cocktail is credited to G. Bongarzoni.
Comment: Gin, lemon and Chartreuse. Not to everybody's taste.

GOOMBAY SMASH

★★★★☆

Glass: Collins
Garnish: Lime wedge
Method: SHAKE all ingredients with ice and strain into ice-filled glass.

2   shots   Pusser's Navy Rum (54.5%)
½ shot   De Kuyper Triple Sec
¾ shot   Coconut rum liqueur
3   shots   Fresh pressed pineapple juice
¼ shot   Freshly squeezed lime juice

Origin: The Goombay Smash is a speciality of Miss Emily's Blue Bee Bar in the Bahamas. Mrs Emily Cooper is now deceased but her daughter, Violet Smith, presides over her secret recipe.
Comment: Smashes are usually short drinks that include muddled mint, but this potent Tiki-style drink features rum, coconut and fruit.

GRAND 'O'

★★★★☆

Glass: Collins
Garnish: Lemon wedge & seasonal berries
Method: POUR soda water into ice-filled glass to half fill. Add lemon juice, orange juice and Grand Marnier. **TOP** with soda.

2¼ shots	Soda (club soda)
2¼ shots	Freshly squeezed orange juice
1 dash	Freshly squeezed lemon juice
1½ shots	Grand Marnier Cordon Rouge
1 wedge	Lemon (optional)

Comment: A fruity, zesty, light summery cocktail. Tip - pouring the soda first makes this refreshingly juicy drink easier to mix due to the specific gravities of the ingredients.

GRAND COSMOPOLITAN

★★★★★

Glass: Martini
Garnish: Orange zest twist (flamed)
Method: SHAKE all ingredients with ice and fine strain into chilled glass.

1 shot	Ketel One Vodka
1 shot	Grand Marnier Cordon Rouge
1½ shots	Cranberry juice
½ shot	Freshly squeezed lime juice
1 dash	Angostura Aromatic Bitters (optional)

Comment: The rich flavours of Grand Marnier shine through what is indeed a 'grand' Cosmopolitan.

GRAND DESIGNS

★★★★☆

Glass: Martini
Garnish: Rosemary sprig
Method: MUDDLE rosemary in base of shaker. Add other ingredients, **SHAKE** with ice and fine strain into chilled glass.

1 inch	Rosemary sprig
1½ shots	Rutte Dry Gin
1 shot	St-Germain elderflower liqueur
¼ shot	Martini Extra Dry vermouth
¾ shot	Fresh pressed pineapple juice

Origin: Created in 2008 for Grand Designs Live exhibition by yours truly, at the Cabinet Room, London, England.
Comment: Easy drinking and slightly sweet, dried and made altogether grander by the rosemary.

GRAND ESPIRIT

★★★★☆

Glass: Collins
Garnish: Orange & strawberry slices
Method: POUR soda into ice-filled glass to half fill. Add garnish, Grand Marnier and elderflower. **TOP** with more soda water.

3½ shots	Soda (club soda)
1 shot	Grand Marnier Cordon Rouge
¾ shot	Elderflower cordial

Comment: A long, refreshing orange and elderflower summery drink.

GRAND GINGER

★★★☆☆

Glass: Collins
Garnish: Lime wedge
Method: POUR all ingredients into ice-filled glass and lightly **STIR**.

1½ shots	Grand Marnier Cordon Rouge
1 wedge	Lime (fresh whole)
Top with	Ginger ale
3 dash	Peychaud's aromatic bitters

Comment: Ginger ale adds a spiced intensity to the rich Grand Marnier in this refreshing long drink.

GRAND MARGARITA

★★★★☆

Glass: Coupe
Garnish: Lime wedge & salt rim (optional)
Method: SHAKE all ingredients with ice and fine strain into chilled glass.

1½ shots	Patrón reposado tequila
1 shot	Grand Marnier Cordon Rouge
¾ shot	Freshly squeezed lime juice

Comment: A balanced and flavoursome Margarita with the rich cognac and orange notes of Grand Marnier adding to this drinks depth of flavour.

GRAND MIMOSA

★★★★☆

Glass: Flute
Garnish: Strawberry
Method: SHAKE first two ingredients with ice and strain into chilled glass. **TOP** with champagne.

1 shot	Grand Marnier Cordon Rouge
2 shots	Freshly squeezed orange juice
Top with	G.H. Mumm Brut Cordon Rouge champagne

Origin: The Mimosa was created in 1925 at the Ritz Hotel, Paris, and named after the Mimosa plant - probably because of its trembling leaves, rather like the gentle fizz of this mixture. The Grand Mimosa as shown here benefits from the addition of Grand Marnier liqueur.
Comment: As the name suggests, the orange of Grand Marnier heavily influences this drink. Basically a Buck's Fizz with more oomph.

GRAND MOJITO

★★★★☆

Glass: Collins
Garnish: Lime wedge
Method: POUR ingredients into glass and half fill with crushed ice. **CHURN** (stir) with bar spoon. Fill glass with more crushed ice and **CHURN** some more. Keep adding ice and churning until drink fills glass. Serve with straws.

1½ shots	Grand Marnier Cordon Rouge
½ shot	Freshly squeezed lime juice
8 fresh	Mint leaves

Comment: Grand Marnier adds its distinctive rich orange flavour to this twist on a Mojito.

GRAND PASSION

★★★☆☆

Glass: Martini
Garnish: Passion fruit
Method: Cut passion fruit in half and scoop out flesh into shaker. Add other ingredients. **SHAKE** with ice and fine strain into chilled glass.

1	fresh	Passion fruit
2	shots	Bacardi Carta Blanca light rum
1	shot	Pressed apple juice
½	shot	Sugar syrup (2 sugar to 1 water)
3	dash	Angostura Aromatic Bitters
½	fresh	Egg white

Comment: Are you lacking passion in your life? There's plenty in this fruity little number.

GRAND SAZERAC

★★★★☆

Glass: Old-fashioned
Garnish: None
Method: POUR absinthe into ice-filled glass and TOP with water. Leave the mixture to stand in the glass. Separately, SHAKE liqueur, bourbon and bitters with ice. Finally discard contents of absinthe-coated glass and fine strain contents of shaker into absinthe washed glass. (Note that there is no ice in the finished drink.)

½ shot Le Fée Parisienne absinthe
Top with Chilled water
1½ shots Grand Marnier Cordon Rouge
1½ shots bourbon whiskey
2 dash Angostura Aromatic Bitters
3 dash Peychaud's aromatic bitters

Origin: Created in 2004 by yours truly, London, England.
Comment: An orange twist on the classic Sazerac.

GRAND SIDECAR

★★★★½

Glass: Coupe
Garnish: Half sugar rim (if you must) and orange zest twist
Method: SHAKE all ingredients with ice and fine strain into chilled glass.

2	shots	Grand Marnier Cordon Rouge
1	shot	Freshly squeezed lemon juice
½	shot	Chilled water (omit if wet ice)

Origin: Created June 2005 by yours truly, London, England.
Comment: A riff on the classic Sidecar that's even simpler to make but equally tasty. Grand Marnier Cordon Rouge consists of 55% cognac so there is no need to add cognac to make a great Sidecar, simply add lemon juice. This drink benefits from a touch of dilution so also works well served strained over ice in an old-fashioned glass.

GRAND SLAM

★★★★☆

Glass: Martini
Garnish: Strawberry
Method: SHAKE all ingredients with ice and fine strain into chilled glass.

2	shots	Swedish Punch liqueur
1	shot	Martini Extra Dry vermouth
1	shot	Martini Rosso vermouth

Origin: Vintage cocktail of unknown origin.
Comment: This after dinner libation is slightly sweet but incredibly aromatic.

GRAND SOUR

★★★★☆

Glass: Old-fashioned
Garnish: Orange wheel
Method: DRY SHAKE all ingredients (without ice). SHAKE again with ice and fine strain into ice-filled glass.

2	shots	Grand Marnier Cordon Rouge
1	shot	Freshly squeezed lemon juice
½	shot	Freshly squeezed orange juice
½	fresh	Egg white (optional)

Comment: The rich cognac and oranges flavours of Grand Marnier shine in this balanced and flavoursome sour.

GRAND TONIC

★★★☆☆

Glass: Collins
Garnish: Lemon wedge
Method: POUR ingredients into ice-filled glass and stir.

1½	shots	Grand Marnier Cordon Rouge
1	wedge	Lemon
Top with		Tonic Water

Comment: Tonic water adds a slight bitterness to the rich Grand Marnier in this refreshing long drink

GRANDE CHAMPAGNE COSMO

★★★★½

Glass: Martini
Garnish: Orange zest twist
Method: SHAKE all ingredients with ice and fine strain into chilled glass.

1½	shots	Martell VSOP Médaillon cognac
¾	shot	Grand Marnier Cordon Rouge
½	shot	Freshly squeezed lemon juice
1	shot	Cranberry juice
½	fresh	Egg white

Comment: 'Grande Champagne' refers to the top cru of the Cognac region: this drink is suitably elite.

GRANDE ELIXIR COCKTAIL (NEW)

★★★★☆

Glass: Coupe
Garnish: Lemon zest twist
Method: SHAKE all ingredients with ice and strain into chilled glass.

1½ shots   Capucana cachaça
¾ shot   Yellow Chartreuse liqueur
½ shot   Honey water (3 honey to 1 water)
½ shot   Freshly squeezed lemon juice

Origin: Adapted from a drink originally served at Franklin Southie (now closed) in Boston, USA.
Comment: The name refers to the inclusion of Yellow Chartreuse which combines well with cachaça in this drink with honey and lemon juice.

GRANNY'S

★★★★☆

Glass: Martini
Garnish: Apple wedge
Method: SHAKE all ingredients with ice and fine strain into chilled glass.

1¾ shots   Bacardi Carta Blanca light rum
½ shot   Apple Schnapps liqueur
¼ shot   Cinnamon schnapps
1½ shots   Pressed apple juice

Comment: Apple, rum and cinnamon were made for each other.

GRAPE COCKTAIL #1 ⊙━━

★★★★☆

Glass: Martini
Garnish: White grapes
Method: MUDDLE grapes in base of shaker. Add other ingredients, **SHAKE** with ice and fine strain into chilled glass.

12 fresh   Seedless white grapes
2 shots   Ketel One Vodka
¼ shot   Sugar syrup (2 sugar to 1 water)

Origin: Created in 2004 by yours truly, London, England.
Comment: Simple but remarkably tasty.

GRAPE COCKTAIL #2

★★★★☆

Glass: Martini
Garnish: Red grapes
Method: MUDDLE grapes in base of shaker. Add other ingredients, **SHAKE** with ice and fine strain into chilled glass

12 fresh   Seedless white grapes
2 shots   Ketel One Vodka
¼ shot   Green Chartreuse liqueur

Comment: Green Chartreuse adds extra complexity to what would otherwise be simply be vodka laced grape juice.

GRAPE DELIGHT

★★★★☆

Glass: Martini
Garnish: Red grapes
Method: MUDDLE grapes in base of shaker. Add rest of ingredients, **SHAKE** with ice and fine strain into chilled glass.

12 fresh   Red grapes
2 shots   Rutte Dry Gin
½ shot   Sloe Gin liqueur
½ shot   Pressed apple juice
¼ shot   Sugar syrup (2 sugar to 1 water)
¼ shot   Freshly squeezed lime juice
1 dash   Angostura Aromatic Bitters

Comment: This rust coloured drink is fruity and delicate.

GRAPE EFFECT ⊙━━

★★★★☆

Glass: Martini
Garnish: Red & white grapes
Method: MUDDLE grapes in base of shaker. Add other ingredients, **SHAKE** with ice and fine strain into chilled glass.

12 fresh   Seedless white grapes
2 shots   Bacardi Carta Blanca light rum
1 shot   St-Germain elderflower liqueur

Comment: Delicately flavoured and heavily laced with rum.

GRAPE ESCAPE ⊙━━

★★★★½

Glass: Collins
Garnish: Mint sprig
Method: MUDDLE grapes and mint in base of shaker. Add cognac and sugar, **SHAKE** with ice and strain into glass filled with crushed ice. **TOP** with champagne, stir and serve with straws.

8 fresh   Seedless white grapes
5 fresh   Mint leaves
2 shots   Martell VSOP Médaillon cognac
½ shot   Sugar syrup (2 sugar to 1 water)
Top with   G.H. Mumm Brut
           Cordon Rouge champagne

Origin: Created in 2000 by Brian Lucas and Max Warner at Long Bar at The Sanderson, London, England.
Comment: A cracking drink - subtle and refreshing.

GRAPEFRUIT DAIQUIRI #1 ⊙━━

★★★★☆

Glass: Martini
Garnish: Luxardo Maraschino cherry
Method: SHAKE all ingredients with ice and fine strain into chilled glass.

2 shots   Bacardi Carta Blanca light rum
1½ shots   Freshly squeezed pink grapefruit juice
¾ shot   Sugar syrup (2 sugar to 1 water)

Comment: The flavours of rum and grapefruit combine perfectly - clean and fresh.

A B C D E F G H I J K L M N O P Q R S T U V W X Y Z

GRAPEFRUIT JULEP o—x

★★★★⯪

Glass: Collins
Garnish: Mint sprig
Method: STIR honey with vodka in base of shaker until honey dissolves. Add other ingredients, SHAKE with ice and strain into glass filled with crushed ice.

1 spoon Runny honey
2 shots Ketel One Vodka
4 fresh Mint leaves
½ shot Freshly squeezed lime juice
¾ shot Freshly squeezed pink grapefruit juice
½ shot Pomegranate / grenadine syrup (2:1)

Origin: Created by Dale DeGroff, New York City, USA.
Comment: Wonderfully refreshing. Bring on the sun.

GRAPPACINO

★★★⯪☆

Glass: Martini
Garnish: Coffee beans
Method: SHAKE all ingredients with ice and fine strain into chilled glass.

2 shots Bepi Tosolini Grappa di Moscato
½ shot Disaronno Originale amaretto
½ shot Sugar syrup (2 sugar to 1 water)
1 shot Espresso coffee (freshly made & hot)

Origin: Adapted from a drink created in 2006 by George Sinclair.
Comment: The character of the grappa shines through and is complemented by the amaretto and coffee.

GRAPPARITA

★★★⯪☆

Glass: Coupe
Garnish: Lime wedge
Method: SHAKE all ingredients with ice and fine strain into chilled glass.

2 shots Bepi Tosolini Grappa di Moscato
1 shot Pallini Limoncello
1 shot Freshly squeezed lemon juice
½ fresh Egg white

Origin: Adapted from a drink discovered in 2005 at Alfredo's of Rome, New York City, USA. The original called for a sour mix.
Comment: Grappa replaces tequila and lemon liqueur triple sec in this Italian twist in the classic Margarita.

GRAPPLE MARTINI

★★★★☆

Glass: Martini
Garnish: White grapes
Method: MUDDLE grapes in base of shaker. Add other ingredients, SHAKE with ice and fine strain into chilled glass.

7 fresh Seedless white grapes
2 shots Ketel One Vodka
¾ shot Sauvignon blanc white wine
1 shot Pressed apple juice
¼ shot Sugar syrup (2 sugar to 1 water)

Origin: Adapted from a recipe created in 2003 by Chris Setchell at Las Iguanas, UK.
Comment: A rounded, fruity Martini-style drink.

GRASSHOPPER

★★★⯪☆

Glass: Martini
Garnish: Mint leaf
Method: SHAKE all ingredients with ice and fine strain into chilled glass.

1 shot Green crème de menthe liqueur
1 shot White crème de cacao liqueur
1 shot Single cream / half-and-half
1 shot Milk

Origin: Created at Tujague's, the second oldest restaurant in New Orleans, which was opened in 1856 by Guillaume Tujague. Some time before he died in 1912, Guillaume sold the restaurant to Philibert Guichet, who won second prize in a prestigious New York cocktail competition for this drink.
Comment: It's hard not to like this creamy, minty after dinner treat.

GRATEFUL DEAD

★★★⯪☆

Glass: Sling
Garnish: Lime wedge
Method: SHAKE first 7 ingredients with ice and strain into ice-filled glass. TOP with soda and serve with straws.

½ shot Ketel One Vodka
½ shot Rutte Dry Gin
½ shot Bacardi Carta Blanca light rum
½ shot De Kuyper Triple Sec
½ shot Midori Green Melon liqueur
1 shot Freshly squeezed lime juice
½ shot Sugar syrup (2 sugar to 1 water)
Top with Soda (club soda)

Origin: An LA Iced Tea with Midori in place of berry liqueur.
Comment: Don't be put off by the lime green colour. This fruity, sweet 'n' sour drink is actually quite pleasant.

GREAT NORTHERN (NEW)

★★★★☆

Glass: Old-fashioned
Garnish: Half orange slice
Method: SHAKE all ingredients with ice and strain into glass filled with crushed ice.

2 shots Lysholm Linie Aquavit
¾ shot Lillet Blanc
½ shot De Kuyper Triple Sec
¾ shot Freshly squeezed lemon juice
½ shot Honey water (3 honey to 1 water)

Origin: Created in 2011 by Jessica Gonzalez at Death & Company, New York City, USA.
Comment: Your choice of honey will greatly influence this drink which harnesses the character of aquavit to great effect with white wine and citrusy notes.

GREEK CELERY COCKTAIL (NEW)

★★★★☆

Glass: Coupe
Garnish: Grind of pepper & celery stick
Method: SHAKE all ingredients with ice and fine strain into chilled glass.

1 ⅔ shots Skinos Mastiha
1 shot Rutte Dry Gin
⅔ shot Freshly extracted celery juice

Origin: A simplified version of a drink promoted by Skinos mastiha by yours truly in August 2015 at the Cabinet Room, London, England.
Comment: Celery and mastiha pair well, while gin adds a spirituous bite and botanical complexity. A small grind of pepper to finish adds a nuance of spice.

GREEK MARTINI (NEW)

★★★★☆

Glass: Martini
Garnish: Float mint sprig
Method: STIR all ingredients with ice and fine strain into chilled glass.

2 shots Rutte Dry Gin
½ shot Skinos Mastiha
¾ shot Martini Extra Dry vermouth
⅛ shot Ouzo 12

Origin: Created by yours truly in August 2015 at the Cabinet Room, London, England. (If only I were on a Greek island.)
Comment: Mastiha (which after all is botanically flavoured spirit) combines wonderfully with gin and dry vermouth. A splash of ouzo adds more Greek interest.

GREEK PIÑA COLADA

★★★★☆

Glass: Pineapple shell (frozen)
Garnish: Lime wedge
Method: BLEND ingredients with 12oz scoop of crushed ice. Pour into glass and serve immediately with straws.

2 shots Bacardi Carta Oro rum
1½ shots Yoghurt liqueur
2 wedge Pineapple (fresh)
½ shot Pineapple (ananas) liqueur
1 shot Coconut rum liqueur

Origin: Created in 2011 by yours truly at the Cabinet Room, London, England.
Comment: A yoghurt and rum based pineapple and coconut drink, and if your blender is sufficiently powerful, with tiny fragments of pineapple shrapnel.

GREEN BEAST (FRESH VERSION)

★★★½☆

Glass: Collins
Garnish: Cucumber slice
Method: MUDDLE cucumber in base of shaker. Add remaining ingredients, SHAKE with ice and strain into ice-filled glass.

3 slice English cucumber peeled
1 shot Le Fée Parisienne absinthe
½ shot Sugar syrup (2 sugar to 1 water)
1 shot Freshly squeezed lime juice
2¼ shots Chilled water

Origin: Adapted from a drink created in 2010 for Pernod Absinthe by Charles Vexenat, Paris, France.
Comment: A whole shot of absinthe tamed by lime, sugar and plenty of water. The cucumber is an essential freshening element.

GREEN BEETLE

★★★½☆

Glass: Martini
Garnish: Lemon zest twist
Method: POUR absinthe into ice-filled glass, TOP with water and leave to stand. Separately SHAKE other ingredients with ice. DISCARD contents of glass (absinthe, water and ice) and STRAIN contents of shaker into absinthe-coated glass.

½ shot Le Fée Parisienne absinthe
Top with Chilled water
2 shots Patrón reposado tequila
½ shot Agave syrup
½ shot Pallini Limoncello

Origin: Created by Alex Richer at Bar Red, London, England.
Comment: Tequila and lemon aromatized by absinthe.

GREEN DEACON

★★★½☆

Glass: Martini
Garnish: Grapefruit zest twist (discarded)
Method: MIST glass with spray or rinse of absinthe. Separately **SHAKE** all other ingredients with ice and **STRAIN** into absinthe-coated glass.

½ shot Le Fée Parisienne absinthe
1½ shots Rutte Dry Gin
¾ shot Sloe Gin liqueur
1 shot Freshly squeezed pink grapefruit juice

Origin: Created in 2009 by Jim Meehan at PDT, New York City, USA.
Comment: Actually red and not green, this is a most unusual combination of absinthe, gin, sloe gin and grapefruit.

GREEN DESTINY

★★★½☆

Glass: Old-fashioned
Garnish: Kiwi slice
Method: MUDDLE cucumber and kiwi in base of shaker. Add other ingredients, **SHAKE** with ice and fine strain into glass filled with crushed ice.

1	inch	English cucumber peeled
½	fresh	Kiwi fruit
2	shots	Zubrówka bison vodka
1½	shots	Pressed apple juice
¼	shot	Sugar syrup (2 sugar to 1 water)

Origin: Created in 2001 by Andrew Tiunos at Hakk, Warsaw, Poland.
Comment: Looks green and even tastes green, but pleasantly so.

GREEN DRAGON

★★★½☆

Glass: Martini
Garnish: Mint sprig
Method: SHAKE all ingredients with ice and fine strain into chilled glass.

2	shots	Rutte Dry Gin
½	shot	Green crème de menthe liqueur
¼	shot	Kümmel
¼	shot	Freshly squeezed lemon juice
3	dash	Peach bitters
½	shot	Chilled water (omit if wet ice)

Origin: Adapted from Harry Craddock's 1930 'The Savoy Cocktail Book'.
Comment: Mint, juniper, caraway and fennel make for an unusual cocktail that's conducive to fresh breath.

GREEN EYES

★★★½☆

Glass: Martini
Garnish: Lime wedge
Method: SHAKE all ingredients with ice and fine strain into chilled glass.

2	shots	Ketel One Citroen vodka
½	shot	Blue curaçao liqueur
1	shot	Freshly squeezed orange juice
½	shot	Freshly squeezed lemon juice
¼	shot	Almond (orgeat) syrup

Comment: A cross between a Blue Cosmo and a short Screwdriver.

GREEN FAIRY

★★★★☆

Glass: Martini
Garnish: Lemon zest twist
Method: SHAKE all ingredients with ice and fine strain into chilled glass.

1	shot	Le Fée Parisienne absinthe
1	shot	Freshly squeezed lemon juice
1	shot	Chilled water
¾	shot	Sugar syrup (2 sugar to 1 water)
1	dash	Angostura Aromatic Bitters
½	fresh	Egg white

Origin: Created in the 1990s by Dick Bradsell, London, England.
Comment: An Absinthe Sour style drink served straight-up.

GREEN FIZZ

★★★☆☆

Glass: Collins
Garnish: Lemon slice & mint sprig
Method: SHAKE first four ingredients with ice and strain into chilled glass. **TOP** with soda.

2	shots	Rutte Dry Gin
½	shot	Giffard Menthe Pastille liqueur
1	shot	Freshly squeezed lemon juice
¼	shot	Sugar syrup (2 sugar to 1 water)
Top with		Soda (club soda)

Origin: A mid-19th century classic.
Comment: Fresh, cleansing and refreshing - as only a minty Fizz can be.

GREEN FLY

★★★½☆

Glass: Shot
Garnish: None
Method: Refrigerate ingredients then **LAYER** in chilled glass by carefully pouring in the following order.

½	shot	Midori Green Melon liqueur
½	shot	Giffard Menthe Pastille liqueur
½	shot	Green Chartreuse liqueur

Origin: Created by Alex Turner at Circus, London, England.
Comment: A strong shot comprising three layers of different green liqueurs.

GREEN GLAZIER

★★★★☆

Glass: Martini
Garnish: Lime zest twist
Method: STIR all ingredients with ice and strain into chilled glass.

2	shots	Martell VSOP Médaillon cognac
¾	shot	Green Chartreuse liqueur
¼	shot	White crème de cacao liqueur
2	dash	Angostura Aromatic Bitters

Origin: Created in 2008 by Jamie Boudreau at Vessel, Seattle, USA.
Comment: This Martini-style drink doesn't take any prisoners. Go easy.

GREEN HORN

★★★⯪☆

Glass: Martini
Garnish: Pineapple wedge & Luxardo Maraschino cherry
Method: SHAKE all ingredients with ice and fine strain into chilled glass.

1½	shots	Bacardi Carta Ocho aged rum
1	shot	Fresh pressed pineapple juice
1	shot	Midori Green Melon liqueur
½	fresh	Egg white

Comment: Far more interesting and serious than the green hue from the melon liqueur would suggest.

GREEN MELON SOUR

★★★☆☆

Glass: Old-fashioned
Garnish: Lemon slice & cherry on stick (sail)
Method: SHAKE all ingredients with ice and strain into ice-filled glass.

2	shots	Midori Green Melon liqueur
½	shot	Freshly squeezed lemon juice
½	shot	Freshly squeezed lime juice

Comment: Neon green in colour and a tad on the sweet side, but each to their own.

GREEN PARK

★★★★⯪

Glass: Coupe
Garnish: Basil leaf
Method: Lightly **MUDDLE** basil in base of shaker (just to bruise). Add other ingredients, **SHAKE** with ice and strain back into shaker. **DRY SHAKE** (without ice) and fine strain into chilled glass.

6	fresh	Basil leaves
1½	shot	Old tom gin
1	shot	Freshly squeezed lemon juice
½	shot	Sugar syrup (2 sugar to 1 water)
3	dash	Celery bitters
½	fresh	Egg white

Comment: Lime green in colour under a frothy head, lemon fresh and botanical with gin, basil and a hint of celery.
Origin: Created in 2011 by Erik Lorincz at the American Bar, The Savoy, London, England.

GREEN POINT (NEW)

★★★★⯪

Glass: Coupe
Garnish: Orange zest twist
Method: STIR all ingredients with ice and strain into chilled glass.

2	shot	Straight rye whiskey
½	shot	Yellow Chartreuse
½	shot	Martini Rosso sweet vermouth
1	dash	Angostura Aromatic Bitters
1	dash	Orange bitters

Comment: Stirred and boozy with rye whiskey punch and spice smoothed by herbal Yellow Chartreuse and sweet vermouth.
Origin: Created in 2006 by Michael McIlroy at Milk & Honey, New York City, USA. Michael's original recipe calls for a lemon zest twist but we prefer with an orange zest twist.

GREEN SWIZZLE

★★★★⯪

Glass: Collins
Garnish: Crown with 3 dashes Angostura bitters over the drink's ice cap, a lime wedge and mint sprig
Method: POUR ingredients into chilled glass and two-thirds fill with crushed ice. **SWIZZLE** with a swizzle stick (or churn with a barspoon). Add more crushed ice to fill and **SWIZZLE** some more. Serve with straws.

1½	shots	Bacardi Carta Blanca light rum
½	shot	White overproof rum
¼	shot	Le Fée Parisienne absinthe
1	shot	Taylor's Velvet Falernum liqueur
⅛	shot	Green crème de menthe liqueur
½	shot	Freshly squeezed lime juice

Origin: The Green Swizzle was popular between 1890s and the 1930s during a period when the grand hotels of the Caribbean, such as the Queen's Park Hotel in Trinidad, were in their prime. This drinks legendary status is partly due to its featuring in 'The Rummy Affair of Old Biffy' by P.G. Wodehouse. Bertie Wooster sings its praises after enjoying a few at the Panter's Bar of the West Indian stand at the 1924 British Empire Exposition at Wembley, London.

We bow to David Wondrich, who in his 2015 'Updated and Revised Imbibe' says, "It is impossible to give a definitive recipe for the Green Swizzle" and he goes on to explain that there are versions based on rum, whiskey, old tom gin and jenever. While the recipe has numerous variations, it is certain that this swizzle was originally made green by dashes of absinthe bitters, rather than the green crème de menthe used in some modern interpretations of the drink. That said we like the way the minty liqueur combines with the absinthe that we've used as a wormwood bitters substitute. As for the base spirit, given the Green Swizzle's Caribbean heritage, white rum seems most appropriate (aged rum dirties the drink's pale green hue).
Comment: Robustly flavoured ingredients brought together harmoniously in a tall, most refreshing swizzle. Worthy of its legendary status.

GREENBELT

★★★⯪☆

Glass: Collins
Garnish: White grapes
Method: MUDDLE grapes in base of shaker. Add other ingredients, **SHAKE** with ice and fine strain into ice-filled glass.

12	fresh	Seedless white grapes
2	shots	BarSol Mosto Verde Italia pisco
1	shot	St-Germain elderflower liqueur
Top with		G.H. Mumm Brut Cordon Rouge champagne

Origin: Created in 2007 by yours truly, London, England.
Comment: Tastes as green as it looks. Floral and refreshing.

GRETA GARBO

★★★★☆

Glass: Coupe
Garnish: Star anise
Method: **SHAKE** all ingredients with ice and fine strain into chilled glass.

2	shots	**Bacardi Carta Blanca light rum**
¼	shot	**Luxardo Maraschino liqueur**
½	shot	**Sugar syrup (2 sugar to 1 water)**
1	shot	**Freshly squeezed lime juice**
⅛	shot	**Pernod anise**

Origin: The origins of this cocktail are unknown but it is named after the Swedish film actress and Hollywood star. Born Greta Lovisa Gustafsson on the 18th September 1905, Greta Garbo received three Academy Award nominations for Best Actress and an honorary one in 1954. She was ranked the fifth greatest female star of all time by the American Film Institute in 1999 behind Katharine Hepburn, Bette Davis, Audrey Hepburn, and Ingrid Bergman.

Garbo's career launched with the 1924 Swedish film The Saga of Gosta Berling. Although her role was minor, her performance caught the attention of Louis B. Mayer, chief executive of Metro Goldwyn Mayer (MGM) who signed her to his studio in 1925. The next year she appeared in MGM's silent film, Torrent, then Flesh and the Devil in 1926 which propelled her to international stardom. Garbo's first talking film was Anna Christie (1930) which MGM marketed with the catch-phrase "Garbo talks!" Garbo retired from the screen after the failure of Two-Faced Woman in 1941 at the age of 35 having appeared in 28 films. An avid art collector, she never married, had no children and lived alone shunning publicity. Greta Garbo died 15th April 1990.
Comment: A Daiquiri with delicate notes of maraschino and anise.

GREYHOUND

★★★☆☆

Glass: Collins
Garnish: Orange slice
Method: **POUR** ingredients into ice-filled glass and stir.

2	shots	**Ketel One Vodka**
Top with		**Freshly squeezed pink grapefruit juice**

Comment: A sour Screwdriver.

GREYHOUND'S TOOTH

★★★★½

Glass: Coupe
Garnish: Lemon zest twist
Method: **SHAKE** all ingredients with ice and fine strain into chilled glass.

¾	shot	**Bénédictine D.O.M. liqueur**
1½	shots	**Ketel One Vodka**
¾	shot	**Freshly squeezed pink grapefruit juice**
¼	shot	**Freshly squeezed lemon juice**
2	dash	**Grapefruit bitters**

Origin: Created in 2010 by Brandon Clements, San Francisco, USA.
Comment: Fresh grapefruit flavours form the backbone of this summer-fresh cocktail.

GROG

★★★★★

Glass: Old-fashioned
Garnish: Lime wedge
Method: **SHAKE** all ingredients with ice and strain into ice-filled glass.

2	shots	**Pusser's Navy Rum (54.5%)**
½	shot	**Freshly squeezed lime juice**
½	shot	**Light muscovado sugar syrup (2 sugar to 1 water)**
2	shots	**Chilled water**
2	dash	**Angostura Aromatic Bitters**

Origin: For over 300 years the British Navy issued a daily 'tot' of rum, sometimes with double issues before battle. In 1740, as an attempt to combat drunkenness, Admiral Vernon gave orders that the standard daily issue of half a pint of neat, high-proof rum be replaced with two servings of a quarter of a pint, diluted 4:1 with water. The Admiral was nicknamed 'Old Grogram' due to the waterproof grogram cloak he wore, so the mixture he introduced became known as 'grog'. Lime juice was often added to the grog in an attempt to prevent scurvy, lending British sailors their 'limey' nickname.

The 'tot' tradition, which started in Jamaica in 1665, was finally broken on 31st July 1970, a day now known as Black Tot Day, although by then the 'tot' had been reduced to a meagre two ounces.

We hate to let truth ruin a good story but drinks historians now say that grog emanates from an earlier period than Old Grogram.
Comment: Strong, flavoursome navy rum with a splash of scurvy-inhibiting lime. Properly mixed at the right dilution, this is a great drink. However, too many and you'll be groggy in the morning.

GROSVENOR COCKTAIL (NEW)

★★★★½

Glass: Coupe
Garnish: Lemon zest twist
Method: **STIR** all ingredients with ice and strain into chilled glass.

1½	shots	**Kamm & Sons**
1	shot	**Carpano Punt E Mes**
⅛	shot	**Islay single malt Scotch whisky**

Origin: Adapted from a recipe by Alex Kammerling. He originally used an extra 1/2 shot of Kamm & Sons but as it is his brand we'd not criticise him for a generous pour.
Comment: On the bitter side of bittersweet this is a great aperitif cocktail.

GROUNDS FOR DIVORCE

★★★½☆

Glass: Coupe
Garnish: Pineapple wedge
Method: **MUDDLE** pineapple in base of shaker. Add other ingredients, **SHAKE** with ice and fine stain into chilled glass.

4	wedge	**Pineapple (cored, skinned and chopped)**
2	shots	**Patrón reposado tequila**
½	shot	**Licor 43 liqueur**
½	shot	**Freshly squeezed lime juice**

Origin: Adapted from a recipe created by Jasper de Graaf.
Comment: Vanilla and herbal notes with pineapple and tequila.

THE GTO COCKTAIL

★★★★☆

Glass: Collins
Garnish: Pineapple wedge
Method: SHAKE all ingredients with ice and strain into ice-filled glass.

2	shots	Bourbon whiskey
½	shot	Disaronno Originale amaretto
½	shot	Freshly squeezed lemon juice
3	shots	Fresh pressed pineapple juice

Origin: Adapted from a recipe discovered in 2004 at Jones, Los Angeles, USA.
Comment: A fruity punch-like drink.

GUARD'S COCKTAIL

★★★★☆

Glass: Martini
Garnish: Orange zest twist
Method: SHAKE all ingredients with ice and fine strain into chilled glass.

1½	shots	Rutte Dry Gin
¾	shot	Martini Rosso vermouth
⅛	shot	Grand Marnier Cordon Rouge
1	dash	Angostura Orange Bitters

Origin: Vintage cocktail of unknown origins.
Comment: Old Guard but this Sweet Martini made sweeter with a dash of orange liqueur well deserves a place on modern cocktail lists.

GUARDABOSQUES

★★★★☆

Glass: Old-fashioned
Garnish: Pineapple wedge
Method: SHAKE ingredients with ice and strain into ice-filled glass.

1½	shots	Patrón reposado tequila
1	shot	Midori Green Melon liqueur

Origin: A popular cocktail in Mexico.
Comment: Don't let the lime-green hue of this drink put you off. It tastes considerably more adult than it looks.

GUILLOTINE

★★★★☆

Glass: Flute
Garnish: Seasonal berries
Method: POUR first two ingredients into glass and TOP with champagne.

½	shot	Lejay crème de cassis de Dijon
½	shot	Poire William eau de vie
Top with		G.H. Mumm Brut Cordon Rouge champagne

Comment: Add some life to your bubbly.

GUN CLUB PUNCH NO.1

★★★★☆

Glass: Cartridge mug or Collins
Garnish: Pineapple wedge, Luxardo Maraschino cherry & mint sprig
Method: BLEND all ingredients with 12oz scoop crushed ice. Serve with straws.

1	shot	Bacardi Carta Blanca light rum
1	shot	Pusser's Navy Rum (54.5%)
1	shot	Freshly squeezed lime juice
1½	shots	Fresh pressed pineapple juice
¼	shot	De Kuyper Triple Sec
¼	shot	Pomegranate / grenadine syrup (2:1)

Origin: Victor Bergeron specified that this drink should be served in one of his bespoke green cartridge mugs (pictured here). This recipe comes from 'Trader Vic's Bartender's Guide' (1972 revised edition).
Comment: This Trader Vic classic is balanced rather than sweet. Fruit juice and ice tone down rum's powerful blast.

GUN METAL BLUE COCKTAIL (NEW)

★★★★☆

Glass: Coupe
Garnish: Orange zest twist (coin sized)
Method: SHAKE all ingredients with ice and strain into chilled glass.

1½ shots Del Maguey VIDA mezcal
½ shot Blue curaçao liqueur
¾ shot Freshly squeezed lime juice
¼ shot Crème de pêche (peach) liqueur
⅓ shot Cinnamon sugar syrup (2:1)
¾ shot Chilled water (omit if wet ice)

Origin: Created in February 2015 by Mike Shain and Nicholas Bennett at Porchlight, New York City, USA. At Porchlight the original is made with house-made cinnamon syrup infused with gentian root to add a light bitterness.
Comment: Orange, peach and cinnamon subtly flavour this mezcal based margarita.

GUSTO

★★★★☆

Glass: Collins
Garnish: Apple slice
Method: MUDDLE grapes in base of shaker. Add other ingredients, SHAKE with ice and fine strain into ice-filled glass.

7 fresh Seedless white grapes
2 shots Patrón reposado tequila
¾ shot Agavero liqueur
2 shots Pressed apple juice

Origin: Created in 2003 by Thomas Gillgren at The Kingly Club, London, England.
Comment: A pleasing long drink flavoured with apple, grape and tequila.

GYPSY #1

★★★★☆

Glass: Martini
Garnish: Lime zest twist
Method: SHAKE all ingredients with ice and fine strain into chilled glass.

1½ shots	Rutte Dry Gin
¾ shot	St-Germain elderflower liqueur
¼ shot	Green Chartreuse liqueur
½ shot	Freshly squeezed lime juice

Origin: Created in 2007 by Dominic Venegas at Bourbon & Branch, San Francisco, USA.
Comment: Dominic describes this drink as "a little homage to the 'Last Word' cocktail".

GYPSY COCKTAIL

★★★★☆

Glass: Martini
Garnish: Rosemary sprig
Method: MUDDLE rosemary and raisins in base of shaker. Add other ingredients, SHAKE with ice and fine strain into chilled glass.

1	sprig	Rosemary sprig
10	dried	Raisins
2	shots	Rutte Dry Gin
½	shot	Sugar syrup (2 sugar to 1 water)
1	shot	Chilled water (reduce if wet ice)

Origin: Adapted from a recipe created by Jason Fendick in 2002 for Steam, London, England.
Comment: Jason's original recipe called for raisin infused gin and I'd recommend you make this drink that way if time permits.

GYPSY QUEEN #1

★★★★☆

Glass: Coupe
Garnish: Lemon zest twist (discarded)
Method: STIR all ingredients with ice and strain into chilled glass.

1½ shots Ketel One Vodka
½ shot Bénédictine D.O.M. liqueur
½ shot Martell VSOP Médaillon cognac
1 dash Angostura Aromatic Bitters

Origin: This recipe is adapted from one by drinks historian, David Wondrich (thanks Dave). The Gypsy originated in New York City's famed Russian Tea Room, which in 1938 published a vodka cocktail booklet which included this cocktail.
Comment: Vodka both fortifies and brings out subtle bready cereal notes in this complexly spiced cocktail.

GYPSY QUEEN #2

★★★★☆

Glass: Martini
Garnish: Orange zest twist
Method: STIR all ingredients with ice and strain into chilled glass.

1½ shots Ketel One Vodka
¾ shot Bénédictine D.O.M. liqueur
¾ shot Freshly squeezed orange juice
¼ shot Freshly squeezed lemon juice

Origin: A long lost classic.
Comment: Tangy, herbal, predominantly ora not overly sweet.

HABANERO

★★★★☆

Glass: Martini
Garnish: Orange zest twist
Method: MUDDLE ginger and chilli in base of shaker. Add other ingredients, SHAKE with ice and fine-strain into chilled glass.

1	slice	Red chilli (thin slice)
1	slice	Fresh root ginger (thumbnail sized)
2	shots	Bacardi Carta Blanca light rum
1	shot	Drambuie liqueur
¾	shot	Freshly squeezed lime juice
2	spoon	Honey sugar syrup
2	dash	Angostura Orange Bitters
½	fresh	Egg white

Origin: Created in 2008 by Giuliano Morandin at The Bar at The Dorchester Hotel, Hotel, London, England.
Comment: A Daiquiri-style drink with honey, ginger and chilli.

HABERDASHER

★★★★★

Glass: Wine
Garnish: Cocoa & mint leaf
Method: STIR first 3 ingredients with ice and strain into chilled glass. DRY SHAKE Chartreuse, cream and milk (without ice) and LAYER by carefully pouring over surface of drink.

1½ shots Bourbon whiskey
1 shot De Kuyper Dark crème de cacao
¼ shot Fernet Branca
¾ shot Green Chartreuse liqueur
¾ shot Single cream / half-and-half
¾ shot Milk

Origin: Discovered in January 2013 at Pouring Ribbons, New York City, USA.
Comment: Chocolaty bourbon with a freshening herbal blast of Fernet Branca, smoothed by sipping through a Chartreuse cream head. The ultimate after-dinner drink.

THE HAC

★★★★½

Glass: Coupe
Garnish: Pineapple wedge
Method: **MUDDLE** cardamom in base of shaker. Add other ingredients, **SHAKE** with ice and fine strain into chilled glass.

1 fresh Cardamom pod
1½ shots Patrón reposado tequila
½ shot Fresh pressed pineapple juice
½ shot Freshly squeezed lime juice
¼ shot Agave syrup
1 dash Angostura Orange Bitters

Origin: Discovered in 2009 at Cloud 23, Manchester, England.
Comment: Perhaps better billed as being a 'Pineapple and Cardamom Margarita'.

HAIR OF THE DOG

★★★★☆

Glass: Martini
Garnish: Dust with grated nutmeg
Method: **STIR** honey with Scotch until honey dissolves. Add other ingredients, **SHAKE** with ice and fine strain into chilled glass.

3 spoon Runny honey
2 shots Dewar's 12 Year Old Scotch whisky
1 shot Single cream / half-and-half
1 shot Milk

Origin: Traditionally drunk as a pick-me-up hangover cure.
Comment: This drink's name and reputation as a hangover cure may lead you to assume it tastes unpleasant. In fact, honey, whisky and cream combine wonderfully.

HAKKATINI

★★★★☆

Glass: Martini
Garnish: Orange zest twist
Method: **SHAKE** all ingredients with ice and fine strain into chilled glass.

1 shot Ketel One Vodka
1 shot Grand Marnier Cordon Rouge
¼ shot Campari Bitter
¾ shot Pressed apple juice

Origin: Adapted from a drink discovered in 2003 at Hakkasan, London, England.
Comment: Balanced bitter sweet orange and apple.

STAR RATINGS EXPLAINED

★★★★★+	OUTSTANDING	★★★★★	EXCEPTIONAL
★★★★½	EXCELLENT	★★★★☆	RECOMMENDED
★★★½☆	COMMENDED	★★★☆☆	MEDIOCRE
★★½☆☆	DISAPPOINTING	★★☆☆☆	PRETTY AWFUL
★½☆☆☆	SHAMEFUL	★☆☆☆☆	DISGUSTING

HAND GRENADE

★★★☆☆

Glass: Collins
Garnish: Whole lime with scored skin
Method: **SHAKE** all ingredients with ice and strain into glass filled with crushed ice.

1½ shots Rutte Dry Gin
1½ shots Bacardi Carta Blanca light rum
1½ shots Ketel One Vodka
1½ shots Midori Green Melon liqueur

Origin: This recipe bears little similarity to the notorious Hand Grenade served by the three Tropical Isle Bars and the Funky Pirate bar in New Orleans, USA. Marketed as 'New Orleans' most powerful drink' and served in long plastic half-yard hand-grenade shaped vessels this green melon flavoured proprietary drink is available as a pre-mix by mail order from www.tropicalisle.com. In the USA the operators of Tropical Isle have trademarked Hand Grenade so preventing other establishments not licensed by Tropical Isle from selling cocktails of this name.
Comment: A blend of white spirits sweetened and melon flavoured by the addition of green-coloured liqueur. Classy!

HANKY PANKY COCKTAIL

★★★★☆

Glass: Martini
Garnish: Orange zest twist
Method: **STIR** all ingredients with ice and strain into chilled glass.

1¾ shots Rutte Dry Gin
1¾ shots Martini Rosso vermouth
⅛ shot Fernet Branca
¼ shot Freshly squeezed orange juice

Origin: Created in the early 1900s by Ada 'Coley' Coleman at The Savoy's American Bar, London, for actor Sir Charles Hawtrey (1858–1923).

The original from Harry Craddock's 1930 'The Savoy Cocktail Book' is as follows:

"Hank Panky Cocktail
2 dashes Fernet Branca
1/2 Italian vermouth
1/2 Dry gin
Shake well and strain into cocktail glass. Squeeze orange peel on top".

Ada was quoted in a 1925 edition of The People newspaper as saying, "The late Charles Hawtrey... was one of the best judges of cocktails that I knew. Some years ago, when he was overworking, he used to come into the bar and say, "Coley, I am tired. Give me something with a bit of punch in it." It was for him that I spent hours experimenting until I had invented a new cocktail. The next time he came in, I told him I had a new drink for him. He sipped it, and, draining the glass, he said, "By Jove! That is the real hanky-panky!" And Hanky Panky it has been called ever since." Coley was the first Bar Manager of the Savoy's famous American Bar and the Hanky-Panky is her most famous creation. She perfected her craft at Claridge's Hotel and left to start at the Savoy in July 1903, where she stayed until her retirement in December 1924. During her tenure at the Savoy she served drinks to the likes of Mark Twain, the Prince of Wales and Prince Wilhelm of Sweden.
Comment: This is basically a Sweet Martini influenced by the addition of bittersweet and aromatic Fernet Branca. Although not classically used in the original recipe, the Hanky Panky is greatly improved by the addition of a dash of freshly squeezed orange juice. This slightly clouds the appearance of the drink but the hint of fruit freshens and balances the heavy Fernet Branca.

The addition of orange juice crept into our recipe for the Hanky Panky around 2010 but sadly we did not record who or what occasion inspired this variation.

HAPPY NEW YEAR

★★★☆☆

Glass: Flute
Garnish: Orange slice
Method: SHAKE first three ingredients with ice and fine strain into chilled glass. TOP with champagne.

¼	shot	Martell VSOP Médaillon cognac
¾	shot	Tawny port
¾	shot	Freshly squeezed orange juice
Top with		G.H. Mumm Brut Cordon Rouge champagne

Origin: Created in 1981 by Charles Schumann, Munich, Germany.
Comment: Reminiscent of fizzy, fruity claret.

HARD LEMONADE ⦿━☞

★★★★☆

Glass: Collins
Garnish: Lemon slice
Method: SHAKE first three ingredients with ice and strain into ice-filled glass. TOP with soda and serve with straws.

2	shots	Ketel One Vodka
2	shots	Freshly squeezed lemon juice
1	shot	Sugar syrup (2 sugar to 1 water)
Top with		Soda (club soda)

Origin: Discovered in 2004 at Spring Street Natural Restaurant, New York City, USA.
Comment: Refreshing lemonade with a kick. Great for a hot afternoon.

THE HARLEM

★★★★☆

Glass: Martini
Garnish: Luxardo Maraschino cherry
Method: SHAKE all ingredients with ice and fine strain into chilled glass.

2	shots	Rutte Dry Gin
¼	shot	Luxardo Maraschino liqueur
2	shots	Fresh pressed pineapple juice

Origin: Thought to date back to the Prohibition era and the Cotton Club in Harlem.
Comment: Soft and fruity. Careful, it's harder than you think.

HAROLD AND MAUDE

★★★★⯪

Glass: Coupe
Garnish: Orange zest twist
Method: SHAKE all ingredients with ice and fine strain into ice-filled glass.

1	shot	Dewar's 12 Year Old Scotch whisky
1	shot	Bacardi Carta Ocho aged rum
½	shot	Freshly squeezed lemon juice
¼	shot	Rose syrup
⅛	shot	Lavender sugar syrup

Origin: Adapted from a drink created in 2009 by Chase Mallen at Raines Law Rooms, New York City, USA.
Comment: Balanced, complex and very, very serious.

HARPOON COCKTAIL ⦿━☞

★★★⯪☆

Glass: Old-fashioned
Garnish: Lime wedge
Method: POUR ingredients into ice-filled glass and stir.

1½ shots Ketel One Vodka
2 shots Cranberry juice
¼ shot Freshly squeezed lime juice

Origin: Thought to be the forerunner to the Cosmopolitan. A 1968 bottle label from Ocean Spray's archives lists the Harpoon as a "new cocktail". It was originally launched as being 2 ounces Ocean Spray cranberry and 1 ounce vodka or light rum served "over the rocks or tall with soda. Suggested garnish: a splash of lime or lemon optional." In 1970, it was updated to also list gin as a possible base spirit.
Comment: Innocuously light in both flavour and alcohol. Add a shot of triple sec and you are well on your way to making a Cosmopolitan.

HARVARD

★★★★☆

Glass: Martini
Garnish: Lemon zest twist
Method: STIR all ingredients with ice and strain into chilled glass. TOP with a shot or so of chilled soda.

1½	shots	Martell VSOP Médaillon cognac
2	shots	Martini Rosso vermouth
2	dash	Angostura Orange Bitters (optional)
Top with		Soda from siphon

Origin: Recipe adapted from George J. Kappeler's 1895 'Modern American Drinks'.

In his 1931 book 'Old Waldorf Bar Days', Albert Stevens Crockett notes of this drink, "Named after a school for young men, whose site is contiguous to the Charles River, in a suburb of Boston. Alumni who drunk it sometimes lost the 'Harvard accent'."
Comment: Old-school, but approachably so. Dry and herbal. A great aperitif.

HARVARD COCKTAIL #2 (NEW)

★★★★☆

Glass: Coupe
Garnish: Orange zest twist
Method: STIR all ingredients with ice and strain into chilled glass.

1½	shots	Martell VSOP Médaillon cognac
1	shot	Byrrh Grand Quinquina
1	dash	Angostura Orange Bitters

Origin: Adapted from a drink created in 2015 by Tony Conigliaro at 69 Colebrooke Row, London, England.
Comment: Byrrh combines well with cognac in this variation on the classic Harvard.

HARVARD COOLER

★★★★☆

Glass: Collins
Garnish: Lime wedge
Method: SHAKE first 3 ingredients with ice and strain into ice-filled glass. TOP with soda, stir and serve with straws.

2	shots	Calvados brandy
1	shot	Freshly squeezed lime juice
½	shot	Sugar syrup (2 sugar to 1 water)
Top with		Soda (club soda)

Comment: Refreshing and not too sweet. Lime and sugar enhance the appley spirit.

HARVEY WALLBANGER

★★★★☆

Glass: Collins
Garnish: Orange slice
Method: POUR all ingredients into ice-filled glass.

2 shots Ketel One Vodka
½ shot Galliano L'Autentico liqueur
3½ shots Freshly squeezed orange juice

Origin: Legend has it that 'Harvey' was a surfer at Manhattan beach, California. His favourite drink was a Screwdriver with added Galliano. One day in the late sixties, while celebrating winning a surfing competition, he staggered from bar to bar, banging his surfboard on the walls, and so a contemporary classic gained its name.

However, an article in Bartender Magazine credits the creation to Bill Donner, the host of a house party held in the mid-sixties in Newport Beach, California. One of the guests, Harvey, was found banging his head the next morning, complaining of the hangover this drink induced.

Comment: Like the Screwdriver, the Harvey Wallbanger has sadly waned in popularity in recent years, probably due to it being served with packaged orange juice. When made with freshly squeezed orange juice and recently revived Galliano L'Autentico this is worthy of a renaissance.

HAVANA COBBLER

★★★★☆

Glass: Old-fashioned
Garnish: Lime twist or wedge
Method: SHAKE all ingredients with ice and strain into glass filled with crushed ice.

2	shots	Bacardi Carta Blanca light rum
1	shot	Tawny port
½	shot	Stone's green ginger wine
¼	shot	Sugar syrup (2 sugar to 1 water)

Comment: An unusual, spiced, Daiquiri-like drink.

HAVANA SPECIAL

★★★★☆

Glass: Old-fashioned
Garnish: Lemon zest twist
Method: SHAKE all ingredients with ice and strain into glass filled with crushed ice.

2	shots	Bacardi Carta Blanca light rum
½	shot	Luxardo Maraschino liqueur
1¾	shots	Fresh pressed pineapple juice

Comment: Daiquiri-like without the sourness. Fragrant and all too easy to drink.

HAVANATHEONE

★★★★☆

Glass: Coupe
Garnish: Mint leaf
Method: SHAKE all ingredients with ice and fine strain into chilled glass.

10	fresh	Mint leaves
2	spoon	Runny honey
2	shots	Bacardi Carta Blanca light rum
½	shot	Freshly squeezed lime juice
¾	shot	Pressed apple juice

Origin: Discovered in 2003 at Hush, London, England.
Comment: A flavoursome Daiquiri featuring honey, apple and mint.

HAWAIIAN COCKTAIL

★★★★☆

Glass: Martini
Garnish: Pineapple wedge & Luxardo Maraschino cherry
Method: SHAKE all ingredients with ice and fine strain into chilled glass.

1½	shots	Bacardi Carta Blanca light rum
½	shot	Disaronno Originale amaretto
½	shot	Southern Comfort liqueur
¾	shot	Freshly squeezed orange juice
1½	shots	Fresh pressed pineapple juice

Origin: Discovered in Las Vegas in 2004.
Comment: Sweet, tangy and fruity.

HAWAIIAN COSMOPOLITAN

★★★★☆

Glass: Martini
Garnish: Pineapple wedge
Method: SHAKE all ingredients with ice and fine strain into chilled glass.

2	shots	Ketel One Vodka
1	shot	Sour apple liqueur
1	shot	Pressed apple juice
½	shot	Freshly squeezed lime juice

Origin: Created in 2002 by Wayne Collins, UK.
Comment: Fresh, tangy and distinctly tropical.

HAWAIIAN EYE

★★★★☆

Glass: Collins
Garnish: Pineapple wedge & Luxardo Maraschino cherry
Method: BLEND all ingredients with two 12oz scoops of crushed ice. Serve with straws.

1	shot	Bacardi Carta Blanca light rum
1	shot	Bacardi Carta Oro rum
½	shot	Taylor's Velvet Falernum liqueur
½	shot	Freshly squeezed lime juice
½	shot	Sugar syrup (2 sugar to 1 water)

Origin: A Tiki drink created in 1963 by Tony Ramos at China Trader, California, USA, for the cast of the TV series of the same name.
Comment: Tropical, rum laced cooler.

HAWAIIAN MARTINI

★★★★☆

Glass: Martini
Garnish: Pineapple wedge & Luxardo Maraschino cherry
Method: SHAKE all ingredients with ice and fine strain into chilled glass.

1½	shots	Rutte Dry Gin
½	shot	Martini Extra Dry vermouth
½	shot	Martini Rosso vermouth
1½	shots	Fresh pressed pineapple juice

Origin: Adapted from a drink discovered in 2005 at the Four Seasons, Milan, Italy.
Comment: An aptly named fruity twist on the classic Martini.

HAWAIIAN SEABREEZE

★★★★☆

Glass: Collins
Garnish: Pineapple wedge
Method: SHAKE all ingredients with ice and strain into ice-filled glass.

2	shots	Ketel One Vodka
2½	shots	Cranberry juice
1½	shots	Fresh pressed pineapple juice

Comment: Easygoing, foam topped relative of the Seabreeze.

HAWAIIAN STONE SOUR

★★★★★

Glass: Old-fashioned
Garnish: Pineapple slice and cherry.
Method: SHAKE all ingredients with ice and fine strain into ice-filled glass.

1½	shots	Bourbon whiskey
¾	shot	Freshly squeezed lemon juice
1	shot	Fresh pressed pineapple juice
½	shot	Sugar syrup (2 sugar to 1 water)

Origin: Created in 2000 by Dale DeGroff at Blackbird Bar, New York City, USA.
Comment: The thinking man's Piña Colada.

HAYDENISTIC

★★★★☆

Glass: Martini
Garnish: Lime zest twist
Method: STIR all ingredients with ice and strain into chilled glass.

2	shots	Ketel One Vodka
⅛	shot	St-Germain elderflower liqueur
⅛	shot	Taylor's Velvet Falernum liqueur

Origin: Created in 2007 by Hayden Lambert at The Merchant Hotel, Belfast, Northern Ireland.
Comment: Extremely subtle, like a very complex Wet Vodkatini.

HAZELNUT ALEXANDER

★★★★☆

Glass: Martini
Garnish: Dust with chocolate powder
Method: SHAKE all ingredients with ice and strain back into shaker. **DRY SHAKE** (without ice) and fine strain into chilled glass.

1¾	shots	Martell VSOP Médaillon cognac
½	shot	De Kuyper Dark crème de cacao
¾	shot	Hazelnut liqueur
½	shot	Milk
½	shot	Single cream / half-and-half
2	dash	Angostura Aromatic Bitters

Origin: Created in 2005 by James Mellnor at Maze, London, England.
Comment: Great twist on a classic - the use of bitters is inspired.

HEAD SHOT

★★☆☆☆

Glass: Shot
Garnish: None
Method: Refrigerate ingredients then **LAYER** in chilled glass by carefully pouring in the following order.

¾	shot	Black sambuca liqueur
¾	shot	Green Chartreuse liqueur

Comment: Please drink responsibly.

HEARN COCKTAIL (NEW)

★★★★★

Glass: Coupe
Garnish: Orange zest twist
Method: STIR all ingredients with ice and strain into chilled glass.

1½	shot	Teeling Small Batch Irish whiskey
1½	shot	Martini Rosso vermouth
½	shot	Green Chartreuse
4	dash	The Dead Rabbit Orinoco Bitters
2	dash	Le Fée Parisienne absinthe
2	dash	Orange bitters

Comment: Stirred and boozy with Green Chartreuse and bitters adding herbal spice to Irish whiskey.
Origin: Adapted from a recipe created by Jack McGarry at The Dead Rabbit, New York City, USA.

HEARST MARTINI

★★★★☆

Glass: Martini
Garnish: Orange zest twist
Method: STIR all ingredients with ice and strain into chilled glass.

2	shots	Rutte Dry Gin
1	shot	Martini Rosso vermouth
1	dash	Angostura Orange Bitters
1	dash	Angostura Aromatic Bitters

Origin: This was supposedly a favourite of hacks who worked for the American newspaper magnate, William Randolph Hearst, and is believed to have been created at New York's Waldorf-Astoria. It is nicknamed 'The Disgruntled Journalist' and indeed, is not dissimilar to a Journalist with extra bitters.
Comment: A fantastically wet, sweet and aromatic Martini.

HEATHER JULEP

★★★★½

Glass: Julep Tin
Garnish: Mint sprigs
Method: SHAKE all ingredients with ice and strain into glass filled with crushed ice. CHURN (stir) the drink using a bar spoon. Top the glass with more crushed ice so as to fill it and churn again. Serve with straws.

12 fresh Mint leaves
2½ shots Dewar's 12 Year Old Scotch whisky
½ shot Drambuie liqueur
½ shot Sugar syrup (2 sug to 1 water)

Origin: Adapted from a drink discovered in 2001 at Teatro, London, England.
Comment: A Scottish twist on the classic bourbon based Mint Julep.

HEAVEN SCENT

★★★½☆

Glass: Martini
Garnish: Orange zest twist
Method: SHAKE all ingredients with ice and fine strain into chilled glass.

1½	shots	Vanilla infused Ketel One vodka
1½	shots	Old Krupnik
½	shot	Freshly squeezed lemon juice
¾	shot	Chilled water (omit if wet ice)

Origin: Discovered in 2003 at Oxo Tower Bar, London, England.
Comment: Honey, vanilla and lemon - reminiscent of a chilled, straight-up toddy.

HEAVENS ABOVE

★★★½☆

Glass: Collins
Garnish: Pineapple wedge
Method: SHAKE all ingredients with ice and strain into glass filled with crushed ice.

2	shots	Bacardi Carta Blanca light rum
¼	shot	De Kuyper Dark crème de cacao
¼	shot	Coffee liqueur
3	shots	Fresh pressed pineapple juice

Origin: A Tiki style drink adapted from a drink featured in Jeff Berry's 'Intoxica' and originally created circa 1970 at Top of Toronto, CN Tower, Toronto, Canada.
Comment: Slightly sweet, fruity rum - hard not to like.

HEDGEROW SLING

★★★½☆

Glass: Sling
Garnish: Lemon slice & seasonal berries
Method: SHAKE first four ingredients with ice and strain into glass filled with crushed ice. TOP with soda and then DRIZZLE blackberry liqueur over drink. Serve with straws.

1	shot	Rutte Dry Gin
1	shot	Sloe Gin liqueur
1	shot	Freshly squeezed lemon juice
½	shot	Sugar syrup (2 sugar to 1 water)
Top with		Soda (club soda)
¼	shot	Lejay Crème de Mûre liqueur

Origin: Created by Brian Duell at Detroit, London, England.
Comment: Rich, long, berry drink.

THE HEE BEE JEE BEES

★★★★½

Glass: Coupe
Garnish: Lime wedge
Method: SHAKE all ingredients with ice and fine strain into chilled glass.

1 shot 42 Below Manuka Honey Vodka
1 shot Patrón reposado tequila
¾ shot Agave Sec Liqueur
⅓ shot Freshly squeezed lime juice
3 drop Bob's Lavender bitters

Origin: Created in 2010 by yours truly at the Cabinet Room, London, England and named after Julio Bermejo & Jacob Briars. Julio is an tequila ambassador and Jacob was promoting 42 Below honey vodka.
Comment: A Margarita with a touch of honey vodka and agave enriched orange liqueur.

HEISENBERG COCKTAIL (NEW)

★★★★⯪

Glass: Coupe
Garnish: Blue coloured salt rim
Method: SHAKE all ingredients with ice and fine strain into chilled glass. (Most appropriately served in a science beaker.)

1⅓ shots Patrón anejo tequila
½ shot Del Maguey VIDA mezcal
⅓ shot Luxardo Maraschino liqueur
⅔ shot Freshly squeezed lime juice
¼ shot Lavender sugar syrup
¼ shot Blue curaçao liqueur
⅛ shot Sugar syrup (2 sugar to 1 water)

Origin: Adapted from a drink created in September 2013 at Mark's Bar, Soho, London to celebrate the last episode of Breaking Bad inspired by the show's blue crystal meth.
Comment: Like a suitably complex chemistry experiment this Margarita-like cocktail has seven ingredients with mezcal adding smoky notes to tequila and a trio of liqueurs balancing lime sourness.

HEMINGWAY

★★★☆☆

Glass: Flute
Garnish: Star anise
Method: POUR anis into chilled glass. TOP with champagne.

1 shot Pernod anise
Top with G.H. Mumm Brut Cordon Rouge champagne

Origin: Created at Cantineros' Club, the famous Cuban bar school.
Comment: Why dilute your anis with water when you can use champagne.

HEMINGWAY MARTINI

★★★★☆

Glass: Martini
Garnish: Luxardo Maraschino cherry
Method: SHAKE all ingredients with ice and fine strain into chilled glass.

2 shots Ketel One Oranje vodka
¼ shot Vanilla schnapps
1 shot Freshly squeezed pink grapefruit juice
¼ shot Martini Extra Dry vermouth
¼ shot Maraschino syrup (from cherry jar)

Origin: Adapted from a drink created in 2005 by Claire Smith, London, England.
Comment: A fresh and refreshing orange and vanilla influenced Vodkatini.

HEMINGWAY SPECIAL DAIQUIRI (PAPA DOBLE)

★★★★⯪

Glass: Martini (large 10oz)
Garnish: Lime wedge
Method: SHAKE all ingredients with ice and fine strain into chilled glass.

3½ shots Bacardi Carta Blanca light rum
1 shot Freshly squeezed pink grapefruit juice
¾ shot Luxardo Maraschino liqueur
1 shot Freshly squeezed lime juice
½ shot Sugar syrup (2 sugar to 1 water)

Origin: Created by Constantino (Constante) Ribalaigua Vert, the legendary head bartender of La Floridita, Havana, Cuba for Ernest Hemingway, after the great man wandered into the bar to use the toilet. When Hemingway tried the Floridita's standard frozen Daiquiri, he is quoted as saying, "That's good but I prefer it without sugar and with double rum" - so the Hemingway Special was born.

Hemingway suffered from haemochromotosis (a rare hereditary disease that can lead to diabetes) from which his father also suffered, hence his aversion to sugar. The original version was exactly as Hemingway requested a Daiquiri without sugar and heavy on the rum, basically rum shaken with a splash of lime juice. Years later after he took over the position of Head Bartender at La Floridita, Antonio Meilan added maraschino and grapefruit juice into the drink. Today sugar is commonly also added to balance this drink and make it more palatable to people with less sour palates than Hemingway.

Hemingway was affectionately known as 'Papa' in Cuba and this drink was originally named 'Daiquiri Like Papa' and then later 'Papa Doble'. After Meilan added maraschino and grapefruit the drink changed its name again to the Hemingway Special we recognise today.
Comment: A true Hemingway Special should be served without the addition of sugar. However, Hemingway had a hardened palate and more delicate drinkers may prefer the recipe above.

THE HERITAGE (NEW)

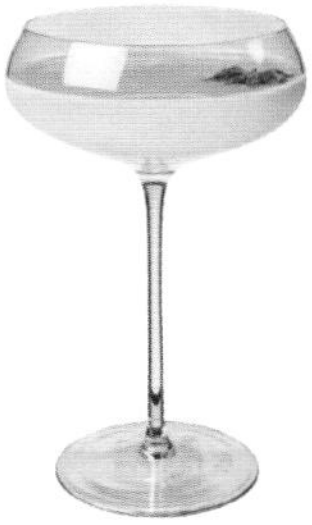

★★★★⯪

Glass: Martini
Garnish: Float star anise
Method: SHAKE all ingredients with ice and fine strain into chilled glass.

1 shot Ketel One Vodka
1 shot Grand Marnier Cordon Rouge
1 shot Pressed apple juice
½ shot Freshly squeezed lemon juice
¼ shot Anise syrup
¼ shot Sugar syrup (2 sugar to 1 water)

Origin: Adapted from a recipe created in May 2014 by Danish bartender (and winner of Diageo World Class 2012 Western Europe Final), Hasse Johansen from Apothex Bar. This cocktail was first made to celebrate the birthday of the creator of Ketel One Vodka, Carolus Nolet. If you'd like to make one and toast Carolus, his birthday is on the 15th of May.
Comment: Vodka fortifies and supports a well-balanced blend of orange zest, apple, lemon and star anise.

HESITATION

★★★☆☆

Glass: Martini
Garnish: Lemon zest twist
Method: SHAKE all ingredients with ice and fine strain into chilled glass.

2 shots Swedish Punch liqueur
1 shot Bourbon whiskey
¼ shot Freshly squeezed lemon juice
½ shot Chilled water

Origin: Vintage cocktail of unknown origin.
Comment: Lightly spiced and slightly on the sweet side.

HEY HEY COCKTAIL

★★★★☆

Glass: Coupe
Garnish: Lemon zest twist
Method: SHAKE all ingredients with ice and fine strain into chilled glass.

1 shot Martell VSOP Médaillon cognac
1 shot De Kuyper Triple Sec
1 shot Lillet Blanc
1 shot Freshly squeezed lemon juice

Origin: Hey Hey is a song by Eric Clapton and also a long-running variety television program on Australian television. However, this cocktail is thought to predate both. The origin of the Hey Hey cocktail is unknown but its original calling for 'Kina Lillet' dates the drink before 1986 as this is when the product's name was changed to Lillet Blanc.
Comment: A sidecar-like cocktail with a good balance between sweet (triple sec) and sour (lemon juice), fortified by cognac and smoothed by Lillet Blanc.

HI FALUTIN

★★★★★

Glass: Coupe
Garnish: Lemon zest twist
Method: STIR all ingredients with ice and strain into chilled glass.

1½ shots Bourbon whiskey
1 shot Swedish Punch liqueur
1 shot Byrrh Grand Quinquina

Origin: Adapted from a drink created in 2012 at Tooker Alley Bar, Brooklyn, USA by owner Del Pedro. To quote the menu, "This brash American Whippersnapper has been nattily clad by a classy old-world tailor. A puttin'-on-aits, high-steppin', diamond-pink-ed, cane-twirlin' dandy of a cocktail. Whippersnapper American Whiskey, Swedish Punsch, Byrrh and lemon essence."
Comment: Forceful and Manhattan-like in style but with sweet delicate influences from France and Sweden.

HI LADIES! 0⇀

★★★★☆

Glass: Coupe
Garnish: Mint sprig
Method: SHAKE all ingredients with ice and fine strain into chilled glass.

2 shots Ketel One Vodka
8 fresh Mint leaves
¾ shot Freshly squeezed lime juice
½ shot Sugar syrup (2 sugar to 1 water)

Origin: Adapted from a drink in Ted Saucier's 1951 book, 'Bottoms Up!'.
Comment: Basically this very tasty number is a 'Vodka Mojito' served straight-up.

HI LIFE SPRITZ (NEW)

★★★★☆

Glass: Collins
Garnish: Lime wedge squeezed and dropped in drink
Method: STIR three ingredients with ice and strain into ice-filled glass. **TOP** with soda and lightly stir.

1½ shots Rutte Dry Gin
1½ shots Chardonnay (Chablis) white wine
1½ shots St-Germain elderflower liqueur
Top with Soda (club soda)

Origin: Created on 30th May 2014 by yours truly at the Cabinet Room, London, England for British Airways' BA High Life Magazine.
Comment: Borrowing its name from both BA High Life magazine and the Hi-ball glass it is served in, this refreshing long drink combines the botanical complexity of gin with honeyed elderflower liqueur balanced by white wine acidity.

HIBISCUS MARGARITA

★★★★☆

Glass: Martini
Garnish: Wild hibiscus flower
Method: SHAKE all ingredients with ice and fine strain into chilled glass.

2 shots Patrón reposado tequila
1 shot Freshly squeezed lime juice
1 shot Hibiscus tea syrup

Comment: Hibiscus combines wonderfully with tequila in this flavoursome Margarita.

HIGH SOCIETY COCKTAIL (NEW)

★★★★☆

Glass: Coupe
Garnish: Mint leaf pegged to rim
Method: THROW all ingredients with ice and strain into chilled glass.

2 shots Dewar's 12 Year Old Scotch whisky
⅓ shot Giffard Menthe Pastille liqueur
⅛ shot Fernet Branca

Origin: Adapted from a 2015 recipe by Maxime Verrier at Pollen Street Social, London who named this drink, inspired by the classic Stinger and Brandy Cocktail, after the eponymous 1956 movie ' High Society' starring Frank Sinatra. The Stinger cocktail also appeared in the film.
Comment: Minty fresh Scotch whisky with herbal complexity courtesy of Fernet Branca.

HIGHBALL (GENERIC NAME) 0—⟍

★★★★⯪

Glass: Collins
Garnish: Orange, lime or lemon slice (as appropriate to the spirit or the carbonate)
Method: POUR spirit into ice-filled glass and **TOP** with a carbonated soft drink (ginger ale, soda or tonic water). Stir gently so as not to kill the fizz.

2 shots Brandy, whisk(e)y, gin, rum etc.
Top with Ginger ale, soda, tonic water or other carbonated mixer

Origin: Scotch & Soda, Gin & Tonic, Whiskey & Ginger, Vodka & Tonic and Rum & Coke are all examples of Highball cocktails. Highballs are a type of simple cocktail with only two ingredients, normally a spirit and a carbonate, served in a tall ice-filled glass (often referred to as a highball glass).

Unlike Rickeys, Collinses and Fizzes, Highballs do not contain citrus fruit juice.

In his 1934 'The Official Mixer's Guide', Patrick Gavin Duffy comments, "It is one of my fondest hopes that the highball will again take its place as the leading American Drink. I admit to being prejudiced about this - it was I who first brought the highball to America, in 1895. Although the distinction is claimed by the Parker House in Boston, I was finally given due credit for this innovation in the New York Times of not many years ago."

That New York Times reference appears to be a letter written by Duffy on 22nd October 1927 to the Editor in response to an editorial piece in the paper. He starts, "An editorial in The Times says that the Adams House, Boston, claims to have served the first Scotch highball in this country. This claim is unfounded." He goes on to tell of how in 1894 he opened a little café next the old Lyceum in New York City and that in the Spring of that year, an English actor and regular patrón, E. J. Ratcliffe, one day asked for a Scotch and soda. At that time Duffy did not carry Scotch but this request and the growing number of English actors frequenting his bar led Duffy to order five cases of Usher's from Park & Tilford. Duffy claims that when the shipment arrived he "sold little but Scotch highballs", consisting of 'Scotch, a lump of ice and a bottle of club soda'. His letter finishes, "Shortly afterward every actor along Broadway, and consequently every New Yorker who frequented the popular bars, was drinking Scotch highballs. In a few years other Scotch distillers introduced their brands and many were enriched by the quantity consumed in this country. Actors on tour, and members of the Ancient and Honorable Artillery of Boston, who came here annually to attend the Old Guard Ball, brought the new drink to the Adams House."

Duffy's letter to The New York Times mentions Adam House in Boston while the reference in his subsequent book talks of 'Parker House'. Both are plausible Boston locations but does this confusion mean we should not take any of Duffy's claims for being the first to make Scotch Highballs in America seriously?

The Times merely published Duffy's letter to the editor, the paper did not substantiate or even 'give credit' to his claims.

In his 2003 'The Joy of Mixology', Gary Regan explains that "Highball is an old railroad term for the ball indicator connected to a float inside a steam train's water tank which told the conductor that there was enough water in the tank and so the train could proceed. Apparently when the train was set to depart, the conductor would give the highball - two short whistle blows and one long". Gary explains that this term was apt as the drinks consist of two shots of liquor and a long pour of mixer.
Comment: Simple, but simplicity can be beautiful.

HIGHLAND SAZERAC

★★★★⯪

Glass: Old-fashioned
Garnish: Lemon zest twist
Method: POUR Chartreuse into glass and twirl to coat inside with liqueur, fill glass with ice and stand to one side. Separately, **STIR** other ingredients with ice in mixing glass. **DISCARD** contents of glass (Chartreuse and ice), fill with fresh ice and strain contents of mixing glass.

½	shot	Green Chartreuse liqueur
1½	shots	Martell VSOP Médaillon cognac
½	shot	Speyside single malt whisky
¼	shot	Sugar syrup (2 sugar to 1 water)
3	dash	Peychaud's aromatic bitters
2	dash	Angostura Aromatic Bitters

Origin: Adapted from a recipe by Don Lee, PDT, New York, USA.
Comment: A dash of malt gives a Highland influence to the Sazerac, also given a herbal note due to a generous splash of Chartreuse.

HIGHLAND SLING

★★★★☆

Glass: Sling
Garnish: Apple wedge
Method: SHAKE all ingredients with ice and strain into ice-filled glass.

1½	shots	Dewar's 12 Year Old Scotch whisky
1	shot	Chambord Liqueur
½	shot	De Kuyper XO Apricot Brandy
½	shot	Galliano L'Autentico liqueur
2	shots	Pressed apple juice

Comment: A surprisingly good combination of diverse flavours.

HIGHLANDER

★★★★⯪

Glass: Coupe
Garnish: Orange zest twist
Method: STIR all ingredients with ice and fine strain into chilled glass.

2	shots	Dewar's 12 Year Old Scotch whisky
1	shot	Martini Rosso vermouth
1	dash	Angostura Orange Bitters

Origin: Adapted from a drink discovered in 2010 at Campbell Apartment, New York City, USA.

Comment: A sweet Manhattan with orange bitters.

THE HIVE

★★★★☆

Glass: Martini
Garnish: Orange zest twist
Method: STIR honey with vodka until honey dissolves. Add other ingredients, **SHAKE** with ice and fine strain into chilled glass.

2	spoon	Runny honey
1	shot	Ketel One Vodka
1	shot	Old Krupnik
2	shots	Freshly squeezed pink grapefruit juice

Origin: Discovered in 2004 at Circus, London, England.
Comment: Sour grapefruit balanced by sweet honey.

HOBSON'S CHOICE (MOCKTAIL) 🗝

★★★☆☆

Glass: Collins
Garnish: Lime wedge
Method: SHAKE all ingredients with ice and strain into ice-filled glass.

2½ shots Freshly squeezed orange juice
2½ shots Pressed apple juice
1   shot Freshly squeezed lime juice
¼   shot Pomegranate / grenadine syrup (2:1)

Comment: A fruity, non-alcoholic cocktail.

HOCUS POCUS

★★★★½

Glass: Coupe
Garnish: Orange zest twist
Method: STIR all ingredients with ice and strain into chilled glass.

2   shots Rutte Dry Gin
¾   shot Carpano Antica Formula
¾   shot Orange Curaçao liqueur
⅛   shot Fernet Branca

Origin: Adapted from a drink discovered in 2010 at Forty Four, New York City, USA. Hocus Pocus by the Dutch rock band Focus was a chart-topper both sides of the Atlantic in 1971. Famous for its yodelling, whistling, accordion and flute this is a tune that has to heard to be believed.
Comment: Bittersweet with gin's botanical complexity and orange zest freshness.

HOFFMAN HOUSE

★★★★☆

Glass: Martini
Garnish: Lemon zest twist
Method: SHAKE all ingredients with ice and fine strain into chilled glass.

2½ shots Rutte Dry Gin
½   shot Martini Extra Dry vermouth
2   dash Angostura Orange Bitters

Origin: Apparently the house cocktail at Manhattan's Hoffman House in the 1880s.
Comment: A shaken Wet (5:1) Martini with orange bitters.

THE HOLLAND HOUSE #1 (KAPPELER'S RYE BASED)

★★★½☆

Glass: Coupe
Garnish: Orange zest twist
Method: STIR all ingredients with ice and fine strain into chilled glass.

2   shots Straight rye whiskey
½   shot De Kuyper Triple Sec
2   dash Peychaud's aromatic bitters
½   shot Chilled water (omit if wet ice)

Origin: Recipe adapted from George J. Kappeler's 1895 book ' Modern American Drinks: How To Mix and Serve All Kinds of Cups and Drinks'. Kappeler stipulates, "Mixing-glass half-full fine ice, two dashes Peychaud bitters, one-half pony Eau de Vie d'Oranges,

one and a half pony old rye whiskey, a piece lemon peel. Mix. Moisten the edge of cocktail glass with lemon, dip in sugar. Strain the cocktail into prepared glass."

There are numerous versions of the Holland House but Kappeler was head barman at the Holland House Hotel so was well placed to recount how the hotel's signature cocktail was made.

Orange eau de vie, or distillate of oranges is not readily available but clear sweetened orange distillate in the shape of triple sec is, hence we have used as a substitute in this drink.
Comment: Spicy rye whiskey sweetened and given an orange accent by a splash of triple sec and heightened with a couple of dashes of Peychaud's bitters.

THE HOLLAND HOUSE #2 (CRADDOCK'S LONDON DRY BASED)

★★★★☆

Glass: Coupe
Garnish: Lemon zest twist
Method: MUDDLE pineapple in base of shaker. Add other ingredients, SHAKE with ice and fine strain into chilled glass.

4 wedge Pineapple (fresh)
2 shots Rutte Dry Gin
¾ shot Martini Extra Dry vermouth
¼ shot Luxardo Maraschino liqueur
½ shot Freshly squeezed lemon juice

Origin: Recipe adapted from Harry Craddock's 1930 book, ' The Savoy Cocktail Book'. Prior to heading up the American Bar at The Savoy Hotel in London, Craddock worked in New York's Holland House Hotel where this was the signature cocktail.

Craddock's Holland House recipe is very different to that of George J. Kappeler, who preceded Craddock at The Holland House and wrote his cocktail book 35 years earlier.
Comment: Pineapple, maraschino, gin and vermouth makes for a dry fruit Aviation-style drink.

THE HOLLAND HOUSE #3 (GENEVER BASED)

★★★★☆

Glass: Coupe
Garnish: Lemon zest twist
Method: STIR all ingredients with ice and fine strain into chilled glass.

1¾ shot Rutte Old Simon genever
¾   shot Martini Extra Dry vermouth
½   shot Freshly squeezed lemon juice
¼   shot Luxardo Maraschino liqueur

Comment: Genever adds its own complexity to this Dutch version of the classic Holland House.
Origin: This genever based version of The Holland House was practically unknown before 2008 but it has since been rescued from obscurity.

HOLLYWOOD o━━

★★★★★

Glass: Flute
Garnish: Dust with grated nutmeg
Method: DRY SHAKE all ingredients without ice to emulsify. **SHAKE** again with ice and fine strain into chilled glass.

1½ shots Bacardi Carta Blanca light rum
½ shot Freshly squeezed pink grapefruit juice
⅛ shot Pomegranate / grenadine syrup (2:1)
½ fresh Egg white

Comment: This drink is deliciously different. Rum, grapefruit and pomegranate smoothed with egg white and spice with nutmeg.

HONEY & MARMALADE DRAM o━━

★★★★½

Glass: Martini
Garnish: Orange zest twist
Method: STIR honey with Scotch in base of shaker until honey dissolves. Add other ingredients, **SHAKE** with ice and fine strain into chilled glass.

2 shots Dewar's 12 Year Old Scotch whisky
4 spoon Runny honey
1 shot Freshly squeezed lemon juice
1 shot Freshly squeezed orange juice

Origin: Recipe adapted from the Honeysuckle Daiquiri.
Comment: This citrusy drink seems to enrich and enhance the flavour of Scotch.

HONEY APPLE COCKTAIL

★★★★☆

Glass: Martini
Garnish: Lemon zest twist
Method: SHAKE all ingredients with ice and fine strain into chilled glass.

1½ shots Zubrówka bison vodka
¾ shot Old Krupnik
1¼ shots Pressed apple juice
¼ shot Freshly squeezed lemon juice

Comment: A classically Polish blend of flavours.

HONEY BEE o━━

★★★★☆

Glass: Martini
Garnish: Lemon zest twist
Method: STIR honey with rum in base of shaker until honey dissolves. Add other ingredients, **SHAKE** with ice and fine strain into chilled glass.

2 shots Bacardi Carta Blanca light rum
3 spoon Runny honey
½ shot Freshly squeezed lemon juice
¾ shot Chilled water

Origin: Adapted from 1949 copy of Esquire's 'Handbook for Hosts'.
Comment: Honey balances lemon juice in this rum cocktail.

HONEY BEE MINE (NEW)

★★★★★

Glass: Coupe
Garnish: Lemon zest twist (discarded) & honeycomb on rim
Method: STIR honey with rum in base of shaker to dissolve honey. Add vanilla essence, **SHAKE** with ice and fine strain into chilled glass. **TOP** with champagne.

2 shots Bacardi Carta Blanca light rum
3 spoon Runny honey
⅛ shot Vanilla extract
¾ shot G.H. Mumm Cordon Rouge Champagne

Origin: Created February 2014 by yours truly at the Cabinet Room, London, England.
Comment: Honey and vanilla laced with white rum and charged with champagne. Perfect for Valentine's Day.

HONEY BERRY SOUR

★★★★☆

Glass: Old-fashioned
Garnish: Lemon wedge
Method: SHAKE all ingredients with ice and strain into ice-filled glass.

1½ shots Old Krupnik
¾ shot Lejay crème de cassis de Dijon
1 shot Freshly squeezed lemon juice
¼ shot Sugar syrup (2 sugar to 1 water)
½ fresh Egg white

Origin: Created by Tim Hallilaj, London, England.
Comment: More sweet than sour but berry nice.

HONEY BUBBLE o━━

★★★★½

Glass: Flute
Garnish: Mint sprig in top of hulled strawberry
Method: STIR honey with gin in base of shaker until honey dissolves. **ADD** other ingredients, **SHAKE** with ice and strain into ice-filled glass.

2 spoon Runny honey
1 shot Rutte Dry Gin
Top with Prosecco sparkling wine

Comment: Light and delicate, a great aperitif cocktail.

HONEY COBBLER

★★★★½

Glass: Goblet
Garnish: Mint sprig and berries
Method: STIR honey with Scotch in base of shaker until honey dissolves. **ADD** other ingredients, **SHAKE** with ice and strain into ice-filled glass.

2 spoon Runny honey
1½ shots Dewar's 12 Year Old Scotch whisky
1 shot Claret red wine
¼ shot Lejay crème de cassis de Dijon

Comment: Dry wine tannins and smoky scotch balance rich honey and blackcurrant liqueur.

HONEY DAIQUIRI

★★★★½

Glass: Martini
Garnish: Lime wedge
Method: **STIR** honey with rum in base of shaker until honey dissolves. Add other ingredients, **SHAKE** with ice and fine strain into chilled glass.

2 spoon Runny honey
2 shots Bacardi Carta Blanca light rum
½ shot Freshly squeezed lime juice
½ shot Chilled water

Comment: Sweet honey replaces sugar syrup in this natural Daiquiri. Try experimenting with different honeys. We favour orange blossom honey.

HONEY LIMEAID (MOCKTAIL)

★★★★☆

Glass: Collins
Garnish: Lime wedge
Method: Stir honey with lime juice in base of shaker until honey dissolves. **SHAKE** with ice and strain into ice-filled glass. **TOP** with soda.

7 spoon Runny honey
1½ shots Freshly squeezed lime juice
Top with Soda (club soda)

Origin: Discovered in 2005 at Hotel Quinta Real, Guadalajara, Mexico.
Comment: A refreshing Mexican variation on Real Lemonade.

HONEY VODKA COLLINS

★★★★☆

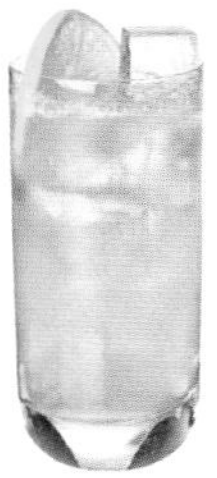

Glass: Collins
Garnish: Lemon slice
Method: **STIR** honey with vodka in base of shaker until honey dissolves. **ADD** other ingredients, **SHAKE** with ice and strain into ice-filled glass.

2 spoon Runny honey
2 shots Ketel One Vodka
1 shot Freshly squeezed lemon juice
Top with Soda (club soda)

Comment: The honey and lemon combo are reminiscent of a toddy but here served long and iced with cleansing vodka.

HONEY VODKA SOUR

★★★★☆

Glass: Old-fashioned
Garnish: Lemon or lime wedge
Method: **SHAKE** all ingredients with ice and strain into ice-filled glass.

2 shots Old Krupnik
1½ shots Freshly squeezed lemon juice
½ shot Sugar syrup (2 sugar to 1 water)
½ fresh Egg white
3 dash Angostura Aromatic Bitters

Comment: A vodka sour with true honey character.

HONEY WALL

★★★★☆

Glass: Martini
Garnish: Orange zest twist (flamed)
Method: **STIR** all ingredients with ice and strain into chilled glass.

1¼ shots Bacardi Carta Blanca light rum
1¼ shots Tuaca liqueur
1¼ shots Dark crème de cacao liqueur

Origin: Adapted from a drink created in 2002 by Dick Bradsell at Downstairs at Alfred's, London, England.
Comment: Strong, rich and chocolatey.

HONEYMOON

★★★★½

Glass: Martini
Garnish: Orange zest twist
Method: **SHAKE** all ingredients with ice and fine strain into chilled glass.

¾ shot Bénédictine D.O.M. liqueur
1½ shots Calvados brandy
¼ shot De Kuyper Triple Sec
½ shot Freshly squeezed lemon juice
½ fresh Egg white

Origin: A 1930s classic created in a long since departed New York bar called Brown Derby.
Comment: A romantic combination of apple, orange, lemon and herbs.

HONEYSUCKLE DAIQUIRI

★★★★★

Glass: Martini
Garnish: Mint leaf
Method: **STIR** honey with rum in base of shaker until honey dissolves. Add lemon and orange juice, **SHAKE** with ice and fine strain into chilled glass.

2 shots Bacardi Carta Blanca light rum
4 spoon Runny honey
1 shot Freshly squeezed lemon juice
1 shot Freshly squeezed orange juice

Origin: Adapted from a recipe in David A. Embury's 1948 'Fine Art of Mixing Drinks'.
Comment: Honey, I love it!

THE HONEYSUCKLE ORCHARD

★★★★☆

Glass: Martini
Garnish: Lemon wedge
Method: **STIR** honey with vodka in base of shaker until honey dissolves. Add other ingredients, **SHAKE** with ice and fine strain into chilled glass.

1 spoon Runny honey
2 shots Zubrówka bison vodka
1½ shots Pressed apple juice
¼ shot Freshly squeezed lemon juice

Origin: Discovered in 2005 at The Stanton Social, New York City, USA.
Comment: A back to nature Polish Martini - all the better for it.

A B C D E F G H I J K L M N O P Q R S T U V W X Y Z

HONG KONG FUEY

★★★★½☆

Glass: Collins
Garnish: Lime wedge & Luxardo Maraschino cherry
Method: SHAKE first eight ingredients with ice and strain into ice-filled glass. TOP with lemonade, stir and serve with straws.

½ shot Ketel One Vodka
½ shot Rutte Dry Gin
½ shot Bacardi Carta Blanca light rum
½ shot Patrón reposado tequila
¾ shot Midori Green Melon liqueur
¼ shot Green Chartreuse liqueur
¼ shot Freshly squeezed lemon juice
¼ shot Rose's lime cordial
Top with Lemonade/Sprite/7-Up

Comment: You may recall Hong Kong Phooey, the 1970s Hanna-Barbera animated children's TV series featuring the mild-mannered janitor Penry and his superhero alter ego. This party drink is little better than Penry's kung fu but deadly all the same.

HONI HONI

★★★★½☆

Glass: Old-fashioned
Garnish: Pineapple wedge, Luxardo Maraschino cherry & mint sprig
Method: SHAKE all ingredients with ice and fine strain into glass filled with crushed ice.

2 shots Bourbon whiskey
½ shot De Kuyper Triple Sec
¾ shot Freshly squeezed lime juice
½ shot Almond (orgeat) syrup
¼ shot Sugar syrup (2 sugar to 1 water)

Origin: Adapted from Victor Bergeron's 'Trader Vic's Bartender's Guide' (1972 revised edition). The name of this vintage Tiki drink means 'Kiss Kiss'.
Comment: A Mai Tai based on whiskey rather than rum.

HONOLULU

★★★★☆

Glass: Old-fashioned
Garnish: Pineapple wedge & Luxardo Maraschino cherry
Method: BLEND all ingredients with 12oz scoop of crushed ice and serve with straws.

1½ shots Bacardi Carta Blanca light rum
1 shot Fresh pressed pineapple juice
½ shot Freshly squeezed lemon juice
¼ shot Sugar syrup (2 sugar to 1 water)
¼ shot Pomegranate / grenadine syrup (2:1)

Origin: Adapted from Victor Bergeron's 'Trader Vic's Bartender's Guide' (1972 revised edition).
Comment: Cooling, fruity and pretty light on alcohol - perfect for a hot afternoon in Honolulu.

HONOLULU COCKTAIL NO.1 ⌐━

★★★★½☆

Glass: Martini
Garnish: Pineapple wedge & Luxardo Maraschino cherry
Method: SHAKE all ingredients with ice and fine strain into chilled glass.

2 shots Rutte Dry Gin
¼ shot Freshly squeezed orange juice
¼ shot Fresh pressed pineapple juice
¼ shot Freshly squeezed lemon juice
¼ shot Sugar syrup (2 sugar to 1 water)

Origin: Adapted from Harry Craddock's 1930 'The Savoy Cocktail Book'.
Comment: Gin is hardly Hawaiian, but its bite works well in this tropically fruity cocktail.

HONOLULU COCKTAIL NO.2

★★★★½☆

Glass: Martini
Garnish: Luxardo Maraschino cherry
Method: STIR all ingredients with ice and strain into chilled glass.

¾ shot Rutte Dry Gin
¾ shot Bénédictine D.O.M. liqueur
¾ shot Luxardo Maraschino liqueur
¾ shot Chilled water (omit if wet ice)

Origin: Adapted from Harry Craddock's 1930 'The Savoy Cocktail Book'.
Comment: Spicy maraschino dominates this old-school after dinner cocktail.

HONOLULU JUICER

★★★★½☆

Glass: Collins
Garnish: Pineapple wedge & Luxardo Maraschino cherry
Method: SHAKE all ingredients with ice and strain into glass filled with crushed ice.

1 shot Bacardi Carta Blanca light rum
1½ shots Southern Comfort liqueur
2 shots Fresh pressed pineapple juice
¾ shot Rose's lime cordial
¾ shot Freshly squeezed lemon juice
¼ shot Sugar syrup (2 sugar to 1 water)

Origin: A classic Tiki drink.
Comment: A practically tropical, rum laced, fruity number.

HOOPLA ⌐━

★★★★☆

Glass: Martini
Garnish: Orange zest twist
Method: SHAKE all ingredients with ice and fine strain into chilled glass.

1 shot Martell VSOP Médaillon cognac
1 shot De Kuyper Triple Sec
¾ shot Martini Extra Dry vermouth
¾ shot Freshly squeezed lemon juice
½ fresh Egg white

Comment: Not far removed from a Sidecar.

Column letters down left margin: A B C D E F G H I J K L M N O P Q R S T U V W X Y Z

HOP TOAD #1 🗝

★★★★☆

Glass: Martini
Garnish: Apricot slice
Method: SHAKE all ingredients with ice and fine strain into chilled glass.

1¼ shots	**Bacardi Carta Blanca light rum**
1¼ shots	**De Kuyper XO Apricot Brandy**
1¼ shots	**Freshly squeezed lime juice**
½ shot	**Chilled water** (omit if wet ice)

Origin: First published in Tom Bullock's 'Ideal Bartender', circa 1917.
Comment: Resembles an apricot Daiquiri that's heavy on the lime yet balanced.

HOP TOAD #2

★★★★☆

Glass: Martini
Garnish: Apricot slice
Method: SHAKE all ingredients with ice and fine strain into chilled glass.

1¾ shots	**Bacardi Carta Ocho aged rum**
1 shot	**De Kuyper XO Apricot Brandy**
¾ shot	**Freshly squeezed lime juice**
½ shot	**Chilled water** (omit if wet ice)

Comment: Alcoholic apricot jam with a lovely twang of aged rum.

HOP TOAD #3 🗝

★★★★☆

Glass: Martini
Garnish: Lemon zest twist
Method: SHAKE all ingredients with ice and fine strain into chilled glass.

1½ shots	**De Kuyper XO Apricot Brandy**
¾ shot	**Freshly squeezed lemon juice**
¾ shot	**Chilled water** (omit if wet ice)

Origin: Adapted from Harry Craddock's 1930 'The Savoy Cocktail Book'.
Comment: Fresh apricot dessert - all it lacks is a dollop of whipped cream.

HORNITOS LAU

★★★★☆

Glass: Collins
Garnish: Mint sprig
Method: Lightly **MUDDLE** mint (just to bruise) in base of shaker. Add other ingredients, **SHAKE** with ice and strain into glass filled with crushed ice. **CHURN** (stir) drink and add more crushed ice so drink meets rim of glass.

12 fresh	**Mint leaves**
2 shots	**Patrón reposado tequila**
1½ shots	**Licor 43 liqueur**
½ shot	**Freshly squeezed lime juice**

Origin: Created in 2005 by Jaspar Eyears at Bar Tiki, Mexico City, Mexico.
Comment: Jaspar recommends making a batch in their glasses and refreezing them with the straws already in the glass, like the old colonels and their julep freezers in Kentucky.

HORSE'S NECK WITH A KICK 🗝

★★★☆☆

Glass: Collins
Garnish: Lemon peel (whole)
Method: POUR ingredients into ice-filled glass and stir.

2 shots	**Bourbon whiskey**
3 dash	**Angostura Aromatic Bitters**
Top with	**Ginger ale**

Origin: A Horse's Neck without a kick is simply ginger ale and bitters.
Comment: Whiskey and ginger with added shrubbery.

THE HORSESHOE SLING

★★★★☆

Glass: Collins
Garnish: Seasonal fruit
Method: SHAKE first five ingredients with ice and strain into ice-filled glass. **TOP** with champagne.

2 shots	**Patrón reposado tequila**
¾ shot	**Freshly squeezed lime juice**
½ shot	**Bénédictine D.O.M. liqueur**
½ shot	**Cherry Heering Liqueur**
1½ shots	**Fresh pressed pineapple juice**
Top with	**G.H. Mumm Cordon Rouge Champagne**

Origin: Adapted from a drink created by Gary Regan, New York, USA.
Comment: Like its creator, this is upfront and refreshingly different.

HOT BUTTERED RUM COCKTAIL

★★★★☆

Glass: Toddy
Garnish: Cinnamon stick & lemon slice (studded with cloves)
Method: Place bar spoon loaded with honey in warmed glass. Add other ingredients and **STIR** until honey and butter are dissolved.

2 spoon	**Runny honey**
1 knob	**Unsalted butter**
2 shots	**Bacardi Carta Oro rum**
1 spoon	**Freshly grated nutmeg**
Top with	**Boiling water**

Comment: In his ' The Fine Art of Mixing Drinks', David Embury says, "The Hot Spiced Rum is bad enough, but the lump of butter is the final insult. It blends with the hot rum just about as satisfactorily as warm olive oil blends with champagne!"

It's rare for us to question Embury but we rather like this slightly oily, warming, spicy toddy. This drink is even better when you use heated dry cider in place of boiling water.

HOT BUTTERED WHISKEY

★★★★☆

Glass: Toddy
Garnish: Dust with grated nutmeg
Method: Place bar spoon in warmed glass. Add ingredients and **STIR** until butter dissolves.

1	knob	Unsalted butter
2	shots	Bourbon whiskey
¾	shot	Sugar syrup (2 sugar to 1 water)
Top with		Boiling water

Comment: Warming and smooth - great on a cold day or whenever you fancy a warming treat.

HOT GIN TODDY (NEW)

★★★★☆

Glass: Toddy
Garnish: Orange zest horses neck
Method: Place bar spoon in empty (ideally warmed glass). **POUR** all ingredients into glass and then **STIR**.

2	shots	Old Tom gin
¼	shot	Sugar syrup (2 sugar to 1 water)
1	shot	Chilled water
3	shots	Boiling water

Comment: Warmed and sweetened gin with a hint of orange. (Others prefer a grapefruit zest garnish but there is no accounting.)

HOT GROG

★★★★☆

Glass: Toddy
Garnish: Lemon zest twist
Method: Place bar spoon loaded with honey in warmed glass. Add other ingredients and **STIR** until honey dissolves.

3	spoon	Runny honey
1	shot	Pusser's Navy Rum (54.5%)
¼	shot	Freshly squeezed lime juice
2½	shots	Boiling water

Comment: Warming, honeyed, pungent rum with a hint of lime.

HOT RED BLOODED FRENCHMAN

★★★★☆

Glass: Toddy
Garnish: Orange zest twist
Method: Place bar spoon in warmed glass. Add other ingredients and **STIR**.

1	shot	Grand Marnier Cordon Rouge
2	shots	Claret red wine
½	shot	Freshly squeezed orange juice
½	shot	Freshly squeezed lemon juice
¼	shot	Sugar syrup (2 sugar to 1 water)
Top with		Boiling water

Comment: Warm, fruity red wine - great on a cold night.

HOT RUM PUNCH

★★★⯪☆

Glass: Toddy
Garnish: Dust with grated nutmeg
Method: Place bar spoon in warmed glass. Add ingredients and **STIR**.

1	shot	Bacardi Carta Oro rum
1	shot	Martell VSOP Médaillon cognac
½	shot	Romate Fino sherry
¼	shot	Sugar syrup (2 sugar to 1 water)
1	shot	Freshly squeezed lime juice
Top with		Boiling water

Origin: Punch was one of the many rum-based drinks popular in the 18th century when taverns would serve cold punch and warm it up upon request by dunking a red-hot iron in it. This version is said to have been a favourite drink of Mozart the composer.
Comment: A great winter warmer.

HOT SHOT

★★★☆☆

Glass: Shot
Garnish: None
Method: **LAYER** by carefully pouring ingredients in the following order.

¾	shot	Galliano L'Autentico liqueur
¾	shot	Espresso coffee (freshly made & hot)
½	shot	Single cream / half-and-half

Origin: A huge drink in Scandinavia during the early 90s.
Comment: The Scandinavian answer to Irish coffee.

HOT TODDY #1

★★★★⯪

Glass: Toddy
Garnish: Lemon wedge & cinnamon stick
Method: Place bar spoon loaded with honey in warmed glass. Add other ingredients and **STIR** until honey dissolves.

1	spoon	Runny honey
2	shots	Dewar's 12 Year Old Scotch whisky
½	shot	Freshly squeezed lemon juice
½	shot	Sugar syrup (2 sugar to 1 water)
3	dried	Clove
Top with		Boiling water

Origin: Lost in time but Dickens refers to a "Whisky Toddy" in 'The Pickwick Papers'.
Comment: The smoky flavours in the Scotch add spice to this warming drink that's great when you're feeling down with a cold or the flu.

HOT TODDY #2

★★★★⯪

Glass: Toddy
Garnish: Lemon zest twist
Method: Place bar spoon loaded with honey in warmed glass. Add other ingredients and **STIR** until honey dissolves.

1	spoon	Runny honey
2	shots	Dewar's 12 Year Old Scotch whisky
3	dried	Clove
¼	spoon	Freshly grated nutmeg
Top with		Hot English breakfast tea

Comment: Tea and Scotch combine wonderfully in this hot and spicy winter warmer.

HOT TODDY #3 🗝

★★★☆☆

Glass: Toddy
Garnish: Lemon wedge & cinnamon stick
Method: Place bar spoon in warmed glass. Add ingredients and **STIR**.

2	shots	Martell VSOP Médaillon cognac
½	shot	Freshly squeezed lemon juice
¼	shot	Sugar syrup (2 sugar to 1 water)
Top with		Boiling water

Comment: Warms the cockles with cognac and a good dose of citrus.

HOT TOMMY 🗝

★★★★☆

Glass: Toddy
Garnish: Lime zest twist
Method: Place spoon in glass. **POUR** first 3 ingredients into glass. **TOP** up with boiling water and **STIR** until agave nectar dissolves.

2	shots	Patrón reposado tequila
½	shot	Freshly squeezed lime juice
½	shot	Agave syrup
Top with		Boiling water

Origin: Created in December 2009 by Alan Brown of Menzel's Bar, who says of this drink "Over the busy festive period, feeling full of flu and cold I decided to make a hot toddy to soothe my symptoms. Having no honey to hand I tried using agave nectar instead. This led me to the idea of using tequila and lime instead of lemon (to complement the tequila) with the agave and boiling water. The name for the drink is a Hot Tommy, a nod to the Tommy's Margarita, which makes use of both tequila and agave."
Comment: A Mexican twist on the original winter pick-me-up.

HOT TUB 🗝

★★★★☆

Glass: Martini
Garnish: Pineapple wedge
Method: **SHAKE** first three ingredients with ice and fine strain into chilled glass. **TOP** with prosecco.

1½	shots	Ketel One Vodka
1	shot	Fresh pressed pineapple juice
¼	shot	Chambord Liqueur
Top with		Prosecco sparkling wine

Origin: Adapted from a drink discovered in 2004 at Teatro Boston, USA.
Comment: Basically a French Martini with bubbles.

HOT WINE LEMONADE

★★★☆☆

Glass: Toddy
Garnish: Lemon zest twist
Method: **POUR** first three ingredients into warmed glass and top up with boiling water.

2	shots	Claret red wine
1½	shots	Freshly squeezed lemon juice
¾	shot	Sugar syrup (2 sugar to 1 water)
Top with		Boiling water

Origin: Rediscovered classic.
Comment: This citrusy mulled wine is simply made with hot red wine and freshly squeezed lemon juice.

HOULA HOULA COCKTAIL 🗝

★★★☆☆

Glass: Martini
Garnish: Orange zest twist
Method: **SHAKE** all ingredients with ice and fine strain into chilled glass.

2	shots	Rutte Dry Gin
½	shot	De Kuyper Triple Sec
1	shot	Freshly squeezed orange juice
½	shot	Chilled water (omit if wet ice)

Origin: Adapted from Harry Craddock's 1930 'The Savoy Cocktail Book'.
Comment: Orange generously laced with gin.

HOYT'S DAIQUIRÍ

★★★★☆

Glass: Martini
Garnish: Lime slice (seared)
Method: Sear two halves of lime with a chef's blow torch and squeeze into a shaker. **SHAKE** all remaining ingredients with ice and fine strain into chilled glass.

2 shots Bacardi Carta Blanca light rum
1 shot Burnt lime juice
¼ shot Jägermeister
½ shot Vanilla sugar syrup
½ fresh Egg white

Origin: Created in 2008 by Meimi Sanchez at Bramble, Edinburgh, Scotland.
Comment: Most unusual and interesting. Recognisably a Daiquiri but with creamy mouth-feel and great depth of flavour.

HUAPALA 🗝

★★★★☆

Glass: Martini
Garnish: Lemon wedge
Method: **SHAKE** all ingredients with ice and fine strain into chilled glass.

1	shot	Bacardi Carta Blanca light rum
1	shot	Rutte Dry Gin
½	shot	Freshly squeezed lemon juice
¼	shot	Pomegranate / grenadine syrup (2:1)
½	shot	Chilled water (omit if wet ice)

Origin: Adapted from Victor Bergeron's 'Trader Vic's Bartender's Guide' (1972 revised edition).
Comment: In his book Vic prefaces this cocktail with the comment, "Nice, easy drink". It's basically a lemon Daiquiri with gin and grenadine.

A B C D E F G H I J K L M N O P Q R S T U V W X Y Z

HUCKLE MY BUFF

★★★★★

Glass: Toddy
Garnish: Freshly grated nutmeg
Method: Gently **BLEND** all ingredients on a slow speed then warm in a saucepan, gently stirring with a whisk (or microwave for 30 seconds and stir), then pour into warmed glass. If you make several servings in one batch, keep warm and serve from a sous-vide or heated soup kettle at to 60°C.

1	fresh	Egg yolk
5	shots	Harveys Porter 1859
1	shot	Martell VSOP Médaillon cognac
¼	shot	King's Ginger Liqueur
¾	shot	Light muscovado sugar syrup (2 sugar to 1 water)

Origin: Our adaptation of a recipe presented by Jamie Oliver and Jimmy Doherty on Friday 9th August 2013 at the Cabinet Room, London as their entry to the diffordsguide Beer-tail Competition for London Cocktail Week 2013.

Also known as Huckle-my-butt and Huckle-and-buff, Huckle-my-buff is an early 18th century hot drink combining gin or cognac and beer. Jamie and Jimmy resurrected the Huckle-my-buff and gave it a modern twist with the use of nitrous oxide and a sous-vide in place of the traditional red-hot poker.

The Jamie and Jimmy recipe was as follows: whisk 1 fresh egg yolk then slowly whisk in 20 grams muscovado sugar, 35ml cognac, 150ml Harvey's Stout beer and 0.8ml ginger juice. Pour mixture into a soda syphon, close and charge with nitrous oxide (laughing gas/N2O). Gently warm the filled cream whipper to 60°C in a sous-vide (water bath). Discharge warmed syphon into glass. Finish with freshly grated nutmeg.
Comment: To quote Jamie Oliver, "the Huckle-my-buff is not a Dodo but a Phoenix".

HULA HULA

★★★★☆☆

Glass: Martini
Garnish: Pineapple wedge & Luxardo Maraschino cherry
Method: **SHAKE** all ingredients with ice and fine strain into chilled glass.

1½	shots	Rutte Dry Gin
1	shot	De Kuyper Triple Sec
1½	shots	Freshly squeezed orange juice

Origin: Adapted from a drink created by Ray Buhen, one of Don The Beachcomber's original bartenders. In 1961 Ray opened his own Tiki-Ti Bar in Los Angeles, which today is run by his son and grandson.
Comment: Gin and juice - orange with a splash of orange liqueur.

HULK

★★☆☆☆

Glass: Old-fashioned
Garnish: None
Method: **LAYER** ingredients in ice-filled glass by carefully pouring in the following order.

2	shots	Hpnotiq liqueur
1	shot	Martell VSOP Médaillon cognac

Comment: Turns green when mixed. A crying waste of good cognac.

HUMMINGBIRD

★★★☆☆

Glass: Hurricane
Garnish: Banana chunk
Method: **BLEND** all ingredients with 12oz scoop crushed ice and serve with straws.

1½ shots	Bacardi Carta Blanca light rum
½ shot	Coffee liqueur
1 shot	Crème de banane liqueur
1 shot	Coco Re'al Cream of Coconut
1 fresh	Banana (peeled)

Origin: The house cocktail at the Hummingbird Beach Resort, Soufriere, St. Lucia.
Comment: With flavours of rum, coconut, banana and coffee, this tall, frozen drink tastes rather like dessert.

HUNK COCKTAIL

★★★★½

Glass: Martini
Garnish: Luxardo Maraschino cherry
Method: **SHAKE** all ingredients with ice and fine strain into chilled glass.

2	shots	Vanilla infused Ketel One vodka
1¾	shots	Fresh pressed pineapple juice
½	shot	Freshly squeezed lime juice
¼	shot	Sugar syrup (2 sugar to 1 water)

Origin: The drink Carrie and co discovered in the summer of 2003. In this series the Sex and the City stars dropped Cosmopolitans in favour of Hunks - no change there then.
Comment: Pineapple and vanilla combine wonderfully. American readers may notice more than a passing resemblance to a Key Lime Pie served without the Graham Cracker rim.

HUNTER COCKTAIL

★★★★☆

Glass: Coupe
Garnish: Luxardo Maraschino cherry
Method: **STIR** all ingredients with ice and strain into chilled glass.

2½ shots Bourbon whiskey
½ shot Cherry Heering Liqueur
⅛ shot Luxardo Maraschino liqueur
3 drop Angostura Orange Bitters

Origin: Unknown, but the popularity of the Hunter Cocktail has been much helped by its being recommended by the famous bartender Hidetsugu Ueno to visitors to his High Five bar in Ginzo, Tokyo, Japan.
Comment: An after dinner cocktail with a good slug of bourbon, sweetened by rich cherry.

HURRICANE #1

★★★★☆

Glass: Hurricane
Garnish: Pineapple wedge & Luxardo Maraschino cherry
Method: SHAKE all ingredients with ice and strain into ice-filled glass.

1½ shots	Bacardi Carta Blanca light rum
1 shot	Pusser's Navy Rum (54.5%)
1 shot	Freshly squeezed orange juice
1 shot	Fresh pressed pineapple juice
½ shot	Freshly squeezed lime juice
¼ shot	Passion fruit syrup
¾ shot	Rose's lime cordial

Origin: Named after the shape of a hurricane lamp and served in the tall, shapely glass of the same name. Thought to have originated in 1939 at The Hurricane Bar, New York City, but made famous at Pat O'Brien's in New Orleans. Some old cocktail books list a much earlier Hurricane made with cognac, absinthe and vodka.
Comment: A strong, tangy, refreshing drink packed with fruit and laced with rum.

HURRICANE #2

★★★☆☆

Glass: Hurricane
Garnish: Orange slice & cherry on stick (sail)
Method: Cut passion fruit in half and scoop flesh into shaker. Add other ingredients, **SHAKE** with ice and strain into ice-filled glass.

1 fresh	Passion fruit
1½ shots	Gosling's Black Seal dark rum
1½ shots	Bacardi Carta Blanca light rum
1 shot	Freshly squeezed orange juice
1 shot	Fresh pressed pineapple juice
½ shot	Freshly squeezed lime juice
¼ shot	Passion fruit syrup
¼ shot	Pomegranate / grenadine syrup (2:1)

Comment: Sweet, tangy and potentially dangerous.

HURRICANE #3

★★★☆☆

Glass: Hurricane
Garnish: Pineapple wedge & cherry
Method: SHAKE all ingredients with ice and strain into ice-filled glass.

1 shot	Gosling's Black Seal dark rum
1 shot	Bacardi Carta Blanca light rum
½ shot	Galliano L'Autentico liqueur
2 shots	Fresh pressed pineapple juice
2 shots	Freshly squeezed orange juice
¾ shot	Freshly squeezed lime juice
¾ shot	Passion fruit syrup
2½ dash	Angostura Aromatic Bitters

Origin: Adapted from a 2006 recipe by Chris McMillian, New Orleans, USA.
Comment: A veritable tropical fruit salad laced with rum.

HURRICANE NO.1 (ORIGINAL RECIPE)

★★★☆☆

Glass: Hurricane
Garnish: Pineapple wedge & Luxardo Maraschino cherry
Method: SHAKE all ingredients with ice and strain into ice-filled glass.

4 shots	Pot still Jamaican rum
2 shots	Passion fruit syrup
2 shots	Freshly squeezed lemon juice

Origin: Recipe adapted from Jeff Berry's 1998 'Beachbum Berry's Grog Log' and purported to be the 1960s recipe used at Pat O'Brien's in New Orleans. The recipe was adapted to a rum and juice combination where it was served in 1939 at the World's Fair in New York at the Hurricane bar.
Comment: The flavour of the passion fruit syrup predominates. Ok if you like that kind of thing.

HYPNOTIC MARGARITA

★★★★☆

Glass: Coupe
Garnish: Lime wedge
Method: SHAKE all ingredients with ice and fine strain into chilled glass.

1½ shots	Patrón silver tequila
½ shot	De Kuyper Triple Sec
½ shot	Hpnotiq liqueur
½ shot	Freshly squeezed lime juice

Origin: Created in 2005 by Gary Regan at Painter's, Cornwall-on-Hudson, New York, USA.
Comment: Liqueurs combine harmoniously with lime and tequila in this tangy, fruity Margarita. However, I remain unconvinced by Hpnotiq.

I B DAMM'D

★★★★☆

Glass: Martini
Garnish: Peach wedge on rim
Method: SHAKE all ingredients with ice and fine strain into chilled glass.

2 shots	Rutte Old Simon oude jenever
½ shot	St-Germain elderflower liqueur
¼ shot	Peachtree peach schnapps
1¾ shots	Pressed apple juice

Origin: Discovered in 2003 at Oxo Tower Bar, London, England.
Comment: Subtle combination of fruit and floral flavours.

I'LL TAKE MANHATTAN

★★★★☆

Glass: Martini
Garnish: Luxardo Maraschino cherry
Method: STIR all ingredients with ice and strain into chilled glass.

2 shots	Bourbon whiskey
½ shot	Cherry Heering Liqueur
1 shot	Martini Rosso vermouth
2 dash	Angostura Aromatic Bitters

Origin: Adapted from a drink discovered in 2005 at The Stanton Social, New York City, USA.
Comment: Cherry is more than a garnish in this twist on the classic Manhattan.

ICE 'T' KNEE

★★★★½

Glass: Martini
Garnish: Orange zest twist
Method: STIR all ingredients with ice and strain into chilled glass.

2 shots Ketel One Vodka
1½ shots Cold jasmine tea
¾ shot Icewine

Origin: Created in 2004 by yours truly, London, England
Comment: Honeyed palate topped off with tannin and jasmine.

ICE MAIDEN

★★★★☆

Glass: Martini
Garnish: Orange zest twist
Method: STIR all ingredients with ice and strain into chilled glass.

1½ shots Rutte Dry Gin
1 shot Icewine
¾ shot Sauvignon blanc white wine
¾ shot Chilled water (reduce if wet ice)

Origin: Created in 2004 by yours truly, London, England.
Comment: A subtle Martini with the honeyed flavours of icewine melding with botanicals in the gin and balanced by the acidity of the white wine.

ICED SAKE MARTINI

★★★★½

Glass: Martini
Garnish: Cucumber slices
Method: STIR all ingredients with ice and strain into chilled glass.

2 shots Ketel One Vodka
2 shots Junmai ginjō sake
¼ shot Icewine

Origin: Created in 2004 by yours truly, London, England.
Comment: The icewine adds interesting and wonderfully honeyed notes to this Sake Martini.

ICED TEA

★★★½☆

Glass: Collins
Garnish: Lime wedge
Method: SHAKE first six ingredients with ice and strain into glass filled with crushed ice. **TOP** with cola.

½ shot Martell VSOP Médaillon cognac
½ shot Gosling's Black Seal dark rum
½ shot De Kuyper Triple Sec
½ shot Freshly squeezed lime juice
½ shot Freshly squeezed orange juice
2 shots Cold English breakfast tea
Top with Coca-Cola

Origin: Created in 1990 by Charles Schumann, Munich, Germany.
Comment: Sweetened and fortified fruity cola.

ICED TEA MARTINI

★★★★☆

Glass: Martini
Garnish: Lemon zest twist
Method: SHAKE all ingredients with ice and strain into chilled glass.

2 shots Rutte Dry Gin
1 shot Cold Earl Grey tea
½ shot Martini Extra Dry vermouth
½ shot Sugar syrup (2 sugar to 1 water)

Origin: Created in 2006 by yours truly, London, England.
Comment: Tannic and bittersweet. A refreshing after dinner drink.

ICEY APPLE MARTINI

★★★★☆

Glass: Martini
Garnish: Orange zest twist
Method: STIR all ingredients with ice and strain into chilled glass.

2 shots Rutte Dry Gin
¾ shot Icewine
¾ shot Pressed apple juice
¼ shot Martini Extra Dry vermouth

Origin: Created in 2004 by yours truly and updated in October 2013.
Comment: Delicate with subtle flavours.

IDEAL

★★★★☆

Glass: Martini
Garnish: Almonds
Method: SHAKE all ingredients with ice and fine strain into chilled glass.

1 shot Rutte Dry Gin
1 shot Martini Extra Dry vermouth
1 shot Martini Rosso vermouth
¼ shot Freshly squeezed pink grapefruit juice
⅛ shot Luxardo Maraschino liqueur

Origin: Recipe adapted from a 1937 Bar Florida menu (later renamed Floridita), Havana, Cuba.
Comment: Aromatic and herbal with grapefruit sourness balancing sweeter notes.

IGUANA

★★★½☆

Glass: Shot
Garnish: None
Method: SHAKE all ingredients with ice and fine stain into chilled glass.

½ shot Ketel One Vodka
½ shot Patrón reposado tequila
½ shot Coffee liqueur

Comment: Coffee and tequila's successful relationship is enhanced by the introduction of vodka.

IGUANA WANA

★★★☆☆

Glass: Old-fashioned
Garnish: Orange slice
Method: SHAKE all ingredients with ice and strain into ice-filled glass.

1	shot	Ketel One Vodka
¾	shot	Peachtree peach schnapps
2½	shots	Freshly squeezed orange juice

Comment: Orange juice and peach schnapps, laced with vodka.

ILLICIT AFFAIR ⊙━━

★★★⯪☆

Glass: Old-fashioned
Garnish: Orange slice
Method: SHAKE all ingredients with ice and strain into ice-filled glass.

2	shots	Ketel One Vodka
1¾	shots	Freshly squeezed orange juice
1¾	shots	Cranberry juice

Comment: Fruity, easy drinking.

ILLUSION

★★★★☆

Glass: Collins
Garnish: Watermelon wedge
Method: SHAKE all ingredients with ice and strain into ice-filled glass.

2	shots	Ketel One Vodka
¾	shot	De Kuyper Triple Sec
¾	shot	Midori Green Melon liqueur
2½	shots	Fresh pressed pineapple juice

Comment: This medium-sweet, lime green drink is one for a summer's day by the pool.

IMPROVED HOLLAND GIN COCKTAIL

★★★★☆

Glass: Coupe
Garnish: Lemon zest twist
Method: STIR all ingredients with ice and strain into chilled glass.

2	shots	Rutte Old Simon oude jenever
¼	shot	Luxardo Maraschino liqueur
2	dash	Angostura Aromatic Bitters
¼	spoon	Le Fée Parisienne absinthe
½	spoon	Sugar syrup (2 sugar to 1 water)
½	shot	Chilled water

Origin: The classic Holland House "improved" due to the use of jenever.
Comment: Salmon-pink with subtle juniper, rounded by maraschino liqueur, Angostura bitters and absinthe.

IN AND OUT MARTINI ⊙━━

★★★⯪☆

Glass: Martini
Garnish: Chilled olive on stick or lemon zest twist
Method: Gently **SHAKE** vermouth with ice. Strain and discard vermouth to leave the ice in the shaker coated with vermouth. Add gin, **SHAKE** again with coated ice and strain into chilled glass.

½	shot	Martini Extra Dry vermouth
2½	shots	Rutte Dry Gin

Origin: This drinks origin is unknown but former U.S. President Richard Nixon is said to have preferred his Martini made this way.
Comment: A well-diluted shaken Dry Martini. However, seems like a waste of good vermouth.

IN-SEINE

★★★★⯪

Glass: Old-fashioned
Garnish: White grapes on stick
Method: POUR absinthe into ice-filled old-fashioned glass, **TOP** with water and set aside. Separately, in mixing glass, **STIR** other ingredients with ice. Dump contents (absinthe and ice) of old-fashioned glass and charge with fresh ice. Then **STRAIN** contents (cognac, bourbon and elderflower liqueur) of mixing glass into absinthe rinsed and ice charged old-fashioned glass.

¼	shot	Le Fée Parisienne absinthe
Top with		water
1	shot	Martell VSOP Médaillon cognac
1	shot	Bourbon whiskey
1	shot	St-Germain elderflower liqueur

Comment: Elderflower liqueur mellows and boosts floral notes in the cognac while the merest dash of absinthe dries and adds a robust hint of aniseed.
Origin: Created in 2006 by yours truly (Simon Difford) at The Cabinet Room, London, England.

The name is a reference to the Parisian district of St-Germain lying on the left bank of the River Seine and also a nod to the use of absinthe and its pre-war ban in France, partly due to the belief that it induced insanity.

INCOGNITO ⊙━━

★★★⯪☆

Glass: Martini
Garnish: Apricot slice or physalis fruit
Method: SHAKE all ingredients with ice and fine strain into chilled glass.

1½	shots	Martell VSOP Médaillon cognac
1	shot	De Kuyper XO Apricot Brandy
1½	shots	Martini Extra Dry vermouth
3	dash	Angostura Aromatic Bitters

Comment: Dry with hints of sweet apricot - unusual.

INCOME TAX COCKTAIL

★★★★☆

Glass: Martini
Garnish: Orange zest twist
Method: SHAKE all ingredients with ice and fine strain into chilled glass.

2	shots	Rutte Dry Gin
¼	shot	Martini Extra Dry vermouth
¼	shot	Martini Rosso vermouth
1	shot	Freshly squeezed orange juice
2	dash	Angostura Aromatic Bitters

Origin: A vintage cocktail adapted from the classic Bronx Cocktail, created in 1906 by Johnny Solon, a bartender at New York's Waldorf-Astoria Hotel, and named after the newly opened Bronx Zoo.
Comment: A Bronx with the addition of two dashes of Angostura.

INDIAN ROSE

★★★★☆

Glass: Martini
Garnish: Rose petal
Method: SHAKE all ingredients with ice and fine strain into chilled glass.

2½	shots	Rutte Dry Gin
¼	shot	De Kuyper XO Apricot Brandy
¼	shot	Rose water
¼	shot	Rose syrup
½	shot	Chilled water (omit if wet ice)

Origin: Adapted from a drink discovered in 2005 at Mie N Yu, Washington DC, USA.
Comment: Subtle rose hue and flavour

INDOCHINE

★★★★☆

Glass: Martini
Garnish: Fresh ginger slice
Method: SHAKE all ingredients with ice and fine strain into chilled glass.

2	shots	Ketel One Vodka
1	shot	King's Ginger Liqueur
¾	shot	Fresh pressed pineapple juice

Origin: Adapted from a drink promoted at the end of 2007 by the makers of Canton ginger liqueur.
Comment: Slightly sweet and very frothy. Easy drinking with a ginger kick.

INK COCKTAIL #2

★★★★☆

Glass: Martini
Garnish: Orange zest twist
Method: SHAKE all ingredients with ice and fine strain into chilled glass.

2	shots	Ketel One Vodka
½	shot	Blue curaçao liqueur
1½	shots	Cranberry juice

Origin: Discovered in 2005 at Halo, Atlanta, USA.
Comment: Surprisingly subtle and pleasant in flavour.

INSOMNIAC

★★★★½

Glass: Martini
Garnish: Coffee beans
Method: SHAKE all ingredients with ice and fine strain into chilled glass.

¾	shot	Ketel One Vodka
¾	shot	Hazelnut liqueur
¾	shot	Coffee liqueur
1	shot	Espresso coffee (freshly made & hot)
½	shot	Single cream / half-and-half
½	shot	Milk

Comment: Wonderfully balanced, creamy and caffeine laced.

INTERNATIONAL INCIDENT

★★★★☆

Glass: Martini
Garnish: Dust with grated nutmeg
Method: SHAKE all ingredients with ice and fine strain into chilled glass.

¾	shot	Ketel One Vodka
¾	shot	Disaronno Originale amaretto
1½	shots	Baileys Irish cream liqueur
¾	shot	Coffee liqueur
¾	shot	Hazelnut liqueur

Comment: Rich and creamy.

INTIMATE MARTINI

★★★★☆

Glass: Martini
Garnish: Orange zest twist
Method: STIR all ingredients with ice and strain into chilled glass.

2	shots	Ketel One Vodka
1	shot	De Kuyper XO Apricot Brandy
½	shot	Martini Extra Dry vermouth
3	dash	Angostura Orange Bitters

Comment: Sweet apricot dried and balanced by vermouth and bitters. Surprisingly complex and pleasant.

IONIAN SPRITZ COCKTAIL (NEW)

★★★★☆

Glass: Goblet
Garnish: Orange slice
Method: POUR ingredients into ice-filled glass and lightly stir.

3	shots	Prosecco sparkling wine
2	shots	Skinos Mastiha
1	shot	Soda (club soda)

Origin: Created in August 2015 by yours truly at the Cabinet Room, London, England.
Comment: The Greeks and Italians are separated by the Ionian Sea, in this Spritz both countries come together with Italian Prosecco and Greek Mastiha.

IRISH ALEXANDER

★★★★☆

Glass: Martini
Garnish: Crumbled Cadbury's Flake bar
Method: SHAKE all ingredients with ice and strain back into shaker. **DRY SHAKE** (without ice) and fine strain into chilled glass.

1½ shot	Irish cream liqueur
1½ shot	Martell VSOP Médaillon cognac
½ shot	Single cream / half-and-half

Comment: Rich, thick and creamy.

IRISH COCKTAIL

★★★★☆

Glass: Martini
Garnish: Shamrock (or mint leaf)
Method: STIR all ingredients with ice and strain into chilled glass.

1½ shots	Bourbon whiskey
1 shot	Tuaca liqueur
½ shot	Grand Marnier Cordon Rouge
¼ shot	Vanilla sugar syrup

Origin: Adapted from a drink discovered in 2001 at Detroit, London, England.
Comment: There's nothing Irish about this drink, but it's good all the same.

Irish Coffee

Sometimes called a Gaelic Coffee and properly known by its Irish name 'Caife Gaelach', the Irish Coffee is traditionally served in a handled or stemmed heatproof glass known as a toddy glass. It comprises hot filter coffee, Irish whiskey and sugar (preferably brown sugar) topped with lightly whipped cream. The sweetened whiskey laced coffee is drunk through the creamy head.

A good Irish coffee should be topped with a luxurious moustache inducing inch thick layer of cream. To ensure your cream floats rather than sinks into the coffee, lightly whip, shake, or blend your cream before pouring over the bowl of a spoon. It also helps if the cream and the spoon are gently warmed. Sweetening the coffee with sugar also amplifies the drinks flavours and helps the cream float. We prefer to use homemade muscovado sugar syrup in our Irish Coffee recipe.

The history of alcoholic hot coffee drinks served in a glass topped with cream dates back to the mid-19th Century with the best-known examples being the Fiaker and Pharisäer served in Viennese coffee houses. By the turn of the 20th century variations called Kaisermelange, Maria Theresia and Biedermeier-Kaffee could also be found on menus at Viennese coffee houses. Combining coffee and spirits was also popular in 19th century France where such drinks were called a Gloria.

The relatively modern Irish Coffee was created in the 1940s by Joe Sheridan, a chef turned bartender originally from Castlederg, County Tyrone while working at Foynes' Port. Sheridan added whiskey to hot coffee to warm a group of American passengers disembarking from a Pan Am flying boat at Foynes on a cold and wet winter evening. The passengers are said to have asked if they were being served Brazilian coffee to which Sheridan answered, "It's an Irish coffee".

Early planes lacked sufficient flying range to make Atlantic crossings and from 1937 onwards, flying boats were used to make the journey with Foynes' Port on the west coast of Ireland the last refuelling point for the Sikorsky S-42 and Boeing 314 planes. The first non-stop New York service started on 22 June 1942 and took 25 hours 40 minutes. The planes were comparatively primitive and the flight was arduous so the restorative boozy coffees were well received by cold weary travellers.

The demise of Foynes Port was sealed in 1942 with the opening of nearby Shannon Airport, built on bog land on the northern bank of the Estuary. Foynes Flying Boat Museum is all that remains of the old port but the tradition of serving Irish Coffees to transatlantic travellers continued at the new airport, and it is here, in 1947, that Stanton Delaplane, a travel writer for the San Francisco Chronicle, enjoyed his first Irish Coffee.

Back home in San Francisco, at one of his favourite local bars, Buena Vista Café, late on 10th November 1952, Delaplane recounted travel stories to Jack Koepple, the bar owner, and the two of them set about trying to recreate Sheridan's Irish Coffee. Despite numerous attempts the drink did not quite taste right and the cream would not float. This prompted Koepple to travel to Shannon Airport to see how the drink was made.

Upon returning back to San Francisco he continued his experimentation and also discussed the issues he was having floating the cream with the city's mayor, who was also a dairy owner. Koepple discovered that the cream better whipped and so floated when it was two days old rather than being fresh. After further experimentation Koepple arrived at the method, recipe and 6oz heat-treated goblet still used at the Buena Vista today, where some 2,000 Irish Coffees are reputedly sold every day.

IRISH COFFEE

★★★★☆

Glass: Toddy
Garnish: Dust with freshly grated nutmeg &/or float 3 coffee beans
Method: Select a heat-treated heat-proof glass and warm by filling with very hot water and leave to stand. Separately prepare cream by lightly warming and whipping (we recommend using Aeroccino by Nespresso to whip your cream). Empty the now warmed glass. **POUR** whiskey, sugar syrup and hot coffee into warmed glass until it is about three-quarters full and stir. Float whipped cream over the back of a warmed spoon.

1½ shots Teeling Small Batch Irish whiskey
½ shot Light muscovado sugar syrup (2 sugar to 1 water)
Top with Filter coffee (hot)
Float lightly whipped Single cream / half-and-half

Comment: Like most great ideas, this one is very simple. Coffee with a whiskey kick.

IRISH COFFEE COCKTAIL

★★★★☆

Glass: Martini
Garnish: Coffee beans
Method: SHAKE all ingredients with ice and fine strain into chilled glass.

1½ shots	Teeling Small Batch Irish whiskey
2 shots	Espresso coffee (freshly made & hot)
½ shot	Light muscovado sugar syrup (2 sugar to 1 water)
1 shot	Single cream / half-and-half

Origin: Created in 2003 by yours truly in London, England.
Comment: Forget sipping warm java through a cold head of cream. This Martini version of the classic Irish Coffee offers all the flavour without the moustache.

IRISH ESPRESSO'TINI

★★★★☆

Glass: Martini
Garnish: Coffee beans
Method: SHAKE all ingredients with ice and fine strain into chilled glass.

2   shots   Baileys Irish cream liqueur
1¼ shots   Vanilla infused Ketel One vodka
1¼ shots   Espresso coffee (freshly made & hot)

Comment: Richly flavoured with a pleasantly bitter finish.

IRISH FLAG

★★★☆☆

Glass: Shot
Garnish: None
Method: Refrigerate ingredients then **LAYER** in chilled glass by carefully pouring in the following order.

½   shot   Green crème de menthe liqueur
½   shot   Baileys Irish cream liqueur
½   shot   Grand Marnier Cordon Rouge

Origin: The Irish tricolour is the national flag of the Republic of Ireland. Its three equal stripes represent the political landscape. Orange stands for the Protestants because of William of Orange, the Protestant king of England who defeated the Roman Catholic James II in 1690. Green stands for the Catholic nationalists of the south and white for the the hope of peace between Catholics and Protestants.
Comment: Tricoloured orange and mint smoothed with cream liqueur.

IRISH MAID (NEW)

★★★★☆

Glass: Old-fashioned
Garnish: Cucumber slice
Method: MUDDLE cucumber in base of shaker. Add other ingredients, **SHAKE** with ice and strain into ice-filled glass.

2   slice   Cucumber
2   shot   Teeling Small Batch Irish Whiskey
½   shot   St-German elderflower liqueur
⅔   shot   Freshly squeezed lemon juice
⅓   shot   Sugar syrup (2 sugar to 1 water)

Comment: Fresh, juicy cucumber and elderflower with Irish whiskey and zesty lemon.
Origin: Adapted from a recipe created by Jack McGarry at The Dead Rabbit, New York City, USA.

IRONBOUND (NEW)

★★★★☆

Glass: Old-fashioned
Garnish: Lemon zest twist
Method: STIR all ingredients with ice and strain into ice-filled glass.

1   shot   Capucana cachaça
1   shot   Applejack brandy (bonded)
½   shot   Bénédictine D.O.M. liqueur
⅛   shot   Light muscovado sugar syrup (2 sugar to 1 water)
2   dash   Peychaud's aromatic bitters

Origin: Who'd have thought cachaça and apple brandy would make such good bedfellows with herbal liqueur and Peychaud's? They do.
Comment: Adapted from a drink created by Mayur Subbarao of New York, USA.

ISLAND BREEZE

★★★☆☆

Glass: Collins
Garnish: Grapefruit wedge
Method: SHAKE all ingredients with ice and strain into ice-filled glass.

2   shots   Coconut rum liqueur
2½ shots   Cranberry juice
1½ shots   Freshly squeezed pink grapefruit juice

Origin: Named after the Twelve Islands Shipping Company, The Caribbean producers of Malibu.
Comment: Great balance of sweet and sour flavours.

ISLANDER

★★★★☆

Glass: Coupe
Garnish: Lemon zest twist
Method: STIR all ingredients with ice and strain into a chilled glass.

2   shots   Martini Rosso vermouth
¾   shot   Dewar's 12 Year Old Scotch whisky
¼   dash   Pernod anise

Origin: Adapted from a recipe by Gary 'Gaz' Regan, Ardent Spirits, New York.
Comment: Vermouth based and bitter-sweet with hints of liquorice and malty, smoky notes.

STAR RATINGS EXPLAINED

★★★★★+ OUTSTANDING		★★★★★ EXCEPTIONAL
★★★★☆ EXCELLENT		★★★★☆ RECOMMENDED
★★★☆☆ COMMENDED		★★★☆☆ MEDIOCRE
★★☆☆☆ DISAPPOINTING		★★☆☆☆ PRETTY AWFUL
★☆☆☆☆ SHAMEFUL		★☆☆☆☆ DISGUSTING

ISLAY OLD FASHIONED (NEW)

★★★★½

Glass: Old-fashioned
Garnish: Lemon zest twist
Method: STIR whisky with three ice cubes (dry to the touch frozen ice, not wet ice) in a glass. Add sugar syrup, bitters and two more ice cubes. STIR some more and add another two ice cubes. STIR a bit more, and if you have room, add more ice.

2½ shots Islay single malt Scotch whisky
⅓ shot Light muscovado sugar syrup (2 sugar to 1 water)
3 dash Peychaud's aromatic bitters

Origin: In late 2014, Eliot Cole sent us an email saying "one of my favourite drinks ever was an Old Fashioned made with Laphroaig (possibly quarter cask)... it was made at Hotel Delmano in Williamsburg, Brooklyn." Thanks to Eliot we took to the bar and with a nod to David Embury's preference for Peychard's bitters with whiskys in my mind made this tasty Old Fashioned.
Comment: Islay single malt is for many the king of all whiskeys so it should be celebrated in more cocktails – particularly Old Fashioneds.

ITALIAN JOB #2

★★★★☆

Glass: Sling
Garnish: Orange zest twist
Method: SHAKE first three ingredients with ice and strain into glass filled with crushed ice. TOP with wine and serve with straws.

1 shot Tuaca liqueur
1 shot Disaronno Originale amaretto
1 shot Cranberry juice
Top with Shiraz red wine

Origin: Discovered in 2002 at Rapscallion, London, England.
Comment: Mix layers with straw prior to drinking for vanillaed, almond, fruity wine.

ITALIAN MARGARITA

★★★★½

Glass: Martini
Garnish: Lime wedge
Method: SHAKE all ingredients with ice and fine strain into chilled glass.

2 shots Patrón reposado tequila
½ shot De Kuyper Triple Sec
½ shot Disaronno Originale amaretto
1 shot Freshly squeezed lime juice

Origin: Discovered in 2005 at the Club Bar, The Peninsula Beverly Hills, USA.
Comment: A liberal dash of amaretto adds very Italian subtexts of apricot and almond to your classic Margarita.

ITALIAN MILK PUNCH

★★★★☆

Glass: Snifter
Garnish: Dust with grated nutmeg
Method: SHAKE all ingredients and fine strain into chilled glass.

1½ shots Italian Brandy
¼ shot Galliano L'Autentico liqueur
½ shot Disaronno Originale amaretto
⅛ shot Bepi Tosolini Grappa di Moscato
3½ shots Milk

Origin: A riff on the classic Milk Punch created in 2011 by yours truly at the Cabinet Room, London, England.
Comment: The distinctive flavour of moscato grappa shines through in this milky drink, with amaretto adding rich almond notes and Galliano a touch of peppermint and aniseed.

ITALIAN SOUR

★★★☆☆

Glass: Old-fashioned
Garnish: Lemon slice & cherry on stick (sail)
Method: SHAKE all ingredients and strain into ice-filled chilled glass.

½ shot Galliano L'Autentico liqueur
½ shot Strega liqueur
½ shot Campari Bitter
1 shot Freshly squeezed lemon juice
1 dash Angostura Aromatic Bitters
½ fresh Egg white

Comment: Perhaps a little too many powerful Italian flavours for one drink.

ITALIAN SUN

★★★★☆

Glass: Martini
Garnish: Lemon zest twist
Method: SHAKE all ingredients with ice and fine strain into chilled glass.

2 shots Sauvignon blanc white wine
1½ shots Pallini Limoncello
¾ shot Hazelnut liqueur
½ shot Freshly squeezed lemon juice

Origin: Created in 2002 by Dan Spink at Browns, St Martin's Lane, London, England.
Comment: Tastes rather like a bon bon (a round, sugar coated, lemon flavoured sweet).

IVO 🔑

★★★★½

Glass: Coupe
Garnish: Luxardo Maraschino cherry
Method: STIR all ingredients with ice and strain into chilled glass.

2 shots Bourbon whiskey
1 shot Martini Extra Dry vermouth
½ shot Chambord Liqueur
1 dash Angostura Aromatic Bitters

Origin: Named after Quo Vadis London logo, where yours truly asked Emma Ramos to make this drink for Charlotte Ashburner, Chambord's UK Brand Manager in December 2009.
Comment: A fruity twist on the Manhattan.

JA-MORA

★★★★☆

Glass: Flute
Garnish: Raspberries
Method: **SHAKE** first four ingredients with ice and fine strain into chilled glass. **TOP** with champagne.

1 shot Ketel One Vodka
½ shot Chambord Liqueur
½ shot Freshly squeezed orange juice
½ shot Pressed apple juice
Top with G.H. Mumm Cordon Rouge Champagne

Origin: Created by Jamie Terrell and Andres Masso in 1998. Named after 'mora', the Spanish for raspberry. The 'j' and 'a' stand for the names of its two creators.
Comment: Ja-mora of this fruity champagne cocktail you drink, ja-mora you'll like it.

JACK COLLINS

★★★★½

Glass: Collins
Garnish: Lemon slice
Method: **SHAKE** first 3 ingredients with ice and strain into ice-filled glass. **TOP** with soda, stir and serve with straws.

2 shots Calvados brandy
1 shot Freshly squeezed lemon juice
½ shot Sugar syrup (2 sugar to 1 water)
Top with Soda (club soda)

Origin: A Collins named after its applejack (apple brandy) base.
Comment: Apple brandy makes a great base spirit in this refreshing classic.

JACK DEMPSEY

★★★½☆

Glass: Martini
Garnish: Luxardo Maraschino cherry
Method: **SHAKE** all ingredients with ice and fine strain into chilled glass.

1½ shots Bacardi Carta Blanca light rum
1½ shots Rutte Dry Gin
¼ shot Freshly squeezed lemon juice
¼ shot Sugar syrup (2 sugar to 1 water)
¾ shot Chilled water (omit if wet ice)

Comment: Dilution makes or breaks this subtle, gin laced drink.

JACK FROST #1

★★★½☆

Glass: Old-fashioned
Garnish: Orange zest twist
Method: **SHAKE** all ingredients with ice and strain into ice-filled glass.

1½ shots Jack Daniel's Old No.7 Brand
½ shot Drambuie liqueur
¾ shot Freshly squeezed orange juice
½ shot Freshly squeezed lemon juice
¼ shot Pomegranate / grenadine syrup (2:1)

Comment: Tangy and fruity with the whiskey base dominating.

JACK FROST #2

★★★½☆

Glass: Coupe
Garnish: Sugar rim
Method: **SHAKE** all ingredients with ice and strain into ice-filled glass.

1½ shots Martell VSOP Médaillon cognac
1½ shots Chambord Liqueur
1½ shots Cranberry juice
½ shot Freshly squeezed lime juice

Comment: Fruits of the forest and cranberry burst forth from this cognac laced, slightly sweet drink.

JACK MAPLES

★★★½☆

Glass: Martini
Garnish: Dust with cinnamon powder
Method: **SHAKE** all ingredients with ice and fine strain into chilled glass.

2 shots Calvados brandy
¼ shot Maple syrup
1 dash Angostura Orange Bitters

Comment: Maple syrup smooths apple brandy, even as it enhances its character.

JACK POT

★★★★½

Glass: Coupe
Garnish: Strawberry with mint sprig on rim

Method: **STIR** all ingredients with ice and fine strain into chilled glass.

½ shot Drambuie liqueur
¼ shot Dewar's 12 Year Old Scotch whisky
¼ shot Islay single malt Scotch whisky
¼ shot Teeling Small Batch Irish whiskey
¼ shot Welsh single malt whisky
¾ shot Rutte Dry Gin
1½ shots Fuller's Chiswick Bitter
¼ shot Pressed apple juice

Origin: Created in August 2013 by yours truly at the Cabinet Room, London, England.
Comment: Creating this cocktail started with a desire to make a properly British cocktail to toast those special occasions when a fellow Brit wins a sporting event. Fittingly a different whisky in the drink represents England, Ireland, Scotland and Wales. London dry gin, British ale and Drambuie are all obviously British, and with names such as Cox, Granny Smith and Kingston Black, apples are intrinsically a Great British fruit, as indeed is the strawberry (think of Wimbledon), so the obvious garnish.

Handily Drambuie contains Scotch whisky so naturally mixes well with the other whiskies and apple juice is a favourite fruit among bartenders to use in whisky cocktails.

The name is inspired by the Union Jack and also what I thought when I'd successfully combined all the above into one tasty cocktail.

JACK PUNCH

★★★★☆

Glass: Collins
Garnish: Pineapple wedge
Method: Cut passion fruit in half and scoop flesh into shaker. Add other ingredients, **SHAKE** with ice and strain into ice-filled glass.

1	fresh	**Passion fruit**
2	shots	**Jack Daniel's Old No.7 Brand**
½	shot	**Licor 43 liqueur**
3	shots	**Fresh pressed pineapple juice**
⅛	shot	**Sugar syrup (2 sugar to 1 water)**
3	dash	**Angostura Aromatic Bitters**

Origin: Adapted from a recipe created in 2002 at Townhouse, London, England.
Comment: Vanilla hints in the whiskey and liqueur combine to dominate this fruity long drink.

JACK ROSE COCKTAIL

★★★★☆

Glass: Martini
Garnish: Lemon wedge
Method: **SHAKE** all ingredients with ice and fine strain into chilled glass.

2	shots	**Calvados brandy**
¾	shot	**Freshly squeezed lemon juice**
¼	shot	**Pomegranate / grenadine syrup (2:1)**
¼	shot	**Sugar syrup (2 sugar to 1 water)**
2	dash	**Angostura Aromatic Bitters** (optional)
½	shot	**Chilled water** (omit if wet ice)

Origin: Like many great classics this drink is served with numerous plausible origins:

1. The Jack Rose is named after the Jacqueminot rose, which in turn takes its name from the French general, Jean-François Jacqueminot. According to Albert S. Crockett's 1935 'The Old Waldorf-Astoria Bar Book', it is so called because of its pink colour, the exact shade of a Jacqueminot rose, when properly concocted.

2. Some credit this drink's creation to the Colt's Neck inn in New Jersey, which was originally owned by a member of the Laird's family of applejack distillers. His name was Jack and 'Rose' is said to be a reference to the drink's reddish-pink hue. However, this theory has been discredited by Lisa Laird-Dunn, a ninth generation Laird family ancestor.

3. Others simply claim 'Jack' is short for 'applejack' and again hold that 'Rose' a reference to the drink's colour.

4. According to the Police Gazette of 1905, "Frank J. May, better known as Jack Rose, is the inventor of a very popular cocktail by that name, which has made him famous as a mixologist. Jack Rose, apparently also a wrestler, held bar at Gene Sullivan's Café, 187 Pavonia Avenue, Jersey City, New Jersey".

5. However, the most popular theory relates to a late 19th century New York small-time gangster called Jack Rose who was the informant in a notorious 1912 murder case. 'Bald' Jack Rose, whose favourite beverage is said to have been applejack brandy with lemon and grenadine, was heavily implicated in the 1912 shooting of Herman 'Beansy' Rosenthal, the owner of several New York gambling dens who was in throws of blowing the lid on police and municipal links to organised crime. Rosenthal had already squealed to the press and on the evening of July 15, after the lengthy delivery of his affidavit, left D.A. Charles Whitman's office at around midnight. Fatally he then headed to the Metropole Café at the Hotel Metropole on West 43rd Street, a favourite late night gambler's haunt, for a nightcap. As he exited the Metropole he was killed by four bullets, one to the chest and three to his head. The hit was pinned on a Lieutenant Charles Becker of the NYPD's antigambling squad and Rose was star witness in what was then the trial of the century. Becker went to the electric chair while Rose apparently went into the catering business, lending his name to his favourite drink.

6. Or, alternatively, it could be named after Jack Rose, an early 20th century brand of small cigars which sold for five cents a pack. Interestingly, these little cigars became known by the nickname 'squealers' after the Rosenthal case.
Comment: An apple brandy sour sweetened with grenadine. Better when shaken with egg white.

JACK TAR

★★★★½

Glass: Old-fashioned
Garnish: Lime wedge
Method: **SHAKE** all ingredients and strain into ice-filled glass.

1	shot	**Pusser's Navy Rum (54.5%)**
½	shot	**Bourbon whiskey**
½	shot	**Rutte Dry Gin**
¼	shot	**Freshly squeezed lime juice**
¼	shot	**Freshly squeezed lemon juice**
¼	shot	**Light muscovado sugar syrup (2 sugar to 1 water)**

Origin: Jack is a generic name for all British sailors, derived from Jack Tar in the 18th and 19th centuries. Sailors in those years used high-grade tar in their clothing and hair for waterproofing. The term, "Jack-of-all-trades," described a sailor who could turn his hand to anything, is widely used today.
Comment: Characterful rum leads with gin and whiskey playing supporting roles with hints of citrus.

JACK-IN-THE-BOX

★★★★☆

Glass: Martini
Garnish: Pineapple wedge
Method: **SHAKE** all ingredients with ice and fine strain into chilled glass.

2	shots	**Calvados brandy**
1½	shots	**Fresh pressed pineapple juice**
¼	shot	**Sugar syrup (2 sugar to 1 water)**
2	shots	**Angostura Aromatic Bitters**

Comment: Smooth 'n' easy apple and pineapple with spirity spice.

JACKIE O'S ROSE

★★★★☆

Glass: Martini
Garnish: Lime wedge
Method: **SHAKE** all ingredients with ice and fine strain into chilled glass.

2	shots	**Bacardi Carta Blanca light rum**
½	shot	**De Kuyper Triple Sec**
1	shot	**Freshly squeezed lime juice**
½	shot	**Sugar syrup (2 sugar to 1 water)**
½	spoon	**Rose water**

Comment: In its simplest form this is a Daiquiri with added triple sec and rose water - or a Margarita with rum. Whatever, it's a good balance of sweet and sour.

JACKTINI

★★★★☆

Glass: Martini
Garnish: Lemon zest twist
Method: **SHAKE** all ingredients and fine strain into chilled glass.

1	shot	**Jack Daniel's Old No.7 Brand**
1	shot	**Mandarine Napoléon liqueur**
1¾	shots	**Freshly squeezed lemon juice**
½	shot	**Sugar syrup (2 sugar to 1 water)**

Comment: A citrus bite and a smooth Tennessee draw enhanced with rich mandarin liqueur.

JACUZZI

★★★★☆

Glass: Flute
Garnish: Orange slice
Method: SHAKE first three ingredients with ice and fine strain into chilled glass. **TOP** with champagne.

1	shot	Peachtree peach schnapps
½	shot	Rutte Dry Gin
1	shot	Freshly squeezed orange juice
Top with		G.H. Mumm Cordon Rouge Champagne

Comment: A sweet, peachy champagne cocktail.

JADE DAIQUIRI

★★★★☆

Glass: Martini
Garnish: Mint leaf
Method: SHAKE all ingredients with ice and fine strain into chilled glass.

2	shots	Bacardi Carta Blanca light rum
¼	shot	De Kuyper Triple Sec
¼	shot	Giffard Menthe Pastille liqueur
½	shot	Freshly squeezed lime juice
¼	shot	Sugar syrup (2 sugar to 1 water)

Comment: A Daiquiri with a splash of orange and mint liqueurs. Fresh breath enhancing.

JADE GARDEN

★★★★☆

Glass: Collins
Garnish: Lemon slice
Method: SHAKE all ingredients with ice and strain into ice-filled glass.

2 shots Ketel One Vodka
1 shot St-Germain elderflower liqueur
½ shot Cold jasmine tea
1½ shots Pressed apple juice
½ shot Freshly squeezed lemon juice

Origin: Adapted from a drink created in 2004 by Michael Butt and Giles Looker of Soulshakers, England.
Comment: Not too dry, nor too sweet, but tasty, balanced and refreshing.

JAFFA COCKTAIL

★★★★☆

Glass: Martini
Garnish: Mini Jaffa Cake
Method: SHAKE all ingredients with ice and fine strain into chilled glass.

1	shot	De Kuyper Triple Sec
1	shot	Dark crème de cacao liqueur
½	shot	Ketel One Oranje vodka
½	shot	Freshly squeezed lemon juice
1	shot	Freshly squeezed orange juice
3	dash	Angostura Orange Bitters
1	fresh	Eggs (white & yolk)

Origin: Created by yours truly in 2004.

McVitie's Jaffa Cakes have a tangy orange jelly centre on a hardish sponge base, covered in dark chocolate. Back in 1991 these tasty little snacks beat off UK Customs & Excise who sought to reclassify them as chocolate biscuits, which, unlike cakes, are categorised as luxuries and so subjected to Value Added Tax.
Comment: Sweet, dessert-style cocktail.

JÄGERBOMB

★★☆☆☆

Glass: Shot
Garnish: None
Method: POUR Jägermeister into shot glass and separately POUR Red Bull into old-fashioned glass. Instruct drinker to drop shot of Jägermeister into a glass of Red Bull.

| 3 | shots | Red Bull |
| 1 | shot | Jägermeister |

Origin: In Germany this drink is called a 'Turbojäger', a 'Flying Hirsch' with flying referencing Red Bull's marketing slogan "Red Bull gives you wings" and Hirsch (German for 'stag') the Jägermeister logo. In Mexico, it is called a 'Perla Negra' (Black Pearl) and in Finland, a 'Akkuhappo' (meaning 'battery acid').

A Jäger-train is a theatrical method of preparing a number of Jägerbombs at once. To do this set up a row of old-fashioned glasses with one extra glass than the number of drinkers at the end. Pour half-a-can of Red Bull into each of the old-old fashioned glasses. Pour Jägermeister into shot glasses and balance on the rims where each of the two old-fashioned glasses meet. Starting one end knock the first shot glass into the old-fashioned glass beneath and the rest should follow domino style.
Comment: Famous and infamous.

THE JÄGERITA

★★★☆☆

Glass: Martini
Garnish: Lime wedge
Method: SHAKE all ingredients with ice and fine strain into chilled glass.

2	shots	Jägermeister
1	shot	De Kuyper Triple Sec
1	shot	Freshly squeezed lime juice
¼	shot	Sugar syrup (2 sugar to 1 water)

Origin: Created by David Cordoba and demonstrated at Difford's Cabinet Room in September 2008.
Comment: The bartender's favourite shot meets the bartender's favourite cocktail.

JALISCO

★★★★☆

Glass: Martini
Garnish: White grapes
Method: MUDDLE grapes in base of shaker. Add other ingredients, SHAKE with ice and fine strain into chilled glass.

12	fresh	Seedless white grapes
2½	shots	Patrón reposado tequila
½	shot	Sugar syrup (2 sugar to 1 water)
3	dash	Angostura Orange Bitters

Origin: Created in 2003 by Shelim Islam at GE Club, London, England. Pronounced 'Hal-is-co', this cocktail takes its name from the Mexican state that is home to the town of Tequila and the spirit of the same name.
Comment: It's amazing how well grapes combine with tequila.

JALISCO ESPRESSO

★★★★½

Glass: Martini
Garnish: Coffee beans
Method: SHAKE all ingredients with ice and fine strain into chilled glass.

2	shots	Patrón reposado tequila
1	shot	Espresso coffee (freshly made & hot)
1	shot	Coffee liqueur

Origin: Adapted from a drink created in 2005 by Henry Besant & Andres Masso, London, England, and named after the Mexican state where the tequila industry is centred.
Comment: A tequila laced wake up call.

JALISCO FLOWER

★★★★½

Glass: Flute
Garnish: Grapefruit zest twist
Method: SHAKE first three ingredients with ice and fine strain into chilled glass. TOP with champagne. Lightly stir and serve.

½	shot	Patrón reposado tequila
¾	shot	St-Germain elderflower liqueur
1	shot	Freshly squeezed ruby grapefruit juice
Top with		G.H.Mumm Cordon Rouge Champagne

Origin: Created in 2008 by Vincenzo Marianella at Doheny, Los Angeles, USA.
Comment: Subtle, fruity and one of my favourite champagne cocktails.

JAM ROLL

★★½☆☆

Glass: Shot
Garnish: None
Method: Refrigerate ingredients then LAYER in chilled glass in the following order.

½	shot	Chambord Liqueur
½	shot	Hazelnut liqueur
½	shot	Baileys Irish cream liqueur

Origin: Created in 2003 at Liquid Lounge, Marbella, Spain.
Comment: A very sweet jam roll laced with alcohol.

JAMAICAN ME CRAZY

★★★½☆

Glass: Hurricane
Garnish: Passion fruit & mint sprig
Method: SHAKE all ingredients with ice and strain into glass filled with crushed ice.

1½	shots	Passion fruit juice
2	shots	Bacardi Carta Blanca light rum
1	shot	Coconut rum liqueur
2	shots	Freshly squeezed orange juice
2	shots	Cranberry juice
1½	shots	Freshly squeezed lime juice
¾	shot	Pomegranate / grenadine syrup (2:1)

Comment: A rum laced (originally Jamaican), fruity, Tiki-style cocktail.

JAMAICAN MULE

★★★½☆☆

Glass: Collins
Garnish: Lime wedge
Method: POUR ingredients into ice-filled glass and lightly stir.

2	shots	Bacardi OakHeart Spiced Rum
½	shot	Freshly squeezed lime juice
½	shot	Sugar syrup (2 sugar to 1 water)
Top with		Gosling's Stormy Ginger Beer

Comment: A long, rum based drink with a spicy ginger taste.

JAMAICAN SUNSET

★★★★☆

Glass: Collins
Garnish: Orange slice
Method: SHAKE all ingredients with ice and strain into ice-filled glass.

1½	shots	White overproof rum
1½	shots	Cranberry juice
3	shots	Freshly squeezed orange juice

Comment: Made with vodka as a base this drink would be called a Madras. Overproof rum adds both strength and flavour.

JAMBALAYA

★★★½☆

Glass: Collins
Garnish: Orange slice & peach schnapps
Method: SHAKE all ingredients with ice and strain into glass filled with crushed ice.

2	shots	Patrón reposado tequila
1	shot	Peachtree peach schnapps
2	shots	Freshly squeezed orange juice
½	shot	Freshly squeezed lime juice
¼	shot	Pomegranate / grenadine syrup (2:1)

Comment: Peachy tropical fruit laced with tequila.

JAMBOUREE

★★★★☆

Glass: Martini
Garnish: Orange zest twist
Method: STIR preserve with bourbon in base of shaker until mostly dissolved. Add other ingredients, **SHAKE** with ice and fine strain into chilled glass.

2 spoon Apricot jam (preserve)
2 shots Bourbon whiskey
½ shot Grand Marnier Cordon Rouge
½ shot Freshly squeezed lemon juice
¾ shot Chilled water (omit if wet ice)

Comment: Rich and jammy flavours balanced by bourbon and lemon juice.

JAMES JOYCE

★★★★☆

Glass: Martini
Garnish: Luxardo Maraschino cherry
Method: SHAKE all ingredients with ice and fine strain into chilled glass.

1½ shots	Teeling Small Batch Irish whiskey
¾ shot	De Kuyper Triple Sec
¾ shot	Martini Rosso vermouth
½ shot	Freshly squeezed lime juice

Origin: Created in 2001 by the American drinks author Gary Regan. This recipe is taken from his book, 'The Joy of Mixology'.
Comment: A balanced adult sour blend.

JAMIE'S MOJITO (NEW)

★★★★½

Glass: Collins
Garnish: Mint sprig
Method: POUR first 4 ingredients into glass. **ADD** lime wedges & mint and crushed ice. **CHURN** (stir), **TOP** with Prosecco and **CHURN** again.

1	shot	Bacardi Carta Blanca light rum
1	shot	Martini Bianco
¾	shot	Freshly squeezed lime juice
½	shot	Sugar syrup (2 sugar to 1 water)
3	wedge	Lime (fresh whole)
12	fresh	Mint leaves
Top with		Prosecco sparkling wine

Origin: Adapted from a popular drink on the menu of Jamie's Italian restaurant and bar chain.
Comment: A light mojito made more complex with bianco vermouth.

JAMMIE DODGER ⚷

★★☆☆☆

Glass: Shot
Garnish: Biscuit rim
Method: POUR liqueur into glass and then float cream on top.

¾	shot	Chambord Liqueur
¼	shot	Single cream / half-and-half

Origin: The origin of this drink is unknown but it is named after and inspired by the classic British biscuit produced by Burton's Foods. Jammie Dodgers were launched in 1960 and consist of two circular discs of shortbread biscuit with raspberry-flavoured plum jam sandwiched between with a heart-shaped hole in the upper biscuit to reveal the jam. In recent years the original heart-shaped embossing on the shortbread has been replaced by splashes.
Comment: The sugar and fat will get you before the alcohol does.

JANIE JONES

★★★★½☆

Glass: Collins
Garnish: Luxardo Maraschino cherry
Method: SHAKE first three ingredients with ice and strain into ice-filled glass. **TOP** with soda.

2	shots	Rutte Dry Gin
½	shot	King's Ginger Liqueur
2	shots	Pressed apple juice
Top with		Soda (club soda)

Origin: Created in 2010 by Mike Atkinson at the Badem House, Goa, India and named after the classic 1970's punk song by British band 'The Clash'. The two maraschino cherries represent Janie Jones herself who famously appeared at a London film premiere in 1964 wearing a topless dress.
Comment: A long gin laced apple and ginger cocktail.

JAPANESE COCKTAIL

★★★★☆

Glass: Coupe
Garnish: Lemon zest twist
Method: SHAKE all ingredients with ice and fine strain into chilled glass.

2	shots	Martell VSOP Médaillon cognac
¼	shot	Almond (orgeat) syrup
¾	shot	Chilled water (reduce if wet ice)
2	dash	Angostura Aromatic Bitters

Origin: Adapted from a recipe first published in 'Professor' Jerry Thomas' 1862 'Bartender's Guide', this is one of the few drinks in the book which is believed to be of his own creation.

It is thought that he created and named the drink in 1860 to commemorate the first Japanese mission to the USA. While in New York, the delegates stayed at the Metropolitan Hotel, just a block away from Jerry Thomas' bar at 622 Broadway. And as David Wondrich writes in his 2015 'Updated and Revised Imbibe!', "I can't imagine that in their strolls around the neighbourhood, they wouldn't have stopped in to see the Professor for a quick one. And if you were Jerry Thomas, wouldn't you come up with something special to mark the occasion?"
Comment: Lightly sweetened and diluted cognac flavoured with almond and a hint of spice.

JAPANESE MAPLE

★★★★⯪

Glass: Coupe
Garnish: Mist with Angostura
Method: DRY SHAKE (without ice) all ingredients. SHAKE again with ice and fine strain into chilled glass.

1¾ shots Yamazaki 12yo Japanese whisky
¾ shot   Freshly squeezed lemon juice
½ shot   Maple syrup
½ fresh   Egg white

Origin: Created in 2009 by Damian Windsor at The Roger Room, Los Angeles, USA.
Comment: This excellent Japanese whisky based sour is balanced with maple syrup.

JAPANESE PEAR

★★★★☆

Glass: Martini
Garnish: Pear slice
Method: SHAKE all ingredients with ice and fine strain into chilled glass.

1½ shots Ketel One Vodka
½ shot   Poire William eau de vie
1 shot   Junmai ginjō sake
¼ shot   Sugar syrup (2 sugar to 1 water)

Origin: Adapted in 2002 from a recipe from Grand Pacific Blue Room, Sydney, Australia.
Comment: Originally made with Poire William liqueur, hence this version calls for a little sugar.

JAPANESE SLIPPER

★★★★☆

Glass: Martini
Garnish: Salt rim
Method: SHAKE all ingredients with ice and fine strain into chilled glass.

2 shots   Patrón reposado tequila
1 shot   Midori Green Melon liqueur
1 shot   Freshly squeezed lime juice

Comment: A melon Margarita.

JASMINE (NEW)

★★★★☆

Glass: Martini
Garnish: Lemon zest twist
Method: SHAKE all ingredients with ice and fine strain into chilled glass.

1½ shot   Rutte Dry Gin
¼ shot   De Kuyper Triple sec
¼ shot   Campari Bitter
¾ shot   Freshly squeezed lemon juice
1 spoon   Sugar syrup (2 sugar to 1 water)

Comment: This bittersweet riff on the Pegu Club will appeal to drinkers who have acquired the taste for Campari.
Origin: Created in the mid 90s by Paul Harrington at Townhouse, Emeryville, California, USA. The Jasmine was promoted by its inclusion in his 1998 book 'Cocktail'.

JASMINE & ELDERFLOWER MARTINI

★★★★☆

Glass: Martini
Garnish: Mint leaf
Method: SHAKE all ingredients with ice and fine strain into chilled glass.

2 shots   Ketel One Vodka
1 shot   St-Germain elderflower liqueur
¼ shot   Cold jasmine tea
⅛ shot   Martini Extra Dry vermouth

Origin: Created in 2006 by yours truly, London, England.
Comment: Delicate and floral yet dry and serious. The tannins in the tea complement and balance the drink.

JASMINE LASSI COCKTAIL

★★★⯪☆

Glass: Coupe
Garnish: Lime zest twist
Method: MUDDLE cardamom in base of shaker. Add other ingredients, SHAKE with ice and fine strain into chilled glass.

1 whole   Cardamom pod
1½ shots Ketel One Vodka
1½ shots Yoghurt liqueur
¾ shot   Cold jasmine tea

Origin: Created in 2012 by yours truly at the Cabinet Room, London, England.
Comment: Fragrant cardamom and jasmine cooled with yoghurt and ice. Best consumed with a Madras.

JAYNE MANSFIELD

★★★★⯪

Glass: Flute
Garnish: Strawberry on rim
Method: MUDDLE strawberries in base of shaker. Add next three ingredients, SHAKE with ice and fine strain into glass. TOP with champagne.

4 fresh   Small ripe strawberries (hulled)
1 shot   Bacardi Carta Blanca light rum
1 shot   Lejay Crème de Fraise
¼ shot   Sugar syrup (2 sugar to 1 water)
Top with   G.H. Mumm Cordon Rouge Champagne

Origin: Named after the Hollywood actress.
Comment: Champagne is made to go with strawberries.

JEAN GABIN

★★★★☆

Glass: Toddy
Garnish: Dust with grated nutmeg
Method: POUR first three ingredients into glass. Add maple syrup and STIR until maple syrup dissolves.

1½ shots Gosling's Black Seal dark rum
¾ shot   Calvados brandy
5 shots   Milk (steamed foaming)
1 spoon   Maple syrup

Origin: Created in 1986 by Charles Schumann, Munich, Germany.
Comment: Beats hot chocolate as a nightcap.

JEAN LAFITTE COCKTAIL

★★⯨☆☆

Glass: Coupe
Garnish: Orange zest twist
Method: SHAKE all ingredients with ice and fine strain into chilled glass.

2 shots Bacardi Carta Ocho aged rum
¼ shot Le Fée Parisienne absinthe
¼ shot De Kuyper Triple Sec
⅛ shot Sugar syrup (2 sugar to 1 water)
1 fresh Egg yolk
1 dash Peychaud's aromatic bitters

Origin: My adaptation of the New Orleans classic named after the infamous privateer and hero of the Battle of New Orleans.
Comment: Not dissimilar to spicy, fortified advocaat.

JEAN MARC

★★★★☆

Glass: Collins
Garnish: Mint sprig
Method: MUDDLE mint and ginger in base of shaker. Add next two ingredients, **SHAKE** with ice and fine strain into ice-filled glass. **TOP** with Appletiser, stir and serve with straws.

2 slice Fresh root ginger (thumbnail sized)
4 fresh Mint leaves
1½ shots Green Chartreuse liqueur
¼ shot Apple Schnapps liqueur
Top with Appletiser

Origin: Created in 2003 by yours truly after judging a Chartreuse cocktail competition in London and realising which flavours best combine with Chartreuse. Named after my friend the then President Directeur General of Chartreuse.
Comment: Chartreuse combines well with apple, ginger and mint in this summertime drink.

JELLY BELLY BEANY

★★★★☆

Glass: Martini
Garnish: Jelly Bean sweets
Method: SHAKE all ingredients with ice and fine strain into chilled glass.

1½ shots Bacardi Carta Blanca light rum
1 shot Peachtree peach schnapps
1 shot Coconut rum liqueur
2 dash Angostura Orange Bitters
½ shot Chilled water (omit if wet ice)

Origin: Created in 2002 at Hush, London, England.
Comment: It's a sweetie but you're going to enjoy chewing on it.

JENEVER PUNCH

★★★★⯨

Glass: Goblet
Garnish: Grated nutmeg
Method: SHAKE first 4 ingredients with ice and strain into ice-filled glass. **TOP** up with soda.

1½ shots Rutte Old Simon oude jenever
1 shot Freshly squeezed lemon juice
½ shot Light muscovado sugar syrup (2 sugar to 1 water)
2 dash Luxardo Maraschino liqueur
Top with Soda (club soda)

Comment: A more complex riff of a Collins with malty genever and brown sugar flavours considerably adding to the drink.

JENEVER SOUR

★★★★☆

Glass: Old-fashioned
Garnish: Luxardo Maraschino cherry
Method: SHAKE all ingredients with ice and strain into ice-filled glass.

2 shots Rutte Old Simon oude jenever
1 shot Freshly squeezed lemon juice
½ shot Sugar syrup (2 sugar to 1 water)
½ fresh Egg white

Comment: One of the more delicately flavoured sours.

JEREZ

★★★★☆

Glass: Old-fashioned
Garnish: None
Method: STIR all ingredients with ice and strain into ice-filled glass.

½ shot Romate Fino sherry
½ shot Romate Pedro Ximénez sherry
1 shot Peachtree peach schnapps
1 shot Sauvignon blanc white wine
1 shot La Vieille Prune plum brandy
1 dash Angostura Aromatic Bitters

Origin: This drink heralds from one of the noble houses in Spain - well that's what the sherry PR told us, anyway, we've changed the recipe slightly.
Comment: Sherry depth and stoned fruit flavours.

JERSEY SOUR

★★★★★

Glass: Old-fashioned
Garnish: Lemon zest twist
Method: SHAKE all ingredients with ice and fine strain into chilled glass.

2 shots Calvados brandy
1 shot Freshly squeezed lemon juice
½ shot Sugar syrup (2 sugar to 1 water)
½ fresh Egg white

Origin: The classic name for an Applejack sour.
Comment: Apple brandy is possibly the best spirit on which to base a sour.

JEWEL COCKTAIL

★★★☆☆

Glass: Martini
Garnish: Luxardo Maraschino cherry
Method: STIR all ingredients with ice and strain into chilled glass.

1	shot	Rutte Dry Gin
1	shot	Green Chartreuse liqueur
1	shot	Martini Rosso vermouth
1	dash	Angostura Orange Bitters
½	shot	Chilled water (omit if wet ice)

Comment: Powerful in both alcohol and flavour. An old-school drink to challenge modern palates.

JOAN BENNETT

★★★☆☆

Glass: Collins
Garnish: Pineapple wedge
Method: SHAKE all ingredients with ice and strain into glass filled with crushed ice.

2	shots	Bacardi Carta Blanca light rum
1	shot	Parfait Amour liqueur
2½	shots	Fresh pressed pineapple juice

Origin: Adapted from a Tiki drink featured in Jeff Berry's 'Intoxica' and originally created in 1932 at Sloppy Joe's Bar, Havana, Cuba. Named after Hollywood ingénue, Joan Bennett, who in the same year starred in Fox's Careless Lady. Years later she hit the news when her husband, producer Walter Wanger, shot her agent in the crotch after catching them in bed together. Oo-err!
Comment: Fruity and floral, but an unfortunate colour.

JOCKEY CLUB

★★★★☆

Glass: Martini
Garnish: Orange zest twist
Method: SHAKE all ingredients with ice and fine strain into chilled glass.

2	shots	Rutte Dry Gin
½	shot	Disaronno Originale amaretto
½	shot	Freshly squeezed lemon juice
¾	shot	Chilled water (omit if wet ice)
1	dash	Angostura Orange Bitters
1	dash	Angostura Aromatic Bitters

Origin: This classic drink from the 1930s originally called for crème de noyaux.
Comment: Peachy almond with gin.

JODI MAY 🔑

★★★★☆

Glass: Collins
Garnish: Orange slice
Method: SHAKE all ingredients with ice and fine strain into chilled glass.

1½	shots	Bourbon whiskey
½	shot	De Kuyper Triple Sec
2½	shots	Freshly squeezed orange juice
1½	shots	Cranberry juice
¼	shot	Freshly squeezed lime juice

Origin: Adapted from a drink discovered in 2003 at World Service, Nottingham, England.
Comment: Long, fruity and laced with whiskey.

JOHN COLLINS 🔑

★★★★☆

Glass: Collins
Garnish: Orange slice & Luxardo Maraschino cherry on stick (sail)
Method: SHAKE first 3 ingredients with ice and strain into ice-filled glass. **TOP** with soda, stir and serve with straws.

2	shots	Rutte Dry Gin
1	shot	Freshly squeezed lemon juice
½	shot	Sugar syrup (2 sugar to 1 water)
Top with		Soda (club soda)

Comment: A refreshing balance of sour lemon and sugar, laced with gin and lengthened with soda.

JOHN DALY

★★★★☆

Glass: Collins
Garnish: Lemon slice
Method: SHAKE all ingredients with ice and strain into ice-filled glass.

1½	shots	Ketel One Citroen vodka
¼	shot	De Kuyper Triple Sec
1½	shots	Freshly squeezed lemon juice
¾	shot	Sugar syrup (2 sugar to 1 water)
2	shots	Cold English breakfast tea

Origin: Named after the American professional golfer noted for his victory in the 1991 PGA Championship and colourful personal life.
Comment: Essentially an alcoholic iced tea, this is bittersweet and refreshing - perfect for a hot afternoon.

JOLT'INI

★★★★☆

Glass: Martini
Garnish: Coffee beans
Method: SHAKE all ingredients with ice and fine strain into chilled glass.

1¾	shots	Vanilla infused Ketel One vodka
½	shot	Coffee liqueur
1¼	shots	Espresso coffee (freshly made & hot)
¼	shot	Vanilla sugar syrup

Origin: Discovered in 2005 at Degrees, Washington DC, USA.
Comment: A flavoursome wake up call of espresso coffee laced with vanilla vodka.

JOSE COLLINS 🔑

★★★★☆

Glass: Collins
Garnish: Orange slice & cherry on stick (sail)
Method: SHAKE first three ingredients with ice and strain into ice-filled glasses. **TOP** with soda, stir and serve with straws.

2	shots	Patrón reposado tequila
1	shot	Freshly squeezed lemon juice
½	shot	Sugar syrup (2 sugar to 1 water)
Top with		Soda (club soda)

Comment: The classic long balance of sweet and sour with tequila adding Mexican spirit.

JOSEPHINE BAKER

★★★½☆

Glass: Martini
Garnish: Dust with cinnamon powder
Method: SHAKE all ingredients with ice and fine strain into chilled glass.

1½ shots **Martell VSOP Médaillon cognac**
1½ shots **Tawny port**
1 shot **De Kuyper XO Apricot Brandy**
¼ shot **Sugar syrup (2 sugar to 1 water)**
1 fresh **Lemon zest**
1 fresh **Egg yolk**

Origin: Recipe adapted from a 1937 Bar Florida menu, Havana, Cuba. This cocktail is named in honour of Josephine Baker (1906-1975), an American-born dancer, singer, and actress. She dropped out of school at just 12-years-old and lived as a street child amongst the slums of St. Louis until her street-corner dancing attracted attention and at 15 she was recruited for the St. Louis Chorus vaudeville show. Baker then became a hit in New York City during the Harlem Renaissance, reputedly "the highest-paid chorus girl in vaudeville".

In October 1925 she moved to Paris and starred at the Théâtre de Champs-Élysées where she appeared practically nude. Her erotic dancing earned her the nicknames Bronze Venus, Black Pearl and Créole Goddess.

Baker was a staunch supporter of the Civil Rights Movement in the United States and for assisting the French Resistance during World War II which earned her French military honour, the Croix de guerre.
Comment: A smooth apricot and brandy dessert-style cocktail with hints of wine and cold tea.

THE JOURNALIST

★★★★☆

Glass: Martini
Garnish: Luxardo Maraschino cherry
Method: SHAKE all ingredients with ice and fine strain into chilled glass.

2 shots **Rutte Dry Gin**
¼ shot **De Kuyper Triple Sec**
½ shot **Martini Extra Dry vermouth**
½ shot **Martini Rosso vermouth**
¼ shot **Freshly squeezed lemon juice**
2 dash **Angostura Aromatic Bitters**

Comment: Like some journalists I've met, this gin Martini is bitter and sour.

JOY DIVISION (NEW)

★★★★½

Glass: Coupe
Garnish: Lemon zest twist
Method: STIR all ingredients with ice and strain into chilled glass.

2 shot **Rutte Dry Gin**
1 shot **Martini Extra Dry vermouth**
½ shot **De Kuyper Triple sec**
3 dash **Le Fée Parisienne absinthe**

Comment: A 2:1 Dry Martini with slug of triple sec and dashes of absinthe contributing zesty orange and subtle aniseed respectively.
Origin: Recipe created in 2008 by Phil Ward at Death & Co., New York, USA.

JUBILANT

★★★★½

Glass: Martini
Garnish: Orange slice
Method: SHAKE all ingredients with ice and fine strain into chilled glass.

1½ shots **Rutte Dry Gin**
¾ shot **Bénédictine D.O.M. liqueur**
½ shot **Freshly squeezed lemon juice**
½ shot **Freshly squeezed orange juice**
½ fresh **Egg white**

Origin: A long lost classic.
Comment: Wonderfully balanced, aromatic, herbal and fruity.

JUDGEMENT DAY

★★★★☆

Glass: Martini
Garnish: Spray of Pimento Dram
Method: SHAKE with ice and fine strain into chilled glass.

1 shot **BarSol Mosto Verde Italia pisco**
⅛ shot **Le Fée Parisienne absinthe**
½ shot **Freshly squeezed lime juice**
½ shot **Freshly squeezed lemon juice**
¼ shot **Sugar syrup (2 sugar to 1 water)**
½ fresh **Egg white**

Origin: On 16th May 2008, superstar bartender Charles Vexenat was unjustly jailed in New Orleans during Tales of the Cocktail after his friend Dre dropped a bottle in the Old Absinthe House. Fortunately for Charles he was saved a second day in the slammer by Melanie Asher, owner of Macchu Pisco who bailed them out. This cocktail, created at PDT, New York City, is Charles's tribute to Melanie.
Comment: Charles was pretty sour about his experience when he created this very aromatic sour.

JUDY (MOCKTAIL)

★★★½☆

Glass: Collins
Garnish: Lime wedge
Method: SHAKE all ingredients with ice and strain into ice-filled glass.

2 shots **Freshly squeezed pink grapefruit juice**
3 shots **Fresh pressed pineapple juice**
½ shot **Freshly squeezed lemon juice**
½ shot **Rose's lime cordial**

Comment: A refreshing, not sweet, driver's option. Consider adding a couple of dashes of Angostura aromatic bitters although be aware that these contain some alcohol.

STAR RATINGS EXPLAINED

★★★★★+	OUTSTANDING	★★★★★	EXCEPTIONAL
★★★★½	EXCELLENT	★★★★☆	RECOMMENDED
★★★½☆	COMMENDED	★★★☆☆	MEDIOCRE
★★½☆☆	DISAPPOINTING	★★☆☆☆	PRETTY AWFUL
★½☆☆☆	SHAMEFUL	★☆☆☆☆	DISGUSTING

JULEP (GENERIC NAME) 🔑

★★★★★

Glass: Collins
Garnish: Mint sprig
Method: Lightly **MUDDLE** mint leaves with spirit in base of shaker (just enough to bruise). (At this stage, if time allows, you should refrigerate the shaker, mint and spirit, and the glass in which the drink is to be served, for at least two hours.) Add other ingredients to shaker, **SHAKE** with ice and strain into glass filled with crushed ice. **CHURN** (stir) the drink with the crushed ice using a bar spoon. Top with more crushed ice to fill glass and churn again. Serve with straws.

12 fresh Mint leaves
2½ shots Brandy, whisk(e)y, gin, rum etc.
¾ shot Sugar syrup (2 sugar to 1 water)
3 dash Angostura Aromatic Bitters

Origin: Juleps are tall drinks generally served in Collins or ideally in julep cups, and based on a spirit, liqueur or fortified wine. They are most often served with fresh mint over crushed ice.

The name ultimately derives from the Arabic word 'julab', meaning rosewater. Although this had been used to describe any sweetened drink, up to and including medicines. The Julep is thought to have originated in Persia, or thereabouts, and it travelled to Europe (some say Southern France) where the rose petals were substituted for indigenous mint. The drink is then believed to have crossed the Atlantic where cognac was replaced with peach brandy and then whiskey - the Mint Julep we recognise today.

The first known written reference to a cocktail-style Julep was by a Virginian gentleman in 1787.
Comment: The key to this drink is serving it ice cold and giving the flavours in the mint time to marry with the spirit. Hence, Juleps are ideally prepared hours in advance of serving. Adjust sugar to balance if using a fortified wine in place of a spirit.

JULEP MARTINI

★★★★☆

Glass: Martini
Garnish: Mint leaf
Method: Lightly **MUDDLE** mint in base of shaker (just to bruise). Add other ingredients, **SHAKE** with ice and fine strain into chilled glass.

8 fresh Mint leaves
2½ shots Bourbon whiskey
½ shot Sugar syrup (2 sugar to 1 water)
¾ shot Chilled water (omit if wet ice)

Origin: Adapted from a recipe created in the mid 1990s by Dick Bradsell.
Comment: A short variation on the classic Julep: sweetened bourbon and mint.

JULES DELIGHT

★★★★☆

Glass: Coupe
Garnish: Strawberry
Method: **MUDDLE** strawberries in base of shaker. Add other ingredients, **SHAKE** with ice and fine strain into chilled glass.

3 fresh Small ripe strawberries (hulled)
2 shots Ketel One Vodka
¼ shot White balsamic vinegar
¾ shot Pressed apple juice
¼ shot Freshly squeezed lemon juice
½ shot Sugar syrup (2 sugar to 1 water)

Origin: Created in 2005 by Julien 'Papa Jules' Gualdoni at Trailer Happiness, London, England.
Comment: Sweet fortified strawberries with a cleansing balsamic vinegar bite.

JULIET & ROMEO (NEW) 🔑

★★★★☆

Glass: Coupe
Garnish: Float 3 drops rose water, 3 drops Angostura bitters & mint leaf
Method: **MUDDLE** cucumber in base of shaker. Add other ingredients, **SHAKE** with ice and fine strain into chilled glass.

3 slice Cucumber
8 fresh Mint leaves
1 pinch Salt
2 shot Rutte Dry Gin
¾ shot Freshly squeezed lime juice
½ Sugar syrup (2 sugar to 1 water)

Comment: You smell rose water but taste gin, lime, cucumber and mint. A refreshing summery cocktail.
Origin: Created in 2007 by Toby Maloney at The Violet Hour in Chicago, USA.

JULIETTE

★★★☆☆

Glass: Collins
Garnish: Pineapple wedge & Luxardo Maraschino cherry
Method: **SHAKE** all ingredients with ice and strain into ice-filled glass.

1 shot Martell VSOP Médaillon cognac
1 shot Belle de Brillet pear liqueur
¼ shot Chambord Liqueur
2½ shots Cranberry juice
1 shot Fresh pressed pineapple juice

Comment: Fruity, medium sweet, cognac laced cooler.

JUMBLED FRUIT JULEP

★★★★☆

Glass: Collins
Garnish: Strawberry & mint sprig
Method: **MUDDLE** strawberries and then mint in base of shaker (just to bruise mint). Add other ingredients, **SHAKE** with ice and strain into glass filled with crushed ice.

4 fresh Mint leaves
3 fresh Small ripe strawberries (hulled)
2 shots Ketel One Vodka
1 shot Pressed apple juice
½ shot Passion fruit syrup
½ shot Freshly squeezed lime juice

Origin: Created in 2005 by Michael Butt and Giles Looker of Soulshakers, England.
Comment: A fruity twist on the classic Julep.

JUMPIN' JACK FLASH

★★★★☆

Glass: Martini
Garnish: Pineapple wedge
Method: **SHAKE** all ingredients with ice and fine strain into chilled glass.

1½ shots Jack Daniel's Old No.7 Brand
½ shot Crème de banane liqueur
½ shot Galliano L'Autentico liqueur
¾ shot Freshly squeezed orange juice
¾ shot Fresh pressed pineapple juice

Comment: Whiskey further mellowed and sweetened by a tasty combo of liqueurs and juices.

JUNE BUG

★★★⯪☆

Glass: Hurricane
Garnish: Pineapple wedge & Luxardo Maraschino cherry
Method: SHAKE all ingredients with ice and strain into glass filled with crushed ice. Serve with straws.

1	shot	Midori Green Melon liqueur
1	shot	Crème de banane liqueur
1	shot	Coconut rum liqueur
4	shots	Fresh pressed pineapple juice
1	shot	Freshly squeezed lime juice

Comment: Sweet & fruity.

JUNGLE BIRD

★★★★☆

Glass: Old-fashioned
Garnish: Orange slice & cherry on stick (flag)
Method: SHAKE all ingredients with ice and strain into glass filled with crushed ice.

1½	shots	Gosling's Black Seal dark rum
½	shot	Campari Bitter
½	shot	Freshly squeezed lime juice
½	shot	Sugar syrup (2 sugar to 1 water)
2	shots	Fresh pressed pineapple juice

Origin: Adapted from a drink featured in Jeff Berry's 'Intoxica' and originally created circa 1978 at the Aviary Bar, Kuala Lumpur, Malaysia.
Comment: Bittersweet and fruity with good rum notes.

JUNGLE JUICE

★★★⯪☆

Glass: Collins
Garnish: Orange slice
Method: SHAKE all ingredients with ice and strain into ice-filled glass.

1	shot	Ketel One Vodka
1	shot	Bacardi Carta Blanca light rum
½	shot	De Kuyper Triple Sec
1	shot	Cranberry juice
1	shot	Freshly squeezed orange juice
1	shot	Fresh pressed pineapple juice
¾	shot	Freshly squeezed lime juice
¼	shot	Sugar syrup (2 sugar to 1 water)

Comment: If this is the juice of the jungle, I'm a monkey's uncle. That said, as long fruity drinks go this is not bad at all.

JUNIPORT FIZZ

★★★★☆

Glass: Collins (small 8oz)
Garnish: Mint sprig
Method: SHAKE first 4 ingredients with ice and strain into empty chilled glass. **TOP** with soda from a siphon.

1½	shots	Rutte Dry Gin
½	shot	Tawny port
¾	shot	Freshly squeezed lemon juice
½	shot	Sugar syrup (2 sugar to 1 water)
Top with		Soda from siphon

Origin: Created in 2007 by Julian de Feral at Milk & Honey, London, England.
Comment: This straightforward fizz benefits from the unusual combination of gin and port.

JUPITER MARTINI

★★★⯪☆

Glass: Martini
Garnish: Orange zest twist
Method: SHAKE all ingredients with ice and fine strain into chilled glass.

2	shots	Rutte Dry Gin
⅛	shot	Parfait Amour liqueur
¾	shot	Martini Extra Dry vermouth
⅛	shot	Freshly squeezed orange juice
½	shot	Chilled water (omit if wet ice)

Origin: A classic which is thought to have originated sometime in the 1920's.
Comment: Bone dry and aromatic, this drink's colour is the grey hue of an overcast sky.

THE JUXTAPOSITION

★★★★☆

Glass: Martini
Garnish: Pineapple wedge
Method: STIR honey with vodka in base of shaker until honey dissolves. Add other ingredients, **SHAKE** with ice and fine strain into chilled glass.

2	spoon	Runny honey
2	shots	Cranberry flavoured vodka
1	shot	Fresh pressed pineapple juice
¾	shot	Freshly squeezed lime juice
3	dash	Angostura Aromatic Bitters

Origin: Adapted from a long drink created in 2003 by Michael Butt and Giles Looker of Soulshakers, England.
Comment: Tangy, complex and smoothed by foaming pineapple.

K.G.B.

★★⯪☆☆

Glass: Shot
Garnish: None
Method: LAYER in glass by pouring carefully in the following order.

½	shot	Coffee liqueur
½	shot	Galliano L'Autentico liqueur
½	shot	Martell VSOP Médaillon cognac

Comment: The initials of this simple peppermint and coffee shooter stand for Kahlúa, Galliano and brandy.

KAMANIWANALAYA

★★★⯪☆

Glass: Collins
Garnish: Pineapple wedge & Luxardo Maraschino cherry
Method: SHAKE all ingredients with ice and strain into ice-filled glass.

1½	shots	Bacardi Carta Blanca light rum
½	shot	Pusser's Navy Rum (54.5%)
1	shot	Disaronno Originale amaretto
3	shots	Fresh pressed pineapple juice

Comment: Try saying the name after a few of these rum laced, tropical pineapple concoctions.

A B C D E F G H I J K L M N O P Q R S T U V W X Y Z

KAMIKAZE ⬦━

★★★★☆

Glass: Shot
Garnish: None
Method: SHAKE all ingredients with ice and fine strain into chilled glass.

1	shot	Patrón reposado tequila
½	shot	De Kuyper Triple Sec
½	shot	Freshly squeezed lime juice

Comment: A bite-sized Margarita.

KANGAROO DRY MARTINI ⬦━

★★★★★

Glass: Martini
Garnish: Lemon zest twist
Method: STIR all ingredients with ice and strain into chilled glass.

| 2 | shots | Ketel One Vodka |
| ½ | shot | Martini Extra Dry vermouth |

Origin: Bartending legend has it that 'Kangaroo' was the original name for a Vodkatini and the evidence usually put forward to corroborate this is the drinks listing in later editions of David A. Embury's 'Fine Art of Mixing Drinks'. However, the original 1948 edition omits this drink but does list a Vodka Martini served both 'dry' and 'perfect'.
Comment: Temperature is key to the enjoyment of this modern classic. Consume while icy cold.

KANU-NO

★★★★☆

Glass: Old-fashioned
Garnish: Orange zest twist
Method: STIR all ingredients with ice and strain into ice-filled glass.

2¼	shots	Bacardi Carta Ocho aged rum
¼	shot	Romate Oloroso sherry
⅛	shot	Cream sherry (med/swt)
⅛	shot	Ruby port

Origin: Adapted from a drink created in 2007 by Mr Ueno at Star Bar, Ginza, Tokyo. Originally served straight-up.
Comment: The rum's sherry notes are heightened by the addition of port and sherry.

KARAMEL SUTRA MARTINI

★★★☆☆

Glass: Martini
Garnish: Fudge
Method: SHAKE all ingredients with ice and fine strain into chilled glass.

1½	shots	Vanilla infused Ketel One vodka
1½	shots	Tuaca liqueur
1	shot	Toffee liqueur

Origin: Adapted from a drink discovered in 2003 at the Bellagio, Las Vegas, USA.
Comment: Liquid confectionery that bites back.

KATINKA ⬦━

★★★★⯪☆

Glass: Martini
Garnish: Lime wedge
Method: SHAKE all ingredients with ice and fine strain into chilled glass.

1½	shots	Ketel One Vodka
½	shot	De Kuyper XO Apricot Brandy
1	shot	Freshly squeezed lime juice
½	shot	Sugar syrup (2 sugar to 1 water)

Comment: Medium sweet, yet also tart and tangy.

KATRINA COCKTAIL

★★★☆☆

Glass: Old-fashioned
Garnish: Dust with grated nutmeg
Method: SHAKE all ingredients with ice and fine strain into chilled glass.

2	shots	Patrón reposado tequila
¼	shot	Coffee liqueur
⅛	shot	Le Fée Parisienne absinthe
¼	shot	Chambord Liqueur
1	shot	Pressed apple juice

Origin: Adapted from a drink created in 2005 at Pirates Alley Café, New Orleans, and named after the hurricane which devastated the city in 2005. The name is an acronym of its original ingredients: Kahlúa, Absinthe, Tequila, Raspberry, Ice, Nutmeg and Apple juice.
Comment: Spicy, fruity tequila served in a style synonymous with the Crescent City - full on!

KAVA

★★★★☆

Glass: Collins
Garnish: Pineapple wedge & Luxardo Maraschino cherry
Method: SHAKE all ingredients with ice and strain into chilled glass.

1½	shots	Bacardi Carta Blanca light rum
½	shot	Bacardi Carta Oro rum
1	shot	Fresh pressed pineapple juice
1	shot	Freshly squeezed lemon juice
¼	shot	Sugar syrup (2 sugar to 1 water)
¼	shot	Pomegranate / grenadine syrup (2:1)

Origin: Adapted from a drink featured in Jeff Berry's 'Intoxica' and originally created circa 1942 by Trader Vic.
Comment: A wonderfully fruity, fluffy and kitsch Tiki drink.

KEE-WEE MARTINI

★★★★☆

Glass: Martini
Garnish: Kiwi slice
Method: Cut kiwi fruit in half, scoop out flesh into base of shaker and **MUDDLE**. Add other ingredients, **SHAKE** with ice and fine strain into chilled glass.

1	fresh	Kiwi fruit
2	shots	Rutte Dry Gin
¼	shot	Freshly squeezed lemon juice
½	shot	Sugar syrup (2 sugar to 1 water)

Origin: My version of this ubiquitous drink.
Comment: The citrus hints in the kiwi combine brilliantly with those in the gin and fresh lemon juice.

KENTUCKY COLONEL

★★★★☆

Glass: Old-fashioned
Garnish: Peach slice & mint sprig
Method: SHAKE all ingredients with ice and strain into glass filled with crushed ice.

1½ shots Bourbon whiskey
¼ shot De Kuyper Triple Sec
1 shot Peach purée
¼ shot Southern Comfort liqueur
½ shot Freshly squeezed lemon juice
½ shot Sugar syrup (2 sugar to 1 water)

Origin: Created by Morgan Watson of Apartment, Belfast, Northern Ireland.
Comment: Peach and bourbon with hints of orange and spice.

KENTUCKY DREAM

★★★★☆

Glass: Old-fashioned
Garnish: Lemon zest twist
Method: STIR vanilla liqueur and bitters with two ice cubes in a glass. Add half the bourbon and two more ice cubes. Stir some more and add another two ice cubes and the rest of the bourbon. Add the last two ingredients and more ice cubes and stir lots more. The melting and stirring of the ice cubes is essential to the dilution and taste of the drink.

½ shot Vanilla schnapps
2 shots Bourbon whiskey
½ shot De Kuyper XO Apricot Brandy
1 shot Pressed apple juice
2 dash Angostura Aromatic Bitters

Origin: Created in 2002 by Wayne Collins for Maxximum UK.
Comment: Tames bourbon and adds hints of apricot, vanilla and apple.

KENTUCKY JEWEL ⎯⚷

★★★★☆

Glass: Martini
Garnish: Seasonal berries
Method: SHAKE all ingredients with ice and strain into chilled glass.

1½ shots Bourbon whiskey
¼ shot De Kuyper Triple Sec
¼ shot Chambord Liqueur
2 shots Cranberry juice

Origin: Adapted from a drink created in 2004 by Jonathan Lamm, The Admirable Crichton, London, England.
Comment: Easy sipping, fruity bourbon.

KENTUCKY MAC

★★★½☆

Glass: Old-fashioned
Garnish: Mint sprig
Method: MUDDLE ginger and mint in base of shaker. Add other ingredients, SHAKE with ice and strain into glass filled with crushed ice.

2 slice Fresh root ginger (thumbnail sized)
2 fresh Mint leaves
1½ shots Bourbon whiskey
1 shot King's Ginger Liqueur
2 shots Pressed apple juice

Origin: Created in 1999 by Jamie Terrell, London, England.
Comment: Spicy, yet smooth and easy to sip.

KENTUCKY MUFFIN ⎯⚷

★★★½☆

Glass: Old-fashioned
Garnish: Blueberries
Method: MUDDLE blueberries in base of shaker. Add other ingredients, SHAKE with ice and strain into glass filled with crushed ice. Stir and serve with straws.

12 fresh Blueberries
2 shots Bourbon whiskey
1 shot Pressed apple juice
½ shot Freshly squeezed lime juice
½ shot Sugar syrup (2 sugar to 1 water)

Origin: Created in 2000 at Mash, London, England.
Comment: Blueberries, lime and apple combine with and are fortified by bourbon.

KENTUCKY PEAR

★★★★½

Glass: Martini
Garnish: Pear slice
Method: SHAKE all ingredients with ice and fine strain into chilled glass.

1 shot Bourbon whiskey
1 shot Belle de Brillet pear liqueur
1 shot Pressed pear juice
1 shot Pressed apple juice

Origin: Created in 2003 by Jes at The Cinnamon Club, London, England.
Comment: Pear, apple, vanilla and whiskey are partners in this richly flavoured drink.

KENTUCKY TEA ⎯⚷

★★★½☆

Glass: Collins
Garnish: Lime wedge
Method: SHAKE first 4 ingredients with ice and fine strain into ice-filled glass. TOP with ginger ale.

2 shots Bourbon whiskey
1 shot De Kuyper Triple Sec
1 shot Freshly squeezed lime juice
½ shot Sugar syrup (2 sugar to 1 water)
Top with Ginger ale

Comment: Spicy whiskey and ginger.

KEY LIME

★★★★☆

Glass: Coupe
Garnish: Lime wedge
Method: BLEND all ingredients without ice and serve.

1½	shots	Vanilla infused Ketel One vodka
1½	shots	Lime flavoured vodka
½	shot	Sugar syrup (2 sugar to 1 water)
½	shot	Rose's lime cordial
3	scoop	Vanilla ice cream

Comment: Tangy, smooth and rich! Alcoholic ice-cream for grown-ups.

KEY LIME PIE #1

★★★★☆

Glass: Martini
Garnish: Pie rim
Method: SHAKE first three ingredients with ice and fine strain into chilled, rimmed glass. **SHAKE** cream and Licor 43 without ice so as to mix and whip. **FLOAT** cream mix on surface of drink.

2	shots	Coconut rum liqueur
1	shot	De Kuyper Triple Sec
1	shot	Freshly squeezed lime juice
2	shots	Single cream / half-and-half
½	shot	Licor 43 liqueur

Origin: Created by Michael Waterhouse, owner of Dylan Prime, New York City, USA.
Comment: This extremely rich drink is great when served as a dessert alternative.
To make the pie rim, wipe outside edge of rim with cream mix and dip into crunched up Graham Cracker or digestive biscuits.

KEY LIME PIE #2

★★★★☆

Glass: Martini
Garnish: Pie rim
Method: Shake all ingredients with ice and fine strain into chilled, rimmed glass. To make the pie rim, wipe outside edge of rim with cream mix and dip into crunched up Graham Cracker or digestive biscuits.

2 shots Vanilla infused Ketel One vodka
1¾ shots Fresh pressed pineapple juice
½ shot Freshly squeezed lime juice
¼ shot Rose's lime cordial

Comment: Beautiful balance of pineapple, vanilla, sweet and sour.

KEY LIME PIE #3

★★★★☆

Glass: Martini
Garnish: Pie rim
Method: SHAKE all ingredients with ice and fine strain into chilled, rimmed glass.

2	shots	Ketel One Citroen vodka
½	shot	Vanilla schnapps
1½	shots	Fresh pressed pineapple juice
½	shot	Freshly squeezed lime juice
¼	shot	Rose's lime cordial

Origin: Recipe adapted from one by Claire Smith in 2005, London, England.
Comment: My favourite rendition of this dessert-in-a-glass cocktail.
To make the pie rim - wipe with cream mix and dip into crushed Graham Crackers or digestive biscuits.

KEY WEST COOLER

★★★⯪☆

Glass: Collins
Garnish: Lime wedge
Method: SHAKE all ingredients with ice and strain into ice-filled glass.

2	shots	Ketel One Vodka
1	shot	Coconut rum liqueur
1½	shots	Cranberry juice
1½	shots	Freshly squeezed orange juice

Origin: Named after the island near the southernmost tip of the Florida Keys in Florida, USA.
Comment: A coconut laced Breeze that's perfectly suited to the poolside.

KEYSER SÖZE COCKTAIL (NEW)

★★★★☆

Glass: Coupe
Garnish: Orange zest twist
Method: SHAKE all ingredients with ice and strain into chilled glass.

¾	shot	Martell VSOP Médaillon cognac
¾	shot	Rutte Dry Gin
¾	shot	Suze Saveur d'Autrefois
¾	shot	Freshly squeezed lemon juice
½	shot	Sugar syrup (2 sugar to 1 water)

Origin: Keyser Söze is a fictional character and the main antagonist in the 1995 film The Usual Suspects, while Suze, spelt with a 'u', is the bittersweet gentian flavoured liqueur and main antagonist in this cocktail.
Comment: Gin and cognac sit surprisingly well together as base ingredients with gentian and citrus freshness.

KILL BILL COCKTAIL (NEW)

★★★⯪☆

Glass: Old-fashioned
Garnish: Mint sprig
Method: POUR all ingredients into ice-filled glass and lightly stir.

¾	shot	Ketel One Vodka
¾	shot	Kwai Feh lychee liqueur
Top with		Ginger ale

Comment: There is little danger of killing bill with this slightly sweet, lychee and ginger drink which is laced with less than one shot of vodka.

KILLER PUNCH

★★★½☆

Glass: Collins
Garnish: Lime wedge
Method: **SHAKE** all ingredients with ice and strain into ice-filled glass.

1 shot Ketel One Vodka
½ shot Midori Green Melon liqueur
½ shot Disaronno Originale amaretto
½ shot Freshly squeezed lime juice
3½ shots Cranberry juice

Comment: Pretty soft, sweet and fruity as killers go.

KING COLE COCKTAIL

★★★★☆

Glass: Martini
Garnish: Orange & pineapple slices
Method: **STIR** all ingredients with ice and strain into chilled glass.

2 shots Bourbon whiskey
¼ shot Fernet Branca
½ shot Sugar syrup (2 sugar to 1 water)
½ shot Chilled water (omit if wet ice)

Origin: Adapted from Harry Craddock's 1930 'The Savoy Cocktail Book'.
Comment: My Fernet loving friends in San Francisco will appreciate this herbal number.

KING OF ORANGE (NEW)

★★★★☆

Glass: Coupe
Garnish: Orange zest twist to resemble a crown
Method: **SHAKE** all ingredients with ice and fine strain into chilled glass.

1½ shots Ketel One Vodka
¾ shot Grand Marnier Cordon Rouge
½ shot Campari Bitter
½ shot Freshly squeezed lemon juice

Origin: Created in 2012 by Dutch bartender Fjalar Goud in honour of King's Day, celebrated across the Netherlands annually on 27th April.
Comment: Slightly on the bitter side of bittersweet with the richness of Grand Marnier balancing Campari and lemon juice.

KING'S JUBILEE

★★★★★

Glass: Coupe
Garnish: Lemon zest twist
Method: **SHAKE** all ingredients with ice and fine strain into chilled glass.

2 shots Bacardi Carta Blanca light rum
¾ shot Luxardo Maraschino liqueur
½ shot Freshly squeezed lemon juice

Origin: Recipe adapted from W.J. Tarling's 1937 'Cafe Royal Cocktail Book - Coronation Edition' in which Tarling credits this drink's creation to Harry Craddock, the then head bartender of the American Bar at London's Savoy Hotel.
Comment: If there is such a thing as a 'Rum Aviation', then this is surely it.

KINGSTON NEGRONI (NEW)

★★★★☆

Glass: Old-fashioned
Garnish: Orange slice
Method: **STIR** all ingredients with ice and strain into ice-filled glass.

1 shot Pot still Jamaican rum
1 shot Martini Rosso vermouth
1 shot Campari Bitter

Origin: Created in 2013 by Joaquín Simó, New York City, USA
Comment: The huge character of pungent rum is matched with a bittersweet liqueur and sweet vermouth combo. Not for everyone but a Negroni riff worth trying.

Kir and Kir Royale cocktail

Sometimes called the 'Kir Cocktail' but more properly termed 'Kir aperitif' or simply Kir, this drink consists of just two ingredients, crème de cassis and chilled Bourgogne Aligoté white wine, poured into a glass.

The origins of Kir are said to date back to 1904 when a waiter named Faivre first had the idea of mixing white wine with crème de cassis at the Café George, 42 Rue de Montchapet at the corner of Rue de Constantine, Dijon, France. (Now Café Le Montchapet.)

Faivre's new drink became known as the 'Cassis Blanc' but is now better known simply as 'Kir' due to its being promoted by a colourful politician and WWII resistance hero by the name of Canon Félix Kir. During his tenure as Mayor of the French city of Dijon he sought to promote regional products at official functions. The Cannon popularised the concoction of locally made crème de cassis and Bourgogne Aligoté white wine and it quickly became known as Canon Kir's aperitif, then Father Kir's and finally as just Kir.

Félix Kir led quite a life. He was a Catholic priest at the outbreak of the Second World War, but became a major resistance fighter against the German occupation earning him the French Honour Cross. In 1945 he became a member of the French Parliament as a 'député' and the mayor of Dijon, an office to which he was re-elected four times and held until his death (aged 92) in 1968.

Bourgogne Aligoté is an Appellation d'origine contrôlée (AOC) white wine produced from the Aligoté grape variety in the France's Burgundy region. Bourgogne Aligoté tends to be light and acidic in style and usually unoaked. The appellation allows up to 15% Chardonnay to be blended into Bourgogne Aligoté so we suggest substituting with a unoaked Chardonnay if you are unable to source Bourgogne Aligoté. However, Chardonnay tends to lack the high acidity characteristic of Bourgogne Aligoté which so perfectly balances the sweet rich crème de cassis.

Champagne and other sparkling wines are often mixed with crème de cassis to produce the Kir Royal Cocktail but it's worth noting that depending on the brand, brut champagne also usually lacks the acidity needed to balance the rich crème de cassis, so consider using a brut nature or ultra brut champagne.

In 1951, when the Kir was becoming well-known, Roger Damidot, the then owner of the Lejay-Lagoute brand of crème de cassis and the largest liqueur producer in the region, asked the mayor for his the authorisation to use his name [Kir] commercially.

Probably flattered, the mayor agreed and on 20-November 1951, on a French National Assembly letterhead, wrote: "Canon Félix Kir, Member of Parliament and

Mayor of Dijon, gives exclusively to the house of Lejay-Lagoute, currently represented by Roger Damidot, the right to use his name for blackcurrant liqueur advertising purposes, in the form he sees fit and notably designate a 'vin blanc cassis'." Armed with this letter, Lejay-Lagoute patented the brand name 'Kir' in March 1952.

Years later, after seeing the increasing popularity of kir as an aperitif, the cannon sought to offer other cassis makers the same privilege but due to Lejay-Lagoute having already registered the Kir trademark he was too late. Numerous court challenges ensued, propelling the case to the highest French court, 'Cour de Cassation' where on 27-October 1992 it confirmed Lejay-Lagoute as having exclusive rights to the Kir trademark.

Following their legal triumph Lejay-Lagoute registered Kir Royal and Lejay-Lagoute now produce a pre-mixed bag-in-box Kir and a pre-mixed bottled cassis and sparkling wine called 'Kir Royal'.

If made with crémant, cava or another sparkling wine other than champagne then this drink becomes a 'kir pétillant'. (Pétillant is French for sparkling.)

KIR APERITIF

★★★★½

Glass: Goblet
Garnish: None
Method: POUR half the chilled wine into chilled glass. POUR cassis into glass and TOP with rest of the chilled wine.

2½ shots   Bourgogne Aligoté wine white
¾   shot   Lejay crème de cassis de Dijon
2½ shots   Bourgogne Aligoté wine white

Origin: The Kir aperitif is thought to have first been mixed in 1904 by a waiter called Faivre at the Café George, 42 Rue de Montchapet, Dijon, France. It is named after Canon Félix Kir, who as the Mayor of Dijon promoted the drink by serving at civic functions.
Comment: Traditionally made 1/3 cassis to 2/3 wine, that's too sweet for most modern palates. We recommend a ratio of one part cassis to between five and seven parts Bourgogne Aligoté white wine (13.5% to 20% cassis). The above formula is closer to 7:1 and at this concentration the mix of blackcurrant and wine is clean, crisp and not too sweet.

KIR COCKTAIL

★★★★½

Glass: Martini
Garnish: Seasonal berries
Method: STIR all ingredients with ice and strain into chilled glass.

1½ shots   Ketel One Vodka
¾   shot   Bourgogne Aligoté wine white
⅔   shot   Lejay crème de cassis de Dijon
⅛   shot   BarSol Mosto Verde Italia pisco
            (optional)

Origin: Created in 2004 by yours truly, London, England. This cocktail was inspired by the classic Kir, popularised by Canon Kir, Mayor of Dijon, France (1946-1968). At his receptions he served an aperitif made with the locally produced crème de cassis and Bourgogne Aligoté white wine. The concoction eventually became known as Kir aperitif.
Comment: Canon Félix Kir's traditional white wine and cassis aperitif with added vodka 'oomph'. A barspoon of pisco adds complexity to this cocktail but if available instead use Marc de Bourgogne, the eau-de-vie Canon Kir would have chosen.

KIR ROYALE COCKTAIL

★★★★☆

Glass: Flute
Garnish: Seasonal berries (blackcurrants)
Method: POUR cassis into glass and TOP with champagne.

½   shot   Lejay crème de cassis de Dijon
Top with   G.H. Mumm Cordon Rouge Champagne

Origin: A sparkling version of the Kir Aperitif which is thought to have first been mixed in 1904 at Café George in Dijon, France. It is named after Canon Félix Kir who promoted the mixture while Mayor of Dijon.
Comment: Champagne replaces Bourgogne Aligoté white wine in this 'Royal' rendition of Mayor Canon Kir's classic aperitif. Easy to make, easy to drink.

KIR SPRITZ (NEW)

★★★★½☆

Glass: Wine
Garnish: Lemon zest twist & blackcurrants/blackberries
Method: POUR ingredients into ice-filled glass in the following order.

3   shots   G.H. Mumm Cordon Rouge Champagne
1½ shots   Lejay crème de cassis de Dijon
Top with   Soda (club soda)

Comment: Rich blackcurrant fruit dried by the acidity of champagne and freshened with a splash of sparkling water.

KIRSCH COSMO

★★★★½

Glass: Martini
Garnish: Orange zest twist

Method: SHAKE all ingredients with ice and fine strain into chilled glass.

1   shot   Kirschwasser eau de vie
1   shot   De Kuyper Triple Sec
1½ shots   Cranberry juice
½   shot   Freshly squeezed lime juice

Origin: Adapted from a drink created in 2013 by Hannah Lanfear at Boisdale, Canary Wharf, London.
Comment: As the name suggests this is a riff on the classic Cosmopolitan using kirsch eau de vie in place of vodka.

KIWI BATIDA

★★★☆☆

Glass: Collins
Garnish: Kiwi slice
Method: Cut kiwi in half and scoop flesh into blender. Add other ingredients and BLEND with 18oz scoop crushed ice until smooth. Serve with straws.

2½ shots   Capucana cachaça
1   fresh   Kiwi fruit
1   shot   Sugar syrup (2 sugar to 1 water)

Comment: The kiwi fruit flavour is a little lacking so this drink is improved by using kiwi-flavoured sugar syrup.

KIWI BELLINI

★★★★☆

Glass: Flute
Garnish: Kiwi slice
Method: Cut kiwi in half, scoop out flesh into base of shaker. Add next three ingredients, **SHAKE** with ice and fine strain into chilled glass. **TOP** with prosecco.

1	fresh	Kiwi fruit
1¼ shots		Ketel One Vodka
¼	shot	Freshly squeezed lemon juice
¼	shot	Sugar syrup (2 sugar to 1 water)
Top with		Prosecco sparkling wine

Origin: Adapted from a drink discovered at Zuma, London, England, in 2004.
Comment: Lemon fresh kiwi, fortified with vodka and charged with prosecco.

KIWI COCKTAIL (SIMPLE)

★★★★☆

Glass: Martini
Garnish: Kiwi slice
Method: Cut kiwi fruit in half, scoop out flesh into base of shaker and **MUDDLE**. Add other ingredients, **SHAKE** with ice and fine strain into chilled glass.

1	fresh	Kiwi fruit
2	shots	Ketel One Vodka
½	shot	Sugar syrup (2 sugar to 1 water)

Comment: You may need to adjust the sugar depending on the ripeness of your fruit.

KIWI COLLINS

★★★★☆

Glass: Collins
Garnish: Kiwi slice
Method: Cut kiwi fruit in half, scoop out flesh into base of shaker and **MUDDLE**. Add next three ingredients, **SHAKE** with ice and fine strain into ice-filled glass. **TOP** with soda water.

1	fresh	Kiwi fruit
2	shots	Ketel One Vodka
1½ shots		Freshly squeezed lemon juice
½	shot	Sugar syrup (2 sugar to 1 water)
Top with		Soda (club soda)

Origin: Formula by yours truly.
Comment: A fruity adaptation of a Vodka Collins.

KIWI CRUSH

★★★★☆

Glass: Martini
Garnish: Kiwi slice
Method: Cut kiwi fruit in half, scoop out flesh into base of shaker and **MUDDLE**. Add other ingredients, **SHAKE** with ice and fine strain into chilled glass.

1	fresh	Kiwi fruit
2	shots	Ketel One Citroen vodka
1	shot	Pressed apple juice
½	shot	Freshly squeezed lemon juice
¼	shot	Almond (orgeat) syrup

Origin: Adapted from a recipe by Claire Smith in 2005, London, England.
Comment: Spirit laced kiwi, citrus and almond.

KLONDIKE

★★★½☆

Glass: Collins
Garnish: Orange slice
Method: POUR ingredients into ice-filled glass and stir.

2	shots	Bourbon whiskey
2	shots	Freshly squeezed orange juice
Top with		Ginger ale

Origin: Recipe adapted from A. S. Crockett's 1935 'The Old Waldorf-Astoria Bar Book'.
Comment: A simple drink but the three ingredients combine well.

KNICKERBOCKER MARTINI

★★★½☆

Glass: Martini
Garnish: Orange zest twist
Method: STIR all ingredients with ice and strain into chilled glass.

1¾ shots		Rutte Dry Gin
¾	shot	Martini Extra Dry vermouth
½	shot	Martini Rosso vermouth

Origin: Thought to have been created at the Knickerbocker Hotel, New York City, USA.
Comment: Aromatic vermouth dominates this flavoursome Martini variant.

KNICKERBOCKER SPECIAL

★★★★☆

Glass: Martini
Garnish: Pineapple wedge & Luxardo Maraschino cherry
Method: SHAKE all ingredients with ice and fine strain into chilled glass.

2	shots	Bacardi Carta Blanca light rum
½	shot	Grand Marnier Cordon Rouge
½	shot	Fresh pressed pineapple juice
½	shot	Freshly squeezed orange juice
½	shot	Freshly squeezed lemon juice
¼	shot	Raspberry syrup (1 juice to 1 sugar)

Origin: The Knickerbocker first appears in Jerry Thomas' 1862 *The Bartender's Guide*.
Comment: Easy drinking rum and orange curaçao, flavoured with pineapple and raspberry.

KNOCKOUT MARTINI

★★★½☆

Glass: Martini
Garnish: Star anise
Method: STIR all ingredients with ice and strain into chilled glass.

1½ shots		Rutte Dry Gin
1½ shots		Martini Extra Dry vermouth
¼	shot	Le Fée Parisienne absinthe
¼	shot	Giffard Menthe Pastille liqueur

Comment: A Wet Martini with hints of aniseed and mint. Stir well as it benefits from dilution.

A B C D E F G H I J K L M N O P Q R S T U V W X Y Z

KOI YELLOW

★★★★☆

Glass: Martini
Garnish: Rose petal
Method: SHAKE all ingredients with ice and fine strain into chilled glass.

2 shots Raspberry flavoured vodka
½ shot De Kuyper Triple Sec
1 shot Freshly squeezed lemon juice
½ shot Sugar syrup (2 sugar to 1 water)

Origin: The signature drink at Koi Restaurant, Los Angeles, USA.
Comment: Sherbet raspberry Martini with a sweet and citrus sour finish.

KONINGSDAG COCKTAIL (NEW)

★★★★☆

Glass: Coupe
Garnish: Coriander sprig
Method: SHAKE all ingredients with ice and fine strain into chilled glass.

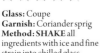

1½ shots Ketel One Vodka
¾ shot Orange Curaçao liqueur
¼ shot King's Ginger Liqueur
1½ shots Freshly extracted carrot juice
5 drop Bob's Bitters Coriander bitters

Origin: Created by yours truly in April 2015 in celebration of Koningsdag, a festival held in the Netherlands on 27th April each year when the Dutch dress in orange and party to commemorate their monarch's birthday. Any excuse to party!
Comment: This very Dutch celebratory cocktail is made using Dutch Ketel One vodka, Dutch orange curacao, Dutch-made King's Ginger liqueur. The all-important orange hue and subtle flavour comes from carrot juice. For the truly orange King's Day experience make with 50% Ketel One vodka and 50% Ketel One Oranje, or even replace vodka with 100% Ketel One Oranje.

KOOL HAND LUKE

★★★★☆

Glass: Rocks
Garnish: Lime wedge
Method: MUDDLE lime in base of glass to release juices. POUR other ingredients into glass, add crushed ice and CHURN (stir). Serve with straws.

1 fresh Lime (fresh whole) (cut into segments)
2 shots Pot still Jamaican rum
1 shot Sugar syrup (2 sugar to 1 water)
2 dash Angostura Aromatic Bitters

Comment: This looks like a Caipirinha and has a similar balance of sweet, sour and spirit. The bitters bring out the spice in the rum, which is every bit as pungent as cachaça.

KOOLAID

★★★★☆

Glass: Collins
Garnish: Lime wedge
Method: SHAKE all ingredients with ice and strain into ice-filled glass.

1½ shots Ketel One Vodka
¾ shot Midori Green Melon liqueur
¾ shot Disaronno Originale amaretto
½ shot Freshly squeezed lime juice
2 shots Cranberry juice
1 shot Freshly squeezed orange juice

Origin: A drink with unknown origins that emerged and morphed during the 1990s.
Comment: Tangy liquid marzipan with hints of melon cranberry and orange juice.

KOPSTOOT

★★★★☆

Glass: Shot and Beer
Garnish: None
Method: POUR genever into shot glass and beer into beer glass. To enjoy, simply sip a shot of ice-cold genever from a small, tulip-shaped glass, then follow with a sip of beer.

½ shot Rutte Old Simon oude jenever (chilled)
½ pint Belgium dubbel abbey ale

Origin: The traditional Dutch way to drink genever, Kopstoot (pronounced 'Cop-Stout') translates as 'a blow for your head'.
Comment: In the worthy pursuit of responsible drinking I must stress that when enjoying a Kopstoot you should repeatedly take a sip from each glass – savour the combination rather than shooting the genever in one gulp.

KRAKOW TEA

★★★★☆

Glass: Collins
Garnish: Lime wedge & mint sprig
Method: Lightly MUDDLE mint in base of shaker (just to bruise). SHAKE all ingredients with ice and fine strain into ice-filled glass.

12 fresh Mint leaves
2 shots Zubrówka bison vodka
1 shot Cold camomile tea
3½ shots Pressed apple juice
¼ shot Freshly squeezed lime juice
¼ shot Sugar syrup (2 sugar to 1 water)

Origin: Created in 2002 by Domhnall Carlin at Apartment, Belfast, Northern Ireland.
Comment: Refreshing and floral with a dry, citrus finish.

KRETCHMA

★★★½☆

Glass: Martini
Garnish: Dust with chocolate powder
Method: **SHAKE** all ingredients with ice and fine strain into chilled glass.

2 shots Ketel One Vodka
¾ shot White crème de cacao liqueur
½ shot Freshly squeezed lemon juice
⅛ shot Pomegranate / grenadine syrup (2:1)

Origin: Adapted from a recipe in David Embury's 'The Fine Art of Mixing Drinks'.
Comment: Fortified Turkish Delight.

L'AMOUR EN FUITE

★★★★☆

Glass: Old-fashioned
Garnish: Orange zest twist
Method: **POUR** absinthe into ice-filled glass, **TOP** with water and leave to stand. Separately **STIR** gin, vermouth and elderflower liqueur with ice. **DISCARD** contents of glass (absinthe, water and ice) and **STRAIN** contents of mixing glass into absinthe-coated glass.

½ shot Le Fée Parisienne absinthe
1½ shots Rutte Dry Gin
¾ shot Martini Extra Dry vermouth
¼ shot St-Germain elderflower liqueur

Origin: Created in 2007 by Jamie Boudreau, Seattle, USA, originally using Lillet. The name comes from a 1979 French film.
Comment: Serious yet approachably subtle with hints of vermouth and elderflower dominated by absinthe and gin.

L.A. ICED TEA

★★★½☆

Glass: Sling
Garnish: Lime wedge
Method: **SHAKE** first 7 ingredients with ice and strain into ice-filled glass. **TOP** with soda.

½ shot Ketel One Vodka
½ shot Rutte Dry Gin
½ shot Bacardi Carta Blanca light rum
½ shot De Kuyper Triple Sec
½ shot Midori Melon liqueur
1 shot Freshly squeezed lime juice
½ shot Sugar syrup (2 sugar to 1 water)
Top with Soda (club soda)

Comment: Long and lime green with subtle notes of melon and fresh lime.

LA BICYCLETTE

★★★½☆

Glass: Coupe
Garnish: Lemon zest twist
Method: **STIR** all ingredients with ice and strain into chilled glass.

2 shots Rutte Dry Gin
½ shot Martini Rosso vermouth
¼ shot St-Germain elderflower liqueur
2 dash Peach bitters

Origin: Adapted from a drink created in 2008 by Jamie Boudreau, Seattle, USA.
Comment: A light and fragrant Sweet Martini style drink with elderflower liqueur and peach bitters.

LA DOLCE VITA

★★★★½

Glass: Martini
Garnish: Lemon zest twist
Method: **MUDDLE** grapes in base of shaker. Add vodka, honey and bitters, **SHAKE** with ice and fine strain into chilled glass. **TOP** with prosecco.

4 fresh Seedless white grapes
1 shot Ketel One Vodka
1 spoon Runny honey
1 dash Angostura Orange Bitters
Top with Prosecco sparkling wine

Origin: Created in 2002 by Tony Conigliaro at Isola, London, England
Comment: Complex, yet easy to quaff with grape juice, vodka, honey and a touch of fizz.

LA FEUILLE MORTE

★★★½☆

Glass: Collins
Garnish: None
Method: **POUR** first 3 ingredients into glass. Serve iced water separately in a small jug (known in France as a 'broc') so the customer can dilute to their own taste. (I recommend five shots). Lastly, add ice to fill glass.

1 shot Ricard Pastis
½ shot Pomegranate / grenadine syrup (2:1)
½ shot Mint (menthe) syrup
Top with Chilled water

Origin: Pronounced 'Fueel-Mort', the name literally means 'The dead leaf', a reference to its colour.
Comment: A traditional French way to serve pastis.

LA PERLA

★★★★★

Glass: Coupe
Garnish: Lemon zest twist
Method: **STIR** all ingredients with ice and strain into chilled glass.

1½ shots Patrón reposado tequila
1½ shot San León Manzanilla Sherry
¾ shot Pear liqueur

Comment: Simple yet complex, this beautifully balanced cocktail has faint saltiness from the manzanilla, delicate pear fruit and well integrated fortifying tequila.
Origin: Created in 2005 by Jacques Bezuidenhaut at Tres Agaves, San Francisco, USA.

LA POIRE DES BENEDICTINES (NEW)

★★★★★

Glass: Coupe
Garnish: Pear wedge speared with cube of Roquefort cheese
Method: **STIR** all ingredients with ice and strain into chilled glass.

¾ shot Pear flavoured vodka
¾ shot Bénédictine D.O.M. liqueur
¾ shot Martell VSOP Médaillon cognac
¼ shot Chilled water

Origin: Adapted from a drink promoted by Grey Goose in 2013.
Comment: Pear and cognac are a match made in heaven. Bénédictine adds honeyed sweetness and herbal complexity to this after dinner cocktail.

LA ROSA MARGARITA

★★★★☆

Glass: Coupe
Garnish: Lime wedge
Method: **SHAKE** all ingredients with ice and fine strain into chilled glass.

2 shots Patrón reposado tequila
¾ shot Lejay Crème de Mûre liqueur
1 shot Cold hibiscus tea (strong brewed)
½ shot Freshly squeezed lime juice

Comment: A fruity yet dry crimson-coloured Margarita

LA SANG

★★★★☆

Glass: Collins
Garnish: Chopped fruit
Method: **SHAKE** all ingredients with ice and strain into ice-filled glass.

2 shots Martell VSOP Médaillon cognac
2 shots Shiraz red wine
2 shots Freshly squeezed orange juice
¼ shot Sugar syrup (2 sugar to 1 water)

Origin: French for 'blood', this cocktail is a twist on the classic Spanish Sangria, which also means 'blood'.
Comment: The tannin in the wine balances the fruit and sweetness nicely.

LA TOUR EIFFEL

★★★★☆

Glass: Flute
Garnish: Lemon zest twist
Method: **STIR** all ingredients with ice and fine strain into chilled glass.

2½ shots Martell VSOP Médaillon cognac
½ shot De Kuyper Triple Sec
½ shot Suze Saveur d'Autrefois
1 dash Le Fée Parisienne absinthe

Origin: Adapted from a drink created in 2007 by Gary Regan after a Sazerac-fuelled trip to New Orleans. He was inspired by how the Sazerac might have been if it had originally been created in France rather than New Orleans.
Comment: Bitter sweet cognac-influenced palate with lingering flavours of liquorice root, honey, pine and eucalyptus from the Suze.

LA VENDANGEUSE (NEW)

★★★★☆

Glass: Coupe
Garnish: Lemon zest twist (discarded) & grapes on stick
Method: **MUDDLE** grapes in base of shaker. Add other ingredients, **SHAKE** with ice and fine strain into chilled glass.

7 fresh Seedless white grapes
1½ shots Lillet Blanc
1 shot Rutte Dry Gin
¾ shot Freshly squeezed lemon juice
⅓ shot Sugar syrup (2 sugar to 1 water)

Comment: Depending on the ripeness of your grapes, and the sweetness of your palate, you may want to stretch to 1/2 shot sugar syrup. Strike the right balance and you'll be rewarded with a medley of white grapes, white wine and botanical gin freshness with faint, cleansing zesty citrus.

THE LADY WEARS RED

★★★★☆

Glass: Martini
Garnish: Champagne foam
Method: **SHAKE** all ingredients with ice and fine-strain chilled glass. **FLOAT** champagne foam made by macerating orange zests in champagne overnight, adding gelatin and charging with N2O siphon.

1½ shots Bacardi Carta Blanca light rum
½ shot Aperol Aperitivo
¼ shot Grand Marnier Cordon Rouge
¼ shot De Kuyper Triple Sec
⅛ shot Romate Fino sherry
⅛ shot Martini Extra Dry vermouth
⅛ shot Taylor's Velvet Falernum liqueur
¾ shot Freshly squeezed lime juice
¼ shot Sugar syrup (2 sugar to 1 water)
1 dash Grapefruit bitters
1 dash Angostura Orange Bitters

Origin: Adapted from a drink created in 2008 by Ben Carlotto at The Voodoo Rooms, Edinburgh, Scotland. The original recipe calls for homemade dry orange syrup made by macerating orange zests in a blend of different sugars with Lillet Blanc and fino sherry. It also calls for homemade citrus bitters, a complex mixture of kaffir lime leaves, various citrus elements, and spices like cardamom and cassia.
Comment: This 'Lady' is high maintenance but she delivers a complex reward.

LADY'S SIDECAR

★★★★½

Glass: Martini
Garnish: Orange zest twist
Method: **SHAKE** all ingredients with ice and fine strain into chilled glass.

1½ shots Martell VSOP Médaillon cognac
1 shot De Kuyper Triple Sec
1 shot Freshly squeezed lemon juice
¼ shot Freshly squeezed orange juice

Comment: The addition of orange juice and an orange zest twist supposedly gives this otherwise classic Sidecar a feminine twist.

LAGO COSMO

★★★½☆

Glass: Martini
Garnish: Orange zest twist
Method: SHAKE all ingredients with ice and fine strain into chilled glass.

1½ shots Cranberry flavoured vodka
¾ shot De Kuyper Triple Sec
1¾ shots Freshly squeezed orange juice
¼ shot Freshly squeezed lime juice
½ shot Sugar syrup (2 sugar to 1 water)

Origin: Discovered in 2003 at Nectar at Bellagio, Las Vegas, USA.
Comment: A Cosmo with cranberry vodka in place of citrus vodka and orange juice in place of cranberry juice.

LARCHMONT

★★★★½

Glass: Martini
Garnish: Orange zest twist
Method: SHAKE all ingredients with ice and fine strain into chilled glass.

1½ shots Bacardi Carta Blanca light rum
½ shot Grand Marnier Cordon Rouge
½ shot Freshly squeezed lime juice
¼ shot Sugar syrup (2 sugar to 1 water)
½ shot Chilled water (omit if wet ice)

Origin: Created by David A. Embury, who in his 1948 'Fine Art of Mixing Drinks' writes of this drink: "As a grand finale to cocktails based on the Rum Sour, I give you one of my favorites which I have named after my favorite community".
Comment: I share Embury's appreciation of this fine and delicate drink, although I think of it more as a type of Orange Daiquiri.

LAST STRAW

★★★★☆

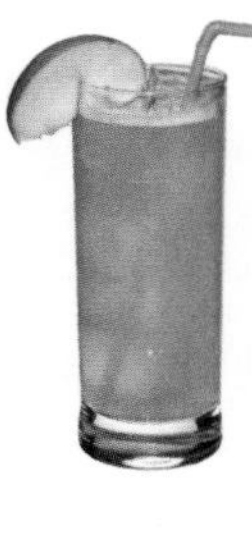

Glass: Collins
Garnish: Apple wedge
Method: SHAKE all ingredients with ice and strain into ice-filled glass.

1½ shots Calvados brandy
1½ shots St-Germain elderflower liqueur
1½ shots Medium dry cider
1½ shots Pressed apple juice

Origin: Created in 2006 by yours truly. We used the last straw we had left to sample the first one.
Comment: Three stages of the apple's alcoholic journey, juice, cider and brandy, are sweetened and aromatised by elderflower liqueur.

Last Word cocktail

Made with gin, Green Chartreuse, maraschino liqueur and freshly pressed lime juice, traditionally in equal parts, shaken with ice and served straight-up. The Last Word is thought to date from immediately prior to prohibition but owes its present day popularity to being reincarnated in 2004 by Murray Stenson during his tenure at the Zig Zag Cafe in Seattle, USA.

The earliest known written reference to the Last Word is in Ted Saucier's 1951 cocktail book ' Bottoms Up!' where under the drink's name he wrote "Courtesy Detroit Athletic Club, Detroit. This cocktail was first introduced here around thirty years ago by Frank Fogarty, who was very well known in vaudeville. He was called the 'Dublin Minstrel,' and was a very fine monologue artist."

Depending on how accurate we assume "around thirty years" prior to the 1951 publication date is, this puts the drinks origins around 1920, immediately before or after Prohibition. The consensus seems to be that this this is one of the few great cocktails to emerge from the period before Prohibition.

The Detroit Athletic Club, or the DAC, was established in 1887 by a group of young athletes with a clubhouse on Detroit's Woodward Avenue. The DAC was reborn in 1913 by a group of prominent Detroit automotive and industrial leaders who built the magnificent six-story Clubhouse on Madison Avenue which opened in 1915, where it is said Fogarty introduced the Last Word.

Known as the 'The Dublin Minstrel', Frank Fogarty was a famous American theatre entertainer who was born in County Tipperary, Ireland but from the age of two grew up and lived on Warren Street, Brooklyn. He broke into vaudeville (akin to today's stand-up comedy) in 1911 when he performed at the Orpheum in Brooklyn and became famous for his monologues, winning the New York Morning Telegraph contest for the most popular vaudeville performer in 1912. He typically opened his performance with a song and finished it with a recitation and this could well be where the drink's Last Word name emanates. Fogarty was quite a speaker, who also dabbled in politics being elected president of the vaudeville actors union in 1914.

The Last Word continued to be popular during and after Prohibition and so found its way into in Ted Saucier's book. However, like so many cocktails the Last Word fell out of favour to be forgotten. That was until 2004, when Murray Stenson, a bartender at the Zig Zag Café in Seattle, USA found the recipe in a 1952 copy of Saucier's book. Murray added the cocktail to the menu at the Zig Zag Café where it was well received by regulars.

As Tan Vinh wrote in the The Seattle Times on 11th March 2009, "The drink became a cult hit around Seattle, then Portland and was eventually picked up at cocktail dens in New York City, where many bartending trends are set. The Last Word then started to appear on drink menus in Chicago and San Francisco and spread to several cities in Europe - especially around London and Amsterdam - and beyond"

Over on America's East Coast, when Audrey Saunders opened Manhattan's Pegu Club in 2005, the Last Word was one of the cocktails championed by her team, including Phil Ward, the man responsible for the Final Ward, the best-known of the many modern riffs on the Last Word.

THE LAST WORD COCKTAIL

★★★★★

Glass: Coupe
Garnish: Lime twist (discarded) and Luxardo Maraschino cherry
Method: SHAKE all ingredients with ice and fine strain into chilled glass.

1 shot Rutte Dry Gin
⅔ shot Green Chartreuse liqueur
⅔ shot Luxardo Maraschino liqueur
⅔ shot Freshly squeezed lime juice
½ shot Chilled water (omit if wet ice)

Comment: Chartreuse devotees will love this balanced, tangy drink. I'm one.

LATEST WORD (NEW)

★★★★⯪

Glass: Coupe
Garnish: Lime zest twist
Method: SHAKE all ingredients with ice and fine strain into chilled glass.

¾	shot	Rutte Old Simon oude jenever
¾	shot	Green Chartreuse liqueur
¾	shot	Luxardo Maraschino liqueur
¾	shot	Freshly squeezed lime juice

Comment: A Last Word made to classic equal parts proportions but with genever replacing London dry gin. The more robust flavour of genever stands up well to the other very characterful ingredients.

LAVENDER & BLACK PEPPER COCKTAIL

★★★★☆

Glass: Martini
Garnish: None
Method: Pour the syrup into an ice filled mixing glass. Add the vodka and black pepper. **STIR** and super-fine strain into chilled glass.

2½	shots	Ketel One Vodka
¼	shot	Lavender sugar syrup
2	grind	Black pepper

Origin: Adapted from a recipe created in 2006 by Richard Gillam at the Kenilworth Hotel, Warwickshire, England.
Comment: Subtly sweetened and lavender flavoured vodka, with a bump and grind of spicy pepper.

LAVENDER HONEY SOUR

★★★★☆

Glass: Flute
Garnish: Dried lavender
Method: STIR honey with whiskey in base of shaker to dissolve honey. Add other ingredients, **SHAKE** with ice and fine strain into chilled glass.

1½	shots	Teeling Small Batch Irish whiskey
2	spoon	Runny honey
½	shot	Bénédictine D.O.M. liqueur
1	shot	Freshly squeezed lemon juice
½	fresh	Egg white
3	dash	Peychaud's aromatic bitters

Origin: Created by Dre Masso at Lonsdale 2006, Notting Hill, London England.
Comment: An Irish whiskey sour sweetened with runny honey and herbal Bénédictine with Peychaud's adding aromatics.

LAVENDER MARGARITA

★★★★★

Glass: Coupe
Garnish: Lime wedge
Method: SHAKE all ingredients with ice and fine strain into chilled glass.

2	shots	Patrón reposado tequila
1	shot	Freshly squeezed lime juice
½	shot	Lavender sugar syrup

Origin: Created in 2006 by yours truly at the Cabinet Room, London, England.
Comment: Lavender lime and tequila combine harmoniously.

LAVENDER MARTINI

★★★★⯪

Glass: Martini
Garnish: Lemon zest twist
Method: STIR all ingredients with ice and strain into chilled glass.

2½	shots	Ketel One Vodka (infused with lavender)
¾	shot	Parfait Amour liqueur
¼	shot	Martini Extra Dry vermouth

Origin: Created in 2006 by yours truly.
Comment: Infusing lavender in liquor tends to make it bitter but the Parfait Amour adds sweetness as well as flavour and colour.

LAZARUS

★★★★⯪

Glass: Martini
Garnish: Coffee beans
Method: SHAKE all ingredients with ice and fine strain into chilled glass.

1	shot	Ketel One Vodka
½	shot	Martell VSOP Médaillon cognac
1	shot	Coffee liqueur
1	shot	Espresso coffee (freshly made & hot)

Origin: Created in 2000 by David Whitehead at Atrium, Leeds, England.
Comment: A flavoursome combination of spirit and coffee.

LAZY MAN FLIP

★★★★⯪

Glass: Sour or Martini/Coupette
Garnish: Orange zest twist (discarded) & dust with grated nutmeg
Method: SHAKE all ingredients with ice and fine strain into chilled glass.

1½	shots	Ruby port
¾	shot	Calvados brandy
¾	shot	Single cream / half-and-half
¼	shot	Sugar syrup (2 sugar to 1 water)
1	fresh	Egg yolk

Origin: Created in 2007 by Chris Jepson at Milk and Honey, London, England.
Comment: Obviously creamy but not too sweet with a great balance between the port and the calvados.

LE DIJONNAIS MARTINI

★★★★☆

Glass: Coupe
Garnish: Cocktail onion
Method: STIR all ingredients with ice and fine strain into chilled glass.

1½	shots	Galander Fine Mustard liqueur
½	shot	Martini Extra Dry vermouth
⅛	shot	Rutte Dry Gin
2	dash	Celery bitters

Origin: Created by Gonzo de Sousa Monteiro, Berlin, Germany.
Comment: A most unusual cocktail based on a most unusual product - mustard liqueur.

LE FIZZ COCKTAIL (NEW)

★★★★☆

Glass: Flute
Garnish: Stirrer and lime zest twist
Method: **SHAKE** first three ingredients with ice fine strain into chilled glass. **TOP** with chilled soda.

1½ shots Ketel One Vodka
¾ shot St-Germain elderflower liqueur
⅔ shot Freshly squeezed lime juice
2 shots Soda (club soda)

Origin: Created in 2013 by Joe McCanta, London, England.
Comment: A poor man's champagne cocktail. Refreshing and, providing consumed whilst still cold, unknowingly boozy.

LE FUME

★★★★☆

Glass: Coupe
Garnish: Orange zest twist
Method: **STIR** all ingredients with ice and fine strain into chilled glass.

2 shots Ketel One Vodka
½ shot Islay single malt Scotch whisky
¼ shot Lapsang souchong sugar syrup
½ shot Chilled water

Origin: Adapted from a drink discovered in 2011 at Le Salon Bar at L'Atelier de Joël Robuchon, London, England.
Comment: Peat smoked Islay whisky meets pinewood smoked Chinese tea, fortified with vodka.

LE GRAND (NEW)

★★★★½

Glass: Coupe
Garnish: Lemon zest twist
Method: **STIR** first three ingredients with ice and strain into chilled glass. **TOP** with champagne.

1⅔ shots Byrrh Grand Quinquina
1 shot Martell VSOP Médaillon cognac
1 spoon Pomegranate / grenadine syrup (2:1)
Top with G.H. Mumm Cordon Rouge Champagne

Origin: Adapted from a recipe created in 2015 by Samuel Rose at Panda & Sons, Edinburgh, Scotland.

LE GRAND FEU

★★★☆☆

Glass: Martini
Garnish: Mint sprig
Method: **SHAKE** all ingredients with ice and fine strain into chilled glass.

1½ shots Martell VSOP Médaillon cognac
1½ shots Vanilla schnapps
½ shot Baileys Irish cream liqueur
¾ shot Cold chai tea

Origin: Adapted from a recipe by Tony Venci, La Femme Bar, MGM Grand Hotel, Las Vegas, USA.
Comment: Cognac smoothed with vanilla and cream, spiced with chai tea.

LE JARDIN (NEW)

★★★★☆

Glass: Coupe
Garnish: Lavender sprig
Method: **SHAKE** first 7 ingredients with ice and fine strain into chilled glass. **TOP** with champagne.

¾ shot Rutte Dry Gin
⅛ shot Luxardo Maraschino liqueur
⅛ shot Sugar syrup (2 sugar to 1 water)
4 fresh Blueberries
½ shot Freshly squeezed lemon juice
⅓ shot Pressed apple juice
1 dash Bob's Lavender bitters
2½ shots G.H. Mumm Brut Rosé Champagne

Origin: Created in January 2014 for Laurent-Perrier by Sean Ware of the London Cocktail Club, London, England.
Comment: This salmon pink cocktail combines gin, maraschino liqueur, fresh blueberries, lemon juice and apple juice with rose champagne to create a refreshing harmonious blend. The inspiration behind the drink is a quote by Nicolas Gilsoul, "A garden, like champagne, is a filter, a medium through which the person walking in it awakens his senses and reveals the depth of his emotions."

LE MINUIT

★★★★☆

Glass: Martini
Garnish: Orange zest twist
Method: **SHAKE** all ingredients with ice and fine strain into chilled glass.

½ shot Le Fée Parisienne absinthe
1 shot Sauvignon blanc white wine
1 shot Pressed apple juice
⅛ shot Sugar syrup (2 sugar to 1 water)
1 dash Angostura Orange Bitters

Origin: Adapted from a drink created in 2001 by Tony Conigliaro at Isola, Knightsbridge, London, England.
Comment: Absinthe based but incredibly subtle. Absinthe combines wonderfully with wine and apple.

LE SANG ET SABLE (NEW)

★★★½☆

Glass: Coupe
Garnish: Lemon zest twist (discarded) & Luxardo maraschino cherry
Method: **SHAKE** all ingredients with ice and strain into chilled glass.

1½ shots Martell VSOP Médaillon cognac
½ shot Dubonnet Red
½ shot Cherry Heering Liqueur
⅓ shot Blood orange juice
⅓ shot Freshly squeezed lemon juice
¾ shot Chilled water (omit if wet ice)

Origin: Adapted from a recipe by Toby Cecchini, New York City, USA.
Comment: Reminiscent of a French cognac-based Blood & Sand.

LEAP YEAR MARTINI

★★★☆☆

Glass: Martini
Garnish: Lemon zest twist
Method: SHAKE all ingredients with ice and fine strain into chilled glass.

2	shots	Rutte Dry Gin
½	shot	Grand Marnier Cordon Rouge
½	shot	Martini Rosso vermouth
¼	shot	Freshly squeezed lemon juice

Origin: Harry Craddock created this drink for the Leap Year celebrations at the Savoy Hotel, London, on 29th February 1928 and recorded it in his 1930 Savoy Cocktail Book.
Comment: This drink, which is on the dry side, needs to be served ice cold.

LEAVE IT TO ME MARTINI

★★★☆☆

Glass: Martini
Garnish: Lemon zest twist
Method: SHAKE all ingredients with ice and fine strain into chilled glass.

1½	shots	Rutte Dry Gin
½	shot	De Kuyper XO Apricot Brandy
¾	shot	Martini Rosso vermouth
½	shot	Freshly squeezed lemon juice
¼	shot	Pomegranate / grenadine syrup (2:1)

Origin: Adapted from a recipe in Harry Craddock's 1930 Savoy Cocktail Book.
Comment: Gin, apricot, vermouth and lemon create an old-fashioned but well balanced drink.

THE LEAVENWORTH

★★★★☆

Glass: Martini
Garnish: Orange zest twist
Method: STIR all ingredients with ice and strain into chilled glass.

2 shots Bacardi Carta Ocho aged rum
1 shot Cherry Heering Liqueur
10 drop Tiki's Falernum Bitters

Origin: Created in 2008 by Francesco Lafranconi of Southern Wine & Spirits, USA.
Comment: This great cocktail is dramatically influenced by the style of rum used. Francesco's original recipe calls for English Harbour rum.

LEFT BANK MARTINI

★★★★★

Glass: Martini
Garnish: Lime zest twist
Method: SHAKE all ingredients with ice and fine strain into chilled glass.

2	shots	Rutte Dry Gin
½	shot	St-Germain elderflower liqueur
½	shot	Chardonnay (Chablis) white wine
¼	shot	Martini Extra Dry vermouth

Origin: Created in 2006 by yours truly at the Cabinet Room, London, England. I updated this recipe in 2013. Older? Yes. Wiser? Perhaps. Drier palate? Definitely. Hence, seven years after creating this drink I reduced the elderflower liqueur from 3/4 shot to 1/2 shot and I also reduced the vermouth from 1/2 to a 1/4.
Comment: An aromatic, dry blend. Modern bartending convention would suggest that this drink should be stirred. However, it's much better shaken. Go easy with the spray of lime zest oils - this delicate drink is easily over powered with any more than a fine mist.

LEKKER LEKKER

★★★☆☆

Glass: Martini
Garnish: Apple slice
Method: SHAKE all ingredients with ice and fine strain into chilled glass.

1	shot	Zubrówka bison vodka
¾	shot	Hazelnut liqueur
½	shot	Freshly squeezed lemon juice
2	shot	Pressed apple juice
½	shot	Sugar syrup (2 sugar to 1 water)

Origin: Created by Tom Lawman at Snafu, Aberdeen. Lekker Lekker (pronounced 'Laker Laker') is Afrikaans for 'very nice', which is what Tom's South African friend exclaimed when he tasted this drink.
Comment: Most unusual with apple, hazelnut and lemon freshness.

LEMON BEAT

★★★★☆

Glass: Rocks
Garnish: Lemon slice
Method: STIR honey with cachaça in the base of shaker to dissolve honey. Add other ingredients, SHAKE with ice and strain into ice-filled glass.

2	spoon	Runny honey
2	shots	Capucana cachaça
1	shot	Freshly squeezed lemon juice

Comment: Simple but effective. Use quality cachaça and honey and you'll have a great drink.

STAR RATINGS EXPLAINED

★★★★★+ OUTSTANDING	★★★★★ EXCEPTIONAL
★★★★☆ EXCELLENT	★★★★☆ RECOMMENDED
★★★☆☆ COMMENDED	★★★☆☆ MEDIOCRE
★★☆☆☆ DISAPPOINTING	★★☆☆☆ PRETTY AWFUL
★☆☆☆☆ SHAMEFUL	★☆☆☆☆ DISGUSTING

A
B
C
D
E
F
G
H
I
J
K
L
M
N
O
P
Q
R
S
T
U
V
W
X
Y
Z

LEMON CAIPIROVSKA

★★★★☆

Glass: Old-fashioned
Garnish: None
Method: MUDDLE lemon in base of shaker, add other ingredients and **SHAKE** with 6oz scoop crushed ice. Pour into glass without straining and serve with straws.

¾	fresh	Lemon (chopped wedges)
2	shots	Ketel One Citroen vodka
¾	shot	Sugar syrup (2 sugar to 1 water)
1	dash	Angostura Aromatic Bitters

Origin: Created in 2002 by Tony Conigliaro at Isola, London, England.
Comment: A lemon-tastic Caipirovska.

LEMON CHIFFON PIE

★★★★☆

Glass: Coupe
Garnish: Grated lemon zest
Method: BLEND all ingredients with crushed ice and serve with straws.

1	shot	Bacardi Carta Blanca light rum
1	shot	White crème de cacao liqueur
1	shot	Freshly squeezed lemon juice
2	scoop	Vanilla ice cream

Comment: Creamy and tangy - like a lemon pie. Consume in place of dessert.

LEMON CURD COCKTAIL

★★★★☆

Glass: Martini
Garnish: Lemon wedge
Method: SHAKE all ingredients with ice and fine strain into chilled glass.

2	shots	Ketel One Citroen vodka
3	spoon	Lemon curd
½	shot	Freshly squeezed lemon juice

Origin: Created in 2001 by yours truly, London, England.
Comment: This almost creamy cocktail is named after and tastes like its primary ingredient.

LEMON DROP

★★★½☆

Glass: Shot
Garnish: Sugar coated lemon slice
Method: SHAKE all ingredients with ice and fine strain into chilled glass.

½	shot	Ketel One Vodka
½	shot	De Kuyper Triple Sec
½	shot	Freshly squeezed lemon juice

Comment: Lemon and orange combine to make a fresh tasting citrus shot.

LEMON DROP COCKTAIL

★★★★☆

Glass: Martini
Garnish: Lemon zest twist
Method: SHAKE all ingredients with ice and fine strain into chilled glass.

2	shots	Ketel One Citroen vodka
¼	shot	De Kuyper Triple Sec
¾	shot	Freshly squeezed lemon juice
½	shot	Sugar syrup (2 sugar to 1 water)

Comment: Sherbety lemon - well balanced and very refreshing.

LEMON LIME & BITTERS (MOCKTAIL*)

★★★½☆

Glass: Collins
Garnish: Lime wedge
Method: POUR lime and lemonade into ice-filled glass and lightly stir. **DASH** bitters onto surface of drink and serve with straws so drinker can stir in Angostura.

½ shot Freshly squeezed lime juice
Top with Lemonade/Sprite/7-Up
4 dash Angostura Aromatic Bitters

Origin: Very popular in its homeland, Australia.
Comment: *NOTE: Contains minute levels of alcohol due to use of Angostura bitters but is considered an alcohol free cocktail.

LEMON MERINGUE PIE'TINI

★★★★☆

Glass: Martini
Garnish: Pie rim
Method: SHAKE first three ingredients with ice and fine strain into chilled and rimmed glass. **DRY SHAKE** cream and Licor 43 (without ice) so as to mix and whip. **FLOAT** cream by pouring over back of spoon.

1	shot	Pallini Limoncello
1	shot	Sugar syrup (2 sugar to 1 water)
1	shot	Freshly squeezed lemon juice
2	shots	Single cream / half-and-half
½	shot	Licor 43 liqueur

Origin: Created by Michael Waterhouse at Dylan Prime, New York City, USA.
Comment: Rich and syrupy base sipped through a vanilla cream topping.
To make the pie rim, wipe outside edge of rim with cream mix and dip into crunched up Graham Cracker or digestive biscuits.

LEMON SORBET

★★★★☆

Glass: Martini
Garnish: Grated lemon zest
Method: Heat water in pan and add sugar. Simmer and stir until sugar dissolves, add lemon juice and grated lemon rind and continue to simmer and stir for a few minutes. Take off the heat and allow to cool. Fine strain into a shallow container and stir in liqueur and orange bitters. Beat egg whites and fold into mix. Place in freezer and store for up to 3-4 days before use.

¾	shot	Chilled water
1	cupful	Granulated sugar
½	cupful	Freshly squeezed lemon juice
5	fresh	Lemon zest
¼	cupful	Pallini Limoncello
2	spoon	Angostura Orange Bitters
2	fresh	Egg white

Comment: Our favourite recipe for this dessert and occasional cocktail ingredient.

LEMON TART (NEW)

★★★★☆

Glass: Coupe
Garnish: Lemon zest twist (discarded) & half lemon wheel on rim
Method: SHAKE all ingredients with ice and strain back into shaker. SHAKE again without ice (dry shake) and fine strain into chilled glass.

1	shot	Rutte Dry Gin
½	shot	Suze Saveur d'Autrefois
½	shot	Freshly squeezed lemon juice
¼	shot	Sugar syrup (2 sugar to 1 water)
½	shot	Egg white

Comment: This bitter-sweet aperitif cocktail harnesses the herbal bitterness of gentian root with gin's botanical notes and sweetened freshly squeezed lemon juice.

LEMONADE SPRITZ (MOCKTAIL) (NEW)

★★★★☆

Glass: Collins
Garnish: Lemon slice
Method: SHAKE first 3 ingredients with ice and strain into ice-filled glass. TOP with soda.

8 fresh Mint leaves
1¼ shots Freshly squeezed lemon juice
⅛ shot Sugar syrup (2 sugar to 1 water)
3½ shots Soda (club soda)

Origin: Adapted from a popular drink on the menu of Jamie's Italian restaurant and bar chain.
Comment: A minty real lemonade. A seriously refreshing non-alcoholic summery drink.

LEMONGRAD

★★★★☆

Glass: Collins
Garnish: Lemon wedge
Method: SHAKE first four ingredients with ice and strain into ice-filled glass. TOP with tonic and lightly stir.

2	shots	Ketel One Vodka
½	shot	Ketel One Citroen vodka
½	shot	Freshly squeezed lemon juice
½	shot	St-Germain elderflower liqueur
Top with		Tonic Water

Origin: Created in 2002 by Alex Kammerling, London, England.
Comment: A great summer afternoon drink. Fresh lemon with elderflower and quinine.

LEMONGRASS COSMO

★★★★☆

Glass: Martini
Garnish: Lemon zest twist
Method: MUDDLE lemongrass in base of shaker. Add other ingredients, SHAKE with ice and fine strain into chilled glass.

1	inch	Lemongrass stem (chopped)
1	shot	Ketel One Citroen vodka
1	shot	De Kuyper Triple Sec
1½	shots	Cranberry juice
½	shot	Freshly squeezed lemon juice

Origin: Adapted from a drink discovered in 2005 at Opia, Hong Kong, China.
Comment: Lemongrass adds complexity to this balanced Cosmo.

LEMONHEAD

★★★★☆

Glass: Martini
Garnish: Lemon zest twist
Method: MUDDLE lemongrass in base of shaker. Add other ingredients, SHAKE with ice and fine strain into chilled glass.

2	inch	Lemongrass stem (chopped)
2¼	shots	Ketel One Vodka
¼	shot	Martini Extra Dry vermouth
1	shot	Freshly squeezed lemon juice
½	shot	Sugar syrup (2 sugar to 1 water)

Origin: Created in 2006 by yours truly, originally as a Lemon Martini. Every cocktail was named martini back then.
Comment: Delicately lemony and vodka laced.

LEMONY

★★★★☆

Glass: Martini
Garnish: Luxardo Maraschino cherry
Method: SHAKE all ingredients with ice and fine strain into chilled glass.

2	shots	Rutte Dry Gin
½	shot	Yellow Chartreuse liqueur
½	shot	Pallini Limoncello
½	shot	Freshly squeezed lemon juice
½	shot	Chilled water (omit if wet ice)

Comment: Lemon subtly dominates this complex, herbal drink.

LENINADE

★★★★☆

Glass: Collins
Garnish: Orange zest twist (discarded) and lemon slice
Method: SHAKE first five ingredients with ice and strain into ice-filled glass. **TOP** with soda.

1½ shots	Ketel One Citroen vodka
½ shot	De Kuyper Triple Sec
¾ shot	Freshly squeezed lemon juice
½ shot	Pomegranate / grenadine syrup (2:1)
2 dash	Angostura Orange Bitters (optional)
Top with	Soda (club soda)

Origin: Created by Dick Bradsell at Fred's, London, England, in the late 1980s. His original recipe (1½ shots citrus vodka, ¼ shot triple sec, 1 shot lemon juice, ¼ shot sugar syrup and 3 dash orange bitters) was served short and straight-up with sugar syrup rather than grenadine. Yours truly added the grenadine and made the Leninade a long drink in July 2013 after reader feedback on diffordsguide.com said the name was suggestive of a long red vodka-based drink.
Comment: Orange undertones add citrus depth to the lemon explosion.

THE LIBERTINE

★★★★☆

Glass: Old-fashioned
Garnish: Candied lime
Method: SHAKE first four ingredients with ice and fine strain into ice-filled glass. **TOP** with ginger beer and lightly stir.

1½ shots	Kaffir lime flavoured vodka
¾ shot	Green Chartreuse liqueur
¾ shot	St-Germain elderflower liqueur
½ shot	Freshly squeezed lime juice
1 shot	Gosling's Stormy Ginger Beer

Origin: Created in 2008 by Joe Parrilli at Bacar, San Francisco, USA.
Comment: Huge flavours delicately combine in this surprisingly approachable drink.

LIMA SOUR

★★★★☆

Glass: Old-fashioned
Garnish: Lemon zest twist
Method: BLEND all ingredients with one 12oz scoop of crushed ice. Serve with straws.

2 shots	BarSol Mosto Verde Italia pisco
½ shot	Luxardo Maraschino liqueur
¾ shot	Freshly squeezed pink grapefruit juice
¾ shot	Freshly squeezed lime juice
¾ shot	Sugar syrup (2 sugar to 1 water)

Origin: Created before 1947 by Jerry Hooker.
Comment: A refreshing blend of pisco, maraschino and citrus.

LIMEADE (MOCKTAIL)

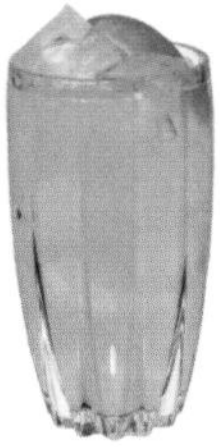

★★★★☆

Glass: Collins
Garnish: Lime wedge
Method: SHAKE all ingredients with ice and fine strain into ice-filled glass.

2 shots	Freshly squeezed lime juice
1 shot	Sugar syrup (2 sugar to 1 water)
3 shots	Chilled water

Comment: A superbly refreshing alternative to lemonade.

LIMERICK

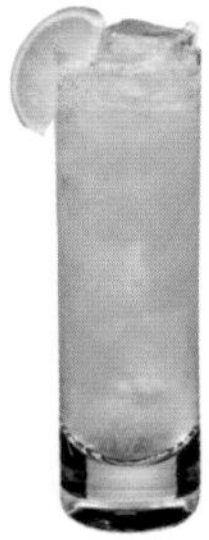

★★★★☆

Glass: Collins
Garnish: Lime wedge
Method: SHAKE first three ingredients with ice and strain into ice-filled glass. **TOP** with soda water and lightly stir.

2 shots	Teeling Small Batch Irish whiskey
1 shot	Freshly squeezed lime juice
½ shot	Sugar syrup (2 sugar to 1 water)
Top with	Soda (club soda)

Origin: Basically a Irish whiskey Ricky.
Comment: A long stretched and so refreshing Irish whiskey lime sour.

LIMEY GIMLET

★★★★★

Glass: Coupe
Garnish: Lime zest twist (discarded) & lime wedge
Method: SHAKE all ingredients with ice and fine strain into chilled glass.

1 shot	Rose's lime cordial
1 shot	Rutte Dry Gin
½ shot	Bacardi Carta Blanca light rum
½ shot	Freshly squeezed lime juice

Origin: Created in 2010 by yours truly at the Cabinet Room, London, England.
Comment: The two naval spirits sit harmoniously together in this delicately flavoured Gimlet.

LIMONCELLO MARTINI

★★★★☆

Glass: Martini
Garnish: Lemon zest twist
Method: SHAKE all ingredients with ice and fine strain into chilled glass.

1½ shots	Ketel One Vodka
1½ shots	Pallini Limoncello
1 shot	Freshly squeezed lemon juice

Origin: Adapted from a drink created in 2005 by Francesco at Mix, New York City, USA.
Comment: If you like the liqueur, you'll love the cocktail.

LINCOLN CLUB COOLER

★★★☆☆

Glass: Collins
Garnish: Lime wedge
Method: POUR ingredients into ice-filled glass and gently stir.

2 shots Bacardi Carta Oro rum
Top with Ginger ale

Origin: Adapted from a drink originally published in George J. Kappeler's 1895 'Modern American Drinks'. Kappeler originally called for St. Croix rum.
Comment: Basically a rum and ginger ale Highball but Lincoln Club Cooler has more of a ring to it.

LINSTEAD

★★★★☆

Glass: Coupe
Garnish: Lemon zest twist
Method: SHAKE all ingredients with ice and fine strain into chilled glass.

2 shots Dewar's 12 Year Old Scotch whisky
1½ shots Fresh pressed pineapple juice
¼ shot Sugar syrup (2 sugar to 1 water)
⅛ shot Le Fée Parisienne absinthe

Comment: Absinthe and pineapple come through first, with Scotch last. A great medley of flavours.

LION'S TAIL (NEW)

★★★★★

Glass: Coupe
Garnish: Lime zest twist
Method: SHAKE all ingredients with ice and strain into chilled glass.

2 shots Bourbon whiskey
⅓ shot Allspice pimento dram liqueur
½ shot Freshly squeezed lime juice
1 spoon Sugar syrup (2 sugar to 1 water)
1 dash Angostura Aromatic Bitters

Origin: Adapted from a recipe that first appeared in 'Café Royal Cocktail Book', published in London in 1937. However, the drinks creator is likely to have been an American bartender driven to London by Prohibition. "Twisting the lion's tail" was an American slang expression for provoking the British which emerged during the period of American Anglophobia between the World Wars.
Comment: A heavily Allspice Dram liqueur influenced, Daiquiri-like, bourbon-based cocktail.

LIQUORICE ALL SORT

★★★★☆

Glass: Collins
Garnish: Liquorice Allsorts
Method: SHAKE first four ingredients with ice and strain into ice-filled glass. **TOP** with lemonade.

1 shot Black sambuca liqueur
1 shot Crème de banane liqueur
1 shot Lejay Crème de Fraise
1 shot Blue curaçao liqueur
Top with Lemonade/Sprite/7-Up

Origin: George Bassett (1818-1886), a manufacturer of liquorice sweets, did not invent the Liquorice Allsort that carries his name. That happened 15 years after George died when a salesman accidentally dropped a tray of sweets, they fell in a muddle and the famous sweet was born.
Comment: This aptly named, semi-sweet drink has a strong liquorice flavour with hints of fruit.

LIQUORICE SHOT

★★★☆☆

Glass: Shot
Garnish: None
Method: SHAKE all ingredients with ice and fine strain into chilled glass.

½ shot Ketel One Vodka
½ shot Luxardo sambuca dei cesari
⅓ shot Lejay crème de cassis de Dijon

Comment: For liquorice fans.

LIQUORICE WHISKY SOUR

★★★★☆

Glass: Old-fashioned
Garnish: Dust with grated liquorice
Method: SHAKE all ingredients with ice and strain into ice-filled glass.

2 shots Dewar's 12 Year Old Scotch whisky
¼ shot Liquorice liqueur
1 shot Freshly squeezed lemon juice
½ shot Sugar syrup (2 sugar to 1 water)
½ fresh Egg white
1 dash Angostura Aromatic Bitters

Origin: Created in 2006 by Tony Conigliaro at Shochu Lounge, London, England.
Comment: Liquorice dramatically changes the classic Sour, working harmoniously with the Scotch. I have also tried with bourbon and the result is not nearly so pleasing.

STAR RATINGS EXPLAINED

★★★★★⁺	OUTSTANDING	★★★★★	EXCEPTIONAL
★★★★☆	EXCELLENT	★★★★☆	RECOMMENDED
★★★☆☆	COMMENDED	★★★☆☆	MEDIOCRE
★★☆☆☆	DISAPPOINTING	★★☆☆☆	PRETTY AWFUL
★☆☆☆☆	SHAMEFUL	★☆☆☆☆	DISGUSTING

LISA'S SPECIAL DAIQUIRI

★★★★★

Glass: Martini
Garnish: Grapefruit zest twist
Method: SHAKE all ingredients with ice and fine strain into chilled glass.

2½ shots	Bacardi Carta Blanca light rum (vanilla infused)
½ shot	Freshly squeezed lime juice
½ shot	Vanilla sugar syrup
1 shot	Freshly squeezed pink grapefruit juice

Origin: Created in 2003 by yours truly for a fan of both Daiquiris and pink grapefruit juice.
Comment: Reminiscent of a Hemingway Special, this flavoursome, vanilla laced Daiquiri has a wonderfully tangy, bitter sweet finish.

LITTLE ITALY

★★★★☆

Glass: Coupe
Garnish: Maraschino cherry
Method: STIR all ingredients with ice and strain into chilled glass.

1 shot	Straight rye whiskey
¾ shot	Martini Rosso sweet vermouth
½ shot	Cynar

Comment: This rye whiskey-based, Manhattan-like, bittersweet cocktail makes for a great aperitivo.
Origin: Created in 2005 by Audrey Saunders at Pegu

LITTLE SMITH

★★★★☆

Glass: Coupe
Garnish: Float dried apple slice
Method: SHAKE all ingredients with ice and fine strain into chilled glass.

1 shot	Zubrówka bison vodka
1 shot	Calvados brandy
½ shot	Taylor's Velvet Falernum liqueur
1 shot	Pressed apple juice
1 fresh	Wasabi leaf

Origin: Discovered in 2011 at Ubar, Copenhagen, Denmark.
Comment: Slightly sweet but this apple cocktail is light and delicately spiced.

LITTLE VENICE

★★★★☆

Glass: Martini
Garnish: Orange zest twist (discarded) & Luxardo Maraschino cherry
Method: STIR all ingredients with ice and strain into chilled glass.

2 shots	Junmai ginjō sake
1 shot	Bourbon whiskey
1 shot	Martini Rosso vermouth

Origin: Discovered in 2007 at Yakitoria, London, England.
Comment: Simple and yet beautiful. Just the way a great drink should be.

LIVINGSTONE 🗝

★★★★☆

Glass: Martini
Garnish: Lemon zest twist
Method: SHAKE all ingredients with ice and fine strain into chilled glass.

2 shots	Rutte Dry Gin
1 shot	Martini Extra Dry vermouth
¼ shot	Sugar syrup (2 sugar to 1 water)

Origin: This 1930's classic was named after Doctor Livingstone, the famous African missionary.
Comment: The classic gin and vermouth Martini made more approachable with a dash of sugar.

LO MISMO 🗝

★★★☆☆

Glass: Old-fashioned
Garnish: Lime zest twist
Method: POUR ingredients into ice-filled glass.

| 2 shots | Bacardi Carta Blanca light rum |
| Top with | Soda (club soda) |

Origin: The Mismo was a craze said to be started by a group of Americans at the Cosmopolitan Club in Santiago in 1899. When ordering drinks, one of their Cuban colleagues asked for a Bacardi rum and seltzer (soda). His friend, also Cuban, called for 'Lo mismo' - Spanish for 'the same'. Not speaking Spanish, but eager to fit in, the Americans all also asked for 'lo mismos'. The next day, the Americans returned and ordered another round of 'Mismos' from the same barman. The name stuck.

"It spread with remarkable rapidity", reported the New York Tribune soon after. Now every barkeeper in Santiago knows what you are after if you ask for a 'Mismo'.
Comment: Light rum and soda makes for a fabulously subtle and refreshing drink. Don't serve too long or the dilution will kill it.

LOCH ALMOND

★★★★☆

Glass: Collins
Garnish: Amaretti biscuit
Method: POUR all ingredients into ice-filled glass, stir and serve with straws.

1½ shots	Dewar's 12 Year Old Scotch whisky
1½ shots	Disaronno Originale amaretto
Top with	Ginger ale

Comment: If you haven't got to grips with Scotch but like amaretto, try this spicy almond combination.

LOLITA MARGARITA 🗝

★★★★☆

Glass: Coupe
Garnish: Lime wedge
Method: STIR honey with tequila in base of shaker to dissolve honey. Add other ingredients, SHAKE with ice and fine strain into chilled glass.

2 spoon	Runny honey
2 shots	Patrón reposado tequila
1 shot	Freshly squeezed lime juice
2 dash	Angostura Aromatic Bitters

Origin: Named after the novel by Vladimir Nabokov which chronicles a middle-aged man's infatuation with a 12 year old girl. Nabokov invented the word 'nymphet' to describe her seductive qualities.
Comment: A fittingly seductive Margarita.

LONDON CALLING

★★★☆☆

Glass: Martini
Garnish: Orange zest twist
Method: STIR all ingredients with ice and strain into chilled glass.

2	shots	Rutte Dry Gin
1¼	shots	Sloe Gin liqueur
½	shot	Martini Rosso vermouth
2	dash	Angostura Orange Bitters

Origin: Discovered in 2003 at Oxo Tower Bar & Brasserie, London, England.
Comment: A traditionally styled sweet Martini with a dry, fruity finish.

LONDON COCKTAIL

★★★☆☆

Glass: Martini
Garnish: Orange zest twist
Method: SHAKE all ingredients with ice and fine strain into chilled glass.

2½	shots	Rutte Dry Gin
⅛	shot	Le Fée Parisienne absinthe
⅛	shot	Sugar syrup (2 sugar to 1 water)
2	dash	Angostura Orange Bitters
½	shot	Chilled water (omit if wet ice)

Origin: Adapted from a recipe in Harry Craddock's 1930 'Savoy Cocktail Book'.
Comment: Chilled, diluted and sweetened gin invigorated by a hint of absinthe.

LONDON COSMOPOLITAN 🗝

★★★★☆

Glass: Martini
Garnish: Orange zest twist (discarded)
Method: SHAKE all ingredients with ice and fine strain into chilled glass.

1	shot	Rutte Dry Gin
1	shot	De Kuyper Triple Sec
1½	shots	Cranberry juice
½	shot	Freshly squeezed lime juice

Origin: A subtle 2008 twist on the classic by yours truly at the Cabinet Room, London, England.
Comment: Basically a Cosmopolitan but made with London dry gin instead of citrus vodka.

LONDON GYPSY

★★★★☆

Glass: Coupe
Garnish: Grapefruit zest twist
Method: STIR all ingredients with ice and strain into chilled glass.

2	shots	Rutte Dry Gin
1	shot	Bénédictine D.O.M. liqueur
3	dash	Angostura Aromatic Bitters

Comment: The botanicals in the gin and the herbal Benedictine combine well in this drink which is balanced by the addition of bitters.

LONDON SCRAMBLE

★★★★☆

Glass: Old-fashioned
Garnish: Lemon zest twist & blackberries
Method: SHAKE first four ingredients with ice and fine strain into glass filled with crushed ice. **DRIZZLE** créme de mûre over drink (will slowly bleed through the cocktail).

2	shots	Patrón silver tequila
½	shot	Freshly squeezed lemon juice
½	shot	Freshly squeezed lime juice
½	shot	Agave syrup
¼	shot	Lejay Crème de Mûre liqueur

Origin: Created in 2007 by Dre Masso & Henry Besant from the Worldwide Cocktail Club, London.
Comment: A tequila Bramble of which I'm sure Dick Bradsell (the legendary bartender behind the original Bramble) would be most approving.

LONDON SOUR (NEW)

★★★★☆

Glass: Collins
Garnish: Orange slice & mint sprig
Method: SHAKE all ingredients with ice and strain into ice-filled glass.

2	shots	Dewar's 12 Year Old Scotch whisky
2½	shots	Freshly squeezed orange juice
½	shot	Freshly squeezed lemon juice
⅛	shot	Almond (orgeat) syrup
⅛	shot	Sugar syrup (2 sugar to 1 water)

Origin: Created by Trader Vic himself for the opening of the Hyde Park Hilton, London branch of his eponymous restaurant chain in 1963.
Comment: Our thanks to Brent Evans for pointing us towards this tasty cocktail which he describes as "Scotch whisky blended with fresh oranges, lemons and a whisper of almond." We tried with egg white, usually our preference in a sour, but prefer this one without the resulting foam. We also found upping the orange juice and serving long preferable.

LONDONER (WARD'S RECIPE) (NEW)

★★★★☆

Glass: Coupe
Garnish: Flamed orange zest twist
Method: STIR all ingredients with ice and strain into chilled glass.

2	shots	Rutte Dry Gin
½	shot	Martini Rosso vermouth
½	shot	Grand Marnier Cordon Rouge
2	dash	Angostura Orange Bitters

Origin: Adapted from a recipe created by Philip Ward while at Pegu Club, New York City, USA and bought to our attention by the super imbiber and scribe that is Gaz Regan.
Comment: As a born and bred Londoner I'm slightly miffed that a New Yorker has applied the name of our great city to a drink using French and Italian products, but as its Phil Ward and a great gin-based drink, I'll forgive him and mix up another.

LONDONER (WOOD'S RECIPE) (NEW)

★★★★☆

Glass: Coupe
Garnish: Flamed orange zest twist
Method: SHAKE all ingredients with ice and fine strain into chilled glass.

2	shots	Rutte Dry Gin
½	shot	Lejay Crème de Mûre liqueur
1	shot	Freshly squeezed pink grapefruit juice
¼	shot	Freshly squeezed lime juice

Origin: Adapted from a recipe created by Joe Wood, Cocktail Stars, England and bought to our attention by Gaz Regan.
Comment: Rich raspberry fruit liqueur balanced by pink grapefruit and lime juice, with gin fortifying and adding complexity. The flavour is reminiscent of a Bramble served straight-up.

THE LONE RANGER 🗝

★★★★☆

Glass: Collins
Garnish: Lemon zest twist
Method: SHAKE first 3 ingredients with ice and strain into ice-filled glass. TOP with champagne.

1½	shots	Patrón silver tequila
¾	shot	Freshly squeezed lemon juice
½	shot	Sugar syrup (2 sugar to 1 water)
Top with		G.H. Mumm Cordon Rouge Champagne

Origin: Created in 2012 by Jeffrey Morgenthaler, Oregon, USA.
Comment: Very slightly sweet tequila and lemon, lengthened and dried with brut champagne.

LONELY BULL

★★★★☆

Glass: Old-fashioned
Garnish: Dust with grated nutmeg
Method: SHAKE all ingredients with ice and strain into ice-filled glass.

1½	shots	Patrón reposado tequila
1½	shots	Coffee liqueur
¾	shot	Single cream / half-and-half
¾	shot	Milk

Comment: Like a creamy iced coffee - yum.

LONG BEACH ICED TEA

★★★★☆

Glass: Sling
Garnish: Lemon slice
Method: SHAKE all ingredients with ice and strain into ice-filled glass. Serve with straws.

½	shot	Coffee liqueur
½	shot	Patrón reposado tequila
½	shot	Bacardi Carta Blanca light rum
½	shot	Rutte Dry Gin
½	shot	Ketel One Vodka
1	shot	Freshly squeezed lime juice
½	shot	Sugar syrup (2 sugar to 1 water)
2	shots	Cranberry juice

Comment: One of the more grown-up 'Iced Tea' cocktails.

LONG FLIGHT OF STAIRS

★★★★½

Glass: Collins
Garnish: Apple or pear slice
Method: SHAKE all ingredients with ice and strain into ice-filled glass. Serve with straws.

1	shot	Pear flavoured vodka
1	shot	Calvados brandy
1	shot	Belle de Brillet pear liqueur
2½	shots	Pressed apple juice

Origin: Created in 2005 by yours truly as a homage to the G.E. Club's 'Stairs Martini'.
Comment: A seriously tasty, strong, long drink. The name is a reversal of the London rhyming slang 'apples and pears' (stairs).

LONG ISLAND ICED TEA COCKTAIL 🗝

★★★☆☆

Glass: Sling
Garnish: Lemon wedge
Method: SHAKE first 8 ingredients with ice and strain into ice-filled glass. TOP with cola, stir and serve with straws.

½	shot	Bacardi Carta Blanca light rum
½	shot	Rutte Dry Gin
½	shot	Ketel One Vodka
½	shot	De Kuyper Triple Sec
½	shot	Patrón reposado tequila
½	shot	Sugar syrup (2 sugar to 1 water)
½	shot	Freshly squeezed lemon juice
½	shot	Freshly squeezed lime juice
Top with		Coca-Cola

Origin: This infamous drink reached the height of its popularity in the early 1980s. Of the many stories surrounding its origin, perhaps the most credible attributes its creation to sometime in the late 1970s by Robert (Rosebud) Butt at Oak Beach Inn in Babylon, New York. This area of New York State is known as 'Long Island' and the drink looks like iced tea disguising its contents – a fact that has many claiming its true origins lie with Prohibition.
Comment: A cooling, combination of five different spirits with a hint of lime and a splash of cola.

LONG ISLAND SPICED TEA

★★★☆☆

Glass: Collins
Garnish: Lime wedge
Method: SHAKE first seven ingredients with ice and strain into ice-filled glass. TOP with cola, stir and serve with straws.

½	shot	Bacardi OakHeart Spiced Rum
½	shot	Rutte Dry Gin
½	shot	Ketel One Vodka
½	shot	Patrón reposado tequila
½	shot	De Kuyper Triple Sec
1	shot	Freshly squeezed lime juice
½	shot	Sugar syrup (2 sugar to 1 water)
Top with		Coca-Cola

Comment: A contemporary spicy twist on an American classic.

THE LONG SHOT

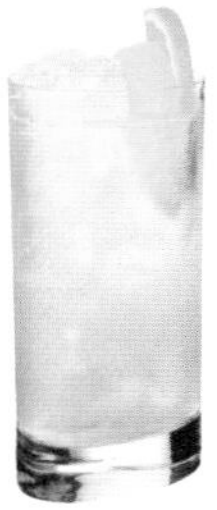

Glass: Collins
Garnish: Orange slice & lemon wedge
Method: **SHAKE** first five ingredients with ice and strain ice-filled glass. **TOP** with soda, lightly stir and serve with straws.

1½ shots	Patrón reposado tequila
½ shot	Orange Curaçao liqueur
¼ shot	Sugar syrup (2 sugar to 1 water)
¾ shot	Freshly squeezed lemon juice
1 dash	Angostura Aromatic Bitters
Top with	Soda (club soda)

Origin: Created in 2007 by Julian de Feral at Milk & Honey, London, England.
Comment: A simple variation on William Schmidt's Alabazam.

LONSDALE

Glass: Collins
Garnish: Basil leaf & apple slice
Method: **STIR** honey syrup with gin until honey dissolves. **TEAR** basil leaves and add to shaker with all other ingredients. **SHAKE** with ice and fine strain into chilled glass.

2 shots Rutte Dry Gin
½ shot Honey sugar syrup
3 fresh Basil leaves
¾ shot Freshly squeezed lemon juice
2½ shots Pressed apple juice

Origin: Created by Alexandra Fiot at The Lonsdale, London, England.
Comment: Not dry, not sweet, just balanced, long and refreshing.

LOOKS FAMILIAR

Glass: Old-fashioned
Garnish: Orange zest twist
Method: **STIR** malt with ice and then strain and discard excess to leave the ice and mixing glass coated. Add other ingredients and **STIR** with the coated ice. Strain into ice-filled glass.

½ shot	Islay single malt Scotch whisky
2 shots	Patrón silver tequila
½ shot	Agave syrup
2 dash	Angostura Aromatic Bitters
¼ shot	Amer Picon

Origin: Created by Jake Burger at Jake's Bar, Leeds, England.
Comment: I defy you not to love this herbal bitter-sweet tequila laced concoction.

LORRAINE #1

Glass: Old-fashioned
Garnish: Orange zest twist
Method: **STIR** all ingredients with ice and strain into ice-filled glass.

1½ shots	Rutte Dry Gin
1 shot	Martini Extra Dry vermouth
½ shot	Grand Marnier Cordon Rouge

Origin: Created by Joe Gilmore to mark Charles de Gaulle's first state visit to Britain in the 1950s and named after the Cross of Lorraine, symbol of the Order of Liberation. The original recipe called for one whole shot of Grand Marnier.
Comment: A Wet Martini served on the rocks, sweetened and flavoured with a slug of orange liqueur.

LORRAINE #2

Glass: Martini
Garnish: Lime zest twist
Method: **SHAKE** all ingredients and fine strain into chilled glass.

¾ shot	Kirschwasser eau de vie
¾ shot	Ketel One Vodka
¾ shot	Bénédictine D.O.M. liqueur
½ shot	Freshly squeezed lime juice
⅛ shot	Sugar syrup (2 sugar to 1 water)

Comment: Sweet and sour with fruity, herbal notes.

LOTUS ESPRESSO

Glass: Martini
Garnish: Coffee beans
Method: **SHAKE** all ingredients with ice and fine strain into chilled glass.

2 shots	Ketel One Vodka
½ shot	Coffee liqueur
½ shot	Maple syrup
1 shot	Espresso coffee (freshly made & hot)

Origin: Adapted from a drink discovered in 2005 at Lotus Bar, Sydney, Australia.
Comment: Coffee to the fore but with complex, earthy bitter-sweet notes.

LOUD SPEAKER MARTINI

Glass: Martini
Garnish: Lemon zest twist
Method: **SHAKE** all ingredients with ice and fine strain into chilled glass.

1½ shots	Rutte Dry Gin
1½ shots	Martell VSOP Médaillon cognac
½ shot	Martini Rosso vermouth
¼ shot	Freshly squeezed lemon juice
¼ shot	Sugar syrup (2 sugar to 1 water)

Origin: Adapted from a recipe in the 1930 'Savoy Cocktail Book' by Harry Craddock.
Comment: I've added a dash of sugar to the original recipe which I found too dry.

LOUISIANA TRADE

★★★☆☆

Glass: Old-fashioned
Garnish: Lime wedge
Method: SHAKE all ingredients with ice and strain into glass filled with crushed ice.

2	shots	Southern Comfort liqueur
1	shot	Freshly squeezed lime juice
¼	shot	Sugar syrup (2 sugar to 1 water)
½	shot	Maple syrup

Origin: Created in 2001 by Mahdi Otmann at Zeta, London, England.
Comment: Peach and apricot with the freshness of lime and the dense sweetness of maple syrup.

LOUISVILLE SOUR COCKTAIL (NEW)

★★★★☆

Glass: Old-fashioned
Garnish: Lemon zest twist & dash Angostura aromatic bitters
Method: SHAKE all ingredients with ice and strain back into shaker. **DRY SHAKE** (without ice) and strain into ice-filled glass.

1	shot	Bourbon whiskey
1	shot	Tobacco liqueur
1	shot	Freshly squeezed lemon juice
½	shot	Sugar syrup (2 sugar to 1 water)
1	dash	Angostura Aromatic Bitters
½	fresh	Egg white

Origin: Created in 2013 by Amanda Humphrey of Maxxium UK for Maker's Mark.
Comment: A hint of tobacco liqueur perfectly suits this sour named after bourbon's spiritual home.

LOVE HEART (NEW)

★★★★☆

Glass: Flute
Garnish: Half strawberry on rim with Love Heart sweet pegged to rim
Method: POUR into chilled glass and lightly stir.

1½	shots	Ketel One Vodka
½	shot	Lejay Crème de Fraise
½	shot	Parfait Amour liqueur
Top with		G.H. Mumm Cordon Rouge Champagne

Origin: Created in February 2014 by yours truly at the Cabinet Room, London, England.
Comment: This lavender pink drink is everything you (or your partner) might want for a Valentine's tipple. It is the right colour, includes parfait amour liqueur (meaning perfect love) and the all-important champagne sparkle. Good luck.

In case he/she asks, parfait amour is a lilac coloured curaçao (orange) liqueur flavoured with rose petals, vanilla pods and almonds.

LOVE JUNK

★★★☆☆

Glass: Old-fashioned
Garnish: Apple wedge
Method: SHAKE all ingredients with ice and strain into ice-filled glass.

2	shots	Ketel One Vodka
½	shot	Midori Green Melon liqueur
½	shot	Peachtree peach schnapps
1½	shots	Pressed apple juice

Comment: A light, crisp, refreshing blend of peach, melon and apple juice, laced with vodka.

LOVE ME FLIP

★★★★★

Glass: Goblet
Garnish: Grate tonka bean over drink.
Method: BEAT egg yolk with sugar in base of shaker. Add other ingredients, **SHAKE** with ice and fine strain into chilled glass.

1	fresh	Egg yolk
2	shots	Bacardi Carta Ocho aged rum
1	shot	Yoghurt liqueur
½	shot	Romate Pedro Ximénez sherry
3	drop	Angostura Aromatic Bitters
¼	shot	Sugar syrup (2 sugar to 1 water)

Origin: Created in 2010 by Erik Lorincz at The Connaught Hotel. London, England.
Comment: The grated Tonka bean adds a vanilla aroma to the surface of this drink.

LOVE UNIT

★★★★☆

Glass: Martini
Garnish: Basil leaf & bell pepper
Method: MUDDLE pepper in base of shaker. Add other ingredients, **SHAKE** with ice and fine strain into chilled glass.

2 slice Red bell pepper
7 fresh Basil leaves (thai)
1 shot Bacardi Carta Blanca light rum
1 shot Bacardi Carta Blanca (vanilla infused)
¾ shot Freshly squeezed lime juice
½ shot Freshly squeezed pink grapefruit juice
½ shot Sugar syrup (2 sugar to 1 water)

Origin: Created by Ryan Magarian, Seattle, USA.
Comment: Delicate, complex and balanced with enough fruit and veg to make your five-a-day.

LOVED UP

★★★★⯪☆

Glass: Martini
Garnish: Seasonal berries
Method: SHAKE all ingredients with ice and fine strain into chilled glass.

1½	shots	Patrón reposado tequila
½	shot	De Kuyper Triple Sec
½	shot	Chambord Liqueur
½	shot	Freshly squeezed lime juice
1	shot	Freshly squeezed orange juice
¼	shot	Sugar syrup (2 sugar to 1 water)

Origin: Adapted from a cocktail discovered in 2002 at the Merc Bar, New York City, where the original name was listed as simply 'Love'.
Comment: Tequila predominates in this rusty coloured drink, which also features orange and berry fruit.

LUCIEN GAUDIN

★★★★☆

Glass: Martini
Garnish: Orange zest twist
Method: STIR all ingredients with ice and strain into chilled glass.

1½ shots Rutte Dry Gin
¾ shot De Kuyper Triple Sec
¾ shot Campari Bitter
¾ shot Martini Extra Dry vermouth

Origin: This vintage cocktail is named after Lucien Gaudin, a French fencer who achieved gold medals with two different weapons at the 1924 Olympics in Paris and the 1928 Olympics in Amsterdam.
Comment: A must try for anyone who loves Negronis.

LUCKY LILY MARGARITA

★★★★⯪

Glass: Coupe
Garnish: Pineapple wedge dusted with pepper on rim.
Method: STIR honey with tequila in base of shaker to dissolve honey. Add other ingredients, **SHAKE** with ice and super-fine strain into chilled glass.

2	spoon	Runny honey
2	shots	Patrón reposado tequila
1	shot	Fresh pressed pineapple juice
¾	shot	Freshly squeezed lime juice
5	grind	Black pepper

Origin: Adapted from a drink discovered in 2006 at All Star Lanes, London, England.
Comment: Spicy tequila and pineapple tingle with balance and flavour.

LUCKY LINDY

★★★★⯪☆

Glass: Collins
Garnish: Lemon slice
Method: STIR honey with bourbon in base of shaker so as to dissolve honey. Add lemon juice, **SHAKE** with ice and strain into ice-filled glass. **TOP** with lemonade, lightly stir and serve with straws.

3	spoon	Runny honey
2	shots	Bourbon whiskey
½	shot	Freshly squeezed lemon juice
Top with		Lemonade/Sprite/7-Up

Origin: Adapted from a drink discovered in 2003 at The Grange Hall, New York City, USA.
Comment: A long refreshing drink that combines whiskey, citrus and honey - a long chilled toddy without the spice.

LUSH

★★★★☆

Glass: Flute
Garnish: Raspberries
Method: POUR vodka and liqueur into chilled glass, **TOP** with champagne and lightly stir.

1	shot	Ketel One Vodka
½	shot	Chambord Liqueur
Top with		G.H. Mumm Cordon Rouge Champagne

Origin: Created in 1999 by Spike Marchant at Alphabet, London, England.
Comment: It is, are you?

LUTKINS SPECIAL MARTINI

★★★★⯪☆

Glass: Martini
Garnish: Orange zest twist
Method: SHAKE all ingredients with ice and fine strain into chilled glass.

1½	shots	Rutte Dry Gin
½	shot	De Kuyper XO Apricot Brandy
1	shot	Martini Extra Dry vermouth
¾	shot	Freshly squeezed orange juice

Origin: Adapted from a recipe in Harry Craddock's 1930 'Savoy Cocktail Book'.
Comment: I've tried many variations on the above formula and none that are special.

LUX DAIQUIRI

★★★★☆

Glass: Martini
Garnish: Luxardo Maraschino cherry
Method: BLEND all ingredients with one 12oz scoop of crushed ice and serve in chilled glass.

3	shots	Bacardi Carta Blanca light rum
½	shot	Luxardo Maraschino liqueur
¾	shot	Freshly squeezed lime juice
¼	shot	Maraschino syrup (from cherry jar)
¼	shot	Sugar syrup (2 sugar to 1 water)

Origin: Created by yours truly. This was one of the two cocktails with which I won a Havana Club Daiquiri competition in 2002. It's named after Girolamo Luxardo, creator of the now famous liqueur, 'Luxardo Maraschino'. Lux is also Latin for light.
Comment: A classic frozen Daiquiri heavily laced with maraschino cherry.

LUXURY MOJITO

★★★★☆

Glass: Collins
Garnish: Mint sprig
Method: MUDDLE mint in glass with sugar and lime juice. Fill glass with crushed ice, add rum, Angostura and champagne, then stir.

12 fresh	Mint leaves
¼ shot	Sugar syrup (2 sugar to 1 water)
1 shot	Freshly squeezed lime juice
2 shots	Bacardi Carta Ocho aged rum
3 dash	Angostura Aromatic Bitters
Top with	G.H. Mumm Cordon Rouge Champagne

Comment: A Mojito made with aged rum and topped with champagne instead of soda water: more complex than the original.

LYCHEE & ELDERFLOWER SPRITZ (NEW)

★★★★☆

Glass: Old-fashioned
Garnish: Half fresh lychee
Method: POUR prosecco and liqueurs into glass. Add ice. Top with soda.

3 shots	Prosecco sparkling wine
1 shot	Kwai Feh lychee liqueur
1 shot	St-Germain elderflower liqueur
Top with	Soda (club soda)

Origin: Created in 2013 by yours truly for Jamie's Italian Bar.
Comment: As the apt name suggests, this slightly sweet spritz is flavoured with lychee and elderflower liqueurs. East meets west in Italy.

LYCHEE MARTINI

★★★★☆

Glass: Martini
Garnish: Lychee
Method: STIR all ingredients with ice and fine strain into chilled glass.

2 shots	Ketel One Vodka
½ shot	Kwai Feh lychee liqueur
1 shot	Lychee syrup (from tinned fruit)
½ shot	Martini Extra Dry vermouth

Origin: Thought to have been first made in 2001 at Clay, a Korean restaurant in New York City, USA.
Comment: If you like lychee you'll love this delicate Martini.

LYCHEE RICKEY

★★★☆☆

Glass: Collins (small 8oz)
Garnish: Length of lime peel
Method: SHAKE first three ingredients with ice and strain into ice-filled glass. TOP with soda water.

2 shots	Rutte Dry Gin
1 shot	Kwai Feh lychee liqueur
½ shot	Freshly squeezed lime juice
Top with	Soda (club soda)

Origin: Adapted from a drink discovered in 2005 at Club 97, Hong Kong, China.
Comment: The lychee liqueur dominates this surprisingly dry Rickey.

LYNCHBURG LEMONADE

★★★★☆

Glass: Collins
Garnish: Lemon slice
Method: SHAKE first 3 ingredients with ice and strain into ice-filled glass. TOP with lemonade.

1½ shots	Jack Daniel's Old No.7 Brand
1 shot	De Kuyper Triple Sec
1 shot	Freshly squeezed lemon juice
Top with	Lemonade/Sprite/7-Up

Origin: Created for the Jack Daniel's distillery in - yep, you guessed it - Lynchburg, Tennessee.
Comment: Tangy, light and very easy to drink.

M.G.F.

★★★★½

Glass: Martini
Garnish: Orange zest twist
Method: SHAKE all ingredients with ice and fine strain into chilled glass.

1 shot	Ketel One Oranje vodka
1 shot	Ketel One Citroen vodka
1 shot	Freshly squeezed pink grapefruit juice
1 shot	Freshly squeezed lemon juice
½ shot	Sugar syrup (2 sugar to 1 water)

Origin: Discovered in 2003 at Claridge's Bar, London, England.
Comment: Short and sharp.

MAC ORANGE

★★★½☆

Glass: Old-fashioned
Garnish: Orange zest twist
Method: SHAKE all ingredients with ice and fine strain into chilled glass.

2 shots	Dewar's 12 Year Old Scotch whisky
1 shot	Stone's green ginger wine
1 shot	Freshly squeezed orange juice
¼ shot	Sugar syrup (2 sugar to 1 water)
3 dash	Angostura Orange Bitters

Comment: A Whisky Mac with orange topping off the ginger.

MAÇÃ COCKTAIL

★★★★☆

Glass: Martini
Garnish: Apple slice & mint sprig
Method: SHAKE all ingredients with ice and fine strain into chilled glass.

2 shots	Capucana cachaça
½ shot	St-Germain elderflower liqueur
1½ shots	Pressed apple juice
½ shot	Freshly squeezed lime juice

Origin: Adapted from a recipe created in 2007 by Jamie Terrell, New York, USA while he was working for Sagatiba. Maçã means apple in Portuguese.
Comment: Subtle combination of cachaça, fresh lime, apple juice and elderflower.

MACHINE HEAD

★★★★☆

Glass: Coupe
Garnish: Luxardo Maraschino cherry & orange zest twist
Method: POUR all ingredients except tea into mixing glass. **SMOKE** tea using a chefs smoker and direct smoke into mixing glass. Cover to capture smoke for a minute or so. Remove cover, **STIR** with ice and strain into chilled glass.

1	shot	Martell VSOP Médaillon cognac
1	shot	Bacardi Carta Blanca light rum
1	shot	Bourbon whiskey
1	shot	Benoit Serres créme de violette
1	dash	Angostura Orange Bitters
1	dash	Angostura Aromatic Bitters
1	dash	Xocolatl Mole bitters
3	pinch	Lychee Rose Tea (for smoker)

Origin: Adapted from a drink created in 2010 by Jamie Boudreau at Vessel, Seattle, USA.
Comment: Overdo the smoke and your cocktail will start to resemble a cigar. Too little and you may find a tad sweet.

MACKA

★★★☆☆

Glass: Collins
Garnish: Lemon slice
Method: SHAKE first 4 ingredients with ice and strain into ice-filled glass. **TOP** with soda.

2	shots	Rutte Dry Gin
½	shot	Martini Extra Dry vermouth
½	shot	Martini Rosso vermouth
½	shot	Lejay crème de cassis de Dijon
Top with		Soda (club soda)

Comment: A long fruity drink for parched palates.

THE MACKINNON

★★★★☆

Glass: Martini
Garnish: Lemon zest twist
Method: SHAKE all ingredients with ice and fine strain into chilled glass.

2	shots	Bacardi Carta Oro rum
1	shot	Drambuie liqueur
½	shot	Freshly squeezed lemon juice

Origin: Named after the MacKinnon family, the makers of Drambuie.
Comment: Honeyed rum with herbal and citrus nuances.

MAD MONK MILKSHAKE

★★★☆☆

Glass: Collins
Garnish: Cord around glass
Method: SHAKE all ingredients with ice and strain into ice-filled glass.

1	shot	Baileys Irish cream liqueur
2	shots	Hazelnut liqueur
¼	shot	Coffee liqueur
2	shots	Milk
1	shot	Single cream / half-and-half

Comment: Long, creamy and slightly sweet with hazelnut and coffee.

MADE MAN

★★★★☆

Glass: Coupe
Garnish: Luxardo Maraschino cherry on stick
Method: STIR all ingredients with ice and strain into chilled glass.

1½	shot	Straight rye whiskey
½	shot	Yellow Chartreuse
½	shot	Cherry Herring liqueur
⅛	shot	Fernet Branca
½	shot	Chilled water (omit if wet ice)

Comment: Fernet Branca adds an almost smoky note to the rye, Yellow Chartreuse and cherry brandy combo. A great bittersweet after diner digestive.
Origin: Adapted from a drink created by Ali Reynolds at Hawksmoor, London, England where this drink is described as being "A variation on the Manhattan that Mad Men and Goodfellas would have enjoyed at the end of a hard day's work."

MADRAS

★★★☆☆

Glass: Collins
Garnish: Orange slice
Method: SHAKE all ingredients with ice and strain into ice-filled glass.

2	shots	Ketel One Vodka
3	shots	Cranberry juice
2	shots	Freshly squeezed orange juice

Comment: A seabreeze with orange juice in place of grapefruit, making it slightly sweeter.

MADROSKA

★★★☆☆

Glass: Collins
Garnish: Orange slice
Method: SHAKE all ingredients with ice and strain into ice filled glass.

2	shots	Ketel One Vodka
2½	shots	Pressed apple juice
1½	shots	Cranberry juice
1	shot	Freshly squeezed orange juice

Origin: Created in 1998 by Jamie Terrell, London, England.
Comment: A Madras with more than a hint of apple juice.

MAE WEST COCKTAIL

★★★★☆

Glass: Martini
Garnish: Melon slice
Method: STIR all ingredients with ice and strain into chilled glass.

2	shots	Ketel One Vodka
½	shot	Disaronno Originale amaretto
¼	shot	Midori Green Melon liqueur
1½	shots	Cranberry juice

Comment: A rosé coloured, semi-sweet concoction with a cherry, chocolate flavour.

MAESTRO

★★★★☆

Glass: Martini
Garnish: Balsamic covered strawberry
Method: **SHAKE** all ingredients with ice and fine strain into chilled glass.

2 shots Ketel One Vodka
1 shot Lejay Crème de Fraise
1 shot Freshly squeezed orange juice
⅛ shot Maple syrup
1 dash Balsamic vinegar of moderna

Origin: Created by Salvatore Calabrese at Salvatore At Fifty, London, England.
Comment: Strawberry and balsamic are a great combo - here served with orange juice, vodka and maple syrup.

MAGIC BUS

★★★½☆

Glass: Martini
Garnish: Lime wedge
Method: **SHAKE** all ingredients with ice and fine strain into chilled glass.

1 shot Patrón reposado tequila
1 shot De Kuyper Triple Sec
1 shot Cranberry juice
1 shot Freshly squeezed orange juice

Comment: Orange and cranberry laced with tequila.

MAHUKONA

★★★½☆

Glass: Sling
Garnish: Pineapple cubes, Luxardo Maraschino cherry & mint sprig
Method: **BLEND** all ingredients with 6oz scoop crushed ice and strain into glass half-filled with crushed ice. Serve with straws.

1 shot Bacardi Carta Blanca light rum
½ shot De Kuyper Triple Sec
1 shot Fresh pressed pineapple juice
½ shot Freshly squeezed lemon juice
¼ shot Sugar syrup (2 sugar to 1 water)
2 dash Angostura Aromatic Bitters

Origin: Adapted from Victor Bergeron's 'Trader Vic's Bartender's Guide' (1972 revised edition).
Comment: Citrus fresh and refreshing, not at all a sweetie.

MAI TAI #2 (BEAUMONT-GANTT'S FORMULA)

★★★★☆

Glass: Old-fashioned
Garnish: Mint sprig
Method: Lightly muddle mint in base of shaker (just to bruise). Add other ingredients, **SHAKE** with ice and strain glass filled with crushed ice.

12 fresh Mint leaves
1½ shots Pot still Jamaican rum
1 shot Bacardi Carta Blanca light rum
¾ shot De Kuyper Triple Sec
½ shot Taylor's Velvet Falernum liqueur
1 shot Freshly squeezed lime juice
1 shot Freshly squeezed pink grapefruit juice
2 dash Angostura Aromatic Bitters

Origin: It is claimed that Ernest Raymond Beaumont-Gantt first served this drink in 1933 at his Don The Beachcomber's bar in Hollywood, California. This is some ten years earlier than Bergeron's Mai Tai moment in cocktail history.
Comment: Whichever of the two created the drink; it is Trader Vic that made it famous and it is his recipe that endures.

MAI TAI (TRADER VIC'S) COCKTAILS

★★★★½

Glass: Old-fashioned
Garnish: Lime, mint sprig, pineapple cube & Luxardo Maraschino cherry
Method: **SHAKE** all ingredients with ice and strain into glass filled with crushed ice.

2 shots Bacardi Carta Ocho aged rum
½ shot Orange Curaçao liqueur
¾ shot Freshly squeezed lime juice
¼ shot Almond (orgeat) syrup
¼ shot Sugar syrup (2 sugar to 1 water)

Origin: In 1934, Victor Jules Bergeron, or Trader Vic as he became known, opened his first restaurant in Oakland, San Francisco. He served Polynesian food with a mix of Chinese, French and American dishes cooked in wood-fired ovens. But he is best known for the rum based cocktails he created.

One evening, in 1944, he tested a new drink on two friends from Tahiti, Ham and Carrie Guild. After the first sip, Carrie is said to have exclaimed, "mai tai-roa aé", which in Tahitian means 'out of this world - the best!'. So Bergeron named his drink the Mai Tai.

The original Mai Tai was based on 17 year old Jamaican J.Wray & Nephew rum, which Vic in his own guide describes as being "surprisingly golden in colour, medium bodied, but with the rich pungent flavour particular to the Jamaican blends". Vic states he used "rock candy" syrup, an old term for the type of strong sugar syrup we prescribe - two parts sugar to one part water. The term 'rock candy' referred to the fact that you could dangle a piece of string in the syrup to encourage crystallisation and make rock candy.

When supplies of the Jamaican 17-year-old rum dwindled, Vic started using a combination of dark Jamaican rum and Martinique rum to achieve the desired flavour. Sheer demand in his chain of restaurants later necessitated the introduction of a Mai Tai pre-mix (still available from tradervics.com).

Others, particularly Ernest Raymond Beaumont-Gantt, then owner of a Hollywood bar called Don the Beachcomber's, have also laid claim to the creation of this drink. But as Vic says in his own Bartender's Guide, "Anybody who says I didn't create this drink is a dirty stinker."

This recipe is adapted from Victor Bergeron's 'Trader Vic's Bartender's Guide' (1972 revised edition), the original 1944 formula is:

2 ounces of 17-year old J. Wray & Nephew Rum
Juice from one fresh lime, 1/2 ounce Holland DeKuyper Orange Curacao, 1/4 ounce Trader Vic's Rock Candy Syrup, 1/2 ounce French Garier Orgeat Syrup
Shake vigorously over shaved ice and garnish with a mint sprig.
Comment: We love Daiquiris and this is basically a classic Daiquiri with a few bells and whistles.

MAID IN CUBA

★★★★☆

Glass: Coupe
Garnish: Slice of cucumber
Method: POUR absinthe into ice-filled glass, TOP with water and leave to stand. Separately SHAKE other ingredients with ice (Don't muddle cucumber). DISCARD contents of glass (absinthe, water and ice) and STRAIN contents of shaker into absinthe-coated glass. TOP with splash of soda.

¼	shot	Le Fée Parisienne absinthe
2	shots	Bacardi Carta Blanca light rum
¾	shot	Freshly squeezed lime juice
½	shot	Sugar syrup (2 sugar to 1 water)
7	fresh	Mint leaves
2	slice	English cucumber peeled
Top with		Soda (club soda)

Origin: Created in 2012 by Tom Walker at The Savoy's American Bar in London, England for Bacardi's Legacy Cocktail Competition. Tom went on to win the UK leg of this global competition with this drink.
Comment: A classic Daiquiri shaken with mint and cucumber strained into an absinthe washed glass and spritzed with soda.

MAIDA VALE

★★★★☆

Glass: Coupe
Garnish: Luxardo Maraschino cherry
Method: STIR all ingredients with ice and strain into chilled glass.

2	shots	Bourbon whiskey
½	shot	Straight rye whiskey
½	shot	Martini Rosso vermouth
½	shot	Martini Bianco
¼	shot	Grand Marnier Cordon Rouge
2	dash	Angostura Aromatic Bitters

Origin: Created in January 2011 by Andy Green of Unripe, London, England.
Comment: Originally named the Unripe Manhattan after the website of its creator, this Manhattan-style cocktail benefits from the spice of rye whiskey with sweet and bianco vermouth and a dash of orange curaçao.

MAIDEN'S BLUSH 0━🗝

★★★★☆

Glass: Coupe
Garnish: Lemon zest twist
Method: SHAKE all ingredients with ice and fine strain into chilled glass.

2	shots	Rutte Dry Gin
½	shot	De Kuyper Triple Sec
½	shot	Pomegranate / grenadine syrup (2:1)
¼	shot	Freshly squeezed lemon juice
½	shot	Chilled water (omit if wet ice)

Origin: Adapted from a recipe in Harry Craddock's 1930 'Savoy Cocktail Book'.
Comment: Pale pink, subtle and light.

MAIDEN'S PRAYER 0━🗝

★★★★☆

Glass: Martini
Garnish: Orange zest twist
Method: SHAKE all ingredients with ice and fine strain into chilled glass.

1½	shots	Rutte Dry Gin
1	shot	De Kuyper Triple Sec
1	shot	Freshly squeezed orange juice
½	shot	Freshly squeezed lemon juice

Origin: Adapted from a recipe in Harry Craddock's 1930 'Savoy Cocktail Book'.
Comment: Fresh, zesty orange with a pleasing twang of alcohol.

MAINBRACE 0━🗝

★★★★☆

Glass: Martini
Garnish: Orange zest twist
Method: SHAKE all ingredients with ice and fine strain into chilled glass.

1¼	shots	Rutte Dry Gin
1¼	shots	De Kuyper Triple Sec
1¼	shots	Freshly squeezed pink grapefruit juice

Comment: Tangy grapefruit laced with gin and a hint of orange. Tart finish.

MAISON CHARLES DAIQUIRI 0━🗝

★★★★☆

Glass: Martini
Garnish: Sugar & mint rim
Method: Lightly MUDDLE (just to bruise) mint in base of shaker. Add other ingredients, SHAKE with ice and fine strain into chilled glass.

8	fresh	Mint leaves
2	shots	Bacardi Carta Blanca light rum
½	shot	Freshly squeezed lime juice
½	shot	Sugar syrup (2 sugar to 1 water)
½	shot	Chilled water (omit if wet ice)

Origin: Pronounced 'May-Sawn Sharl', this recipe is adapted from David A. Embury's 1948 'Fine Art of Mixing Drinks'.
Comment: Reminiscent of concentrated Mojito.

MAJOR BAILEY #1 0━🗝

★★★★☆

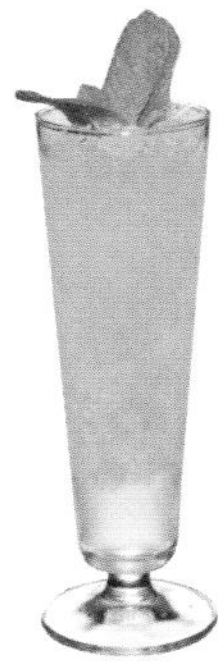

Glass: Sling
Garnish: Mint sprig
Method: Lightly MUDDLE (only to bruise) mint with gin in base of shaker. Add other ingredients, SHAKE with ice and fine strain into glass half filled with crushed ice. CHURN (stir) drink with ice using a barspoon. Top the glass to the brim with more crushed ice and churn again. Serve with straws.

12	fresh	Mint leaves
2	shots	Rutte Dry Gin
¼	shot	Freshly squeezed lime juice
¼	shot	Freshly squeezed lemon juice
½	shot	Sugar syrup (2 sugar to 1 water)

Origin: Adapted from a recipe in the 1947 'Trader Vic's Bartender Guide' by Victor Bergeron.
Comment: As Victor says of this gin based Julep, "This is a hell of a drink."

MAJOR BAILEY #2 🗝

★★★★½

Glass: Sling
Garnish: Mint sprig
Method: BLEND all ingredients with one 12oz scoop of crushed ice and serve with straws.

2	shots	Bacardi Carta Blanca light rum
1	shot	De Kuyper Triple Sec
1	shot	Fresh pressed pineapple juice
½	shot	Freshly squeezed lemon juice
¼	shot	Sugar syrup (2 sugar to 1 water)

Origin: Adapted from a drink created by Victor Bergeron.
Comment: Made well this is a long, fruity, brilliant frozen Daquiri.

MALCOM LOWRY

★★★★☆

Glass: Old-fashioned
Garnish: Lime wedge
Method: SHAKE all ingredients with ice and strain into ice-filled glass.

1	shot	Patrón reposado tequila
½	shot	White overproof rum
¼	shot	De Kuyper Triple Sec
½	shot	Freshly squeezed lime juice
¼	shot	Sugar syrup (2 sugar to 1 water)

Origin: Created by drinks author David Broom. Named after Malcom Lowry's 1947 novel 'Under the Volcano' which explores a man's battle with alcoholism in Mexico.
Comment: A suitably 'hard' and flavoursome Daiquiri-like drink.

MALECON COCKTAIL (NEW)

★★★★½

Glass: Coupe
Garnish: float chunk of block ice (or ice cube)
Method: SHAKE all ingredients with ice and fine strain into chilled glass.

1⅔	shots	Bacardi Carta Blanca light rum
½	shot	Ruby port
⅓	shot	Romate Oloroso sherry
1	shot	Freshly squeezed lime juice
½	shot	Sugar syrup (2 sugar to 1 water)
1	dash	Peychaud's aromatic bitters

Origin: Created in 2011 by Erik Lorincz at the American Bar, The Savoy, London, England.
Comment: Best described as a fortified wine rich Daiquiri.

MALTY DRY MARTINI

★★★★★

Glass: Martini
Garnish: Chilled olive or lemon zest twist
Method: STIR all ingredients with ice and strain into chilled glass.

2½	shots	Rutte Old Simon oude jenever
½	shot	Martini Extra Dry vermouth

Origin: A Martini which emerged in 2008.
Comment: Using a genuinely malty oude jenever produces a deliciously retro take on the modern Dry Martini.

MAMBO

★★★½☆

Glass: Collins
Garnish: Orange slice
Method: SHAKE all ingredients with ice and strain into ice-filled glass.

1	shot	Ketel One Vodka
1	shot	De Kuyper Triple Sec
1	shot	De Kuyper XO Apricot Brandy
¼	shot	Campari Bitter
3	shots	Freshly squeezed orange juice

Origin: Created by Nichole Colella.
Comment: A slightly bitter, tangy, orange, cooling drink.

MAMIE TAYLOR 🗝

★★★½☆

Glass: Collins
Garnish: Lime wedge
Method: POUR all ingredients into ice-filled glass and lightly STIR.

2	shots	Dewar's 12 Year Old Scotch whisky
¼	shot	Freshly squeezed lime juice
Top with		Ginger ale

Origin: Bartenders apparently became so sick of making Mamie Taylors in the 1900s that they hiked up the price of the cocktail to discourage customers from ordering it. It dates from 1899 when it was invented in Rochester, New York and it spread like wildfire. The name is a bit of a mystery but there are several versions of a tale which links the drink to a Broadway star of the same name. 30 years after its creation the Mamie Taylor appears in Albert Stevens Crockett's 1935 'The Old Wardorf-Astoria Bar Book' but sadly never managed to recover from Prohibition and has since faded from the limelight.
Comment: A Scotch and ginger with a splash of lime juice.

MAÑANA DAIQUIRI 🗝

★★★★☆

Glass: Coupe
Garnish: Apricot slice
Method: SHAKE all ingredients with ice and fine strain into chilled glass.

2	shots	Bacardi Carta Blanca light rum
½	shot	De Kuyper XO Apricot Brandy
¼	shot	Pomegranate / grenadine syrup (2:1)
¼	shot	Freshly squeezed lemon juice
½	shot	Chilled water (omit if wet ice)

Origin: Mañana, literally meaning 'tomorrow' in Spanish but more usually used to mean some indefinite time in the future. This recipe is adapted from David A. Embury's 1948 "Fine Art of Mixing Drinks".
Comment: Salmon pink in colour, the Mañana has a subtle and delicate rum laced apricot flavour.

MANCHESTER SPECIAL RUM PUNCH

★★★☆☆

Glass: Old-fashioned
Garnish: Grapefruit slice
Method: STIR honey with rum until honey dissolves. Add other ingredients, **SHAKE** with ice and strain into glass filled with crushed ice.

2	shots	Pot still Jamaican rum
2	spoon	Runny honey
1	shot	Freshly squeezed pink grapefruit juice
2	dash	Angostura Aromatic Bitters

Origin: Originally made at the Manchester Hotel, Mandeville, Jamaica. The Manchester Hotel lies in a lush tropical setting in the centre of Jamaica high in the cool mountains of Manchester.
Comment: Fruity punch.

MANDARINE COLLINS

★★★☆☆

Glass: Collins
Garnish: Orange slice
Method: SHAKE first three ingredients with ice and strain into ice-filled glass. **TOP** with soda.

1½ shots	Rutte Dry Gin
1 shot	Mandarine Napoléon liqueur
1 shot	Freshly squeezed lemon juice
Top with	Soda (club soda)

Comment: A tangy, long refreshing drink with an intense mandarin flavour.

MANDARINE SIDECAR

★★★★☆

Glass: Martini
Garnish: Sugar rim (optional) & lemon zest twist
Method: SHAKE all ingredients with ice and fine strain into chilled glass.

1½ shots	Martell VSOP Médaillon cognac
1 shot	Mandarine Napoléon liqueur
1 shot	Freshly squeezed lemon juice
⅛ shot	Sugar syrup (2 sugar to 1 water)
¾ shot	Chilled water (omit if wet ice)

Comment: Wonderfully tart and strong in flavour.

MANDARINE SONGBIRD

★★★☆☆

Glass: Collins
Garnish: Orange slice
Method: SHAKE first 3 ingredients with ice and fine strain into ice-filled glass. **TOP** with ginger beer.

2	shots	Mandarine Napoléon liqueur
½	shot	Freshly squeezed lemon juice
¾	shot	Freshly squeezed orange juice
Top with		Gosling's Stormy Ginger Beer

Comment: Long, spicy orange.

MANDARINE SOUR

★★★★☆

Glass: Old-fashioned
Garnish: Lemon slice
Method: SHAKE all ingredients with ice and strain into ice-filled glass.

2	shots	Mandarine Napoléon liqueur
1	shot	Freshly squeezed lemon juice
¼	shot	Sugar syrup (2 sugar to 1 water)
½	fresh	Egg white

Comment: Sour, but with a strong mandarin sweetness.

MANDARINTINI

★★★★☆

Glass: Martini
Garnish: Orange slice
Method: SHAKE all ingredients with ice and fine strain into chilled glass.

1½ shots	Ketel One Oranje vodka
½ shot	Grand Marnier Cordon Rouge
¼ shot	Campari Bitter
1½ shots	Pressed apple juice

Origin: Adapted from a drink discovered in 2005 at Aqua Spirit, Hong Kong, China.
Comment: This bittersweet palate cleanser looks like pink grapefruit juice.

MANDARITO

★★★★☆

Glass: Old-fashioned
Garnish: Mint sprig
Method: Lightly **MUDDLE** mint (just to bruise) in base of glass. Add next 4 ingredients, half fill glass with crushed ice and **CHURN** (stir). Fill glass to brim with more crushed ice and churn some more. **TOP** with soda, stir and serve with straws.

12 fresh	Mint leaves
1 shot	Ketel One Vodka
1½ shots	Mandarine Napoléon liqueur
1 shot	Freshly squeezed lime juice
⅛ shot	Sugar syrup (2 sugar to 1 water)
Top with	Soda (club soda)

Comment: A vodka Mojito with mandarine accents.

MANGO COLLINS

★★★★☆

Glass: Collins
Garnish: Lemon slice
Method: SHAKE first three ingredients with ice and strain into ice-filled glass. **TOP** with soda, stir and serve with straws.

2	shots	Rutte Dry Gin
2	shots	Mango purée
1½ shots	Freshly squeezed lemon juice
Top with	Soda (club soda)

Comment: Lemon juice and gin combine with mango in this refreshing tall drink.

MANGO DAIQUIRI

★★★★☆

Glass: Martini
Garnish: Lime wedge
Method: SHAKE all ingredients with ice and fine strain into chilled glass.

2	shots	Bacardi Carta Blanca light rum
2	shots	Mango purée
½	shot	Freshly squeezed lime juice

Comment: Tropical yet potent and refreshing.

MANGO MARGARITA (FROZEN)

★★★★☆

Glass: Coupe
Garnish: Mango slice
Method: BLEND all ingredients with 6oz scoop of crushed ice. Serve with straws.

2	shots	Patrón reposado tequila
¾	shot	Mango purée
1	shot	De Kuyper Triple Sec
½	shot	Freshly squeezed lime juice
¼	shot	Sugar syrup (2 sugar to 1 water)

Comment: Mango first and Margarita second.

MANGO MARGARITA (SERVED 'STRAIGHT UP')

★★★★☆

Glass: Coupe
Garnish: Lime wedge
Method: SHAKE all ingredients with ice and fine strain into chilled glass.

2	shots	Patrón reposado tequila
1	shot	Mango purée
1	shot	De Kuyper Triple Sec
1	shot	Freshly squeezed lime juice

Comment: The character of the tequila is not overwhelmed by the fruit.

Manhattan cocktail

Like so many cocktails, the origins of the Manhattan are lost in time. And, as neither the name nor the ingredients are so unusual as to prevent inadvertent duplication, the mystery is likely to remain unsolved.

The first known written mention of the Manhattan is in a September 1882 article of the Olean, New York, 'Sunday Morning Herald'. "It is but a short time ago that a mixture of whiskey, vermouth and bitters came into vogue." The same article causes some confusion when it goes on to discuss the name of this concoction, "It went under various names - Manhattan cocktail, Turf Club cocktail, and Jockey Club cocktail."

The first full written recipe for the Manhattan appeared two years later in O.H. Byron's 1884 book, 'The Modern Bartenders' Guide'.

Until fairly recently, it was wrongly and widely believed that the Manhattan was first created in November 1874 at New York City's Manhattan Club for Lady Randolph Churchill (née Jenny Jerome), at a banquet to celebrate the successful gubernatorial campaign of Samuel Jones Tilden. (The Manhattan Club was opposite the site that now houses the Empire State Building.) However, drinks historian David Wondrich has pointed out that the celebratory banquet in question was held in November 1874, during the period when Lady C was in England, giving birth to Winston - indeed, the banquet was held on the day Winston was christened at Blenheim.

A plausible story comes from a book published in 1923, 'Valentine's Manual of New York'. In this a William F. Mulhall who was a bartender at New York's Hoffman House in the 1880s recounts, "The Manhattan cocktail was invented by a man named Black who kept a place ten doors below Houston Street on Broadway in the [eighteen] sixties - probably the most famous drink in the world in its time."

Yet another story involves a Col. Joe Walker on a yachting trip in New York. This last story is the most recent I have come across and is courtesy of Barry Popik's barrypopik.com where Barry notes an entry in the Daily Journal, Racine, Wisconsin, 8 March 1899. The article purports that Col. Joe Walker ran the then-famous Crescent Hall Saloon in New Orleans, at the corner of Canal and St. Charles Streets and that some years before he went on a little yachting trip with a party of friends while in New York.

"By some oversight the liquid refreshments in the icebox were confined to Italian vermouth and plain whisky, and it occurred to the colonel that a palatable drink might be made by mixing the two. The results were so good that he experimented a little on his return to New Orleans, and soon perfected the Manhattan cocktail, as it is known today. It was christened in honor of his friends on Manhattan Island, and the fame of the decoction soon spread all over the country. The true Manhattan cocktail is always made with Italian vermouth, but at half the places where they undertake to serve them, French [dry] vermouth is substituted, and the fine flavor is altogether destroyed. French vermouth is a sort of wine, while Italian vermouth is a cordial, pure and simple. They are as different as milk and molasses. A cocktail made from the French brand is no more a Manhattan cocktail than it is a Spanish omelette." [sic]

One of the first printed references to the Manhattan appears in William Schmidt's 1891 'The Flowing Bowl'. The recipe calls for gum, includes a dash of absinthe and suggests "a little maraschino may be added".

Harry Johnson's 1900 'Bartenders' Manual' includes the following recipe:

"Manhattan Cocktail
(Use a large bar glass)
Fill the glass up with ice;
1 or 2 dashes of gum syrup, very carefully;
1 or 2 dashes of bitters (orange bitters);
1 dash of curacao or absinthe, if required;
1/2 wine-glass of whiskey;
1/2 wine glass of vermouth;
Stir up well; strain into fancy cocktail glass; squeeze a piece of lemon peel on top, and serve; leave it for the customer to decide, whether to use absinthe or not. This drink is very popular at the present day. It is the bartender's duty to ask the customer, whether he desires his drink dry or sweet."

Over the decades the gum syrup and absinthe has been omitted from the Manhattan while the maraschino has morphed into the garnish. It is also more common for Angostura aromatic bitters to be used in place of orange bitters - perhaps mostly due to Angostura being more commonplace over the decades. However, it should be noted that various bartenders favour the use of different bitters, including Abbott's Bitters.

Frustratingly the recipes in the early bar books above simply state 'whiskey' but the Manhattan was probably originally made with rye whiskey, rather than bourbon, as New York was a rye-drinking city. Today it is common to use bourbon, although purists tend to favour bonded rye whiskey. Some folks even prefer Tennessee or Canadian whiskey.

Once you've decided on your choice of whiskey comes the decision of what vermouth to use. Firstly, you'll need to establish if you are making a Dry Manhattan, which calls for dry vermouth, a Perfect Manhattan which uses dry and sweet vermouths, or a Sweet Manhattan with just sweet vermouth. Not to mention the brand.

While the Dry Manhattan is usually garnished with a twist, the more commonplace Perfect and Sweet Manhattans are generally garnished with a maraschino cherry. Maraschino and American whiskey (bourbon or rye) are a match made in heaven - so much so, that I am one of those people who likes a small spoon of cherry syrup from the jar added to the mixing glass so subtly sweetening and influencing the drink.

Convention has it that a Manhattan should be stirred and served in a cocktail glass (coupe or martini) but the drink also works well served over ice in an old-fashioned glass. Some even prefer their Manhattans shaken rather than stirred. Each to their own.

MANHATTAN DRY 🔑

★★★★⯪

Glass: Martini
Garnish: Lemon or orange zest twist
Method: STIR all ingredients with ice and strain into chilled glass.

2½ shots Bourbon whiskey
1 shot Martini Extra Dry vermouth
3 dash Angostura Aromatic Bitters

Comment: A bone dry Manhattan for those with dry palates.

MANHATTAN ISLAND

★★★★⯪

Glass: Martini
Garnish: Luxardo Maraschino cherry
Method: STIR all ingredients with ice and fine strain into chilled glass.

2 shots Martell VSOP Médaillon cognac
1 shot Martini Rosso vermouth
3 dash Angostura Aromatic Bitters
⅛ shot Luxardo Maraschino liqueur

Comment: A twist on the classic Harvard, or brandy based Manhattan.

MANHATTAN PERFECT 🔑

★★★★★

Glass: Martini
Garnish: Orange zest twist (discarded) & Luxardo Maraschino cherry
Method: STIR all ingredients with ice and strain into chilled glass.

2½ shots Bourbon whiskey
½ shot Martini Rosso vermouth
½ shot Martini Extra Dry vermouth
3 dash Angostura Aromatic Bitters

Comment: The medium dry version of the Manhattan.

MANHATTAN SWEET

★★★★★

Glass: Martini
Garnish: Orange zest twist (discarded) & Luxardo Maraschino cherry
Method: STIR all ingredients with ice and strain into chilled glass.

2½ shots Bourbon whiskey
⅛ shot Maraschino syrup (from cherry jar)
1 shot Martini Rosso vermouth
3 dash Angostura Aromatic Bitters

Comment: I must confess to preferring my Manhattans served 'sweet', or 'perfect' at a push. The Manhattan is complex, challenging and moreish. Best of all, it's available in a style to suit every palate.

MANHATTAN TRANSFER (NEW)

★★★★★

Glass: Coupe
Garnish: Orange zest twist (discarded) & Luxardo maraschino cherry
Method: STIR all ingredients with ice and strain into chilled glass.

1½ shots Straight rye whiskey
1 shot Martini Extra Dry vermouth
1 shot Amaro liqueur
1 dash Angostura Orange Bitters

Origin: Adapted from a recipe created in 2013 by Phil Ward at Mayahuel, New York City, USA.
Comment: Amaro Italian bitter liqueur (originally Ramazzotti) takes the place of Angostura aromatic bitters and adds bitter-sweetness in this riff on a Dry Manhattan.

MANICURE

★★★★☆

Glass: Coupe
Garnish: Apple wedge
Method: STIR all ingredients with ice and fine strain into chilled glass.

1 shot Calvados brandy
1 shot Dewar's 12 Year Old Scotch whisky
1 shot Drambuie liqueur

Origin: Created in 2010 by a collaboration between Emma Ramos and yours truly at the Cabinet Room, London, England.
Comment: Due to the use of Calvados this drink was going to be called 'FRENCH NAIL CARE' but thankfully this led to the name 'Manicure'.

MANKY PANKY COCKTAIL (NEW)

★★★★⯪

Glass: Coupe
Garnish: Orange zest twist
Method: SHAKE all ingredients with ice and strain into chilled glass.

1 shot Rutte Dry Gin
¾ shot Chambord Liqueur
¾ shot Shiraz red wine
¼ shot Fernet Branca
¾ shot Blood orange juice

Origin: Created 5th February 2014 by yours truly at the Cabinet Room, London, England. A fruity riff on the classic Hanky-Panky, created in the early 1900s by Ada 'Coley' Coleman at The Savoy's American Bar.
Comment: Red berries, red wine and ruby orange subtly fortified with gin and the underlying herbal notes of Fernet Branca.

MANTINI

★★★★⯪

Glass: Martini
Garnish: Olive wrapped in bacon
Method: STIR all ingredients with ice and strain into chilled glass.

2½ shots Rutte Dry Gin
½ shot Fuller's Chiswick Bitter

Comment: A gin martini-style drink made with beer in place of vermouth. A suitably manly garnish is also called for.

MAPLE LEAF

★★★★☆

Glass: Old-fashioned
Garnish: Lemon zest twist
Method: SHAKE all ingredients with ice and strain into ice-filled glass.

2	shots	Bourbon whiskey
½	shot	Freshly squeezed lemon juice
⅓	shot	Maple syrup

Comment: This trio combine wonderfully with maple to the fore.

MAPLE OLD-FASHIONED COCKTAIL

★★★★☆

Glass: Martini
Garnish: Orange zest twist
Method: STIR one shot of the bourbon with two ice cubes in a glass. Add maple syrup and Angostura and two more ice cubes. Stir some more and add another two ice cubes and the rest of the bourbon. Stir lots more so as to melt the ice, then add fresh ice to complete the drink. The melting and stirring in of ice cubes is essential to the dilution and taste of this drink.

2	shots	Bourbon whiskey
2	dash	Angostura Aromatic Bitters
½	shot	Maple syrup

Origin: Discovered in 2004 at Indigo Yard, Edinburgh, Scotland.
Comment: Maple syrup replaces sugar in this reworking of the classic Old-fashioned.

MAPLE POMME

★★★★☆

Glass: Collins
Garnish: Apple wedge
Method: SHAKE first four ingredients with ice and strain into ice-filled glass. TOP with ginger ale, lightly stir and serve with straws.

2	shots	Dewar's 12 Year Old Scotch whisky
½	shot	Freshly squeezed lemon juice
1	shot	Pressed apple juice
½	shot	Maple syrup
Top with		Ginger ale

Origin: Adapted from a short drink created in 2005 by Tonin Kacaj at Maze, London, England.
Comment: Scotch based drink for warm weather.

MARAMA RUM PUNCH

★★★★☆

Glass: Sling
Garnish: Mint sprig & lime wedge
Method: Lightly MUDDLE mint (just to bruise). Add next five ingredients, SHAKE with ice and strain into ice-filled glass. TOP with lemonade, lightly stir and serve with straws.

12	fresh	Mint leaves
1½	shots	White overproof rum
½	shot	De Kuyper Triple Sec
½	shot	Freshly squeezed lime juice
½	shot	Almond (orgeat) syrup
3	dash	Angostura Aromatic Bitters
Top with		Lemonade/Sprite/7-Up

Comment: A tangy, well-balanced punch.

MARGARET DUFFY

★★★★☆

Glass: Martini
Garnish: Lemon zest twist
Method: STIR all ingredients with ice and strain into chilled glass.

2	shots	Swedish Punch liqueur
1	shot	Martell VSOP Médaillon cognac
2	dash	Angostura Aromatic Bitters
½	shot	Chilled water (omit if wet ice)

Origin: Vintage cocktail of unknown origin.
Comment: Spiced and sweetened cognac.

Margarita Cocktail

Part of the 'sour' cocktail family, the Margarita traditionally consists of three ingredients; tequila, triple sec orange liqueur and lime juice, often served in a glass with salt on the rim. Margaritas are mostly shaken and served either straight-up in the eponymous margarita glass (coupette) or over ice in an old-fashioned glass. They may also be blended with ice and served 'frozen'.

Margarita recipe
Classically a margarita consists of 2 parts tequila, 1 part triple sec liqueur and 1 part lime juice. This tends to produce a drink which is a little on the sour side of balanced (depending on your limes and liqueur sweetness). Hence it is common to subtly up the degree of sweetness by adding a spoon or two of sugar syrup. I prefer adding agave syrup in place of sugar and my Difford's Margarita recipe is a classic 2:1:1 with a spoon of agave syrup.

The 2:1:1 Margarita formula - with or without an additional spoon or two of sugar/agave syrup (to taste) works well either served straight-up or on-the-rocks. However, if blending to serve 'frozen' then the drink will benefit from dramatically raising the degree of sweetness by increasing either the amount of liqueur, sugar or agave used.

I like to add half a pinch of salt to a Margarita rather than salting the rim. Although barely detectable by the drinker, this small amount of salt subtlety enhances the drink's flavour.

A salted rim on a Margarita delivers a hit of salt that is too intense and masks the flavour of the drink. However, the salt rim is so synonymous with the Margarita that drinkers expect it - even if they do drink from the same area of the glass to avoid another hit of salt. So consider only salting just half or two thirds of the rim to give the drinker the option of avoiding the salt altogether.

When salting a rim run a lime wedge around the outside of the glass' rim and then roll the rim in salt rather than dipping the rim into juice and then salt. The dipping method coats the inside of the glass with salt which is inevitably washed into the cocktail so polluting it with too much salt.

While triple sec liqueur is the classic sweetener in a Margarita, other liqueurs are often used and thanks to drinks industry legend, Julio Bermejo, and his Tommy's Margarita, liqueurs are either totally or partly replaced as a sweetener by the use of agave syrup.

Tommy's Margaritas made with agave syrup in place of orange liqueur are not strictly Margaritas at all, they are Tequila Sours. A Margarita is defined by the combination of tequila and lime juice with the liqueur not only balancing the sourness of the lime but also contributing subtle orange notes.

I understand that people would rather use agave as a sweetener in place of the beet or cane sugar in a triple sec liqueur so back in 2008 Bruno Giffard and I created Agave Sec liqueur. This is a triple sec sweetened only with agave syrup and without sugar. It is formulated to replicate the sweetness of a triple sec such as Cointreau and allows a true, subtly orange flavoured sugar-free Margarita to be made.

Margaritas are classically made with Mexican limes - Key lime (Citrus aurantifolia) or Persian lime (Citrus latifolia) varieties with the ubiquitous availability of Persian limes making their use by far the most common. However, Margaritas made with equal parts lime and lemon juice are more delicate and I'd argue better. It's perhaps worth mentioning that the first known printed Margarita recipe, in the December 1953 Esquire Magazine, calls for an ounce of tequila, a dash of triple sec and the juice of half a lime or lemon.

Margarita origins and history
Margarita is the Spanish word for 'daisy'. (Incidentally, 'daisy' is thought to be a corruption of 'day's eye' due to the flower head of the daisy closing at night and opening in the morning.) And its probable that the Margarita cocktail is simply a tequila-based Daisy - a style of drink made with citrus juice, sweetened with a syrup or liqueur, and fortified with a base spirit that dates back to Victorian times.

The Daisy was a category of cocktail popular in the early 20th century with the 19 July 1939 edition of the Albuquerque Journal describing the Daisy as being "ubiquitous", while the first specific mention of a Tequila Daisy appeared in the Moville Mail on 23rd July 1936 (pg. 4, cols. 1-3) in a piece titled "Graham's Sightseeing". James Graham was the newspaper's editor and owner and in the piece he recounts his visit to Tijuana and Augua (sic) Caliente, Mexico.

"When we parked, the driver told us of places of interest that are now not so interesting as in the days of Prohibition in the States. Then there were 150 bars open, now there are nine. One of these is run by an Irishman named Madden. The driver had told us of his skill in mixing drinks. One of his inventions has given his saloon the name of "The Home of the Famous Tequila Daisy." As a newspaper man seeking information, I entered the joint and told Mr. Madden my curiosity was aroused regarding The Daisy. He was not as talkative as his prototype, Mr. Dooley, but I imagine he looks like that gentleman, the creature of the imagination of the late Peter Finlay Dunne. After a while he told me The Daisy was not an invention, as no skill was employed in its creation, it was a mistake. "In mixing a drink I grabbed the wrong bottle and the customer was so delighted that he called for another and spread the good news far and wide," said Mr. Madden."

Shortly after, in the 19th August 1936 edition of the Syracuse Herald (pg. 24, col. 3), an advertisement for "Leo Lighter and His All-Girl Band" mentions "Syracuse's newest and refreshing drink Tequila Daisy". If Leo Lighter and His All-Girl Band and Tequila Daisies weren't enough the ad also promises "Eddie Vanzill" the "Dancing Waiter" as an "Added Attraction".

The 1937 *Café Royal Cocktail Book* by William J. Tarling includes a British antecedent of the Margarita called a 'Picador'. This predates the first known mention of the Margarita by 16 years with the recipe in proportions identical to that recognised today as a Margarita. So the Margarita is obviously a British invention!

The first (suitably flowery) printed mention of a Margarita cocktail is in the December 1953 issue of Esquire magazine: "She's from Mexico, Señores, and she is lovely to look at, exciting and provocative". The recipe given is one-ounce tequila, a dash of triple sec and the juice of half a lime or lemon. It's worth mentioning that Margarita as an American girl's name reached its peak of popularity in the 1930s and 40s so there were plenty of Margaritas around in the 1950s when it would appear the Margarita cocktail was christened. Margarita is also the name of an island, Isla de Margarita (Margarita Island) a popular holiday destination in the Caribbean north of Venezuela, two-and-a-half hours from Miami.

There are many people who either claim to have invented or named the Margarita cocktail. The following are the most notable, in rough chronological order, rather than by probability:

1. **Vernon Underwood** was president of Young's Market Company, which in the 1930s had started distributing Cuervo tequila in America. He is said to have asked Johnny Durlesser, head bartender of the Tail O' The Cock in Los Angeles, to create something using his newly acquired spirit, then named the new drink after his wife Margaret (Margarita).

2. **Sara Morales**, an expert in Mexican folklore, claimed the Margarita was created in 1930 by Doña Bertha, owner of Bertha's Bar in Taxco, Mexico.

3. **Daniel (Danny) Negrete** is said to have created the drink in 1936 when he was the manager of Garci Crespo Hotel in Puebla, Mexico. His girlfriend, Margarita, apparently liked salt in her drinks and the story goes that he created the drink for her as a present. In 1944 Danny moved to Tijuana, Mexico, and became a bartender at the Agua Caliente Racetrack, a place which claims to be the birthplace of the Margarita in the early 1930s.

4. **Francisco 'Pancho' Morales** said he created the Margarita whilst working in a bar called Tommy's Place in Ciudad Juarez, Mexico, after being asked to make a 'Magnolia' on the 4th July 1942. Unable to remember the recipe he is said to have created the now famous drink. Who knows, the customer's name may even have been Margarita.

5. **Carlos 'Danny' Herrera** is also said to have created the cocktail either in 1947 or 1948 at his Rancho La Gloria bar in Rosarito, Mexico, for an actress called Marjorie King who drank no spirit but tequila. He added Cointreau and lime, and the unique salt rim that caught people's attention at the bar, then named his creation Margarita, the Spanish for Marjorie.

6. The socialite **Margaret Sames** held a Christmas party in Acapulco, Mexico, in 1948, where she is said to have created the first Margarita. She thought nothing of it until, when flying home to San Antonio from Acapulco airport, she saw a bar advertising 'Margarita's Drink', a cocktail with exactly the same ingredients as her own.

MARGARITA (FROZEN)

★★★★☆

Glass: Martini
Garnish: Luxardo Maraschino cherry
Method: BLEND all ingredients with 12oz scoop of crushed ice. Serve heaped in the glass and with straws.

1½ shots Patrón reposado tequila
¾ shot De Kuyper Triple Sec
¾ shot Freshly squeezed lime juice
½ shot Sugar syrup (2 sugar to 1 water)

Comment: Citrus freshness with the subtle agave of tequila served frozen.

MARGARITA ON-THE-ROCKS (DIFFORD'S RECIPE)

★★★★★

Glass: Old-fashioned
Garnish: Salt rim (optional) & lime wedge
Method: SHAKE all ingredients with ice and strain into ice-filled glass.

1½ shots Patrón reposado tequila
¾ shot De Kuyper Triple Sec
¾ shot Freshly squeezed lime juice
1 spoon Agave syrup
½ pinch Salt
1 dash Bob's Lavender bitters (optional)

Origin: The traditional Margarita recipe is 2 parts tequila, 1 part triple sec and 1 part lime juice. This produces a drink which is a tad on the sour side with the triple sec not quite balancing the lime. We like to add a spoon of agave syrup to boost flavour and improve the drink's balance.
Comment: This is how we prefer our margaritas to be served. Tangy citrus and tequila with a hint of balancing sweetness and a faint salty undertone. We also prefer the subtlety of half a pinch of salt in the drink to a salt laden glass rim.

MARGARITA STRAIGHT-UP (STANDARD RECIPE)

★★★★½

Glass: Margarita
Garnish: Salt rim & lime wedge
Method: SHAKE all ingredients with ice and fine strain into chilled glass.

2 shots Patrón reposado tequila
1 shot De Kuyper Triple Sec
1 shot Freshly squeezed lime juice
1 spoon Agave syrup
3 drop Bob's Lavender bitters (optional)

Comment: For the perfect salt rim, liquidise sea salt to make it finer, then run a lime wedge around the outside edge of the glass before dipping the rim in salt. Rimming only half the glass with salt gives the drinker the option of enjoying the cocktail with or without salt.

MARGARITA WITH SALT FOAM FLOAT 0━☞

★★★★⯪☆

Glass: Margarita
Garnish: Lime wedge
Method: Combine first three ingredients, **POUR** into cream whipping siphon and **CHARGE** with nitrous oxide. Shake and place siphon in a refrigerator for one hour prior to making drink. **SHAKE** next three ingredients with ice and fine strain into chilled glass. **SQUIRT** salt foam over surface of drink from siphon.

4	spoon	Salt
1	pint	Chilled water
2	fresh	Egg white
2	shots	Patrón reposado tequila
1	shot	Freshly squeezed lime juice
1	shot	De Kuyper Triple Sec

Comment: Classic Margarita with a salty foam topping.

MARGUERITE COCKTAIL

★★★★☆

Glass: Coupe
Garnish: Orange zest twist
Method: STIR all ingredients with ice and strain into chilled glass.

1½	shot	Rutte Dry Gin
1½	shot	Martini Extra Dry vermouth
⅛	shot	Orange curaçao liqueur
2	dash	Orange bitters

Origin: The earliest known Marguerite Cocktail recipe appears in Harry Johnson's 1900 Bartenders' Manual.

"Marguerite Cocktail
(Use a large bar glass)
Fill glass 3/4 full of fine-shaved ice;
2 or 3 dashes of orange bitters;
2 or 3 dashes of anisette;
1/2 wine glass of French vermouth;
1/2 wine glass of Plymouth gin;
Stir up well with a spoon, strain into a cocktail glass, putting in a cherry, squeeze piece of lemon peel on top and serve."

Then in his 1903 *Bartenders Encyclopedia*, Tim Daly omits the anisette in his recipe for the Marguerite:

"Marguerite Cocktail
Use a mixing glass.
Half fill with fine ice.
2 dashes of orange bitters.
1 dash of orange curacoa.[sic]
½ wine glass of French vermouth.
½ wine glass of Plymouth gin.
Stir well with spoon, strain into a cocktail glass, twist a piece of lemon peel on top, and serve."

The Marguetite, then turns drier and by the 1904 Stuart's Fancy Drinks it becomes 2/3 Plymouth gin [a dry gin] to 1/3 French [dry] vermouth. Basically a modern day 2:1 Dry Martini.
Comment: An equal parts (Fifty-Fifty) Dry Martini with a hint of orange due to the use of orange curaçao, orange bitters and an orange zest twist.

MARIA THERESA MARGARITA 0━☞

★★★★☆

Glass: Martini
Garnish: Lime wedge
Method: STIR honey with tequila in base of shaker to dissolve honey. Add other ingredients, **SHAKE** with ice and fine strain into chilled glass.

2	spoon	Runny honey
2	shots	Patrón reposado tequila
1	shot	Cranberry juice
½	shot	Freshly squeezed lime juice

Origin: Adapted from a Tiki drink created by Victor Bergeron (Trader Vic).
Comment: Originally sweetened with sugar syrup, this is better smoothed with honey.

MARIE ROSE

★★★★☆

Glass: Martini
Garnish: Rosemary sprig
Method: Strip leaves from rosemary and **MUDDLE** with grapes in base of shaker. Add other ingredients, **SHAKE** with ice and fine strain into chilled glass.

½	sprig	Rosemary sprig
8	fresh	Seedless white grapes
2	shots	Rutte Dry Gin
¾	shot	St-Germain elderflower liqueur
¼	shot	Freshly squeezed lime juice

Origin: Created in 2007 by Renan Lejeune at Zeta Bar, London, England.
Comment: Rosemary spiced gin with grape juice and elderflower: very aromatic.

MARKET DAIQUIRÍ

★★★★☆

Glass: Coupe
Garnish: Pear slice
Method: SHAKE all ingredients with ice and fine strain into chilled glass.

2	fresh	Mint leaves
2	shots	Bacardi Carta Blanca light rum
½	shot	Pear purée
¼	shot	Almond (orgeat) syrup
½	shot	Freshly squeezed lime juice

Origin: Created in 2008, by Dez O'Connell, London, England
Comment: A classic Daiquiri influenced by the addition of pear, mint and almonds.

MARMALADE COCKTAIL 0━☞

★★★★☆

Glass: Martini
Garnish: Orange zest twist
Method: STIR marmalade with gin in base of shaker so as to dissolve marmalade. **ADD** other ingredients, **SHAKE** with ice and fine strain into chilled glass.

4	spoon	English orange marmalade
2	shots	Rutte Dry Gin
½	shot	Freshly squeezed lemon juice

Origin: Adapted from a recipe in the 1930 Savoy Cocktail Book by Harry Craddock (the original recipe serves six people).
Comment: Harry wrote of his own drink, "By its bitter-sweet taste this cocktail is especially suited to be a luncheon aperitif."

MARMALADE SOUR

★★★★⯪☆

Glass: Old-fashioned
Garnish: Orange zest twist
Method: SHAKE all ingredients with ice and fine strain into ice-filled glass.

2 spoon **English orange marmalade**
2 shots **Capucana cachaça**
½ shot **Freshly squeezed lemon juice**
2 dash **Angostura Orange Bitters**
½ fresh **Egg white**

Origin: Adapted from a drink created in 2010 by Jamie Boudreau at Vessel, Seattle, USA.
Comment: Tangy sweet and sour marmalade flavours combine with the distinctive grassy notes of cachaça.

MARMARITA 0━━☞

★★★★☆

Glass: Coupe
Garnish: Marmite (yeast extract) rim
Method: SHAKE all ingredients with ice and fine strain into chilled glass.

2 shots **Patrón reposado tequila**
1 shot **De Kuyper Triple Sec**
1 shot **Freshly squeezed lime juice**

Origin: Created in 2005 by Simon (Ginger) Warneford at Blanch House, Brighton, England.
Comment: A Margarita with a Marmite rim. After all, yeast extract is slightly salty.

MARNY COCKTAIL

★★★★⯪

Glass: Martini
Garnish: Orange zest twist
Method: SHAKE all ingredients with ice and fine strain into chilled glass.

2 shots **Rutte Dry Gin**
1 shot **Grand Marnier Cordon Rouge**
2 dash **Angostura Orange Bitters**
½ shot **Chilled water**

Origin: Adapted from a recipe in Harry Craddock's 1930 Savoy Cocktail Book.
Comment: This appropriately named, simple drink is one of my favourite Grand Marnier cocktails.

MARQUEE 0━━☞

★★★★☆

Glass: Martini
Garnish: Raspberries
Method: SHAKE all ingredients with ice and fine strain into chilled glass.

1½ shots **Bourbon whiskey**
½ shot **Chambord Liqueur**
1½ shots **Cranberry juice**
½ shot **Freshly squeezed lemon juice**
¼ shot **Sugar syrup** (2 sugar to 1 water)

Origin: Created in 1998 by Giovanni Burdi at Match EC1, London, England.
Comment: Raspberry and bourbon combine perfectly in this short, slightly sweet, fruity drink.

MARSALA MARTINI (NEW)

★★★★★

Glass: Coupe
Garnish: Pickled almond
Method: STIR all ingredients with ice and strain into chilled glass.

2 shots **Rutte Dry Gin**
⅓ shot **Marsala superiore secco wine**
⅓ shot **Martini Extra Dry vermouth**
⅛ shot **Disaronno Originale amaretto**

Origin: Created by Tony Conigliaro at 69 Colebrooke Row.
Comment: Tony C's original recipe calls for 50ml London dry gin, 10ml marsala dolce (sweet marsala), 5ml dry vermouth and 3 dashes 69 Colebrooke Row made almond bitters. Sadly we didn't have the 69 Colebrooke Row lab kit or the patience to use it, so we subbed amaretto for almond bitters and then dried the combo by using dry marsala in place of sweet marsala.

MARTÍ'S MARTINI

★★★☆☆

Glass: Martini
Garnish: None
Method: STIR ingredients with ice and fine strain into chilled glass.

1½ shots **Bacardi Carta Blanca light rum**
¼ shot **Galliano L'Autentico liqueur**
¼ shot **Genepi des Peres Chartreux**
½ shot **Martini Extra Dry vermouth**
½ shot **Chilled water** (omit if wet ice)

Origin: Created in 2008 by Oli Gillespie at Bibendum Wine Ltd, London, England and named after José Martí (1853-1895) - a leader of the Cuban independence movement, writer and renowned poet.
Comment: Herbal, medium dry, rum-based, Martini-style drink.

MARTINEZ #1 (ORIGINAL JENEVER)

★★★★★

Glass: Martini
Garnish: Orange zest twist
Method: STIR all ingredients with ice and strain into chilled glass.

1½ shots **Rutte Old Simon oude jenever**
1½ shots **Martini Rosso vermouth**
⅛ shot **Orange Curaçao liqueur**
2 dash **Angostura Aromatic Bitters**

Origin: Probably the forerunner of the Martini, the first known recipe for this drink appears in O.H. Byron's 1884 'The Modern Bartender' where it is listed as a variation to the Manhattan. Its first written standalone listing in a recipe book appears in Harry Johnson's 1888 'Bartender's Manual'.

Although the drink appears in his 1887 Bartenders' Guide (as a variation), there is no evidence that Jerry Thomas invented the Martinez and significantly he omits the drink from the earlier 1862 edition of his 'Bartender's Guide'.

Many claim that one Julio Richelieu created the drink in 1874 for a goldminer and that the drink is named after the Californian town of Martinez, where that unnamed goldminer enjoyed this libation.
Comment: This medium dry Martini is somewhat more approachable than a Dry Martini.

MARTINEZ #4 (LONDON DRY)

★★★★☆

Glass: Martini
Garnish: Orange zest twist
Method: **STIR** ingredients with ice and fine strain into chilled glass.

- 2 shots **Rutte Dry Gin**
- ½ shot **Martini Rosso vermouth**
- ¼ shot **Martini Extra Dry vermouth**
- ⅛ shot **Luxardo Maraschino liqueur**
- 1 dash **Angostura Aromatic Bitters**

Comment: Aromatic, complex and very dry.

MARTINEZ (MADE WITH OLD TOM)

★★★★★½

Glass: Martini
Garnish: Orange zest twist (discarded) & Luxardo Maraschino cherry
Method: **STIR** ingredients with ice and fine strain into chilled glass.

- 2 shots **Old Tom gin**
- ¼ shot **Martini Extra Dry vermouth**
- ¾ shot **Martini Rosso vermouth**
- ¼ shot **Luxardo Maraschino liqueur**
- 1 dash **Angostura Aromatic Bitters**

Comment: Use an authentic tasting distilled old tom gin that's balanced rather than overly sweet and you'll have a fabulous cocktail.

We've used dry vermouth to balance the sweet vermouth but if you're looking for simplicity and less ingredients then you might want to omit the dry vermouth and balance by reducing the sweet vermouth and maraschino while also doubling the bitters as follows:

2 shot Old Tom Gin, 2/3 shot Sweet vermouth, 1/8 shot Maraschino
2 dashes of orange bitters

MARTINEZ (ORANGE)

★★★★☆

Glass: Martini
Garnish: Orange zest twist
Method: **STIR** ingredients with ice and fine strain into chilled glass.

- 2 shots **Rutte Dry Gin**
- ½ shot **Martini Rosso vermouth**
- ¼ shot **Orange Curaçao liqueur**
- 2 dash **Angostura Orange Bitters** (optional)

Comment: Stir well as dilution helps to tame this old-school classic in which bitter orange predominates.

MARTINEZ COCKTAIL (MODERN RECIPE USING GENEVER)

★★★★★

Glass: Martini
Garnish: Orange zest twist
Method: **STIR** ingredients with ice and fine strain into chilled glass.

- 2 shots **Rutte Old Simon oude jenever**
- ½ shot **Martini Extra Dry vermouth**
- ½ shot **Martini Rosso vermouth**
- ⅛ shot **Luxardo Maraschino liqueur**

Origin: This formula for the vintage classic emerged and became popular in London during early 2008 with the introduction of Antica Formula.

MARTINI PERFECT

★★★½☆

Glass: Martini
Garnish: Orange zest twist
Method: **SHAKE** all ingredients with ice and fine strain into chilled glass.

- 1¼ shots **Rutte Dry Gin**
- 1¼ shots **Martini Extra Dry vermouth**
- 1¼ shots **Martini Rosso vermouth**
- 1 dash **Angostura Orange Bitters**

Origin: Adapted from a recipe in the 1930 edition of the 'Savoy Cocktail Book' by Harry Craddock.
Comment: The high proportion of vermouth makes this Martini almost sherry-like.

MARTINI ROYALE

★★★½☆

Glass: Martini
Garnish: Lemon zest twist
Method: **STIR** vodka and crème de cassis with ice and strain into chilled glass. **TOP** with chilled champagne.

- 1½ shots **Ketel One Vodka**
- ½ shot **Lejay crème de cassis de Dijon**
- Top with **G.H. Mumm Cordon Rouge Champagne**

Origin: Created in 2001 by Dick Bradsell at Monte's, London, England.
Comment: The Kir Royale meets the vodkatini in this pink but powerful drink.

MARTINI SPECIAL

★★★★½

Glass: Martini
Garnish: Orange zest twist
Method: Fill glass with ice and **POUR** absinthe and Angostura over ice. **TOP** with chilled mineral water and leave to stand. **SHAKE** gin, vermouth and orange water with ice. **DISCARD** contents of standing glass and fine strain shaken drink into washed glass.

- ¼ shot **Le Fée Parisienne absinthe**
- 4 dash **Angostura Aromatic Bitters**
- Top with **Chilled water**
- 2 shots **Rutte Dry Gin**
- ¾ shot **Martini Rosso vermouth**
- ⅛ shot **Orange flower water**

Origin: Adapted from a recipe in Harry Craddock's 1930 Savoy Cocktail Book.
Comment: Aromatic, very dry and very serious - yet has a frothy head.

MARTINI THYME

★★★★☆

Glass: Martini
Garnish: Olives on thyme sprig
Method: MUDDLE thyme in base of shaker. Add other ingredients, **SHAKE** with ice and fine strain into chilled glass.

2	sprig	Lemon thyme (remove stalks)
1	shot	Rutte Dry Gin
¾	shot	Green Chartreuse liqueur
¼	shot	Sugar syrup (2 sugar to 1 water)

Origin: A combination of two very similar drinks, that both originally called for thyme infused gin. The first I discovered at The Lobby Bar (One Aldwych, London) and the other came from Tony Conigliaro at Isola, London, England.
Comment: A wonderfully fresh herbal Martini with the distinctive taste of Chartreuse. You'll either love it or hate it.

MARVIN'S LAST WORD (NEW)

★★★★☆

Glass: Coupe
Garnish: Lime zest twist
Method: SHAKE all ingredients with ice and fine strain into chilled glass.

¾	shot	Rutte Dry Gin
¾	shot	Skinos Mastiha
¾	shot	Green Chartreuse liqueur
¾	shot	Freshly squeezed lime juice

Origin: The distinctive notes of mastiha and Chartreuse shine in this Greek riff on the classic Last Word.
Comment: Created at the 42 Bar in Athens, Greece – a bar where the work of Douglas Adams influences many of the drink names. In Adams' thought provoking and amusing 'The Hitchhiker's Guide to the Galaxy' the number 42 is the "answer to the ultimate question of life, the universe, and everything", while 'Marvin' is a paranoid, depressive android.

MARY PICKFORD COCKTAIL

★★★★★

Glass: Martini
Garnish: Luxardo Maraschino cherry
Method: SHAKE all ingredients with ice and fine strain into chilled glass.

2	shots	Bacardi Carta Blanca light rum
1½	shots	Fresh pressed pineapple juice
¼	shot	Pomegranate / grenadine syrup (2:1)
⅛	shot	Luxardo Maraschino liqueur

Origin: Created in the 1920s (during Prohibition) by Fred Kaufman at the Hotel Nacional de Cuba, for the silent movie star and wife of Douglas Fairbanks.

Mary was in Cuba filming a movie with her husband and Charlie Chaplin and this is recounted on page 40 of Basil Woon's 1928 book ' When It's Cocktail Time in Cuba', "The Mary Pickford, invented during a visit to Havana of the screen favourite by Fred Kaufman, is two-thirds pineapple-juice and one-third Bacardi, with a dash of grenadine. Both cocktails [The Presidenté is also mentioned] are sweetish and should be well shaken. The pineapple juice must be fresh-squeezed." Thus it would appear that a dash of maraschino liqueur is a later addition.
Comment: When made correctly, this pale pink cocktail has a perfect balance between the fruit flavours and the spirit of the rum.

MARY QUEEN OF SCOTS

★★★★☆

Glass: Martini
Garnish: Sugar rim & Luxardo Maraschino cherry
Method: SHAKE all ingredients with ice and fine strain into chilled glass.

1½	shots	Dewar's 12 Year Old Scotch whisky
¾	shot	Green Chartreuse liqueur
¾	shot	Drambuie liqueur

Origin: Discovered in 2006 an Kyle Branch's Cocktail Hotel blog (www.cocktailhotel.blogspot.com). Mary Stuart, Mary Queen of Scots was born on December 8th 1542 at Linlithgow Place in West Lothian. On February 8th 1587, she was executed in the Great Hall of Fotheringhay.
Comment: Slightly sweet but herbal, serious and strong.

MARY ROSE

★★★★☆

Glass: Martini
Garnish: Lime zest twist (discarded) & rosemary sprig
Method: MUDDLE rosemary in base of shaker. Add other ingredients, **SHAKE** with ice and fine strain into chilled glass.

1	fresh	Rosemary sprig
2	shots	Rutte Dry Gin
1	shot	Green Chartreuse liqueur
½	shot	Sugar syrup (2 sugar to 1 water)
½	shot	Chilled water (omit if wet ice)

Origin: Created in 1999 by Philip Jeffrey at the Great Eastern Hotel, London, England. Named after King Henry VIII's warship, sunk during an engagement with the French fleet in 1545 and now on display in Portsmouth.
Comment: Herbal, herbal and herbal with a hint of spice.

MASTIHA & TONIC (NEW)

★★★★☆

Glass: Collins
Garnish: Celery stick
Method: POUR ingredients into ice-filled glass and lightly stir.

2 shots Skinos Mastiha
4 shots Tonic Water

Comment: The very distinctive taste of mastiha with freshening tonic water.

MASTIHA MOJITO (NEW)

★★★★☆

Glass: Collins
Garnish: Mint sprigs
Method: SHAKE all ingredients with ice and fine strain into ice-filled glass. CHURN (stir) with bar spoon. Fill glass with more crushed ice and CHURN some more. Keep adding ice and churning until drink fills glass. Serve with straws.

12 fresh   Mint leaves
1 shot   Bacardi Carta Blanca light rum
1½ shots Skinos Mastiha
¾ shot   Freshly squeezed lime juice

Comment: Mastiha adds a distinctively Greek fresh flavour to this otherwise fairly classic mojito.

MASTIHA SOUR (NEW)

★★★★☆

Glass: Old-fashioned
Garnish: Orange or lemon zest
Method: SHAKE all ingredients with ice and strain back into shaker. DRY SHAKE (without ice) and strain into ice-filled glass.

2 shots Skinos Mastiha
¾ shot   Freshly squeezed lemon juice
¼ shot   Sugar syrup (2 sugar to 1 water)
½ fresh   Egg white

Comment: Some use a whole shot of lemon juice and correspondingly a tad more sugar. It's also common to add a dash of Angostura bitters but we prefer the refreshing flavour of mastiha unhindered.

MAT THE RAT

★★★★⯪☆

Glass: Collins
Garnish: Lime wedge
Method: SHAKE first 4 ingredients with ice and strain into ice-filled glass. TOP with lemonade, lightly stir and serve with straws.

2 shots Bacardi Carta Blanca light rum
½ shot   De Kuyper Triple Sec
1½ shots Freshly squeezed orange juice
½ shot   Freshly squeezed lime juice
Top with Lemonade/Sprite/7-Up

Origin: A popular drink in UK branches of TGI Friday's where it was created.
Comment: Whether or not Mat was a rat, we shall never know. However, the drink that's named after him is long and thirst quenching.

MATADOR #1 ⚷

★★★★☆

Glass: Collins
Garnish: Pineapple wedge
Method: SHAKE all ingredients with ice and strain into ice-filled glass.

2 shots Patrón reposado tequila
1 shot   De Kuyper Triple Sec
1 shot   Freshly squeezed lime juice
2 shots Fresh pressed pineapple juice

Comment: A long Margarita-style drink. The lime and tequila work wonders with the pineapple.

MATADOR #2 (TOMMY'S STYLE) ⚷

★★★★☆

Glass: Martini
Garnish: Pineapple wedge
Method: SHAKE all ingredients with ice and fine strain into chilled glass.

2 shots Patrón reposado tequila
1 shot   Freshly squeezed lime juice
½ shot   Agave syrup
1½ shots Fresh pressed pineapple juice

Comment: A pineapple Margarita with agave syrup in place of a sweet liqueur.

MAURESQUE

★★★★☆

Glass: Collins
Garnish: None
Method: POUR absinthe and almond syrup into glass. Serve iced water separately in a small jug (known in France as a 'broc') so the customer can dilute to their own taste (I recommend five shots). Lastly, add ice to fill glass.

1 shot   Le Fée Parisienne absinthe
1 shot   Almond (orgeat) syrup
Top with Chilled water

Origin: Pronounced 'Mor-Esk', this classic drink is very popular in the South of France, where it is now commonly made with pastis in place of absinthe. It was originally created by French soldiers serving in the Bataillon d'Afrique during the Algerian campaign of the 1830s and 40s, and was alternatively known as Bureau Arabe after the military department which dealt with local affairs and was said to act like 'an iron fist in a velvet glove'.
Comment: Long, refreshing aniseed, liquorice and almond.

MAURICE COCKTAIL

★★★★⯪☆

Glass: Martini
Garnish: Orange zest twist
Method: SHAKE all ingredients with ice and fine strain into chilled glass.

1½ shots Rutte Dry Gin
¼ shot   Le Fée Parisienne absinthe
¾ shot   Martini Extra Dry vermouth
¾ shot   Martini Rosso vermouth
¾ shot   Freshly squeezed orange juice

Origin: Adapted from a recipe in Harry Craddock's 1930 Savoy Cocktail Book.
Comment: A Bronx Cocktail with the addition of an aromatic burst of absinthe – you'll notice the difference.

MAXIM'S COFFEE (HOT)

★★★★☆

Glass: Toddy
Garnish: Coffee beans
Method: POUR all ingredients into warmed glass and STIR.

1 shot   Martell VSOP Médaillon cognac
½ shot   Bénédictine D.O.M. liqueur
¼ shot   Galliano L'Autentico liqueur
Top with Filter coffee (hot)

Comment: An interesting herbal cognac laced coffee.

MAYA MARGARITA

★★★★☆

Glass: Coupe
Garnish: Pink river salt rim & lime wedge
Method: **SHAKE** all ingredients with ice and fine strain into chilled glass.

1 shot Patrón silver tequila
½ shot Agave Sec Liqueur
⅓ shot Grand Marnier Cordon Rouge
1 shot Freshly squeezed lime juice
½ shot Freshly squeezed orange juice
¼ shot Calamansi juice (optional)

Origin: Created in 2010 by Rob Jameson at Maya Bar, Shanghai, China.
Comment: A tasty Margarita with Grand Marnier, Agave Sec liqueur and orange juice.

MAYAN

★★★☆☆

Glass: Old-fashioned
Garnish: Coffee beans
Method: **SHAKE** all ingredients with ice and strain into ice-filled glass.

1½ shots Patrón reposado tequila
½ shot Coffee liqueur
2½ shots Fresh pressed pineapple juice

Comment: Tequila, coffee and pineapple juice combine in this medium dry short drink.

MAYAN WHORE

★★★★☆

Glass: Sling
Garnish: Pineapple wedge
Method: **SHAKE** first three ingredients with ice and strain into ice-filled glass. **TOP** with soda, **DO NOT STIR** and serve with straws.

2 shots Patrón reposado tequila
¾ shot Coffee liqueur
1½ shots Fresh pressed pineapple juice
Top with Soda (club soda)

Comment: An implausible ménage à trois: coffee, tequila and pineapple, served long.

MAYFAIR COCKTAIL #1

★★★★☆

Glass: Martini
Garnish: Orange zest twist
Method: **MUDDLE** cloves in base of shaker. Add other ingredients, **SHAKE** with ice and fine strain into chilled glass.

2 shots Rutte Dry Gin
1 shot De Kuyper XO Apricot Brandy
2 dried Clove
1 shot Freshly squeezed orange juice
⅛ shot Sugar syrup (2 sugar to 1 water)

Origin: Adapted from a recipe in Harry Craddock's 1930 Savoy Cocktail Book. Apparently this drink celebrates a fair that took place in the month of May during the rein of King Charles II.
Comment: Spiced apricot laced with gin. Slightly sweet.

MAYFAIR COCKTAIL #2

★★★★☆

Glass: Martini
Garnish: Orange zest twist
Method: **MUDDLE** cloves in base of shaker. Add other ingredients, **SHAKE** with ice and fine strain into chilled glass.

2 shots Rutte Dry Gin
1 shot De Kuyper XO Apricot Brandy
2 dried Clove
1 shot Freshly squeezed orange juice
¼ shot Allspice pimento dram liqueur

Comment: Gin with spicy cloves and hints of apricot and orange.

THE MAYFLOWER MARTINI

★★★★☆

Glass: Martini
Garnish: Lemon zest twist
Method: **SHAKE** all ingredients with ice and fine strain into chilled glass.

1½ shots Rutte Dry Gin
½ shot St-Germain elderflower liqueur
½ shot De Kuyper XO Apricot Brandy
½ shot Pressed apple juice
½ shot Freshly squeezed lemon juice

Origin: Adapted from a drink created in 2002 by Wayne Collins, London, England.
Comment: Fragrant balance of English fruits and flowers.

THE MED (NEW)

★★★★☆

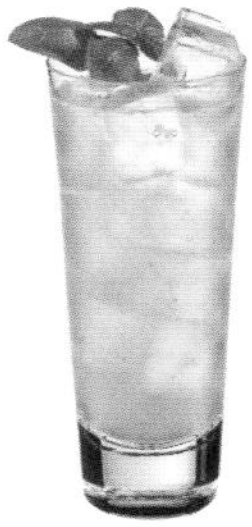

Glass: Collins
Garnish: Basil sprig
Method: **MUDDLE** basil in base of shaker. Add next 3 ingredients, **SHAKE** with ice and fine strain into ice-filled glass. **TOP** with soda.

7 fresh Basil leaves
1⅔ shots Skinos Mastiha
⅔ shot Freshly squeezed lemon juice
⅛ shot Sugar syrup (2 sugar to 1 water)
Top with Soda (club soda)

Comment: A long summery drink with basil and the distinctive flavour of Greek mastiha.

MEDICINA LATINA (NEW)

★★★★★

Glass: Old-fashioned
Garnish: Candied ginger and spray of mezcal
Method: **SHAKE** all ingredients with ice and strain into ice-filled glass.

2 shot Patrón silver tequila
⅓ shot Honey sugar syrup
⅛ shot Ginger sugar syrup

Comment: Tequila and ginger smoothed with a hint of honey. A cleansing after dinner cocktail.
Origin: Created in 2009 by Marcos Tello at The Varnish in, Los Angeles, USA

MEDIOCRE (NEW)

★★★★½

Glass: Coupe
Garnish: Pineapple wedge
Method: SHAKE all ingredients with ice and fine strain into chilled glass.

1½	shot	Vanilla infused Bacardi Carta Blanca rum
1	shot	Mead
1¼	shot	Pressed pineapple juice
¼	shot	Honey water
1	dash	Bob's Vanilla Bitters

Comment: Ripe pineapple, rich vanilla and honey laced with rum. The use of mead in this drink inspired the 'Mediocre' name.
Origin: Created by yours truly (Simon Difford) at the Cabinet Room, London, England.

MEDITERRANEAN SOUR (NEW)

★★★★★

Glass: Old-fashioned
Garnish: Orange zest twist
Method: SHAKE all ingredients with ice and fine strain into ice-filled glass.

2	shots	Skinos Mastiha
⅔	shot	Freshly squeezed lemon juice
⅓	shot	Sugar syrup (2 sugar to 1 water)
1	dash	Angostura Aromatic Bitters
½	fresh	Egg white

Comment: This tasty sour features the distinctive flavour of Mastiha.

MEDIUM MARTINI 🔑

★★★★½

Glass: Martini
Garnish: Orange zest twist
Method: STIR all ingredients with ice and strain into chilled glass

1½	shots	Rutte Dry Gin
¾	shot	Martini Extra Dry vermouth
¾	shot	Martini Rosso vermouth

Origin: Adapted from a recipe in Harry Craddock's 1930 'Savoy Cocktail Book.'
Comment: A classic Martini served perfect and very wet. I prefer mine shaken which is the method Harry specifies in his guide.

MELBA COCKTAIL

★★★★☆

Glass: Coupe
Garnish: Mint leaf
Method: SHAKE all ingredients with ice and fine strain into chilled glass.

1½	shots	Bacardi Carta Blanca light rum
1	shot	Swedish Punch liqueur
½	spoon	Le Fée Parisienne absinthe
½	shot	Freshly squeezed lime juice
1	spoon	Pomegranate / grenadine syrup (2:1)

Comment: A dry Daiquiri-like drink with pomegranate, a touch of absinthe and pine fresh notes.

MELON BALL SHOT

★★★☆☆

Glass: Shot
Garnish: None
Method: SHAKE all ingredients with ice and fine strain into chilled glass.

½	shot	Ketel One Vodka
½	shot	Midori Green Melon liqueur
¾	shot	Freshly squeezed orange juice

Comment: A vivid green combination of vodka, melon and orange.

MELON COLLIE MARTINI

★★★★☆

Glass: Martini
Garnish: Crumbled Cadbury's Flake bar
Method: SHAKE all ingredients with ice and fine strain into chilled glass.

1	shot	Bacardi Carta Blanca light rum
¾	shot	Midori Green Melon liqueur
¼	shot	White crème de cacao liqueur
½	shot	Coconut rum liqueur
¾	shot	Milk
¾	shot	Single cream / half-and-half

Origin: Created in 2003 by Simon King at MJU, Millenniun Hotel, London, England.
Comment: Something of a holiday disco drink but tasty all the same.

MELON DAIQUIRI #1 (SERVED 'UP')

★★★★☆

Glass: Martini
Garnish: Melon slice or melon balls
Method: Cut melon into 8 segments and deseed. Cut cubes of flesh from skin of one segment and MUDDLE in base of shaker. Add other ingredients, SHAKE with ice and fine strain into chilled glass.

⅛	fresh	Cantaloupe melon
2	shots	Bacardi Carta Blanca light rum
½	shot	Midori Green Melon liqueur
½	shot	Freshly squeezed lime juice
⅛	shot	Sugar syrup (2 sugar to 1 water)

Comment: A classic Daiquiri with the gentle touch of melon.

MELON DAIQUIRI #2 (SERVED FROZEN)

★★★★☆

Glass: Martini
Garnish: Melon slice or melon balls
Method: Cut melon into 8 segments and deseed. Cut cubes of flesh from skin of one segment and place in blender. Add other ingredients and BLEND with half scoop of crushed ice. Serve with straws.

⅛	fresh	Cantaloupe melon
2	shots	Bacardi Carta Blanca light rum
½	shot	Midori Green Melon liqueur
½	shot	Freshly squeezed lime juice

Comment: A cooling, fruity Daiquiri.

MELON MAPLE FIZZ (NEW)

★★★★☆

Glass: Collins
Garnish: Slice of melon & lemon twist
Method: MUDDLE melon in base of shaker. Add other ingredients, SHAKE with ice and fine strain into ice-filled glass. TOP with soda water.

4	cube	Honeydew melon
1	shot	Rutte Dry Gin
1	shot	Midori Green Melon liqueur
½	shot	Freshly squeezed lemon juice
½	shot	Maple syrup
½	fresh	Egg white
Top with		Soda (club soda)

Origin: Created in 2014 by Manuel Terron, Midori Global Brand ambassador.
Comment: Light, fruity and refreshing. Not overly sweet.

MELON MARGARITA #1 (SERVED 'UP')

★★★★☆

Glass: Coupe
Garnish: Melon slice or melon balls
Method: Cut melon into 8 segments and deseed. Cut cubes of flesh from skin of one segment and MUDDLE in base of shaker. Add other ingredients, SHAKE with ice and fine strain into chilled glass.

⅛	fresh	Cantaloupe melon
2	shots	Patrón reposado tequila
1	shot	Midori Green Melon liqueur
1	shot	Freshly squeezed lime juice

Comment: Looks like stagnant pond water but tastes fantastic.

MELON MARGARITA #2 (SERVED FROZEN)

★★★½☆

Glass: Coupe
Garnish: Melon slice or melon balls
Method: Cut melon into 8 segments and deseed. Cut cubes of flesh from skin of one segment and place in blender. Add other ingredients and BLEND with 6oz scoop crushed ice. Serve with straws.

⅛	fresh	Cantaloupe melon
2	shots	Patrón reposado tequila
1	shot	Midori Green Melon liqueur
½	shot	Freshly squeezed lime juice

Comment: Melon and tequila always combine well - here in a frozen Margarita.

MELON MARTINI (FRESH FRUIT)

★★★★☆

Glass: Martini
Garnish: Melon slice
Method: Cut melon into eight segments and deseed. Cut cubes of flesh from skin of one segment and MUDDLE in base of shaker. Add other ingredients, SHAKE with ice and fine strain into chilled glass.

⅛	fresh	Cantaloupe melon
2	shots	Ketel One Vodka
¼	shot	Sugar syrup (2 sugar to 1 water)

Comment: Probably the most popular of all the fresh fruit martinis.

MELON MARTINI (MIDORI)

★★★☆☆

Glass: Martini
Garnish: Lime wedge
Method: SHAKE all ingredients with ice and fine strain into chilled glass.

2¼	shots	Ketel One Vodka
1	shot	Midori Green Melon liqueur
½	shot	Freshly squeezed lime juice
¼	shot	Sugar syrup (2 sugar to 1 water)

Comment: Bright green, lime and melon with more than a hint of vodka.

MELONCHOLY MARTINI

★★★★☆

Glass: Martini
Garnish: Mint sprig
Method: SHAKE all ingredients with ice and fine strain into chilled glass.

1	shot	Ketel One Vodka
1	shot	Midori Green Melon liqueur
½	shot	De Kuyper Triple Sec
½	shot	Coconut rum liqueur
1	shot	Fresh pressed pineapple juice
¼	shot	Freshly squeezed lime juice
¾	shot	Single cream / half-and-half

Origin: Created in 2002 by Daniel O'Brien at Ocean Bar, Edinburgh, Scotland.
Comment: Sweet, but the flavours in this smooth, tangy, lime-green drink combine surprisingly well.

MENEHUNE JUICE

★★★★☆

Glass: Old-fashioned
Garnish: Lime wedge, mint sprig & Menehune
Method: SHAKE all ingredients with ice and strain into glass filled with crushed ice. Serve with straws.

2	shots	Bacardi Carta Blanca light rum
½	shot	De Kuyper Triple Sec
¼	shot	Almond (orgeat) syrup
¾	shot	Freshly squeezed lime juice
¼	shot	Sugar syrup (2 sugar to 1 water)

Origin: Adapted from a recipe in the 1947-72 'Trader Vic's Bartender's Guide' by Victor Bergeron.
Comment: Slightly sweet and strong. According to Vic, "One sip and you may see a Menehune."

MERCHANT OF VENICE

★★★★½

Glass: Flute
Garnish: Lemon zest twist
Method: STIR honey with vodka in base of shaker to dissolve. Add other ingredients and DRY SHAKE (without ice). SHAKE again with ice and fine strain into chilled glass.

2	shots	Ketel One Vodka
2	spoon	Runny honey
½	shot	Aperol Aperitivo
½	shot	Freshly squeezed lemon juice
½	fresh	Egg white

Origin: Discovered in 2010 at Eclipse Bar, Barcelona, Spain.
Comment: The richness and flavour of honey along with the distinctive taste of Aperol jointly balance lemon citrus notes in this majestic vodka-based drink.

MERRY WIDOW #1

★★★⯨☆

Glass: Martini
Garnish: Lemon zest twist
Method: STIR all ingredients with ice and strain into chilled glass.

1½	shots	Rutte Dry Gin
1½	shots	Martini Extra Dry vermouth
¼	shot	Bénédictine D.O.M. liqueur
¼	shot	Le Fée Parisienne absinthe
3	dash	Angostura Aromatic Bitters
½	shot	Chilled water (omit if wet ice)

Origin: Adapted from a recipe in Harry Craddock's 1930 Savoy Cocktail Book.
Comment: Aromatic, complex, strong and bitter.

MERRY WIDOW #2

★★★⯨☆

Glass: Martini
Garnish: Orange zest twist
Method: STIR all ingredients with ice and strain into chilled glass.

1¼	shots	Ketel One Vodka
1¼	shots	Dubonnet Red
1¼	shots	Martini Extra Dry vermouth
1	dash	Fresh orange

Comment: Complex, aromatic and complex - for toughened palates.

MERRY-GO-ROUND MARTINI

★★★★☆

Glass: Martini
Garnish: Chilled olive on stick or lemon zest twist
Method: STIR all ingredients with ice and fine strain into chilled glass.

2	shots	Rutte Dry Gin
½	shot	Martini Extra Dry vermouth
½	shot	Martini Rosso vermouth

Origin: Long lost classic variation on the Dry Martini.
Comment: Stir this 'perfect' Martini around and then get merry.

MERYL LYNCHBURG

★★★★☆

Glass: Collins
Garnish: Lemon zest twist
Method: SHAKE first four ingredients with ice and strain into ice filled glass (or mug), TOP with soda water

2	shots	Jack Daniel's Old No.7 Brand
¾	shot	Agave Sec Liqueur
½	shot	Freshly squeezed lemon juice
2	dash	Whiskey Barrel Aged Bitters
Top with		Soda (club soda)

Origin: Discovered in 2009 at Underdog Bar, Clapham, London, England.
Comment: A long refreshing 'sugar' free whiskey iced tea-style drink.

MESA FRESCA

★★★★☆

Glass: Collins
Garnish: Lime slice
Method: SHAKE all ingredients with ice and strain into ice-filled glass.

2	shots	Patrón reposado tequila
3	shots	Freshly squeezed pink grapefruit juice
1	shot	Freshly squeezed lime juice
½	shot	Sugar syrup (2 sugar to 1 water)

Origin: Discovered in 2005 at Mesa Grill, New York City, USA.
Comment: Sweet and sour tequila and grapefruit.

MET MANHATTAN

★★★★☆

Glass: Martini
Garnish: Orange zest twist
Method: SHAKE all ingredients with ice and fine strain into chilled glass.

2	shots	Bourbon whiskey
1	shot	Grand Marnier Cordon Rouge
½	shot	Butterscotch liqueur
2	dash	Angostura Orange Bitters

Origin: The Met bar, Metropolitain Hotel, London, England.
Comment: Smooth and rounded bourbon with a hint of orange toffee.

METROPOLE

★★★★⯨

Glass: Coupe
Garnish: Luxardo Maraschino cherry
Method: STIR all ingredients with ice and strain into chilled glass.

2	shots	Martell VSOP Médaillon cognac
1	shot	Martini Extra Dry vermouth
2	dash	Peychaud's aromatic bitters
1	dash	Angostura Orange Bitters
¼	shot	Sugar syrup (2 sugar to 1 water)

Origin: Named after The Hotel Metropole, located just off Times Square at 147 West 43rd Street. This was the first hotel in New York City to have running water in every room but had a less than salubrious reputation due to the clientele its all-night licensed street-level Café Metropole attracted. As Albert Stevens Crockett says in his 1935, 'The Old Waldorf Bar Days', "Attributed to a once well known and somewhat lively hotel, whose bar was a long centre of life after dark in the Times Square district."

In the early morning hours of 16th July 1912 Herman Rosenthal, the owner of several New York gambling dens, was murdered as he left Café Metropole (a crime recounted in the story of the Jack Rose). Just one week after the murder, The Hotel Metropole went bankrupt, later to become became the Hotel Rosoff.
Comment: I've slightly tweaked this recipe from the original as it cried out for sweetness but it remains a dry cognac Manhattan.

METROPOLITAN

★★★⯪☆

Glass: Martini
Garnish: Orange zest twist (flamed)
Method: SHAKE all ingredients with ice and fine strain into chilled glass.

1	shot	Raspberry flavoured vodka
1	shot	De Kuyper Triple Sec
1½	shots	Cranberry juice
½	shot	Freshly squeezed lime juice
¼	shot	Rose's lime cordial

Origin: Created in 1993 by Chuck Coggins at Marion's Continental Restaurant & Lounge, New York City. Marion's was originally opened in 1950 by fashion model Marion Nagy, who came to the States after seeking asylum while swimming for Hungary in the Paris Peace Games after WWII.
Comment: A Cosmo with more than a hint of blackcurrant.

MEXICAN ⌐⊸

★★★★☆

Glass: Martini
Garnish: Pineapple wedge
Method: SHAKE all ingredients with ice and fine strain into chilled glass.

2	shots	Patrón reposado tequila
1½	shots	Fresh pressed pineapple juice
¼	shot	Pomegranate / grenadine syrup (2:1)

Comment: Fresh pineapple makes this drink.

MEXICAN 55 ⌐⊸

★★★★☆

Glass: Collins
Garnish: Lime wedge
Method: SHAKE first 4 ingredients with ice and strain into ice-filled glass. TOP with champagne.

1½	shots	Patrón reposado tequila
1	shot	Freshly squeezed lemon juice
½	shot	Sugar syrup (2 sugar to 1 water)
2	dash	Angostura Aromatic Bitters
Top with		G.H. Mumm Cordon Rouge Champagne

Origin: An adaptation of the classic French 75 created in 1988 at La Perla, Paris, France. The name comes from Fidel Castro's statement that bullets, like wine, came in vintages and Mexican 55 was a good year [for bullets].
Comment: Suitably hard, yet surprisingly refreshing and sophisticated.

MEXICAN COFFEE (HOT) ⌐⊸

★★★⯪☆

Glass: Toddy
Garnish: Coffee beans
Method: Place bar spoon in glass. POUR first three ingredients into glass and stir. FLOAT cream.

1	shot	Patrón reposado tequila
¼	shot	Sugar syrup (2 sugar to 1 water)
Top with		Filter coffee (hot)

Float lightly whipped Single cream / half-and-half

Comment: Tequila's answer to the Irish Coffee.
Tip: Lightly whip or simply shake cream in container before pouring over the bowl of a spoon. It also helps if the cream is gently warmed.

MEXICAN MANHATTAN ⌐⊸

★★★★☆

Glass: Martini
Garnish: Luxardo Maraschino cherry
Method: STIR all ingredients with ice and strain into chilled glass.

2	shots	Patrón reposado tequila
1	shot	Martini Rosso vermouth
3	dash	Angostura Aromatic Bitters

Comment: You've tried this with bourbon, now surprise yourself with an aged tequila.

MEXICAN MARTINI (AÑEJO MARGARITA)

★★★★⯪

Glass: Martini
Garnish: Jalapeño stuffed olives
Method: SHAKE all ingredients with ice and fine strain into chilled glass.

2	shots	Patrón añejo tequila
1	shot	Freshly squeezed lime juice
½	shot	De Kuyper Triple Sec
¼	shot	Agave syrup

Comment: Basically a top-shelf Margarita garnished with Jalapeño stuffed olives.

MEXICAN MELON BALL

★★★⯪☆

Glass: Collins
Garnish: Melon balls
Method: Cut melon into eight segments and deseed. Cut cubes of flesh from skin of one segment and MUDDLE in base of shaker. Add other ingredients, SHAKE with ice and fine strain into ice-filled glass.

⅛	fresh	Cantaloupe melon
2	shots	Patrón reposado tequila
2	shots	Freshly squeezed orange juice
¼	shot	Sugar syrup (2 sugar to 1 water)

Origin: Adapted from a drink discovered at the Flying V Bar & Grill, Tuscon, Arizona, USA.
Comment: Orange and melon laced with tequila.

MEXICAN MULE ⌐⊸

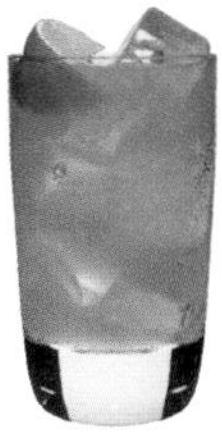

★★★★⯪

Glass: Collins
Garnish: Lime wedge
Method: SHAKE first 3 ingredients with ice and strain into ice-filled glass. TOP with ginger beer, lightly stir and serve with straws.

1½	shots	Patrón reposado tequila
¾	shot	Freshly squeezed lime juice
¼	shot	Sugar syrup (2 sugar to 1 water)
Top with		Gosling's Stormy Ginger Beer

Comment: A tequila based version of the Moscow Mule.

A B C D E F G H I J K L M N O P Q R S T U V W X Y Z

MEXICAN NAIL

★★★★½

Glass: Old-fashioned
Garnish: Lime zest twist
Method: STIR all ingredients with ice and strain into ice-filled glass.

1½ shots   Patrón reposado tequila
1   shot   Drambuie liqueur
¼   shot   Islay single malt Scotch whisky

Origin: Created in 2010 by yours truly at the Cabinet Room, London, England.
Comment: Very complex with obvious whisky and tequila notes made more interesting with subtle spice and chocolatey notes.

MEXICAN SURFER ⊶

★★★★☆

Glass: Martini
Garnish: Lime wedge
Method: SHAKE all ingredients with ice and fine strain into chilled glass.

2   shots   Patrón reposado tequila
1½ shots   Fresh pressed pineapple juice
½   shot   Rose's lime cordial

Comment: Frothy topped, easy to make, and all too easy to drink.

MEXICAN TEA (HOT) ⊶

★★★★½

Glass: Toddy
Garnish: Lime slice
Method: Place bar spoon in warmed glass. **POUR** all ingredients into glass and stir.

2   shots   Patrón reposado tequila
½   shot   Sugar syrup (2 sugar to 1 water)
Top with   Hot English breakfast tea

Comment: Tiffin will never be the same again.

MEXICANO (HOT)

★★★★½

Glass: Toddy
Garnish: Dust with grated nutmeg & cinnamon
Method: POUR tequila and liqueur into warmed glass and top with coffee. **FLOAT** cream over drink.

1   shot   Patrón reposado tequila
½   shot   Grand Marnier Cordon Rouge
Top with   Filter coffee (hot)
Float   lightly whipped
     Single cream / half-and-half

Comment: A spicy, flavour-packed hot coffee. Lightly whip or simply shake cream in container before pouring over the bowl of a spoon. It also helps if the cream is gently warmed.

MEXICO CITY

★★★★½

Glass: Coupe
Garnish: Lime wedge
Method: SHAKE all ingredients with ice and fine strain into chilled glass.

1½ shots   Patrón reposado tequila
¾   shot   Grand Marnier Cordon Rouge
½   shot   Freshly squeezed lime juice
½   shot   Cranberry juice
¼   shot   Sugar syrup (2 sugar to 1 water)

Origin: Adapted from a cocktail discovered in 2002 at the Merc Bar, New York City.
Comment: This pinky-red Margarita benefits from a hint of cranberry.

MEZCAL MARGARITA

★★★★★

Glass: Old-fashioned
Garnish: Lime wedge
Method: SHAKE all ingredients with ice and fine strain into ice-filled glass.

1½ shots   Del Maguey VIDA mezcal
¾   shot   De Kuyper Triple Sec
¾   shot   Freshly squeezed lime juice
⅛   shot   Agave syrup
½   pinch   Salt

Comment: A smokin' Margarita.

MEZCAL NEGRONI (NEW)

★★★★☆

Glass: Old-fashioned
Garnish: Orange zest twist
Method: POUR all ingredients into ice-filled glass and **STIR**.

1½ shots   Del Maguey VIDA mezcal
1½ shots   Campari Bitter
1½ shots   Martini Rosso vermouth

Comment: This smoky mezcal influenced Negroni is an interesting take on the classic which will be appreciated by mezcal aficionados.

MEZZO E MEZZO

★★★★½

Glass: Old-fashioned
Garnish: Lemon zest twist
Method: POUR ingredients into ice-filled glass and briefly stir.

1½ shots   Nardini Rosso
1½ shots   Rabarbaro
2   shots   Soda (club soda)

Origin: Originally and properly made with equal parts Nardini Rosso, Nardini Rabarbaro and soda water, this drink originates from the famous Grapperia Nardini on the Ponte Vecchio where Nardini Rosso was first served with soda water in the 1920s. In the 1970s a drinker tried Nardini Rosso with a dash of Nardini's rhubarb liqueur. The combination became increasingly popular, and as its popularity grew, so the dash became larger until the mixture reached equal parts Nardini Rosso and Rabarbaro.
Comment: Slightly on the bitter side of bittersweet, this classic aperitivo is light and palate cleansing. Best made with equal parts Nardini Rosso, Nardini Rabarbaro and soda.

MIAMI BEACH 0⚷

★★★★☆

Glass: Martini
Garnish: Pineapple wedge & Luxardo Maraschino cherry
Method: SHAKE all ingredients with ice and fine strain into chilled glass.

2 shots **Rutte Dry Gin**
1½ shots **Fresh pressed pineapple juice**
¼ shot **Sugar syrup (2 sugar to 1 water)**

Comment: Fruity and well proportioned - like the babes on Miami Beach. Sorry.

MIAMI DAIQUIRI

★★★★☆

Glass: Martini
Garnish: Mint leaf
Method: SHAKE all ingredients with ice and fine strain into chilled glass.

2 shots **Bacardi Carta Blanca light rum**
¼ shot **Giffard Menthe Pastille liqueur**
½ shot **Freshly squeezed lime juice**
⅛ shot **Sugar syrup (2 sugar to 1 water)**
¾ shot **Chilled water (omit if wet ice)**

Comment: The merest hint of mint in a refreshing Daiquiri with a dry finish.

MIAMI MARTINI

★★★★☆

Glass: Martini
Garnish: Watermelon slice
Method: SHAKE all ingredients with ice and fine strain into chilled glass.

1 wedge **Fresh watermelon**
2 shots **Ketel One Vodka**
¼ shot **Campari Bitter**
½ shot **Freshly squeezed lemon juice**
¾ shot **Sugar syrup (2 sugar to 1 water)**
2 dash **Angostura Orange Bitters**

Origin: Adapted from a recipe by Alexandra Fiot at The Lonsdale, London, England.
Comment: Light, refreshing and all too quaffable. Campari and orange bitters add depth of flavour.

MICHELADA

★★★⯪☆

Glass: Collins
Garnish: Coarse salt rim
Method: SALT the rim of a chilled beer mug by rubbing it with a lime wedge and dipping rim in the coarse salt. Squeeze the lime into the mug. Add the Worcestershire sauce and Tabasco. Pour in the beer and serve.

½ shot **Freshly squeezed lime juice**
3 dash **Tabasco hot pepper sauce**
2 spoon **Worcestershire sauce**
Top with **Budweiser Budvar**

Origin: Loosely translates as 'my beer' – 'mi' means 'my' and 'chela' is Mexican slang for pint. This drink, which is popular in Mexico, is thought to have originated there sometime in the 1940s. There are many variations of this drink. It is sometimes served with ice but usually with light Mexican lager. Even the spicy ingredients vary with soya sauce often omitted, but the hot pepper sauce is a constant.

In Mexico City itself, a Michelada almost always refers to something much simpler than this: 1 shot fresh lime juice in a glass with a salted rim, into which a light lager is poured. Very common too is the Michelato made with 2 shots Clamato (a clam-flavoured sweet tomato juice), then topped up with the beer, hot sauce (usually Valentina) and black pepper.
Comment: On a hot day, if a beer is not refreshing enough then a Michelada may hit the spot. In Mexico Valentina is the preferred brand of hot pepper sauce.

MIDNIGHT IN NYC

★★★★☆

Glass: Coupe
Garnish: Lemon zest twist
Method: SHAKE all ingredients with ice and fine strain into chilled glass.

1 shot **Bourbon whiskey**
1 shot **Shiraz red wine**
½ shot **Freshly squeezed lemon juice**
¼ shot **Pomegranate / grenadine syrup (2:1)**

Origin: Adapted from a recipe by Trudy Thomas, Liquid Remedy Inc, Phoenix, AZ.
Comment: The success of this cocktail is very dependent on the red wine you use. A lighter earthier style will work better than a big fruity red.

MIDNIGHT MOON

★★★⯪☆

Glass: Coupe
Garnish: Half apple slice to represent a crescent moon & orange zest twist (discarded).
Method: STIR first three ingredients with ice and strain into chilled glass. TOP with champagne.

½ shot **Martell VSOP Médaillon cognac**
½ shot **Disaronno Originale amaretto**
½ shot **White crème de cacao liqueur**
3 shots **G.H.Mumm Cordon Rouge Champagne**

Origin: Adapted from a recipe by Colin Peter Field, Hemingway Bar, Ritz Paris, France.
Comment: A slightly sweet bubbly crowd pleaser of a cocktail.

MIDNIGHT OVER TENNESSEE

★★★★⯪

Glass: Martini
Garnish: Dust with chocolate powder
Method: SHAKE first three ingredients with ice and fine strain into chilled glass. Separately SHAKE cream and crème de menthe and carefully strain over drink to layer.

2 shots **Jack Daniel's Old No.7 Brand**
½ shot **Coffee liqueur**
½ shot **Dark crème de cacao liqueur**
½ shot **Green crème de menthe liqueur**
½ shot **Single cream / half-and-half**

Origin: Created in 2006 by Leon Edwards at Restaurant Bar & Grill, Manchester, England.
Comment: A great looking tasty dessert cocktail. Whiskey, coffee and chocolate sipped through a layer of minty cream.

MIDTOWN MUSE (NEW)

★★★★☆☆

Glass: Martini
Garnish: Flamed orange twist
Method: STIR all ingredients with ice and strain into chilled glass.

1½	shots	Lowland single malt scotch whisky
⅔	shot	Midori Green Melon liqueur
⅓	shot	Licor 43 liqueur
1	dash	Angostura Aromatic Bitters
¾	shot	Chilled water (omit if wet ice)

Origin: Created in 2014 by Manuel Terron, Midori Global Brand ambassador.
Comment: Melon and vanilla liqueurs lightly sweeten and flavour the subtle maltiness of Lowland whisky.

MIKE ROMANOFF ⚬━▷

★★★★☆☆

Glass: Martini
Garnish: Orange zest twist
Method: SHAKE all ingredients with ice and fine strain into chilled glass.

2	shots	Ketel One Vodka
⅛	shot	De Kuyper Triple Sec
⅛	shot	De Kuyper XO Apricot Brandy
¾	shot	Freshly squeezed lime juice
¼	shot	Sugar syrup (2 sugar to 1 water)

Origin: Michael Romanoff (1890-1971) was a Hollywood impresario. Born Hershel Geguzin in Lithuania he immigrated to New York City aged ten and changed his name to Harry F. Gerguson. He moved to Hollywood where he took on the Michael Romanoff persona, claiming to be born Prince Michael Alexandrovitch Dimitri Obolensky Romanoff, nephew of Tsar Nicholas II.

Scotland Yard described the former British and French convict as a "rogue of uncertain nationality." He was another actor in a town of actors and when a filmmaker needed a 'technical adviser' for a movie set in Europe, Romanoff was the obvious well paid expert. He was a popular Hollywood figure and he opened Romanoff's, a Beverly Hills restaurant popular with movie stars in the 1940s and 1950s.

Humphrey Bogart was a good friend of Romanoff and a regular at the restaurant. Hollywood legend has it that one day in 1955 Bogie was lunching with Frank Sinatra, Judy Garland and Jimmy Van Heusen when Mrs Bogart, A.K.A. Lauren Bacall walked into the restaurant and on seeing the group exclaimed, "I see the rat pack is all here". Thus Romanoff's became the place where the Rat Pack term was first coined and also where this drink was created.

David Niven was also a close friend and in his book 'Bring on the Empty Horses' he devotes chapter eight, 'The Emperor', to the colourful Romanoff.
Comment: A Vodka Daisy sweetened with triple sec, apricot brandy and a touch of sugar.

MILANESE BREAKFAST MARTINI

★★★★☆

Glass: Coupe
Garnish: None
Method: STIR marmalade with gin in base of shaker to dissolve marmalade. Add Campari and lemon juice, **SHAKE** with ice and fine strain into chilled glass. **TOP** with Prosecco.

1	shot	Rutte Dry Gin
1	spoon	English orange marmalade
⅛	shot	Campari Bitter
½	shot	Freshly squeezed lemon juice
Top with		Prosecco sparkling wine

Origin: Adapted from a drink created by Dawid Steenkamp at Jamie Oliver's Barbecoa, London, England and inspired by a Negroni and Salvatore's 'Breakfast Martini'. Originally named 'Breakfast in Milan'.
Comment: A fruity but dry aperitif drink served 'up' but with a hint of sparkle from prosecco.

MILANO

★★★★☆

Glass: Old-fashioned
Garnish: Orange slice
Method: STIR all ingredients with ice and strain into ice-filled glass.

1	shot	Ketel One Vodka
1	shot	Campari Bitter
1	shot	Martini Rosso vermouth

Comment: A Negroni with vodka.

MILANO TORINO COCKTAIL (NEW)

★★★★☆

Glass: Old-fashioned
Garnish: Orange slice or wedge
Method: POUR ingredients into ice-filled glass and stir.

2	shots	Campari Bitter
2	shots	Martini Rosso vermouth

Origin: Created at Milan's Caffè Camparino in the 1860's, the Milano-Torino name is after the ingredients: Campari is from Milan (Milano in Italian) and sweet vermouth traditionally comes from Turin (Torino in Italian). Later soda water was added to the Milano-Torino to create the Americano. The Milano-Torino also morphed into the Negroni with gin added.
Comment: The drink that led to both the Negroni and the Americano.

MILK & HONEY COCKTAIL

★★★★☆

Glass: Martini
Garnish: Dust with grated nutmeg
Method: STIR Scotch with honey in base of shaker to dissolve honey. Add other ingredients, **SHAKE** with ice and fine strain into chilled glass.

2	shots	Dewar's 12 Year Old Scotch whisky
3	spoon	Runny honey
½	shot	Old Krupnik
¾	shot	Single cream / half-and-half
¾	shot	Milk

Origin: Created in 2002 by yours truly, London, England.
Comment: The rich flavour of Scotch is tamed by honey and cream.

MILK PUNCH

★★★★☆

Glass: Collins
Garnish: Dust with grated nutmeg
Method: SHAKE all ingredients with ice and strain into glass filled with crushed ice.

1	shot	Martell VSOP Médaillon cognac
½	shot	Gosling's Black Seal dark rum
½	shot	Vanilla sugar syrup
2	shots	Milk
1	shot	Single cream / half-and-half

Comment: The cream, vanilla and sugar tame the cognac and rum.

MILLENNIUM COCKTAIL

★★★★★

Glass: Coupe
Garnish: Orange zest twist & dust with grated nutmeg
Method: SHAKE all ingredients with ice and fine strain into chilled glass.

1½	shots	Martell VSOP Médaillon cognac
1½	shots	Fresh pressed pineapple juice
1	shot	Orange Curaçao liqueur
1	dash	Angostura Aromatic Bitters

Origin: Created by Dale DeGroff, New York City, USA.
Comment: Somewhat reminiscent of a cognac laced Hawaiian pizza. Yum!

MILLION DOLLAR COCKTAIL 0⟶

★★★★½

Glass: Martini
Garnish: Lemon zest twist
Method: SHAKE all ingredients with ice and fine strain into chilled glass.

2	shots	Rutte Dry Gin
1	shot	Martini Rosso vermouth
½	shot	Fresh pressed pineapple juice
¼	shot	Pomegranate / grenadine syrup (2:1)
½	fresh	Egg white

Origin: This Million Dollar Cocktail is thought to have been created around 1910 by Ngiam Tong Boon at The Long Bar, Raffles Hotel, Singapore. Boon is more famous for the Singapore Sling.
Comment: Serious, yet superbly smooth and a bit fluffy.

MILLION DOLLAR MARGARITA

★★★★½

Glass: Old-fashioned
Garnish: Lime wedge
Method: SHAKE all ingredients with ice and strain into ice-filled glass.

1½	shots	Patrón reposado tequila
1½	shots	Grand Marnier Cordon Rouge
½	shot	Freshly squeezed lime juice

Origin: Discovered in 2006 at Maison 140 Hotel, Los Angeles, USA where we paid a mere $41.14 plus tip for the drink.
Comment: The proportions of this Margarita accentuate the liqueur.

MILLIONAIRE 0⟶

★★★★☆

Glass: Coupe
Garnish: Orange slice
Method: SHAKE all ingredients with ice and fine strain into chilled glass.

2 shots Bourbon whiskey
½ shot De Kuyper Triple Sec
½ shot Freshly squeezed lemon juice
¼ shot Pomegranate / grenadine syrup (2:1)
½ fresh Egg white (optional)

Origin: There are numerous cocktails that go by the name Millionaire and this particular recipe is credited to London's Ritz Hotel, sometime pre 1925.
Comment: Whiskey, orange liqueur and pomegranate in sweet harmony. Depending on your grenadine, this will either look a dirty yellow or have a faint red hue.

MILLY MARTINI

★★★★☆

Glass: Martini
Garnish: Pineapple wedge
Method: Lightly MUDDLE basil (just to bruise) in base of shaker. Add other ingredients, SHAKE with ice and fine strain into chilled glass.

5	fresh	Basil leaves
2	shots	Rutte Dry Gin
2	shots	Fresh pressed pineapple juice
½	shot	Sugar syrup (2 sugar to 1 water)
2	dash	Angostura Orange Bitters

Origin: Created in 2003 by Shelim Islam at the GE Club, London, England.
Comment: Gin and pineapple with a pleasing hint of basil.

MILO

★★★★½☆

Glass: Martini
Garnish: Raspberries
Method: SHAKE all ingredients with ice and fine strain into chilled glass.

4 fresh Raspberries
2 shots Rutte Dry Gin
½ shot De Kuyper Triple Sec
¼ shot Sugar syrup (2 sugar to 1 water)
1 dash Peychaud's aromatic bitters

Origin: Created in 2002 by Tony Conigliaro at Isola, London, England.
Comment: Reminiscent of a Raspberry Cosmopolitan, only drier and stronger.

MIMOSA

★★★★⯪

Glass: Flute
Garnish: Orange zest twist
Method: **POUR** a shot of champagne into glass, then **POUR** orange juice and liqueur. **TOP** with champagne.

½ shot Grand Marnier Cordon Rouge
1 ¾ shots Freshly squeezed orange juice
Top with G.H. Mumm Cordon Rouge Champagne

Origin: Created in 1925 at the Ritz Hotel in Paris and named after the tropical flowering shrub. In his 1948 'Fine Art of Mixing Drinks', David A. Embury writes of this drink, "Just another freak champagne mixture. It is not half bad and the ladies usually like it. Use a good quality domestic champagne, medium dry."
Comment: A liqueur-infused take on the Buck's Fizz. Great when made with freshly squeezed orange juice.

MINT & HONEY DAIQUIRI 0━

★★★★⯪

Glass: Martini
Garnish: Mint sprig
Method: **STIR** honey and rum in base of shaker until honey dissolves. Add other ingredients, **SHAKE** with ice and fine strain into chilled glass.

2	spoon	Runny honey
2	shots	Bacardi Carta Blanca light rum
3	fresh	Mint leaves
½	shot	Freshly squeezed lime juice
½	shot	Chilled water (omit if wet ice)

Origin: Created in 2006 by yours truly.
Comment: A fresh-breath-tastic twist on the classic Daiquiri.

MINT COCKTAIL

★★★★⯪

Glass: Martini
Garnish: Mint leaf
Method: Lightly **MUDDLE** (just to bruise) mint in base of shaker. Add other ingredients, **SHAKE** with ice and fine strain into chilled glass.

12	fresh	Mint leaves
2	shots	Rutte Dry Gin
1	shot	Sauvignon blanc white wine
¼	shot	Giffard Menthe Pastille liqueur
¼	shot	Sugar syrup (2 sugar to 1 water)

Origin: Adapted from a recipe in Harry Craddock's 1930 'Savoy Cocktail Book'.
Comment: A great grassy, minty digestif with a good balance between acidity and sweetness.

MINT COLLINS 0━

★★★★☆

Glass: Collins
Garnish: Mint sprig
Method: Lightly **MUDDLE** (just to bruise) mint in base of shaker. Add next three ingredients, **SHAKE** with ice and fine strain into chilled glass. **TOP** with soda, lightly stir and serve with straws.

12	fresh	Mint leaves
2	shots	Rutte Dry Gin
1	shot	Freshly squeezed lemon juice
½	shot	Sugar syrup (2 sugar to 1 water)
Top with		Soda (club soda)

Origin: Adapted from a recipe in the 1942-72 Trader Vic's Bartender's Guide by Victor Bergeron.
Comment: Exactly what the name promises.

MINT DAIQUIRI 0━

★★★★⯪

Glass: Martini
Garnish: Mint leaf
Method: Lightly **MUDDLE** (just to bruise) mint in base of shaker. Add other ingredients, **SHAKE** with ice and fine strain into chilled glass.

12	fresh	Mint leaves
2	shots	Bacardi Carta Blanca light rum
½	shot	Freshly squeezed lime juice
¼	shot	Sugar syrup (2 sugar to 1 water)
½	shot	Chilled water (omit if wet ice)

Origin: Created in 2006 by yours truly.
Comment: A short, concentrated Mojito.

MINT FIZZ

★★★⯪☆

Glass: Collins
Garnish: Mint sprig
Method: Lightly **MUDDLE** mint (just to bruise) in base of shaker. Add other ingredients apart from soda, **SHAKE** with ice and fine strain into ice-filled glass. **TOP** with soda, lightly stir and serve with straws.

7	fresh	Mint leaves
2	shots	Rutte Dry Gin
¼	shot	Giffard Menthe Pastille liqueur
1	shot	Freshly squeezed lime juice
½	shot	Sugar syrup (2 sugar to 1 water)
Top with		Soda (club soda)

Comment: Long, refreshing citrus and mint fizz.

MINT JULEP (MEXICAN STYLE)

★★★⯪☆

Glass: Martini
Garnish: Luxardo Maraschino cherry
Method: **PLACE** lemon zest and mint in shaker. Add other ingredients, **SHAKE** with ice and fine strain into ice-filled glass.

1	fresh	Lemon zest
8	fresh	Mint leaves
1	shot	Martell VSOP Médaillon cognac
1	shot	Tawny port
¼	shot	Luxardo Maraschino liqueur

Origin: Recipe adapted from a 1937 Bar Florida (later renamed Floridita) menu, Havana, Cuba.
Comment: Mint, cognac, port, lemon and maraschino - all subtly contribute to this Cuban take on Mexico.

MINT JULEP COCKTAIL

★★★★★

Glass: Julep Tin
Garnish: Mint sprig dusted with icing sugar
Method: **SHAKE** all ingredients with ice and fine strain into julep cup half filled with crushed ice. **CHURN** (stir) the drink with the crushed ice using a bar spoon. Top up the cup with more crushed ice and **CHURN** again. Repeat this process until the drink fills the cup and serve.

12 fresh Mint leaves
2½ shots Bourbon whiskey
¾ shot Sugar syrup (2 sugar to 1 water)
3 dash Angostura Aromatic Bitters

Origin: Like so many cocktails, the humble Mint Julep's origins are the subject of heated debate. Today it is closely identified with America's Deep South, famously served at the Kentucky Derby. However, the name derives from the Arabic word 'julab', meaning rosewater, and the first known written reference to a cocktail-style Julep was by a Virginia gentleman in 1787. At that time it could be made with rum, brandy or whiskey, but by 1900 whiskey had become the preferred base spirit. Indeed in his 1862 'The Bartender's Guide: How to Mix Drinks', Jerry Thomas calls for cognac, a dash of Jamaican rum and a garnish of berries and orange slices. He also lists a Julep variation made with gin and one calling for ripe pineapple as well as the now ubiquitous whiskey version.

Common perceived wisdom has it that the Julep originated in Persia, or thereabouts, and it travelled to Europe (some say Southern France) where the rose petals were substituted for indigenous mint. The drink is then believed to have crossed the Atlantic where cognac was replaced with peach brandy and then whiskey, the Mint Julep we recognise today.

The remodelled U.S. style mint julep reached Britain in 1837, thanks to the novelist Captain Frederick Marryat, who complained of being woken at 7am by a slave brandishing a Julep. He popularised the drink through his descriptions of American Fourth of July celebrations and praise such as the following:

"I must descant a little upon the mint julep, as it is, with the thermometer at 100°, one of the most delightful and insinuating potations that was ever invented, and may be drunk with equal satisfaction when the thermometer is as low as 70°... As the ice melts, you drink. I once overheard two ladies in the room next to me, and one of them said, 'Well, if I have a weakness for any one thing, it is for a 'mint julep!' - a very amiable weakness, and proving her good sense and taste. They are, in fact, like the American ladies, irresistible."

When making a Mint Julep it is important to only bruise the mint as crushing the leaves releases the bitter, inner juices. Also be sure to discard the stems, which are also bitter.

It is imperative that the drink is served ice cold. Cocktail etiquette dictates that the shaker containing the mint and other ingredients should be placed in a refrigerator with the serving vessel (preferably made of metal rather than glass) for at least two hours prior to adding ice, shaking and serving.

Variations on the Mint Julep include substituting the bourbon for rye whiskey, rum, gin, brandy, calvados or applejack brandy. Another variation calls for half a shot of aged rum to be floated on top of the bourbon-based julep.
Comment: This superb drink is better if the shaker and its contents are placed in the refrigerator for several hours prior to mixing with ice. This allows the mint flavours to infuse in the bourbon.

MINT MARTINI

★★★★½

Glass: Martini
Garnish: Mint leaf
Method: Lightly **MUDDLE** (just to bruise) mint in base of shaker. Add other ingredients, **SHAKE** with ice and fine strain into chilled glass.

12 fresh Mint leaves
1½ shots Ketel One Vodka
¼ shot Green crème de menthe liqueur
½ shot Martini Extra Dry vermouth
1½ shots Sauvignon blanc white wine
¼ shot Sugar syrup (2 sugar to 1 water)

Origin: Created in 2005 by yours truly, London, England.
Comment: An after-dinner palate cleanser.

MINTY LIMEADE (MOCKTAIL)

★★★★½

Glass: Collins
Garnish: Mint sprigs
Method: Lightly **MUDDLE** (just to bruise) mint in base of shaker. Add next three ingredients, **SHAKE** with ice and fine strain into ice-filled glass. **TOP** with lemonade, lightly stir and serve with straws.

12 fresh Mint leaves
1½ shots Freshly squeezed lime juice
1 shot Pressed apple juice
¾ shot Sugar syrup (2 sugar to 1 water)
Top with Lemonade/Sprite/7-Up

Origin: Created in 2006 by yours truly, London, England.
Comment: Superbly refreshing, mint and lime served long.

MINTY PENTONES COCKTAIL (NEW)

★★★★½

Glass: Old-fashioned
Garnish: Mint sprig
Method: **STIR** all ingredients with ice and strain into glass filled with crushed ice.

1½ shots Rutte Dry Gin
1½ shots Cranberry juice
½ shot Giffard Menthe Pastille liqueur
½ shot Skinos Mastiha
4 drop Bob's Bitters Peppermint bitters

Origin: Created by yours truly in August 2015 at the Cabinet Room, London, England and named after one of my favourite New Orleans' bands, 'Mark and the Pentones', whose album was playing at the time of the drinks creation.
Comment: Gin's botanical complexity combined with minty and mastiha freshness and a pink hint of cranberry fruitiness makes for a cleansing after dinner digestive.

MINTY WHITE LADY COCKTAIL (NEW)

★★★★⯪

Glass: Coupe
Garnish: Lemon zest twist (discarded) & mint sprig
Method: SHAKE all ingredients with ice and strain back into shaker. **DRY SHAKE** (without ice) and strain into chilled glass.

1	shot	Rutte Dry Gin
¾	shot	De Kuyper Triple Sec
¾	shot	Giffard Menthe Pastille liqueur
¾	shot	Freshly squeezed lemon juice
4	drop	Bob's Bitters Peppermint bitters
½	fresh	Egg white

Origin: A minty riff on the classic White Lady created by yours truly in August 2015 at the Cabinet Room, London, England.
Comment: White crème de menthe and peppermint bitters bring minty freshness to this not so innocent lady in white.

MISS MARTINI 0⎯⛶

★★★⯪☆

Glass: Martini
Garnish: Raspberries
Method: MUDDLE raspberries in base of shaker. Add other ingredients, **SHAKE** with ice and fine strain into chilled glass.

7 fresh Raspberries
2 shots Ketel One Vodka
½ shot Chambord Liqueur
¼ shot Milk
¼ shot Single cream / half-and-half
⅛ shot Sugar syrup (2 sugar to 1 water)

Origin: Created in 1997 by Giovanni Burdi at Match EC1, London, England.
Comment: A pink, fruity, creamy concoction.

MISS MOONSHINE (NEW)

★★★★⯪

Glass: Coupe
Garnish: Rosemary sprig
Method: STIR all ingredients and strain into chilled glass.

1⅔	shots	Poteen/Poitín
⅔	shot	Lillet Blanc
⅓	shot	Suze Saveur d'Autrefois
⅓	shot	St-Germain elderflower liqueur
⅓	shot	Rosemary sugar syrup (2:1)
2	dash	Angostura Orange Bitters

Origin: Created in 2014 by Louis Lebaillif at Hawksmoor Air Street, London, England.
Comment: Gentian, elderflower and rosemary combine harmoniously, over a Poitín base with aromatised wine.

MISSIONARY'S DOWNFALL

★★★★★

Glass: Collins
Garnish: Mint sprig
Method: Lightly **MUDDLE** mint (just to bruise) in base of shaker. Add other ingredients, **SHAKE** with ice and strain into glass filled with crushed ice.

12	fresh	Mint leaves
2	shots	Bacardi Carta Blanca light rum
½	shot	Peachtree peach schnapps
1½	shots	Freshly squeezed lime juice
2	shots	Fresh pressed pineapple juice
½	shot	Sugar syrup (2 sugar to 1 water)

Origin: Created in the 1930's by Don The Beachcomber at his restaurant in Hollywood, California, USA.
Comment: Superbly balanced and refreshing rum, lime, mint and a hint of peach.

MISSISSIPPI PUNCH 0⎯⛶

★★★★☆

Glass: Collins
Garnish: Lemon slice
Method: SHAKE all ingredients with ice and strain into glass filled with crushed ice.

1½	shots	Bourbon whiskey
¾	shot	Martell VSOP Médaillon cognac
¾	shot	Freshly squeezed lemon juice
1	shot	Sugar syrup (2 sugar to 1 water)
2	shots	Chilled water

Comment: Balanced and refreshing.

MISSISSIPPI SCHNAPPER 0⎯⛶

★★★⯪☆

Glass: Martini
Garnish: Orange zest twist
Method: SHAKE all ingredients with ice and fine strain into chilled glass.

2	shots	Bourbon whiskey
¾	shot	Martell VSOP Médaillon cognac
½	shot	De Kuyper Triple Sec
¼	shot	Freshly squeezed lime juice
¼	shot	Sugar syrup (2 sugar to 1 water)

Origin: Created in 1999 by Dan Cottle at Velvet, Manchester, England.
Comment: Orange predominates with peach sweetness balanced by whiskey and lime.

MISTER STU

★★★⯪☆

Glass: Collins
Garnish: Pineapple wedge
Method: SHAKE all ingredients with ice and strain into ice-filled glass. Serve with straws.

2	shots	Patrón reposado tequila
½	shot	Disaronno Originale amaretto
½	shot	Coconut rum liqueur
1½	shots	Fresh pressed pineapple juice
1½	shots	Freshly squeezed orange juice

Comment: There's a touch of the disco about this foamy drink, but it is still complex and interesting.

MITCH MARTINI

★★★★☆

Glass: Martini
Garnish: Lemon zest twist
Method: SHAKE all ingredients with ice and fine strain into chilled glass.

2	shots	Zubrówka bison vodka
1	shot	Pressed apple juice
¼	shot	Peachtree peach schnapps
¼	shot	Passion fruit syrup

Origin: Created in 1997 by Giovanni Burdi at Match EC1, London, England.
Comment: One of London's contemporary classics. Far from a proper Martini, this is fruity and sweet, but not overly so.

MIXED BERRY JULEP

★★★★½

Glass: Collins
Garnish: Blackberries & mint sprig
Method: Lightly MUDDLE berries in base of glass. Add mint, bourbon, cognac, and sugar syrup into glass, add crushed ice and CHURN (stir) with bar spoon. Top up the glass with more crushed ice and CHURN again. Repeat this process until the drink fills the glass and serve.

12	fresh	Mint leaves
2	fresh	Blackberries
3	fresh	Raspberries
1	shot	Bourbon whiskey
1	shot	Martell VSOP Médaillon cognac
¾	shot	Sugar syrup (2 sugar to 1 water)

Origin: Created by Dre Masso in Colombia 2009.
Comment: A fruity, minty crowd pleasing Julep.

MIZUWARI

★★★★★

Glass: Collins
Garnish: Lemon zest twist (discarded) & mint sprig
Method: Fill glass with ice and STIR until water formed in base of glass. Add more ice and continue stirring to cool glass. STRAIN water from glass, pour whisky into glass and top ice to brim. STIR whisky and ice, adding more ice to keep level at brim. Lastly, add water and briefly stir some more.

| 2 | shots | Dewar's 12 Year Old Scotch whisky |
| Top with | | Chilled water |

Origin: Pronounced "Miz-Zoo-Ware-E", this literally translates as "mizu" = water and "wari" = divide, thus the whisky is simply cut with water and served over ice. The ratio is personal to both the drinker and bartender and varies between 1:2.5 and 1:4 whisky to water. It is common in Japan for diners to drink mizu wari in place of wine with their meals and the light whisky flavours combine excellently with Japanese food. Extremely thin, delicate glasses are used and the thickness and quality of glass is considered key to mizu wari in Japan.
Comment: This is simply whisky and water, but as with the Japanese tea ceremony, observing the time and care taken over it making and the prolonged anticipation contributes greatly to the finished drink. And you thought an Old Fashioned took a long time.

MOCHA MARTINI

★★★★½

Glass: Martini
Garnish: Dust with chocolate powder
Method: SHAKE first four ingredients with ice and fine strain into chilled glass. FLOAT cream in centre of drink.

1½	shots	Bourbon whiskey
1	shot	Espresso coffee (freshly made & hot)
½	shot	Baileys Irish cream liqueur
½	shot	Dark crème de cacao liqueur
½	shot	Single cream / half-and-half

Comment: Made with great espresso, this drink is a superb, richly flavoured balance of sweet and bitter.

MOCK MARGARITA (MOCKTAIL)

★★★½☆

Glass: Old-fashioned
Garnish: Salt rim & lime wedge
Method: SHAKE all ingredients with ice and strain into ice-filled glass.

1½ shots Freshly squeezed lime juice
½ shot Freshly squeezed lemon juice
1 shot Agave syrup
Top with Ginger ale

Origin: Adapted from a drink created in 2010 by Cheri Loughlin AKA The Intoxicologist, USA.
Comment: While this is a long way from a fine 100% agave tequila based Margarita, the flavour is surprisingly reminiscent of an alcoholic Margarita.

THE MODERN COCKTAIL

★★★½☆

Glass: Coupe
Garnish: Luxardo Maraschino cherry
Method: SHAKE all ingredients with ice and fine strain into chilled glass.

1½	shots	Dewar's 12 Year Old Scotch whisky
1½	shots	Sloe Gin liqueur
½	shot	Freshly squeezed lemon juice
⅛	shot	Sugar syrup (2 sugar to 1 water)
1	dash	Le Fée Parisienne absinthe
1	dash	Angostura Orange Bitters

Origin: Adapted form a drink created in the early 20th century by Charlie Mahoney, head bartender at New York's Hoffman House Hotel.
Comment: A pleasantly fruity cocktail with equal parts scotch and sloe liqueur shaken with lemon juice and a dash of absinthe.

A B C D E F G H I J K L M N O P Q R S T U V W X Y Z

MODERNISTA

★★★½☆

Glass: Martini
Garnish: Lemon zest twist
Method: **SHAKE** all ingredients with ice and fine strain into chilled glass.

2 shots Rutte Dry Gin
½ shot Gosling's Black Seal dark rum
¼ shot Pernod anise
1 shot Swedish Punch liqueur
¼ shot Freshly squeezed lemon juice
1 dash Angostura Orange Bitters

Origin: Adapted from a drink created by Ted Haigh (AKA Dr. Cocktail) and derived from the 'Modern Cocktail'. See Ted's book, 'Vintage Spirits & Foreign Cocktails'.
Comment: A massive flavour hit to awaken your taste buds.

Mojito Cocktail

The exact origins of the Mojito and its name are lost in the mists of time. Some trace it back to 1586 and a medicinal drink named after Sir Francis Drake, one of a band of privateers sponsored by England's Queen Elizabeth I to plunder Spanish cities in the New World and seize their riches.

In 1586, Drake dropped anchor off the Cuban shore with a cargo of Spanish treasure which was valued at twice the Queen's annual income. King Philip II of Spain had warned his governor in Cuba of Drake's approach, and of his intentions to take the Aztec gold stored in the city's royal treasury. Havana was well-prepared. But everyone was amazed when, after several days of waiting, Captain Drake sailed away from the richest port in the West Indies after firing only a few shots.

Drake left Havana and its gold intact, but his visit was a major event, something perhaps worthy of naming a drink after. Known as the Draque, Drak or Drac this consisted of aguardiente (a crude cane spirit that was the forerunner of rum), sugar, lime and mint.

Some say the drink was not originally Cuban and it was actually invented upon board Drake's ship which carried mint to mix with cane spirit, sugar and lime to make a drink to relieve fever and colds. What is for certain is that the Draque was drunk for its perceived medicinal value. During one of the worst cholera epidemics ever to hit Havana, the author Ramon de Paula wrote, "Every day at eleven o' clock I consume a little Draque made from aguardiente (local cane spirit) and I am doing very well."

The drink stayed that way until the mid 1800s. Then, at the same time as Don Facundo Bacardi Massó was establishing the Bacardi Company, the original recipe for the Draque changed. As Frederick Villoch described in 1940 '...when aguardiente was replaced with rum, the Draque was to be called a Mojito.'

However, some maintain the Mojito was invented after Americans visiting Cuba's thriving bar culture between the wars, and especially during Prohibition, introduced the locals to the Mint Julep.

The origins of the name 'Mojito' are equally misty. Some say it comes from 'mojar', a Spanish verb suggesting wetness. Others claim it comes from the African word 'mojo', meaning to place a little spell. Either way, Cuba's oldest cocktail is superbly refreshing and is one of the world's best-selling cocktails.

Bodeguita del Medio bar in Havana is by urban myth credited with making the first Mojito and this is also apparently where Ernest Hemingway went for his. Here a framed hand-written note, personally written and signed by Hemmingway reads, "My Mojito in La Bodeguita My Daiquiri in El Floridita." However, none of his books mention either the Mojito or La Bodeguita, nor does any letter or other piece of writing attributed to Hemmingway.

MOJITO COCKTAIL

★★★★★

Glass: Collins
Garnish: Mint sprig
Method: Lightly **MUDDLE** mint (just to bruise) in base of glass. Add rum, lime juice and sugar. Half fill glass with crushed ice and **CHURN** (stir) with bar spoon. Fill glass with more crushed ice and **CHURN** some more. **TOP** with soda, stir and serve with straws.

12 fresh Mint leaves
2 shots Bacardi Carta Blanca light rum
¾ shot Freshly squeezed lime juice
½ shot Sugar syrup (2 sugar to 1 water)
Top with Soda (club soda)

Comment: When well made, this Cuban cousin of the Mint Julep is one of the world's greatest and most refreshing cocktails.

MOJITO COCKTAIL (DIFFORD'S METHOD)

★★★★★

Glass: Collins
Garnish: Mint sprig
Method: **SHAKE** all ingredients with ice and fine strain into ice-filled glass. **CHURN** (stir) with bar spoon. Fill glass with more crushed ice and **CHURN** some more. Keep adding ice and churning until drink fills glass. Serve with straws.

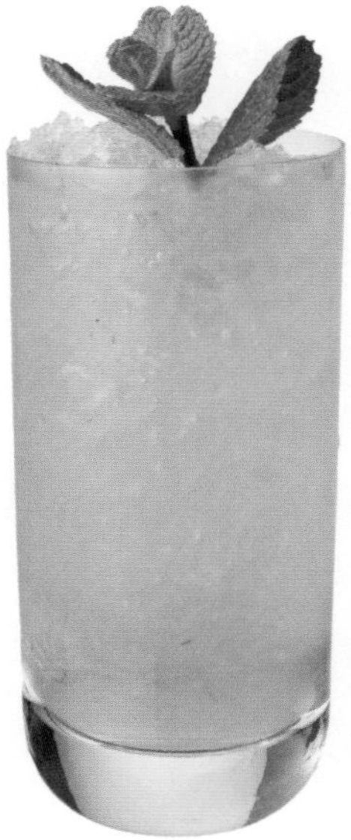

12 fresh Mint leaves
2½ shots Bacardi Carta Blanca light rum
¾ shot Freshly squeezed lime juice
½ shot Sugar syrup (2 sugar to 1 water)
⅛ shot Giffard Menthe Pastille liqueur
2 dash Angostura Aromatic Bitters

Origin: Recipe by yours truly, the man who likes his Mojito shaken and stirred.
Comment: All the flavour of the Mojito but without unattractive mint leaves trapped in crushed ice. This only works when fresh, cold crushed ice is used. Otherwise the drink will be overly diluted.

MOJITO DE CASA

★★★★☆

Glass: Collins
Garnish: Mint sprig
Method: Lightly **MUDDLE** mint (just to bruise) in base of glass. Add tequila, lime juice and sugar. Half fill glass with crushed ice and **CHURN** (stir) with bar spoon. Fill glass with more crushed ice and churn some more. **TOP** with soda, stir and serve.

12 fresh Mint leaves
2 shots Patrón reposado tequila
¾ shot Freshly squeezed lime juice
½ shot Sugar syrup (2 sugar to 1 water)
Top with Soda (club soda)

Origin: Created at Mercadito, New York City, USA.
Comment: A tequila based Mojito.

MOJITO PARISIEN ⚷

★★★★⯪

Glass: Collins
Garnish: Mint sprig
Method: Lightly **MUDDLE** mint (just to bruise) in base of glass. Add other ingredients, half fill glass with crushed ice and **CHURN** (stir) with bar spoon. Fill glass to brim with more crushed ice and churn some more. Serve with straws.

12	fresh	Mint leaves
2	shots	Bacardi Carta Blanca light rum
1½	shots	St-Germain elderflower liqueur
1	shot	Freshly squeezed lime juice

Origin: Created in 2006 by yours truly.
Comment: Those with a sweet tooth may want to add a dash of sugar syrup to taste.

MOLLY'S MILK

★★★★☆

Glass: Coupe
Garnish: Dust with grated nutmeg
Method: STIR first two ingredients with ice and strain into chilled glass. **FLOAT** whipped cream on drink.

1½ shots	Teeling Small Batch Irish whiskey
1½ shots	Irish Mist Liqueur
Float lightly whipped Single cream / half-and-half	

Origin: Adapted from a drink created in 1997 by Dale DeGroff at Molly Malone's Pub, Prague, Czech Republic.
Comment: Herbal, honeyed Irish whiskey drunk through a creamy head.

MOMISETTE

★★★★☆

Glass: Collins
Garnish: None
Method: POUR pastis and almond syrup into glass. Serve with bottle of sparkling water so the customer can dilute to their own taste. (I recommend five shots.) Lastly, add ice to fill glass.

1	shot	Ricard Pastis
¼	shot	Almond (orgeat) syrup
Top with	Sparkling mineral water	

Origin: A traditional French drink, the name of which literally translates as 'tiny mummy'.
Comment: Complex balance of anis, almond and liquorice.

MOMO SPECIAL ⚷

★★★★☆

Glass: Collins
Garnish: Mint sprig
Method: Lightly **MUDDLE** mint (just to bruise) in base of shaker. Add next 3 ingredients, **SHAKE** with ice and strain into ice-filled glass. **TOP** with soda, lightly stir and serve with straws.

12	fresh	Mint leaves
2	shots	Ketel One Vodka
½	shot	Freshly squeezed lime juice
½	shot	Sugar syrup (2 sugar to 1 water)
Top with	Soda (club soda)	

Origin: Created in 1998 by Simon Mainoo at Momo, London, England.
Comment: Enrich the minty flavour by macerating the mint in the vodka some hours before making.

MONA LISA

★★★★☆

Glass: Collins
Garnish: Orange slice
Method: SHAKE first 3 ingredients with ice and strain into ice-filled glass. **TOP** with tonic water.

1	shot	Green Chartreuse liqueur
3	shots	Freshly squeezed orange juice
2	dash	Angostura Aromatic Bitters
Top with	Tonic Water	

Comment: Chartreuse fans will appreciate this drink, which is also an approachable way for novices to acquire a taste for the green stuff.

MONARCH MARTINI

★★★★☆

Glass: Martini
Garnish: Lemon zest twist
Method: MUDDLE mint (just to bruise) in base of shaker. Add other ingredients, **SHAKE** with ice and fine strain into chilled glass.

7	fresh	Mint leaves
2	shots	Rutte Dry Gin
½	shot	St-Germain elderflower liqueur
½	shot	Freshly squeezed lemon juice
¼	shot	Sugar syrup (2 sugar to 1 water)
2	dash	Peach bitters

Origin: Created in 2003 by Douglas Ankrah at Townhouse, London, England.
Comment: Wonderfully floral and minty - worthy of a right royal drinker.

MONET'S MOMENT

★★★★☆

Glass: Goblet
Garnish: Orange zest twist (discarded)
Method: STIR all ingredients with ice and strain into ice-filled glass (preferably with one large hand-cracked cube)

1½ shots Martell VSOP Médaillon cognac
1 shot Byrrh Grand Quinquina
⅛ shot Le Fée Parisienne absinthe
¼ shot Sugar syrup (2 sugar to 1 water)
1 dash Creole bitters

Origin: Created in 2013 by Erik Lorincz, Head Bartender at the American Bar, Savoy Hotel, London. He was inspired after seeing a work by Claude Monet that hangs in the suite where the French impressionist originally sketched the pastels piece entitled Waterloo Bridge in 1901. Erik was inspired by the moment when Monet entered his suite and decided to sketch the view from his window of the capital's iconic landmark.
Comment: Cognac and aromatised wine lifted with a splash of absinthe. Complex and refreshing.

THE MONEY PENNY

★★★★★

Glass: Martini
Garnish: Grapefruit zest twist
Method: SHAKE all ingredients with ice and fine strain into chilled glass.

2 shots Rutte Dry Gin
¾ shot Freshly squeezed pink grapefruit juice
½ shot Martini Extra Dry vermouth
¼ shot Sugar syrup (2 sugar to 1 water)
1 dash Grapefruit bitters

Origin: Discovered in 2010 at the Blue Owl, New York City, USA.
Comment: Fresh grapefruit and gin soured with a splash of grapefruit and balanced with the merest touch of sugar.

MONK'S HABIT

★★★☆☆

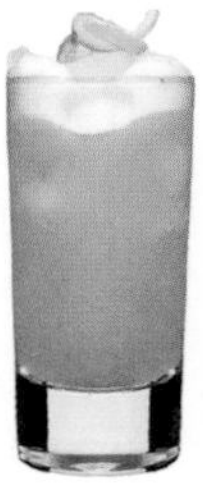

Glass: Collins
Garnish: Orange slice
Method: SHAKE all ingredients with ice and strain into ice-filled glass.

1½ shots Bacardi Carta Blanca light rum
½ shot De Kuyper Triple Sec
1 shot Hazelnut liqueur
3 shots Fresh pressed pineapple juice
¼ shot Pomegranate / grenadine syrup (2:1)

Comment: Fruit and nut laced with rum. Slightly sweet.

MONKEY GLAND #1

★★★★⯪

Glass: Martini
Garnish: Orange zest twist
Method: SHAKE all ingredients with ice and fine strain into chilled glass.

2 shots Rutte Dry Gin
1½ shots Freshly squeezed orange juice
⅛ spoon Le Fée Parisienne absinthe
⅛ shot Pomegranate / grenadine syrup (2:1)
⅛ shot Sugar syrup (2 sugar to 1 water)

Origin: Created in the late 1920's by Harry MacElhone at his Harry's New York Bar in Paris, France. The Monkey Gland takes its name from the work of Dr Serge Voronoff who, convinced that testosterone was vital to a long and healthy life, transplanted monkey testicles onto elderly Frenchmen.
Comment: Approach with caution. Unlike the experiments of Serge Voronoff, nothing about this drink is designed to enhance virility.

MONKEY GLAND #2

★★★★☆

Glass: Old-fashioned
Garnish: Orange slice
Method: SHAKE all ingredients with ice and fine strain into ice-filled glass.

2 shots Rutte Dry Gin
½ shot Bénédictine D.O.M. liqueur
1¼ shots Freshly squeezed orange juice
¼ shot Pomegranate / grenadine syrup (2:1)

Comment: A somewhat off-putting name for a very palatable cocktail.

MONKEY SHINE

★★★★☆

Glass: Martini
Garnish: Cinnamon & sugar rim
Method: SHAKE all ingredients with ice and fine strain into chilled glass.

2 shots Bacardi Carta Blanca light rum
1 shot Coconut rum liqueur
1 shot Fresh pressed pineapple juice

Origin: An adaptation of a drink discovered in 2003 at the Bellagio Resort & Casino, Las Vegas.
Comment: The sweet, tropical fruitiness of this drink is set off by the spicy rim.

MONKEY WRENCH

★★★⯪☆

Glass: Collins
Garnish: None
Method: POUR rum into ice-filled glass. Top with grapefruit juice, stir and serve with straws.

2 shots Bacardi Carta Oro rum
Top with Freshly squeezed pink grapefruit juice

Comment: Simple but pleasant.

MONSIEUR LECROIX

★★★⯪☆

Glass: Martini
Garnish: Lime zest twist
Method: STIR all ingredients with ice and strain into chilled glass.

2 shots Chocolate Spirit
1 shot Martell VSOP Médaillon cognac
½ shot Grand Marnier Cordon Rouge
2 dash Angostura Orange Bitters

Origin: Adapted from a drink created in 2010 by Klaus St. Rainer at Schumann's Bar, Munich, Germany.
Comment: Chocolate and cognac with the merest splash of orange liqueur still leaving this drink on the dry side.

MONSTRE VERTE COCKTAIL

★★★⯪☆

Glass: Old-fashioned
Garnish: Basil leaf
Method: POUR aniseed into ice-filled glass and **TOP** with chilled water. Separately **SHAKE** rest of ingredients with ice. **DISCARD** contents of glass and refill with fresh ice. Then fine strain contents of shaker into the now absinthe coated glass.

¼ shot Le Fée Parisienne absinthe
1½ shots Rutte Dry Gin
½ shot Green Chartreuse liqueur
¼ shot Freshly squeezed lime juice
¼ shot Sugar syrup (2 sugar to 1 water)
4 fresh Basil leaves

Origin: Created in 2011 by Jamie Boudreau, Seattle, USA
Comment: A drink for fans of Chartreuse and aniseed.

MONTE CARLO IMPERIAL

★★★½☆

Glass: Martini
Garnish: Mint leaf
Method: SHAKE first 3 ingredients with ice and fine strain into chilled glass. **TOP** with champagne.

1½ shots	Rutte Dry Gin
½ shot	Giffard Menthe Pastille liqueur
½ shot	Freshly squeezed lemon juice
Top with	G.H. Mumm Cordon Rouge Champagne

Origin: Adapted from a recipe in Harry Craddock's 1930 Savoy Cocktail Book.
Comment: A classic, minty digestif.

MONTE CASSINO

★★★★½

Glass: Coupe
Garnish: Lemon zest twist
Method: SHAKE all ingredients with ice and fine strain into chilled glass.

¾ shot	Straight rye whiskey
¾ shot	Bénédictine D.O.M. liqueur
¾ shot	Yellow Chartreuse liqueur
¾ shot	Freshly squeezed lemon juice
½ shot	Chilled water (omit if wet ice)

Origin: Adapted from a drink created in 2010 by Damon Dyer at Louis 649, New York City. Damon won the Bénédictine 500th Anniversary Cocktail Competition with this drink. Named after Monte Cassino, a rocky hill 80 miles southeast of Rome, Italy which is best-known for its historic monastery, built on the site where St. Benedict of Nursia established the Benedictine Order circa 529. The hilltop abbey was destroyed by Allied bombing during the World War II but was subsequently rebuilt and reconsecrated in 1964 by Pope Paul VI.
Comment: The robust flavours of rye combine harmoniously with the other ingredients in this riff on the classic Last Word.

MONTEGO BAY

★★★½☆

Glass: Old-fashioned
Garnish: Lime wedge
Method: SHAKE all ingredients with ice and strain into ice-filled glass.

1½ shots	Martinique blanc rhum agricole
½ shot	De Kuyper Triple Sec
½ shot	Freshly squeezed lime juice
¼ shot	Sugar syrup (2 sugar to 1 water)
2 dash	Angostura Aromatic Bitters

Origin: Adapted from a recipe in the 1947-72 Trader Vic's Bartender's Guide by Victor Bergeron.
Comment: The name suggest Jamaica but the recipe requires agricole rum. This pungent style of rum is not Jamaican.

THE MONTFORD

★★★★½

Glass: Coupe
Garnish: Lemon zest twist
Method: STIR all ingredients with ice and strain into chilled glass.

2 shots	Rutte Dry Gin
¾ shot	Lillet Blanc
½ shot	Noilly Ambre vermouth
2 dash	Angostura Orange Bitters

Origin: Adapted from a drink created by Dan Warner at the Beefeater Distillery, London, England.
Comment: A wonderfully wet martini with the addition of Lillet and orange bitters.

MONTGOMERY SLUGGER

★★★★½

Glass: Coupe
Garnish: Orange zest twist
Method: POUR absinthe into ice-filled glass, **TOP** with water and leave to stand. Separately **STIR** other ingredients with ice. **DISCARD** contents of glass (absinthe, water and ice) and **STRAIN** contents of stirring glass into absinthe-coated glass.

½ shot	Le Fée Parisienne absinthe
Top with	Chilled water
1½ shots	Bourbon whiskey
½ shot	Carpano Antica Formula
¼ shot	Coffee liqueur
¼ shot	Taylor's Velvet Falernum liqueur
¼ shot	Nocello walnut liqueur
2 dash	Angostura Aromatic Bitters
1 pinch	Salt

Origin: Adapted from a drink discovered in January 2013 at Maison Premiere, Williamsburg, New York.
Comment: A chocolaty nutty coffee.

MONTRÉAL

★★★★☆

Glass: Coupe
Garnish: Orange twist
Method: STIR all ingredients with ice and fine strain into chilled glass.

1½ shots	Straight rye whiskey
¾ shot	Martini Rosso vermouth
⅛ shot	Pernod anise
3 dash	Peychaud's aromatic bitters

Origin: Adapted from a recipe in Sips & Apps by Kathy Casey, Chronicle Books, Spring 2009.
Comment: A sweet rye Manhattan with French Creole influence.

MONZA

★★★★☆

Glass: Collins
Garnish: Apple slice
Method: Cut passion fruit in half and scoop flesh into shaker. Add other ingredients, **SHAKE** with ice and strain into ice-filled glass.

1 fresh	Passion fruit
2 shots	Ketel One Vodka
2 shots	Campari Bitter
2 shots	Pressed apple juice
¼ shot	Sugar syrup (2 sugar to 1 water)

Origin: A classic cocktail promoted by Campari and named after the Italian Grand Prix circuit.
Comment: If you like Campari you'll love this.

MOO'LATA

★★★★★

Glass: Martini
Garnish: Lime wedge
Method: SHAKE all ingredients with ice and fine strain into chilled glass.

2 shots Dewar's 12 Year Old Scotch whisky
¼ shot Dark crème de cacao liqueur
¼ shot White crème de cacao liqueur
½ shot Freshly squeezed lime juice
¼ shot Sugar syrup (2 sugar to 1 water)

Origin: Created in January 2011 by yours truly at the Cabinet Room, London, England after mistakenly taking a bottle of Scotch from the speed well to make a Mulata Daiquiri. It proved a tasty mistake.
Comment: Scotch soured with lime and sweetened with a touch of chocolate liqueur.

MOOD INDIGO

★★★★☆

Glass: Martini
Garnish: Violet blossom or mint sprig
Method: SHAKE all ingredients with ice and fine strain into chilled glass.

1½ shots Rutte Dry Gin
½ shot Martell VSOP Médaillon cognac
½ shot Benoit Serres créme de violette
½ fresh Egg white
⅛ shot Sugar syrup (2 sugar to 1 water)
½ shot Chilled water (omit if wet ice)

Origin: Named after the jazz standard that was a hit for Nat King Cole.
Comment: Smooth, delicate and floral: the gin and brandy add just enough bite.

MOON COCKTAIL (NEW)

★★★★½

Glass: Coupe
Garnish: Lemon zest twist
Method: STIR all ingredients with ice and strain into chilled glass.

2 shots Rutte Dry Gin
¾ shot Romate Amontillado sherry
1 spoon Crème de peche liqueur
¼ shot Honey sugar syrup

Comment: Gin and sherry combine harmoniously in this stirred boozy cocktail with a touch of honey and peach.
Origin: Created in 2008 by Thomas Waugh at Death & Co., New York City, USA.

MOON RIVER

★★★½☆

Glass: Martini
Garnish: Mint leaf
Method: SHAKE all ingredients with ice and fine strain into chilled glass.

1½ shots Rutte Dry Gin
½ shot De Kuyper XO Apricot Brandy
½ shot De Kuyper Triple Sec
¼ shot Galliano L'Autentico liqueur
½ shot Freshly squeezed lemon juice
½ shot Chilled water (omit if wet ice)

Origin: Adapted from a drink discovered in 2005 at Bar Opiume, Singapore.
Comment: There's a hint of aniseed in this fruity, sweet and sour drink.

MOONDREAM

★★★★☆

Glass: Coupe
Garnish: Peach slice
Method: STIR all ingredients with ice and strain into chilled glass.

3 shots Rutte Dry Gin
1 shot San León Manzanilla sherry
¼ shot Martini Extra Dry vermouth
¼ shot Crème de pêche (peach) liqueur

Origin: Created in 2007 by Thomas Waugh at Alembic, San Francisco, USA.
Comment: Also try with subtle styles of dry vermouth such as Dolin.

MOONLIGHT COCKTAIL (GAZ REGAN'S)

★★★★½

Glass: Flute
Garnish: Orange zest twist
Method: SHAKE all ingredients with ice and fine strain into chilled glass.

1½ shots Rutte Dry Gin
¾ shot De Kuyper Triple Sec
½ shot Benoit Serres créme de violette
¼ shot Freshly squeezed lime juice
¼ shot Freshly squeezed lemon juice

Origin: This riff on the classic Aviation was created by Gaz Regan and first published in his The Cocktailian column in the San Francisco Chronicle on 27 September 2007. Gaz wrote, "After making my new baby I took it for a stroll around my deck and gazed up at the moon. It was off-white that evening, but it had a faint purplish hue to it. Just like my drink. The Moonlight Cocktail was born."
Comment: Basically an Aviation but with triple sec in place of maraschino and lime instead of lemon juice. Gaz used lime juice because he didn't have any lemons but in this adaptation of his recipe I've mellowed the citrus sourness by using both lime and lemon juice.

MOONLIGHT COCKTAIL (HARRY CRADDOCK'S RECIPE)

★★★★☆

Glass: Martini
Garnish: Lemon zest twist
Method: SHAKE all ingredients with ice and fine strain into chilled glass.

1½ shots Rutte Dry Gin
¼ shot Kirschwasser eau de vie
1 shot Sauvignon blanc white wine
1¼ shots Freshly squeezed pink grapefruit juice

Origin: Adapted from a recipe in Harry Craddock's 1930 Savoy Cocktail Book.
Comment: Craddock describes this as 'a very dry cocktail'. It is, but pleasantly so.

MOONRAKER

★★★½☆

Glass: Martini
Garnish: Luxardo Maraschino cherry
Method: SHAKE all ingredients with ice and fine strain into chilled glass.

1½ shots Martell VSOP Médaillon cognac
¾ shot Peachtree peach schnapps
¼ shot Pernod anise
1½ shots Dubonnet Red

Origin: Adapted from a recipe in the 1947-72 Trader Vic's Bartender's Guide by Victor Bergeron.
Comment: A diverse range of flavours come together surprisingly well.

MOONSHINE MARTINI

★ ★ ★ ★ ⯨

Glass: Coupe
Garnish: Luxardo Maraschino cherry
Method: **STIR** all ingredients with ice and strain into chilled glass.

1½ shots	Rutte Dry Gin
½ shot	Luxardo Maraschino liqueur
1 shot	Martini Extra Dry vermouth
⅛ shot	Le Fée Parisienne absinthe

Origin: Adapted from a recipe in the 1930 Savoy Cocktail Book by Harry Craddock.
Comment: A wet Martini with balanced hints of maraschino and absinthe.

MOONWALK COCKTAIL

★ ★ ★ ⯨ ☆

Glass: Flute
Garnish: Orange zest twist (spray & discard) & 1/4 orange slice on rim.
Method: **POUR** ingredients into chilled glass. **TOP** with champagne. (Build in glass like a classic Champagne Cocktail.)

¾ shot	Grand Marnier Cordon Rouge
2 dash	Orange flower water
3 dash	Grapefruit bitters
Top with	G.H. Mumm Cordon Rouge Champagne

Origin: Adapted from a recipe created in 1969 by Joe Gilmore at London's American Bar at the Savoy Hotel, London, England to commemorate the moon landings.

Speaking to Difford's Guide in January 2012 Joe said, "The moon landings were a big deal to everyone at the time and I thought I've got to make a cocktail for this." Joe, who watched the moon landings repeated on TV when his shift was over, went on to say, "I never got to serve Neil Armstrong personally, but I sent one in a flask to NASA and apparently it was the first drink he had when he landed. He wrote a letter to me at the Savoy to say thank you."
Comment: Delicately sweetened Champagne with cognac and citrus flavours.

MORAVIAN COCKTAIL

★ ★ ★ ☆ ☆

Glass: Old-fashioned
Garnish: Orange slice & cherry on stick (sail)
Method: **STIR** all ingredients with ice and strain into ice-filled glass.

¾ shot Slivovitz plum brandy
¾ shot Becherovka
(Carlsbad Becher)
1½ shots Martini Rosso vermouth

Origin: Discovered in 2005 at Be Bop Bar, Prague, Czech Republic.
Comment: The hardcore, Czech answer to the Italian Negroni. A drink for those who have acquired a taste for Becherovka.

MORNING GLORY

★ ★ ★ ★ ☆

Glass: Old-fashioned
Garnish: Lemon zest twist
Method: **SHAKE** all ingredients with ice and strain into ice-filled glass.

1 shot	Martell VSOP Médaillon cognac
¾ shot	Grand Marnier Cordon Rouge
⅛ shot	Le Fée Parisienne absinthe
½ shot	Freshly squeezed lemon juice
¼ shot	Sugar syrup (2 sugar to 1 water)
2 dash	Angostura Aromatic Bitters
½ shot	Chilled water (omit if wet ice)

Origin: My interpretation of a classic.
Comment: Sophisticated and complex - one for sipping.

MORNING GLORY FIZZ

★ ★ ★ ⯨ ☆

Glass: Collins (small 8oz)
Garnish: Lime slice
Method: Vigorously **SHAKE** first 5 ingredients with ice and strain into chilled glass (without ice). **TOP** with soda water from a siphon.

2 shots	Dewar's 12 Year Old Scotch whisky
¾ shot	Freshly squeezed lemon juice
½ shot	Sugar syrup (2 sugar to 1 water)
½ fresh	Egg white
1 dash	Le Fée Parisienne absinthe
Top with	Soda from siphon

Origin: Recipe adapted from George Kappeler's 1895 'Modern American Drinks'.
Comment: This classic, sour and aromatic cocktail is traditionally considered a morning after pick-me-up.

MOSCOW LASSI

★ ★ ★ ☆ ☆

Glass: Collins
Garnish: Cucumber slices
Method: **MUDDLE** cucumber in base of shaker. Add other ingredients. **SHAKE** with ice and fine strain into ice-filled glass.

2 inch	English cucumber peeled
1½ shots	Ketel One Vodka
1 shot	Mango purée
2 shots	Pressed apple juice
¼ shot	Sugar syrup (2 sugar to 1 water)
3 spoon	Natural yoghurt

Origin: Created in 2001 by Jamie Stephenson at Graucho Grill, Manchester, England.
Comment: One to serve with your Indian takeaway.

Moscow Mule

"The vodka drink with a kick" is simply vodka and ginger beer with a squeeze of lime served over ice, traditionally served in a copper mug. The Moscow Mule was created in 1941 - 1946 (the date and place of creation are disputed).

John G. Martin had recently (in 1939) acquired the rights to Smirnoff vodka for Heublein, a small Connecticut based liquor and food distributor. Meanwhile, Jack Morgan, a friend of his and owner of Hollywood's famous British pub, the Cock'n'Bull Saloon on Sunset Strip, was trying to launch his own brand of ginger beer but sales were not going well. Legend has it that the two men met at New York City's Chatham Bar and hit on the idea of mixing Martin's vodka with Morgan's ginger beer and adding a squeeze of lime (perhaps inspired by the Cuba Libre) to create the Moscow Mule.

Others, most notably Eric Felton in a 2007 article in the Wall Street Journal, say the drink was invented back in Hollywood at the Cock'n' Bull by Wes Price, its head bartender. Price is said to have created the drink in an attempt to clear an overstock of ginger beer from the pub's basement. He served the new drink to actor Broderick Crawford and so the drink caught on from there.

Wes Price, apparently resigned from the Cock'n' Bull in 1953 and is quoted as saying "I wasn't truly appreciated. I never got an extra cent for my invention".

What is sure is that the combination of vodka and ginger beer helped both Morgan and Martin shift their products but the drinks success is greatly due to its being served in a five ounce copper mug specially engraved with a kicking mule. This intuitive was driven by a girlfriend of Morgan's who'd recently inherited a copper factory which made the previously poorly selling copper mugs. The success of the Moscow Mule was most fortuitous for all three friends.

By 1947 when Edwin H. Land invented the Polaroid Land Camera, the Moscow Mule was already established on the drinks menus of numerous bars. Martin, bought himself one of the instant cameras and went from bar to bar photographing bartenders holding a bottle Smirnoff Vodka in one hand and a copper mule mug in the other. He gave one photograph to the bartender and used a second to show the next neighbouring bar what they were missing out on. The Moscow Mule and the use of the Polaroid Camera was a stroke of marketing genius.

MOSCOW MULE

★★★★☆

Glass: Copper mug or Collins glass
Garnish: Lime slice & mint sprigs
Method: POUR ingredients into ice-filled mug/glass. TOP with crushed ice.

2 shots Ketel One Vodka
½ shot Freshly squeezed lime juice
Top with Gosling's Stormy Ginger Beer

Comment: A long, vodka based drink with spice provided by ginger beer and Angostura.

MOSCOW MULE (DIFFORD'S RECIPE) (NEW)

★★★★☆

Glass: Copper mug or Collins glass
Garnish: Lime slice and mint sprigs
Method: SHAKE first four ingredients with ice and strain into ice-filled mug/glass. TOP with ginger beer and crushed ice.

2	shots	Ketel One Vodka
½	shot	Freshly squeezed lime juice
¼	shot	King's Ginger Liqueur
1	dash	Angostura Aromatic Bitters
Top with		Gosling's Stormy Ginger Beer

Origin: Adaptation of a classic by yours truly in December 2014.
Comment: A dash of bitters adds extra interest to this classic with a dash of ginger liqueur boosting the ginger flavour and adding the merest touch of sweetness to balance the use of bitters.

MOSQUITO

★★★★☆

Glass: Old-fashioned
Garnish: Mint sprig
Method: SHAKE all ingredients with ice and fine strain into ice-filled glass.

6	fresh	Mint leaves
2	shots	BarSol Mosto Verde Italia pisco
1	shot	Freshly squeezed lime juice
¾	shot	Sugar syrup (2 sugar to 1 water)

Origin: Adapted from a 2008 recipe created by Hans Hilburg at El Pisquerito, Cuzco, Peru.
Comment: A short pisco based Mojito.

MOTHER RUM

★★★★½

Glass: Old-fashioned
Garnish: Cinnamon stick
Method: STIR all ingredients with ice and strain into ice-filled glass.

2	shots	Bacardi Carta Ocho aged rum
¼	shot	White crème de cacao liqueur
¼	shot	Maple syrup

Origin: Created in 2006 by Milo Rodriguez at Crazy Bear, London, England.
Comment: To quote Milo, this drink is 'warm and comforting, just like the drinks my mother made.'

MOTOX

★★★★☆

Glass: Martini
Garnish: Coriander leaf
Method: MUDDLE ginger and coriander in base of shaker. Add other ingredients, SHAKE with ice and fine strain into chilled glass.

1	slice	Fresh root ginger (thumbnail sized)
10	fresh	Coriander (cilantro) leaves
1½	shot	Ketel One Citroen vodka
½	shot	Pallini Limoncello
1	shot	Fresh pressed pineapple juice
1	shot	Pressed apple juice

Origin: Adapted from a drink discovered in 2005 at Mo Bar, Landmark Mandarin Oriental Hotel, Hong Kong.
Comment: Each sip is fruity, lemon fresh and followed by a hot ginger hit.

MOUNTAIN

★★★★☆

Glass: Coupe
Garnish: Luxardo Maraschino cherry
Method: SHAKE all ingredients with ice and fine strain into chilled glass.

2	shots	Bourbon whiskey
¾	shot	Martini Extra Dry vermouth
¾	shot	Martini Rosso vermouth
½	shot	Egg white

Comment: A perfect Manhattan smoothed by egg white.

MOUNTAIN COCKTAIL

★★★★☆

Glass: Martini
Garnish: Luxardo Maraschino cherry
Method: SHAKE all ingredients with ice and fine strain into chilled glass.

1½	shots	Bourbon whiskey
½	shot	Martini Extra Dry vermouth
½	shot	Martini Rosso vermouth
½	shot	Freshly squeezed lemon juice
½	fresh	Egg white

Origin: This vintage cocktail is thought to have been originally made at New York's Hoffman House.
Comment: Bone dry - I prefer with the addition of half spoon sugar syrup.

MOUNTAIN MAN COCKTAIL (NEW)

★★★★☆

Glass: Old-fashioned
Garnish: Crystallised ginger
Method: SHAKE all ingredients with ice and strain into ice-filled glass.

2	shots	Bourbon whiskey
¼	shot	Crème de pêche (peach) liqueur
¾	shot	Freshly squeezed lemon juice
¼	shot	Maple syrup
¼	shot	Ginger sugar syrup
½	fresh	Egg white

Origin: Created in 2015 by Natasha David at Nitecap, New York City, USA.
Comment: A peachy whiskey sour with a ginger kick.

MOUNTAIN SIPPER

★★★★☆

Glass: Old-fashioned
Garnish: Orange zest twist
Method: SHAKE all ingredients with ice and strain into ice-filled glass.

2	shots	Bourbon whiskey
1	shot	De Kuyper Triple Sec
1	shot	Cranberry juice
1	shot	Freshly squeezed pink grapefruit juice
⅛	shot	Sugar syrup (2 sugar to 1 water)

Comment: Fruity citrus flavours balance the richness of the whiskey.

MR ANTHONY (NEW)

★★★★☆

Glass: Old-fashioned
Garnish: Lemon zest twist
Method: SHAKE all ingredients with ice and strain into ice-filled glass.

1	shot	Rutte Old Simon oude jenever
1	shot	Islay single malt Scotch whisky
2	spoon	Runny honey
¼	shot	King's Ginger Liqueur
¾	shot	Freshly squeezed lemon juice

Origin: Adapted from a drink discovered in February 2014 at Mystique, Amsterdam, Netherlands.
Comment: A genever based Penicillin - smoke and honey with subtle spice and plenty of Scottish attitude.

MR KAPPES

★★★★☆

Glass: Coupe
Garnish: Lemon zest twist
Method: STIR all ingredients with ice and fine strain into chilled glass.

2	shots	Kirschwasser eau de vie
1	shot	Lillet Blanc
1	shot	Romate Pedro Ximénez sherry

Origin: Created in 2009 by Diana Haider, Frankfurt, Germany.
Comment: A quality Germanic brand of Kirschwasser is key to this complex drink.

MR PRESIDENT

★★★★☆

Glass: Coupe
Garnish: Orange zest twist
Method: STIR all ingredients with ice and fine strain into chilled glass.

1¼	shots	Bacardi Carta Blanca light rum
¾	shot	Martini Rosso vermouth
½	shot	Campari Bitter

Origin: Adapted from a drink created in 2010 by Andy Pearson, London, England for Barak Obama.
Comment: A combination of the El-Presidente and Negroni. A drink Campari lovers will appreciate.

MRS ROBINSON #1

★★★★☆

Glass: Old-fashioned
Garnish: Raspberries
Method: MUDDLE raspberries in base of shaker. Add next 4 ingredients, SHAKE with ice and strain into ice-filled glass. TOP with soda, lightly stir and serve with straws.

8	fresh	Raspberries
2	shots	Bourbon whiskey
1	shot	Lejay Crème de Framboise liqueur
¼	shot	Freshly squeezed lemon juice
¼	shot	Sugar syrup (2 sugar to 1 water)
Top with		Soda (club soda)

Origin: Created in 2000 by Max Warner at Long Bar, Sanderson, London, England.
Comment: Rich raspberry fruit laced with bourbon.

MRS ROBINSON #2

★★★⯪☆

Glass: Martini
Garnish: Orange slice
Method: SHAKE all ingredients with ice and fine strain into chilled glass.

2½ shots   Ketel One Vodka
½   shot   Galliano L'Autentico liqueur
1   shot   Freshly squeezed orange juice

Origin: Discovered in 2006 on Kyle Branch's Cocktail Hotel blog. (www.cocktailhotel.blogspot.com).
Comment: A short Harvey Wallbanger.

MUDSLIDE

★★★★☆

Glass: Hurricane
Garnish: Crumbled Cadbury's Flake bar
Method: BLEND all ingredients with a 12oz scoop of crushed ice and serve with straws.

1½ shots   Baileys Irish cream liqueur
1½ shots   Ketel One Vodka
1½ shots   Coffee liqueur
3   scoop   Vanilla ice cream

Comment: A simply scrumptious dessert drink with whiskey cream and coffee.

MUJER VERDE

★★★★☆

Glass: Martini
Garnish: Lime zest twist
Method: SHAKE all ingredients with ice and fine strain into chilled glass.

1   shot   Rutte Dry Gin
½   shot   Green Chartreuse liqueur
½   shot   Yellow Chartreuse liqueur
½   shot   Freshly squeezed lime juice
¼   shot   Sugar syrup (2 sugar to 1 water)
¾   shot   Chilled water (omit if wet ice)

Origin: Discovered in 2006 at Absinthe, San Francisco, where 'D Mexican' resurrected this drink from his hometown of Guadalajara.
Comment: The name means 'Green Lady'... and she packs a Chartreuse punch.

MULATA DAIQUIRI

★★★★⯪

Glass: Martini
Garnish: Lime wedge
Method: SHAKE all ingredients with ice and fine strain into chilled glass.

2   shots   Bacardi Carta Ocho aged rum
¼   shot   Dark crème de cacao liqueur
¼   shot   White crème de cacao liqueur
½   shot   Freshly squeezed lime juice
¼   shot   Sugar syrup (2 sugar to 1 water)

Origin: Thought to have been created by Constantino (Constante) Ribalaigua Vert at Havana's Floridita bar but in the Cuban book, 'Bartender's Sixth Sense' the cocktail is said to have been created in the 1940s by one Jose Maria Vazquez.

The drink was originally made with Bacardi Elixir, a liqueur made by infusing plums in rum. Crème de cacao liqueur has been used a substitute since the 1970s. Production of Bacardi Elixir ended when Bacardi was forced to leave Cuba but a small batch of around 60 bottles were made to celebrate Bacardi Legacy Competition in April 2013.
Comment: A classic Daiquiri with aged rum and a hint of chocolate.

MULATA DAISY

★★★★☆

Glass: Coupe
Garnish: Chocolate powder rim
Method: MUDDLE fennel seeds in base of shaker. Add other ingredients, **SHAKE** with ice and fine strain into chilled glass.

1½ spoon   Fennel seeds
1¾ shots   Bacardi Carta Blanca light rum
1   shot   Dark crème de cacao liqueur
¾   shot   Freshly squeezed lime juice
¼   shot   Galliano L'Autentico liqueur

Origin: Created in 2008 by Ago Perrone at The Connaught, London, England. This drink won the 2009 Bacardi Legacy Final.
Comment: Delicately spiced and subtly chocolatey.

THE MULBERRY

★★★★⯪

Glass: Old-fashioned
Garnish: Mint sprig
Method: STIR jam and gin in base of shaker to dissolve jam. Add mint, Pimm's and lemon juice, **SHAKE** with ice and fine strain into ice-filled glass. **TOP** with elderflower pressé.

1½ shots   Rutte Dry Gin
1   spoon   Mulberry jam
7   fresh   Mint leaves
1   shot   Pimm's No.1 Cup
½   shot   Freshly squeezed lemon juice
Top with   Elderflower pressé

Origin: Created in 2006 at The Manor House Hotel, Moreton-in-Marsh, Gloucestershire, England. The Manor House Hotel make their mulberry jam using fruit from the Mulberry Tree which grows in the hotels grounds and is thought to be over 350 years old.
Comment: Jammy mulberry fruit, Pimm's and gin freshened with mint and lemon, served on the rocks.

MULE'S HIND LEG

★★★★⯪

Glass: Martini
Garnish: Apricot slice
Method: SHAKE all ingredients with ice and fine strain into chilled glass.

1   shot   Rutte Dry Gin
1   shot   Bénédictine D.O.M. liqueur
1   shot   Calvados brandy
¾   shot   De Kuyper XO Apricot Brandy
¼   shot   Maple syrup
½   shot   Chilled water (omit if wet ice)

Origin: My version of a classic 1920's recipe.
Comment: Apricot and maple syrup dominate this medium sweet drink.

MULLED APPLE BLACK (NEW)

★★★★⯪

Glass: Toddy
Garnish: Blackberries on stick
Method: HEAT all ingredients and pour into warmed glass.

1½ shots Calvados brandy
3½ shots Pago Blackcurrant
1 shot   Claret red wine

Origin: Created in February 2015 by yours truly at the Cabinet Room, London, England.
Comment: Fruity rich and warming with apple (calvados) and blackberry.

MULLED WINE

★★★★☆

Glass: Toddy
Garnish: Cinnamon stick
Method: POUR ingredients into pre-warmed glass and stir.

5 dried   Clove
1 pinch Freshly grated nutmeg
1 pinch Ground cinnamon
1½ shots Tawny port
1½ shots Shiraz red wine
1 wedge Fresh orange
½ shot   Freshly squeezed lemon juice
2 spoon Runny honey
½ shot   Grand Marnier Cordon Rouge
Top with Boiling water

Comment: Warming, soothing and potent. Better if several servings are made at the same time and the ingredients mixed together and warmed in a saucepan.

MURE & LAVANDER BATIDA (NEW)

★★★★☆

Glass: Collins
Garnish: Blackberries
Method: BLEND all ingredients with crushed ice and serve with straws.

1⅔ shots Capucana cachaça
1⅔ shots Coconut water
½ shot   Lavender sugar syrup
¼ shot   Freshly squeezed lime juice
6 fresh   Blackberries

Origin: Recipe by Jorge Balbontin, Vantguard, Barcelona, Spain.
Comment: As the name suggests this creamy Batida is flavoured with blackberries and lavender.

STAR RATINGS EXPLAINED

★★★★★+ OUTSTANDING	★★★★★ EXCEPTIONAL
★★★★⯪ EXCELLENT	★★★★☆ RECOMMENDED
★★★⯪☆ COMMENDED	★★★☆☆ MEDIOCRE
★★⯪☆☆ DISAPPOINTING	★★☆☆☆ PRETTY AWFUL
★⯪☆☆☆ SHAMEFUL	★☆☆☆☆ DISGUSTING

MY SHERRY AMORE

★★★★☆

Glass: Coupe
Garnish: Grapefruit zest twist
Method: SHAKE all ingredients with ice and fine strain into chilled glass.

1¾ shots Rutte Dry Gin
1 shot   Aperol Aperitivo
¾ shot   Freshly squeezed pink grapefruit juice
¼ shot   Romate Fino sherry
2 dash   Peychaud's aromatic bitters

Origin: Created in 2011 by Nick Van Tiel and named after the 1969 soul classic by Motown singer-songwriter Stevie Wonder. Originally titled 'Oh My Marcia', the song was originally about Wonder's girlfriend whilst he was at the Michigan School for the Blind in Lansing, Michigan. After they broke up, the lyrics and title were changed to 'My Cherie Amour'.
Comment: A bitter-sweet, salmon pink, light, delicate balance of gin, herbal complexity, grapefruit and dry sherry.

MYRTLE BANK SPECIAL RUM PUNCH

★★★★⯪

Glass: Old-fashioned
Garnish: Luxardo Maraschino cherry
Method: SHAKE all ingredients with ice and strain into ice-filled glass.

2 shots Pot still Jamaican rum
1 shot Freshly squeezed lime juice
⅛ shot Cherry Heering Liqueur
½ shot Sugar syrup (2 sugar to 1 water)
½ shot Chilled water (omit if wet ice)

Origin: Originally made at the Myrtle Bank Hotel, Kingston, Jamaica. Built in the mid-1800s, the Myrtle Bank, was converted from a shipyard into a select boarding house. After the hotel was destroyed in the 1907 earthquake it was reconstructed in 1918 and was then the largest hotel in Jamaica with 205 rooms and a filtered salt water pool.
Comment: A rich fruity Daiquiri with tangy molasses.

NACIONAL DAIQUIRI #1

★★★★⯪

Glass: Martini
Garnish: Luxardo Maraschino cherry
Method: SHAKE all ingredients with ice and fine strain into chilled glass.

2 shots Bacardi Carta Blanca light rum
¾ shot   De Kuyper XO Apricot Brandy
½ shot   Freshly squeezed lime juice
¾ shot   Chilled water (omit if wet ice)

Origin: An old classic named after the Hotel Nacional, Havana, Cuba, where it was created.
Comment: A sophisticated complex apricot Daiquiri.

NACIONAL DAIQUIRI #2

★★★★½

Glass: Martini
Garnish: Luxardo Maraschino cherry
Method: SHAKE all ingredients with ice and fine strain into chilled glass.

2 shots Bacardi Carta Blanca light rum
½ shot De Kuyper XO Apricot Brandy
1½ shots Fresh pressed pineapple juice
½ shot Freshly squeezed lime juice

Comment: An apricot Daiquiri with extra interest courtesy of pineapple.

NAILED

★★★★½☆

Glass: Shot
Garnish: None
Method: Carefully pour so as to LAYER ingredients in the following order.

½ shot Drambuie liqueur
½ shot Dewar's 12 Year Old Scotch whisky

Origin: Created in 2010 by yours truly at the Cabinet Room, London, England.
Comment: A shamelessly obvious twist on the classic Rusty Nail.

NAKED & FAMOUS (NEW)

★★★★★

Glass: Coupe
Garnish: Lime wedge
Method: STIR all ingredients with ice and strain into chilled glass.

¾ shot Del Maguey VIDA Mezcal
¾ shot Aperol
¾ shot Yellow Chartreuse
¾ shot Freshly squeezed lime juice

Comment: Salmon pink in colour. Mezcal adds earthy complexity to this bittersweet, citrusy fresh, aperitivo cocktail.
Origin: Created in 2011 by Joaquín Simó at Death & Co., New York City, USA.

NANTUCKET

★★★½☆

Glass: Collins
Garnish: Lime wedge
Method: SHAKE all ingredients with ice and strain into ice-filled glass.

2 shots Bacardi Carta Blanca light rum
3 shots Cranberry juice
2 shots Freshly squeezed pink grapefruit juice

Origin: Popularised by the Cheers bar chain, this is named after the beautiful island off Cape Cod.
Comment: Essentially a Seabreeze with rum in place of vodka.

NAPOLEON MARKET

★★★★½

Glass: Martini
Garnish: Lemon zest twist
Method: SHAKE all ingredients with ice and fine strain into chilled glass.

2 shots Rutte Dry Gin
¼ shot De Kuyper Triple Sec
¼ shot Fernet Branca
½ shot Dubonnet Red
½ shot Chilled water (omit if wet ice)

Origin: Adapted from a recipe in Harry Craddock's 1930 'Savoy Cocktail Book'.
Comment: A beautifully balanced, very approachable, rust coloured Martini.

NARANJA

★★★★☆

Glass: Old-fashioned
Garnish: Orange zest twist
Method: STIR one shot of rum with two ice cubes in a glass. Add sugar syrup, vermouth, bitters and two more ice cubes. STIR some more and add another two ice cubes and the rest of the rum. STIR lots more and add more ice.

2 shots Bacardi Carta Blanca light rum
⅛ shot Cinzano Orancio Vermouth
¼ shot Sugar syrup (2 sugar to 1 water)
2 dash Angostura Orange Bitters

Origin: Created in 2008 by Chris Edwardes at Hanbury Club, Brighton, England.
Comment: Rum based twist on the classic Old-Fashioned.

NARANJA DAIQUIRI

★★★★☆

Glass: Martini
Garnish: Orange slice
Method: SHAKE all ingredients with ice and fine strain into chilled glass.

1¾ shots Bacardi Carta Blanca light rum
¾ shot Grand Marnier Cordon Rouge
1 shot Freshly squeezed orange juice
½ shot Freshly squeezed lime juice
⅛ shot Sugar syrup (2 sugar to 1 water)

Comment: The Latino version of an orange Daiquiri.

NATHALIA

★★★½☆

Glass: Old-fashioned
Garnish: Orange zest twist
Method: STIR all ingredients with ice and strain into ice-filled glass.

2 shots Martell VSOP Médaillon cognac
¾ shot Yellow Chartreuse liqueur
¾ shot Crème de banane liqueur
1 dash Angostura Orange Bitters

Origin: Adapted from a drink discovered in 2006 at English Bar, Regina Hotel, Paris, France.
Comment: Herbal bananas and cognac. Be warned, the subtle sweetness conceals its strength

NAUTILUS

★★★★☆

Glass: Collins
Garnish: Mint sprig
Method: SHAKE all ingredients with ice and strain into ice-filled glass. Serve with straws.

2	shots	Patrón reposado tequila
2	shots	Cranberry juice
1	shot	Freshly squeezed lime juice
½	shot	Sugar syrup (2 sugar to 1 water)

Origin: Adapted from a drink created by Victor Bergeron (Trader Vic).
Comment: Basically a Margarita lengthened with cranberry juice.

NAVIGATOR

★★★★☆

Glass: Martini
Garnish: Lemon zest twist
Method: SHAKE all ingredients with ice and fine strain into chilled glass.

2	shots	Rutte Dry Gin
¾	shot	Pallini Limoncello
1¼	shots	Freshly squeezed pink grapefruit juice

Origin: Created in 2005 by Jamie Terrell, London, England.
Comment: This fruity, grapefruit-led drink is pleasantly bitter and sour.

NAVY GROG

★★★★☆

Glass: Old-fashioned
Garnish: Lemon wedge
Method: STIR honey with rum in base of shaker to dissolve honey. Add next 3 ingredients, SHAKE with ice and strain into ice-filled glass.

3	spoon	Runny honey
1½	shots	Pusser's Navy Rum (54.5%)
¼	shot	Freshly squeezed lime juice
2	dash	Angostura Aromatic Bitters
2½	shots	Chilled water

Comment: An extremely drinkable, honeyed cocktail.

NEAL'S BARBADOS COSMOPOLITAN

★★★★☆

Glass: Martini
Garnish: Orange zest twist
Method: SHAKE all ingredients with ice and fine strain into chilled glass.

1¼	shots	Bacardi Carta Oro rum
¾	shot	De Kuyper Triple Sec
½	shot	Freshly squeezed lime juice
1½	shots	Cranberry juice

Origin: Discovered in 2006 at Bix, San Francisco, USA.
Comment: Your standard Cosmo made more complex by a slug of warm Caribbean spirit.

NEGRONI AND THE GOAT (NEW)

★★★★☆

Glass: Old-fashioned
Garnish: Orange zest twist
Method: STIR all ingredients with ice and strain into ice-filled glass.

1½	shots	Rutte Dry Gin
¾	shot	Aperol Aperitivo
¾	shot	Carpano Antica Formula
½	shot	Amaro liqueur

Origin: This riff on a Negroni was originally served straight-up in a coup and comes from The Girl and the Goat restaurant in Chicago, USA where it was created in 2014.
Comment: Negroni in name and Negroni in style with the sweetness of Aperol countered by the use of amaro.

Negroni cocktail

James Bond drank a negroni when he wasn't in the mood for a martini, and when Orson Welles tried his first one in 1947 he commented, "The bitters are excellent for your liver, the gin is bad for you. They balance each other."

The origins of many cocktails are often the subject of debate but in the case of the Negroni it's an interchange that has become quite heated. Negroni is a very old family name and it's a family that seems to have different branches, or not as the case may be, not to mention the fact that Italian and French pride is at stake.

By most popular accounts, the Negroni affords its origins in an aperitivo popular in Northern Italy at the beginning of the twentieth century. Gaz Regan in ' The Negroni ' writes "thanks to Dom Costa, we know that the Negroni was from the loins of the Americano, the Americano was based on the Milano-Torino, and in turn, the Milano-Torino was a variation on the Torino-Milano". The Milano-Torino incidentally taking its name from the geographical origins of its two main ingredients: equal parts Campari (from Milan) and Amaro Cora (from Turin).

The Milano-Torino is said to have been invented in the 1860s at the Caffè Camparino in Milan which was owned by Gaspare Campari. The drink was popular with Americans who during this period of economic improvement and cheaper travel were out and about in the world exerting their influence, which in this instance included requesting the addition of a dash of soda water in their Milano-Torinos, thus giving birth to the Americano.

However, both Dale Degroff in ' The Essential Cocktail' and Anistatia Miller & Jared Brown in ' A Spirituous Journey' take the view that the Milano-Torino already contained soda and it was simply renamed as the Americano because Americans liked it. There are other reasons given as to why the drink took that name, but this is not a history of the Americano.

The story then runs that in 1919, one Italian born Count Camillo Negroni, a reputed wide boy and regular customer at the Casoni Bar (later named Caffè Giacosa) on Tornabuoni Street in Florence, Italy, one day asked for a bit more kick in his Americano. The bartender, Fosco Scarselli responded by switching the soda water for gin and the combination became the Count's usual order. Other patrons of the bar soon started to ask for "one of Count Negroni's drinks" and after a while the drink simply became known as a Negroni.

The flamboyant count is said to have returned to Florence when prohibition was initiated in America having spent time as a cowboy in the wild-west and gambler in New York. It seems a shame to squash a romantic story but Colonel Hector Andres Negroni, in what has turned into quite a vitriolic argument, is emphatic that there is "no Count Camillo Negroni in the Negroni Family Genealogy, which dates back to the 11th Century... the true inventor of the Negroni Cocktail was General Pascal Oliver Comte de Negroni". He makes this remark as a customer review on Amazon feedback for Luca Picchi's book ' Sulle tracce del conte. La vera storia del cocktail Negroni'. Luca Picchi is head bartender at the caffé Rivoire in Piazza della Signora round the corner from Caffè Giacosa and "knows more about the Negroni's history than anyone else" according to Alice Lascelles in her 2015 ' Ten Cocktails' .

The Colonel is not alone with his view. In an article entitled "New Evidence Negroni was Invented in Africa - Sorry Italy" published by 'Drinking Cup' we are told that General Pascal Oliver Comte de Negroni was a Frenchman who fought in the Franco-Prussian War of 1870 and that during a soirée with his friends "introduced the Lunéville Officers Club to his signature "vermouth-based cocktail", a drink now believed to the true source of the Negroni cocktail" It would appear that this wing of the Negroni family are able to produce letters in support of their claims for a vermouth based cocktail.

As far as hard evidence for the early existence of the Negroni in its own right goes we turn to gaz 'finger stirring' Regan, who in his 'The Joy of Mixology', says that the first printed recipes he was able to find for "one of the world's finest drinks" are in two 1955 publications: 'The U.K.B.G Guide to Drinks' compiled by the United Kingdom Bartenders' Guild and 'Cocktail and Oscar Haimo's Wine Digest' published in New York.

Andrew Willet, in his blog 'Elemental Mixology' has sourced a reference to the Negroni in Horace Suttons 1950 book 'Footloose in Italy', "in the book he suggests a couple of drinks he found to be native to Italy - the Negroni and the Cardinale". Sutton's account of the Negroni however additionally includes seltzer. The earliest recipe we could source was in Jacinto Sanfeliu Brucart's 1949 book 'El Bar: Evolución y arte del cocktail' which has a Negroni recipe that is ¼ gin, ¼ Italian vermouth and ½ Campari. And then of course there is the reputed Orson Welles quote of 1947, which he is said to have made in correspondence with the Coshocton Tribune while filming Black Magic in Rome.

Much earlier than any printed references to the Negroni, there are printed recipes for cocktails that are almost the same as the Negroni, and in one instance exactly the same.

Doug Ford in his blog 'Cold Glass' writes "there had been a gin-heavy Campari blend called the Camparinete since the 19th century; I wouldn't be surprised to learn that Campari re-jiggered that drink's proportions, attached a plausible story, and the rest was what passes for history." We'd love to hear from Doug on his source for this recipe.

Jim Meehan in his 'The PDT Cocktail Book' writes that "The combination of gin, sweet vermouth and Campari, showed up in French and Spanish cocktail books such as J S Brucart's 1943 'Cien Cocktails' and 'L'Heure du Cocktail' before being recognized universally as the Negroni. The Camparinete in Cien Cocktails is ¼ Campari, ¼ Italian vermouth and ½ dry gin. No garnish." We found an earlier reference to the Camparinete (which is why we have gone with this spelling rather than Camparinette) in Boothby's 1934 'World Drinks and How to Mix Them' the recipe is in the same ratios as the Cien Cocktail recipe: ½ jigger gin, ¼ jigger It. Vermouth, ¼ jigger Campari, served with a twist of lemon peel.

But most fascinating of all, the recipe for the Campari Mixte in 'L'heure du Cocktail' published in 1929 is equal parts gin, Campari, and Italian vermouth with a lemon zest which is quite clearly a Negroni. This recipe is the earliest reference to a drink with the same ingredients as a Negroni mixed in equal parts we could find.

It is worth interjecting at this point that two years earlier a cocktail called the Boulevardier, which was made for Erskine Gwynne by Harry McElhone at his Harry's New York Bar in Paris, appears in his 1927 book, 'Barflies and Cocktails'. Like Harry, Erskine Gwynne was an American expatriate, but he was also a socialite, nephew of railroad tycoon Alfred Vanderbilt and most importantly for this story, edited a monthly magazine called The Boulevardier, hence the drink's name. With its one and a half shots of Bourbon whiskey, single shot of sweet Vermouth and single shot of Campari Bitter this is remarkably close to a Negroni with the bourbon replacing the gin.

Just to throw another cat in with the pigeons, Andrew Willet ('Elemental Mixology') sees links to the Negroni in George Kappeler's 1895 recipe for the Dundorado Cocktail published in 'Modern American Drinks in Chicago':

Andrew Willet writes "Calisaya bitters were (and are again) also cinchona bitters - featuring Cinchona calisaya. Campari features Cinchona officinalis. Calisaya bitters are a bit less-sweet than Campari bitters. With this in mind, we find that the Dundorado Cocktail is very close to the Camparinete Cocktail, differing only in which type of London-style gin it is based upon, which variant of cinchona bitters it is bittered with, and in the proportion of those bitters to the other liquors." Perhaps.

Glowing red in hue, the Negroni manages to be both sophisticated and simple at the same time, and is definitely for a grown up palate – for many it's simply too bitter. It has a challengingly complex flavour, makes the perfect aperitif and, though popular the world over, is absolutely de rigeur during aperitivo hour in Milan.

In line with our preference, most Negroni recipes call for the ingredients to be mixed in equal parts. In his 2003 'The Joy of Mixology' Gary Regan emphatically states, "don't experiment with the proportions here - the balance is of primary importance.... and using equal parts of each ingredient is absolutely necessary to achieve perfection." However, by 2012 Gary had become 'gaz' and in 'Negroni a gaz regan notion' he says, "you can slap my wrist and call me Deborah if it doesn't also work no matter what ratios you use." He adds, "I tend toward around 4 parts gin to one part each of sweet vermouth and Campari".

Not Deborah but Alice Lascelles adds in her 'Ten Cocktails', "if you're feeling really cocky, you can even alter the balance of the formula without putting yourself in mortal danger – just make sure you always observe that holy trinity of earthy/spicy (vermouth), bittersweet/syrupy (Campari or similar Italian bitter) and strong/clean gin, vodka or even blanco tequila can work – although gin is always best, I think."

Some misguided fools call for the Negroni to be shaken but it should of course be stirred, although there is something about this no nonsense drink that does not suit fussing about with mixing glasses and strainers, so we prefer that the ingredients are assembled and mixed directly over ice in the glass. Indeed, perhaps follow gaz Regan's example and simply stir in the glass with your finger (though perhaps not when serving others).

Some bartenders choose to serve Negronis straight up in a chilled coupe in which case it's essential to give this noble drink a good stir with the ice to provide enough dilution to open up its many botanicals. Bitter and dry, but very tasty, it takes its depth from the vermouth, is centred by the bittersweet Campari and is made to sing through the life of the gin.

NEGRONI COCKTAIL

★★★★★

Glass: Old-fashioned
Garnish: Orange zest twist
Method: **POUR** all ingredients into ice-filled glass and **STIR**.

1½ shots Rutte Dry Gin
1½ shots Campari Bitter
1½ shots Martini Rosso vermouth

Comment: Bitter and dry, but very tasty. This no namby-pamby drink is traditionally assembled and mixed directly in the glass. There is something about a Negroni that does not suit fussing about with mixing glasses and strainers. To garnish with a lemon slice is a heinous crime but I am quite partial to a fat orange wedge.

NEGRONI SBAGLIATO

★★★½☆

Glass: Old-fashioned
Garnish: Orange slice
Method: **POUR** all ingredients into ice-filled glass and **STIR**.

1 shot Martini Rosso vermouth
1 shot Campari Bitter
2 shots Spumante (or brut champagne)

Origin: Pronounced 'spal-yacht-oh' which in Italian means 'mistake', this drink was created in the late 1980s by Mirko Stocchetti at his Bar Basso in Milan when making a Negroni he mistakenly reached for a bottle of spumante instead of gin. They are still served at Basso today in enormous chalice like glasses with single, giant, rectangular ice cube.
Comment: This light style Negroni has the bitterness but lacks the punch and character of the original.

NEGRONI SPUMANTE

★★★★★

Glass: Old-fashioned
Garnish: Orange zest twist
Method: **POUR** first 3 ingredients into ice-filled glass. **TOP** with spumante and lightly **STIR**.

1 shot Martini Rosso vermouth
1 shot Campari Bitter
1 shot Rutte Dry Gin
Top with Spumante (or brut champagne)

Comment: A Negroni lengthened with sparkling wine. Every Negroni drinker should try this variation

NEGRONI TREDICI

★★★★⯪

Glass: Old-fashioned
Garnish: Lemon zest twist (discarded) & orange wedge
Method: STIR all ingredients with ice and strain into chilled glass.

2	shots	Rutte Dry Gin
¼	shot	Cynar
¼	shot	Campari Bitter
1	shot	Martini Rosso vermouth

Origin: Adapted from a drink created in 2009 by Toby Maloney of Alchemy Consulting, USA.
Comment: Campari fans will love this Negroni twist.

NEGUS (HOT)

★★★★☆

Glass: Toddy
Garnish: Dust with grated nutmeg
Method: Place bar spoon in warmed glass. **POUR** all ingredients into glass and **STIR**.

3	shots	Tawny port
1	shot	Freshly squeezed lemon juice
½	shot	Sugar syrup (2 sugar to 1 water)
Top with		Boiling water

Origin: Colonel Francis Negus was the MP for Ipswich, England from 1717 to 1732. He created this diluted version of the original Bishop.
Comment: A tangy, citrusy hot drink.

NELSON'S BLOOD #2

★★★★★

Glass: Collins
Garnish: Lime wedge
Method: SHAKE all ingredients with ice and strain into ice.

2	shots	Pusser's Navy Rum (54.5%)
2	shots	Cranberry juice
1	shot	Freshly squeezed orange juice
1	shot	Freshly squeezed lime juice
½	shot	Sugar syrup (2 sugar to 1 water)
3	dash	Angostura Aromatic Bitters

Origin: A cocktail promoted by the marketers of Pusser's Rum.
Comment: The pungent flavours of naval rum contribute to this tasty, fruity rum punch with will warm your cockles – m' hearties!

NELSON'S BLOOD COCKTAIL

★★★★☆

Glass: Coupe
Garnish: Lemon zest twist
Method: STIR all ingredients with ice and strain into chilled glass.

| 1½ | shots | Martell VSOP Médaillon cognac |
| 1½ | shots | Ruby port |

Origin: After the Battle of Trafalgar (21 October 1805) when the British Royal Navy demonstrated its navy supremacy by conquering the combined fleets of the French and Spanish Navies the Franco-Spanish fleet lost twenty-two ships without a single British vessel being lost. However, the English lost Admiral Lord Nelson who was mortally wounded during the battle aboard HMS Victory.

To preserve Nelson's body during the return voyage to England, the ship's surgeon ordered that his body be placed in a barrel of French brandy. Although this was lashed to the deck and guarded, stories abound of sailors drinking the brandy out of respect for their commander, Nelson.
Comment: This carpet scary, appropriately named, blood red cocktail balances the rich fruitiness of port with the fortifying complexity of cognac. A popular drink in classic British pubs.

NESSIE COCKTAIL (NEW)

★★★★⯪

Glass: Coupe
Garnish: Orange zest twist curled to resemble Nessie
Method: STIR all ingredients with ice and strain into chilled glass.

1½	shots	Dewar's 12 Year Old Scotch whisky
¼	shot	Islay single malt Scotch whisky
¾	shot	Martini Rosso vermouth
¼	shot	Nocello walnut liqueur
⅛	shot	Romate Pedro Ximénez sherry
2	dash	Whiskey Barrel Aged Bitters

Origin: Created in January 2015 by yours truly in tribute to the Loch Ness Monster, a.k.a. Nessie, who reputedly inhabits Loch Ness in the Scottish Highlands.
Comment: A Rob Roy (Scotch Manhattan) with nocello walnut liqueur and Pedro Ximénez sherry.

NETHERLAND COCKTAIL

★★★★☆

Glass: Coupe
Garnish: Orange zest twist
Method: SHAKE all ingredients with ice and fine strain into chilled glass.

2	shots	Martell VSOP Médaillon cognac
⅔	shot	Orange Curaçao liqueur
1	dash	Angostura Orange Bitters

Origin: Created in the early 1900s as the house cocktail at the New Netherland Hotel, on Fifth Avenue (at 59th Street) New York City, which was for a period the tallest hotel in the world.
Comment: There will be those that call for this cocktail to be stirred. If you are going to deviate from the original, our advice would be to make this frothier by adding a dash of egg white.

THE NEUTRAL GROUND

★★★★⯪

Glass: Coupe
Garnish: Orange zest twist
Method: STIR all ingredients with ice and strain into chilled glass.

2	shots	Straight rye whiskey
½	shot	Romate Amontillado sherry
½	shot	Bénédictine D.O.M. liqueur
3	dash	Angostura Aromatic Bitters

Origin: Created in 2008 by Rhiannon Enlil at Bar Tonique, New Orleans, USA and named after the median area on Canal Street in New Orleans that formerly separated the American district from the Spanish/French district (now known as the French quarter).
Comment: Sweet Manhattan - like with sherry and spiced notes.

NEVADA DAIQUIRI

★★★★☆

Glass: Martini
Garnish: Lime wedge
Method: **SHAKE** all ingredients with ice and fine strain into chilled glass.

2 shots Bacardi Carta Blanca light rum
1 shot Freshly squeezed pink grapefruit juice
½ shot Freshly squeezed lime juice
½ shot Sugar syrup (2 sugar to 1 water)

Comment: A pungent Daiquiri with the intense flavour of Navy Rum.

NEVINS COCKTAIL

★★★½☆

Glass: Martini
Garnish: Lemon zest twist
Method: **SHAKE** all ingredients with ice and fine strain into chilled glass.

1½ shots Bourbon whiskey
½ shot De Kuyper XO Apricot Brandy
½ shot Freshly squeezed pink grapefruit juice
¼ shot Freshly squeezed lemon juice
1 dash Angostura Aromatic Bitters

Comment: Whiskey and apricot combine beautifully with a light burst of citrus in this easy sipper.

NEW AMSTERDAM

★★★★½

Glass: Coupe
Garnish: Lemon zest twist
Method: **STIR** all ingredients with ice and fine strain into chilled glass.

2 shots Rutte Old Simon oude jenever
1 shot Kirschwasser eau de vie
1 spoon Sugar syrup (2 sugar to 1 water)
2 dash Peychaud's aromatic bitters

Origin: Adapted from a drink created in 2009 by Jim Meehan at PDT, New York City, USA.
Comment: A delicately flavoured and lightly balanced genever based drink with hints of Kirsch and aromatic Peychard's bitters.

NEW ORLEANS GIN FIZZ

★★★★★

Glass: Collins
Garnish: Lemon slice & mint sprig
Method: 1 / Flash **BLEND** first 7 ingredients without ice (to emulsify mix). Then pour contents of blender into shaker and **SHAKE** with ice. Strain into chilled glass (no ice in glass) and **TOP** with soda from siphon.
ALTERNATIVELY: 2 / Vigorously **DRY SHAKE** first 7 ingredients until bored/tired. Add ice to shaker, **SHAKE** again and strain into chilled glass (without ice). **TOP** with soda water from siphon.

2¼ shots Old Tom gin
½ shot Freshly squeezed lemon juice
½ shot Freshly squeezed lime juice
¾ shot Sugar syrup (2 sugar to 1 water)
⅛ shot Orange flower water
1 fresh Egg white
1 shot Single cream / half-and-half
Top with Soda from siphon

Origin: Said to be the original name and recipe of the Ramos Gin Fizz, created in 1888 by Henry C. Ramos at the Imperial Cabinet Saloon on the corner of Gravier and Carondelet Streets in New Orleans. Today, a New Orleans Gin Fizz is made with Old Tom gin while a Ramos Gin Fizz is made with London dry gin. While today's Ramos Gin Fizz always has added rose water and sometimes vanilla essence, the New Orleans Gin Fizz usually relies on the use of Old Tom gin for its flavour nuances.
Comment: The full flavour of Old Tom gin adds an extra dimension to this classic Gin Fizz. Indeed, it is properly the original Gin Fizz.

NEW ORLEANS MINUTE COCKTAIL (NEW)

★★★★½

Glass: Coupe
Garnish: Lemon and orange zests (discarded) & 3 coffee beans floated on drink
Method: **POUR** mezcal into chilled glass and swirl to coat. Discard excess mezcal. **STIR** other ingredients with ice and strain into mezcal rinsed glass.

¼ shot Del Maguey VIDA mezcal
1⅔ shots Patrón reposado tequila
⅔ shot Carpano Antica Formula
½ shot Luxardo Maraschino liqueur
⅛ shot Sugar syrup (2 sugar to 1 water)
2 dash Angostura Orange Bitters

Origin: Created by Sune Urth at Ruby, Copenhagen and adapted from the original New York Minute created by Luke Whearty at Der Raum, Melbourne.
Comment: Perhaps not a Bourbon Street staple but characterful nonetheless with tequila, mezcal, aromatised wine, maraschino and orange bitters.

NEW YORK FLIP

★★★★½

Glass: Wine
Garnish: Dust with grated nutmeg
Method: Vigorously **SHAKE** all ingredients with ice and fine strain into chilled glass.

1½ shots Bourbon whiskey
½ shot Tawny port
1 fresh Eggs (white & yolk)
½ shot Sugar syrup (2 sugar to 1 water)

Origin: One of the most famous flip-style drinks.
Comment: Flipping good. Easy and light.

NEW YORK MINUTE (NEW)

★★★★★☆

Glass: Coupe
Garnish: Lemon and orange zest (discarded) & 3 coffee beans floating on drink
Method: STIR all ingredients with ice and strain into chilled glass.

1¾	shots	Patrón reposado tequila
⅔	shot	Carpano Antica Formula
½	shot	Luxardo Maraschino liqueur
⅛	shot	Sugar syrup (2 sugar to 1 water)
1	dash	Whiskey Barrel Aged Bitters

Origin: Adapted from a drink discovered in 2014 at Duck & Cover, Copenhagen, Denmark but originally created by Luke Whearty at Der Raum, Melbourne.
Comment: Honeyed tequila and aromatic maraschino with complex herbal vinous notes.

NEW YORK SOUR COCKTAIL (NEW)

★★★★½

Glass: Old-fashioned
Garnish: Lemon zest twist
Method: SHAKE all ingredients with ice and strain back into shaker. DRY SHAKE (without ice) and strain into ice-filled glass. DRIZZLE red wine around surface of drink.

2	shots	Bourbon whiskey
1	shot	Freshly squeezed lemon juice
½	shot	Sugar syrup (2 sugar to 1 water)
1	dash	Angostura Aromatic Bitters
½	fresh	Egg white
¾	shot	Claret red wine

Origin: Thought to have been first made in the 1880s by a bartender in Chicago this drink was originally named the Continental Sour and then Southern Whiskey Sour before becoming the New York Sour, probably after a bartender in Manhattan started serving the drink and made it popular.
Comment: A classic bourbon-based Whiskey Sour made more interesting – both visually and in flavour by the addition of a little red wine.

NEW YORK, NEW YORK

★★★½☆

Glass: Coupe
Garnish: Luxardo Maraschino cherry
Method: STIR all ingredients with ice and strain into chilled glass.

1½	shots	Bourbon whiskey
¾	shot	Apple Schnapps liqueur
¾	shot	Martini Rosso vermouth
1	dash	Whiskey Barrel Aged Bitters

Origin: Discovered January 2011 at the King Cole Bar & Lounge, New York City, USA.
Comment: This simple spirit drink is similar to an apple flavoured Sweet Manhattan.

NEW YORKER

★★★★☆

Glass: Martini
Garnish: Orange zest twist
Method: SHAKE all ingredients with ice and fine strain into chilled glass.

2	shots	Bourbon whiskey
1	shot	Claret red wine
½	shot	Freshly squeezed lemon juice
½	shot	Sugar syrup (2 sugar to 1 water)

Comment: Sweet 'n' sour whiskey and wine.

NEXT TO LAST WORD (NEW)

★★★★☆

Glass: Coupe
Garnish: Lime zest twist
Method: SHAKE all ingredients with ice and fine strain into chilled glass.

¾	shot	Rutte Dry Gin
¾	shot	Luxardo Maraschino liqueur
¾	shot	St-Germain elderflower liqueur
¾	shot	Freshly squeezed lemon juice

Comment: A floral riff on the classic Last Word with maraschino to the fore.

NIAGARA FALLS

★★★½☆

Glass: Flute
Garnish: Physalis (cape gooseberry)
Method: SHAKE first four ingredients with ice and strain into chilled glass. TOP with ginger ale and lightly stir.

1	shot	Ketel One Vodka
1	shot	Grand Marnier Cordon Rouge
½	shot	Freshly squeezed lemon juice
¼	shot	Sugar syrup (2 sugar to 1 water)
Top with		Ginger ale

Comment: Ginger ale and orange complement each other, fortified by vodka.

NICE PEAR

★★★★½

Glass: Martini
Garnish: Pear slice
Method: SHAKE all ingredients with ice and fine strain into chilled glass.

1	shot	Martell VSOP Médaillon cognac
½	shot	Belle de Brillet pear liqueur
½	shot	Poire William eau de vie
2	shots	Pressed pear juice
¼	shot	Sugar syrup (2 sugar to 1 water)

Origin: Created in 2002 by yours truly, London, Martini.
Comment: Spirited, rich and fruity.

NICK & NORA

★★★★⯪

Glass: Coupe
Garnish: Olive
Method: STIR all ingredients with ice and strain into chilled glass.

2¼ shots   Rutte Dry Gin
¾ shot   Martini Extra Dry vermouth

Origin: Created in the 1930s and named after Nick and Nora Charles, the flirtatious married couple at the center of the 1934 Thin Man comic detective film starring William Powell and Myrna Loy. In the film Nick is a hard drinking retired detective and Nora a wealthy heiress.
Comment: The classic three to one Martini.

NICKY FINN

★★★★☆

Glass: Martini
Garnish: Lemon zest twist
Method: SHAKE all ingredients with ice and fine strain into chilled glass.

1 shot   Martell VSOP Médaillon cognac
1 shot   De Kuyper Triple Sec
¼ shot   Pernod anise
1 shot   Freshly squeezed lemon juice

Origin: Adapted from a recipe in 'Cocktail: The Drink's Bible for the 21st Century' by Paul Harrington and Laura Moorhead.
Comment: Basically a Sidecar spiked with an aniseedy dash of Pernod.

NICKY'S FIZZ

★★★★⯪☆

Glass: Collins
Garnish: Orange slice
Method: SHAKE first two ingredients with ice and strain into ice-filled glass. TOP with soda, lightly stir and serve with straws.

2 shots   Rutte Dry Gin
2 shots   Freshly squeezed pink grapefruit juice
Top with   Soda from siphon

Comment: A dry, refreshing, long drink.

NIGHT VISION (NEW)

★★★★☆

Glass: Flute
Garnish: Baby carrot on rim
Method: SHAKE first 3 ingredients with ice and fine strain into chilled glass. TOP with soda.

1 shot   Capucana cachaça
1 shot   Freshly extracted carrot juice
⅓ shot   Agave syrup
Top with   Tonic Water

Origin: Adapted from a drink originally called "Natural" created in 2015 by Jorge Balbontin of Vantguard, Barcelona, Spain.

Carrots are packed full of Vitamin A, in the form of beta carotene, so are good for the health of our eyes but contrary to popular belief carrots don't help you see in the dark. This urban myth stems from WWII. During the 1940 Blitzkrieg, the Luftwaffe struck the southeast of England under the cover of darkness but The Royal Air Force had the upper hand in the dark skies due to new radar technology. First installed in RAF aircraft in 1939, the secret on-board Airborne Interception Radar (AI) could spot enemy bombers before they reached the English Channel. Not wanting the Germans to develop similar technology, to explain the success of the British pilots, the Ministry of Information spread the myth that they could see in the dark due to eating carrots.
Comment: Cachaça, carrot and tonic water make for a very interesting combo in this drink which is "naturally" sweetened with agave syrup. Perhaps more health shop/juice bar than speakeasy but unusually tasty all the same.

NINE-20-SEVEN

★★★★☆

Glass: Flute
Garnish: Vanilla pod
Method: POUR ingredients into chilled glass and lightly stir.

¼ shot   Vanilla infused Ketel One vodka
¼ shot   Licor 43 liqueur
Top with   G.H. Mumm Cordon Rouge Champagne

Origin: Created in 2002 by Damien Caldwell at Home Bar, London, England. Damian was lost for a name until a customer asked for the time.
Comment: Champagne with a hint of vanilla.

THE NINTH WARD

★★★★☆

Glass: Martini
Garnish: Lemon zest twist
Method: SHAKE all ingredients with ice and fine strain into chilled glass.

1½ shots   Bourbon whiskey
¼ shot   St-Germain elderflower liqueur
½ shot   Taylor's Velvet Falernum liqueur
¾ shot   Freshly squeezed lime juice
2 dash   Peychaud's aromatic bitters

Origin: Adapted from a drink created by Brother Cleve, Boston, USA for Tales of the Cocktail 2008. The drink is a play on the classic Ward Eight and a homage to one of the New Orleans neighbourhoods hardest hit by Hurricane Katrina.
Comment: Bourbon with a hint of elderflower, cloves and lime.

NIPPON MARTINI

★★★★⯪☆

Glass: Coupe
Garnish: Lemongrass leaf knot
Method: STIR all ingredients with ice and strain into chilled glass.
Alternatively, you can use the THROW technique.

1½ shots   Yamazaki 12yo Japanese whisky
1 shot   Martini Rosso vermouth
¼ shot   King's Ginger Liqueur

Origin: Adapted from a recipe by Martini's Guiseppe Gallo.
Comment: A delicate balance of whisky, sweet vermouth and a touch of ginger spice.

NO. 10 LEMONADE

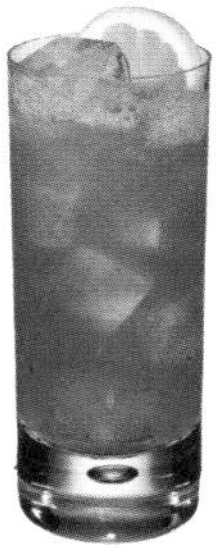

★★★★⯪

Glass: Collins
Garnish: Lemon slice
Method: MUDDLE blueberries in base of shaker. Add next three ingredients, SHAKE with ice and fine strain into ice-filled glass. TOP with soda.

12 fresh	Blueberries
2 shots	Bacardi Carta Blanca light rum
1½ shots	Freshly squeezed lemon juice
¾ shot	Sugar syrup (2 sugar to 1 water)
Top with	Soda (club soda)

Origin: Adapted from a drink discovered in 2006 at Double Seven, New York City, USA.
Comment: Basically a long blueberry Daiquiri.

NOBLE EUROPE

★★★★⯪

Glass: Old-fashioned
Garnish: Orange slice
Method: SHAKE all ingredients with ice and strain into glass filled with crushed ice.

1½ shots	Tokaji Hungarian wine
1 shot	Ketel One Vodka
1 shot	Freshly squeezed orange juice
1 dash	Vanilla extract

Origin: Created in 2002 by Dan Spink at Brown's, St Martin's Lane, London, England.
Comment: A delicious cocktail that harnesses the rich, sweet flavours of Tokaji.

NOBLESSE

★★★★☆

Glass: Coupe
Garnish: Lime wedge
Method: SHAKE all ingredients with ice and fine strain into chilled glass.

¾ shot	Martell VSOP Médaillon cognac
¾ shot	Bénédictine D.O.M. liqueur
½ shot	Freshly squeezed lime juice
1 shot	Cranberry juice

Origin: Recipe adapted from Gary Regan's 'Ardent Spirits', November 2010.
Comment: A light, sweet and sour, herbal and fruity aperitif cocktail.

NOLA DAIQUIRI

★★★⯪☆

Glass: Old-fashioned
Garnish: Pineapple wedge
Method: SHAKE all ingredients with ice and fine strain into chilled glass.

1¾ shots	Bacardi Carta Blanca light rum
¾ shot	St-Germain elderflower liqueur
⅛ shot	Freshly squeezed lemon juice
⅛ shot	Angostura Orange Bitters
1 dash	Peychaud's aromatic bitters

Origin: Created in 2007 by Lynnette Marrero at Freeman's, New York City, USA.
Comment: Light rum and elderflower with the merest hint of orange and lemon juice.

NOME

★★★★☆

Glass: Martini
Garnish: Mint leaf
Method: STIR all ingredients with ice and strain into chilled glass.

1½ shots	Rutte Dry Gin
1 shot	Yellow Chartreuse liqueur
1½ shots	Romate Fino sherry

Origin: A classic cocktail whose origin is unknown.
Comment: This dyslexic gnome is dry and interesting.

NOON

★★★★☆

Glass: Martini
Garnish: Orange zest twist
Method: SHAKE all ingredients with ice and strain into chilled glass.

1½ shots	Rutte Dry Gin
¾ shot	Martini Extra Dry vermouth
¾ shot	Martini Rosso vermouth
¾ shot	Freshly squeezed orange juice
2 dash	Angostura Aromatic Bitters
½ fresh	Egg white

Comment: This classic cocktail is smooth and aromatic.

THE NOONER (NEW)

★★★★★

Glass: Coupe
Garnish: Flamed orange zest twist
Method: SHAKE all ingredients with ice and fine strain into chilled glass.

2 shot	Bourbon whiskey
¼ shot	Giffard Vanille de Madagascar liqueur
¼ shot	Maple syrup
¼ shot	King's Ginger liqueur
2 dash	Orange bitters
½ shot	Chilled water (omit)

Comment: Charles Joly's original recipe called for Nevan liqueur (sadly no longer made) and fresh ginger. This simplified version has as a flavour reminiscent of the original combining 'made for each other flavours' in the shape of bourbon, vanilla, maple syrup, ginger and orange.
Origin: Adapted from a recipe created in 2013 by Charles Joly at The Aviary, Chicago, USA.

NORTH POLE MARTINI

★★★★☆

Glass: Martini
Garnish: None
Method: SHAKE first four ingredients with ice and fine strain into chilled glass. FLOAT cream over drink.

2 shots	Rutte Dry Gin
1 shot	Luxardo Maraschino liqueur
½ shot	Freshly squeezed lemon juice
½ fresh	Egg white
Float	Single cream / half-and-half

Origin: Adapted from a recipe in the 1947-72 'Trader Vic's Bartender's Guide' by Victor Bergeron.
Comment: An Aviation smoothed by egg white and cream.

NORTHERN GLOW

★★★★⯪

Glass: Old-fashioned
Garnish: Pink grapefruit zest

Method: SHAKE all ingredients with ice and fine strain into chilled glass.

1½ shots	**Rutte Dry Gin**
½ shot	**De Kuyper Triple Sec**
1 shot	**Freshly squeezed pink grapefruit juice**
⅓ shot	**Freshly squeezed lemon juice**
⅓ shot	**Sugar syrup (2 sugar to 1 water)**
3 dash	**Rhubarb bitters** (optional)

Origin: Adapted from a drink discovered in July 2013 at Plum & Split Milk, London, England.
Comment: A White Lady with grapefruit juice and so an extra dash of sugar to balance. Tasty.

NORTHERN LIGHTS

★★★★☆

Glass: Martini
Garnish: Float star anise
Method: SHAKE all ingredients with ice and fine strain into chilled glass.

1½ shots **Zubrówka bison vodka**
¾ shot **Apple Schnapps liqueur**
½ shot **Pernod anise**
1 shot **Pressed apple juice**
½ shot **Freshly squeezed lime juice**
½ shot **Sugar syrup (2 sugar to 1 water)**

Origin: Created in 2003 by Stuart 'Holiday' Hudson at MJU Bar, Millennium Hotel, London, England.
Comment: Wonderfully refreshing: apple and anis served up on a grassy vodka base.

NORTHERN SUN

★★★★☆

Glass: Collins
Garnish: Pear slice
Method: MUDDLE ginger in base of shaker. Add other ingredients, **SHAKE** with ice and fine strain into ice-filled glass.

2	slice	**Fresh root ginger (thumbnail sized)**
2	shots	**Bacardi Carta Ocho aged rum**
3	shots	**Pressed pear juice**
1	shot	**Cranberry juice**
¼	shot	**Freshly squeezed lime juice**
¼	shot	**Maple syrup**

Origin: Recipe adapted 2008 from LCBO Magazine and comes courtesy of Sean Murray, Aurora, Ontario, Canada.
Comment: Subtle and easy. Hard to believe this drink contains two measures of rum.

NOSHINO MARTINI

★★★★☆

Glass: Martini
Garnish: Cucumber slices
Method: STIR all ingredients with ice and strain into chilled glass.

1½ shots **Junmai ginjō sake**
1½ shots **Shochu**

Origin: Adapted from a drink discovered in 2007 at Shochu Lounge, London, England.
Comment: If good quality sake and shochu are used then this can be a great drink. However, it lacks the alcoholic bite I associate with a true Martini, so I much prefer this drink when vodka is used in place of shochu.

NOT SO COSMO (MOCKTAIL) 🗝

★★★⯪☆

Glass: Martini
Garnish: Orange zest twist
Method: SHAKE all ingredients with ice and fine strain into chilled glass.

1	shot	**Freshly squeezed orange juice**
1	shot	**Cranberry juice**
1	shot	**Freshly squeezed lime juice**
1	shot	**Freshly squeezed lemon juice**

Origin: Discovered in 2003 at Claridge's Bar, London, England.
Comment: This non-alcoholic cocktail may look like a Cosmo, but it doesn't taste like one.

NOVEMBER SEABREEZE (MOCKTAIL) 🗝

★★★⯪☆

Glass: Collins
Garnish: Lime wedge
Method: SHAKE first three ingredients with ice and strain into ice-filled glass. **TOP** with soda, gently stir and serve with straws.

2	shots	**Cranberry juice**
2	shots	**Pressed apple juice**
1	shot	**Freshly squeezed lime juice**
Top with		**Soda (club soda)**

Comment: A superbly refreshing fruity drink, whatever the time of year.

NUCLEAR DAIQUIRI

★★★★☆

Glass: Martini
Garnish: Lime wedge
Method: SHAKE all ingredients with ice and fine strain into chilled glass.

1	shot	**White overproof rum**
¾	shot	**Green Chartreuse liqueur**
1	shot	**Freshly squeezed lime juice**
¼	shot	**Taylor's Velvet Falernum liqueur**
½	shot	**Chilled water** (omit if wet ice)

Origin: Created in 2005 by Gregor de Gruyther at LAB bar, London, England.
Comment: A great way to inflict mutually assured destruction, although there will be fallout the morning after.

NUEZ DAIQUIRI

★★★★☆

Glass: Coupe
Garnish: Walnut
Method: SHAKE all ingredients with ice and fine strain into chilled glass.

2	shots	Bacardi Carta Blanca light rum
1	shot	Nocello walnut liqueur
¾	shot	Freshly squeezed lime juice
½	shot	Pressed apple juice

Origin: Named after the Spanish for walnut.
Comment: A Daiquiri with nutty notes.

NUTTY NASHVILLE

★★★★☆

Glass: Martini
Garnish: Lemon zest twist
Method: STIR honey with bourbon in base of shaker to dissolve honey. Add other ingredients, SHAKE with ice and fine strain into chilled glass.

2	spoon	Runny honey
2	shots	Bourbon whiskey
1	shot	Hazelnut liqueur
1	shot	Old Krupnik

Origin: Created in 2001 by Jason Fendick at The Rockwell, Trafalgar Hotel, London, England.
Comment: Bourbon and hazelnut smoothed and rounded by honey.

NUTTY PEAR (NEW)

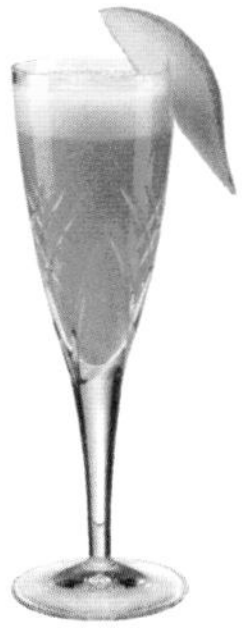

★★★★½

Glass: Flute
Garnish: Pear slice on rim
Method: SHAKE first 3 ingredients with ice and strain into chilled glass over champagne.

1½	shots	Calvados brandy
¼	shot	Disaronno Originale amaretto
1	shot	Pear purée
2	shots	G.H. Mumm Cordon Rouge Champagne

Origin: Created in September 2014 by yours truly at the Cabinet Room, London, England.
Comment: As the name suggests pear and almond are the main flavours with calvados providing backbone and hints of apple, while champagne dries and adds flavoursome effervescence.

NUTTY RUSSIAN

★★★½☆

Glass: Old-fashioned
Garnish: Walnut halves on rim
Method: STIR all ingredients with ice and strain into ice-filled glass.

2	shots	Ketel One Vodka
1	shot	Hazelnut liqueur
1	shot	Coffee liqueur

Comment: A Black Russian with hazelnut liqueur.

NUTTY SUMMER

★★★★½

Glass: Martini
Garnish: Three drops of Angostura bitters
Method: SHAKE all ingredients with ice and fine strain into chilled glass.

1½	shots	Warninks Advocaat liqueur
¾	shot	Disaronno Originale amaretto
¾	shot	Coconut rum liqueur
¾	shot	Fresh pressed pineapple juice
½	shot	Single cream / half-and-half

Origin: Created in 2001 by Daniel Spink at Hush Up, London, England.
Comment: A flavoursome after-dinner tipple for summer.

O'HENRY

★★★½☆

Glass: Collins
Garnish: Lemon slice
Method: SHAKE first two ingredients with ice and strain into ice-filled glass. TOP with ginger ale, lightly stir and serve with straws.

2	shots	Bourbon whiskey
1	shot	Bénédictine D.O.M. liqueur
Top with		Ginger ale

Origin: Discovered in 2006 at Brandy Library, New York City, USA.
Comment: Herbal whiskey and ginger.

OAXACA OLD-FASHIONED

★★★★½

Glass: Old-fashioned
Garnish: Orange zest twist (flamed)
Method: STIR tequila with three ice cubes in a glass. Add other ingredients and STIR with more ice. Top up ice and STIR some more.

1½	shots	Patrón reposado tequila
½	shot	Del Maguey VIDA mezcal
1	spoon	Agave syrup
1	dash	Angostura Aromatic Bitters

Origin: Created 2007 by Philip Ward at Death & Co., New York City, USA and now one of many tequila and mezcal-based drinks at Phil's own bar Mayahuel, also in Manhattan.
Comment: An agave influenced old-fashioned with a wonderful hit of smokiness from the mezcal.

OBITUARY

★★★★☆

Glass: Martini
Garnish: Olive
Method: STIR all ingredients with ice and strain into chilled glass.

2	shots	Rutte Dry Gin
⅛	shot	Le Fée Parisienne absinthe
¼	shot	Martini Extra Dry vermouth

Comment: What a way to go. A Dry Martini with a dash of the green fairy.

OCEANBREEZE

★★★★☆

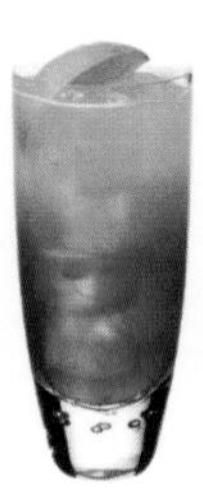

Glass: Collins
Garnish: Lime wedge
Method: POUR cranberry juice into ice-filled glass. **SHAKE** other ingredients with ice and carefully strain into glass to **LAYER** over the cranberry juice. Serve with straws.

2 shots Ketel One Vodka
2½ shots Cranberry juice
1½ shots Freshly squeezed pink grapefruit juice
½ shot Fresh pressed pineapple juice

Origin: Created in 2007 by yours truly for Ocean Spray.
Comment: Refreshingly juicy.

OCEANS 21

★★★★☆

Glass: Martini
Garnish: Orange zest twist (flamed)
Method: SHAKE all ingredients with ice and fine strain into chilled glass.

1 shot Calvados brandy
½ shot Grand Marnier Cordon Rouge
1½ shots Cranberry juice

Comment: Apple, cranberry and orange.

ODDBALL MANHATTAN DRY

★★★★☆

Glass: Martini
Garnish: Luxardo Maraschino cherry
Method: STIR all ingredients with ice and strain into chilled glass.

2½ shots Bourbon whiskey
½ shot Yellow Chartreuse liqueur
1 shot Martini Extra Dry vermouth
3 dash Angostura Aromatic Bitters

Comment: Not as oddball as it sounds, the Chartreuse combines harmoniously.

OESTERSOE COLA (NEW)

★★★½☆

Glass: Old-fashioned
Garnish: Lemon zest twist
Method: SHAKE all ingredients with ice and strain into ice-filled glass.

1½ shots Ketel One Vodka
¾ shot Pimm's No.1 Cup
⅔ shot Crème de pêche (peach) liqueur
⅛ shot Liquorice liqueur
¾ shot Freshly squeezed lemon juice

Origin: Our thanks to Joel Savard for sending us this drink which he discovered in 2014 at Copenhagen's Lidkoeb (Lidkøb) cocktail bar. This drink's name, Østersø Cola, translates as Baltic Cola.
Comment: Fruit and balanced rather than sweet or dry and with a subtle but interesting liquorice note.

OH CECILIE!

★★★★½

Glass: Old-fashioned
Garnish: Grapefruit zest twist
Method: STIR all ingredients with ice and strain into ice-filled glass.

1½ shots Rutte Dry Gin
¾ shot Aperol Aperitivo
¾ shot Martini Rosso vermouth
¼ shot Amer Picon
1 dash Angostura Aromatic Bitters

Origin: Created in 2010 by Carl Wrangel at the Oak Room, Copenhagen, Denmark and named after his girlfriend.
Comment: A tasty Danish rift on the Negroni.

OH GOSH!

★★★★★

Glass: Martini
Garnish: Lemon zest twist
Method: SHAKE all ingredients with ice and fine strain into chilled glass.

1½ shots Bacardi Carta Blanca light rum
1 shot De Kuyper Triple Sec
½ shot Freshly squeezed lime juice
¼ shot Sugar syrup (2 sugar to 1 water)
½ shot Chilled water (omit if wet ice)

Origin: Created by Tony Conigliaro in 2001 at Isola, London, England. A customer requested a Daiquiri with a difference - when this was served he took one sip and exclaimed "Oh Gosh!".
Comment: A very subtle orange twist on the classic Daiquiri.

OIL SLICK

★★½☆☆

Glass: Shot
Garnish: None
Method: Refrigerate ingredients then **LAYER** in chilled glass by carefully pouring in the order listed.

¾ shot Baileys Irish cream liqueur
¾ shot Black sambuca liqueur

Comment: Whiskey, cream and liquorice.

OLD CUBAN

★★★★½

Glass: Martini
Garnish: Mint leaf
Method: Lightly **MUDDLE** mint in base of shaker (just to bruise). Add next four ingredients, **SHAKE** with ice and fine strain into chilled glass. **TOP** with champagne.

6 fresh Mint leaves
2 shots Bacardi Carta Ocho aged rum
¾ shot Freshly squeezed lime juice
½ shot Sugar syrup (2 sugar to 1 water)
2 dash Angostura Aromatic Bitters
¾ shot G.H.Mumm Cordon Rouge Champagne

Origin: Created in 2004 by Audrey Saunders, New York, USA.
Comment: A luxurious, minty Daiquiri topped with a splash of champagne.

OLD FASHIONED CADDY

★★★★☆

Glass: Old-fashioned
Garnish: Orange slice & cherry on stick (sail)
Method: SHAKE all ingredients with ice and strain into ice-filled glass.

2	shots	Dewar's 12 Year Old Scotch whisky
½	shot	Cherry Heering Liqueur
½	shot	Martini Rosso vermouth
2	dash	Angostura Aromatic Bitters

Origin: Created in 2005 by Wayne Collins, London, England.
Comment: Rich, red and packed with flavour.

Old Fashioned cocktail

Traditionally made with bourbon or rye whiskey, lightly sweetened with sugar and aromatised with bitters this most classic of vintage cocktails is served over ice in a heavy bottomed tumbler named after the drink and garnished with an orange zest twist.

The Old-Fashioned is just that, a very old, established cocktail, but over many decades this vintage classic has changed name, originally being known as the Whisky Cocktail. It has also evolved with both the methods deployed to make it and its ingredients influenced by bartending fashions. This has resulted in six different methods/ingredients being used:

1. Bourbon or rye whiskey
Jerry Thomas inclusion of the Whiskey Cocktail in his 1862 ' The Bar-Tender's Guide', the world's first cocktail book, calls for a "wine-glass of whiskey". In those days that "whiskey" would probably have been rye whiskey with bourbon developing in the decades after prohibition. Consequently some traditionalists insist an Old-Fashioned should be made with rye, but bourbon is equally correct and the choice of whiskey should be entirely up to the personal taste of the drinker. Bourbon makes a mellow, slightly sweeter drink, while rye adds more spice and kick.

Be aware of the alcoholic strength of your whiskey. In my Old-Fashioned I like to use a combination of 1½ shot bourbon at 45% alc./vol. and 1 shot straight rye whiskey at 50% alc./vol. (When you shake a bottle of straight rye it should hold a foam for a good few seconds or I consider it too weak for my Old-fashioned.)

2. Sugar cube or sugar syrup
Older recipes for the Old-Fashioned tend to call for sugar syrup or gum syrup but over the ages a trend for sweetening with a sugar cube has emerged. This is placed in the base of the glass, dampened with aromatic bitters, and usually a splash of water, and is then pulverised and stirred into a syrup with the flat end of a bartender's spoon. All that time and effort to make syrup when pre-made sugar syrup could instead be simply poured in. As David A. Embury writes in his seminal ' The Fine Art of Mixing Drinks', "You can make perfect Old-Fashionds only using sugar syrup."

I almost understand the desire to use a cube when 1:1 (50 brix) 'simple' sugar syrup is the only sugar syrup available in a bar but not when homemade 2:1 (70 brix) sugar is available. When making your sugar syrup consider using unrefined Demerara sugar or a combination of this and white caster sugar.

3. Muddling of fruit
In the U.S. orange and lemon segments, and often a maraschino cherry or two, are regularly muddled into Old-Fashioned cocktails. The practice probably originated during Prohibition as a means of disguising rough spirits and thankfully this practice never caught on in England. As Crosby Gaige wrote in 1944, "Serious-minded persons omit fruit salad from Old-Fashioneds." However, an Old-Fashioned in not complete without an orange zest twist with some also liking an additional lemon zest twist, but that would seem to be heading back to fruit salad territory.

4. Stir in the glass or in a mixing glass
Back in 1862, Jerry Thomas called for a Whiskey Cocktail to be shaken and if you're a lover of Fruit Salads (see above) then you may as well shake your Old-Fashioned. However, correct society, good manners and leading bartenders now dictate that an Old-Fashioned should be stirred, and stirred, and stirred some more. The stirring action is essential to attaining the correct dilution. This can be achieved in a mixing glass but I prefer to stir directly in the serving glass, gradually adding more ice as I stir.

5. What bitters?
There is no doubt (well at least I have none) that an Old-Fashioned is improved by the use of aromatic bitters but the question is what bitters. Originally Broker's bitters were used but almost by default, due to their being one of the only aromatic bitters to survive, Angostura Aromatic Bitters are now most commonly used. Thankfully, a huge range of bitters are once again available including reproductions of both Broker's and Abbotts bitters, both of which work well in Old-Fashioneds.

6. Ice
If using a mixing glass to prepare an Old-Fashioned then the drink looks much more appealing and holds its dilution better if strained over a single large chunk of ice. Otherwise I recommend my usual double frozen ice (from ice-machine to freezer and freezer to ice well.)

Conclusion
I've experimented with all off the above and find myself reverting back to the method David A. Embury stipulates to make his Old-Fashioned De Luxe and the method endorsed by Dick Bradsell when the Old-Fashioned become popular in London in the mid 1990s. Stirred and stirred directly in the glass with ice gradually added.

My favoured Old-Fashioned recipe calls for both bourbon and rye. For the reasons given above I favour sugar syrup over sugar cubes and use a little more sugar than most, but then I also use a dash more of bitters and a glug more whiskey than most so I guess I'm in line with the proportions used by most.

The story of the Old-Fashioned

Like many veritable classics, the origins of this cocktail are shrouded in the mists of time. So for clarity we commissioned an expert, Robert Simonson, author of Old-Fashioned: ' The Story of the World's First Classic Cocktail, with Recipes and Lore' to write the following.

"The Old-Fashioned Whiskey Cocktail (the drink's full name) is the primordial drink, dating from the earliest days of the cocktail era. It follows the classic cocktail formula as laid down in 1806: spirit, a bit of sugar, a bit of water, and bitters. It is rare among mixed drinks in that, over the following two centuries, it never completely faded from view. However, the drink did go through a roller-coaster's worth of twists and turns.

For the first several decades of its life, the drink went by the name of simply Whiskey Cocktail. During this period, it was served 'up' and without ice, and was considered a 'matutinal' cocktail—that is, it was commonly drunk in the morning as an eye-opener. By the 1840's, it picked up in popularity as a favored drink among the well-heeled young 'dudes' of the time.

Beginning in the 1870's, bartenders, bewitched by the new liqueurs available to them, began making "Improved" Whiskey Cocktails, spiked with dashes of absinthe, curacao, maraschino liqueur, Chartreuse and other potions. This led to a revolt among old-school imbibers, who began to call out for "Old-Fashioned Whiskey Cocktails"- that is, the standard formula of whiskey, bitters, sugar, water. Thus, the name by which we now know the drink came into being.

Various people and bars have, over the years, claimed to have invented the Old-Fashioned, the most noted and persistent boast coming from Louisville's private Pendennis Club, which was founded in 1881. All have been debunked. As the Old-Fashioned began life as a "cocktail" in its most elemental form, any meaningful authorship of the drink will likely never be established.

For reasons that are unclear, The Old-Fashioned took a different form than the old Whiskey Cocktail. It was now served in the glass in which it was prepared (a short, heavy-bottomed glass which came to be known as an Old-Fashioned glass); was made with lump sugar, not syrup, which was pulverized into syrup by the use of a muddler (now an all-important tool in the creation of the cocktail); and was served on the rocks. It was now enjoyed as a sipping drink, not the knock-back it was of old. It kept to this form in the late 19th century and early 20th century, and was wildly popular.

Following the repeal of Prohibition in 1933, the Old-Fashioned again underwent an alteration. The cocktail was now commonly made with fruit, typically an orange slice and maraschino cherry, though pineapple was also often drafted into use. Sometimes, the fruit was muddled at the bottom of the glass. Again, the causes of this change are obscure. A creditable theory posits that fruit was added during Prohibition to disguise the taste of the poor liquor being used. One thing is for certain: every one of the flood of cocktail books that came out in the 1930s featured recipes for the Old-Fashioned that called for fruit. Bartenders, newly returned to service after 13 years of inactivity, duly followed the formula.

The drink enjoyed another burst of popularity in the decades following Repeal, particularly among women, who were now accustomed to drinking in public. However, by the 1970s, with the rise of vodka and disco drinks, the Old-Fashioned began to fall into eclipse. By the end of the 20th century, it was a drink mainly associated with older people.

A few geographical pockets kept the drink's name alive. It never fell from its pedestal in the United States' Midwest. However, in that area (particularly in the state of Wisconsin), it was prepared in its own sui generis way, with muddled fruit, domestic brandy and curious garnishes such as pickled mushrooms. In the UK, which never adopted the American fruited version of the cocktail, it was also never forgotten. However, bartenders favored an unusual 'stirred-down' version of the drink, in which the whiskey and ice were added gradually, and preparation could last as long as five minutes. This method has been traced back to Dick Bradsell, who credits his early mentor Ray Cooke with instructing him to make it that way. Both Cooke and Bradsell are acolytes of David Embury's "The Fine Art of Making Drinks," in which a lengthy execution of the Old-Fashioned is advocated.

The Old-Fashioned returned to its 1880's form during the first decade of this century, when cocktail historians and bartenders uncovered old cocktail manuals and the recipes they contained. The best cocktail bars began serving the drink, sans-fruit, and the Old-Fashioned once again entered an era of wide popularity, among young and old drinkers alike. Literally hundreds of new variations on the Old-Fashioned formula also began to crop up. Among these, a few emerged as modern classics, including Phil Ward's tequila and mezcal-laced Oaxaca Old-Fashioned and Don Lee's bacon-flavored Benton's Old-Fashioned."

In his 1931 'Old Waldorf Bar Days', Albert Stevens Crocket, writes of the Old-Fashioned, "This was brought to the Old Waldorf in the days of the 'sit-down' Bar, and was introduced by, or in the honor of, Col. James E. Pepper, of Kentucky, a proprietor of a celebrated whiskey of the period. It was said to have been the invention of a bartender at the famous Pendennis Club in Louisville, of which Col. Pepper was a member."

Crocket would appear to corroborate the Old-fashioned being created by a bartender at the Pendennis Club in Louisville. The club maintains that the bartender was Martin Cuneo, and that he made the drink for a Kentucky Colonel (and bourbon distiller) named James E. Pepper sometime between 1889 and 1895. In those days the clubhouse was situated at the old Belknap family mansion located between Third and Fourth Streets on the south side of Walnut Street (now Muhammad Ali Blvd.) in Louisville. This was torn down and replaced by the current opulent Georgian clubhouse, located about a block to the east, at 218 West Walnut Street, which opened in late 1928.

As Robert writes above, there are numerous references to the Old-Fashioned that pre-date that drink Martin Cuneo made for Colonel Pepper, so the Pendennis Club cannot be the drink's birthplace. The club accepts that the drink's origin pre-dates 1889/1895 but maintains that Martin Cuneo created the version of the Old-Fashioned with added muddled fruit and sugar syrup.

So it's certain that the Old-Fashioned was not created at the Pendennis but perhaps the fruity version of the drink, which became the regular way the drink was served for decades in America, was invented at the Pendennis?

I have a fondness for the Pendennis and have enjoyed drinking Old-Fashioneds at the club so I'd very much like to believe that at least the fruity version of the Old-Fashioned originated there. Sadly, apart from a 2009 paper produced by the Club there is no known evidence to support this and the recipe given by Crocket in 'Old Waldorf Bar Days' has no mention of muddled fruit so discrediting the only supportive evidence there is. More damming is the 1914 'Drinks' book published by Jacques Straub, a former manager at the Pendennis Club, which omits fruit in the Old-Fashioned entry and makes no mention of the cocktail being created at the club where he worked for two decades.

OLD FASHIONED COCKTAIL (DIFFORD'S RECIPE)

★★★★★

Glass: Old-fashioned
Garnish: Orange zest twist
Method: **STIR** bourbon with three ice cubes (dry to the touch frozen ice, not wet ice) in a glass. Add rye whiskey, sugar syrup, bitters and two more ice cubes. **STIR** some more and add another two ice cubes. **STIR** a bit more, and if you have room, add more ice.

1½ shots **Bourbon whiskey**
1 shot **Straight rye whiskey**
⅓ shot **Sugar syrup (2 sugar to 1 water)**
3 dash **Angostura Aromatic Bitters**

Origin: As with the Martini, the glass this cocktail is served in has taken the name of the drink. Its origin stems from the adaptation and renaming of a similar drink known as the Whisky Cocktail which was shaken and served up. Who did the adapting and renaming is unknown.
Comment: The melting and stirring in of ice cubes is essential to the dilution, chilling and so the taste of this sublime classic.

OLD FASHIONED COCKTAIL (US MUDDLED FRUIT VERSION)

★★★★½

Glass: Old-fashioned
Garnish: Orange zest twist & Luxardo Maraschino cherry
Method: **MUDDLE** orange and cherries in base of shaker. Add other ingredients, **SHAKE** with ice and fine strain into ice-filled glass.

2 whole **Maraschino cherries & syrup**
½ slice **Fresh orange** (cut into segments)
½ slice **Lemon** (cut into segments)
2½ shots **Bourbon whiskey**
¼ shot **Maraschino syrup (from cherry jar)**
¼ shot **Sugar syrup (2 sugar to 1 water)**
2 dash **Angostura Aromatic Bitters**

Origin: In the US orange and lemon segments, and sometimes even a maraschino cherry, are regularly muddled when making an Old Fashioned. The practice probably originated during Prohibition as a means of disguising rough spirits. This practice is almost unknown in England and as Crosby Gaige wrote in 1944, "Serious-minded persons omit fruit salad from Old Fashioneds."
Comment: This drink is often mixed in the glass in which it is to be served. Shaking better incorporates the flavours produced by muddling and fine straining removes the orange peel and cherry skin.

OLD FLAME

★★★★☆

Glass: Martini
Garnish: Orange zest twist (flamed)
Method: **SHAKE** all ingredients with ice and fine strain into chilled glass.

1 shot **Rutte Dry Gin**
½ shot **De Kuyper Triple Sec**
½ shot **Martini Rosso vermouth**
¼ shot **Campari Bitter**
1½ shots **Freshly squeezed orange juice**

Origin: Created by Dale DeGroff, New York, USA.
Comment: Bittersweet, orchard fresh orange charged with gin.

OLD MILL (NEW)

★★★★☆

Glass: Old-fashioned
Garnish: Cinnamon stick
Method: STIR all ingredients with ice and strain into ice-filled glass.

1½ shots Calvados brandy
½ shot   Islay single malt Scotch whisky
1   shot   Stone's green ginger wine
⅓   shot   Sugar syrup (2 sugar to 1 water)
2   dash Peychaud's aromatic bitters

Origin: Adapted from a drink created in 2014 by Andrea Buttier, an Italian bartender from Bologna working at The Loft, Clapham Common. Andrea originally used Laphroaig 10 year old for his malt with equal parts calvados, 1 shot Stones ginger wine, ½ shot simple syrup and 2 dashes Peychaud bitters.
Comment: Peaty Islay malt and calvados combine in this spicy and warming on-the-rocks cocktail.

OLD PAL

★★★½☆

Glass: Old-fashioned
Garnish: Orange slice
Method: STIR all ingredients with ice and strain into ice-filled glass.

1¼ shots Canadian blended whisky
1¼ shots Campari Bitter
1¼ shots Martini Extra Dry vermouth

Origin: Adapted from Harry Craddock's 1930 'Savoy Cocktail Book'.
Comment: A dry, bitter sipper for the more hardened palate.

OLE

★★★½☆

Glass: Martini
Garnish: Orange slice
Method: SHAKE all ingredients with ice and fine strain into chilled glass.

2   shots Martell VSOP Médaillon cognac
¾   shot   Licor 43 liqueur
1½ shots Freshly squeezed orange juice

Comment: Vanilla, orange and brandy combine well.

OLYMPIC

★★★★½

Glass: Martini
Garnish: Orange zest twist
Method: SHAKE all ingredients with ice and fine strain into chilled glass.

1¼ shots Martell VSOP Médaillon cognac
1¼ shots Grand Marnier Cordon Rouge
1¼ shots Freshly squeezed orange juice

Origin: Adapted from a recipe in Harry Craddock's 1930 'Savoy Cocktail Book'.
Comment: The perfect balance of cognac and orange juice.

ONION RING MARTINI

★★★☆☆

Glass: Martini
Garnish: Onion ring
Method: MUDDLE onion in base of shaker. Add other ingredients, **SHAKE** with ice and fine strain into chilled glass.

2   fresh Red onion rings
1   shot   Junmai ginjō sake
2   shots Rutte Dry Gin
3   dash Angostura Orange Bitters
⅛   shot   Sugar syrup (2 sugar to 1 water)

Origin: Reputed to have been created at the Bamboo Bar, Bangkok, Thailand.
Comment: Certainly one of the most obscure Martini variations - drinkable, but leaves you with onion breath.

OOOH GINGER

★★★★☆

Glass: Martini
Garnish: Candied ginger
Method: STIR all ingredients with ice and fine strain into chilled glass.

2   shots Patrón añejo tequila
½   shot   King's Ginger Liqueur
½   shot   Martini Extra Dry vermouth

Origin: Created in March 2008 by Dick Bradsell and yours truly at the Cabinet Room, London, England.
Comment: Subtle ginger spice flavours this dry tequila martini.

OPAL

★★★★½

Glass: Martini
Garnish: Orange zest twist
Method: SHAKE all ingredients with ice and fine strain into chilled glass.

2   shots Rutte Dry Gin
½   shot   De Kuyper Triple Sec
1¼ shots Freshly squeezed orange juice
¼   shot   Sugar syrup (2 sugar to 1 water)
⅛   shot   Orange flower water

Origin: Adapted from the 1920s recipe.
Comment: Fresh, fragrant flavours of orange zest and gin.

THE OPENING ACT

★★★★½

Glass: Collins
Garnish: Mint sprig
Method: SHAKE first four ingredients with ice and strain into ice-filled glass. **TOP** with tonic water.

2   shots King's Ginger Liqueur
½   shot   Campari Bitter
½   shot   Freshly squeezed lime juice
1   dash Angostura Orange Bitters
Top with Tonic Water

Origin: Created by Andrew Pollard for the 2010 Domaine de Canton Bartender of the Year competition winning 'Best Overall Cocktail'.
Comment: Campari and ginger topped with tonic, a surprisingly good combo. Adult and balanced. A great long drink.

A
B
C
D
E
F
G
H
I
J
K
L
M
N
O
P
Q
R
S
T
U
V
W
X
Y
Z

OPENING SHOT

★★★⯪☆

Glass: Shot
Garnish: None
Method: SHAKE all ingredients with ice and fine strain into chilled glass.

1	shot	Bourbon whiskey
½	shot	Martini Rosso vermouth
⅛	shot	Pomegranate / grenadine syrup (2:1)

Comment: Basically a miserly Sweet Manhattan.

OPERA

★★★★☆

Glass: Martini
Garnish: Orange zest twist
Method: SHAKE all ingredients with ice and fine strain into chilled glass.

2	shots	Rutte Dry Gin
¼	shot	Luxardo Maraschino liqueur
2	shots	Dubonnet Red
3	dash	Angostura Orange Bitters

Origin: Adapted from the classic 1920's cocktail.
Comment: Dubonnet smoothes the gin while maraschino adds floral notes.

ORANG-A-TANG

★★★★☆

Glass: Sling
Garnish: Orange slice
Method: SHAKE first five ingredients with ice and strain into ice-filled glass. **FLOAT** layer of rum over drink.

1½	shots	Ketel One Vodka
¾	shot	De Kuyper Triple Sec
2	shots	Freshly squeezed orange juice
½	shot	Freshly squeezed lime juice
¼	shot	Pomegranate / grenadine syrup (2:1)
½	shot	Wood's 100 rum

Comment: Orange predominates in this long, tangy, topical cooler.

ORANGE BLOOM MARTINI

★★★★⯪

Glass: Martini
Garnish: Luxardo Maraschino cherry
Method: SHAKE all ingredients with ice and fine strain into chilled glass.

2	shots	Rutte Dry Gin
1	shot	De Kuyper Triple Sec
1	shot	Martini Rosso vermouth

Origin: Adapted from a recipe in the 1930s edition of the 'Savoy Cocktail Book' by Harry Craddock.
Comment: Strong, fruity, zesty orange laced with gin.

ORANGE BLOSSOM

★★★⯪☆

Glass: Old-fashioned
Garnish: Orange zest twist
Method: SHAKE all ingredients with ice and strain into ice-filled glass.

1½	shots	Rutte Dry Gin
½	shot	De Kuyper Triple Sec
1½	shots	Freshly squeezed orange juice
½	shot	Freshly squeezed lime juice
⅛	shot	Pomegranate / grenadine syrup (2:1)

Comment: Gin sweetened with liqueur and grenadine, and soured with lime.

ORANGE BRULÉE

★★★★★

Glass: Martini
Garnish: Dust with chocolate powder
Method: SHAKE first three ingredients with ice and fine strain into chilled glass. **FLOAT** thin layer of cream over drink and turn glass to spread evenly.

1½	shots	Disaronno Originale amaretto
1½	shots	Grand Marnier Cordon Rouge
¾	shot	Martell VSOP Médaillon cognac
¼	shot	Single cream / half-and-half

Origin: Created in 2005 by Xavier Laigle at Bar le Forum, Paris, France.
Comment: A great looking, beautifully balanced after-dinner drink.

ORANGE DAIQUIRI #1

★★★★⯪

Glass: Old-fashioned
Garnish: Orange zest twist
Method: SHAKE all ingredients with ice and fine strain into ice-filled glass.

2	shots	Bacardi Carta Blanca light rum
¾	shot	Freshly squeezed orange juice
½	shot	Freshly squeezed lime juice
¼	shot	Sugar syrup (2 sugar to 1 water)

Comment: Far more serious that it looks. Sweet and sour in harmony.

ORANGE DAIQUIRI #2

★★★★⯪

Glass: Martini
Garnish: Orange zest twist
Method: SHAKE all ingredients with ice and fine strain into chilled glass.

2	shots	Clément Creole Shrubb liqueur
½	shot	Freshly squeezed lime juice
¾	shot	Chilled water (omit if wet ice)

Origin: Conceived in 1998 by yours truly, after visiting the London Dockland's based company which was then importing Créole Shrubb. I took a bottle to London's Met Bar where Ben Reed made me my first Orange Daiquiri.
Comment: Créole Shrubb is an unusual liqueur made by infusing orange peel in casks of mature Martinique rum.

ORANGE MARTINI

★★★★☆

Glass: Martini
Garnish: Orange zest twist
Method: SHAKE all ingredients with ice and fine strain into chilled glass.

2	shots	Rutte Dry Gin
1	shot	Freshly squeezed orange juice
½	shot	Martini Rosso vermouth
¼	shot	Sugar syrup (2 sugar to 1 water)
3	dash	Angostura Orange Bitters

Origin: Adapted from the Orange Cocktail and Orange Martini Cocktail in the 1930's edition of the 'Savoy Cocktail Book' by Harry Craddock.
Comment: A sophisticated, complex balance of orange and gin.

ORANGE MOJITO

★★★★½

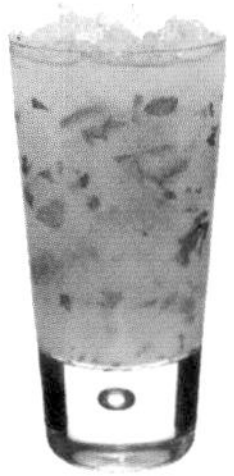

Glass: Collins
Garnish: Mint sprig
Method: Lightly **MUDDLE** mint (just to bruise) in base of glass. Add other ingredients and half fill glass with crushed ice. **CHURN** (stir) with bar spoon. Fill with more crushed ice and churn some more. **TOP** with soda, stir and serve with straws.

8	fresh	Mint leaves
1½	shots	Ketel One Oranje vodka
½	shot	Mandarine Napoléon liqueur
½	shot	Bacardi Carta Blanca light rum
1	shot	Freshly squeezed lime juice
½	shot	Sugar syrup (2 sugar to 1 water)
Top with		Soda (club soda)

Origin: Created in 2001 by Jamie MacDonald while working in Sydney, Australia.
Comment: Mint and orange combine to make a wonderfully fresh drink.

ORANGE NEGRONI

★★★★☆

Glass: Old-fashioned
Garnish: Orange zest twist
Method: POUR all ingredients into ice-filled glass and stir.

1	shot	Ketel One Oranje vodka
1	shot	Campari Bitter
1	shot	Martini Rosso vermouth

Comment: Orange and Campari always combine well especially when supported by sweet vermouth.

ORANGE SPUR

★★★★☆

Glass: Coupe
Garnish: Star anise
Method: STIR all ingredients with ice and strain into chilled glass.

2	shots	Ketel One Vodka
½	shot	Marie Brizard Anisette
½	shot	Aperol Aperitivo
2	dash	Angostura Aromatic Bitters

Origin: Created in 2008 by Don Lee at PDT, New York City, USA.
Comment: Stir well - this bittersweet drink benefits from dilution.

ORANJEY COCKTAIL

★★★★☆

Glass: Martini
Garnish: Orange zest twist
Method: STIR all ingredients with ice and strain into chilled glass.

1	shot	Ketel One Vodka
1	shot	Ketel One Oranje vodka
½	shot	De Kuyper Triple Sec
¼	shot	Martini Rosso vermouth
⅛	shot	Campari Bitter
¼	shot	Freshly squeezed orange juice

Comment: Dry, and yes, very orangey with bittersweet orange complexity.

ORCHARD BREEZE

★★★★½

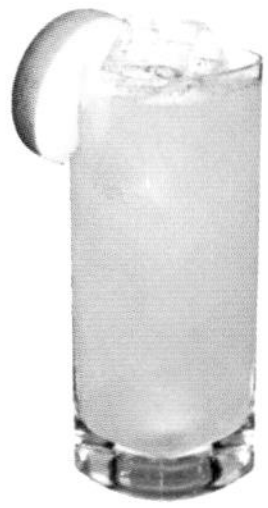

Glass: Collins
Garnish: Apple slice
Method: SHAKE all ingredients with ice and strain into ice-filled glass.

2	shots	Ketel One Vodka
1	shot	St-Germain elderflower liqueur
1	shot	Sauvignon blanc white wine
2½	shots	Pressed apple juice
¼	shot	Freshly squeezed lime juice

Origin: Adapted from a drink created in 2002 by Wayne Collins for Maxximum UK.
Comment: A refreshing, summery combination of white wine, apple, lime and elderflower laced with vodka.

ORCHARD CRUSH

★★★★½

Glass: Old-fashioned
Garnish: Seasonal berries
Method: SHAKE all ingredients with ice and strain into an ice-filled glass.

1	spoon	Damson jam (preserve)
2	shots	Calvados brandy
1	shot	Freshly squeezed lemon juice
¼	shot	Sugar syrup (2 sugar to 1 water)

Origin: Created in 2008 by Jeffrey Morgenthaler at Bel Ami Lounge, Oregon, USA.
Comment: Apple brandy and damson jam combine brilliantly in this tangy but not at all sweet cocktail.

ORIENTAL

★★★★☆

Glass: Martini
Garnish: Orange zest twist
Method: SHAKE all ingredients with ice and fine strain into chilled glass.

2	shots	Straight rye whiskey
1	shot	Martini Rosso vermouth
1	shot	Grand Marnier Cordon Rouge
½	shot	Freshly squeezed lime juice

Origin: Adapted from 1930 the 'Savoy Cocktail Book' in which author Harry Craddock writes of this drink, "In August, 1924, an American Engineer nearly died of fever in the Philippines, and only the extraordinary devotion of Dr. B- saved his life. As an act of gratitude the Engineer gave Dr. B- the recipe of this cocktail."
Comment: Be warned this dry, orangey bourbon based cocktail packs a punch.

A B C D E F G H I J K L M N O P Q R S T U V W X Y Z

ORIENTAL GRAPE COCKTAIL

★★★★☆

Glass: Martini
Garnish: White grapes
Method: **MUDDLE** grapes in base of shaker. Add other ingredients, **SHAKE** with ice and fine strain into chilled glass.

2 shots Ketel One Vodka
7 fresh Seedless white grapes
1½ shots Junmai ginjō sake
⅛ shot Sugar syrup (2 sugar to 1 water)

Origin: Created in 2004 by yours truly.
Comment: Sake adds some oriental intrigue to what would otherwise be a plain old grape cocktail.

ORIENTAL TART

★★★★☆

Glass: Martini
Garnish: Lychee
Method: **SHAKE** all ingredients with ice and fine strain into chilled glass.

1½ shots Rutte Dry Gin
1 shot Kwai Feh lychee liqueur
2 shots Freshly squeezed pink grapefruit juice

Origin: Created in 2004 by yours truly.
Comment: A sour, tart, fruity cocktail with more than a hint of lychee.

ORIGINAL SIN

★★★★½

Glass: Martini
Garnish: Star anise
Method: **POUR** absinthe into ice-filled glass and top with water. Leave the mixture to stand in the glass. Separately, **STIR** all ingredients with ice. Finally discard contents of absinthe-coated glass and fine strain contents of shaker into absinthe washed glass.

½ shot Le Fée Parisienne absinthe
2 shots Ketel One Vodka
¾ shot Junmai ginjō sake
⅛ shot Honey sugar syrup

Origin: Created in 2009 by Spike Marchant and yours truly at the Cabinet Room, London, England.
Comment: Sake and vodka with a delicate hint of honey.

ORINOCO COCKTAIL (NEW)

★★★★½

Glass: Coupe
Garnish: Dust with cacao powder
Method: **SHAKE** all ingredients with ice and strain into chilled glass.

2 shots Capucana cachaça
1½ shots Pressed apple juice
⅓ shot Romate Fino sherry
¼ shot White crème de cacao liqueur
⅓ shot Almond (orgeat) syrup

Origin: Adapted from an originally blended drink created in 2015 by Sergio Padilla at Boca Chica, Barcelona, Spain.
Comment: Dry sherry, chocolate and coconut add subtle nuances to a base of cachaça and apple juice.

OSMO

★★★★☆

Glass: Martini
Garnish: Orange zest twist
Method: **SHAKE** all ingredients with ice and fine strain into chilled glass.

2 shots Junmai ginjō sake
½ shot De Kuyper Triple Sec
¼ shot Freshly squeezed lime juice
1½ shots Cranberry juice

Origin: Adapted from a drink discovered in 2005 at Mo Bar, Landmark Mandarin Oriental Hotel, Hong Kong.
Comment: A sake based Cosmopolitan.

THE OTHER WOMAN (NEW)

★★★★½

Glass: Coupe
Garnish: Spray absinthe mist over drink (or pre-rinse glass)
Method: **SHAKE** all ingredients with ice and fine strain into chilled glass.

1⅔ shots Byrrh Grand Quinquina
¾ shot Rutte Dry Gin
⅔ shot Freshly squeezed lemon juice
½ shot Almond (orgeat) syrup
2 dash Peychaud's aromatic bitters

Origin: Adapted from a recipe created in 2015 by Lucy Horncastle at Nola Bar, London, England.

OTHER WORD (NEW)

★★★★½

Glass: Old-fashioned
Garnish: Lime zest twist
Method: **SHAKE** all ingredients with ice and strain into ice-filled glass.

1½ shots Del Maguey VIDA mezcal
¾ shot Yellow Chartreuse liqueur
¼ shot Agave syrup
¼ shot Freshly squeezed lime juice
⅛ shot Luxardo Maraschino liqueur

Origin: Discovered at Varnish, Los Angeles, USA.
Comment: Mezcal dominates this Californian riff on the Last Word.

OYSTER BAY

★★★★☆

Glass: Coupe
Garnish: Olive on stick
Method: **STIR** all ingredients with ice and strain into chilled glass.

2 shots Dewar's 12yo Scotch whisky
⅓ shot Martini Extra Dry vermouth
⅓ shot Orange Curaçao liqueur
⅛ shot Freshly squeezed lemon juice
1 dash Angostura Orange Bitters

Origin: Named after Oyster Bay, Long Island. Famous for being the location of Sagamore Hill, US President Theodore Roosevelt's summer White House.
Comment: Citrus notes and dry vermouth subtly influence Scotch in this refined, masculine cocktail.

P.S. I LOVE YOU

★★★★☆

Glass: Martini
Garnish: Crumbled Cadbury's Flake bar
Method: SHAKE all ingredients with ice and strain back into shaker. SHAKE again without ice (dry shake) and strain into chilled glass.

¾	shot	Baileys Irish cream liqueur
¾	shot	Disaronno Originale amaretto
¾	shot	Bacardi Carta Oro rum
½	shot	Coffee liqueur
¾	shot	Single cream / half-and-half

Comment: P.S. You'll love this creamy, slightly sweet dessert cocktail.

PABLO À PARIS COCKTAIL (NEW)

★★★★☆

Glass: Old-fashioned
Garnish: Orange slice
Method: STIR all ingredients with ice and strain into ice-filled glass.

⅔	shot	8 year old rhum agricole
⅔	shot	Suze Saveur d'Autrefois
1	shot	Martini Extra Dry vermouth
2	dash	Le Fée Parisienne absinthe

Origin: Adapted from a drink created in March 2015 by Julian de Féral of the Gorgeous Group for Culinaire Bazaar, Paris, France.

Inspired by Picasso and the time he spent in Paris, where at the turn of the 20th century he painted one of his most important and influential masterpieces, Les Demoiselles d'Avognon. As well as being fond of absinthe, Picasso painted a cubist interpretation of a Suze bottle. To quote Julian, "the use of rhum agricole draws parallels between the African influence on Picasso and the culture in Caribbean French colonies." Julian's original recipe calls for Barbancourt 8 rhum agricole, Suze and Dolin Blanc.
Comment: A dry and angular aperitif with robust flavours of aged rhum agricole and gentian liqueur, lengthened and tamed by dry vermouth with dashes of absinthe.

PABLO ALVAREZ DE CAÑAS SPECIAL

★★★★☆

Glass: Coupe
Garnish: Pineapple cubes, Luxardo Maraschino cherry & orange slice
Method: Place lemon zest in shaker, add other ingredients, SHAKE with ice and strain into ice-filled glass.

1	fresh	Lemon zest
1	shot	Martell VSOP Médaillon cognac
1	shot	Romate Fino sherry
⅛	shot	Cherry Heering Liqueur
⅛	shot	Sugar syrup (2 sugar to 1 water)

Origin: Recipe adapted from 1937 Bar Florida (later renamed Floridita) menu.
Comment: Sherry is most prevalent on the palate, but all the other ingredients, including the lemon zest, also contribute to this subtle, balanced and altogether a most unusual cocktail.

PADDINGTON BEAR MARTINI COCKTAIL (NEW)

★★★★½

Glass: Martini
Garnish: Orange zest twist
Method: SHAKE all ingredients with ice and fine strain into chilled glass.

2	spoon	English orange marmalade
1¾	shots	Rutte Dry Gin
¾	shot	BarSol Mosto Verde Italia pisco
½	shot	Martini Bianco

Origin: Created on the 28th November 2014 by yours truly to celebrate the premiere of Paddington Bear the movie. Paddington is a Peruvian bear who has a penchant for marmalade sandwiches – hence the use of both marmalade and Peruvian pisco in this Martini.
Comment: Tangy orange marmalade with gin and pisco rounded with bianco vermouth.

PADOVANI 〇──🔑

★★★★☆

Glass: Old-fashioned
Garnish: Lemon zest twist
Method: STIR all ingredients with ice and strain into ice-filled glass.

| 2 | shots | Dewar's 12yo Scotch whisky |
| ¾ | shot | St-Germain elderflower liqueur |

Origin: Created in 2006 by yours truly and named after a fellow whisky fan, Xavier Padovani. At the time I was working on the launch of St-Germain and Xav was brand ambassador for Monkey Shoulder whisky.

The original recipe was equal parts, after all I was trying to sell St-Germain at the time. The reduction of liqueur to allow the Scotch to shine through is the work of the chaps at Le Lion in Hamburg, Germany where they also use single malt and so have appropriately renamed this a 'Single Padovani'.
Comment: Peaty Scotch combines wonderfully with floral, delicate elderflower liqueur.

PAGO PAGO COCKTAIL

★★★★☆

Glass: Coupe
Garnish: Pineapple wedge on rim
Method: MUDDLE pineapple in base of shaker. ADD other ingredients, SHAKE with ice and fine strain into chilled glass.

2	wedge	Pineapple (fresh)
1½	shots	Bacardi Carta Oro rum
½	shot	Green Chartreuse liqueur
½	shot	White crème de cacao liqueur
½	shot	Freshly squeezed lime juice
½	shot	Chilled water

Origin: Adapted from Jeff Berry's 'Beachbum Berry Remixed', and according to Jeff originally from a 1940 book called 'The How and When'.
Comment: A Pineapple Daiquiri with two liqueurs giving a herbal chocolate influence.

PAINKILLER

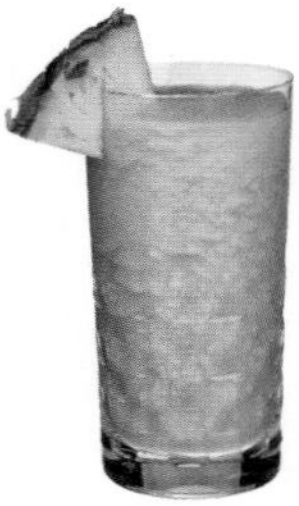

★★★★½

Glass: Collins
Garnish: Pineapple wedge & Luxardo Maraschino cherry
Method: BLEND all ingredients with 12oz scoop of ice.

2	shots	Pusser's Navy Rum (54.5%)
2	shots	Fresh pressed pineapple juice
1	shot	Freshly squeezed orange juice
1	shot	Coco Re'al Cream of Coconut

Origin: From the soggy dollar bar on the island of Jost Van Dyke in the British Virgin Islands. The bar's name is logical, as most of the clientele are sailors and there is no dock. Hence they have to swim ashore, often paying for drinks with wet dollars.
Comment: Full-flavoured and fruity.

PAISLEY MARTINI

★★★★☆

Glass: Martini
Garnish: Lemon zest twist
Method: STIR all ingredients with ice and strain into chilled glass.

2½ shots	Rutte Dry Gin
¼ shot	Dewar's 12yo Scotch whisky
½ shot	Martini Extra Dry vermouth

Comment: A dry Martini for those with a penchant for Scotch.

PALE CHARLIE

★★★★☆

Glass: Collins
Garnish: Grapefruit zest twist
Method: SHAKE first 5 ingredients with ice and strain into ice-filled glass. TOP with ale.

¾	shot	Sloe Gin liqueur
¾	shot	De Kuyper XO Apricot Brandy
¾	shot	Freshly squeezed pink grapefruit juice
¾	shot	Freshly squeezed lime juice
2	dash	Le Fée Parisienne absinthe
3	shots	Camden Pale Ale

Origin: Created in 2013 by Michele Mariotti at The American Bar at The Savoy Hotel, London. Michele was one of five finalists in the diffordsguide Beer-tail Competition for London Cocktail Week 2013 held on Friday 9th August 2013 at the Cabinet Room, London, England.

Michele's drink was inspired by Charie Chaplin's stay at the Savoy in 1889.
Comment: Zesty, fruity and refreshing with berry and stone fruit accompanying lime and grapefruit with hoppy pale ale.

PALERMO

★★★★☆

Glass: Martini
Garnish: Vanilla pod
Method: SHAKE all ingredients with ice and fine strain into chilled glass.

1½ shots	Bacardi Carta Blanca light rum (infused with vanilla)
1 shot	Sauvignon blanc white wine
1¼ shots	Fresh pressed pineapple juice
¼ shot	Sugar syrup (2 sugar to 1 water)

Origin: Adapted from a cocktail discovered in 2001 at Hotel du Vin, Bristol, England.
Comment: This smooth cocktail beautifully combines vanilla rum with tart wine and the sweetness of the pineapple juice.

PALL MALL MARTINI

★★★★☆

Glass: Martini
Garnish: Orange zest twist
Method: SHAKE all ingredients with ice and fine strain into chilled glass.

1	shot	Rutte Dry Gin
1	shot	Martini Extra Dry vermouth
1	shot	Martini Rosso vermouth
¼	shot	White crème de cacao liqueur
1	dash	Angostura Orange Bitters

Comment: A classic Martini served 'perfect' with the tiniest hint of chocolate.

PALM BEACH

★★★½☆

Glass: Martini
Garnish: Luxardo Maraschino cherry
Method: SHAKE all ingredients with ice and fine strain into chilled glass.

2½ shots	Rutte Dry Gin
½ shot	Martini Rosso vermouth
1 shot	Freshly squeezed pink grapefruit juice

Origin: A classic from the 1940s.
Comment: Dry, aromatic and packs one hell of a punch.

PALMETTO COCKTAIL

★★★★☆

Glass: Martini
Garnish: Orange zest twist
Method: STIR all ingredients with ice and stain into chilled glass.

1½ shots	Bacardi Carta Ocho aged rum
1½ shots	Martini Rosso vermouth
2 dash	Angostura Orange Bitters

Origin: Adapted from Harry Craddock's 1930 The Savoy Cocktail Book, which calls for this cocktail to be shaken.
Comment: The orange bitters are key to balancing and adding depth to the equal parts aged rum and sweet vermouth. However, go easy with those dashes or bitter orange will dominate this complex cocktail.

PALOMA

★★★★⯪

Glass: Collins
Garnish: Lime wedge & salt rim
Method: SHAKE first 4 ingredients with ice and strain into ice-filled glass. **TOP** with grapefruit soda and lightly stir.

2	shots	Patrón reposado tequila
2	shots	Freshly squeezed pink grapefruit juice
½	shot	Freshly squeezed lime juice
¼	shot	Agave syrup
Top with		Grapefruit Soda

Origin: Paloma is Spanish for 'dove' and this well-known cocktail in Mexico was created by the legendary Don Javier Delgado Corona, owner/bartender of La Capilla (The Chapel) in Tequila, Mexico.
Comment: Reminiscent of a long, fruity, Margarita.

PALOMA (SIMPLE)

★★★★☆

Glass: Collins
Garnish: Lime wedge & salt rim
Method: POUR ingredients into ice-filled glass and gently stir.

2 shots Patrón reposado tequila
½ shot Freshly squeezed lime juice
Top with Grapefruit Soda

Origin: Paloma is Spanish for 'dove' and this well-known cocktail in Mexico was created by the legendary Don Javier Delgado Corona, owner/bartender of La Capilla (The Chapel) in Tequila, Mexico. Still mixing, even in his eighties, Don Javier is noted for stirring his drinks with a huge knife.
Comment: Long, fruity and refreshing.

PALOMINO FLOR

★★★★⯪

Glass: Coupe
Garnish: Short pale yellow stalk and leaf from celery heart
Method: MUDDLE celery in base of shaker. Add other ingredients, **SHAKE** with ice and fine strain into chilled glass.

½	shot	Freshly extracted celery juice
2	shots	Bacardi Carta Blanca light rum
⅔	shot	Martini Bianco
⅓	shot	Romate Fino sherry
⅛	shot	St-Germain elderflower liqueur

Origin: Jody Monteith at The Liquorists, Manchester, England.
Comment: A subtle vegetal note comes from the celery in this unusual aperitif cocktail.

PANACHÉE

★★★☆☆

Glass: Collins
Garnish: None
Method: POUR first two ingredients into glass. Serve iced water separately in a small jug (known in France as a 'broc') so the drinker can dilute to their own taste (we recommend four-and-a-half shots). Lastly, add ice to glass.

1	shot	Le Fée Parisienne absinthe
1	shot	Marie Brizard Anisette
Top with		Chilled water

Origin: This is one of the earliest known absinthe mixtures. Today if you order a 'panachée' at a French café, you will receive beer with lemonade (shandy).
Comment: Anisette sweetens the absinthe and adds a refreshing burst of herbal aniseed.

PANCHO VILLA

★★★★☆

Glass: Martini
Garnish: Pineapple wedge
Method: SHAKE all ingredients with ice and fine strain into chilled glass.

1	shot	Bacardi Carta Blanca light rum
1	shot	Rutte Dry Gin
1	shot	De Kuyper XO Apricot Brandy
¼	shot	Cherry Heering Liqueur
¼	shot	Fresh pressed pineapple juice
½	shot	Chilled water (omit if wet ice)

Origin: Adapted from a recipe in the 1942-72 'Trader Vic's Bartender's Guide' by Victor Bergeron.
Comment: To quote Victor Bergeron, "This'll tuck you away neatly - and pick you up and throw you right to the floor".

PAPA BEAR

★★★★⯪

Glass: Coupe
Garnish: Honeycomb rim
Method: SHAKE all ingredients with ice and fine strain into chilled glass.

1 spoon Honey sugar syrup
1½ shots Martell VSOP Médaillon cognac
1½ shots Old Krupnik
¾ shot Freshly squeezed lemon juice

Origin: Created in 2008 by Tim Homewood, Dirty Martini Bar, London, England. Named after an old family friend who passed away. He was known to all of his children as 'daddy bear' so Papa Bear seemed appropriate.
Comment: Delicately spiced and honeyed cognac.

PAPA GHIRARDELLI

★★★½☆

Glass: Collins
Garnish: Orange slice
Method: SHAKE first five ingredients with ice and strain into ice-filled glass. TOP with soda.

1½ shots   BarSol Mosto Verde Italia pisco
½ shot   Campari Bitter
¾ shot   Martini Rosso vermouth
½ shot   Bénédictine D.O.M. liqueur
½ shot   Freshly squeezed lemon juice
Top with   Soda (club soda)

Origin: Adapted from a drink which was the signature cocktail of San Fanscisco Cocktail Week 21-27 September 2010.
Comment: This cocktail is named after the founder of Ghirardelli Chocolate Company, Domingo Ghirardelli, an Italian-born man who moved to Peru and ran a successful confectioners business and, following the gold rush, ultimately ended up in San Francisco. He went on to found Ghirardely & Girard (later changed to the Ghirardelli Chocolate Company), which has been in continuous operation since 1852. In his own way, Ghirardelli helped build and shape San Francisco, and his company has become synonymous with the city. Ghirardelli Square, which his company-built, has been an official City landmark since 1965.

PAPER PLANE (NEW)

★★★★½

Glass: Coupe
Garnish: Lemon zest twist
Method: SHAKE all ingredients with ice and fine strain into chilled glass.

¾ shot   Bourbon whiskey
¾ shot   Amaro Montenegro
¾ shot   Aperol
¾ shot   Freshly squeezed lemon juice

Comment: This pink/rust red drink is bittersweet with underlying bourbon character and lemon zestiness.
Origin: Created in 2007 by Sam Ross at The Violet Hour, Chicago, USA. He first made this drink with Amaro Nonino Quintessentia and Campari but switched Campari for Aperol soon after creating the drink when he started making it at New York's Milk & Honey.

PAPPY HONEYSUCKLE

★★★★½

Glass: Martini
Garnish: Physalis (cape gooseberry)
Method: STIR honey with whiskey in base of shaker to dissolve honey. Add other ingredients, SHAKE with ice and fine strain into chilled glass.

1½ shots   Teeling Small Batch Irish whiskey
1¼ shots   Sauvignon blanc white wine
2 spoon   Runny honey
1½ shots   Pressed apple juice
¼ shot   Freshly squeezed lemon juice
¼ shot   Passion fruit syrup

Origin: Created in 2002 by Shelim Islam at the GE Club, London, England.
Comment: Fresh and fruity with honeyed sweetness.

PARADISE #1

★★★½☆

Glass: Martini
Garnish: Orange zest twist
Method: SHAKE all ingredients with ice and fine strain into chilled glass.

2 shots   Rutte Dry Gin
1 shot   De Kuyper XO Apricot Brandy
1 shot   Freshly squeezed orange juice
¼ shot   Freshly squeezed lemon juice

Origin: Proportioned according to a recipe in the 1930 edition of the 'Savoy Cocktail Book' by Harry Craddock.
Comment: Orange predominates in this strong complex cocktail.

PARADISE #2

★★★½☆

Glass: Martini
Garnish: Orange zest twist
Method: Cut passion fruit in half and scoop flesh into shaker. Add other ingredients, SHAKE with ice and fine strain into chilled glass.

2 shots   Rutte Dry Gin
¾ shot   De Kuyper XO Apricot Brandy
1¾ shots   Freshly squeezed orange juice
3 dash   Angostura Aromatic Bitters

Origin: A 1920s recipe revitalised by Dale DeGroff, New York, USA.
Comment: When well-made, this wonderfully fruity cocktail beautifully harnesses and balances its ingredients.

PARADISE #3

★★★★½

Glass: Martini
Garnish: Orange zest twist
Method: Wash and cut passion fruit in half, SCOOP out the seeds and flesh into shaker. Add other ingredients, SHAKE with ice and fine strain into chilled glass.

1 fresh   Passion fruit
2 shots   Rutte Dry Gin
¾ shot   De Kuyper XO Apricot Brandy
¾ shot   Freshly squeezed orange juice

Comment: Thick, almost syrupy. Rich and fruity.

PARIS MANHATTAN

★★★★½

Glass: Martini
Garnish: Luxardo Maraschino cherry
Method: STIR all ingredients with ice and strain into chilled glass.

2 shots   Bourbon whiskey
1 shot   St-Germain elderflower liqueur
½ shot   Martini Extra Dry vermouth
2 dash   Angostura Aromatic Bitters

Origin: Created in 2006 by yours truly, originally titled 'Elderflower Manhattan'.
Comment: Elderflower replaces sweet vermouth in this floral riff on a Manhattan.

PARIS SOUR

★★★★☆

Glass: Old-fashioned
Garnish: Lemon zest twist
Method: SHAKE all ingredients with ice and strain into ice-filled glass.

2	shots	Bourbon whiskey
1¼	shots	Dubonnet Red
¼	shot	Sugar syrup (2 sugar to 1 water)
½	shot	Freshly squeezed lemon juice
½	fresh	Egg white

Origin: Created in 2005 by Mark at Match Bar, London, England.
Comment: A wonderfully accommodating whiskey sour - it's easy to make and a pleasure to drink.

PARISIAN MARTINI #1

★★★★☆

Glass: Martini
Garnish: Lemon zest twist
Method: SHAKE all ingredients with ice and fine strain into chilled glass.

1¼	shots	Rutte Dry Gin
1¼	shots	Martini Extra Dry vermouth
1¼	shots	Lejay crème de cassis de Dijon

Origin: A drink created in the 1920s to promote créme de cassis. This recipe is adapted from one in Harry Craddock's 'Savoy Cocktail Book'.
Comment: Full-on rich cassis is barely tempered by gin and dry vermouth.

PARISIAN MARTINI #2 0⚷

★★★★⯪

Glass: Martini
Garnish: Lime zest twist
Method: STIR all ingredients with ice and strain into chilled glass.

2	shots	Ketel One Vodka
1	shot	St-Germain elderflower liqueur
¼	shot	Martini Extra Dry vermouth

Origin: Created in 2006 by yours truly.
Comment: Floral, yet dry and aromatic.

PARISIAN SIDECAR 0⚷

★★★★⯪

Glass: Martini
Garnish: Lemon zest twist
Method: SHAKE all ingredients with ice and fine strain into chilled glass.

1½	shots	Martell VSOP Médaillon cognac
1½	shots	St-Germain elderflower liqueur
1	shot	Freshly squeezed lemon juice

Origin: Created in 2006 by yours truly.
Comment: An elderflower flavoured Sidecar.

PARISIAN SPRING PUNCH

★★★★⯪

Glass: Collins
Garnish: Lemon zest twist
Method: SHAKE first four ingredients with ice and strain into ice-filled glass. TOP with champagne and serve with straws.

1	shot	Calvados brandy
½	shot	Martini Extra Dry vermouth
¼	shot	Freshly squeezed lemon juice
¼	shot	Sugar syrup (2 sugar to 1 water)
Top with		G.H. Mumm Cordon Rouge Champagne

Comment: Dry apple and champagne - like upmarket cider.

PARK AVENUE

★★★★⯪

Glass: Martini
Garnish: Luxardo Maraschino cherry
Method: SHAKE all ingredients with ice and fine strain into chilled glass.

2	shots	Rutte Dry Gin
½	shot	Grand Marnier Cordon Rouge
½	shot	Martini Rosso vermouth
1	shot	Fresh pressed pineapple juice

Origin: A classic from the 1940s.
Comment: Very fruity and well-balanced rather than dry or sweet.

PARK LANE 0⚷

★★★★⯪

Glass: Martini
Garnish: Orange zest twist
Method: SHAKE all ingredients with ice and strain back into shaker. DRY SHAKE (without ice) and fine strain into chilled glass.

2	shots	Rutte Dry Gin
¾	shot	De Kuyper XO Apricot Brandy
¾	shot	Freshly squeezed orange juice
⅛	shot	Pomegranate / grenadine syrup (2:1)
½	fresh	Egg white

Comment: This smooth, frothy concoction hides a mean kick.

PARLE-VOUS IRISH COCKTAIL (NEW)

★★★★⯪

Glass: Coupe
Garnish: Orange zest twist & freshly grated nutmeg
Method: STIR all ingredients with ice and strain into chilled glass. (Consider adding a chunk of ice to the glass.)

1	shot	Martell VSOP Médaillon cognac
1	shot	Teeling Small Batch Irish whiskey
½	shot	Grand Marnier Cordon Rouge
½	shot	Bénédictine D.O.M. liqueur
½	shot	Chilled water (omit if wet ice)

Origin: Created in 2015 by Chris Strong at The Luggage Room, London, England.
Comment: An after-dinner sipper of a cocktail with cognac and Irish whiskey stirred with rich orange and herbal liqueurs.

PARMA NEGRONI

★★★★☆

Glass: Collins
Garnish: Orange slice
Method: SHAKE first five ingredients with ice and strain into ice-filled glass. **TOP** with tonic water, lightly stir and serve with straws.

1	shot	Rutte Dry Gin
1	shot	Campari Bitter
1	shot	Freshly squeezed pink grapefruit juice
½	shot	Sugar syrup (2 sugar to 1 water)
2	dash	Angostura Aromatic Bitters
Top with		Tonic Water

Origin: Discovered in 2005 at Club 97, Hong Kong, China.
Comment: Negroni drinkers will love this fruity adaptation.

PARMA VIOLET SPRITZ (NEW)

★★★★☆

Glass: Old-fashioned
Garnish: Small pack of Parma Violet sweets
Method: POUR prosecco and liqueur into glass. Add ice. Top with soda.

3	shots	Prosecco sparkling wine
2	shots	Benoit Serres créme de violette
Top with		Soda (club soda)

Origin: Created in 2013 by yours truly for Jamie's Italian Bars.
Comment: Inspired by and garnished with mini Parma Violet sweets, this spritz is flavoured with crème de violette liqueur.

PASSION FRUIT CAIPRINHA

★★★★☆

Glass: Old-fashioned
Garnish: None
Method: MUDDLE lime wedges in base of sturdy glass (being careful not to break the glass). Cut the passion fruit in half and scoop out the flesh into the glass. **POUR** cachaça and sugar syrup into glass, add crushed ice and **CHURN** (stir) with barspoon. Serve with straws.

1	fresh	Passion fruit
1	fresh	Lime (chopped wedges)
2	shots	Capucana cachaça
¾	shot	Sugar syrup (2 sugar to 1 water)

Comment: A tasty fruit Caipirinha. You may end up sipping this from the glass as the passion fruit pips tend to clog straws.

PASSION FRUIT COCKTAIL #1

★★★★☆

Glass: Martini
Garnish: Float half passion fruit
Method: Cut passion fruit in half and scoop out flesh into shaker. Add other ingredients, **SHAKE** with ice and fine strain into chilled glass.

1½	fresh	Passion fruit
1½	shots	Rutte Dry Gin
½	shot	De Kuyper Triple Sec
¼	shot	Freshly squeezed lemon juice
½	shot	Passion fruit syrup

Origin: Created in 2004 by yours truly.
Comment: Full-on passion fruit with gin and citrus.

PASSION FRUIT COCKTAIL #2

★★★★☆

Glass: Martini
Garnish: Star fruit
Method: Cut passion fruit in half and scoop out flesh into shaker. Add other ingredients, **SHAKE** with ice and fine strain into chilled glass.

2	fresh	Passion fruit
2	shots	Ketel One Vodka
½	shot	Passion fruit syrup

Comment: A fruity, easy drinking concoction.

PASSION FRUIT COCKTAIL #3

★★★★☆

Glass: Martini
Garnish: Float half passion fruit or physalis (cape gooseberry) on rim
Method: Cut passion fruit in half and scoop out flesh into shaker. Add other ingredients, **SHAKE** with ice and fine strain into chilled glass.

1½	fresh	Passion fruit
2	shots	Ketel One Vodka
½	shot	Sugar syrup (2 sugar to 1 water)

Comment: Simple but tasty, harnessing the flavour of passion fruit.

PASSION FRUIT COLLINS

★★★★☆

Glass: Collins
Garnish: Lemon slice
Method: Cut passion fruit in half and scoop out flesh into shaker. Add next three ingredients, **SHAKE** with ice and fine strain into ice-filled glass. **TOP** with soda, stir and serve with straws.

2	fresh	Passion fruit
2	shots	Rutte Dry Gin
1½	shots	Freshly squeezed lemon juice
½	shot	Passion fruit syrup
Top with		Soda (club soda)

Comment: This fruity adaptation of the classic Collins may be a tad sharp for some: if so, add a dash more sugar.

PASSION FRUIT DAIQUIRI

★★★★☆

Glass: Martini
Garnish: Lime wedge
Method: Cut passion fruit in half and scoop out flesh into shaker. Add other ingredients, **SHAKE** with ice and fine strain into chilled glass.

2	fresh	Passion fruit
2	shots	Bacardi Carta Blanca light rum
½	shot	Freshly squeezed lime juice
½	shot	Sugar syrup (2 sugar to 1 water)

Comment: The rum character comes through in this tropically fruity cocktail.

PASSION FRUIT MARGARITA

★★★★☆

Glass: Coupe
Garnish: Salt rim & lime wedge
Method: Cut passion fruit in half and scoop out flesh into shaker. Add other ingredients, **SHAKE** with ice and fine strain into chilled glass.

1	fresh	Passion fruit
2	shots	Patrón reposado tequila
1	shot	De Kuyper Triple Sec
1	shot	Freshly squeezed lime juice
¼	shot	Passion fruit syrup

Comment: The flavour of tequila is very evident in this fruity adaptation.

PASSION FRUIT RUM PUNCH

★★★★☆

Glass: Collins
Garnish: Passion fruit
Method: Cut passion fruit in half and scoop out flesh into shaker. Add next four ingredients, **SHAKE** with ice and strain into glass filled with crushed ice. **CHURN** (stir) and then top with champagne

1½	fresh	Passion fruit
1½	shots	White overproof rum
¾	shot	Freshly squeezed lime juice
½	shot	Sugar syrup (2 sugar to 1 water)
½	shot	Passion fruit syrup
Top with		G.H. Mumm Cordon Rouge Champagne

Origin: Created in 2004 by yours truly.
Comment: Rum and fruit combine in this punchy tropical style drink.

PASSION KILLER

★★★☆☆

Glass: Shot
Garnish: None
Method: Refrigerate ingredients then **LAYER** in chilled glass by carefully pouring in the following order.

½	shot	Midori Green Melon liqueur
½	shot	Passoa Liqueur
½	shot	Patrón reposado tequila

Comment: Tropical fruit and tequila.

PASSION PUNCH

★★★★☆

Glass: Collins
Garnish: Passion fruit
Method: Cut passion fruit in half and **SCOOP** flesh into blender. Add other ingredients and **BLEND** with 12oz scoop crushed ice. Serve with straws.

1	fresh	Passion fruit
2	shots	Rutte Dry Gin
¼	shot	Martell VSOP Médaillon cognac
¾	shot	Freshly squeezed lime juice
¾	shot	Sugar syrup (2 sugar to 1 water)
2	dash	Angostura Aromatic Bitters

Origin: Adapted from a recipe in the 1947-72 'Trader Vic's Bartender's Guide' by Victor Bergeron.
Comment: To quote the Trader, "A robust libation with the opulence of 'down under."

PASTIS WHISKY SOUR

★★★★☆

Glass: Old-fashioned
Garnish: Lemon slice & cherry on stick (sail)
Method: **SHAKE** all ingredients with ice and strain into ice-filled glass.

2	shots	Dewar's 12yo Scotch whisky
½	shot	Ricard Pastis
1	shot	Freshly squeezed lemon juice
½	shot	Sugar syrup (2 sugar to 1 water)
½	fresh	Egg white
3	dash	Angostura Aromatic Bitters

Origin: Created in 2006 by yours truly, London, England.
Comment: Pastis adds a pleasing hint of anise and liquorice to the classic Whisky Sour.

PASTRY WAR MARGARITA (NEW)

★★★★☆

Glass: Coupe
Garnish: Lime wedge
Method: **SHAKE** all ingredients with ice and fine strain into chilled glass.

1	shot	Patrón reposado tequila
½	shot	Del Maguey VIDA mezcal
½	shot	Amaro liqueur
½	shot	St-Germain elderflower liqueur
½	shot	Freshly squeezed lime juice
1	pinch	Salt

Origin: Adapted from a drink discovered at Bastille Cafe & Bar, Seattle, USA.
Comment: Mezcal, amaro, elderflower liqueur and salt add attitude and complexity to this Margarita-styled cocktail.

PATRICK GAVIN DUFFY'S PUNCH

★★★★☆

Glass: Collins
Garnish: Mint sprig
Method: **SHAKE** all ingredients with ice and strain into ice-filled glass.

3	shots	Martell VSOP Médaillon cognac
1½	shots	Bénédictine D.O.M. liqueur
¼	shot	Sugar syrup (2 sugar to 1 water)
2½	shots	Freshly squeezed orange juice

Comment: Over four shots of alcohol per serve means this sure packs a tasty punch.

PAVLOVA SHOT ⦿━

★★★★☆

Glass: Shot
Garnish: None
Method: Refrigerate ingredients then **LAYER** in chilled glass by carefully pouring in the following order.

| ¾ | shot | Chambord Liqueur |
| ¾ | shot | Ketel One Vodka |

Comment: Pleasant, sweet shot.

PEACH & APRICOT SPRITZ (NEW)

★★★★☆

Glass: Old-fashioned
Garnish: Fresh peach wedge
Method: POUR prosecco and liqueurs into glass. Add ice. Top with soda.

3	shots	Prosecco sparkling wine
1	shot	Peachtree peach schnapps
1	shot	De Kuyper XO Apricot Brandy
Top with		Soda (club soda)

Origin: Created in 2013 by yours truly for Jamie's Italian Bars.
Comment: This Prosecco-based spritz is fruity but not overly sweet. Peach and apricot sit brilliantly with the sparling wine, think Bellini with a hint of apricot.

PEACH DAIQUIRI

★★★★☆

Glass: Martini
Garnish: Peach slice
Method: SHAKE all ingredients with ice and fine strain into chilled glass.

2	shots	Bacardi Carta Blanca light rum
1	shot	Peachtree peach schnapps
½	shot	Freshly squeezed lime juice
½	shot	Chilled water (omit if wet ice)

Comment: A classic Daiquiri with hint of peach liqueur.

PEANUT BUTTER & JELLY SHOT

★★★☆☆

Glass: Shot
Garnish: None
Method: SHAKE all ingredients with ice and fine strain into a chilled glass.

½	shot	Baileys Irish cream liqueur
½	shot	Chambord Liqueur
½	shot	Hazelnut liqueur

Comment: Does indeed taste a little like peanut butter and jelly (jam in the UK).

PEAR & CARDAMOM SIDECAR

★★★★½

Glass: Martini
Garnish: Pear slice
Method: MUDDLE cardamom in base of shaker. Add other ingredients, SHAKE with ice and fine strain into chilled glass.

2	whole	Cardamom pod
1	shot	Martell VSOP Médaillon cognac
¾	shot	De Kuyper Triple Sec
¾	shot	Belle de Brillet pear liqueur
¾	shot	Freshly squeezed lemon juice
⅛	shot	Sugar syrup (2 sugar to 1 water)
½	shot	Chilled water (omit if wet ice)

Origin: Adapted from a drink created in 2002 by Jason Scott at Oloroso, Edinburgh, Scotland.
Comment: A wonderful meld of aromatic ingredients.

PEAR & ELDERFLOWER COCKTAIL

★★★★☆

Glass: Martini
Garnish: Pear slice
Method: SHAKE all ingredients with ice and fine strain into chilled glass.

2	shots	Ketel One Vodka
¾	shot	St-Germain elderflower liqueur
1½	shots	Pressed pear juice

Origin: Created in 2001 by Angelo Vieira at St. Martins, London, England.
Comment: Pear and elderflower fortified with vodka.

PEAR DROP

★★★½☆

Glass: Shot
Garnish: None
Method: SHAKE all ingredients with ice and fine strain into chilled glass.

½	shot	Ketel One Citroen vodka
½	shot	Kwai Feh lychee liqueur
½	shot	Belle de Brillet pear liqueur

Comment: Sweet, sticky and strong.

PEAR DROP COCKTAIL

★★★★☆

Glass: Martini
Garnish: Pear Drop sweet
Method: SHAKE all ingredients with ice and fine strain into chilled glass.

1¼	shots	Belle de Brillet pear liqueur
1	shot	Poire William eau de vie
1	shot	Pallini Limoncello
1	shot	Pressed pear juice

Origin: Created in 2002 by yours truly.
Comment: Not as sticky as the sweet it takes its name from but full-on tangy pear.

PEAR MARTINI

★★★★½

Glass: Martini
Garnish: Pear slice
Method: STIR all ingredients with ice and fine strain into chilled glass.

1½	shots	Pear flavoured vodka
1½	shots	St-Germain elderflower liqueur
⅛	shot	Martini Extra Dry vermouth

Comment: Vermouth adds depth of flavour to aromatic pear vodka and floral elderflower liqueur.

PEAR SHAPED #1 (DELUXE VERSION)

★★★★⯪

Glass: Martini
Garnish: Pear slice
Method: Cut passion fruit in half and scoop out flesh into base of shaker. Add other ingredients, **SHAKE** with ice and fine strain into chilled glass.

1	fresh	Passion fruit
1½	shots	Dewar's 12yo Scotch whisky
1	shot	Belle de Brillet pear liqueur
1	shot	Pressed apple juice
1	shot	Pressed pear juice
¼	shot	Freshly squeezed lime juice

Comment: Wonderful balance of flavours but pear predominates with a dry yet floral finish.

PEAR SHAPED #2 (POPULAR VERSION)

★★★★☆

Glass: Collins
Garnish: Pear wedge
Method: **SHAKE** all ingredients with ice and strain into ice-filled glass.

2	shots	Dewar's 12yo Scotch whisky
1	shot	Pear and cognac liqueur
3	shots	Pressed apple juice
½	shot	Freshly squeezed lime juice
¼	shot	Vanilla sugar syrup

Origin: Adapted from a drink created in 2003 by Jamie Terrell at Dick's Bar, Atlantic, London, England.
Comment: Scotch, pear and apple combine wonderfully in this medium-sweet long drink.

PEAR TREE COCKTAIL

★★★★⯪

Glass: Martini
Garnish: Pear slice
Method: **SHAKE** first two ingredients with ice and fine strain into chilled glass. **TOP** with champagne.

1½	shots	Pear flavoured vodka
1½	shots	St-Germain elderflower liqueur
Top with		G.H. Mumm Cordon Rouge Champagne

Comment: Aromatic pear vodka and elderflower liqueur paired with biscuity champagne.

PEARL BUTTON (NEW)

★★★★☆

Glass: Collins
Garnish: Half grapefruit slice
Method: **SHAKE** first 3 ingredients with ice and strain into ice-filled glass. **TOP** with lemonade.

2	shots	Capucana cachaça
¾	shot	Lillet Blanc
½	shot	Freshly squeezed lime juice
2½	shots	Lemonade (English-style)

Origin: Adapted from a drink created in 2013 by John Deragon at PDT, New York City, USA. John's original recipe calls for San Pellegrino Limonata in place of lemonade.
Comment: Cachaça, Lillet Blanc and citrus combine in this dry, refreshing drink.

PEARLINSTRUM

★★★★☆

Glass: Coupe
Garnish: Lime zest twist
Method: **SHAKE** all ingredients with ice and fine strain into chilled glass.

½	shot	Martini Extra Dry vermouth
½	shot	St-Germain elderflower liqueur
1½	shots	Pear flavoured vodka
1½	shots	Ketel One Vodka

Origin: Created in 2012 by yours truly at the Cabinet Room, London, England.
Comment: A delicate harmony of pear and elderflower.

PEDRO COLLINS 🔑

★★★★☆

Glass: Collins
Garnish: Orange slice & cherry on stick (sail)
Method: **SHAKE** first three ingredients with ice and strain into ice-filled glass. **TOP** with soda, lightly stir and serve with straws.

2	shots	Bacardi Carta Blanca light rum
1	shot	Freshly squeezed lime juice
½	shot	Sugar syrup (2 sugar to 1 water)
Top with		Soda (club soda)

Comment: This rum based Tom Collins is basically a long Daiquiri with soda.

PEGGY MARTINI

★★★☆☆

Glass: Martini
Garnish: Orange zest twist
Method: **SHAKE** all ingredients with ice and fine strain into chilled glass.

2	shots	Rutte Dry Gin
1	shot	Martini Extra Dry vermouth
¼	shot	Le Fée Parisienne absinthe
¼	shot	Dubonnet Red
½	shot	Chilled water

Origin: Adapted from a recipe in the 1930s edition of the 'Savoy Cocktail Book' by Harry Craddock.
Comment: Very dry and aromatic. Sadly this will appeal to few palates.

PEGU CLUB #1

★★★★☆

Glass: Martini
Garnish: Lime wedge
Method: **SHAKE** all ingredients with ice and fine strain into chilled glass.

2	shots	Rutte Dry Gin
1	shot	De Kuyper Triple Sec
½	shot	Freshly squeezed lime juice
¼	shot	Sugar syrup (2 sugar to 1 water)
1	dash	Angostura Aromatic Bitters
1	dash	Angostura Orange Bitters
½	shot	Chilled water (omit if wet ice)

Origin: Created in the 1920s at the Pegu Club, an expat gentlemen's club in British colonial Rangoon, Burma. The recipe was first published in Harry MacElhone's 1927 'Barflies and Cocktails'.
Comment: We've added a dash of sugar to the original recipe to reduce the tartness of this gin based Margarita-like concoction.

PEGU CLUB #2

★★★★⯪

Glass: Martini
Garnish: Lime wedge
Method: SHAKE all ingredients with ice and fine strain into chilled glass.

2	shots	Rutte Dry Gin
1	shot	Grand Marnier Cordon Rouge
½	shot	Freshly squeezed lime juice
1	dash	Angostura Aromatic Bitters
1	dash	Angostura Orange Bitters
½	shot	Chilled water (omit if wet ice)

Comment: This version of the Burmese classic is richer in orange.

PENDENNIS COCKTAIL

★★★★☆

Glass: Martini
Garnish: Luxardo Maraschino cherry
Method: SHAKE all ingredients with ice and fine strain into chilled glass.

2	shots	Rutte Dry Gin
1	shot	De Kuyper XO Apricot Brandy
½	shot	Freshly squeezed lime juice
1	dash	Peychaud's aromatic bitters
¾	shot	Chilled water (omit if wet ice)

Origin: This classic is named after the Pendinnis Club in Louisville, Kentucky, which is popularly supposed to be the birthplace of the Old-Fashioned.
Comment: Tangy, subtle, sweet, and sour.

PENICILLIN COCKTAIL

★★★★★⯪

Glass: Old-fashioned
Garnish: Candied ginger
Method: SHAKE all ingredients with ice and strain into ice-filled chilled glass.

3	spoon	Honey water (3 honey to 1 water)
1½	shots	Islay single malt Scotch whisky
1	shot	Dewar's 12yo Scotch whisky
¼	shot	King's Ginger Liqueur
¾	shot	Freshly squeezed lemon juice

Origin: Adapted from a 2005 recipe by Sam Ross at Milk & Honey, New York City, USA.
Comment: Smoke and honey with subtle spice and plenty of Scottish attitude.

PENTHOUSE COCKTAIL

★★★★☆

Glass: Coupe
Garnish: Luxardo Maraschino cherry
Method: SHAKE all ingredients with ice and fine strain into chilled glass.

2	shots	Bourbon whiskey
¼	shot	Luxardo Maraschino liqueur
¾	shot	Freshly squeezed lime juice
½	shot	Sugar syrup (2 sugar to 1 water)

Origin: Created by Carl Wrangel at the Oak Room, Copenhagen, Denmark.
Comment: A bourbon sour with a touch of maraschino adding an almondy cherry note.

PEPIN RIVERO SPECIAL

★★★⯪☆

Glass: Coupe
Garnish: Chocolate powder rim
Method: SHAKE all ingredients with ice and fine strain into chilled glass.

1½	shots	Rutte Dry Gin
1	shot	White crème de cacao liqueur
1	shot	Milk

Origin: Created by Constantino (Constante) Ribalaigua Vert at the Floridita bar in Havana, Cuba. This recipe is adapted from a 1937 Bar Florida (later renamed Floridita) menu. The name refers to Pepin Rivero, who took over the Cuban El Diario de la Marina newspaper upon the death of his father Don Nicolas Rivero in 1944.
Comment: White chocolate come coconut ice-cream, only vaguely rescued from fluffiness by gin spirit.

PEPPER & VANILLA

★★★★⯪

Glass: Martini
Garnish: Yellow pepper strip
Method: SHAKE all ingredients with ice and fine strain into chilled glass.

1	shot	Vanilla infused Ketel One vodka
¾	shot	Pepper-infused Ketel One vodka
¾	shot	Tuaca liqueur
1	shot	Licor 43 liqueur
1	shot	Yellow bell pepper juice

Origin: Created in 2002 by yours truly, London, England and originally somewhat dodgily named Pepper & Vanilla'tini. Incidentally, Pieprz i wanilia (which translates as Pepper and Vanilla) was a popular Polish television program broadcast by TVP. This travel documentary program was broadcast for over 20 years with 300 episodes.
Comment: Vanilla and pepper seem to complement each other in a sweet and sour kind of way.

PEPPERED MARY

★★★★☆

Glass: Collins
Garnish: Peppered rim & cherry tomato
Method: SHAKE all ingredients with ice and strain into ice-filled glass.

2	shots	Pepper-infused Ketel One vodka
2	shots	Yellow bell pepper juice
2	shots	Tomato juice
½	shot	Freshly squeezed lemon juice
7	drop	Tabasco hot pepper sauce
1	spoon	Worcestershire sauce

Comment: A Bloody Mary with sweet and spicy pepper.

PERFECT ALIBI

★★★★☆

Glass: Martini
Garnish: Mint leaf
Method: MUDDLE ginger in base of shaker. Add other ingredients, SHAKE with ice and fine strain into ice-filled glass.

2	inch	Fresh root ginger (thumbnail sized)
½	shot	Old Krupnik
1½	shots	Bärenjäger honey liqueur
½	shot	Sugar syrup (2 sugar to 1 water)
3	shots	Cold jasmine tea

Origin: Created in 2001 by Douglas Ankrah for Akbar, London, England.
Comment: A very unusual and pleasant mix of flavours.

PERFECT FAIRY

★★★½☆

Glass: Wine
Garnish: Freshly grated nutmeg
Method: BLEND all ingredients with one 12oz scoop crushed ice and serve.

1	shot	Le Fée Parisienne absinthe
1	shot	Crème de pêche (peach) liqueur
1	shot	Freshly squeezed lemon juice
1	fresh	Egg white

Origin: Adapted from a drink created in 2011 by Charles Vexenat for Pernod Absinthe.
Comment: This white drink with the merest tint of absinthe green balances lemon, peach liqueur and lemon juice, rounded and made fluffy with egg white.

PERFECT GUEST

★★★★½

Glass: Coupe
Garnish: Lemon zest twist
Method: STIR all ingredients with ice and strain into chilled glass.

1½	shots	Ketel One Vodka
⅔	shot	Lillet Blanc
⅓	shot	St-Germain elderflower liqueur
1	dash	Celery bitters

Origin: Created by Giuseppe Santamaria during for the Spanish World Class 2012 bartender competition.
Comment: Clean grainy vodka forms the back bone of this floral and herbal delicate dessert Vodkatini-style drink.

PERFECT JOHN

★★★★☆

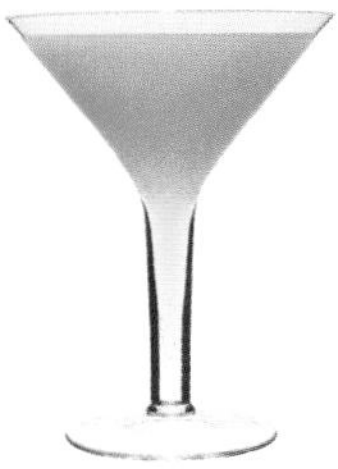

Glass: Martini
Garnish: Orange zest twist
Method: SHAKE all ingredients with ice and fine strain into chilled glass.

1	shot	Ketel One Vodka
¾	shot	De Kuyper Triple Sec
¼	shot	Galliano L'Autentico liqueur
1½	shots	Freshly squeezed orange juice

Comment: A straight up Harvey Wallbanger with triple sec.

PERFECT LADY

★★★★½

Glass: Martini
Garnish: Lemon zest twist (spray and discard) & peach slice
Method: SHAKE all ingredients with ice and fine strain into chilled glass.

2	shots	Rutte Dry Gin
¾	shot	Crème de pêche (peach) liqueur
¾	shot	Freshly squeezed lemon juice
½	fresh	Egg white

Origin: Created in 1936 by Sidney Cox, a bartender at the Grosvenor House, London for The British Empire Cocktail Competition where it took the 1st Prize. That same year a constitutional crisis in the British Empire was caused by King-Emperor Edward VIII's proposal to marry Wallis Simpson, a twice-divorced American socialite. Religious, legal, political, and moral objections were raised due to Mrs Simpson being twice divorced and the marriage was opposed by the King's governments in the United Kingdom and the autonomous Dominions of the British Commonwealth. Despite the opposition, Edward declared his love for Mrs Simpson and his refusal to give her up led to his abdication in December 1936.

He was succeeded by his brother Albert, who took the regal name George VI. Disgraced due to renouncing the throne, Edward was given the title His Royal Highness the Duke of Windsor. He married Mrs Simpson the following year and they remained married until his death 35 years later. She was obviously his 'Perfect Lady'.
Comment: This White Lady riff uses peach liqueur in place of triple sec to make a lighter, fruitier elaboration.

PERFECT REGENT

★★★★½

Glass: Coupe
Garnish: Seasonal berries
Method: SHAKE all ingredients with ice and fine strain into chilled glass.

2	shots	Martell VSOP Médaillon cognac
¼	shot	Martini Rosso vermouth
¼	shot	Martini Extra Dry vermouth
½	shot	Lejay crème de cassis de Dijon

Origin: Recipe adapted in 2008 by yours truly.
Comment: Fruity and easy, perhaps not what you would expect.

PERFECT SUMMIT MANHATTAN

★★★★★

Glass: Coupe
Garnish: Luxardo Maraschino cherry
Method: STIR all ingredients with ice and strain into a chilled glass.

2½	shots	Bourbon whiskey
¾	shot	Martini Extra Dry vermouth
¾	shot	Muscat wine
⅛	shot	Orange Curaçao liqueur
2	dash	Whiskey Barrel Aged Bitters

Origin: Adapted from a recipe by Pilar Zeglin, Summit Restaurant Bar, Cincinnati, USA and courtesy of Ardent Spirits.
Comment: A riff on a Dry Manhattan given extra depth by the addition of dessert wine and whiskey bitters.

PERFECTLY PAIRED COCKTAIL (NEW)

★★★★½

Glass: Flute
Garnish: Dust with cinnamon & pear slice on rim
Method: **SHAKE** first 3 ingredients with ice and strain into chilled glass. **TOP** with champagne.

1 shot Pear purée
1 shot Capucana cachaça
½ shot Licor 43 liqueur
Top with G.H. Mumm Cordon Rouge Champagne

Origin: Created in 2015 by yours truly at the Cabinet Room, London, England.
Comment: This autumnal champagne cocktail has notes of pear tart dessert with orchard fruit, vanilla and cinnamon laced with sugar cane spirit.

PERFECTLY STRAIGHT BLOOD & SAND (NEW)

★★★★★☆

Glass: Coupe
Garnish: Orange zest twist (discarded) & cherry
Method: **SHAKE** all ingredients with ice and fine strain into chilled glass.

½ shot Dewar's 12yo Scotch whisky
½ shot Islay single malt Scotch whisky
½ shot Cherry Heering Liqueur
½ shot Kirschwasser eau de vie
½ shot Martini Rosso vermouth
½ shot Martini Extra Dry vermouth
1 shot Freshly squeezed orange juice

Origin: Created by yours truly at the Cabinet Room, London, England in August 2014.
Comment: If I were in Asia where the number eight is lucky then I'd have also used equal parts orange juice and blood orange juice to keep the number of ingredients lucky. I'm usually a maximum of five ingredients in a cocktail kind-a-guy but this Blood & Sand riff is balanced and tasty.

PERIODISTA DAIQUIRI

★★★★☆

Glass: Martini
Garnish: Lime wedge
Method: **SHAKE** all ingredients with ice and fine strain into chilled glass.

1½ shots Bacardi Carta Blanca light rum
½ shot Grand Marnier Cordon Rouge
½ shot De Kuyper XO Apricot Brandy
½ shot Freshly squeezed lime juice
½ shot Chilled water (omit if wet ice)

Comment: Basically an orange and apricot Daiquiri.

PERISCOPE

★★★★★

Glass: Martini
Garnish: Grapefruit zest twist
Method: **SHAKE** all ingredients with ice and fine strain into chilled glass.

1½ shots Rutte Dry Gin
1 shot St-Germain elderflower liqueur
⅛ shot Freshly squeezed lemon juice
⅛ shot Freshly squeezed lime juice
½ fresh Egg white

Origin: Created by Matt Gee at Milk & Honey, New York City, USA.
Comment: Fabulously light, almost creamy, and very refreshing.

PERNELLE

★★★★½

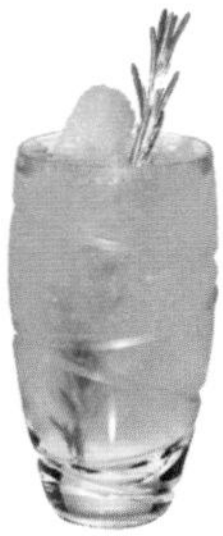

Glass: Collins
Garnish: Lemon zest twist & rosemary sprig
Method: **SHAKE** first four ingredients with ice and strain into glass filled with crushed ice. **TOP** with soda and serve with straws.

1 shot Ketel One Vodka
1 shot St-Germain elderflower liqueur
1 shot Poire William eau de vie
1 shot Freshly squeezed lemon juice
Top with Soda (club soda)

Origin: Created in 2007 by Colin Asare-Appiah, London, England for U'Luvka vodka. This is named after the wife of the 14th century alchemist Nicolas Flamel, who supported him in his search for the Philosopher's Stone.
Comment: This long clear drink has a grassy, alpine aroma and a fresh pine finish.

PERONI NEGRONI

★★★½☆

Glass: Shot and Beer
Garnish: None
Method: **STIR** gin, Campari and vermouth with ice and fine strain into chilled shot glass. Carefully position the shot glass in the beer glass. Then carefully **POUR** Peroni into beer glass so not quite reaching the top of the shot glass, being careful not to splash any beer into shot glass. Instruct drinker to drink from beer glass and so inevitably also shot glass. Use sturdy glassware.

½ shot Rutte Dry Gin
½ shot Campari Bitter
½ shot Martini Rosso vermouth
⅛ bottle Peroni lager

Origin: Created by the team at 8 Bar, Falmouth, Cornwall.
Comment: Negroni is a great chaser to beer so why not consume in unison.

PERPETUAL COCKTAIL

★★★★⯪

Glass: Coupe
Garnish: Orange zest twist
Method: SHAKE all ingredients with ice and fine strain into chilled glass.

1	shot	Martini Rosso vermouth
1	shot	Martini Extra Dry vermouth
½	shot	Benoit Serres créme de violette
¼	shot	White crème de cacao liqueur

Origin: Recipe adapted from Hugo R. Ensslin's 1917 book 'Recipes for Mixed Drinks'.
Comment: A tad on the sweet side and flavoured with chocolate, red berries and violets over a base of sweet and dry vermouth.

PERROQUET

★★★☆☆

Glass: Collins
Garnish: None
Method: POUR pastis and mint syrup into glass. Serve iced water separately in small jug (known in France as a 'broc') so the customer can dilute to their own taste (I recommend five shots). Lastly, add ice to fill glass.

1	shot	Ricard Pastis
¼	shot	Mint (menthe) syrup
Top with		Chilled water

Origin: Very popular throughout France, this drink is named after the parrot due to the bird's brightly coloured plumage.
Comment: The traditional French café drink with a hint of sweet mint.

PERRY COCKTAIL

★★★★☆

Glass: Martini
Garnish: Pear slice
Method: SHAKE first three ingredients with ice and fine strain into chilled glass. TOP with champagne.

1	shot	Poire William eau de vie
1	shot	Belle de Brillet pear liqueur
2	shots	Pressed pear juice
Top with		G.H. Mumm Cordon Rouge Champagne

Origin: Created in 2002 by yours truly.
Comment: Pear with a hint of sparkle.

PERUVIAN ELDER SOUR

★★★★⯪

Glass: Martini
Garnish: Lime wedge
Method: SHAKE all ingredients with ice and fine strain into chilled glass.

½	shot	Freshly squeezed lime juice
1	shot	St-Germain elderflower liqueur
2	shots	BarSol Mosto Verde Italia pisco

Origin: Drinks writer gaz regan created this in 2006 in New York, USA.
Comment: This tasty sour combines the aromatics of pisco and elderflower in an intriguing variation on the Margarita. Consider smoothing with fresh egg white.

PETANQUE COCKTAIL (NEW)

★★★★⯪

Glass: Coupe
Garnish: Luxardo Maraschino cherry
Method: STIR all ingredients with ice and strain into chilled glass.

2½ shots Romate Fino sherry
1 shot Disaronno Originale amaretto
2 dash Peychaud's aromatic bitters

Origin: Adapted from a drink created in 2014 by Andrew Bohrer at Mistral Kitchen, Seattle, USA, and named after the French game where hollow metal balls are thrown as close as possible to a small wooden jack ball. Andrew used 2 shots of Toro Albalá Fino Eléctrico sherry but we thought 2½ shots of fino better balanced the rich amaretto.
Comment: The game this drink is named after is French while the main ingredients are Italian and Spanish, but they do play Pétanque in the Basque region of Spain. They also play football, sorry soccer in the States where both the creator of this drink and the biters used in it come from.

PETER PAN MARTINI #1

★★★☆☆

Glass: Martini
Garnish: Orange zest twist
Method: SHAKE all ingredients with ice and fine strain into chilled glass.

1	shot	Rutte Dry Gin
1	shot	Martini Extra Dry vermouth
1	shot	Freshly squeezed orange juice
3	dash	Peach bitters

Origin: Adapted from a recipe in the 1930 edition of the 'Savoy Cocktail Book' by Harry Craddock. The original recipe called for equal parts, including the bitters - surely a mistake.
Comment: Smoother, lighter and easier than most classic cocktails - perhaps a little too much so.

PETER PAN MARTINI #2

★★★☆☆

Glass: Martini
Garnish: Orange zest twist
Method: SHAKE all ingredients with ice and fine strain into chilled glass.

2	shots	Rutte Dry Gin
1	shot	Martini Extra Dry vermouth
1	shot	Freshly squeezed orange juice
3	dash	Peach bitters

Origin: Adapted from a recipe in the 1930 edition of the 'Savoy Cocktail Book' by Harry Craddock.
Comment: Orange predominates in this complex cocktail.

PETO MARTINI

★★★★⯪

Glass: Martini
Garnish: Orange zest twist
Method: SHAKE all ingredients with ice and fine strain into chilled glass.

2	shots	Rutte Dry Gin
1	shot	Martini Extra Dry vermouth
1	shot	Martini Rosso vermouth
¼	shot	Freshly squeezed orange juice
⅛	shot	Luxardo Maraschino liqueur

Origin: Adapted from a recipe in the 1930 edition of the 'Savoy Cocktail Book' by Harry Craddock.
Comment: An aromatic classic Martini served 'perfect' with a hint of orange juice and maraschino.

PETRUCHIO COCKTAIL

★★★★☆

Glass: Coupe
Garnish: None
Method: SHAKE all ingredients with ice and fine strain into chilled glass.

1	shot	Rutte Dry Gin
1	shot	Aperol Aperitivo
½	shot	Freshly squeezed lemon juice
¼	shot	Sugar syrup (2 sugar to 1 water)
2	dash	Angostura Orange Bitters
1	fresh	Egg white

Origin: Created in 2010 by Jamie Boudreau at Vessel, Seattle, USA.
Comment: Gin-based and bitter-sweet, this bright orange drink has a foamy head which may mislead some into thinking it is sweet and easy.

PHARMACEUTICAL STIMULANT

★★★★☆

Glass: Medical cup or Old-fashioned
Garnish: Coffee beans
Method: SHAKE all ingredients with ice and strain into ice-filled glass.

2	shots	Ketel One Vodka
½	shot	Coffee liqueur
¼	shot	Sugar syrup (2 sugar to 1 water)
1½	shots	Espresso coffee (freshly made & hot)

Comment: A real wake-up call and the drink that led to many an Espresso Martini.

PHISH HOOK

★★★★☆

Glass: Coupe
Garnish: None
Method: STIR all ingredients with ice and fine strain into glass.

2	shots	Straight rye whiskey
½	shot	St-Germain elderflower liqueur
¼	shot	Carpano Punt E Mes
⅛	shot	Luxardo Maraschino liqueur

Origin: Adapted from a January 2010 recipe courtesy of Jamie Boudreau's spiritsandcocktails.wordpress.com
Comment: Rye whiskey tamed and flavoured by elderflower, Punt E Mes and maraschino.

PICADOR

★★★★★

Glass: Martini
Garnish: Lime zest twist
Method: SHAKE all ingredients with ice and fine strain into chilled glass.

2	shots	Patrón reposado tequila
1	shot	De Kuyper Triple Sec
1	shot	Freshly squeezed lime juice

Origin: Yes, you're right! This drink is exactly the same as a classically proportioned Margarita. It was published in W. J. Tarling's 1937 Cafe Royal Cocktail Book, 16 years before the first written reference to a Margarita. Conjecture suggests that this British recipe was copied by whichever American gave the Margarita its name.
Comment: The name might be more masculine but it still tastes just like a classic Margarita.

PICCA

★★★★☆

Glass: Martini
Garnish: Luxardo Maraschino cherry
Method: SHAKE all ingredients with ice and fine strain into chilled glass.

1½	shots	Dewar's 12yo Scotch whisky
1	shot	Galliano L'Autentico liqueur
1	shot	Martini Rosso vermouth
¾	shot	Chilled water (omit if wet ice)

Comment: Bittersweet whisky.

PICCADILLY MARTINI

★★★★⯪

Glass: Martini
Garnish: Lemon zest twist
Method: SHAKE all ingredients with ice and fine strain into chilled glass.

2	shots	Rutte Dry Gin
1	shot	Martini Extra Dry vermouth
⅛	shot	Le Fée Parisienne absinthe
⅛	shot	Pomegranate / grenadine syrup (2:1)

Origin: Adapted from a recipe in the 1930 edition of the 'Savoy Cocktail Book' by Harry Craddock.
Comment: A classic Martini tempered by a hint of pomegranate and absinthe.

PICHUNCHO MARTINI

★★★★⯪

Glass: Martini
Garnish: Orange zest twist
Method: SHAKE all ingredients with ice and fine strain into chilled glass.

2¼	shots	BarSol Mosto Verde Italia pisco
1½	shots	Martini Rosso vermouth
¼	shot	Sugar syrup (2 sugar to 1 water)

Origin: Based on the traditional Chilean drink: pisco and vermouth served on the rocks.
Comment: This drink craves the best pisco and the best sweet vermouth. Find those and measure carefully and it's sublime.

PICKLE BACK

★★★⯪☆☆

Glass: Shot
Garnish: None
Method: POUR ingredients into two separate chilled glasses. Instruct drinker to drink whiskey followed by cucumber chaser.

| 1 | shot | Teeling Small Batch Irish whiskey |
| 1 | shot | Pickle brine |

Origin: Created in 2006 at Brooklyn's Bushwick Country Club after the neighbouring business, McClure's Pickles, stored some of their pickles in the bar's basement.

Apparently this inspired bartender, Reggie Cunningham, to serve Old Crow Bourbon with a shot of McClure's spicy pickle brine. The Ruotolo brother took the drink to their Whiskey Town in New York's East Village with Irish whiskey replacing bourbon.
Comment: Now, we do like a juicy wally (gherkin) with our cod'n'chips but necking the brine in which they are packed is another thing. Our American cousins have some strange habits - drive on the right, carry the ball when playing football and bowl underarm. So these eccentricities should be remembered when I tell you that the drinking of cucumber brine as part of this drink is popular in New York City.

PICOTIN (NEW)

★★★★⯪

Glass: Coupe
Garnish: Luxardo Maraschino cherry
Method: SHAKE all ingredients with ice and strain into a chilled glass.

¾	shot	Suze Saveur d'Autrefois
¾	shot	Lysholm Linie Aquavit
⅔	shot	Freshly squeezed lemon juice
½	shot	Cocchi Americano Bianco
⅓	shot	Luxardo Maraschino liqueur

Origin: Discovered in 2015 at Joyeux Bordel, London, England. Created by Florian Dubois.
Comment: Bright yellow and on the bitter side of bittersweet with aquavit, lemon, gentian and maraschino liqueurs.

PIERRE COLLINS 🔑

★★★★☆

Glass: Collins
Garnish: Orange slice & cherry on stick (sail)
Method: SHAKE first three ingredients with ice and strain into ice-filled glass. **TOP** with soda, lightly stir and serve with straws.

2	shots	Martell VSOP Médaillon cognac
1	shot	Freshly squeezed lemon juice
½	shot	Sugar syrup (2 sugar to 1 water)
Top with		Soda (club soda)

Comment: A Tom Collins made with cognac. The cognac's character shines through.

PILGRIM COCKTAIL

★★★★⯪☆

Glass: Martini
Garnish: Dust with freshly grated nutmeg
Method: SHAKE all ingredients with ice and fine strain into chilled glass.

1½	shots	Bacardi Carta Oro rum
½	shot	Grand Marnier Cordon Rouge
1	shot	Freshly squeezed orange juice
¾	shot	Freshly squeezed lime juice
¼	shot	Allspice pimento dram liqueur
2	dash	Angostura Aromatic Bitters

Comment: Whether you serve this hot or cold, it's a delicately spiced drink to warm the cockles.

PIMM'S COCKTAIL

★★★★⯪

Glass: Martini
Garnish: Lemon & orange zest twists (discarded) & strawberry on rim
Method: SHAKE first four ingredients with ice and strain into chilled glass. **TOP** with champagne.

2	shots	Pimm's No.1 Cup
½	shot	Rutte Dry Gin
¼	shot	Freshly squeezed lemon juice
¼	shot	Sugar syrup (2 sugar to 1 water)
Top with		G.H. Mumm Cordon Rouge Champagne

Comment: Luxuriate in this quintessentially English tipple.

PIMM'S CUP (OR CLASSIC PIMM'S)

★★★★⯪☆

Glass: Collins
Garnish: Mint sprig
Method: POUR Pimm's into glass half filled with ice. Add fruit and fill glass with more ice. **TOP** with ginger ale, lightly stir and serve with straws.

2	shots	Pimm's No.1 Cup
1	slice	Fresh orange
1	slice	Lemon
1	slice	English cucumber peeled
1	fresh	Small ripe strawberries (hulled)
⅛		Top with Lemonade (English-style) (or ginger ale)

Origin: This quintessential English summer tipple is usually credited to James Pimm, who in 1823-4 began trading as a shellfish-monger in London's Lombard Street. He later moved to nearby number 3 Poultry, also in the City of London, where he established Pimm's Oyster Warehouse. It is here, in 1840, that he is said to have first served this drink.

Others dispute this, maintaining that James Pimm only unwittingly lent his name to the drink. They say the true credit lies with his successor, Samuel Morey, who is recorded as having taken out a retail liquor licence in 1860. This would appear to be when the oyster bar first offered its customers spirits.

Many establishments of the day mixed house spirits to serve with liqueurs and juices as 'cups', in reference to the tankards in which they were sold. Naturally the 'cup' made at Pimm's Oyster Bar was named after the establishment which retained the goodwill of its founder.

Pimm's restaurant became very popular and changed hands a couple more times. Eventually Horatio David Davies, a wine merchant and owner of cafes in London bought the business. He became Sir Horatio, a Member of Parliament and between 1897-1898, Lord Mayor of London. He formed Pimm's into a private company in 1906, which, was controlled by family trusts for another 57 years after his death.

The precise date that the drink Pimm's was first sold outside restaurants and bars controlled by the Pimm's company is unknown. However, it is certain that the original product, No.1, "The Original Gin Sling," was based on gin and flavoured with numerous botanicals including quinine

A second Pimm's product based on Scotch (Pimm's No.2 Cup) was launched and a third (Pimm's No.3 Cup) was based on brandy. Pimm's became popular in Britain in the 1920s and took off internationally after the Second World War. Other versions were then introduced: Pimm's No.4 based on rum, Pimm's No.5 on rye, Pimm's No.6 on vodka and Pimm's No.7 on tequila.

Comment: You've not properly experienced an English summer until you've drunk one of these whilst sheltering from the rain.

PIMM'S ROYALE

★★★½☆☆

Glass: Flute
Garnish: Seasonal berries & cucumber peel
Method: POUR Pimm's into chilled glass and TOP with champagne.

1	shot	Pimm's No.1 Cup
Top with		G.H. Mumm Cordon Rouge Champagne

Comment: Dry, subtle and refreshing.

PIMM'S SPRITZ (NEW)

★★★★☆

Glass: Rocks
Garnish: Orange slice & mint
Method: POUR all ingredients into ice-filled glass and lightly stir.

2	shots	Prosecco sparkling wine
2	shots	Pimm's No.1 Cup
2	shots	Lemonade (English-style)

Origin: Created on 30th May 2014 by yours truly at the Cabinet Room, London, England for British Airways' BA High Life Magazine.
Comment: As the name suggests, this cocktail is inspired by and combines elements of both the classic Venetian Spritz and England's Pimm's Cup. The result is a lightly sparkling and very refreshing aperitif cocktail.

PIÑA COCKTAIL 🔑

★★★★☆

Glass: Martini
Garnish: Pineapple wedge
Method: SHAKE all ingredients with ice and fine strain into chilled glass.

2	shots	Ketel One Vodka
1¾	shots	Fresh pressed pineapple juice
¼	shot	Freshly squeezed lime juice
⅛	shot	Sugar syrup (2 sugar to 1 water)

Comment: Rich pineapple but not too sweet.

Piña Colada Cocktail

The name 'Piña Colada' directly translates from Spanish as 'strained pineapple', a reference to the freshly pressed and strained pineapple juice that should ideally be used in the drink's preparation.

Three Puerto Rican bartenders contest the ownership of their country's national drink. Ramon 'Monchito' Marrero Pérez claims to have first made it at the Caribe Hilton Hotel's Beachcomber Bar in San Juan on 15th August 1952, using the then newly available Coco Lopez cream of coconut. Ricardo Garcia, who also worked at the Caribe, says that it was he who invented the drink. And Ramon Portas Mingot says he created it in 1963 at the Barrachina Restaurant, 104 Fortaleza Street, Old San Juan.

It could be that all three Puerto Rican's played their part in the Piña Colada's creation. Perhaps Ricardo Garcia tweaked a cocktail originally created by his colleague. It is plausible that the cocktail was christened 'Piña Colada at the Barrachina Restaurant a decade after first being created at the Caribe Hilton, after all it is not mentioned in cocktail books until the late 1960s. The Barrachina Restaurant displays a plaque supporting Ramon Portas Mingot's claim to the drinks creation to this day.

Truth is, rum, pineapple and coconut have been mixed together pretty much since rum was first distilled and the first written reference to a drink named Piña Colada would appear to be in an issue of Travel Magazine dated December 1922. However, this recipe does not include coconut and was more a shaken Pineapple Daiquiri served long, and made with Bacardi Rum, pineapple juice, lime and sugar. Now commonly referred to as a Cuban-style Piña Colada, this drink perhaps more befits the 'strained pineapple' name than what most people today consider a Piña Colada.

So the Puerto Ricans merely added cream of coconut and it is commonly accepted that the modern Piña Colada was adapted from an existing creation at the Caribe Hilton Hotel. Like the Barrachina Restaurant, the Caribe Hilton has since promoted itself as the home of the Piña Colada and today credits Ramon Marrero Pérez with its invention.

The Caribe Hilton Hotel sits on a 17-acre peninsula outside San Juan and was the first luxury hotel to open in the region, becoming a popular destination for the rich and famous who helped spread word of the Piña Colada. Today, the hotel is more 'package tourist' than luxurious and you may prefer the Conrad Hilton across the causeway which traverses the lagoon, but even this is hardly what you'd consider a destination for "the rich and famous".

To make a 'Puerto Rican' style Piña Colada you'll need a sticky goo called 'cream of coconut', not to be confused with coconut cream. Cream of coconut is made by mixing coconut juice, sugar, emulsifier, cellulose, thickeners, citric acid and salt and is usually sold in 15oz/425ml cans which make 14 to 25 drinks depending on how sweet you like your Piña Coladas. Once opened the can's contents should be stored in a refrigerator: this may thicken the product, so gentle warming may be required prior to use.

The original brand of cream of coconut is Coco Lopez which was developed in 1948 in Puerto Rico by Don Ramon Lopez-Irizarry – hence the Puerto Rican connection and the believable 1952 date for the creation of the modern day Piña Colada at the Caribe Hilton Hotel. Some say the drink did not acquire its name until the 1960s – perhaps that's where Ramon Portas Mingot and the Barrachina restaurant come into play.

It seems there's a set day in the calendar to celebrate most things and readers may want to mark their diaries with National Piña Colada Day which is celebrated each 10th July on the island of Puerto Rico and to a lesser degree across the USA.

PINA COLADA (DIFFORD'S RECIPE) (NEW)

★★★★★

Glass: Collins
Garnish: Parasol, pineapple wedge & Luxardo Maraschino cherry
Method: BLEND all ingredients with 12oz scoop ice and serve with straws.

2 shots Bacardi Carta Blanca light rum
½ shot Capucana cachaça
3½ shots Fresh pressed pineapple juice
¾ shot Coco Re'al Cream of Coconut
½ shot Freshly squeezed lime juice
¼ shot Single cream / half-and-half
1 pinch Salt

Comment: A splash of cachaça adds some Latin flavour, lime adds citrusy bite and cream makes this Pina Colada creamy white.

PINA COLADA COCKTAIL (CUBAN STYLE)

★★★★☆

Glass: Collins or Pineapple shell
Garnish: Lime wedge
Method: SHAKE all ingredients with ice and strain into ice-filled glass.

2 shots Bacardi Carta Ocho aged rum
4 shots Fresh pressed pineapple juice
¼ shot Freshly squeezed lime juice
¼ shot Sugar syrup (2 sugar to 1 water)

Origin: The name 'Piña Colada' means 'strained pineapple', a reference to the freshly pressed and strained pineapple juice used in this drink's preparation.

Basically a coconut flavoured Daiquiri, this recipe dating from 1922 represents the first written reference to a Piña Colada and is what we now refer to as a 'Cuban Style Piña Colada' - one without the addition of coconut.
Comment: This Colada has no coconut, but it is smooth, balanced and rather tasty.

PINA COLADA COCKTAIL (PUERTO RICAN STYLE)

★★★★½

Glass: Pineapple shell (frozen)
Garnish: Parasol, pineapple wedge & Luxardo Maraschino cherry
Method: BLEND all ingredients with one 12oz scoop ice & serve with straws.

2 shots Bacardi Carta Oro rum
3 shots Fresh pressed pineapple juice
⅔ shot Coco Re'al Cream of Coconut
½ shot Freshly squeezed lime juice

Comment: A wonderful creamy, fruity concoction that's not half as sticky as the world would have you believe. Too much ice will detract from the creaminess and kill the drink.

PIÑA COLADA VIRGIN (MOCKTAIL)

★★★☆☆

Glass: Hurricane
Garnish: Pineapple wedge & Luxardo Maraschino cherry
Method: BLEND all ingredients with a scoop of crushed ice and serve with straws.

4 shots Fresh pressed pineapple juice
1½ shots Coco Re'al Cream of Coconut
¾ shot Single cream / half-and-half
¾ shot Milk

Comment: A Piña Colada with its guts ripped out.

PINEAPPLE & CARDAMOM DAIQUIRI

★★★★½

Glass: Martini
Garnish: Pineapple wedge
Method: MUDDLE cardamom in base of shaker. Add other ingredients, **SHAKE** with ice and fine strain into chilled glass.

4 whole Cardamom pod
2 shots Bacardi Carta Blanca light rum
1¾ shots Fresh pressed pineapple juice
¼ shot Freshly squeezed lime juice
¼ shot Sugar syrup (2 sugar to 1 water)

Origin: Adapted from Henry Besant's excellent Pineapple & Cardamom Martini.
Comment: One of the tastiest Daiquiris we've tried.

PINEAPPLE & CARDAMOM MARTINI

★★★★★

Glass: Martini
Garnish: Pineapple wedge
Method: MUDDLE cardamom in base of shaker. Add other ingredients, **SHAKE** with ice and fine strain into a chilled glass.

4 whole Cardamom pod
2 shots Ketel One Vodka
2 shots Fresh pressed pineapple juice
¼ shot Sugar syrup (2 sugar to 1 water)

Origin: Created in 2002 by Henry Besant at The Lonsdale, London, England.
Comment: This is about as good as it gets: a spectacular pairing of fruit and spice.

PINEAPPLE & GINGER COCKTAIL

★★★★☆

Glass: Martini
Garnish: Pineapple wedge
Method: MUDDLE ginger in base of shaker. Add other ingredients, **SHAKE** with ice and fine strain into chilled glass.

2 slice Fresh root ginger (thumbnail sized)
2 shots Ketel One Vodka
2 shots Fresh pressed pineapple juice
⅛ shot Sugar syrup (2 sugar to 1 water)

Comment: Smooth, rich pineapple flavour with hints of vodka and ginger

PINEAPPLE & SAGE MARGARITA

★★★★⯪

Glass: Coupe
Garnish: Pineapple wedge
Method: SHAKE all ingredients with ice and fine strain into chilled glass.

5	fresh	Sage leaves
2	shots	Patrón reposado tequila
1	shot	Fresh pressed pineapple juice
½	shot	Freshly squeezed lime juice
¼	shot	Agave syrup

Origin: Adapted from a drink created in 2005 at Green & Red Bar London, England.
Comment: Herbal tequila and sweet pineapple in harmony.

PINEAPPLE BLOSSOM ⬦⟶

★★★★☆

Glass: Martini
Garnish: Pineapple wedge
Method: SHAKE all ingredients with ice and fine strain into chilled glass.

2	shots	Dewar's 12yo Scotch whisky
1	shot	Fresh pressed pineapple juice
½	shot	Freshly squeezed lemon juice
½	shot	Sugar syrup (2 sugar to 1 water)

Comment: Richly flavoured but drier than you might expect.

PINEAPPLE DAIQUIRI #1 (ON-THE-ROCKS) ⬦⟶

★★★★⯪

Glass: Old-fashioned
Garnish: Pineapple wedge & Luxardo Maraschino cherry
Method: SHAKE all ingredients with ice and fine strain into ice-filled glass.

2	shots	Bacardi Carta Blanca light rum
1	shot	Fresh pressed pineapple juice
½	shot	Freshly squeezed lime juice
¼	shot	Sugar syrup (2 sugar to 1 water)

Comment: Rum and pineapple are just meant to go together.

PINEAPPLE DAIQUIRI #2 (FROZEN) ⬦⟶

★★★★⯪

Glass: Martini (large 10oz)
Garnish: Pineapple wedge & Luxardo Maraschino cherry
Method: BLEND all ingredients with a scoop of crushed ice. Served heaped in the glass and with straws.

2	shots	Bacardi Carta Blanca light rum
1½	shots	Fresh pressed pineapple juice
½	shot	Freshly squeezed lime juice
¾	shot	Sugar syrup (2 sugar to 1 water)

Comment: A tad fluffy but very tasty.

PINEAPPLE FIX

★★★★☆

Glass: Old-fashioned
Garnish: Pineapple wedge
Method: SHAKE all ingredients with ice and strain into ice-filled glass.

2	shots	Bacardi Carta Ocho aged rum
1	shot	Fresh pressed pineapple juice
1	shot	Freshly squeezed lemon juice
½	shot	Sugar syrup (2 sugar to 1 water)

Comment: Rum and pineapple are a match made in heaven, here with lemon adding citrus freshness.

PINEAPPLE FIZZ

★★★★★

Glass: Collins
Garnish: Lime wedge & Luxardo Maraschino cherry
Method: SHAKE first four ingredients with ice and fine strain in chilled glass. TOP with soda, lightly stir and serve with straws.

2	shots	Bacardi Carta Oro rum
1½	shots	Fresh pressed pineapple juice
1	shot	Freshly squeezed lime juice
½	shot	Sugar syrup (2 sugar to 1 water)
Top with		Soda (club soda)

Comment: A Pineapple Daiquiri lengthened with soda. Surprisingly tasty and refreshing.

PINEAPPLE LASSI COCKTAIL

★★★★☆

Glass: Coupe
Garnish: Pineapple wedge
Method: MUDDLE cardamom and then pineapple in base of shaker. Add other ingredients, SHAKE with ice and fine strain into chilled glass.

3	whole	Cardamom pod
3	wedge	Pineapple (fresh) (cored, skinned and chopped)
1½	shots	Ketel One Vodka
1½	shots	Yoghurt liqueur

Origin: Created in 2011 by yours truly at the Cabinet Room, London, England.
Comment: Creamy yoghurty cardamom and pineapple laced with vodka.

PINEAPPLE MARGARITA ⬦⟶

★★★★☆

Glass: Coupe
Garnish: Pineapple wedge
Method: SHAKE all ingredients with ice and fine strain into chilled glass.

2	shots	Patrón reposado tequila
¾	shot	De Kuyper Triple Sec
1½	shots	Fresh pressed pineapple juice

Comment: A Tequila Margarita with a pineapple fruit kick

PINEAPPLE MOJITO

★★★★⯨

Glass: Collins
Garnish: None
Method: Lightly **MUDDLE** mint (just to bruise) in glass. **POUR** other ingredients into glass and half fill with crushed ice. **CHURN** (stir) with barspoon. Fill glass with more crushed ice, churn and serve with straws.

12	fresh	Mint leaves
2	shots	Bacardi Carta Blanca light rum
¾	shot	Licor 43 liqueur
2	shots	Fresh pressed pineapple juice
1	shot	Freshly squeezed lime juice

Origin: Discovered in 2003 at Apartment 195, London, England.
Comment: A fruity, vanilla-ed twist on the classic Mojito

PINEAPPLE SMOOTHIE (MOCKTAIL)

★★★⯨☆

Glass: Collins
Garnish: Pineapple wedge
Method: BLEND all the ingredients with 12oz scoop crushed ice. Serve with straws.

2	spoon	Natural yoghurt
2	spoon	Runny honey
4	shots	Fresh pressed pineapple juice

Comment: Fluffy in every sense of the word.

PINECONE (NEW)

★★★★⯨

Glass: Coupe
Garnish: Clove studded pineapple wedge
Method: MUDDLE cloves in base of shaker to crush. Add other ingredients, **SHAKE** with ice and fine strain into chilled glass.

2	dried	Cloves
1½	shot	BarSol Mosto Verde Italia pisco
1	shot	Crowded Hive Mead
1	shot	Pressed pineapple juice
½	shot	Licor 43 liqueur
1	spoon	Zirbenz pine liqueur

Comment: Honey and pineapple, laced with aromatic pisco and spiced with clove.
Origin: Created by yours truly (Simon Difford) at the Cabinet Room, London, England.

PINI

★★★★⯨

Glass: Martini
Garnish: Luxardo Maraschino cherry
Method: SHAKE all ingredients with ice and fine strain into chilled glass.

2	shots	BarSol Mosto Verde Italia pisco
½	shot	Martell VSOP Médaillon cognac
¼	shot	White crème de cacao liqueur
¼	shot	Sugar syrup (2 sugar to 1 water)
½	shot	Chilled water (omit if wet ice)

Comment: Use a great pisco and you'll have a wonderfully complex drink.

PINK CHIHUAHUA

★★★★⯨

Glass: Coupe
Garnish: Lime wedge on rim
Method: SHAKE all ingredients with ice and strain back into shaker. **DRY SHAKE** (without ice) and fine strain into chilled glass.

2 shots	Patrón silver tequila
½ shot	Freshly squeezed lime juice
¼ shot	Freshly squeezed lemon juice
½ shot	Pomegranate / grenadine syrup (2:1)
¼ shot	Almond (orgeat) syrup
½ fresh	Egg white

Origin: Created in 2010 by Dick Bradsell at The Pink Chihuahua at El Camion, London, England. This fluffy little pink drink is named Chihuahua (Spanish: Chihuahueño) after the smallest breed of dog and also the state of Mexico. At El Camion, the front door is painted with an artist's impression of a pink Chihuahua.
Comment: Yes, this appropriately named drink is pink and fluffy – due to being sweetened with pomegranate syrup in place of triple sec and given a foamy head by the addition of egg white.

PINK CLOUD

★★★☆☆

Glass: Martini
Garnish: None
Method: SHAKE all ingredients with ice and fine strain into chilled glass.

1	shot	Disaronno Originale amaretto
1	shot	Pomegranate / grenadine syrup (2:1)
1	shot	White crème de cacao liqueur
¾	shot	Evaporated milk (sweetened)

Origin: Adapted from a recipe in the 1947-72 'Trader Vic's Bartender's Guide' by Victor Bergeron.
Comment: To make this sweet after dinner drink I've used amaretto and pomegranate syrup in place of crème de noyaux. This almond flavoured liqueur made from apricot and peach stones is not currently available in the UK. US readers should use 2 shots of crème de noyaux in place of the first two ingredients.

PINK DAIQUIRI

★★★★☆

Glass: Martini
Garnish: Lime wedge
Method: SHAKE all ingredients with ice and fine strain into chilled glass.

2	shots	Bacardi Carta Blanca light rum
½	shot	Pomegranate / grenadine syrup (2:1)
¼	shot	Luxardo Maraschino liqueur
½	shot	Freshly squeezed lime juice
3	dash	Angostura Aromatic Bitters
½	shot	Chilled water (omit if wet ice)

Origin: A classic from the 1930s.
Comment: The quality of the pomegranate syrup will make or break this delicate Daiquiri.

PINK GIN

★★★★☆

Glass: Martini
Garnish: Lemon zest twist
Method: STIR all ingredients with ice and fine strain into chilled glass.

2 shots Rutte Dry Gin
1 shot Chilled water (reduce if wet ice)
2 dash Angostura Aromatic Bitters

Origin: Gin was a favourite of the Royal Navy - along with rum, which was served as a daily ration right up until the 70s. It was often mixed with healthy ingredients to make them more palatable. Pink gin was originally used against stomach upsets, as Angostura aromatic bitters were considered medicinal. Traditionally this drink was made in a bitters washed glass without the use of ice.
Comment: Normally I'd advocate liberal use of bitters but this refined and subtle drink benefits from frugality.

PINK GIN & TONIC

★★★★☆

Glass: Collins
Garnish: Lime slice
Method: POUR gin and Angostura bitters into ice-filled glass, **TOP** with tonic, lightly **STIR** and serve with straws.

2 shots Rutte Dry Gin
4 dash Angostura Aromatic Bitters
Top with Tonic Water

Comment: Basically a G&T with an extra pep of flavour from Angostura, this has a wider appeal than the original Pink Gin.

PINK GRAPEFRUIT MARGARITA

★★★★☆

Glass: Coupe
Garnish: Lime wedge
Method: SHAKE all ingredients with ice and fine strain into chilled glass

2 shots Patrón reposado tequila
1 shot Freshly squeezed pink grapefruit juice
½ shot Freshly squeezed lime juice
¼ shot Sugar syrup (2 sugar to 1 water)

Comment: Delivers exactly what the name promises.

PINK HOUND

★★★★☆

Glass: Martini
Garnish: Lemon zest twist
Method: SHAKE all ingredients with ice and fine strain into chilled glass.

2 shots Rutte Dry Gin
1½ shots Freshly squeezed pink grapefruit juice
¼ shot Pomegranate / grenadine syrup (2:1)

Comment: A flavoursome balance of sweet and sour.

PINK KHALEESI (NEW)

★★★★☆

Glass: Coupe
Garnish: 3 pink peppercorns
Method: MUDDLE peppercorns in base of shaker. Add other ingredients, **SHAKE** with ice and fine strain into chilled glass.

1 spoon Pink peppercorns
1 shot Ketel One Vodka
1 shot Skinos Mastiha
¼ shot Freshly squeezed lemon juice
¼ shot Sugar syrup (2 sugar to 1 water)
2 dash Peychaud's aromatic bitters

Comment: Pretty in pink but with a hint of spice and the distinctive Greek flavour of mastiha.

PINK LADY

★★★★½

Glass: Martini
Garnish: Luxardo Maraschino cherry
Method: SHAKE all ingredients with ice and fine strain into chilled glass.

2 shots Rutte Dry Gin
½ fresh Egg white
¼ shot Pomegranate / grenadine syrup (2:1)
½ shot Freshly squeezed lemon juice

Origin: A classic cocktail named after a successful 1912 stage play.
Comment: Despite the colour, this is sharp and alcoholic.

PINK LEMONADE (MOCKTAIL)

★★★☆☆

Glass: Collins
Garnish: Lemon slice
Method: SHAKE first three ingredients with ice and strain into ice-filled glass. **TOP** with soda and serve with straws.

2 shots Freshly squeezed lemon juice
¼ shot Sugar syrup (2 sugar to 1 water)
½ shot Pomegranate / grenadine syrup (2:1)
Top with Soda (club soda)

Origin: Discovered in 2004 in New York City.
Comment: A tall, pink, tangy alcohol free cocktail.

PINK PALACE

★★★★½

Glass: Martini
Garnish: Lemon zest twist
Method: SHAKE all ingredients with ice and fine strain into chilled glass.

2 shots Rutte Dry Gin
½ shot Grand Marnier Cordon Rouge
½ shot Freshly squeezed lime juice
¼ shot Pomegranate / grenadine syrup (2:1)

Origin: The signature drink at the Polo Lounge, Beverly Hills Hotel, Los Angeles, USA. The hotel, which is lovingly termed the 'Pink Palace' inspired The Eagles' Hotel California and graces the album cover.
Comment: A great drink but rarely done justice at the Polo Lounge.

PINK SIN MARTINI

★★★☆☆

Glass: Martini
Garnish: Dust with cinnamon powder
Method: SHAKE all ingredients with ice and fine strain into chilled glass.

1½ shots	Ketel One Vodka
1 shot	White crème de cacao liqueur
¾ shot	Cinnamon schnapps
1 shot	Cranberry juice

Comment: This looks a little like a Cosmo but delivers sweet cinnamon and chocolate.

PINK SQUIRREL

★★★☆☆

Glass: Martini
Garnish: Mint leaf
Method: SHAKE all ingredients with ice and fine strain into chilled glass.

1 shot	Crème de noyaux liqueur
1 shot	White crème de cacao liqueur
½ shot	Single cream / half-and-half
½ shot	Milk

Origin: Adapted from Victor Bergeron's 'Trader Vic's Bartender's Guide' (1972 revised edition).
Comment: Crème de noyaux, a pink almond liqueur, is now very hard to obtain: if in doubt, substitute with amaretto and grenadine.

PINK TUTU

★★★★☆

Glass: Old-fashioned
Garnish: Orange slice
Method: SHAKE all ingredients with ice and strain into ice-filled glass.

1 shot	Peachtree peach schnapps
½ shot	Ketel One Vodka
½ shot	Campari Bitter
1½ shots	Freshly squeezed pink grapefruit juice
¼ shot	Sugar syrup (2 sugar to 1 water)

Origin: Created in 1999 by Dominique of Café Rouge, Leeds, England.
Comment: A cocktail that's both bitter and sweet.

PINKY PINCHER

★★★★☆

Glass: Old-fashioned
Garnish: Mint sprig, orange & lemon slices
Method: SHAKE all ingredients with ice and strain into ice-filled glass.

2 shots	Bourbon whiskey
1 shot	Freshly squeezed orange juice
1 shot	Freshly squeezed lemon juice
¼ shot	Sugar syrup (2 sugar to 1 water)
¼ shot	Almond (orgeat) syrup

Origin: Adapted from a drink created by Victor Bergeron (Trader Vic).
Comment: Fruity, sweetened bourbon.

PINO PEPE ⊶

★★★★☆

Glass: Pineapple shell (frozen)
Garnish: Mint sprig
Method: BLEND all ingredients with 12oz scoop crushed ice. POUR into glass (or pineapple shell) and serve with straws. If using a pineapple shell, serve with ice cubes.

1 shot	Bacardi Carta Blanca light rum
1 shot	Ketel One Vodka
½ shot	De Kuyper Triple Sec
2 shots	Fresh pressed pineapple juice
½ shot	Freshly squeezed lime juice
¼ shot	Freshly squeezed lemon juice
½ shot	Sugar syrup (2 sugar to 1 water)

Origin: Adapted from a recipe in the 1947-72 'Trader Vic's Bartender's Guide' by Victor Bergeron.
Comment: To quote Trader Vic, "Lethal but smooth - pineapple at its best".

PIRATE DAIQUIRI

★★★★☆

Glass: Martini
Garnish: Lime wedge
Method: SHAKE all ingredients with ice and fine strain into chilled glass.

¾ shot	White overproof rum
¾ shot	Pusser's Navy Rum (54.5%)
½ shot	Cinnamon schnapps
½ shot	Freshly squeezed lime juice
¼ shot	Pomegranate / grenadine syrup (2:1)
¾ shot	Chilled water (omit if wet ice)

Origin: Created in 2004 by yours truly.
Comment: Why the name? Well, the rums are hard and nautical, the lime protects against scurvy, the liqueur contains gold and the syrup is red as blood.

PISCO BELL RINGER

★★★★☆

Glass: Coupe
Garnish: None
Method: RINSE chilled glass with apricot brandy (swirl liqueur round inside of glass to coat and then shake out excess). SHAKE other ingredients with ice and fine strain into apricot rinsed glass.

⅛ shot	De Kuyper XO Apricot Brandy
2 shots	BarSol Mosto Verde Italia pisco
½ shot	Freshly squeezed lemon juice
¼ shot	Sugar syrup (2 sugar to 1 water)
1 dash	Angostura Orange Bitters
2 dash	Peychaud's aromatic bitters

Origin: Yet again I must thank drinks historian David Wondrich for unearthing this drink and its history. It was created by a bartender named Jim Maloney and first appeared in his 1903 'How to Mix Drinks'. Maloney patented the name 'Bell-Ringers' as referring to cocktails served in glasses rinsed with apricot brandy.
Comment: Go easy on the bitters and this will be a delicate, aromatic pisco cocktail.

PISCO COLLINS

★★★★☆

Glass: Collins
Garnish: Orange slice & cherry on stick (sail)
Method: SHAKE first three ingredients with ice and strain into ice-filled glass. TOP with soda, lightly stir and serve with straws.

2	shots	BarSol Mosto Verde Italia pisco
1	shot	Freshly squeezed lime juice
½	shot	Sugar syrup (2 sugar to 1 water)
Top with		Soda (club soda)

Comment: The most aromatic and flavoursome of the Collins family.

PISCO KID (NEW)

★★★★½

Glass: Coupe
Garnish: Orange zest twist (discarded) & Nestle's Milkybar or other white chocolate
Method: STIR all ingredients with ice and strain into chilled glass.

2 shots BarSol Mosto Verde Italia pisco
¾ shot De Kuyper White Crème de Cacao
½ shot Sauvignon blanc white wine
¼ shot Romate Fino sherry
½ shot Chilled water

Origin: Created by yours truly at the Cabinet Room, London, England.
Comment: This short pisco-based spirituous stirred drink was inspired by memories of Nestle's Milkybars and the 1980s British TV ads featuring the Milkybar Kid promoting the white chocolate bars. White crème de cacao's sweetness is balanced by dry sherry and the acidity of Sauvignon Blanc wine which also adds grassy floral notes and complexity. The discarded orange zest twist makes the first sip a white chocolate orange experience.

PISCO NARANJA

★★★★☆

Glass: Collins
Garnish: Orange slice
Method: SHAKE all ingredients with ice and strain into ice-filled glass.

2	shots	BarSol Mosto Verde Italia pisco
1	shot	Grand Marnier Cordon Rouge
3	shots	Freshly squeezed orange juice

Origin: I based this recipe on the traditional Chilean combination of pisco and orange juice.
Comment: Aromatic brandy and orange juice pepped and sweetened with a slug of orange liqueur.

Pisco Punch cocktail

Described by Rudyard Kipling as being "Compounded of the shavings of cherub's wings", the Pisco Punch was made famous at San Francisco's legendary Bank Exchange bar where the recipe was a closely guarded secret – to the extent that all we really know for sure is that it was made with pisco. However, many recipes and stories of the drink regale.

This exquisite drinks creation is usually credited to Professor Jerry Burns of the Bank Exchange. However, its origin could lie in the late 1800s, when the drink was served aboard steamships stopping in Peru, Puerto Vallarta, Mexico and San Diego en route to San Francisco and its gold rush economy. Those same ships ensured a plentiful supply of lemons, pineapples and the all-important pisco needed for San Francisco's bartenders to produce Pisco Punch cocktails.

The Bank Exchange Billiard Saloon was on the ground floor on the southwest corner of the Montgomery Block, on the corner of Montgomery and Washington Streets, San Francisco, near where the Transamerica Pyramid now stands. The bar opened in 1853 and survived the earthquake and fire of 1906. For over 50 years its popularity never waned and only Prohibition brought about its sad and unjust demise in 1919.

Resplendent in marble and mahogany, and lit by magnificent crystal chandeliers, the Bank Exchange was lavishly appointed and the main attraction in the city's most important building. Duncan Nicol, the last proprietor built a separate lounge for women, making it the first lounge in the American West where 'non-working' women could drink unimpeded as equals to the men. The Bank Exchange and its legendary Pisco Punch were enjoyed by the rich and famous.

Much of the Bank Exchange's notoriety was due to the Pisco Punch, so much so that the establishment gained the nickname 'Pisco John's'. Due to the bar's nickname, John Torrence, one of its early owners, is credited with the creation of the Pisco Punch but the last owner, Duncan Nicol (or Nichol, or Nichols) is also often identified with the drink's creation. In his 2007 book, 'Wings of Cherubs', Guillermo Toro-Lira surmises that Duncan Nicol was in fact 'Pisco John' and he was so nicknamed after his telephone number. The 1903 San Francisco telephone directory lists the first part telephone numbers as words, and the number for both John Nichol and the Bank Exchange as 'John 3246'

Mark Twain drank at the Bank Exchange with a flamboyant fireman named Tom Sawyer whom he'd acquainted while working as a reporter at the San Francisco Call. The stories that Tom Sawyer recounted at the bar inspired the literary 'Adventures' for the Tom Sawyer character in Twain's books.

After drinking at the Bank Exchange, Rudyard Kipling immortalised Pisco Punch in his 1889 ' From Sea to Sea' as being "compounded of the shavings of cherub's wings, the glory of a tropical dawn, the red clouds of sunset and the fragments of lost epics by dead masters".

In 1937, Harold Ross, founder of The New Yorker magazine, wrote "In the old days in San Francisco there was a famous drink called Pisco Punch, made from Pisco, a Peruvian brandy... pisco punch used to taste like lemonade but had a kick like vodka, or worse."

It is said that the Bank Exchange's Pisco Punch recipe was handed down from one owner to the next in absolute secrecy. Duncan Nicol, the Scottish immigrant who co-owned/owned the bar outright for a total of 32 years (1887 to 1919), either inherited the precious recipe from the previous owner, George Brown, or created the recipe himself - we'll probably never know for sure.

Whether or not Duncan Nicol was the originator of the Pisco Punch, it appears he was very secretive over the precious recipe, preparing batches of a gum arabic, sugar and pineapple pre-mix in the basement so that neither his patrons or staff could discover the exact recipe. Nicol died in 1926 at the age of 72, presumably taking the recipe with him.

Like so many classic cocktails, the original Pisco Punch recipe is lost to time and Duncan Nicol's grave, so is the subject of much drink historian's conjecture. However, where there's drink involved secrets tend to be divulged.

John Lannes was the manager of the Bank Exchange in its latter years and in 1919 took over ownership of the bar from Duncan Nicol, only to find the Prohibition was to force its closure the next year. In 1964, a William Bronson discovered John Lannes' Pisco Punch recipe in a letter written by a lawyer in 1941, and in 1973 Bronson published the recipe in the California History Society Quarterly:

1. Cut a ripe pineapple into 1 inch squares and place in bowl of gum syrup to soak overnight. This both flavours the gum syrup and when strained, produces sugar coated pineapple cubes with which to garnish each glass of Pisco Punch.

2. In the morning mix the following in a large container;
½ pint (8 oz) of the pineapple flavoured gum syrup
1 pint (16 oz) distilled water
¾ pint (10 oz) lemon juice
1 bottle (24 oz) Peruvian pisco

However, in the recipe above Lannes omits a secret ingredient, perhaps in deference to Nicol or perhaps because Nicol never revealed it to him. Back in 2003 I adapted Lannes' recipe to produce a simple but refreshing Pisco Punch.

John Lannes recipe and most modern interpretations of the Pisco Punch use a pineapple and gomme arabic marinade in place of sugar syrup. To make the marinade:
1. Cut the leafy head off your pineapple.
2. Thoroughly clean pineapple under hot water.
3. Core and remove the rind.
4. Cut the pineapple into inch (25mm) thick rings and then into cubes.
5. Place cubes in deep container, cover with gomme arabic and seal.
6. Leave marinade for 24 hours turning occasionally.
7. Strain, bottle the syrup and set aside the pineapple wedges to use as a garnish for your Pisco Punch.

In his book 'Wings of Cherubs', Guillermo Toro-Lira outlines historical evidence suggesting that the Pisco Punch made by Nicol at the Bank Exchange contained cocaine. The drug was widely available during the late 1800s and was a common ingredient in tonics, not to mention coca cola. Perhaps cocaine was the secret to the drink's lasting appeal – something perhaps supported by quotes referring to the Pisco Punch from the period, such as "it makes a gnat fight an elephant".

Toro-Lira says that "the most popular cocaine laced drink at the time was Vin Mariani (Mariani Wine) first concocted by the Italian Angelo Mariani in France in 1863." Vin Mariani was Bordeaux wine infused with coca leaf.

Duggan McDonnell, the owner San Francisco's Cantina bar and the Encanto Pisco brand, believes Vin Mariani was the secret ingredient in Nicol's Punch. McDonnell references "the glory of a tropical dawn, the red clouds of sunset" in Rudyard Kipling's famous Pisco Punch quote, pointing out that the quote implies that the drink had a reddish tint. Vin Mariani was red and so would have affected the appearance of the otherwise golden pineapple coloured drink.

Sadly, Vin Mariani hasn't been available since the early 20th century, partly due to its cocaine content hence McDonnell's Pisco Punch recipe uses Lillet Rouge in place of Vin Mariani which contributes much to the flavour and also adds the desired colour of the "red clouds of sunset".

Inspired by Alfredo Micheli's recipe (see below) I believe cloves are the key to a great Pisco Punch with the aromatic spice combining brilliantly with both pineapple and pisco. Either smash a couple of cloves in the base of your shaker before adding the other ingredients, or add to the marinade above.

My Pisco Punch recipe uses gomme arabic, clove and pineapple juice. It is essential that the pineapple juice is freshly extracted using a centrifugal extractor. I find with fresh pineapple juice there is no need to make the marinade, although if I have time and the inclination I use a combination of pineapple juice and the marinade. I've experimented with lime and lemon juice and both work well but I favour lemon juice or even a 50/50 combination of the two citrus juices. A splash of freshly squeezed orange juice also contributes greatly to the punch.

Alfredo Micheli, who went by the nickname Mike, was employed at the Bank Exchange and is said to have spied on Duncan Nichol as he prepared the pre-mixed batch ingredients in the bar's basement. After he believed he'd learnt the secret he left the Bank Exchange to start bartending at a newly opened competitor to the Bank Exchange, Paoli's on Montgomery Street. Alfredo's Pisco Punch recipe relies on a pineapple marinade as described above, but with the addition of clove.

Jack Koeppler, the bartender at the Buena Vista Café in San Francisco who's also famous for being the first bartender in America to serve Irish Coffee, was given a white grape based and absinthe influenced Pisco Punch recipe by the son of its creator, a fellow San Franciscan by the name of Mr Prosser.

In his book 'Wings of Cherubs', Guillermo Toro-Lira examines the Pisco Punch recipe John Lannes gave to Crawford Green in 1941 and concludes that it "reveals a break-up of bartending mixing rules". Toro-Lira re-balances the recipe and due to evidence he has unearthed deduces the original Bank Exchange Pisco Punch recipe used limes and not lemons as is stated in Lannes' recipe.

Toro-Lira also says that in order to minimize waste and eke out the most flavour from the expensive pineapples "Nicol may have added a relatively small step during the production of his punch. One which could have further contributed to the punch's renowned smoothness and overall appeal." Many Pisco Punch recipes, including Lannes', stipulate the use of distilled water. Toro-Lira asserts that this is inspired by the Peruvian drink called 'Chicha de piña' which has been prepared since the 1700's by soaking the rind of a clean pineapple for 24 hours in water. He says that "Nicol could have easily prepared the Chicha by soaking the pineapple rind - which was a waste of his punch preparation process – in distilled water and then use this as the water component of the punch."

I've made Guillermo Toro-Lira's Revisited Pisco Punch recipe using both Chicha and plain water. It's very simple and makes a good drink, even better when made with Chicha.
3 shots Pisco
2 shots Pineapple gum arabic syrup
1 shots Freshly squeezed Lime juice
4 shots Chilled water (or chicha water)

PISCO PUNCH (DIFFORD'S RECIPE)

★ ★ ★ ★ ★

Glass: Old-fashioned
Garnish: Pineapple wedge
Method: MUDDLE cloves in base of shaker. Add next 5 ingredients, SHAKE with ice and strain into ice-filled glass. TOP with champagne.

2	dried	Clove
2	shots	BarSol Mosto Verde Italia pisco
1	shot	Fresh pressed pineapple juice
½	shot	Freshly squeezed orange juice
½	shot	Freshly squeezed lemon juice
½	shot	Sugar syrup (2 sugar to 1 water)
½	shot	G.H. Mumm Cordon Rouge Champagne

Origin: Formula by yours truly in 2003, London, England.
Comment: A tangy, balanced combination of rich flavours. The quality of pisco used is crucial to the success of a Pisco Punch.

PISCO PUNCH (LANNES' RECIPE)

★ ★ ★ ★ ☆

Glass: Collins
Garnish: Pineapple wedge
Method: SHAKE first four ingredients with ice and strain into glass filled with crushed ice. TOP with soda.

2½ shots	BarSol Mosto Verde Italia pisco
½ shot	Freshly squeezed lemon juice
1 shot	Fresh pressed pineapple juice
½ shot	Sugar syrup (2 sugar to 1 water)
Top with	Soda (club soda)

Origin: This recipe is adapted from John Lannes' recipe, owner of the famous Bank Exchange when it closed in 1920.
Comment: Pisco's character shines through the sweetened pineapple fruit in this long, refreshing classic.

PISCO PUNCH (MICHELI'S RECIPE)

★★★★⯨

Glass: Goblet
Garnish: Pineapple wedge
Method: **MUDDLE** orange and pineapple in base of shaker. Add pisco and pineapple marinade. **SHAKE** with ice and fine strain into ice-filled glass. **TOP** with no more than two shots of soda water.

2	slice	Fresh orange
3	fresh	Marinated pineapple wedges
2	shots	BarSol Mosto Verde Italia pisco
¾	shot	Pineapple marinade
Top with		Soda (club soda)

Origin: Alfredo Micheli (who went by the nickname Mike) was employed at the Bank Exchange and spied on Duncan Nichol to learn how to make this legendary drink. After he believed he'd learnt the secret he left to start serving at a newly opened competitor to the Bank Exchange, Paoli's on Montgomery Street.
Comment: This Pisco Punch is very fruity and slightly on the sweet side but is so tasty that it justifies it's legendary reputation.

PISCO PUNCH (PROSSER'S RECIPE)

★★★★★

Glass: Martini
Garnish: White grapes
Method: **MUDDLE** grapes in base of shaker. Add other ingredients, **SHAKE** with ice and fine strain into chilled glass.

20	fresh	Seedless white grapes
2½	shots	BarSol Mosto Verde Italia pisco
1	shot	Fresh pressed pineapple juice
⅛	shot	Le Fée Parisienne absinthe

Origin: Jack Koeppler, the bartender at the Buena Vista Café in San Francisco who's also famous for being the first bartender in America to serve Irish Coffee, was given this recipe by the son of it's creator, a fellow San Franciscan by the name of Mr Prosser.

I adapted this recipe from Mr Prosser's recipe, which originally comprised: 2 shots white grape juice, 2 shots pisco, 1 spoon pineapple juice and 1 spoon absinthe.
Comment: An aromatic take on the Pisco Punch.

Pisco Sour cocktail

The national drink of both Peru and Chile and both countries lay claim to the origins of the Pisco Sour and indeed the spirit it is made from, but as I explain below the earliest known Pisco Sour recipe is of Peruvian origin.

All the Peruvian bartenders I met blend rather than shake their Pisco Sours. Indeed, it is a brilliant blended cocktail and if you want to try this method then add a touch more sugar than if you are shaking and blend with scoop of crushed ice. However, I prefer my Pisco Sours shaken.

While some like to omit the egg white, like most sours it's better made with, although half a small egg white is plenty. I'm an advocate of sugar syrup over caster sugar in all drinks, the Pisco Sour included, but there are plenty of misguided folks who'd argue to the contrary.

More worthy of debate is the choice of pisco. My Peruvian friends favour pisco made from the Quebranta grape or even acholado (a blend of varieties). However, I prefer to use Peruvian pisco made from the more aromatic Italia grape, preferably mosto verde Italia pisco.

Convention has it that the Pisco Sour is garnished with three drops of bitters dropped symmetrically onto its foaming head. This not only adds to the visual appearance, the aroma of the bitters also helps mask the wet dog-like smell of egg white. Angostura Aromatic Bitters are fine but for authenticity consider using Peruvian Amargo Chuncho bitters which are based on various Amazonian barks and herbs. Some also dust the surface of the drink, or the rim of the glass, with cinnamon.

Somewhat controversially, if the use of Italia pisco were not enough, I also like to add a dash of orange flower water to my Pisco Sours. I also tend to serve them straight-up in a frozen heavy bottomed old-fashioned glass to help retain the drinks cold temperature but a frozen coupe also works well.

Like so many vintage cocktails, the documented origins of the Pisco Sour have changed over recent years as evidence of earlier origins has been discovered. Back in the mid-1980s, a Chilean newspaper, El Comercio de Iquique, reported that the pisco sour was created in 1872 by Elliot Stubb, an English steward from a sailing ship named Sunshine, who opened a bar in the then Peruvian port of Iquique (now in northern Chile). However, closer scrutiny shows a quote attributed to Stubb was actually about the whiskey sour, the forerunner to the pisco sour, the origins of which lie even earlier in the United States.

In 2009, Luis Guillermo Toro-Lira Stahl and Michael P. Morris published a document 'Clarifying the legends in the history of pisco sour'. This traced the origins of the Pisco Sour to Victor Vaughen Morris Jones (Victor Morris), the grandfather of one of the authors.

Victor Morris, originated from Salt Lake City, Utah, but immigrated to Peru in 1903, initially working as a cashier for the Cerro de Pasco Railroad railway company in the town of Cerro de Pasco. Legend, and indeed members of his family, say that while working here at the inauguration of the line from Oroyo, Morris created the Pisco Sour after running out of whiskey for the Whiskey Sours he was making for the reported 5,000 people in attendance.

Morris moved to Lima, where, backed by long term friend Daniel C. Babbitt, on 1st April 1916 he opened the appropriately named Morris' Bar at 847 Calle Boza. Here, Morris, who was also known by his nickname Gringo, became noted for his Pisco Sours and the bar prospered.

The bar's original 82 page visitor book, titled 'Morris' Bar Register', still in the hands of the Morris family, records more than 2,200 signatures, their names showing that it was a high end establishment attracting many visiting Americans including diplomats, businessmen, lawyers and journalists. Notable names in the journal include: Emiliano Figueroa, former president of Chile and ambassador to Peru; millionaire Roger W. Straus and Elmer Faucett, founder of the Company of Faucett Aviation. Perhaps most interesting is John Lannes from the Bank Exchange in San Francisco, famous for the Pisco Punch.

Numerous remarks from visitors in this register testify to the delicious nature of Morris' pisco sours. As does a July 1924 notice for the Morris' Bar in the South Pacific Mail, a newspaper from the Chilean port of Valparaiso published weekly in English by Nelson Rounsevell, a friend of Morris who had also worked in Cerro de Pasco. The advert asks, "Have you registered at the Morris Bar LIMA? It goes on the say the register at the bar can be helpful to contact [English-speaking] acquaintances and ends with "has been known for many years for their 'Pisco Sours'."

An earlier mention of the Pisco Sour in the 22nd April 1921 edition of the Peruvian magazine Mundial, describes the drink as a white-coloured beverage and attributes its invention to "Mister Morris."

The 1929 Lima directory - The City of the Viceroys, lists the Pisco Sour as one of Morris Bar's cocktails under the heading "visitelo y pida alguna especialidad".

Sadly for Victor it appears that bartenders working at Morris' Bar left, taking his recipe with them to nearby establishments with bars such as the Hotel Bolivar (opened December 1924) and the Lima Country Club (opened February 1927). The competition for wealthy foreign guests obviously had detrimental effect on his bar's success. Victor's fortunes and his health declined eventually leading to his declaring voluntary bankruptcy and the closing of the Morris Bar in 1929. He died a few months later, on 11th June, of cirrhosis aged 56. In December, Morris' wife, Maria Vargas emigrated to San Francisco, California with their three children.

With its large turnover of guests, the bar at The Hotel Bolivar which was largely staffed by ex-Morris' bartenders, is widely credited for spreading the popularity of the Pisco Sour. The drinks survival is also attributed to Mario Alfonso Bruijet

Burgos, a bartender who worked at Morris' Bar from 1924 and continued serving Pisco Sours at the Hotel Maury until his retirement. Some say that it is Bruijet who added bitters to the recipe after his move to the Maury.

With a few twists, turns and variations, the above was the accepted origin of the Pisco Sour. That was until 22nd February 2012, when Peruvian writer Raúl Rivera Escobar uploaded a scan of a pamphlet published in Lima in 1903 by S.E. Ledesma to an internet page. Titled ' Nuevo Manual de Cocina a la Criolla' , 'New Manual of Creole Cooking', on page 32, among the food recipes, this includes a recipe simply titled 'Cocktail', containing an "egg white, a cup of pisco, a teaspoon of sugar and a few drops of lime juice to taste". Obviously a Pisco Sour, this is the earliest known recipe.

Nuevo Manual de Cocina a la Criolla proves that Victor Morris didn't create the Pisco Sour and also shows that Mario Bruijet was not responsible for adding egg white to the recipe while working at Hotel Maury, as previously suggested by some.

So the Pisco Sour dates from before 1903 and looks to be of Peruvian rather than Chilean origin. We shall probably never know who was first to take a Whiskey Sour recipe and use pisco as the base spirit. Or indeed who was first to add bitters to it. It's a wonderful coincidence that Victor Morris also emigrated to Peru in 1903.

The drinks recent popularity outside of its native Peru and Chile is attributed to Joe Baum who promoted the drink in the 1960s at La Fonda Del Sol in New York.

PISCO SOUR (DIFFORD'S RECIPE)

★★★★⯪

Glass: Old-fashioned
Garnish: Three drops of Angostura bitters
Method: SHAKE all ingredients with ice and fine strain into chilled glass.

2	shots	BarSol Mosto Verde Italia pisco
¾	shot	Freshly squeezed lime juice
½	shot	Sugar syrup (2 sugar to 1 water)
½	fresh	Egg white
1	dash	Orange flower water

Comment: Traditionally this is drunk is blended with crushed ice, but I prefer it served straight-up. Be sure to drink it quickly while it's cold.

PISCOLA

★★★⯪☆

Glass: Collins
Garnish: Lime wedge
Method: POUR pisco and bitters into ice-filled glass, top with cola, stir and serve with straws.

2½ shots	BarSol Mosto Verde Italia pisco
3	dash	Angostura Aromatic Bitters
Top with	Coca-Cola

Origin: A popular long drink in its native Chile.
Comment: A 'brandy' and cola with a hint of angostura bitters. Try and see why the Chileans enjoy it.

PLANTATION PUNCH

★★★⯪☆

Glass: Collins
Garnish: Orange slice & mint sprig
Method: SHAKE first five ingredients with ice and strain into ice-filled glass. TOP with soda.

1	shot	Bacardi Carta Blanca light rum
1½ shots	Southern Comfort liqueur
¾	shot	Freshly squeezed lemon juice
¼	shot	Sugar syrup (2 sugar to 1 water)
2	dash	Angostura Aromatic Bitters
Top with	Soda (club soda)

Comment: Southern Comfort drives this tropical punch.

PLANTER'S PUNCH

★★★★☆

Glass: Collins
Garnish: Orange slice & mint sprig
Method: SHAKE all ingredients with ice and strain into ice-filled glass.

1½ shots	Pot still Jamaican rum
1	shot	Freshly squeezed lime juice
½	shot	Sugar syrup (2 sugar to 1 water)
3	dash	Angostura Aromatic Bitters
2	shots	Chilled water

Origin: Invented in the late 19th century by the founder of Myers's rum, Fred L. Myers. The recipe on the back of each bottle is known as the 'Old Plantation formula' and uses classic rum punch proportions of 1 sour (lime), 2 sweet (sugar), 3 strong (rum) and 4 weak (water). Rather than this or the American formula (1 sour, 2 sweet, 3 weak, and 4 strong), I've followed David A. Embury's recommendation of 1 sweet, 2 sour, 3 strong and 4 weak.
Comment: A tangy punch which harnesses the rich flavours of Myers's rum.

PLANTER'S PUNCHLESS (MOCKTAIL)

★★★☆☆

Glass: Collins
Garnish: Lime wedge
Method: SHAKE first three ingredients with ice and strain into ice-filled glass. TOP with lemonade, lightly stir and serve with straws.

2	shots	Pressed apple juice
¾	shot	Freshly squeezed lime juice
¼	shot	Pomegranate / grenadine syrup (2:1)
Top with	Lemonade / Sprite / 7-Up

Comment: A pleasant, if uninspiring, driver's option.

PLANTEUR

★★★★☆

Glass: Collins
Garnish: Orange slice
Method: SHAKE all ingredients with ice and strain into ice-filled glass.

2	shots	Martinique blanc rhum agricole
¼	shot	Pomegranate / grenadine syrup (2:1)
3½ shots	Freshly squeezed orange juice

Comment: Handle with extreme care.

A
B
C
D
E
F
G
H
I
J
K
L
M
N
O
P
Q
R
S
T
U
V
W
X
Y
Z

PLAYA DEL MAR ⚷

★★★★☆

Glass: Martini
Garnish: Pineapple wedge
Method: SHAKE all ingredients with ice and fine strain into chilled glass.

1	shot	Patrón reposado tequila
½	shot	De Kuyper Triple Sec
1	shot	Cranberry juice
¾	shot	Fresh pressed pineapple juice
½	shot	Freshly squeezed lime juice
¼	shot	Sugar syrup (2 sugar to 1 water)

Origin: This cocktail was created in 1997 by Wayne Collins at Navajo Joe, London, England. The name translates as a 'Beach of the Sea'.
Comment: A fruity complex taste with a hint of tequila.

PLAYMATE COCKTAIL

★★★★⯪

Glass: Martini
Garnish: Orange zest twist and 2 drops of bitter on foamy head (spread with a cocktail stick)
Method: SHAKE all ingredients with ice and fine strain into chilled glass.

¾	shot	Martell VSOP Médaillon cognac
¾	shot	Grand Marnier Cordon Rouge
¾	shot	De Kuyper XO Apricot Brandy
¾	shot	Freshly squeezed orange juice
½	fresh	Egg white
2	dash	Angostura Aromatic Bitters

Comment: Apricot and orange laced with cognac. Smooth and easy drinking.

PLEASED AS PUNCH

★★★⯪☆

Glass: Goblet
Garnish: Mint sprig
Method: SHAKE first five ingredients with ice and fine strain into ice-filled glass. **TOP** with champagne and lightly stir.

1	shot	Ketel One Citroen vodka
½	shot	St-Germain elderflower liqueur
¾	shot	Freshly squeezed lemon juice
¼	shot	Sugar syrup (2 sugar to 1 water)
5	fresh	Mint leaves
Top with		G.H. Mumm Cordon Rouge Champagne

Origin: Adapted from a drink created in 2012 by Chris Hopkins, USA.
Comment: Refreshing lemony citrus with a splash of elderflower liqueur, enlivened with champagne.

PLUM DAIQUIRI

★★★★☆

Glass: Martini
Garnish: Lime wedge
Method: CUT plum into quarters, remove stone and peel. **MUDDLE** plum in base of shaker. Add other ingredients, **SHAKE** with ice and fine strain into chilled glass.

1	fresh	Plum (stoned, peeled & chopped)
2	shots	Bacardi Carta Blanca light rum
½	shot	Freshly squeezed lime juice
½	shot	Sugar syrup (2 sugar to 1 water)

Comment: Depending on the ripeness of the plums, you may need to adjust the quantity of sugar.

PLUM SOUR

★★★★⯪

Glass: Old-fashioned
Garnish: Orange zest twist
Method: MUDDLE plum in base of shaker. Add other ingredients, **SHAKE** with ice and fine strain into ice-filled glass.

1	fresh	Plum (stoned, peeled & chopped)
2	shots	Ketel One Vodka
1	shot	Freshly squeezed lemon juice
½	shot	Sugar syrup (2 sugar to 1 water)
½	fresh	Egg white

Comment: Soft, ripe plums are key to this fruity sour.

POET'S DREAM

★★★★⯪

Glass: Martini
Garnish: Lemon zest twist
Method: STIR all ingredients with ice and strain into chilled glass.

1	shot	Rutte Dry Gin
½	shot	Bénédictine D.O.M. liqueur
1	shot	Martini Extra Dry vermouth
2	dash	Angostura Orange Bitters
½	shot	Chilled water (omit if wet ice)

Origin: Adapted from an original recipe in the 1949 edition of 'Esquire's Handbook for Hosts'.
Comment: Subtle, honeyed and herbal.

POGO STICK ⚷

★★★★☆

Glass: Martini
Garnish: Mint sprig
Method: BLEND all ingredients with 12oz scoop crushed ice. Serve with straws.

2	shots	Rutte Dry Gin
½	shot	Fresh pressed pineapple juice
½	shot	Freshly squeezed pink grapefruit juice
½	shot	Freshly squeezed lime juice
½	shot	Sugar syrup (2 sugar to 1 water)

Origin: Adapted from a recipe in the 1947-72 'Trader Vic's Bartender's Guide' by Victor Bergeron.
Comment: To quote Trader Vic, "A refreshing blend of gin with pineapple and grapefruit juice... a real romper".

POINSETTIA ⚷

★★★⯪☆

Glass: Flute
Garnish: Orange slice
Method: POUR first two ingredients into chilled glass. **TOP** with champagne.

½	shot	De Kuyper Triple Sec
1	shot	Cranberry juice
Top with		G.H. Mumm Cordon Rouge Champagne

Comment: Fruity champagne.

POLISH MARTINI

★★★★☆

Glass: Martini
Garnish: Apple slice
Method: SHAKE all ingredients with ice and fine strain into chilled glass.

¾	shot	Ketel One vodka
¾	shot	Bison grass vodka
⅔	shot	Krupnik spiced honey liqueur
1	shot	Pressed apple juice

Comment: In Poland Bison Grass vodka and apple juice are a classic combo, here also with an additional splash of Polish honey liqueur.
Origin: Created by Dick Bradsell, for his (Polish) father-in-law, Victor Sarge. The original formula was equal parts, but that was also with sweet clear pasteurized apple juice.

POLLY'S SPECIAL

★★★★☆

Glass: Martini
Garnish: Grapefruit wedge
Method: SHAKE all ingredients with ice and fine strain into chilled glass.

2	shots	Dewar's 12yo Scotch whisky
1	shot	Freshly squeezed pink grapefruit juice
1	shot	Grand Marnier Cordon Rouge
⅛	shot	Sugar syrup (2 sugar to 1 water)

Origin: Adapted from a recipe in the 1947-72 'Trader Vic's Bartender's Guide' by Victor Bergeron.
Comment: Sweet, sour, flavoursome and balanced.

POMEGRANATE COCKTAIL

★★★★☆

Glass: Martini
Garnish: Orange zest twist
Method: SHAKE all ingredients with ice and fine strain into chilled glass.

2	shots	Ketel One Vodka
1½	shots	Pomegranate juice
½	shot	Pomegranate / grenadine syrup (2:1)

Origin: Adapted from a drink discovered in 2005 at Lotus Bar, Sydney, Australia.
Comment: This drink was originally based on gin but we find that juniper and pomegranate clash.

POMEGRANATE MARGARITA

★★★★☆

Glass: Coupe
Garnish: Lime wedge
Method: SHAKE all ingredients with ice and fine strain into chilled glass.

2	shots	Patrón reposado tequila
1	shot	Pomegranate juice
¼	shot	Pomegranate / grenadine syrup (2:1)
½	shot	Freshly squeezed lime juice

Origin: Recipe by yours truly in 2006.
Comment: Pomegranate and tequila combine harmoniously in this Margarita.

POMME ET SUREAU

★★★★☆

Glass: Collins
Garnish: Apple wedge
Method: POUR first 2 ingredients into ice-filled glass, **TOP** with soda and lightly stir.

1	shot	Calvados brandy
2	shots	St-Germain elderflower liqueur
Top with		Soda (club soda)

Origin: Created in 2006 by yours truly. The name is French for 'apple and elderflower'.
Comment: Light, long and refreshing apple and elderflower.

POMPANSKI MARTINI

★★★★☆

Glass: Martini
Garnish: Orange zest twist
Method: SHAKE all ingredients with ice and fine strain into chilled glass.

1¾	shots	Ketel One Vodka
½	shot	De Kuyper Triple Sec
1½	shots	Freshly squeezed pink grapefruit juice
¼	shot	Sugar syrup (2 sugar to 1 water)
1	spoon	Martini Extra Dry vermouth

Comment: Dry and zesty with the sharp freshness of grapefruit and a hint of orange.

PONCE DE LEON

★★★★☆

Glass: Flute
Garnish: None
Method: SHAKE first four ingredients with ice and fine strain into chilled glass. **TOP** with champagne.

½	shot	Bacardi Carta Blanca light rum
½	shot	Martell VSOP Médaillon cognac
½	shot	De Kuyper Triple Sec
½	shot	Freshly squeezed pink grapefruit juice
Top with		G.H. Mumm Cordon Rouge Champagne

Origin: A long lost classic.
Comment: A well-balanced classic champagne cocktail.

PONCHA

★★★★☆

Glass: Collins
Garnish: Orange wedge
Method: STIR honey with aguardiente in base of shaker to dissolve honey. Add other ingredients, **SHAKE** with ice and strain into ice filled glass.

2	spoon	Runny honey
2½	shots	Torres Aqua d'Or aguardiente
1	shot	Freshly squeezed lemon juice
¼	shot	Sugar syrup (2 sugar to 1 water)
1½	shots	Freshly squeezed orange juice
1½	shots	Freshly squeezed pink grapefruit juice

Origin: My adaptation of a traditional drink from the island of Madeira.
Comment: This citrus refresher is reputedly an excellent cold remedy.

PONCHE DE ALGARROBINA

★★★½☆

Glass: Goblet
Garnish: Dust with cinnamon powder
Method: BLEND all ingredients with 12oz scoop crushed ice. Serve with straws.

2	shots	BarSol Mosto Verde Italia pisco
1	fresh	Egg yolk
1	shot	Condensed milk
1	spoon	Algarrobo extract (or malt extract from health food shops)

Origin: We discovered this traditional Peruvian drink at Tito's Restaurant, London, England. Algarrobo is extracted from the fruits of the tree of the same name and is a sticky honey-like liquid which tastes a little like malt extract.
Comment: A creamy frozen drink with real character. Tip: It pays to add the condensed milk and algarrobo (or malt extract) after starting the blender.

PONTBERRY MARTINI

★★★★☆

Glass: Martini
Garnish: Blackberries
Method: SHAKE all ingredients with ice and fine strain into chilled glass.

1½	shots	Ketel One Vodka
½	shot	Lejay Crème de Mûre liqueur
2	shots	Cranberry juice

Origin: Created by Dick Bradsell in the late 90s for the opening of Agent Provocateur in Pont Street, London, England.
Comment: A light, fruity, easy drinking cocktail.

POOH'TINI

★★★★½

Glass: Martini
Garnish: Lemon zest twist
Method: STIR honey with vodka in base of shaker to dissolve honey. Add other ingredients, **SHAKE** with ice and fine strain into chilled glass.

2	spoon	Runny honey
2	shots	Zubrówka bison vodka
1½	shots	Cold camomile tea
½	shot	Old Krupnik

Origin: Adapted from a drink discovered in 1999 at Lot 61, New York City.
Comment: Grassy honey with spicy, slightly tannic, camomile finish.

POP MY CHERRY

★★★★½☆

Glass: Martini
Garnish: Dust with chocolate powder
Method: SHAKE all ingredients with ice and fine strain into chilled glass.

1	shot	Cherry Heering Liqueur
½	shot	Disaronno Originale amaretto
½	shot	Ketel One Vodka (infused with vanilla)
1	shot	Milk
1	shot	Single cream / half-and-half

Origin: Adapted from a drink created by in 2010 by Sarah Mason, United Kingdom.
Comment: A crowd pleasing cherry and almond dessert-style cocktail.

POPEYE SOUR (NEW)

★★★★☆

Glass: Coupe
Garnish: Spinach leaf
Method: MUDDLE spinach in base of shaker. Add other ingredients, **SHAKE** with ice and strain back into shaker. **DRY SHAKE** (without ice) and fine strain into chilled glass.

8	fresh	Baby spinach leaves
1⅔	shots	Capucana cachaça
¼	shot	Del Maguey VIDA mezcal
⅓	shot	King's Ginger Liqueur
⅔	shot	Freshly squeezed lime juice
⅓	shot	Almond (orgeat) syrup
¼	fresh	Egg white

Origin: Adapted from a drink created by Juanillo Falcon at Creps al Born, Barcelona, Spain.
Comment: Spinach gives this cachaça-based cocktail a vibrant green colour while its flavour is influenced by lime, ginger and rich almond.

PORN STAR MARTINI

★★★★☆

Glass: Coupe
Garnish: Float half fresh passion fruit
Method: Wash and cut passion fruit in half, **SCOOP** out the seeds and flesh into shaker. (Keep last passion fruit half for garnish). Add next four ingredients (all but champagne), **SHAKE** with ice and fine strain into chilled glass. **POUR** champagne into chilled shot glass to serve on the side. Instruct drinker to sip alternately from each glass.

1½	fresh	Passion fruit
2	shots	Vanilla infused Ketel One vodka
½	shot	Passoa Liqueur
½	shot	Vanilla sugar syrup
½	shot	Freshly squeezed lime juice
2	shots	G.H. Mumm Cordon Rouge Champagne

Origin: Adapted from a drink created in 2002 by Douglas Ankrah at The Townhouse bar in Knightsbridge, London. Douglas also founded London's LAB bar which is also often associated with this drink.
Comment: A fruity sweet crowd-pleaser with champagne served on the side.

PORT & STARBOARD

★★½☆☆

Glass: Shot
Garnish: None
Method: Refrigerate ingredients then **LAYER** in chilled glass by carefully pouring in the following order.

| ½ | shot | Pomegranate / grenadine syrup (2:1) |
| ½ | shot | Giffard Menthe Pastille liqueur |

Origin: Named after and inspired by the red and green running lights which respectively mark the 'Port' (left-hand) and 'Starboard' (right-hand) sides of a ship. The red light is called Port side because port wine is red. The original name for the opposite side was Larboard, but over the years was corrupted to Starboard.
Comment: Easy to layer but hard to drink. Very sweet.

PORT FLIP

★★★½☆

Glass: Martini
Garnish: Dust with grated nutmeg
Method: SHAKE all ingredients with ice and fine strain into chilled glass.

1	shot	Martell VSOP Médaillon cognac
3	shots	Tawny port
⅛	shot	Sugar syrup (2 sugar to 1 water)
1	fresh	Eggs (white & yolk)

Comment: Old-school and something of a meal in a glass.

PORT LIGHT

★★★½☆

Glass: Martini
Garnish: Passion fruit
Method: STIR honey with bourbon in base of shaker to dissolve honey. Cut passion fruit in half and scoop flesh into shaker. Add other ingredients, **SHAKE** with ice and fine strain into chilled glass.

2	spoon	Runny honey
2	shots	Bourbon whiskey
2	fresh	Passion fruit
1	shot	Freshly squeezed lemon juice
½	shot	Pomegranate / grenadine syrup (2:1)
½	fresh	Egg white

Origin: Adapted from a drink created by Victor Bergeron (Trader Vic)
Comment: Strong and very fruity. Too many will put your lights out.

PORT NO.2

★★★½☆

Glass: Martini
Garnish: Orange zest twist
Method: STIR all ingredients with ice and strain into chilled glass.

2	shots	Tawny port
½	shot	Orange Curaçao liqueur
2	dash	Angostura Orange Bitters
1	dash	Angostura Aromatic Bitters

Origin: Vintage cocktail of unknown origin.
Comment: Sangria for grown-ups.

PORT OF SPAIN COCKTAIL (NEW)

★★★★☆

Glass: Coupe
Garnish: Lemon zest twist
Method: SHAKE all ingredients with ice and strain back into shaker. **DRY SHAKE** (without ice) and fine strain into chilled glass.

1	shot	Straight rye whiskey
½	shot	Angostura Aromatic Bitters
½	shot	Allspice pimento dram liqueur
¾	shot	Freshly squeezed lemon juice
¾	shot	Pomegranate / grenadine syrup (2:1)
½	fresh	Egg white

Origin: Adapted from a drink created in 2013 by Kyle Mathis at Taste Bar, St. Louis, Missouri, USA.
Comment: Unusual in its bold use of a half shot of Angostura Bitters. In Knee High Bar in Seattle, USA I've tried this cocktail made with a massive one-and-a-half shots. However, half a shot seems more than generous.

PORT SANGAREE

★★★½☆

Glass: Sour
Garnish: Orange zest twist
Method: STIR all ingredients with ice and strain into chilled glass.

2	shots	Tawny port
1	shot	Chilled water
¼	shot	Sugar syrup (2 sugar to 1 water)

Origin: Vintage cocktail of unknown origin.
Comment: Wine-like, light and easy.

PORT WINE COCKTAIL

★★★½☆

Glass: Martini
Garnish: Orange zest twist
Method: STIR all ingredients with ice and strain into chilled glass.

| 1 | shot | Martell VSOP Médaillon cognac |
| 3 | shots | Tawny port |

Origin: A classic from the early 1900s.
Comment: Port and brandy served straight-up and dressed up.

PORTOBELLO STAR MANHATTAN (PERFECT)

★★★★★

Glass: Coupe
Garnish: Cherry on stick
Method: STIR all ingredients with ice and strain into chilled glass.

2	shots	Straight rye whiskey
½	shot	Martini Extra Dry vermouth
½	shot	Carpano Antica Formula
1	dash	Abbott's Bitters

Origin: Jake Burger introduced his take on the Perfect Manhattan at the Portobello Star, Notting Hill, London, England in 2011 after working with Robert Petrie of Bob's Bitters fame to make a reproduction of Abbott's Bitters. Jake uses Jim Beam rye whiskey, Noilly Prat Blanc Original dry vermouth, Carpano Antica Formula and Abbott's Bitters.
Comment: Rye based (originally Jim Beam) perfectly served with dry vermouth and Antica Formula

POTTED PARROT

★★★½☆

Glass: Sling
Garnish: Parrot on stick & mint sprig
Method: SHAKE all ingredients with ice and strain into a glass filled with crushed ice.

2	shots	Bacardi Carta Blanca light rum
½	shot	De Kuyper Triple Sec
2	shots	Freshly squeezed orange juice
1	shot	Freshly squeezed lemon juice
¼	shot	Sugar syrup (2 sugar to 1 water)
¼	shot	Almond (orgeat) syrup

Origin: Adapted from a recipe in the 1947-72 'Trader Vic's Bartender's Guide' by Victor Bergeron. Popular in Trader Vic's restaurants.
Comment: Tangy orange, not too sweet.

POUSSE-CAFÉ

★★☆☆☆

Glass: Shot
Garnish: None
Method: Refrigerate ingredients then **LAYER** in chilled glass by carefully pouring in the following order.

¼	shot	Pomegranate / grenadine syrup (2:1)
¼	shot	Coffee liqueur
¼	shot	Green crème de menthe liqueur
¼	shot	De Kuyper Triple Sec
¼	shot	Bourbon whiskey
¼	shot	White overproof rum

Origin: A pousse-café is now a term for any multi-layered cocktail. The term originally seems to have been a general term for a mixture of liqueurs and/or spirits served after dinner, and most probably originated in France.
Comment: More a test of patience and a steady hand than a drink.

PRADO

★★★★☆

Glass: Martini
Garnish: Lime wedge
Method: SHAKE all ingredients with ice and fine strain into chilled glass.

2	shots	Patrón reposado tequila
1	shot	Freshly squeezed lime juice
½	shot	Luxardo Maraschino liqueur
½	shot	Egg white

Comment: Rather like a cross between an Aviation and a Margarita.

PRAECOCIA COCKTAIL

★★★★★

Glass: Coupe
Garnish: Luxardo Maraschino cherry
Method: STIR all ingredients with ice and strain into chilled glass.

1½ shots Bourbon whiskey
¾ shot Carpano Punt E Mes
¼ shot De Kuyper XO Apricot Brandy
1 dash Angostura Aromatic Bitters

Origin: Created in 2010 by Jamie Boudreau at Vessel, Seattle, USA. Jamie describes his 1½ spirits to ¾ vermouth and ¼ modifier as the 'Mister Potato Head of Ratios'.
Comment: Bourbon and apricot are an established match made in Heaven, and everybody who drinks Manhattans will recognise how well sweet vermouth and bitters work with bourbon.

PRAIRIE OYSTER #1 (MOCKTAIL)

★★☆☆☆

Glass: Coupe
Garnish: None
Method: Taking care not to break the egg yolk, **PLACE** it in the centre of the hollow in the glass. **SHAKE** the rest of the ingredients with ice and strain over egg. Instruct drinker to down in one.

1	fresh	Egg yolk
¼	shot	Malt vinegar
1	spoon	Worcestershire sauce
1	spoon	Tomato ketchup
5	drop	Tabasco hot pepper sauce

Origin: Recipe adapted from Harry Craddock's 1930 'Savoy Cocktail Book'. This drink is thought to have originally been created in Germany in the 1870s. Jeeves makes something similar for Bertie Wooster in a P.G. Wodehouse tale.
Comment: Like many supposed hangover cures, this works on the kill or cure basis. It tastes slightly better than it looks.

PRAIRIE OYSTER #2 (MODERN & ALCOHOLIC)

★★★☆☆

Glass: Coupe
Garnish: None
Method: Taking care not to break the egg yolk, **PLACE** it in the centre of the hollow in the glass. **SHAKE** the rest of the ingredients with ice and strain over egg. Instruct drinker to down in one.

1	fresh	Egg yolk
1	shot	Martell VSOP Médaillon cognac
¼	shot	Worcestershire sauce
¼	shot	Tomato juice
5	drop	Tabasco hot pepper sauce
2	pinch	Salt
2	grind	Black pepper
½	shot	Malt vinegar

Comment: This 'pick-me-up' (A.K.A. hangover cure) may be a somewhat daunting prospect irrespective of the present state of your constitution.

PRALINE PECAN PIE

★★★★☆

Glass: Coupe
Garnish: Orange zest twist
Method: SHAKE all ingredients with ice and fine strain into chilled glass.

2	shots	Bourbon whiskey
½	shot	Martini Rosso vermouth
½	shot	Praline Original Pecan Liqueur
2	dash	Angostura Aromatic Bitters

Origin: Created in December 2010 by Cheri Loughlin, The Intoxicologist, USA.
Comment: Reminiscent of a pecan-flavoured Sweet Manhattan.

PRE SIESTA

★★★★⯪

Glass: Martini
Garnish: Orange zest twist
Method: SHAKE all ingredients and fine strain into chilled glass.

2 shots **Patrón reposado tequila**
½ shot **Aperol Aperitivo**
¾ shot **De Kuyper Triple Sec**
3 dash **Angostura Orange Bitters**

Origin: Created in 2007 by Little Rich Hunt at Mahiki, London, England.
Comment: Orange liqueurs and bitters flavour this tequila-based, salmon-pink, dry and hard cocktail.

PREAKNESS COCKTAIL

★★★★⯪

Glass: Coupe
Garnish: Lemon zest twist
Method: STIR all ingredients with ice and strain into chilled glass.

2 shots Straight rye whiskey
1 shot Martini Rosso vermouth
¼ shot Bénédictine D.O.M. liqueur
2 dash Angostura Aromatic Bitters

Origin: Thanks to a 2009 article by Dave Wondrich in The Malt Advocate we know that this cocktail was created in 1936 by a chap called George who was the head bartender at Baltimore's Emerson Hotel. The Preakness Stakes is an American horse race held on the third Saturday in May annually at the Pimlico Race Course in Baltimore. George was the winner of a contest to come up with an official cocktail for the first Preakness Ball held that year. Incidentally, The Pimlico Racetrack is said to be named after "Ben Pimlico's Tavern" which once stood in the area.
Comment: A Bénédictine-influenced twist on the Sweet Manhattan.

PREAKNESS MANHATTAN

★★★★⯪

Glass: Martini
Garnish: Lemon zest twist
Method: STIR all ingredients with ice and strain into chilled glass.

1½ shots **Bourbon whiskey**
¼ shot **Martell VSOP Médaillon cognac**
½ shot **Bénédictine D.O.M. liqueur**
½ shot **Martini Rosso vermouth**
3 dash **Angostura Aromatic Bitters**

Comment: A Sweet Manhattan with a herbal touch of Bénédictine and cognac.

PRECURSORY COCKTAIL

★★★★⯪

Glass: Coupe
Garnish: Lemon zest twist (discarded) & orange slice
Method: SHAKE all ingredients with ice and fine strain into chilled glass.

1½ shots **Tawny port**
1½ shots **Carpano Antica Formula**
¼ shot **Sugar syrup (2 sugar to 1 water)**
⅛ shot **Freshly squeezed lemon juice**
3 dash **Angostura Aromatic Bitters**
3 dash **Angostura Orange Bitters** (optional)

Origin: Adapted from a drink created in 2009 by Tim Philips at Milk & Honey, London, England.
Comment: The winning cocktail from CLASS magazine Bartender of the Year 2009.

PRESBYTERIAN ⌐🗝

★★★⯪☆

Glass: Collins
Garnish: Lemon slice
Method: POUR all ingredients into ice-filled glass and lightly **STIR**.

2 shots **Dewar's 12yo Scotch whisky**
2 shots **Soda (club soda)**
Top with **Ginger ale**

Origin: A traditional British serve using Dewar's 12yo Scotch whisky.
Comment: Basically a Scotch and soda with a delicate hint of ginger spice, the Presbyterian cocktail is traditionally made using Scotch whisky rather than bourbon, rye or Irish whiskey.

The name Presbyterian may come from presbýteros (πρεσβύτερος), the Greek word for 'elder', which incidentally is used 72 times in the New Testament, but the modern Presbyterian Church after which this cocktail is named, originated primarily in Scotland. Indeed Presbyterian Church government is enacted in the 1707 Acts of Union which created the kingdom of Great Britain.

THE PRESERVE COCKTAIL

★★★⯪☆

Glass: Old-fashioned
Garnish: Mint sprig & 3 raspberries
Method: SHAKE all ingredients with ice and fine strain into chilled glass.

8 fresh Raspberries
1½ shots Bourbon whiskey
½ shot Lejay Crème de Mûre liqueur
½ shot Freshly squeezed lemon juice
½ shot Sugar syrup (2 sugar to 1 water)

Origin: Created in 2010 by Gareth Edge at Opal Lounge, Edinburgh, Scotland.
Comment: Slightly sweetened bourbon laced with raspberry jam - at least that's how it tastes.

A B C D E F G H I J K L M N O P Q R S T U V W X Y Z

PRESIDENT

★★★★☆

Glass: Martini
Garnish: Orange zest twist
Method: SHAKE all ingredients with ice and fine strain into chilled glass.

2 shots **Bacardi Carta Blanca light rum**
1 shot **Freshly squeezed orange juice**
¼ shot **Freshly squeezed lemon juice**
¼ shot **Pomegranate / grenadine syrup (2:1)**
½ shot **Chilled water** (omit if wet ice)

Origin: Adapted from a recipe from Harry Craddock's 1930 the 'Savoy Cocktail Book'.
Comment: A delicately fruity orange Daiquiri.

PRESIDENT VINCENT

★★★½☆

Glass: Martini
Garnish: Lime zest twist
Method: SHAKE all ingredients with ice and fine strain into chilled glass.

2 shots **Bacardi Carta Blanca light rum**
½ shot **Martini Extra Dry vermouth**
½ shot **Freshly squeezed lime juice**
¼ shot **Sugar syrup (2 sugar to 1 water)**

Origin: Probably originates from the 1930s.
Comment: A dry, spicy take on the Daiquiri.

PRESIDENTE

★★★★☆

Glass: Coupe
Garnish: Orange zest twist (discarded) & Luxardo Maraschino cherry
Method: SHAKE all ingredients with crushed ice and strain into chilled glass.

1½ shots **Bacardi Carta Blanca light rum**
¼ shot **De Kuyper Triple Sec**
1½ shots **Martini Extra Dry vermouth**

Origin: Thought to have created during the 1920s in Vista Alegre, Havana, Cuba. This recipe is adapted from a 1937 Bar Florida (later renamed Floridita) menu, Havana, Cuba. On page 40 of his 1928 book 'When it's cocktail time in Cuba', Basil Woon says of this drink, "It is the aristocrat of cocktails and is the one preferred by the better class of Cuban."
Comment: Bone dry, light and delicate. The sweetness and colour of the maraschino cherry makes this drink.

PRESIDENTE MENOCAL SPECIAL

★★★★☆

Glass: Martini
Garnish: Mint sprig & Luxardo Maraschino cherry
Method: SHAKE all ingredients with ice and fine strain into chilled glass.

7 fresh **Mint leaves**
2 shots **Bacardi Carta Blanca light rum**
¼ shot **Sugar syrup (2 sugar to 1 water)**
⅛ shot **Freshly squeezed lime juice**

Origin: Created by Constantino (Constante) Ribalaigua Vert at the Floridita bar in Havana, Cuba. This recipe is adapted from a 1937 Bar Florida (later renamed Floridita) menu. The name refers to Mario García Menocal, who was president of Cuba from 1912 to 1920.
Comment: What hot Cuban summers are made for.

PRESTIGE COCKTAIL

★★★★½

Glass: Martini
Garnish: Pineapple wedge & spiral lime peel
Method: SHAKE all ingredients with ice and strain into chilled glass.

1¾ shots **Bacardi Carta Ocho aged rum**
1 shot **Fresh pressed pineapple juice**
½ shot **Martini Extra Dry vermouth**
½ shot **Taylor's Velvet Falernum liqueur**
½ shot **Freshly squeezed lime juice**

Origin: Created in 2002 by Dale Degroff, New York City, USA.
Comment: Slightly sweet but very more-ish. Aged rum, pineapple, clove and lime.

PRICKLY PEAR MULE

★★★★☆

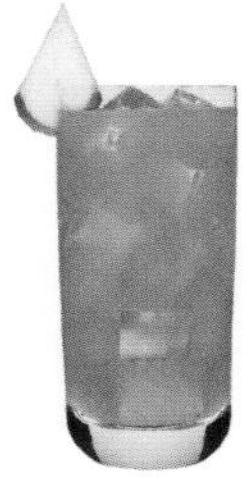

Glass: Collins
Garnish: Pear slice
Method: SHAKE first 5 ingredients with ice and strain into ice-filled glass. **TOP** with ginger beer.

1¼ shots **Belle de Brillet pear liqueur**
1¼ shots **Poire William eau de vie**
3 shots **Pressed pear juice**
¼ shot **Freshly squeezed lemon juice**
2 dash **Angostura Aromatic Bitters**
Top with **Gosling's Stormy Ginger Beer**

Origin: Created in 2002 by yours truly.
Comment: Subtle pear with ginger spice. Fill the glass with ice and go easy on the ginger beer which can predominate and overpower the pear.

PRINCE CHARLIE

★★★★☆

Glass: Martini
Garnish: Lemon zest twist
Method: SHAKE all ingredients with ice and fine strain into chilled glass.

1 shot **Martell VSOP Médaillon cognac**
1 shot **Drambuie liqueur**
1 shot **Freshly squeezed lemon juice**
¾ shot **Chilled water** (omit if wet ice)

Origin: A long lost classic.
Comment: Cognac and honey with sweet and sourness in harmony.

PRINCE OF WALES

★★★½☆

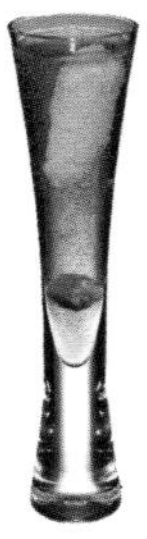

Glass: Flute
Garnish: Lemon zest twist
Method: RUB sugar cube with lemon zest, coat with bitters and drop into glass. **POUR** cognac and liqueur over soaked cube and **TOP** with champagne.

1 cube **Brown sugar**
2 dash **Angostura Aromatic Bitters**
½ shot **Martell VSOP Médaillon cognac**
½ shot **Grand Marnier Cordon Rouge**
Top with **G.H.Mumm Cordon Rouge Champagne**

Comment: More interesting than a Classic Champagne Cocktail.

THE PRINCE OF WALES COCKTAIL II

★★★⯪☆

Glass: Coupe
Garnish: Orange slice
Method: MUDDLE pineapple in base of shaker. Add next 5 ingredients (all but champagne), **SHAKE** with ice and fine strain into chilled glass. **TOP** with champagne.

1	wedge	Pineapple (fresh)
2	shots	Straight rye whiskey
⅛	shot	Luxardo Maraschino liqueur
⅛	shot	Sugar syrup (2 sugar to 1 water)
1	inch	Lemon zest
1	dash	Angostura Aromatic Bitters
Top with		G.H. Mumm Cordon Rouge Champagne

Origin: Recipe adapted from David Wondrich's 2007 masterpiece 'Imbibe'' in which David tells the story of his Highness Albert Edward, Prince of Wales, son of Queen Victoria and his mastering of his riff on the Improved Whisky Cocktail.

Born 9th November 1841, he was not crowned King Edward VII until 9th August 1902 (ascended 22nd January 1901) and by all accounts made the most of his 60 years as understudy by becoming a playboy and travelling the world - there are worse ways to while away your years. In 1860, he became the first British royal to visit North America and it is thought that this cocktail resulted from the trip.
Comment: Rich whiskey and maraschino with subtle pineapple balanced by a dash of brut champagne.

THE PRINCE OF WALES PUNCH

★★★★☆

Glass: Collins
Garnish: Raspberries
Method: MUDDLE pineapple in base of shaker. Add next five ingredients, **SHAKE** with ice and fine strain into ice-filled glass. Float the port on drink.

¼	ring	Pineapple (fresh)
		(cored, skinned and chopped)
1½	shots	Martell VSOP Médaillon cognac
¾	shot	Bacardi Carta Ocho aged rum
½	shot	Grand Marnier Cordon Rouge
¼	shot	Luxardo Maraschino liqueur
1½	shots	Freshly squeezed orange juice
½	shot	Tawny port

Origin: Adapted from Jerry Thomas' 1862 'The Bar-Tender's Guide (How to Mix Drinks or The Bon-Vivant's Companion)'.
Comment: Fruity yet complex with the oak maturation of both spirits and liqueurs adding depth of flavour.

PRINCESS MARINA

★★★★☆

Glass: Martini
Garnish: Orange zest twist
Method: SHAKE all ingredients with ice and fine strain into chilled glass.

1	shot	Rutte Dry Gin
½	shot	Calvados brandy
½	shot	Dubonnet Red
½	shot	De Kuyper Triple Sec
½	shot	Swedish Punch liqueur
¾	shot	Chilled water

Origin: Created in the late 1920s/early 1930s and named after the Princess Marina, the late mother of The Duke of Kent, Prince Michael of Kent and Princess Alexandra.
Comment: Delicate yet loaded with alcohol and flavour.

PRINCESS MARY

★★★★☆

Glass: Martini
Garnish: Dust with chocolate powder
Method: SHAKE all ingredients with ice and fine strain into chilled glass.

1½	shots	Rutte Dry Gin
1	shot	White crème de cacao liqueur
1	shot	Single cream / half-and-half

Origin: Created in London during 1922 by Scottish bartender Harry MacElhone to celebrate H.R.H. Princess Mary's marriage to Lord Lascelles. The original recipe featured equal parts of all three ingredients: 1/3 gin, 1/3 white crème de cacao and 1/3 fresh cream. The year after, Harry MacElhone purchased his eponymously named bar in Paris.
Comment: Slightly sweet, very creamy - drink after dinner.

PRINCESS MARY'S PRIDE

★★★☆☆

Glass: Martini
Garnish: Orange zest twist
Method: SHAKE all ingredients with ice and fine strain into chilled glass.

2	shots	Calvados brandy
1	shot	Dubonnet Red
1	shot	Martini Extra Dry vermouth

Origin: Created by Harry Craddock on 28th February 1922 to mark the wedding celebrations of H.R.H. Princess Mary. Recipe from 1930's 'Savoy Cocktail Book'.
Comment: Apple brandy to the fore, followed by aromatised wine.

PRINCESS PRIDE

★★★⯪☆

Glass: Martini
Garnish: Orange zest twist
Method: SHAKE all ingredients with ice and fine strain into chilled glass.

2	shots	Calvados brandy
1	shot	Dubonnet Red
1	shot	Martini Rosso vermouth

Origin: Adapted from a recipe in the 1947-1972 'Trader Vic's Bartender's Guide' by Victor Bergeron.
Comment: Vic's improved version of the Princess Mary's Pride cocktail.

PRINCETON

★★★★☆

Glass: Martini
Garnish: Lemon zest twist
Method: SHAKE all ingredients with ice and fine strain into chilled glass.

2	shots	Rutte Dry Gin
1	shot	Tawny port
¼	shot	Sugar syrup (2 sugar to 1 water)
2	dash	Angostura Orange Bitters

Origin: An old classic originally made with old tom gin and without the sugar syrup.
Comment: Overproof wine with a herbal orange garnish.

PRINCETON MARTINI

★★★★☆

Glass: Martini
Garnish: Lime zest twist
Method: **SHAKE** all ingredients with ice and fine strain into chilled glass.

2	shots	**Rutte Dry Gin**
½	shot	**Martini Extra Dry vermouth**
¼	shot	**Rose's lime cordial**
½	shot	**Chilled water** (omit if wet ice)

Comment: The Dry Martini meets the Gimlet. They should meet more often.

PROCRASTINATION COCKTAIL

★★★★☆

Glass: Coupe
Garnish: Lemon zest twist
Method: **STIR** all ingredients with ice and strain into chilled glass.

2	shots	**Rutte Dry Gin**
½	shot	**Martini Extra Dry vermouth**
¾	shot	**Pallini Limoncello**
⅛	shot	**Green Chartreuse liqueur**

Origin: Recipe created by Paul Clarke, the Seattle-based cocktail enthusiast behind the excellent cocktailchronicles.com.
Comment: A wet martini flavoured with copious amounts of limoncello (which sweetens and surprisingly adds subtle lemon favours) and a dash of Chartreause which shines through.

PROSPECTOR

★★★★½

Glass: Coupe
Garnish: Orange zest twist (flamed)
Method: **STIR** all ingredients with ice and strain into chilled glass.

2	shots	**Dewar's 12yo Scotch whisky**
¾	shot	**Verdelho madeira (medium dry)**
¾	shot	**Bénédictine D.O.M. liqueur**
1	dash	**Whiskey Barrel Aged Bitters**

Origin: Adapted from a drink created in 2010 by Thomas Waugh at Prospect, San Francisco, USA.
Comment: Complex and strong with all three ingredients balancing and enhancing each other.

PRUNE FACE

★★★★☆

Glass: Old-fashioned
Garnish: Orange zest twist
Method: **POUR** bourbon into a glass with four ice cubes and **STIR** until ice has at least half melted. Add other ingredients and additional ice and stir some more.

2	shots	**Bourbon whiskey**
¾	shot	**Vieille de prune eau de vie**
¼	shot	**Mandarine Napoléon liqueur**
¼	shot	**Sugar syrup (2 sugar to 1 water)**

Origin: Created in 2002 by Dan Warner at Zander, London, England and named after our friend's nickname for his stepmother.
Comment: Why muddle cherries into your Old Fashioned when you can add a hint of prune?

PRUNEAUX

★★★★☆

Glass: Martini
Garnish: Prunes
Method: **SHAKE** all ingredients with ice and fine strain into chilled glass.

1½	shots	**Rutte Dry Gin**
1	shot	**Romate Amontillado sherry**
½	shot	**Romate Pedro Ximénez sherry**
¾	shot	**Freshly squeezed orange juice**
¾	shot	**Prune syrup (from tinned fruit)**

Origin: Adapted from a recipe in Harry Craddock's 1930 'Savoy Cocktail Book'.
Comment: Sherried prunes further fortified by gin.

PUCCINI

★★★½☆

Glass: Flute
Garnish: Mandarin segment
Method: **MUDDLE** segments in base of shaker. Add liqueur, **SHAKE** with ice and fine strain into chilled glass. **TOP** with prosecco and lightly stir.

8	segments	**Fresh mandarin**
¾	shot	**Mandarine Napoléon liqueur**
Top with		**Prosecco sparkling wine**

Origin: Named after the composer of Madame Butterfly, this cocktail is popular in Venice and other areas of northern Italy. It is often made without the mandarine liqueur.
Comment: The use of mandarine (tangerine) instead of orange makes the Puccini slightly sharper than a simple mimosa.

PULP FICTION

★★★★☆

Glass: Collins
Garnish: Apple slice
Method: **SHAKE** all ingredients with ice and strain into ice-filled glass. **TOP** with lemonade.

2 shots Martell VSOP Médaillon cognac
2 shots Pressed apple juice
1 shot Apple Schnapps liqueur
Top with Lemonade/Sprite/7-Up

Origin: Discovered in 2001 at Teatro, London, England.
Comment: Originally made with apple pulp, this drink has a zingy apple taste.

PUNCH & JUDY

★★★★⯪☆

Glass: Collins
Garnish: Lime wheel & dust with grated nutmeg
Method: SHAKE all ingredients with ice and strain into ice-filled glass.

6	fresh	Mint leaves
1	shot	Martell VSOP Médaillon cognac
½	shot	Bacardi Carta Blanca light rum
½	shot	Rutte Dry Gin
½	shot	Orange Curaçao liqueur
1½	shots	Fresh pressed pineapple juice
½	shot	Freshly squeezed lime juice
½	shot	Freshly squeezed orange juice
½	shot	Agave syrup
2	dash	Angostura Aromatic Bitters

Origin: Adapted from the official cocktail of the 2008 Tales of the Cocktail created by Charlotte Voisey, USA.
Comment: A veritable fruit bowl and spirits rail of a punch in a glass.

PUNCH (GENERIC NAME)

★★★★★

Glass: Collins
Garnish: Lime slice
Method: SHAKE all ingredients with ice and fine strain into glass filled with crushed ice.

¾	shot	Freshly squeezed lemon or lime juice
1½	shots	Sugar syrup (2 sugar to 1 water)
2¼	shots	Brandy, whisk(e)y, gin, rum etc.
3	shots	Fruit juice or water
3	dash	Angostura Aromatic Bitters

Origin: Long before the Martini, the V-shaped glass and the cocktail shaker, the drink of choice at society gatherings was punch and the punch bowl was the centre of activity at every party.

Punch had existed in India for centuries before colonialists brought it back to Europe some time in the latter half of the 1600s. The name derives from the Hindi word for five, 'panch', and refers to the five key ingredients: alcohol, citrus, sugar, water and spices. In India, it was made with arrack (the Arabic word for liquor and a local spirit distilled from palm sap or sugar cane). Back in Britain it was common for punches to be spiced with nutmeg or tea.

The classic proportions of a punch follow a mnemonic, 'one of sour, two of sweet, three of strong and four of weak.' It refers to lime juice, sugar, rum and water - the fifth element, spice was added to taste.

The basic punch principle of balancing sweet and sour with spirit and dilution remains key to making a good cocktail to this day. Indeed, the essential punch ingredients - spirit, citrus, sugar and water - lie at the centre of most modern day cocktails including the Daiquiri, Sour, Margarita, Caipirinha and Sidecar. Today's bartenders are now also reintroducing the fifth punch ingredient by muddling or macerating herbs and spices in their cocktails.
Comment: Two traditional punches remain on today's cocktail lists, the 'Rum Punch' and the 'Hot Whisky Punch', now better known as the 'Hot Toddy'. Also bear in mind that the Gin Punch probably led to the creation of the Collins.

PUNCH BACK

★★★★☆

Glass: Collins
Garnish: Pineapple wedge on rim with cherries on stick
Method: SHAKE all ingredients with ice and strain into ice-filled glass.

1½	shots	Bacardi Carta Oro rum
1	shot	Capucana cachaça
¾	shot	Freshly squeezed lemon juice
¾	shot	Sugar syrup (2 sugar to 1 water)
2	shots	Coconut water
1	dash	Angostura Aromatic Bitters

Origin: Created in May 2013 by yours truly at the Cabinet Room, London, for the National Aids Trust.
Comment: Cachaça is the raw, spirity love interest in this rum based coconut and lime punch.

PURGATORY

★★★★⯪

Glass: Martini
Garnish: Lemon zest twist
Method: SHAKE all ingredients with ice and strain into chilled glass.

2½	shots	Straight rye whiskey
¾	shot	Bénédictine D.O.M. liqueur
¾	shot	Green Chartreuse liqueur

Origin: Created in 2007 by Ted Kilgore at Monarch Restaurant, Maplewood, USA. Adapted from an adapted recipe by Gary Regan and first published in his column in The San Francisco Chronicle. Apparently, Kilgore created this drink as a pick-me-up.
Comment: Too many and you're in it.

PURGATORY A LA FRANÇAISE

★★★★☆

Glass: Old-fashioned
Garnish: Lemon zest twist
Method: STIR all ingredients with ice and strain into glass.

1	shot	Martell VSOP Médaillon cognac
¾	shot	Islay single malt Scotch whisky
¾	shot	Yellow Chartreuse liqueur
¾	shot	Carpano Punt E Mes

Origin: Adapted from a drink discovered in 2010 at Curio Parlour, Paris, France.
Comment: This Islay smoke influenced drink makes for a great night cap.

THE PURITAN

★★★★★

Glass: Martini
Garnish: Orange zest twist
Method: STIR all ingredients with ice and strain into chilled glass.

1¾	shots	Rutte Dry Gin
½	shot	Martini Extra Dry vermouth
¼	shot	Yellow Chartreuse liqueur
1	dash	Angostura Orange Bitters
½	shot	Chilled water (omit if wet ice)

Origin: An often overlooked classic which is thought to have originated at the end of the nineteenth century.
Comment: Vermouth enhances the aromatics; Chartreuse and orange bitters add a hint of sweetness and complexity; gin underpins the whole.

THE PURL

★★★☆☆

Glass: Pint
Garnish: None
Method: POUR ingredients into chilled glass.

2   shots   **Old Tom gin**
Top with   **Fuller's Chiswick Bitter**

Origin: In 18th century London Gin tended to be mixed two to one with water and sold by the quarter pint. The Purl, simply gin and ale, was another popular mix. Sometimes the beer was warmed first to make a 'hot purl', apparently popular with Thames boatman of the day.
Comment: Somebody seems to have spiked my beer!

PURPLE COSMO

★★★★☆

Glass: Martini
Garnish: Orange zest twist
Method: STIR all ingredients with ice and strain into chilled glass.

2   shots   **Ketel One Citroen vodka**
¾   shot   **Parfait Amour liqueur**
1½ shots   **Cranberry juice (white)**
¼   shot   **Freshly squeezed lime juice**

Comment: If shaken this becomes more of grey cosmo. The flavour and colour make for an interesting twist.

PURPLE FLIRT #1

★★★★☆

Glass: Martini
Garnish: Orange zest twist
Method: SHAKE all ingredients with ice and fine strain into chilled glass.

1½ shots   **Ketel One Vodka**
¾   shot   **Black sambuca liqueur**
2   shots   **Cranberry juice**

Comment: This purple drink is surprisingly balanced with subtle hints of liquorice.

PURPLE FLIRT #2

★★★☆☆

Glass: Old-fashioned
Garnish: Orange slice & cherry on stick (sail)
Method: SHAKE all ingredients with ice and strain into ice-filled glass.

1   shot   **Gosling's Black Seal dark rum**
¼   shot   **Blue curaçao liqueur**
1   shot   **Fresh pressed pineapple juice**
½   shot   **Freshly squeezed lemon juice**
¼   shot   **Pomegranate / grenadine syrup (2:1)**
½   fresh   **Egg white**

Comment: This popular drink is more brown than purple. It tastes ok, anyway.

PURPLE HAZE

★★★⯪☆

Glass: Shot
Garnish: None
Method: SHAKE first three ingredients with ice and strain into glass. POUR liqueur down the inside the glass. This will fall to the bottom and form a purple haze.

1½ shots   **Ketel One Vodka**
½   shot   **Freshly squeezed lime juice**
¼   shot   **Sugar syrup (2 sugar to 1 water)**
⅛   shot   **Chambord Liqueur**

Comment: A sweet and sour shot with a sweet, berry base.

PURPLE HOOTER

★★★⯪☆

Glass: Collins
Garnish: Lime wedge
Method: SHAKE first three ingredients with ice and strain into ice-filled glass. TOP with soda.

2   shots   **Ketel One Vodka**
1   shot   **Chambord Liqueur**
1   shot   **Freshly squeezed lime juice**
Top with   **Soda (club soda)**

Comment: Tangy, fruity, long and refreshing.

PURPLE PEAR MARTINI

★★★★☆

Glass: Martini
Garnish: Pear slice
Method: SHAKE all ingredients with ice and fine strain into chilled glass.

¾   shot   **Zubrówka bison vodka**
¾   shot   **Poire William eau de vie**
¾   shot   **Benoit Serres créme de violette**
1   shot   **Lillet Blanc**

Origin: Created in 2002 by yours truly.
Comment: This floral drink suits its name.

PURPLE TURTLE

★★★☆☆

Glass: Shot
Garnish: None
Method: SHAKE all ingredients with ice and fine strain into chilled glass.

½   shot   **Patrón reposado tequila**
½   shot   **Sloe Gin liqueur**
½   shot   **Blue curaçao liqueur**

Comment: An aquamarine shoot with tequila, sloe gin and blue curaçao.

PUSSYFOOT (MOCKTAIL)

★★★★½

Glass: Collins
Garnish: Orange slice
Method: MUDDLE mint in base of shaker. Add other ingredients, **SHAKE** with ice and fine strain into ice-filled glass.

7	fresh	Mint leaves
4	shots	Freshly squeezed orange juice
½	shot	Freshly squeezed lemon juice
½	shot	Freshly squeezed lime juice
½	shot	Pomegranate / grenadine syrup (2:1)
1	fresh	Egg yolk

Origin: Created in 1920 by Robert Vermeire at the Embassy Club, London, England. This non-alcoholic is named after 'Pussyfoot' (William E.) Johnson who was an ardent supporter of prohibition.
Comment: Probably the best non-alcoholic cocktail ever.

PYRAMID PUNCH

★★★★★

Glass: Collins
Garnish: Pineapple wedge
Method: MUDDLE cloves in base of shaker. Add other ingredients, **SHAKE** with ice and strain into ice-filled glass.

2	dried	Clove
2	shots	BarSol Mosto Verde Italia pisco
1	shot	St-Germain elderflower liqueur
2	shots	Fresh pressed pineapple juice
½	shot	Freshly squeezed pink grapefruit juice

Origin: Created in 2006 by yours truly. This is a riff on the classic Pisco Punch which was made famous before Prohibition at San Francisco's legendary Bank Exchange Bar. The Transamerica Pyramid skyscraper now stands on the site of The Bank Exchange, at the corner of Washington & Montgomery Streets, hence this drink's name and wedge-shaped garnish.
Comment: Tangy, fruity and packed with flavour. Clove spice, fragrant floral pisco and elderflower with a hint of sweet pineapple and sour grapefruit.

THE QUAD

★★★★½

Glass: Coupe
Garnish: Orange zest twist
Method: SHAKE all ingredients with ice and fine strain into chilled glass.

1½	shots	Ketel One Oranje
1	shot	De Kuyper Triple Sec
¼	shot	Campari Bitter
1	shot	Freshly squeezed orange juice

Origin: Created in 2010 by yours truly at the Cabinet Room, London, England.
Comment: Four different orange flavoured ingredients combine in this complex fruity cocktail.

QUARTER DECK

★★★★☆

Glass: Martini
Garnish: Orange zest twist
Method: SHAKE all ingredients with ice and fine strain into chilled glass.

2	shots	Bacardi Carta Blanca light rum
1	shot	Romate Pedro Ximénez sherry
¼	shot	Freshly squeezed lemon juice
¾	shot	Chilled water (omit if wet ice)

Origin: Long lost classic.
Comment: Hints of prune, toffee and maple syrup. Very complex.

QUARTERBACK

★★★★☆

Glass: Martini
Garnish: Orange zest twist
Method: SHAKE all ingredients with ice and fine strain into chilled glass.

1	shot	Yellow Chartreuse liqueur
1	shot	De Kuyper Triple Sec
1	shot	Single cream / half-and-half
1	shot	Milk

Comment: This white, creamy drink has a flavoursome bite.

QUEBEC

★★★★☆

Glass: Martini
Garnish: Orange zest twist
Method: STIR all ingredients and strain into chilled glass.

2	shots	Canadian blended whisky
2	shots	Dubonnet Red
2	dash	Angostura Orange Bitters

Origin: Created in 2004 by Gonçalo de Sousa Monteiro at Victoria Bar, Berlin, Germany.
Comment: Canadian whisky with French accents of aromatised wine - trés Quebecois.

QUEEN MARTINI

★★★★☆

Glass: Martini
Garnish: Luxardo Maraschino cherry
Method: SHAKE all ingredients with ice and fine strain into chilled glass.

1½	shots	Rutte Dry Gin
½	shot	Martini Extra Dry vermouth
½	shot	Martini Rosso vermouth
½	shot	Freshly squeezed orange juice
½	shot	Fresh pressed pineapple juice

Comment: A 'perfectly' fruity Martini that's fit for a....

QUEEN'S PARK HOTEL SUPER COCKTAIL (NEW)

★★★★½

Glass: Coupe
Garnish: Lime zest twist
Method: SHAKE all ingredients with ice and strain into chilled glass.

1½	shots	Bacardi Carta Oro rum
½	shot	Martini Rosso vermouth
½	shot	Freshly squeezed lime juice
½	shot	Pomegranate / grenadine syrup (2:1)
4	shots	Angostura Aromatic Bitters

Origin: Recipe adapted from ' If Crab No Walk: A Traveller in the West Indies', a 1932 book written by British travel writer Owen Rutter, who writes of the Queen's Park Hotel, Port of Spain, Trinidad, "The cooking is good; the servants, though slow, are attentive; there is an excellent ballroom, a first-rate band, and a good bar: 'the Long Bar with the Brass Rail,' where you may drink the Queen's Park Hotel Super Cocktail."
Comment: Perhaps best described as being a Trinidadian Daiquiri due to its heavy use of Angostura Bitters. Obviously it would also have originally been made with Trinidad gold rum, Canning's Caroni Rum according to Owen Rutter. Preferably make your own pomegranate (grenadine) syrup.

QUEEN'S PARK SWIZZLE

★★★★½

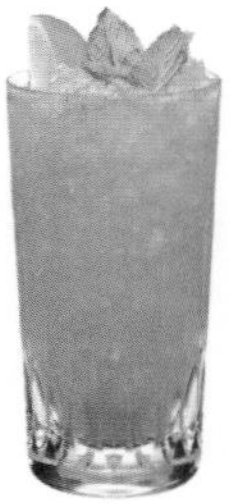

Glass: Collins
Garnish: Lime wedge & mint sprig
Method: Lightly MUDDLE mint (just to bruise) in base of glass. Use your barspoon to raise the bruised mint up and around the inside of the glass so as to coat with fragrant mint oils. Add other ingredients and two-thirds fill glass with crushed ice. SWIZZLE with a swizzle stick or CHURN (stir) with a bar spoon. Fill glass with more crushed ice and repeat. Serve with straws.

8	fresh	Mint leaves
2	shots	Bacardi Carta Oro rum
¾	shot	Freshly squeezed lime juice
½	shot	Light muscovado sugar syrup (2 sugar to 1 water)
2	dash	Angostura Aromatic Bitters

Origin: Created at the Queen's Park Hotel, Port of Spain, Trinidad. The hotel opened on the 15th January 1895 and it is likely that this cocktail emanated soon after.
Comment: This close relation to the Mojito is drier, more complex and less minty than its sibling.

QUELLE VIE

★★★½☆

Glass: Martini
Garnish: Orange zest twist
Method: STIR all ingredients with ice and fine strain into chilled glass.

2	shots	Martell VSOP Médaillon cognac
½	shot	Kümmel
¾	shot	Chilled water (omit if wet ice)

Origin: Adapted from a recipe in the 1930 'Savoy Cocktail Book' by Harry Craddock.
Comment: To quote Harry Craddock, "Brandy gives you courage and Kümmel makes you cautious, thus giving you the perfect mixture of bravery and caution, with the bravery predominating."

QUINCE MUSTARD MARGARITA

★★★★½

Glass: Old-fashioned
Garnish: Lime wedge & cracked black pepper
Method: SHAKE all ingredients with ice and fine strain into chilled glass.

1	spoon	Quince mustard jam
2	grind	Black pepper
1½	shots	Patrón reposado tequila
½	shot	De Kuyper Triple Sec
1	shot	Freshly squeezed lime juice
⅛	shot	Sugar syrup (2 sugar to 1 water)

Origin: Created by Ryan Magarian, Seattle, USA.
Comment: A wonderfully quince influenced Margarita.

QUINCE SOUR

★★★★☆

Glass: Old-fashioned
Garnish: Lemon slice & cherry on stick (sail)
Method: STIR quince jam with vodka in base of shaker to dissolve jam. Add other ingredients, SHAKE with ice and fine strain into ice-filled glass.

3	spoon	Quince mustard jam
2	shots	Ketel One Vodka
1	shot	Freshly squeezed lemon juice
½	fresh	Egg white

Comment: The sweet quince both flavours and balances the sour.

QUINCY JONES (NEW)

★★★★½

Glass: Coupe
Garnish: Orange zest twist
Method: STIR all ingredients with ice and strain into chilled glass.

1⅔	shots	Byrrh Grand Quinquina
⅓	shot	Islay single malt Scotch whisky
⅔	shot	Clove & quince sugar syrup (housemade)
2	dash	Dead Rabbit Orinoco Bitters

Origin: Adapted from a recipe created in 2015 by Miran Chauhan at Bon Vivant, Edinburgh, Scotland.

THE QUINGENTI

★★★★½

Glass: Martini
Garnish: Lemon zest twist
Method: SHAKE all ingredients with ice and fine strain into chilled glass.

2	shots	Martell VSOP Médaillon cognac
½	shot	Apple Schnapps liqueur
½	shot	Martini Extra Dry vermouth
¼	shot	Sugar syrup (2 sugar to 1 water)

Origin: A created in 2008 by yours truly at the Cabinet Room, London, England to celebrate Courvoisier's Future 500 initiative. As every schoolboy knows, quingenti is Latin for five-hundred.
Comment: Cognac with apple notes and a touch of herbal complexity by way of dry vermouth.

R U BOBBY MOORE?

★★★★★☆

Glass: Martini
Garnish: Apple wedge
Method: STIR honey with Scotch and vodka in base of shaker until honey dissolves. Add other ingredients, **SHAKE** with ice and fine strain into chilled glass.

3	spoon	Runny honey
1	shot	Dewar's 12yo Scotch whisky
1	shot	Zubrówka bison vodka
¾	shot	Sauvignon blanc white wine
1	shot	Pressed apple juice

Origin: Created in 2002 by yours truly and named after the rhyming slang for 'are you bloody sure?' My dictionary of rhyming slang claims 'Bobby Moore' means 'door' - well, not in South London it doesn't.

During the 1960s, Robert Frederick Chelsea 'Bobby' Moore OBE (1941-1993) was the England football team captain and West Ham United defender.
Comment: It's common to pair Scotch and Zubrówka with apple, but combining all three together with wine and honey really works.

RAC COCKTAIL

★★★★☆

Glass: Martini
Garnish: Orange zest twist (discarded) & Luxardo Maraschino cherry
Method: STIR all ingredients with ice and strain into chilled glass.

2	shots	Rutte Dry Gin
1	shot	Martini Extra Dry vermouth
1	shot	Martini Rosso vermouth
⅛	shot	Pomegranate / grenadine syrup (2:1)
1	dash	Angostura Orange Bitters

Origin: The house cocktail at the Royal Automobile Club in London's Pall Mall. King Edward VII awarded this private members' club its royal title in 1907.
Comment: A one to one Perfect Martini with extra grenadine sweetness and orange bitters adding complexity.

RAGING BULL

★★★★☆

Glass: Shot
Garnish: None
Method: Refrigerate ingredients then **LAYER** in chilled glass by carefully pouring in the order listed.

½	shot	Coffee liqueur
½	shot	Black sambuca liqueur
½	scoop	Patrón reposado tequila

Comment: Coffee and sambuca make a great combination, as do coffee and tequila.

RAGTIME

★★★★★☆

Glass: Coupe
Garnish: Orange zest twist
Method: Rinse mixing glass with absinthe (sazerac style). **STIR** rest of ingredients with ice and strain into chilled glass.

½	shot	Le Fée Parisienne absinthe
1½	shots	Straight rye whiskey
1	shot	Amaro liqueur
1	shot	Aperol Aperitivo
1	dash	Peychaud's aromatic bitters

Origin: Adapted from a drink created in 2009 by Jeremy James Thompson at Raines Law Rooms, New York City, USA.
Comment: This bitter-sweet drink benefits from the strength of bonded rye whiskey and was originally made with Rittenhouse.

RAITA COCKTAIL

★★★★☆

Glass: Coupe
Garnish: Cucumber slices
Method: MUDDLE cardamom, cumin and then cucumber in base of shaker. Add other ingredients, **SHAKE** with ice and fine strain into chilled glass.

2	dried	Cardamom pod
½	spoon	Cumin seeds
1½	inch	English cucumber peeled
1½	shots	Rutte Dry Gin
1½	shots	Yoghurt liqueur
1	pinch	Salt
3	fresh	Mint leaves

Origin: Created in 2011 by yours truly at the Cabinet Room, London, England.
Comment: Fresh cucumber, mint and yoghurt with a hint of cardamom and cumin spice, laced with vodka.

RAMOS CHOCOLATE FIZZ COCKTAIL (NEW)

★★★★★☆

Glass: Flute
Garnish: Chocolate truffle on rim
Method: HARD SHAKE first 6 ingredients without ice. **SHAKE** again with ice and fine strain into chilled glass. **TOP** with champagne slowly poured into glass from a height to create thick foamy head.

1½	shots	Rutte Dry Gin
1½	shots	White crème de cacao liqueur
⅛	shot	Orange flower water
⅛	shot	Vanilla extract
1	fresh	Egg white
1	shot	Single cream / half-and-half
1	shot	G.H. Mumm Cordon Rouge Champagne

Origin: Created 4th February 2014 by yours truly at the Cabinet Room as a Valentine's Day drink for Handbag.com
Comment: Creamy chocolate vanilla fudge with faint orange and a hint of gin.

Ramos Gin Fizz cocktail

Created in 1888 by Henry Charles Ramos at the Imperial Cabinet Saloon on the corner of Gravier and Carondelet Streets in New Orleans. Henry, then better known as Carl, took over the bar, along with his brother Charles Henry Ramos, from Emile Sunier, who had in turn acquired the premises from Pat Morgan who used to champion Imperial Cabinet branded whiskey, hence the bar's name.

Originally named the New Orleans Fizz, Henry used to call his famous creation the *One And Only One*. The creamy, yet almost fluffy cocktail was an immediate success, propelling the bar's popularity to the extent that it would often have 20 bartenders and "shaker boys" dedicated to just making Ramos Gin Fizz cocktails, but they would still struggle to meet demand. That's perhaps understandable when you hear that devotees say it takes 12 minutes to shake, requiring several bartenders to shake in relay, not least because the shaker becomes so cold and frosted that it must be wrapped in a cloth to be comfortably held.

Driven by the success of his creation, in 1907 Henry opened his own larger bar, taking over Tom Anderson's Stag Saloon, a few blocks down at 712 Gravier Street on the corner of St Charles Avenue, opposite the entrance to the St. Charles Hotel.

In his *Famous New Orleans Drinks and How to Mix 'Em*, Stanley Clisby Arthur writes that at The Stag, "the corps of busy shaker boys behind the bar was one of the sights of the town during Carnival, and in the 1915 Mardi Gras, 35 shaker boys nearly shook their arms off, but were still unable to keep up with the demand."

In 1935, the Fairmont Hotel in New Orleans, just a couple of blocks away from where Henry created the drink, purchased the rights to the Ramos Gin Fizz from Henry's son and trademarked the drink. (Confusingly, what is now the Fairmont Hotel originally opened in 1893 as The Hotel Grunewald, then became The Fairmont, then The Roosevelt before reopening after Hurricane Katrina as The Fairmont. To allay confusion, I've stuck to Fairmont regardless of period.)

The Fairmont Hotel promoted the drink, the popularity of which was also helped by the governor of Louisiana, Huey P. Long's fondness of it. So much so, that in July 1935, he took a bartender, named Sam Guarino, from the Fairmont Hotel to the New Yorker Hotel in New York City to train the staff there how to make the drink, so he could have it whenever he stayed in New York. The Museum of the American Cocktail has newsreel footage of this.

Bartenders at the Fairmont Hotel's Sazerac Bar continue to proudly make the drink and tell the story of Henry Ramos to this day.

The recipe
With the onset of Prohibition on 27th October 1919, at the stroke of midnight, Henry announced, "I've sold my last Gin Fizz." Henry was forced to close his bar and the recipe remained a closely guarded secret. That was until a staff writer for the *The New Orleans Item-Tribune* by the name of Don Higgins had "the brass bound nerve to ask it of him."

The reporter interviewed Henry "in his roomy, cool old Creole home at 726 North Rampart Street" where he is reported to have said, "Now I will give you the formula for the One And Only One, the Ramos Original Gin Fizz. But in publishing it you must say that if success does not attend the first mixture, a second should be tried. And be sure to use an airtight shaker and to shake and shake and shake until there is not a bubble left but the drink is smooth and snowy white and of the consistency of good rich milk. The secret in success lies in the good care you take and in your patience, and be certain to use good material."

Higgins' piece about meeting Henry was re-published some years later on 23rd September 1928, five days after Henry's death as "A tribute to one of New Orleans' greatest treasures" and this included the following recipe.

Ramos' Original Gin Fizz
One tablespoonful powdered sugar
Three or four drops of orange flower water
One-half lime (juice)
One-half lemon (juice)
One jigger of Old Tom Gin

The white of one egg
One-half glass of crushed ice
About two tablespoonsful of rich milk or cream
A little Seltzer water (about an ounce) to make it pungent
Together well shaken and strained (drink freely)

Some say that vanilla extract was the secret ingredient which prevented others successfully copying the Ramos Gin Fizz, while others hold it was not originally used. In his 1937 Famous New Orleans Drinks and How to Mix 'Em, Stanley Clisby Arthur writes, "Veteran barkeepers differ violently - practically come to blows - over the inclusion of the two innocent drops of *extract of vanilla*. Old-timers who worked for Henry Ramos in the past declare the original Ramos included no vanilla. Others hold that the twin drops of extract wrung from the heart of the vanilla bean either make or break a real gin fizz - make it taste like heaven or the reverse."

Arthur goes on, "Therefore, when you mix your fizz, add the two vanilla drops or leave them out, just as you please." I have chosen to use three drops of vanilla extract in our Ramos Gin Fizz recipe.

RAMOS GIN FIZZ

★★★★★

Glass: Collins
Garnish: Lemon slice & mint sprig
Method: **SHAKE** first 8 ingredients with ice and strain back into shaker. **DRY SHAKE** without ice and strain into chilled glass (no ice in glass). **TOP** with soda from siphon.

Some recipes for a Ramos Gin Fizz, and indeed Henry's original recipe, calls for old tom gin, in which case you may need to reduce the amount of sugar syrup depending on your old tom.

2	shot	Rutte Dry Gin
½	shot	Freshly lemon juice
½	shot	Freshly lime juice
¾	shot	Sugar syrup (2 sugar to 1 water)
⅛	shot	Orange flower water
3	drop	Vanilla extract (optional)
½	fresh	Egg white
1	shot	Single cream / half-and-half
Top up with Soda from siphon		

Comment: One of the great classic cocktails. The perfect balance of sweet and sour is enhanced by the incredibly smooth, almost fluffy mouthfeel.

RANDY

★★★★☆

Glass: Old-fashioned
Garnish: Orange zest twist
Method: **STIR** all ingredients with ice and strain into ice-filled glass.

1½	shots	Martell VSOP Médaillon cognac
½	shot	Grand Marnier Cordon Rouge
1½	shots	Tawny port
¼	shot	Vanilla sugar syrup

Origin: Created in 2003 by yours truly.
Comment: Named after the London rhyming slang for port and brandy, its base ingredients. The love interest comes courtesy of orange and vanilla.

RANDY OLD-FASHIONED (NEW)

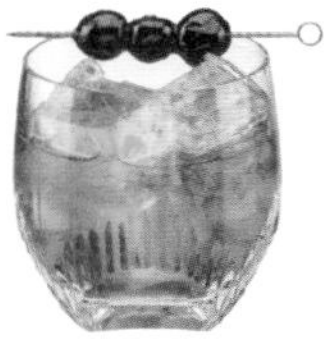

Glass: Old-fashioned
Garnish: Luxardo Maraschino cherries on stick
Method: **STIR** all ingredients with ice and strain into ice-filled glass.

2	shots	Martell VSOP Médaillon cognac
1	shot	Tawny port
¼	shot	Maple syrup
2	dash	Le Fée Parisienne absinthe
2	dash	Peychaud's aromatic bitters

Origin: Created December 2014 by yours truly at the Cabinet Room, London, England.
Comment: Port and brandy (rhymes 'Randy') are traditionally consumed at Christmas and used to be a popular British pub combo. I've used maple syrup in place of brown sugar syrup to lightly sweeten this festive after dinner combo. The Sazerac was the inspiration for the choice of bitters and use of absinthe.

RANGLUM

Glass: Old-fashioned
Garnish: Lime wedge
Method: **SHAKE** all ingredients with ice and strain into ice-filled glass.

1½	shot	Gosling's black seal rum
⅓	shot	White overproof rum
⅓	shot	Taylor's Velvet Falernum liqueur
½	shot	Freshly squeezed lime juice

Comment: Estery rum notes predominate with zesty lime and faint sweet clove spice. A Tiki-style drink for a full-on sunny afternoon or to lift a dull winter's day.
Origin: Created in 2006 by Gonçalo de Sousa Monteiro at Victoria Bar, Berlin, Germany. Gonçalo created this drink whilst listening to Ernest Langlin, so used a combination of the guitarist's surname and falernum to name his new libation.

RAPSCALLION

Glass: Coupe
Garnish: Lemon zest twist (discarded) and olive on a stick

Method: **POUR** pastis into chilled glass, **TOP** with chilled water and leave to stand. Separately **STIR** other ingredients with ice. **DISCARD** contents of glass (pastis, water and ice) and **STRAIN** contents of stirring glass into pastis-coated glass.

¼	shot	Ricard Pastis
1½	shots	Speyside single malt whisky
½	shot	Islay single malt Scotch whisky
½	shot	Romate Pedro Ximénez sherry
¾	shot	Chilled water

Origin: Adapted from a drink created in 2007 by Adeline Shepard and Craig Harper at Ruby Bar, Copenhagen.
Comment: Smoky island malts tamed by the Christmas pudding flavours of Pedro Ximénez with pastis adding notes of enlivening anise. To quote Ruby's menu, "An unabashedly smoky, Scottish version of the Manhattan. Talisker single malt whisky [we used blended Scotch and Lagavulin] and stirred over pedro ximenez sweet sherry with a Ricard pastis rinse. A well-loved signature Ruby Cocktail."

RASPBERRY CAIPIRINHA

Glass: Old-fashioned
Garnish: None
Method: **MUDDLE** lime and raspberries in base of glass. Add the other ingredients and fill glass with crushed ice. **CHURN** drink with barspoon and serve with short straws.

¾	fresh	Lime (fresh whole) (chopped wedges)
8	fresh	Raspberries
2	shots	Capucana cachaça
¾	shot	Sugar syrup (2 sugar to 1 water)

Comment: A fruity twist on the popular Caipirinha.

RASPBERRY COCKTAIL #1 🔫

Glass: Martini
Garnish: Raspberries
Method: **MUDDLE** raspberries in base of shaker. Add other ingredients, **SHAKE** with ice and fine strain into chilled glass.

10	fresh	Raspberries
2½	shots	Ketel One Vodka
½	shot	Sugar syrup (2 sugar to 1 water)

Comment: The simplest of raspberry Martinis but still tastes good.

RASPBERRY COCKTAIL #2

Glass: Martini
Garnish: Raspberries
Method: **MUDDLE** raspberries in base of shaker. Add other ingredients, **SHAKE** with ice and fine strain into chilled glass.

7	fresh	Raspberries
2	shots	Rutte Dry Gin
1	shot	Lejay Crème de Framboise liqueur
2	dash	Angostura Orange Bitters (optional)

Origin: Created in 1997 by Dick Bradsell, London, England and originally named Raspberry Martini.
Comment: Great raspberry flavour integrated with gin.

RASPBERRY COLLINS

Glass: Collins
Garnish: Raspberries & lemon slice
Method: **MUDDLE** raspberries in base of shaker. Add next five ingredients, **SHAKE** with ice and strain into ice-filled glass. **TOP** with soda, lightly stir and serve with straws.

10	fresh	Raspberries
2	shots	Rutte Dry Gin
½	shot	Lejay Crème de Framboise liqueur
1½	shots	Freshly squeezed lemon juice
½	shot	Sugar syrup (2 sugar to 1 water)
3	dash	Angostura Orange Bitters (optional)
Top with		Soda (club soda)

Origin: Created in 1999 by Cairbry Hill, London England.
Comment: This fruity drink is the most popular modern adaptation of the classic Collins.

RASPBERRY COSMOPOLITAN

★★★★½☆

Glass: Martini
Garnish: Raspberries
Method: SHAKE all ingredients with ice and fine strain into chilled glass.

1½	shots	Ketel One Citroen vodka
¾	shot	Lejay Crème de Framboise liqueur
1	shot	Cranberry juice
½	shot	Freshly squeezed lime juice

Comment: Your classic Cosmo but with raspberry liqueur replacing orange liqueur.

RASPBERRY DAIQUIRI

★★★★½☆

Glass: Coupe
Garnish: 3 Raspberries
Method: BLEND all ingredients with 1/2 scoop (6oz) crushed ice and serve in chilled glass.

1½	shots	Bacardi Carta Blanca light rum
1½	shots	Lejay Crème de Framboise liqueur
1	shot	Freshly squeezed lime juice

Comment: A crowd pleasing, slightly sweet blended fruity Daiquiri.

RASPBERRY DEBONNAIRE

★★★★½☆

Glass: Collins
Garnish: Raspberries & lemon slice
Method: MUDDLE raspberries in base of shaker. Add next five ingredients. **SHAKE** with ice and strain into ice-filled glass. **TOP** with soda and lightly stir.

10	fresh	Raspberries
2	shots	Ketel One Vodka
1½	shots	Freshly squeezed lemon juice
½	shot	Lejay Crème de Framboise liqueur
½	shot	Sugar syrup (2 sugar to 1 water)
3	dash	Angostura Orange Bitters (optional)
Top with		Soda (club soda)

Comment: If based on gin rather than vodka this would be a Raspberry Collins.

RASPBERRY FRANGIPANE SPRITZ (NEW)

★★★★★½

Glass: Old-fashioned
Garnish: Raspberry on rim
Method: POUR ingredients into ice-filled glass and lightly stir.

3	shots	Prosecco sparkling wine
1¼	shots	Lejay Crème de Framboise liqueur
¼	shot	Disaronno Originale amaretto
¼	shot	Vanilla schnapps
⅛	shot	Coconut rum liqueur
⅛	shot	Butterscotch liqueur
Top with		Soda (club soda)

Origin: Created in 2013 by yours truly for Jamie's Italian Bars.
Comment: Just like the eponymously named dessert this slightly sweet spritz is flavoured with raspberry, almond, vanilla and coconut. Butterscotch liqueur adds a biscuity note.

RASPBERRY LASSI COCKTAIL

★★★★☆

Glass: Coupe
Garnish: Raspberries & dust with cracked black pepper
Method: SHAKE all ingredients with ice and fine strain into chilled glass.

8	fresh	Raspberries
1½	shots	Ketel One Vodka
1	shot	Yoghurt liqueur
½	shot	Lejay Crème de Framboise liqueur

Origin: Created in 2011 by yours truly at the Cabinet Room, London, England.
Comment: Rich creamy vanilla yoghurt with fresh raspberries and raspberry liqueur fortified with vodka.

RASPBERRY LYNCHBURG

★★★★☆

Glass: Collins
Garnish: Raspberries
Method: SHAKE first three ingredients with ice and strain into ice-filled glass. **TOP** with lemonade and **DRIZZLE** liqueur around surface of drink. It will fall through the drink leaving coloured threads.

2	shots	Jack Daniel's Old No.7 Brand
¾	shot	Freshly squeezed lime juice
¼	shot	Sugar syrup (2 sugar to 1 water)
Top with		Lemonade/Sprite/7-Up
½	shot	Chambord Liqueur

Origin: Created in 1992 by Wayne Collins at Road house, London, England.
Comment: This variation on a Lynchburg Lemonade has a sweet and sour flavour laced with whiskey.

RASPBERRY MARGARITA 🔑

★★★★☆

Glass: Coupe
Garnish: Lime wedge
Method: MUDDLE raspberries in base of shaker. Add other ingredients, **SHAKE** with ice and fine strain into chilled glass.

7	fresh	Raspberries
2	shots	Patrón reposado tequila
1	shot	De Kuyper Triple Sec
1	shot	Freshly squeezed lime juice
⅛	shot	Sugar syrup (2 sugar to 1 water)

Comment: Just as it says - a raspberry flavoured Margarita.

RASPBERRY MOCHA'TINI

★★★★☆

Glass: Martini
Garnish: Raspberries
Method: SHAKE all ingredients with ice and fine strain into chilled glass.

1½	shots	Raspberry flavoured vodka
¾	shot	Dark crème de cacao liqueur
¾	shot	Lejay Crème de Framboise liqueur
1	shot	Espresso coffee (freshly made & hot)

Origin: Discovered in 2002 at Lot 61, New York City, USA.
Comment: Sweet chocolate and raspberry tempered by dry coffee and vodka.

RASPBERRY MULE

★★★★☆

Glass: Collins
Garnish: Lime wedge
Method: MUDDLE raspberries in base of shaker. Add next three ingredients, **SHAKE** with ice and fine strain into ice-filled glass. **TOP** with ginger beer, lightly stir and serve with straws.

12	fresh	Raspberries
2	shots	Ketel One Vodka
1	shot	Freshly squeezed lime juice
½	shot	Sugar syrup (2 sugar to 1 water)
Top with		Gosling's Stormy Ginger Beer

Comment: The fruity alternative to a Moscow Mule.

RASPBERRY SMOOTHIE (ALCOHOLIC)

★★★★☆

Glass: Sling
Garnish: Raspberries
Method: BLEND ingredients with a scoop of crushed ice. Pour into glass and serve immediately with straws.

2	shots	Ketel One Vodka
1½	shots	Yoghurt liqueur
3	spoon	Runny honey
8	fresh	Raspberries
½	shot	Lejay Crème de Framboise liqueur
1	shot	Pressed apple juice

Origin: Created in 2011 by yours truly at the Cabinet Room, London, England.
Comment: This soft pink, creamy yoghurt drink is loaded with raspberry fruit and laced with vodka.

RASPBERRY WATKINS

★★★★☆

Glass: Sling
Garnish: Raspberries
Method: SHAKE first four ingredients with ice and strain into ice-filled glass. **TOP** with soda, lightly stir and serve with straws.

2	shots	Ketel One Vodka
½	shot	Chambord Liqueur
½	shot	Freshly squeezed lime juice
¼	shot	Pomegranate / grenadine syrup (2:1)
Top with		Soda (club soda)

Comment: A light, long, fizzy and refreshing drink.

RASPUTIN

★★★☆☆

Glass: Collins
Garnish: Lime wedge
Method: SHAKE all ingredients with ice and strain into ice-filled glass.

2	shots	Raspberry flavoured vodka
2½	shots	Cranberry juice
1½	shots	Freshly squeezed pink grapefruit juice

Comment: This fruity adaptation of an Arizona Breeze is raspberry rich.

RAT PACK MANHATTAN

★★★★☆

Glass: Martini
Garnish: Orange zest twist & Luxardo Maraschino cherry
Method: Chill glass, add Grand Marnier, swirl to coat and then **DISCARD. STIR** other ingredients with ice and strain into liqueur coated glass.

½ shot **Grand Marnier Cordon Rouge**
1½ shots **Bourbon whiskey**
¾ shot **Martini Rosso vermouth**
¾ shot **Martini Extra Dry vermouth**
3 dash **Angostura Aromatic Bitters**

Origin: Created in 2000 by Wayne Collins at High Holborn, London, England. Originally Wayne used different whiskies to represent each of the Rat Pack crooners. The wash of Grand Marnier was for Sammy Davis, the wild card of the bunch.
Comment: A twist on the classic Manhattan.

RATTLESNAKE

★★★★☆

Glass: Martini
Garnish: Lemon zest twist
Method: SHAKE all ingredients with ice and fine strain into chilled glass.

2	shots	Bourbon whiskey
¼	shot	Freshly squeezed lemon juice
¼	shot	Sugar syrup (2 sugar to 1 water)
⅛	shot	Le Fée Parisienne absinthe
½	shot	Egg white
½	shot	Chilled water (omit if wet ice)

Origin: Adapted from a recipe purloined from a 1930 edition of the 'Savoy Cocktail Book' by Harry Craddock.
Comment: To quote Craddock, "So called because it will either cure rattlesnake bite, or kill rattlesnakes, or make you see them".

RAY GUN

★★★☆☆

Glass: Flute
Garnish: Orange zest twist
Method: POUR Chartreuse and blue curaçao into chilled glass. **TOP** with champagne.

½	shot	Green Chartreuse liqueur
¾	shot	Blue curaçao liqueur
Top with		G.H. Mumm Cordon Rouge Champagne

Comment: Not for the faint-hearted.

RAY'S HARD LEMONADE

★★★★☆

Glass: Collins
Garnish: Mint sprig
Method: Lightly **MUDDLE** (just to bruise) mint in base of shaker. Add next 4 ingredients, **SHAKE** with ice and fine strain into ice-filled glass. **TOP** with soda, lightly stir and serve with straws.

7	fresh	Mint leaves
2	shots	Ketel One Vodka
1	shot	Freshly squeezed lemon juice
2	shots	Freshly squeezed lime juice
1½	shots	Sugar syrup (2 sugar to 1 water)
Top with		Soda (club soda)

Origin: Discovered in 2004 at Spring Street Natural Restaurant, New York City, USA.
Comment: Alcoholic lemonade with mint? A vodka mojito? However you describe it, it works.

REAL LEMONADE (MOCKTAIL)

★★★★☆

Glass: Collins
Garnish: Lemon slice
Method: **POUR** ingredients in ice-filled glass and lightly **STIR**. Serve with straws.

2	shots	Freshly squeezed lemon juice
1	shot	Sugar syrup (2 sugar to 1 water)
Top with		Soda (club soda)

Comment: The classic English summertime refresher.

REALITY CHECK

★★★★★

Glass: Rum barrel mug or pint glass
Garnish: Lime zest twist
Method: **MUDDLE** raspberries in base of large shaker tin. Add ice and other ingredients then **THROW** (strain from a height into a second strainer). Repeat four times and then strain into ice-filled glass.

5	fresh	Raspberries
⅔	shot	Ketel One Vodka
⅔	shot	Becherovka (Carlsbad Becher)
¼	shot	Freshly squeezed lime juice
2¾	shots	Budweiser Budvar
⅓	shot	Sugar syrup (2 sugar to 1 water)
1	dash	Angostura Aromatic Bitters

Origin: Created in 2013 by Simone Caporale at the Artesian Bar, Langham Hotel, London, England. Simone was one of five finalists in the Difford's Guide Beer-tail Competition held on Friday 9th August 2013 at the Cabinet Room, London, England.
Comment: Raspberry fruit, herbal complexity and dry hoppy beer with a splash of zesty lime. Fabulously refreshing.

REBUJITO COCKTAIL (NEW)

★★★★⯪

Glass: Collins
Garnish: Lemon and lime slices
Method: **POUR** ingredients into ice-filled glass and stir.

| 3½ | shots | Lemonade/Sprite/7-Up |
| 2½ | shots | Romate Fino sherry |

Origin: Named after the Spanish word 'arrebujar' meaning to mix, the recipe for a Rebujito changes from region to region in Spain and is often as simple as equal parts fino sherry and soda or equal parts fino sherry and Sprite or Seven-up. It is popular in Seville and the south of Spain, particularly during April's Seville Fair (La feria de Abril).
Comment: Dry characterful sherry with sweet zesty lemonade – a combo made for a hot summer's day.

RED ANGEL

★★★★☆

Glass: Martini
Garnish: Orange zest twist
Method: **STIR** all ingredients with ice and strain into chilled glass.

2	shots	Shiraz red wine
1	shot	Grand Marnier Cordon Rouge
¼	shot	Luxardo Maraschino liqueur
½	shot	Chilled water (omit if wet ice)

Origin: Created in 2001 by Tony Conigliaro at Isola, Knightsbridge, London, England.
Comment: A subtly flavoured cocktail with a dry, almost tannic edge.

RED APPLE

★★★★☆

Glass: Martini
Garnish: Luxardo Maraschino cherry
Method: **SHAKE** all ingredients with ice and fine strain into chilled glass.

1½	shots	Bourbon whiskey
½	shot	Sour apple liqueur
2	shots	Cranberry juice

Comment: As Apple Martinis go, this one is rather good.

RED BREAST

★★★⯪☆

Glass: Collins
Garnish: Raspberries
Method: **POUR** first three ingredients into ice-filled glass and lightly stir. **DRIZZLE** raspberry liqueur over surface of drink.

2	shots	Dewar's 12yo Scotch whisky
½	shot	Freshly squeezed lime juice
Top with		Gosling's Stormy Ginger Beer
½	shot	Lejay Crème de Framboise liqueur

Origin: Created in 2004 by Wayne Collins, London, England.
Comment: Scotch, lime juice and ginger beer, flavoured and made a tad pink by raspberry liqueur.

RED GEMMA (NEW)

★★★★☆

Glass: Flute
Garnish: Raspberry on rim
Method: STIR first 3 ingredients with ice and strain into chilled glass. **TOP** with Champagne and gently stir.

1	shot	Rutte Dry Gin
1	shot	Chambord Liqueur
1	shot	Shiraz red wine
3	shots	G.H. Mumm Cordon Rouge Champagne

Origin: Created 5th February 2014 by yours truly at the Cabinet Room, London, England and named after Gemma Monaghan, who incidentally is a blond Mancunian who supports Liverpool FC.
Comment: Red berry flavours with light red wine tannins, liqueur sweetness and botanical depth courtesy of gin, all refreshed with fizz. Berry fizz!

RED HOOK

★★★★☆

Glass: Coupe
Garnish: Luxardo Maraschino cherry
Method: STIR all ingredients with ice and strain into chilled glass.

2	shots	Straight rye whiskey
½	shot	Punt E Mes
½	shot	Luxardo Maraschino liqueur

Comment: This boozy Manhattan-like drink was inspired by the Brooklyn Cocktail, hence it is named after a neighbourhood of Brooklyn.
Origin: Created in 2003 by Enzo Enrico at Milk & Honey, New York City, USA.

RED HOOKER

★★★☆☆

Glass: Martini
Garnish: Peach slice
Method: SHAKE all ingredients with ice and fine strain into chilled glass.

1	shot	Peach purée
2	shots	Patrón reposado tequila
¾	shot	Lejay Crème de Framboise liqueur
¾	shot	Freshly squeezed lemon juice

Comment: An appropriately named red, fruity drink with more than a hint of tequila.

RED LION COCKTAIL (EMBURY'S FORMULA)

★★★★☆

Glass: Martini
Garnish: Orange slice
Method: SHAKE all ingredients with ice and fine strain into chilled glass.

2	shots	Rutte Dry Gin
¼	shot	Grand Marnier Cordon Rouge
½	shot	Freshly squeezed lime juice
¼	shot	Pomegranate / grenadine syrup (2:1)
¾	shot	Chilled water (reduce if wet ice)

Origin: Adapted from a recipe in David A. Embury's 1948 'Fine Art of Mixing Drinks'.
Comment: Embury was a Daiquiri fan and this is reminiscent of a Daiquiri in both style and proportions.

RED LION COCKTAIL (MODERN RECIPE)

★★★★☆

Glass: Martini
Garnish: Orange slice
Method: SHAKE all ingredients with ice and fine strain into chilled glass.

1¼	shots	Rutte Dry Gin
1¼	shots	Grand Marnier Cordon Rouge
1	shot	Freshly squeezed orange juice
1	shot	Freshly squeezed lemon juice
⅛	shot	Pomegranate / grenadine syrup (2:1)

Origin: The classic drink is said to have been created for the Chicago World Fair in 1933. However, it won the British Empire Cocktail Competition that year and was more likely created by W J Tarling for Booth's gin and named after the brand's Red Lion Distillery in London, England.
Comment: The colour of a summer's twilight with a rich tangy orange flavour.

RED MANHATTAN

★★★★☆

Glass: Coupe
Garnish: Luxardo Maraschino cherry
Method: STIR all ingredients with ice and strain into chilled glass.

2 shots Bourbon whiskey
1 shot Martini Rosso vermouth
¼ shot Claret red wine
⅛ shot Luxardo Maraschino liqueur
2 dash Angostura Aromatic Bitters

Origin: Created in November 2010 by yours truly at the Cabinet Room, London, England.
Comment: The tannins from the splash of red wine add complexity and depth of flavour to this Sweet Manhattan.

RED MARAUDER

★★★★☆

Glass: Martini
Garnish: Raspberries
Method: SHAKE all ingredients with ice and fine strain into chilled glass.

2	shots	Martell VSOP Médaillon cognac
½	shot	Chambord Liqueur
1½	shots	Cranberry juice
¼	shot	Freshly squeezed lime juice

Origin: Originally created for Martell, long term sponsors of the Grand National, this is named after the horse that won in 2001.
Comment: Slightly sweet and fruity with a hint of raspberry and cognac's distinctive flavour.

RED MELON'TINI

★★★½☆

Glass: Martini
Garnish: Watermelon wedge
Method: Cut watermelon into 16 segments, chop the flesh from one segment into cubes and **MUDDLE** in base of shaker. Add other ingredients, **SHAKE** all ingredients with ice and fine strain into chilled glass.

1	segment	Fresh watermelon (chopped)
2	shots	Pepper-infused Ketel One vodka
¼	shot	Sugar syrup (2 sugar to 1 water)
4	grind	Black pepper

Origin: Discovered in 2002 at the Fifth Floor Bar, Harvey Nichol's, London, England.
Comment: Watermelon peppered with vodka and the subtlest peppery finish.

RED NECK MARTINI

★★★★☆

Glass: Martini
Garnish: Orange zest twist
Method: **SHAKE** all ingredients with ice and fine strain into chilled glass.

2	shots	Dewar's 12yo Scotch whisky
1	shot	Dubonnet Red
1	shot	Cherry Heering Liqueur

Origin: Created by Sylvain Solignac in 2002 at Circus Bar, London, England.
Comment: Aromatic and not too sweet - the flavour of the Scotch shines through.

RED OPAL COCKTAIL (NEW)

★★★★½

Glass: Coupe
Garnish: Orange zest twist
Method: **SHAKE** all ingredients with ice and fine strain into chilled glass.

2	shots	Rutte Dry Gin
½	shot	De Kuyper Triple Sec
1¼	shots	Freshly squeezed orange juice
¼	shot	Sugar syrup (2 sugar to 1 water)
⅛	shot	Orange flower water

Origin: Adapted from the 1920s classic Opal recipe.
Comment: The combination of gin, triple sec and blood orange juice results in clementine-like flavours with subtle flavours of orange flower water.

RED ROVER

★★★★☆

Glass: Old-fashioned
Garnish: Orange slice
Method: **SHAKE** all ingredients with ice and strain into ice-filled glass.

3	shots	Shiraz red wine
1	shot	Pusser's Navy Rum (54.5%)
½	shot	Chambord Liqueur

Comment: Carpet-scaring red with the body of red wine but the palate of a cocktail.

RED RUM COCKTAIL

★★★★½

Glass: Martini
Garnish: Redcurrants
Method: **MUDDLE** redcurrants a base of shaker. Add other ingredients, **SHAKE** all ingredients with ice and fine strain into chilled glass.

24	fresh	Redcurrants
2	shots	Bacardi Carta Ocho aged rum
½	shot	Sloe Gin liqueur
½	shot	Freshly squeezed lemon juice
½	shot	Vanilla sugar syrup

Origin: Created by Jason Scott in 2002 at Oloroso, Edinburgh, Scotland.

This cocktail, which is red and contains rum, is named after 'Red Rum', the only horse in history to win England's Grand National three times (on his other two attempts he came second). He became a British hero, made an appearance on the BBC Sports Personality of the Year show and paraded right up to his death at the age 30 in 1995.
Comment: A beautifully fruity, adult balance of bittersweet flavours.

RED SNAPPER

★★★★★

Glass: Collins
Garnish: Salt & pepper rim
Method: **SHAKE** all ingredients with ice and strain into ice-filled glass. Serve with straws.

2	shots	Rutte Dry Gin
4	shots	Tomato juice
½	shot	Freshly squeezed lemon juice
7	drop	Tabasco hot pepper sauce
4	dash	Worcestershire sauce
2	pinch	Celery salt
2	grind	Black pepper

Origin: Today, the term Red Snapper means a Bloody Mary made with gin instead of vodka. But the first known recipes, from the 1940s, describe a 50-50 blend of vodka and tomato juice, with spices, just like an early Bloody Mary: one book even states that the Red Snapper is identical to the Bloody Mary.
Comment: Looks like a Bloody Mary but features gin's aromatic botanicals.

REDBACK

★★★☆☆

Glass: Shot
Garnish: Luxardo Maraschino cherry
Method: **POUR** sambuca into glass, then pour advocaat down the side of the glass.

½	shot	Warninks Advocaat liqueur
1	shot	Black sambuca liqueur

Comment: An impressive looking shot.

REEF JUICE

★★★★☆

Glass: Collins
Garnish: Pineapple wedge
Method: SHAKE all ingredients with ice and strain into ice-filled glass.

1½	shots	Pusser's Navy Rum (54.5%)
½	shot	Ketel One Vodka
1	shot	Crème de banane liqueur
½	shot	Freshly squeezed lime juice
2½	shots	Fresh pressed pineapple juice
½	shot	Pomegranate / grenadine syrup (2:1)

Origin: Charles Tobias, proprietor of Pusser's, created this drink at the Beach Bar in Fort Lauderdale, Florida. It was a favourite of a friend who crashed his boat on the reef.
Comment: Tangy, fruity and dangerously moreish.

REGGAE RUM PUNCH

★★★★½

Glass: Collins
Garnish: Pineapple wedge & Luxardo Maraschino cherry
Method: SHAKE all ingredients with ice and strain into ice-filled glass.

1¾	shots	White overproof rum
½	shot	Lejay Crème de Framboise liqueur
¾	shot	Freshly squeezed lime juice
1	shot	Fresh pressed pineapple juice
1½	shots	Freshly squeezed orange juice
¾	shot	Pomegranate / grenadine syrup (2:1)

Origin: The most popular punch in Jamaica, where it is sold under different names with slightly varying ingredients. It always contains orange, pineapple and most importantly, overproof rum.
Comment: Jamaicans have a sweet tooth and love their rum. This drink combines sweetness, strength and a generous amount of fruit.

REGGATTA DE BLANC (NEW)

★★★★½

Glass: Old-fashioned
Garnish: Green grapes on stick
Method: STIR all ingredients with ice and strain into ice-filled glass.

1	shot	BarSol Mosto Verde Italia pisco
1	shot	Calvados brandy
1	shot	Sauvignon blanc white wine
½	shot	Suze Saveur d'Autrefois
⅛	shot	Sugar syrup (2 sugar to 1 water)

Origin: Created in August 2015 by yours truly at the Cabinet Room, London, England.
Comment: Dry and boozy.

"White Reggae" was the second, and seminal, album by the English rock band 'The Police'. The album's French name reflects the heavy influence of the country's products in this cocktail. Happily for approval by our naming committee (my missus), most of the ingredients are also decidedly "Blanc".

REMEMBER THE MAINE

★★★★½

Glass: Old-fashioned
Garnish: Lemon zest twist
Method: POUR the absinthe into ice-filled glass, top up with water and set to one side. Separately, **POUR** other ingredients into a ice-filled mixing glass and **STIR** well. **DISCARD** absinthe, water and ice from serving glass. Finally strain contents of mixing glass into the absinthe rinsed glass.

1	shot	Le Fée Parisienne absinthe
Top with		Chilled water
2	shots	Bourbon whiskey
¾	shot	Cherry Heering Liqueur
¾	shot	Martini Rosso vermouth

Origin: Adapted from a recipe by Charles H. Baker Junior. In his 1939 'The Gentleman's Companion' he writes of this drink, "a Hazy Memory of a Night in Havana during the Unpleasantnesses of 1933, when Each Swallow Was Punctuated with Bombs Going off on the Prado, or the Sound of 3" Shells Being Fired at the Hotel NACIONAL, then Haven for Certain Anti-Revolutionary Officers".

The drink is named after the press slogan, which allegedly provoked the 1898 Spanish-American War.
Comment: Charles H. Baker says of this twist on a Sazerac, "Treat this one with the respect it deserves, gentleman."

REMSEN COOLER 🗝

★★★★☆

Glass: Collins
Garnish: Lemon peel (whole)
Method: POUR ingredients into ice-filled glass and serve with straws.

2½	shots	Dewar's 12yo Scotch whisky
Top with		Soda from siphon

Origin: Adapted from a recipe purloined from David Embury's classic book, 'The Fine Art of Mixing Drinks', and so named because it was originally made with the now defunct Remsen Scotch whisky. Embury claims this is "the original cooler".
Comment: Scotch and soda for the sophisticate.

RESOLUTE 🗝

★★★★☆

Glass: Martini
Garnish: Lemon zest twist
Method: SHAKE all ingredients with ice and fine strain into chilled glass.

1¾	shots	Rutte Dry Gin
1	shot	De Kuyper XO Apricot Brandy
½	shot	Freshly squeezed lemon juice
½	shot	Chilled water (omit if wet ice)

Origin: Adapted from a recipe purloined from a 1930 edition of the 'Savoy Cocktail Book' by Harry Craddock.
Comment: Simple but tasty. All three flavours work in harmony.

RÉVEILLON COCKTAIL (NEW)

★★★★½

Glass: Old-fashioned
Garnish: Cinnamon stick
Method: STIR all ingredients with ice and strain into chilled glass.

1½ shots   Calvados brandy
1   shot   Carpano Antica Formula
½   shot   Poire William pear liqueur
¼   shot   Allspice pimento dram liqueur
1   dash   Whiskey Barrel Aged Bitters

Origin: Adapted from a drink created in 2005 by Chuck Taggart, the Los Angeles based New Orleanian cocktail loving disc jockey behind TheGumboPages.com. In French and Portuguese speaking lands a réveillon is a long dinner, and often a social gathering, held on the evenings preceding Christmas Day and New Year's Day. In the same way that Americans seem to celebrate St Patrick's Day more fervently than the Irish, réveillon is particularly celebrated in the city New Orleans, either due to the city's strong French heritage or it being a damn good excuse for a nosh-up and party.

Réveillon, comes from the French word, réveil meaning 'waking' (or 'alarm clock' according to the very literal Google Translate). Why the name! Well any good party should last through the early hours. Right.

Chuck Taggart, one of the creators of this cocktail, reports that after trying the drink for the first time at a 2005 Christmas party, Ted Haigh (AKA DrCocktail.com) declared, "Oh, this is delightful!" adding, "It's like sucking on Santa!"
Comment: Bittersweet and spicy with underlying warming apple spirit. Originally designed to be served 'up' in a Nick & Nora glass we think it's better suited to being served on-the-rocks, preferably a chunk of block ice. The original formula called for more apple brandy and a lot less aromatized wine.

REVERSE MARTINI

★★★★★

Glass: Martini
Garnish: Chilled olive on stick or lemon zest twist
Method: STIR all ingredients with ice and strain into chilled glass.

2   shots   Martini Extra Dry vermouth
1   shot   Rutte Dry Gin

Comment: Simply a Dry Martini with the proportions reversed to make a dripping Wet Martini.

REVERSE VESPER MARTINI (NEW)

★★★★½

Glass: Martini
Garnish: Lemon zest twist
Method: SHAKE all ingredients with ice and fine strain into chilled glass.

2   shots   Lillet Blanc
⅔   shot   Ketel One Vodka
⅓   shot   Rutte Dry Gin

Comment: More a subtly fortified wine than a true "three and under the guest" Martini but delightfully so with sherry-like wine notes and faint botanical influences. Subtly refined. Despite the 'Vesper' name some will say that this should be stirred. Shake boldly on, but with good ice.

REVERSED VESPER & TONIC

★★★★★

Glass: Martini
Garnish: Lemon zest twist
Method: SHAKE all ingredients with ice and fine strain into chilled glass.

1   shot   Rutte Dry Gin
1   shot   Ketel One Vodka
1   shot   Lillet Blanc
⅛   shot   Becherovka (Carlsbad Becher)
⅛   shot   Pomegranate / grenadine syrup (2:1)
½   shot   Tonic Water

Origin: Created in 2008 by yours truly at the Cabinet Room, London, England.

James Bond named his favourite style of Martini after the beautiful Russian agent Vesper Lynd. This version is 'Reversed' due to the dramatically increased ratio of Lillet Blanc. Fittingly my drink mixes east and west ingredients with the introduction of Becherovka. And where there is Becherovka there should be tonic water.
Comment: Martini in style but with the hard edges smoothed and a hint of eastern spice added. Scarily, it took 14 attempts and 13 wasted drinks to arrive at the above formula but it seemed like an idea worth pursuing.

RHETT BUTLER

★★★★☆

Glass: Old-fashioned
Garnish: Lime wedge
Method: SHAKE all ingredients with ice and strain into ice-filled glass.

1   shot   Grand Marnier Cordon Rouge
1   shot   Southern Comfort liqueur
2   shots   Cranberry juice
1   shot   Freshly squeezed lime juice

Comment: A simple and well-balanced classic drink.

RHINE WINE COBBLER

★★★★½

Glass: Goblet
Garnish: A grape, orange and pineapple slice
Method: MUDDLE grapes and pineapple in base of shaker and fine strain (without shaking) into glass filled with crushed ice. POUR other ingredients into glass and cobble (churn/stir) with barspoon to thoroughly mix.

3   fresh   Seedless white grapes
2   wedge   Pineapple (fresh)
               (cored, skinned and chopped)
3   shots   Reisling wine
½   shot   Freshly squeezed orange juice
½   shot   Sugar syrup (2 sugar to 1 water)

Origin: Recipe adapted from Harry Johnson's 1882 'Bartender's Manual'.
Comment: Light, grapey, fruit and very refreshing. One for a summer's afternoon.

RHINESTONE COWGIRL

★★★⯪☆

Glass: Collins
Garnish: Orange slice
Method: SHAKE all ingredients with ice and strain into chilled glass.

2	shots	Bourbon whiskey
2	shots	Cranberry juice
1	shot	Freshly squeezed lemon juice
½	shot	Sugar syrup (2 sugar to 1 water)
¾	shot	Lejay crème de cassis de Dijon

Comment: Tangy, citrus, cranberry and berry fruit laced with sweetened bourbon.

RHODE ISLAND RED

★★★★☆

Glass: Collins
Garnish: Lemon & lime zest twists
Method: SHAKE first five ingredients with ice and strain into ice-filled glass. TOP with ginger beer, lightly stir and serve with straws.

2	shots	Patrón reposado tequila
½	shot	Chambord Liqueur
¾	shot	Freshly squeezed lemon juice
½	shot	Agave syrup
1	dash	Angostura Orange Bitters
Top with		Gosling's Stormy Ginger Beer

Origin: Created in 2009 by Vincenzo Marianella at Copa d'Oro, Santa Monica, USA.
Comment: Tequila with a hint of berry fruit, slightly sweetened with agave nectar, spiced and made long with ginger beer.

RHUBARB & CUSTARD COCKTAIL

★★★★☆

Glass: Martini
Garnish: Dust with grated nutmeg
Method: SHAKE all ingredients with ice and fine strain into chilled glass.

1¼	shots	Rutte Dry Gin
1¼	shots	Warninks Advocaat liqueur
1¼	shots	Rhubarb syrup (from tinned fruit)

Origin: Created by yours truly in 2002. Rhubarb and Custard is a great British dessert and was a cult children's TV cartoon in the 1970s. It featured a naughty pink cat called Custard and a green dog named Rhubarb who, like many British men, spent a lot of time in his garden shed.
Comment: As sharp, sweet, creamy and flavourful as the dessert it imitates.

RHUBARB & HONEY BELLINI

★★★★☆

Glass: Flute
Garnish: Orange zest twist
Method: SHAKE rhubarb syrup and honey liqueur with ice and fine strain into chille glass. TOP with Prosecco and gently stir.

1¼	shots	Rhubarb & orange preserve
1¼	shots	Old Krupnik
Top with		Prosecco sparkling wine

Origin: A simplified adaptation of a drink created in 2003 by Tony Conigliaro at London's Shumi.
Comment: The implausible combination works surprisingly well.

RHUBARB & LEMONGRASS COCKTAIL

★★★⯪☆

Glass: Martini
Garnish: Lemongrass
Method: MUDDLE lemongrass in base of shaker. Add other ingredients, SHAKE all ingredients with ice and fine strain into chilled glass.

4	inch	Lemongrass stem (chopped)
2	shots	Rutte Dry Gin
1½	shots	Rhubarb syrup (from tinned fruit)
⅛	shot	Sugar syrup (2 sugar to 1 water)

Origin: Based on a cocktail discovered in 2003 at Zuma, London, England.
Comment: Fragrant, exotic lemon flavours combine well with rhubarb to make a surprisingly refreshing drink.

RHUBARB LUCCA NEGRONI

★★★★⯪

Glass: Old-fashioned
Garnish: Orange zest twist (discarded) and rhubarb stirrer
Method: POUR all ingredients into ice-filled glass and STIR.

1	shot	Rutte Dry Gin
1	shot	Campari Bitter
½	shot	Carpano Antica Formula
½	shot	Rabarbaro

Origin: Created in 2011 by Jonathan Abarbanel at Quo Vadis, London, England. Jonathan originally used Rhubarb-infused London dry gin.
Comment: A rhubarb-influenced rift on the classic Negroni.

RIBALAIGUA DAIQUIRI #3

★★★★☆

Glass: Martini
Garnish: Mint leaf
Method: SHAKE all ingredients with ice and fine strain into chilled glass.

2	shots	Bacardi Carta Blanca light rum
½	shot	Luxardo Maraschino liqueur
1	shot	Freshly squeezed pink grapefruit juice
½	shot	Chilled water (omit if wet ice)

Origin: Named for Constatino Ribalaigua, who introduced Hemingway to the Daiquiri at El Floridita, Havana, Cuba.
Comment: This unusual Daiquiri leads with sweet maraschino and finishes with sour grapefruit.

RICHMOND GIMLET

★★★★☆

Glass: Martini
Garnish: Mint leaf
Method: SHAKE all ingredients with ice and fine strain into chilled glass.

8	fresh	Mint leaves
2	shots	Rutte Dry Gin
¾	shot	Freshly squeezed lime juice
½	shot	Sugar syrup (2 sugar to 1 water)
½	shot	Chilled water (omit if wet ice)

Origin: Adapted from a recipe created in 2008 by Jeffrey Morgenthaler at Bel Ami Lounge, Oregon, USA.
Comment: A properly grown-up Gimlet.

THE RIGHT HAND (NEW)

★★★★★

Glass: Old-fashioned
Garnish: Orange slice
Method: STIR all ingredients with ice and strain into ice-filled glass.

2 shots Bacardi Carta Ocho aged rum
1 shot Martini Rosso vermouth
1 shot Campari Bitter
2 dash Xocolatl Mole bitters

Origin: Created in 2007 by Michael McIlroy at Milk & Honey, New York City, USA.
Comment: This rum based Negroni may make you wonder why you've been drinking gin Negronis all these years.

ROA AE

★★★½☆

Glass: Collins
Garnish: Pineapple wedge
Method: SHAKE all ingredients with ice and strain into ice-filled glass.

1½ shots	Bacardi Carta Blanca light rum
½ shot	De Kuyper XO Apricot Brandy
½ shot	Grand Marnier Cordon Rouge
½ shot	Belle de Brillet pear liqueur
3 shots	Fresh pressed pineapple juice
¾ shot	Freshly squeezed lime juice

Origin: Discovered in 2003 at Booly Mardy's, Glasgow, Scotland. Cocktail aficionados will be familiar with the Tahitian phase 'Mai Tai - Roa Ae', or 'out of this world - the best', which gave Mai Tai it's name. This cocktail means simply 'the best'.
Comment: Not quite the best, but this long, fruity thirst quencher isn't half bad.

RITZ COCKTAIL

★★★★☆

Glass: Martini
Garnish: Flamed orange zest twist
Method: STIR first four ingredients with ice and strain into chilled glass. TOP with a splash of champagne.

¾	shot	Martell VSOP Médaillon cognac
½	shot	De Kuyper Triple Sec
¼	shot	Luxardo Maraschino liqueur
¼	shot	Freshly squeezed lemon juice
Top with		G.H. Mumm Cordon Rouge Champagne

Origin: Created by Dale DeGroff, New York City, USA.
Comment: Citrus freshness with a cognac backbone, lightened and dried with champagne.

THE ROADRUNNER

★★★★☆

Glass: Martini
Garnish: Lemon zest twist
Method: SHAKE all ingredients with ice and fine strain into chilled glass.

2	shots	Patrón reposado tequila (infused with vanilla)
¾	shot	Freshly squeezed lemon juice
2	dash	Angostura Aromatic Bitters
½	shot	Maple syrup
½	fresh	Egg white

Origin: Discovered in 2005 at The Cuckoo Club, London, England.
Comment: Citrus and tequila with a hint of maple and vanilla, smoothed with egg white.

RIZZO

★★★★☆

Glass: Martini
Garnish: Apple slice
Method: SHAKE all ingredients with ice and fine strain into chilled glass.

1	shot	Calvados brandy
1	shot	Rutte Dry Gin
¾	shot	Freshly squeezed pink grapefruit juice
½	shot	Freshly squeezed lime juice
¼	shot	Passion fruit syrup
¼	shot	Pomegranate / grenadine syrup (2:1)

Origin: Created in 2006 by Gregor de Gruyther at Ronnie Scott's, London, England, and named for Betty Rizzo, the leader of the Pink Ladies in the film Grease.
Comment: The tangy, sharp grapefruit reveals hints of apple spirit smoothed by grenadine.

ROB ROY COCKTAIL

★★★★☆

Glass: Martini
Garnish: Lemon zest twist (discarded) & Luxardo Maraschino cherry
Method: STIR all ingredients with ice and strain into chilled glass.

2	shots	Dewar's 12yo Scotch whisky
1	shot	Martini Rosso vermouth
2	dash	Angostura Aromatic Bitters
⅛	shot	Maraschino syrup (from cherry jar) (optional)

Origin: Created in 1894 at New York's Waldorf-Astoria Hotel (the Empire State Building occupies the site today) and named, not after the Scottish folk hero and outlaw Robert Roy MacGregor, but after the Broadway show that was showing at the time.
Comment: A Sweet Manhattan made with Scotch in place of bourbon. The dry, peaty whisky and bitters ensure it's not too sweet.

ROB ROY COCKTAIL (EMBURY'S RECIPE)

★★★★½

Glass: Martini
Garnish: Orange zest twist (discarded) & Luxardo Maraschino cherry
Method: STIR all ingredients with ice and strain into chilled glass.

2	shots	Dewar's 12yo Scotch whisky
1	shot	Martini Rosso vermouth
2	dash	Peychaud's aromatic bitters
½	shot	Chilled water (omit if wet ice)

Origin: This variation on the classic Rob Roy is recommended by author David Embury in his influential Fine Art of Mixing Drinks.
Comment: The Scotch answer to the Manhattan with added complexity courtesy of Peychaud's aromatic bitters.

ROBIN HOOD #1

★★★★☆

Glass: Martini
Garnish: Apple wedge
Method: SHAKE all ingredients with ice and fine strain into chilled glass.

1¾	shots	Bacardi Carta Blanca light rum
1¼	shots	Apple Schnapps liqueur
¾	shot	Rose's lime cordial
½	shot	Freshly squeezed lime juice

Origin: Adapted from a drink created in 2002 by Tony Conigliaro at The Lonsdale, London, England.
Comment: American readers might consider this a Apple Martini based on rum.

ROC-A-COE

★★★½☆

Glass: Martini
Garnish: Luxardo Maraschino cherry
Method: STIR all ingredients with ice and strain into chilled glass.

1½	shots	Rutte Dry Gin
2	shots	Romate Amontillado sherry
⅛	shot	Sugar syrup (2 sugar to 1 water)
½	shot	Chilled water

Origin: Adapted from Harry Craddock's 1930 ' The Savoy Cocktail Book'.
Comment: Aromatic and balanced.

ROCK 'N' RYE

★★★★½

Glass: Old-fashioned
Garnish: Orange zest twist (discarded) & Luxardo Maraschino cherry
Method: SHAKE all ingredients with ice and strain into ice-filled glass.

2½	shots	Straight rye whiskey
½	shot	Freshly squeezed orange juice
⅛	shot	Freshly squeezed lemon juice
¼	shot	Maraschino syrup (from cherry jar)
¼	shot	Sugar syrup (2 sugar to 1 water)

Comment: Great rye whiskey notes with hints of orange and cherry. Slightly sweet but all too easy.

ROCKY LEFT BANK

★★★★★½

Glass: Old-fashioned
Garnish: Lime zest twist
Method: SHAKE all ingredients with ice and strain into ice-filled glass.

1½	shots	Rutte Dry Gin
1½	shots	St-Germain elderflower liqueur
1½	shots	Chardonnay (Chablis) white wine

Origin: Created in 2006 by yours truly at the Cabinet Room, London, England.
Comment: Slightly sweet, crowd pleasing combo of gin, elderflower and white wine.

ROCKY MOUNTAIN ROOTBEER

★★★★☆

Glass: Collins
Garnish: Lime wedge
Method: POUR vodka and liqueur into ice-filled glass, TOP up with cola and lightly stir.

2	shots	Ketel One Vodka
¾	shot	Galliano L'Autentico liqueur
Top with		Coca-Cola

Comment: Does indeed taste reminiscent of alcoholic root beer.

ROCOCOA

★★★½☆

Glass: Coupe
Garnish: Half vanilla pod
Method: STIR all ingredients with ice and strain into chilled glass.

2	shots	Bacardi Carta Blanca light rum
⅓	shot	White crème de cacao liqueur
⅛	shot	Islay single malt Scotch whisky
2	dash	Bob's Chocolate bitters (omit if wet ice)
½	shot	Chilled water (omit if wet ice)

Origin: Adapted from a drink created by Scott Tyrer at Bibis Italianissimo, Leeds, England.
Comment: Subtly smoky chocolate and light rum.

THE ROFFIGNAC

★★★★☆

Glass: Collins
Garnish: Lime wedge
Method: SHAKE first two ingredients with ice and strain into ice-filled glass. TOP with soda, lightly stir and serve with straws.

2	shots	Martell VSOP Médaillon cognac
1	shot	Lejay Crème de Framboise liqueur
Top with		Soda (club soda)

Origin: This classic cocktail is named after Count Louis Philippe Joseph de Roffignac, Mayor of New Orleans 1820-1828. Roffignac is noted for introducing street lights to the city and laying cobblestones on the roads in the French Quarter.
Comment: This bright red, fruity drink is simple but moreish.

ROGER

★★★⯪☆

Glass: Martini
Garnish: Peach slice
Method: SHAKE all ingredients with ice and fine strain into chilled glass.

2 shots Ketel One Vodka
2 shots Peach purée (white)
½ shot Freshly squeezed lemon juice
¼ shot Sugar syrup (2 sugar to 1 water)

Origin: A popular drink in Venice, where it is made using the peach purée mix prepared for bellinis.
Comment: Thick and very fruity - one for a summer's afternoon.

ROMAN HIGHBALL (NEW)

★★★★⯪

Glass: Collins
Garnish: Candied ginger or fresh ginger
Method: SHAKE first 3 ingredients with ice and strain into ice-filled glass. TOP with soda.

1½ shots Amaro liqueur
¾ shot King's Ginger Liqueur
½ shot Freshly squeezed lime juice
Top with Soda (club soda)

Origin: Adapted from a recipe created by Danny Gil at Weather Up, New York City, USA.
Comment: A refreshing, long and Pimm's Cup-like. A great drink to come home to.

ROMAN PUNCH

★★★★☆

Glass: Collins
Garnish: Lemon slice
Method: SHAKE all ingredients with ice and strain into glass filled with crushed ice. CHURN (stir) drink and top up ice if necessary. Serve with straws. (If serving with cubed rather than crushed ice add 1½ shots of chilled water before shaking.

1½ shots Bénédictine D.O.M. liqueur
1½ shots Martell VSOP Médaillon cognac
¾ shot White overproof rum
¾ shot Freshly squeezed lemon juice

Comment: Spirited and refreshing with herbal notes.

ROOSEVELT COCKTAIL

★★★★⯪

Glass: Martini
Garnish: Orange zest twist
Method: SHAKE all ingredients with ice and fine strain into chilled glass.

1¾ shots Bacardi Carta Ocho aged rum
¾ shot Martini Extra Dry vermouth
¼ shot Freshly squeezed orange juice
¼ shot Sugar syrup (2 sugar to 1 water)

Comment: Hit the right proportions with freshly squeezed orange juice and this drink is sublime.

ROOSEVELT COCKTAIL #2 (NEW)

★★★★⯪

Glass: Coupe
Garnish: Luxardo Maraschino cherry
Method: STIR all ingredients with ice and strain into chilled glass.

2 shot Straight rye whiskey
½ shot Romate Pedro Ximenez Sherry
1 dash Angostura Aromatic bitters
1 dash Walnut bitters

Comment: Rye whiskeys' strength and spice cuts through and dries the rich sultana notes of PX sherry with the bitters, particularly the walnut bitters, adding flavour and complexity.

ROOSEVELT MARTINI 0⚷

★★★★⯪

Glass: Martini
Garnish: Two olives on stick
Method: STIR all ingredients with ice and strain into chilled glass.

2½ shots Rutte Dry Gin
½ shot Martini Extra Dry vermouth

Origin: Named after Franklin Delano Roosevelt (1882-1945), the 32nd President of the United States. Roosevelt is remembered for leading his country into World War II to fight alongside the Allies against Germany and Japan: he died just as victory was in sight.
Comment: A regular Martini, but garnished with two olives instead of one.

ROSARITA MARGARITA

★★★★☆

Glass: Coupe
Garnish: Lime wedge & salt rim (optional)
Method: SHAKE all ingredients with ice and fine strain into chilled glass.

1½ shots Patrón reposado tequila
¾ shot Grand Marnier Cordon Rouge
½ shot Cranberry juice
½ shot Rose's lime cordial
¾ shot Freshly squeezed lime juice
⅓ shot Sugar syrup (2 sugar to 1 water)

Origin: Created in 1999 by Robert Plotkin and Raymon Flores of BarMedia, USA.
Comment: This peachy coloured Margarita is well-balanced and flavoursome.

THE ROSE #1 (ORIGINAL)

★★★★⯪

Glass: Martini
Garnish: Luxardo Maraschino cherry
Method: STIR all ingredients with ice and strain into chilled glass.

2 shots Martini Extra Dry vermouth
1 shot Kirsch liqueur
½ shot Raspberry syrup (1 juice to 1 sugar)

Origin: Created in 1920 by Johnny Milta at the Chatham Hotel, Paris. This recipe is adapted from one in 'The Fine Art of Mixing Drinks' by David Embury.
Comment: This salmon pink drink is wonderfully aromatic.

THE ROSE #2

★★★★⯪☆

Glass: Martini
Garnish: Luxardo Maraschino cherry
Method: STIR all ingredients with ice and fine strain into chilled glass.

2	shots	Rutte Dry Gin
1	shot	Cherry Heering Liqueur
1	shot	Martini Extra Dry vermouth

Origin: Adapted from a recipe in Harry Craddock's 1930 'Savoy Cocktail Book'.
Comment: Cherry and gin dried with vermouth.

THE ROSE #3

★★★★⯪

Glass: Martini
Garnish: Luxardo Maraschino cherry
Method: SHAKE all ingredients with ice and fine strain into chilled glass.

1½	shots	Kirsch liqueur
1½	shots	Martini Extra Dry vermouth
½	shot	Pomegranate / grenadine syrup (2:1)

Origin: Adapted from a recipe in Harry Craddock's 1930 'Savoy Cocktail Book'.
Comment: Delicate, aromatic cherry - not too sweet.

ROSE MEMOIRE (NEW)

★★★★☆

Glass: Coupe
Garnish: Redcurrants or red berry
Method: SHAKE first 2 ingredients with ice and fine strain into chilled glass. TOP with champagne.

2	spoon	Redcurrant jelly
1	shot	Clementine juice
3	shots	G.H. Mumm Brut Rosé Champagne

Origin: Created in January 2014 for Laurent-Perrier by Sean Ware of the London Cocktail Club, London, England.
Comment: This unusual riff on the classic mimosa unusually calls for redcurrant jelly and sweet clementine juice, topped with rosé champagne.

ROSE PETALINI

★★★★☆

Glass: Martini
Garnish: Rose petal
Method: STIR all ingredients with ice and strain into chilled glass.

1½	shots	Rose petal liqueur
1½	shots	Rutte Dry Gin
1	shot	Lychee syrup (from tinned fruit)
3	dash	Peychaud's aromatic bitters

Origin: Discovered in 2005 at Rain, Amsterdam, The Netherlands.
Comment: Peychaud's bitters give this fragrant cocktail a delicate pink hue.

ROSE-HYP COCKTAIL

★★★★★

Glass: Martini
Garnish: Edible flower
Method: THROW all ingredients with ice and strain into chilled glass.

2	shots	Rutte Dry Gin
¾	shot	St-Germain elderflower liqueur
½	shot	Martini Extra Dry vermouth
¼	shot	Rose petal liqueur

Origin: Dry (but not bone dry), aromatic and floral.
Comment: Created in 2006 by yours truly in London, England.

ROSELYN MARTINI 🗝

★★★★⯪

Glass: Martini
Garnish: Luxardo Maraschino cherry
Method: SHAKE all ingredients with ice and fine strain into chilled glass.

2	shots	Rutte Dry Gin
1	shot	Martini Extra Dry vermouth
¼	shot	Pomegranate / grenadine syrup (2:1)

Origin: Adapted from a recipe in Harry Craddock's 1930 'Savoy Cocktail Book'.
Comment: Subtle and beautifully balanced. A wet Martini made 'easy' by a dash of pomegranate syrup.

ROSIE LASSI COCKTAIL

★★★★☆

Glass: Coupe
Garnish: Rose petal
Method: SHAKE all ingredients with ice and fine strain into chilled glass.

2	shots	Ketel One Vodka
1½	shots	Yoghurt liqueur
¼	shot	Rose petal liqueur

Origin: Created in 2011 by yours truly at the Cabinet Room, London, England.
Comment: Creamy vanilla yoghurt with floral rose liqueur fortified with vodka.

ROSITA

★★★★⯪

Glass: Old-fashioned
Garnish: Lemon zest twist
Method: POUR ingredients into ice-filled glass and stir.

1½	shots	Patrón reposado tequila
1	shot	Campari Bitter
½	shot	Martini Extra Dry vermouth
½	shot	Martini Rosso vermouth
1	dash	Angostura Aromatic Bitters

Origin: The origin of this drink remains unknown but its popularity (like many things in this industry) can be blamed squarely on Gary 'gaz' Regan, even though for some years he was in denial.

A B C D E F G H I J K L M N O P Q **R** S T U V W X Y Z

The Rosita was introduced to gaz by a fellow cocktail geek back in 2005; who in turn had discovered the recipe in an article written by Terry Sullivan, a fellow drinks writer. Gaz questioned Sullivan as to where he found the recipe, but he could not remember so gaz let the matter drop until 2007 when he made the drink as an aperitif for a few friends round for dinner. Gaz's guests asked the origins of the drink and this led gaz to contact Sullivan again.

This time Sullivan remembered and told gaz that he had found it in 'The Bartender's Bible'. Now many of you will already be smiling as The Bible, published in 1991, was gaz Regan's first book.

Gaz has imbibed and written about thousands of cocktails over the years so it is understandable that he overlooked his own book. After an embarrassed oh-yeah moment he started rummaging around in the back of the closet of his guest room where an oversized envelope still held his working notes for the book. So it transpired that gaz purloined the recipe from a 1988 edition of 'Mr. Boston Official Bartender's Guide', but he had added a typical gaz touch, namely a dash of bitters, and predictably a bit more tequila.
Comment: A bittersweet, tequila based, Negroni-like drink.

ROSSINI

★★★★☆

Glass: Flute
Garnish: Strawberry
Method: **MUDDLE** strawberries in base of shaker. Add liqueur, **SHAKE** with ice and fine strain into chilled glass. **TOP** with prosecco and gently stir.

4 fresh Small ripe strawberries (hulled)
¾ shot Lejay Crème de Fraise liqueur
Top with Prosecco sparkling wine

Origin: Named for the 19th century Italian opera composer, Gioachino Antonio Rossini. This is one of the most popular Bellini variants in Venice.
Comment: Strawberries seem to complement Prosecco even better than white peaches.

ROSSINI SPRITZ (NEW)

★★★★☆

Glass: Old-fashioned
Garnish: Strawberry (1/2 strawberry)
Method: **POUR** prosecco and Rossini mix into glass. Add ice. Top with soda.

3 shots Prosecco sparkling wine
1½ shots Strawberry puree
½ shot Lejay Crème de Fraise liqueur
Top with Soda (club soda)

Origin: Created in 2013 by yours truly for Jamie's Italian Bars.
Comment: Perhaps best described as a Strawberry Bellini, sweet strawberry flavours are tamed with the gentle acidity of Prosecco.

ROSY COCKTAIL

★★★★☆

Glass: Martini
Garnish: Orange zest twist
Method: **STIR** all ingredients with ice and strain into chilled glass.

2 shots Ketel One Citroen vodka
¾ shot De Kuyper Triple Sec
¾ shot Dubonnet Red

Comment: An aptly named drink with hints of spice, citrus peel, honey and mulled wine.

ROULETTE

★★★★☆

Glass: Martini
Garnish: Orange zest twist
Method: **SHAKE** all ingredients with ice and fine strain into chilled glass.

1½ shots Calvados brandy
¾ shot Bacardi Carta Blanca light rum
¾ shot Swedish Punch liqueur
½ shot Chilled water (omit if wet ice)

Origin: Adapted from a recipe in Harry Craddock's 1930 'Savoy Cocktail Book'.
Comment: Balanced apple and spice.

ROY ROGERS (MOCKTAIL)

★★½☆☆

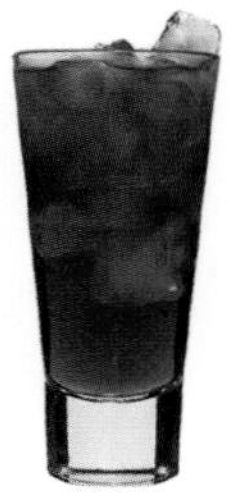

Glass: Collins
Garnish: Lime wedge
Method: **POUR** grenadine and cola into ice-filled glass and stir. Serve with straws.

¼ shot Pomegranate / grenadine syrup (2:1)
Top with Coca-Cola

Comment: Cola with an added ingredient - not sure if it makes enough difference.

ROYAL BERMUDA YACHT CLUB DAIQUIRI

★★★★☆

Glass: Martini
Garnish: Lime wedge
Method: **SHAKE** all ingredients with ice and fine strain into chilled glass.

2½ shots Bacardi Carta Oro rum
½ shot Taylor's Velvet Falernum liqueur
¼ shot De Kuyper Triple Sec
¾ shot Freshly squeezed lime juice

Origin: Created at the eponymous club, established in Bermuda in 1844 and largely frequented by British Army Officers. This recipe is adapted from one in 'Trader Vic's Bartender's Guide'.
Comment: A full-flavoured, tangy Daiquiri.

ROYAL COSMOPOLITAN

★★★★☆

Glass: Martini
Garnish: Orange zest twist
Method: **SHAKE** first four ingredients with ice and fine strain into chilled glass. **TOP** with champagne.

1 shot Ketel One Citroen vodka
½ shot De Kuyper Triple Sec
1 shot Cranberry juice
¼ shot Freshly squeezed lime juice
Top with G.H. Mumm Cordon Rouge Champagne

Origin: Created in 2003 by Wayne Collins, London, England.
Comment: The classic Cosmopolitan with a layer of fizz on top adding a biscuity complexity. Sex And The City meets Ab Fab.

ROYAL GINGERSNAP

★★★★☆

Glass: Old-fashioned
Garnish: Cinnamon & sugar rim with orange zest twist (flamed)
Method: MUDDLE the cherry in base of shaker. Add other ingredients, **SHAKE** with ice and fine strain into ice-filled glass.

1	whole	Maraschino cherries & syrup
2	shots	Canadian blended whisky
1	spoon	English orange marmalade
¼	shot	King's Ginger Liqueur
½	shot	Freshly squeezed orange juice
2	dash	Angostura Aromatic Bitters

Origin: Created by Dale DeGroff, this recipe is adapted from his 2008 book 'The Essential Cocktail'.
Comment: Variation on Old-Fashioned

ROYAL MOJITO

★★★★★

Glass: Collins
Garnish: Mint sprig
Method: Lightly **MUDDLE** mint (just to bruise) in base of glass. Add rum, lime juice and sugar. Half fill glass with crushed ice and **CHURN** (stir) with bar spoon. Fill glass with more crushed ice and **CHURN** some more. **TOP** with champagne, stir and serve with straws.

12	fresh	Mint leaves
2	shots	Bacardi Carta Blanca light rum
¾	shot	Freshly squeezed lime juice
¼	shot	Sugar syrup (2 sugar to 1 water)
Top with		G.H. Mumm Cordon Rouge Champagne

Comment: A mojito topped with champagne instead of soda water. There's posh.

ROYAL SMILE

★★★★☆

Glass: Martini
Garnish: Lemon zest twist
Method: SHAKE all ingredients with ice and fine strain into chilled glass.

1	shot	Rutte Dry Gin
1	shot	Calvados brandy
½	shot	Freshly squeezed lemon juice
¼	shot	Pomegranate / grenadine syrup (2:1)
½	shot	Chilled water (omit if wet ice)

Origin: Purloined from David Embury's classic book, 'The Fine Art of Mixing Drinks'.
Comment: This balanced sweet and sour could put a smile on anyone's face. Unless one is not amused!

ROYAL TOAST

★★★★☆

Glass: Coupe
Garnish: Luxardo Maraschino cherry
Method: STIR all ingredients with ice and strain into chilled glass.

1½	shots	Ketel One Vodka
¾	shot	Cherry Heering Liqueur
1	shot	Martini Extra Dry vermouth

Origin: Adapted from a UKBG recipe from 1937 which was originally equal parts.
Comment: Rich cherry liqueur flavours are balanced by dry vermouth and lifted by vodka.

ROYALIST COCKTAIL

★★★★☆

Glass: Coupe
Garnish: Peach slice on rim
Method: STIR all ingredients with ice and strain into chilled glass.

1½	shots	Martini Extra Dry vermouth
1	shot	Bourbon whiskey
¾	shot	Bénédictine D.O.M. liqueur
1	dash	Peach bitters

Origin: Adapted from a recipe by W.J. Tarling and featured in his 1937 'The Café Royal Cocktail Book'. Tarling originally called for his drink to be shaken rather than stirred and used 1/2 Dry Martini vermouth, 1/4 bourbon, 1/4 Bénédictine.
Comment: A Manhattan-style cocktail but with dry vermouth and considerably more of it, Bénédictine and peach bitters.

RUBY DAIQUIRI

★★★★☆

Glass: Martini
Garnish: Grapefruit wedge
Method: SHAKE all ingredients with ice and fine strain into chilled glass.

2	shots	Bacardi Carta Blanca light rum
¼	shot	Disaronno Originale amaretto
⅛	shot	Almond (orgeat) syrup
¼	shot	Freshly squeezed lime juice
¼	shot	Freshly squeezed pink grapefruit juice

Origin: Created in 2008 by Wrigley (Oz) Osbourne at Goldbrick House, Bristol, England.
Comment: A well-balanced, almond influenced Daiquiri.

THE RUBY GOLD

★★★★☆

Glass: Coupe
Garnish: Float raspberry and dust with grated nutmeg
Method: DRY SHAKE (without ice) all ingredients. Add ice, **SHAKE** again with ice and fine strain into chilled glass.

1¾	shots	Tawny port
⅔	shot	Straight rye whiskey
½	shot	Suze Saveur d'Autrefois
¼	shot	Sugar syrup (2 sugar to 1 water)
1	fresh	Egg yolk

Origin: Created in 2010 by Rufus at the Hide Bar, London. England.
Comment: A rich after dinner, dessert-style cocktail.

RUBY MARTINI #1

★★★★☆

Glass: Martini
Garnish: Lemon slice
Method: SHAKE all ingredients with ice and fine strain into chilled glass.

1½	shots	Ketel One Citroen vodka
1	shot	De Kuyper Triple Sec
1	shot	Freshly squeezed pink grapefruit juice
¼	shot	Sugar syrup (2 sugar to 1 water)

Origin: Several appearances in episodes of the hit US TV series, Sex And The City, helped this drink become fashionable in 2002, particularly in New York City. It is thought to have originated at the Wave restaurant in Chicago's W Hotel.
Comment: A sour, citrus-led variation on the Cosmopolitan.

RUDE COSMOPOLITAN

★★★★⯪

Glass: Martini
Garnish: Orange zest twist
Method: SHAKE all ingredients with ice and fine strain into chilled glass.

1	shot	Patrón reposado tequila
1	shot	De Kuyper Triple Sec
1½	shots	Cranberry juice
½	shot	Freshly squeezed lime juice
2	dash	Angostura Orange Bitters (optional)

Comment: Don't let the pink appearance of this Cosmopolitan (made with tequila in place of vodka) fool you into thinking it's a fluffy cocktail. It's both serious and superb.

RUDE GYPSY

★★★★☆

Glass: Coupe
Garnish: Lime zest twist
Method: STIR all ingredients with ice and strain into chilled glass.

2	shots	Patrón reposado tequila
1	shot	Bénédictine D.O.M. liqueur
1	dash	Angostura Aromatic Bitters

Comment: Slightly sweet but wonderfully herbal and slightly spicy.

RUM OLD FASHIONED

★★★★★

Glass: Old-fashioned
Garnish: Orange zest twist
Method: STIR rum with three ice cubes in a glass. Add sugar, falernum, bitters and two more ice cubes. **STIR** lots more and add more ice.

2	shots	Bacardi Carta Ocho aged rum
½	shot	White overproof rum
¼	shot	Taylor's Velvet Falernum liqueur
1	dash	Angostura Aromatic Bitters
⅛	shot	Sugar syrup (2 sugar to 1 water)

Origin: Created in 2009 by Goncalo de Sousa Monteiro, Berlin, Germany.
Comment: The flavour of the overproof rum greatly adds to the character of this Old Fashioned.

Rum Punch

Simply consisting of rum, citrus juice, sugar, water and spice/bitters, the rum punch one of the world's oldest drinks. As David Wondrich says in 'Imbibe!', "For nearly two hundred years, from the 1670s to the 1850s, the Kingdom of Mixed Drinks was ruled by the Bowl of Punch."

Punch as a concept, a drink loosely following the adage of 'one of sour, two of sweet, three of strong and four of weak' first appears not with rum but with wine, in 1576. This is its first print reference, but sadly for keen cocktail historians, we will never know who mixed the first bowl of punch, it was probably long before this. We will never know what the original spirit was, what citrus was first used, what type of sugar. But we do know that it was in India that this drink was imbibed by English explorers and travellers, and soon spread out across the centuries with England's rapidly growing empire.

Punch remained the choice of tipple for English aristocrats for hundreds of years to come. There was something about the sharing nature of it, everyone consuming together, that was perfect at gatherings. And as the lower classes attempted to emulate

those punch-imbibing rich folks, it became the drink to be seen drinking.

Recipes from this age are somewhat sketchy but we know most punches combined spirits with tea, sugar, citrus and nutmeg. These were not the cheapest of ingredients to come by, as Wondrich says in ' Punch: The Delights (and Dangers) of the Flowing Bowl' "The lemons alone cost the equivalent of eight dollars each. In 1690s London a three-quart bowl of Rum Punch would set you back half a week's living wage." Punch bowls started becoming an accessory to acquire and show off. There are accounts of the ostentatiously rich commissioning punch bowls large enough for three children to play in and melting down coinage to make them.

And it was rum that became the most popular choice for both England's punch-guzzling aristocracy and as the drink of the sea. Soon after England acquired its sugar producing territories, The Royal Navy swapped its daily allowance of a gallon of beer or pint of wine for half a pint of Jamaican rum. Not only did this smaller portion take up much less room on board but it didn't spoil on the long journeys. As rum was being produced throughout England's new found lands, from New England in America to Mauritius off the coast of Africa, it made its way back to Londoners who were suffering dwindling supplies of brandy as England waged its constant wars against France and Spain. When the boats docked from the Caribbean, as William Dampier wrote in his 1697 ' A New Voyage Around the World', they were "always well stored with rum, sugar and lime juice to make punch, to hearten their men when they are at work."

In the tropics themselves, as Jeff Berry writes in his introduction to ' Potions of the Caribbean', "Rum mixed with sugar and lime made the nasty, brutish, short life of the average Caribbean combatant worth living." Or as Wondrich wrote "But whether it's the Ti Punch of Martinique, where the citrus has been reduced to a mere squeezing of lime peel, the Peanut Punch popular in Trinidad or Jamaica, or the generic Rum Punch, made with a bottled tutti-frutti mix that you'll find throughout the region, the drink is invariably based on rum."

Despite movie franchises such as ' Pirates of the Caribbean' depicting Caribbean cutthroats swigging straight from bottles of rum, the men of the 17th and 18th centuries who resided on the islands, be they ruffians or not, actually preferred a bowl of Rum Punch. There are numerous accounts of merchant seamen being lured with Rum Punch only to find themselves surrounded by pirates. Indeed it was the infamous Captain Kidd who negotiated a privateer contract over Rum Punch with the then commander-in-chief of England's Caribbean forces.

The punch they drank is possibly known today, as pointed out by Richard Zacks in his book ' The Pirate Hunter' which cites an eyewitness to this meeting in 1688. The punch was supposedly made of "rum, water, lime-juice, egg yolk, sugar with a little nutmeg scrap'd on top." Jeff Berry has translated this 320 year old recipe, replacing ice for water.

Captain Kidd's Punch
For an individual serve, shake over ice and strain into a punch cup. Grate nutmeg on top.
2 ounces gold Barbados rum
1 ounce gold muscovado sugar
½ ounce fresh lime juice
1 raw egg
Nutmeg

From the tropics back to Europe, and growing throughout the new world, Rum Punch was managing to hold its spot as a favourite indulgence. Traditions surrounding a flowing bowl of punch were steeped in history and companionship. It was the ultimate sharing drink, to be consumed at leisure and enjoyed right to the last drop. It's even been written that the founding fathers and friends drank 76 bowls at the celebration following the signing of the Declaration of Independence.

The Meeting House Punch is a recipe from this time, 1789, just 13 years after the Declaration of Independence, which was intended for the entire town of Medfield, Massachusetts. According to Jeff Berry it called for "four barrels of beer, twenty five gallons of West India rum, thirty gallons of New England rum, thirty four pounds of loaf sugar, twenty five pounds of brown sugar and four hundred and sixty five lemons."

Sadly times changed and as the Victorian era ushered in a new style of drinking, less and for shorter periods of time, the punch bowls were left to gather dust. It was in a magazine entitled ' Household Words' edited by Charles Dickens, and so potentially written by the great man himself, that a piece was published, 'A Bowl of Punch', which bemoaned the fact that punch bowls which once lined the shelves in bars ready to be called upon were now stacked up and uncalled for.

Punch also fell victim to the pace at which we started to live our lives. Sitting around in bars sipping out of a huge bowl of libation became too much a luxury, too much a statement of leisure. In a world where the busier we seem to be, the more important our status, slow unhurried drinking is a thing of the past. Indeed by the time the grandfather of bartending, Mr Jerry Thomas wrote his guide punches were already a thing of the past. As David Wondrich points out, although he had many recipes in his book they were probably fostered on him by publishers and were in fact obsolete.

Nowadays we enjoy our Rum Punch by the glass, and although still a delightful cocktail, it's never as good as when shared with friends and family out of a stunning bowl.

Oleo-Saccharum
In 'Punch!' David Wondrich identifies four main areas of punch-making which became refined throughout the centuries of our ancestors combing spirits, sugar and citrus together. These are the handling of the citrus oil, the handling of the citrus juice the order of assembly and the proportions of the ingredients. And the first pillar of punch-making has to be the oleo-saccharum.

The oil of a citrus fruit, and in this case we're speaking almost exclusively about lemons, is a very fragrant element which can, used in the right way, impart a lot of flavour to punch. In fact it was Jerry Thomas who wrote "to make punch of any sort in perfection, the ambrosial essence of the lemon must be extracted."

The easiest way to extract this oil is with sugar. The following technique works well with oranges as well, but if lime is the citrus of choice for your Rum Punch recipe then abstain, its peel is bitter and won't help the drink at all.

Oleo-Saccharum is Latin (or rather dog Latin) for oil-sugar, and is a method used in punch-making since at least 1670 which is where we find the first recorded mention. It basically means infusing the sugar with the citrus oils. Jerry Thomas recommended rubbing lumps of sugar on the rind to break the oils open and simultaneously infuse the sugar. However, this doesn't work nowadays as our modern sugar isn't hard enough. As Wondrich found out "I've tried it with every kind of modern sugarloaf, cube and crystal I could procure and only ended up with a mass of crumbled, faintly scented sugar and a lemon undimmed in its yellowness. In this, our ancestors had the advantage on us."

The simplest, although a tad time consuming, method is to peel the lemons, aiming to get as little pith as possible and muddle in a bowl with the sugar. Vacuum packs can be used to speed up the infusion process, as outlined by Jeffrey Morgenthalar in his excellent 2014 'The Bar Book'.

RUM PUNCH

★★★★★

Glass: Collins
Garnish: Orange slice & cherry on stick (sail)
Method: **SHAKE** all ingredients with ice and fine strain into glass filled with crushed ice.

2¼ shots White overproof rum
¾ shot Freshly squeezed lime juice
1½ shots Sugar syrup (2 sugar to 1 water)
3 dash Angostura Aromatic Bitters
3 shots Chilled water

Origin: The classic proportions of this drink are 'one of sour, two of sweet, three of strong and four of weak,' referring to lime juice, sugar syrup, rum and water respectively.
Comment: In Jamaica, the spiritual home of the Rum Punch, they like their rum overproof (more than 57% alc./vol.) and serving over crushed ice dilutes and tames this very strong spirit.

RUM PUNCH-UP

★★★★½

Glass: Martini
Garnish: Lime wedge
Method: **SHAKE** all ingredients with ice and fine strain into chilled glass.

1½ shots White overproof rum
½ shot Freshly squeezed lime juice
½ shot Sugar syrup (2 sugar to 1 water)
2 dash Angostura Aromatic Bitters
1 shot Chilled water (reduce if wet ice)

Origin: Adapted from a drink discovered in 2006 at Albannach, London, England.
Comment: Exactly what the name promises - a rum punch served straight-up. Daiquiri style.

RUM RUNNER

★★★★☆

Glass: Hurricane
Garnish: Pineapple wedge & Luxardo Maraschino cherry
Method: **SHAKE** all ingredients with ice and strain into glass filled with crushed ice.

1½ shots Pusser's Navy Rum (54.5%)
½ shot Lejay Crème de Mûre liqueur
1 shot Crème de banane liqueur
1 shot Freshly squeezed lime juice
2 shots Fresh pressed pineapple juice
½ shot Pomegranate / grenadine syrup (2:1)

Comment: Fruity, sharp and rounded.

RUM SOUR

★★★★☆

Glass: Old-fashioned
Garnish: Orange zest twist
Method: **SHAKE** all ingredients with ice and strain into ice-filled glass.

2 shots Bacardi Carta Ocho aged rum
1 shot Freshly squeezed orange juice
1 shot Freshly squeezed lime juice
½ shot Sugar syrup (2 sugar to 1 water)
½ fresh Egg white

Comment: Smooth and sour - well balanced.

RUM SWIZZLE

★★★★★

Glass: Collins
Garnish: Mint sprig & orange slice
Method: **POUR** ingredients into chilled glass and two-thirds fill with crushed ice. **SWIZZLE** with a swizzle stick (or churn with a barspoon). Add more crushed ice to fill and **SWIZZLE** some more. Serve with straws.

2 shots Bacardi Carta Ocho aged rum
⅔ shot Taylor's Velvet Falernum liqueur
½ shot Freshly squeezed lime juice
¼ shot Freshly squeezed lemon juice
½ shot Light muscovado sugar syrup (2 sugar to 1 water)
1 dash Angostura Aromatic Bitters

Origin: This drink emerged in the early 1800s in Guyana when British ex-pats mixed this drink on the terrace of the Georgetown club.
Comment: Dark rich sugar, equally dark and richly flavoured rum, sweetened and spiced with the clove and cinnamon flavours of falernum and freshened with citrus juice. All served long with crushed ice.

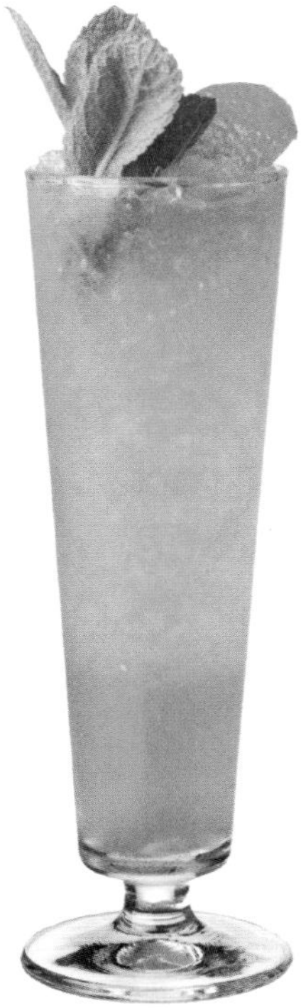

RUMBA

★★★★☆

Glass: Old-fashioned
Garnish: Lime wedge
Method: SHAKE all ingredients with ice and strain into glass filled with crushed ice. Serve with straws.

¾ shot **White overproof rum**
1 shot **Rutte Dry Gin**
1 shot **Freshly squeezed lime juice**
¼ shot **Sugar syrup (2 sugar to 1 water)**
½ shot **Pomegranate / grenadine syrup (2:1)**
½ shot **Chilled water** (omit if wet ice)

Origin: Recipe adapted from David Embury's classic book, 'The Fine Art of Mixing Drinks'.
Comment: To quote Embury, "Whoever thought up this snootful of liquid dynamite certainly liked his liquor hard!"

RUSSIAN

★★★⯪☆

Glass: Martini
Garnish: Orange zest twist
Method: SHAKE all ingredients with ice and fine strain into chilled glass.

1½ shots **Rutte Dry Gin**
1 shot **Ketel One Vodka**
1 shot **White crème de cacao liqueur**

Origin: Adapted from a recipe in Harry Craddock's 1930 'Savoy Cocktail Book'.
Comment: Gin and vodka with a sweet hint of chocolate.

RUSSIAN BRIDE

★★★★☆

Glass: Martini
Garnish: Dust with chocolate powder
Method: SHAKE all ingredients with ice and fine strain into chilled glass.

2 shots **Vanilla infused Ketel One vodka**
¾ shot **Coffee liqueur**
¼ shot **White crème de cacao liqueur**
½ shot **Single cream / half-and-half**
½ shot **Milk**

Origin: Created in 2002 by Miranda Dickson, A.K.A. the Vodka Princess, for the UK's Revolution bar chain, where some 500,000 were sold each year.
Comment: A little on the sweet side for some but vanilla, coffee and chocolate smoothed with cream is a tasty combination.

RUSSIAN COCKTAIL

★★★⯪☆

Glass: Coupe
Garnish: Luxardo Maraschino cherry
Method: SHAKE all ingredients with ice and fine strain into chilled glass.

1½ shots **Ketel One Vodka**
¾ shot **Cherry Heering Liqueur**
¼ shot **Kirschwasser eau de vie**

Origin: We have David Wondrich to thank for re-discovering this drink, believed to be the first vodka cocktail to appear in print in a 1911 book called 'Beverage Deluxe'. The drink itself is thought to originally come from the St. Charles Hotel in New Orleans, USA.
Comment: Sweet brandy meets dry cherry eau-de-vie in this serious vodka laced cocktail.

RUSSIAN NAIL

★★★⯪☆

Glass: Old-fashioned
Garnish: Dust with grated nutmeg
Method: SHAKE all ingredients with ice and strain into ice-filled glass.

2 shots **Dewar's 12yo Scotch whisky**
¾ shot **Drambuie liqueur**
¾ shot **Coffee liqueur**
½ shot **Single cream / half-and-half**
½ shot **Milk**

Origin: Created in 2010 by a collaboration between Jamie Stephenson and yours truly at the Cabinet Room, London, England.
Comment: A marriage of the Rusty Nail and White Russian cocktails.

RUSSIAN QUALUDE SHOT

★★★☆☆

Glass: Shot
Garnish: None
Method: Refrigerate ingredients then **LAYER** in chilled glass by carefully pouring in the order listed.

½ shot **Galliano L'Autentico liqueur**
½ shot **Green Chartreuse liqueur**
½ shot **Ketel One Vodka**

Comment: An explosive herb and peppermint shot.

RUSSIAN SPRING PUNCH

★★★★½

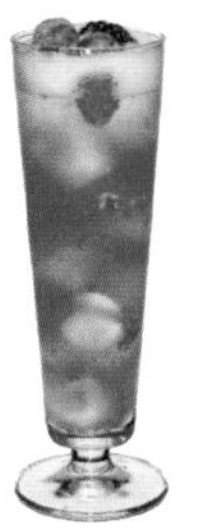

Glass: Sling
Garnish: Lemon slice & seasonal berries
Method: **SHAKE** first 6 ingredients with ice and strain into glass filled with crushed ice. **TOP** with champagne, lightly stir and serve with straws.

7 fresh Raspberries
1½ shots Ketel One Vodka
¼ shot Lejay Crème de Framboise liqueur
¼ shot Lejay crème de cassis de Dijon
¾ shot Freshly squeezed lemon juice
¼ shot Sugar syrup (2 sugar to 1 water)
Top with G.H.Mumm Cordon Rouge Champagne

Origin: Created in the 1990s by Dick Bradsell, London, England. In the Dec-Jan 1998 edition of CLASS magazine (page 6), Dick wrote of this drink, "Many springs ago, I conceived the Russian Spring Punch which is basically a spiked Kir Royal over ice. This conforms to the original punch formula of 1 sweet, 2 sour, 3 strong, 4 weak except the most of the 'weak' bit (normally soda or juice) is replaced with champagne, turning the recipe into a sledgehammer of a cocktail.

"To make, fill a Collins glass with ice. Add 50ml best vodka, 25ml lemon juice, two teaspoons of cassis and two teaspoons of sugar syrup. Top with champagne and stir. Garnish with a lemon slice and some berries.

"At its premiere, I, the hostess and the ill-fated guests were unaware of its extreme potency. Within hours, the party had descended into what appeared to be a re-enactment from the battle of Waterloo with the prone bodies of the guests littering the dance floor, bedrooms and stairways. The whole shambles was voted a great success by the few who could remember it the next day and I still suggest the Spring Punch as the ultimate party icebreaker for those who don't dabble in exotic drugs."
Comment: Well-balanced, complex and refreshing.

RUSTY

★★★★

Glass: Old-fashioned
Garnish: Orange zest twist
Method: **STIR** all ingredients with ice and strain into ice-filled glass.

1½ shots Bacardi Carta Ocho aged rum
1½ shots Romate Amontillado sherry
¼ shot Islay single malt Scotch whisky
¼ shot Sugar syrup (2 sugar to 1 water)

Origin: Created in December 2008 by yours truly at the Cabinet Room, London, England. Originally made using Zacapa rum.
Comment: Sherry and rum combine harmoniously with the smoky Islay malt highlighting spicy notes.

RUSTY COMPASS COCKTAIL (NEW)

★★★★½

Glass: Old-fashioned
Garnish: Orange zest twist
Method: **STIR** all ingredients with ice and strain into ice-filled glass.

1½ shots Islay single malt Scotch whisky
¾ shot Drambuie liqueur
½ shot Cherry Heering Liqueur

Origin: Based on a drink originally made with Compass Box The Peat Monster Malt Scotch Whisky and served straight-up in coupe.
Comment: Peaty Islay single malt whisky lightly sweetened and flavoured with heather honey herbal whisky liqueur and cherry brandy, stirred and served on-the-rocks with an orange zest twist adding zestiness.

RUSTY MARGARITA

★★★★½

Glass: Old-fashioned
Garnish: Lime wedge
Method: **SHAKE** all ingredients with ice and strain into ice-filled glass.

2 shots Patrón reposado tequila
1 shot Drambuie liqueur
1 shot Freshly squeezed lime juice

Origin: Created in December 2010 by yours truly at the Cabinet Room, London, England.
Comment: The rich honeyed notes from Drambuie combine wonderfully with tequila and add an extra dimension to this this tasty Margarita.

RUSTY NAIL COCKTAIL

★★★★

Glass: Old-fashioned
Garnish: Lemon zest twist
Method: **STIR** ingredients with ice and strain into ice-filled glass.

2 shots Dewar's 12yo Scotch whisky
¾ shot Drambuie liqueur

Origin: Created in 1942 at a Hawaiian bar for the artist Theodore Anderson but popularized in the 1950's at Club 21 in New York City.
Comment: The liqueur smooths and wonderfully combines with Scotch whisky. The proportions of Scotch to Drambuie vary wildly and are a matter of taste. However, somewhere around 3:1 appears to be preferred by most.

RUSTY TACK COCKTAIL

★★★★½

Glass: Old-fashioned
Garnish: Lemon zest twist
Method: **STIR** all ingredients with ice and strain into ice-filled glass.

2 shots Dewar's 12yo Scotch whisky
½ shot Drambuie liqueur
½ shot King's Ginger Liqueur

Origin: Adapted from a drink discovered in 2010 in New York City, USA.
Comment: A ginger twist on the rusty nail.

RUSTY TO THE CORE

★★★★½

Glass: Coupe
Garnish: Apple slice
Method: **SHAKE** all ingredients with ice and fine strain into chilled glass.

1½ shots Calvados brandy
¾ shot Drambuie liqueur
¼ shot Islay single malt Scotch whisky
1 shot Pressed apple juice
¼ shot Freshly squeezed lemon juice

Origin: Created in 2010 by Julian de Feral at Lutyens Bar, London, England for his autumn menu.
Comment: Honeyed herbal Drambuie with an apple brandy base, freshened with lemon juice and given a wisp of smokiness by a splash of Islay malt.

S. TEA G. 🔑

★★★½☆

Glass: Collins
Garnish: Lemon slice
Method: SHAKE first three ingredients with ice and strain into ice-filled glass. **TOP** with tonic water.

1½ shots	Rutte Dry Gin
1½ shots	St-Germain elderflower liqueur
1 shot	Cold English breakfast tea
Top with	Tonic Water

Origin: Created in 2006 by yours truly.
Comment: Floral, long and refreshing.

SAGE COCKTAIL

★★★★☆

Glass: Martini
Garnish: Sage leaf
Method: Lightly **MUDDLE** (just to bruise) sage in base of shaker. Add other ingredients, **SHAKE** with ice and fine strain into chilled glass.

3 fresh	Sage leaves
1½ shots	Ketel One Vodka
1½ shots	Martini Extra Dry vermouth
¾ shot	Pressed apple juice

Comment: Delicate sage and a hint of apple, dried with vermouth and fortified with vodka.

SAGE MARGARITA

★★★★☆

Glass: Coupe
Garnish: Sage leaf
Method: Lightly **MUDDLE** (just to bruise) sage in base of shaker. Add other ingredients, **SHAKE** with ice and fine strain into chilled glass.

3 fresh	Sage leaves
2 shots	Patrón reposado tequila
1 shot	De Kuyper Triple Sec
1 shot	Freshly squeezed lime juice
⅛ shot	Sugar syrup (2 sugar to 1 water)

Comment: Exactly as promised - a sage flavoured Margarita.

SAIGON COOLER 🔑

★★★★½☆

Glass: Collins
Garnish: Raspberries
Method: MUDDLE raspberries in base of shaker. Add other ingredients, **SHAKE** with ice and fine strain into chilled glass.

7 fresh	Raspberries
2 shots	Rutte Dry Gin
½ shot	Chambord Liqueur
3 shots	Cranberry juice
¾ shot	Freshly squeezed lime juice

Origin: Created at Bam-Bou, London, England.
Comment: Well balanced sweet 'n' sour with a rich fruity flavour.

SAILOR'S SWIZZLE (NEW)

★★★★½

Glass: Collins
Garnish: A few dashes Angostura bitters over ice cap crowned with lime zest strings
Method: POUR ingredients into chilled glass and two-thirds fill with crushed ice. **SWIZZLE** with a swizzle stick (or churn with a barspoon). Add more crushed ice to fill and **SWIZZLE** some more. Serve with straws.

1½ shots	Bacardi Carta Oro rum
⅔ shot	Ruby port
⅛ shot	Allspice pimento dram liqueur
¾ shot	Freshly squeezed lime juice
½ shot	Sugar syrup (2 sugar to 1 water)

Origin: Created in 2012 by Erik Lorincz at the American Bar, London, England.
Comment: Port wine is further fortified with golden rum and delicately spiced with Pimento Dram in this long swizzled punch.

THE SAINT (NEW)

★★★★½

Glass: Coupe
Garnish: Quarter slice grapefruit on rim
Method: SHAKE all ingredients with ice and strain into chilled glass.

1½ shot	Bourbon whiskey
¾ shot	Freshly squeezed lemon juice
¼ shot	Ginger sugar syrup
½ shot	Lillet Blanc
½ shot	Pink grapefruit liqueur (pamplemouse)

Comment: A riff on the classic Brown Derby, this is a refreshing bourbon sour with zesty citrus and subtle warming earthy ginger.
Origin: Created in 2015 by Karen Grill at Sassafras Saloon, Los Angeles, USA.

SAINT CLEMENTS (MOCKTAIL)

★★★☆☆

Glass: Collins
Garnish: Lime wedge
Method: POUR ingredients into ice-filled glass, lightly stir and serve with straws.

| 3 shots | Freshly squeezed orange juice |
| Top with | Bitter lemon |

Comment: Slightly more interesting than orange juice.

STAR RATINGS EXPLAINED

★★★★★+ OUTSTANDING	★★★★★ EXCEPTIONAL
★★★★½ EXCELLENT	★★★★☆ RECOMMENDED
★★★½☆ COMMENDED	★★★☆☆ MEDIOCRE
★★½☆☆ DISAPPOINTING	★★☆☆☆ PRETTY AWFUL
★½☆☆☆ SHAMEFUL	★☆☆☆☆ DISGUSTING

SAINT-MARC DAIQUIRI (NEW)

★★★★½

Glass: Coupe
Garnish: Lime slice
Method: **SHAKE** all ingredients with ice and fine strain into chilled glass.

2 shots **Bacardi Carta Blanca light rum**
½ shot **Bénédictine D.O.M. liqueur**
⅛ shot **Le Fée Parisienne absinthe**
¾ shot **Freshly squeezed lime juice**
¼ shot **Sugar syrup (2 sugar to 1 water)**
½ shot **Chilled water** (omit if wet ice)

Origin: Adapted from a drink discovered in 2014 at Bastille Cafe & Bar, Seattle, USA.
Comment: It's a Daiquiri but with monastic Bénédictine and less than holy absinthe influences – perhaps it's the saffron in the Bénédictine, perhaps it's the star anise in the absinthe, but the result is truly a spiritual experience. It's simply divine.

SAISON L'HIVER (NEW)

★★★★½

Glass: Flute
Garnish: Seasonal berries on rim
Method: **MUDDLE** clove in base of shaker. Add next 3 ingredients, **SHAKE** with ice and fine strain into chilled glass. **TOP** with champagne.

1 dried **Clove**
⅓ shot **Honey water (3 honey to 1 water)**
½ shot **Sloe Gin liqueur**
½ shot **Freshly squeezed lemon juice**
Top with **G.H. Mumm Brut Rosé Champagne**

Origin: Created in September 2014 by yours truly (Simon Difford) at the Cabinet Room, London, England.
Comment: The rich wintery flavours of sloe gin and honey are balanced by lemon juice with clove providing seasonal spice and rosé champagne lifting and refreshing all.

SAKE MARTINI

★★★★½

Glass: Coupe
Garnish: Apple slice
Method: **STIR** all ingredients with ice and fine stain into chilled glass.

2 shots **Rutte Dry Gin**
2 shots **Junmai ginjō sake**
⅛ shot **Martini Extra Dry vermouth**

Comment: Dry, subtle, and depending on your choice of sake, possibly amazing.

SAKE'POLITAN

★★★★☆

Glass: Martini
Garnish: Orange zest twist
Method: **SHAKE** all ingredients with ice and fine strain into chilled glass.

2¼ shots **Junmai ginjō sake**
¾ shot **De Kuyper Triple Sec**
¾ shot **Cranberry juice**
¼ shot **Freshly squeezed lime juice**
2 dash **Angostura Orange Bitters** (optional)

Comment: A Cosmo with more than a hint of sake.

SAKE-TINI #1

★★★★☆

Glass: Martini
Garnish: Cucumber slices
Method: **STIR** all ingredients with ice and strain into chilled glass.

1 shot **Rutte Dry Gin**
½ shot **Grand Marnier Cordon Rouge**
2½ shots **Junmai ginjō sake**

Comment: Sake and a hint of orange liqueur add the perfect aromatic edge to this Martini-style drink.

SAKE-TINI #2

★★★★☆

Glass: Martini
Garnish: Orange zest twist
Method: **SHAKE** all ingredients with ice and fine strain into chilled glass.

1½ shots **Ketel One Vodka**
1 shot **Plum wine**
½ shot **Junmai ginjō sake**
1 shot **Cranberry juice**

Origin: Discovered at Nobu Berkeley, London, England.
Comment: Salmon-coloured, light and fragrant with plum wine and sake to the fore.

SAKINI

★★★★☆

Glass: Martini
Garnish: Olive on stick
Method: **STIR** all ingredients with ice and strain into chilled glass.

2½ shots **Ketel One Vodka**
1 shot **Junmai ginjō sake**

Comment: Very dry. The sake creates an almost wine-like delicacy.

SAKURA MARTINI (NEW)

★★★★½

Glass: Coupe
Garnish: Salted cherry blossom (or olive)
Method: **STIR** all ingredients with ice and strain into chilled glass.

2½ shots **Junmai ginjō sake**
1 shot **Rutte Dry Gin**
¼ spoon **Luxardo Maraschino liqueur**

Origin: Created by Kenta Goto in 2015, this is the house Martini at his 'Bar Goto' in New York City, USA.
Comment: This Reverse Martini-style drink features a floating salted cherry blossom as a garnish. This is not just for looks, the hint of saltiness it lends this delicate drink replaces that which an olive typically brings to a Martini.

SALFLOWER SOUR

★★★★☆

Glass: Martini
Garnish: Orange zest twist
Method: SHAKE all ingredients with ice and fine strain into chilled glass.

2 shots St-Germain elderflower liqueur
¾ shot Freshly squeezed orange juice
¾ shot Freshly squeezed lime juice
1 dash Angostura Orange Bitters
½ fresh Egg white

Origin: Created on 12th April 2007 by Salvatore Calabrese at Fifty, London, England.
Comment: Classic sweet and sour enhanced by floral notes.

SALTECCA

★★★☆☆

Glass: Martini
Garnish: Lemon zest twist
Method: STIR all ingredients with ice and fine strain into chilled glass.

2 shots Patrón reposado tequila
½ shot Romate Fino sherry
⅛ shot Caper brine (from jar)
½ shot Sugar syrup (2 sugar to 1 water)

Comment: Reminiscent of salted water after boiling vegetables but you have got to try these things.

THE SALTY BIRD

★★★★½

Glass: Coupe
Garnish: Dehydrated pineapple
Method: SHAKE all ingredients with ice and strain into ice-filled glass.

1½ shots Bacardi Carta Blanca light rum
¾ shot Campari Bitter
1½ shots Fresh pressed pineapple juice
½ shot Freshly squeezed lime juice
¼ shot Sugar syrup (2 sugar to 1 water)
1 pinch Salt

Origin: Created by bartender Lauren Schell and promoted by Campari in 2013.
Comment: Salty Bird hardly suggests a sweet fruity drink but perfectly befits this bittersweet rum laced pineapple and Campari sipper.

SALTY DOG

★★★★☆

Glass: Martini
Garnish: Salt rim
Method: SHAKE all ingredients with ice and fine strain into chilled glass.

2 shots Ketel One Vodka
⅛ shot Luxardo Maraschino liqueur
2¼ shots Freshly squeezed pink grapefruit juice

Origin: Created in the 1960s.
Comment: For a more interesting drink, try basing this classic on gin rather than vodka.

SALTY LYCHEE MARTINI

★★★★☆

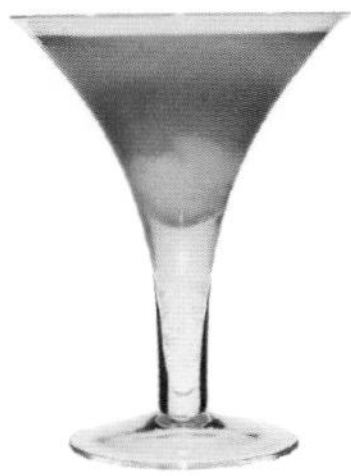

Glass: Martini
Garnish: Lychee
Method: STIR all ingredients with ice and strain into chilled glass.

2 shots Romate Fino sherry
1 shot Rose petal liqueur
1 shot Kwai Feh lychee liqueur

Origin: I created this drink in 2002 after trying Dick Bradsell's Lychee & Rose Petal Martini.
Comment: Light pink in colour and subtle in flavour with the salty tang of Fino sherry.

SALTY MARTINI (NEW)

★★★★★

Glass: Coupe
Garnish: Large caperberry on pick
Method: STIR all ingredients with ice and strain into chilled glass.

2½ shot Ketel One Vodka
¼ shot Martini Extra Dry vermouth
¼ shot Romate fino sherry
⅛ shot Caper brine (from jar)

Comment: As the name suggests, fino sherry and caper brine add saltiness but this 'Salty Martini' also has a distinct nuttiness from the sherry. We'd suggest both a long stir for generous dilution, and serving with grilled almonds.
Origin: Adapted from a recipe created in 2009 by Salvatore Calabrese at Fifty, London England.

SALVATORE MEETS BACARDI (NEW)

★★★★½

Glass: Martini
Garnish: None
Method: SHAKE first 4 ingredients with ice and fine strain into chilled glass. **TOP** with champagne.

2 shots Bacardi Carta Blanca light rum
⅔ shot Pallini Limoncello
1 shot Freshly squeezed lime juice
⅓ shot Sugar syrup (2 sugar to 1 water)
Top with G.H.Mumm Cordon Rouge Champagne

Origin: Created in 2015 by Salvatore Calabrese at his bar in the Playboy Club, London, Engand.
Comment: A refreshing zesty lemon Daiquiri topped with a splash of champagne.

SAN FRANCISCO

★★★½☆

Glass: Collins
Garnish: Pineapple wedge
Method: SHAKE all ingredients with ice and strain into ice-filled glass.

2 shots Ketel One Vodka
½ shot De Kuyper Triple Sec
½ shot Crème de banane liqueur
1½ shots Freshly squeezed orange juice
1½ shots Fresh pressed pineapple juice
¼ shot Pomegranate / grenadine syrup (2:1)

Comment: Long, fruity, slightly sweet and laced with vodka.

SANDSTORM

★★★★☆

Glass: Collins
Garnish: Pineapple wedge
Method: SHAKE all ingredients with ice and strain into ice-filled glass.

1½ shots	Rutte Dry Gin
1 shot	Grand Marnier Cordon Rouge
½ shot	Vanilla schnapps
1½ shots	Freshly squeezed pink grapefruit juice
1½ shots	Fresh pressed pineapple juice
¼ shot	Sugar syrup (2 sugar to 1 water)
¼ shot	Freshly squeezed lime juice
¼ shot	Rose's lime cordial

Origin: Created in 2003 by James Cunningham at Zinc, Glasgow, Scotland, and is named for its cloudy yellow colour.
Comment: A long, fruity drink featuring well balanced sweet and sourness.

SANDY THE SHOWGIRL (NEW)

★★★★★

Glass: Coupe
Garnish: Lime zest twist
Method: STIR all ingredients with ice and strain into ice-filled glass.

1½ shots Patrón Añejo tequila
½ shot Del Maguey VIDA mezcal
½ shot Luxardo Maraschino liqueur
1 spoon Agave syrup
8 drop Bob's Lavender bitters
¾ shot Chilled water

Origin: Created in April 2015 by yours truly. The name was inspired by Neil Young's 1969 song about a promiscuous woman, Cow Girl In The Sand.
Comment: Tequila based with complex mezcal smokiness, rich maraschino cherry and floral lavender bitters. It's a drink that likes dilution so consider serving on the rocks. Sandy's that kinda girl.

SANDYGAFF

★★★½☆

Glass: Boston
Garnish: None
Method: POUR ale into glass, top with ginger ale and lightly stir.

⅔ fill glass with Guinness stout
Top with Ginger ale

Origin: Adapted from a recipe purloined from David Embury's classic book, 'The Fine Art of Mixing Drinks'.
Comment: Better than your average lager shandy.

SANGAREE (SANGRE)

★★★★½

Glass: Flute
Garnish: Dust with grated nutmeg
Method: SHAKE gin and sugar with ice and strain into chilled glass. Lastly **POUR** the port wine which will sink through drink and mix, leaving a thin clear layer at the top.

2 shots	Old Tom gin
¼ shot	Sugar syrup (2 sugar to 1 water)
1 shot	Tawny port

Origin: The Sangaree takes its name from the Spanish word for blood, Sangre. The drink's origins date back to the early 1700s and it first appears in writing in a 1736 issue of the ' British Gentleman's Magazine ', "... a punch seller in the Strand had devised a new punch made of strong Madeira wine and called Sangre".
Comment: Either drink through the layers or stir before consuming. Fabulously old-school in style, this sweetened port and old tom gin drink resembles chilled mulled wine.

SANGAREE (SANGRIA)

★★★★☆

Glass: Collins
Garnish: Dust with grated nutmeg
Method: SHAKE first six ingredients with ice and strain into ice-filled glass. **TOP** with soda and lightly stir. Serve with straws.

½ shot	Martell VSOP Médaillon cognac
½ shot	Grand Marnier Cordon Rouge
3 shots	Shiraz red wine
1 shot	Freshly squeezed orange juice
¼ shot	Freshly squeezed lemon juice
½ shot	Sugar syrup (2 sugar to 1 water)
1 shot	Soda (club soda)

Origin: This version of the Spanish Sangria was popular in 19th century America. The only real difference is that while a Sangria is usually made in batches, Sangaree are single serve.
Comment: Basically just red wine and orange liqueur, diluted with water, lemon juice and sugar. But tasty!

SANGRE DULCE COCKTAIL (NEW)

★★★★½

Glass: Coupe
Garnish: Dehydrated blood orange slice
Method: SHAKE all ingredients with ice and fine strain into chilled glass.

1⅔ shots	Del Maguey VIDA mezcal
1 shot	Blood orange juice
¼ shot	Cinnamon sugar syrup (2:1)
¼ shot	Fernet Branca

Origin: Created in 2013 by Regina Butler at Blackbird Bar in San Francisco, USA.
Comment: Mezcal, cinnamon and bittersweet Fernet are big hitting flavours which combine brilliantly in this characterful yet harmonious cocktail.

SANGRIA COCKTAIL

★★★★☆

Glass: Martini
Garnish: Orange slice
Method: SHAKE all ingredients with ice and fine strain into chilled glass.

1	shot	Shiraz red wine
1½	shots	Martell VSOP Médaillon cognac
¾	shot	Freshly squeezed orange juice
½	shot	Apple Schnapps liqueur
½	shot	Lejay Crème de Framboise liqueur

Origin: Created in 2003 by Angelo Vieira at The Light Bar, St. Martins Hotel, London, England.
Comment: Brandy based and fruit laced - just like it's namesake.

SANGRITA

★★★★½

Glass: Shot
Garnish: None
Method: SHAKE ingredients with ice and strain into shot glass. Serve with a shot of tequila. The drinker can either down the tequila and chase it with sangrita or sip the two drinks alternately.

½	shot	Tomato juice
½	shot	Pomegranate juice
¼	shot	Freshly squeezed orange juice
½	shot	Freshly squeezed lime juice
⅛	shot	Pomegranate / grenadine syrup (2:1)
2	drop	Tabasco hot pepper sauce
2	dash	Worcestershire sauce
1	pinch	Salt
1	grind	Black pepper

Origin: The name means 'little blood' in Spanish and the drink is served with tequila in every bar in Mexico.
Comment: In Mexico the quality of the homemade Sangrita can make or break a bar. This recipe is spicey and slightly sweet and perfect for chasing tequila.

SANGUINELLO COCKTAIL (NEW)

★★★★☆

Glass: Old-fashioned
Garnish: Blood orange slice
Method: SHAKE all ingredients with ice and strain into ice-filled glass.

1 shot Campari Bitter
1 shot Pallini Limoncello
1 shot Blood orange juice

Origin: This well-established Italian classic is named after one of the three most common varieties of blood oranges, the Sanguinello orange is native to Spain.
Comment: Bitter Campari notes are balanced by sweet, lemony limoncello liqueur with blood orange juice adding citrus freshness.

SANTA MARTA DAIQUIRI (NEW)

★★★★★+

Glass: Coupe
Garnish: Lime wedge
Method: SHAKE first 3 ingredients with ice and fine strain into chilled glass. FLOAT spoon of kirsch eau de vie on surface of drink.

2⅓	shot	Bacardi Carta Blanca white rum
¾	shot	Freshly squeezed lime juice
½	shot	Sugar syrup (2 sugar to 1 water)
½	shot	Chilled water (omit if wet ice)
⅙	shot	Kirsch eau-de-vie.

Comment: A float of Kirsch eau-de-vie adds wonderfully fruity aromatics to an otherwise classic Natural Daiquiri.
Origin: This adaptation of a Natural Daiquiri was discovered by Joerg Meyer in 2011 in the 1948 edition of the Cuban Cantinero bartender's own journal, *El Arte del Cantinero Los Vinos Y Los Licores*.

SANTIAGO DAIQUIRI ⚬━

★★★★★

Glass: Martini
Garnish: Luxardo Maraschino cherry
Method: SHAKE all ingredients with ice and fine strain into chilled glass.

2	shots	Bacardi Carta Blanca light rum
1	shot	Freshly squeezed lemon juice
½	shot	Pomegranate / grenadine syrup (2:1)
½	shot	Chilled water (omit if wet ice)

Origin: Adapted from a recipe in Harry Craddock's 1930 'Savoy Cocktail Book'. Made with Barcardi rum this becomes the Barcardi Cocktail.
Comment: This Daiquiri is particularly delicate in its balance between sweet and sour.

SANTORINI (NEW)

★★★★☆

Glass: Old-fashioned
Garnish: Orange zest twist
Method: STIR all ingredients with ice and strain into ice-filled glass.

2	shots	Martini Rosso vermouth
1	shot	Dewar's 12yo Scotch whisky
¼	shot	Ouzo 12

Origin: Created in December 2014 by yours truly as an adaption of a drink called an Islander created by Gary Regan which uses Pernod anis. Santorini is an island in the southern Aegean Sea and I was inspired to use a combination of whisky and ouzo as I was presenting the mixability of scotch to Greek bartenders in Athens.
Comment: Scotch whisky and sweet vermouth combine harmoniously with ouzo providing subtle and complementary aniseed notes.

SARATOGA COCKTAIL #1

★★★⯪☆

Glass: Coupe
Garnish: Lemon slice
Method: Vigorously **SHAKE** all ingredients with just two cubes of ice and strain into chilled glass.

1	shot	Martell VSOP Médaillon cognac
1	shot	Straight rye whiskey
1	shot	Martini Rosso vermouth
2	dash	Angostura Aromatic Bitters

Origin: Recipe adapted from Jerry Thomas' 1862 'The Bartenders Guide'.
Comment: Frothy topped yet hardcore.

SARATOGA COCKTAIL #2

★★★★☆

Glass: Coupe
Garnish: Luxardo Maraschino cherry
Method: **SHAKE** all ingredients with ice and fine strain into chilled glass.

2	shots	Martell VSOP Médaillon cognac
¼	shot	Luxardo Maraschino liqueur
½	shot	Fresh pressed pineapple juice
½	shot	Freshly squeezed lemon juice
1	dash	Angostura Aromatic Bitters
½	shot	Chilled water (omit if wet ice)

Comment: Dry and robust with cognac character combining well with maraschino and raspberry.

SARGASSO

★★★★☆

Glass: Coupe
Garnish: Orange zest twist
Method: **STIR** all ingredients with ice and strain into chilled glass.

2	shots	Martinique V.S.O.P rum
¾	shot	Romate Oloroso sherry
½	shot	Aperol Aperitivo
2	dash	Angostura Aromatic Bitters

Origin: Created in 2008 by Don Lee at PDT, New York City, USA.
Comment: This orange-red bitter sweet drink has a dry oaky complexity.

SATAN'S WHISKERS (CURLED) 🗝

★★★★⯪

Glass: Martini
Garnish: Orange zest twist
Method: **SHAKE** all ingredients with ice and fine strain into chilled glass.

1	shot	Rutte Dry Gin
1	shot	Martini Extra Dry vermouth
1	shot	Martini Rosso vermouth
½	shot	De Kuyper Triple Sec
1	shot	Freshly squeezed orange juice
1	dash	Angostura Aromatic Bitters

Origin: Adapted from a recipe in Harry Craddock's 1930 'Savoy Cocktail book.'
Comment: This variation on the 'Straight' Satan's Whiskers is made curly by the use of triple sec. It seems strangely counter intuitive as you'd think the slightly richer Grand Marnier would be what made it curly.

SATAN'S WHISKERS (ENROULÉE)

★★★★⯪

Glass: Martini
Garnish: Orange zest twist
Method: **SHAKE** all ingredients with ice and fine strain into chilled glass.

1½	shots	Rutte Dry Gin
½	shot	Martini Extra Dry vermouth
½	shot	Martini Rosso vermouth
½	shot	Mandarine Napoléon liqueur
¼	shot	Freshly squeezed orange juice
2	dash	Angostura Aromatic Bitters

Origin: Created in 2011 by Gary 'gaz' Regan, New York, USA.
Comment: Enroulée is the French word for 'curled' and this particular version of Satan's Whiskers is 'curled' by the use of mandarine liqueur in place of the Grand Marnier found in the 'straight' version.

SATAN'S WHISKERS (MARCELLED)

★★★★⯪

Glass: Martini
Garnish: Orange zest twist
Method: **SHAKE** all ingredients with ice and fine strain into chilled glass.

1½	shots	Rutte Dry Gin
¾	shot	Martini Rosso vermouth
1¼	shots	Freshly squeezed orange juice
⅛	shot	Taylor's Velvet Falernum liqueur
2	dash	Angostura Orange Bitters

Origin: Adapted from a drink created in 2011 by William "Chili Bill" Eichinger at Finnegan's Wake, San Francisco, USA and courtesy of Gaz Regan's Ardent Spirits.
Comment: This variation on the classic Satan's Whiskers calls for it not to be 'curled' (as is the case when you use triple sec), but to be 'marcelled', apparently a deep soft wave in one's hair (for those that still have some) created with curling tongs and popular in the '20s and '30s.

SATAN'S WHISKERS (STRAIGHT)

★★★★⯪

Glass: Martini
Garnish: Orange zest twist
Method: **SHAKE** all ingredients with ice and fine strain into chilled glass.

1	shot	Rutte Dry Gin
1	shot	Martini Extra Dry vermouth
1	shot	Martini Rosso vermouth
½	shot	Grand Marnier Cordon Rouge
1	shot	Freshly squeezed orange juice
1	shot	Angostura Orange Bitters (optional)

Origin: Adapted from a recipe in Harry Craddock's 1930 'Savoy Cocktail Book'.
Comment: A variation on the Bronx. Perfectly balanced tangy orange.

SATIN SHEET

★★★★☆

Glass: Martini
Garnish: Lime wedge
Method: SHAKE all ingredients with ice and fine strain into chilled glass.

2 shots Patrón reposado tequila
1 shot Freshly squeezed lime juice
½ shot Taylor's Velvet Falernum liqueur
¼ shot Sugar syrup (2 sugar to 1 water)

Comment: A spiced margarita-style drink.

SATSUMA COCKTAIL

★★★★☆

Glass: Martini
Garnish: Orange zest twist
Method: SHAKE all ingredients with ice and fine strain into chilled glass.

1½ shots Ketel One Oranje vodka
¾ shot Grand Marnier Cordon Rouge
1¾ shots Pressed apple juice
1 dash Angostura Aromatic Bitters

Origin: Adapted from a drink discovered in 2002 at the Fifth Floor Bar, Harvey Nichol's, London, England.
Comment: Tastes like its namesake - hard to believe it's almost half apple.

SATURN MARTINI

★★★★⯪

Glass: Martini
Garnish: White grapes
Method: MUDDLE grapes in base of shaker. STIR honey with vodka and grapes to dissolve honey. Add wine, SHAKE with ice and fine strain into chilled glass.

7 fresh Seedless white grapes
1½ shots Ketel One Citroen vodka
2 shots Runny honey
1½ shots Sauvignon blanc white wine

Origin: Created in 2001 by Tony Conigliaro at Isola, Knightsbridge, London, England.
Comment: Delicate, beautifully balanced and subtly flavoured.

SAÚCO MARGARITA 🗝

★★★★⯪

Glass: Margarita
Garnish: Lime wedge & salt rim (optional)
Method: SHAKE all ingredients with ice and fine strain into chilled glass.

1½ shots Patrón reposado tequila
1½ shots St-Germain elderflower liqueur
¾ shot Freshly squeezed lime juice

Origin: Created in 2006 by yours truly and named after 'flor saúco', which is Spanish for elderflower.
Comment: The floral notes of elderflower combine wonderfully with the herbaceous tequila and citrusy lime.

SAVANNAH

★★★⯪☆

Glass: Martini
Garnish: Orange zest twist
Method: SHAKE all ingredients with ice and fine strain into chilled glass.

2½ shots Rutte Dry Gin
¾ shot Freshly squeezed orange juice
½ shot White crème de cacao liqueur
½ fresh Egg white

Origin: Adapted from a recipe in the 1949 edition of 'Esquire's Handbook for Hosts'.
Comment: Gin and orange with a hint of chocolate - smoothed with egg white.

SAVOY SPECIAL #1

★★★★☆

Glass: Martini
Garnish: Orange zest twist
Method: SHAKE all ingredients with ice and fine strain into chilled glass.

2 shots Rutte Dry Gin
1 shot Martini Extra Dry vermouth
¼ shot Pomegranate / grenadine syrup (2:1)
⅛ shot Le Fée Parisienne absinthe
½ shot Chilled water (omit if wet ice)

Origin: Adapted from Harry Craddock's 1930 'Savoy Cocktail Book'.
Comment: Wonderfully dry and aromatic.

SAY SAY

★★★⯪☆

Glass: Coupe
Garnish: Lemon zest twist
Method: MUDDLE tomatoes in base of shaker. Add other ingredients, SHAKE with ice and fine strain into chilled glass.

3 fresh Cherry tomatoes (chopped)
1½ shots Bacardi Carta Blanca light rum
½ shot St-Germain elderflower liqueur
½ shot Pomegranate / grenadine syrup (2:1)
¾ shot Freshly squeezed lemon juice

Origin: Adapted from a drink created in 2008 by J.P. Keating, Saba, Dublin, Republic of Ireland.
Comment: This may have tomatoes in but it is no Bloody Mary. Possibly a tad on the sweet side, but complex none the less.

Sazerac Cocktail

Traditionally based on cognac or rye whiskey, as David A. Embury says of the Sazerac in his seminal 1948 'Fine Art of Mixing Drinks', "essentially it is merely an Old Fashioned made with Peychaud bitters instead of Angostura and flavoured with a dash of absinthe." Created in New Orleans it is the city's official cocktail and is one of America's oldest cocktails.

The Sazerac was originally made with cognac but due to the phylloxera plague hitting cognac supplies in the 1870s rye whiskey was substituted. As bourbon started to dominate American whiskey so many bartenders started making Sazeracs with bourbon rather than rye. However, there are many who fervently object to the use of bourbon, including Legendary New Orleans bartender, Stanley Clisby Arthur, who in his 1937 ' Famous New Orleans Drinks & how to mix'em' wrote "for while Bourbon may do for a julep it just won't do for a real Sazerac."

I like Sazeracs made with rye whisky. I also like them made with bourbon and/or cognac. All three spirits make a good Sazerac, each very different. The rye is obviously more robust and spicier while the bourbon is softer and cognac softer still. After trying all three I profess to preferring rye or a combination of all three – equal parts of each – a tad schizo perhaps, but each spirit contributes some of their personality resulting in a very complex Sazerac.

A Sazerac is simply not a Sazerac without Peychaud Bitters but many recipes, including Stanley Clisby Arthur's also call for a dash of Angostura Aromatic Bitters. I have been guilty of using three dashes of Angostura in the past, but I was also guilty of making my Sazeracs with a blend of bourbon and cognac, and a Sazerac made with these softer spirits can benefit from heavy bittering. However, one dash will suffice, especially when using rye as your base spirit. Don't be tempted to forgo the Angostura altogether as it adds a special something to the drink.

Regular Difford's Guide readers will know my bias towards sugar syrup over granulated sugar, let alone a sugar cube and for support I turn to Embury who writes, "Traditionally, the Sazerac, like the Old-Fashioned, is made by first saturating a lump of sugar with bitters and then muddling it. In the interest of simplicity and better drinks, however, we have abandoned loaf sugar in favour of sugar syrup."

The action of dampening a sugar cube with a splash of water and bitters then muddling creates a syrup, albeit one with crystals of undissolved sugar for the drinker to crunch upon. Surely Embury is right and using a quality, homemade sugar syrup makes more sense and a better Sazerac.

The balance of sugar and bitters makes or breaks a Sazerac. The sugar should just take the edge of the spirit and the bitters but not produce a sweet drink.

Again to quote Embury, "The Sazerac is a sharp, pungent, thoroughly dry cocktail. To most people, however, the combination of absinthe and whisky [sic] is not particularly pleasing. While whisky lovers do not like the sharp, biting taste that the absinthe imparts, absinthe lovers prefer their absinthe straight, dripped, frappéed, or mixed with gin rather than whisky. Even among my various New Orleans friends I have yet to find a Sazerac addict."

Made using the classical proportions and methods the Sazerac can indeed be a "thoroughly dry cocktail", perhaps a tad too dry and punchy. Achieving the correct fine balance of sugar and bitters is crucial but so is the dilution. Over stir or use wet ice and the drink will be too dilute. Use ice straight from the freezer and even with a prolonged stir you are unlikely to achieve spot on dilution. Therefore, to be certain of controlled consistent dilution, I prescribe stirring with properly frozen ice and half a shot of chilled water.

The oils from a twist of lemon zest make this drink but a fine spray is enough. Too much and lemon starts to overpower the flavour. I don't drop the zest into the drink as there is something off-putting about the lemon touching your lips as you sip the drink. As Stanley Clisby Arthur says, "do not commit the sacrilege of dropping the peel into the drink." He goes on to say, "some bartenders put a cherry in a Sazerac; very pretty but not necessary."

Although considered a sacrilege by many and classically a misdemeanour, I believe this drink great served shaken rather than stirred. However, bowing to peer pressure I have formerly stirred my Sazeracs. I now sit between both camps and instead throw rather than stir my Sazeracs. Throwing aerates and opens but does not leave the unattractive foamy top that shaking does.

History
Brandy-based cocktails were being served in New Orleans before the Sazerac was created and these early mixed drinks almost certainly included bitters, possibly Stoughton's Bitters, a long extinct medicinal stomach bitters. The ingredients for the Sazerac have varied over the years, however, its flavour has remained distinctive due to one essential ingredient: Peychaud's aromatic bitters, created by one Antoine Amedee Peychaud.

His story starts in 1795 when he arrives in New Orleans as a refugee after his father was forced to flee the island of San Domingo, and his family's coffee plantation, after the slaves rebelled. Antoine grew up to become a pharmacist and bought his own drug and apothecary store at 437 Rue Royale (then No. 123 Royal Street) in 1834. Here he created an 'American Aromatic Bitter Cordial' and marketed it as a medicinal tonic. Such potions were fashionable at the time and there were many similar products.

Antoine also served his bitters mixed with brandy and other liquors and it has been falsely claimed that the word 'cocktail' originated with Antoine and the measure, known as a 'coquetier', he used to prepare drinks. However, the term cocktail first appeared in print in an upstate New York newspaper in 1806 when Antoine was but a child.

Meanwhile, sometime around 1850, Sewell T. Taylor, another New Orleans entrepreneur gave up being a bar owner to move into the liquor business, becoming the local agent for a French cognac company, 'Sazerac-du-Forge et Fils' of Limoges. His bar, the Merchant's Exchange Coffee House at 13 Exchange Alley, was taken over by either a Aaron Bird or John B. Schiller.

Exchange Alley used to run between Royal Street and Exchange Place in the French Quarter where the Wyndham Hotel now stands. A service road under the hotel still links the two streets. It is here, at the Exchange Coffee House, sometime between 1850 and 1859, that the Sazerac Cocktail was created, based on and named after Taylor's Sazerac cognac with Peychaud's aromatic bitters and sugar. The cocktail became the bar's main specialty.

In 1869/70, Thomas H. Handy, the bar's bookkeeper, took over the Sazerac Coffeehouse and renamed it the Sazerac Coffeehouse after its house cocktail. Meanwhile Antoine Peychaud fell upon hard times and sold the pharmacy store, along with the formula and brand name of his bitters which Handy acquired in 1873. Having purchased the bar and the bitters required to make its house cocktail Handy then faced a predicament as cognac, the main ingredient to the Sazerac Cocktail, became hard to obtain.

The phylloxera aphid, a bug which attacks the roots of vines, devastated French vineyards in the late 1860s-1870s and so practically halted cognac production, forcing Handy to change the recipe of the Sazerac Cocktail. He still used the all-important Peychaud's bitters but substituted American distilled Maryland Club rye whiskey, retaining a dash of cognac. Around this time, perhaps before the change to rye whiskey, a splash of the newly fashionable absinthe was added to the Sazerac. As the cognac became more scarce, so it gradually disappeared from the drink.

To quote from Stanley Clisby Arthur's 1937 ' Famous New Orleans Drinks & how to mix'em' , "The absinthe innovation has been credited to Leon Lamothe who in 1858 was a bartender for Emile Seignouret, Charles Cavaroc & Co., a wine importing firm located in the old Seignouret mansion still standing at 520 Royal Street. More likely it was about 1870, when Lamothe was employed at Pina's restaurant in Burgundy Street that he experimented with absinthe and made the Sazerac what it is today."

Before his death in 1889, Handy disclosed the recipe for his house cocktail to William T. 'Cocktail Bill' Boothby who published it in his 1908 book, ' The World's Drinks and How to Mix Them' .

Sazerac (Boothby's recipe)
' ¾ jigger Whiskey
2 dashes Peychaud
Absinthe to wet glass
½ spoon Sugar syrup
1 slice Lemon peel
Chill cocktail glass, wet with few drops absinthe and toss out. Stir other ingredients well with ice, strain into prepared glass and serve with ice water chaser.'

In the 1890s, the Sazerac Company began to bottle and market the Sazerac Cocktail, now made with rye whiskey instead of cognac. The cocktail, which continued to be served at the Sazerac Bar was further adapted in 1912 when absinthe was banned in the US. The Sazerac company started to produce a product called Herbsaint as an absinthe substitute and although absinthe is once again legal in the USA, most bars in New Orleans continue to make their Sazerac Cocktails with Herbsaint rather than absinthe.

The Sazerac Bar reopened after Prohibition at 300 Carondelet Street. In 1949, Seymour Weiss, the Vice President and Managing Director of the nearby Roosevelt Hotel purchased the rights to use the name Sazerac Bar from the Sazerac Company. He renovated a former Wine and Spirits store on Baronne Street and on 26th September 1949 opened the new Sazerac Bar. Weiss published that the new bar would abolish its 'men only' rule and welcome women. The move was marketing genius and women flocked to the launch, leading to the event becoming known as 'Storming the Sazerac'.

In 1959, the Sazerac Bar on Baronne Street was closed and the name transferred to the hotel's Main Bar which had opened in 1938. Here the Sazerac Bar remains popular and can be considered the spiritual and actual home of the Sazerac with around 40,000 Sazeracs served there every year. (To allay confusion, the hotel originally opened in 1893 as The Hotel Grunewald, then became The Fairmont, then The Roosevelt before reopening after Hurricane Katrina as The Fairmont.)

In 2007, Ann Tuennerman, of The New Orleans Culinary and Cultural Preservation Society, lobbied the Louisiana legislature to "Save the Sazerac". The following March, state senator Edwin R. Murray filed a Senate Bill designating the Sazerac as Louisiana's official state cocktail. The bill was defeated on 8th April 2008 but after further debate and lobbying, on 23 June 2008, the Louisiana Legislature passed a bill proclaiming the Sazerac as New Orleans official cocktail.

SAZERAC COCKTAIL (DIFFORD'S RECIPE)

★★★★★

Glass: Old-fashioned
Garnish: Lemon zest twist (discarded)
Method: POUR absinthe into ice-filled glass, **TOP** with water and leave to stand. Separately **THROW** other ingredients with ice. **DISCARD** contents of glass (absinthe, water and ice) and **STRAIN** thrown drink into absinthe-coated glass.

½	shot	Le Fée Parisienne absinthe
2⅓	shots	Chilled water
¾	shot	Martell VSOP Médaillon cognac
¾	shot	Straight rye whiskey
¾	shot	Bourbon whiskey
⅓	shot	Sugar syrup (2 sugar to 1 water)
3	dash	Peychaud's aromatic bitters
1	dash	Angostura Aromatic Bitters
⅓	shot	Chilled water (omit if wet ice)

Comment: If you are concerned about chucking expensive absinthe down the drain then consider straining into a shot glass and serve on the side. The five to one proportion used to rinse the glass produces a tasty chaser.

SAZERAC COCKTAIL (NEW ORLEANS STYLE) (NEW)

★★★★☆

Glass: Rocks
Garnish: Lemon zest twist
Method: Ice glass and set to one side. Separately, in another glass stir other ingredients with ice. Discard ice in the now chilled set aside glass and rinse with absinthe (or Herbsaint). Then strain drink into absinthe/Herbsaint washed glass.

1½	shots	Straight rye whiskey
¼	shot	Sugar syrup (2 sugar to 1 water)
3	dash	Peychaud's aromatic bitters

Comment: While bartenders in other cities have complicated the Sazerac by using a combination of spirits (us included), in New Orleans they keep it simple: straight rye whisky with a dash of sugar, stirred and strained into an Herbsaint washed glass.

SCARLETT O'HARA

★★★☆☆

Glass: Martini
Garnish: Lime wedge
Method: SHAKE all ingredients with ice and strain into ice-filled glass.

1½	shots	Southern Comfort liqueur
1½	shots	Cranberry juice
¾	shot	Freshly squeezed lime juice

Origin: This drink helped put Southern Comfort on the proverbial drink map and was created in 1939 and named after the heroine of the film Gone With The Wind, released that year.
Comment: The tang of lime and the dryness of cranberry balance the apricot sweetness of Southern Comfort.

SCOFFLAW

★★★★☆

Glass: Martini
Garnish: Lemon zest twist
Method: SHAKE all ingredients with ice and fine strain into chilled glass.

1½	shots	Bourbon whiskey
1½	shots	Martini Extra Dry vermouth
½	shot	Freshly squeezed lemon juice
¼	shot	Pomegranate / grenadine syrup (2:1)
1	dash	Angostura Orange Bitters

Origin: During the height of Prohibition The Boston Herald ran a competition asking readers to coin a new word for "a lawless drinker of illegally made or illegally obtained liquor". Out of 25,000 entries, 'Scofflaw' was chosen and on 15th January 1924 the $200 prize was shared between two people who had submitted the word. This cocktail was created Jock at Harry's American Bar, Paris, to celebrate the new term.
Comment: This rust coloured drink is made or broken by the quality of the pomegranate syrup used.

SCORPION

★★★★☆

Glass: Collins
Garnish: Orange slice & mint sprig
Method: BLEND all ingredients with 12oz crushed ice and serve with straws

1½	shots	Bacardi Carta Blanca light rum
¾	shot	Martell VSOP Médaillon cognac
2	shots	Freshly squeezed orange juice
1	shot	Freshly squeezed lemon juice
½	shot	Almond (orgeat) syrup

Origin: Created by Victor Bergeron and this recipe adapted from his 'Trader Vic's Bartender's Guide' (1972 revised edition).
Comment: Well balanced, refreshing spirit and orange. Not sweet.

SCOTCH MILK PUNCH 🔑

★★★½☆

Glass: Martini
Garnish: Dust with grated nutmeg
Method: SHAKE all ingredients with ice and fine strain into chilled glass.

2	shots	Dewar's 12yo Scotch whisky
½	shot	Sugar syrup (2 sugar to 1 water)
¾	shot	Single cream / half-and-half
¾	shot	Milk

Comment: A creamy, malty affair.

SCOTCH NEGRONI

★★★★☆

Glass: Old-fashioned
Garnish: Orange slice
Method: STIR all ingredients and strain into ice-filled glass.

1	shot	Dewar's 12yo Scotch whisky
1	shot	Campari Bitter
1	shot	Martini Rosso vermouth

Comment: On the bitter side of bittersweet and faintly smoky.

SCOTCH SOUR ⚷

★★★★★

Glass: Old-fashioned
Garnish: Lemon & orange zest twists
Method: SHAKE all ingredients with ice. Strain back into shaker and DRY SHAKE (without ice). Strain into ice-filled glass.

2	shots	Dewar's 12yo Scotch whisky
1	shot	Freshly squeezed lemon juice
½	shot	Sugar syrup (2 sugar to 1 water)
½	fresh	Egg white

Comment: This drink is sadly often overlooked in favour of the bourbon based Whiskey Sour.

THE SCOTT

★★★★☆

Glass: Martini
Garnish: Lemon zest twist
Method: STIR all ingredients with ice and strain into chilled glass.

2	shots	Dewar's 12yo Scotch whisky
½	shot	Drambuie liqueur
1	shot	Martini Extra Dry vermouth

Origin: Discovered in 2006 at The Clift Hotel, San Francisco, USA.
Comment: This golden drink is dry and sophisticated, yet honeyed and approachable.

SCOTTISH BREAKFAST

★★★★☆

Glass: Old-fashioned
Garnish: Dust with cinnamon powder
Method: SHAKE all ingredients with ice and strain into ice-filled glass.

1½	shots	Dewar's 12yo Scotch whisky
½	shot	Calvados brandy
½	shot	Maple syrup
1	shot	Single cream / half-and-half
⅛	shot	Sugar syrup (2 sugar to 1 water)

Origin: Created in 2009 by Erik Castro at Rickhouse, San Francisco, USA.
Comment: Scotch sweetened with maple syrup, flavoured with calvados and smoothed with cream.

SCOTTISH GYPSY

★★★★☆

Glass: Coupe
Garnish: Lemon zest twist
Method: STIR all ingredients with ice and strain into chilled glass.

2	shots	Dewar's 12yo Scotch whisky
1	shot	Bénédictine D.O.M. liqueur
3	dash	Angostura Aromatic Bitters

Comment: Scotch and Bénédictine complement each other in this herbal cocktail which is balanced by the addition of bitters.

SCREAMING BANANA BANSHEE

★★★½☆

Glass: Hurricane
Garnish: Banana chunk
Method: BLEND all ingredients with 12oz scoop of crushed ice and serve with straws.

2	shots	Ketel One Vodka
1	shot	Crème de banane liqueur
1	shot	White crème de cacao liqueur
1½	shots	Single cream / half-and-half
1½	shots	Milk
½	fresh	Banana (peeled)

Origin: Without the vodka this is a plain 'Banana Banshee'.
Comment: An alcoholic milkshake - not too sweet.

SCREAMING ORGASM

★★½☆☆

Glass: Hurricane
Garnish: Dust with chocolate powder
Method: SHAKE all ingredients with ice and strain into glass filled with crushed ice.

1¼	shots	Ketel One Vodka
1¼	shots	Coffee liqueur
1¼	shots	Disaronno Originale amaretto
1¼	shots	Baileys Irish cream liqueur
1¼	shots	Single cream / half-and-half
1¼	shots	Milk

Origin: A dodgy drink from the 1980s.
Comment: Probably as fattening as it is alcoholic, this is a huge, creamy dessert in a glass.

SCREWDRIVER (DIFFORD'S RECIPE)

★★★★☆

Glass: Collins
Garnish: Orange slice
Method: SHAKE all ingredients with ice and strain into ice-filled glass.

2½	shots	Ketel One Vodka
3		Top with Freshly squeezed orange juice
¼	shot	Sugar syrup (2 sugar to 1 water)
3	dash	Angostura Orange Bitters

Origin: This cocktail first appeared in the 1950s in the Middle East. Parched US engineers working in the desert supposedly added orange juice to their vodka and stirred it with the nearest thing to hand, usually a screwdriver.
Comment: The temperature at which this drink is served and the freshness of the orange juice are crucial to its success but perhaps better made into a Harvey Wallbanger.

SEABREEZE #1 (SIMPLE) ⚷

★★★½☆

Glass: Collins
Garnish: Lime slice
Method: SHAKE all ingredients with ice and strain into ice-filled glass.

2	shots	Ketel One Vodka
3	shots	Cranberry juice
1½	shots	Freshly squeezed pink grapefruit juice

Origin: Thought to have originated in the early 1990s in New York City.
Comment: Few bartenders bother to shake this simple drink, instead simply pouring and stirring in the glass.

SEABREEZE #2 (LAYERED) 0━━

★★★☆☆

Glass: Collins
Garnish: Lime wedge
Method: POUR cranberry juice into ice-filled glass. SHAKE other ingredients with ice and carefully strain into glass to LAYER over the cranberry juice.

2	shots	Ketel One Vodka
3	shots	Cranberry juice
1½	shots	Freshly squeezed pink grapefruit juice
½	shot	Freshly squeezed lime juice

Comment: This layered version requires mixing with straws before drinking.

SEELBACH

★★★☆☆

Glass: Flute
Garnish: Orange zest twist
Method: POUR first four ingredients into chilled glass. TOP with champagne.

1	shot	Bourbon whiskey
½	shot	De Kuyper Triple Sec
2	dash	Peychaud's aromatic bitters
2	dash	Angostura Aromatic Bitters
Top with		G.H. Mumm Cordon Rouge Champagne

Origin: Created circa 1917 and named after its place of origin, the Seelbach Hotel, 500 South 4th Street, Louisville, Kentucky, USA. The original recipe is reputed to have called for seven dashes of each of the aromatic bitters. I find even 7 drops of each a tad excessive. Like many other vintage American whiskey based cocktails, purists often prefer to use rye whiskey in place of bourbon.

The Old Seelbach Bar has been restored to its authentic, early 1900s decor and continues to serve its signature drink to this day. Gary Regan once described the expansive bourbon selection stocked on the bar back here as "one of the finest stretches of mahogany in the country." If visiting the Seelbach be sure to check out the beautiful tiled function room with its vaulted ceiling in the basement.
Comment: A champagne cocktail fortified with bourbon and triple sec liqueur.

SENSATION

★★★★☆

Glass: Martini
Garnish: Luxardo Maraschino cherry
Method: Lightly MUDDLE mint (just to bruise) in base of shaker. Add other ingredients, SHAKE with ice and fine strain into chilled glass.

12	fresh	Mint leaves
2	shots	Rutte Dry Gin
¾	shot	Luxardo Maraschino liqueur
¾	shot	Freshly squeezed lemon juice
⅛	shot	Sugar syrup (2 sugar to 1 water)
½	shot	Chilled water (omit if wet ice)

Origin: Adapted from a recipe in Harry Craddock's 1930 'Savoy Cocktail Book'.
Comment: Fresh, fragrant and balanced.

SENTIMENTAL MELODY

★★★☆☆

Glass: Martini
Garnish: Orange zest twist (flamed)
Method: STIR grapefruit preserve and rum in base of a shaker to dissolve the jam. Add other ingredients, SHAKE with ice and fine strain into chilled glass.

2	spoon	Grapefruit preserve
2	shots	Bacardi Carta Blanca light rum
¼	shot	De Kuyper Triple Sec
½	shot	St-Germain elderflower liqueur
¾	shot	Cranberry juice
¼	shot	Pomegranate juice
½	shot	Freshly squeezed lime juice

Origin: Adapted from a recipe created in 2008 by Peter Dorelli, London, England.
Comment: A twisted Daiquiri with rich berry fruit.

SERENDIPITY #2

★★★★☆

Glass: Old-fashioned
Garnish: Mint sprig
Method: SHAKE first 4 ingredients with ice and fine strain into ice-filled glass. TOP with champagne.

8	fresh	Mint leaves
1½	shots	Calvados brandy
1½	shots	Pressed apple juice
¼	shot	Sugar syrup (2 sugar to 1 water)
Top with		G.H. Mumm Cordon Rouge Champagne

Origin: Our adaptation of Colin Field's signature drink. Collin first served this drink on 31 December 1994 at the Hemingway Bar of the Paris Ritz Hotel for Jean-Louis Constanza. Upon tasting it, Jean-Louis exclaimed, "Serendipity."
Comment: Spirity, minty apple invigorated by a splash of champagne.

SETTLE PETAL

★★★★☆

Glass: Martini
Garnish: Rose petal
Method: STIR all ingredients with ice and strain into chilled glass.

2	shots	Rutte Dry Gin
1	shot	Cucumber flavoured vodka
½	shot	Rose water
½	shot	Vanilla sugar syrup

Origin: Created in 2003 by Andy Fitzmorris at Eclipse, Notting Hill, London, England.
Comment: An aptly named floral cocktail.

SEVENTH HEAVEN #2

★★★★☆

Glass: Martini
Garnish: Mint leaf
Method: SHAKE all ingredients with ice and fine strain into chilled glass.

2	shots	Rutte Dry Gin
¾	shot	Luxardo Maraschino liqueur
1½	shots	Freshly squeezed pink grapefruit juice

Origin: Adapted from the Seventh Heaven No.2 recipe in Harry Craddock's 1930 'The Savoy Cocktail Book'.
Comment: Grapefruit citrus bitterness balances rich floral maraschino liqueur in this gin-based cocktail.

SEX ON THE BEACH #1

★★★½☆☆

Glass: Collins
Garnish: Orange slice & cherry on stick (sail)
Method: **SHAKE** all ingredients with ice and strain into ice-filled glass.

2	shots	Ketel One Vodka
½	shot	Peachtree peach schnapps
½	shot	Chambord Liqueur
1½	shots	Freshly squeezed orange juice
1½	shots	Cranberry juice

Origin: An infamous cocktail during the 1980s.
Comment: Sweet fruit laced with vodka.

SEX ON THE BEACH #2

★★★☆☆

Glass: Old-fashioned
Garnish: Orange slice & cherry on stick (sail)
Method: **SHAKE** all ingredients with ice and strain into ice-filled glass.

2	shots	Ketel One Vodka
½	shot	Midori Green Melon liqueur
½	shot	Chambord Liqueur
1½	shots	Fresh pressed pineapple juice

Comment: Sweeter than most.

SEX ON THE BEACH #3

★★½☆☆

Glass: Shot
Garnish: None
Method: Refrigerate ingredients then **LAYER** in chilled glass by carefully pouring in the order listed.

½	shot	Chambord Liqueur
½	shot	Midori Green Melon liqueur
½	shot	Freshly squeezed lime juice
½	shot	Fresh pressed pineapple juice

Comment: A sweet and sour shot, combining raspberry, melon, lime and pineapple.

SGROPPINO / SORBETTO

★★★★½

Glass: Flute
Garnish: Lemon zest twist
Method: **BLEND** all ingredients without additional ice and serve in chilled glass.

½	shot	Ketel One Vodka
¼	shot	Single cream / half-and-half
1½	shots	Prosecco sparkling wine
2	scoop	Lemon sorbet

Origin: Pronounced 'scroe-pee-noe', this hybrid of cocktail and dessert is often served after meals in Venice. The name comes from a vernacular word meaning 'untie', a reference to the belief that it relaxes your stomach after a hearty meal.
Comment: Smooth and all too easy to quaff. A great dessert.

SHADY GROVE COOLER

★★★½☆

Glass: Collins
Garnish: Lime wedge
Method: **SHAKE** first three ingredients with ice and strain into ice-filled glass. **TOP** with ginger ale, lightly stir and serve with straws.

2	shots	Rutte Dry Gin
1	shot	Freshly squeezed lime juice
½	shot	Sugar syrup (2 sugar to 1 water)
Top with		Ginger ale

Comment: Long and refreshing with lime freshness and a hint of ginger.

SHAKERATO

★★★★½☆

Glass: Martini
Garnish: Orange zest twist
Method: **SHAKE** all ingredients with ice and fine strain into chilled glass.

1½	shots	Campari Bitter

Comment: Campari lovers only need apply.

SHAKY PETE'S GINGER BREW

★★★★☆

Glass: Rum barrel mug or pint glass
Garnish: None
Method: Blitz **BLEND** the first three ingredients with two ice cubes for ten seconds. Fine strain into chilled glass and **TOP** with beer. See Origin for Pete's original homemade ginger syrup.

1½	shots	Rutte Dry Gin
2	shots	Freshly squeezed lemon juice
2	shots	Ginger sugar syrup
4	shots	Fuller's Chiswick Bitter

Origin: Adapted from a drink created in 2012 by Pete Jeary (aka Shaky Pete) at Hawksmoor, Seven Dials, London, England. Pete's original recipe calls for homemade ginger syrup made by blending 1 kg ginger (peeled and chopped), 1 kg caster sugar and 500ml water fine strained into bottles. Pete uses London Pride beer.
Comment: Imagine a ginger flavoured shandy with a kick – pretty much describes this gin laced lemon and ginger flavoured beer-tail.

SHAMROCK #1

★★★★½☆

Glass: Martini
Garnish: Orange zest twist (discarded)
Method: **STIR** all ingredients with ice and strain into chilled glass.

2½	shots	Bourbon whiskey
¼	shot	Green crème de menthe liqueur
1	shot	Martini Rosso vermouth
2	dash	Angostura Aromatic Bitters

Origin: Purloined from David Embury's classic book, 'The Fine Art of Mixing Drinks'.
Comment: Basically a sweet Manhattan with a dash of green crème de menthe.

SHAMROCK #2

★★★★☆

Glass: Martini
Garnish: Mint leaf
Method: **STIR** all ingredients with ice and strain into chilled glass.

1½ shots Teeling Small Batch Irish whiskey
1½ shots Martini Extra Dry vermouth
½ shot Green Chartreuse liqueur
½ shot Green crème de menthe liqueur
½ shot Chilled water (omit if wet ice)

Origin: Adapted from a recipe in Harry Craddock's 1930 'Savoy Cocktail Book'.
Comment: A great drink for St Patrick's Day.

SHANDYGAFF

★★★☆☆

Glass: Pint
Garnish: None
Method: **POUR** ale into glass, **TOP** with ginger ale.

⅔ fill glass with Budweiser Budvar
Top with Ginger ale

Origin: This drink and its name originated in England and dates back to at least the late 19th century. The name comes from the London slang for a pint of beer, 'shant of gatter' (shanty being a public house, gatter meaning water). The ginger ale serves as a flavoursome way to water down the strength of the beer, thus the literal translation, 'pub water'.

In the first chapter of 'The History of Mr. Polly', H. G. Wells describes a shandygaff as being, "two pints of beer and two bottles of ginger beer foaming in a huge round-bellied jug." In London the beer is now usually diluted with lemonade and this drink is now simply known as a shandy. When ordering in a pub you are expected to call for 'lager shandy' or 'bitter shandy', the latter specifying the drink should be based on traditional real ale.

Today the term 'Shandygaff' is forgotten in London but popular in the Caribbean where this drink is made with beer and ginger ale or ginger beer.
Comment: Tastier than your average 'lager shandy'.

SHARK BITE

★★★½☆

Glass: Hurricane
Garnish: None
Method: **BLEND** first three ingredients with 18oz scoop crushed ice and pour into glass. **POUR** grenadine around edge of the drink. Do not stir before stirring.

2 shots Pusser's Navy Rum (54.5%)
3 shots Freshly squeezed orange juice
½ shot Freshly squeezed lime juice
¾ shot Pomegranate / grenadine syrup (2:1)

Comment: Strong rum and orange juice. A tad sweet but easy to drink.

SHARK'S TOOTH NO.1

★★★½☆

Glass: Sling
Garnish: Lime wedge
Method: **SHAKE** first five ingredients with ice and strain into ice-filled glass. **TOP** with soda and serve with straws.

2½ shots White overproof rum
½ shot Freshly squeezed lime juice
½ shot Freshly squeezed lemon juice
¼ shot Sugar syrup (2 sugar to 1 water)
¼ shot Pomegranate / grenadine syrup (2:1)
Top with Soda (club soda)

Origin: Adapted from Victor Bergeron's 'Trader Vic's Bartender's Guide' (1972 revised edition) where he writes, "One of the first drinks we ever made".
Comment: Salmon-pink in colour and heavily influenced by the flavoursome overproof rum.

SHARK'S TOOTH NO.3

★★★½☆

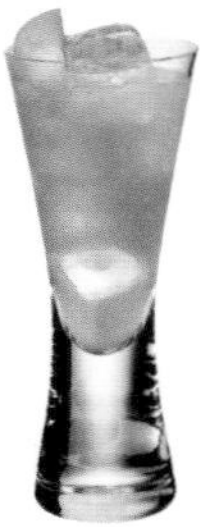

Glass: Sling
Garnish: Lime wedge
Method: **SHAKE** first three ingredients with ice and strain into ice-filled glass. **TOP** with soda and serve with straws.

2½ shots Bacardi Carta Blanca light rum
1 shot Freshly squeezed lemon juice
½ shot Pomegranate / grenadine syrup (2:1)
Top with Soda (club soda)

Origin: Adapted from Victor Bergeron's 'Trader Vic's Bartender's Guide' (1972 revised edition).
Comment: Sounds hard; looks pink. Tastes reminiscent of a dilute Bacardi Cocktail.

SHARMAN-COX DAIQUIRI

★★★★☆

Glass: Coupe
Garnish: Orange zest twist (discarded) & lime wedge
Method: **DRY SHAKE** all ingredients (without ice). **SHAKE** again with ice and fine strain into chilled glass.

2 shots Bacardi Carta Blanca light rum
⅓ shot Blue curaçao liqueur
¼ shot Freshly squeezed lime juice
¼ shot Freshly squeezed lemon juice
¼ shot Sugar syrup (2 sugar to 1 water)
½ fresh Egg white

Origin: Adapted from a drink created in 2013 at the Rum Kitchen, Notting Hill, London. The name 'Cox' is the common theme to this drink: 1) It is inspired by the Perfect Lady, a classic cocktail created in 1936 by Sidney Cox, a bartender at the Grosvenor House, London for The British Empire Cocktail Competition where it took the 1st Prize. 2) The original Daiquiri, said to be created in 1898 by Jennings Cox, an American mining engineer working at a tin mine near the Cuban town of Daiquiri. 3) Most importantly, this drink was created and named to honour the fabulous Hannah Sharman-Cox of London Cocktail Week fame.
Comment: A foam-topped blue twist on the classic daiquiri served in a coupette glass, which as every schoolboy knows are shaped after Marie Antoinette's breasts.

SHERRY COBBLER

★★★★½

Glass: Collins
Garnish: Lemon & orange wedges
Method: **MUDDLE** fruit in base of shaker. Add other ingredients, **SHAKE** with ice and fine strain into a glass filled with crushed ice.

¼ slice **Pineapple (fresh)**
½ slice **Fresh orange**
3½ shots **Romate Fino sherry**
¼ shot **Luxardo Maraschino liqueur**
¼ shot **Freshly squeezed lemon juice**
¼ shot **Sugar syrup (2 sugar to 1 water)**

Origin: The origins of this cocktail are unknown but it is one of the oldest classic cocktails. This recipe is adapted from Jerry Thomas' 1862 'How to Mix Drinks - the Bon Vivant's Companion'.

In his 1882 'Bartender's Manual', Harry Johnson writes of the Sherry Cobbler, "This drink is without doubt the most popular beverage in the country, with ladies as well as with gentlemen."
Comment: This age old cocktail is said to have been the drink for which the waxed paper straw was invented. To quote Harry Johnson, from his 1882 'Bartender's Manual', "It is a very refreshing drink for old and young."

SHERRY SOUR

★★★★½

Glass: Old-fashioned
Garnish: Luxardo Maraschino cherry
Method: **SHAKE** all ingredients with ice and strain into ice-filled glass.

2 shots **Romate Palo cortado sherry**
¾ shot **Freshly squeezed lemon juice**
½ shot **Sugar syrup (2 sugar to 1 water)**
½ fresh **Egg white**

Origin: Discovered in 2007 at Suba, New York, USA.
Comment: The huge flavour of sherry is freshened by lemon juice and rounded by egg white.

SHIRLEY TEMPLE (MOCKTAIL)

★★★☆☆

Glass: Collins
Garnish: Luxardo Maraschino cherry & lemon slice
Method: **POUR** ingredients into ice filled glass, lightly stir and serve with straws.

¼ shot **Pomegranate / grenadine syrup (2:1)**
¼ shot **Freshly squeezed lemon juice**
Top with **Ginger ale**

Comment: I've added a splash of lemon juice to the usual recipe. It's still not that exciting.

SHOWBIZ

★★★★☆

Glass: Martini
Garnish: Blackcurrants
Method: **SHAKE** all ingredients with ice and fine strain into chilled glass.

1½ shots **Ketel One Vodka**
¾ shot **Lejay Creme de Cassis de Dijon**
1½ shots **Freshly squeezed pink grapefruit juice**

Comment: Sweet cassis soured with grapefruit and fortified with vodka.

SI-MAO

★★★★☆

Glass: Shot
Garnish: None
Method: **SHAKE** all ingredients with ice and fine strain into chilled glass.

1 shot **Jack Daniel's Old No.7 Brand**
½ shot **Crème de banane liqueur**
¼ shot **Freshly squeezed orange juice**
¼ shot **Freshly squeezed lemon juice**

Origin: Adapted from a drink discovered in 2010 at Nobu Berkeley, London, England.
Comment: A whiskey laced shot with a hint of banana.

SICILIAN NEGRONI COCKTAIL

★★★★½

Glass: Old-fashioned
Garnish: Orange slice
Method: **SHAKE** all ingredients with ice and strain into ice-filled glass.

1½ shots **Rutte Dry Gin**
1½ shots **Campari Bitter**
1½ shots **Blood orange juice** (blood)

Origin: Discovered in 2006 at The Last Supper Club, San Francisco, USA.
Comment: Blood orange juice replaces sweet vermouth in this fruity Negroni.

SICILIAN ORANGE SPRITZ (NEW)

★★★★☆

Glass: Old-fashioned
Garnish: Slice blood orange
Method: **POUR** prosecco and liqueur into glass. Add ice. Top with soda.

3 shots **Prosecco sparkling wine**
2 shots **Blood orange liqueur**
Top with **Soda (club soda)**

Origin: Created in 2013 for Jamie's Italian bar.
Comment: Zesty, bittersweet blood orange with Prosecco effervescence.

SIDE ERR

★★★★½

Glass: Old-fashioned
Garnish: Apple slice
Method: **POUR** ingredients into ice-filled glass and stir.

1 shot **Calvados brandy**
¼ shot **Zubrówka bison vodka**
½ spoon **Islay single malt Scotch whisky**
2¾ shots **Medium dry cider**

Origin: Created in August 2011 by yours truly at the Cabinet Room, London, England.
Comment: This apple delight combines apple brandy, Bison Grass vodka, cider (ideally Devonshire English cider) with a smoky whiff of Islay whisky.

Sidecar Cocktail

The Sidecar is a classic cocktail made with cognac, triple sec orange liqueur and lemon juice. Traditionally made to be on the slightly sour side of balanced, it is often served in a glass with a sugared rim to compensate. However, modern bartenders tend to forgo the sugared rim and balance when mixing with the addition of a dash of sugar syrup or other sweetener.

The proportions of this drink are debated as much as its origin. Perhaps due to ease rather than balance, the equal parts formula (1 x brandy, 1 x triple sec and 1 x lemon juice) was the earliest published recipe (Harry McElhone's 1919 'ABC of Cocktails' and Robert Vermeire's 1922 'Cocktails: How to Mix Them', and still seems popular to this day.

In his 1948 'Fine Art of Mixing Drinks', David A. Embury writes of the 'equal parts' Sidecar, "This is the most perfect example of a magnificent drink gone wrong". He argues that "Essentially the Sidecar is nothing but a Daiquiri with brandy in the place of rum and Cointreau in the place of sugar syrup" and so the Daiquiri formula should be followed (2 x brandy, 1/2 x triple sec and 1/4 lemon juice). This may work for a Daiquiri but makes for an overly dry Sidecar.

In his 1930 'The Savoy Cocktail Book', Harry Craddock calls for 2 x brandy, 1 x Cointreau and 1 x lemon juice.

MacElhone and Vermiere's equal parts recipe are referred to by some as belonging to "the French school" while the Savoy's 2:1:1 formula is said to be from the "English school". My Sidecar recipe takes the middle ground between The Savoy and the 'equal parts' camp. I also find this drink benefits from a dash of Pineau des Charentes or sugar syrup to help balance the citrus and, if using just-out-the freezer ice, a little water for extra dilution.

There have been periods when it has been fashionable to coat the rim of the glass in which this drink is served with sugar. The earliest written reference to this is in 1934. Thankfully sugar rims are now out of vogue and, as Embury writes in his book, "A twist of lemon may be used if desired and the peel dropped into the glass. Otherwise no decoration."

History
In his 1948 'Fine Art of Mixing Drinks', David A. Embury says of the Sidecar's origin: "It was invented by a friend of mine at a bar in Paris during World War I and was named after the motorcycle sidecar in which the good captain customarily was driven to and from the little bistro where the drink was born and christened."

Embury doesn't name the bar but it's commonly assumed that he meant Harry's New York Bar and that the cocktail was created by its owner, Harry MacElhone. However, in early editions (1919 and 1922) of Harry's own 'ABC of Cocktails' he credits the drink to Pat McGarry "the Popular bar-tender at Buck's Club, London", but in later editions appears to take credit for the drink himself.

In his 1922 'Cocktails How To Mix Them', Robert Vermeire writes, "This cocktail is very popular in France. It was first introduced in London by McGarry, the celebrated bar-tender of Buck's Club."

Like so many classic cocktails we shall probably never know who created/named the Sidecar cocktail but it would appear to have Parisian origins and to have been popularised by McGarry at London's Bucks Club.

STAR RATINGS EXPLAINED

★★★★★+	OUTSTANDING	★★★★★	EXCEPTIONAL
★★★★½	EXCELLENT	★★★★☆	RECOMMENDED
★★★½☆	COMMENDED	★★★☆☆	MEDIOCRE
★★½☆☆	DISAPPOINTING	★★☆☆☆	PRETTY AWFUL
★½☆☆☆	SHAMEFUL	★☆☆☆☆	DISGUSTING

SIDECAR COCKTAIL (DIFFORD'S RECIPE)

★★★★½

Glass: Coupe
Garnish: Lemon zest twist (some like with a sugared rim)
Method: **SHAKE** all ingredients with ice and fine strain into chilled glass.

1½ shots **Martell VSOP Médaillon cognac**
1 shot **De Kuyper Triple Sec**
¾ shot **Freshly squeezed lemon juice**
½ shot **Chevessac Pineau Des Charentes Extra Vieux**
½ shot **Chilled water** (omit if wet ice)

Comment: Complex and balanced but still a 'sour'. Those with a sweet tooth may prefer with a sugar rim.

SIDECAR NAMED DESIRE

★★★★☆

Glass: Coupe
Garnish: Lemon zest twist
Method: **SHAKE** all ingredients with ice and fine strain into chilled glass.

1½ shots **Calvados brandy**
¾ shot **Apple Schnapps liqueur**
¾ shot **Freshly squeezed lemon juice**
¼ shot **Sugar syrup (2 sugar to 1 water)**

Comment: Take a classic Sidecar and add some love interest - apples!

SIDECARRIAGE

★★★★☆

Glass: Martini
Garnish: Lemon zest twist
Method: **SHAKE** all ingredients with ice and fine strain into chilled glass.

1½ shots **Calvados brandy**
1½ shots **St-Germain elderflower liqueur**
1 shot **Freshly squeezed lemon juice**

Origin: Created in 2006 by yours truly, London, England.
Comment: Hints of cider come through in this calvados based Sidecar with an elderflower twist.

SIDEKICK

★★★★☆

Glass: Martini
Garnish: Orange slice
Method: **SHAKE** all ingredients with ice and fine strain into chilled glass.

2 shots **Martell VSOP Médaillon cognac**
¾ shot **De Kuyper Triple Sec**
1 shot **Freshly squeezed orange juice**
½ shot **Freshly squeezed lime juice**

Origin: Adapted from a drink discovered in 2003 at Temple Bar, New York City, USA.
Comment: Rich pear and orange with a stabilising hint of sour lime.

SILENT SEVEN (NEW)

★★★★☆

Glass: Old-fashioned
Garnish: Orange zest twist
Method: SHAKE all ingredients with ice and strain into ice-filled glass.

2	shots	Jack Daniel's Old No.7 Brand
⅔	shot	De Kuyper Triple Sec
⅔	shot	Freshly squeezed lemon juice
¼	shot	Sugar syrup (2 sugar to 1 water)

Origin: A riff on the classic 'Silent Third' cocktail first published in the 1937 ' Cafe Royal Cocktail Book'. Originally made with Scotch whisky but perhaps not so silent with rock 'n' roll Tennessee whiskey.

SILENT THIRD 🔑

★★★★☆

Glass: Martini
Garnish: Lemon zest twist
Method: SHAKE all ingredients with ice and fine strain into chilled glass.

1½ shots	Dewar's 12yo Scotch whisky
1 shot	De Kuyper Triple Sec
¾ shot	Freshly squeezed lemon juice
½ shot	Chilled water (omit if wet ice)

Origin: A classic cocktail first published in the 1937 Cafe Royal Cocktail book.
Comment: Basically a Sidecar made with Scotch in place of cognac.

SILK PANTIES

★★★☆☆

Glass: Martini
Garnish: Peach slice
Method: SHAKE all ingredients with ice and fine strain into chilled glass.

2	shots	Ketel One Vodka
1	shot	Peachtree peach schnapps
2	dash	Peach bitters (optional)

Origin: Created sometime in the 1980s.
Comment: This drink may be sweet but despite the silly name it is more serious than you might expect.

SILK ROAD

★★★★½

Glass: Coupe
Garnish: Grapefruit zest twist
Method: SHAKE all ingredients with ice and fine strain into chilled glass.

1½ shots	Rutte Dry Gin
⅓ shot	Bénédictine D.O.M. liqueur
⅓ shot	De Kuyper XO Apricot Brandy
½ shot	Freshly squeezed lime juice
½ shot	Sugar syrup (2 sugar to 1 water)
2 dash	Angostura Aromatic Bitters

Origin: Adapted from a drink created in 2012 by Timothy Carroll at Barrio North, London, England.
Comment: As the name suggests, the Silk Road harnesses the exotic herbs and spices found in the gin and Bénédictine to deliver a harmonious, flavoursome drink with a silky delivery.

SILK STOCKING COCKTAIL

★★★★★

Glass: Martini
Garnish: Dust with cinnamon powder
Method: SHAKE all ingredients with ice and fine strain into chilled glass.

2	shots	Patrón silver tequila
¾	shot	White crème de cacao liqueur
¼	shot	Pomegranate / grenadine syrup (2:1)
¾	shot	Single cream / half-and-half

Origin: A vintage classic. This recipe is from Ryan Chetiyawardana in 2009, who shared his recipe at the Cabinet Room, London during the finals of World Class.
Comment: So smooooooth but still retains a tequila bite and a hint of chocolate and fruit.

SILVER BRONX 🔑

★★★★☆

Glass: Martini
Garnish: Luxardo Maraschino cherry
Method: SHAKE all ingredients with ice and fine strain into chilled glass.

2	shots	Rutte Dry Gin
¼	shot	Martini Extra Dry vermouth
¼	shot	Martini Rosso vermouth
1	shot	Freshly squeezed orange juice
1	fresh	Egg white

Origin: A vintage cocktail adapted from the classic Bronx Cocktail, created in 1906 by Johnny Solon, a bartender at New York's Waldorf-Astoria Hotel, and named after the newly opened Bronx Zoo.
Comment: A Bronx made 'silver' by the addition of egg white.

SILVER BULLET

★★★★☆

Glass: Martini
Garnish: Lemon zest twist
Method: SHAKE all ingredients with ice and fine strain into chilled glass.

2	shots	Rutte Dry Gin
½	shot	Kümmel
½	shot	Freshly squeezed lemon juice
¼	shot	Sugar syrup (2 sugar to 1 water)
⅓	shot	Chilled water (omit if wet ice)

Origin: Thought to have been created in the 1920s.
Comment: Caraway and fennel flavour this unusual sweet 'n' sour drink.

SILVER FIZZ 🔑

★★★★☆

Glass: Collins (small 8oz)
Garnish: Lemon slice
Method: SHAKE first four ingredients with ice and strain into chilled glass (no ice). **TOP** with soda from siphon.

2	shots	Brandy, whisk(e)y, gin, rum etc.
1	shot	Freshly squeezed lemon or lime juice
½	shot	Sugar syrup (2 sugar to 1 water)
½	shot	Egg white
Top with	Soda from siphon

Origin: A mid 19th century classic.
Comment: I prefer my fizzes with the addition of egg white. Why not try a Derby Fizz, which combines spirits and liqueurs?

SILVER MARTINI

★★★½☆

Glass: Martini
Garnish: Luxardo Maraschino cherry
Method: SHAKE all ingredients with ice and fine strain into chilled glass.

1½	shots	Rutte Dry Gin
1½	shots	Martini Extra Dry vermouth
¼	shot	Luxardo Maraschino liqueur
2	dash	Angostura Orange Bitters

Origin: Adapted from a recipe in Harry Craddock's 1930 'Savoy Cocktail Book'.
Comment: Dry and aromatic - for serious imbibers only.

SIN CYN COCKTAIL (NEW)

★★★★★

Glass: Old-fashioned
Garnish: Orange zest twist
Method: POUR ingredients into ice-filled glass and lightly STIR.

1	shot	Speyside single malt whisky
1	shot	Cynar
1	shot	Martini Rosso vermouth

Origin: Created by Paul Dellevigne at the Red Owl Tavern, Philadelphia, USA.
Comment: A single malt whisky laced twist on a Boulevardier with Cynar replacing Campari.

Singapore Sling

Convention has it that the Singapore Sling was created sometime between 1899 and 1915 by Chinese-born Ngiam Tong Boon at the Long Bar in Raffles Hotel, Singapore.

Raffles Hotel is named after the colonial founder of Singapore, Sir Stamford Raffles, and was the Near East's ex-pat central. As Charles H. Baker Jr. wrote in his 1939 'Gentleman's Companion', "Just looking around the terrace porch we've seen Frank Buck, the Sultan of Johor, Aimee Semple McPherson, Somerset Maugham, Dick Halliburton, Doug Fairbanks, Bob Ripley, Ruth Elder and Walker Camp - not that this is any wonder". Raffles still sticks out of modern-day Singapore like a vast, colonial Christmas cake.

The first known reference to a sling in Singapore newspapers comes in 1897 and indeed a Gin Sling was a popular drink at the time. It is the red-pink colour that distinguishes the ingredients used in a Singapore Gin Sling and a 'Pink Sling is mentioned in a Singapore newspaper in 1903.

The weight of evidence suggests that it was indeed Chinese-born Ngiam Tong Boon who created the Singapore Sling while working at the Long Bar at Raffles Hotel, so this dates the drinks invention sometime between 1899, when Boon started work at the hotel after its expansion, and 1915, when Boon died after leaving the hotel to travel back to Hainan, China.

So there is little controversy as to who created the Singapore Sling, where he created it and (roughly) when, but there is huge debate over the original name and ingredients.

Early bar books include recipes for both Singapore Slings and Straits Slings – Singapore was part of the British cluster of colonies which in 1836 was grouped with Penang and Malacca to form the Straits Settlements and it seems certain that Boon's drink was similarly named the 'Straits Sling'. In the Long Bar itself it seems

likely that people simply ordered a 'Gin Sling' and were served Boon's 'house' version of the drink.

The name appears to have changed sometime between 1922, when Robert Vermeire describes the Straits Sling as a "well-known Singapore drink" in his 'Cocktails and How to Mix Them', and the early 1930s. In his 1930 'The Savoy Cocktail Book', Harry Craddock includes both the Singapore Sling and Straits Sling, the latter being closer to what we recognise today as being a Singapore Sling.

Singapore Sling
From Harry Craddock's 1930 Savoy Cocktail Book
' "The Juice of ¼ Lemon
¼ Dry Gin.
½ Cherry Brandy.
Shake well and strain into medium size glass, and fill with soda water. Add 1 lump ice."'

Straits Sling
From Harry Craddock's 1930 Savoy Cocktail Book
' (for 6 people)
"Place in a shaker 4 glasses of Gin, 1 glass of Bénédictine, 1 glass of Cherry Brandy, the Juice of 2 Lemons, a teaspoon of Angostura Bitters, and one of Orange Bitters. Shake sufficiently, and serve in large glasses, filled up with Soda water."'

Noel Coward, who first visited Raffles in 1930, records drinking simply "gin slings" and it appears the drink most widely known as a Singapore Sling was originally a classic gin sling with cherry brandy and optional Bénédictine D.O.M. liqueur.

The operators of the modern day Raffles Hotel claim the original recipe is as follows and this is printed on the hotel's menus and hand-out cards.

Raffles Hotel Singapore Sling "original recipe"
' 15 ml Heering Cherry liqueur
30 ml Gin
7.5 ml Cointreau triple sec
7.5 ml Bénédictine D.O.M.
15 ml Lime juice
120 ml Pineapple juice
10 ml Grenadine
1 dash Angostura aromatic bitters'

The hotel was occupied by invading Japanese in 1942 and Allied Forces used it as a transit camp for prisoners of war in 1945, so it is not surprising that no record of Boon's original recipe survives. Indeed, the hotel's only source for the recipe they tout as being the original is a note scrawled by a visitor to the bar in 1936 after asking one of the bartenders how to make the drink. If this was the bar's standard or original spec is far from certain. It's also worth mentioning that a soda called Holy Joe's Singapore Sling was sold in the USA around the same time.

It was almost 40 years after the inquisitive drinker recorded this recipe that manager Roberto Pregarz took over as GM of Raffles and set about re-launching what had become a tired hotel as a luxurious landmark with the Singapore Sling part of a successful PR campaign. Sceptics to the authenticity of this recipe, particularly the inclusion of pineapple juice and grenadine, argue that pink, fruity Tiki-style drinks were fashionable at the time of the re-launch (1970s) and these ingredients could have been added to Boon's original recipe to make the Singapore Sling better suited to the tastes of the day. Further, while pineapple grows in Singapore, oranges were imported so pineapple could have been added to increase the drink's profitability.

The hotel counters such claims with a statement they attained from Ngiam Dee Saun, Boon's nephew, confirming that the Tiki-style recipe was indeed his uncle's 60 year old recipe. He happened to work at Raffles at the time so arguably had a vested interest.

Pink gin slings could have been ubiquitous in early 20th century Singapore and Boon may have created his own version by simply adding grenadine and pineapple juice, the latter also appears in his Million Dollar Cocktail. However, the equal-parts recipe recorded by globetrotting Charles H. Baker in his 1939 The Gentleman's Companion omits both grenadine and pineapple juice. He wrote of the Singapore Sling:

"The original formula is 1/3 each of dry gin, cherry brandy and Bénédictine; shake it for a moment, or stir it in a bar glass, with 2 fairly large lumps of ice to chill. Turn into a small 10 oz highball glass with one lump of ice left in and fill up to individual taste with chilled club soda. Garnish with the spiral peel of 1 green lime. In other ports in the Orient drinkers often use C & C ginger ale instead of soda, or even stone bottle ginger beer."

While contemporary sources are clear that it was cherry brandy that distinguishes the Singapore Sling from other kinds of gin sling, a great debate rages over the type of cherry brandy used. Was it a cherry 'brandy' liqueur and if so was Cherry Heering the brand used, as stated by Raffles. Or was it actually a cherry eau de vie (Kirschwasser)? This conjecture is partly based on Robert Vermeire's 1922 recipe for Straits Sling which calls for "dry cherry brandy" while in his 1948 Fine Art of Mixing Drinks, David A. Embury calls for "Cherry Brandy (Kirsch)". (Neither recipe features either grenadine or pineapple juice.)

Almost all historic and modern Singapore/Straits Sling recipes call for Bénédictine liqueur and it's worth mentioning they are referring to Bénédictine D.O.M. rather than the Bénédictine & Brandy (B&B) version now popular in the U.S. which was not launched until 1938.

For years it was hard to take any reference by Raffles to the original Singapore Sling recipe seriously as the hotel's famous Long Bar made its Singapore Slings using a premix, also sold in packets in its gift shop. Incidentally, the Long Bar itself was relocated from the lobby to the first floor of the then newly built shopping arcade in 1991. Thankfully Richard Gillam, a British bartender living in Singapore was instrumental in Raffles abandoning the pre-mix in favour of freshly made Singapore Slings. So since 2012 the hotel has made Singapore Slings according to the recipe it describes as the original. However, in our experience, they are fruity, sweet and best avoided. Sadly today's Long Bar is something of a tourist trap rather than a bar with real substance.

SINGAPORE SLING (BAKER'S FORMULA)

★★★★☆

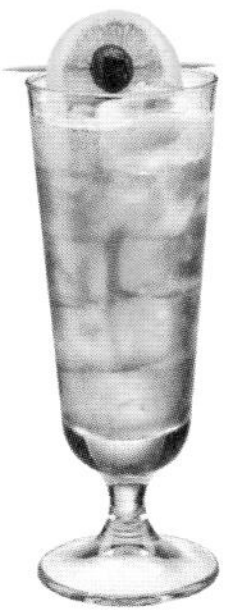

Glass: Collins
Garnish: Lemon slice & cherry on stick (sail)
Method: **SHAKE** first three ingredients with ice and strain into ice-filled glass. **TOP** with soda, lightly stir and serve with straws.

2 shots Old Tom gin
½ shot Bénédictine D.O.M. liqueur
½ shot Cherry Heering Liqueur
Top with Soda (club soda)

Comment: Lacks the citrus of other Singapore Slings but the strength of the gin and dilution cuts and so balances the sweetness of the liqueurs.

SINGAPORE SLING (DIFFORD'S RECIPE) (NEW)

★★★★☆

Glass: Sling
Garnish: Lemon slice & cherry on stick (sail)
Method: **SHAKE** first nine ingredients with ice and strain into ice-filled glass. **TOP** with soda and lightly stir.

1½ shots Rutte Dry Gin
⅓ shot Cherry Heering Liqueur
⅕ shot Bénédictine D.O.M. liqueur
⅕ shot De Kuyper Triple Sec
½ shot Fresh pressed pineapple juice
1 shot Freshly squeezed lemon juice
⅛ shot Sugar syrup (2 sugar to 1 water)
1 dash Angostura Aromatic Bitters
1 dash Angostura Orange Bitters
Top with Soda (club soda)

Comment: This doesn't follow classic 'Singapore Sling' proportions or ingredients, nor does it follow what the modern day Raffles day hotel claims is the original formula, but it steals elements from all of these to produce a tall, fruity, balanced cocktail.

SINGAPORE SLING (RAFFLES FORMULA)

★★★☆☆

Glass: Sling
Garnish: Lemon slice & cherry on stick (sail)
Method: **SHAKE** first eight ingredients with ice and strain into ice-filled glass. **TOP** with soda, lightly stir and serve with straws.

1 shot Rutte Dry Gin
½ shot Cherry Heering Liqueur
¼ shot Bénédictine D.O.M. liqueur
¼ shot De Kuyper Triple Sec
2½ shots Fresh pressed pineapple juice
½ shot Freshly squeezed lime juice
¼ shot Pomegranate / grenadine syrup (2:1)
1 dash Angostura Aromatic Bitters
Top with Soda (club soda)

Comment: Tangy and very fruity.

SINGAPORE SLING (USING OLD TOM GIN)

★★★★☆

Glass: Sling
Garnish: Lemon slice & cherry on stick (sail)
Method: **SHAKE** first six ingredients with ice and strain into ice-filled glass. **TOP** with soda and lightly stir.

2 shots Old Tom gin
½ shot Bénédictine D.O.M. liqueur
½ shot Cherry Heering Liqueur
1 shot Freshly squeezed lemon juice
2 dash Angostura Aromatic Bitters
2 dash Angostura Orange Bitters
Top with Soda (club soda)

Comment: Slightly on the dry and sour side, this is decidedly more complex than most Singapore Sling recipes.

SIR CHARLES PUNCH

★★★★☆

Glass: Old-fashioned
Garnish: Orange zest twist
Method: **STIR** all ingredients with ice and strain into ice-filled glass.

1 shot Tawny port
½ shot Martell VSOP Médaillon cognac
½ shot Grand Marnier Cordon Rouge
⅛ shot Sugar syrup (2 sugar to 1 water)

Origin: Adapted from a recipe in the 1949 edition of 'Esquire's Handbook for Hosts', which suggests serving it at Christmas.
Comment: Short but full of personality.

SIR THOMAS

★★★★☆

Glass: Martini
Garnish: Luxardo Maraschino cherry
Method: **STIR** all ingredients with ice and strain into chilled glass.

2 shots Bourbon whiskey
½ shot De Kuyper Triple Sec
½ shot Cherry Heering Liqueur
½ shot Martini Rosso vermouth

Origin: Created in 2005 by Tom Ward, London, England.
Comment: Akin to a fruit laced Sweet Manhattan.

SIR WALTER COCKTAIL

★★★☆☆

Glass: Martini
Garnish: Lemon zest twist
Method: SHAKE all ingredients with ice and fine strain into chilled glass.

¾	shot	Bacardi Carta Blanca light rum
¾	shot	Martell VSOP Médaillon cognac
¼	shot	Grand Marnier Cordon Rouge
¼	shot	Pomegranate / grenadine syrup (2:1)
¾	shot	Freshly squeezed lemon juice
2	dash	Angostura Aromatic Bitters

Origin: Adapted from Victor Bergeron's 'Trader Vic's Bartender's Guide' (1972 revised edition).
Comment: This blend of rum and cognac has more than a hint of Tiki fruitiness.

SKETCHER'S PET

★★★★½

Glass: Flute
Garnish: Orange slice
Method: SHAKE all ingredients with ice and fine strain into chilled glass.

2 shots Ketel One Vodka
1 shot Freshly squeezed orange juice
¾ shot De Kuyper XO Apricot Brandy
¼ shot Passion fruit syrup
½ shot Single cream / half-and-half

Origin: Created in January 2010 by Zdenek Kestanek at Quo Vadis, London, England for Petek Sketcher.
Comment: A sweet creamy, fruity dessert style cocktail.

SKID ROW

★★★★☆

Glass: Coupe
Garnish: Orange zest twist (flamed)
Method: STIR all ingredients with ice and strain into chilled glass.

2	shots	Rutte Old Simon oude jenever
½	shot	De Kuyper XO Apricot Brandy
½	shot	Yellow Chartreuse liqueur
1	dash	Angostura Aromatic Bitters
1	dash	Angostura Orange Bitters

Origin: Adapted from a drink created in 2009 by Eric Alperin at The Varnish, Los Angeles, USA.
Comment: Complex and strong in alcohol, bitter-sweet with apricot liqueur and amaro and Dutch jenever.

SLEEPY HOLLOW

★★★★☆

Glass: Old-fashioned
Garnish: Lemon slice
Method: Lightly MUDDLE mint in base of shaker (just to bruise). Add other ingredients, SHAKE with ice and fine strain into glass filled with crushed ice. Serve with straws.

10	fresh	Mint leaves
2	shots	Rutte Dry Gin
½	shot	De Kuyper XO Apricot Brandy
1	shot	Freshly squeezed lemon juice
½	shot	Sugar syrup (2 sugar to 1 water)

Origin: An adaptation of a drink created in the early 1930s and named after Washington Irving's novel and its enchanted valley with ghosts, goblins and headless horseman.
Comment: Hints of lemon and mint with gin and apricot fruit. Very refreshing.

SLING (GENERIC NAME)

★★★★☆

Glass: Sling
Garnish: Lemon slice
Method: SHAKE first three ingredients with ice and strain into ice-filled glass. TOP with soda or ginger ale.

2	shots	Brandy, whisk(e)y, gin, rum etc.
½	shot	Freshly squeezed lemon juice
¼	shot	Sugar syrup (2 sugar to 1 water)
Top with	Soda (club soda) (or ginger ale)

Origin: The word 'Sling' comes from the German 'schlingen', meaning 'to swallow', and Slings based on a spirit mixed with sugar and water were popularly drunk in the late 1800s.

Slings are similar to Toddies and like Toddies can be served hot. (Toddies, however, are never served cold.) The main difference between a Toddy and a Sling is that Slings are not flavoured by the addition of spices. Also, Toddies tend to be made with plain water, while Slings are charged with water, soda water or ginger ale.

The earliest known definition of 'cocktail' describes it as a bittered sling.
Comment: Sugar balances the citrus juice, the spirit fortifies and the carbonate lengthens.

SLOANE SQUARE COCKTAIL (NEW)

★★★★½

Glass: Coupe
Garnish: Orange zest twist
Method: STIR all ingredients with ice and strain into chilled glass.

2	shots	Oban 14yo malt whisky
¾	shot	Patrón reposado tequila
⅔	shot	Bénédictine D.O.M. liqueur
2	dash	Angostura Orange Bitters

Origin: An unusual pairing of Highland single malt scotch and tequila with herbal complexity courtesy of Bénédictine liqueur, freshened with orange zestiness.
Comment: Adapted from a 2013 recipe by Paige McCune of aroundortwo.com

SLOE GIN FIZZ

★★★½☆

Glass: Sling
Garnish: Lemon & cucumber slices
Method: SHAKE first five ingredients with ice and strain into ice-filled glass. **TOP** with soda, stir and serve with straws.

1	shot	Rutte Dry Gin
1½	shots	Sloe Gin liqueur
1	shot	Freshly squeezed lime juice
¼	shot	Sugar syrup (2 sugar to 1 water)
½	fresh	Egg white
Top with		Soda (club soda)

Comment: A sour gin fizz with dark, rich sloe gin.

SLOE MOTION

★★★½☆

Glass: Flute
Garnish: Lemon zest twist
Method: POUR liqueur into chilled glass and **TOP** with champagne.

| ¾ | shot | Sloe Gin liqueur |
| Top with | | G.H. Mumm Cordon Rouge Champagne |

Comment: Sloe gin proves to be an excellent complement to champagne.

THE SLOPE

★★★★★

Glass: Coupe
Garnish: Dried apricot on rim
Method: STIR all ingredients with ice and strain into chilled glass.

2½	shot	Straight rye whiskey
¾	shot	Punt E Mes
¼	shot	De Kuyper XO Apricot brandy
1	dash	Angostura Aromatic bitters

Comment: Stirred, strong and boozy - Manhattan/Brooklyn-like. Rye whisky-based with aromatised wine complexity and apricot brandy adding a touch of fruity sweetness. This riff on a Manhattan is a late night sipper.
Origin: Created in 2009 by Julie Reiner at Clover Club, Brooklyn, NY, USA,

SLOPPY JOE

★★★★☆

Glass: Martini
Garnish: Lime wedge
Method: SHAKE all ingredients with ice and fine strain into chilled glass.

1	shot	Bacardi Carta Blanca light rum
¼	shot	De Kuyper Triple Sec
1	shot	Martini Extra Dry vermouth
1	shot	Freshly squeezed lime juice
½	shot	Sugar syrup (2 sugar to 1 water)
¼	shot	Pomegranate / grenadine syrup (2:1)

Comment: Nicely balances sweet and sourness.

SLOW COMFORTABLE SCREW

★★★★☆

Glass: Collins
Garnish: Orange slice
Method: SHAKE all ingredients with ice and strain into ice-filled glass.

1½	shots	Ketel One Vodka
½	shot	Sloe Gin liqueur
½	shot	Southern Comfort liqueur
3½	shots	Freshly squeezed orange juice

Comment: A Screwdriver (vodka and orange) with sloe gin and Southern Comfort. Long and refreshing. Spiked fresh orange juice with hints of sloe berry fruit and Southern Comfort.

SLOW COMFORTABLE SCREW AGAINST THE WALL

★★★★½

Glass: Collins
Garnish: Orange slice
Method: SHAKE first 4 ingredients with ice and strain into ice-filled glass. **FLOAT** Galliano.

1½	shots	Ketel One Vodka
½	shot	Sloe Gin liqueur
½	shot	Southern Comfort liqueur
3½	shots	Freshly squeezed orange juice
¼	shot	Galliano L'Autentico liqueur

Comment: Galliano adds the wall (as in Harvey Wallbanger) and some herbal peppermint to this Slow Comfortable Screw.

SLOW SCREW

★★★★☆

Glass: Collins
Garnish: Orange slice
Method: SHAKE all ingredients with ice and strain into ice-filled glass.

1½	shots	Ketel One Vodka
¾	shot	Sloe Gin liqueur
3½	shots	Freshly squeezed orange juice

Comment: A Screwdriver (vodka and orange juice) with sloe gin. Long and refreshing.

SLUTTY MARY

★★★★½

Glass: Collins
Garnish: Salt/pepper rim and garnish with lime, coriander and celery.
Method: ROLL (turn shaker over repeatedly rather than shake) all ingredients with ice and strain into ice-filled glass.
To make paste, blend:
1 can of La Costena Chipotle Chili in Adobo Sauce
2 large bunches of fresh coriander
1 tablespoon of salt
1 tablespoon of black pepper
100ml Agavero tequila liqueur
500ml Worcestershire sauce

2	spoon	Homemade paste
2	shots	Patrón silver tequila
½	shot	Freshly squeezed lime juice
3	shots	Tomato juice

Origin: Adapted from a drink created by Carl Wrangel at the Oak Room, Copenhagen, Denmark.
Comment: A Bloody Maria given extra spice with chipotle chilli.

SMARTINI

★★★★☆

Glass: Martini
Garnish: Smarties
Method: **SHAKE** all ingredients with ice and fine strain into chilled glass.

2 shots Ketel One Vodka
1 shot White crème de cacao liqueur
¼ shot Sugar syrup (2 sugar to 1 water)
¾ shot Chilled water (omit if wet ice)
3 dash Angostura Orange Bitters

Comment: Citrus with a crispy chocolate edge. A sweetie.

SMOKE AND MIRRORS #1

★★★★½

Glass: Coupe
Garnish: Orange zest twist
Method: **POUR** ingredients into mixing glass, **SMOKE** (with applewood smoke), then **STIR** with ice and strain into chilled glass.

1½ shots Speyside single malt whisky
½ shot Bénédictine D.O.M. liqueur
½ shot Byrrh Grand Quinquina
3 dash Angostura Aromatic Bitters

Origin: Created in 2011 by Erik Lorincz at the Savoy's American Bar, London, England where this drink is 'smoked' into a decanter in front of the customer and served at the table.
Comment: His aperitif-style cocktail has subtle smoky peatiness with herbal complexity provided by Bénédictine and Byrrh.

SMOKE AND MIRRORS #2

★★★★½

Glass: Coupe
Garnish: Lemon zest twist
Method: **STIR** all ingredients with ice and strain into chilled glass.

2 shots Islay single malt Scotch whisky
¾ shot De Kuyper XO Apricot Brandy
¼ shot Amaro liqueur
2 dash Angostura Aromatic Bitters

Origin: Adapted from a drink discovered in 2010 at Raines Law Rooms, New York City, USA.
Comment: A hardcore but sublime drink. Beware - accurate proportions make or break this drink.

SMOKE OF SCOTLAND

★★★★☆

Glass: Martini
Garnish: Grapefruit zest twist (flamed)
Method: **STIR** all ingredients with ice and strain into chilled glass.

2 shots Islay single malt Scotch whisky
½ shot Martini Extra Dry vermouth
½ shot St-Germain elderflower liqueur
⅛ shot Cynar

Origin: Created in 2007 by Vincenzo Marianella at Providence, Los Angeles, USA.
Comment: Smoky, with floral and tropical fruit notes from the elderflower liqueur and added complexity from the vermouth and Cynar.

SMOKED APPLETINI

★★★★☆

Glass: Martini
Garnish: None
Method: **STIR** all ingredients with ice. Smoke with apple and pecan (or other wood) and fine strain into chilled glass.

1½ shots 42 Below Manuka Honey Vodka
½ shot Islay single malt Scotch whisky
½ shot Taylor's Velvet Falernum liqueur
1 shot Pressed apple juice
⅓ shot Freshly squeezed lemon juice

Origin: Adapted from a drink created in 2012 by Michael Stringer, Flip-It! Mixology, London.
Comment: Apple and honey with hints of lemon and clove spice.

SMOKED MAPLE

★★★★½

Glass: Coupe
Garnish: Orange zest twist
Method: **SHAKE** all ingredients with ice and fine strain into chilled glass.

2 shots Islay single malt Scotch whisky
¼ shot De Kuyper XO Apricot Brandy
1 spoon Maple syrup
¼ shot Freshly squeezed orange juice

Origin: Adapted from a cocktail discovered in 2009 at Dylanbar, Dublin, Ireland.
Comment: This smoky cocktail won't be to everybody's taste but an Islay malt fan will approve.

SMOKED SALTY SOUR (NEW)

★★★★☆

Glass: Old-fashioned
Garnish: Lemon zest twist
Method: **SHAKE** all ingredients with ice and fine strain into ice-filled glass.

1 shot Dewar's 12yo Scotch whisky
1 shot Islay single malt Scotch whisky
½ shot Green Chartreuse liqueur
1 shot Freshly squeezed lemon juice
½ shot Light muscovado sugar syrup (2 sugar to 1 water)
1 dash Peychaud's aromatic bitters
1 pinch Salt
½ fresh Egg white

Origin: Adapted from a drink created in 2014 by Dennis Wolf at Bar Raclette, Puerto Rico.
Comment: Salty Islay peaty malt and Green Chartreuse influence this Scotch whisky sour.

SMOKESTACK LIGHTNING

★★★★½

Glass: Coupe
Garnish: Lime wedge
Method: **SHAKE** all ingredients with ice and fine strain with ice.

1¾ shots Patrón reposado tequila
¼ shot Islay single malt Scotch whisky
½ shot Agave syrup
¾ shot Freshly squeezed lime juice

Origin: Created in 2009 by yours truly for Tales of the Cocktail 2009.
Comment: Margarita-like with a wisp of Islay smoke.

SMOKEY BOAT (NEW)

★★★★½

Glass: Coupe
Garnish: Dried apple slice
Method: **SHAKE** all ingredients with ice and fine strain into chilled glass.

1	shot	**Islay single malt Scotch whisky**
1	shot	**Calvados brandy**
1½	shots	**Pressed apple juice**
⅓	shot	**Vanilla sugar syrup**
2	dash	**Peychaud's aromatic bitters**

Origin: Adapted from a drink created in 2014 by Andrea Buttier, an Italian bartender from Bologna working at The Loft, Clapham Common. Andrea originally used Laphroaig 10 year old for his malt with equal parts calvados, 2 shots apple juice, 2/3rd shot vanilla syrup and 1 dash peychards.
Comment: Andrea created this drink "for enjoying the flavour of smoky whisky with calvados adding to apple fruitiness." The amount of Peychaud's used makes or breaks this drink so beware of how generous your 'dash' is.

SMOKEY JOE

★★★★★

Glass: Coupe
Garnish: Beef flavoured hula hoops
Method: **STIR** all ingredients with ice and strain into chilled glass.

2	shots	**Junmai ginjō sake**
½	shot	**Martell VSOP Médaillon cognac**
¼	shot	**Islay single malt Scotch whisky**
1	shot	**Sauternes dessert wine**

Origin: Created in August 2008 by yours truly at the Cabinet Room, London, England.
Comment: Sake sweetened with Sauternes and flavoured with cognac and Islay whisky.

SMOKY OLD BASTARD

★★★★½

Glass: Old-fashioned
Garnish: Lemon zest twist
Method: **STIR** bourbon, tea bag and four ice cubes in glass for 60 seconds. Remove tea bag, add maple syrup and bitters, and **STIR** some more. Add more ice and the rest of the bourbon. **STIR** lots more and add more ice.

2	shot	**Bourbon whiskey**
1	bag	**Lapsang Souchong tea**
¼	shot	**Maple syrup**
2	dash	**Boker's bitters**

Comment: Lapsang souchong flavours and dry tannins are balanced by maple syrup and fortified with bourbon.
Origin: Created in 2011 by Craig Toone at Glovers Bar, Merseyside, England who says of his drink, "Smoky" obviously refers to the distinctive tea flavour and the bastard refers to the bastardisation of the classic drink" [Old Fashioned].

SMOKIN ROSE

★★★★☆

Glass: Martini
Garnish: Luxardo Maraschino cherry
Method: **SHAKE** all ingredients with ice and strain into chilled glass.

2	shots	**Bacardi Carta Blanca light rum**
½	shot	**Rose petal liqueur**
⅛	shot	**Islay single malt Scotch whisky**
⅛	shot	**Sugar syrup (2 sugar to 1 water)**
¼	shot	**Pressed apple juice**
½	shot	**Freshly squeezed lime juice**
1	dash	**Angostura Aromatic Bitters**

Origin: Created in 2008 by yours truly at the Cabinet Room, London, England.
Comment: A Daiquiri riff with Islay malt, rose petal liqueur and vanilla.

SMOKIN' HOT PALOMA (NEW)

★★★★☆

Glass: Collins
Garnish: Cinnamon & chili salt rim
Method: **SHAKE** first 5 ingredients with ice and strain into ice-filled glass. **TOP** with grapefruit soda.

1 shot Del Maguey VIDA mezcal
¾ shot Chili liqueur
1½ shots Freshly squeezed pink grapefruit juice
½ shot Freshly squeezed lime juice
¼ shot Agave syrup
Top with Grapefruit Soda

Origin: Adapted from a drink discovered in 2015 at Building on Bond, Brooklyn, NYC, UK
Comment: Mezcal provides a subtle hint of smokiness while chili liqueur adds hot spice. The other guests to Paloma's party bring fruity honeyed sweetness.

SMOKIN' PALOMA (NEW)

★★★★☆

Glass: Collins
Garnish: Cinnamon & chili salt rim
Method: **SHAKE** first 4 ingredients with ice and strain into ice-filled glass. **TOP** with grapefruit soda.

1½	shots	**Del Maguey VIDA mezcal**
1½	shots	**Freshly squeezed pink grapefruit juice**
½	shot	**Freshly squeezed lime juice**
⅓	shot	**Agave syrup**
Top with		**Grapefruit Soda**

Origin: Adapted from a drink discovered in 2015 at Building on Bond, Brooklyn, NY, USA.
Comment: Mezcal adds subtle smoky complexity to a classic Paloma.

SMOKING STALLION

★★★★☆

Glass: Martini
Garnish: Dill sprig
Method: STIR all ingredients with ice and fine strain into chilled glass.

1	sprig	Fresh dill
2	shots	Ketel One Vodka
½	shot	Martini Extra Dry vermouth
⅛	shot	Islay single malt Scotch whisky
⅛	shot	Maple syrup

Origin: Created in 2008 by Bart Van Ween at a Dutch World Class.
Comment: Subtly herbal and dry with a hint of whisky smokiness.

SMOKY APPLE MARTINI

★★★½☆

Glass: Martini
Garnish: Luxardo Maraschino cherry
Method: SHAKE all ingredients with ice and fine strain into chilled glass.

2½	shots	Dewar's 12yo Scotch whisky
1	shot	Sour apple liqueur
½	shot	Rose's lime cordial

Comment: Scotch adds some peaty character to this twist on the Sour Apple Martini.

SMOKY MARTINI #1

★★★★★

Glass: Martini
Garnish: Olive on stick
Method: STIR all ingredients with ice and strain into chilled glass.

2	shots	Rutte Dry Gin
¼	shot	Islay single malt Scotch whisky
½	shot	Martini Extra Dry vermouth

Comment: Smoky Islay malt combines with London dry gin to give a smoky, almost sweet character to a traditional Dry Martini.

SMOKY MOCHA SPRITZ (NEW)

★★★★☆

Glass: Old-fashioned
Garnish: Two segments of dark Toblerone chocolate on the rim
Method: POUR all ingredients into ice-filled glass and stir.

3	shots	Prosecco sparkling wine
1	shot	White crème de cacao liqueur
1½	shots	Beavertown Smog Rocket Smoked Porter

Origin: Created on 30th January 2014 by yours truly at the Cabinet Room, London, England.
Comment: Coffee and chocolate flavours with a faint smokiness, invigorated with sparkling wine.

SMOKY TEARS COCKTAIL (NEW)

★★★★½

Glass: Coupe
Garnish: Grapefruit wedge
Method: SHAKE all ingredients with ice and strain into chilled glass.

1½	shots	Del Maguey VIDA mezcal
1½	shots	Skinos Mastiha
¾	shot	Freshly squeezed pink grapefruit juice
⅛	shot	Sugar syrup (2 sugar to 1 water)

Comment: Best described as being a mezcal, mastiha and pink grapefruit Margarita. It's a great combo. Mastiha freshness with a hint of smoky mezcal is balanced by slightly acidic pink grapefruit juice.

SMOKY WHISKY SOUR (NEW)

★★★★½

Glass: Old-fashioned
Garnish: Lemon zest twist & Angostura bitters drawn across foam.
Method: SHAKE all ingredients with ice and strain back into shaker. **DRY SHAKE** (without ice) and strain into ice-filled glass.

1	shot	Islay single malt Scotch whisky
1	shot	Dewar's 12yo Scotch whisky
1	shot	Freshly squeezed lemon juice
¾	shot	Maple syrup
1	dash	Angostura Aromatic Bitters
½	fresh	Egg white

Origin: Created in November 2014 by yours truly at the Cabinet Room, London, England.
Comment: Islay single malt and maple syrup add a distinctive smoky character to this otherwise classic Scotch Whisky Sour.

SMOOTH & CREAMY

★★★★☆

Glass: Martini
Garnish: Dust with grated nutmeg
Method: SHAKE all ingredients with ice and fine strain into chilled glass.

1½	shots	Bacardi Carta Oro rum
1	shot	Coconut rum liqueur
¼	shot	Crème de banane liqueur
¾	shot	Single cream / half-and-half
¾	shot	Milk

Comment: Creamy and moreish.

SNAKEBITE

★★★☆☆

Glass: Collins
Garnish: None
Method: POUR lager into glass and **TOP** with cider.

| ½ | fill glass with Budweiser Budvar |
| Top with | Medium dry cider |

Comment: The students special.

456

SNOOD MURDEKIN

★★★☆☆

Glass: Shot
Garnish: None
Method: SHAKE first three ingredients with ice and strain into chilled glass. FLOAT cream over drink.

½	shot	Ketel One Vodka
½	shot	Chambord Liqueur
½	shot	Coffee liqueur
¼	shot	Single cream / half-and-half

Origin: Created in the late 90s by Dick Bradsell at Detroit, London, England for Karin Wiklund and named for the sad, flute-playing Moomin Troll.
Comment: Moreish combination of coffee and raspberries topped with cream.

SNOOPY

★★★★☆

Glass: Old-fashioned
Garnish: Orange zest twist
Method: SHAKE all ingredients with ice and fine strain into ice-filled glass.

1½	shots	Bourbon whiskey
¾	shot	Grand Marnier Cordon Rouge
1	shot	Galliano L'Autentico liqueur
½	shot	Campari Bitter
¼	shot	Freshly squeezed lemon juice

Comment: Tangy fruit with a balancing hint of citrus and bitterness.

SNOW WHITE DAIQUIRI 🔑

★★★★☆

Glass: Martini
Garnish: Pineapple wedge
Method: SHAKE all ingredients with ice and strain back into shaker. Then DRY SHAKE (without ice) and fine strain into chilled glass.

2	shots	Bacardi Carta Blanca light rum
½	shot	Fresh pressed pineapple juice
½	shot	Freshly squeezed lime juice
¼	shot	Sugar syrup (2 sugar to 1 water)
½	fresh	Egg white

Origin: My yours truly adaptation of a classic cocktail.
Comment: The pineapple and egg white ensure that this delightful Daiquiri has an appropriately white frothy head.

SNOWBALL

★★★★☆

Glass: Collins
Garnish: Lime zest twist or lime slice
Method: POUR lemonade and lime juice into ice-filled glass and then the advocaat which will mostly sink though the other ingredients. Lightly stir to integrate while retaining the lemonade's carbonation.

3½	shots	Lemonade (English-style)
¾	shot	Freshly squeezed lime juice
2	shots	Warninks Advocaat liqueur

Origin: Thought to have originated in Britain in the late 1940s or early 1950s, reaching its peak of popularity in the 1970s.
Comment: Fresh lime juice and lemonade freshens and invigorates creamy advocaat.

SNOWBALL (DIFFORD'S RECIPE) (NEW)

★★★★★

Glass: Flute
Garnish: Lime zest twist (discarded) & dust with chocolate powder
Method: POUR champagne into ice-filled glass. SHAKE last three ingredients with ice and strain over champagne.

2	shots	G.H. Mumm Cordon Rouge Champagne
1	shot	Romate Fino sherry
½	shot	Rose's lime cordial
2	shots	Warninks Advocaat liqueur

Origin: A riff on the classic Snowball by yours truly, London, England.
Comment: Rich thick and creamy egg yolk freshened with dry sherry, zesty lime cordial and invigorated with champagne.

SNOWFALL COCKTAIL

★★★★★

Glass: Martini
Garnish: Vanilla pod
Method: Cut vanilla pod along its length and MUDDLE in base of shaker. Add other ingredients, SHAKE with ice and fine strain into chilled glass.

¼	whole	Vanilla pod
1½	shots	Vanilla infused Ketel One vodka
1½	shots	Single cream / half-and-half
½	shot	Sugar syrup (2 sugar to 1 water)

Origin: Originally called a Snowfall Martini and discovered in 2002 at Lot 61, New York City, USA.
Comment: An alcoholic version of a vanilla milkshake with tiny black specs from the vanilla.

SNYDER MARTINI

★★★★☆

Glass: Martini
Garnish: Orange zest twist
Method: SHAKE all ingredients with ice and fine strain into chilled glass.

2	shots	Rutte Dry Gin
1	shot	Martini Extra Dry vermouth
¼	shot	Grand Marnier Cordon Rouge

Origin: Adapted from a recipe in Harry Craddock's 1930 'Savoy Cocktail Book'.
Comment: Dry, hardcore and yet mellow.

SO-SO MARTINI

★★★★☆

Glass: Martini
Garnish: Apple slice
Method: SHAKE all ingredients with ice and fine strain into chilled glass.

1	shot	Rutte Dry Gin
1	shot	Martini Extra Dry vermouth
½	shot	Calvados brandy
½	shot	Pomegranate / grenadine syrup (2:1)

Origin: Adapted from a recipe in Harry Craddock's 1930 'Savoy Cocktail Book'. Harry McElhone's 1929 'ABC of Cocktails' credits this drink to "Mr P. Soso, the popular manager of Kit-Kat Club, London."
Comment: This beautifully balanced, appley drink is so much more than so-so.

SOCIALITE

★★★☆☆

Glass: Old-fashioned
Garnish: None
Method: SHAKE all ingredients with ice and strain into glass filled with crushed ice

1	shot	Grand Marnier Cordon Rouge
1	shot	Vanilla infused Ketel One vodka
1	shot	Pallini Limoncello
1	shot	Freshly squeezed lemon juice
½	shot	Vanilla sugar syrup

Origin: Discovered in 2001 at Lab Bar, London, England.
Comment: Rich citrus with lashings of vanilla.

SODDEN GRAPE

★★★★☆

Glass: Martini
Garnish: White grapes
Method: MUDDLE grapes in base of shaker. Add other ingredients, **SHAKE** with ice and fine strain into chilled glass.

7	fresh	Seedless white grapes
2	shots	Zubrówka bison vodka
¾	shot	Icewine

Origin: Created in 2004 by yours truly, London, England.
Comment: A 'sod' is a piece of turf. Here 'sodden' refers to the Bison grass, the flavour of which combines well with the grapes and icewine.

SOL ARDIENTE

★★★★☆

Glass: Coupe
Garnish: Crushed red peppercorns
Method: MUDDLE peppercorns in base of shaker. Add next four ingredients, **SHAKE** with ice and fine strain into chilled glass. **TOP** with splash soda.

1	spoon	Pink peppercorns
2	shots	Bacardi Carta Blanca light rum
1	shot	Fresh pressed pineapple juice
1	shot	Freshly squeezed lime juice
½	shot	Sugar syrup (2 sugar to 1 water)
Top with		Soda (club soda)

Origin: Created in 2008 by Anthony Farrell, San-greal Bartending Ltd, Belfast, Northern Ireland. The name translates from Spanish as 'Burning Sun'.
Comment: Red pepper and pineapple influences this twisted Daiquiri.

SOLENT SUNSET

★★★☆☆

Glass: Collins
Garnish: Pineapple wedge & Luxardo Maraschino cherry
Method: SHAKE all ingredients with ice and strain into ice-filled glass.

2	shots	Pusser's Navy Rum (54.5%)
¼	shot	Pomegranate / grenadine syrup (2:1)
¾	shot	Freshly squeezed lime juice
3	shots	Fresh pressed pineapple juice

Comment: A naval style tropical rum punch for those occasional hot sunny days on the Solent (the stretch of sea which separates the Isle of Wight from mainland Britain).

SORREL RUM PUNCH

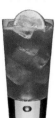

★★★★☆

Glass: Collins
Garnish: Lime wedge
Method: SHAKE all ingredients with ice and strain into glass filled with crushed ice. Serve with straws.

2¼	shots	White overproof rum
3	shots	Sorrelade (see sorrelade recipe)
¾	shot	Freshly squeezed lime juice
1½	shots	Sugar syrup (2 sugar to 1 water)

Origin: A classic Jamaican punch using the classic proportions of 'one of sour, two of sweet, three of strong and four of weak.'
Comment: This drink harnesses the flavour of sorrelade and combines it with the traditional strength and bitter sweetness of rum punch. Jamaica in a glass.

SORRELADE (MOCKTAIL)

★★★☆☆

Glass: Collins
Garnish: Lime wedge
Method: (Bulk recipe.) **SOAK** dried sorrel in water with ginger, ground cloves, and honey for 12 hours. Bring this mixture to the **BOIL** then leave to cool and **SOAK** for a further 12 hours, **STRAIN** and then keep refrigerated.

70	gram	Hibiscus Flower (Red) Petals
1¼	litre	Chilled water
30	gram	Fresh root ginger (thumbnail sized)
12	dried	Clove
3	spoon	Runny honey

Origin: Jamaican sorrel, also known by it's scientific name 'Hibiscus Sabdariffa', is a plant propagated for its red petals. In Jamaica these are used to make this refreshing drink. (Jamaican sorrel is not related to the English Garden herb of the same name.)
Comment: Sorrelade looks a little like cranberry juice and like cranberry juice has a bittersweet, slightly spicy taste.

SOUR (GENERIC NAME)

★★★☆☆

Glass: Old-fashioned
Garnish: Lemon slice & Luxardo Maraschino cherry on stick (sail)
Method: SHAKE all ingredients with ice and strain into ice-filled glass.

2	shots	Brandy, whisk(e)y, gin, rum etc.
1	shot	Freshly squeezed lemon juice
½	shot	Sugar syrup (2 sugar to 1 water)
3	dash	Angostura Aromatic Bitters
½	fresh	Egg white

Origin: Sours are aptly named drinks. Their flavour comes from either lemon or lime juice, which is balanced with sugar.

Sours can be based on practically any spirit but the bourbon based Whiskey Sour is by far the most popular. Many (including us) believe this drink is only properly made when smoothed with a little egg white.

Sours are served either straight-up in a sour glass (rather like a small flute) or on the rocks in an old-fashioned glass. They are traditionally garnished with a cherry and an orange slice, or sometimes a lemon slice.
Comment: This 4:2:8 formula is a tad sourer than the classic 3:4:8 which translates as: three quarter part of the sour ingredient (lemon juice), one part of the sweet ingredient (sugar syrup) and two parts of the strong ingredient (spirit). So if you find my formula too sour than best follow the classic proportions in future.

SOUR APPLE MARTINI #1 (POPULAR US VERSION)

★★★½☆

Glass: Martini
Garnish: Luxardo Maraschino cherry
Method: **SHAKE** all ingredients with ice and fine strain into chilled glass.

1½ shots Ketel One Vodka
1½ shots Sour apple liqueur
¼ shot Rose's lime cordial

Comment: A hugely popular drink across North America in the Noughties.

SOUR APPLE MARTINI (DELUXE U.S. VERSION)

★★★★½

Glass: Martini
Garnish: Apple slice
Method: **SHAKE** all ingredients with ice and fine strain into chilled glass.

2 shots Ketel One Vodka
1 shot Sour apple liqueur
½ shot Freshly squeezed lime juice
¼ shot Sugar syrup (2 sugar to 1 water)
½ fresh Egg white

Comment: A sophisticated version of a contemporary classic.

SOUR CHERRY SPRITZ (NEW)

★★★★☆

Glass: Rocks
Garnish: Cherry on drink
Method: **POUR** prosecco and liqueurs into glass. Add ice. Top with soda.

3 shots Prosecco sparkling wine
1 shot De Kuyper Triple Sec
1 shot Cherry Heering Liqueur
Top with Soda (club soda)

Origin: Created in 2013, this is a popular drink at Jamie's Italian Bars.
Comment: The name aptly describes the drink.

SOURISE

★★★★½

Glass: Coupe
Garnish: Raspberries
Method: **DRY SHAKE** all ingredients (without ice). **SHAKE** again with ice and fine strain into chilled glass.

5 fresh Raspberries
2 shots Martell VSOP Médaillon cognac
¼ shot Almond (orgeat) syrup
½ shot Freshly squeezed lemon juice
¼ shot Sugar syrup (2 sugar to 1 water)
½ shot Egg white

Origin: Created in 2010 by David Wondrich and named 'Sourise' after the French for 'smile'.
Comment: Almond, cognac and raspberry harmoniously sit together to flavour this sour-style cocktail.

SOURPUSS MARTINI

★★★★☆

Glass: Martini
Garnish: Physalis (cape gooseberry)
Method: **SHAKE** all ingredients with ice and fine strain into chilled glass.

1 shot Ketel One Citroen vodka
½ shot Midori Green Melon liqueur
½ shot Sour apple liqueur
2 shots Pressed apple juice

Origin: Created in 2001 by Colin 'Big Col' Crowden at Time, Leicester, England.
Comment: A lime-green, flavoursome cocktail that balances sweet and sour.

SOUTH BEACH

★★★★☆

Glass: Martini
Garnish: Orange zest twist
Method: **SHAKE** all ingredients with ice and fine strain into chilled glass.

1 shot Disaronno Originale amaretto
1 shot Campari Bitter
2½ shots Freshly squeezed orange juice
¼ shot Sugar syrup (2 sugar to 1 water)

Origin: Created in 1992 by Dale DeGroff, New York City, USA.
Comment: An unusual bittersweet combination with a strong orange and almond flavour.

SOUTH CHINA BREEZE

★★★★☆

Glass: Collins
Garnish: Orange slice
Method: **SHAKE** all ingredients with ice and strain into ice-filled glass.

2 shots Ketel One Vodka
1½ shots Lychee syrup (from tinned fruit)
3 shots Freshly squeezed pink grapefruit juice
3 dash Angostura Aromatic Bitters

Comment: Orange and grapefruit with an oriental influence by way of lychee.

STAR RATINGS EXPLAINED

★★★★★+	OUTSTANDING	★★★★★	EXCEPTIONAL
★★★★½	EXCELLENT	★★★★☆	RECOMMENDED
★★★½☆	COMMENDED	★★★☆☆	MEDIOCRE
★★½☆☆	DISAPPOINTING	★★☆☆☆	PRETTY AWFUL
★½☆☆☆	SHAMEFUL	★☆☆☆☆	DISGUSTING

SOUTH IRELAND SOUR

★★★★☆

Glass: Coupe
Garnish: Mint leaf
Method: **DRY SHAKE** all ingredients (without ice). Add ice, **SHAKE** again and fine strain into chilled glass.

1	shot	Feijoa flavoured vodka
1	shot	Guinness stout
½	shot	Sugar syrup (2 sugar to 1 water)
1	shot	Freshly squeezed lemon juice
½	fresh	Egg white

Origin: Created by Jacob Briars at Cocktail World Cup 2007 as a reaction to an Irish bartender who said 42 Below Feijoa Vodka was "undrinkable", to which Jacob responded "in large parts of the world people thought the same about Guinness." So as a joke Jacob made this surprisingly tasty cocktail.
The name is a geographical in-joke. The Irishman was from Cork, in southern Ireland. Cork is part of Munster, and they were in Queenstown, in New Zealand's South Island, which was once known as New Munster. With their flat vowel pronunciation, Kiwis say Island and Ireland in exactly the same way.
Comment: Smells of sticking plasters and uses Feijoa and Guinness. Only a Kiwi could create such a drink. Give it a try, it's not as crazy as it sounds.

SOUTH OF HEAVEN COCKTAIL (NEW)

★★★★★☆

Glass: Coupe
Garnish: Lemon zest & mint sprig
Method: **STIR** all ingredients with ice and strain into chilled glass.

1⅔	shots	Skinos Mastiha
1	shot	Martini Bianco
½	shot	Fernet Branca
3	dash	Celery bitters

Origin: Adapted from a recipe created in 2013 by George Megalokonomos at Food Mafia, Athens, Greece. This was the winning cocktail in the Mediterranean Cocktails Challenge 2013.
Comment: Bittersweet and refreshing with the very distinctive flavours of mastiha and Fernet.

SOUTH PACIFIC BREEZE

★★★★☆

Glass: Collins
Garnish: Pineapple wedge
Method: **POUR** gin and Galliano into ice-filled glass. **TOP** with lemonade to just below the rim. **DRIZZLE** blue curaçao around top of drink (it will sink leaving strings of blue). Serve with straws.

1½	shots	Rutte Dry Gin
¾	shot	Galliano L'Autentico liqueur
Top with		Lemonade/Sprite/7-Up
¾	shot	Blue curaçao liqueur

Comment: Quite sweet but flavoursome - looks great.

SOUTHERN MULE

★★★☆☆

Glass: Collins
Garnish: Lime wedge
Method: **SHAKE** first three ingredients with ice and strain into ice filled glass. **TOP** with ginger beer, lightly stir and serve with straws.

2 shots Southern Comfort liqueur
½ shot Freshly squeezed lime juice
3 dash Angostura Aromatic Bitters
Top with Gosling's Stormy Ginger Beer

Comment: Tangy, fruity and spiced with ginger.

SOUTHERN PUNCH

★★★☆☆

Glass: Collins
Garnish: Pineapple wedge
Method: **SHAKE** all ingredients with ice and strain into ice-filled glass.

½	shot	Bourbon whiskey
1½	shots	Southern Comfort liqueur
2	shots	Fresh pressed pineapple juice
1	shot	Freshly squeezed lemon juice
½	shot	Sugar syrup (2 sugar to 1 water)
½	shot	Pomegranate / grenadine syrup (2:1)

Comment: Tropical flavours with the warmth of liquor trailed by a fresh lemon finish.

SOUTHSIDE ⚷

★★★★☆

Glass: Martini
Garnish: Mint leaf
Method: **SHAKE** all ingredients with ice and fine strain into chilled glass.

7	fresh	Mint leaves
2	shots	Rutte Dry Gin
1	shot	Freshly squeezed lime juice
½	shot	Sugar syrup (2 sugar to 1 water)

Origin: This vintage cocktail is purported to have originated at New York's Twenty-One Club. A long version served over crushed ice is said to have come from the southside of Chicago during Prohibition where it was drunk by the Southside mobsters, while on the other side of town hoodlums enjoyed the Northside (gin and ginger ale).
Comment: Gin and mint with a splash of lime. Refreshingly balanced.

SOUTHSIDE FIZZ ⚷

★★★★⯪☆

Glass: Collins (small 8oz)
Garnish: Mint sprig
Method: Lightly **MUDDLE** mint in base of shaker (just to bruise). Add next three ingredients, **SHAKE** with ice and fine strain into (empty) chilled glass. **TOP** with soda.

7	fresh	Mint leaves
2	shots	Rutte Dry Gin
1	shot	Freshly squeezed lemon juice
½	shot	Sugar syrup (2 sugar to 1 water)
Top with		Soda from siphon

Origin: A minty Collins.
Comment: Thought to have been created at the Southside Sportsman's Club in Long Island, New York in the 1890s when the style of drink known as a Fizz was at the height of its popularity.

This recipe adapted from Harry Craddock's 1930 'The Savoy Cocktail Book'.

SOUTHSIDE RICKEY (NEW) ⚷

★★★★★

Glass: Collins
Garnish: Lime and mint sprigs
Method: **SHAKE** all ingredients with ice and strain into ice-filled glass.

2	shots	Rutte Dry Gin
1	shot	Freshly squeezed lime juice
¾	shot	Sugar syrup (2 sugar to 1 water)
5	fresh	Mint leaves
Top with		Soda (club soda)

Origin: Created in 2014 by Meaghan Dorman at Raines Law Rooms, New York, USA.
Comment: A gin based Mojito served over cracked ice meets the classic Southside. The result is refreshing and easy drinking.

SOUTHSIDE ROYALE ⚷

★★★★⯪☆

Glass: Martini
Garnish: Mint leaf
Method: Lightly **MUDDLE** (just to bruise) mint in base of shaker. Add next three ingredients, **SHAKE** with ice and fine strain into chilled glass. **TOP** with a splash of champagne.

7	fresh	Mint leaves
2	shots	Rutte Dry Gin
1	shot	Freshly squeezed lemon juice
½	shot	Sugar syrup (2 sugar to 1 water)
Top with		G.H. Mumm Cordon Rouge Champagne

Origin: Created during Prohibition, either at a New York City speakeasy called Jack & Charlie's, or at Manhattan's Stork Club, or by Chicago's Southside gang to make their bootleg liquor more palatable.
Comment: A White Lady with fresh mint and champagne

SOYER AU CHAMPAGNE

★★★★⯪☆

Glass: Martini
Garnish: None
Method: **PLACE** scoop of ice cream in base of glass. **SHAKE** next three ingredients with ice and strain over ice cream. **TOP** with champagne and serve while foaming with straws that the drinker should use to mix.

1	scoop	Vanilla ice cream
½	shot	Martell VSOP Médaillon cognac
½	shot	Grand Marnier Cordon Rouge
½	shot	Luxardo Maraschino liqueur
Top with		G.H. Mumm Cordon Rouge Champagne

Origin: Adapted from a recipe in the 1949 edition of 'Esquire's Handbook For Hosts'. Apparently this was "one of the most popular drinks at Christmas in the continental cafés".
Comment: A unique dessert of a drink.

SPANISH EYES (NEW)

★★★★⯪

Glass: Coupe
Garnish: Orange zest (discarded) & float star anise
Method: **SHAKE** all ingredients with ice and fine strain into chilled glass.

¾ shot Patrón reposado tequila
¾ shot Byrrh Grand Quinquina
¾ shot Zoco Pacharan
⅛ shot Del Maguey VIDA mezcal
¾ shot Freshly squeezed orange juice
4 drop Bob's Chocolate bitters

Origin: Created in August 2015 by yours truly at the Cabinet Room, London, England. Why Spanish eyes? Tequila distillers speak Spanish, Byrrh is made close to the Spanish boarder, pacharan is very Spanish, as are the best oranges. Plus my missus is half Spanish so has brown eyes and this drink is brownish.
Comment: Reminiscent of a Mexican Blood & Sand, refreshing and complex.

SPARKLING PERRY

★★★★☆

Glass: Flute
Garnish: Pear slice
Method: **SHAKE** first 3 ingredients with ice and fine strain into chilled glass. **TOP** with champagne and lightly stir.

¾	shot	Poire William eau de vie
¾	shot	Belle de Brillet pear liqueur
1	shot	Pressed pear juice
Top with		G.H. Mumm Cordon Rouge Champagne

Origin: Created in December 2002 by yours truly.
Comment: Reminiscent of perry (pear cider).

SPECIAL

★★★★☆

Glass: Martini
Garnish: Grapefruit wedge
Method: SHAKE all ingredients with ice and fine strain into chilled glass.

1½ shots Dewar's 12yo Scotch whisky
1 shot Freshly squeezed pink grapefruit juice
1 shot Grand Marnier Cordon Rouge
⅛ shot Sugar syrup (2 sugar to 1 water)

Comment: Grand Marnier and grapefruit juice provide a flavoursome sweet and sour combination fortified with malty Scotch notes.

SPECIAL BREW MARTINI (NEW)

★★★★★

Glass: Coupe
Garnish: Lemon zest twist
Method: STIR all ingredients with ice and strain into chilled glass.

1¼ shots Ketel One Vodka
1¼ shots Byrrh Grand Quinquina
1¼ shots Junmai ginjō sake
1 dash Le Fée Parisienne absinthe

Origin: Created 21st February 2015 by yours truly at the Cabinet Room, London, England.
Comment: Hopefully it's 'Special'! 'Brew' refers to both the use of Byrrh (pronounced beer) and sake (which is brewed). To be a true 'Martini' a cocktail should have both gin and vermouth – we tried gin but vodka worked so much better. Byrrh doesn't qualify as a vermouth as while an aromatised wine it lacks wormwood – an omission made up for in this drink with a dash of absinthe.

SPENCER COCKTAIL

★★★★☆

Glass: Martini
Garnish: Orange zest twist (discarded) & Luxardo Maraschino cherry
Method: SHAKE all ingredients with ice and fine strain into chilled glass.

2 shots Rutte Dry Gin
1 shot De Kuyper XO Apricot Brandy
¼ shot Freshly squeezed orange juice
1 dash Angostura Aromatic Bitters

Origin: Adapted from a recipe in Harry Craddock's 1930 'The Savoy Cocktail Book'.
Comment: To quote Craddock, "Very mellifluous: has a fine and rapid action: for morning work."

SPEYSIDE COCKTAIL

★★★★☆

Glass: Martini
Garnish: Lemon zest twist
Method: MUDDLE grapes in base of shaker. Add other ingredients, **SHAKE** with ice and fine strain into chilled glass.

7 fresh Seedless white grapes
2 shots Dewar's 12yo Scotch whisky
¾ shot De Kuyper XO Apricot Brandy
¾ shot Freshly squeezed pink grapefruit juice

Origin: Discovered in 2004 (originally named Speyside Martini) at Indigo Yard, Edinburgh, Scotland.
Comment: Scotch, grape juice, apricot liqueur and grapefruit may seem an unlikely combo but they get on well together.

SPICED PEAR

★★★★½

Glass: Old-fashioned
Garnish: Pear slice
Method: SHAKE all ingredients with ice and strain into ice-filled glass.

1 shot Pear liqueur
1 shot Bacardi OakHeart Spiced Rum
1 shot Pressed pear juice
½ shot Freshly squeezed lime juice
½ shot Sugar syrup (2 sugar to 1 water)

Origin: Created in 2002 by James Stewart, Edinburgh, Scotland
Comment: Just as it says on the tin - spiced pear.

SPICY FIFTY (NEW)

★★★★½

Glass: Martini
Garnish: Fresh chilli on rim
Method: MUDDLE chilli in base of **SHAKER**. Add other ingredients, **SHAKE** with ice and fine strain into chilled glass.

1⅔ shots Vanilla infused Ketel One vodka
½ shot Elderflower cordial
⅓ shot Honey sugar syrup
⅔ shot Freshly squeezed lime juice
2 slice Chilli

Origin: Created by Salvatore Calabrese at his bar Fifty, London, England.
Comment: Chilli spice smoothed by honey with vanilla vodka and lime juice.

SPIKED APPLE CIDER (HOT)

★★★★☆

Glass: Toddy
Garnish: None
Method: MUDDLE cloves in base of shaker. Add cognac and apple juice. **SHAKE** without ice and fine strain into glass. **WARM** in microwave then **FLOAT** double cream over drink.

2 dried Clove
2 shots Martell VSOP Médaillon cognac
3 shots Pressed apple juice
Float Single cream / half-and-half

Origin: Adapted from a drink discovered in 2006 at Double Seven, New York City, USA.
Comment: Warming and lightly spiced under a creamy head.

SPITFIRE

★★★★☆

Glass: Martini
Garnish: Lemon zest twist
Method: SHAKE all ingredients with ice and fine strain into chilled glass.

2	shots	Martell VSOP Médaillon cognac
½	shot	Sauvignon blanc white wine
1	shot	Freshly squeezed lemon juice
½	shot	Sugar syrup (2 sugar to 1 water)
½	fresh	Egg white

Origin: Created in 2006 by Tony Conigliaro at Shochu Lounge, London, England.
Comment: A brandy sour with a splash of dry white wine.

SPORRAN BREEZE

★★★★☆

Glass: Collins
Garnish: Apple slice
Method: SHAKE all ingredients with ice and strain into ice-filled glass. Serve with straws.

2	shots	Dewar's 12yo Scotch whisky
4	shots	Pressed apple juice
½	shot	Passion fruit syrup

Origin: Created in 2002 by Phillip Jeffrey at the GE Club, London, England.
Comment: A deliciously fresh blend of malty fruit.

SPRITZ AL BITTER (CAMPARI SPRITZ)

★★★★½☆

Glass: Old-fashioned
Garnish: Orange zest twist
Method: POUR ingredients into ice-filled glass and lightly stir.

3	shots	Prosecco sparkling wine
1½	shots	Campari Bitter
Top with		Soda (club soda)

Origin: Popular in northern Italy, especially in Venice and the Veneto region where it is pronounced 'Spriss'. (From the German verb Spritzen, meaning spray or splash). This aperitif cocktails origins date back to the end of the 19th century when Venice was still part of the Austrian Empire. During this period German soldiers drank the local wines of Veneto in taverns where they were billeted but they often diluted these with water to achieve a similar alcohol content to the beer they were more accustomed to drinking. Hence, the Spritzer, a combination of equal parts white wine and soda water.

In Veneto, the Spritz Al Bitter is made with the traditional white wines of the Veneto region, Pinot Grigio, Soave or Prosecco. The bitter liqueur used varies according to personal taste with Campari perhaps the driest.

Other popular bitter liqueurs used include Aperol, Gran Classico, Select or Cynar. It is usually garnished with a slice of orange but sometimes an olive depending on the liqueur used. According to Gruppo Campari, In Veneto, around 300,000 Spritzes are consumed every day, that's more that's 200 Spritzes a minute.

In the 2000 American comedy film 'Meet the Parents' starring Robert de Niro, Barbra Streisand, and Dustin Hoffman, the latter offers De Niro an Italian Spritz instead of his usual Tom Collins.
Comment: Basically a Spritzer with a generous splash of campari - dry and very refreshing.

SPRITZER

★★★½☆

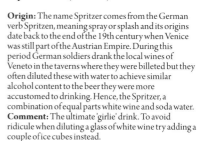

Glass: Goblet
Garnish: Lemon zest twist
Method: POUR ingredients into chilled glass and lightly stir. No ice!

| 3 | shots | Sauvignon blanc white wine |
| Top with | | Soda (club soda) |

Origin: The name Spritzer comes from the German verb Spritzen, meaning spray or splash and its origins date back to the end of the 19th century when Venice was still part of the Austrian Empire. During this period German soldiers drank the local wines of Veneto in the taverns where they were billeted but they often diluted these with water to achieve similar alcohol content to the beer they were more accustomed to drinking. Hence, the Spritzer, a combination of equal parts white wine and soda water.
Comment: The ultimate 'girlie' drink. To avoid ridicule when diluting a glass of white wine try adding a couple of ice cubes instead.

SPUTNIK #1

★★★½☆

Glass: Martini
Garnish: Orange zest twist
Method: SHAKE all ingredients with ice and fine strain into chilled glass.

1	shot	Ketel One Vodka
1	shot	Peachtree peach schnapps
1½	shots	Freshly squeezed orange juice
1	shot	Single cream / half-and-half

Comment: Blasts of fruit cut through this soft creamy drink.

SPUTNIK #2

★★★★☆

Glass: Old-fashioned
Garnish: Orange slice
Method: SHAKE all ingredients with ice and strain into ice filled glass.

1	shot	Bacardi Carta Blanca light rum
1	shot	Martell VSOP Médaillon cognac
2	shots	Freshly squeezed orange juice
½	shot	Sugar syrup (2 sugar to 1 water)

Origin: A cocktail served in underground clubs all over the former Eastern Bloc. It was originally made with cheap Cuban rum, Georgian brandy and tinned orange juice.
Comment: Orange, cognac and rum meld well. Fruity and refreshing.

SQUASHED FROG

★★★☆☆

Glass: Shot
Garnish: None
Method: Refrigerate ingredients then LAYER in chilled glass by carefully pouring in the order listed.

½	shot	Pomegranate / grenadine syrup (2:1)
½	shot	Midori Green Melon liqueur
½	shot	Warninks Advocaat liqueur

Comment: Very sweet. However, the taste is not as offensive as the name might suggest.

ST KITTS (MOCKTAIL)

★★★★☆

Glass: Collins
Garnish: Lime wedge
Method: SHAKE first three ingredients with ice and strain into ice-filled glass. **TOP** with ginger ale, lightly stir and serve with straws.

3 shots **Fresh pressed pineapple juice**
½ shot **Freshly squeezed lime juice**
¼ shot **Pomegranate / grenadine syrup (2:1)**
Top with **Ginger ale**

Comment: Rust coloured and refreshing.

ST LAWRENCE

★★★½☆

Glass: Martini
Garnish: Lemon zest twist
Method: SHAKE all ingredients with ice and fine strain into chilled glass.

2½ shots **Bourbon whiskey**
½ shot **Maple syrup**
¾ shot **Freshly squeezed lemon juice**

Origin: Adapted from a drink discovered in 2011 at Bar Rouge, Copenhagen, Denmark.
Comment: Bourbon soured with lemon juice and sweetened with maple syrup.

ST-GERMAIN COCKTAIL (ELDERFLOWER SPRITZ)

★★★★½

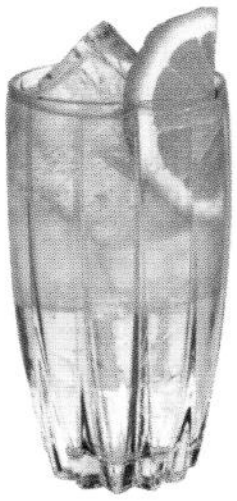

Glass: Collins
Garnish: Lime slice
Method: POUR wine and then elderflower liqueur into ice-filled glass. **TOP** with soda (or champagne), lightly stir and serve with straws.

2 shots **Sauvignon blanc white wine**
1½ shots **St-Germain elderflower liqueur**
Top with **Soda (club soda)**

Origin: Created in 2006 by yours truly ahead of the launch of St-Germain elderflower liqueur. It went on to become the brand's signature drink
Comment: A long, easy drinking summer cooler.

STAFFORDSHIRE DELIGHT

★★★★☆

Glass: Collins
Garnish: Pineapple wedge
Method: SHAKE all ingredients with ice and strain into ice-filled glass.

2 shots **Bacardi Carta Oro rum**
½ shot **Fernet Branca**
½ shot **Almond (orgeat) syrup**
½ shot **Freshly squeezed lime juice**
1½ shots **Fresh pressed pineapple juice**
1 dash **Angostura Aromatic Bitters**

Origin: Adapted from a drink created in 2010 by Thomas Dalloway, United Kingdom.
Comment: A modern day pick-me-up / hair-of-the-dog with a rich, enlivening bitter sweet bite.

STAIRS COCKTAIL

★★★★★

Glass: Martini
Garnish: Pear slice
Method: SHAKE all ingredients with ice and fine strain into chilled glass.

2 shots **Ketel One Vodka**
1 shot **Pressed pear juice**
1 shot **Pressed apple juice**
¼ shot **Freshly squeezed lemon juice**
¼ shot **Sugar syrup (2 sugar to 1 water)**
2 dash **Angostura Orange Bitters**

Origin: Created in 2000 by Ian Baldwin at the GE Club, London, England.
Comment: In London's cockney rhyming slang 'apples and pears' means stairs. Thus this tasty cocktail is appropriately named.

STANLEY COCKTAIL

★★★★☆

Glass: Martini
Garnish: Lemon zest twist
Method: SHAKE all ingredients with ice and fine strain into chilled glass.

1½ shots **Rutte Dry Gin**
1½ shots **Bacardi Carta Blanca light rum**
½ shot **Freshly squeezed lemon juice**
½ shot **Pomegranate / grenadine syrup (2:1)**

Origin: Adapted from a recipe in Harry Craddock's 1930 'Savoy Cocktail Book'.
Comment: Salmon pink and reminiscent of a Daiquiri with a splash of gin.

THE STAR

★★★★☆

Glass: Martini
Garnish: Olive on stick
Method: STIR all ingredients with ice and fine strain into chilled glass.

1½ shots **Calvados brandy**
1½ shots **Martini Rosso vermouth**
1 dash **Angostura Aromatic Bitters**

Origin: Recipe adapted from Harry Craddock's 1930 'Savoy Cocktail Book'. Said to have been created in the 1870s by a bartender at the legendary Manhattan Club, which once stood at the north corner of 34th Street and 5th Avenue, New York City.
Comment: Like many old classics, this drink needs dilution so stir until you're bored and thirsty.

STARRY NIGHT

★★★★½

Glass: Coupe
Garnish: Star anise
Method: STIR all ingredients with ice and strain into chilled glass.

2 shots **Chardonnay (Chablis) white wine**
½ shot **Poire William eau de vie**
½ shot **Luxardo Maraschino liqueur**

Origin: Created in 2008 by Jamie Boudreau at Vessel, Seattle, USA.
Comment: Delicate pear and aromatic maraschino over a wine base.

STARS & STRIPES SHOT

★★⯪☆☆

Glass: Shot
Garnish: None
Method: Refrigerate ingredients then **LAYER** in chilled glass by carefully pouring in the order listed.

½ shot   **Lejay crème de cassis de Dijon**
½ shot   **Luxardo Maraschino liqueur**
½ shot   **Green Chartreuse liqueur**

Origin: Adapted from a recipe in Harry Craddock's 1930 'Savoy Cocktail Book'.
Comment: The taste is too sweet and the colours aren't quite right. A shame.

STEEL BOTTOM

★★★☆☆

Glass: Collins
Garnish: None
Method: POUR ingredients into glass, lightly stir and serve with straws.

1 shot   **White overproof rum**
Top with   **Budweiser Budvar**

Origin: A very popular drink in Jamaica.
Comment: For those who like their beer turbo charged.

STEEP FLIGHT

★★★★★

Glass: Collins
Garnish: Apple or pear slice
Method: SHAKE all ingredients with ice and fine strain into ice-filled glass.

1 shot   **Calvados brandy**
1 shot   **Ketel One Vodka**
1 shot   **Martell VSOP Médaillon cognac**
3 shots   **Pressed apple juice**

Origin: Created in 2005 by yours truly. This cocktail was awarded a Gold in the Long Drink category at Drinks International Bartender's Challenge on 31st May 2006.
Comment: 'Apples and pears' is the cockney rhyming slang for stairs, hence the flavours in this particular flight.

STEPHEN MARSHALL

★★★⯪☆

Glass: Old-fashioned
Garnish: Orange zest twist
Method: STIR all ingredients with ice and strain into ice-filled glass.

1 shot   **Rutte Dry Gin**
1 shot   **Campari Bitter**
¾ shot   **Hazelnut liqueur**
1 shot   **Martini Rosso vermouth**

Origin: Created in 2012 and named for its inventor, the flamboyant, music-loving Whisky Ambassador, and a man who likes a Negroni and, it would appear, hazelnut liqueur.
Comment: A Negroni with hazelnut liqueur. Some will ask: why? Negroni-loving drinkers of hazelnut liqueur might ask: why not?

STICKY TOFFEE FIZZ (NEW)

★★★★☆

Glass: Flute
Garnish: Toffee sauce around rim
Method: SHAKE first three ingredients with ice and strain into chilled glass. **TOP** with champagne.

1 shot Bacardi OakHeart Spiced Rum
½ shot Butterscotch liqueur
½ shot Caramel liqueur
Top with G.H. Mumm Cordon Rouge Champagne

Origin: Inspired by a drink at London's Light Bar. Created by yours truly in September 2014 at the Cabinet Room, London, England.
Comment: Given the name and the ingredients of this indulgent champagne cocktail it is surprisingly dry and complex.

THE STIG

★★★★★

Glass: Old-fashioned
Garnish: Lime zest twist
Method: STIR all ingredients with ice and strain into ice-filled glass.

¾ shot   **Calvados brandy**
¾ shot   **BarSol Mosto Verde Italia pisco**
1 shot   **St-Germain elderflower liqueur**
1 shot   **Sauvignon blanc white wine**

Origin: Created in 2006 by yours truly at the Cabinet Room, London, England. Named partly for the 'St-G' on the screw cap of St-Germain elderflower liqueur and partly after 'The Stig', the mysterious racing driver on the BBC's Top Gear show.
Comment: Whiter than white but yet mysterious.

STILETTO

★★★★⯪☆

Glass: Collins
Garnish: Lime wedge
Method: SHAKE all ingredients with ice and strain into ice-filled glass.

2 shots   **Bourbon whiskey**
1 shot   **Disaronno Originale amaretto**
2½ shots   **Cranberry juice**
½ shot   **Freshly squeezed lime juice**
¼ shot   **Sugar syrup (2 sugar to 1 water)**

Comment: Long and fruity with a hint of bourbon and almond.

STINGER

★★★★☆

Glass: Old-fashioned
Garnish: Mint sprig
Method: STIR all ingredients with ice and strain into glass filled with crushed ice. Serve with straws.

2 shots   Martell VSOP Médaillon cognac
¾ shot   Giffard Menthe Pastille liqueur

Origin: In the classic film 'High Society', Bing Crosby explains to Grace Kelly how the Stinger gained its name. "It's a Stinger. It removes the sting."

In his 2015 ' Updated & Revised Imbibe', David Wondrich recounts a 1923 newspaper gossip page story which credits the invention of The Stinger to Reginald Vanderbilt, an American millionaire and father of fashion designer Gloria Vanderbilt.

According to the piece "Reggie" was a keen cocktail maker and "was observed in all its pomp and glory in the bar of [his] home, and he himself was the high priest, the host, the mixer." The bar in his Fifth Avenue mansion was apparently modelled after the one in the William the Conqueror tavern in Normandy and "the 'Stinger' was his own invention, a short drink with a long reach, a subtle blending of ardent nectars, a boon to friendship, a dispeller of care."

So keen a cocktail maker was Reggie that he died from liver failure due to alcohol abuse on 4th September 1925.
Comment: Classically the Stinger is shaken and served straight-up in a chilled coupe. However, we think it makes for a more refreshing peppermint and cognac digestif when served over crushed ice.

STONE & GRAVEL

★★★★☆

Glass: Old-fashioned
Garnish: None
Method: POUR ingredients into glass filled with crushed ice and stir.

1 shot   White overproof rum
3 shots   Stone's green ginger wine

Origin: A popular drink in Jamaica.
Comment: Simple, strong and surprisingly good.

STONE FENCE

★★★★☆

Glass: Pint
Garnish: Apple slice
Method: POUR ingredients into ice-filled glass and stir. Serve with straws.

2 shots   Straight rye whiskey
Top with   Medium dry cider

Origin: Although the origin of this simple mixed drink and its name are unknown history chronicles its being served at taverns since at least the early 1800s.
Comment: Dry cider fortified and made drier by whiskey.

THE STONE PLACE

★★★★☆

Glass: Coupe
Garnish: Dust with grated nutmeg
Method: SHAKE all ingredients with ice and fine strain into chilled glass.

2½ shots   Bacardi Carta Ocho aged rum
¾ shot   Freshly squeezed lemon juice
¾ shot   Freshly squeezed orange juice
¼ shot   Pomegranate / grenadine syrup (2:1)

Origin: Adapted from a drink created in 2010 by Willy Shine at Forty Four, New York City, USA. This twist on the Ward 8 is named after the street where Shine's parents, who were big Ward 8 imbibers, used to live.
Comment: Rum loves fruit and this pink drink has lots of both.

STORK CLUB

★★★★☆

Glass: Martini
Garnish: Orange zest twist
Method: SHAKE all ingredients with ice and fine strain into chilled glass.

1 shot   Rutte Dry Gin
1 shot   De Kuyper Triple Sec
1 shot   Freshly squeezed orange juice
½ shot   Freshly squeezed lime juice
2 dash   Angostura Orange Bitters (optional)

Comment: Orange and gin with a souring splash of lime juice.

STOUT FELLOW

★★★★☆

Glass: Coupe
Garnish: Dust with grated 85% cacao chocolate.
Method: SHAKE all ingredients with ice and fine strain into chilled glass.

2 shots   Guinness stout
1 shot   Pot still Jamaican rum
1 shot   Coffee liqueur
⅛ shot   Dark crème de cacao liqueur

Origin: Created in 2013 by Matthew Coates (M.C.) at Jake's Bar and Still Room, Leeds, England. Matthew was one of five finalists in the diffordsguide Beer-tail Competition for London Cocktail Week 2013 held on Friday 9th August 2013 at the Cabinet Room, London, England.

Matthew told us, "The inspiration behind my cocktail comes from my love of all of its components – rum, beer (Guinness) and coffee. I call my drink 'a stout fellow' because it's strong and hearty but also warming and 'friendly'. It also refers to the old Guinness advertising of 'Guinness for strength' encompassing more than one meaning of the word stout."
Comment: In a similar style to an Espresso Martini but with very different ingredients including Guinness stout and coffee liqueur in place of espresso coffee.

STRAITS SLING

★★★½☆

Glass: Sling
Garnish: Orange slice & cherry on stick (sail)
Method: SHAKE first six ingredients with ice and strain into ice-filled glass. **TOP** with soda, lightly stir and serve with straws.

2	shots	Rutte Dry Gin
½	shot	Bénédictine D.O.M. liqueur
½	shot	Kirschwasser eau de vie
1	shot	Freshly squeezed lemon juice
2	dash	Angostura Orange Bitters
Top with		Soda (club soda)

Origin: Straits Sling is thought to be the original name of the Singapore Sling and in his 1922 ' Cocktails and How to Mix Them' Robert Vermeire gives the following recipe for the drink:

2 dashes of Orange Bitters
2 dashes of Angostura Bitters
The juice of half a lemon
1/8 gill of Bénédictine
1/8 gill of Dry Cherry Brandy
1/8 gill of Gin
Pour into a tumbler and fill up with cold Soda Water.

In his 1948 Fine Art of Mixing Drinks, David A. Embury calls for "Cherry Brandy (Kirsch)" in his Singapore Sling and this Straits Sling recipe is adapted from this recipe.
Comment: Dry cherry and gin come to the fore in this long refreshing drink.

STRATOSPHERE

★★★★☆

Glass: Flute
Garnish: Lemon zest twist (discarded) & two cloves
Method: POUR liqueur into glass and **TOP** with champagne.

| ¼ | shot | Benoit Serres créme de violette |
| Top with | | G.H. Mumm Cordon Rouge Champagne |

Origin: Recipe adapted from The Stork Club Bar Book published 1946 in which Lucius Beebe writes, "Leo Spitzel, captain, asserts that a Stratosphere Cocktail will do wonders for you."
Comment: The thinking woman's Kir Royal.

STRAWBERRY & BALSAMIC COCKTAIL

★★★★☆

Glass: Martini
Garnish: Strawberry
Method: MUDDLE strawberries in base of shaker. Add other ingredients, **SHAKE** with ice and fine strain into chilled glass.

5	fresh	Small ripe strawberries (hulled)
2½	shots	Ketel One Vodka
⅛	shot	Balsamic vinegar of moderna
½	shot	Sugar syrup (2 sugar to 1 water)

Origin: Created in Che, St James's Street, London, England and originally named Strawberry & Balsamic Martini, this drink was popular in London's bars during in 2002.
Comment: The balsamic adds a little extra interest to the fortified strawberries.

STRAWBERRY BLONDE

★★★★☆

Glass: Collins
Garnish: Strawberry
Method: MUDDLE strawberries in base of shaker. Add next three ingredients, **SHAKE** with ice and fine strain into ice-filled glass. **TOP** with soda and serve with straws.

2	fresh	Small ripe strawberries (hulled)
2	shots	Ketel One Vodka
1½	shots	Freshly squeezed lemon juice
¾	shot	Sugar syrup (2 sugar to 1 water)
Top with		Soda (club soda)

Origin: Created in 2008 by yours truly at the Cabinet Room, London, England.
Comment: This long, refreshing orange-red drink is basically a vodka-laced strawberry flavoured real lemonade.

STRAWBERRY BLONDE MARTINI

★★★½☆

Glass: Martini
Garnish: Basil leaf
Method: MUDDLE basil in mixing glass. Add other ingredients, **STIR** with ice and fine strain into chilled glass.

4	fresh	Basil leaves
2½	shots	Raspberry flavoured vodka
½	shot	Lejay Crème de Fraise liqueur
½	shot	Martini Extra Dry vermouth
⅛	shot	Sugar syrup (2 sugar to 1 water)

Origin: Adapted from a recipe discovered in 2003 at Oxo Tower Bar, London, England
Comment: Berry vodka dominates with hints of strawberry and basil.

STRAWBERRY COCKTAIL

★★★★☆

Glass: Martini
Garnish: Strawberry on rim
Method: MUDDLE strawberries in base of shaker. Add other ingredients, **SHAKE** with ice and fine strain into chilled glass.

5	fresh	Small ripe strawberries (hulled)
2	shots	Ketel One Vodka
½	shot	Sugar syrup (2 sugar to 1 water)
2	grind	Black pepper

Origin: Originated in London during the late 1990s under the name Strawberry Martini.
Comment: Rich strawberries fortified with vodka and a hint of pepper spice.

STRAWBERRY COSMO

★★★½☆

Glass: Martini
Garnish: Strawberry
Method: SHAKE all ingredients with ice and fine strain into chilled glass.

2	shots	Ketel One Citroen vodka
¾	shot	Lejay Crème de Fraise liqueur
1¼	shots	Cranberry juice
½	shot	Freshly squeezed lime juice

Comment: Strawberry liqueur replaces the usual orange liqueur in this riff on a Cosmopolitan.

STRAWBERRY DAIQUIRI

★★★★☆

Glass: Martini
Garnish: Strawberry
Method: **MUDDLE** strawberries in base of shaker. Add other ingredients, **SHAKE** with ice and fine strain into chilled glass.

- 7 fresh **Small ripe strawberries (hulled)**
- 2 shots **Bacardi Carta Blanca light rum**
- ½ shot **Freshly squeezed lime juice**
- ¼ shot **Sugar syrup (2 sugar to 1 water)**

Origin: A popular drink in Cuba where it is known as a Daiquiri de Fresa.
Comment: Makes strawberries and cream appear very dull.

STRAWBERRY DAIQUIRI (FROZEN)

★★★½☆

Glass: Martini
Garnish: Strawberry
Method: **BLEND** all ingredients with a 6oz scoop of crushed ice.

- 2 shots **Bacardi Carta Blanca light rum**
- ¾ shot **Freshly squeezed lime juice**
- ½ shot **Sugar syrup (2 sugar to 1 water)**
- 5 fresh **Small ripe strawberries (hulled)**

Comment: Strawberry Mivvi for grown-ups.

STRAWBERRY ÉCLAIR

★★★★☆

Glass: Shot
Garnish: None
Method: **SHAKE** all ingredients with ice and fine strain into chilled glass.

- ½ shot **Lejay Crème de Fraise liqueur**
- ½ shot **Hazelnut liqueur**
- ¼ shot **Freshly squeezed lime juice**

Origin: This drink heralds from Australia where it was a popular shot in the 1990s.
Comment: Far from sophisticated but appropriately named.

STRAWBERRY FIELDS (NEW)

★★★★½

Glass: Coupe
Garnish: Five drops of balsamic vinegar and a dusting of freshly ground black pepper
Method: **MUDDLE** strawberry in base of shaker. Add vodka, honey syrup, lemon juice and egg white and **SHAKE** with ice. Strain back into shaker, **DRY SHAKE** (without ice) and strain into chilled glass.

- 2 fresh **Small ripe strawberries (hulled)**
- 1½ shots **Ketel One Vodka**
- ½ shot **Freshly squeezed lemon juice**
- ½ shot **Honey water (3 honey to 1 water)**
- ½ fresh **Egg white**

Origin: Created by Trina Nishimura in 2014.
Comment: This refreshing vodka-based strawberry cocktail balances tart lemon juice with rich honey. Drops of balsamic and a dusting of black pepper add complexity.

STRAWBERRY JIVE

★★★½☆

Glass: Old-fashioned
Garnish: Mint sprig
Method: **MUDDLE** strawberries in base of shaker. **SHAKE** next six ingredients with ice and fine strain into ice-filled glass. **TOP** with soda.

- **2 fresh Small ripe strawberries (hulled)**
- **2 shots Rutte Dry Gin**
- **4 fresh Mint leaves**
- **1 fresh Basil leaves**
- **¼ shot Sugar syrup (2 sugar to 1 water)**
- **1 shot Freshly squeezed orange juice**
- **½ shot Freshly squeezed lemon juice**
- **Top with Soda (club soda)**

Origin: Adapted from a drink created in 2011 by Dale DeGroff, New York, USA.
Comment: Strawberry, lemon and orange fruit with herbal mint and basil, laced with gin and freshened with soda.

STRAWBERRY MARGARITA

★★★★☆

Glass: Martini
Garnish: Strawberry
Method: **MUDDLE** strawberries in base of shaker. Add other ingredients, **SHAKE** with ice and fine strain into chilled glass.

- 2 shots **Patrón reposado tequila**
- 1 shot **Freshly squeezed lime juice**
- ¾ shot **Sugar syrup (2 sugar to 1 water)**
- 5 fresh **Small ripe strawberries (hulled)**

Comment: Fresh strawberries combine well with tequila in this fruity margarita.

STRAWBERRY ON ACID

★★★★½

Glass: Flute
Garnish: Balsamic covered strawberry
Method: **MUDDLE** strawberries in base of shaker. Add other ingredients, **SHAKE** with ice and fine strain into chilled glass. **TOP** with champagne.

- 3 fresh **Small ripe strawberries (hulled)**
- 1½ shots **Ketel One Vodka**
- ¾ shot **Lejay Crème de Fraise liqueur**
- ⅛ shot **Balsamic vinegar of moderna**
- 1 pinch **Black pepper**
- Top with **G.H. Mumm Cordon Rouge Champagne**

Origin: Adapted from a drink discovered in 2010 at Bordeaux Quay, Bristol, England.
Comment: Fruity, slightly sweet strawberry, balanced and made interesting by vodka, balsamic vinegar and black pepper tingle.

STRUDEL MARTINI

★★★★⯪

Glass: Martini
Garnish: Dust with cinnamon powder
Method: SHAKE all ingredients with ice and fine strain into chilled glass.

1½	shots	Ketel One Vodka
½	shot	Romate Pedro Ximénez sherry
¾	shot	Pressed apple juice
½	shot	Milk
½	shot	Single cream / half-and-half

Origin: Created in 2002 by Jason Borthwick, Tiles, Edinburgh, Scotland.
Comment: Still think sherry is just for Granny?

STUPID CUPID

★★★☆☆

Glass: Martini
Garnish: Lemon zest twist
Method: SHAKE all ingredients with ice and fine strain into chilled glass.

2	shots	Ketel One Citroen vodka
½	shot	Sloe Gin liqueur
1	shot	Freshly squeezed lime juice
½	shot	Sugar syrup (2 sugar to 1 water)

Comment: Citrusy with subtle hints of Sloe gin.

SUBMARINE KISS

★★★★⯪

Glass: Flute
Garnish: Lemon zest twist (discarded)
Method: POUR liqueur into base of chilled glass. SHAKE the rest of ingredients with ice and strain back into shaker. SHAKE again without ice (dry shake) and slowly fine strain into liqueur primed glass so contents of shaker float over liqueur.

⅓ shot Benoit Serres créme de violette
2 shots Rutte Dry Gin
½ shot Freshly squeezed lemon juice
¼ shot Sugar syrup (2 sugar to 1 water)
½ fresh Egg white

Origin: In 1915 this drink was reported in the New York 'Day by Day' newspaper as follows, "Sailors who come to Broadway for a touch of high life have invented a new drink called The Submarine Kiss. The liquid combination is a milky white above and purple below and the submarine effect is secured after drinking about three."
Comment: Looks stunning and gives the drinker the option to sip or swirl to mix the sweet liqueur base into the body of the drink.

SUBOURBON

★★★★☆

Glass: Collins
Garnish: Blackberries
Method: SHAKE all ingredients with ice and fine strain into ice-filled glass.

2	fresh	Blackberries
1½	shots	Bourbon whiskey
¾	shot	Carpano Antica Formula
2	shots	Cranberry juice
2	dash	Angostura Aromatic Bitters

Origin: Adapted from a drink created in 2010 by David Steenkamp at Jamie Oliver's Barbecoa, London, England. Originally also with a dash of crème de mûre (blackberry) liqueur so sweeter and fruitier.
Comment: A fruity (blackberry and cranberry) long bourbon laced drink with a flavour reminiscent of a fruity, sweet manhattan.

SUBURBAN

★★★★☆

Glass: Old-fashioned
Garnish: Orange zest twist
Method: STIR all ingredients with ice and strain into ice-filled glass.

1½	shots	Bourbon whiskey
¾	shot	Bacardi Carta Ocho aged rum
¾	shot	Tawny port
1	dash	Angostura Aromatic Bitters
1	dash	Angostura Orange Bitters

Origin: Created at New York's old Waldorf-Astoria Hotel (the Empire State Building occupies the site today) for James R Keene, a racehorse owner whose steeds ran in the Suburban Handicap at Brooklyn's Sheepshead Bay track.
Comment: An interesting alternative to an Old-Fashioned

SUCCULENT BLOOD (NEW)

★★★★★

Glass: Coupe
Garnish: Dehydrated blood orange slice
Method: SHAKE all ingredients with ice and fine strain into chilled glass.

2	shots	Del Maguey VIDA mezcal
1	shot	Blood orange juice
¼	shot	Cinnamon sugar syrup (2:1)
⅛	shot	Taylor's Velvet Falernum liqueur

Origin: Created in February 2014 by yours truly after misreading the recipe for a Sangre Dulce by Regina Butler at Blackbird Bar in San Francisco. I used Velvet Falernum in place of Fernet Vallet but liked the result. Mezcal is distilled from agave plants which are categorised 'Succulents', plants which are thickened and fleshy, allowing them to retain water in arid climates.
Comment: Mezcal and blood orange juice with sweet spice added with cinnamon syrup and clove rich falernum.

SUFFERING BASTARD

★★★★☆

Glass: Old-fashioned
Garnish: Pineapple cubes, Luxardo Maraschino cherry, lime wedge, cucumber peel & mint sprig
Method: SHAKE all ingredients with ice and strain glass filled with crushed ice.

1	shot	Bacardi Carta Blanca light rum
2	shots	Martinique blanc rhum agricole
½	shot	Orange Curaçao liqueur
¼	shot	Almond (orgeat) syrup
½	shot	Sugar syrup (2 sugar to 1 water)
1	shot	Freshly squeezed lime juice

Origin: Adapted from Victor Bergeron's 'Trader Vic's Bartender's Guide' (1972 revised edition).
Comment: Pungent, heavily rum laced yet all too easy.

SUITABLY FRANK

★★★★☆

Glass: Shot
Garnish: None
Method: Refrigerate ingredients then LAYER in chilled glass by carefully pouring in the listed order.

½	shot	Licor 43 liqueur
½	shot	Cherry Heering Liqueur
½	shot	Ketel One Vodka

Comment: Frankly - it's a good shot.

SUMMER BREEZE 🗝

★★★★☆

Glass: Collins
Garnish: Apple slice
Method: SHAKE all ingredients with ice and strain into ice-filled glass.

2	shot	Ketel One Vodka
1	shot	St-Germain elderflower liqueur
1½	shot	Cranberry juice
1½	shot	Pressed apple juice

Comment: Cranberry, apple and elderflower fortified with vodka.
Origin: Adapted from a drink created in 1998 by Dick Bradsell, London, England.

SUMMER ROSE COCKTAIL

★★★★☆

Glass: Martini
Garnish: Rose petal
Method: STIR first 3 ingredients with ice and strain into chilled glass. POUR grenadine into the centre of the drink. This should settle to form a red layer in the base of the glass.

1½	shots	Ketel One Vodka
¾	shot	White crème de cacao liqueur
½	shot	Kwai Feh lychee liqueur
½	shot	Pomegranate / grenadine syrup (2:1)

Origin: Created in 2003 by Davide Lovison at Isola Bar, London, England.
Comment: Unless you've a sweet tooth don't mix the red and white layers - sip from the chocolate and lychee top and stop when you hit red.

SUMMERTIME COCKTAIL

★★★★☆

Glass: Martini
Garnish: Kumquat
Method: SHAKE all ingredients with ice and fine strain into chilled glass.

1½	shots	Rutte Dry Gin
1	shot	Grand Marnier Cordon Rouge
¼	shot	Pomegranate / grenadine syrup (2:1)
1½	shots	Freshly squeezed orange juice

Comment: Smooth, gin laced fruit for a summer's day.

SUMMIT

★★★☆☆

Glass: Old-fashioned
Garnish: Cucumber peel
Method: Lightly MUDDLE lime zest and ginger slices in base of mixing glass. Add other ingredients, STIR with ice and fine strain into ice-filled glass.

1	twist	Lime (fresh whole) (zest)
1	slice	Fresh root ginger (thumbnail sized)
1½	shots	Martell VSOP Médaillon cognac
2	shots	Lemonade/Sprite/7-Up

Origin: Created in January 2008 when around 20 of the world's top mixologists gathered at The International Cognac Summit at the invitation of the BNIC.
Comment: A cocktail created by a committee rather than any one bartender. "How many bartenders does it take to change a light bulb?" jokes are appropriate.

SUMO IN A SIDECAR

★★★★★

Glass: Martini
Garnish: Orange zest twist
Method: SHAKE all ingredients with ice and fine strain into chilled glass.

1	shot	De Kuyper XO Apricot Brandy
2½	shots	Junmai ginjō sake
½	shot	Freshly squeezed lemon juice

Comment: Hints of sake but retains the Sidecar style.

SUN KISSED VIRGIN (MOCKTAIL)

★★★☆☆

Glass: Sling
Garnish: Physalis (cape gooseberry)
Method: SHAKE all ingredients with ice and strain into ice-filled glass.

2	shots	Freshly squeezed orange juice
2	shots	Fresh pressed pineapple juice
1	shot	Freshly squeezed lime juice
½	shot	Almond (orgeat) syrup

Comment: Golden, slightly sweet and very fruity - just like a Sun Kissed Virgin should be.

THE SUN SALUTATION

★★★½☆

Glass: Collins
Garnish: Mint sprig
Method: MUDDLE mint in base of shaker. Add next three ingredients, **SHAKE** with ice and fine strain into ice-filled glass. **TOP** with soda.

10	fresh	Mint leaves
1	shot	Ketel One Vodka
1½	shots	Kwai Feh lychee liqueur
¾	shot	Freshly squeezed lemon juice
Top with		Soda (club soda)

Origin: Adapted from a recipe by David Nepove, Enrico's Bar & Restaurant, San Francisco.
Comment: Mint and lychee, long and refreshing.

SUNDOWNER #1

★★★★☆

Glass: Martini
Garnish: Orange zest twist
Method: SHAKE all ingredients with ice and fine strain into chilled glass.

2	shots	Martell VSOP Médaillon cognac
½	shot	Grand Marnier Cordon Rouge
½	shot	Freshly squeezed orange juice
½	shot	Freshly squeezed lemon juice
¾	shot	Chilled water (omit if wet ice)

Origin: This cocktail is popular in South Africa where it is made with locally produced brandy and a local orange liqueur called Van der Hum.
Comment: Cognac and orange served straight-up.

SUNDOWNER #2

★★★★☆

Glass: Old-fashioned
Garnish: Mint sprig
Method: SHAKE all ingredients with ice and strain into ice-filled glass.

¾	shot	Grand Marnier Cordon Rouge
1½	shots	Southern Comfort liqueur
2	shots	Sauvignon blanc white wine

Origin: Adapted from a cocktail created in 2002 by Gary Regis at Bed Bar, London, England.
Comment: Subtle meld of summer and citrus flavours.

SUNNY DISPOSITION COCKTAIL (NEW)

★★★★½

Glass: Coupe
Garnish: Lemon zest twist
Method: SHAKE all ingredients with ice and fine strain into chilled glass.

2	shots	Patrón silver tequila
½	shot	Suze Saveur d'Autrefois
½	shot	De Kuyper XO Apricot Brandy
½	shot	Freshly squeezed lemon juice
⅛	shot	Sugar syrup (2 sugar to 1 water)
1	dash	Dr. Adam Elmegirab's Boker's Bitters

Comment: Slightly on the bitter side of bittersweet with gentian, jammy apricot and lemon juice over a tequila base.

SUNSET STRIP (NEW)

★★★★½

Glass: Coupe
Garnish: Grapefruit zest twist
Method: SHAKE all ingredients with ice and fine strain into chilled glass.

1½	shot	Bourbon whiskey
1	shot	Aperol
1	shot	Pink grapefruit (pamplemousse rosé) liqueur

Comment: Eric Tecosky's original recipe for this drink called for 1.25oz of Jack Daniels Single Barrel in place of the bourbon used here. Being a mix of spirits and liqueurs it was stirred, as you'd expect of such a combination. However, somewhat reminiscent of Shakerato, the Sunset Strip seems to benefit from the aeration and extra dilution provided by shaking, hence this is the method we've chosen.
Origin: Adapted from 2015 recipe created by Eric Tecosky at Jones Hollywood, Los Angeles, USA.

SUNSHINE COCKTAIL #1 🗝

★★★★½

Glass: Martini
Garnish: Pineapple wedge
Method: SHAKE all ingredients with ice and fine strain into chilled glass.

1½	shots	Bacardi Carta Blanca light rum
1½	shots	Martini Extra Dry vermouth
1½	shots	Fresh pressed pineapple juice
⅛	shot	Pomegranate / grenadine syrup (2:1)

Origin: Adapted from a recipe in the 1949 edition of 'Esquire's Handbook for Hosts'.
Comment: Light, fruity and a tad on the sweet side, but could well brighten up your day.

SUNSHINE COCKTAIL #2

★★★★☆

Glass: Martini
Garnish: Lemon zest twist
Method: SHAKE all ingredients with ice and fine strain into chilled glass.

1½	shots	Bacardi Carta Blanca light rum
¼	shot	Lejay crème de cassis de Dijon
1½	shots	Martini Extra Dry vermouth
¼	shot	Freshly squeezed lemon juice

Origin: Adapted from a recipe in Harry Craddock's 1930 'The Savoy Cocktail Book'.
Comment: More a sunset but fruity, flavoursome and well-balanced all the same.

SUNSTROKE 🗝

★★★★☆

Glass: Martini
Garnish: Orange zest twist
Method: SHAKE all ingredients with ice and fine strain into chilled glass.

1	shot	Ketel One Vodka
1	shot	De Kuyper Triple Sec
2	shots	Freshly squeezed pink grapefruit juice

Comment: Fruity but balanced. One to sip in the shade.

SURF & TURF COCKTAIL (NEW)

★★★★½

Glass: Coupe
Garnish: Lemon zest twist
Method: **STIR** all ingredients with ice and strain into chilled glass.

1½ shots Old Tom gin
¾ shot Martini Extra Dry vermouth
½ shot Romate Fino sherry
¼ shot Orange Curaçao liqueur
1 dash Angostura Aromatic Bitters
½ shot Chilled water (omit if wet ice)

Origin: Created 8th September 2014 by yours truly at the Cabinet Room, London, England.
Comment: Fino sherry adds a slight salty 'surf' note to this riff on the classic Turf Club Cocktail.

THE SURFER

★★★★☆

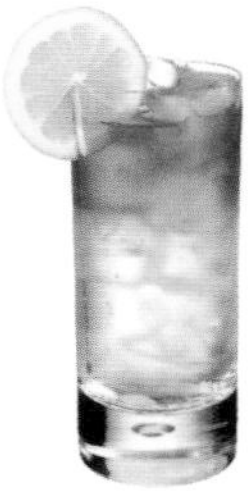

Glass: Collins
Garnish: Lemon slice
Method: **POUR** lemonade into ice-filled glass to two-thirds full. **FLOAT** cognac over lemonade. Serve with straws and instruct drinker to stir ingredients before drinking.

4 shots Lemonade (English-style)
2 shots Martell VSOP Médaillon cognac

Origin: Created in 2008 by yours truly. The original Cognac Surfer is made by floating cognac on mineral water.
Comment: Simple but tasty and very refreshing. The use of good ice and a quality lemonade is essential to this drink's success.

SURFER ON A.C.D.

★★★½☆

Glass: Shot
Garnish: None
Method: **SHAKE** first two ingredients with ice and fine strain into chilled glass. **FLOAT** Jagermeister.

½ shot Coconut rum liqueur
¼ shot Jägermeister
¾ shot Fresh pressed pineapple juice

Comment: The spirity herbal topping counters the sweet coconut and pineapple base.

SUZIE COCKTAIL (NEW)

★★★★★

Glass: Old-fashioned
Garnish: Pineapple wedge on rim
Method: **SHAKE** all ingredients with ice and strain into ice-filled glass.

1½ shots BarSol Mosto Verde Italia pisco
⅓ shot Suze Saveur d'Autrefois
1¼ shots Fresh pressed pineapple juice
½ shot Sauvignon blanc white wine
⅓ shot Sugar syrup (2 sugar to 1 water)

Origin: Created in August 2015 by yours truly at the Cabinet Room, London, England.
Comment: Pisco, pineapple and Sauvignon Blanc wine are a match made in heaven, while Suze provides complex underlying gentian bittersweet notes.

SWAMP WATER

★★★★☆

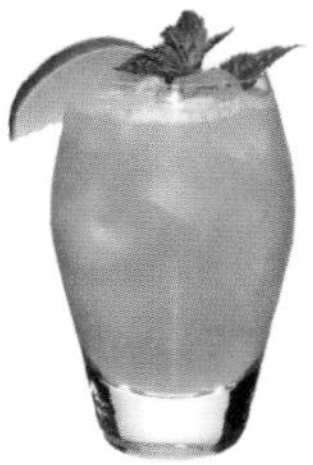

Glass: Collins
Garnish: Lime wedge & mint sprig
Method: **SHAKE** all ingredients with ice and strain into ice-filled glass.

1½ shots Green Chartreuse liqueur
4 shots Fresh pressed pineapple juice
½ shot Freshly squeezed lime juice

Comment: Long and refreshing - the herbal taste of Chartreuse combined with the fruitiness of pineapple.

SWEDISH ALE PUNCH

★★★★½

Glass: Collins
Garnish: Grapefruit slice
Method: **SHAKE** first 3 ingredients with ice and fine strain into chilled glass. **TOP** with beer.

2 shots Bourbon whiskey
1 shot Swedish Punch liqueur
1 shot Freshly squeezed pink grapefruit juice
Top with Fuller's Chiswick Bitter

Origin: Created in 2011 by yours truly at the Cabinet Room, London, England.
Comment: The grapefruit hop notes in the beer are amplified by fresh grapefruit juice while the beer's cereal notes are fortified with bourbon. Meanwhile, Swedish Punch both sweetens and adds flavour.

Swedish Punch (also known as Arrack Punch, Caloric Punch or Punsch) is a style of liqueur popular in Sweden and other Nordic countries. It's based on Batavia arrack (and other spices) which was first introduced from Java by the East Indian Company in 1773.

SWEDISH MARGARITA

★★★★½

Glass: Coupe
Garnish: Lime wedge
Method: **SHAKE** all ingredients with ice and fine strain into chilled glass.

2 shots Patrón reposado tequila
1 shot Swedish Punch liqueur
½ shot Freshly squeezed lime juice
¼ shot Freshly squeezed lemon juice

Origin: Created in 2010 by yours truly at the Cabinet Room, London, England.
Comment: A Swedish punch influenced Margarita. Tangy and oily.

SWEDISH RUM PUNCH

★★★★☆

Glass: Old-fashioned
Garnish: Lime wedge
Method: **SHAKE** all ingredients with ice and strain into ice-filled glass.

1½ shots Bacardi Carta Ocho aged rum
¾ shot Swedish Punch liqueur
½ shot Freshly squeezed lime juice

Origin: Created in 2008 by yours truly.
Comment: A flavoursome Daiquiri-style with the subtle spice of Swedish punch.

SWEET MARTINI

★★★★⯪

Glass: Martini
Garnish: Luxardo Maraschino cherry
Method: STIR all ingredients with ice and strain into chilled glass.

2½ shots   Rutte Dry Gin
½   shot   Martini Rosso vermouth

Comment: A gin martini made with sweet vermouth - sweet in name but drier than the cherry garnish might indicate.

SWEETIE PIE

★★★★☆

Glass: Coupe
Garnish: Apple wedge
Method: SHAKE all ingredients with ice and fine strain into chilled glass.

2   shots   Bacardi Carta Ocho aged rum
¼   shot   Allspice pimento dram liqueur
1½ shots   Pressed apple juice
2   dash   Angostura Aromatic Bitters
1   pinch   Salt

Origin: Adapted from a drink created by Lydia Reissmueller at Eletaria, New York City, USA.
Comment: Bitter sweet and most intriguing.

SWIZZLES COCKTAIL

★★★★⯪

Glass: Collins
Garnish: Crown with few dashes Angostura bitters on drinks ice peak, plus juniper berries
Method: POUR all ingredients into chilled glass and two-thirds fill with crushed ice. **SWIZZLE** with a swizzle stick (or churn with a barspoon). Add more crushed ice to fill and **SWIZZLE** some more. Serve with straws.

2   shots   Rutte Dry Gin
1   shot   Freshly squeezed lime juice
⅔   shot   Sugar syrup (2 sugar to 1 water)
1   dash   Angostura Aromatic Bitters

Origin: Adapted from Harry Craddock's 1930 'The Savoy Cocktail Book'.
Comment: Somewhat reminiscent of a frozen gimlet – the combination of gin and lime shines in this freshening swizzle.

TABU

★★★⯪☆

Glass: Coconut shell or Collins glass
Garnish: Pineapple cubes, Luxardo Maraschino cherry & mint sprig
Method: BLEND all ingredients with 12oz scoop crushed ice.

1   shot   Bacardi Carta Blanca light rum
1   shot   Ketel One Vodka
1½ shots   Fresh pressed pineapple juice
½   shot   Freshly squeezed lemon juice
¼   shot   Sugar syrup (2 sugar to 1 water)

Origin: Adapted from Victor Bergeron's 'Trader Vic's Bartender's Guide' (1972 revised edition) where Vic states the drink 'originated in Seattle'.
Comment: Ice-cold fresh pineapple laced with rum and vodka with a splash of citrus.

TABULA RASA

★★★⯪☆

Glass: Old-fashioned
Garnish: Orange zest twist
Method: POUR ingredients into ice-filled glass and stir.

1   shot   Chocolate Spirit
¾   shot   Campari Bitter
¾   shot   Carpano Antica Formula

Origin: Created in 2009 by Klaus St Rainer at Schumann's Bar, Munich, Germany.
Comment: A chocolate Negroni-style drink. Bitter chocolate laced with alcohol.

TAHITIAN HONEY BEE

★★★★☆

Glass: Martini
Garnish: Lemon zest twist
Method: STIR honey with rum in base of shaker so as to dissolve honey. Add lemon juice, **SHAKE** with ice and fine strain into chilled glass.

2   shots   Bacardi Carta Blanca light rum
2   spoon   Runny honey
½   shot   Freshly squeezed lemon juice

Origin: Adapted from Victor Bergeron's 'Trader Vic's Bartender's Guide' (1972 revised edition).
Comment: Basically a honey Daiquiri - very tasty it is too.

TAILOR MADE

★★★★☆

Glass: Martini
Garnish: Grapefruit zest twist
Method: STIR honey with bourbon in base of shaker to dissolve honey. Add other ingredients, **SHAKE** with ice and fine strain into chilled glass.

1   spoon   Runny honey
1½ shots   Bourbon whiskey
¼   shot   Taylor's Velvet Falernum liqueur
1   shot   Freshly squeezed pink grapefruit juice
1   shot   Cranberry juice

Origin: Created by Dale DeGroff in New York City, USA.
Comment: Light, balanced fruit and bourbon.

TANGLEFOOT

★★★★☆

Glass: Coupe
Garnish: Orange zest twist
Method: SHAKE all ingredients with ice and fine strain into chilled glass.

2   shots   Bacardi Carta Blanca light rum
1   shot   Swedish Punch liqueur
½   shot   Freshly squeezed lemon juice
½   shot   Freshly squeezed orange juice

Comment: Light rum, lemon and orange juice served short with a tang of Swedish punch.

TANGO MARTINI #1

★★★½☆

Glass: Martini
Garnish: Orange zest twist
Method: SHAKE all ingredients with ice and fine strain into chilled glass.

1½ shots	Rutte Dry Gin
½ shot	De Kuyper Triple Sec
½ shot	Martini Rosso vermouth
½ shot	Martini Extra Dry vermouth
1 shot	Freshly squeezed orange juice

Origin: Adapted from a recipe in Harry Craddock's 1930 Savoy Cocktail Book. Harry McElhone's 1929 'ABC of Cocktails' credits this drinks creation to Harry, a bartender at Palermo, Rue Fontaine, Paris.
Comment: Balanced and complex with hints of gin and orange.

TANGO MARTINI #2

★★★★☆

Glass: Martini
Garnish: Orange zest twist
Method: SHAKE all ingredients with ice and fine strain into chilled glass.

1¾ shots	Rutte Dry Gin
¾ shot	Passoa Liqueur
2 shots	Freshly squeezed pink grapefruit juice
¼ shot	Sugar syrup (2 sugar to 1 water)

Origin: Adapted from a drink discovered in 2003 at the Bellagio, Las Vegas, USA.
Comment: Floral and balanced.

TANTRIS SIDECAR NO.1

★★★★☆

Glass: Martini
Garnish: Lemon zest twist
Method: SHAKE all ingredients with ice and fine strain into chilled glass.

1 shot	Martell VSOP Médaillon cognac
½ shot	Calvados brandy
½ shot	De Kuyper Triple Sec
¼ shot	Green Chartreuse liqueur
¼ shot	Fresh pressed pineapple juice
½ shot	Freshly squeezed lemon juice
¼ shot	Sugar syrup (2 sugar to 1 water)

Origin: Adapted from a recipe created in 2000 by Audrey Saunders at Beacon, New York City, USA.
Comment: A Sidecar with extra interest courtesy of Chartreuse, pineapple and Calvados.

TAPERED NAIL

★★★★½

Glass: Old-fashioned
Garnish: Pineapple wedge
Method: STIR all ingredients with ice and strain into ice-filled glass.

2 shots	Bacardi Carta Ocho aged rum
1 shot	Drambuie liqueur
¼ shot	Islay single malt Scotch whisky

Origin: Created in 2010 by yours truly at the Cabinet Room, London, England.
Comment: Rum takes over from Scotch as base spirit in this Nail but Islay malt adds interest and keeps it a true Nail (being any drink with Drambuie and Scotch whisky).

TARTE TATIN COCKTAIL

★★★★☆

Glass: Martini
Garnish: Dust with cinnamon powder
Method: SHAKE first 3 ingredients with ice and strain into chilled glass. Separately, SHAKE cream and egg white with ice and strain back into shaker. DRY SHAKE (without ice) and carefully pour over back of spoon so as to LAYER over drink.

1½ shots	Vanilla infused Ketel One vodka
¾ shot	Apple Schnapps liqueur
¾ shot	Caramel liqueur
1 shot	Single cream / half-and-half
½ shot	Egg white

Origin: Created in 2003 by yours truly, London, England.
Comment: A creamy top hides a vanilla, apple and caramel combo. Inspired by the dessert created by the Tatin sisters, a tart of caramelised apples cooked under a pastry lid.

TARTINI

★★★★☆

Glass: Martini
Garnish: Raspberries
Method: MUDDLE raspberries in base of shaker. Add other ingredients, SHAKE with ice and fine strain into chilled glass.

2 shots	Ketel One Vodka
½ shot	Chambord Liqueur
1½ shots	Cranberry juice
12 fresh	Raspberries

Origin: Adapted from a cocktail discovered at the Soho Grand Hotel, New York City, USA during the 1990s.
Comment: Richly raspberry flavoured.

TATANKA

★★★★½

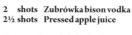

Glass: Old-fashioned
Garnish: Apple slice
Method: SHAKE all ingredients with ice and strain into ice-filled glass.

2 shots	Zubrówka bison vodka
2½ shots	Pressed apple juice

Origin: This Polish drink takes its name from the film 'Dances With Wolves'. Tatanka is a Native American word for buffalo and refers to the Bison grass flavoured vodka the cocktail is based on.
Comment: The taste of this excellent drink (which is equally good served straight-up) is a little reminiscent of Earl Grey tea.

TATANKA ROYALE

★★★★☆

Glass: Flute
Garnish: Apple slice
Method: SHAKE first two ingredients with ice and fine strain into chilled glass. TOP with champagne.

1 shot	Zubrówka bison vodka
1 shot	Pressed apple juice
Top with	G.H.Mumm Cordon Rouge Champagne

Origin: Discovered in 2004 at Indigo Yard, Edinburgh, Scotland.
Comment: Champagne with a subtle, grassy hint of apple.

TEAQUILA

★★★★☆

Glass: Glass teacup & saucer (or Collins over ice)
Garnish: Lemon slice
Method: SHAKE all ingredients with ice and fine strain into chilled glass.

2 shots   Cold English breakfast tea
1½ shots   Patrón silver tequila
½ shot   Honey Vodka
½ shot   Sugar syrup (2 sugar to 1 water)
½ shot   Freshly squeezed lemon juice
2 dash   Angostura Orange Bitters (optional)

Origin: Created in 2011 by Mark Cooke and the rest of the team at North Bar, Leeds, England.
Comment: A Mexican iced tea sweetened with honey.

TEDDY BEAR

★★★★☆

Glass: Martini
Garnish: Pear slice
Method: SHAKE all ingredients with ice and fine strain into chilled glass.

1½ shots Pear liqueur
¾ shot Apple Schnapps liqueur
1½ shots Pressed apple juice
1 pinch Ground cinnamon

Origin: Created in 2002 at The Borough, Edinburgh, Scotland. Originally named after a well-known cockney duo but renamed after the cockney rhyming slang for pear.
Comment: Light (low in alcohol) and tad on the sweet side, apple and pear with a hint of cinnamon spice.

TENNER MARTINI

★★★★⯪

Glass: Martini
Garnish: Grapefruit zest twist
Method: STIR all ingredients with ice and strain into chilled glass.

2 shots   Rutte Dry Gin
1 shot   Martini Extra Dry vermouth
2 dash   Grapefruit bitters

Comment: Very wet, aromatic Martini.

TENNESSEE BERRY MULE

★★★★☆

Glass: Collins
Garnish: Raspberries
Method: MUDDLE raspberries in base of shaker. Add next four ingredients, SHAKE with ice and strain into ice-filled glass. TOP with ginger beer, lightly stir and serve with straws.

8 fresh   Raspberries
1½ shots   Jack Daniel's Old No.7 Brand
1 shot   Disaronno Originale amaretto
1½ shots   Cranberry juice
½ shot   Freshly squeezed lime juice
Top with   Gosling's Stormy Ginger Beer

Origin: Adapted in 2003 from a recipe Alex Kammerling created for TGI Friday's UK. Named partly for the ingredients and partly as a reference to Jack Daniel's proprietor (and nephew), Lemuel Motlow, who took up mule trading during Prohibition.
Comment: A berry rich cocktail laced with whiskey, flavoured with Amaretto and topped with ginger beer.

TENNESSEE ICED TEA

★★★★☆

Glass: Sling
Garnish: Lemon wedge on rim
Method: SHAKE first six ingredients with ice and strain into ice-filled glass. TOP with cola and serve with straws.

1 shot   Jack Daniel's Old No.7 Brand
½ shot   Bacardi Carta Blanca light rum
½ shot   Ketel One Vodka
½ shot   De Kuyper Triple Sec
⅔ shot   Freshly squeezed lemon juice
¼ shot   Sugar syrup (2 sugar to 1 water)
Top with   Coca-Cola

Comment: Whiskey and cola with extra interest courtesy of several other spirits and lemon juice.

TENNESSEE RUSH

★★★★☆

Glass: Collins
Garnish: Lime wedge
Method: SHAKE all ingredients with ice and strain into ice-filled glass.

2 shots   Jack Daniel's Old No.7 Brand
1 shot   Mandarine Napoléon liqueur
2½ shots   Cranberry juice
½ shot   Freshly squeezed lime juice

Comment: This ruby red cocktail is long, fruity, refreshing and not too sweet.

STAR RATINGS EXPLAINED

★★★★★+	OUTSTANDING	★★★★★	EXCEPTIONAL
★★★★⯪	EXCELLENT	★★★★☆	RECOMMENDED
★★★⯪☆	COMMENDED	★★★☆☆	MEDIOCRE
★★⯪☆☆	DISAPPOINTING	★★☆☆☆	PRETTY AWFUL
★⯪☆☆☆	SHAMEFUL	★☆☆☆☆	DISGUSTING

TENNESSEE SOUR (NEW)

★★★★☆

Glass: Old-fashioned
Garnish: Lemon zest twist
Method: SHAKE all ingredients with ice and strain into ice-filled glass.

2 shots Jack Daniel's Old No.7 Brand
1 shot Freshly squeezed lemon juice
½ shot Sugar syrup (2 sugar to 1 water)
1 dash Angostura Aromatic Bitters
½ fresh Egg white

Origin: The Whiskey Sour was first published in Jerry Thomas' 'How to Mix Drinks or the Bon Vivant's Companion' in 1862. The Jack Daniels distillery was established and registered just four years later.

TEQRONI

★★★★½

Glass: Old-fashioned
Garnish: Orange zest twist
Method: POUR all ingredients into ice-filled glass and stir.

1 shot Patrón silver tequila
1 shot Aperol Aperitivo
1 shot Martini Rosso vermouth

Origin: Unknown, but as the same suggests this is simply a tequila-based Negroni.
Comment: Lighter and slightly sweeter than a classic gin-based Negroni with Campari. However, this Italian and Mexican trio make for pleasing cross continental bedfellows.

TEQUILA BASIL LEMONADE

★★★★½

Glass: Collins
Garnish: Lemon wedge & basil leaf
Method: SHAKE first 4 ingredients with ice and fine strain into ice-filled glass. TOP with soda and gently stir.

2 shots Patrón reposado tequila
3 fresh Basil leaves
½ shot Sugar syrup (2 sugar to 1 water)
¾ shot Freshly squeezed lemon juice
Top with Soda (club soda)

Origin: Created in 2011 by Chris Stave.
Comment: Just as it says on the tin, tequila charged with lemonade and flavoured with basil.

TEQUILA FIZZ

★★★½☆

Glass: Sling
Garnish: Orange zest twist
Method: SHAKE first four ingredients with ice and strain into ice-filled glass. TOP with lemonade.

2 shots Patrón reposado tequila
1 shot Freshly squeezed orange juice
1 shot Freshly squeezed lime juice
½ shot Sugar syrup (2 sugar to 1 water)
Top with Lemonade/Sprite/7-Up

Comment: Refreshing with lingering lime.

TEQUILA GIMLET

★★★☆☆

Glass: Martini
Garnish: Lime wedge
Method: STIR all ingredients with ice and strain into chilled glass.

2½ shots Patrón reposado tequila
¾ shot Rose's lime cordial

Comment: Tequila flavoured and slightly sweetened by lime cordial.

TEQUILA MOCKINGBIRD

★★★½☆

Glass: Martini
Garnish: Mint leaf
Method: SHAKE all ingredients with ice and fine strain into chilled glass.

2 shots Patrón reposado tequila
½ shot Green crème de menthe liqueur
½ shot Freshly squeezed lime juice
⅓ shot Sugar syrup (2 sugar to 1 water)

Origin: Named after Harper Lee's 1960 novel 'To Kill a Mockingbird', this is thought to have been created some time in the 1960s. Genius.
Comment: Minty tequila.

TEQUILA OLD FASHIONED (NEW)

★★★★★

Glass: Old-fashioned
Garnish: Orange zest twist
Method: STIR one shot of tequila with three ice cubes (dry to the touch frozen ice, not wet ice) in a glass. Add sugar syrup and Angostura bitters and two more ice cubes. STIR some more and add another two ice cubes and the rest of the tequila. STIR some more, and if you have room, add more ice.

2½ shots Patrón añejo tequila
¼ shot Agave syrup
3 dash Angostura Aromatic Bitters

Comment: A hint of agave syrup sweetness and dilution from the stirred ice knock back the spirit's fire while opening and releasing flavours.

TEQUILA SLAMMER

★★★☆☆

Glass: Shot
Garnish: None
Method: POUR tequila into glass and then carefully LAYER with champagne. The drinker should hold and cover the top of the glass with the palm of their hand so as to grip it firmly and seal the contents inside. Then they should briskly pick the glass up and slam it down (obviously not so hard as to break the glass), then gulp the drink down in one while it is still fizzing.

1 shot Patrón reposado tequila
1 shot G.H. Mumm Cordon Rouge Champagne

Origin: Originally topped with ginger ale and not champagne, this infamous libation is thought to have started out as a Hell's Angel drink - it needs no ice and can be carried in a bike bag.

The simplest slammer is a lick of salt, a shot of tequila and then a bite of lemon (or lime).

A Bermuda Slammer involves straight tequila, salt, a slice of lemon and a partner: one has to lick the salt off the other one's neck and bite the lemon (held between their partner's teeth) before downing a shot of tequila.
Comment: To quote Victor Bergeron (Trader Vic), "You know, this rigmarole with a pinch of salt and lemon juice and tequila - in whatever order - was originally for a purpose: It's hot in Mexico. People dehydrate themselves. And they need more salt. Here, it's not so hot, and we don't need salt in the same way. So you can drink tequila straight right out of the bottle, if you want to."

TEQUILA SMASH

★★★★½

Glass: Old-fashioned
Garnish: Mint sprig
Method: SHAKE all ingredients with ice and fine strain into ice-filled glass.

7 fresh Mint leaves
2 shots Patrón reposado tequila
¼ shot Agave syrup

Origin: Adapted from the classic Brandy Smash.
Comment: Simple, not too sweet - a great way to appreciate quality tequila.

TEQUILA SOUR

★★★★½

Glass: Old-fashioned
Garnish: Lime zest twist
Method: SHAKE all ingredients with ice and fine strain into ice-filled glass.

2 shots Patrón reposado tequila
1 shot Freshly squeezed lime juice
½ shot Sugar syrup (2 sugar to 1 water)
½ fresh Egg white

Comment: A standard sour but with tequila zing.

TEQUILA SUNRISE

★★★★½

Glass: Collins
Garnish: Orange slice
Method: SHAKE first two ingredients with ice and strain into ice-filled glass. POUR grenadine in a circle around the top of the drink (it will sink to create a sunrise effect).

2 shots Patrón reposado tequila
¾ shot Pomegranate / grenadine syrup (2:1)
3 shots Freshly squeezed orange juice

Comment: Everyone has heard of this drink, but those who have tried it will wonder why it's so famous.

TEQUILA SUNSET

★★★★☆

Glass: Sling
Garnish: Lemon slice
Method: STIR honey with tequila in base of shaker until honey dissolves. Add other ingredients, SHAKE with ice and strain into ice-filled glass. TOP with soda.

7 spoon Runny honey
2 shots Patrón reposado tequila
2 shots Freshly squeezed lemon juice

Comment: A good sweet and sour balance with subtle honey hints.

TEQUILA'TINI

★★★★½

Glass: Martini
Garnish: Lime zest twist
Method: SHAKE all ingredients with ice and fine strain into chilled glass.

2 shots Patrón reposado tequila
1 shot Martini Extra Dry vermouth
½ shot Sugar syrup (2 sugar to 1 water)
3 dash Angostura Aromatic Bitters

Comment: If you like tequila and strong drinks - this is for you.

TERESA

★★★☆☆

Glass: Martini
Garnish: Lime wedge
Method: SHAKE all ingredients with ice and fine strain into chilled glass.

2 shots Campari Bitter
1 shot Freshly squeezed lime juice
¾ shot Lejay Crème de Cassis de Dijon

Origin: Created by Rafael Ballesteros of Spain, this recipe is taken from 'The Joy of Mixology' by Gary Regan.
Comment: Bold, sweet and sour.

TEST PILOT

★★★★☆

Glass: Old-fashioned
Garnish: Lime zest twist
Method: SHAKE all ingredients with ice and fine strain into ice-filled glass.

1½ shots   Bacardi Carta Ocho aged rum
¾ shot   Bacardi Carta Blanca light rum
¼ shot   De Kuyper Triple Sec
¼ shot   Taylor's Velvet Falernum liqueur
¼ shot   Freshly squeezed lemon juice

Origin: Adapted from a recipe in the 1947-72 Trader Vic's Bartender's Guide by Victor Bergeron.
Comment: A fruity, sophisticated Daiquiri with hints of almond and spicy clove, served short over ice.

TESTAROSSA

★★★☆☆

Glass: Collins
Garnish: Orange slice
Method: POUR all ingredients into ice-filled glass, lightly stir and serve with straws.

1½ shots   Ketel One Vodka
1½ shots   Campari Bitter
Top with   Soda (club soda)

Comment: Campari and soda with some oomph.

TEX COLLINS

★★★★☆

Glass: Collins
Garnish: Lemon slice
Method: STIR honey with gin in base of shaker to dissolve honey. Add grapefruit juice, SHAKE with ice and strain into ice-filled glass. TOP with soda water.

2   shots   Rutte Dry Gin
2   spoon   Runny honey
2   shots   Freshly squeezed pink grapefruit juice
Top with   Soda (club soda)

Origin: Adapted from a recipe in the 1949 edition of 'Esquire's Handbook for Hosts'.
Comment: A dry, tart blend of grapefruit and gin.

TEXAS ICED TEA

★★★★☆

Glass: Sling
Garnish: Lemon wedge
Method: SHAKE first six ingredients with ice and strain into ice-filled glass. TOP with cola.

1   shot   Patrón reposado tequila
½   shot   Bacardi Carta Blanca light rum
½   shot   Ketel One Vodka
½   shot   De Kuyper Triple Sec
¾   shot   Freshly squeezed lemon juice
¼   shot   Sugar syrup (2 sugar to 1 water)
Top with   Coca-Cola

Comment: Our favourite of the Iced Tea family of drinks. The tequila shines through.

TEXSUN

★★★☆☆

Glass: Martini
Garnish: Lemon zest twist
Method: SHAKE all ingredients with ice and fine strain into chilled glass.

1½ shots   Bourbon whiskey
1½ shots   Martini Extra Dry vermouth
1½ shots   Freshly squeezed pink grapefruit juice

Origin: Adapted from a recipe in the 1949 edition of 'Esquire's Handbook for Hosts'.
Comment: Bone dry with fruity herbal hints.

THAI GREEN COCKTAIL (NEW)

★★★★☆

Glass: Old-fashioned
Garnish: 3 sprigs coriander
Method: MUDDLE first 3 ingredients in base of shaker. SHAKE all ingredients with ice and fine strain into ice-filled glass.

1 inch Lemongrass stem (chopped)
7 fresh Coriander seeds
3 sprig Coriander (cilantro) leaves
2 shots Ketel One Vodka
½ shot Freshly squeezed lime juice
½ shot Coconut syrup

Origin: Created in September 2014 by yours truly at the Cabinet Room, London, England to accompany Spiced Beef and Chilli Blinis.
Comment: Extracting the juice from the stems and leaves of the coriander is key to both the colour and flavour of this fresh tasting cocktail, inspired by some of the flavours of a Thai Green Curry - only without the chilli heat.

THAI LEMONADE (MOCKTAIL)

★★★☆☆

Glass: Collins
Garnish: Lime wedge
Method: MUDDLE coriander in base of shaker. Add next two ingredients, SHAKE with ice and fine strain into ice-filled glass. TOP with ginger beer.

5   sprigs   Fresh coriander
2   shots   Freshly squeezed lime juice
½   shot   Almond (orgeat) syrup
Top with   Gosling's Stormy Ginger Beer

Origin: Adapted from a drink created in 2005 by Charlotte Voisey, London, England.
Comment: Lime lemonade with Thai influences courtesy of ginger, almond and coriander.

THAI RED DAIQUIRI

★★★★☆

Glass: Old-fashioned
Garnish: Red pepper slice
Method: MUDDLE pepper in base of shaker. Add other ingredients, **SHAKE** with ice and fine strain into chilled glass.

½ slice **Red bell pepper**
3 fresh **Basil leaves** (thai)
2 shots **Bacardi Carta Ocho aged rum**
½ fresh **Coconut water**
½ shot **Freshly squeezed lime juice**
¼ sprig **Sugar syrup (2 sugar to 1 water)**

Origin: Aged rum, delicately spiced by red pepper and basil.
Comment: Created in December 2008 by yours truly at the Cabinet Room, London, England.

THERE IT IS... (NEW)

★★★★★

Glass: Old-fashioned
Garnish: Blood orange slice
Method: SHAKE all ingredients with ice and strain into ice-filled glass.

1 shot **Dewar's 12yo Scotch whisky**
1 shot **Rutte Old Simon oude jenever**
½ shot **Luxardo Maraschino liqueur**
1 shot **Blood orange juice**

Origin: Created by yours truly in March 2014 at the Cabinet Room, London, England.
Comment: Jenever is basically a blend of whisky and gin and in this drink combines wonderfully with Scotch as a base to which maraschino and blood orange flavour and lengthen.

THOMAS BLOOD MARTINI

★★★☆☆

Glass: Martini
Garnish: Apple wedge
Method: STIR honey with vodka in base of shaker until honey dissolves. Add other ingredients, **SHAKE** with ice and fine strain into chilled glass.

2 spoon **Runny honey**
1 shot **Ketel One Vodka**
1 shot **Old Krupnik**
1 shot **Apple Schnapps liqueur**
1 shot **Freshly squeezed lemon juice**

Comment: An appealing, honey led melange of sweet and sour.

THREE MILER

★★★★☆

Glass: Martini
Garnish: Lemon zest twist
Method: SHAKE all ingredients with ice and fine strain into chilled glass.

1½ shots **Martell VSOP Médaillon cognac**
1½ shots **Bacardi Carta Blanca light rum**
½ shot **Pomegranate / grenadine syrup (2:1)**
½ shot **Freshly squeezed lemon juice**

Origin: Adapted from the Three Miller Cocktail in the 1930 'Savoy Cocktail Book'.
Comment: A seriously strong drink, in flavour and in alcohol.

THREESOME

★★★½☆

Glass: Martini
Garnish: Pineapple wedge
Method: SHAKE all ingredients with ice and fine strain into chilled glass.

1½ shots **Calvados brandy**
1 shot **De Kuyper Triple Sec**
½ shot **Pernod anise**
1½ shots **Fresh pressed pineapple juice**

Origin: Adapted from a drink discovered in 2002 at Circus Bar, London, England.
Comment: Why stop at three when you can have a foursome? An interesting meld of apple, orange, anise and pineapple.

THRILLER COCKTAIL

★★★½☆

Glass: Martini
Garnish: Orange zest twist
Method: SHAKE all ingredients with ice and fine strain into chilled glass.

2 shots Dewar's 12yo Scotch whisky
¾ shot Rutte Dry Gin
¾ shot Freshly squeezed orange juice
¼ shot Sugar syrup (2 sugar to 1 water)

Comment: Spiced Scotch with a hint of orange.

THRILLER FROM VANILLA

★★★★☆

Glass: Martini
Garnish: Half vanilla pod
Method: SHAKE all ingredients with ice and fine strain into chilled glass.

¾ shot **Vanilla infused Ketel One vodka**
¾ shot **Rutte Dry Gin**
½ shot **De Kuyper Triple Sec**
2 shots **Freshly squeezed orange juice**

Origin: Adapted from a drink discovered in 2003 at Oporto, Leeds, England. The 'Thriller in Manila' was the name given to the 1975 heavyweight fight between Muhammad Ali and Smokin' Joe Frazier.
Comment: Orange and creamy vanilla fortified with a hint of gin.

THUIR SOUR (NEW)

★★★★⯨

Glass: Coupe
Garnish: Orange zest twist
Method: SHAKE all ingredients with ice and strain back into shaker. **DRY SHAKE** (without ice) and fine strain into chilled glass.

1	shot	Byrrh Grand Quinquina
½	shot	De Kuyper XO Apricot Brandy
¾	shot	Freshly squeezed lemon juice
⅓	shot	Sugar syrup (2 sugar to 1 water)
¼	fresh	Egg white
¾	shot	Chilled water (omit if wet ice)

Origin: Adapted from a drink created in 2015 by Stuart Bale of 69 Colebrooke Row, London during a visit to Thuir in the South of France where Byrrh has been made since the 1870s. When Stuart asked what Thuir was famous for, apart from Byrrh, the locals claimed their apricots were the best in the world. Hence Stuart's use of Byrrh and crème d'apricot in this cocktail.
Comment: Perfectly balanced sweet and sour apricot with faint red wine notes.

THUNDERBIRD

★★★★☆

Glass: Martini
Garnish: Pineapple wedge
Method: SHAKE all ingredients with ice and fine strain into chilled glass.

1½	shots	Bourbon whiskey
¾	shot	Disaronno Originale amaretto
1	shot	Fresh pressed pineapple juice
1	shot	Freshly squeezed orange juice

Comment: Tangy bourbon with fruity almond.

TI PUNCH

★★★★☆

Glass: Old-fashioned
Garnish: Lime zest twist
Method: POUR the rum and sugar into glass. Then SQUEEZE the lime disc between finger and thumb before dropping into the drink. This expresses the oil from the skin and little of the juice into the Ti Punch. Lastly STIR and consider adding two or three ice cubes.

1½	shots	Martinique blanc rhum agricole
¼	shot	Martinique cane sugar syrup
1	slice	Lime (fresh whole)

Origin: Named Ti from the French word 'Petit', this is literally a small rum punch: unlike most rum punches, it is not lengthened with water or juice. It is popular in the French islands of Martinique, Guadeloupe, Réunion and Maurice where it's often drunk straight down without adding ice and chased by a large glass of chilled water (called a 'crase' in Martinique). These islands are also home to Rhum Agricole (a style of rum distilled only from sugar cane juice and usually bottled at 50% alc./vol.)
Comment: This drink only works with authentic agricole rum and sugar cane juice. On its native islands it is usual to use rhum blanc (unaged white agricole rum) during the day and rhum vieux (aged agricole rum) during the evening. Note: Traditionally the limes used to make this drink are not cut into slices or wedges. Instead a round disc is cut from the side of the fruit. These are cut large enough that some of the fruits pulp backs the peel on the disc.

TIGER'S MILK

★★★⯨☆

Glass: Old-fashioned
Garnish: Dust with grated nutmeg
Method: SHAKE all ingredients with ice and strain into ice-filled glass.

2	shots	Martell VSOP Médaillon cognac
2	drop	Vanilla extract
1	pinch	Ground cinnamon
¼	shot	Sugar syrup (2 sugar to 1 water)
¾	shot	Milk
¾	shot	Single cream / half-and-half
½	fresh	Egg white

Origin: Adapted from a recipe purloined from Charles H. Baker Jr's classic book, 'The Gentleman's Companion'. He first discovered this drink in April 1931 at Gerber's Snug Bar, Peking, China.
Comment: Creamy cognac and spice.

TIJUANA BRASS 0━

★★★★⯨

Glass: Old-fashioned
Garnish: Cucumber foam
Method: SHAKE first three ingredients with ice and fine strain into ice-filled glass. Top with cucumber foam (fill a cream whipper two-thirds full with equal parts liquified cucumber juice, 1:1 simple syrup and egg white, charge with two CO2 cartridges and chill).

2	shots	Patrón reposado tequila
¾	shot	Agave syrup
1	shot	Freshly squeezed lime juice

Origin: Created in 2009 by Damian Windsor at The Roger Room, Los Angeles, USA.
Comment: Pronounced "Tea-You-One-Na" this is basically a Tommy's Margarita topped with cucumber foam.

TIKI MARGARITA

★★★★⯨

Glass: Old-fashioned
Garnish: Mint leaf, lime & pineapple wedges
Method: SHAKE all ingredients with ice and strain into glass filled with crushed ice.

2	shots	Patrón reposado tequila
½	shot	Almond (orgeat) syrup
1	shot	Freshly squeezed lime juice

Origin: Created in 2005 by Crispin Somerville and Jasper Eyears at Bar Tiki, Mexico City.
Comment: A simple almond twist on the classic Margarita - fantastic.

TILT

★★★★☆

Glass: Sling
Garnish: Pineapple leaf
Method: SHAKE first five ingredients with ice and strain into glass filled with crushed ice. **TOP** with bitter lemon.

1½	shots	Pineapple flavoured vodka
½	shot	Coconut rum liqueur
1½	shots	Fresh pressed pineapple juice
1	shot	Freshly squeezed pink grapefruit juice
¼	shot	Vanilla sugar syrup
Top with		Bitter lemon

Comment: Totally tropical taste.

TIP TOP COCKTAIL

★★★★⯪

Glass: Coupe
Garnish: Lemon zest twist
Method: STIR all ingredients with ice and strain into chilled glass.

2	shots	Martini Extra Dry vermouth
¾	shot	Bénédictine D.O.M. liqueur
2	dash	Angostura Aromatic Bitters

Origin: Recipe adapted from Albert S. Crockett's 1935 'Old Waldorf Bar Days'.
Comment: The lemon zest twist is essential to the fine balance of this vermouth (note; no spirit) cocktail.

TIPPERARY COCKTAIL NO.1

★★★★⯪

Glass: Coupe
Garnish: Orange zest twist (discarded) & Luxardo Maraschino cherry
Method: STIR all ingredients with ice and strain into chilled glass.

1½	shot	Teeling Small Batch Irish whiskey
½	shot	Green Chartreuse
1	shot	Martini Rosso sweet vermouth
½	shot	Chilled water (omit if wet ice)

Comment: Chartreuse fans will love this serious drink. The uninitiated will hate it.
Origin: Adapted from a recipe which first appeared in Hugo R. Ensslin's 1916 *Recipes for Mixed Drinks* where he stipulates equal parts. It also appears in Harry McElhone's 1922 *ABC of Mixing Cocktails*, although McElhone's recipe calls for ½ ounce Green Chartreuse, 2 ounces Irish whiskey and 1 ounce sweet vermouth by the time Harry Craddock publishes his 1930 *The Savoy Cocktail Book* the recipe returns to its original equal parts formulation and is joined by a second unrelated recipe also called Tipperary No.2.

TIPPERARY #2 0️⃣🔫

★★★★⯪

Glass: Martini
Garnish: Mint leaf
Method: Lightly MUDDLE mint in base in shaker (just to bruise). Add other ingredients, SHAKE with ice and fine strain into chilled glass.

7	fresh	Mint leaves
2	shots	Rutte Dry Gin
1	shot	Martini Extra Dry vermouth
¼	shot	Freshly squeezed orange juice
¼	shot	Pomegranate / grenadine syrup (2:1)

Origin: This drink first appears (along side Tipperary No.1) in Harry Craddock's 1930 *The Savoy Cocktail Book* where he stipulates 2 mint sprigs, 1 dry gin, 1 dry vermouth, ½ grenadine and ½ orange juice. We've adapted our recipe from David Embury's later, *The Fine Art of Mixing Drinks*.
Comment: Delicate with subtle hints of mint, orange and gin.

TIRAMISU MARTINI

★★★★⯪

Glass: Martini
Garnish: Dust with chocolate powder
Method: SHAKE all ingredients with ice and fine strain into chilled glass.

1	shot	Martell VSOP Médaillon cognac
½	shot	Coffee liqueur
½	shot	Dark crème de cacao liqueur
1	shot	Single cream / half-and-half
½	fresh	Egg yolk
1	spoon	Mascarpone cheese

Origin: Created by Adam Ennis in 2001 at Isola, London, England.
Comment: The chef meets the bartender in the rich dessert cocktail.

TNT (TEQUILA 'N' TONIC) 0️⃣🔫

★★★★☆

Glass: Collins
Garnish: Lime wedge
Method: POUR all ingredients into ice-filled glass and STIR.

1½	shots	Patrón reposado tequila
½	shot	Freshly squeezed lime juice
Top with		Tonic Water

Origin: Adapted from Victor Bergeron's 'Trader Vic's Bartender's Guide' (1972 revised edition).
Comment: A simple but very tasty way to enjoy tequila.

TO BE ORANGED COCKTAIL (NEW)

★★★★⯪

Glass: Coupe
Garnish: Orange zest (discarded) & orange wedge on rim
Method: SHAKE all ingredients with ice and fine strain into chilled glass.

1¼	shots	Patrón reposado tequila
1¼	shots	Byrrh Grand Quinquina
1¼	shots	Freshly squeezed orange juice
4	drop	Bob's Chocolate bitters

Origin: Created in August 2015 by yours truly at the Cabinet Room, London, England.
Comment: To be arranged - In the meantime shake your tangerine with this pleasing earthy tequila and zesty fruity number.

TOAST & ORANGE COCKTAIL

★★★★☆

Glass: Martini
Garnish: Orange zest twist
Method: SHAKE all ingredients with ice and fine strain into chilled glass.

2	shots	Bourbon whiskey
1	spoon	English orange marmalade
3	dash	Peychaud's aromatic bitters
⅛	shot	Sugar syrup (2 sugar to 1 water)

Comment: Bourbon rounded and enhanced by bitter orange and Peychaud's bitters.

TOASTED ALMOND

★★★★☆

Glass: Martini
Garnish: Dust with chocolate powder
Method: SHAKE all ingredients with ice and fine strain into chilled glass.

1	shot	Ketel One Vodka
1	shot	Disaronno Originale amaretto
¾	shot	Coffee liqueur
¾	shot	Single cream / half-and-half
¾	shot	Milk

Comment: Slightly sweet but smooth, creamy and definitely toasted.

TOBLERONE

★★★★½

Glass: Martini
Garnish: Segments of Toblerone chocolate on rim
Method: STIR honey with vodka in base of shaker until honey dissolves. Add other ingredients, SHAKE with ice and strain back into shaker. DRY SHAKE (without ice) and strain into chilled glass.

2	spoon	Runny honey
1½	shots	Vanilla infused Ketel One vodka
½	shot	Disaronno Originale amaretto
1¼	shots	Dark crème de cacao liqueur
¾	shot	Single cream / half-and-half
½	fresh	Egg white

Origin: Created in 2003 by yours truly and originally named the Triangular Martini after the triangular Toblerone chocolate bar, which incidentally was invented in 1908 by the Swiss chocolate maker Theodor Tobler.

The chocolate bar's name is a blend of Tobler with Torrone, the Italian word for honey-almond nougat, one of its main ingredients.
Comment: Nibble at the garnish as you sip honeyed, chocolate and almond flavoured liquid candy.

TOFFEE APPLE

★★★★☆

Glass: Sling
Garnish: Apple wedge
Method: SHAKE all ingredients with ice and strain into ice-filled glass.

1	shot	Calvados brandy
2	shots	Caramel liqueur
1	shot	Pressed apple juice
¼	shot	Freshly squeezed lime juice

Origin: Created in 2002 by Nick Strangeway, London, England.
Comment: The taste is just as the name suggests.

TOKYO BLOODY MARY

★★★★☆

Glass: Collins
Garnish: Celery stick
Method: SHAKE all ingredients with ice and strain into ice-filled glass.

2	shots	Junmai ginjō sake
3½	shots	Tomato juice
½	shot	Freshly squeezed lemon juice
¼	shot	Tawny port
7	drop	Tabasco hot pepper sauce
3	dash	Worcestershire sauce
1	pinch	Celery salt
1	grind	Black pepper

Comment: Sake adds an interesting dimension to the traditionally vodka based Bloody Mary.

TOKYO ICED TEA

★★★½☆

Glass: Sling
Garnish: Lemon slice
Method: SHAKE first seven ingredients with ice and strain into ice-filled glass. TOP with lemonade, lightly stir and serve with straws.

½	shot	Bacardi Carta Blanca light rum
½	shot	Rutte Dry Gin
½	shot	Ketel One Vodka
½	shot	Patrón reposado tequila
½	shot	De Kuyper Triple Sec
½	shot	Midori Green Melon liqueur
1	shot	Freshly squeezed lime juice
Top with		Lemonade/Sprite/7-Up

Comment: You will be surprised how the half shot of melon liqueur shows through the many other ingredients.

TOLLEYTOWN PUNCH

★★★★☆

Glass: Collins
Garnish: Orange & lemon slices
Method: SHAKE first four ingredients with ice and strain into ice-filled glass. TOP with ginger ale.

2	shots	Jack Daniel's Old No.7 Brand
2	shots	Cranberry juice
½	shot	Fresh pressed pineapple juice
½	shot	Freshly squeezed orange juice
Top with		Ginger ale

Origin: A drink promoted by Jack Daniel's. Tolleytown lies just down the road from Lynchburg, USA.
Comment: A fruity long drink with a dry edge that also works well made in bulk and served from a punch bowl.

TOM & JERRY

★★★★½

Glass: Toddy
Garnish: Dust with freshly grated nutmeg
Method: 1) Pre-warm six 20cl (6.75oz) toddy glasses or Tom & Jerry mugs with hot water. 2) Using a whisk, **BEAT** the yolks in a mixing bowl "until they are thin as water." Add sugar, Jamaican rum, spices and **STIR** thoroughly with whisk. 3) In a separate bowl, use a whisk to **BEAT** the egg whites "to a stiff froth." 4) Use a tablespoon to **FOLD** the frothy egg whites into the spiced and beaten yolk mixture. This produces the gloopy base mixture known as 'Tom & Jerry batter.' 5) To make individual drinks, to each of the warmed glasses or mugs, **POUR** cognac and rum, and add two table spoons of Tom & Jerry batter. **STIR** each glass/mug thoroughly with a barspoon while topping with boiling water. 6) Each should end up with frothy head ready to receive the garnish of grated nutmeg. Serve and enjoy.

2	fresh	Egg whites
2	fresh	Egg yolks
6	spoon	Caster sugar
½	shot	Pot still Jamaican rum
2	pinch	Cinnamon
2	pinch	Clove
3	pinch	Nutmeg
1½	shot	Martell VSOP Médaillon
½	shot	Bacardi Carta Ocho aged rum
Top with		Boiling water

Comment: A warming and filling winter's meal in itself. This recipe will fill six small toddy glasses or Tom & Jerry mugs (each 20cl capacity to brim), and given the faff involved you might as well double or treble the recipe and make for a crowd, or enjoy several each.
Origin: Due to his own claims of being this drink's inventor, the Tom & Jerry was for many years created to Jerry Thomas at the Planter's House Hotel in St Louis. However, the Tom & Jerry's real origins predate the flamboyant 'Professor'.

Although there are many earlier written references to this drink, the cocktail appeared in Jerry Thomas' first 1862 edition of *How To Mix Drinks* as follows:

Tom and Jerry
(Use punch-bowl for the mixture.)

> 5 lbs. sugar.
> 12 eggs.
> ½ small glass of Jamaican rum.
> 1½ teaspoonful of ground cinnamon.
> ½ teaspoon of ground cloves.
> ½ teaspoon of ground allspice.

Beat the whites of the eggs to a stiff froth, and the yolks until they are thin as water, then mix together and add the spice and rum, thicken with sugar until the mixture attains the consistency of a light batter.
To deal out Tom and Jerry to customers:
Take a small bar glass, and to one table-spoonful of the above mixture, add one wine-glass of brandy, and fill the glass with boiling water, grate a little nutmeg on top.
Adepts at the bar, in serving Tom and Jerry, sometimes adopt a mixture of 1/2 brandy, 1/4 Jamaican rum, and 1/4 Santa Cruz rum, instead of brandy plain. This compound is usually mixed and kept in a bottle, and a wine-glassful is used in each tumbler of Tom and Jerry. This drink is sometimes called Copenhagen, and sometimes Jerry Thomas."

Jerry Thomas became synonymous with the Tom and Jerry cocktail. Indeed, in his own recipe above, he says the drink sometimes takes his own name. And during his career he repeatedly claimed the drink as his own, including an often quoted 1880 interview by a reporter named Alan Dale, an interview repeated almost word for word in Thomas' New York Times obituary, which appears as follows courtesy of David Wondrich's 2015 *Imbibe!*:

"One day in... 1847 a gentleman asked me to give him an egg beaten up in sugar. I prepared the article, and then... I thought to myself, 'How beautiful the egg and sugar would be with brandy to it!' I ran to the gentleman and, says I, 'If you'll only bear with me for five minutes I'll fix you up a drink that'll do your heartstrings good.' He wasn't at all averse to having the condition of his heartstrings improved, so back I went, mixed the egg and sugar, which I had beaten up into a kind of batter, with some brandy, then I poured in some hot water and

stirred vigorously. The drink realised my expectations. It was the one thing I'd been dreaming of for months... I named the drink after myself, kinder familiarly: I had two small white mice in those days, one of them I called Tom and the other Jerry, so I combined the abbreviations in the drink, as Jeremiah P. Thomas would have sounded rather heavy, and that wouldn't have done for a beverage."

Despite this and many other claims, Jerry Thomas most definitely did not create the Tom & Jerry. Again (as is so often the case in matters of cocktail history) we turn to David Wondrich and his excellent *Imbibe!* where he reprints an article first published 20th March 1827 in the *Salem Gazette (Massachusetts)*. Appearing three years prior to Jerry Thomas' birth, this damming evidence clearly references the Tom and Jerry, both by name and ingredients.

"At the police court in Boston, last week, a lad about 13 years of age was tried for stealing a watch, and acquitted. In the course of the trial, it appeared that the prosecutor [the plaintiff] sold to the lad, under the name of "Tom and Jerry," a composition of saleratus [baking soda], eggs, sugar, nutmeg, ginger, allspice and rum. A female witness testified that the boy... appeared to be perfectly deranged, probably in consequence of the 'hell-broth' that he had been drinking."

The above, and other pre-Jerry Thomas references to the Tom & Jerry uncovered by David Wondrich suggest the drink originated in America's New England area, although its true inventor remains unknown. Fact is, if it were not for Jerry Thomas championing the drink, the Tom & Jerry itself would probably also be unknown.

TOM ARNOLD 0——

★★★★☆

Glass: Collins
Garnish: Lemon slice
Method: **SHAKE** all ingredients with ice and strain into ice-filled glass.

1½	shots	Ketel One Vodka
1½	shots	Freshly squeezed lemon juice
¾	shot	Sugar syrup (2 sugar to 1 water)
2	shots	Cold English breakfast tea

Origin: This is one of a series of tea-based drinks that were originally named after golfers. It takes its name from the actor and comedian who starred in 'National Lampoon's Golf Punk'.
Comment: Traditional lemonade laced with vodka and lengthened with tea to make a light and refreshing drink.

TOM COLLINS

★★★★½

Glass: Collins
Garnish: Orange slice & cherry on stick (sail)
Method: **SHAKE** first three ingredients with ice and strain into ice-filled glass. **TOP** with soda, lightly stir and serve with straws.

2	shots	Old Tom gin
1	shot	Freshly squeezed lemon juice
½	shot	Sugar syrup (2 sugar to 1 water)
Top with		Soda (club soda)

Comment: A medium-dry Gin Collins.

TOMAHAWK 0——

★★★★½☆

Glass: Collins
Garnish: Pineapple wedge
Method: **SHAKE** all ingredients with ice and strain into ice-filled glass.

1	shot	Patrón reposado tequila
1	shot	De Kuyper Triple Sec
2	shots	Cranberry juice
2	shots	Fresh pressed pineapple juice

Comment: A simple recipe and an effective drink.

TOMATE

★★★☆☆

Glass: Collins
Garnish: None
Method: POUR pastis and grenadine into glass.
SERVE iced water separately in a small jug (known in France as a 'broc') so the customer can dilute to their own taste (I recommend five shots). Lastly Add **ICE** to fill glass.

1	shot	Ricard Pastis
¼	shot	Pomegranate / grenadine syrup (2:1)
Top with		Chilled water

Origin: Very popular throughout France. Pronounced 'Toh-Maht', the name literally means 'tomato' and refers to the drink's colour.
Comment: The traditional aniseed and liquorice French café drink with a sweet hint of fruit.

TOMATINI

★★★★☆

Glass: Coupe
Garnish: Pepper half rim & cherry tomato
Method: MUDDLE tomato in base of shaker. Add other ingredients, **SHAKE** with ice and fine strain into chilled glass.

1	fresh	Cherry tomatoes (chopped)
2	shots	Ketel One Vodka
½	shot	White balsamic vinegar
½	shot	Freshly squeezed lemon juice
⅓	shot	Sugar syrup (2 sugar to 1 water)
1	pinch	Black pepper

Origin: Created by Jimmy Barrat, Dubai for World Class 2012 bartender's competition.
Comment: A sweet and sour sipper that has to be tried. Delicate and yet assertive, this is an 'out there' recipe!

TOMMI'S COCKTAIL (NEW)

★★★★☆

Glass: Coupe
Garnish: Orange zest twist (discarded) & Luxardo maraschino cherry
Method: STIR all ingredients with ice and strain into chilled glass.

1½	shots	Del Maguey VIDA mezcal
1	shot	Aperol Aperitivo
½	shot	Luxardo Maraschino liqueur

Origin: Adapted from a drink discovered in 2014 at Wahaca's Mezcalería Cocktail Bar, London, England.
Comment: A delicately bittersweet aperitif cocktail which heros complex smoky mezcal.

TOMMY'S MARGARITA ⊙━⚷

★★★★★

Glass: Margarita
Garnish: Lime wedge
Method: SHAKE all ingredients with ice and fine strain into chilled glass.

2	shots	Patrón reposado tequila
1	shot	Freshly squeezed lime juice
½	shot	Agave syrup

Origin: Created by Julio Bermejo and named after his family's Mexican restaurant and bar in San Francisco, the self-proclaimed "premier tequila bar on earth".

Tomas and Elmy Bermejo set up Tommy's in 1965 and Julio is one of their five children, all of whom are involved in what is truly a family business. Julio has become a legend in the drinks industry for the Tommy's Margarita and his knowledge of tequila.

Tommy's Margarita now appears on the menus of bars all around the world and in turn, the small family restaurant where the drink was created has become something of a mecca for bartenders and bar flies wanting to experience the now famous drink in the bar where it was invented. Their journey is a well-rewarded. At Tommy's the classic Margarita trio of tequila, sugar and triple sec is enhanced by using agave syrup in place of the triple sec and the use of hand-squeezed Persian limes. The drink is served accompanied by plentiful tortillas and salsa. The bar's shelves groan with the largest selection of 100% agave spirit in the USA and drinkers are encouraged to sample how different tequilas taste in the bar's signature cocktail.
Comment: The flavour of agave is king in this simple Margarita, made without the traditional orange liqueur.

TONGUE TWISTER

★★★★½

Glass: Old-fashioned
Garnish: Luxardo Maraschino cherry
Method: SHAKE all ingredients with ice and strain into glass filled with crushed ice.

¾	shot	Bacardi Carta Blanca light rum
¾	shot	Patrón reposado tequila
¾	shot	Ketel One Vodka
½	shot	Coco Re'al Cream of Coconut
3	shots	Fresh pressed pineapple juice
½	shot	Milk
½	shot	Single cream / half-and-half
¼	shot	Pomegranate / grenadine syrup (2:1)

Origin: Adapted from a drink featured in May 2006 on tikibartv.com
Comment: This creamy, sweet Tiki number is laced with three different spirits.

TONIC BOOM ⊙━⚷

★★★★☆

Glass: Old-fashioned
Garnish: None
Method: POUR tonic water into old-fashioned glass. Then **POUR** gin into shot glass. Instruct drinker to hold gin-filled shot glass directly over surface of tonic water and drop shot into old-fashioned glass and consume.

6	shots	Tonic Water
1	shot	Rutte Dry Gin

Origin: Created in 2010 by Edward 'Teddy' McPartland at The Portobello Star, London, England.
Comment: Essentially a gin and tonic bomb. To quote a Portobello Star regular, "the thinking man's Jager Bomb".

TONKA

★★★★☆

Glass: Martini
Garnish: Orange zest twist (flamed)
Method: STIR all ingredients with ice and strain into chilled glass.

2	shots	Yamazaki 12yo Japanese whisky
1	shot	Carpano Antica Formula
½	shot	Chocolate Spirit
2	dash	Angostura Orange Bitters

Origin: Created in 2010 by Klaus St. Rainer at Schumann's Bar Munich, Germany.
Comment: A chocolaty, Japanese whisky-based Manhattan-like drink.

TOOTIE FRUITY LIFESAVER

★★★½☆

Glass: Pineapple shell (frozen)
Garnish: Lemon zest twist
Method: SHAKE all ingredients with ice and strain into ice-filled glass. Serve with straws.

1½ shots	Ketel One Vodka
¾ shot	Crème de banane liqueur
¾ shot	Galliano L'Autentico liqueur
1 shot	Cranberry juice
1 shot	Fresh pressed pineapple juice
1 shot	Freshly squeezed orange juice

Comment: It's certainly fruity but is it aptly named?

TOP BANANA SHOT

★★★½☆

Glass: Shot
Garnish: None
Method: Refrigerate ingredients then LAYER in chilled glass by carefully pouring in the order listed.

½ shot	Coffee liqueur
½ shot	White crème de cacao liqueur
½ shot	Crème de banane liqueur
½ shot	Ketel One Vodka

Comment: Banana, chocolate and coffee.

TOREADOR ᴏ━┳

★★★★☆

Glass: Martini
Garnish: Lime zest twist
Method: SHAKE all ingredients with ice and fine strain into chilled glas.

2 shots	Patrón reposado tequila
1 shot	De Kuyper XO Apricot Brandy
1 shot	Freshly squeezed lime juice

Origin: This twist in the Margarita was published in W. J. Tarling's 1937 'Cafe Royal Cocktail Book', 16 years before the first written reference to a Margarita. He also lists another drink called a Picador which is identical to the later Margarita.
Comment: Apricot brandy replaces triple sec in what otherwise follows the same recipe to a classic Margarita.

TORONTO COCKTAIL (NEW)

★★★★½

Glass: Coupe
Garnish: Orange zest twist (discarded) and Luxardo Maraschino cherry
Method: STIR all ingredients with ice and strain into chilled glass.

1¾ shots	Canadian blended whisky
¼ shot	Fernet Branca
¼ shot	Sugar syrup (2 sugar to 1 water)
1 dash	Angostura Aromatic Bitters
½ shot	Chilled water (omit if wet ice)

Origin: A previously forgotten classic resurrected in 2006 by Jamie Boudreau, Seattle, USA. The Toronto appears in David A. Embury's 1948 'Fine Art of Mixing Drinks' but its earliest written incarnation is as the 'Fernet Cocktail' in Robert Vermeire's 1922 'Cocktails - How to Mix Them'.

Vermeire's recipe is "1 dash of Angostura Bitters, 2 dashes of plain Sugar or Gum Syrup, 1/4 gill of Fernet Branca, 1/4 gill of Cognac Brandy, or Rye Whisky to taste. Stir up well with a spoon, strain into a cocktail-glass, and squeeze lemon peel on top." Although Vermeire titles the drink the 'Fernet Cocktail', under the recipe he finishes, "This cocktail is much appreciated by the Canadians of Toronto".

Embury's 1848 Toronto Recipe calls for "1 part Sugar syrup, 2 parts Fernet Branca, 6 parts Canadian Whisky and 1 dash Angostura" and he writes "This cocktail may be made in Old-Fashioned glasses or may be stirred with large cubes of ice and strained into cocktail glasses. In either case, decorate with a twist of orange peel."
Comment: The merest dash of sugar syrup tames and amplifies the flavour of rye whiskey with Fernet and bitters to making this a Manhattan-style cocktail. However, Canadians will be quick to remind you that this drink has little to do with New York.

TOTAL RECALL

★★★★½☆

Glass: Collins
Garnish: Lime wedge
Method: SHAKE all ingredients with ice and strain into ice-filled glass.

¾ shot	Patrón reposado tequila
¾ shot	Bacardi Carta Oro rum
¾ shot	Southern Comfort liqueur
1½ shots	Cranberry juice
1½ shots	Freshly squeezed orange juice
¾ shot	Freshly squeezed lime juice

Comment: A long, burgundy coloured drink with a taste reminiscent of blood orange.

TRE MARTINI ᴏ━┳

★★★★☆

Glass: Martini
Garnish: Lemon zest twist
Method: SHAKE all ingredients with ice and fine strain into chilled glass.

2 shots	Bacardi Carta Blanca light rum
½ shot	Chambord Liqueur
1½ shots	Pressed apple juice

Origin: Created in 2002 by Asa Nevestveit at Sosho, London, England.
Comment: A simple, well balanced, fruity drink, laced with rum.

TREACLE NO.1

★★★★½

Glass: Old-fashioned
Garnish: Lemon zest twist
Method: STIR half of the rum, sugar syrup and bitters with two ice cubes in glass. Add rest of rum, another couple of ice cubes and STIR again. Fill glass with ice and STIR again. Finally FLOAT apple juice.

2 shots	Pot still Jamaican rum
¼ shot	Sugar syrup (2 sugar to 1 water)
½ shot	Pressed apple juice
2 dash	Angostura Aromatic Bitters

Origin: This twist on the Old-Fashioned was created by Dick Bradsell. Like the original, it takes a few minutes to make and there are no shortcuts. The apple juice Dick originally used is the cheap clear stuff rather than the posh pressed cloudy apple juice. In this drink, cheap is best.
Comment: Richly flavoured, almost like molasses.

TREACLE NO.2

★★★★☆

Glass: Old-fashioned
Garnish: Orange zest twist
Method: STIR one shot of rum with two ice cubes in a glass. Add sugar syrup, bitters and two more ice cubes. **STIR** some more and add another two ice cubes and the rest of the rum. **STIR** lots more and add more ice.

2	shots	**Bacardi Carta Ocho aged rum**
⅓	shot	**Romate Pedro Ximénez sherry**
¼	shot	**Light muscovado sugar syrup (2 sugar to 1 water)**
1	dash	**Angostura Aromatic Bitters**

Origin: Adapted from a 2011 reworking on Bradsell's original recipe by Fraser Campbell at The Alchemist Bar, Melbourne, Australia.
Comment: Made to appeal to drinkers who actually want a cocktail that tastes like Treacle. And it does.

TRES AMIGOS DAIQUIRI

★★★★½

Glass: Coupe
Garnish: Lime wedge
Method: SHAKE all ingredients with ice and fine strain into chilled glass.

1	shot	**Patrón silver tequila**
1	shot	**Patrón añejo tequila**
¼	shot	**Pusser's Navy Rum (54.5%)**
½	shot	**Freshly squeezed lime juice**
¼	shot	**Sugar syrup (2 sugar to 1 water)**

Origin: Adapted from Craig Toone's (8:2:1) interpretation of a cocktail that was doing the rounds in Manchester in 2003, originally under the name 'Triple Rum Daiquiri'.
Comment: Actually this is a navy rum influenced Margarita made to Daiquiri proportions, but whatever it's called, it's damn good.

TRES COMPADRES MARGARITA

★★★★½

Glass: Coupe
Garnish: Lime wedge & salt rim (optional)
Method: SHAKE ingredients with ice and fine strain into chilled glass.

1¼	shots	**Patrón reposado tequila**
½	shot	**De Kuyper Triple Sec**
½	shot	**Chambord Liqueur**
½	shot	**Rose's lime cordial**
¾	shot	**Freshly squeezed lime juice**
¾	shot	**Freshly squeezed orange juice**
¾	shot	**Freshly squeezed pink grapefruit juice**

Origin: Created in 1999 by Robert Plotkin and Raymon Flores of BarMedia, USA.
Comment: A well balanced, tasty twist on the standard Margarita.

TRIBBBLE

★★★★☆

Glass: Shot
Garnish: None
Method: Refrigerate ingredients then **LAYER** in chilled glass by carefully pouring in the following order.

½	shot	**Butterscotch liqueur**
½	shot	**Crème de banane liqueur**
½	shot	**Baileys Irish cream liqueur**

Origin: A drink created by bartenders at TGI Friday's UK in 2002.
Comment: Named Tribbble with three 'B's' due to its three layers: butterscotch, banana and Baileys.

TRIDENT (NEW)

★★★★☆

Glass: Old-fashioned
Garnish: Lemon zest twist
Method: STIR all ingredients with ice and strain into ice-filled glass.

1	shot	**San León Manzanilla sherry**
1	shot	**Cynar**
1	shot	**Lysholm Linie Aquavit**
2	dash	**Peach bitters**

Origin: This riff on a Negroni was created in 2002 by Robert Hess. The Trident name apparently was inspired by the fact that each of the three main ingredients come from different sea-faring countries.
Comment: Bone dry and boozy, this cocktail is aimed at those who have a penchant for both sherry and aquavit, not to mention bittersweet artichoke liqueurs - hardly mass market then. Nor are Aston Martin cars but I want one.

Be warned - use the wrong sherry and this drink falls apart - don't be tempted to sub Manzanilla with a fino.

TRIFLE COCKTAIL

★★★½☆

Glass: Martini
Garnish: Hundreds & Thousands
Method: SHAKE all ingredients with ice and fine strain into chilled glass.

1⅔	shots	**Raspberry flavoured vodka**
⅓	shot	**Chambord Liqueur**
1⅓	shots	**Drambuie liqueur**

Origin: Created by Ian Baldwin at GE Club, London, England.
Comment: A cocktail that tastes like its namesake.

TRILBY #1

★★★★☆

Glass: Martini
Garnish: Orange zest twist
Method: STIR all ingredients with ice and strain into chilled glass.

1	shot	**Dewar's 12yo Scotch whisky**
⅛	shot	**Le Fée Parisienne absinthe**
1	shot	**Parfait Amour liqueur**
1	shot	**Martini Rosso vermouth**
¾	shot	**Chilled water** (omit if wet ice)
2	dash	**Angostura Orange Bitters**

Comment: An aromatic old classic of unknown origin.

TRILBY #2

★★★★☆

Glass: Martini
Garnish: Lemon zest twist
Method: STIR all ingredients with ice and strain into chilled glass.

3	shots	Martini Extra Dry vermouth
¼	shot	De Kuyper Triple Sec
1	dash	Peychaud's aromatic bitters
½	shot	Dewar's 12yo Scotch whisky

Comment: Salmon pink in colour and distinctly different in style. One of those drinks you just have to try.

TRINIDAD ESPECIAL (NEW)

★★★★☆

Glass: Coupe
Garnish: Lime zest twist
Method: SHAKE all ingredients with ice and fine strain into chilled glass.

1 shot Angostura Aromatic Bitters
⅓ shot BarSol Mosto Verde Italia pisco
1 shot Almond (orgeat) syrup
⅔ shot Freshly squeezed lime juice

Origin: Created by Italian Barman, Valentino Bolognese and the winning drink in the Angostura European Cocktail Competition held at Mood Bar, Paris in January 2008.
Comment: This deep reddy-brown bittersweet drink is based upon sweet almond syrup balancing bitter notes from the Angostura and lime tartness. With a whole shot of Angostura this cocktail is most unusual.

TRINIDAD SOUR (NEW)

★★★☆☆

Glass: Coupe
Garnish: None
Method: SHAKE all ingredients with ice and fine stain into chilled glass.

1½	shots	Angostura Aromatic Bitters
½	shot	Straight rye whiskey
1½	shots	Almond (orgeat) syrup
¾	shot	Freshly squeezed lemon juice

Origin: Created in 2009 by Giuseppe Gonzalez, at Clover Club Bar, Brooklyn, USA and inspired by the competition-wining Trinidad Especial by Valentino Bolognese.
Comment: This deep lurid reddy-brown cocktail won't be to everybody's taste but that's only to be expected with one-and-a-half shots of Angostura.

TRINITY

★★★⯪☆

Glass: Martini
Garnish: Orange zest twist (discarded) & Luxardo Maraschino cherry
Method: STIR all ingredients with ice and strain into chilled glass.

2½	shots	Dewar's 12yo Scotch whisky
¼	shot	De Kuyper XO Apricot Brandy
1	shot	Martini Extra Dry vermouth
¼	shot	Giffard Menthe Pastille liqueur
1	dash	Angostura Orange Bitters

Origin: Recipe purloined from David Embury's classic book, 'The Fine Art of Mixing Drinks'.
Comment: A Dry Manhattan based on Scotch with a dash of apricot liqueur and a touch of créme de menthe.

TRIPLE 'C' COCKTAIL

★★★★☆

Glass: Martini
Garnish: Chocolate powder rim
Method: SHAKE all ingredients with ice and fine strain into chilled glass.

2	shots	Vanilla infused Ketel One vodka
1	shot	Dark crème de cacao liqueur
1¼	shots	Cranberry juice

Origin: Created in 2001 by yours truly and originally called the Chocolate Covered Cranberry Martini - every drink in V-shaped glass was called a 'Martini' in those days.
Comment: Rich vanilla, dark chocolate and cranberry juice. Indulgent and best after dinner.

TRIPLE A (NEW)

★★★★☆

Glass: Coupe
Garnish: Lemon zest twist
Method: SHAKE all ingredients with ice and fine strain into chilled glass.

1	shot	Le Fée Parisienne absinthe
1	shot	Chilled water
1	shot	Pressed apple juice
½	shot	Almond (orgeat) syrup
¼	shot	Freshly squeezed lime juice

Origin: Created in 2010 by Dick Bradsell, London, England
Comment: So named due to this drink being flavoured with absinthe, apple and almond.

TRIPLE ORANGE

★★★★☆

Glass: Martini
Garnish: Orange zest twist
Method: SHAKE all ingredients with ice and fine strain into chilled glass.

1	shot	Ketel One Vodka
1	shot	Grand Marnier Cordon Rouge
¼	shot	Campari Bitter
1½	shots	Freshly squeezed orange juice
½	fresh	Egg white

Origin: Created in 1998 by yours truly.
Comment: This aperitif cocktail has a trio of orange flavours with the bitter orange of Campari adding character and balance.

TRIPLEBERRY

★★★★☆

Glass: Martini
Garnish: Seasonal berries
Method: SHAKE all ingredients with ice and fine strain into chilled glass.

7	fresh	Raspberries
2	shots	Ketel One Vodka
½	shot	Lejay Crème de Fraise liqueur
¼	shot	Shiraz red wine
½	shot	Lejay Crème de Cassis de Dijon

Origin: Created in 2006 by yours truly.
Comment: Rich berry fruit fortified with vodka and tamed by the tannins from a splash of red wine.

TROPIC

★★★★☆

Glass: Collins
Garnish: Lemon slice
Method: SHAKE all ingredients with ice and strain into ice-filled glass.

1	shot	Bénédictine D.O.M. liqueur
2	shots	Sauvignon blanc white wine
2	shots	Freshly squeezed pink grapefruit juice
½	shot	Freshly squeezed lemon juice

Origin: Based on a recipe believed to date back to the 1950s.
Comment: A light, satisfying cooler.

TROPIC THUNDER

★★★★☆

Glass: Coupe
Garnish: Dust with freshly ground black pepper
Method: SHAKE all ingredients with ice and fine strain into chilled glass.

1½	shots	Rutte Dry Gin
¾	shot	Crème de pêche (peach) liqueur
½	shot	Freshly squeezed lemon juice
1	shot	Fresh pressed pineapple juice

Origin: Created by Sean Henry at Epernay Champagne Bar, Leeds, England and to quote Sean is "named Tropic Thunder" as it aptly describes what to expect on the palate.
Comment: Gin, peach, lemon juice and pineapple juice may not seem the most obvious combination but it's a combo that works.

TROPICAL BREEZE

★★★☆☆

Glass: Collins
Garnish: Lime wedge
Method: SHAKE all ingredients with ice and strain into ice-filled glass.

1½	shots	Ketel One Vodka
1	shot	Passoa Liqueur
2½	shots	Cranberry juice
1½	shots	Freshly squeezed pink grapefruit juice

Comment: A sweet, fruity Seabreeze.

TROPICAL CAIPIRINHA

★★★★½

Glass: Old-fashioned
Garnish: Lime wedge
Method: SHAKE all ingredient with ice and strain into glass filled crushed ice.

1	shot	Capucana cachaça
1	shot	Coconut rum liqueur
1	shot	Fresh pressed pineapple juice
1	shot	Freshly squeezed lime juice
¼	shot	Sugar syrup (2 sugar to 1 water)

Origin: Created in 2003 by yours truly.
Comment: In drink circles, tropical usually spells sweet. This drink has a tropical flavour but a definite adult sourness.

TROPICAL DAIQUIRI

★★★★☆

Glass: Martini
Garnish: Pineapple wedge
Method: SHAKE all ingredients with ice and fine strain into chilled glass.

2	shots	Gosling's Black Seal dark rum
¼	shot	Pomegranate / grenadine syrup (2:1)
1	shot	Fresh pressed pineapple juice
½	shot	Freshly squeezed lime juice

Origin: Adapted from a recipe in David Embury's classic book 'The Fine Art of Mixing Drinks'.
Comment: A seriously tangy Daiquiri.

TULIP COCKTAIL

★★★★☆

Glass: Martini
Garnish: Lemon zest twist
Method: SHAKE all ingredients with ice and fine strain into chilled glass.

1	shot	Calvados brandy
½	shot	De Kuyper XO Apricot Brandy
1	shot	Martini Rosso vermouth
½	shot	Freshly squeezed lemon juice
½	shot	Chilled water (omit if wet ice)

Origin: Adapted from a recipe in Harry Craddock's 1930 'Savoy Cocktail Book'.
Comment: Rich but balanced with bags of fruit: apple, apricot and lemon.

Turf Club Cocktail

A sibling, or at least cousin, of the Martinez and the Martini, the Turf Club is, or could be, the first cocktail to combine gin and vermouth. It makes its first written appearance in the 1884 'How To Mix Drinks – Bar-Keeper's Handbook' as the "Turf Club" with later books most often merely titling the drink "Turf".

The name Turf Club refers to the gentlemen's clubs of the late 1800s - early 1900s which operated as a combined restaurant, bar, meeting place and gambling den for the gentleman of the day. Captains of industry and the aristocracy have always liked horse racing and where men gather to watch racing there is bound to be betting. Many a 'turf accountant' (bookmaker) frequented such clubs and many a Turf Cocktail was consumed.

One of the most famous of these gentlemen's clubs, The Turf Club, stood at the corner of Madison Avenue and 26th Street in New York. The building, Jerome Mansion, was a building with some pedigree, being the former home of Lady Randolph Churchill, the American mother of Winston Churchill – a man I suspect would have appreciated a well-made Turf Club cocktail.

The oldest mention of the Turf Club cocktail is in George Winter's 1884 How To Mix Drinks-Bar-Keeper's Handbook. George J. Kappeler's 1895 'Modern American Drinks' also includes a Turf Cocktail but his recipe uses old tom gin rather than Plymouth Gin and omits both vermouth and maraschino liqueur. Harry Johnson tellingly doesn't list the Turf cocktail in the 1882 first edition of his Bartenders' Manual but does include it as the last drink in his revised 1900 "New and Improved" Edition. Robert Vermeire's 1932 'Cocktails: How to Mix Them', repeats the Harry Johnson formula, also crediting Johnson as being the drink's creator.

According to Albert Stevens Crockett's 1935 The Old Waldorf-Astoria Bar Book, the Turf Cocktail served at the venerable old hotel was actually 2/3rds jenever to 1/3 sweet vermouth (as below) but I find these proportions make an overly dry drink so I've slightly upped the proportion of vermouth to gin in my adaptation.

Charles H. Baker, Jr's 1946' The Gentleman's Companion: An Exotic Drinking Book' is more a travel log with recipes than a bartender's guide so accordingly he has a fair bit more to say on the Turf cocktail than the other authors quoted above, documenting three versions of the drink and where he encountered them:

The Improved Turf Cocktail, No. 1 (Baker 1946)
A modification of own from Dirty Dick's, Nassau, B.I., 1937
We first sampled this drink in Nassau quite some time back, having flown over Pan-American Airways, after the official tourist season was finished, with a 6-year bride and 4 friends, to do a bit of sailing and swimming and basking on undiscovered white sand beaches by vitriol blue coral water that is clearer than anywhere else in the whole universe. A gentleman of colour suggested this as a dry, appetizing taste-thrill at Dirty Dick's, and found it to be merely Holland gin and vermouth - nothing else except Angostura - in a 2 to 1 ratio....
After a bit of later experiment on self and friends we discovered that the addition of ½ a green lime - strained juice - and ½ tsp of grenadine or bar sugar works miracles with this drink."

Turf Cocktail No. II (Baker 1946)
From the Taj Mahal Hotel, on Apollo Bunder, in Bombay, Saturday, February 14th 1931, to be exact;
Served after the Running of the Maharajah of Rajpipla Gold Cup at the Western India Turf Club, Ltd.
We had won all of sixty-seven rupees on this gold-cup, 23,000 rupees race, and were feeling very horsy and turfy, and tired of the eternal chotapegs - just plain Scotch and not-too-cold soda, without ice, of the last few days - and were open for suggestions. G.J. Mack, local Manager for General Motors Export, suggested a Turf Cocktail, of a recognised mix, and after a barrage of Hindustani this resulted, much to everyone's amazement: 1 jigger of dry gin, 1 pony French vermouth, 1 tsp of absinthe, or Pernod Veritas; donate 1 tsp of maraschino and a dash of Abbots bitters. Stir in a bar glass like a Martini and serve in a Manhattan glass, ungarnished."

Turf Cocktail No. III (Baker 1946)
From the Havana Country Club, Winter of 1930
This is virtually the same as No.II, only using old Tom gin for a base, orange bitters, and everything else the same."

TURF CLUB COCKTAIL (CROCKETT'S RECIPE) (NEW)

★★★★½

Glass: Coupe
Garnish: Lemon zest twist
Method: STIR all ingredients with ice and strain into chilled glass.

1 ¾ shots   Rutte Old Simon oude jenever
1 ¼ shots   Martini Rosso vermouth
1   dash   Angostura Aromatic Bitters

Origin: Made with a quality oude jenever this is almost nutty and makes for an interesting aperitif.
Comment: According to his 1935 'The Old Waldorf-Astoria Bar Book', Albert Stevens Crockett's recipe was actually 2/3rds jenever to 1/3 sweet vermouth but produces an overly dry drink so I've slightly upped the proportion of vermouth to gin.

TURF CLUB COCKTAIL (JOHNSON'S RECIPE) (NEW)

★★★★½

Glass: Coupe
Garnish: Lemon zest twist (discarded) & Luxardo Maraschino cherry
Method: STIR all ingredients with ice and strain into chilled glass.

1½ shots   Rutte Dry Gin
1½ shots   Martini Extra Dry vermouth
¼ shot   Luxardo Maraschino liqueur
1   dash   Le Fée Parisienne absinthe
1   dash   Angostura Orange Bitters

Origin: Adapted by yours truly from Harry Johnson's 1882 Bartenders' Manual.
Comment: Despite the maraschino liqueur this Martini-style cocktail is dry and punchy.

TURF CLUB COCKTAIL (KAPPELER'S RECIPE) (NEW)

★★★★½

Glass: Coupe
Garnish: Orange zest twist
Method: STIR all ingredients with ice and strain into chilled glass.

2 shots Old Tom gin
3 dash Angostura Orange Bitters
1 dash Le Fée Parisienne absinthe
⅛ shot Sugar syrup (2 sugar to 1 water)
¾ shot Chilled water (omit if wet ice)

Origin: Adapted by yours truly from George J. Kappeler's 1895 Modern American Drinks.
Comment: Reminiscent of a Martini but sans vermouth, sweetened with dash of sugar and balanced by heavy use of bitters.

TURF CLUB COCKTAIL (WINTER'S RECIPE)

★★★★½

Glass: Coupe
Garnish: Orange zest twist
Method: STIR all ingredients with ice and strain into chilled glass.

1½ shots   Old Tom gin
1½ shots   Martini Rosso vermouth
2   dash   Angostura Aromatic Bitters

Origin: Adapted by yours truly from George Winter's 1884 How To Mix Drinks–Bar-Keeper's Handbook. His original recipe calls for "Peruvian bitters" and 3 dashes of Cortesano Amargo Bitters Aromatic work well if you have them. Alternatively use slightly less Angostura aromatic bitters.
Comment: Simple but very tasty, equal parts old tom gin and sweet vermouth with aromatic bitters.

TURKISH DELIGHT COCKTAIL

★★★★☆

Glass: Martini
Garnish: Turkish Delight
Method: STIR honey and vodka in base of shaker until honey dissolves. Add other ingredients, **SHAKE** with ice and fine strain into chilled glass.

2	spoon	Runny honey
1	shot	Ketel One Vodka
1	shot	Vanilla infused Ketel One vodka
½	shot	White crème de cacao liqueur
⅛	shot	Rose water
¾	shot	Chilled water (omit if wet ice)
½	fresh	Egg white

Origin: Created in 2003 by yours truly, London, England.
Comment: Rosewater, honey, chocolate and vanilla provide a distinct flavour of Turkish Delight - fortified with vodka.

TURQUOISE DAIQUIRI

★★★½☆

Glass: Martini
Garnish: Lime wedge
Method: SHAKE all ingredients with ice and fine strain into chilled glass.

1½ shots	Bacardi Carta Blanca light rum
½ shot	De Kuyper Triple Sec
½ shot	Blue curaçao liqueur
¾ shot	Freshly squeezed lime juice
1 shot	Fresh pressed pineapple juice

Comment: A blue-rinsed Daiquiri with orange and pineapple - with tequila instead of rum it would be a twisted Margarita.

TUSCAN MULE

★★★½☆

Glass: Collins
Garnish: Lime wedge
Method: SHAKE first two ingredients with ice and strain into ice-filled glass. **TOP** with ginger beer, lightly stir and serve with straws.

2 shots	Tuaca liqueur
¾ shot	Freshly squeezed lime juice
Top with	Gosling's Stormy Ginger Beer

Origin: Adapted from a drink created in 2003 by Sammy Berry, Brighton, England.
Comment: A spicy long drink smoothed with vanilla.

TUXEDO COCKTAIL

★★★★☆

Glass: Martini
Garnish: Lemon zest twist & Luxardo Maraschino cherry
Method: STIR all ingredients with ice and fine strain into chilled glass.

1¾ shots	Old Tom gin
1¾ shots	Martini Extra Dry vermouth
3 dash	Angostura Orange Bitters
1 dash	Le Fée Parisienne absinthe
⅛ shot	Luxardo Maraschino liqueur

Origin: Recipe adapted from Harry Johnson's 'Bartenders' Manual' first published in 1882. The drink was not created at the Tuxedo Club as is often suspected as this did not open until 1886. The Tuxedo Club being a private member-owned country club near the village of Tuxedo Park, Orange County, New York State, USA.

While the club can't claim to have created this cocktail, it is credited with being the birthplace of the tuxedo jacket - well at least where its American name originated.

The origins of the gentleman's black tie dinner dress dates from 1860, when Henry Poole & Co. of London's Savile Row made a short smoking jacket for the Prince of Wales (later Edward VII) as an informal alternative to white tie dress, then the standard formal wear.

In the spring of 1886, the Prince invited James Potter, a rich New Yorker to Sandringham. When Potter sought the Prince's advice on dinner dress, he sent Potter to his tailor's, Henry Poole. Back in New York Potter wore his newly acquired dinner suit at the Tuxedo Park Club which had recently opened. Other members of the club copied him and so the tailless dinner jacket acquired the club's name.
Comment: Equal parts old tom gin and vermouth flavoured with the merest hint of maraschino, absinthe and orange bitters.

TVR

★★★☆☆

Glass: Collins
Garnish: Lime wedge
Method: POUR ingredients into ice-filled glass. Lightly stir and serve with straws.

1 shot	Patrón reposado tequila
1 shot	Ketel One Vodka
Top with	Red Bull

Origin: A 90s drink named after its ingredients (tequila, vodka, Red Bull), and which is also the name of a British sports car.
Comment: Very much 'driven' by the flavour of Red Bull. Use an anejo tequila to balance the initial sweetness on the palate.

TWENTIETH CENTURY MARTINI

★★★½☆

Glass: Martini
Garnish: Lemon zest twist
Method: SHAKE all ingredients with ice and fine strain into chilled glass.

1½ shots	Rutte Dry Gin
½ shot	White crème de cacao liqueur
¾ shot	Martini Extra Dry vermouth
½ shot	Freshly squeezed lemon juice

Origin: Thought to have been created in 1939 by one C.A. Tuck and named after the express train that travelled between New York City and Chicago.
Comment: Chocolate and lemon juice. 21st century tastes have definitely moved on.

STAR RATINGS EXPLAINED

★★★★★+	OUTSTANDING	★★★★★	EXCEPTIONAL
★★★★½	EXCELLENT	★★★★☆	RECOMMENDED
★★★½☆	COMMENDED	★★★☆☆	MEDIOCRE
★★½☆☆	DISAPPOINTING	★★☆☆☆	PRETTY AWFUL
★½☆☆☆	SHAMEFUL	★☆☆☆☆	DISGUSTING

TWINKLE ⚷

★★★★½

Glass: Martini
Garnish: Lemon zest twist
Method: SHAKE first two ingredients with ice and fine strain into chilled glass. **TOP** with Prosecco (or champagne).

3 shots   Ketel One Vodka
¾ shot   St-Germain elderflower liqueur
Top with   G.H. Mumm Cordon Rouge Champagne

Origin: Created in 2002 by Tony Conigliaro at The Lonsdale, London, England.
Comment: It's hard to believe this floral, dry, golden tipple contains three whole shots of vodka.

TWISTED SOBRIETY

★★★★☆

Glass: Flute
Garnish: Pear slice on rim
Method: STIR first two ingredients with ice and fine strain into chilled glass. **TOP** with champagne.

1 shot   Martell VSOP Médaillon cognac
1 shot   Poire William eau de vie
Top with   G.H. Mumm Cordon Rouge Champagne

Comment: Fortified champagne with a hint of pear.

TWO 'T' FRUITY

★★★★☆

Glass: Martini
Garnish: Tooty Frooties
Method: SHAKE all ingredients with ice and fine strain into chilled glass.

2½ shots   Ketel One Vodka
3 dash   Angostura Orange Bitters
¾ shot   Passion fruit syrup

Origin: Created in 2002 at Hush, London, England.
Comment: Simple is beautiful - this drink is both. The rawness of vodka is balanced with sweet passion fruit and hints of orange bitters.

TWO-ONE-TWO (212)

★★★½☆

Glass: Collins
Garnish: Grapefruit zest twist
Method: SHAKE all ingredients with ice and fine strain into chilled glass.

2 shots   Freshly squeezed ruby grapefruit juice
1 shot   Aperol Aperitivo
2 shots   Patrón reposado tequila

Origin: Created in 2008 by Willy Shine at Contemporary Cocktails Inc. in New York City. The name is a reference to NYC's 212 area code as well as the ounces in the recipe. Willy is also the Partida Tequila Ambassador for NYC so I should point out that this is the brand originally called for in his recipe.
Comment: Earthy taste with freshness coming fro the grapefruit.

ULTIMA PALABRA (NEW)

★★★★★

Glass: Coupe
Garnish: Thyme sprig
Method: SHAKE all ingredients with ice and fine strain into chilled glass.

¾ shot   Del Maguey VIDA mezcal
¾ shot   Green Chartreuse
¾ shot   Luxardo Maraschino liqueur
¾ shot   Pressed pineapple juice
¾ shot   Freshly squeezed lime juice
½ shot   Chilled water (omit if wet ice)

Comment: This riff on the Last Word is named after the direct Spanish translation of Last Word, hence the use of mezcal in place of gin. Pineapple juice, another distinguishing feature of this riff on the classic, works brilliantly – adding a fruity sweetness and complexity.
Origin: Created by Simone De Luca at High Road House Club in Chiswick, London, England. Recipe courtesy of Gary 'gaz' Regan's Ardent Spirits.

UNCLE VANYA

★★★★☆

Glass: Martini
Garnish: Lime wedge
Method: SHAKE all ingredients with ice and fine strain into chilled glass.

1¾ shots   Ketel One Vodka
1 shot   Lejay Crème de Mûre liqueur
1 shot   Freshly squeezed lime juice
½ shot   Sugar syrup (2 sugar to 1 water)
½ fresh   Egg white

Origin: Named after Anton Chekhov's greatest play - a cheery tale of envy and despair. A popular drink in Britain's TGI Friday bars, its origins are unknown.
Comment: Simple but great - smooth, sweet 'n' sour blackberry, although possibly a tad on the sweet side for some.

UNICAR ⚷

★★★★☆

Glass: Coupe
Garnish: Orange zest twist
Method: SHAKE all ingredients with ice and fine strain into chilled glass.

2½ shots   Martell VSOP Médaillon cognac
¾ shot   Freshly squeezed lemon juice
½ shot   Sugar syrup (2 sugar to 1 water)

Origin: Inspired by a drink discovered in May 2010 at Babel Bar, Hotel du Rome, Berlin, Germany. Named after a combination of 'Sidecar' and 'Ugni-blanc', the grape from which cognac is most commonly made.
Comment: A mismade but fabulously balanced Sidecar inspired this drink.

STAR RATINGS EXPLAINED

★★★★★+ OUTSTANDING   ★★★★★ EXCEPTIONAL
★★★★½ EXCELLENT   ★★★★☆ RECOMMENDED
★★★½☆ COMMENDED   ★★★☆☆ MEDIOCRE
★★½☆☆ DISAPPOINTING   ★★☆☆☆ PRETTY AWFUL
★½☆☆☆ SHAMEFUL   ★☆☆☆☆ DISGUSTING

UNION CLUB

★★★★☆

Glass: Martini
Garnish: Orange zest twist
Method: **SHAKE** all ingredients with ice and fine strain into chilled glass.

2 shots Bourbon whiskey
¼ shot De Kuyper Triple Sec
½ shot Freshly squeezed lime juice
⅛ shot Almond (orgeat) syrup
⅛ shot Pomegranate / grenadine syrup (2:1)
½ fresh Egg white

Origin: Adapted from a recipe purloined from David Embury's classic book, 'The Fine Art of Mixing Drinks'.
Comment: Balanced sweet and sour with bourbon to the fore.

UNION CLUB COCKTAIL

★★★★☆

Glass: Coupe
Garnish: Orange zest twist
Method: **SHAKE** all ingredients with ice and fine strain into chilled glass.

2 shots Bourbon whiskey
½ shot Luxardo Maraschino liqueur
½ shot Campari Bitter
1½ shots Freshly squeezed orange juice

Origin: Created in 2008 by Jamie Boudreau at Tini Bigs, Seattle, USA and named after a gambling joint Wyatt Earp opened in Seattle in 1899.
Comment: Maraschino and Campari balance perfectly. Fruity yet dry and complex.

UNIVERSAL SHOT

★★★☆☆

Glass: Shot
Garnish: None
Method: Refrigerate ingredients then **LAYER** in chilled glass by carefully pouring in the order listed.

½ shot Midori Green Melon liqueur
½ shot Freshly squeezed pink grapefruit juice
½ shot Ketel One Vodka

Comment: Sweet melon liqueur toned down by grapefruit and fortified by vodka.

UNUSUAL NEGRONI COCKTAIL

★★★½☆

Glass: Old-fashioned
Garnish: Orange zest twist
Method: **STIR** all ingredients with ice and strain into ice filled glass.

1 shot Rutte Dry Gin
1 shot Aperol Aperitivo
1 shot Lillet Blanc

Origin: Adapted from a drink created in 2011 by Charlotte Voisey, USA.
Comment: A very soft rendition of a classic Negroni.

UP IN THE AIR

★★★★☆

Glass: Coupe
Garnish: Apple and lemon slice
Method: **SHAKE** all ingredients with ice and fine strain into chilled glass.

2 shots Ketel One Vodka
½ shot Pressed apple juice
½ shot Freshly squeezed lemon juice
¼ shot Almond (orgeat) syrup

Origin: Adapted from a drink discovered in 2011 at the Chapel Bar, Berlin, Germany.
Comment: Apple, almond and lemon juice fortified with vodka in this richly flavoured sweet and sour cocktail.

UPSIDE-DOWN RASPBERRY CHEESECAKE

★★★★☆

Glass: Martini
Garnish: Crumbled Digestive biscuit
Method: First Layer: **MUDDLE** raspberries in base of shaker. Add Chambord, **SHAKE** with ice and fine strain into centre of glass.

Second Layer: Grate lemon zest into shaker. Add rest of ingredients, **SHAKE** all ingredients with ice and strain into glass over spoon so as to **LAYER** over raspberry base.

4 fresh Raspberries
½ shot Chambord Liqueur
½ fresh Lemon zest (grated)
2 shots Vanilla infused Ketel One vodka
½ shot Vanilla schnapps
½ shot Sugar syrup (2 sugar to 1 water)
5 spoon Mascarpone cheese
1 shot Single cream / half-and-half

Origin: Created in 2003 by yours truly after adapting Wayne Collins' original cheesecake recipe.
Comment: Surprisingly, the biscuity top continues to float as you sip the vanilla cream layer right down to the point when you hit the raspberry base.

URBAN HOLISTIC

★★★½☆

Glass: Martini
Garnish: Lemon zest twist
Method: **SHAKE** first two ingredients with ice and fine strain into chilled glass. **TOP** with ginger ale.

2 shots Junmai ginjō sake
1 shot Martini Extra Dry vermouth
Top with Ginger ale

Origin: Adapted from a drink discovered in 2005 at Mo Bar, Landmark Mandarin Oriental Hotel, Hong Kong, China.
Comment: East meets West in this dry refreshing cocktail.

URBAN OASIS

★★★½☆

Glass: Martini
Garnish: Orange zest twist
Method: SHAKE all ingredients with ice and fine strain into chilled glass.

1½ shots	Ketel One Oranje vodka
½ shot	Raspberry flavoured vodka
¼ shot	Chambord Liqueur
1½ shots	Fresh pressed pineapple juice

Origin: Discovered in 2003 at Paramount Hotel, New York City, USA.
Comment: Alcoholic orange and raspberry sherbet - how bad is that? A crowd pleasing drink.

USB COCKTAIL

★★★★★

Glass: Martini
Garnish: Vanilla pod
Method: SHAKE all ingredients with ice and fine strain into chilled glass.

1½ shots	Martell VSOP Médaillon cognac (infused with vanilla)
1¼ shots	Sauvignon blanc white wine
1½ shots	Fresh pressed pineapple juice
¼ shot	Sugar syrup (2 sugar to 1 water)

Origin: Created in 2003 by yours truly, London, England.

Inspired by the Palermo cocktail discovered in 2001 at Hotel du Vin, Bristol, England and named after the grape varieties Ugni and Sauvignon Blanc. Ugni Blanc is the most common grape variety in Cognac, and Sauvignon Blanc is the grape variety in the wine which best seems to suit this drink.
Comment: A relatively dry cocktail where the vanilla combines beautifully with the cognac and the acidity of the wine balances the sweetness of the pineapple juice.

UTTERLY BUTTERLY

★★★★½☆

Glass: Collins
Garnish: Apple wedge
Method: STIR peanut butter with vodka in base of shaker. Add other ingredients, **SHAKE** with ice and fine strain into ice-filled glass.

1	spoon	Smooth peanut butter
2	shots	Ketel One Vodka
¼	shot	Cinnamon schnapps
½	shot	Coconut rum liqueur
1½	shots	Pressed apple juice
1½	shots	Fresh pressed pineapple juice
¾	shot	Freshly squeezed lime juice

Comment: Yup, your eyes are not deceiving you and nor will your taste buds - it's made with peanut butter. Refreshingly different.

VALENCIA COCKTAIL NO. 2

★★★★☆

Glass: Flute
Garnish: Orange zest twist
Method: POUR first three ingredients into chilled glass. **TOP** with champagne.

½	shot	De Kuyper XO Apricot Brandy
¼	shot	Freshly squeezed orange juice
4	dash	Angostura Orange Bitters (optional)
Top with		G.H. Mumm Cordon Rouge Champagne

Origin: Adapted from the Valencia Cocktail No. 2 in The Savoy Cocktail Book.
Comment: Floral and fruity - makes Bucks Fizz look a tad sad.

VALENCIA MARTINI

★★★★½☆

Glass: Martini
Garnish: Orange zest twist
Method: STIR all ingredients with ice and strain into chilled glass.

2½ shots	Rutte Dry Gin
½ shot	Romate Fino sherry

Comment: A Martini-style drink but using fino sherry instead of vermouth. Crisp and dry.

VALENTINO

★★★★☆

Glass: Coupe
Garnish: Lemon zest twist
Method: STIR all ingredients with ice and strain into a chilled glass.

2	shots	Rutte Dry Gin
½	shot	Campari Bitter
1	shot	Martini Rosso vermouth

Comment: A variation on the Negroni. More gin and less Campari, make for an unusual bittersweet Martini.

VAMPIRO

★★★★☆

Glass: Old-fashioned
Garnish: Lime wedge
Method: SHAKE all ingredients with ice and strain into ice-filled glass.

2	shots	Patrón reposado tequila
1	shot	Tomato juice
1	shot	Freshly squeezed orange juice
½	shot	Freshly squeezed lime juice
½	shot	Pomegranate / grenadine syrup (2:1)
7	drop	Tabasco hot pepper sauce
1	pinch	Salt
1	grind	Black pepper

Origin: The national drink of Mexico where it's often made with pomegranate juice in place of tomato juice and without the grenadine.
Comment: Something of a supercharged Bloody Mary with tequila and a hint of sweet grenadine.

VANCOUVER

★★★⯪☆

Glass: Martini
Garnish: Lemon zest twist
Method: STIR all ingredients with ice and fine strain into chilled glass.

1½	shots	Rutte Dry Gin
¾	shot	Martini Rosso vermouth
¼	shot	Bénédictine D.O.M. liqueur
1	dash	Angostura Orange Bitters

Comment: A herbal medium dry Martini.

VANDERBILT

★★★★⯪

Glass: Martini
Garnish: Lemon zest twist
Method: SHAKE all ingredients with ice and fine strain into chilled glass.

2¼	shots	Martell VSOP Médaillon cognac
¾	shot	Cherry Heering Liqueur
⅛	shot	Sugar syrup (2 sugar to 1 water)
2	dash	Angostura Aromatic Bitters

Origin: Adapted from a recipe in Harry Craddock's 1930 'Savoy Cocktail Book'.
Comment: Tangy, rich cherry and hints of vanilla fortified with brandy.

VANILLA & GRAPEFRUIT DAIQUIRI 0—🗝

★★★★⯪

Glass: Martini
Garnish: Grapefruit zest twist (discarded) & vanilla pod
Method: SHAKE all ingredients with ice and fine strain into chilled glass.

2½	shots	Bacardi Carta Blanca light rum (infused with vanilla)
½	shot	Freshly squeezed lime juice
½	shot	Sugar syrup (2 sugar to 1 water)
1	shot	Freshly squeezed pink grapefruit juice

Origin: Created in 2003 by yours truly, London, England.
Comment: Reminiscent of a Hemingway Special, this flavoursome, vanilla laced Daiquiri has a wonderfully tangy bittersweet finish.

VANILLA & RASPBERRY COCKTAIL

★★★★☆

Glass: Martini
Garnish: Raspberries
Method: MUDDLE raspberries in base of shaker. Add other ingredients, **SHAKE** with ice and fine strain into chilled glass.

12	fresh	Raspberries
2	shots	Vanilla infused Ketel One vodka
¼	shot	Shiraz red wine
¼	shot	Sugar syrup (2 sugar to 1 water)
½	shot	Chilled water (omit if wet ice)

Origin: Created in 2006 by yours truly, London, England.
Comment: Exactly that - vanilla and raspberries.

VANILLA DAIQUIRI 0—🗝

★★★★⯪

Glass: Martini
Garnish: Lime wedge
Method: SHAKE all ingredients with ice and fine strain into chilled glass.

2	shots	Bacardi Carta Blanca light rum (infused with vanilla)
½	shot	Freshly squeezed lime juice
¼	shot	Sugar syrup (2 sugar to 1 water)
¾	shot	Chilled water (omit if wet ice)

Comment: The classic 'Natural Daiquiri' with a hint of vanilla.

VANILLA LAIKA

★★★⯪☆

Glass: Collins
Garnish: Seasonal berries
Method: SHAKE all ingredients with ice and strain into glass filled with crushed ice.

1½	shots	Vanilla infused Ketel One vodka
¾	shot	Lejay Crème de Mûre liqueur
¼	shot	Freshly squeezed lemon juice
¾	shot	Sugar syrup (2 sugar to 1 water)
4	shots	Pressed apple juice

Origin: Created by Jake Burger in 2002 at Townhouse, Leeds, England. Laika was a Russian dog and the first canine in space.
Comment: Vanilla berry fruit in a tall, refreshing drink.

VANILLA MARGARITA 0—🗝

★★★★☆

Glass: Old-fashioned
Garnish: Lime wedge
Method: SHAKE all ingredients with ice and fine strain into ice-filled chilled glass.

2	shots	Patrón reposado tequila (infused with vanilla)
1	shot	De Kuyper Triple Sec
1	shot	Freshly squeezed lemon juice

Origin: Discovered in 1998 at Café Pacifico, London, England.
Comment: A classic Margarita with a hint of vanilla.

VANILLA SENSATION

★★★★☆

Glass: Martini
Garnish: Apple slice
Method: SHAKE all ingredients with ice and fine strain into chilled glass.

2	shots	Vanilla infused Ketel One vodka
1	shot	Sour apple liqueur
½	shot	Martini Extra Dry vermouth

Origin: Created in 2003 but by whom is unknown.
Comment: A pleasing vanilla twist on an Apple Martini.

VANILLA VODKA SOUR

★★★★☆

Glass: Flute
Garnish: Lemon & orange zest twists
Method: SHAKE all ingredients with ice and fine strain into chilled glass.

2	shots	Vanilla infused Ketel One vodka
¾	shot	Licor 43 liqueur
¾	shot	Freshly squeezed lemon juice
½	fresh	Egg white

Comment: A Vodka Sour with a blast of spicy vanilla.

VANILLA'TINI

★★★½☆

Glass: Martini
Garnish: Half vanilla pod
Method: STIR all ingredients with ice and strain into chilled glass.

2½ shots	Vanilla infused Ketel One vodka
½ shot	Hazelnut liqueur
1½ shots	Lemonade/Sprite/7-Up

Origin: Discovered in 2003 at Paramount Hotel, New York City, USA.
Comment: Vanilla, hazelnut and a hint of creamy citrus.

VANITINI

★★★½☆

Glass: Martini
Garnish: Pineapple wedge
Method: SHAKE all ingredients with ice and fine strain into chilled glass.

2	shots	Vanilla infused Ketel One vodka
2	shots	Sauvignon blanc white wine
¾	shot	Sour pineapple liqueur
¼	shot	Lejay Crème de Mûre liqueur

Comment: Vanilla and pineapple dried by the acidity of the wine, and sweetened and flavoured by blackberry liqueur.

VANTE COCKTAIL

★★★★½

Glass: Martini
Garnish: Orange zest twist
Method: MUDDLE cardamom in base of shaker. Add other ingredients, SHAKE with ice and fine strain into chilled glass.

4	fresh	Cardamom pod
1½ shots	Vanilla infused Ketel One vodka
1½ shots	Sauvignon blanc white wine
1	shot	Licor 43 liqueur
¼	shot	Fresh pressed pineapple juice

Origin: Created in 2003 by yours truly, London, England.
Comment: Bold, aromatic and complex flavours.

VAVAVOOM

★★★★☆

Glass: Flute
Garnish: None
Method: POUR ingredients into chilled glass. **TOP** with champagne.

½	shot	De Kuyper Triple Sec
½	shot	Freshly squeezed lemon juice
¼	shot	Sugar syrup (2 sugar to 1 water)
Top with	G.H. Mumm Cordon Rouge Champagne

Origin: Adapted from a drink created in 2002 by Yannick Miseriaux at The Fifth Floor Bar, Harvey Nichols, London, England, and named after the Renault television advertisements.
Comment: This drink does indeed give champagne that vavavoom.

VELVET ELVIS

★★★½☆

Glass: Old-fashioned
Garnish: Lime wedge
Method: SHAKE first three ingredients with ice and strain into ice-filled glass. **TOP** with lemon-lime soda.

1½ shots	Jack Daniel's Old No.7 Brand
1	shot	Chambord Liqueur
½	shot	Freshly squeezed lime juice
Top with	Lemonade/Sprite/7-Up

Comment: The merest bit on the sweet side, fruity with a hint of whiskey.

VELVET FOG

★★★★½

Glass: Martini
Garnish: Orange zest twist (discarded) & dust with grated nutmeg
Method: SHAKE all ingredients with ice and fine strain into chilled glass.

1½ shots	Ketel One Vodka
¾	shot	Taylor's Velvet Falernum liqueur
1¼ shots	Freshly squeezed lime juice
¾	shot	Freshly squeezed orange juice
2	dash	Angostura Aromatic Bitters

Origin: Created by Dale DeGroff, New York City, USA.
Comment: Tangy, fresh and bittersweet.

VELVET HAMMER

★★★½☆

Glass: Martini
Garnish: Dust with grated nutmeg
Method: SHAKE all ingredients with ice and fine strain into chilled glass.

1	shot	Ketel One Vodka
¾	shot	De Kuyper Triple Sec
¾	shot	White crème de cacao liqueur
¾	shot	Single cream / half-and-half
¾	shot	Milk
¼	shot	Pomegranate / grenadine syrup (2:1)

Comment: Lots of velvet with a little bit of hammer courtesy of a shot of vodka.

VELVET MAKER (NEW)

★★★★½

Glass: Coupe
Garnish: Pink grapefruit zest twist
Method: **SHAKE** all ingredients with ice and fine strain into chilled glass.

2 shots Vanilla infused Ketel One vodka
½ shot Martini Extra Dry vermouth
½ shot Freshly squeezed pink grapefruit juice
⅓ shot Vanilla sugar syrup
2 dash Grapefruit bitters

Origin: Created by yours truly and named after Velvet Maker, the filly who won the 15:05 at the wonderfully named Fairyhouse racecourse in Ireland on 31st January 2015 - the day I first made made this drink.
Comment: Vanilla infused vodka and zesty grapefruit with dry vermouth balancing and botanical complexity.

VELVET OLD FASHIONED (NEW)

★★★★½

Glass: Old-fashioned
Garnish: Orange zest twist
Method: **STIR** half of the Scotch with three ice cubes (dry to the touch frozen ice, not wet ice) in a glass. Add sherry, sugar syrup and Angostura and two more ice cubes. **STIR** some more and add another two ice cubes and the rest of the Scotch. **STIR** some more, and if you have room, add more ice.

2½ shots Dewar's 12yo Scotch whisky
¼ shot Romate Pedro Ximénez sherry
¼ shot Light muscovado sugar syrup (2 sugar to 1 water)
2 dash Angostura Aromatic Bitters

Comment: The use of a good Pedro Ximénez sherry and achieving the correct level of dilution by repeated stirring is key to the success of this drink. With perfect dilution the sherry and whisky combine brilliantly.

VELVET THREESOME

★★★★½

Glass: Coupe
Garnish: Orange zest twist
Method: **STIR** all ingredients with ice and fine strain into chilled glass.

¾ shot Calvados brandy
¾ shot Martell VSOP Médaillon cognac
¾ shot BarSol Mosto Verde Italia pisco
½ shot Licor 43 liqueur
¼ shot Martini Extra Dry vermouth

Origin: Created in 2010 by yours truly at the Cabinet Room, London, England.
Comment: A trio of brandies with a dash of herbal vanilla, rounded with vermouth.

VENETIAN

★★★★

Glass: Old-fashioned
Garnish: Orange zest twist (spray & discard)
Method: **STIR** all ingredients with ice and fine strain into ice filled glass.

2 shots Aperol Aperitivo
2 shots Sauvignon blanc white wine
1 spoon Cartron No. 7 liqueur
1 spoon Elderflower cordial
1 spoon Picon Biere

Origin: Created in 2009 by Rich Hunt at Quo Vadis, London, England. It is based on the flavours of the spritz, but there are no bubbles of any kind.
Comment: Burnished copper red and bitter sweet with Aperol, wine and a dash of elderflower, fruit liqueur and bitters.

VENETO

★★★½

Glass: Martini
Garnish: Lemon zest twist
Method: **SHAKE** all ingredients with ice and fine strain into chilled glass.

2 shots Martell VSOP Médaillon cognac
½ shot Luxardo sambuca dei cesari
½ shot Freshly squeezed lemon juice
⅛ shot Sugar syrup (2 sugar to 1 water)
½ shot Egg white

Comment: A serious, Stinger-like drink.

VENUS COCKTAIL

★★★½

Glass: Martini
Garnish: Raspberries
Method: **MUDDLE** raspberries in base of shaker. Add other ingredients, **SHAKE** with ice and fine strain into chilled glass.

7 fresh Raspberries
2 shots Rutte Dry Gin
1 shot De Kuyper Triple Sec
¼ shot Sugar syrup (2 sugar to 1 water)
3 dash Peychaud's aromatic bitters

Comment: Raspberry with hints of bitter orange and gin - surprisingly dry.

VENUS IN FURS

★★★½

Glass: Collins
Garnish: Seasonal berries & lemon slice
Method: **SHAKE** all ingredients with ice and strain into ice-filled glass.

1 shot Raspberry flavoured vodka
1 shot Ketel One Citroen vodka
3½ shots Pressed apple juice
3 dash Angostura Aromatic Bitters

Origin: A cocktail which emerged in London's bars early in 2002.
Comment: Juicy flavours with a hint of spice make for a refreshing, quaffable drink.

VERDI COCKTAIL

★★★★☆

Glass: Martini
Garnish: Pineapple wedge
Method: **SHAKE** all ingredients with ice and fine strain into chilled glass.

- 1¾ shots **Ketel One Vodka**
- ½ shot **Midori Green Melon liqueur**
- ½ shot **Peachtree peach schnapps**
- 1 shot **Fresh pressed pineapple juice**
- 1 shot **Pressed apple juice**
- ¼ shot **Freshly squeezed lime juice**

Origin: Adapted from a drink discovered in 2002 at the Fifth Floor Bar, Harvey Nichols, London, England.
Comment: A melange of fruits combine in a gluggable short drink.

VERT'ICAL BREEZE

★★★½☆

Glass: Collins
Garnish: Lemon wedge
Method: **SHAKE** all ingredients with ice and strain into ice-filled glass.

- 1½ shots **Le Fée Parisienne absinthe**
- 3 shots **Cranberry juice**
- 3 shots **Freshly squeezed pink grapefruit juice**

Comment: For those who don't speak French, 'vert' means green - the colour of absinthe. Vertical suggests take-off - try it and see.

VERY FRENCH MARTINI (NEW)

★★★★½

Glass: Coupe
Garnish: Raspberry
Method: **SHAKE** all ingredients with ice and fine strain into glass.

- 1½ shots **Martell VSOP Médaillon cognac**
- ½ shot **Chambord Liqueur**
- 1½ shots **Fresh pressed pineapple juice**

Origin: Created in January 2015 by yours truly and Matthias Lataille at the Cabinet Room, London, England.
Comment: Cognac, pineapple juice and black raspberry liqueur. OK, so France is not known for its pineapples but I said 'very' not 'totally' French.

VERY RUSTY DAIQUIRI

★★★★☆

Glass: Coupe
Garnish: Lime wedge
Method: **SHAKE** all ingredients with ice and fine strain into chilled glass.

- 2 shots **Bacardi Carta Ocho aged rum**
- ½ shot **Drambuie liqueur**
- ½ shot **Freshly squeezed lime juice**

Origin: Created in December 2010 by yours truly at the Cabinet Room, London, England.
Comment: Honey and spice notes from Drambuie add interest to this Aged Daiquiri.

VESPER DRY MARTINI

★★★★★

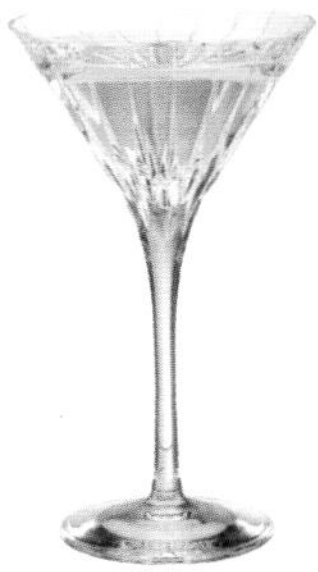

Glass: Martini
Garnish: Lemon zest twist
Method: **SHAKE** all ingredients with ice and fine strain into chilled glass.

- 2 shots **Rutte Dry Gin**
- ⅔ shot **Ketel One Vodka**
- ⅓ shot **Lillet Blanc**

Origin: This variation on the Dry Martini is said to have been created by Gilberto Preti at Duke's Hotel, London, for the author Ian Fleming. He liked it so much that he included it in his first James Bond novel, 'Casino Royale', published in 1953.

In chapter seven Bond explains to a Casino bartender exactly how to make and serve the drink: "In a deep champagne goblet. Three measures of Gordon's, one of vodka, half a measure of Kina Lillet [now called Lillet Blanc]. Shake it very well until it's ice-cold, then add a large slice of lemon peel."

When made, 007 compliments the bartender, but tells him it would be better made with a grain-based vodka. He also explains his Martini to Felix Leiter, the CIA man, saying, "This drink's my own invention. I'm going to patent it when I can think of a good name."

In chapter eight, Bond meets the beautiful agent Vesper Lynd. She explains why her parents named her Vesper and Bond asks if she'd mind if he called his favourite Martini after her. Like so many of Bond's love interests Vesper turns out to be a double agent and the book closes with his words, "The bitch is dead now."
Comment: Many bartenders advocate that a Martini should be stirred and not shaken, some citing the ridiculous argument that shaking will "bruise the gin." If you like your Martinis shaken then avoid the possible look of distaste from your server and order a Vesper. This particular Dry Martini is always shaken, an action that aerates the drink, and makes it colder and more dilute than simply stirring. It also gives the drink a slightly clouded appearance and can leave small shards of ice on the surface of the drink - easily prevented by the use of a fine strainer when pouring.

VIAGRA FALLS

★★★½☆

Glass: Martini
Garnish: Orange zest twist
Method: **SHAKE** all ingredients with ice and fine strain into chilled glass.

- ¾ shot **Le Fée Parisienne absinthe**
- 1½ shots **Sour apple liqueur**
- 1¾ shots **Chilled water**
- 2 dash **Angostura Orange Bitters**

Origin: Created by Jack Leuwens, London, England.
Comment: Aniseed and apple - sure to get your pecker up.

VICTORIAN LEMONADE

★★★½☆

Glass: Collins
Garnish: Lemon slice
Method: Lightly **MUDDLE** mint (just to bruise) in base of shaker. Add other ingredients, **SHAKE** with ice and fine strain into ice-filled glass.

- 12 fresh **Mint leaves**
- 1½ shots **Rutte Dry Gin**
- 1 shot **Freshly squeezed lemon juice**
- ¾ shot **Sugar syrup (2 sugar to 1 water)**
- 2½ shots **Chilled water**

Comment: Gin laced, mint flavoured, traditional lemonade.

VIEUX CARRÉ COCKTAIL

★★★★½

Glass: Old-fashioned
Garnish: Lemon zest twist
Method: STIR all ingredients with ice and strain into ice-filled glass.

1	shot	Bourbon whiskey
1	shot	Martell VSOP Médaillon cognac
¼	shot	Bénédictine D.O.M. liqueur
1	shot	Martini Rosso vermouth
1	dash	Angostura Aromatic Bitters
1	dash	Peychaud's aromatic bitters

Origin: Created in 1938 by Walter Bergeron, the then head bartender at what is now the Carousel bar at the Monteleone Hotel, New Orleans, USA. Pronounced 'Voo-Ka-Ray', it is named after the French term for New Orlean's French Quarter and literally translates as 'old square'.
Comment: Like an ultra-smooth and complex Sweet Manhattan served on the rocks.

VIEUX NAVINE

★★★★☆

Glass: Coupe
Garnish: Luxardo Maraschino cherry
Method: STIR all ingredients with ice and strain into chilled glass.

1	shot	Calvados brandy
1	shot	Bourbon whiskey
1	shot	Martini Rosso vermouth
1	shot	Whiskey Barrel Aged Bitters
1	dash	Maple bitters

Origin: Adapted from a drink created in 2010 by Patrick Brennan at Prospect, San Francisco, USA.
Comment: An apple spirit influenced Sweet Manhattan style cocktail.

VIOLET AFFINITY

★★★★½

Glass: Coupe
Garnish: Lemon zest twist
Method: STIR all ingredients with ice and strain into chilled glass.

1½	shots	Benoit Serres créme de violette
¾	shot	Martini Extra Dry vermouth
¾	shot	Martini Rosso vermouth

Origin: Our adaptation of the classic Affinity.
Comment: Amazingly delicate and complex for such a simple drink.

VIOLET NEGRONI COCKTAIL (NEW)

★★★★½

Glass: Old-fashioned
Garnish: Orange zest twist
Method: POUR all ingredients into ice-filled glass and STIR.

1	shot	Rutte Dry Gin
2	shots	Byrrh Grand Quinquina
½	shot	Suze Saveur d'Autrefois

Origin: Created in 2013 by Mathieu Sabbagh of Pernod Ricard.
Comment: Bittersweet with a strong hint of gentian. A great aperitif.

VODKA COLLINS

★★★★☆

Glass: Collins
Garnish: Orange slice & cherry on stick (sail)
Method: SHAKE first three ingredients with ice and strain into ice-filled glass. TOP with soda, lightly stir and serve with straws.

2	shots	Ketel One Vodka
1	shot	Freshly squeezed lemon juice
½	shot	Sugar syrup (2 sugar to 1 water)
Top with		Soda (club soda)

Origin: The exact origins of this drink are unknown but it is certain that Vodka Collins' were being served in New York after the repeal of Prohibition in 1933.
Comment: A Tom Collins with vodka - a refreshing balance of sweet and sour.

VODKA DAISY

★★★☆☆

Glass: Goblet
Garnish: Lemon wedge
Method: SHAKE all ingredients with ice and strain into glass filled with crushed ice. CHURN (stir) drink with ice and serve with straws.

2	shots	Ketel One Vodka
1	shot	Freshly squeezed lemon juice
½	shot	Pomegranate / grenadine syrup (2:1)
½	shot	Sugar syrup (2 sugar to 1 water)

Comment: Slightly sweet with gentle fruitiness.

VODKA ESPRESSO

★★★★½

Glass: Old-fashioned
Garnish: Float 3 coffee beans in the centre of the drink, arranged in a flower petal formation.
Method: SHAKE all ingredients with ice and fine strain into ice-filled glass.

1⅔	shot	Ketel One vodka
1½	shot	Espresso coffee
⅔	shot	Coffee liqueur
¼	shot	Sugar syrup (2 sugar to 1 water)

Comment: Vodka and coffee combine in this tasty wake up call.
Origin: Created by Dick Bradsell in 1983 at the Soho Brasserie, Dick's original recipe called for 10ml Kahlua and 10ml Tia Maria rather than simply 20ml coffee liqueur.
Variant: Pharmaceutical Stimulant, Espresso Martini.

VODKA GIMLET

★★★★☆

Glass: Martini
Garnish: Lime wedge
Method: STIR all ingredients with ice and strain into chilled glass.

2½	shots	Ketel One Vodka
1¼	shots	Rose's lime cordial

Comment: Sweetened lime fortified with vodka.

VODKA RICKEY

★★★½☆

Glass: Collins (small 8oz)
Garnish: Length of lime peel
Method: SHAKE first three ingredients with ice and strain into ice-filled glass. **TOP** with soda.

2	shots	Ketel One Vodka
½	shot	Freshly squeezed lime juice
¼	shot	Sugar syrup (2 sugar to 1 water)
Top with		Soda (club soda)

Comment: Lacks interest but balanced and hard to fault as a simple and refreshing drink.

VODKA SOUR

★★★★☆

Glass: Old-fashioned
Garnish: Lemon slice & cherry on stick (sail)
Method: SHAKE all ingredients with ice and strain into ice-filled glass.

2	shots	Ketel One Vodka
1	shot	Freshly squeezed lemon juice
½	shot	Sugar syrup (2 sugar to 1 water)
3	dash	Angostura Aromatic Bitters
½	fresh	Egg white

Comment: A great vodka based drink balancing sweet and sour.

VODKATINI / VODKA DRY MARTINI

★★★★½

Glass: Martini
Garnish: Chilled olive on stick or lemon zest twist
Method: SHAKE all ingredients with ice and fine strain into chilled glass.

| 2½ | shots | Ketel One Vodka |
| ¼ | shot | Martini Extra Dry vermouth |

Origin: Exactly where the Vodkatini fits in the vexed question of the origins of the Dry Martini are unknown but it is certain that 'Vodka Martinis' were being served in New York after the repeal of Prohibition in 1933.
Comment: Temperature is key to the enjoyment of this modern classic. Consume while icy cold.

VOLGA BOATMAN

★★★★½☆

Glass: Martini
Garnish: Orange zest twist
Method: SHAKE all ingredients with ice and fine strain into chilled glass.

1½	shots	Ketel One Vodka
¾	shot	Kirschwasser eau de vie
1½	shots	Freshly squeezed orange juice

Origin: Recipe adapted from David Embury's classic 'Fine Art of Mixing Drinks'. Named after the epic (and somewhat camp) Cecil b. De Mille movie, which took its name from a Russian folksong hymning the Volga - Europe's longest river.
Comment: A Screwdriver served straight up with a twist of cherry.

VOODOO

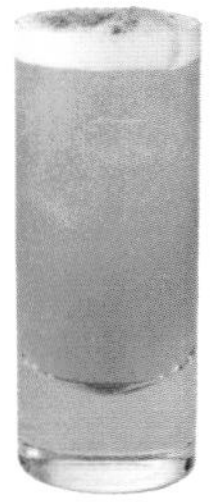

★★★★☆

Glass: Collins
Garnish: Dust with cinnamon powder.
Method: SHAKE all ingredients with ice and strain into ice-filled glass.

2	shots	Bacardi Carta Ocho aged rum
¾	shot	Martini Rosso vermouth
2½	shots	Pressed apple juice
½	shot	Freshly squeezed lime juice
¼	shot	Sugar syrup (2 sugar to 1 water)

Origin: Created in 2002 by Alex Kammerling, London, England.
Comment: The rich flavour of the aged rum marries well with apple and lime juice.

VOODOO I DO

★★★★☆

Glass: Old-fashioned
Garnish: Pineapple wedge & Luxardo Maraschino cherry
Method: MUDDLE pineapple in base of shaker. Add other ingredients, **SHAKE** with ice and fine strain into ice-filled glass.

1 ring Pineapple (fresh)
2 shots Patrón reposado tequila
¼ shot De Kuyper Triple Sec
½ shot De Kuyper XO Apricot Brandy
½ shot Freshly squeezed lime juice

Origin: Adapted from a drink created in 2011 by Michael Layer at the Chapel Bar, Berlin, Germany.
Comment: Pineapple, tequila, orange and apricot with a touch of sour lime all presented in an harmonious Tiki-style concoction.

VOWEL COCKTAIL

★★★★½

Glass: Martini
Garnish: Orange zest twist
Method: SHAKE all ingredients with ice and fine strain into chilled glass.

1¼	shots	Dewar's 12yo Scotch whisky
1	shot	Kümmel
1	shot	Martini Rosso vermouth
¾	shot	Freshly squeezed orange juice
2	dash	Angostura Aromatic Bitters

Origin: Adapted from a recipe in 'Vintage Spirits & Forgotten Cocktails' by Ted Haigh (AKA Dr Cocktail).
Comment: Caraway from the Kümmel subtly dominates this aromatic drink.

VOYAGER VODKA MARTINI

★★★★⯨

Glass: Coupe
Garnish: Frozen green grape on stick (place on stick then freeze)
Method: STIR all ingredients with ice and fine strain into chilled glass.

2½	shots	Ketel One Vodka
½	shot	Martini Extra Dry vermouth
½	shot	Junmai ginjō sake
⅛	shot	BarSol Mosto Verde Italia pisco

Origin: Created in 2013 by yours truly at the Cabinet Room, London, England.
Comment: Why have your Martini dampened by just vermouth, when the Japanese and South Americans have so much to give?

WAH-WAH

★★★★☆

Glass: Martini
Garnish: Orange zest twist
Method: SHAKE all ingredients with ice and fine strain into chilled glass.

1½	shots	BarSol Mosto Verde Italia pisco
1	shot	St-Germain elderflower liqueur
¾	shot	Aperol Aperitivo
¾	shot	Freshly squeezed pink grapefruit juice
1	dash	Angostura Aromatic Bitters

Origin: Created in 2007 at Range, San Francisco, USA.
Comment: Bittersweet and complex with hints of elderflower and grapefruit.

WALDORF COCKTAIL NO.1

★★★★☆

Glass: Martini
Garnish: Lemon zest twist
Method: STIR all ingredients with ice and strain into chilled glass

2	shots	Bourbon whiskey
1	shot	Martini Rosso vermouth
⅛	shot	Le Fée Parisienne absinthe
2	dash	Angostura Aromatic Bitters

Origin: The eponymous cocktail from the Waldorf Hotel occupied a site on New York's Fifth Avenue. The Empire State Building now occupies the hotel's original site and a landmark Art-Deco building at 301 Park Avenue has long been known as the Waldorf-Astoria Hotel.

Consisting of equal parts whiskey (probably originally rye whiskey), sweet vermouth and absinthe with a dash of bitters. This is the earlier of the two classic versions of this vintage cocktail which appeared in Jacques Straub's 1914 book 'Drinks" and later in A. S. Crockett's 1935 ' The Old Waldorf-Astoria Bar Book'.

We adapted this recipe to suit modern palates and ingredients.
Comment: A Sweet Manhattan dried by the merest hint of bitter absinthe.

WALDORF COCKTAIL NO.2

★★★★☆

Glass: Martini
Garnish: Lemon zest twist
Method: SHAKE all ingredients with ice and fine strain into chilled glass.

2	shots	Swedish Punch liqueur
1½	shots	Rutte Dry Gin
¾	shot	Freshly squeezed lime juice

Origin: This is the later of the two versions of this vintage cocktail from New York's Waldorf-Astoria Hotel. It appears in the 1939 Café Royale book and in the 1955 'United Kingdom Bartender's Book'. Both books offer a choice between using lemon or lime juice. The original recipe calls for two parts Swedish punch to one part gin but with the punches I've tried this makes for an overly sweet drink.
Comment: Lime works better than lemon but like the Astor, using a combination of lime and lemon makes for a better drink.

WALDORF DAIQUIRI

★★★★⯨

Glass: Coupe
Garnish: A walnut, apple wedge and chunk of blue cheese on the side
Method: MUDDLE celery in base of shaker. Add other ingredients, SHAKE with ice and fine strain into chilled glass.

2	inch	Freshly extracted celery juice
2	shots	Bacardi Carta Ocho aged rum
½	shot	White crème de cacao liqueur
¼	shot	Sugar syrup (2 sugar to 1 water)
½	shot	Freshly squeezed lemon juice
½	shot	Pressed apple juice

Origin: Adapted from a drink created in 2010 by Julian de Feral at Lutyens Bar, London, England.
Comment: Walnut, celery and apple are essential elements to both a Waldorf Salad and this tasty Daiquiri.

WALNUT ALEXANDER

★★★★☆

Glass: Martini
Garnish: Dust with grated nutmeg
Method: SHAKE all ingredients with ice and fine strain into chilled glass.

2	shots	Martell VSOP Médaillon cognac
½	shot	Nocello walnut liqueur
¼	shot	Sugar syrup (2 sugar to 1 water)
½	shot	Milk
½	shot	Single cream / half-and-half

Origin: Created in 2008 by yours truly at the Cabinet Room, London, England.
Comment: One to accompany the nutty chocolates from the after-dinner selection box.

WALNUT MARTINI

★★★★☆

Glass: Martini
Garnish: Walnut
Method: STIR all ingredients with ice and strain into chilled glass.

2	shots	Ketel One Vodka
½	shot	Tuaca liqueur
½	shot	Nocello walnut liqueur
½	shot	Martini Extra Dry vermouth

Origin: Created in 2005 by yours truly.
Comment: Nutty but nice.

WALTZING MATILDA

★★★★☆

Glass: Collins
Garnish: Orange slice
Method: Cut passion fruit in half and scoop out flesh into shaker. Add next three ingredients, SHAKE with ice and fine strain into ice-filled glass. TOP with ginger ale.

1	fresh	Passion fruit
1	shot	Rutte Dry Gin
2	shots	Sauvignon blanc white wine
⅛	shot	Grand Marnier Cordon Rouge
Top with		Ginger ale

Origin: Adapted from a recipe from David Embury's classic book, 'The Fine Art of Mixing Drinks'.
Comment: Passion fruit, gin, wine and ginger ale all combine well in this refreshing drink.

WANTON ABANDON

★★★★☆

Glass: Martini
Garnish: Strawberry on rim
Method: MUDDLE strawberries in shaker. Add next three ingredients, SHAKE with ice and fine strain into chilled glass. TOP with champagne.

5	fresh	Small ripe strawberries (hulled)
2	shots	Ketel One Vodka
¾	shot	Freshly squeezed lemon juice
½	shot	Sugar syrup (2 sugar to 1 water)
1	shot	G.H. Mumm Cordon Rouge Champagne

Comment: A crowd-pleaser - looks great and its fruity, balanced flavour will offend few.

WARD EIGHT ⚷

★★★★☆

Glass: Coupe
Garnish: Orange slice & cherry on stick (sail)
Method: SHAKE all ingredients with ice and fine strain into chilled glass.

2¼ shots		Bourbon whiskey
¾	shot	Freshly squeezed lemon juice
¾	shot	Freshly squeezed orange juice
¼	shot	Pomegranate / grenadine syrup (2:1)
½	shot	Chilled water

Origin: Ward Eight was a voting district of Boston and famed for its political corruption. This drink was first served by Tom Hussion in November 1898 at Boston's Locke-Ober Café, in honour of Martin Lomasney, who owned the café and was running for election in Ward Eight.
Comment: This is a spirited, sweet and sour combination - like most politicians.

WARSAW

★★★⯪☆

Glass: Martini
Garnish: Orange zest twist
Method: STIR all ingredients with ice and fine strain into chilled glass.

2	shots	Ketel One Vodka
½	shot	Polska Wisniowka cherry liqueur
¼	shot	De Kuyper Triple Sec
2	dash	Angostura Aromatic Bitters
¾	shot	Chilled water (omit if wet ice)

Comment: Subtle cherry notes with orange.

WARSAW COOLER

★★★★⯪

Glass: Collins
Garnish: Mint sprig & orange zest twist
Method: STIR honey with vodka in base of shaker until honey dissolves. Add other ingredients, SHAKE with ice and strain into ice-filled glass.

2	spoon	Runny honey
1½ shots		Zubrówka bison vodka
½	shot	Bacardi OakHeart Spiced Rum
¼	shot	De Kuyper Triple Sec
½	shot	Sugar syrup (2 sugar to 1 water)
¾	shot	Freshly squeezed lemon juice
2	shots	Pressed apple juice

Origin: Created in 2002 by Morgan Watson of Apartment, Belfast, Northern Ireland.
Comment: Orange, honey, apple and spice laced with Polish Bison grass vodka.

WARSAW PACT

★★★★☆

Glass: Martini
Garnish: Mint leaf
Method: SHAKE all ingredients with ice and fine strain into chilled glass.

5	fresh	Mint leaves
2	shots	Zubrówka bison vodka
½	shot	Disaronno Originale amaretto
1½ shots		Pressed apple juice

Origin: Adapted from a drink discovered in 2007 at Paparazzi, Warsaw, Poland.
Comment: Fruit and mint flavours combine in this beautifully balanced complex yet easy cocktail.

WASABI MARTINI

★★★★⯪

Glass: Martini
Garnish: Yaki nori seaweed
Method: Squeeze a pea-sized quantity of wasabi paste onto a barspoon and STIR with vodka until wasabi dissolves. Add other ingredients, SHAKE with ice and fine strain into chilled glass.

2	shots	Ketel One Vodka
1	pea	Wasabi paste
¾	shot	Freshly squeezed lemon juice
½	shot	Sugar syrup (2 sugar to 1 water)

Origin: Created in 2004 by Philippe Guidi at Morton's, London, England.
Comment: Wonderfully balanced with spicy heat and a zesty finish.

WASH HOUSE

★★★★☆

Glass: Martini
Garnish: Thyme sprig
Method: Lightly **MUDDLE** basil (just to bruise) in base of shaker. Add other ingredients, **SHAKE** with ice and fine strain into chilled glass.

4	fresh	Basil leaves
2	shots	Ketel One Vodka
½	shot	Freshly squeezed lime juice
½	shot	Sugar syrup (2 sugar to 1 water)
½	shot	Chilled water

Origin: Adapted from a recipe by Neyah White at Nopa, San Francisco, USA. The building that now houses Nopa was once a laundry, hence the name.
Comment: Delicately herbal - simple but refreshing.

WASHINGTON APPLE

★★★★⯪

Glass: Collins
Garnish: Apple slice
Method: **SHAKE** first four ingredients with ice and fine strain into ice-filled glass. **DRIZZLE** grenadine over drink. Serve with straws.

2	shots	Ketel One Vodka
½	shot	Sour apple liqueur
3	shots	Pressed apple juice
¼	shot	Freshly squeezed lime juice
¼	shot	Pomegranate / grenadine syrup (2:1)

Origin: Created by Wayne Collins, London, England.
Comment: A long version of the popular Sour Apple Martini.

WATERLOO (NEW)

★★★★⯪

Glass: Martini
Garnish: Light orange zest twist (discarded) & float pickled almond
Method: **STIR** all ingredients with ice and fine strain into chilled glass.

2 shots Rutte Old Simon genever
½ shot Mandarine Napoleon liqueur
⅛ shot Jägermeister

Comment: A dry, lightly bitter, aperitif cocktail highlighting the bready notes in genever and the bright zesty freshness of Mandarine Napoleon. Jägermeister adds bitter complexity.
Origin: Created by Simon Difford at the Cabinet Room, London, England.

Named after the Battle of Waterloo which was fought on Sunday 18th June 1815 near the town of Waterloo in present-day Belgium, then part of the Netherlands. The French army commanded by Napoleon Bonaparte was defeated by an Anglo-allied army commanded by the Duke of Wellington fitting alongside a Prussian army commanded by Gebhard Leberecht von Blücher, Prince of Wahlstatt. Napoleon's defeat at Waterloo brought his reign as French Emperor to a sudden end.

WATERLOO SUNSET

★★★★☆

Glass: Flute
Garnish: Raspberries
Method: **STIR** first two ingredients with ice and strain into chilled glass. **TOP** with champagne. Add raspberry liqueur.

1	shot	Rutte Dry Gin
½	shot	St-Germain elderflower liqueur
Top with		G.H. Mumm Cordon Rouge Champagne
¼	shot	Chambord Liqueur

Origin: Created in 2008 by Dan Warner, then the Beefeater Global Ambassador, hence originally made using said gin.
Comment: Fruity, pink champagne. Girls are going to love it.

WATERMELON & BASIL COCKTAIL

★★★★☆

Glass: Martini
Garnish: Watermelon wedge
Method: Cut watermelon into 16 segments, chop the flesh from one segment into cubes and **MUDDLE** in base of shaker. Add other ingredients, **SHAKE** with ice and fine strain into chilled glass.

1	slice	Fresh watermelon (chopped)
7	fresh	Basil leaves
2	shots	Rutte Dry Gin
½	shot	Sugar syrup (2 sugar to 1 water)

Comment: Refreshing watermelon with interesting herbal hints from the basil and gin.

WATERMELON & BASIL SMASH

★★★★☆

Glass: Collins
Garnish: Watermelon wedge
Method: Cut watermelon into 16 segments, chop the flesh from one segment into cubes and **MUDDLE** in base of shaker. Add other ingredients, **SHAKE** with ice and fine strain into ice-filled glass. **TOP** with ginger ale.

1	slice	Fresh watermelon
8	fresh	Basil leaves
2	shots	Patrón reposado tequila
¾	shot	Pallini Limoncello
Top with		Ginger ale

Comment: Sweet and sour, long and refreshing with subtle hints of basil, ginger and tequila amongst the fruit.

WATERMELON BATIDA (NEW)

★★★★☆

Glass: Collins
Garnish: Watermelon wedge on rim
Method: **MUDDLE** watermelon in base of shaker. Add other ingredients, **SHAKE** with ice and fine strain into ice-filled glass.

1	cupful	Fresh watermelon (chopped)
2	shots	Capucana cachaça
2	shots	Evaporated milk (sweetened)
⅔	shot	Agave syrup
2	shots	Coconut water

Origin: Recipe by Jorge Balbontin, Vantguard, Barcelona, Spain.
Comment: Watermelon adds fruity notes to this creamy Batida.

A B C D E F G H I J K L M N O P Q R S T U V W X Y Z

WATERMELON COSMO

★★★★⯪☆

Glass: Martini
Garnish: Watermelon wedge
Method: Cut watermelon into 16 segments, chop the flesh from one segment into cubes and **MUDDLE** in base of shaker. Add other ingredients, **SHAKE** with ice and fine strain into chilled glass.

1	slice	Fresh watermelon
2	shots	Ketel One Citroen vodka
¾	shot	Freshly squeezed lime juice
¾	shot	Cranberry juice
⅛	shot	Rose's lime cordial
½	shot	Midori Green Melon liqueur
2	dash	Angostura Orange Bitters

Origin: Created in 2003 by Eric Fossard at Cecconi's, London, England.
Comment: Looks like a standard Cosmo but tastes just as the name suggests.

WATERMELON MAN

★★★★⯪☆

Glass: Collins
Garnish: Lime wedge
Method: **SHAKE** first five ingredients with ice and strain into ice-filled glass. Top with soda and serve with straws.

2	shots	Ketel One Vodka
1	shot	Watermelon liqueur
¼	shot	Sugar syrup (2 sugar to 1 water)
½	shot	Freshly squeezed lime juice
1	shot	Pomegranate / grenadine syrup (2:1)
Top with		Soda (club soda)

Origin: Named after the Herbie Hancock track and popularised by a club night promoter called Cookie in Berlin during the mid-1990s. He started serving this cocktail at his club nights and now practically every bar in Berlin offers it. Try the original at his Cookie Club.
Comment: Sweet and far from sophisticated, but better than the fodder peddled at most clubs.

WATERMELON MARGARITA (NEW)

★★★★☆

Glass: Margarita
Garnish: Watermelon wedge
Method: **MUDDLE** watermelon in base of shaker. Add other ingredients, **SHAKE** with ice and fine strain into chilled glass.

1 cupful Fresh watermelon (chopped)
2 shots Patrón reposado tequila
¾ shot Freshly squeezed lime juice
½ shot Watermelon sugar syrup
½ pinch Salt

Comment: Just as it says on the tin – this is a very fruity Margarita.

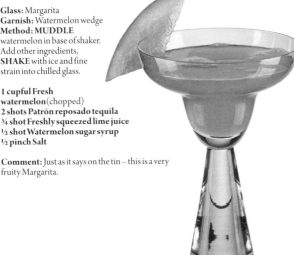

WATERMELON MARTINI

★★★★☆

Glass: Coupe
Garnish: Watermelon wedge
Method: Cut watermelon into 16 segments, chop the flesh from one segment into cubes and **MUDDLE** in base of shaker. Add other ingredients, **SHAKE** with ice and fine strain into chilled glass.

1	slice	Fresh watermelon
2	shots	Ketel One Vodka
½	shot	Sugar syrup (2 sugar to 1 water)

Comment: So fruity, you could almost convince yourself this is a health drink.

WATERS OF CHAOS

★★★★☆

Glass: Old-fashioned
Garnish: Ti-Punch style lime slice
Method: **SHAKE** all ingredients with ice and strain into ice-filled glass.

1½ shots Rutte Old Simon oude jenever
¼ shot White overproof rum
¼ shot Green Chartreuse liqueur
¾ shot Freshly squeezed lime juice
½ shot Sugar syrup (2 sugar to 1 water)
½ shot Chilled water (omit if wet ice)

Origin: Created by yours truly at the Cabinet Room, London, England and named after the words of the track Argha Noah by Nightmares on Wax.
Comment: Robust flavours of overproof rum and Chartreuse combine with Dutch jenever in this Daiquiri-like cocktail.

WEBBER COCKTAIL (NEW)

★★★★☆

Glass: Martini
Garnish: Red apple fan
Method: **SHAKE** all ingredients with ice and fine strain into chilled glass.

1½	shots	Ketel One Citroen vodka
½	shot	Lejay crème de cassis de Dijon
1	shot	Pressed apple juice
⅓	shot	Sugar syrup (2 sugar to 1 water)

Origin: Created in September 2011 by Jack Webber for the British Brown's Bar & Restaurant chain, it's since become a favourite on the Brown's menu where it's listed under 'Browns Signature Cocktails'.
Comment: This blackcurrant fruity cocktail will appeal to those who like their drinks a tad on the sweet side with citrus flavoured vodka adding backbone.

WEBSTER MARTINI 🗝

★★★★⯪☆

Glass: Coupe
Garnish: Lime zest twist
Method: SHAKE all ingredients with ice and fine strain into chilled glass.

2 shots Rutte Dry Gin
½ shot De Kuyper XO Apricot Brandy
1 shot Martini Extra Dry vermouth
½ shot Freshly squeezed lime juice

Origin: Adapted form a recipe in Harry Craddock's 1930 'Savoy Cocktail Book'. Craddock wrote of this drink "A favourite cocktail at the bar of the S.S. Mauretania."
Comment: Balanced rather than sweet. The old-school Dry Martini meets the contemporary fruit driven Martini.

WEESKI (NEW)

★★★★⯪

Glass: Coupe
Garnish: Orange zest twist
Method: STIR all ingredients with ice and strain into chilled glass.

2 shot Teeling Small Batch Irish whiskey
1 shot Lillet Blanc
¼ shot De Kuyper Triple sec
1 dash Orange bitters

Comment: Irish whiskey with herbal complexity and zesty orange.
Origin: Created in 2004 by David Wondrich in Brooklyn, New York City, USA.

WEISSEN SOUR

★★★★⯪

Glass: Collins
Garnish: Lemon slice
Method: STIR marmalade with bourbon in base of shaker to dissolve marmalade. Add lemon juice and bitters, SHAKE with ice and fine strain into ice-filled glass. TOP with beer.

2 shots Bourbon whiskey
1 spoon English orange marmalade
¾ shot Freshly squeezed lemon juice
2 dash Angostura Orange Bitters
Top with Weisse (wheat) beer

Origin: Adapted from a recipe created in 2010 by Kevin Diedrich at the Burritt Room, San Francisco, USA.
Comment: Wheaty bourbon with wheat beer and marmaladey citrus notes - they all go hand in hand and so work harmoniously in this unusual long drink.

WELL-FORTIFIED (NEW)

★★★★⯪

Glass: Coupe
Garnish: Orange zest twist
Method: STIR all ingredients with ice and strain into chilled glass.

1½ shot Moscatel
1¼ shot Ketel One vodka
¾ shot Martini Extra Dry vermouth
½ shot Romate fino sherry
¼ shot Bison grass vodka

Comment: A Bamboo meets a Vodka Martini in this boozy, vodka-laced aromatic aperitif cocktail, so named due to this cocktail packing a trio of fortified wines.
Origin: Created by yours truly (Simon Difford) at The Cabinet Room, London, England.

WELL OILED MAI TAI

★★★★⯪☆

Glass: Old-fashioned
Garnish: Half lime shell, cherry, pineapple cube & mint sprig
Method: SHAKE all ingredients with ice and strain into glass filled with crushed ice.

2 shots Bacardi Carta Ocho aged rum
¼ shot Taylor's Velvet Falernum liqueur
½ shot Almond (orgeat) syrup
¾ shot Freshly squeezed lime juice
2 dash Angostura Aromatic Bitters

Origin: Adapted from a drink created by Craig Toone at Kuckoo Boutique Bar, Newton-le-Willows, England. Craig's drink was inspired by the Tiki Margarita and he told us. "I looked at cross breeding two other well-known classics. Therefore I present the bastard love child of a Mai Tai and Corn & Oil... Genes carried forward are falernum in place of triple sec and a dash of Angostura bitters to the basic Trader Mai Tai recipe."
Comment: A heavily spiced riff on a classic Mai Tai.

THE WENTWORTH

★★★★☆

Glass: Martini
Garnish: Orange zest twist
Method: SHAKE all ingredients with ice and fine strain into chilled glass.

1¼ shots Bourbon whiskey
1¼ shots Dubonnet Red
1¼ shots Cranberry juice

Origin: Created in 2003 by Sharon Cooper at the Harvest Restaurant, Pomfret, Connecticut, USA.
Comment: The pleasing tang of bourbon adds backbone to this fruity herbal cocktail.

WET COCKTAIL (NEW)

★★★★⯪

Glass: Collins
Garnish: Lemon zest twist
Method: SHAKE all ingredients with ice and strain into glass filled with crushed ice.

1⅓ shots Capucana cachaça
⅓ shot Almond (orgeat) syrup
¼ shot Freshly squeezed lemon juice
1 pinch Ground cinnamon
Top with Ginger ale

Origin: Created in 2015 by Jorge Balbontin of Vantguard, Barcelona, Spain.
Comment: Superbly refreshing. The pinch of cinnamon adds delicate spice which combines well with cachaça and ginger ale.

WHAT THE HELL ⚬━━

★★★★☆

Glass: Martini
Garnish: Lime wedge
Method: SHAKE all ingredients with ice and fine strain into chilled glass.

2 shots Rutte Dry Gin
1 shot De Kuyper XO Apricot Brandy
¾ shot Martini Extra Dry vermouth
¼ shot Freshly squeezed lime juice
⅛ shot Sugar syrup (2 sugar to 1 water)

Comment: Gin and dry apricots.

WHAT'S UP, DOC? (NEW)

★★★★☆

Glass: Old-fashioned
Garnish: Baby carrot & mint sprig
Method: SHAKE all ingredients with ice and strain into ice-filled glass.

1½ shots Rutte Dry Gin
1½ shots Freshly extracted carrot juice
½ shot King's Ginger Liqueur
½ shot Freshly squeezed lemon juice
⅛ shot Cinnamon sugar syrup (2:1)

Origin: We discovered this drink at The Wayland in Manhattan's East Village. The What's Up, Doc? cocktail became popular across New York City in 2014 with numerous versions using different base spirits such as rye whiskey and grappa.

"Eh, What's up Doc?" is the catch phrase of Bugs Bunny, the nonchalant cartoon character who starred in the series of animated short films produced by Warner Bros.
Comment: Carrot juice gives this drink an orange hue and combines surprisingly well with gin. Extra flavour and spice comes courtesy of ginger liqueur, lemon juice and cinnamon.

WHISKEY COLLINS ⚬━━

★★★★⯪

Glass: Collins
Garnish: Orange slice & cherry on stick (sail)
Method: SHAKE first four ingredients with ice and strain into ice-filled glass. **TOP** with soda water, lightly stir and serve with straws.

2 shots Bourbon whiskey
¾ shot Freshly squeezed lemon juice
½ shot Sugar syrup (2 sugar to 1 water)
3 dash Angostura Aromatic Bitters
Top with Soda (club soda)

Comment: A whiskey based twist on the classic Tom Collins.

WHISKEY DAISY #1 ⚬━━

★★★⯪☆

Glass: Martini
Garnish: Lemon zest twist
Method: SHAKE all ingredients with ice and fine strain into chilled glass.

1¾ shots Bourbon whiskey
½ shot De Kuyper Triple Sec
¼ shot Pomegranate / grenadine syrup (2:1)
¾ shot Freshly squeezed lemon juice

Comment: This venerable, bourbon led classic has a strong citrus flavour.

WHISKEY DAISY #2

★★★⯪☆

Glass: Goblet
Garnish: Lemon & orange zest twists
Method: SHAKE first four ingredients with ice and fine strain into glass filled with crushed ice. **TOP** with small dash soda.

1½ shots Bourbon whiskey
1 spoon Honey sugar syrup
½ shot Grand Marnier Cordon Rouge
¾ shot Freshly squeezed lemon juice
Top with Soda (club soda)

Origin: Recipe adapted from Harry Johnson's 1888 'Bartender's Manual'.
Comment: Light, fresh and fruity. Perfect for a summer's afternoon.

WHISKEY SMASH (NEW) ⚬━━

★★★★⯪

Glass: Old-fashioned
Garnish: Lemon slice & mint sprig
Method: SHAKE all ingredients with ice and fine strain into ice-filled glass.

10 fresh Mint leaves
2 shots Bourbon whiskey
¾ shot Freshly squeezed lemon juice
½ shot Sugar syrup (2 sugar to 1 water)

Comment: A mint flavoured version of the Whiskey Sour.
Origin: Created 1998-1999 by Dale DeGroff at The Rainbow Room, New York City, USA.

WHISKEY SOUR #1 (CLASSIC FORMULA) ⊶

★★★★☆

Glass: Old-fashioned
Garnish: Lemon slice & cherry on stick (sail)
Method: SHAKE all ingredients with ice and strain into ice-filled glass.

2 shots Bourbon whiskey
¾ shot Freshly squeezed lemon juice
1 shot Sugar syrup (2 sugar to 1 water)
3 dash Angostura Aromatic Bitters
½ fresh Egg white

Origin: This recipe follows the classic sour proportions (3:4:8) three quarter part of the sour ingredient (lemon juice) one part of the sweet ingredient (sugar syrup) and two parts of the strong ingredient (whiskey).
Comment: I find the classic formulation more sweet than sour and prefer the 4:2:8 ratio.

WHISKEY SOUR (DIFFORD'S RECIPE) ⊶

★★★★★

Glass: Old-fashioned
Garnish: Lemon slice & cherry on stick (sail)
Method: SHAKE all ingredients with ice and strain into ice-filled glass.

2 shots Bourbon whiskey
1 shot Freshly squeezed lemon juice
½ shot Sugar syrup (2 sugar to 1 water)
3 dash Angostura Aromatic Bitters
½ fresh Egg white

Origin: A 4:2:8 sour formula.
Comment: Smooth with a hint of citrus sourness and an invigorating blast of whiskey.

WHISKEY SQUIRT

★★★★☆

Glass: Collins
Garnish: Peach slice
Method: SHAKE first three ingredients with ice and strain into ice-filled glass. TOP with soda from a siphon. Serve with straws.

2 shots Peach purée
2 shots Bourbon whiskey
¼ shot Grand Marnier Cordon Rouge
Top with Soda from siphon

Origin: Adapted from a recipe purloined from David Embury's classic book, 'The Fine Art of Mixing Drinks'.
Comment: Peach combines wonderfully with bourbon and this drink benefits from that marriage.

WHISKY BUTTER (NEW)

★★★★½

Glass: Coupe
Garnish: Mini Christmas pudding/cake
Method: SHAKE first 4 ingredients with ice and fine strain into chilled glass. FLOAT drizzle of Islay malt on surface of drink.

1½ shots Dewar's 12yo Scotch whisky
1 shot Romate Fino sherry
¼ shot Yellow Chartreuse liqueur
¾ shot Warninks Advocaat liqueur
¼ shot Islay single malt Scotch whisky

Origin: Created in December 2014 by yours truly at the Cabinet Room, London, England.
Comment: Creamy and complex Christmasy cocktail. Fino sherry dries, scotch whisky provides backbone and character while advocaat adds dairy-like creaminess. Chartreuse adds faint religious significance – after all Christmas is meant to celebrate the birth of Christ.

WHISKY COBBLER

★★★☆☆

Glass: Goblet
Garnish: Lemon slice & mint sprig
Method: SHAKE all ingredients with ice and strain into glass filled with crushed ice.

2 shots Dewar's 12yo Scotch whisky
½ shot Martell VSOP Médaillon cognac
½ shot Grand Marnier Cordon Rouge

Comment: A hardcore yet sophisticated drink.

WHISKY FIZZ ⊶

★★★★☆

Glass: Collins
Garnish: Lemon slice
Method: SHAKE first three ingredients with ice and strain into ice-filled glass. TOP with soda, lightly stir and serve with straws.

2 shots Dewar's 12yo Scotch whisky
1 shot Freshly squeezed lemon juice
½ shot Sugar syrup (2 sugar to 1 water)
Top with Soda from siphon

Comment: The character of the whisky shines through this refreshing, balanced, sweet and sour drink.

WHISKY FLOWER

★★★★☆

Glass: Old-fashioned
Garnish: Lemon zest twist
Method: DRY SHAKE all ingredients (without ice) SHAKE again with ice and strain into ice-filled glass.

2 shots Islay single malt Scotch whisky
1½ shots St-Germain elderflower liqueur
1 shot Freshly squeezed lemon juice
½ fresh Egg white

Origin: Created by Robert Williams at Mamasan, Glasgow, Scotland.
Comment: Basically an elderflower whisky sour with added interest due to the use of an Islay malt.

WHISKY MAC

★★★½☆

Glass: Old-fashioned
Garnish: None
Method: POUR ingredients into ice-filled glass and lightly stir.

| 2 | shots | Dewar's 12yo Scotch whisky |
| 1 | shot | Stone's green ginger wine |

Comment: Ginger wine smoothes and spices the Scotch.

WHITE CARGO

★★★★½

Glass: Martini
Garnish: Dust with grated nutmeg
Method: SHAKE all ingredients with ice and fine strain into chilled glass.

2	shots	Rutte Dry Gin
1	scoop	Vanilla ice cream
¼	shot	Chardonnay (Chablis) white wine

Origin: Adapted from Harry Craddock's 1930 'The Savoy Cocktail Book'.
Comment: A delicious dessert-style drink.

WHITE COSMO

★★★★☆

Glass: Martini
Garnish: Orange zest twist
Method: SHAKE all ingredients with ice and fine strain into chilled glass.

1	shot	Ketel One Citroen vodka
1	shot	De Kuyper Triple Sec
1½	shots	Cranberry juice (white)
½	shot	Freshly squeezed lime juice

Origin: Emerged during 2002 in New York City.
Comment: Just what it says on the tin.

WHITE KNIGHT

★★★½☆

Glass: Martini
Garnish: Dust with grated nutmeg
Method: SHAKE all ingredients with ice and fine strain into chilled glass.

¾	shot	Dewar's 12yo Scotch whisky
¾	shot	Coffee liqueur
¾	shot	Drambuie liqueur
¾	shot	Milk
¾	shot	Single cream / half-and-half

Comment: This creamy after-dinner drink features Scotch and honey with a hint of coffee. Not too sweet.

White Lady cocktail

Shaken and served straight-up in a coupe glass, the White Lady cocktail is made with gin, triple sec and lemon juice. Many (including yours truly) also add egg white and sugar syrup. It is garnished with a lemon zest twist.

While the merits of adding egg white and sugar may be debated by some the gin, triple sec and lemon trio are beyond reproach, although there are subtle variations as to their proportions. However, when Harry MacElhone, from Dundee, Scotland, first created his White Lady while working at London's Ciro's Club in 1919 it consisted of equal parts triple sec, white crème de menthe and lemon juice. He created the version we know today in 1929 while at his own Harry's New York Bar in Paris, France.

The American Bar at the Savoy Hotel in London claims that the White Lady was first created there by Harry Craddock and a recipe for the drink appears in his 1930 'The Savoy Cocktail Book'. It is said that F. Scott Fitzgerald's wife, Zelda, was drinking at the Savoy and Craddock named the drink after her because she was a platinum blonde.

My preferred recipe follows many others in calling for:
1½ shots London dry gin
¾ shot Triple sec liqueur
¾ shot Freshly squeezed lemon juice

However, the sweetness in the Triple Sec fails to quite balance the lemon's citrus acidity (many triple sec liqueurs have become drier post 2000) so it is desirable to add a dash or even splash of sugar syrup. Whether or how much you add is a matter of personal taste but I favour 1/3 shot (10ml) of 2:1 sugar syrup.

Early recipes, including MacElhone's own 'Harry's ABC of Mixing Cocktails' and Harry Craddock's 1930 'The Savoy Cocktail Book' make no mention of the use of egg white. While the Japanese enjoy raw fish the trend for adding raw egg to sour cocktails is yet to catch on there with modern day Japanese bartenders such as Hidetsugo Ueno San vehemently against egg white being used in any cocktail.

I believe the Japanese omission of egg white is more a cultural judgment than one of taste and egg white definitely rounds a White Lady. It also makes it white. Beneath the attractive fluffy white foam produced by aerating the egg white lies a dirty yellow drink that hardly befits the name. Those against the use of egg white argue that the drink is not named after its colour but the numerous ghostly white ladies of mythology. Maybe, but dirty yellow is not as visually appealing as a fluffy white head.

WHITE LADY COCKTAIL 🗝

★★★★½

Glass: Martini
Garnish: Lemon zest twist
Method: SHAKE all ingredients with ice and strain back into the same shaker to remove the ice. **SHAKE** again without ice (dry shake) and then strain into chilled glass.

1½	shots	Rutte Dry Gin
¾	shot	De Kuyper Triple Sec
¾	shot	Freshly squeezed lemon juice
⅓	shot	Sugar syrup (2 sugar to 1 water)
½	fresh	Egg white (optional)

Comment: A simple but lovely classic drink with a sour finish.

WHITE LION (DAVID EMBURY'S RECIPE)

★★★★☆

Glass: Martini
Garnish: Lime wedge
Method: **SHAKE** all ingredients with ice and fine strain into chilled glass.

- **2 shots Bacardi Carta Blanca light rum**
- **¼ shot De Kuyper Triple Sec**
- **¼ shot Pomegranate / grenadine syrup (2:1)**
- **½ shot Freshly squeezed lime juice**

Origin: Adapted from a recipe purloined from David Embury's classic 1948 book, 'The Fine Art of Mixing Drinks'.
Comment: This fruity Daiquiri is superb when made with quality pomegranate syrup and white rum to emerge with an off-white hue. Other renditions of this classic are ruby red - hardly a 'White' Lion.

WHITE NEGRONI (NEW)

★★★★½

Glass: Old-fashioned
Garnish: Pink grapefruit zest twist
Method: **POUR** all ingredients into ice-filled glass and **STIR**.

- **1 shot Rutte Dry Gin**
- **1 shot Suze Saveur d'Autrefois**
- **1 shot Lillet Blanc**

Origin: Created in 2001 by Wayne Collins at VinExpo. Bordeaux, France using Plymouth Gin for Nick Blacknell, then director of Plymouth Gin. Later, Simon Ford, who was the Plymouth Gin ambassador, introduced the drink to Audrey Saunders in the early days of her Pegu Club where the drink became a hit on the menu.
Comment: Wayne Collins, this drink's creator, originally used equal parts as is usual for a classic Negroni and after trying various other formulations we've found this works best. Wayne also specifies a grapefruit zest twist and this makes the drink. However, be warned, this is a drink for aficionados of bittersweet aperitifs and Suze. We love it!

WHITE RUSSIAN CHRISTMAS (NEW)

★★★★½

Glass: Coupe
Garnish: Serve with mince pie
Method: **SHAKE** all ingredients with ice and fine strain into chilled glass.

- **2 shots Ketel One Vodka**
- **1 spoon Robertson's mincemeat**
- **½ shot Coffee liqueur**
- **¼ shot Gingerbread sugar syrup**
- **1 shot Single cream / half-and-half**

Origin: Created in December 2014 by yours truly at the Cabinet Room, London, England.
Comment: As the apt name suggests, this is a Christmassy white Russian – the festive feel courtesy of mincemeat and gingerbread syrup.

White Russian cocktail

One of the best-known cocktails of the modern era, the White Russian presents vodka and coffee liqueur served on the rocks, sipped through a silky layer of cream or milk.

A White Russian can be as simple as equal measures vodka, coffee liqueur and fresh cream poured over ice. However, it looks better if you shake at least the first two ingredients and then layer cream on the surface of the drink. Or some prefer to shake all three ingredients to make a properly integrated cocktail. While not essential we like to grate some nutmeg over the surface of the drink.

Origins
Named due to its appearance and vodka base - Smirnoff and Stolichnaya being the main vodka brands at the time hence vodka was associated with Russia. The White Russian is obviously related to the Black Russian whose origins are thought to date from 1949. Who first came up with this creamy interpretation and when is unknown.

Mention of the White Russian cocktail in print first appeared in an advertisement for a now long defunct coffee liqueur called 'Coffee Southern' which was run in the Boston Globe on 21st March 1965, and also later in the California's Oakland Tribune on 21 November 1965. Along with the White Russian, the "Try delicious Coffee Sothern" advert also gives the recipes for 'Coffee and Cointreau', 'Southern Grasshopper' and 'Java Sundae' using the liqueur.

The White Russian strutted its way through the 70s disco era before its popularity waned in the 1980s, only to be rescued and made more popular than ever after being the libation of choice of The Dude in the cult 1998 movie The Big Lebowski. Played by Jeff Bridges, throughout the comedy caper film Jeffrey 'The Dude' Lebowski has little interest or passion for anything other than bowling and drinking White Russians which he refers to as a "Caucasian". Over the duration of the film, The Dude consumes seven of the creamy cocktails.

WHITE RUSSIAN COCKTAIL

★★★★☆

Glass: Old-fashioned
Garnish: Dust with grated nutmeg
Method: **SHAKE** vodka and coffee liqueur with ice and strain into ice-filled glass. **FLOAT** lightly whipped cream on top of drink.

- **2 shots Ketel One Vodka**
- **1 shot Coffee liqueur**
- **1 shot Single cream / half-and-half**

Comment: A Black Russian smoothed with cream.

WIBBLE

★★★★½

Glass: Coup
Garnish: Lemon zest twist
Method: **SHAKE** all ingredients with ice and fine strain into chilled glass.

- **1 shot Rutte Dry Gin**
- **1 shot Sloe gin liqueur**
- **1 shot Freshly squeezed grapefruit juice**
- **⅓ shot Freshly squeezed Lemon juice**
- **⅓ shot Lejay crème de mûre (blackberry)**
- **¼ shot Sugar syrup (2 sugar to 1 water)**

Comment: Created in 1999 by Dick Bradsell at The Player, London, England for Nick Blacknell - a conspicuous lover of gin.
Origin: As Dick Bradsell once said to me, "It may make you wobble, but it won't make you fall down." Dick named this cocktail after the 1970s' Weebles children's roly-poly toys which were advertised with the catchphrase, "Weebles wobble, but they don't fall down."

WIDOW'S KISS

★ ★ ★ ★ ★

Glass: Martini
Garnish: Mint leaf
Method: STIR all ingredients with ice and fine strain into chilled glass.

1½	shots	Calvados brandy
¾	shot	Bénédictine D.O.M. liqueur
¾	shot	Yellow Chartreuse liqueur
2	dash	Angostura Aromatic Bitters

Origin: Created before by George J. Kappeler at New York City's Holland House Hotel. This recipe is adapted from his 1895 'Modern American Drinks'.
Comment: Fantastically herbal with hints of apple, mint and eucalyptus. This classic is often made with green Chartreuse but we prefer with half yellow and half green. It's controversial but try this combo shaken rather than stirred.

WILD BLOSSOM

★ ★ ★ ★ ☆

Glass: Martini
Garnish: Grapefruit zest twist
Method: SHAKE all ingredients with ice and fine strain into chilled glass.

2 shots Rutte dry gin
¾ shot St-Germain elderflower liqueur
¾ shot Freshly squeezed pink grapefruit juice
1 shot Cranberry juice

Origin: Adapted from a drink created in 2007 by James Scarito at BLT Market, New York City, USA.
Comment: Aptly named - it is indeed blossom-like, yet also dry and serious.

WILD HONEY

★ ★ ★ ★ ☆

Glass: Martini
Garnish: Dust with grated nutmeg
Method: SHAKE all ingredients with ice and fine strain into chilled glass.

1½	shots	Dewar's 12yo Scotch whisky
½	shot	Vanilla infused Ketel One vodka
¾	shot	Drambuie liqueur
½	shot	Galliano L'Autentico liqueur
½	shot	Milk
½	shot	Single cream / half-and-half

Origin: Created in 2001 by James Price at Bar Red, London, England.
Comment: A serious yet creamy after dinner cocktail with whisky and honey.

WILD IRISH ROSE

★ ★ ★ ★ ✦

Glass: Coupe
Garnish: Lemon zest twist & Luxardo Maraschino cherry
Method: SHAKE first four ingredients with ice and fine strain into chilled glass. **TOP** with soda.

2	shots	Teeling Small Batch Irish whiskey
½	shot	Freshly squeezed lemon juice
¼	shot	Sugar syrup (2 sugar to 1 water)
¼	shot	Pomegranate / grenadine syrup (2:1)
½	shot	Soda (club soda) (optional)

Origin: An adaptation on Dale DeGroff's twist on the classic Jack Rose.
Comment: The gentle bite of Irish whiskey soured with lemon and sweetened with pomegranate syrup. The splash of soda which crowns this drink serves to lighten and add a touch of sparkle.

WILL OF ALAN

★ ★ ★ ★ ✦

Glass: Old-fashioned
Garnish: Lime wedge
Method: DRY SHAKE all ingredients without ice. Add ice, **SHAKE** again and strain into ice-filled glass.

2	shots	Bacardi Carta Ocho aged rum
½	shot	Taylor's Velvet Falernum liqueur
¾	shot	Pineapple (fresh)
¾	shot	Freshly squeezed lime juice
2	dash	Old-fashioned bitters
¼	fresh	Egg white

Origin: Discovered in 2008 at Tonic, Edinburgh, Scotland.
Comment: Fantastic, spiced, tiki-style twisted Daiquiri.

WILLI WONKA COCKTAIL (NEW)

★ ★ ★ ★ ✧

Glass: Old-fashioned
Garnish: White Chocolate square and half strawberry
Method: Muddle strawberries in base of shaker. Add other ingredients, **SHAKE** with ice and strain into glass filled with crushed ice.

2 fresh Small ripe strawberries (hulled)
2 shots Capucana cachaça
⅓ shot Freshly squeezed lime juice
⅛ shot Sugar syrup (2 sugar to 1 water)
⅓ shot White chocolate sugar syrup

Origin: Adapted from a drink created in 2015 by Carlos Londoño at Café Pacifico London.
Comment: Cachaca and strawberry with subtle hints of lime and chocolate.

WILLIAM PORTER

★★★★½

Glass: Coupe
Garnish: None
Method: **STIR** all ingredients with ice and strain into chilled glass.

2	shots	**Dewar's 12yo Scotch whisky**
½	shot	**Martini Rosso vermouth**
¼	shot	**De Kuyper Triple Sec**
⅛	shot	**Freshly squeezed lime juice**
1	dash	**Angostura Orange Bitters**

Origin: Named after William Trotter Porter (1809–1858), an American journalist and editor who founded the Spirit of the Times, a newspaper devoted to sports.
Comment: A delicate, Manhattan-like combo of Scotch, sweet vermouth and triple sec.

WILTON MARTINI

★★★★☆

Glass: Martini
Garnish: Cinnamon dusted apple slice
Method: **SHAKE** all ingredients with ice and fine strain into chilled glass.

1	shot	**Ketel One Vodka**
1	shot	**Calvados brandy**
½	shot	**Apple Schnapps liqueur**
⅛	shot	**Cinnamon schnapps**
1½	shots	**Pressed apple juice**

Origin: A 2003 adaptation of the signature cocktail at The Blue Bar, The Berkeley Hotel, London, England.
Comment: Refined cinnamon and apple.

WIMBLEDON MARTINI

★★★★☆

Glass: Martini
Garnish: Strawberry
Method: **MUDDLE** strawberries in base of shaker. Add other ingredients, **SHAKE** with ice and fine strain into chilled glass.

3	fresh	**Small ripe strawberries (hulled)**
1½	shots	**Bacardi Carta Blanca light rum**
1½	shots	**Lejay Crème de Fraise liqueur**
¼	shot	**Sugar syrup (2 sugar to 1 water)**
½	shot	**Single cream / half-and-half**

Origin: Created in London sometime during the 1990s when every cocktail served in a V-shaped glass was called a Martini.
Comment: Takes some getting through the strainer, but when you do it's simply strawberries and cream.

THE WINDSOR ROSE

★★★★☆

Glass: Martini
Garnish: Rose petal
Method: **SHAKE** all ingredients with ice and fine strain into chilled glass.

1¼	shots	**Ketel One Oranje vodka**
1	shot	**De Kuyper Triple Sec**
1	shot	**Cranberry juice**
½	shot	**Freshly squeezed lime juice**
⅛	shot	**Rose water**

Origin: Adapted from a drink discovered in 2005 at The Polo Club Lounge, New Orleans, USA.
Comment: An orange vodka and rosewater Cosmo.

WINDY MILLER

★★★★☆

Glass: Collins
Garnish: Lemon slice
Method: **SHAKE** first three ingredients with ice and strain into glass filled with crushed ice. **TOP** with lemonade.

1	shot	**Ketel One Citroen vodka**
½	shot	**Le Fée Parisienne absinthe**
1	shot	**Mandarine Napoléon liqueur**
Top with		**Lemonade/Sprite/7-Up**

Origin: Discovered in 2000 at Teatro, London, England.
Comment: British readers over 40 may remember the children's TV series Trumpton, Chigley and Camberwick Green. If you do, then sing between sips, 'Pugh, Pugh, Barney McGrew, Cuthbert, Dibble and Grubb.'

WINK

★★★★½

Glass: Old-fashioned
Garnish: Orange zest twist (discarded)
Method: **POUR** absinthe into ice-filled glass. **TOP** with chilled water and leave to stand. Separately **SHAKE** other ingredients with ice. **DISCARD** contents of glass (absinthe, water and ice) and **STRAIN** drink into empty absinthe-coated glass.

½	shot	**Le Fée Parisienne absinthe**
2	shots	**Rutte Dry Gin**
¼	shot	**De Kuyper Triple Sec**
⅛	shot	**Sugar syrup (2 sugar to 1 water)**
2	dash	**Peychaud's aromatic bitters**

Origin: Created in 2002 by Tony Conigliaro at The Lonsdale, London, England.
Comment: Reminiscent of a Sazerac but with gin and triple sec. Delicate, remarkably fruity and very sippable.

WINTER COCKTAIL

★★★★☆

Glass: Martini
Garnish: Lemon zest twist
Method: **STIR** all ingredients with ice and strain into chilled glass.

2	shots	**Martell VSOP Médaillon cognac**
½	shot	**Sour apple liqueur**
½	shot	**Martini Extra Dry vermouth**
¼	shot	**Sugar syrup (2 sugar to 1 water)**

Comment: Reminiscent of an Apple Cart (a Calvados Sidecar), this is simple, balanced and tastes great.

WISECRACK FIZZ

★★★★½

Glass: Collins
Garnish: Lemon zest twist
Method: **SHAKE** first four ingredients with ice and strain into an ice-filled glass. **TOP** with soda and serve with straws.

1½	shots	**BarSol Mosto Verde Italia pisco**
1	shot	**St-Germain elderflower liqueur**
1	shot	**Freshly squeezed pink grapefruit juice**
½	shot	**Freshly squeezed lemon juice**
Top with		**Soda (club soda)**

Origin: Created in 2007 by Matt Gee at Milk & Honey, New York City, USA.
Comment: Light, balanced and refreshing. The pisco character shines through.

WOLF TICKET

★★★★☆

Glass: Sour or Martini/Coupette
Garnish: Lemon zest twist
Method: **MUDDLE** peach in base of shaker. Add other ingredients, **SHAKE** with ice and fine strain into chilled glass.

½ fresh Ripe peach
(skinned and diced)
1½ shots Bourbon whiskey
¼ shot Crème de pêche (peach) liqueur
½ shot Freshly squeezed lemon juice
½ shot Sugar syrup (2 sugar to 1 water)
1 dash Angostura Aromatic Bitters

Origin: Adapted from a drink created in 2013 by Eric Johnson at the Sycamore Den, a 1970s-inspired cocktail lounge in San Diego's Normal Heights neighbourhood, USA.
Comment: The ripeness and quality of the peach will make or break this drink. If in season white peaches are preferable.

WONKY MARTINI

★★★★☆

Glass: Martini
Garnish: Pink grapefruit zest twist
Method: **STIR** all ingredients with ice and strain into chilled glass.

2 shots Vanilla infused Ketel One vodka
½ shot Tuaca liqueur
¾ shot Martini Rosso vermouth
2 shots Grapefruit bitters

Origin: Created in 2003 by yours truly, London, England.
Comment: A sweet, wet Vodkatini invigorated with vanilla and grapefruit.

WOO WOO

★★★☆☆

Glass: Old-fashioned
Garnish: Lime wedge
Method: **SHAKE** all ingredients with ice and strain into ice-filled glass.

2 shots Ketel One Vodka
¾ shot Peachtree peach schnapps
2½ shots Cranberry juice

Origin: A Fuzzy Navel with cranberry juice instead of orange juice.
Comment: Fruity, dry cranberry laced with vodka and peach. Not nearly as bad as its reputation but still lost in the eighties.

WOOD SAP & SAND COCKTAIL (NEW)

★★★★⯪

Glass: Coupe
Garnish: Mint leaf
Method: Lightly **MUDDLE** mint in base of stirring glass. Add other ingredients, **STIR** with ice and fine strain into chilled glass.

2 fresh Mint leaves
1½ shots Dewar's 12yo Scotch whisky
¾ shot Skinos Mastiha
¾ shot Martini Rosso vermouth
¾ shot Freshly squeezed orange juice

Origin: Created in August 2015 by yours truly at the Cabinet Room, London, England.
Comment: Fresh and refreshing Greek mastiha replaces cherry liqueur in this riff on the classic Blood & Sand.

WOODLAND PUNCH

★★★⯪☆

Glass: Collins
Garnish: Lime wedge
Method: **SHAKE** first four ingredients with ice and strain into ice-filled glass. **TOP** with soda, lightly stir and serve with straws.

2 shots Southern Comfort liqueur
¼ shot Cherry Heering Liqueur
½ shot Freshly squeezed lime juice
2 shots Fresh pressed pineapple juice
Top with Soda (club soda)

Origin: Adapted from a drink created in 1997 by Foster Creppel. This is the signature at his Woodland Plantation, the great house on the west bank of the Mississippi that used to feature on every bottle of Southern Comfort.
Comment: Tart, tangy and refreshing.

WOODSIDE

★★★★☆

Glass: Coupe
Garnish: None
Method: **MUDDLE** pineapple in base of shaker and add other ingredients. **DRY SHAKE** (without ice), then **SHAKE** again with ice and fine strain into chilled glass.

½ ring Pineapple (fresh)
(cored, skinned and chopped)
¾ shot Bacardi Carta Blanca light rum
½ shot Ruby port
¾ shot Martini Extra Dry vermouth
(grapefruit infused)
½ shot Freshly squeezed lemon juice
½ shot Sugar syrup (2 sugar to 1 water)
2 dash Angostura Aromatic Bitters
½ fresh Egg white

Origin: Created in 2009 by Darren Thrower at The Kenilworth, Warwickshire, England and named after Count Basie's "Jumpin' at the Woodside".
Comment: Delicately fruity, light and fluffy.

WOODY COCKTAIL (NEW)

★★★★½☆

Glass: Coupe
Garnish: Mint sprig
Method: MUDDLE mint in base of stirring glass. Add other ingredients, **STIR** with ice and fine strain into chilled glass.

3	fresh	Mint leaves
1½	shots	Ketel One Vodka
1	shot	Skinos Mastiha
1	shot	Birch water
¼	shot	Romate Fino sherry
8	drop	Bob's Bitters Peppermint bitters

Origin: Created in August 2015 by yours truly at the Cabinet Room, London, England.
Comment: Named not after the cheery chap in Cheers or even the Beatles' Norwegian Wood but due to this particularly Woody cocktail containing birch water and mastiha.

WORDSMITH (NEW)

★★★★☆

Glass: Coupe
Garnish: Lime zest twist
Method: SHAKE all ingredients with ice and fine strain into chilled glass.

¾	shot	Pot still Jamaican rum
¾	shot	Green Chartreuse liqueur
¾	shot	Luxardo Maraschino liqueur
¾	shot	Freshly squeezed lime juice

Origin: Created in 2009 by Chuck Taggart, Los Angeles and named by Dave Stolte.
Comment: Punchy pot-still rum with the equally powerful notes of Green Chartreuse supported by Maraschino liqueur with lime zestiness. Powerful in every respect.

WOXUM

★★★★½☆

Glass: Coupe
Garnish: Lemon zest twist
Method: STIR all ingredients with ice and strain into chilled glass.

1½	shots	Applejack brandy (bonded)
½	shot	Martini Rosso vermouth
½	shot	Yellow Chartreuse liqueur

Origin: Recipe is adapted from Albert Stevens Crockett's 1935 'The Old Waldorf-Astoria Bar Book'.
Comment: The flavour of Chartreuse shines through in this slightly sweet, spirit cocktail.

YACHT CLUB

★★★★½☆

Glass: Martini
Garnish: Lemon zest twist
Method: STIR all ingredients with ice and strain into chilled glass.

2	shots	Bacardi Carta Oro rum
¼	shot	De Kuyper XO Apricot Brandy
1	shot	Martini Rosso vermouth

Origin: Adapted from a recipe purloined from David Embury's classic book, 'The Fine Art of Mixing Drinks'.
Comment: Rich and slightly sweet with hints of apricot fruit.

YELLOW BELLY MARTINI

★★★★☆

Glass: Martini
Garnish: Lemon zest twist
Method: SHAKE all ingredients with ice and fine strain into chilled glass.

1	shot	Ketel One Citroen vodka
1	shot	Pallini Limoncello
1	shot	Freshly squeezed lemon juice
⅛	shot	Sugar syrup (2 sugar to 1 water)
½	shot	Chilled water (omit if wet ice)

Origin: A neo-martini from the 1990s.
Comment: Lemon, lemon, lemon. Nice though!

YELLOW PARROT

★★★★☆

Glass: Martini
Garnish: Orange zest twist
Method: SHAKE all ingredients with ice and fine strain into chilled glass.

¼	shot	Le Fée Parisienne absinthe
1	shot	Yellow Chartreuse liqueur
1	shot	De Kuyper XO Apricot Brandy
1	shot	Chilled water (reduce if wet ice)

Origin: Some say this was created in 1935 by Albert Coleman at The Stork Club, New York City, but the drink featured in Harry Craddock's Savoy Cocktail Book five years before that.
Comment: The aniseed of the absinthe combines well with the other ingredients. A bit of a sweety but a strong old bird.

YOKOHAMA

★★★½☆

Glass: Martini
Garnish: Orange zest twist
Method: SHAKE all ingredients and fine strain into chilled glass.

½	shot	Ketel One Vodka
1	shot	Freshly squeezed orange juice
1	shot	Rutte Dry Gin
¼	shot	Le Fée Parisienne absinthe
½	shot	Pomegranate / grenadine syrup (2:1)

Origin: One of the earliest published vodka recipes and credited to Harry McElhone who also created the Monkey Gland #1 to which this cocktail is practically identical, albeit a splash of vodka.
Comment: Gin and orange with a hint of absinthe.

YOU'VE GOT MAIL

★★★★☆

Glass: Collins
Garnish: Orange slice
Method: SHAKE first five ingredients with ice and fine strain into ice-filled glass. **TOP** with champagne.

2	shots	Capucana cachaça
¼	shot	Sugar syrup (2 sugar to 1 water)
½	shot	Freshly squeezed lime juice
½	shot	Freshly squeezed orange juice
¼	shot	Honey sugar syrup
Top with		G.H. Mumm Cordon Rouge Champagne

Origin: Adapted from Dave Wondrich's riff on the classic Airmail.
Comment: Cachaça and citrus balanced by honey and topped with champagne.

A
B
C
D
E
F
G
H
I
J
K
L
M
N
O
P
Q
R
S
T
U
V
W
X
Y
Z

YOUNG MAN COCKTAIL

★★★★☆

Glass: Coupe
Garnish: Luxardo Maraschino cherry
Method: **STIR** all ingredients with ice and strain into chilled glass.

1½ shots Martell VSOP Médaillon cognac
½ shot Martini Rosso vermouth
½ shot Grand Marnier Cordon Rouge
2 dash Angostura Aromatic Bitters

Origin: Adapted from a drink in Harry Craddock's 1930 The Savoy Cocktail Book.
Comment: This particular Young Man is essentially a cognac-based Sweet Manhattan with a splash of orange curaçao – unsurprisingly, the result is slightly sweetened cognac with a hint of orange.

YULE LUVIT

★★★½☆

Glass: Shot
Garnish: Dust with grated nutmeg
Method: Refrigerate ingredients then **LAYER** in chilled glass by carefully pouring in the following order.

¾ shot Bourbon whiskey
¾ shot Hazelnut liqueur

Comment: Actually, 'yule' find it strongly nutty and sweet.

YUM

★★★☆☆

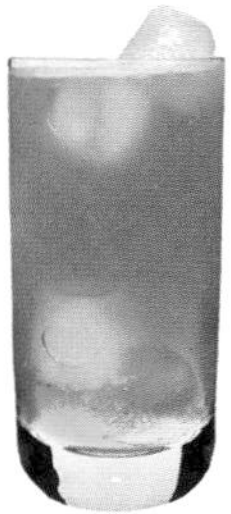

Glass: Collins
Garnish: Lemon wedge
Method: **SHAKE** all ingredients with ice and strain into ice-filled glass.

½ shot Peachtree peach schnapps
1½ shots Mandarine Napoléon liqueur
¼ shot Chambord Liqueur
1 shot Freshly squeezed lemon juice
3 shots Pressed apple juice

Comment: If you like sweet, fruity 'disco drinks' then this is indeed yummy.

Z MARTINI

★★★★★

Glass: Martini
Garnish: Blue cheese stuffed olives
Method: **STIR** all ingredients with ice and strain into chilled glass.

2½ shots Ketel One Vodka
1¼ shots Tawny port

Origin: Discovered in 2004 at Les Zygomates, Boston, USA.
Comment: Grainy vodka with dry, wine-like notes. Top marks for the garnish alone.

ZABAGLIONE COCKTAIL

★★★½☆

Glass: Martini
Garnish: None
Method: Separately **BEAT** egg white until stiff and frothy and yolk until this is as liquid as water, then pour into shaker. Add other ingredients, **SHAKE** with ice and fine strain into chilled glass.

1 fresh Egg white
1 fresh Egg yolk
1½ shots Warninks Advocaat liqueur
½ shot Martell VSOP Médaillon cognac
1 shot Marsala superiore secco wine
¾ shot Freshly squeezed lemon juice

Origin: Created by yours truly in 2003 and inspired by the classic Italian dessert, which incidentally derives its name form the Neapolitan dialect word 'zapillare', meaning 'to foam'.
Comment: Like the dessert, this is sweet and rich with flavours of egg and fortified wine.

ZAC'S DAIQUIRI

★★★★☆

Glass: Martini
Garnish: Lemon zest twist
Method: **SHAKE** all ingredients with ice and strain into chilled glass.

2 shots Bacardi Carta Ocho aged rum
½ shot Freshly squeezed lemon juice
½ shot Pressed apple juice
¼ shot Sugar syrup (2 sugar to 1 water)

Origin: Created in January 2009 by yours truly at the Cabinet Room, London, England.
Comment: Originally made for Zacapa rum which suits lemon rather than lime in a Daiquiri. Daiquiris benefit from dilution and here a dash of apple juice adds a barely perceptible amount of fruit as well.

ZAKUSKI COCKTAIL

★★★★☆

Glass: Martini
Garnish: Cucumber peel
Method: **MUDDLE** cucumber in base of shaker. Add other ingredients, **SHAKE** with ice and fine strain into chilled glass.

1 inch English cucumber peeled
2 shots Ketel One Citroen vodka
½ shot De Kuyper Triple Sec
½ shot Freshly squeezed lemon juice
¼ shot Sugar syrup (2 sugar to 1 water)

Origin: Created in 2002 by Alex Kammerling, London, England.
Comment: Named after the Russian snack.

THE ZAMBOANGA 'ZEINIE' COCKTAIL

★★★★☆

Glass: Martini
Garnish: Lime zest twist (discarded) & cherry
Method: SHAKE all ingredients with ice and fine strain into chilled glass.

2 shots Martell VSOP Médaillon
¼ shot Maraschino syrup (from cherry jar)
1 shot Fresh pressed pineapple juice
½ shot Freshly squeezed lime juice
2 dash Angostura Aromatic Bitters

Origin: Adapted from a recipe purloined from Charles H. Baker Jr's classic book, The Gentleman's Companion. He describes this as "another palate twister from the land where the Monkeys Have No Tails. This drink found its way down through the islands to Mindanao from Manila..."
Comment: Reminiscent of a tropical Sidecar.

ZANZIBAR

★★★½☆

Glass: Old-fashioned
Garnish: Lime zest twist
Method: SHAKE all ingredients with ice and strain into ice-filled glass.

2   shots Gosling's Black Seal dark rum
¼   shot   De Kuyper XO Apricot Brandy
¼   shot   Grand Marnier Cordon Rouge
⅛   shot   Almond (orgeat) syrup
½   shot   Freshly squeezed orange juice
½   shot   Freshly squeezed lime juice

Origin: Discovered in 2005 at Zanzi Bar, Prague, Czech Republic.
Comment: Tangy rum and citrus with fruit and hints of almond.

ZAZA

★★★★☆

Glass: Martini
Garnish: Orange zest twist
Method: SHAKE all ingredients with ice and fine strain into chilled glass.

2   shots Rutte Dry Gin
2   shots Dubonnet Red

Origin: Adapted from a recipe in Harry Craddock's 1930 'Savoy Cocktail Book'. It is named after a French play which was a hit around the verge of the 20th century and was followed by opera and film versions.
Comment: Zaza is a diminutive of Isabelle. But there is nothing diminutive about this simple, yet fantastic drink.

ZELDA COCKTAIL

★★★★☆

Glass: Martini
Garnish: Mint sprig
Method: Lightly MUDDLE mint (just to bruise) in base of shaker. Add other ingredients, SHAKE with ice and fine strain into chilled glass.

5   fresh Mint leaves
2   shots Zubrówka bison vodka
1   shot   Freshly squeezed lime juice
¾   shot   Almond (orgeat) syrup
½   shot   Chilled water (omit if wet ice)

Origin: Created in May 2002 by Phillip Jeffrey at the GE Club, London, England. He made it for a friend called Zelda - the name really wouldn't have worked if she'd been called Tracy.
Comment: Bison grass vodka combines brilliantly with mint and almond.

ZEUS COCKTAIL

★★★★½

Glass: Martini
Garnish: Coffee beans
Method: POUR Fernet Branca into frozen glass, swirl round and DISCARD. MUDDLE raisins with cognac in base of shaker. Add other ingredients, SHAKE with ice and fine strain into chilled glass.

1   shot   Fernet Branca
24   dried Raisins
2   shots Martell VSOP Médaillon cognac
⅛   shot   Coffee liqueur
¼   shot   Maple syrup
1   shot   Chilled water (reduce if wet ice)

Origin: Adapted from Dr Zeus, a cocktail created by Adam Ennis in 2001 at Isola, London, England.
Comment: Rich, pungent and not too sweet.

ZHIVAGO COCKTAIL

★★★★☆

Glass: Martini
Garnish: Float dehydrated apple slice
Method: SHAKE all ingredients with ice and fine strain into chilled glass.

1½ shots Vanilla infused Ketel One vodka
½ shot Bourbon whiskey
½ shot Sour apple liqueur
1 shot Freshly squeezed lime juice
¾ shot Sugar syrup (2 sugar to 1 water)

Origin: Created in 2002 by Alex Kammerling, London, England.
Comment: Sweet and sour - sweet apple, vanilla and bourbon balanced by sour lime juice.

A
B
C
D
E
F
G
H
I
J
K
L
M
N
O
P
Q
R
S
T
U
V
W
X
Y
Z

ZOMBIE #1 (INTOXICA! RECIPE)

★★★★☆

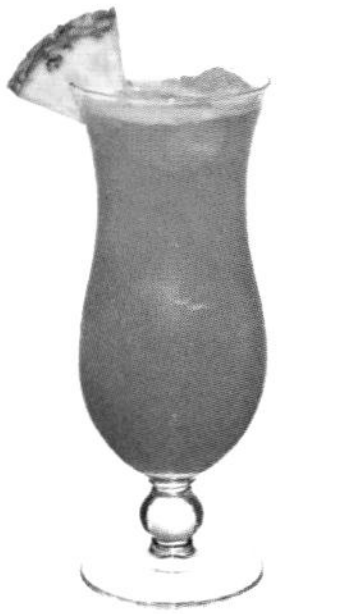

Glass: Hurricane
Garnish: Mint sprig
Method: STIR brown sugar with lemon juice in base of shaker until it dissolves. Add other ingredients, **SHAKE** with ice and strain into ice-filled glass.

1 spoon Brown sugar
1 shot Bacardi Carta Oro rum
1 shot Overproof Demerara rum
1 shot Bacardi Carta Blanca light rum
1 shot Freshly squeezed lemon juice
1 shot Fresh pressed pineapple juice
1 shot Freshly squeezed lime juice
1 dash Angostura Aromatic Bitters
1 shot Passion fruit syrup

Origin: The above recipe for Don the Beachcomber's classic cocktail is based on one published in Intoxica! by Jeff Berry.
Comment: Plenty of flavour and alcohol with tangy rum and fruit.

ZOMBIE #2 (VIC'S FORMULA)

★★★½☆

Glass: Collins
Garnish: Mint sprig
Method: BLEND all ingredients with one 12oz scoop crushed ice. Serve with straws.

¾ shot Bacardi Carta Blanca light rum
¾ shot Bacardi Carta Ocho aged rum
½ shot Grand Marnier Cordon Rouge
¼ shot Pomegranate / grenadine syrup (2:1)
1½ shots Freshly squeezed orange juice
2½ shots Fresh pressed pineapple juice
1 shot Freshly squeezed lemon juice
½ shot Freshly squeezed lime juice

Origin: Adapted from a recipe in the 1947-72 Trader Vic's Bartender's Guide by Victor Bergeron.
Comment: More fruit than alcohol but tangy not sweet.

ZOMBIE COCKTAIL (MODERN RECIPE)

★★★★☆

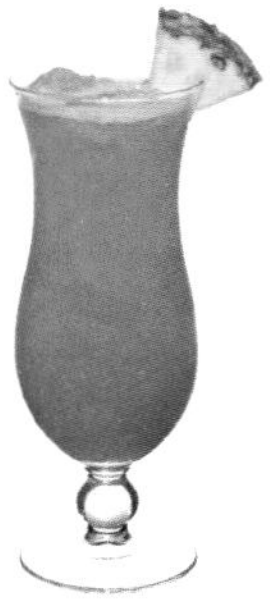

Glass: Hurricane
Garnish: Pineapple wedge
Method: SHAKE first nine ingredients with ice and strain into glass filled with crushed ice. **FLOAT** overproof rum.

¾ shot Bacardi Carta Blanca light rum
¾ shot Pusser's Navy Rum (54.5%)
¾ shot Bacardi Carta Oro rum
½ shot De Kuyper XO Apricot Brandy
½ shot Grand Marnier Cordon Rouge
2½ shots Freshly squeezed orange juice
2½ shots Fresh pressed pineapple juice
1 shot Freshly squeezed lime juice
½ shot Pomegranate / grenadine syrup (2:1)
½ shot White overproof rum

Comment: A heady mix of four different rums with pineapple, orange, lime and grenadine.

ZOOM

★★★★½

Glass: Martini
Garnish: Dust with chocolate powder
Method: SHAKE all ingredients with ice and fine strain into chilled glass.

2½ shots Martell VSOP Médaillon cognac
½ shot Single cream / half-and-half
3 spoon Runny honey
½ shot Milk

Comment: Cognac is smoothed with honey and softened with milk and cream in this classic cocktail.

ZUBROWKA COCKTAIL

★★★★½

Glass: Coupe
Garnish: Lemon zest twist
Method: POUR absinthe into ice-filled glass, top with water and stand to one side. Separately **STIR** other ingredients with ice. Dump contents of glass and strain stirred drink into the absinthe washed glass.

½ shot Le Fée Parisienne absinthe
1½ shots Zubrówka bison vodka
¼ shot Original Danziger Goldwasser Liqueur
1½ shots Martini Rosso vermouth
1 dash Angostura Aromatic Bitters

Origin: Adapted from W. J. Tarling's (Bill Tarling) 1937 'Café Royal Cocktail Book Coronation Edition' in which the invention of this drink is credited to S. T. Yakimovitch.
Comment: The grassy notes of Zubrówka and delicate cinnamon shine through in this well balanced and well integrated delicately spicy vintage cocktail.

ZUZU'S PETALS COCKTAIL (NEW)

★★★★½

Glass: Coupe
Garnish: Lemon zest twist
Method: SHAKE all ingredients with ice and strain into chilled glass.

1½ shots Zubrówka bison vodka
½ shot Suze Saveur d'Autrefois
½ shot St-Germain elderflower liqueur
½ shot Freshly squeezed lime juice
1 shot Luxardo Maraschino liqueur
¼ shot Sugar syrup (2 sugar to 1 water)
2 dash Celery bitters

Comment: Bittersweet with fragrant bison grass vodka and fruity maraschino cherry flavours supported by bitter gentian, rich elderflower and lime juice.

STAR RATINGS EXPLAINED

★★★★★+	OUTSTANDING	★★★★★	EXCEPTIONAL
★★★★½	EXCELLENT	★★★★☆	RECOMMENDED
★★★½☆	COMMENDED	★★★☆☆	MEDIOCRE
★★½☆☆	DISAPPOINTING	★★☆☆☆	PRETTY AWFUL
★½☆☆☆	SHAMEFUL	★☆☆☆☆	DISGUSTING

Everything for the well-stocked bar

BRANDS WE BELIEVE IN

Each year I taste thousands of products brought to market – you can see my ratings and reviews of them all at diffordsguide.com – and I am in the unique position of having made and rated every drink recipe contained in this cocktail encyclopedia.

You'll notice that I have chosen specific brands for some spirits categories throughout the book. I have chosen these brands because, in my opinion, they make great drinks and are available globally at most good liquor stores or supermarkets. None of them are esoteric or expensive, and all represent well-made products that offer good value for money.

In fact, in the speed-rail of The Cabinet Room – my private bar in Bermondsey, London – you'll find these very products that have been included here.

Cheers,
Simon Difford. simon@diffordsguide.com

My Cabinet Room bar when first stocked back in 2007

diffordsguide.com
THE HOME OF DISCERNING DRINKERS

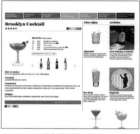

COCKTAILS

BEER, WINE & SPIRITS

CITY BAR GUIDES

PEOPLE & PERSONALITIES

DISTILLERIES & PRODUCERS

BARTENDER'S LOUNGE

Difford's Guide was established in 2001 and since moving online has become one of the world's most complete and authoritative drinks websites.
We are proud to have built a loyal following amongst the top international bartending fraternity, discerning drinkers and keen amateur mixologists alike.

From one of the world's most comprehensive selections of cocktails, beers and spirits to an in-depth look at the fascinating stories and people behind the world's most interesting brands we help discerning drinkers discover what to drink and where to drink it.

Cheers

Simon Difford